INSIGHT GUIDES

WORLD TRAVEL ENCYCLOPEDIA

Surrounded by Tuscan hills: Siena with its beautiful cathedral and the Piazza del Campo.

A magnet for millions of tourists: the fairy castle Neuschwanstein in the Bavarian Alps.

Myanmar: The derelict temple and stupas are remnants of the ancient capital Pagan.

Enchanting landscapes and meandering rivers: Guilin, one of China's most picturesque places.

The magical South Seas: One of Polynesia's most beautiful islands, Moorea, is covered by lush forests.

Sacred ground for Aborigines: Kata Tjuta (Mount Olga), ancient rock formations in Central Australia.

Morocco: Traditional clay brick buildings in Boumaine, a historic town in the Dades Valley.

Tissisat 'smoke from the water' – this is what the Ethiopians call the waterfalls on the Blue Nile.

Surrounded by the Caribbean Sea: The fortress El Morro is Puerto Rico's capital San Juan.

The vibrant heart of Argentina's capital: Plaza de la Republica in Buenos Aires.

Table of Contents

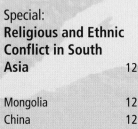 

AFRICA

THE AMERICAS

ALLIANCES AND ORGANISATIONS

Table of Contents

Map locator

NATURAL LANDSCAPES

ATLAS

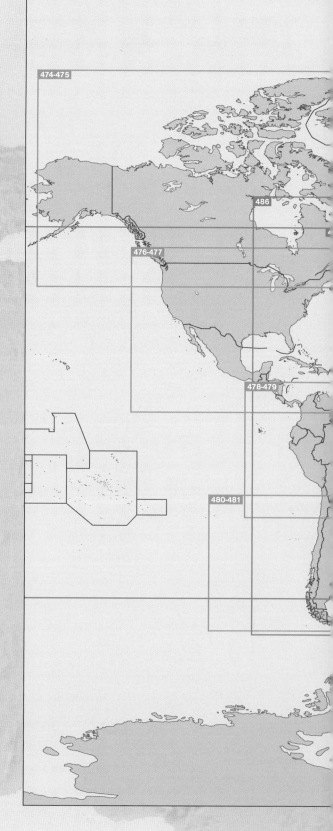

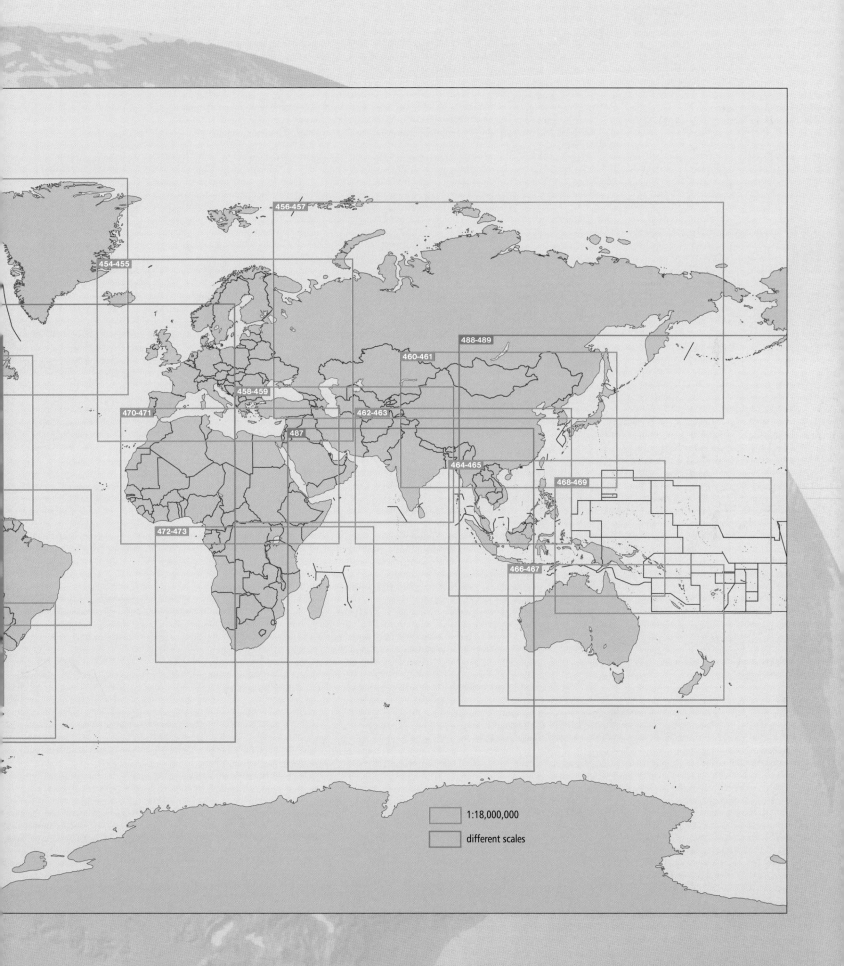

456-457

454-455

488-489

460-461

458-459

470-471

462-463

487

464-465

468-469

472-473

466-467

1:18,000,000

different scales

INDEX OF LOCAL COUNTRY NAMES

This encyclopedia provides a portrait of all the countries in the world in geographical sequence by continents. The alphabetical list gives the English name of each country in the world in the first column, using the official, internationally recognised name in the second column followed by the equivalent page reference.

English	Local	Continent	Page	English	Local	Continent	Page
Afghanistan	Afghānistān	Asia	112	Cuba	Cuba	Central America	280
Albania	Shqipëria	Europe	63	Cyprus	Kypros/Kibris	Europe	66
Algeria	Al-Ġazā'ir/Algérie	Africa	185	Czech Republic	Česká Republika	Europe	52
Andorra	Andorra	Europe	35	Denmark	Danmark	Europe	18
Angola	Angola	Africa	224	Djibouti	Djibouti	Africa	217
Antigua and Barbuda	Antigua and Barbuda	Central America	284	Dominica	Dominica	Central America	285
Argentina	Argentina	South America	305	Dominican Republic	República Dominicana	Central America	282
Armenia	Armenija (Hayastan)	Asia	68	East Timor	Timor-Leste	Asia	150
Australia	Australia	Australia	162	Ecuador	Ecuador	South America	300
Austria	Österreich	Europe	44	Equatorial Guinea	Guinea Ecuatorial	Africa	211
Azerbaijan	Azerbajdzan	Asia	69	Egypt	Al-Mişr/Egypt	Africa	188
Bahamas	Bahamas	Central America	283	El Salvador	El Salvador	Central America	275
Bahrain	Al-Bahrain	Asia	99	Eritrea	Eritrea	Africa	216
Bangladesh	Bangladesh	Asia	115	Estonia	Eesti	Europe	22
Barbados	Barbados	Central America	287	Ethiopia	Îtyopya	Africa	217
Belarus	Belarus	Europe	23	Fiji	Fiji	Australia/Oceania	170
Belgium	België/Belgique	Europe	26	Finland	Suomi/Finland	Europe	19
Belize	Belize	Central America	274	France	France	Europe	28
Benin	Benin	Africa	206	Gabon	Gabon	Africa	212
Bhutan	Bhutan	Asia	118	The Gambia	Gambia	Africa	198
Bolivia	Bolivia	South America	302	Georgia	Gruzija (Sakartvelo)	Asia	67
Bosnia-Herzegovina	Bosna i Hercegovina	Europe	60	Germany	Deutschland	Europe	38
Botswana	Botswana	Africa	226	Ghana	Ghana	Africa	204
Brazil	Brasil	South America	296	Greece	Elláda (Hellás)	Europe	64
Brunei	Brunei	Asia	148	Grenada	Grenada	Central America	286
Bulgaria	Bŭlgarija	Europe	57	Guatemala	Guatemala	Central America	274
Burkina Faso	Burkina Faso	Africa	202	Guinea	Guinée	Africa	200
Burundi	Burundi	Africa	221	Guinea-Bissau	Guinea-Bissau	Africa	199
Cambodia	Kâmpŭchéa	Asia	142	Guyana	Guyana	South America	291
Cameroon	Cameroun/Cameroon	Africa	209	Haiti	Haïti	Central America	281
Canada	Canada	North America	248	Honduras	Honduras	Central America	275
Cape Verde	Cabo Verde	Africa	197	Hungary	Magyarország	Europe	54
Central African Republic	République Centrafricaine	Africa	210	Iceland	Ísland	Europe	21
Chad	Tchad	Africa	208	India	India (Bhărat)	Asia	114
Chile	Chile	South America	308	Indonesia	Indonesia	Asia	149
China	Zhongguo	Asia	122	Iraq	'Irāq	Asia	94
Colombia	Colombia	South America	290	Iran	Îrân	Asia	96
Comoros	Comores	Africa	232	Ireland	Éire/Ireland	Europe	14
Congo	Congo	Africa	212	Israel	Yi'sra'el	Asia	91
Congo, Dem. Rep.	Congo, Rép. Démocratique	Africa	214	Italy	Italia	Europe	46
Costa Rica	Costa Rica	Central America	277	Ivory Coast	Côte d'Ivoire	Africa	203
Croatia	Hrvatska	Europe	60	Jamaica	Jamaica	Central America	281

English	Local	Continent	Page	English	Local	Continent	Page
Japan	Nippon/Nihon	Asia	134	Romania	România	Europe	56
Jordan	Urdunn	Asia	89	Russia	Rossija	Europe	70
Kazakhstan	Kazahstan	Asia	104	Rwanda	Rwanda	Africa	221
Kenya	Kenya	Africa	220	Saint Kitts and Nevis	Saint Kitts and Nevis	Central America	284
Kiribati	Kiribati	Australia/Oceania	169	Saint Lucia	Saint Lucia	Central America	286
Korea, North	Choson	Asia	132	St. Vincent and the Grenadines	St. Vincent and the Grenadines	Central America	286
Korea, South	Taehan-Min'guk	Asia	133	Samoa	Samoa	Australia/Oceania	171
Kuwait	Al-Kuwait	Asia	99	San Marino	San Marino	Europe	48
Kyrgyzstan	Kyrgyzstan	Asia	104	São Tomé and Principe	São Tomé e Príncipe	Africa	211
Laos	Lao	Asia	141	Saudi Arabia	Al-Mamlaka	Asia	98
Latvia	Latvija	Europe	22		al-'Arabiya as-Sa'ūdiya		
Lebanon	Al-Lubnān	Asia	89	Senegal	Sénégal	Africa	198
Lesotho	Lesotho	Africa	230	Serbia	Srbija	Europe	61
Liberia	Liberia	Africa	202	Seychelles	Seychelles	Africa	233
Libya	Lîbîyâ	Africa	187	Sierra Leone	Sierra Leone	Africa	201
Liechtenstein	Liechtenstein	Europe	43	Singapore	Singapore	Asia	147
Lithuania	Lietuva	Europe	22	Slovakia	Slovenská Republika	Europe	54
Luxembourg	Luxembourg	Europe	27	Slovenia	Slovenija	Europe	60
Macedonia	Makedonija	Europe	62	Solomon Islands	Solomon Islands	Australia/Oceania	169
Madagascar	Madagasíkara	Africa	232	Somalia	Soomaaliya	Africa	218
Malawi	Malawi	Africa	225	South Africa	South Africa/Suid-Afrika	Africa	229
Malaysia	Malaysia	Asia	146	Spain	España	Europe	34
Maldives	Maldives (Divehi Rajje)	Asia	117	Sri Lanka	Śrī Laṅkā	Asia	116
Mali	Mali	Africa	195	Sudan	As-Sūdān	Africa	219
Malta	Malta	Europe	49	Suriname	Suriname	South America	292
Marshall Islands	Marshall Islands	Australia/Oceania	168	Swaziland	Swaziland (kaNgwane)	Africa	231
Mauritania	Mawrītāniyah	Africa	194	Sweden	Sverige	Europe	16
Mauritius	Mauritius	Africa	232	Switzerland	Suisse/Schweiz/Svizzera	Europe	42
Mexico	México	Central America	270	Syria	Sūriya	Asia	88
Micronesia	Micronesia	Australia/Oceania	168	Taiwan	Taiwan	Asia	128
Moldova	Moldova	Europe	58	Tajikistan	Tadžikistan	Asia	107
Monaco	Monaco	Europe	30	Tanzania	Tanzania	Africa	222
Mongolia	Mongol Ard Uls	Asia	122	Thailand	Muang Thai	Asia	140
Montenegro	Crna Gora	Europe	62	Togo	Togo	Africa	204
Morocco	Al-Maġrib/Maroc	Africa	184	Tonga	Tonga	Australia/Oceania	171
Mozambique	Moçambique	Africa	226	Trinidad and Tobago	Trinidad and Tobago	Central America	288
Myanmar (Burma)	Myanmar	Asia	140	Tunisia	Tūnisiyah/Tunisie	Africa	186
Namibia	Namibia	Africa	227	Turkey	Türkiye	Europe	66
Nauru	Nauru (Naoero)	Australia/Oceania	169	Turkmenistan	Turkmenistan	Asia	106
Nepal	Nepal	Asia	118	Tuvalu	Tuvalu	Australia/Oceania	170
Netherlands	Nederland	Europe	26	Uganda	Uganda	Africa	220
New Zealand	New Zealand	Australia/Oceania	162	Ukraine	Ukrajina	Europe	58
Nicaragua	Nicaragua	Central America	276	Uruguay	Uruguay	South America	304
Niger	Niger	Africa	196	Uzbekistan	Uzbekistan	Asia	105
Nigeria	Nigeria	Africa	206	Vanuatu	Vanuatu	Australia/Oceania	170
Norway	Norge	Europe	16	Vatican City	Città del Vaticano	Europe	48
Oman	Saltanat 'Umān	Asia	98	Venezuela	Venezuela	South America	290
Pakistan	Pākistān	Asia	112	Vietnam	Viêt-Nam	Asia	142
Palau	Palau	Australia/Oceania	168	United Arab Emirates	Daulat al-Imārāt	Asia	101
Panama	Panamá	Central America	278		al-'Arabiya Al-Muttahida		
Papua New Guinea	Papua New Guinea	Australia/Oceania	168	United Kingdom	United Kingdom	Europe	12
Paraguay	Paraguay	South America	304	United States of America	United States of America	North America	252
Peru	Perú	South America	301	Western Sahara	Al-Saharaw	Africa	184
Philippines	Pilipinas	Asia	150	Yemen	Al-Yaman	Asia	98
Poland	Polska	Europe	52	Zambia	Zambia	Africa	225
Portugal	Portugal	Europe	36	Zimbabwe	Zimbabwe	Africa	224
Qatar	Qaṭar	Asia	100				

Europe

Europe has a total area of 10.5 million sq. km. More than 710 million people, slightly more than one-tenth of the world's population, live on the Earth's most densely populated continent. Europe's wide variety of landscapes include vast plains and lowlands extending over most of the north and east, while the terrain of southern Europe consists largely of low mountains, plateaus and hills. A chain of high mountain ranges, dominated by the Alps (highest peak: Mont Blanc: 4,807 m) and the Pyrenees, stretches from west to east across the continent. Islands and peninsulas constitute no less than one-third of Europe's total land area. The Volga and the Danube are the longest rivers and Lake Ladoga in Russia is the continent's largest inland body of water. Many of the countries of Europe have existed as nation-states for centuries and each one has a wealth of historic and cultural attractions. For centuries, European scientists, scholars and artists contributed to the continent's reputation as the cultural centre of the world.

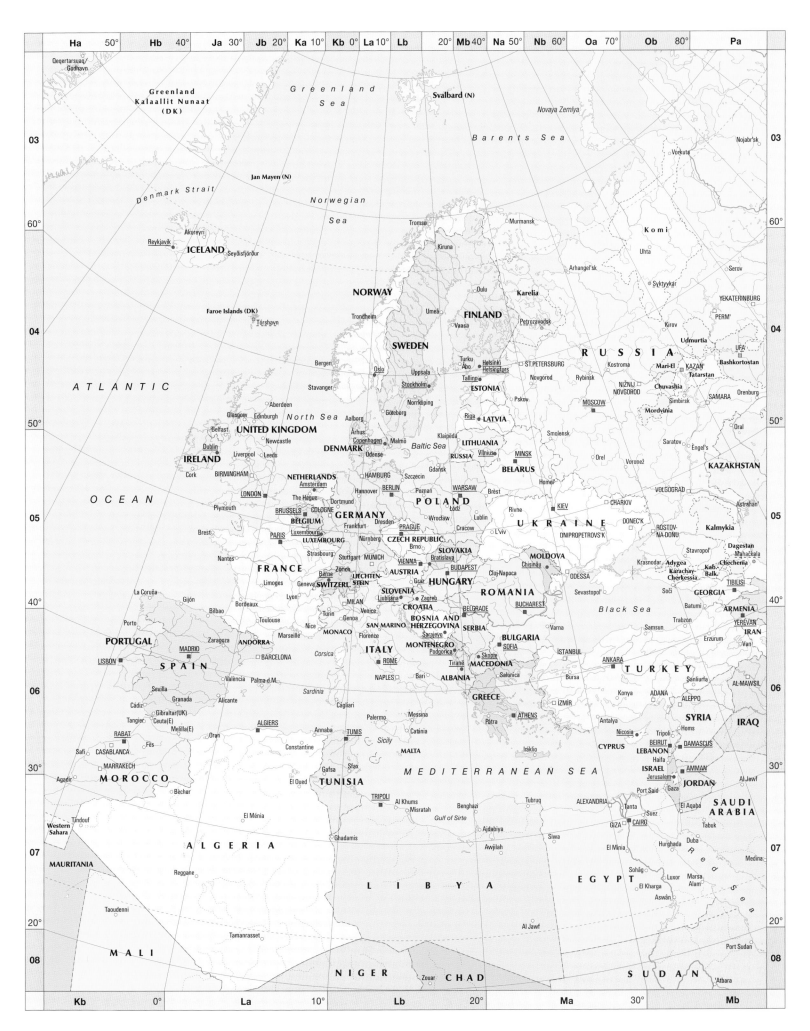

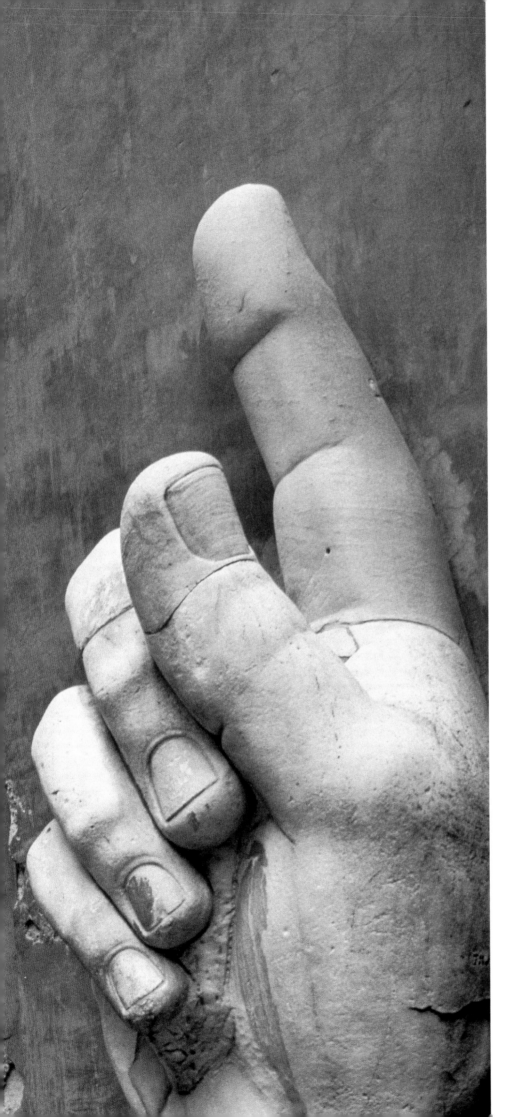

Main photograph:
The remains of a colossal statue of the Roman Emperor Constantine the Great at the Palazzo dei Conservatori in Rome. Constantine changed the course of European history when he declared Christianity to be the official religion of the Roman Empire.

The History of Europe

Early Bronze Age cultures were followed in turn by the Greeks, Etruscans, Romans, the Holy Roman Empire, absolute monarchies, the Enlightenment, the rise of the middle classes and finally the democratic, fascist and socialist

Venice was once known as the 'Queen of the Seas'.

Trafalgar Square, London, a reminder of Britain's naval power.

systems of the twentieth century. Great discoveries and the Industrial Revolution enabled European expansion, and European colonies throughout the world have significantly shaped world history over many centuries. The rise of the USA, Japan and other non-European nations has meant that the Old World has lost some of its global power, yet twenty-first century Europe remains of great cultural, economic and political importance.

Charlemagne (747–814). The Frankish king played an important role in the history of medieval Europe. Charlemagne founded the first major empire in Europe since the fall of Rome, laid the foundations for the French nation-state and initiated important reforms throughout his realm. Medieval Frankish culture combined influences from Germanic, Latin and Christian traditions.

Ancient history

Europe was first settled by hunter-gatherer cultures more than 1.5 million years ago. The first urban settlements emerged between 3000 and 2000 BC. The name 'Europe' probably originated from Ancient Greek mythology. Europa was a Phoenician princess abducted by the god Zeus and taken to the island of Crete where she gave birth to King Minos. Crete was an important bridge between the cultures of Mediterranean Europe and western Asia. Around 1100 BC, Greek culture had spread to Asia Minor and the first Greek city-states were founded. In the turbulent centuries between 800 and 500 BC, the aristocracy replaced monarchs as local rulers as the Greeks established colonies around the Mediterranean. The major political centres of this period were Athens, Sparta, Thebes, Corinth, Argos and Miletus.

Despite the internecine wars between the Greek colonies they shared a cultural identity which was celebrated at the Olympic Games and religious ceremonies such as those held in Delphi.

Greek history between 500 and 336 BC was dominated by conflicts between Athens and Sparta and attacks by foreign nations. Athens became the dominant naval power in Greece and leader of the Delian League after the Athenians led the battle against a Persian army commanded by Xerxes I and helped to end the Carthaginian attacks on Greek colonies in Sicily. Sparta supplanted Athens as the dominant power after its victory in the Peloponnesian War but lost influence after the Delian League was restored.

Rivalries and conflicts between the Greek city-states gave the Macedonian king Phillip II the opportunity to bring the whole of Greece under his control. Phillip II's son, Alexander the Great, led a series of military campaigns and conquests that initiated the Hellenistic Age. Greece, Egypt and most of the Middle East were united in one vast empire by Alexander but after his sudden, early death, his empire was fragmented. His legacy was the spread of Helenistic culture throughout the region, leaving a lasting impact.

After a succession of dynasties and Hellenistic empires, including the Ptolemaic dynasty and the Seleucid Empire, in 146 BC, Greece finally lost its independence and fell to a rapidly expanding new power – the Republic of Rome. According to legend, the city of Rome was founded in 753 BC and ruled by seven kings before it was declared a republic. The Romans defeated the last Etruscan kingdom in 509 BC and by 272 BC had gained control over the whole of Italy south of the Po Valley. Yet, Carthage rather than Rome, was the most powerful naval force in the western Mediterranean during this period. In 146 BC, the Romans finally defeated Carthage after waging three Punic Wars. Despite the Republic's expansion and Germanic invasions became a serious threat to the Roman empire during the reign of Marcus Aurelius. Within the empire, the spread of Christianity was also a threat to the traditional social order and the new religion was brutally suppressed. The Emperor Constantine eventually made Constantinople into a second capital and declared Christianity the official religion of Rome in 379 AD. The Roman Empire was split into a western and an eastern empire in 395. The weak Western Empire, with Rome as its capital, soon lost control over much of its territory; the last western emperor, Romulus Augustus, was deposed in 476. The Eastern Roman (Byzantine) Empire managed to survive in an increasingly weakened state until the Ottoman Turks conquered Constantinople in 1453.

The Middle Ages

After the collapse of the Western Roman Empire, Europe experienced a period of mass migrations as Germanic and Slav tribes moved westwards. The Vandals, Visigoths, Ostrogoths and Lombards all established kingdoms but it was the Franks who created the first major empire in Western Europe since the fall of Rome. The Frankish Merovingian dynasty was succeeded by the Carolingians in 751, under Pippin the Younger, the son of Charles Martel, who led a Christian army to victory over Muslim forces at the Battle of Tours in 732. Charlemagne, the Frankish king who was crowned Emperor of Rome in 800, established a powerful realm, known as the Holy Roman Empire, that covered most of Western Europe.

The western Frankish realm, under the control of the Capetian dynasty, was weakened by internal strife and political disputes. The Eastern Franks appointed Otto I Holy Roman Emperor. He was able to defeat a Magyar invasion and expand his territory. During his reign, the Czechs, Danes and Poles were forced into alliances with the Holy Roman Empire.

The relationship between the popes and Europe's most powerful monarchs was an important factor in the early Middle Ages. In 1076, Pope Gregory VII excommunicated the Holy Roman Emperor Henry IV during one of the many conflicts between the church and Europe's rulers. The Concordat of Worms, signed in 1122, brought only a temporary respite to the political struggles between the popes and the Holy Roman emperors.

Conflicts between Christians and Muslims, including several major wars, also played an important role. In 1492, the last Muslim kingdom in Spain was conquered by Christians. The conquest of the Holy Land and the 'liberation' of Jerusalem were the primary goals of the Crusades, which took place between 1095 and 1275.

The growing cultural differences between Western Europe and Byzantium led to the Great Schism, which divided European Christianity into the Roman Catholic and Eastern Orthodox rites. Several city-states in northern Italy became powerful economically and politically and challenged the power of the Byzantine Empire in the Mediterranean.

In western Christendom, the papacy and Roman Catholicism faced increasing criticism and challenges from new reformist sects; many of these movements were brutally suppressed by the Inquisition. Conflicts, rivalries and wars between European kingdoms lead to political instability and curtailed the power of many secular rulers.

The feudal societies of medieval Europe experienced a dramatic transformation after the fourteenth century, although this process began at different times in different places. France and England gradually emerged as modern nation-states after the Hundred Years' War. Spain and Portugal also emerged as unified nation-states during this period.

1 Religious reformer Martin Luther (1483–1546). **2** Holy Roman Emperor Charles V (1500–1558). **3** Queen Elizabeth I (1533–1603). **4** King Louis XIV of France (1638–1715). **5** Peter the Great, Tsar of Russia (1672–1725). **6** Frederick II of Prussia (1712–1786).

military successes Rome was plagued by internal conflicts that led to several civil wars.

By the time Julius Caesar was assassinated in 44 BC, the Roman senate had lost most of its political influence. Officially, Rome was still a republic but support for an empire ruled by a hereditary monarch continued to grow.

England was ruled by Anglo-Saxon monarchs until William of Normandy's (William the Conqueror) victory at the Battle of Hastings in 1066. The Normans were descendants of the Vikings who had established new kingdoms in areas far from their Scandinavian homelands, including Russia and Southern Italy.

The colourful imagery of the Bayeux Tapestry tells the story of **William of Normandy's** invasion of England and his victory at the Battle of Hastings. The oldest remaining medieval pictorial work of its kind, the Bayeux Tapestry, was probably made in the eleventh century and is 70 m long. The embroidered linen cloth is full of beautiful artistic details and imagery.

The development of banking and the growth of shipping as a source of wealth were signs of the changes taking place in Europe. The effects of the Black Death on the demographics, the discoveries of the New World by Spanish and Portuguese explorers, the Humanist revival of the Renaissance and the Protestant Reformation all marked the end of the Middle Ages in the sixteenth century.

The Early Modern Era

European exploration of the New World and the revolutionary discoveries of scientists such as Galileo and Copernicus were the beginning of a progressive new era in the history of Europe. Spain and Portugal, followed by England, France and the Netherlands, explored the world's oceans and established the first colonies in the New World. The influence of the pope and the Catholic church were significantly weakened by a series of religious wars. The Protestant Reformation and the Catholic Counter-reformation led to the devastating Thirty Years' War that ended in 1648 with the Peace of Westphalia.

Europe was divided between Protestant and Catholic rulers. In 1534, the English king Henry VIII founded the Church of England, a new Protestant established church. While Germany and Italy remained patchworks of small kingdoms and city-states, England became a naval power after the defeat of the Spanish Armada in 1588. The Netherlands were liberated from Spanish rule and rapidly became one of the known world's wealthiest nations. The wars of the seventeenth century enabled the Continent's most powerful nations to expand their influence and military domination. After centuries of conquest, the Ottoman Turks were defeated in Central Europe. France's desire for hegemony was challenged by the other powers. The War of the Spanish Succession (1710–1714) proved that ,at the time, no one nation was capable of dominating Europe. Most of Europe's rulers were absolute monarchs throughout the eighteenth and nineteenth centuries. The Russian Empire emerged as a new power under Tsar Peter the Great.

Two powers struggled for control of Germany in the nineteenth century, Prussia in the north and the Hapsburg Austrian Empire in the south.

Poland found itself at the mercy of its more powerful neighbours who divided the country up between them three times between 1772 and 1795. The extravagance of European aristocracy and the absolutist rule of the monarchs were challenged during the Age of Enlightenment. Prussia and Britain initiated important political reforms and granted their citizens more rights and freedoms. Elsewhere, however, the limited reforms were not enough to contain the people's demands for greater political and personal liberty.

1 The Roman Forum was once the centre of the Roman Empire. Government offices, temples, shops and banks filled this small district in the heart of ancient Rome.

2 Florence was one of the wealthiest cities in Europe in the Middle Ages. Today the city displays its heritage of Renaissance art.

3 Paris, The Louvre was the first royal palace, built around 1200. French kings lived in it for centuries, but it was eventually replaced by the Palace of Versailles. It was finally converted into a museum in 1793.

Modern Europe

The **French Revolution** began when the **Bastille** was stormed on 14 July, 1789. The old Parisian prison was virtually empty and was slated for demolition when crowds of Parisians attacked it. Nevertheless, this symbolic act had a major political impact; Louis XIV was forced to listen to the demands of the Third Estate. For the common people, the Bastille was a symbol of royal tyranny and despotism.

The French Revolution

A guarantee of basic rights, a democratically elected government and limits on government power were demanded of the French monarchy in 1789. The calls for 'liberty, equality, fraternity' became even more insistent after the Bastille was stormed by the mob. A newly created National Assembly granted a series of basic human rights to all citizens, created a constitutional monarchy and limited the power of the clergy.

A republic was declared in 1792 leading to the French Revolutionary Wars, which began with a series of military successes. Foreign threats radicalised France's revolutionary rulers. Louis XIV and his family were executed and the Jacobins under Robespierre initiated the Reign of Terror. The Thermidorian Reaction was a revolt against the excesses and brutality of the revolution and resulted in the creation of a new constitution. The army fell under the control of a Corsican general with political ambitions called Napoleon Bonaparte. Bonaparte had himself proclaimed emperor in 1804. His *code civil* and his many other reforms showed his skills as a military and political leader. By 1810, Napoleon had reached the peak of his power. Europe's existing rulers stirred up resistance to Napoleon's conquests as fear of French hegemony increased. The British navy defeated Napoleon's forces at sea and his army suffered a devastating blow during the Russian campaign of 1812.

Paris was occupied by troops of the nations allied against Napoleon in 1813. The French emperor was forced into exile and the Bourbon dynasty restored, Louis XVIII being made king.

A new order in Europe

In 1815, the great powers of Europe gathered in Vienna to redraw the continent's boundaries under the guidance of the Austrian politician Prince Metternich. The Congress of Vienna was interrupted by Napoleon's escape from exile. His return was short-lived, however, and he suffered a final defeat at the Battle of Waterloo in 1815. In Vienna, the representatives of the European powers supported a return to the social order that had existed prior to the French Revolution. Despite this conservatism, many of the legal and social reforms, of the Napoleonic era were left in place.

The region known as the Austrian Netherlands and the United Provinces were merged to form the Kingdom of the Netherlands. Germany was consolidated into 39 states united in a loose confederation. Support for a united Germany increased significantly in the early nineteenth century, despite political differences and the rivalry between the two most powerful German states, Prussia and Austria.

The 19th century

The Industrial Revolution, which began in England, and the emergence of liberalism and nationalism dominated the development of Europe throughout the nineteenth century. Many of the conservative regimes were successful in resisting or suppressing the demands of the emerging liberal middle classes. Throughout Europe, calls for social reform and national and ethnic unity grew louder. Ottoman rule of Greece ended in 1829 with foreign aid. In Ireland, the nationalists demanded independence from Great Britain and the Poles itemporarily expelled the Russian army from Warsaw. In 1830, the Bourbon dynasty was again deposed in France and the country became a constitutional monarchy under King Louis-Philippe. In Italy, Giuseppe Mazzini formed the 'Giovine Italia', an organization that advocated a united and independent Italian state. Even in the Austro-Hungarian Empire, the Hungarians and Slavs increasingly resisted the domination of the German-speaking Habsburgs.

In Germany, the rise of liberal and nationalist ideals culminated in the 1848 revolution; this inspired a series of uprisings in that year in other countries. Louis-Philippe was deposed in France, Metternich fled Vienna, Prussia's king Frederick was forced to grant a constitution, and a constitutional assembly in Frankfurt began discussing plans for a democratic, united Germany. Eventually most of the revolutions of 1848 were defeated and in many countries the ruling classes were able to successfully resist meaningful reforms. Switzerland and Sardinia were the only countries to ratify reformed liberal constitutions.

Conflicts between the Great Powers

After the mid-nineteenth century, Europe experienced a period of growing national rivalries that led to several wars involving the Continent's dominant powers. Russia exploited the obvious weakness of the Ottoman Empire to expand its influence in Eastern Europe. The British and the French, together with their Turkish and Italian allies, defeated the Russian Empire in the Crimean War (1853–1856). Austria lost control of its territories in northern Italy and Italian nationalists, including Cavour and Garibaldi, led the struggle for the country's unification. Germany was also on the road to national unity during this period. The Prussian prime minister Bismarck supported the nationhood in the form of a 'small Germany'; this called for a united German nation-state that excluded Austria. The birth of the German Empire was officially proclaimed at Versailles in 1871.

Europe's industrialization

The living conditions of Europe's impoverished urban working class reflected the dark side of the Continent's technical advances. The German philosopher Karl Marx advocated radical social change and revolutionary workers' parties emerged throughout Europe. During the same period, the rivalries between the European powers intensified as the countries of Europe became increasingly industrialized. Great Britain, France, Russia and later Italy and Germany were drawn into a race for regional and global influence.

World War I

After the resignation of Chancellor Bismarck in 1890, Emperor Wilhelm II took personal control of Germany's government and armies. His aggressive foreign policy and determination to challenge Great Britain's naval superiority increased the tensions that culminated in World War I, which began in August, 1914. When Ottoman domination ended in south-east Europe, the region experienced a series of brutal wars and suffered political instability. In 1914, the heir to the Austro-Hungarian throne and his wife were assassinated by a young Serbian nationalist in Sarajevo. This caused the Austro-Hungarian Empire to declare war on Serbia.

A complicated web of defence treaties and alliances meant that Austria's declaration of war was quickly followed by military mobilization and numerous declarations of war throughout Europe. Germany, Austria-Hungary, Bulgaria and the Ottoman Empire were ranged against the *Entente*, an alliance of Great Britain, France and Russia.

The war, which many predicted would not last long, quickly turned into a series of bloody battles and dragged on for years. In Russia, the Tsar was deposed and replaced by a moderate government that chose to continue the war until it was overthrown by Lenin's Bolsheviks after the October Revolution in 1917.

The United States' entry into the war on the side of the Entente led to the defeat of Germany and Austro-Hungary in 1918. The military dictatorship that ruled Germany distanced itself from any blame for the defeat and the Emperor abdicated, along with all of Germany's other monarchs. Workers' and veterans' councils assumed power in many parts of Germany until the Weimar Republic restored political order throughout the country.

Napoleon Bonaparte had himself crowned Emperor of France by Pope Pius VII in 1804.

The German philosopher **Karl Marx** (1818–1883) was one of the most radical critics of capitalism and greatly influenced European workers' movements. His political ideology advocating a system of **socialism** led to the development of several new political systems during the twentieth century. **Vladimir Lenin** (1870–1924) adapted Marx's theory for Russian society. His Bolshevik movement was instrumental in overthrowing the Tsar in the Russian Revolution of 1917.

The Treaty of Versailles (1919/1920) was drafted without input from the defeated nations and imposed huge fines on them. When the treaty process was completed very little remained of the fair post-war world order that United States' president Woodrow Wilson had strongly advocated. Germany was forced to surrender territory in the east and west. The Austro-Hungarian and Ottoman empires were dissolved, while Poland, Czechoslovakia, Finland and the Baltic States were granted independence. The League of Nations was created to preserve world peace.

The Post-war era and World War II

In the early post-war era it seemed as if parliamentary democracy had been accepted throughout Europe but an increasing number of authoritarian regimes emerged in the 1920s. Mussolini, leader of the Fascist movement, seized power in Italy in 1922. The situation was made worse by the Wall Street Crash of 1929, which plunged the Western world into a lasting depression. At the height of the economic crisis, in 1933, Adolf Hitler was appointed Chancellor of Germany and Francisco Franco became the dictator of Spain in 1939, after a destructive civil war. In the Soviet Union, Stalin instituted a brutal dictatorship and had his political opponents executed or exiled. Hitler's aggressive foreign policy was largely successful in the early years of his reign. Despite the brutal repression of political opponents and Germany's Jewish population Hitler was allowed to achieve many of his aims with relatively little opposition from the other powers of Europe. It was only after Nazi Germany invaded Poland on 1 September, 1939 that France and Great Britain finally declared war on Germany. It took the German army only a few weeks to conquer Poland. After a successful campaign in Western Europe and North Africa, the German army controlled much of Europe by 1940. The tide of the war turned against Germany as Britain successfully defended itself in the air in the Battle of Britain and the German army was defeated at Stalingrad in 1943. German defeat was almost certain after the United

States entered the war in 1942. The racist policies of the Nazis resulted in the death of six million Jews, most of them in extermination camps, and the death of another six million members of 'inferior' races, such as gypsies, Poles and Russians.

Europe after 1945

The German Army surrendered in May 1945, ending the war in Europe. Germany was divided into four zones of occupation and later into two states.

In 1945, much of Europe was in ruins and the political picture had changed dramatically. Western Europe oriented itself towards the United States while Stalin established a series of communist satellite states in Eastern Europe. The North Atlantic Treaty Organization (NATO) and the Warsaw Pact fconfronted each other in a Cold War armed with an arsenal including nuclear weapons.

In the 1960s, the Vietnam War triggered student riots in Europe and the United States. In Prague, attempts at political reform were crushed by Soviet tanks, as had happened in the 1950s in Poznan, Budapest and East Berlin.

In the 1970s, several Western European politicians, including Germany's Willy Brandt and Sweden's Olof Palme, worked to improve the relationship between the two Cold War factions. The European Community (EC) was founded by the Treaty of Rome. The military dictatorships in Portugal, Spain and Greece were overthrown in the 1970s and the colonial empires all but disappeared. At the same time, however, organised terrorism became a problem in several European countries as so-called liberation movements such as ETA and the IRA used violence to bring about political changes and socialist terror groups such as the Red Brigade in Italy and RAF in Germany targeted their declared enemies.

The Fall of Communism

During the 1980s, the communist regimes of Eastern Europe were challenged by demands for political change. In Poland, the Solidarity movement led to strikes and Mikhail Gorbachev struggled to reform the Soviet Union with his

policies of *glasnost'* and *perestroika*. In 1989, the border between East and West Germany was opened and Germany reunited in 1990. The Communist regimes were toppled in 1990 and both the Soviet Union and the Warsaw Pact were dissolved. Hopes for a new era of peace were dashed by a series of wars in Yugoslavia.

1 The European powers met at the Congress of Berlin in1878 to discuss the influence of Russia and Turkey in southeast Europe.

2 Stalin, Roosevelt and Churchill agreed to the postwar division of Germany and

the creation of the United Nations at the conferences held in Potsdam and Yalta in 1945.

3 In 1970, West German chancellor Willy Brandt knelt in remembrance of the Nazis' victims in the former Warsaw Ghetto.

Main photograph:
The Brandenburg Gate in Berlin
was once a symbol of a divided
city and a divided nation but has
now come to represent a post-Cold
War Europe working towards a
united future.

The Countries of Europe

*Europe at the start of the twenty-first century
is more than just the name of a land mass. After a hundred years of nationalist wars and political division, the old dream of a united Europe has become a reality. The European Union
had 15 members at the start of the twenty-first
century but was greatly expanded in 2004*

La Grande Arche is a highlight of modern Parisian architecture.

21st century art: The Guggenheim Museum in Bilbao, Spain.

*when ten new members, including many for-
mer Communist nations of Eastern Europe,
joined the organisation. The ultimate goal of
the European Union is to unite the diverse
countries and cultures of Europe in a close alliance capable of preserving peace and spreading prosperity across the Continent.*

United Kingdom

Oxford: Situated at the junction of the Cherwell and Thames rivers, Oxford is the historic capital of the English county of Oxfordshire. The site of English-speaking world's oldest university, the city has played an important role in the development of British scholarship, philosophy, literature and the arts. The 34 colleges of England's most beautiful university town continue to attract gifted scholars and students from all over the world.

United Kingdom

Area:	244,820 sq. km
Capital city:	London
Form of government:	Constitutional Monarchy
Administrative divisions:	92 counties and various regional, county, urban district and metropolitan authorities
External territories:	Channel Islands, Isle of Man, Anguilla, Bermuda, British Virgin Islands, Falkland Islands, Gibraltar, Cayman Islands, Montserrat, Pitcairn Island, St. Helena, Turks and Caicos Islands, South Georgia and South Sandwich Islands
Population:	60.4 million (248 inhabitants/sq. km)
Languages:	English (official), Welsh, Gaelic
GDP per capita:	US$30,900
Currency:	1 pound Sterling (£) = 100 pence

Natural geography

Separated from mainland Europe by the North Sea and the **English Channel**, the **United Kingdom** is a **group of islands** consisting of the main island **Great Britain**, several smaller islands and the north of the island of Ireland. England, the largest of the United Kingdom's constituent countries, is dominated by flat coastal plains and **rolling hills** as well as several **low mountain ranges** such as the **Pennines** in the north and the **Cumbrian Mountains** in the northwest. Wales and Scotland are mountainous. Like England, Northern Ireland is largely hilly and mountainous.

Ben Nevis, the United Kingdom's highest mountain, is situated in the **Grampians** in Scotland's Highlands and rises 1,343 m above sea level.

Climate

With the exception of south-east England with its mildly **continental climate**, most of the United Kingdom has a **maritime climate** with mild, wet winters and cool summers.

Population

The United Kingdom stands out as one of the most **ethnically diverse** nations in Europe. While the majority of Britons have **English**, **Welsh**, **Scottish** or **Irish** ancestry many others are the descendants of recent immigrants from other parts of Europe and former British colonies in Africa, Asia and the Caribbean. Around a third of the population is affiliated to one of the two established **Protestant churches** in Britain and around a tenth are **Roman Catholic**. In addition to Christians, the United Kingdom is also home to more than a million **Muslims** and 500,000 **Hindus** as well as to large **Jewish** and **Sikh** communities. English is the country's de facto official language, while Welsh has official status in Wales but is spoken by only a fifth of the Welsh population. Other significant minority languages are Scots, Scottish Gaelic, Irish and Cornish.

History and Politics

Centuries of **Roman control** over most of Britain was followed by a period of invasion and migration as northern European tribes, including the **Saxons**, **Angles** and **Frisians**, gained control and colonised most of what was to become England. In 1066, the Normans, under **William the Conqueror**, successfully invaded southern England. The Anglo-Norman kings who followed William I expanded English territory into large parts of France. After a series of wars, Edward I brought **Wales** under the control of the English crown in 1282. **Scotland** remained an independent kingdom until 1603. It was only in 1707 after the union of the English and Scottish crowns that Great Britain was united under one government. The United Kingdom is not only one of the world's oldest **kingdoms** but it is also considered to be one of the world's oldest **democracies**. In 1215, the English king John I was forced to sign the **Magna Carta** which

primarily **Catholic nationalists** and predominantly **Protestant loyalists** erupted into the Troubles, a period of violent conflict between unionist and Irish nationalists that claimed thousands of lives. In recent years, the Northern Ireland Peace Process has led to a dramatic reduction in sectarian violence, although ethnic tensions remain.

The English victory over the **Spanish Armada** in 1588 opened the way for England to gradually become the world's pre-eminent naval power. It was also during the sixteenth century that England's **empire** began to emerge as new **colonies** and trading outposts were founded on several continents. Eventually, the British Empire would develop into the largest empire in history and encompass vast territories in Africa, south Asia, North America and the Caribbean.

The **decline** of Britain's global empire started after **World War I**. The founding of the **Commonwealth of Nations** in 1931 ushered in a period that would see most British

A view of the Thames and St Paul's: London is the United Kingdom's economic and political centre.

Elizabeth II

*London, 21.4.1926

After the death of her father, King George VI, Elizabeth ascended the throne in 1952 and was crowned Queen of Great Britain and Northern Ireland in 1953. She has four children from her marriage to Prince Philip. She celebrated 50 years on the throne in 2002. She has been unable to quell debate about the future of the British monarchy.

increased the rights of the aristocracy and limited the power of the crown. England's first parliament was held shortly afterwards in 1230, an event which eventually led to the creation of British parliamentary democracy. After 1170, **Ireland** which had previously been dominated by the Vikings, came under Anglo-Norman rule. After centuries of conflict between the Irish and British, the whole of Ireland was united with Great Britain in 1801. In 1922, most of Ireland became independent with only six predominantly Protestant northern counties remaining in a union with Great Britain. The conflict in Northern Ireland between

colonies be granted independence. With the Chinese takeover of **Hong Kong** in 1997 Britain lost control of the last of its heavily populated overseas territories.

The United Kingdom still retains several **small territories** scattered around the globe including the Isle of Man and the Channel Islands near the British mainland as well as more distant territories including **Bermuda** and **Saint Helena** in the Atlantic Ocean, the peninsula of **Gibraltar** at the southern tip of Iberia, **South Georgia** and the **Falklands** in the South Atlantic, and **Pitcairn Island** in the Pacific. Almost half of Britain's overseas territories are

POPULATION DENSITY (People/km²)

- below 50
- 50-75
- 75-100
- 100-250
- 250-500
- 500-1000
- above 1000

SHETLAND ISLANDS

ORKNEY ISLANDS

HEBRIDES

Scotland Aberdeen

NORTH

Edinburgh
Glasgow

SEA

Northern
Belfast
Ireland MAN

UNITED
KINGDOM

IRISH

Dublin SEA Manchester
Liverpool Sheffield

REPUBLIC

Birmingham

OF IRELAND Wales England

Cardiff London

ATLANTIC

OCEAN

Plymouth English Channel

CHANNEL ISLANDS

FRANCE

0 120 km

small islands in the Caribbean – **Anguilla**, **Montserrat**, the **British Virgin Islands**, the **Turks and Caicos Islands** and the **Cayman Islands**.

The United Kingdom's political system is based on an unwritten constitution and other significant legislation, including the Magna Carta and the 1679 Act of Habeas Corpus Act. Britain is governed by a **bicameral parliament**. The **lower house**, the House of Commons, is the more influential chamber and consists of members who are directly elected by electoral constituencies. The **upper house**, the House of Lords, draws its unelected members from a variety of sources, including bishops of the Church of England, hereditary peers from the British aristocracy, and representatives chosen by the country's leading political parties. In recent years, the British government has undertaken steps to reform the House of Lords and transform it into a more representative body. The British **monarch** is the official head of state of the United Kingdom and the Dominions, the countries of the Commonwealth as well as head of Church of England. As a result of government reforms, both Scotland and Wales have been granted greater local political autonomy in recent years. In 1999, Scotland was granted its own parliament for the first time in almost 300 years.

Economy

The economy of the United Kingdom is increasingly dominated by the **service sector**. Almost half of the land mass is used for **agriculture**, including the cultivation of grain, sugar beet, vegetables and livestock. Although less than two per cent of the British work force is employed on the land, food and livestock **exports** remain significant. Even the traditional **fishing** industry is important in certain coastal regions. More than half of the 25

largest corporations in Europe are based in the United Kingdom. Once the world's leading industrial society, the manufacturing sector has lost its importance in recent decades. Only around one-fifth of workers are now employed in manufacturing. Although traditional industries such as mining, automotive, iron and steel, shipbuilding, and machinery have declined since the 1970s, **chemicals, electronics and pharmaceuticals** have experienced strong growth. The United Kingdom possesses the largest **coal and oil reserves** in Western Europe as well as significant natural gas reserves. The service sector accounts for more than three-quarters of the economy and fulled the strong growth Britain experienced in the 1990s. Britain has its own currency, rejecting the euro when it was introduced in 2002.

Transport Infrastructure

The world's first public **railway** was opened in 1833 in England, the birthplace of the industrial revolution. Britain's rail network now encompasses more than 18,000 km of railways, including the **Channel Tunnel** between England and France. Britain's **road network** covers 370,000 km of roads and is one of the densest in the world. Of its 140 **airports**, 21 are international. London's Heathrow Airport is the busiest in Europe. The main **ferry and passenger ship terminals** are Dover, Newhaven, Plymouth, Harwich, Hull, Newcastle, Liverpool, Aberdeen and Holyhead.

United Kingdom, Ireland

Scottish Traditions: *Despite centuries of union with England and Wales, the people of Scotland continue to cherish their country's unique culture and traditions. For many centuries Scottish clans, groups of people related by kinship, played an important role in the culture of country's rural areas. Tartan, unique woven patterns sewn into clothing, often signify specific clans.*

Tourism

The United Kingdom attracts more than 25 million foreign tourists each year. The **Lake District**, **Northumberland National Park** near the Scottish borders, **Snowdonia National Park** in Wales and the **Scottish Highlands** are the most beautiful landscapes. Other attractions include **cathedrals** and churches, **castles** and **stately homes**, the seaside and the major cities. London, with all its **cultural attractions**, remains the most popular destination in the country and one of the world's most visited cities.

Winston Churchill

(Winston Leonard Spencer C.)
*Blenheim Palace, 30.11.1874,
†London, 24.1.1965

Member of parliament for the Liberal and later the Conservative Party, Churchill held ministerial positions in several governments. He was the First Lord of the Admiralty between 1911 and 1915, the year of the disastrous Battle of Gallipoli. He returned to this office again in 1939 before becoming Prime Minister in 1940. His moving speeches were a vital boost to British morale during World War II and his conduct of the war is highly praised by historians. After the war the Conservative party lost control of government but he was re-elected to parliament in 1951 and 1955.

Margaret Thatcher

*Grantham, 13.10.1925

Margaret Thatcher made history in 1979 when she was elected the first woman prime minister of the United Kingdom. Her term as PM was both the longest of any British head of government in the twentieth century and one of the most controversial periods of government in the country's recent history. Her economic policies brought inflation under control but led to a rise in unemployment. Supporters argue that these policies ended economic stagnation, while critics claim they sharpened social divides and devastated British industry. She left office in 1991 and has held the title Baroness Thatcher since 1992.

Natural geography

Ireland is an **island** in the Atlantic Ocean west of the Great Britain, at the western edge of northern Europe. Much of the island's terrain is **hilly** with **low mountains** (Carrauntoohill, 1,041 m) rising in the north and south of the country. The **Great Shannon Basin** is a large low-lying plain covering most of the island's interior.

Ireland has numerous lakes, heaths, bogs and moors. The southwest of the island, primarily County Cork and County Kerry, has a particularly mild climate and lush vegetation due to the effects of the Gulf Stream.

Only one per cent of Ireland is forested, the smallest area of woodland of any country in Western Europe. Due to its fertile **green meadows** and fields the island is popularly known as 'the Emerald Isle'.

Ireland	
Area:	70,285 sq. km
Capital city: Dublin/Baile Átha Cliath	
Form of government: Parliamentary Republic	
Administrative divisions: 4 provinces with 26 counties	
Population: 4 million (55 inhabitants./ sq. km)	
Languages:	Gaelic, English
GDP per capita:	US$34,100
Currency: 1 euro = 100 cents	

Climate

The island of Ireland has a **mild maritime climate** due largely to the Gulf Stream and other ocean currents. Heavy rainfall throughout the year is common in many parts of the island, especially in the west. Summers are generally cool, while winters tend to be mild and wet.

Population

The Republic of Ireland has a largely homogeneous population, 94 per cent being of **Irish** ancestry. Around 96 per cent of the population is Christian, 90 per cent of the population identifying as **Roman Catholics**. In recent years, the country's strong economic growth has attracted an increasing number of migrants, including many from Eastern Europe. The official languages of the Republic of Ireland are Irish and English, though less than five per cent of the Irish speak **Irish** as their first language. The Irish school system, and many other institutions, are similar to those of the United Kingdom, a legacy of the union that once existed between the two nations.

History and Politics

Archaeological evidence indicates that Ireland has been settled for thousands of years. **Celtic** peoples are believed to have arrived no later than in the third century BC. The people converted to Christianity in the fifth century AD. Celtic Ireland was divided into small kingdoms, and it was not until the tenth century that a united **Irish kingdom** emerged. In the time of St Patrick and his successors, culture and education flourished and the island became a base for the

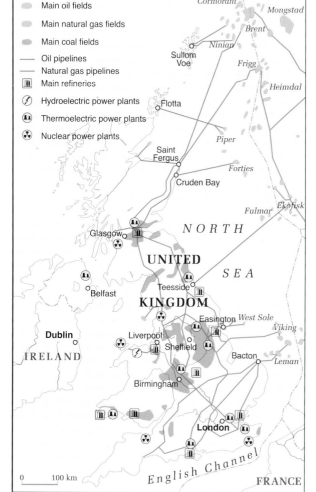

POWER SOURCES

- Main oil fields
- Main natural gas fields
- Main coal fields
- Oil pipelines
- Natural gas pipelines
- ⛿ Main refineries
- ⚡ Hydroelectric power plants
- ⚙ Thermoelectric power plants
- ☢ Nuclear power plants

Edinburgh Castle: once the home of Mary Stuart, Queen of Scots.

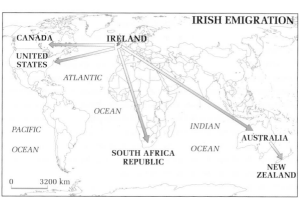

IRISH EMIGRATION

Poblacht Na h'Eireann, an Irish village: *After centuries of poverty, famine, and emigration Ireland has recently undergone a dramatic economic transformation. None the less the Irish have held* *on to many of their cherished traditions and native culture. Although English remains the dominant language in the republic, Irish is affirmed in the constitution as the first official language.*

spread of Christianity to Great Britain and parts of mainland Europe. In 795, the **Vikings** reached the coast of Ireland and began a period of invasion and conquest that lasted until the eleventh century. By the time High King Brian Boru finally drove them out, Ireland had become impoverished. Much of Ireland was conquered by England's Norman king **Henry II** after 1169. This marked the beginning of a long period of English domination and eventually outright control. Under the rule of the English kings, farmers and soldiers from Britain were granted large landholdings at the expense of the native landowners. Attempts to impose **Protestantism** on the Catholic population of Ireland were largely ineffective, although the Catholic upper classes and gentry were largely replaced by Protestants from Scotland and England. A series of Irish revolts against British rule led to reprisals and increased persecution of Catholics. In the nineteenth century, the Potato Famine led to a massive wave of emigration from Ireland. Most went to the United States, while large numbers also settled in Great Britain, Canada and Australia. After decades of political struggle and years of violence most of Ireland's counties separated from the United Kingdom to form the **Irish Free State** in 1922. Six largely Protestant counties in the north chose to remain part of the United Kingdom and became the British province of **Northern Ireland**.
Ireland has a **bicameral parliament** consisting of a directly elected lower house called the Dail Eireann and a Senate whose members are not directly elected but are instead chosen through a variety of methods. The Republic of Ireland's head of state is the directly elected president.

Economy

Ireland is Europe's largest producer of **zinc**. Other mineral resources exploited on the island include peat, copper, lead and oil. Historically, the Irish economy was dominated by **agriculture**, especially livestock husbandry and the production of dairy products. However, like the once thriving fishing industry, agriculture has gradually decreased in

importance. Despite its small size the country's farms are able to produce over 80 per cent of the people's demand for food. In contrast to the agricultural sector, the **service sector** (55 per cent of the country's total GDP) has grown in size and importance in recent years. Ireland's membership in the **European Union** and the development aid it received from that organisation played a major role in the country's incredible economic transformation in the 1990s. Foreign investment was another important factor with almost a quarter of **American foreign investment** in Europe directed to Ireland. The Republic of Ireland, long one of the poorest countries in Western Europe, has become one of the wealthiest nations in the world.

Transport Infrastructure

The **rail network** consists of only about 2,000 km of track. The dominant form of transport is the **car**. Like their British neighbours, the Irish drive on the left. Ireland has four international **airports** and a national airline, Aer Lingus.

Tourism

The Republic of Ireland's most popular tourist attractions are its sparsely populated countryside and historic sights. More than **five million foreign visitors** visit 'the Emerald Isle' each year, providing a major source of income. The centre of the tourist industry is the country's capital and largest city, **Dublin**. The natural attractions include the jagged

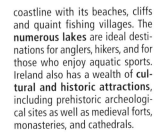

coastline with its beaches, cliffs and quaint fishing villages. The **numerous lakes** are ideal destinations for anglers, hikers, and for those who enjoy aquatic sports. Ireland also has a wealth of **cultural and historic attractions**, including prehistoric archeological sites as well as medieval forts, monasteries, and cathedrals.

1 A coastal lookout: Danluce Castle in Northern Ireland.

2 The crosses at Clonmacnoise monastery are the oldest Christian relics in Ireland.

3 Irish folk music is performed live in public houses throughout Ireland. Many songs

deal with the country's history of foreign domination, poverty and emigration.

4 London: Brightly-lit advertisements have been a feature of Piccadilly Circus since 1890. The famous intersection was planned by John Nash in the early nineteenth century.

Norway: *The enormous oil and gas reserves in the North Sea account for a large part of Norway's gross domestic product. The undersea natural resources are exploited by large offshore oil platforms, which are equipped with drilling equipment, storage tanks and living quarters. Many of the more modern oil rigs are anchored to the seabed. Once extracted oil and gas is transported by pipeline or tanker to onshore refineries.*

Norway	
Area:	324,220 sq. sq. km
Capital city:	Oslo
Form of government:	
Constitutional Monarchy	
Administrative divisions:	
19 provinces	
External territories: Svalbard, Jan Mayen, Bouvet Island, Peter I Island	
Population:	
4.6 million	
(13.8 inhabitants/sq. km)	
Languages:	Norwegian, Sami
GDP per capita:	US$42,400
Currency:	
1 Norwegian krona = 100 øre	

Natural Geography

Norway extends from Cape Lindesnes in the south to the North Cape, a distance of 1725 km and covers much of the western half of the **Scandinavian Peninsula**. The coastline is 2650 km long, while several **fjords** are up to 200 km long, running deep into the country's interior. There are numerous **islands** off Norway ragged coastline. The interior is largely **mountainous** with **glacial plateaus**, high plains, and fairly high mountains. Only the relatively densely populated southwest of Norway contains large areas of **flat land**. The south-east of Norway is covered in vast **forests** extending up to the treeless **tundra** that covers the north much of which lies inside the Arctic Circle. The country's many **lakes** are rich in fish and other marine life. Northern Norway is home to fascinating wildlife, including elk, reindeer and bear.

Climate

The effects of the **Gulf Stream** give coastal Norway a relatively **mild maritime climate**, the mildest on earth for such a northern country. The port of Narvik, remains open all year round, the most northerly year-round harbour in the world. The interior and highlands tend to have a much cooler climate than the coast.

Population

More than 93 per cent of the country's population consists of ethnic **Norwegians**. In addition, Norway also has a **Sami** (Lapp) minority which is concentrated in the north (Lapland), as well as established communities of **Swedes, Danes** and **Russians**. The official national language is Norwegian which has two written forms, Bokmål and Nynorsk. Many Sami people speak dialects of the Sami language. Norwegians enjoy one of the highest standards of living in the world. The government spends over a third of national income on **social services** and **health care**.

History and Politics

United and converted to Christianity in the reign of Harald Fairhair in the ninth century, Norway fell under **Danish rule** in 1387. The union with Denmark lasted more than 400 years and only ended when Denmark ceded Norway to **Sweden** in 1814. In 1905, Norway was granted independence after a referendum. The Norwegian sovereign is the official head of state under the country's constitutional monarchy. Norway, one of the founding members of **NATO**, abandoned its policy of strict **neutrality** after the German occupation during World War II. The constitution, which has been amended several times since it first passed into law in 1814, gives the task of government to the national parliament and assigns the monarch largely symbolic powers. The 165 members of the country's **parliament**, the Storting, are elected directly every four years. In 1994, the Norwegians voted in a referendum against joining the **European Union**. Norway has several **territories**, including the **Svalbard** archipelago and the uninhabited **Bouvet Island, Peter I Island**, and **Jan Mayen Island**.

Economy

Only about three per cent of Norway's land mass is **arable**. Grain and potatoes are the main crops and there are cattle and other livestock. Norway imports more than 50 per cent of its **food**. The Norwegian **fishing** and **fish farming** industries are an important source of **export** income. Norway is one of the biggest fishing nations, and this includes **sealing and whaling**. It is also a large producer of paper, timber and foodstuffs and has important aluminium and iron and steel industries.

The main income stems from the reserves of **oil and natural gas** in the North Sea, most of which belong to Norway and which make it one of the world's largest exporters of heavy crude oil.

Sven Olof Palme
*Stockholm, 30.1.1927, †Stockholm, 28.2.1986

Chairman of the Swedish Social Democratic Party between 1969 and 1986, Sven Olof Palme served as Prime Minister of Sweden for seven years until 1976. His firm opposition to the Vietnam War and nuclear armament during the 1970s brought him respect from outside of his native country. Sven Olof Palme was assassinated in 1986 on a Stockholm street after a visit to a local cinema. His murder, which remains unsolved, was a major shock for the Swedish society.

Transport infrastructure

Norway's mountainous terrain means that the country has no significant **rail network**. Three quarters of the **road network** of the country is surfaced. Norway has two international **airports**, one in Oslo and one in Stavanger.

Tourism

Norway is an expensive but nonetheless popular holiday destination. The country's attractions include **winter sports** facilities in the mountains as well as the stunning landscapes of the country's **fjords** and inland national parks. Other popular sights include the historic stave churches found throughout the country and the old warehouses in **Bergen**, Norway's second city. Oslo has a sculpture park, the national museum, the Oseberg Viking ship and the Kontiki.

Sweden	
Area:	449,964 sq. km
Capital city:	Stockholm
Form of government:	
Constitutional Monarchy	
Administrative divisions:	
24 districts	
Population:	
9 million (20 inhabitants/sq. km)	
Languages:	
Swedish (official), Finnish	
GDP per capita:	US$29,600
Currency:	
1 Swedish krona = 100 öre	

Natural Geography

Sweden covers the eastern and southern half of the **Scandinavian Peninsula**. More than half of the country is afforested and **lakes** occupy more than a tenth of Sweden. In addition to the mainland, Sweden also includes the islands of **Gotland, Öland,** and countless **islets** near the coast. Northern Sweden, which lies between the **Scandinavian mountains** and the **Gulf of Bothnia**, contains numerous rivers, lakes and waterfalls, many of which are used to generate electricity. Southern Sweden consists largely of rolling hills, wide plains and moorland.

Climate

The climate of Sweden varies from south to north and is greatly affected by the **Gulf Stream**, especially along the coast. Much of Sweden's interior, however, has the harsher **continental climate** with summers that are often very warm and bitterly cold winters.

Norway: The craggy mountains on the Lofoten make most of the island uninhabitable.

Population

Around 95 per cent of the population consists of ethnic **Swedes**. Significant minorities include the **Sami** (Lapps) and **Finns** as well a growing number of recent migrants from further afield. At least 83 per cent of the population lives in the cities. Sweden has no official language although Swedish is the dominant language in all of the country's regions. The Swedes have access to excellent **social services** and **health care** as well as the highest levels of **taxation** in the world. **Education** is highly valued in all sectors of Swedish society and no fewer than 95 per cent of all adults have had some form of higher education or training. Sweden has more than 30 universities, including the University of Uppsala, Scandinavia's oldest.

History and Politics

The oldest settlements in Scandinavia appeared before 10,000 BC. The **Vikings**, Scandinavian warriors, raided and conquered territories throughout Europe starting in the eight century AD. The trading routes of the Vikings stretched as far as the Arab world. **Christianity** did not reach Scandinavia until after the eleventh century AD. From 1389 to 1520 Sweden was united with **Norway** and **Denmark** in the Kalmar Union. By the seventeenth century, Sweden had emerged as an important European power and played a significant role in the **Thirty Year's War** (1618 to 1648). However, a devastating defeat in the Great Northern War (1700–1721) led to the end of the Swedish Empire and Swedish dominance of the Baltic Sea.

Sweden declared neutrality during World Wars I and II. Between 1932 and the 1970s, it developed one of the world's most progressive welfare states. The constitution of 1975 defines Sweden as a constitutional monarchy with the sovereign as its head of state. It has a directly elected parliament, the **Riksdag**. The most powerful political party in Sweden is the Social Democratic party, which has been in power for most of the past 70 years. In 1995, Sweden joined the **European Union** but in 2003 Sweden voted against the introduction of the euro as the country's official currency.

Economy

Sweden is one of the wealthiest nations in the world. Although less than a tenth of the country's land is suitable for **agriculture**, Sweden produces around 80 per cent of the food its people consume. The country's vast **forests** as well as its **iron and uranium** reserves support the timber and iron and steel industries. Machinery and machine parts, however, remain the country's most important **exports**. More than 71 per cent of the Swedish work force is employed in the country's robust **service sector**, which accounts for more than a third of the country's gross domestic product. Around one-quarter of the labour force is employed in the **industrial sector** and less than two per cent work in agriculture.

Transport Infrastructure

Sweden has an excellent transport network that covers most of the country. The rail **network**, which is closely integrated into the networks of neighbouring countries, is expected to include several **high-speed train routes** in the

Sweden, Denmark

Stockholm: The Swedish capital is one of the wealthiest and most beautiful cities in Europe. Stockholm is situated on a group of islands and peninsulas between the Baltic Sea and Lake Mälaren. The historic city centre covers the islands Riddarholmen, Helgeandsholmen and Staden. Drottingholm Palace, the residence of Sweden's royal family is near the city centre. King Carl XVI. Gustav is the current reigning monarch of Sweden.

near future. The completion of the impressive 16 km long **Oresund bridge** connects Malmö, the largest city in southern Sweden, to the Danish capital of Copenhagen. Sweden has three international **airports** and is one of the owners of the Scandinavian airline, SAS. The largest **commercial shipping and ferry ports** are Stockholm, Helsingborg and Göteborg.

Tourism

The capital city, **Stockholm, Göteborg**, Sweden's second city and **Malmö** are the most important centres of tourism. Southern Sweden attracts visitors with its beaches, countless lakes, small islands and forests. Central Sweden also has lakes and vast forests as well as the historic university city of **Uppsala**. In northern Sweden, **Lapland**, the home of the Sami people, has pristine, sparsely populated landscapes that are ideal for hiking trips.

Population:
5.4 million
(124 inhabitants/sq. km)

Language:	Danish
GDP per capita:	US$33,500
Currency:	1 euro = 100 cents

Natural Geography

Situated between the North and Baltic seas, Denmark encompasses the peninsula of Jutland and more than **474 islands**, of which only about a quarter are inhabited. **Zeeland**, the largest island, is home to more than 40 per cent of the country's population. The other large islands are **Funen, Lolland, Bornholm** and **Falster**. Only three of Denmark's many islands are situated in the North Sea, **Rømø, Fanø**, and **Mandø**. The landscapes of Jutland include forests, moorlands and heaths as well as coastal wetlands in the west and sands dunes in the north. Nature reserves and conser-

Population

Ethnic **Danes** of Nordic ancestry make up more than 90 per cent of the population. Significant minorities include **Germans** in Jutland, **Swedes, Norwegians** and **Greenlanders**. Recent immigrant communities account for at least five per cent of the Danish population, the majority being from **Turkey**. In addition to Danish, the national official language, German has official status as a minority language in **North Schleswig** on Jutland. The modern Danish **welfare state** guarantees the country's population a high standard of living and excellent social services and health care.

History and Politics

The history of the Danish nation began around 800 AD with the **Viking** warriors who raided the coasts of Europe for generations. By the eleventh century, Vikings

Heligoland to the British. The country was then forced to cede the duchies of Schleswig and Holstein to Prussia after the Danish-Prussian War of 1864. Denmark became **a constitutional monarchy** in 1849 and during the nineteenth century developed into one of the world's most prosperous nations. It declared its neutrality in both **world wars** but was invaded and occupied by German forces in 1940. Denmark has a **unicameral parliament** whose members are elected every four years. The Danish sovereign is the official head of state but the powers granted to the monarchy are largely symbolic. Despite their distance from the Danish mainland, the **Faroes**, a group of 18 rocky islands, 17 of them inhabited, lying between Scotland and Iceland, belong to Denmark. The official language of the islands is Faroese, a Northern Germanic language closely related to Norwegian and Icelandic. Danish, however, plays an impor-

1814, the Faroes remained a part of the Danish kingdom. The Faroes have been an **autonomous province** of Denmark since 1948 and send members to the Danish parliament. Unlike Denmark, the Faroe Islands are not part of the **European Union. Deep-sea fishing** is the islands' most important industry and it has one of the world's largest fishing fleets. A decline in revenue from fishing during the 1990s lead to economic stagnation but the local government has made intensive efforts to diversify the islands' economy. **Fishing** and **mining** are the two most important industries of **Greenland**, an island in the North Atlantic which was a Danish **colony** from the fourteenth century until 1953 and is now a Danish autonomous province. With less than 60,000 inhabitants Greenland, the world's largest island, is also one of the most sparsely populated areas on Earth. That is because more than 80 per cent of

Stockholm: The Swedish kings are buried in Riddarholms church, built in the thirteenth century.

Denmark

Area: 43,094 sq. km;
Greenland 2.176 million sq. km,
Faroe Islands 1,398 sq. km

Capital city:
Copenhagen

Form of government:
Constitutional Monarchy

Administrative divisions:
14 districts

External territories:
Faroe Islands, Greenland

vation areas cover around one-third of the land mass.
Unlike the rest of Scandinavia, Denmark is generally flat.

Climate

Denmark's regions all have a **temperate** climate, although the weather along the Baltic coast tends to be milder than in western Denmark. The average temperature in January, the coldest month, is 0° C rising to 17°C in July, the warmest month.

dominated most of the Baltic and North seas. The rise of the **Hanseatic League** in the late fourteenth century brought Viking control of the Baltic to an end. During the fifteenth century, Denmark was again able to assert its control over much of the Baltic and the surrounding regions. **The Kalmar Union** united the Scandinavian nations under the rule of the Danish crown for more than a century. In 1814, Denmark was forced to surrender control of Norway to Sweden and to give the island of

tant role in the education system. The first settlers in the Faroes arrived from Norway in the early ninth century. Established around 825 AD by early settlers, the Faroese parliament, the **Løgting**, is one of the oldest parliaments in the world. Its members are elected every four years. In 1035, the Faroes came under the control of the Norwegian crown and in 1380 the islands, together with Norway, entered into a union with Denmark. After the union between Norway and Denmark ended in

Greenland is covered by an ice cap throughout the year. The official languages are Greenlandic and Danish. In recent decades, the island has become increasingly self-governing and autonomous.

Economy

Denmark's highly developed economy has shown strong and steady growth in recent years. Although farming dominated the Danish economy into the twentieth century less than five per cent

The once nomadic Sami people have inhabited the grassy moors and tundra of **Lapland** in northern Norway, Sweden, Finland and Russia for at least 2,000 years. The Sami, who have their own languages, divided into several dialects, are now largely integrated into the dominant cultures of their respective home countries.

of Danes are currently employed in **agriculture**. Because the country has few mineral resources Denmark imports most of the natural resources it needs for industry and manufacturing. Major Danish **exports** include agricultural produces, processed foods and drink, shipbuilding, chemicals and machinery as well as products of the country's burgeoning high-tech industries. The **industrial sector** accounts for around 25 per cent of the country's economy. The Danish **service sector**, which accounts for 70 per cent of economic activity, has grown rapidly in recent years.

Transport Infrastructure

Denmark's **rail network** is extensive and well integrated into the country's **shipping and ferries** that connect the various islands and link Denmark to other countries. The largest islands are connected by a series of **bridges**. Zeeland and Funen, the country's largest and most populous islands are connected by the world's second-longest suspension bridge at the time of writing.

Tourism

Millions of tourists visit Denmark each year. In addition to its many **beautiful beaches** and **sailing facilities**, Denmark also has numerous cultural and historic attractions to offer. The major tourist destinations include the vibrant capital city, **Copenhagen** and the historic town of **Roskilde** on the island of Zeeland. **Svendborg** on Funen as well as **Ålborg**, **Århus** and **Esbjerg** on the Jutland peninsula are also tourist attractions, **Odense**, as the birthplace of Hans Christian Andersen, is of particular interest.

Finland

Area:	337,031 sq. km
Capital city:	Helsinki
Form of government:	Republic
Administrative divisions:	
5 provinces and the Åaland Islands	
Population:	
5.2 million	
(15 inhabitants/sq. km)	

Languages:	
Finnish (official), Swedish	
GDP per capita:	US$33,100
Currency:	
1 euro = 100 cents	

Natural Geography

Sparsely populated Finland has a long jagged **coast** that stretches along the Gulf of Bothnia in the west and along the Baltic Sea and Gulf of Finland to the south. Finland owns countless off-shore **islands**, including the largest group, the **Åland Islands**. Around one-tenth of the country is covered by **lakes**, many of which are interconnected by an extensive network of streams

1 Ålesund, one of the most important fishing towns in Norway, is situated at the entrance to the Storfjord.

2 An important harbour for centuries, Copenhagen is Denmark's capitals and one of

Northern Europe's most modern cities.

3 The Swedes cherish their holiday homes. Clusters of these homes are built along most of the coast of Bohuslan province, a region on the shores of the Kattegat.

Finland

*Finland: a country often called 'the land of a thousand lakes' because of the more than 55,000 inland **bodies of water** scattered across its territory. The region around Lake Saimaa in* *south-eastern Finland is a popular and ideal destination for tourists. Lappeenranta, a small city in southern Finland, is a major centre of the tourist industry in Finland.*

and rivers. With the exception of the hilly areas east of the centre of the country, Finland is largely flat. The north includes sections of Lapland's **tundra** and the **Norwegian coastal mountains**. The highest mountain in the region, Haltiantunturi, rises 1,328 m. Large sections of the country are covered by bogs and moors from which peat is harvested in the summer months.

Climate

Most of Finland belongs to the vast belt of coniferous forests that stretches across northern Europe as far as Siberia, while the south-west and the southern islands have a more temperate climate with deciduous vegetation. Finland's **sub-polar continental climate** is characterised by long cold winters with abundant snowfall and warm summers. Helsinki has an average temperature of 6°C in winter 17°C in summer.

History and Politics

The ancestors of the Finns settled the land already before 800 AD. Finland was under **Swedish rule** between the twelfth and eighteenth centuries. It was during this period that **Christianity** was introduced. After numerous wars between Russia and Sweden, the close economic ties to the Soviet Union. The country joined the European Union in 1995. Finland's **constitution**, ratified in 1919, was last altered in 1991. The country has a **unicameral parliament** whose members are elected for four year terms. The president is directly elected by the public for six year terms.

Economy

Finland experienced a period of rapid **industrialisation** after the World War II. During the 1980s, the country experienced another transition from manufacturing to a **services oriented economy**. At least 64 per cent of the Finnish work force is now employed in services and 28 per cent in **industry**, while **forestry and agriculture** employ around eight per cent of workers. Important segments of Finland's industrial sector include the metals, electronics, chemicals, and foodstuffs industries. The country major **export articles** include **paper**, wood, electronics, and machinery. The **oil and natural gas reserves** in northern Finland are currently being exploited in cooperation with Russia. Finland has been a member of the **European Union** since 1995 and one of the founding members of the EU's currency union.

Only eight per cent of Finland is farmland and agriculture plays only a minor role in the nation's economy.

Transport infrastructure

Helsinki is the hub of the Finnish **railway system** which encompasses almost 6,000 km of rail. The country's motorway network is well developed and includes numerous bridges to span the country's many lakes and rivers. Regular **ferry services** travel from Finland to Russia, the Baltic States, and the other Nordic countries. The country's most important international airports are located in Helsinki, Turku, and Tampere.

Tourism

In addition to the country's capital **Helsinki**, Finland's leading tourist destinations include the Åland Islands with their mild climate and the country's countless **lakes**. The cities **Turku** and **Tampere** have numerous cultural and historic attractions.

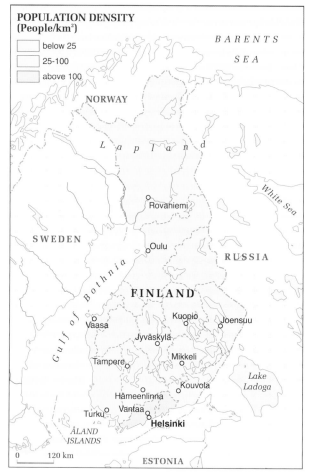

POPULATION DENSITY (People/km²)

- below 25
- 25-100
- above 100

BARENTS SEA

NORWAY

Lapland

White Sea

Rovaniemi

SWEDEN

Oulu

RUSSIA

Gulf of Bothnia

FINLAND

Kuopio
Joensuu
Vaasa
Jyväskylä
Mikkeli
Tampere
Lake Ladoga
Kouvola
Hämeenlinna
Vantaa
Turku
Helsinki
ÅLAND ISLANDS

0   120 km

ESTONIA

Finland's capital, Helsinki, has many historic buildings.

Population

Ethnic **Finns** constitute around 90 per cent of the country's inhabitants. Minorities with Finnish nationality include the large ethnic **Swedish** community (six per cent). The **Sami**, the **Roma**. **Russians** and **Estonians** are the largest ethnic minorities. Finnish and Swedish are the **two official national languages** of Finland. Russian and Sami are also widely spoken in certain regions. More than 80 per cent of the Finnish population are Lutherans.

Swedes surrendered control of Finland to the **Russian Empire** in 1809. Finland was declared a grand duchy of the Russian empire but retained a great deal of local autonomy. The country declared its independence during the **Russian Revolution** of 1917. During the **World War II**, Finland fell within the sphere of influence of both the Soviet Union and Nazi Germany. After a brief war with the Soviet Union, the country was forced to surrender the province **Karelia** to Russia. During the Cold War era Finland adhered to a policy of **neutrality** but maintained

Iceland: The island of ice and fire was created by volcanic activity. Iceland is situated on the Mid-Atlantic Ridge in an area of frequent seismic and volcanic activity. The numerous geysers and solfataras scattered around the island are vivid reminders of the island's geological activity. Iceland's geothermal energy is now used to generate power and warmth for the island's people.

Iceland	
Area:	103,000 sq. km
Capital city:	Reykjavik
Form of government:	Republic
Administrative divisions:	
8 regions	
Population:	
297,000 (3 inhabitants/sq. km)	
Language:	Icelandic
GDP per capita:	US$34,600
Currency:	
1 Icelandic krona = 100 aurar	

Natural Geography

Iceland is a large and ancient volcanic **island** in the North Atlantic situated just below the **Arctic Circle**. Most of the population inhabits the coastal region, while most of the largely **barren interior** is uninhabited. Numerous fjords run inland from the coast. Iceland is situated on a so-called 'hot spot', an area of volcanic activity. Consequently, it has no fewer than 27 **active volcanoes**, many of which are buried beneath glaciers and ice caps.

The island is covered in **geysers**, hot springs and lava fields which give Iceland a continuously changing landscape.

Iceland emerged from the ocean around 16 million years ago at the junction of the North American and Eurasian tectonic plates. More than a tenth of the island's surface is covered by glaciers, including the largest glacier in Europe, the **Vatnajökull**. Occasional volcanic eruptions beneath the surface of the glaciers can cause massive streams of water to be released and pour out from the interior to the coast. Around half of the country's territory consists of **tundra** covered in sub-arctic vegetation.

Climate

Thanks to the **Gulf Stream,** Iceland is situated in a transition area between a **sub-arctic** and a **cool temperate** zone. The air masses that pass over it have a major effect on the weather of distant parts of western and central Europe.

Winters in Iceland are long and bitterly cold. The summers are relatively short and cool but temperatures above 20°C are not uncommon. In the highlands of the interior snow can fall at any time of year, even in summer. Strong winds blow across Iceland throughout the year.

Population

Icelandic, a Germanic language closely related to Norwegian, is spoken by all of the relatively small population. The country has no significant ethnic minority communities other than some American army personnel, Scandinavians and guest workers from Eastern Europe. The Icelanders are the descendants of Norse and Celtic settlers who arrived from the British Isles and Scandinavia. More than 90 per cent of Icelanders are **Protestant**, although church attendance is low.

The standard of education is one of the highest and the illiteracy rate the lowest in the world. In rural districts, **travelling teachers** ensure that even children in the most remote regions have access to **education**. The country's only university is located in Reykjavik, the capital, where almost half the population lives.

The public health and welfare systems of Iceland are among the best in the world; around half of government revenues are invested in them.

History and politics

Roman sailors may have reached the islands in the third century AD and ancient chronicles tell of Irish monks who lived on the island in the sixth century. The first permanent settlers were **explorers from Norway** who arrived in the ninth century. In 930 AD, the Norse settlers on Iceland founded the **Althing**, a **parliament** which is now the oldest in the world.

Christianity was introduced to Iceland around 1000. The island was ruled by Norway in the thirteenth century and Denmark in the fourteenth century. An **independence movement** emerged in the nineteenth century, and Iceland had achieved considerable **autonomy** by 1918. During World War II, the island was occupied by the British and Americans, preventing a German invasion. In 1944, the island's leaders declared **independence** from Denmark. Iceland was a founding member of **NATO**. It maintains no army of it own but is home to large American army bases.

Economy

Iceland's declared territorial waters now extend almost 200 nautical miles from the coast. This has led to tension with other nations, especially the United Kingdom. **Fishing and fish processing** remains the backbone of the economy, employing than a fifth of the labour force. Animal husbandry, especially horse and cattle breeding, remains important and now accounts for around one-tenth of the country's GDP. Iceland's potentially vast **mineral resources** (aluminium, diatomite) will be increasingly exploited. The most important natural resource is its enormous **geothermal and hydroelectric power**. These renewable energy sources come from the geysers and hot springs that have been harnessed to heat greenhouses in which fruit and vegetables are grown. The **tourism industry** has grown in importance in recent years, thanks to the island's natural wonders

Transport infrastructure

The only major road is the 1600-km **ring road** around the island only around one-tenth of which is paved. There is a bus service runs between the country's main population centres, but no **railway**. Regular direct flights connect Iceland to several major cities in North America and Europe. The only international **airport** is in Reykjavik. **Passenger ferries** ply between Greenland, Norway, Great Britain and the Faroes.

Tourism

Iceland is an increasingly popular tourist destination. The rivers are ideal for rafting and the landscapes of the interior appeal to hikers. **Reykjavík**, the northernmost capital in the world, is the starting point for tours of the island. Iceland's political history began in **Thingvellir National Park** near Reykjavik more than a thousand years ago. **Skaftafell National Park** covers the southern half of the Vajnajökull glacier. A series of islands off the west coast are home to large colonies of **birds**.

LAND USE
- Glacier
- Pasture
- Barren land

GEOTHERMAL POWER
- Sources with temperature above 100°C
- Main sources with temperature below 100°C
- Electric power plants

0   75 km

Estonia, Latvia, Lithuania

Riga and Tallinn: Both northern Baltic capitals feature a wealth of historic architecture including medieval and art nouveau buildings. The cities were major Hanseatic ports during the Middle Ages.

Estonia

Area:	45,226 sq. km
Capital city:	Tallinn

Form of government:
Parliamentary Republic
Administrative divisions:
15 regions, 6 urban districts
Population:
1.3m (30 inhabitants/sq. km)
Languages:
Estonian (official), Russian

GDP per capita:	US$16,400

Currency:
1 Estonian kroon = 100 senti

Natural Geography

The northernmost of the three Baltic republics is bounded by the **Gulf of Finland** to the north and the Baltic Sea to the west. Estonia is a largely flat country with countless rivers, lakes, moors and marshes as well as more than **1500 islands** and islets.

Climate

Estonia has a **cool temperate climate**, although the weather in the interior tends to be warmer in summer than at the coast.

Population

Around 65 per cent of the population are ethnic **Estonians**. The largest minorities are **Russians** who constitute 29 per cent of the population and there are smaller communities of **Ukrainians, Belarusians** and **Finns**. Estonia's official language is Estonian, although Russian is widely spoken. The integration of the large Russian minority remains one of the country's major social challenges. Estonia has **two universities**, in Tallinn and in Tartu.

History and Politics

The small country on the Baltic coast fell to the **Danes** in 1219. For most of the centuries that followed Estonia remained under **foreign domination**; in 1561 the region became a territory of **Sweden** and in 1721 it was handed over to the Russian Empire. In 1918, Estonia declared its **independence** but the Soviets under Joseph Stalin occupied Estonia in 1941. After five decades of Soviet

rule, Estonia gained **independence** in 1991. The unicameral parliament, the Riigikogu, is elected every four years.

Economy

A series of economic **reforms** and **privatisations** in the early 1990s allowed Estonia to experience subsequent strong growth. The **export sector** was given a boost when Estonia joined the European Union in 2004. The **service sector**, including the IT industry, now accounts for most of GDP. Favourable taxation has lured investment from other EU member states, especially neighbouring Finland.

Transport Infrastructure

Estonia's only international **airport** is located near the capital, Tallinn. Regular **ferry services** connect Tallinn with Helsinki and Stockholm as well as other cities on the Baltic Sea.

Tourism

Tallinn is the centre of the tourist industry. Several lakes are situated in the region around **Tartu**. The Baltic Sea islands **Saaremaa** and **Hiiumaa** are also popular.

Latvia

Area:	64,589 sq. km
Capital city:	Riga
Form of government:	Republic

Administrative divisions:
33 districts
Population:
2.29m (36 inhabitants/sq. km)
Languages: Latvian (official),

Russian

GDP per capita:	US$12,800

Currency: 1 Lats = 100 santimas

Natural geography

The country is bordered by the **Baltic Sea**, into which extends the **Courland peninsula**. The interior is mainly fertile lowland. The **Western Dvina** flows through the country before draining into the eastern marshes. This region is dotted with numerous **lakes**, and conifers cover 40 per cent of the land.

Population

The population is 56 per cent **Latvian** and 30 per cent **Russian**, with smaller groups of Belarusians, Ukrainians and Poles. Latvia is 55 per cent **Protestant**, and 24 per cent **Catholic**. Nine per cent of the population belong to the **Russian Orthodox** church.

The old town district of Belarus' capital city Minsk.

History and Politics

The **Teutonic Knights** and the merchants of the **Hanseatic League** dominated Latvia during the Middle Ages. Latvia came under the control of Tsarist **Russia** in the eighteenth century. Although it declared its **independence** from Russia in 1918 it became part of the Soviet Union in 1939. In 1991, **Latvia** and the other two Baltic states declared their independence. The last Russian military base on Latvian soil was closed in August 1998.

Economy

Agriculture continues to play an important role in the economy of

many Latvian regions. Vegetables and cereals are cultivated throughout the country. **Fishing** also remains an important industry. **Manufacturing,** including machine tools, spare parts and electronics, account for just under one-third of the country's gross domestic product. Most of the country's former state enterprises have been **privatised**. About 60 per cent of the labour force is employed in the service sector.

Transport Infrastructure

Latvia's only international airport, **Riga International Airport** is situated several miles outside the capital city.

Tourism

Latvia's **national parks** and the historic old city of **Riga** are the most popular tourist attractions and have become increasingly popular since independence.

Lithuania

Area:	65,200 sq. km
Capital city:	Vilnius

Form of government:
Parliamentary Republic
Administrative divisions:
10 districts
Population:
3.6m (55 inhabitants/sq. km)
Languages: Lithuanian (official), Russian

GDP per capita:	US$13,700

Currency: 1 Litas = 100 centas

Natural Geography

Situated between the **Baltic Sea**

and **Belarus**, Lithuania is the southernmost Baltic nation. Marshlands, **plains** and thick forests cover most of the land mass.

Climate

Lithuania's coast has a **cool maritime climate**, while the interior has a **continental climate** with greater seasonal variation in temperature.

Population

Lithuanians constitute at least 80 per cent of the country's population. Significant minorities include communities of ethnic **Russians, Ukrainians** and **Poles**.

History and Politics

The first Lithuanian **kingdom** stretched from the Baltic Sea to the **Black Sea**. Lithuania joined **Poland** to form the Polish-Lithuanian Commonwealth in 1385. The country fell to the **Russian Empire** in 1772. In 1918, Lithuania was declared an **independent republic** but was invaded and annexed by the **Soviet Union** in 1940. In 1990, Lithuania became the first **republic** of the Soviet Union to declare its independence. The 141 members of the country's parliament, the **Sejm**, are directly elected for a five-year term. Lithuania joined the European Union in 2004 with the other Baltic states.

Economy

Agriculture continues to play an important role in the economy accounting for more than a tenth of GDP. Lithuania has few mineral resources, although offshore **oil reserves** in the Baltic Sea are being explored. **Manufacturing** accounts for one-third of economic activity. The **service sector** is the fastest growing segment of the economy.

Transport Infrastructure

Lithuania has two international **airports**, at Vilnius and Kaunas. The main **port** is Klaipeda.

Tourism

The **Courland Spit** is a nature conservation area, and the many **national parks** and capital city, **Vilnius,** are great tourist attractions.

Belarus' cultural roots stretch back to the time of the first settlements by non-Christian Slavic groups. Elements of these cultures survive in the country's traditional culture, including local music and poetry. Brightly coloured paintings are typical of region's traditional art. This influence is clearly apparent is the works of the region's most famous painter, Marc Chagall.

Belarus	
Area:	207,600 sq. km
Capital city:	Minsk
Form of government:	Republic
Administrative divisions:	
6 regions, 1 district (capital city)	
Population:	
10.3m (50 inhabitants/sq. km)	
Languages:	
Belarusian, Russian (official)	
GDP per capita.:	7,600 US$
Currency: 1 Belarusian rouble =	
100 kapiejkas	

Natural geography

Situated on the vast **lowland** that expands through most of **Eastern Europe**, Belarus is an extraordinarily flat country covering wide plains. In addition to plains, the Belarussian landscapes are characterised by numerous rivers, lakes and large marshy forests. The **Pripyet Marsh** in southern Belarus is one of the largest marshes and moor lands in Europe.

Climate

Belarus has a **continental climate** with cold winters.

Population

At least 78 per cent of the population consists of **Belarusians**. **Russians** are the country's largest minority, constituting 14 per cent of the total population. Like many other former members of the Soviet Union, Belarus is experiencing significant demographic changes, including a declining and ageing population.

History and Politics

Because of the relative isolation, the Slavs who inhabited Belarus in the middle ages were able to preserve their distinct culture and language, despite periods of **Polish** and **Lithuanian** domination. The union with **Russia** in the late eighteenth century led to a revival of the country's culture and traditions. In 1919, Belarus was declared a sovereign communist state but joined the **Soviet Union** just three years later. Although of-ficially a democratic republic, Belarus has an **authoritarian government** dominated the president.

Economy

A decline in production, inflation, and **debt** crippled the country's economy after the collapse of the Soviet Union. Despite this, the government has initiated some reforms to modernise the economy though many companies remain under **state control**. **Agriculture** contributes about 16 per cent of the country's gross domestic product. **Industry** accounts for more than 40 per cent of economic activity. Belarus has rich, untapped natural resources.

Transport Infrastructure

The capital city Minsk is the hub of the **rail network** and is situated along the main rail route connecting Moscow and Warsaw. Minsk International Airport is the country's most important air transport hub.

Tourism

Minsk, the capital and its largest city, is the most popular tourist destination, as are the country's many **lakes** and forests.

The European Union

Above: West German chancellor Adenauer, diplomat Walter Hallstein and Italian Prime Minister Segni at a 1957 conference in Rome.

Integration of post-war Europe began with the ratification of the Treaty of Rome by the founding members of the European Union in 1957. European Union successes include the creation of the world's largest trading bloc and the introduction of a common currency, the euro. After decades of focusing on economic concerns, the EU is increasingly moving towards political integration of the member states.

The union of sovereign nations, created after a century of devastating nationalist wars in Europe, was formed from the merger of three previous unions. The European Coal and Steel Community (ECSC) was formed in 1952 when France, Germany, Italy, the Netherlands and the Benelux countries created a single market for coal, iron and steel. The ECSC was absorbed into the European Economic Community (EEC) created in 1957 with the ratification of the Treaty of Rome; it aimed at a single market for all the member states. The European Atomic Energy Community (EURATOM) was created at the same time. Rome

In 1967 the EEC, Euratom and the ECSC merged to the form the European Community (EC). The community quickly expanded and welcomed new members; in 1973 Denmark, the United Kingdom and the Republic of Ireland joined the EC. Greece became the tenth member in 1981 and Spain and Portugal joined in 1986. In the same year, the EC member states agreed to give the organisation's parliament more political power and to further integrate the members' economies.

The Single European Act, an important step for the European free market, was ratified in 1986 and came into effect in 1987.

The modern European Union was created in February 1992 at a summit of European leaders held in the Dutch city of Maastricht. The Maastricht Treaty created a new union, one that had wider political and economic powers. In 1995, three new members joined the union; Finland, Austria and Sweden. Economic and monetary union was achieved in 1999 with the introduction of the euro. Eleven member states (Belgium, Germany, Finland, Austria, Spain, Portugal, the Netherlands, France, Ireland, Italy

The Euro, since 1 January 2002 the shared currency in 12 countries of the EU.

Photos from left to right: EU offices in Brussels, Portuguese EU-politician José Manuel Barroso.

and Luxembourg) chose it to replace their national currencies. A year later, Greece also adopted the euro. On 1 January, 2002 the euro was brought into circulation and become the official currency in these countries. It also became the official currency of several small European states bordering the EU – Andorra, Monaco, San Marino and the Vatican City. Denmark, Sweden and the United Kingdom chose not to adopt the euro.

The European Union now consists of a large network of institutions and agencies. The European Parliament meets in Luxembourg and in Strasbourg, France. The parliament plays an important role in the EU's law-making process and controls the budget. Members of the European Parliament are directly elected for five-year terms by constituents in their home countries. The European Commission is the most powerful organ of the European Union. Decisions made by the Commission are binding upon member states and the other bodies of the European Union. The European Commission, which is based in Brussels, functions as an executive branch of the European Union. The Commission currently consists of 25 commissioners who are each appointed by a different member state and confirmed by the European Parliament. EU commissioners are expected to be independent from their home country's government. They are at the head of the EU's large bureaucracy in Brussels.

The heads of states of the Union's member nations meet at least twice in the country that holds the rotating EU presidency for a half-yearly term. In addition to the Parliament, the EU's legislative branch also includes the Council of the European Union, also known as the Council of Ministers.

The highest judicial body in the European Union is the European Court of Justice. Based in Luxembourg, the court has the power to overturn many decisions and policies of national governments that it considers to be contradictory to EU law. Since June 1998, the Frankfurt-based European Central Bank (ECB) has been in charge of the monetary policy of the Eurozone, the group of EU member states whose currency is the euro.

Further integration of the European Union's member states is planned in the many areas, including foreign policy, defence and internal legislation.

In April 2003, the European Union experienced the greatest expansion in its history when a treaty was ratified admitting ten new member states into the organisation. These are the Baltic states (Latvia, Estonia, Lithuania) former Soviet satellites (Hungary, Poland, the Czech Republic and Slovakia) as well as Slovenia, Malta and Cyprus. These countries officially joined the union on May 2004 bringing the population of the European Union to more than 450 million. Bulgaria and Romania are shortly to be admitted if they meet the economic and social criteria.

The European Parliament in Strasbourg.

The Netherlands: The Dutch have reclaimed a large portion of their country from the sea over many centuries. Former beaches and salt marshes have been transformed into fertile fields producing important crops such as flowers and cereals. The historic windmills scattered around the country were once used to grind wheat and barley and pump water from the fields.

Netherlands

Area:	41,526 sq. km
Capital city:	Amsterdam
(Seat of government: The Hague)	
Form of government:	
Constitutional Monarchy	
Administrative divisions:	
12 provinces, 2 overseas regions	
Population: 16.4 million	
(387 inhabitants/sq. km)	
Language: Dutch	
GDP per capita:	US$30,500
Currency:	1 euro = 100 cents

Natural Geography

More than a quarter of this flat country beside the North Sea on the **Northern European Plain** lies below sea level. Low-lying areas are protected by an extensive network of **dykes**, canals and pumps. The only significant elevations (up to 320 m) are in the south-east. The islands of West Friesland are also Dutch. Almost one-sixth of the country consists of lakes and rivers. Land is still being reclaimed from the sea.

Climate

The temperate **maritime (warm, damp) climate** of the Netherlands is affected by the Gulf Stream.

Population

Citizens of the **Netherlands** of Dutch ancestry comprise more than 90 per cent of the country's population. Significant minorities include communities of Turks, Moroccans and German-speakers as well as those whose trace their ancestry to the former Dutch colonies such as Surinam and Indonesia.

More than a third of the Dutch people have no religious affiliation. About 59 per cent identify as Christians; 36 per cent of the population is **Catholic** and at least 25 per cent are members of **Protestant** churches. Dutch is the official language and Frisian is a recognised minority language in the province of Frisia.

History and Politics

The Low Countries finally threw off the yoke of **Spanish** domination in 1648. By the next century, it had become the **most powerful naval and trading power** in Europe. In 1831, the Austrian Provinces (today's Belgium), declared independence from the Netherlands, but the newly created **Kingdom of the Netherlands** remained a strong world power, thanks to its overseas territories. Despite declaring neutrality in **World War II**, the Netherlands were occupied by Germany. After the war, the Netherlands became a the founding member of **NATO**. The capital, the Hague is the home of the International Courts of Justice.

Since the 1986 constitution, the Caribbean Island of **Aruba** has enjoyed a special status. The neighbouring **Netherlands Antilles**, whose main island is Curaçao, have belonged to the Netherlands since 1634, and have been **self-governing** since 1954.

Economy

The **service sector** dominates the Dutch economy accounting for 70 per cent of the country's GDP. Thanks to its location, the country has always been an important **international trading centre**.

The **agricultural sector** is highly developed. Major exports include tomatoes, cucumbers, peppers and flowers, most of which are now grown in hi-tech greenhouses. The Netherlands are the world's third largest exporter of agricultural produce (after the United States and France). **Fishing** was once a leading export, and remains an important source of income and jobs along the coast. The **industrial sector** is diverse and advanced; important exports from this sector include machinery, cars and trucks, technology and chemicals.

Tourism

The Netherlands' leading tourist destinations include the **North Sea coast** with its beaches and islands as well as the country's main cities, **Amsterdam, The Hague,** and **Leiden,** all of which contain many historical and cultural attractions, including museums housing paintings by the Dutch Old Masters. The **tulip fields** remain a great attraction.

Belgium

Area:	30,528 sq. km
Capital city:	Brussels
Form of government:	
Constitutional Monarchy	
Administrative divisions:	
3 regions (Flanders, Wallonia, Brussels)	
Population:	
10.3 million	
(333 inhabitants/sq. km)	
Languages:	
French, Flemish, German	
GDP per capita:	US$31,800
Currency:	1 euro = 100 cents

Natural Geography

The dunes of the **North Sea coast** protect a series of fertile plains and sandy heaths over most of the north and west, while fertile **low hills** extend through out most of southern Belgium. East of the Meuse (Maas) river, Belgium's terrain is dominated by the rolling hills of the heavily forested Ardennes and the High Fens (Hautes Fagnes).

Population

The Belgians are a nation divided by language; around 56 per cent of the Belgian people are **Dutch-speakers** and 32 per cent are **Francophone Walloons**. There is a German-speaking community in the east near the German border. More than three-quarters of the population is Roman Catholic and at least three percent are Muslims. Smaller communities of Jews and Protestants have a long history in Belgium.

History and Politics

During the late middle ages, the cities of **Flanders** were among the greatest centres of trade and commerce in Europe. However, most of Belgium remained under foreign control for centuries. The **Spanish** controlled most of Belgium in the sixteenth and seventeenth centuries, followed by the **Austrians** and eventually the **French** and the **Dutch**. The country finally became an **independent kingdom** in 1831. Radical changes to the constitution lead to the kingdom's restructuring as a **federal national** with autonomous regions and a complicated political structure. Modern Belgium is now comprised of three culturally and linguistically distinct **regions** (Flanders, Wallonia, and Brussels); each region possessing a great deal of political **autonomy** with their own regional parliaments and courts. Belgium's head of state is the country's **monarch**. The defence alliance **NATO** and the **European Union** both have their headquarters in Brussels.

Economy

Belgium's productive **agricultural sector** accounts for less than two per cent of the country's GDP. Wallonia was one of the first areas in Europe to industrialise, although most of its **heavy industries** such as steel production and coal mining are in decline. The **service sector** currently accounts for at least 70 per cent of the country's economic activity.

Transport Infrastructure

Belgium has one of the world's most extensive **railway networks**. In addition to Brussels International Airport, the country also has four other international airports. **Antwerp** in Flanders has one of the world's busiest harbours. Important **inland harbours** include Brussels, Ghent, and Liege.

Tourism

Bruges and **Ghent** as well as the main cities of **Brussels** and **Antwerp** are popular tourist destinations. Belgian seaside resorts continue to draw visitors. **Hautes Fagnes National Park** is popular with hikers.

Historic buildings on the Grand Place in Belgium's capital city Brussels.

Alkmaar: Until World War II, agriculture dominated the economy of the Netherlands. Even now the country has a strong agricultural sector, producing hothouse fruits and vegetables as well as excellent cheeses. Alkmaar has the country's oldest and most traditional cheese market which is a tourist attraction.*

Luxembourg	

Area: 2,586 sq. km
Capital city: Luxembourg City
Form of government:
Constitutional Monarchy
Administrative divisions:
3 districts with 12 cantons
Population:
469,000 (inhabitants/sq. km)
Languages: Luxembourgish,
French, German
GDP per capita: US$62,700
Currency: 1 euro = 100 cents

Natural Geography

Luxembourg, one of Europe's smallest nations, shares borders with Germany, Belgium, and France. The **hills and forests** of the **Ardennes** dominate the northern part of the country. The south, like neighbouring areas in Germany, has several river valleys. Much of the country is covered by forests and many river valleys are devoted to **wine cultivation**.

Population

At least a third of Luxembourg's population consist of foreign workers, mostly from other European nations, including a significant number from Portugal (39.9 per cent), Italy (13.5 per cent), France (11.2 per cent), Belgium (8.9 per cent), and Germany (6.8 per cent).

History and Politics

Luxembourg became a **duchy** in the fourteenth century and was a member of the German confederation between 1814 and 1866, when it finally become a completely **independent nation**. Luxembourg abandoned its policy of neutrality after its **occupation by German forces** during the World War II. The small nation was a founding member of **NATO** and the **European Union**. Luxembourg head of state is the **Grand Duke**, who has considerable re-serve powers. The sixty members of the nation's parliament are directly elected for five year terms.

Economy

Luxembourg is one of the wealthiest nations in the EU and the world. The country's economy is highly dependent on **foreign trade**. Heavy industry, including **steel and iron production**, was once vital to the economy but has been in decline for decades. The **service sector**, especially the **financial and banking sectors**, is now the backbone of the economy and accounts for 70 per cent of all jobs in Luxembourg. The European Court of Auditors and several other EU institutions have offices in Luxembourg.

Tourism

The lovely countryside and the architecture of the historic cities are tourist attractions. **Luxembourg City** with its well preserved architecture and royal palace is the most popular destination.

France

*Savoir vivre: France is one of the world's leading producers and consumers of **wine** with the average **Frenchman** consuming 63 l of wine annually. Several French regions are well known for their high quality local wines.*

France

Area: 547,030 sq km
Capital city: Paris
Form of government:
Parliamentary Republic
Administrative divisions:
22 regions, 96 départements,
9 independent territories
External territories:
French Guyana, Guadeloupe,
Martinique, Réunion, Mayotte,
Saint Pierre and Miquelon, French
Polynesia, New Caledonia, Wallis
and Futuna
Population: 60.6 million
(110 inhabitants/sq km)
Languages: French (official), and
many dialects, including Alsatian,
Breton, Basque, Occitan and
Languedoc
GDP per capita: US$29,000
Currency: 1 euro = 100 cents

Natural Geography

The hexagon-shaped country stretches between the **English Channel** in the north and the **Mediterranean Sea** in the south and borders the Atlantic Ocean as well as the **Bay of Biscay** in the west. Most of France is largely hilly or consist of flat fertile plains. High mountain ranges on the country's periphery form natural borders to several of France's neighbours; in the south the **Pyrenees** and in the east the **Alps**. River basins encompass much of northern and western France, while the plateaus and mountains

of the **Massif Central** extend through large parts of southern and central France. Several important rivers flow through including the **Loire**, **Rhone**, and the **Seine** rivers.

Climate

The regions along the English Channel and Atlantic Coast, including the provinces of Normandy and Brittany, share a **temperate maritime climate** with abundant precipitation. The interior has a **mild continental climate** with warm summers and cool winters. Southern France has a **Mediterranean climate** with dry and hot summers and mild rainy winters.

Population

French citizens form the vast majority of the country's population. The country, however, has one of the most diverse populations in Europe. A large per cent of French

The Arc de Triomphe: a monument to the glory of Napoleon's army.

citizens are the descendants of recent immigrants, including many people of **Italian, Spanish, East Asian, North African, Caribbean**, and **West African** descent. Around 81 per cent of the French people identify as **Roman Catholics**, although levels of church attendance are relatively low. In addition to Catholics, around five million **Muslims**, at least 900,000 **Protestants**, and more than 700,000 **Jews** live in France. In addition to French, **regional dialects** are widely spoken, mainly Breton, Corsican,

Basque and Alsatian. The French **educational system** is considered to be one of the best in the world. Many students attend one of the more than 90 universities and institutions of higher education, including the elite 'grandes ecoles'.

History and Politics

Once the Roman province of Gaul, invaders from the East overran

France in the fifth century AD. **Clovis I**, who converted to Christianity in the early fifth century, founded the Merovingian Dynasty that ruled much of France for centuries. The Frankish king **Charlemagne** united France with Saxony and Bavaria and had himself declared emperor. France only emerged as a distinct nation with after the division of the Frankish Empire in

Palace of Versailles: The grandiose palace complex was designed by the architects Le Vau and Harouin-Mansart at the behest of Louis XIV, France's absolutist monarch. Connected to the impressive garden Le Nôtre, *the palace was constructed in the late seventeenth century. Between 1682 and 1789, the year of the French Revolution, Versailles as the home of the king was the centre of political power in France.*

centuries, a form of government that reached its peak during the reign of **Louis XIV** during the seventeenth century. The **French Revolution** which began in 1789 was an important development for the emergence of democracy in Europe but ended in the **Reign of Terror**, a period of brutal repressions that left thousands dead. **Napoleon Bonaparte**, a Corsican general, was declared emperor of France in 1804. The **Napoleonic Code**, which influenced legal systems around the world, was introduced during his reign. After many spectacular **victories** Napoleon's armies were defeated at the **Battle of Waterloo** in 1815. The **Congress of Vienna** led to a short-lived **restoration** of the French monarchy. This period ended in revolution in 1848. In 1871, the **Second Empire** of Napoleon III was toppled after France's defeat in the Franco-Prussian War. France fought against Germany during **World War** I; most of the bloodiest battles being fought on French soil. After the war, Alsace and Lorraine were restored to France after almost five decades of German rule. Northern France and the Atlantic coast were occupied by German troops during the **World War II** and a collaborationist regime known as **Vichy**

888. The country was divided into rival **duchies** and **principalities**, while **Normandy** was conquered by the Vikings. In the 987 the **Capet** dynasty united large areas of France and would rule the country on and off until 1848. France emerged victorious from the long **Hundred Years War** (1338–1453) with England. **Joan of Arc** who led to march to expel the English out of Paris is still revered as a French national heroine. The French **nation-state** was ruled by an **absolutist** monarchy for

France ruled the south. General **Charles de Gaulle** dominated the politics and development of France in the post-war decades. Most of France's **colonies** began to demand their independence and the process of decolonisation began. In 1952, Algeria became

the last major French colony to be granted independence after a demoralising war of liberation. The current constitution, ratified in 1958, defines France as democratic presidential republic. France has a **bicameral parliament** that consists of a senate and a **national assembly**. The heads of state are the **president**, who is

1 Located on the coast of Normandy in northern France, the historic abbey built atop Mont-Saint-Michel.

2 The Eiffel Tower, Paris' most famous landmark, rises 320 m high, taller than all the modern office towers built along the Seine in recent decades.

3 The seaside resort town of Menton is built on a group of coastal hills near the Italian border. The French Riviera (Côte d'Azur) is popular destination.

The South of France: Provence's colourful fields of lavender are not only beautiful but also play an important role in southern France's historic perfume industry. Lavender oil from the region is used to produce soaps, cosmetics, and perfumes. During the Middle Ages Christian pilgrims passing through the region on their way to Santiago de Compostela found shelter in the many local monasteries.

elected for a seven-year term, and the **prime minister** who heads the Council of Ministers. The Mediterranean island of **Corsica** was purchased from the Italian city-state Genoa in 1768 and is now the largest French island. After decades of local agitation, Corsica now has a unique political status and enjoys greater local political autonomy than most other French regions.

France's numerous overseas territories are a legacy of the country's history as a colonial empire. These territories include **French Guyana** in South America, the small islands of **Saint-Pierre and Miquelon** off the Newfoundland in Canada, the Caribbean islands of **Martinique** and **Guadeloupe** and the Indian Ocean island **Reunion** near Mauritius as well as **New Caledonia, Wallis and Futuna**, and the islands of **French Polynesia** in the South Pacific.

Economy

After the World War II France made a rapid transition from an **agrarian** economy to one of the world's leading **industrialised nations**. The country was one of the founding members of the **European Economic Community** in the 1960s. More than 50 per cent of mainland France is devoted to **agriculture**. Major agricultural products include grain, sugar beet, potatoes, fruit and wine. Thanks in part to EU subsidies, France is now the world's second **exporter of agricultural produce**, after the United States. The most important **manufacturing sector**, which accounts for 30 percent of GDP, include machine and textile production. The **service sector** now constitutes 70 percent of France's total economic activity and 68 percent of the French workforce is now employed in this sector.

Transport Infrastructure

The **TGV**, France's high speed train system, is the most popular symbol of France's excellent **railway network**. The train connects the country's largest cities at speed up to 300 km per hour. Completed in 1994, the **Channel Tunnel** made high speed train connections between France and Great Britain possible. The country's **network of roads** has a total length of 1.5 million km, more than of which are paved. Charles de Gaulle international airport near Paris is the most important of France's ten **international airports**. A network of historic canals, including many which were built in the Middle Ages, spans France. Rouen and Bordeaux are the country's most important **inland ports** for traffic along the country's rivers and **canals**. The most important **sea ports** in France are Marseilles on the Mediterranean coast and Le Havre on the northern coast.

Tourism

France is often ranked as the most popular tourist destination in the world and each year tens of millions of foreign tourist visit the country.

Paris is both the country's capital and its most popular tourist destination. The city has a wealth of sights including countless historic and cultural attractions such as the Louvre and the Eiffel Tower. The section of the **Loire Valley** between Angers and Orleans contains beautiful landscapes and is famous for its many châteaux and gardens in France.

The **French Riviera**, the coastline between the Spanish and the Italian border, has fashionable resorts such as Cannes, Nice and St. Tropez, charming fishing villages and beautiful beaches.

Winter sports and breathtaking views lure many visitors to the **Pyrenees** and the **French Alps**. Important ski resorts in France include Albertville, Val-d'Isère and Chamonix. Other popular rural destinations are Brittany, Provence and Perigord, with their unspoiled countryside.

Area:	1.95 sq. km
Capital city:	Monaco City
Form of government:	
Constitutional Monarchy	
Administrative divisions:	
Principality	
Population: 32,300	
(16,476 inhabitants/sq. km)	
Languages: French (official),	
Monegasque, Italian	
GDP per capita:	US$32,400
Currency: 1 euro = 100 cents	

Natural Geography

Bordered by **France**, the small principality sits in a small bay on the **Mediterranean**, surrounded by **limestone hills**. Monaco is the world's second smallest independent nation but the country's land area has been significantly expanded through land reclamation in recent decades. Monaco, one of the world's most densely populated states, consists of four districts; Monte Carlo (with beaches and the famous casino), La Condamine (the port), Monaco-Ville (the historic fortified city) and the new district Fontieville, a commercial area created on reclaimed land.

---

*Lille, 22.11.1890,
†Colombey-les-deux-Eglises, 9.11.1970

Charles de Gaulle fought in World War I and achieved the rank of general. After the defeat and occupation of France in 1940, he led the Free French resistance from exile in London. In 1944 de Gaulle returned to France and was appointed leader of the country's provisional government. As founder of the RPF party (Reassemblement du people Francais), he dominated French politics in the early 1950s, but dissolved the party in 1953. After the military revolt in Algeria, he was appointed prime minister and soon after became the first president of the fifth French Republic. Granted wide ranging powers by the new constitution, he ended the war in Algeria and played a major role in the reconciliation between post-war France and Germany. De Gaulle remained president until his resignation in 1969.

The old town and harbour of Cannes in southern France.

*Koblenz, 2.2.1926

He occupied several ministerial posts during the 1960s and founded the National Centre for Independent Republicans in 1966. Giscard was elected president in 1974 but was defeated at the polls by Francois Mitterrand in 1981. He was selected to head the Convention for a European Constitution in 2001 and was admitted to the Académie francaise in 2003.

*Jarnac, 26.10.1916,
†Paris, 8.1.1996

The socialist president occupied various ministerial posts during the 1960s. He was elected secretary of the French Socialist Party in 1971 and was only narrowly defeated in 1974 presidential elections. He was elected President in 1981 and served in that office until 1995, making him the longest serving French President.

POPULATION DENSITY (People/km²)

below 25	100-250
25-50	250-500
50-75	above 500
75-100	

*Monte Carlo: Monaco's most glamourous district lures visitors with its beach and famous historic casino. Because of its low taxes, many wealthy Europeans choose to reside in **Monaco**.*

Native Monegasques now constitute only 15 per cent of the country's population. Several new areas have been reclaimed from the sea to accommodate the demand for building space.

Climate

Monaco has a **Mediterranean climate** with mild winters and warm often dry summers.

Population

Native **Monegasques** now form only around 17 per cent of the principality's population. The rest of the population consists largely of foreign residents including significant numbers of French citizens, who now constitute more than half of the country's population. Many of the more affluent foreign residents move to the principality to take advantage of the Monaco's **low tax levels**. Monaco abolished its income tax laws in 1865. French and the indigenous Monegasque language are both taught in school although French is now the dominant language in the country.

History and Politics

Founded in the thirteenth century as a **Genoese colony**, Monaco first came under the control of the **Grimaldi** dynasty in 1297. The dynasty, one of the longest reigning in Europe, still rules today. Monaco gained **full independence** in 1861 after centuries as a Spanish and later a French protectorate. In 1918, the principality signed a treaty with France that committed the French to defend Monaco against foreign military threats. Monaco also has a customs and currency union with **France** and the euro is the common currency of both countries.
Constitutional reforms in 1911 and 1962 shifted the country's government away from a system of absolute monarchy to one of **constitutional monarchy** with a strong parliament. Members of Monaco's National Council are directly elected for five-year terms. All Monegasque citizens above the age of 21 are eligible to vote. The head of government, who is required by law to be a French citizen, is appointed by the country's **reigning monarch**. Until 2002, a historic agreement between Monaco and France stipulated that should the Grimaldi dynasty fail to produce a male heir sovereignty over Monaco would be given to France. Al-

bert II, the son of Prince Rainier III and Grace Kelly, has reigned as Prince of Monaco since his father's death in 2005.

Economy

Tourism, real estate, and international **banking** are the most important sectors of Monaco's economy. **Light industry**, including the production of cosmetics and electronics, also contributes a significant proportion of GDP. At least 75 per cent of Monaco's small labour force is employed in the **service sector** with remaining 25 per cent employed almost entirely in the **manufacturing** sector.

Transport Infrastructure

Public transport in Monaco consists of several bus and mini-bus routes. Taxis are also available throughout the principality. Only locally registered **cars** are allowed into Monaco's old town, but the district is connected to the rest of city by five **public elevators**. Monaco's train station is integrated into the French **rail network**. The nearest **international airport** is in **Nice**.

Tourism

Monaco's first **casino** opened in 1861 and the current Belle Époque-style building was completed in 1878. Monaco is one of the most popular tourist destinations in Europe. Millions of tourists visit each year, mostly on day trips. Sights include the 19th century cathedral, the **Prince's**

Palace, the small **old town** of Monaco-Ville, and the famous **Oceanographic Museum**. In addition Monaco also offers several **beaches** and facilities for **aquatic sports**. Monte Carlo hosts two of the world's most famous **auto racing events**, the Monaco Grand Prix and Monte Carlo Rally.

1 The mountain village Eze is situated in a breathtaking natural setting on the Côte d'Azur (French Riviera). A small narrow path leads up to the village.

2 During the fourteenth and fifteenth centuries, Avignon was an important cultural centre as the residence of the Popes.

3 Sisteron, the 'pearl of Haute Provence' between the Durance River and the craggy mountains of the coastal Alps.

4 Corsica's interior is a fascinating region with stunning mountainous landscapes and traditional small villages.

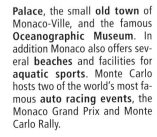

Above: The European Central Bank is based in Frankfurt, a leading global financial centre.

The European Economy

Europe's economies are currently facing three major challenges: the expansion of the European Union, the economic transition of the former communist countries of Eastern Europe and globalisation. The member states of the European Union have become increasingly integrated in recent decades, a process that is likely to continue. The legislative powers once reserved for national governments are devolved to the EU's central legislative bodies and the euro is now the currency of most of Western Europe.

After the collapse of the Soviet Union and the fall of Europe's communist regimes, the nations of central and eastern Europe faced the daunting transition from socialism to capitalism. While Slovenia, the Baltic states, Poland, the Czech Republic, Slovakia and Hungary made necessary reforms and opened their markets to foreign investment, other former socialist states – Russia, the Ukraine and Belarus – were less successful in transforming their economies.

As the nations of Europe opened their economies to one another, the continent also became in-

creasingly open to trade and investment from other regions of the world. International trade organisations such as the OECD, GATT and the WTO worked for open markets and the removal of barriers to international trade.

One consequence of increased global trade and economic integration is the creation of large multinational corporations resulting from the merger of well-known corporations such as the US-German motor company Daimler-Chrysler or the Sony media empire.

The enormous flow of capital to and from Europe is a sign of the

continent's economic importance and wealth. European companies and banks continue to invest heavily in the other regions, including North and South America and the rapidly expanding economies of Asia, especially China and India. At the same time foreign investors, especially from North America and Japan, invest large sums into the economies of Europe each year.

One major obstacle to Europe's economic prosperity the high rate

Europe's hi-tech industries, including aircraft manufacture, are showing rapid growth.

of unemployment. The primary causes of unemployment are the decline of traditional industries as well as high labour costs in the wealthier European nations. While the manufacturing sector has been badly affected by declining demand for manufactured goods and slow growth, even in-

dustries in the service sector have also been affected by this phenomenon. Outsourcing and internet selling has led to job losses in some service sectors. Nevertheless, the service sector remains the fastest growing source of new jobs in all of Europe's economies. Although the agricul-

tural sector in several EU countries is highly productive and employs modern technology, many of Europe's agricultural operations only survive with the help of extensive subsidies from national governments and the European Union. Due to agricultural overproduction and the recent expansion of the EU, the members states ratified Agenda 2000, a plan to gradually reduce the level of subsidies under the European Economic Policy. The expansion of the European Union to include several former communist countries has greatly increased the number of EU citizens employed in agriculture, but the number continues to decline throughout the member states.

The situation of the agricultural sector in Russia, the Ukraine and Belarus remains bleak. Inadequate reforms, corruption, low productivity and a lack of capital

for investment has led to several of these countries now relying on agricultural imports to feed their populations.

Mining has a long history in many regions but has also been affected by changes in recent decades. Coal mining has largely been abandoned in places where it was once the backbone of the economy, including parts of England, Germany and Belgium. This decline is largely the result of cheaper imports from non-European countries, improved recycling technique, and high labour costs. In contrast to the coal mining industry, North Sea oil continues to be a profitable sector of the United Kingdom and Norway's economies. Oil and gas promise a bright future for the Russian economy.

For much of the 20th century, heavy industries such as iron and steel production were the back-

bone of Europe's largest and most industrialised economies. In recent decades, the production of iron and steel and other heavy industries has declined rapidly throughout the continent. The automotive industry is one of the most important exceptions to this trend. Europe's car industry continues to expand although the industry is now largely dominated by a few conglomerates operating across the continent and most of the smaller producers have been taken over.

Airbus Industries, a pan-European consortium, was successfully able to end the U.S. monopoly on civilian aircraft production. ESA, another European consortium, has also been successful in aerospace industry. The telecommunications industry is a high-tech area in which European companies have enjoyed success in recent decades.

Tourism is now one of the fast growing and largest service industries in Europe. While traditionally popular travel destinations such as southern France, Italy, Spain and Austria continue to attract millions of visitors, more people are visiting central and eastern Europe.

Photos left: While other traditional industries in Europe, such as steel production, have declined due to foreign competition, many European car manufacturers continue to expand their operations.

Below: Since the 1990s, public awareness and interest in the stock markets has increased throughout Europe – this is the Paris bourse.

Spain

The Way of St James: Christian pilgrims have been taking the famous Camino de Santiago since the Middle Ages. Travellers from many nations have journeyed along the various routes that lead to the cathedral of Santiago de Compostela which according to tradition contains the tomb of the apostle Saint James.

Area:	504,782 sq. km
Capital city:	Madrid
Form of government:	
Constitutional Monarchy	
Administrative divisions:	
17 autonomous regions,	
50 provinces	
Population: 40.3 million	
(80 inhabitants/sq. km)	
Languages: Spanish (Castillian),	
Catalan, Basque, Galician	
GDP per capita:	US$25,100
Currency: 1 euro = 100 cents	

Natural Geography

Spain occupies four-fifths of the **Iberian Peninsula**, separated from the rest of Europe by the **Pyrenees** (Pico de Aneto, 3,404 m). **Mesetas**, large arid plateaus, occupy much of the country's land area, including most of central Spain. The **Andalusian plain** stretches from the south coast to the mountains of the **Sierra Nevada** (Mulhacén, 3,478 m). Spain's national territory includes the **Balearic Islands** in the Mediterranean and the **Canary Islands** off the coast of West Africa.

Climate

Northern Spain has a **cool, maritime climate** with **abundant rainfall**. Central Spain is a largely arid region with a **continental climate** and **steppe vegetation**. The mountains of the Sierra Nevada shield the south coast from cold north winds.

Population

People who consider themselves to be **Spaniards** constitute 74 per cent of Spain's population. Other important ethnic groups in the country include **Catalonians** (17 per cent), **Galicians** (six per cent) and **Basques** (two per cent). The British and the Moroccans are the two largest foreign communities in Spain. More than 90 per cent of Spain's population are **Roman Catholics**. The official languages include Spanish, also known as Castillian, and several regional languages including Basque, Catalan and Galician. In recent decades, many areas in Spain have witnessed a resurgence of regional identity. Despite having one of the lowest birth rates in Europe, Spain is experiencing a period of steady population growth due to immigration.

History and Politics

Originally inhabited by several **Celtic** and **Iberian** tribes, Spain came under the control of the **Roman Empire** in the first century BC. In the fifth century AD, most of Spain was conquered of the **Visigoths** who then lost control of the country to the Moors, Muslim Arabs and North Africans, in the year 711. For almost the next 800 years, the Moors controlled most of Iberia and a unique new culture was created. Starting in the twelfth century, the Christian kingdoms of northern Spain expanded their territory southwards. After centuries of conflict, **Granada,** the last bastion of Moorish power, fell to Christian forces in 1492. In the same year, **Christopher Columbus** discovered America and opened the door for Spain's emergence as a **world power**. Spanish explorers and adventurers brought enormous wealth from the New World to their home country and conquered vast territories in the name of the Spanish monarchy. During this era, Catholic clergy led the persecution of Spain's non-Christian population, Muslims and Jews. The Jews were expelled in 1492. There followed the **Spanish Inquisition**, designed to root out Christian heretics. The Moriscos, the Spanish Muslims, were expelled in 1568, and in 1579, the Low Countries threw off the Spanish yoke. The defeat of the **Spanish Armada** against England in 1588 marked the end of Spain's domination of Europe. The **War of Spanish Succession** (1701–1714) lead to an international crisis that involved most of Europe's major powers. Spain lost most of its colonies, after a series of revolutionary uprisings in countries of South America in the early nineteenth century.

In 1936, the Spanish king went into exile and Spain was declared a **republic**. Francisco **Franco**, an army general, initiated a coup d'état that lead to the Spanish Civil War Spain and the ultimate victory of Franco's reactionary nationalist forces. Franco supported Mussolini and Hitler, though Spain declared neutrality in World War II. The monarchy was restored in 1975 and **Juan Carlos** became King. The country

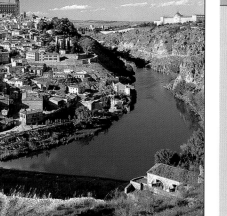

The fort of the ancient city Toledo towers above the old town and the Tagus river.

Francisco Franco

*Ferrol, 4.12.1892,
†Madrid, 20.11.1975

Franco was a general in the Spanish Foreign Legion, stationed in Morocco. He seized power in 1936, causing the Spanish Civil War which he won, thanks to his allies, Nazi Germany and Fascist Italy. His neutrality during World War II, his shrewd Cold War policies, and suppression of all opposition in Spain enabled him to maintain his authoritarian rule until his death.

Juan Carlos I

*Rome, 5.1.1938

Juan Carlos was the son of Don Juan de Bourbon and was named by Franco as his successor to re-establish the monarchy. Juan Carlos acceded to the throne in 1975, after Franco's death. An attempted military coup was thwarted in 1981 when the King made a public television broadcast, and this was a turning point for Spain's move towards democracy and a constitutional monarchy.

*A traditional **Spanish** bullfight usually ends with the death of the bull. In Portugal and southern France the animals are not killed during the fights.*

Mallorca, **Ibiza** and **Gran Canaria**, which are visited by millions of foreign tourists each year. Northern Spain's attractions include the spectacular coasts of the **Basque country**, **Asturias**, and **Galicia**. Catalonia's capital Barcelona, is one of Europe's most visited cities and the seaside resorts of the Costa Brava sand Costa Blanca are popular with foreign tourists. **Valencia** has become increasingly popular and visitors to **Andalusia** can discover the region's Arab heritage in **Seville**, **Malaga**, and **Granada**. The **Pyrenees** and the **Sierra Nevada** offer winter sports.

Andorra

Area:	467.7 sq. km
Capital city:	Andorra la Vella
Form of government:	
Constitutional Monarchy	
Administrative divisions:	
7 districts	
Population:	
70,549 (147 inhabitants/sq. km)	
Languages:	Catalan (official)
Spanish, French	

made a successful transition from dictatorship to constitutional monarchy. The king is now the head of state. Spain's **parliament**, the Cortes, has a lower house and a senate, both elected directly. The senate represents the country's 17 **autonomous regions**. After decades of isolation, Spain is now an important and influential member of the **European Union**.

Economy

Spain has traditionally suffered from high levels of **unemployment** but an economic boom at the turn of the century has

The Basque separatist movement, **ETA**, was founded in 1959 to challenge the Franco regime's suppression of Basque nationalism. ETA led a violent campaign for Basque independence causing the deaths of hundreds and leaving thousands injured. After decades of violence, the organisation declared a unilateral ceasefire in 2006. Spain's last **overseas territories** are Ceuta and Melilla, both enclaves surrounded by Morocco on the north coast of Africa.

Transport Infrastructure

Spain has an excellent **train and motorway network**. The country has more than 20 international **airports** and is the base for dozens of medium-sized and small private airlines, many catering to

brought the level of unemployment closer to the EU average. Almost 60 per cent of Spain's land is devoted to **agriculture**, including large areas under irrigation. Major agricultural produce includes vegetables and fruit (including citrus), grain and wine. **La Rioja** in the interior is one of the leading centres of wine production. **Fishing** remains an important industry; Spain has one of the largest fishing fleets in the world. Spain's **manufacturing industry** is concentrated in the country's northern regions and the capital Madrid. This sector contributes around 30 per cent of the country's gross domestic product. Spain's **service sector** is the most dynamic and largest in the economy and accounts for more than 60 per cent of economic activity. **Tourism** is an important industry in most Spanish regions.

tourists. Spain's most important **ports** are Barcelona, Gijon, and Bilbao. Numerous **ferry services** connect the Spanish mainland to the Balearic and Canary Islands.

Tourism

Spain is one of the most popular destinations in the world. Its attractions include the islands of

Andorra, Portugal

El Escorial: *The enormous complex of El Escorial lies north-west of Madrid at the foot of the Sierra de Guadarrama mountain chain. Designed by Juan de Toledo, it was built between 1563 and 1584 during the reign of King Philip II.*

In addition to several churches and monasteries, the complex houses Spain's royal mausoleum and the summer residence of the country's monarchs. Its architecture and design inspired many monasteries throughout Europe.

GDP per capita:	US$26,800
Currency: 1 euro = 100 cents	

Natural Geography

The tiny mountain principality of Andorra covers three mountain valleys in the eastern **Pyrenees** and is surrounded by mountains rising to 3,000 m above sea level. The **Valira River** and other smaller rivers flow through the country's deep valleys. Andora's elevation ranges between 840 m above sea level in the south to 2,946 m in the north. Andorra la Vella is Europe highest capital.

Climate

The climate in Andorra varies **depending on elevation**, the mountainous areas being distinctly cooler than the valleys. Andorra is one of the **sunniest regions** in the Pyrenees. Average monthly temperatures in the capital range between 5°C in the winter and 22°C in summer.

Population

Native Andorrans who are closely related to their neighbours in **Catalonia** form only a minority of their country's population

(30 per cent). Most of the country's residents are citizens of **Spain** (50 per cent) or **France** (ten per cent). Around 94 per cent of the population are **Roman Catholics**. Resident foreigners are only eligible for Andorra citizenship after 25 years. The country is a tax haven in which permanent residents pay no direct income tax. This has led

to some acrimony in recent years, as French and Spanish citizens have sought refuge in the mountain principality from their respective taxation regimes.

History and Politics

According to a popular legend, Andorra was founded by **Charlemagne**, who granted this tiny

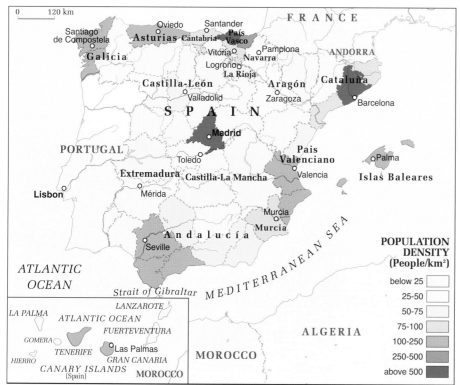

The Alhambra in Granada: former residence of Spain's Moorish rulers.

country independence as a reward for its loyalty to the Holy Roman Empire in his wars against the Moors. Andorra has two official heads of state, the **Bishop of Séo de Urgel** in Spain and the **president of France**, who took over from the French monarchy after the French Revolution. These traditional heads of state now perform purely ceremonial roles. In practice, the country is ruled by its own elected parliament and has a modern constitution. The government is led by an elected council that represents the country's various municipalities.

Economy

Because of the country's mountainous terrain, agriculture plays only a minor role in the economy. Andorra's exports include textiles and tobacco. The economy is dominated, however, by the service sector and invisibles, as befits a tax haven, and these account for 80 per cent of the gross domestic product. **Tourism** is one of the most important industries in the service sector. The country has traditionally been a popular destination for shoppers from neighbouring regions in France and Spain thanks to the tax-free goods on offer, but it also has excellent skiing and other winter sports facilities. Andorra has used the currencies of France and Spain for centuries and when these countries switched to the **euro** it followed suit by adopting the euro as a standard currency.

Transport Infrastructure

Andorra can be easily accessed by road from the **French** and **Spanish** frontiers. The nearest international **airports** are Barcelona in Spain and Toulouse in France.

Tourism

The **landscapes** and tax-free shopping opportunities lure millions of visitors each year. In winter, tourists come for the **skiing**. Andorra's hiking trails guide visitors through the country's mountainous landscapes. The hot springs in **Les Escaldes** health spa are also popular with tourists.

Portugal

Area:	92,391 sq. km
Capital city:	Lisbon
Form of government:	Republic
Administrative divisions: 18 districts, 2 autonomous regions (Azores and Madeira)	
External territory: Macao (until 1999)	
Population: 10.5 million (109 inhabitants/sq. km)	
Language:	Portuguese
GDP per capita:	US$18,400
Currency:	1 euro = 100 cents

Natural Geography

Portugal is a relatively narrow strip of land on the **Atlantic coast of Iberia** with an average width of only 150 km. The foothills of the **Cantabrian Mountains** rise in the country's north and the mountains of **Serra de Estrela** (highest peak: Torre, 1,991 m) extend through central Portugal. The basin of the **Tagus (Tejo) River**, which flows into the Atlantic near Lisbon, extends south to the hot and arid **Alentejo region**. The **Algarve** is the country's southernmost region.

Climate

The **Mediterranean climate** of Portugal is strongly influenced by the winds and currents of the **Atlantic Ocean**. In summer, temperatures in the interior range between 25°C and 27° C. The winter temperature is mild at around 11°C during the coldest months. Portugal's mountainous regions experience the heaviest rainfall.

Population

People of **Portuguese** descent constitute more than 96 per cent of the country's population. Only a third of the population lives in towns and cities. The largest immigrant communities are from former Portuguese colonies, such as Angola and Brazil, and there are growing numbers of Eastern Europeans. Portugal is an overwhelmingly **Catholic** nation, almost 97 per cent of the population professing Roman Catholicism. The **social and education systems** have been improved dramatically since Portugal joined the EU in the 1986.

0   120 km

FRANCE

Santiago de Compostela · Oviedo · Santander · **Asturias** Cantabria · **País Vasco** · Pamplona · ANDORRA

Galicia · Vitória · Navarra · Logroño · **La Rioja** · **Cataluña**

Castilla-León · Valladolid · **Aragón** · Zaragoza · Barcelona

S P A I N

PORTUGAL · **Madrid** · Toledo · **País Valenciano** · Palma

Extremadura · Castilla-La Mancha · Valencia · **Islas Baleares**

Lisbon · Mérida

Murcia · **Murcia**

Andalucía · MEDITERRANEAN SEA

Seville

ATLANTIC OCEAN · Strait of Gibraltar

ALGERIA

POPULATION DENSITY (People/km²)

below 25	
25-50	
50-75	
75-100	
100-250	
250-500	
above 500	

LA PALMA · LANZAROTE · ATLANTIC OCEAN · FUERTEVENTURA · GOMERA · TENERIFE · Las Palmas · GRAN CANARIA · HIERRO · CANARY ISLANDS (Spain)

MOROCCO · MOROCCO

*When the Moors lost their final battle against Spain's King Ferdinand and Queen Isabella in 1492 they left a cultural legacy of beautiful architecture. The former mosque of **Cordoba** is one of the most impressive Moorish structures.*

History and Politics

Dominated by Muslim rulers between the eighth and thirteenth centuries, Portugal was able to secure its **independence** from the **Spanish kingdom of Castille** during the fourteenth century. In the fourteenth and fifteenth centuries, Portuguese **explorers** became the first Europeans to circumnavigate the globe. They sailed down the west coast of Africa, rounded the Cape of Good Hope, and built up trading relationships in Asia and Africa. The **Treaty of Tordesillas** between Spain and Portugal In 1494, granted Portugal a vast territory in the **South America**. By the sixteenth century, however, Great Britain and the Netherlands had surpassed Portugal as a naval power and the country was ruled by **Spain** between 1580 and 1640. **England** captured most Portugal possessions in East Asia in the seventeenth century and Brazil, the country's largest colony, became independent in 1822. In 1911, Portugal became the first European country to depose its **constitutional monarchy.** The new republic suffered from instability and only lasted 15 years before it was toppled by a military coup in 1926. The military **dictatorship** supported Franco's nationalists during the Spanish Civil War but remained neutral during **World War II**. Portugal's remaining **colonies** began to demand greater freedom in the 1960s and after several wars, the country granted independence to its last major colonies. Portugal's decades of dictatorship, under Salazar, came to an end in 1974. The country experienced dramatic changes in the years following the return to democracy; many companies were nationalised and the wealthiest landowners lost many of their properties. The political situation stabilised after Portugal joined the **European Union** in 1986. The parliament is **unicameral,** the members and the country's **president** being directly elected for five-year terms of office. The president is granted considerable powers under the country's **constitution**.

In addition to the mainland, Portuguese territory includes the **Madeira archipelago** and the **Azores**, a group of islands 1,700 km from the mainland in the Atlantic Ocean.

Economy

Agriculture remains an important segment of Portugal's economy. Around 40 per cent of the country's land is devoted to agriculture. The region between the Tejo and Duoro Rivers is an important centre for the cultivation of various agricultural products, including citrus fruit, almonds, figs, peaches, and wine grapes. Maze, potatoes, and beef are important products in the cooler northern region of the country. **Fishing** is an important in many coastal communities in Portugal. The **manufacturing sector** accounts for a quarter of Portuguese GDP. Important manufactured goods include textiles and shoes. Portugal's **service sector** accounts for 60 per cent of the country's economic activity and is the fastest growing sector.

Transport Infrastructure

Portugal has a well developed **rail network** and services are especially extensive between cities and towns on the coast. There is also a good network of **motorways**. The 17-km-long **Vasco da Gama Bridge** in Lisbon, over the Tagus, built in 1998, is the longest bridge in Europe.

Tourism

Portugal is a popular destination for tourists from elsewhere in Europe. The country's are the 850-km-long coastline, as well as the cities of **Lisbon** and **Porto**, are popular destinations, and Northern Portugal and the **mountainous interior** offer excellent hiking and angling . The **Algarve** is especially popular, attracting visitors with beaches, picturesque fishing villages and rocky coastal landscapes. Portugal's **historic towns**, such as Coimbra, are becoming increasingly popular destinations.

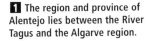

1 The region and province of Alentejo lies between the River Tagus and the Algarve region.

2 Porto was the major port for many centuries; ships left from here for the Americas.

3 Alfama, the oldest district of Lisbon, was spared destruction during a devastating earthquake in 1755. Lisbon was largely rebuilt by the Marquès de Pombal whose statue dominates the city.

4 Tourism is the leading industry in the Algarve, a warm coastal region with beaches and rocky seaside landscapes.

Germany

*The Bundestag, the lower chamber of Germany's parliament, moved into the renovated **Reichstag** in April, 1999. The spectacular new dome was designed by British architect Norman Foster and has become a landmark of the new Berlin.*

Germany

Area:	357,021 sq. km
Capital city:	Berlin
Form of government:	
Parliamentary Federal Republic	
Administrative divisions:	
16 federal states	
Population: 82.4 million	
(230 inhabitants/sq. km)	
Language:	German
GDP per capita:	US$29,700
Currency:	1 euro = 100 cents

Natural Geography

Germany is bordered by the **North Sea** and the **Baltic Sea** in the north and the **Alps** in the south. The country extends 840 km from north to south and 620 km from east to west. A vast plain of **extensive coastal wetlands** stretches throughout most of north-western Germany, and several archipelagos lie off of Germany's flat North Sea coast. These islands include the **East and North Frisian Islands** as well as a collection of tiny islets called **Haligen**. Germany's Baltic Sea coast has a mixture of **rocky and sandy beaches** as well as

Gustav Stresemann

*Berlin, 10.5.1878, †Berlin, 3.10.1929

Berlin-born Stresemann held radical national views throughout the World War I but in his later career as German chancellor worked hard for peace in Europe and for reconciliation between Germany and France. He managed to bring some stability to the weak Weimar Republic and was awarded the Nobel Peace Prize in 1926.

numerous **cliffs**. Several large islands, including **Usedom** and **Rügen**, are located along the country's Baltic coast.
Northwestern Germany's landscapes include a mixture of barren moorlands and fertile heaths, including the famous **Lüneberg Heath**. Northeastern Germany, like the country's northwest, is a largely **flat region**. Mecklenburg's

Lake District contains numerous bodies of water, including Lake Müritz, the second-largest lake in Germany. The southern and central regions of eastern Germany are dominated by the basins of several **major rivers**, including the **Elbe, Havel** and **Oder** Rivers. The plains in the centre of eastern Germany are bounded by several low mountain ranges, including the **Harz Mountains** (Brocken: 1,142 m) and the hill country of **Weserbergland**. To the east of this region lies the largely flat **Thuringian Basin** as well as the hills and low mountains of the **Thuringian Forest**, the **Ore Mountains** and the **Elbe Sandstone Mountains**. Central Germany is a diverse region including

the **Rhineland**, as well as the rolling hills of the **Sauerland**, the **Westerwald** and the **Taunus Mountains**. The scenic valley of the **Moselle** river is bounded by the **Eifel** and **Hunsruck**, two areas of hills and low mountains. Southwest Germany contains such diverse landscapes as the **Rhine basin**, the **Black Forest** (Feldberg, 1,493 m), and the **Swabian Alb**, a

high limestone plateau. **Lake Constance,** lies on the border between Germany, Austria and Switzerland. Germany's largest state, **Bavaria**, covers most of south-east Germany. The landscapes of this region include the hills of the **Franconian Alb** and the **Bavarian Forest**. Southern Bavaria is a diverse region with hilly areas, plains, river valleys and the foothills of the **Alps** which extend south to the Austrian border. Germany's highest mountain, the Zugspitze, rises to 2,962 m above sea level.

Climate

Germany has a **temperate climate** with significant regional variations. In northern Germany the climate is distinctly **maritime and temperate**, while the eastern and southern regions of the country have a **continental climate**. Northern Germany's climate is greatly affected by ocean currents which give the region its **maritime climate** with mild summers and cool, rainy winters. In the coastal north German city

of Hamburg, the average temperature is 4°C in summer and 17°C in winter. In Berlin, the capital, situated inland in eastern Germany, the average summer temperature is 19°C and it is -1° C in winter. The Alpine regions of southern Germany have cold winters, the average winter temperature in Munich is -2°C. The warmest areas in the country are located in the south-west, including the Black Forest and in the Rhine basin.

Population

Ethnic **Germans** form more than 91 per cent of the population. Traditional minority communities with long histories in the country include the Slav **Sorbs** in eastern Germany, the **Danish-speaking minority** in the North German region of Schleswig, the **Frisians** along the North Sea coast and the **Sinti** and **Roma** who lived throughout the country. Traditional minorities form only a small percentage of the country's population and are far less numerous than more recent minority com-

munities. Former 'guest workers' and their descendants form the vast majority of Germany's minority population. Other recent migrants have arrived in Germany as asylum-seekers and economic migrants. **Turks** and **Kurds** form the largest minority group in Germany, at least 2.2 million of them. Other important immigrant communities include **Italians, Greeks, Russians, Poles, Spaniards, Portuguese** and those from the former **Yugoslavia**.

The population of Germany is overwhelmingly Christian with almost equal numbers of **Protestants** and **Roman Catholics**. Around a quarter of Germans are not affiliated to a religious community. **Muslims**, the largest non-Christian group in Germany, form around 3.3 per cent of the population and **Jews** around 0.1 per cent of the population.

Germany has extensive and well-funded **public welfare, pension and healthcare systems**. More than one-tenth of the German national GDP is invested in the national healthcare system. The male **life expectancy** of 77 years is relatively high, while **infant mortality** in Germany is among the lowest in the world.

Chronically **high levels of unemployment** and slow economic growth have posed a major threat to the standard of public services in Germany since the 1990s, due to the reunification. Germany's **public education system** has one of the world's largest and best funded school and university systems. Education is compulsory between the ages of 6 and 18. Adult illiteracy is estimated at less than one per cent. The 337 **higher education institutions** in Germany include 84 universities, 147 polytechnics and as many schools of of art, music and religious seminaries.

Berlin old and new: above, Berlin cathedral and the Charlottenburg Castle, below Potsdamer Platz.

History and Politics

When the Roman Empire collapsed in the fifth century, the area that is now modern Germany was home to various **Germanic, Celtic,** and **Latin-speaking peoples**. In the eighth century most of Germany was conquered and incorporated into the domain ruled by the Frankish king, **Charlemagne**. His **Holy Roman Empire**, which

*The fairy tale castle of **Neuschwanstein** was one of those built at the behest of the Ludwig II, the so-called mad king of Bavaria. Once a drain on the budget of the Bavarian state, the castle is now one of Germany's most popular attractions.*

encompassed mostly German-speaking kingdoms, was founded in the 962 and lasted, until the early nineteenth century, although for most of its history, it was little more than a loose collection of kingdoms, constantly plagued by internecine conflict and rivalries.

Religious divisions played a critical role in the history of Germany in the late Middle Ages. **Martin Luther's** teachings led to the Protestant Reformation and the division of Germany into predominantly Protestant and Catholic regions. During the devastating **Thirty Years' War**, as much as a third of Germany's population perished from Plague and violence. The **rivalries and divisions** in the Holy Roman Empire continued for centuries as various kingdoms vied for domination of the empire and Germany. **Prussia**, with its capital Berlin, had emerged as the most powerful German state by the early nineteenth century.

The **Congress of Vienna** in 1814 radically changed the political picture of Germany. Hitherto, it had consisted of more than 200 kingdoms, principalities and 'free cities'; these were now replaced by 36 kingdoms which united to form the **German Confederation** led by Austria and Prussia. Rivalry between Austria and Prussia, the most powerful kingdoms in the confederation, weakened the alliance greatly and it finally disbanded in 1866 after the Austro-Prussian War. Under the

leadership of the Prussian chancellor von **Bismarck,** most of the German kingdoms joined the Prussian-dominated **North German Confederation**, which was dubbed the **German Empire** in 1870. The Empire experienced a remarkably rapid economic transformation and emerged as one of the world's leading **industrialised countries**. Germany, however, became increasingly **isolated** as a result of its aggressive push for international influence and rapid expansion of its military forces.

Germany entered **World War I** in 1914 in an alliance with the Austro-Hungarian Empire and the Ottoman Empire. The country's defeat in 1918 led to widespread social unrest and forced Kaiser Wilhelm II into exile. With the ratification of a new **constitution** in 1919, Germany became a republic for the first time in its history. The new state, often referred to as the **Weimar Republic,** was created during a time of major social and economic instability.

In 1933, there began the darkest chapter in Germany's history. The **National Socialist (Nazi) party** under the leadership of Adolf Hitler seized power and created a brutal totalitarian and racist regime known as the **Third Reich**. Germany's **invasion of Poland** in 1939 marked the beginning of **World War II**, the deadliest war in history. The Nazi regime in Germany initiated a brutal programme of murder and genocide now known as the **Holocaust** that resulted in the death of millions of civilians, including the majority of Europe's Jewish population. Germany was occupied by the four major allied powers following its surrender in 1945. Post-war disputes between the wartime allies

led to Germany's division into two states. The capital city, Berlin, was also divided into sectors. In May 1949, the occupation zones of the United States the United Kingdom, and France were united to form the Federal Republic of Germany, a democratic republic that covered most of

Germany. Five months later, in October 1945, the western portion of the Soviet occupation zone was declared the **German Democratic Republic** (East Germany). The rest of the Soviet occupation zone was annexed by

the Soviet Union or handed over to Poland.

In 1949, **West Germany** comprised ten federal states and about half of Berlin (West Berlin). The smallest states were the two city-states of the North German

Adolf Hitler

*Braunau, 20.4.1889,
†Berlin, 30.4.1945

Born in the Austro-Hungarian Empire near the Bavarian border, Hitler fought in the German army in World War I. After the war, Hitler was jailed by the Bavarian authorities following a failed coup attempt in Munich. By the late 1920s, he had become leader of the National Socialist (Nazi) party. In 1933, his party was voted into power and he became Chancellor. The fascist ideology and fanatical racism of his dictatorship resulted in World War II and the Holocaust.

*Pfalzgrafstein Castle near the town Kolb sits on a small island in the river **Rhine**, Germany's longest river. The river is both a vital economic resource for the country and a popular tourist attraction.*

port cities of Hamburg and Bremen. Bavaria, the largest German state, was granted the largely ceremonial status of a free state. In addition to these historic entities, several new states were created by the allies, including Schleswig-Holstein, Hesse, North-Rhine Westphalia and Lower Saxony. The original states of Württemberg-Baden, and Württemberg-Hohenzollern merged in 1952 to form the state of Baden-Württemberg. Saarland became the last of the west German states to join the Federal Republic in 1957. Though the residents of West Berlin were granted West German citizenship, the city itself remained officially under the control of the allies until German

Union and other communist countries in Eastern Europe lead to calls for greater political freedom for East Germany. The Berlin Wall, the most visible symbol of Germany's division, was opened on 9 November, 1989. During negotiations in the autumn of 1990 the two German states and the four World War II allied powers agreed to the **reunification** of Germany.

In 1990, the West German currency, the Deutschmark, was introduced into East Germany. On 3 October 1990, the German Democratic Republic was dissolved and five new states joined the **Federal Republic of Germany**; Thuringia (16,171 sq. km), Saxony (18,412 sq. km), Saxony-Anhalt

Although the federal government is the highest and most powerful level of government in Germany, the individual states are granted wide-ranging powers and responsibilities by the German constitution. The country's official head of state is the **federal president**. Each president is elected for a five-year term by a federal assembly consisting of members of Bundestag and delegates from the sixteen states. Although granted important reserve powers, the post of federal president is a largely representative position. Germany's most powerful political official is the **federal chancellor** who appoints **ministers** and leads the federal government. The highest body in the

the sector accounts for less than one per cent of Germany's economy. Germany imports a large percentage its food consumption. The German **industrial sector**, one of the world's most technologically advanced, accounts for 37 per cent of the country's economy. Thanks to high wages and manufacturing costs, however, the German industrial sector concentrates on the production of high-tech and specialised manufacturing. Major **exports** include machinery, the aviation, aerospace and electronics industry, chemicals and motorised vehicles. Germany is the third largest car-maker in the world. Several historically important industries such as shipbuilding,

invested large sums of money in improving the infrastructure and economy of eastern Germany.

Transport Infrastructure

Germany's **road network** is one of the world's most extensive with more than 600,000 km of surfaced roads. The **motorway** (Autobahn) network is 11,250 km long. With more than 538 cars for every 1,000 inhabitants, Germany also has one of the world's highest levels of **private vehicle ownership**. More than 98 per cent of the country's railways are owned by the national rail company Deutsche Bahn. In total, the **rail network** covers 43,586 km of track, of which 18,192 km are

---

Konrad Adenauer

*Cologne, 5.1.1876,
†Rhöndorf, 19.4.1967

As a prominent member of the Catholic Centre party, Adenauer was mayor of Cologne from 1917 to 1933. He was imprisoned several times during the Nazi era but began his political career anew after the end of the war. In 1949, Adenauer became the Federal Republic of Germany's first chancellor. During his tenure, West Germany joined NATO and became a founding member of the EEC (now the European Union). Adenauer left office in 1963.

Dresden has some of Germany's most beautiful historic monuments.

Willy Brandt

born Herbert Frahm
*Lübeck, 18.12.1913,
†Unkel, 8.10.1992

After returning from exile in Scandinavia, Brandt became a prominent figure in Germany's Social Democratic Party (SPD). He served as mayor of West Berlin from 1957 to 1966 and was appointed leader of the SPD in 1964. From 1966 to 1969, he served as Germany's foreign minister. In 1971, he was awarded the Nobel Peace Prize. Brandt resigned in 1974 but remained chairman of the SPD until 1987.

---

reunification in 1990. In 1954, East Germany declared independence, calling itself the German Democratic Republic. East Germany joined the **Warsaw Pact** in 1955, while West Germany joined **NATO** in the same year. West Germany became a founding member of the **European Economic Community**, a predecessor of the EU, in 1957. The construction of the **Berlin Wall** in 1961 led to years of tension between the two Germanies. During the 1970s, West German chancellor **Willy Brandt's** Ostpolitik greatly improved relations between the two countries, leading to greater cultural exchanges and easier travel conditions. During the 1980s, political **reforms** in the Soviet

(20,445 sq. km), Brandenburg (29,478 sq. km), and Mecklenburg-Western Pomerania. The two sections of Berlin were reunited to form one federal state and the city was designated the capital of the reunited republic by the German parliament in 1991. Germany is a democratic federal republic with a **bicameral parliament** in accordance with the country's constitution. Members of the German parliament (**Bundestag**) are elected for four-year terms. The interests of the sixteen states are represented at the federal level by the 69 members of the federal council, the **Bundesrat**. Representation in the Bundesrat is based on the population of each state.

judicial branch of the German government is the **federal constitutional court**. Its panel of judges is appointed by parliament and the federal council for one twelve-year term.

Economy

Germany is one of world's **wealthiest nations** and has the largest economy in Europe. The country is also a leading exporter of agricultural produce, including cereals, fruit, vegetables, and potatoes and wine. Meat and dairy foods are also important products of the country's **agricultural sector**. Less than three per cent of the German labour force is employed in agriculture and

steel production and coal mining have declined dramatically in recent decades.

The **service sector** now accounts for almost two-thirds of economic activity in Germany and is expanding. Germany's banks and insurance companies are among the largest in the world. Germany's retail, media and trade sectors have all expanded in recent decades.

Tourism is an important industry in several regions. Although the country has been reunited for more than fifteen years there remains a considerable **economic gap** between the states of eastern Germany and the rest of the country. Since reunification, the German federal government has

electrified. **High speed trains** connect many of Germany's largest cities. In addition to Deutsche Bahn, there are also a growing number of small train companies operating on regional and commuter routes.

The **navigable waterways** of Germany have a total length of 7,467 km. At least 20 per cent of the all commercial goods transported through Germany are carried on the country's waterways. Major **canals** include the North Sea-Baltic canal in northern Germany and the Rhine-Main-Danube canal. Duisburg in western Germany and Magdeburg in eastern Germany are the most important **inland ports**. Important **coastal habours** include the

Hamburg is the location of Germany's busiest harbour. The busy port relies on modern equipment and large container ships are swiftly loaded and unloaded.

cities of Hamburg, Bremen, Rostock, Lübeck and Wilhelmshaven. Germany's **commercial fleet** has more than 1,600 ships, at least half of which sail under flags of convenience. **Ferry services** connect several ports in northern Germany with various ports along the Baltic and North Sea coasts. The extensive network of **airports** includes 150 national and 14 international airports. **Frankfurt** has one of the world's busiest airports and is the leading air transport hub for central Europe. Lufthansa, once a state enterprise, now privatised, is one of the world's leading airlines.

Tourism

Germany has diverse tourist attractions and is visited by millions of foreign tourists each year.

Major destinations include the country's larger cities, such as **Munich, Berlin,** and **Cologne. Bavaria** is the country's most visited region. The **Bavarian Forest** is popular with hikers. **Alpine lakes,** historic towns, and **beautiful castles,** such as Neuschwanstein, bring large numbers of tourists to the region and the **Bavarian Alps** have excellent tourist facilities.

Baden-Württemberg has several major tourist destinations including the historic towns of **Freiburg** and **Heidelberg,** the **Black Forest** and **Lake Constance.** Medieval castles, terraced vineyards and picturesque towns line the banks of the **Moselle** and the **Rhine** in western Germany. **Trier,** the oldest city in Germany, has some of the most impressive Roman structures north of the Alps.

Historic **Weimar, Dresden** and **Leipzig** are major cultural cities. The Ore Mountains, stretching through western Saxony along the border to the Czech Republic, are popular with ramblers, climbers and hikers.

North Rhine-Westphalia is Germany's most populous state and contains several interesting cities, including **Cologne, Düsseldorf** and **Münster. Lower Saxony's** attractions include the **Lüneberg Heath,** the **Harz Mountains** and the **Weserbergland.** Mecklenburg-Western Pomerania is the most sparsely populated state and, perhaps for this reason, one

of the most popular destinations. The seaside resorts and beaches on the islands of **Rügen, Hiddensee,** and **Usedom,** off the North Sea coast attract their share of visitors. Schleswig-Holstein is worth visiting for the beautiful port city of **Lübeck,** a world heritage site. Naturally, the capital, Berlin, at the historic heart of central Europe attracts many tourists, since it combines important cultural attractions with a scenic landscape of lakes and meadows.

Germany is fortunate in having a relatively low population density in the rural districts, so that it has some of the most unspoiled countryside in Europe.

1 The market square of Bremen is surrounded by historic merchants' houses, the St. Petri cathedral, a statue of the city's symbol, Roland, as well as the famous town hall, one of the finest examples of North German Renaissance architecture.

2 Heidelberg: The Old Bridge crosses the Neckar River into the city's well-preserved old town district.

3 Bavaria: The pilgrimage church of St. Koloman stands near the castle of Hohenschwangau at the foot of the Bavarian Alps.

Switzerland

Local culture and traditions are cherished throughout the cantons of **Switzerland**. Due to their relative isolation from the rest of Europe, the most mountainous regions have been especially successful at preserving many of their unique traditions. But even the lowlands take pride in preserving their regional identities, including local dialects, traditional costumes and festival days.

 Switzerland

Area:	41,290 sq. km
Capital city:	Bern

Form of government:
Democratic Confederation

Administrative divisions:
26 cantons

Population: 7.4 million
(174 inhabitants/sq. km)

Languages: German, French, Italian, Rhaeto-Romansh

GDP per capita:	US$35,000

Currency:
1 Swiss franc =
100 centimes

Natural Geography

Switzerland has three major distinct geographical regions; the **Swiss Alps**, the **Swiss Plateau** and the **Jura Mountains**.
The Swiss part of the Jura Mountains stretches over the north-west of the country, from the French border, and covers around one-tenth of the country's total land area. The Swiss Plateau, a high plain situated at between 400 and 1000 m above sea level, covers the area between the Alps and the Jura Mountains. **Lake Geneva** and **Lake Constance**, the country's two largest lakes, between the two mountain chains. The Alps and Alpine valleys account for most of the rest of the land mass. The northern and southern branches of the Swiss Alps are demarcated by the Rhine and Rhône river valleys. Switzerland has many other waterways, including sections of the **Italian lake** district as well as countless beautiful **Alpine lakes**.

Climate

The Swiss climate varies from a **temperate continental** climate throughout most of the country to an **alpine** climate in the most mountainous regions. In general, the summers are warm with plentiful rainfall, while winters are often bitterly cold; the capital, Bern, occasionally experiences temperatures of -30°C. The Swiss canton of the Tessin (Ticino) near the Italian border is the warmest part of the country.

Population

Around 80 per cent of the population are **Swiss** citizens and the remaining 20 per cent, resident foreigners. Switzerland is ethnically linguistically divided into **Swiss-German-, French-, Italian-,** and **Rhaeto-Romansh-speaking regions**. All four of them have an official status in the country.
At least 40 per cent of the population identify themselves as **Protestants** and 46 per cent are **Roman Catholics**. The wealth of the country is reflected in its excellent public health care and social services, which account for about one-third of the national budget. The well-funded Swiss **education system** is largely the re-sponsibility of the individual cantons. Switzerland's **universities** and other institutions of higher education and research have an excellent reputation, especially in the fields of medicine, pharmaceuticals, medicine and molecular biology.

History and Politics

In 1291, the small states of **Uri, Scwyz** and **Unterwalden** formed an alliance that would eventually grow into the **Swiss Confederation**. In the centuries that followed, the first three canton's declaration of an 'eternal alliance', many new cantons joined the Confederation. After a French invasion in 1798, the Confederation was briefly replaced by a centralised state known as the Helvetic Republic. Switzerland became a **federal union** in 1848 and the current constitution has been in effect since 1874. Foreign policy, national defence, postal services, telecommunications, monetary policy, customs as well as energy and transport are all the responsibility of the federal government. Most other areas of governance are regulated by the country's 20 cantons and six half-cantons. One of the most distinctive aspects of Swiss democracy is the role that **referendums and petitions** play in the country's system of government, as well as its denial of the vote to women until very recent times.

Switzerland's **bicameral parliament** consists of a **national council** and the **council of states**, which represents the cantons. Both houses of the parliament have equal powers and both are responsible for electing the federal council, a seven-member committee which functions as the country's executive branch. The parliament appoints a member of the federal council to hold the office of **federal president**. Unlike in most other countries however, the federal president is only the presiding member of the federal council and not the country's head of state.

Economy

Switzerland is one of the **wealthiest nations** in the world. **Agriculture** accounts for less than three per cent of the country's economy and produce includes cereals, fruit, vegetables and dairy products. Despite its lack of

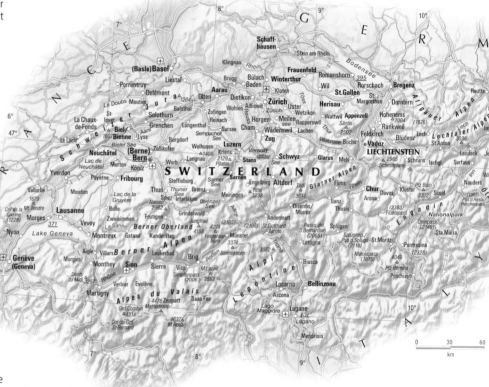

The Matterhorn (4,478 m) in the Valais Alps in one of Switzerland's most famous mountains.

The United Nations (UN) was formed in 1945 as a successor to League of Nations, an international organisation created in 1920. The League of Nations was headquartered in **Geneva** and today many of the organisation's buildings are occupied by bodies of the UN, including the Palais des Nations.

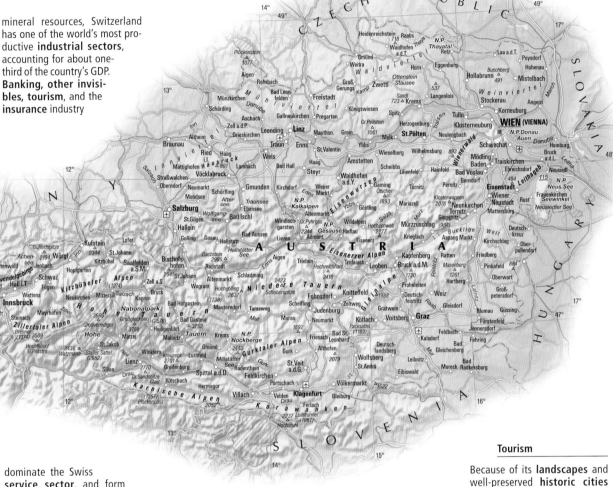

mineral resources, Switzerland has one of the world's most productive **industrial sectors**, accounting for about one-third of the country's GDP. **Banking, other invisibles, tourism**, and the **insurance** industry dominate the Swiss **service sector**, and form the backbone of the national economy accounting for Swiss prosperity.

Transport Infrastructure

The Swiss **rail network** is widely acknowledged to be one of the world's best. Switzerland also has an excellent network of **motorways**, funded largely through petrol taxes. The 17-km-long **St. Gotthard Tunnel** running through the Alps is one of the longest road tunnels in the world. The country has three international **airports** (Basle, Geneva, and Zürich) and several smaller, regional airports.

Tourism

Because of its **landscapes** and well-preserved **historic cities** Switzerland has long been a popular tourist destination. There are no less than 50,000 km of **hiking** trails. The **Bernese Oberland** is one of the most beautiful regions, with its pristine lakes and high mountains. **Valais** and **Grisons** offer **skiing**.

Liechtenstein

Area:	160 sq. km
Capital city:	Vaduz
Form of government:	
Constitutional Monarchy	
Administrative divisions:	
11 municipalities	
Population: 33,400	
(207 inhabitants/sq. km)	
Language:	German
GDP per capita:	US$33,717
Currency:	
1 Swiss franc = 100 centimes	

Natural Geography

Situated high above sea level in the **Alps**, the tiny, land-locked country of Liechtenstein is surrounded by **Austria** and **Switzerland**. The **Rhine** forms the country's northern and western borders.

As the fourth smallest state in Europe, Liechtentstein measures only 25 km from north to south and extends only 6 km from east to west. The area along the Rhine is situated almost 1,000 m lower than the western districts around the country's capital, Vaduz.

Zürich: A view of the historic buildings along the Limmat River.

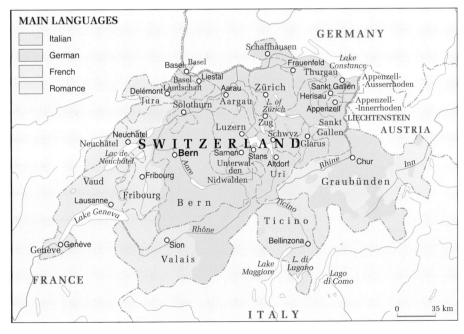

MAIN LANGUAGES
- Italian
- German
- French
- Romance

Liechtenstein, Austria

Vienna is a great Baroque city, but modern architecture still has its place here, as demonstrated by the many Art Nouveau buildings, the clean lines of Adolf Loos, and the fantastic houses of Friedensreich Hundertwasser.

Climate

Liechtenstein has a **continental climate**. Temperatures in the capital can reach a low of -15°C in January, and can climb as high as 28°C in July, the warmest month.

Population

One third of the population of Liechtenstein is **Austrian, Swiss, Italian** or **German**, and the proportion of foreign residents is even higher among the labour force. Almost two-thirds of people working in Liechtenstein come from abroad and many are cross-border commuters from Switzerland and Austria. Like their neighbours in Switzerland, the Liechtensteiner speak an Alemannic dialect of German. **Roman Catholics** constitute 82 per cent of the population, and seven per cent are **Protestant**.

History and Politics

The **principality** was founded in 1719 and became a sovereign state within the **Confederation of the Rhine** in 1806. Liechtenstein maintained a strict policy of neutrality during both World Wars.
Since 1923, the country has shared currency, customs and a postal system with its neighbour **Switzerland**, and Liechtenstein has been represented on the international arena by Switzerland since 1919. The country has been a constitutional hereditary principality with a parliamentary system since 1921. The parliament, known as the **Landtag**, consists of 25 members, elected every four years to advise the Prince.

Economy

No other country in Western Europe has seen such radical changes since World War II. Liechtenstein has moved from a purely agricultural economy to one of the most highly **industrialised** countries – considering the size of the population – in the world. **Agriculture**, mainly animal husbandry and milk production, today represents just one per cent of GDP. Half of the population works in the **service sec-**

tor, while the other half works in **industry** (machine construction, transport and ceramics). The service sector contributes to 50 per cent of GDP and is dominated by trade and the highly developed **banking and trust company** sectors.
Other important sources of revenue are postage stamps and **tourism**.

Transport Infrastructure

There is an open border to Switzerland, and the border to Austria is manned by Swiss border guards. Liechtenstein has no airports, the nearest airport is in Zurich, Switzerland.
The railway station at Schaan provides a connection to the international **rail network**. Liech-

tenstein's 11 districts are connected by a good internal **bus network**.

Tourism

Liechtenstein offers good year-round **skiing and hiking**. The winter sport resorts are **Malbun** (altitude 1,600 m) and **Steg** (altitude 1,300 m). The capital city, **Vaduz**, has many cultural attractions, including an excellent Postal Museum and an

impressive royal art collection. Other cultural highlights are Gutenberg Castle in **Balzers**, Church Hill in **Bendern** and the castle ruins in **Schellenberg**.

Austria	
Area:	83,870 sq. km
Capital city:	Vienna
Form of government:	
Federal Republic	
Administrative divisions:	
9 provinces	
Population:	8.2 million
(97 inhabitants/sq. km)	
Language:	German
GDP per capita:	US$32,900
Currency:	
1 euro = 100 cents	

Natural Geography

The massive peaks of the **Alps**, including the Grossglockner, which reaches a height of 3,797 m, dominate more than half of Austria's land mass. In the east, there is the **Pannonian basin** and the **Hungarian lowlands**, including the **Neusiedler See**, a large lake.
The **Danube** river flows through Austria for a length of 350 km; the river and its tributaries are

flanked by various water-meadows and fields. The mountain regions are covered in dense forest. Wildlife at these high altitudes (ibex, chamois, marmots) are endangered, so that as much as just under 25 per cent of the country is protected as a nature reserve.

Climate

Austria has a **continental climate**, but the weather varies depending on **altitude**. Winters are mostly bitterly cold, while summers, particularly in the south and east of the country, can be moderately warm. Average temperatures in the capital, Vienna, are -2°C in January and 20°C at their warmest in July.

Population

Austrian's population consists of over 90 per cent German-speaking **Austrians**, with minority groups of Croatians, Slovenians, Hungarians, Czechs and Rom (gypsies). **Foreigners** make up roughly nine per cent of the population, of whom the largest groups are from the former Yugoslavia (more than 35 per cent), Turks (20 per cent) and Germans (eight per cent). The population is 78 per cent **Catho-**

lic, five per cent **Protestant** and two per cent **Jewish**. nine per cent of the population have no religious affiliation. Austria's social welfare, pension and health systems are exemplary, but the burden on the state is heavy, with 17 per cent of GDP spent on the **welfare state**. The country has 19 **universities**, of which the most famous is the University of Vienna, founded in 1365.

History and Politics

During the time of the great **tribal wanderings** before the Roman conquest, the area covered by modern-day Austria was at the crossroads of Europe. It was in this region that the **Celts** established the Hallstatt culture, and for the **Romans**, the Danube in

the province of Noricum represented the north-east border of their Empire. From the twelfth century AD, Austria became the heart of the **Habsburg Dynasty**, which at times ruled the German Empire and which had a decisive impact on the history of Europe. The rule of the Habsburgs extended from the Netherlands to Sicily, and after the war against the **Ottoman Empire** in the seventeenth century, it extended ever further eastward. The **Aus-**

Vienna: the Gothic St. Stephen's Cathedral dominates the city.

*High society in **Vienna** revolves around the Opera Ball and the coffee houses, made famous as a meeting place for the artists, politicians and businessmen from the nineteenth century until today.*

trian Empire was founded in 1804, and from 1815 became an ever stronger power in the **German Confederation**. A union with Hungary in 1867 formed the **Dual Monarchy** of the Austro-Hungarian Empire, but this union was often troubled by internal nationality conflicts. The assassination of Archduke Ferdinand, heir to the Emperor, and his wife, in **Sarajevo** in 1914 was one of the triggers for the outbreak of **World War I**. When the war came to an end, the great empire was dismantled and was reduced to a fraction of its former size. A **republic** was founded in 1918, bringing an end to the hierarchical social structure and removing the imperial dynasty. A **constitution** was introduced in 1920, creating a federal state.

In 1938, Austria was annexed by the German **Third Reich**. In 1945, former Austria was divided into four occupied zones until 1955, when an **international treaty** forced the country to declare a policy of 'perpetual neutrality'. The 1920 constitution, which was re-introduced in 1945, provides for a **bicameral parliament**, constituting a lower house, the Nationalrat, and an upper house, the Bundesrat. The nine provinces (Burgenland, Carinthia, Lower Austria, Upper Austria, Salzburg, Styria, Tyrol, Vorarlberg and Vienna) send representatives to these houses. The **President** is directly elected by the people every six years.

Austria has been a member of the **European Union** since 1995, and is one of the founder members of the Economic and Monetary Union. Vienna is the headquarters of several United Nations organisations and of the Organisation for Petroleum Exporting Countries (OPEC).

Economy

Land usage in the country is 42 per cent agriculture and 38 per cent forestry. Austria's **agricultural sector** is based on the cultivation of cereal crops, vines and potatoes. It accounts for only 1.5 per cent of GDP but provides 90 per cent of the country's food. Excess production, mainly of milk and dairy foods, is exported.

The most important raw material is **iron ore**. The **manufacturing** sector accounts for 31 per cent of Gross Domestic Product and the sector employs 30 per cent of the country's labour force. The **Main exports** are machinery, metalworking, electronics, timber and paper, clothing and textiles and vehicles.

Tourism alone accounts for eight per cent of GDP and this makes it one of the most important areas of the **services sector**, which accounts for as much as 67 per cent of GDP.

Transport Infrastructure

Austria is an important **transit country** to and from eastern Europe and has excellent **transport links**. The **road network** extends for 130,000 km, including the **Brenner motorway** across the **Alps** to Italy, one of the best known routes across the numerous alpine passes. Motorways and express roads are toll roads. The **rail network** covers 5,600 km. The entire length of the **Danube** in Austria is navigable, and the most important ports are Linz and Vienna. The country's main **international airport** is **Vienna-Schwechat**.

Tourism

Austria is one of the most popular **tourist destinations** in Europe, especially for its winter sports. The alpine regions of **Salzburg**, **Tyrol**, **Carinthia** and **Vorarlberg** provide countless opportunities for **skiing, hiking and climbing**. The numerous alpine lakes in the **Salzkammergut** and **Carinthia** are very popular, as is the Neusiedler See in **Burgenland**, which has an exceptionally mild climate.

Austria also has many important cultural attractions, including the world's oldest salt mine in **Hallstatt**. The country has numerous monasteries, convents and churches which are well worth a visit. **Linz, Klagenfurt** and **Innsbruck** are picturesque old towns, full of character, and the baroque buildings of **Salzburg** are particularly impressive.

The highlight of a trip to Austria is a visit to the capital, **Vienna**, with its rich culture, important theatres, museums and art collections, and the numerous palaces and castles in the historic centre,

which are a lasting monument to the Habsburg Empire. There is plenty of nightlife, and especially the quaint little inns in the Vienna woods, known as **heurigen**, little inns where the Viennese go in summer to drink new Austrian wine and eat onion bread, while being entertained by musicians, dancing and comedians.

1 The stunning Alpine landscape in the province of Tyrol makes it Austria's number one destination for tourists.

2 Salzburg's skyline contains a wealth of classical and Baroque architecture. The city is a centre of classical music, thanks to its most famous son, Mozart.

3 The Schönbrunn Palace in Vienna was built to match the grandeur of the Palace of Versailles. It was designed by the architect Johann Bernhard Fischer von Erlach, and construction work commenced in the seventeenth century. It was later rebuilt by the Empress Maria Theresa of Austria.

Italy

Castel Sant'Angelo: this complex on the Tiber was originally a mausoleum commissioned by the Emperor Hadrian in 135 AD but was converted into a fortress in 403. It was used by the popes as a fortress, residence and prison. In the thirteenth century, Pope Nicholas III built a battlement connecting the castle to St. Peter's. Legend has is that the Archangel Michael signalled the end of the Plague of 590 by sheathing his sword atop the mausoleum.

Italy	
Area:	301,230 sq. km
Capital city:	Rome
Form of government:	Republic
Administrative divisions: 20 regions; 103 provinces	
Population: 58.1 million (192 inhabitants/sq. km)	
Language:	Italian
GDP per capita:	US$28,300
Currency:	1 Euro = 100 cents

Natural Geography

The mountain range of the **Alps** form the northern border of this predominantly mountainous country with the Ortler as the highest peak (3,899 m). The **Apennines** are joined in the south to the long **Po Valley**. In the north, the Apennines surround the hilly landscape of **Tuscany** and the valley of Umbria. The Apennines split the Italian 'boot' down the centre for about 1,100 km to the extreme south, with one side facing the **Adriatic Sea** and the other facing the **Tyrrhenian Sea**.

The western coastal plains with their numerous bays show clear traces of volcanic activity (**Vesuvius, Etna, Stromboli**). The **Adriatic Coast**, on the other hand, is rather flat. In addition to the larger islands of **Sardinia** and **Sicily** in the southern Mediterranean. Other islands off the coast such as **Ischia, Elba** and **Capri** also belong to the national territory.

Climate

With the exception of the area encompassing the high mountains of the **Alpine region**, the climate is predominantly **Mediterranean** with **dry, hot summers** and **mild, rainy winters**, particularly in the southern regions – although in the south occasional snow showers are also possible in a bad winter. The average temperatures over the whole country are 4–8°C in January and 25–28°C in July.

region and in the Aosta Valley **French** is spoken. **Friulian** and other **local dialects**, which often owe their individuality to Italy's eventful history, are also spoken. Well over 90 per cent of the Italian population are **Roman Catholic**.

History and Politics

From the fourth century BC until the mid-fourth century AD, the **Roman Empire** was the dominant power in Europe. After the decline of the Roman Empire, Rome – and thus Italy – was the centre of the **Papacy**. The political influence and constant conflicts between the Popes and European sovereigns significantly determined the history of the Middle Ages in Europe.

Cultural and political centres in the late Middle Ages became independent **city republics** such as **Venice** and **Milan**. From the sixteenth to the nineteenth century, the regions of today's Italy – which had lost much of their influence – were fought over by all the European powers and fell alternately under **Spanish, Austrian and French rule**. Military opposition to foreign power is inseparably linked with the name of the hero of Italian emancipation, Giuseppe **Garibaldi**. Unification was finally achieved and in 1861 Victor Emmanuel II ascended the Italian throne as the first **King**.

Domestic crises after World War I led in 1922 to a **Fascist** coup and,18 years later, to the accession of the country to the Axis pact. After the fall of **Mussolini** in 1943 and the abdication of the king in 1946, Italy was proclaimed a **republic**. The bicameral parliament consists of the **House of Representatives**, whose members stand for election every five years, and the **Senate**, which consists of about 315 directly elected members and a further ten senators who are elected for life. Both chambers have equal rights and political decisions are made jointly. The **President** of the Republic, who is elected for seven years, has far-reaching power.

In the mid-1990s, numerous cases of **corruption** were uncovered which led to extensive restructuring of the political landscape.

economy was marked by **great state influence**. Just under three per cent of the country's GDP derives from **agriculture** – which is highly modernised in the north, and organised into smallholdings in the south – with the cultivation of fruits, vegetables, wine and grains. Italy is Europe's largest **rice producer**. In order to meet the demand for the production of **pasta**, Italy imports wheat from North and South America. Industry contributes a total of 33 per cent to the GDP. As Italy has few raw materials, mining has traditionally made no important contribution to GDP. Nevertheless, the main industrial emphasis of the Italian economy is in **metal work**. In addition to motor **vehicles**, chemicals, textiles and clothing are among the main exports. **Tourism** is one of the most important economic sectors and makes a large contribution to the **service sector**. The standard of Italy's tourist facilities and services is

The Pantheon in Rome was initially a Roman temple, but was later used as a church and mausoleum.

Population

As many as 95 per cent of the population speak **Italian** as their mother tongue, and five per cent speak minority languages. **German** is widely spoken in the Trentino-South Tyrol

Economy

The large **gap** between the industrialised **north** and the predominantly rural **south**, in which high unemployment predominates, reflects the long period during which Italy's

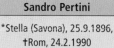
corresponding high. The country was a founder member of the **European Common Market** (EC).

Transport Infrastructure

The **road network** stretches over 317,000 km; major roads

The Spanish Steps in Rome: the stairway to the Trinità dei Monti, constructed by Alessandro Specchi and Francesco de Sanctis from 1723 to 1726.

men. Here, nature-lovers find hiking routes and beautiful natural landscapes. The best known centres are **Meran** and **Cortina d'Ampezzo**.

The national parks in the **Abruzzi** and the Pollino National Park in **Calabria** are among the many **national parks** in Italy – a country in which eight per cent of the land mass is protected.

Bathing and beach holidays are spent on the western **Mediter-** **ranean coasts**, the islands and on the **Adriatic**. The resorts are on the Adriatic coast and in the town of **Rimini** and along the world famous **Ligurian** coast. In addition, the islands of **Elba**, **Ischia**, **Capri** and **Sardinia** are popular holiday destinations. Italy has always been the classic holiday destination for culture lovers: the country is steeped in history from Antiquity to recent times. The most popular attractions are the 'eternal city' of **Rome** which, in addition to impressive buildings from pre-Christian times, such as the Roman Forum and the Colosseum has countless churches, and Renaissance and baroque architectural masterpieces.

are on the whole, subject to a toll charge. In spite of the extensive **rail network** almost 20,000 km long, more than two thirds of all goods are transported by road.

The **inland navigation** system is operated on routes with a length of approximately 2,400 km. **Coastal shipping** is of great importance – a regular ferry service is maintained to the large islands. The largest **ports** in the country are Genoa, Venice, Naples and Leghorn (Livorno). Italy has over 96 **airports**, including eight international airports.

Tourism

Italy is one of the most popular holiday destinations in Europe, not only because of its famous **cuisine** or the pleasant year-round **climate**. The eastern **Alps**, for example the **South Tyrol** and the **Dolomites**, the about the western Alps – the rather remote **Val d'Aosta** – as well as many areas in the Apennines offer numerous opportunities for mountaineers and winter sports-

The centres of Renaissance art are found in **Tuscany**, especially in the cities **Florence**, **Sienna** and **Pisa**.

Venice, the city built on a lagoon – and sinking fast – is considered the most romantic. The cities of **Milan** and **Naples** also attract countless tourists. Southern Italy is not just for sunbathing, it also has archeological remains, especially in the **Naples** area and in **Sicily**.

Vatican City, San Marino

A view of San Gimignano: as a symbol of power and wealth, influential families in the medieval town of San Gimignano built high towers to be used as living space and fortresses. The living space provided by these towers meant that the town walls did not need to be extended. Only 13 of the 77 original towers remain today. Similar towers were once common in Tuscany, but San Gimignano provides the best preserved example.

Vatican City

Area:	0.44 sq. km
Capital city:	Vatican City
Form of government:	
Elective Monarchy	
Population: 921	
(2,070 inhabitants/sq. km)	
Languages:	
Italian, Latin	
Currency: 1 euro =	
100 cents and own currency	

Natural Geography

The smallest sovereign state in the world is surrounded by the Italian capital, **Rome**. The national territory is disjointed: next to the area about St. Peter's Basilica, the Apostolic Palace and the well-tended gardens, there are some **extra-territorial churches** and palaces in Rome as well as the Pope's summer residence at **Castelgandolfo,** which is considered to be part of the Vatican.

residents of the city are **Roman Catholics**, goes without saying.

History and Politics

The Vatican City dates back to the **Donation of Pippin** (Rome, Ravenna, the Adriatic coast), which was made to the Roman Catholic church by the French King Pippin in 754. In European history, the Vatican was always a power base to be taken seriously. In 1929, the Lateran Treaties, made with the Italian state, promised the Vatican City its sovereignty. Today, the political and religious **centres of the Catholic church** are here. The Apostolic Constitution of 1968 was amended for the first time in 1997. The **College of Cardinals** is the highest governing body, whose members – who come from over 60 states – elect the **Pope** from their midst and afterwards function as his advisers. The actual executives of the small country, and at the same time of the whole of the Roman Catholic church throughout

income are the contributions from the dioceses spread throughout the world, as well as the returns from **tourism** and the sale of postage stamps. Moreover, the Vatican mints its own coins, which are valid as currency in addition to the euro; The Vatican publishes its own newspaper and operates a radio station, which broadcasts in all the major languages of the world. It also has a news agency.

Tourism

The majority of visitors are **pilgrims**. **St. Peter's Basilica** and **St. Peter's Square**, the Vatican museums and the galleries with their immense **art treasures**, the **Stanze** containing Raphael's frescoes as well as the **Sistine Chapel** with its world famous frescoes by Michelangelo are the main attractions. The Vatican library contains one of the world's greatest collections of ancient manuscripts and early books and has great attraction for scholars.

Natural Geography

The smallest republic in Europe lies between the Italian regions of **Emilia-Romagna** and **Marche**. San Marino is cut in two by the mountain ridge of **Mount Titano** (739 m) which is the location of the ancient capital. The major rivers are the **Ausa** in the north and the **Marano** in the south east.

Climate

As in central Italy, the **mild climate** has extremes of temperature of +30°C to -2°C.

Population

Only 87 per cent of the population are **Sammarinese**, 13 per cent being **Italian**. The inhabitants are almost without exception **Roman Catholics**.

History and Politics

The **constitution** (the Arengo) of San Marino dates from 1600 but

control of politics. In 1968, Italy's status as the protecting power ended. San Marino joined the **European Common Market** in 1988 and the United Nations four years later. This brought San Marino into the European as well as the world politics. The **parliament** is newly elected every five years; citizens of San Marino who live abroad are also entitled to vote. Two so-called 'captains-regent', who are elected by parliament for a period of office of every six months function as **head of state**.

Economy

The most important economic factors of the mini-state are the sale of its own **stamps and coins** – this contributes to over ten per cent of the total economic turnover – and the extensive **tourism**. In addition, the 3,000 ha of farmland are mostly turned over to growing wheat and vines. Cheeses and olive oil are also produced. The industrial and craft

Pope John Paul II.

born Karol Woityla
*Wadowice, 18.5.1920,
†Rome, 2.4.2005

In 1978, the former Archbishop of Cracow became the first non-Italian Pope since Hadrian VI. He was the most-travelled Pope in history and supported the opposition in the countries of the Soviet bloc, particularly in his native country Poland. He was severely injured in an assassination attempt in 1981 in St. Peter's Square.

In spring, the charming green hills of Tuscany are covered in a blanket of red poppies.

Climate

A **Mediterranean climate** prevails: in summer, the average temperature is 25°C, and in winter 7°C.

Population

The Vatican has about 450 citizens, who do not pay taxes. There are also about 450 residents who have no civil rights as well as about 3,000 employees and 90 Swiss guards, who enjoy civil rights during their period of their service. The fact that all the

the world, are the various departments of the **Roman Curia**, which consist of the Secretariat of State, the Congregations, tribunals, senior officials and other offices; these can be compared to the ministries of a secular government. The pope of the day, who is elected for a lifetime, is their president.

Economy

The Vatican finances itself mainly from the running of its own enormous **treasury** and the so-called **Peter's pence**, which is raised worldwide. Other sources of

San Marino

Area:	61.2 sq. km
Capital city:	San Marino
Form of government:	Republic
Administrative divisions:	
6 Castelli	
(municipalities)	
Population: 28,880	
(459 inhabitants/sq. km)	
Languages: Italian (official),	
Emiliano-Romagnolo	
GDP per capita:	US$34,600
Currency: 1 euro =	
100 cents	

was revised in 1939 and 1971. San Marino is among the **oldest republics** in the world. Inhabited for the first time about 600, today's republic was a **protectorate,** ruled by a count and later a duke, between the ninth and the thirteenth centuries. In 1400, it became an independent state under the protection of the **Dukes of Urbino**. The republic, which was neutral in World War II, was occupied by Germany and then by allied troops in 1944. The post-war years were marked by fundamental agricultural reform and largely state

industries are limited to about 100 **small and medium sized businesses**.

Transport Infrastructure

San Marino has international connections via the **railway station** and **airport** of the seaside resort of Rimini in Italy.

Tourism

The centre of tourism is the **capital**, San Marino, with its historic fortifications, government buildings and famous basilica.

*In the mid-sixteenth century, Crusaders successfully defended the island of **Malta** against the advancing Turkish armies. After the retreat of the Muslims, the foundation stone for a new capital was laid on 28 March 1566.*

*The city was planned by Jean de la Valette and Francesco Laparelli. The result was the city of **Valetta** on the Sciberras peninsula, now the capital, with its grid-like network of streets and a surrounding defensive wall.*

Malta	
Area:	316 sq. km
Capital city:	Valletta
Form of government:	Republic
Administrative divisions:	
6 districts	
Population:	
398,000 (1,267 inhabitants/sq. km)	
Languages:	Maltese, English
GDP per capita:	US$18,800
Currency:	
1 Maltese lira = 100 cents	

Natural Geography

The **island republic in the Mediterranean** consists of the main island of **Malta** and the neighbouring islands of **Gozo** and **Comino**. The main island consists of a limestone plateau, which has neither mountains nor rivers. There are remains of land bridges which existed millions of years ago linking Malta to Italy and north Africa. The country's forests fell victim to ship-building in Antiquity.

Climate

A **Mediterranean climate** prevails with mild air and water temperatures all year round. In Valletta, the average temperature in January is 13°C, rising to 26°C in July.

Population

As many as 96 per cent of the population are **Maltese**; there is also a small **British community**. Malta is among the most densely populated countries in the world. Divorce is prohibited by law in this almost exclusively **Roman Catholic** country.

History and Politics

The areas of **Megalithic Culture** in Gantija and Mnajdra testify to the neolithic settlements that once flourished in the islands. The surrounding naval powers of **Phoenicia**, **Carthage** and **Rome** in pre-Christian times and later the **Saracens** and **Norman**s invaded the island but also passed on their skills to the inhabitants over the centuries. As a possession of the knights of the **Order of St John of Je-**

rusalem **(Knights Hospitaliers)**, whose Grand Master founded the capital, Valetta, between 1530 and 1798, Malta became a bastion of the western world against the **Turks**. In 1800, the islands were conquered by the British and remained a **British colony** until 1964. In 1974, Malta became an independent **Republic**. In 2004, accession to the **European Union** followed.

Economy

Agricultural production is too small for self-sufficiency. Wheat,

barley, potatoes, tomatoes, onions, grapes, citrus fruits and figs are cultivated, mainly with the help of artificial irrigation. About one third of the GDP derives from shoes, clothing, food and metal industries. Malta has important **harbour and ship-yard repair facilities**. The most important economic sector is **tourism**.

Transport Infrastructure

Valetta has an international **air-port**. Additionally there are **regular passenger ship connections** between Italy and most of the rest of Europe. A busy **ferry service** shuttles between the islands, which have a dense, fully developed **road network**.

Tourism

The centre of tourism is the **capital city**, Valetta, with its old part of the town, Fort St. Elmo, palaces and churches. The me-

dieval old town of **Medina** attracts many visitors. **Gozo**, on the other hand, in comparison to Malta. is largely untouched. Megalithic temples and charming fishing villages are found between remote bathing bays. **Como** which is only 2.75 sq. km in area, is a real paradise for divers with its rocky bays.

1 St. Mark's Square contains the Doge's Palace, St. Mark's Campanile, St. Mark's Basilica and the Biblioteca Marciana, and is the grand entrance to the city of Venice.

2 The Amalfi coast surrounding Naples is one of the most beautiful in the world.

3 Preserved by the ash falling from the eruption of Mount Vesuvius in 79 AD, Pompeii gives a fascinating insight into the lives of the Ancient Romans.

4 Baroque architect Gianlorenzo Bernini surrounded the square in front of St. Peter's in Rome with grand colonnades.

Great European Cities

Modern Europe boast a wealth of fascinating great cities. People are leaving the countryside in ever-greater numbers and moving to the centres of Europe: the cities.

European city culture has its origins in the cities of ancient Greece, which first came into being at least 3,000 years ago. These began as fortified towns or palace-cities or sprung up haphazard around army barracks and fortresses. From the year 800 BC onwards, new types of city began to be established in the eastern Mediterranean, mainly ports or trading posts.

After the fifth century BC, centres of population began to develop in a more planned fashion, and roads and streets were laid out according to a geometric pattern. The Romans copied this Etruscan idea and used it as the basis for their great cities.

In the Middle Ages, city growth once more centred on castles and fortresses and craftspeople and traders moved to these cities for the protection they were offered by the religious and secular rulers. Cities rapidly became economic and cultural centres, as well as transport hubs.

Towns and cities were also the catalysts for civic culture. In the Italian city-states and in the port cities that belonged to the Hanseatic League, the inhabitants began to demand rights from the ruling nobility and clergy.

The Renaissance and the baroque periods refined courtly culture in the cities. Roads, public parks and buildings were designed and positioned with artistic consideration, and the dwellings of the wealthy and less wealthy were designed with great architectural care. London and Paris developed into the first 'global cities'.

In the nineteenth century, the face of European cities underwent a radical change. Industrialisation resulted in a rapid increase in population density. Larger areas had to be given over to dwellings and multi-storey tenements were built to house new arrivals from the country. Town councillors and municipalities were faced with social problems, one of the most important being public health. Resolving these problems resulted in impressive sewerage and transport infrastructures, many of which survive to this day. Paris was the first modern city with wide boulevards and avenues and branching side-streets. Economic centralisation in the twentieth century has led to further urbanisation. Today, city centres mainly contain office and administrative buildings, and cities have expanded outwards over large areas into residential suburbs, containing shopping centres and industrial estates.

1 London (pop.: 7.6 million): The Houses of Parliament on the banks of the River Thames. The capital city of the United Kingdom combines British tradition with international modernity.

2 Rome (pop.: 2.72 million): The colonnades of St. Peter's Basilica in the Vatican. Italy's capital is also one of the most important sites for antiquities.

3 Prague (pop.: 1.22 million): The Church of St. Nicholas and the Hradcany Castle above the Vltava. The Czech capital is enjoying renewed prosperity.

4 Istanbul (pop.: 8.2 million): The Topkapi Palace and the Sultan Ahmet Mosque. The economic and cultural centre of Turkey stands on both shores of the Bosphorus.

5 Vienna (pop.: 1.6 million): The Parliament Building on the Ring. Austria's capital has long been the centre of European culture and history.

6 Madrid (pop.: 3.03 million): The Cibeles Fountain in Madrid's busiest square. The city is brimming with art and culture.

7 Moscow (pop.: 10.3 million): Red Square with the Cathedral of St. Basil and the Kremlin. Until the fall of the USSR, Russia's capital was the power centre of eastern Europe.

8 Berlin (pop.: 3.46 million): The glass dome of the Reichstag was completed in 1999. The reunified city is still getting used to its role as the German capital city.

9 Paris (pop.: 2.2 million): A view of Les Invalides and the Eiffel Tower. Paris is the capital and the heart of France, and a world city in the true meaning of the word.

10 Brussels (pop.: 978,400): Baroque Guild Houses on the Grand Place. The home to Belgium's parliament is growing into its role as the EU capital.

Poland, Czech Republic

Gdansk: The port was an autonomous city from the sixteenth to the eighteenth century, bringing great prosperity to the nation. This trading post on the Baltic coast enjoyed a higher turnover than the famous British East India Company. Imposing buildings designed by Flemish and Dutch architects were symbols for the citizens of Gdansk (Danzig) of their wealth, prosperity and education.

Poland

Area:	312,685 sq. km
Capital city:	Warsaw
Form of Government: Republic	
Administrative divisions:	
16 provinces	
Population: 38.6 million	
(124 inhabitants/sq. km)	
Language:	Polish
GDP per capita:	US$12,700
Currency:	
1 zloty = 100 groszy	

Natural Geography

The **Baltic Sea** forms the northern border of Poland. The country consists predominantly of lowlands divided by glacial valleys. The **Baltic Ridge** with the **Great Masurian Lakes** and the **Pomeranian Lakelands** are linked in the south with the **Polish mountains** which are actually rolling hills. They are separated from the **Sudeten** range and the **Carpathians** (Rysy: 2,499 m) by the Upper Silesian Basin on the southern border.

Climate

The **temperate climate** assumes a continental character towards the south. The summers are mild and rainy, the winters severe and very snowy. **Average** temperatures in Warsaw are 4°C in January and 19°C in July.

Population

Almost 98 per cent of the population is **Polish**. There are a few **minority** communities of Ukrainian, Belarusians, Roma and Sinti (gypsies). Germans are the largest minority at 1.3 per cent, of the population. In terms of religious affiliation, 95 per cent of the Polish population is Roman Catholic; there are also Eastern Orthodox and a small group of Protestants.

History and Politics

Polish tribes settled the territory in the ninth century. In the Middle Ages and Renaissance period, Poland was among Europe's great powers, but it was divided three times between 1772, 1793 and 1795 among Prussia, Austria and Russia. Poland did not regain its independence until 1918. The 1921 **constitution** formed the basis for a **parliamentary democracy**, whose timid beginnings came to an abrupt end with the German invasion in 1939. Poland's current borders were established in 1945, when it lost part of its eastern lands to the Soviet Union and extended its western borders up to the **Oder-Neisse line**. This Soviet satellite state was repeatedly unsettled by unrest and rebellion, which culminated in the major strike of 1980 led by the union leader **Lech Walesa**. The freedoms achieved were abolished soon afterwards and **martial law** was imposed. In 1989, Poland threw off the communist yoke and became a democratic republic, creating a **bicameral legislature**, consisting of the Sejm (parliament) and the Senate. Parliament elects the prime minister, while the president is elected directly. Poland has been a **member of NATO since 1999**. A further milestone was the acceptance of Poland into the European Union in 2004.

Economy

Since democratisation and the radical economic reforms which followed entry to the EU, Poland has experienced something of an **economic miracle**. Around 60 per cent of the country's land is still devoted to agriculture, which employs 26 per cent of the population and contributes seven per cent to the GDP. Small farmers own 90 per cent of the farmland on which potatoes, sugar beet, grains, rapeseed, linseed, hops and fruit are grown. Livestock also makes an important economic contribution, pork products being a major export. Although the country's coal, copper and sulphur deposits are considerable, the **mining industry** is still state-owned and is a heavy burden on the budget. **Foreign investment** in Polish industry has reached record levels, and 60 per cent of all employed Poles work in the largely privatised businesses. Polish industrial **exports** consist of metalwork, building materials, electrical items and vehicles. The service sector contributes just under 60 per cent to the GDP.

Transport Infrastructure

Poland has a well developed infrastructure. The **railway network** covers 24,313 km, of which about 9,000 km of track is electrified. The **road network** is more than 375,000 km long, and includes 258 km of motorways. There is **inland shipping** on the Vistula, Oder and Neisse rivers for 3,812 km. The major sea ports are Gdansk (formerly Danzig), Gdynia and Szczecin. There are 68 **airports**, including three international – Warsaw, Cracow and Gdansk.

Tourism

In addition to the **the Baltic Sea**, the **Great Masurian Lakes** and the mountainous region of the **High Tatras**, south of **Cracow**, **Warsaw** and **Wroclaw** as well as the former free state of **Gdansk** are popular tourist destinations. The **Slowinski national park** on the Pomeranian Lakelands and **Bialowieza** national park on Poland's border with Belarus attract hikers. Czestochowa is a site of pilgrimage to the shrine of the Black Madonna. Cracow, the former capital has a magnificent citadel, the Wawel, in which the kings were crowned and many baroque monuments, evidence of its former prosperity. It is also famous for its proximity to the Auschwitz concentration camp, now preserved as a memorial, which attracts visitors.

Czech Republic

Area:	78,866 sq. km
Capital city:	Prague
Form of government: Republic	
Administrative divisions:	
72 regions	
Population: 10.2 million	
(131 inhabitants/sq. km)	
Languages:	
Czech (official), Slovak	
GDP per capita: US$18,100	
Currency:	
1 Czech koruna = 100 haleru	

Natural Geography

The hilly landscape of the heartland, the densely populated **Bohemian Basin**, is surrounded by **the Ore mountains, the Bohemian Forest** and the **Sudetenland**. Rolling hills are also characteristic of the **Moravian Basin** in the east of the country. the highest peak is the **Snezka** (1,602 m). The most important rivers are the **Elbe** and **Vltava**.

Climate

The Czech climate is **continental** with warm summers and cold, damp winters. The average temperature in the capital, Prague, is 20°C in summer and freezing point in winter.

Horse-drawn carriages in the square of Warsaw's old town.

KATOWICE'S INDUSTRIAL CONURBATION IN SILESIA

Mineral
- Fossil coal
- Lead and zinc
- Rock salt

Industry
- Iron metallurgy and metallurgy
- Mechanics industry
- Electronics and electrotechnics
- Chemicals
- Urban and industrial areas

Lech Walesa

*Popowo, 29.9.1943

Lech Walesa was an electrician who assumed leadership of the strike committee of the Lenin shipyard in Gdansk. He became a leading Polish opposition figure and successfully fought for legal, free trade unions in Poland. In 1980, he became chairman of the Solidarity trade union. He was awarded the Nobel Peace Prize in 1983, and served as President of Poland (1990–1996).

Population

Of the population 95 per cent is **Czech**, three per cent **Slovak**, 0.6 per cent **Polish** and 0.5 per cent **German**. Other minorities are **Sinti and Roma** (gypsies) and **Hungarian**. Around 40 per cent of the Czech population do not belong to a religious denomination; 39.2 per cent are Roman Catholic, 4.6 per cent are Protestants, three per cent Orthodox and a further 13.4 per cent belong to other religions. The excellent social system, a legacy from Communist times, is undergoing a radical change.

History and Politics

The ninth century saw the rise of the **Great Moravian Empire**. Eventually, Bohemian became part of the German-dominated Holy Roman Emperor. After the **Hussite rebellion** in the early fifteenth century, and subsequent Protestant kings, the country was conquered by the Habsburgs and absorbed into the Austro-Hungarian empire. **Czechs** and **Slovaks** founded the first Czechoslovak republic which ended with the German invasion that triggered **World War II**. In 1945, the **Czechoslovak People's Republic** arose, known as the Socialist Republic from

1961, became Communist. The 1968 uprising, known as the **'Prague Spring'** was quashed by Soviet troops. The Czech Republic has been an independent **Republic**,

since 1 January 1993, after the split of Czechoslovakia into two states. The Czech Republic has a **bicameral legislature**. One third of the **Senate** is elected every two years, while members of parliament are elected every four years. In 1999, the Czech Republic joined **NATO**, and in 2004,

it joined the European Union.

Economy

Since the **privatisation** of the economy most sectors have prospered. Agriculture provides potatoes, grains, sugar beet and hops and contributes five per

cent to the GDP. There is mining of brown coal, hard coal, iron, silver, copper, uranium and lead; manufactured goods include metal, glass, textiles and paper and contributes 41 per cent of the GDP. Of the labour force, 44 per cent work in the service sector, which contributes 55 per cent of the GDP.

Edvard Benes
*Kozlány, 28.5.1884, †Sezimovo Ústí, 3.9.1948
Edvard Benes was an advocate of Czechoslovak independence from Austro-Hungary. Foreign Minister of Czechoslovakia from 1918 to 1935, and Prime Minister from 1921 to 1922, he became president in 1935, but resigned in 1938. During World War II, he led the government-in-exile, and became president again from 1945 to 1948.

Alexander Dubček
*Uhronec, 27.11.1921, †Prague, 7.11.1992
First secretary of the Central Committee of the Communist Party of Czechoslovakia, he attempted to reform the Communist regime during the famous Prague Spring. His aim was 'Communism with a human face'. This led in 1968 to an invasion by Warsaw Pact troops. After 1989, he became speaker of the Federal Assembly of Czechoslovakia.

Czech Republic, Slovakia, Hungary

*The historic heart of **Prague** is located on a bend on the Vltava River. The city is now a UNESCO world heritage site. The area of the city known as the Malá Strana (literally the 'small quarter') has many medieval buildings, dominated by*

Prague Castle. Many of the city's buildings are of great artistic, cultural and historical interest, including St. Vitus Cathedral and the Old Town and the Nove Mesto, the 'new' town founded in the fourteenth century.

Transport Infrastructure

The **railway network** covers over 9,440 km, of which 2,688 km is electrified. The **road network** is 124,000 km long but only partially surfaced. The international **airport** is in Prague.

Tourism

Tourist centres include the **Bohemian spas** of Karlovy Vary (Carlsbad) and Marianske Lazne (Marienbad), the Bohemian forests and the **Giant Mountains**. The historic cities are **Prague** and **Brno**.

Václav Havel

*Prague, 5.10.1936

This famous Czech dramatist wrote several books as well as plays in the 'Theatre of the Absurd' style. He was spokesman for the Czechoslovak opposition movement 'Charter 77' and was imprisoned several times. After the collapse of Communism in 1989, he was elected President of Czechoslovakia. He resigned in 1992, but when Czechoslovakia split in January 1993, Havel became the first President of the Czech Republic. He retired in February 2003, after exactly ten years as President.

Slovakia

Area:	48,845 sq. km
Capital city:	Bratislava
Form of government:	Republic
Population:	5.4 million
(110 inhabitants/sq. km)	
Languages:	Slovak (official), Hungarian, Czech
GDP per capita:	US$15,700
Currency:	
1 Slovak koruna = 100 halierov	

Natural Geography

Slovakia lies in the mountain system of the **West Carpathians** and consists of numerous valleys between the mountain ranges.

Particularly important regions are the outer arch of the **White Carpathians** and the **West Beskids**, the central zone of the Lesser Carpathians, the Small and High **Tatras** as well the southern volcanic peripheral zone. The small **Danube Lowlands** form the gateway to its Hungarian neighbour.

Climate

The **continental climate** produces cold winters and hot summers. The average temperatures in Bratislava are -3°C in January and 20°C in July.

Population

Of the population, 86 per cent are **Slovak** and 11 per cent **Hungarian**; 1.5 per cent are **Sinti and the Roma** (gypsies). There are other minorities. In terms of religion, 61 per cent of Slovaks are Roman Catholic, 8.4 per cent Protestants and less than ten per cent non-denominational.

History and Politics

The area has been inhabited by **Slavs** since the sixth century. It passed to Hungary in 908 and subsequently became part of the Austro-Hungarian **empire**. After the proclamation of the **Czechoslovak Republic** in 1918,

Slovakia gained **autonomy status** within the framework of the Munich Agreement. During World War II, Slovakia was a Nazi puppet state whose dictator was a Catholic bishop, Father Tiso. In 1948, Slovakia became part of the **Czechoslovak Socialist Republic** following the Communist takeover of Czechoslovakia. In 1969, it became part of the Federation of the Czech and Slovak Republic. In 1989, successful **attempts at reform**, which weakened the leadership of the Communist Party, followed the failure of the reform policy of the 1968 'Prague Spring'.

Following the break-up of the Communist states, an independent constitution came into force in September 1992 and the Slovak Republic was set up on 1 January 1993 as successor to the Czech and Slovak federation. The **unicameral parliament**, the National Council, is elected every four years. In 2004, Slovakia joined the **EU**.

Economy

The economic reform process following the separation from the Czech Republic is still not yet fully completed. **Structural changes** are still to come, but successes achieved have been limited by the financial burden

of the dominant **heavy industries**. These include iron, steel and non-ferrous metal processing and heavy machinery. Other exports are chemicals, rubber, man-made fibres and pharmaceuticals, contributing 31 per cent of the GDP. The **service sector** (64 per cent) is increasing in importance.

Transport Infrastructure

The **railway network** extends over 3,665 km, of which about one third is electrified. The **road network**, which contains 215 km of motorways, covers 36,000 km.

Late baroque buildings from the reign of Maria Theresa of Austria in the centre of Bratislava.

The **Danube**, navigable for 172km, connects the interior with the surrounding countries. The two **ports** are Bratislava and Komarno. Slovakia has eight **airports**, five of them international, Bratislava being the biggest.

Tourism

The most popular tourist destinations are the **spas** of western Slovakia. The best known of these is probably Trenãianske Teplice. The **historical cities** of East Slovakia and the Tatras are popular with sightseers. There are **18 national parks** of which the 'Slovak Paradise' is the most outstanding. Bratislava, the capital, has important historical monuments.

Hungary

Area:	93,030 sq. km
Capital city:	Budapest
Form of government:	
Parliamentary Republic	
Administrative divisions:	
20 regions	
Population:	
10 million	
(110 inhabitants/sq. km)	
Language:	
Hungarian	
GDP per capita: US$15,900	
Currency:	
1 forint = 100 filler	

Imre Nagy

*Kaposvár, 7.6.1896,
†15.6.1958

Imre Nagy was a locksmith by trade. He joined the revolutionary Hungarian workers' movement and had to emigrate to the Soviet Union in 1929. After the end of the German occupation of Hungary, he became Minister for Agriculture in 1944. He became Hungarian Prime Minister in 1953, but was forced to resign by Stalinists in 1955. He returned to office in 1956 and led great reforms. After some initial hesitation, he aligned himself with the uprising against the USSR, which was brutally suppressed. He was executed in 1958.

Natural Geography

The **Hungarian Lowland Plains** to the east of the Danube cover the largest part of Hungary. In the north, lies the **Hungarian Mountain Range** of which the highest peak is Kékes (1,015 m); in the south, there is the hilly region of **Pécs**. The **Puszta steppe**, once very extensive, has remained unchanged in few places. The **Danube**, navigable throughout its length in Hungary flows southwards through the country. The longest river is the **Tisza**. **Lake Balaton**, the largest inland stretch of water in Central Europe, is close to Budapest. Hungary is land-locked, like its Czech and Slovak neighbours.

The Gellért Baths: The natural hot springs on Gellért Hill in Budapest have been used as baths since the thirteenth century. Since the early twentieth century, visitors have been able to relax beneath the huge copper dome.

Climate

The **continental climate** manifests itself in cold, very rainy winters and very warm summers. In winter, the temperatures are near freezing, in summer they can rise to 22°C and above.

Population

Hungary's population is composed predominantly of **Magyars** (90 per cent) with minorities of **Sinti and Roma** (gypsies) (four per cent), **Germans** (2.6 per cent), **Serbs** (two per cent), **Slovaks** and **Romanians**. Two-thirds of Hungarians are Roman Catholic, 20 per cent Calvinists and there are other small religious groups.

History and Politics

In the ninth century, the **Magyars** invaded Hungary, which was a leading power in Europe until the thirteenth century. In the sixteenth century, most of Hungary came under **Ottoman rule**; western Hungary became part of the Austro-Hungarian Empire, which ruled the whole country after the Ottomans were defeated in the seventeenth century. Powerful national movements lead to **independence** in 1867; however, the country remained in the Habsburg **Austro-Hungarian Dual Monarchy** until 1918.

After World War II, in which fascist Hungary fought on the side of Germany, the **Republic of Hungary** was proclaimed in 1946. The people's democracy became a Soviet satellite under a one-party Communist system. In 1989, a peaceful reform process replaced the socialist system of government with a democratic one. In 1990 the first ever democratic elections were held.

The **unicameral parliament** of the National Assembly is elected every four years. Hungary joined **NATO** in 1999 and joined the **European Union** in 2004.

Economy

As a consequence of the privatisation and investment programmes that began in 1995/1996, the economy has experienced a remarkable upturn. A large part of the farmland is used to grow fruit, vegetables, vines and cereals as well as for breeding cattle. The **agricultural sector** contributes only seven per cent, however, to the GDP; the extensive bauxite deposits are of particular economic significance. In the highly developed **industrial sector** (32 per cent of the GDP), the main emphasis is on metal smelting as well as machinery and motorised vehicles; these are now Hungary's main exports. Chemicals, in particular **pharmaceuticals**, are an important export. **Services**, above all tourism, are areas of growth and

importance, contributing as much as 61 per cent to the GDP.

Transport Infrastructure

The **railway network** stretches over a length of 7,606 km; the connection to Austria is managed with Austrian Railways.

The **road network** covers 158,000 km, inclusive of 420 km of motorway, of which around 70,000 km are surfaced. **Inland navigation** is mainly on the Danube and Tisza rivers.

Hungary has over 15 **airports**, among them are two international airports in the capital city Budapest and on Lake Balaton.

Tourism

The centres of tourism are the capital, **Budapest** (once the twin cities of Buda and Pest) with its lovely location on the Danube and numerous historic monuments. **Lake Balaton** is a summer resort where the temperature can reach

as high as 30°C. Fishing on Lake Balaton is an important industry. The famous pike-perch (fogas), found only in the lake, being a national delicacy. The largest national park is the **Puszta Hortobágy (Hungarian Puszta)** which covers 52,000 ha. The wine country, where the famous Tokay is grown and vinified, is also popular.

1 The sculptures along the Charles Bridge lead through the bridge towers and into Prague's old town, the Stare Mesto.

2 The Danube divides Buda on one side from Pest on the other. The twin cities were amalgamated in 1873 to form the Hungarian capital, and are joined by the 375-m-long Széchenyi Chain Bridge, built between 1838 and 1849.

3 The parliament building on the Danube in Budapest was built in the Gothic Revival style in the late 19th century. The National Assembly has its seat in the southern wing.

Romania

Dracula: Bran Castle in **Transylvania** has a gruesome history. It was the residence of Count Dracula, the vampire-hero of Bram Stoker's famous novel. The real Count Dracula was known as Vlad the Impaler for his habit of impaling his victims on stakes.

Romania

Area:	237,500 sq. km
Capital city:	Bucharest
Form of government:	Republic
Adminsitrative divisions:	
41 regions	
Population:	
22.4 million	
(95 inhabitants/sq. km)	
Languages: Romanian (official),	
Hungarian, German	
GDP per capita:	US$8,300
Currency:	
1 leu = 100 bani	

Natural Geography

The **Carpathians** (Moldoveanu: 2,544 m) surround the centre of the country and the **Banat and Apuseni Mountains** join the west **Highlands of Transylvania**. In the west, the country contains part of the **Tisza lowlands**; in the south, the land stretches to the **Danube Delta** and the **Black Sea Coast** with the fertile lowlands of **Walachia**. The hill country of **Moldova** is bounded in the east by the River Prut.

Climate

The climate is predominantly **continental**, ranging from the mild Black Sea Coast to the cold winters and hot summers of the centre of the country. The average temperatures in Bucharest are 3°C in January and 23°C in July, with heavy rainfall in spring and autumn.

Nicolae Ceauşescu

*Scornicesti, 26.1.1918,
†Târgoviste, 25.12.1989

The self-appointed 'Conducator' ('Leader') became an absolute ruler in 1965. His refusal to drag Romania into the 1968 invasion of Czechoslovakia demonstrated that he was not controlled by his Moscow allies, but he was a despotic tyrant who led the country to ruin. At the end of 1989, the uprising against him gained strength and intensity, and he and his wife were eventually executed.

Population

Of the population, 90 per cent are **Romanians,** but there are also Hungarians, and the descendants of German immigrants (Transylvanian Saxons), **Ukrainians, Serbs, Croats**, Russians, as well as around 400,000 **Roma** (gypsies). 70 per cent of the population are Romanian-Orthodox Christian, six per cent are Roman Catholic and six per cent Protestant.

History and Politics

The principalities of **Walachia, Moldavia** and **Transylvania** which were formed in the fourteenth century lost their independence under the Ottoman Empire. The decline of the **Ottoman Empire** brought freedom to Bessarabia, Transylvania and Bukovina. In 1859, the principalities of Moldavia and Walachia joined them and Romania became a **sovereign state** in 1881. After World War II, in which Romania collaborated with the Nazis, it had to cede a part of its territory. The **People's Republic,** proclaimed in 1947 existed until 1960, as a satellite of the Soviet Union. This led to 20 years under the **dictator Nicolae Ceausescu**. Following his fall in 1989, Romania became a **Republic** in 1991. The **bicameral legislature** consists of a senate and parliament, whose members are elected for a term of four years. The head of state, the **President**, is chosen directly by the people for a five-year term.

Economy

Romania is in a transitional phase to a **market economy**. Farming still accounts for 64 per cent of land use. Cereals, maize, fruit and wine contribute 19 per cent of the GDP. The country's **mineral resources** (coal, oil and gas, iron, lead, copper and manganese) form the basis of the chemicals industry and the **metal processing industry**, contributing 36 per cent of GDP. The main manufactured exports are textiles, machinery and metal products. The

*Winding streets through villages lined brightly painted houses are a feature of **Transylvania**. This historic region where most of Romania's German and Hungarian minorities live. Their ancestors were brought here in the twelfth century in order to secure national borders and they still speak their languages.*

Population

85 per cent are **Bulgarian** and Romanian Orthodox and 13 per cent profess Islam. In addition, there are 8.5 per cent Turks, 2.6 per cent **Sinti and Roma** (gypsies), as well as other **Slav minorities**.

History and Politics

The first Bulgarian state was founded in 681 by the nomadic Huns. Around 200 years later, Christianity was adopted. Ottoman **Turkish rule**. which lasted a good 500 years. ended in 1878 when Bulgaria became a kingdom. During World War II, Bulgaria was occupied by the Nazis. In 1947, Bulgaria became a **People's Republic**, and Soviet satellite. Bulgaria has been a **parliamentary republic** since the fall of Communism in 1991. The **national assembly** is elected every four years. The **head of state** is directly elected by the people every five years.

Natural Geography

The Danube plains form the northern border of the country. In the south, there is the fertile North Bulgarian lowlands. Southern Bulgaria is mountainous: the Balkans, Rhodope, Rila (Musala: 2,925 m), Pirin and Vitosha Plateau cover a good third of the land mass.

Climate

The **continental climate**, marked by harsh winters and hot dry summers, is attenuated by the influence of the **Black Sea**.

growing **service sector** provides 45 per cent of Romania's GDP.

Transport Infrastructure

The **railway network** stretches over 11,365 km, of which around 3,800 km is electrified. Only half of the 153,000-km-long **road network** is surfaced. The **inland navigation routes** are 1,724 km long and mainly serve the **Black Sea port** of Constanta.

Tourism

The principal **winter sports facilities** are in the Carpathians. The best known resorts are the towns of **Brasov** and **Poiana**, 1,000 km above sea level. Sulina and Tulcea stand at the gateway to the **Danube Delta conservation area**, which stretches across the border with the Ukraine and contains unique flora and fauna.

The **Black Sea Coast** is the best known holiday destination. The **port of Constanta** dates from pre-Roman times and the nearby **seaside resorts of Mamaia** and **Eforie** offer water sports and spa facilities. The capital city **Bucharest** and **Bukovina** with its famous fifteeenth and sixteenth-century painted churches are also well worth visiting. The Romanian countryside and rural way of life is stil largely unspoilt, and has proved a magnet to tourists.

Bulgaria	

Area:	110,910 sq. km
Capital city:	Sofia
Form of government: Republic	
Administrative divisions:	
8 regions, 1 district (capital city)	
Population: 7.5 million (73 inhabitants/sq. km)	
Language: Bulgarian	
GDP per capita:	US$9,000
Currency: 1 Ley = 100 stotinki	

The Alexander Nevsky Cathedral in Sofia was completed in 1912.

Bulgaria, Moldova, Ukraine

The Roma and Sinti (gypsies) were originally nomads and there are large concentrations of them in **Romania**, **Bulgaria** and the rest of the Balkans. They have now settled across all of Europe. The Roma express their culture mainly through music. 90 per cent of Roma are professing Roman Catholics. Although most Roma communities are no longer nomadic, many Roma live apart from the general population.

Economy

The economy was affected very seriously by the **social changes** of the early 1990s. About 70 per cent of the population live in **poverty**. Extensive **privatisation plans** ought to boost the economy. **Agriculture** – which contributes 12 per cent to the GDP – provides tobacco, fruit, wine, vegetables and attar of roses; animal husbandry is important in the mountain regions. Land reform of the collective farms is still expected. There is an important **mining industry** producing brown coal, iron, lead and zinc. **Industry** contributes a total of 31 per cent to GDP, and includes heavy machinery and metal processing as well as chemicals and textile production. The **service sector**, which accounts for 56 per cent of GDP, is becoming increasingly important as Bulgaria modernises and joins the EU.

Transport Infrastructure

The **railway network** stretches over 4,292 km and is as well planned as the **road network**, which is surfaced over its total length of 36,720 km. **Inland navigation** is of relatively low significance; the major **ports,** in addition to Burgas and Varna– which are also international **airports** – are Lom and Ruse on the **Danube**. Sofia, the capital, also has an international airport.

Tourism

The resorts of the **Black Sea Coast** include Varna with its 'Golden Sands' and the **seaside towns** of Burgas and Nesebar. The **Pirin National Park** welcomes hikers and ramblers. The capital city, **Sofia** whose cathedral is the largest in the Balkans, has many other historic monuments. Winter sports facilities are close to the capital. In addition, the **Rila Monastery** in the mountain range of the same name, as well as the numerous archeological sites, particularly at **Nesebar** and **Kazanlak**, are of great tourist importance. Unquestionably, Bulgaria's most famous attraction is the Valley of the Roses, where attar of roses has been cultivated since early antiquity and is one of Bulgaria's major exports.

	Moldova
Area:	33,700 sq. km
Capital city:	Chisinau
Form of government:	Republic
Administrative divisions:	
40 districts, 10 municipal districts	
Population:	4.4 million
(131 inhabitants/sq. km)	
Languages: Moldovan (official),	
Bulgarian, Gagauz, Russian	
GDP per capita:	US$2,100
Currency: 1 Moldovan leu	
= 100 bani	

Natural Geography

The country of Moldova consists of various rolling hills with peaks of up to 430 m (Balanesti). They are crisscrossed by beautiful river valleys. The northern border of the country forms the **River Dniester**, the western border, the **River Prut**. The largest part of the area is taken up by steppe; there are some stretches of unspoiled deciduous forest.

Climate

The climate of Moldova is **continental**, with warm summers and cold winters. The average temperature in the capital Chisinau is -5°C in January, and 23°C in July.

Bulgaria: Frescoes adorn the walls of the Rila Monastery.

Population

The majority of the population consists of **Moldovans** (64.5 per cent), followed by **Ukrainians** (13.8 per cent), **Russians** (13 per cent) and minorities of **Gagauzians** (3.5 per cent), **Jews** and **Bulgarians**.
Furthermore 98.5 per cent belong to the **Eastern Orthodox Church**, 1.5 per cent are of the **Jewish faith**. There is a small group of **Baptists**. **Moldovan**, the official language, is very similar to Romanian. There have been demands for independence from the predominantly Russian-speaking population of the **Transnistria** region (east of the River Dniester).

History and Politics

In the fourteenth century, the area that is now Moldova was a part of the autonomous **principality of Moldavia**, which was conquered by the **Ottomans** in the sixteenth century. The eastern part, **Bessarabia**, was annexed by **Tsarist Russia** in 1812 and by Romania in 1918. In 1947, the whole of Moldavia was annexed by the **Soviet Union**. The Republic of Moldova declared its **independence** in 1991. A plebiscite was held in 1994 with a proposal to merge Moldova with **Romania**, but this was rejected.

Economy

Moldova has **fertile soil**, which made the country the orchards and vineyards of the former Soviet Union. Moldova has virtually no mineral wealth, and 77 per cent of the land mass is used for **agriculture**. Over half of GDP comes from the cultivation of tobacco and plants for the production of essential oils, as well as table wines and sparkling wines, canned fruit and vegetables.
Of the labour force, 46 per cent work in agriculture, which is increasingly producing goods for export. In the **heavy industries**, which are mainly located on the banks of the Dniester, heavy machinery predominates. A considerable obstacle to changing the formerly planned economy to a market economy remains the irresolute progress of **privatisation** of collective farms.

Transport Infrastructure

The 12,300-km-long road network is extensively surfaced. There are excellent international coach services linking Moldova with Russia, the Ukraine and Romania. The interior of Moldova has access to the **Black Sea** via the Dniester and access to the **Danube** via the Prut. The most important **river ports** are Bender and **Ribnita** as well as **Ungheni**. Moldova's international airport is in the capital, **Chisinau**, which is also a stop on the international railway line that links land-locked Moldova to Romania and Russia.

Tourism

Tourism is not well developed but currently centres on **capital city, Chisinau**. The **fortresses and castles** throughout the country, including the **Soroca fortress** on the Dniester, are sites of great historical interest. The best time to visit Moldova is during the **grape harvest** in October when numerous wine festivals are held.

DNEPR-DONBASS INDUSTRIAL AREAS	0 150 km

⚡	Hydroelectric power plants	▨	Industrial areas
⚙	Thermoelectric power plants	▢	Oil fields
☢	Nuclear power plants	▢	Natural gas
⌂	Main refineries		
—	Oil pipelines		
—	Natural gas pipelines		

	Ukraine
Area:	603,700 sq. km
Capital city:	Kiev
Form of government:	
Republic	
Administrative divisions:	
25 regions, autonomous Republic of Crimea	
Population:	
47.4 million	
(82 inhabitants/sq. km)	
Languages:	
Ukrainian (official), Russian	
GDP per capita:	US$6,800
Currency:	
1 hryvnia = 100 kopiykas	

Bulgaria's Black Sea Coast makes it an attractive tourist and holiday destination. After the collapse of the Soviet Union in 1989, foreign visitor numbers fell dramatically, but the region is now enjoying renewed popularity.

Natural Geography

The landscape of the Ukraine along the **Black Sea** is characterised by an undulating, fertile plain, which gradually flattens to the south. The **black earth area** is extremely fertile. The country's main rivers are the **Dnieper**, with its tributaries, the **Pripjat** and the **Desna**, as well as the **Dniester**. Mountains are found in the south-west, with the foothills of the **Carpathians** and the in the **Crimean Peninsula** (Roman-Kosh: 1,545 m) in the extreme south, jutting into the Black Sea.

Climate

The climate has **continental** characteristics, only Crimea has a **Mediterranean** climate. The rainfall tails off towards southeastern Ukraine. The average temperatures in the capital, Kiev, in the north are between -5°C in January and 19°C in July.

Population

The population consists of 73 per cent **Ukrainians**, 22 per cent **Russians** as well as minorities of **Crimean Tatars** and **Jews**. The Ukrainians are predominantly Christian and profess allegiance to the Eastern Orthodox or to the Greek-Catholic church. There are also Muslims and Jews.

History and Politics

The area covered by the Ukraine was a part of the Slav kingdom centred on Kiyv (Kiev) between the ninth and thirteenth centuries. Falling firstly to the **Mongols**, it was then incorporated into the **Polish-Lithuanian Commonwealth**. Finally, in the seventeenth century, the eastern part fell to **Russia**. After further divisions in the eighteenth century and as a consequence of World War I, the Ukraine became a **Republic of the Soviet Union**. The culture of the Ukrainian Jews, which is centuries old, was exterminated with the occupation by the **German armed forces** from 1941. After the dissolution of the Soviet Bloc and the **Declaration of Independence** by the Ukraine, the country became a member of the **CIS** in 1991. Dissatisfaction within the population led to the peaceful 'Orange' Revolution in 2004. Members of parliament are elected every four years. The **President**, the head of state, is elected directly by the people for a five-year term. The **autonomous Republic of Crimea**, whose population is predominantly Russian, was first ceded to the Ukraine in 1954 and fosters close ties with Russia. Despite its historical ties to Russia, the Ukraine aspires to join the European Union, but its economy and political structure are not yet considered suitable.

Economy

Within the former Soviet Union, the Ukraine was by far the most important **economic power** after Russia. It was always the **'granary'** of the Soviet Union (72 per cent of the land mass is under cultivation) and this, in addition to its mineral wealth and highly diversified **industry** turned the Ukraine into one of the richest of the Soviet Republics. In 1992, the Ukraine, which was **economically isolated** after the dissolution of the Soviet Union, adopted a **liberalisation** approach to the economy, but this was continuously blocked by bureaucracy. Around 14 per cent of today's GDP derives from **agriculture**, of which only a small part has so far been privatised. The **manufacturing sector** is based on heavy industry. There are rich coal and iron ore deposits. Other exports are **machinery and armaments**, which account for most of the profits.

Transport Infrastructure

The **railway network** covers a total of 23,350 km, of which 8,600 km is electrified. The **road network** of 172,565 km is largely surfaced. **Inland navigation** is used on the 4,400 km of the Pripyat and the Dniester. The very well planned network of **air routes** includes 163 airports; Kiev's Borispil is an international airport.

Tourism

The capital city, **Kiev**, is steeped in history and has numerous tourist attractions, including a ski run in the centre of the city, and the magnificent cathedral Lviv (formerly Lvov or Lemburg) also has a picturesque old town. The northern

Black Sea Coast and **Crimea** were the Riviera of the former Soviet Union and their **spa resorts**, such as **Yalta**, and the extensive vineyards are reminiscent of Italy. The historic port of **Odesa** with its classical buildings is a port of call for cruise ships. The Crimea also has sites of archaeological interest from the **Byzantine period**.

1 The Kiev Monastery of the Caves overlooks the Dnieper River and the city.

2 The crenellated towers of Swallow's Nest Castle in Yalta. This part of the Black Sea coast welcomes large numbers of tourists and has a particularly mild climate.

3 A two-storey arcade surrounds the courtyard and the medieval Hrelyu Tower (fourteenth century) at Rila Monastery in Bulgaria. The complex was begun in the ninth century when the hermit St. John of Rila moved there and lived in a cave nearby.

Slovenia, Croatia, Bosnia and Herzegovina

*The church St. Mary of the Lake is one of the landmarks of **Bled**, a picturesque **Slovenian** spa town in a narrow valley in the Karawanken mountains. Bled is not far from the Austrian and Italian borders, the place attracts thousands of foreign tourists from neighbouring countries.*

Slovenia

Area:	20,273 sq. km
Capital city:	Ljubljana
Form of government:	Republic
Population:	2 million
(99 inhabitants/sq. km)	
Language:	Slovenian
GDP per capita:	US$20,900
Currency:	1 tolar = 100 stotin

Natural Geography

Predominantly mountainous Slovenia is characterised by very different landscapes. The **Julian Alps** in the north with the 2,863 m high Triglav as well as the **Karavanke chain**, adjoin the Trnovac and the Franconian forests, which merge into the **Karst field** of Inner Carniola. In the west, there is the Triestine Karst and the 42 km long Adriatic Coast. In Lower Carniola, in the south east there is the **hill country** farmland, bordering in the north with the Sava mountainous district.
The **Sava**, the largest river in Slovenia, crosses the country from the north-west to east.

Climate

Like the landscape, the climate is also varied; it is **Mediterranean** on the coast changing inland to a **continental and Alpine climate**. Around half of the country is afforested.

Population

Slovenia is 92 per cent **Slovenian** and predominantly Roman Catholic. The standard of living is the highest in Eastern Europe thanks to an excellent **social security system**.

History and Politics

Over the long period from 1283 until 1918, the area of Slovenia was ruled by the **Habsburg Empire**. Some parts of the country were then combined with **Croatia**, **Serbia** and **Montenegro** into a **kingdom** while the other parts were ceded to **Italy** and **Austria**. Following the German-Italian occupation of 1941, Slovenia was divided between Germany, Italy and Hungary. Slovenia was re-created in 1945 when it became a constituent of the republic of Yugoslavia. In 1991, Slovenia declared its **independence**. The constitution of 1991 defined Slovenia as a **parliamentary republic** based on the model of Western European democracies. The country was largely spared during the **wars** that so damaged the other former regions of Yugoslavia because of its position at the periphery. Its historic ties to Austria make Slovenia the most 'westernised' of the countries of former Yugoslavia. Slovenia has been a member of the **European Union** since 2004.

Economy

The **service sector** contributes to 60 per cent of GDP compared with **industry** which contributes 35 per cent, principally from brown coal mining, iron and steel, and wood products. **Agriculture and forestry** contribute five per cent, mainly from cattle breeding, cereals, fruit and wine.

Transport Infrastructure

Slovenia has three **ports** (Koper, Izola and Piran) as well as three **airports** (Ljubljana, Maribor and Portoroz). The Slovenian airline is called Adria Airways.

Tourism

Slovenia's tourist destinations, including **winter sports and health resorts** in the Slovenian Alps, **spas** in the Slovenian Styria, and the famous **caves in Karst** and the **Adriatic Coast**. Ljubljana, hosts a major international art show, the Biennale.

Croatia

Area:	56,542 sq. km
Capital city:	Zagreb
Form of government:	Republic
Administrative divisions:	
20 regions, 2 districts	
Population:	4.5 million
(80 inhabitants/sq. km)	
Language:	Croatian
GDP per capita:	US$11,600
Currency:	1 kuna = 100 lipa

Natural Geography

In the west, the country is bounded by the **Adriatic Sea**; the **Dalmatian Coast**, which narrows towards the south-east, ends at the Bay of Kotor. More than **600 islands** lie off the Adriatic Coast to the northeast and have always belonged to Croatia. The largest, Krk, has its own airport. To the north-east, the Dinaric Mountains gradually give way to lowlands between the **Sava, Danube** and **Drava** rivers.

Ljubljana: buildings from the reign of the Habsburgs give the city a distinctly Austrian appearance.

Climate

The **Mediterranean climate** of the Adriatic Coast turns increasingly continental inland.

Population

Of the population, 78 per cent are **Croats**, 12 per cent **Serbs** and there are also Bosnian, Slovenian, Hungarian and other **minorities**. The majority of Croats are **Roman Catholic** (around 77 per cent). In addition to small groups of Muslims and Protestants, about 11 per cent of **Serbs are Orthodox Christians**.

History and politics

After the **southern Slavs** settled in the seventh century, the **Croatian Dynasty** was founded in the ninth century. In 152, part of the country was ruled by the **Habsburgs**, and the rest became part of the **Ottoman Empire**. Between World War I and 1941, Croatia was part of **Yugoslavia**. It became a puppet of the Nazi regime after the invasion, and rejoined Yugoslavia in 1945. The **Declaration of Independence** (the first Constitution of 1990 was amended in 1997) led to a bloody **war**, which ended in 1995.

Economy

A traditionally important economic factor is the highly developed **agriculture** sector (12 per cent). Bauxite and oil deposits are the basis for the metal-processing and the **chemicals industry**. Machine building and ship-building account for the major exports.

The economy is recovering slowly from **the war**. In the same way, **tourism** is also gradually bringing a strong currency to the country which at one time was a much visited holiday destination. Just under two thirds of the GDP is made in the **services sector**.

Tourism

The most attractive destinations are **Zagreb, the capital**, the picturesque sea ports of **Rijeka, Dubrovnik** and **Split**, the famous **Dalmatian coast** and the Krka and Plitvice lakes **National Parks** in Croatia's mountains.

Bosnia and Herzegovina

Area:	52,129 sq. km
Capital city:	Sarajevo
Form of government:	Republic
Population:	4 million
(75 inhabitants/sq. km)	
Languages:	Bosnian, Croatian, Serbian
GDP per capita:	US$6,800
Currency:	
1 convertible mark = 100 fening	

Natural Geography

Most of the land is forested, partly karst and partly **upland regions**. The soil is mostly barren; only a small part of the country – the loess soil of the **Sava** Valley – is suitable for agriculture. The country gets its name from the **Bosna River**, which flows through Sarajevo into the River Sava.

Climate

An **alpine continental climate prevails**, but the coast has a **Mediterranean climate**.

Population

The population of the country is composed of around 40 per cent **Serbs** and **Bosnians**, 17.3 per cent **Croats** and other smaller groups. As to religious faith, 40 per cent are **Muslims**, and 30 per cent **Serbian Orthodox**. The Civil War caused around one million inhabitants to flee abroad and most have not returned. A further one million people became **refugees** in their own country.

History and Politics

The **Kingdom of Bosnia and Herzegovina** was created in the fourteenth century but was conquered in 1463 by the **Ottoman Turks**. It was part of the Ottoman Empire for about 400 years. During this time, many Bosnian Christians converted to Islam. In 1878, the country was incorporated into the **Austro-Hungarian Empire**; in 1918, Bosnia became part of the **Kingdom of Serbia, Slovenia and Croatia**. In 1929, this country was renamed the **Kingdom of Yugoslavia** by King Alexander I.

*The architecture of many **Slovenian** cities is a record of the country's eventful history: some places are built in the baroque style of Austro-Hungary, while others are very Italianate in design – for example, the market square in Piran.*

Following disputes between the Slovenians and Croatians, and despite increasing ethnic problems, Alexander I restructured the country from the ground up. In 1941, the Germans invaded Yugoslavia and forced a large part of the country into the state of **Croatia** which was a puppet state of the Nazis.

In 1945, Bosnia became one of the six republics of the **People's Federal Republic of Yugoslavia**. When this diffuse state broke up in 1991, the majority of Muslim and Croats declared Bosnia to be **independent**. Bosnian Serbs proclaimed the Republic of Serbia and there followed a bitter **ethnic cleansing war** against the Croats and Muslims. After several fruitless efforts to achieve peace, a plan was only successfully drawn up in 1995 separating the country into a Serbian Republic and a Muslim-Croat Federation.

NATO Peace Forces are permanently stationed in Bosnia-Herzegovina, in order to monitor the peace process.

Economy

Production and trade were completely destroyed by the **civil war**. **Agriculture** is only possible on 37 per cent of the land mass but large tracts of fertile land lie fallow because they are sown with about three million landmines. The ruined **industrial plants** are only slowly coming back into operation. Bosnia will have to be dependent on **financial help from abroad** for the rebuilding of its economy for years to come. However, funding only trickles into the country due to ongoing fighting between warring factions and because of the massive obstacles that prevent refugees from returning to the country.

Transport Infrastructure

Road and rail networks were largely destroyed by acts of war and the state railway was destroyed in three attacks. Only recently have the main road arteries through the country come back into use. The roads and bridges, of which around 40 per cent were also destroyed in the war, are now slowly being rebuilt. Sarajevo is the only international **airport**.

Tourism

Despite the fact that Bosnia and Herzegovina still has many problems, the country continues to attract visitors. The unspoiled uplands and alpine forests are a hiker's paradise. The capital Sarajevo has a picturesque Turkish quarter. In the summer, there is a folk festival and an arts festival held by the walls of the Kastel, the ancient fortress in the old town.

Serbia	
Area:	88,361 sq. km
Capital city:	Belgrade
Form of government:	Republic
Population:	10.2 million (115 inhabitants/sq. km)
Languages:	Serbian (official), Albanian
GDP per capita:	US$4,400
Currency:	1 new dinar = 100 para

Natural Geography

Serbia is largely mountainous country with the exception of the **Vojvodina** province and several areas in the Danube and Sava river basins.

Climate

Serbia has a continental climate in its interior and a mediterranean climate on the coast.

Population

Serbs are the largest ethnic group and constitute 83 per cent of the population; in addition there are minorities of Hungarians (four per cent) and **Bosnians** (two per cent). **Albanians** (88 per cent) are the largest ethnic group in Kosovo.

History and Politics

The first Serbian kingdom was founded in the twelfth century and eventually came under Ottoman control. The country gained its independence in the nineteenth century. Serbia was the most populous republic in the socialist Yugoslavia founded after World War II. The collapse of Yugoslavia began in 1990 and ushered in a decade of wars and ethnic conflict that culminated in genocide. The Bosnian War, in which Serbia supported Bosnian Serb secessionists, ended with the Dayton Peace Treaty in 1995. Conflicts between the Kosovo Albanians and the Milosevic regime lead to a wave of repression in the province and eventually a NATO bombing campaign against Yugoslavia. Kosovo was placed under UN control. In 2000, Milosevic was forced from office. Yugoslavia was replaced by a new union of states called Serbia-Montenegro that lasted until 2006, when Montenegro declared its independence.

Economy

Serbia's economy, once one of the strongest in Yugoslavia, was devastated by corruption, war and a decade of international isolation.

Transport Infrastructure

The road network and public transport system are both well developed. Belgrade has an **international airport**.

Tourism

The tourism industry almost disappeared during the 1990s and is only now starting to slowly recovers.

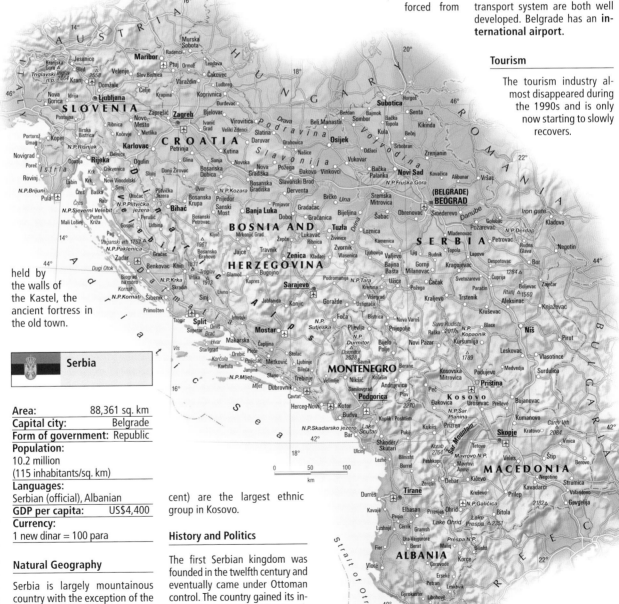

Religion in the Balkans: far left, mosque in Tirana, Albania. Two thirds of Albanians are Muslims, most of the Christians are in the north. Left, the Euphrasius Basilica in the Croatian city of Poreč dates from the sixth century.

Montenegro

Area:	13,812 sq. km
Capital city:	Podgorica
Form of government: Republic	
Population: 620,000 (45 inhabitants/sq. km)	
Languages: Serbian (official), Albanian	
GDP per capita:	US$3100
Currency: 1 euro = 100 cent	

Geography

The country's interior is mountainous with 2,500-m-high summits.

Climate

The climate is predominantly **continental** in the interior, and **Mediteranean along the Adriatic** coast.

History and Politics

The largest ethnic groups are **Montenegrins** (43 per cent) **Serbs** (32 per cent) and **Bosnians** (8 per cent).

History and Politics

Montenegro was united with Serbia for almost 90 years. It declared its independence in 2006.

Economy

The economy stagnated throughout the 1990s. Tourism is an important and growing industry.

Transportation

The road network is relatively well developed. Podgorica has an international airport.

Tourism

Montenegro's pristine coast is its major attraction. The tourism industry is now on the rise again.

Macedonia

Area:	25,333 sq. km
Capital city:	Skopje
Form of government: Republic	
Administrative divisions: 38 municipalities	
Population: 2 million (75 inhabitants/sq. km)	
Languages: Macedonian (official), Albanian, Turkish, Serbian	
GDP per capita:	US$7,400
Currency: 1 Macedonian denar = 100 deni	

Natural Geography

Macedonia is a **mountainous country** with wide **valleys**. Some of the peaks rise to heights of over 2,000 m. More than a third of the country is forested.

Climate

In the south, and in the large Vardar basin in the south-east, a Mediterranean climate predominates; in the rest of the country, a **continental climate** prevails.

Population

The largest population group is Macedonian at around 68 per cent, followed by **Albanians** (22 per cent), **Turks** and **Serbs**. About 67 per cent of the inhabitants are of **Christian Orthodox belief**; almost 30 per cent, mostly Albanians, are **Sunni Muslims**.

History and Politics

From the fourteenth century until 1913 the country was under **Ottoman rule**. The Serbian part of Macedonia was split into three in 1913 but became an independent state structure after the founding of the **People's Republic of Yugoslavia**. In 1991, this former province of Yugoslavia declared independence as the **Republic of Macedonia**. In the same year, the **constitution** was passed. **Parliament** is elected every four years, the **head of state** is elected by the people every five years. Macedonia has faced major hostility from Greece which has its own province of Macedonia and insists that Macedonia call itself FYROM – the Former Yugoslav Republic of Macedonia – to avoid confusion.

Economy

The most fertile farmland is in the Pelagonija Valley, where mostly small independent farmers grow wheat, maize, rye, tobacco, rice, vegetables, poppyseeds, fruit and grapes. **Agriculture** contributes a total of 20 per cent to the GDP.
Iron ore is **mined**. The **industrial sector** contributes 40 per cent of the GDP. The capital, Skopje, has iron and steel foundries and important leather and textiles industries. The **services sector** is gaining in importance.

THE ETHNIC MOSAIC IN THE EX-YUGOSLAVIA

Majority of
- Serbs
- Muslims
- Croatians
- Slovenes
- Montenegrins
- Bulgarians
- Hungarians
- Macedonians
- Albanians
- Mixed areas

The old harbour of Dubrovnik with its cluster of medieval buildings.

Enver Hoxha

*Gjirokastër, 16.10.1908, †Tirana, 11.4.1985

During World War II, Hoxha organised the Communist resistance to the occupying forces. In 1944, he became head of the provisional government, and from the end of the war until 1954, he was Prime Minister of Albania. He removed all opposition and led the country to political isolation. He remained commander-in-chief of the army until his death.

Transport Infrastructure

The **road network** has been extended by a new **motorway**, connecting Istanbul and Albania through Macedonia. There are two international **airports**.

Tourism

The charming city of **Ohrid** and the **lake** of the same name on the Albanian border has numerous medieval orthodox **monasteries in its vicinity**. The **national park** on Lake Prespa as well as the old town of **Skopje** with its Turkish quarter, are the main tourist centres.

*The archeological and ethnographic museum in the Albanian capital of **Tirana** has wonderful exhibits from the Illyrian, Greek, Roman and medieval periods, illustrating Albania's fascinating and eventful history. The building itself is built in the Italian, monumental style of the twentieth century, a perfect example of its type, and demonstrating the Italian influence in Albania.*

Albania	
Area	28,748 sq. km
Capital city:	Tirana
Form of government:	Republic
Administrative divisions: 27 provinces	
Population: 3.5 million (124 inhabitants/sq. km)	
Language:	Albanian
GDP per capita:	US$4,900
Currency: 1 lek = 100 qindarka	

Natural Geography

This mountainous country has over 40 mountain peaks over 2,000 m high, part of the **Dinaric** and **Albanian Alps**. Unnavigable rivers cut deep channels through the gorges of the mostly rough karst mountains. In addition to the large natural lakes such as **Lake Ohrid**, **Lake Prespa** and **Lake Scutari**, Albania also has the Fierza and Koman reservoirs needed for the Drin Hydro-electric Power Station. these three **artificial lakes** also serve as internal waterway. The 175-km-long **coast** consists of a relatively wide strip of alluvial soil.

Climate

The **Mediterranean climate** on the coast gives way to a **continental and alpine climate** in the interior.

Population

Albanians constitute 98 per cent of the population. Two-thirds are **Muslims**. Economic reforms have dragged large sections of the population into poverty.

History and Politics

In 1272, **Charles of Anjou** proclaimed the **Kingdom of Albania**. Albania was originally part of the **Roman Empire** and subsequently the **Byzantine Empire**. In 1502, the country became part of the **Ottoman Empire**, but finally achieved its **independence** in 1912/1913 as the Ottoman Empire collapsed.

Following vain attempts at democratic order and first **Italian**, then **German occupation** in World War II, Albania became a kingdom under King Zog, then a

People's Republic in 1946 under Enver Hoxha, a ruthless dictator. The Communist regime was the most radical in the West, owing allegiance mainly to China. Religion was totally banned!

Since 1990, during the course of the major political upheavals in Eastern Europe, Albania embarked on a policy of reform. In 1991, the first free **elections** were held. Since 1997, the changing governments have had to struggle with the catastrophic consequences of the collapse of the economy and of the state order. In spite of efforts from

international organisations to pacify the country, unrest is the order of the day. Furthermore, in recent years, refugees from **Kosovo** have taken an even heavier toll on the economy and social structure.

Economy

Albania is the **poorest country** in Europe. **Agriculture** contributes to over 55 per cent of GDP (grains, beans, cotton and tobacco). There is very little heavy industry. The **industrial and services sectors** only contribute a total of 44 per cent to GDP.

Transport Infrastructure

Only around a third of the Albanian **road network** is surfaced and much of the roads are unsuitable for motor vehicles, so donkey-carts represent the main form of transport in many areas. There is one European **rail service**; the only **international airport** is in Tirana.

Tourism

Even today, very few tourists visit Albania, despite the fact that the country has numerous **cultural monuments** from the ancient world and the Middle Ages that are well worth seeing and a way of life in the country that is soon to disappear.

1 Paklenica national park: Karst landscapes with their intriguing cave systems are typical of Croatia and Slovenia.

2 The Venetian influence is still apparent in Istria: a campanile rises proudly above the roofs and fishing ports of Valdibora.

3 Houses cling to the cliffs on the picturesque coast of Istria.

4 Macedonia: Lake Ohrid, the largest and deepest lake in the Balkans, offers breathtaking beaches and countless idyllic views over its clear blue water.

Greece

Selling fruit and fish: In Greece, the cultivation of citrus fruit, wine grapes and olives contributes considerably to the economy. The fishing industry is in danger due to over-fishing in the Mediterranean.

Greece

Area:	131,940 sq. km
Capital city:	Athens
Form of government:	
Parliamentary Republic	
Administrative divisions:	
13 regions and the autonomous region of Agion Oros (Mt. Athos)	
Population: 10.6 million	
(80 inhabitants/sq. km)	
Language:	Modern Greek
GDP per capita:	US$22,800
Currency: 1 euro = 100 cents	

Natural Geography

Greece is located at the tip of the Balkan Peninsula. It is bordered to the north by **Albania, Macedonia, Bulgaria** and **Turkey**, and to the south by the **Aegean Sea**. Roughly one fifth of the land mass consists of widely scattered islands. To the west are the **Ionian Islands**, the best known of which are Corfu and Ithaki. The **island of the Aegean** include Evvoia, the Northern Sporades, Lesbos, Khios, Samos, the Cyclades, the Dodecanese, Rhodes, Cythera and Crete. There are a couple of islands, Bozcaada and Imbros, that belong to Turkey. The largest island in the southern Aegean is Crete. The southern tip of mainland Greece is known as the **Peloponnese**. Almost half of the Greek mainland is covered in upland forest. The **Pindus** mountain chain extends along the west coast; the mountains in the east are dominated by **Mount Olympus** (2,917 m). The mountain chains surround the fertile plain of **Thessaly**. Even the Peloponnese and many of the Aegean islands are mountainous. There are alluvial flood plains on the coast. Mainland Greece and the Greek islands have a total of some 14,000 km of coastline, much of it consisting of sheer cliffs. Despite numerous bays, many of which extend deep inland, Greece has very few natural harbours.

Climate

The mountains have a **central European climate**, but the rest of the country enjoys a **Mediterranean climate**. Summers on the coast are dry and hot, and the winters mild and wet. In the mountains to the north, winters are bitter but summers are comparatively mild. Summer temperatures in southern Greece can often rise as high as 45°C.

Population

Approximately 95 per cent of the population is **Greek**. There are small communities of **Macedonians, Turks** and **Bulgarians**, mainly in the north, as well as some **Roma** (gypsies). The majority of the population (98 per cent) belong to the **Greek Orthodox Church**, which is the state religion. Muslims comprise two per cent of the population. More than half of all Greeks (58 per cent) live in towns of more than 10,000 inhabitants. One third of the population resides in the Athens and Piraeus conurbation alone. Rural areas are suffering increasingly as more and more people move to the towns and cities. The **average income** in Greece is amongst the lowest in the European Union. The **health and welfare systems** are underfunded.

History and Politics

The **Mycenaean civilisation** dominated in Greece from 1900 BC but collapsed in the early **Classical period**, ca. 800 BC. Ancient Greece was the **intellectual and cultural centre of the western world**. **Athens** and **Sparta** emerged as leading powers and rivals. The two cities fought each other frequently for control of the land.

Alexander the Great, who was from Macedon, founded a **world empire** and spread Greek civilisation as far as India. After his death in 323 BC, this empire quickly disintegrated.

Greece was a **Roman province** from 148 BC until 396 AD, after which it became part of the **Byzantine Empire**. In 1356, Greece was conquered by the Ottomans. It was not until 1832, after a lengthy **War of Independence**, that Greece gained its independence, and became a kingdom. A **Republic was declared** in 1924 but the monarchy was restored in 1935.

During the **Balkan Wars** of 1912 to 1913, Greece managed to extend its territory, and after **World War I** Greek forces attempted to annex parts of Turkey. Greece was occupied by Germany during **World War II**, causing great suffering. The **monarchy** was re-introduced in 1946.

There was a **military coup** by right-wing generals in 1967, and the monarchy was finally abolished in 1973. The conflict with neighbouring **Turkey** over the status of the island of **Cyprus**, which continues to this day, began with the fall of the military dictatorship. A **democratic republic** was established in 1974. The 1975 constitution provides for a **unicameral parliament**, whose members are elected every four years. A new **President** is elected every five years.

Economy

Despite many plans for privatisation, Greece still has a strongly centralised, state-run economy. Roughly one third of **exports** are of typically Mediterranean

Santorini: The Cyclades are the perfect destination for those who love picturesque villages that blend into the landscape. Cube-shaped houses painted brilliant white stand out against the brilliant blue sky, and scattered, isolated churches break the skyline. The island of Santorini is a perfect example. It is actually part of the crater of an undersea volcano that erupted around 1500 BC. The fertile volcanic soil is ideal for wine cultivation.

agricultural produce, including citrus fruits, olives, wine, currants, cotton and tobacco. There are mineral reserves of iron ore, bauxite, manganese and oil. The **manufacturing sector** contributes 20 per cent of the GDP, but still consists mainly of small businesses. Only two per cent of Greek companies have 30 or more employees.

Main exports are food, shoes, clothing and leather goods. The **service sector**, which makes up roughly 68 per cent of the GDP, is becoming increasingly important. The high percentage is mainly due to shipping and to tourism, which has a long history in Greece. Despite decreasing numbers of ships and tonnage, shipping remains one of the country's most important economic activities. Greece has the fourth largest **merchant navy** in the world. Main trading partners are other member states of the European Union and the USA. In recent years, the country has managed to curb its high levels of national debt and high inflation, and in 2000 successfully met the criteria for entry into the **European Monetary Union.**

Transport Infrastructure

The tracks of the **rail network** are only two-thirds the width of the international gauge, and only a very small part is electrified. The whole network is in need of modernisation and renovation. The **road network** is relatively well constructed.

Andreas Papandreou

*Chios, 5.2.1919,
†Athens, 23.6.1996

The son of the former Greek Prime Minister Georgios Papandreou (1888–1968) became a minister in his father's cabinet in 1965. Two years later, during the military dictatorship, he was imprisoned for a while and exiled. On return from exile, he formed the Panhellenic Liberation Movement (PAK). From 1981 to 1989 and from 1993 until January 1996, he was Prime Minister of Greece.

Nine of the country's 36 **airports** are served by international airlines. Greece also has a dense network of flight connections between the various islands and the mainland. The most important **shipping and passenger ports** are **Piraeus, Patrai, Volos** and **Salonica (Thessaloniki)**. Naturally, there is a network of ferries that ply between the islands, and from the islands to the mainland.

Tourism

Greece is a major holiday destination. Its culture and Mediterranean climate attract more than

seven million tourists annually, year round. The **Ionian** and **Thracian** islands, the **Cyclades**, the **Dodecanese** and **Crete** are the most popular holiday islands. Obviously, Greece is a favourite destination for amateur archaeologists and anyone interested in antiquities. The best-known Ancient Greek archaeological sites are the capital city **Athens** and especially its **Acropolis, Thebes** and **Delphi, Corinth** and **Olympia**. The palace of King Minos on Crete, offering a glimpse of the ancient Minoan civilisation, is another major attraction. Magnificent **Byzantine** architecture can be seen in the orthodox monasteries and churches of Mount Athos on the Chalcidice (Haldidiki) Peninsula. Mount Athos is a self-governing enclave within Greece, and the only territory in Europe which forbids entry to women. Another group of Greek Orthodox monasteries, the impressive **Meteora monasteries,**

are perched inaccessibly on the top of high rocky outcrops in the centre of Greece. Winter sports facilities are enjoyed on **Parnassus** and on **Mt. Olympus.**
Athens, the capital city, suffers from pollution due to its heavy traffic which is affecting the Acropolis, already damaged due to war and plunder.

1 The picturesque island of Mykonos in the Cyclades, and the town of the same name, is a popular tourist destination.

2 The Parthenon, a marble temple dedicated to the goddess Athena, built in the Doric style in 447 to 438 BC tops the Acropolis in Athens.

3 Crusaders stormed the island of Rhodes in the fourteenth century and converted the town of the same name into a fortress.

4 Narrow alleys wind through Oya on Santorini, one of the islands of the Cyclades.

*The Byzantine church **Hagia Sophia** in Istanbul was completed during the reign of the Roman Emperor Justinian in 537, but when the city was conquered by the Ottomans, it was converted into a mosque. In 1935, the building became a museum and national monument. The church's dome has a surface area of 7,570 sq. m and for a long time it was the largest dome in the eastern world, inspiring generations of Muslim and Christian architects.*

 Turkey

Area:	780,580 sq. km
Capital city:	Ankara
Form of government:	Republic
Administrative divisions: 81 provinces	
Population: 69.6 million (87 inhabitants/sq. km)	
Languages: Turkish (official), Kurdish	
GDP per capita:	US$7,900
Currency: 1 Turkish Lira = 100 kurus	

Natural Geography

Turkey is split in half by the **Bosphorus**, the **Sea of Marmara** and the **Dardanelles**. European Turkey (known as **Thrace**) is the smaller land mass, the **Anatolian Peninsula** in Asia accounting for most of the land mass. Turkey extends to the **Pontic Mountains** and the **Black Sea** coast in the north, and the **Taurus Mountains** in the south. Between the two lie the country's broad, high plateaus. The **Aras Mountains** (Mt. Ararat, 5,137 m) lie to the east of the **Tigris** and **Euphrates** rivers.

Climate

Both, the Mediterranean and the Aegean coasts have a **sub-tropical climate**, while the Black Sea coast has a rather **humid climate** with year-round heavy rainfall. Eastern Anatolia's high plateaus have a **continental steppe climate**.

Population

The country's population is 80 per cent **Turkish**, of whom almost all (99.8 per cent) are **Muslim**. Roughly 20 per cent of the population are **Kurds**.

History and Politics

Turkey has been ruled by the Hittites, Greeks, Persians and finally the Romans. The first state in the region of modern Turkey was established in 552 AD.
Turkey first began to flourish towards the late thirteenth century under the rule of the Sultan Osman I. His successor quickly extended the rule of the **Ottoman Empire** as far as the Balkans. In 1453, the fate of the Eastern Roman Empire was sealed when Sultan Mehmet II seized **Constantinople** (modern-day Istanbul). Constantinople then became the capital city of the Ottoman Empire, and the subsequent years were the most glorious in Turkey's history. Ottoman rule extended from **Hungary**, right across the **Balkans, the**

when the **Siege of Vienna** failed in 1683, marking the end of their conquest of Europe. The corruption of the sultanate caused a revolution by the **Young Turks** in 1909. In World War I, Turkey sided with the Germans and Austro-Hungarians and there were terrible battles against the British, notably in the Dardanelles and Gallipoli. The **Turkish Republic** was founded in 1923 with **Kemal Ataturk** as its president. The new regime attempted modernisation. Turkey opted for neutrality in World War II. After a **military coup** in 1980, Turkey received a new constitution. Current internal political problems include human rights abuses, the increasing influence of radical Islam and the conflict with the Kurdish minority. Turkey is currently seeking **EU membership**.

Economy

The most important branches of the **manufacturing sector** (textiles and clothing), which accounts for up to one-third of export income, are privately owned, but **banking, transport** and **communications** are state-owned and a heavy burden on the economy. **Agriculture**, which employs 43 per cent of the population, contributes 15 per cent of the GDP. The main crops are cere-

Transport Infrastructure

Turkey has an excellent transport infrastructure, but **rail and road connections** become fewer the further east one travels. Istanbul, Izmir and Ankara have **International airports**. The major **ports** are Istanbul, Trabzon and Izmir.

Tourism

Istanbul has many tourist attractions, including the Blue Mosque and the Topkapi Palace. The main Mediterranean resorts are Izmir and **Antalya. Ankara** and Trabzon on the **Black Sea** are also important tourist destinations.

 Cyprus

Area:	9,250 sq. km
Capital city:	Nicosia
Form of government: Presidential Republic	
Administrative divisions: 6 districts	
Population: 780,000 (84 inhabitants/sq. km)	
Languages: Greek, Turkish (both official) English	
GDP per capita:	US$21,600
Currency: 1 Cyprus pound = 100 cents	

Kemal Ataturk

born Mustafa Kemal Pasha
*Selanik, 12.3.1881,
†Istanbul, 10.11.1938

After the defeat of the Ottoman Empire in World War I, Mustafa Kemal organised the national resistance to the Greek occupation and liberated modern Turkey. After the abdication of the Sultan in 1923, he became the first President of the Turkish Republic. In terms of domestic issues, he enforced monogamy, female equality, the separation of state and church, the introduction of Latin script for Turkish and fostered closer ties with the West. In 1934, he was awarded the honourary title of Ataturk ('Father of the Turks') by the Turkish National Assembly.

In the European part of Istanbul, the 'Golden Horn' divides the districts of Galata and Beyoglu from the Ottoman old town.

whole of the Middle East including **Mesopotamia** (modern Iraq), as far south as **Egypt**.
In 1526, Sultan Suleiman I (Suleiman the Magnificent) defeated King Lajos I of Hungary, opening the way for the Ottoman onslaught on central Europe. The Ottomans' plans were foiled by

als, fruit, oilseed rape and nuts. Livestock is also an important sector. The **services sector** contributes 57 per cent of the GDP, of which a significant proportion comes from **tourism**. Approximately two million Turks live as 'guest workers' and send money home.

Natural Geography

Cyprus is the third largest **island** in the Mediterranean, lying at the intersection of Europe, Asia and Africa. The south of the island is dominated by the **Troodos Mountains** whose highest peak is Mt. Olympus (1,953 m). The

Mesaoria plain covers the interior bounded in the north by the **Kyrenia Mountains**.

Climate

The country has a **Mediterranean climate** with hot, dry summers and mild, wet winters.

*Meticulous archeological excavation and restoration has restored the city of **Ephesus,** on the west coast of **Turkey**. In ancient times, the city was of immense importance due to its harbour and its Temple of Artemis, one of the Seven Wonders of the Ancient World. Other major monuments include the **Temple of Hadrian**.*

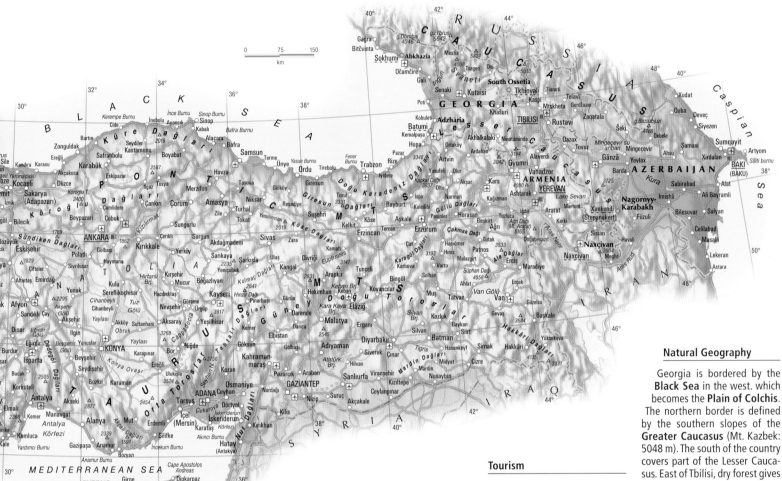

Average temperatures in Nicosia range from 10°C in January to 29°C in July.

Population

The largest proportion of the inhabitants of Cyprus are **Greek Cypriots**, representing 78 per cent of the population, of whom 99.5 per cent live on the Greek part of the island. **Turkish Cypriots** comprise 18 per cent of the population, and 98.7 per cent live in the Turkish part of the island. Cypriots are 78 per cent **Greek Orthodox**, and 18 per cent Sunni **Muslim**.

History and Politics

The island has been ruled by a series of nations, from the Egyptians, the Phoenicians, the Persians, Romans, Arabs, Crusaders and the Venetians. In 1925, it became a **British colony**. Cyprus declared itself an independent **republic** in 1960, but the United Kingdom continues to maintain military bases on the island. The **conflict** between the Greek and Turkish populations erupted into civil war in 1963. After the Turkish invasion of 1973, the island was partitioned in 1974. The **Turkish Republic of Northern Cyprus** is only internationally recognised by Turkey. The **Republic of Cyprus** is governed by a house of representatives, in which only the seats for Greek Cypriots are occupied. Northern Cyprus has its own parliament. Cyprus joined the European Union in 2004, despite the unresolved problems of partition. Shortly after the signing of the accession treaties in the spring of 2003, the Turkish-Cypriot government opened the border between the two sides of the island.

Economy

There is a great discrepancy between the Greek and Turkish parts of the island. In the Republic of Cyprus, 62 per cent of the workforce is employed in the **service sector** (tourism, shipping and banking), contributing 75 per cent of the GDP. **Manufacturing**, including agricultural produce, textiles and vehicle assembly for export, contributes 22 per cent of the GDP. In Northern Cyprus, **agriculture** and tourism are the main sources of income.

Transport Infrastructure

There is no longer a railway on the island. The **road network** covers 12,500 km. There are **International airports** in Nicosia and Paphos. Cyprus has the fourth-largest merchant navy in the world.

Tourism

One of the many attractions is the old city of **Nicosia**. The **Troodos Mountains and the Kyrenia Mountains** contain numerous churches of the Byzantine period. The most popular coastal resorts are Limassol, Kyrenia and Larnaca. There is skiing in Troodos in the winter and one can swim in the Mediterranean on the same day.

✚ Georgia		

Area:	69,700 sq. km
Capital city:	
Tbilisi	
Form of government:	Republic
Administrative divisions:	
79 districts and cities,	
3 autonomous regions	
Population: 5 million	
(72 inhabitants/sq. km)	
Languages: Georgian (official),	
Russian, Armenian	
GDP per capita:	US$652
Currency:	
1 lari = 100 tetri	

Natural Geography

Georgia is bordered by the **Black Sea** in the west. which becomes the **Plain of Colchis**. The northern border is defined by the southern slopes of the **Greater Caucasus** (Mt. Kazbek: 5048 m). The south of the country covers part of the Lesser Caucasus. East of Tbilisi, dry forest gives way to grassy steppes. Up to 80 per cent of the land is mountainous, and the population lives mainly around the river basins.

Climate

The Black Sea coast has a **humid sub-tropical climate**. Average temperatures in Tbilisi range from 6°C to 23°C, but east of the capital city, the climate becomes increasingly **continental**.

Population

Georgians constitute 70 per cent of the population, with 8 per cent **Armenians**, 6.3 per cent **Russians**, 5.7 per cent **Azerbaijanis**, three per cent **Ossetians** and 1.7 per cent are **Abkhazians**. Three-quarters of the population are Christian orthodox, 11 per cent of them Russian Orthodox. Muslims represent 11 per cent of the population and 8 per cent belong to the Armenian Apostolic Church. Georgia has some 250,000 internal refugees as a result of the

*Today, the traders in **Istanbul's** covered bazaar mainly trade with tourists. The bustling atmosphere is typical of souks and markets all over the Middle East. The oldest part of the original bazaar, the Old Bedesten, dates from the time of Mehmed the Conqueror. From here uncovered streets lead to the so-called Egyptian Bazaar.*

struggles for independence in the region.

History and Politics

Georgia in mentioned in ancient **Greek myths**. The land was occupied by the **Romans** from 65 BC, and in the fourth century AD became part of the **Byzantine Empire**. The Georgian kingdom reached the height of its glory in the twelfth and thirteenth centuries, until the land was conquered by the **Mongolians** in the mid-thirteenth century. The country was **divided** between the **Ottomans, Persians** and **Russians** in 1555, and in the eighteenth century, a kingdom of East Georgia was created, which became part of Tsarist Russia between 1801 and 1810. Georgia declared its independence in 1918, and the **Georgian Socialist Soviet Republic** was formed in 1921. Since **independence** in 1991, the pre-

dominately Islamic republics of **Abkhazia** and **South Ossetia** have fought to separate from Georgia. The **Autonomous Republic of Adjara** is 54 per cent populated by Georgian Muslims. In 1993–94, Georgia joined the **Commonwealth of Independent States** (CIS), consisting of members of the former USSR.

Economy

Agriculture represents 30 per cent of Georgia's GDP, and most of the arable land is used for growing turnips, cereals and potatoes. Tropical fruit, tea, tobacco and grapes are important crops and Georgian wines are famous throughout Russia. Georgian tea, a cross between Indian and Chinese, is mainly drunk in Russia. In the sub-tropical coastal region, eucalyptus and bamboo are grown.

Georgia has important mineral resources. Iron ore, oil, coal, copper, manganese, barite, diatomite and semi-precious stones are mined. The manufacturing industry produces food and textiles and contributes 31 per cent of GDP. **Exports** include raw materials and foodstuffs.

Tourism has been important for Georgia, since it was part of the Soviet Union. Tourism continues to flourish and currently employs about one third of the population, representing most of the **service sector**.

Transport Infrastructure

The **infrastructure** has suffered badly from recent civil wars and economic problems. The **rail network** covers 1,583 km but is in poor condition. There are 20,700 km of **roads, however,** much of which are surfaced, though they can be impassible in the winter in the mountains. The **international airport** is in Tiflis (Tbilisi), and the major sea **ports** are Batumi, Poti and the Abkhazian capital city of Sokhumi.

Tourism

The country has 15 **nature conservation areas** and extensive **winter sports and hiking** facilities. **Sokhumi** and **Batumi** on the **Black Sea** coast are popular resorts. There are many **spas and hot springs** in the mountain regions. Important cultural centres are **Tbilisi, Kutaisi** and **Mtskheta**. Georgia's unique cultural heritage is a major attraction for tourists from the West.

Armenia	
Area:	29,800 sq. km
Capital city:	Yerevan
Form of government:	Republic
Administrative divisions:	
11 regions	
Population: 3 million	
(11 inhabitants/sq. km)	

Languages:
Armenian (official), Russian, Kurdish

GDP per capita:	US$5,100
Currency:	1 dram = 100 luma

Natural Geography

The **Armenian Highland** extends across the western reaches of the country. The north is dominated by the peaks of the **Lesser Caucasus**. The highest mountain is Mount Aragats (4,090 m). Armenia lies at an average elevation of 1,800 m. The most fertile areas are found in the southern **Aras Valley**, where climate and soil are favourable for agriculture. Powerful earthquakes are common in Armenia and the country often suffers from prolonged **droughts**.

Climate

Armenia has a **continental climate** and steppe and semi-desert vegetation. Summers are hot, with temperatures in the capital, Yerevan, reaching an average of 25°C, but winters are bitterly cold.

Population

Armenians constitute 96 per cent of the population, and there are also minority populations of **Kurds** and **Russians**. Christianity was introduced in the third century AD, making Armenia the oldest **Christian nation** in the world. Despite former Soviet rule, 94 per cent of the population belongs to the Armenian Apostolic Church. The people of Armenia suffer from the effects of an economic crisis and have a poorly developed **health care and social system**. Their plight is intensified by natural disasters, such as earthquakes, and extreme air and environmental pollution.

History and Politics

The country was conquered in turn by the **Persians, Arabs** and Mongols. In 1828, northern Armenia was conquered by Tsarist **Russia**. The first Armenian Republic was founded in 1918, but was divided in 1922, one part becoming a Soviet republic of the USSR, and the other part ceded to **Turkey**. Armenia declared independence in 1991.

Armenia is demanding autonomy for the **Nagorno-Karabakh**, exclave which lies within the borders of **Azerbaijan** but whose population is overwhelmingly Armenian Christian. This has led to conflicts. Azerbaijan, in turn, lays claim to the enclave of **Nakhichevan**, which is situated within Armenia's borders.

Economy

Armenia's economy is still struggling to cope with the **transition** from the **Soviet centrally planned economy** to a **market economy**. Agriculture represents one third of the country's GDP, based on the cultivation of cereals, tea, vines and tobacco. The **manufacturing industry** was highly developed during the Soviet era and is today beginning to develop once more. Important **exports** are light industry products. The main imports are crude oil, gas and food.

The **services sector** is underdeveloped and contributes to only 20 per cent of GDP. The Armenians have a large diaspora throughout the world, but especially in Turkey and Russia, and they help to fund the country's economy.

Transport Infrastructure

The country's **rail network** covers 825 km, but both the rail and **road network** are in a poor condition. There is an **international airport** in Yerevan.

Tourism

The capital city, **Yerevan,** contains several important museums and is the country's cultural centre. Armenia's greatest treasures are, without doubt, the numerous early Christian monuments. There are magnificent **churches and cliff top monasteries** in the mountains around Yerevan. **Lake Sevan,** at an altitude of 1,600 m, is popular with hikers.

The Blue Mosque in Istanbul gets its name from the blue Iznik tiles covering its walls.

*Much of **Turkey** is farmland, but many farmers have to survive without modern equipment – so the donkey is a very important pack-animal. Agriculture has only been modernised in the fertile lowlands.*

![Azerbaijan flag]	**Azerbaijan**

Area:	86,600 sq. km
Capital city:	Baku
Form of government:	Republic
Administrative divisions: 54 districts, 9 cities, 2 autonomous regions	
Population: 7.9 million (90 inhabitants/sq. km)	
Languages: Azerbaijani (official), Turkish, Russian	
GDP per capita:	US$4,600
Currency: 1 Manat = 100 gepik	

Natural Geography

The **Greater Caucasus** in the north (4,466 m), the **Lesser Caucasus**, the **Karabakh** in the west and the mountain chain in the south, which extends into Iran, cover over half of Azerbaijan's land mass. In the east of the country lie the beginnings of the plains of the **Kura** and **Aras** rivers, which are bordered in the south by the **Caspian Sea**. Parts of this region lie up to 28 m below sea-level. The **Nakhichevan** enclave is separated from the rest of the country by the Sangesur mountains.

Climate

Azerbaijan has a **semi-desert climate**, meaning that agriculture is only possible through the irrigation of large tracts of land. Average temperatures in the capital, Baku, range from 1°C to 34°C.

Population

The population is 90 per cent **Azeri**, 2.5 per cent **Russian** and two per cent **Armenian**. All the Armenians live in the **Nagorno-Karabakh** region. The vast majority of the population is **Muslim**, but there are small groups of **Orthodox Christians**.

History and Politics

The region has been inhabited for millennia, and was once a **Roman province**. It has been a **Muslim country** since the seventh century. After 300 years of **Mongolian** rule, the country first had to fight off the **Ottoman Turks** then deal with attack from **Tsarist Russia**. It was then divided between the

Russians and the Persians in 1813. The **Soviet Republic of Azerbaijan** was established in 1920. Ethnic conflicts in the dispute over the Nagorno-Karabakh region and its union with Armenia in 1988 led Azerbaijan to declare **independence** in 1991 and revived Islamic fundamentalism in the country, although it has not allied itself with other Muslim countries and maintains good relations with Israel and the West.

Economy

Agriculture accounts for 30 per cent of GDP, and much of it provided

by **caviar** from the Caspian Sea. Azerbaijan has rich **reserves** of oil, iron and precious metals. These resources are being developed with the aid of foreign companies. The remaining **manufacturing industry** (chemicals, heavy machinery) is geared towards these resources.

Transport Infrastructure

The public **rail network** covers 2,125 km and the mostly surfaced **road network** covers 57,700 km. The main **port** and **international airport** are located in Baku which is also an important **oil terminal**.

Tourism

Baku is Azerbaijan's cultural centre with numerous mosques, palaces and an interesting old town. The **Seki caravanserai**, in the foothills of the **Caucasus**, is an ancient hostel for travellers, now converted into a delightful hotel. There are ancient **Babylonian monuments** in the south.

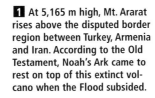

1 At 5,165 m high, Mt. Ararat rises above the disputed border region between Turkey, Armenia and Iran. According to the Old Testament, Noah's Ark came to rest on top of this extinct volcano when the Flood subsided.

2 Turkey is not a well-known wine producer, but the regions around the Sea of Marmara and the Aegean yield excellent red and white wines.

3 Bodrum is an historic town, whose narrow streets are filled with tourists in the summer. In antiquity, the town was known as Halicarnassus and was the site of the tomb of King Mausolus – one of the seven wonders of the Ancient World. The castle on the headland dates from the time of the Crusades (fourteenth century).

4 The thirteenth century Metechi Church sits atop a craggy peak above the Georgian capital city of Tbilisi.

Russia

St. Petersburg: one of the world's greatest art collections is housed in the Hermitage. Since the collapse of the Soviet Union, foreign tourists are once again flocking to the city (formerly Leningrad) which has a long tradition of attracting visitors. In the mid-nineteenth century, Leo von Klenze, court architect of Bavarian King Ludwig I, designed the buildings that surround the Winter Palace.

Russia	
Area:	17,075,200 sq. km
Capital city:	Moscow
Form of government: Federal Presidential Republic	
Administrative divisions: 89 territories of the federation	
Population: 143.4 million (8 inhabitants/sq. km)	
Languages: Russian (official), more than 100 other languages	
GDP per capita: US$10,700	
Currency: 1 rouble = 100 kopecks	

Natural Geography

Russia is the **largest state** on Earth in terms of area, covering some 11 per cent of the surface of the planet. It extends from the **Baltic** and the **Black Sea** in the south to the **Pacific** and the **Bering Straits** and from the **Arctic Ocean** to the inner Asian uplands. There is a time difference

the north and north-east the gigantic afforested regions of the **Taiga belt** covering large parts of Siberia merge into the **Arctic Tundra**; there are peninsulas off the north-east **coast**, such as Kola and Kamchatka and islands such as Sakhalin, which is part of the Japanese archipelago. To the south-east, the wide **steppes** give way to **desert**.

In total, more than one-fifth of the **afforested areas** of Earth are situated within the territory of the Russian Federation. They include the great mixed woodlands of western Russia as well as the huge coniferous forests (boreal forests) of the Taiga in the north. The **Kamchatka** peninsula on the Pacific and the **Kuril Islands** at the extreme east of the country are full of seismic activity. Of the 3,000 **volcanoes** on Kamchatka, thirty are still active; the highest of these peaks is Klyuchevskaya Sopka (4,750 m). Ten **rivers** more than 2,200 km in length flow through Russia, of

Climate

The Russian climate is as varied as the enormous extent of the country. It ranges from the **steppe climate** in the central-south through the **dry continental climate** of most of the European part of Russia, with very hot summers and snowy winters, to the **sub-Arctic and Arctic** temperatures of Siberia. The whole of the north is characterised by a **tundra and polar climate**.

The **coldest place on** Earth is at Oimyakon, Eastern Siberia. Temperatures of -69.8°C have been recorded here. Just under half of the total land mass of Russia is under permafrost. The Black Sea coast and south-central Asia, however, are typically **sub-tropical**, with temperatures of between 6°C in the winter and an average of 23°C in the summer. Temperatures in Moscow in January are -9°C on average, and temperatures of -30°C and below are by no means uncommon. In July,

Russia as well as in the Urals and along the route of the Trans-Siberian Railway. As a result of the deliberate **russification** of the Soviet Union, an estimated 25 million Russians live in the Commonwealth of Independent States, the successor countries of the Soviet Union and in the Baltic states. After decades of **state atheism** in the former USSR, most Russians today profess no religion. The largest number of adherents is claimed by the Russian Orthodox church, while the country also includes a large number of Muslims, as well as minorities of Jews, Catholics, animists and Buddhists. **Other sects** (such as Mun and Aum) are also widely represented. The **health, pensions and social security sys-**

Monument to Nicholas I and St. Isaac's Cathedral in St. Petersburg.

of more than ten hours between the Bering Straits and the Baltic. The **Urals** (Mount Narodnaya: 1895 m) divides the interior of Russia into the **Eastern European Uplands** and the **Western Siberian Lowlands**, an enormous wetland area about the size of Central Europe, fed by the rivers **Ob** and **Yenissey**.

The **Caucasus** (Mount Elbrus: 5633 m) forms the south-eastern border of the country, which is enclosed in the east and southeast by hills and mountains. In

which the longest is the **Ob** with its tributary the **Irtysh**, which rises in the Altai mountains and flows into the **Karal Sea**. The two rivers combined are 5,410 km long.

At 3,351 km, the **Volga** is Europe's longest river. The largest lake, which lies close to the Caspian Sea, is the 600-km-long **Lake Baikal**, south of the Central Siberian mountain range. It has a maximum depth of 1,620 m, making it the deepest freshwater lake on Earth.

the temperature rises to an average of 20°C.

Population

The majority of the population, of whom only 20 per cent live in the Asian part of Russia, are **Russians** (81.5 per cent); minorities include **Tatars** (3.8 per cent), **Ukrainians** (three per cent), **Chuvashes** and hundreds of other ethnic groups, including 0.6 per cent of **German origin**. The **main settlement areas** are in the European part of

tems, were built up under the Soviet Union and until recently were heavily subsidised. They are now in a state of flux, and as a result there is great difficulty in achieving effective adjustment to the fundamentally altered social and economic conditions. About one-fifth of the population, particularly old people, live below the national **poverty line**, and the number is growing, though recent increases in the price of oil and gas, major Russian exports, have improved matters.

History and Politics

As early as the first millennium BC the **ancient Slavs** came from the East and settled in the area around the Dnieper. On the **trade route** between the Baltic and the Black Sea, there developed **Kievan Rus**, a country that was christianised as early as 988. It was to become the largest state in Europe until it was overrun by the **Mongols** in 1230. Before this, it gained in standing and influence through its trade with Byzantium. **Novgorod** remained for a long time the only city-state to withstand the onslaught of the Mongols. It was the principality of Moscow, obscure hitherto, that in 1380 vanquished the Golden Hordes and unified the existing **Russian city-states**. In 1547 the Grand Duke of Muscovy, Ivan IV, had himself crowned the **first Tsar** of all the

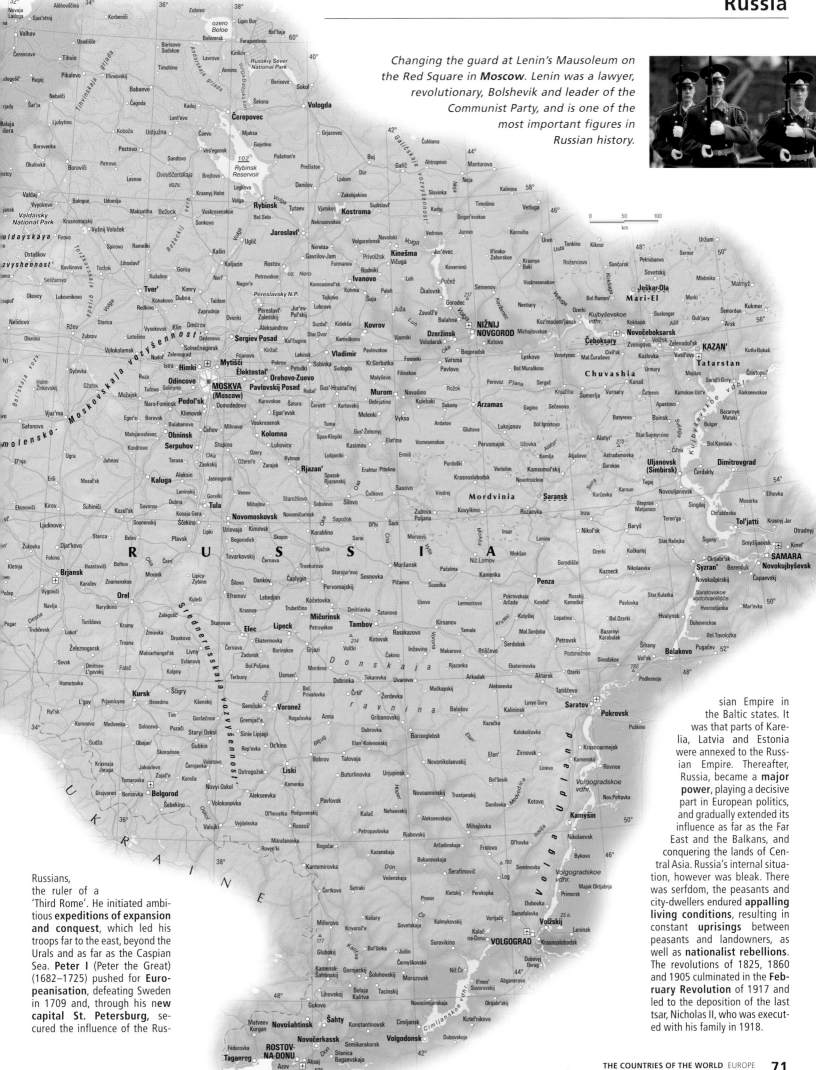

Changing the guard at Lenin's Mausoleum on the Red Square in **Moscow**. Lenin was a lawyer, revolutionary, Bolshevik and leader of the Communist Party, and is one of the most important figures in Russian history.

Russians, the ruler of a 'Third Rome'. He initiated ambitious **expeditions of expansion and conquest**, which led his troops far to the east, beyond the Urals and as far as the Caspian Sea. **Peter I** (Peter the Great) (1682–1725) pushed for **Europeanisation**, defeating Sweden in 1709 and, through his **new capital St. Petersburg,** secured the influence of the Russian Empire in the Baltic states. It was that parts of Karelia, Latvia and Estonia were annexed to the Russian Empire. Thereafter, Russia, became a **major power**, playing a decisive part in European politics, and gradually extended its influence as far as the Far East and the Balkans, and conquering the lands of Central Asia. Russia's internal situation, however was bleak. There was serfdom, the peasants and city-dwellers endured **appalling living conditions**, resulting in constant **uprisings** between peasants and landowners, as well as **nationalist rebellions**. The revolutions of 1825, 1860 and 1905 culminated in the **February Revolution** of 1917 and led to the deposition of the last tsar, Nicholas II, who was executed with his family in 1918.

Russia

*Moscow: the underground is an important method of transport in the capital city of the **Russian Federation**. Since 1935 it has guaranteed speedy connections between different parts of the city. Many of the stations are spectacularly decorated, as seen here at Komsomolskaya. This is yet another sign of Moscow's importance as the political, economic and cultural centre of the former USSR.*

In the **October Revolution** of 1917, the Provisional Government was replaced in a coup by the Workers' Councils, the Bolsheviks, who seized executive power under the leadership of **Vladimir Ilyich Lenin** and **Lev Davidovich Trotsky**. The Communist Party set up a **'dictatorship of the proletariat'**. After the the Red Army won back numerous provinces that had used this opportunity to secede from Russia, the **Union of Soviet Socialist Republics (USSR)** was founded in 1922. Nationalities were officially granted the right to self-determination. Under the USSR's next ruler, **Josef Vissarionovich Stalin**, industrialisation was driven forward from 1924 on a massive scale, and agriculture was collectivised, but at the same

Finland and as far as Manchuria. The Berlin blockade of 1948 marked the beginning of the **Cold War** with the USA; in 1949 the USSR became an **atomic power**. On Stalin's death, the process of **destalinisation** was begun, and limited cooperation with the USA started. In spite of several crises, such as the Cuban Missile Crisis of 1962, a rapprochement with the West continued. **Leonid Ilyich Brezhnev** suppressed the **struggle for independence** of the satellite states such as Czechoslovakia, Poland and Hungary, and made efforts to secure the postwar borders. The enormous cost of the **arms race** took its toll, and the economy suffered a downturn. Gradually, a **dissident movement** took shape, which finally led in 1985 to the election of

nia in August 1991, the Ukraine in 1991, Lithuania and Tadjikistan in September 1991 and Kazakhstan in December 1991).
With the **resignation of Gorbachev** at the end of 1991, the old USSR was finally dissolved. Its successor was the **Russian Federation**, consisting of 21 autonomous republics: Adygea, Altai, Bashkortostan, Buryatia, Khavkassia, Dagestan, Ingushetia, Kabardino-Balkaria, Kalmykia, Karachay-Cherkessia, Karelia, Komi, Mari El, Mordova, North Ossetia, Sakha, Tatarstan, Chechnya, Chuvashia, Tuva and Udmurtia. Added to these were Birobidjan, the Jewish autonomous region on the Chinese border, the autonomous region of the Nenets on the Barents Sea, the autonomous region of the Chukchi on the

the **Federation Council**, to which each of the total of 89 administrative regions (republics, regions and districts) sends two deputies. The **President**, directly elected by the people is accorded extensive authority.
A **potential for conflict** in the future lies in the aspirations to independence of some republics which have led in recent years to violent military clashes in Chechnya, Ossetia and Tatarstan. In the **Commonwealth of Independent States (CIS)**, the union of the twelve former Soviet republics of Armenia, Azerbaijan, Georgia, Kazakhstan, Kyrgyzstan, Moldova, Russia, Tadjikistan, Turkmenistan, Ukraine, Uzbekistan and Belarus, Russia, as the successor to the Soviet Union, plays a leading role.

can be undertaken on only 12 per cent of the land mass, has been largely privatised and contributes seven per cent to the country's GDP, but the **country's domestic needs** are not yet entirely met by the cultivation of potatoes, grain, sugar beet and cabbage along with the livestock and dairy industries.
The strongly diversified **industrial sector**, which has been privatised to a great extent (machine construction, aeronautics, armaments, mining, iron and steel foundries, vehicle manufacture, chemistry, forestry, timber and paper production), is based on the immense supply of raw materials, but they are currently unable to generate sufficient profits.
The **service sector** is of growing importance. Until recently it contributed 52 per cent of the GNP. A large share of the economy of the country, even though difficult to assess, is represented by the so-called **black economy**, which is not included in official statistics because of the large amount of missing tax payments.
The huge rise in the price of oil and gas, of which Russia has taken full advantage, has been a great boost to the economy. Despite its present relative underdevelopment, thanks to its natural resources, Russia is forecast to become one of the world's leading industrial powers by the mid-twenty-first century.
Major pollution, due to neglect during the Communist era, is a serious threat. One of the former regime's misguided policies was the diversion of the rivers that fed the Aral Sea in Central Asia. It has caused the sea to dry up almost completely.

Nikita Khrushchev

*Kalinovka, 17.4.1894,
†Moscow, 11.9.1971

After Stalin's death in 1953, Khrushchev joined the internal power struggle. At the Twentieth Party Congress in 1956, he exposed Stalin's crimes and became premier of the Soviet Union in 1958. His attempt to produce a 'thaw' in the Cold War was overshadowed by the Berlin blockade, the Hungarian Uprising, the Berlin Wall, the Cuban missile crisis and the split with China. He was deposed by Brezhnev in 1964.

Ice statues in front of St. Basil's Cathedral in Moscow.

Mikhail Gorbachev

*Privolnoje, 2.3.1931

After being named General Secretary of the CPSU, Gorbachev led a process of democratisation of the Soviet Union under his 'perestroika' and 'glasnost' programmes. He also ended the atomic arms race. The collapse of the political and economic systems of the Eastern Bloc also led to the breakup of the USSR, of which he was president until 1991. He received the Nobel Peace Prize in 1990.

time the government also set up labour camps to which dissents were deported and ordered millions of executions of alleged enemies of the state.
In 1939, Stalin concluded a **non-aggression pact** with Germany using this opportunity to gain time and to annex the Baltic states and eastern Poland. When the German Wehrmacht eventually attacked the Soviet Union in 1941 Russia entered the **World War II**. The Red Army valiantly defended its territory making great sacrifices until it was finally victorious, entering the German Reich and occupying Berlin in 1945. After World War II, the Soviet sphere of influence extended over the whole of Eastern Europe through

Mikhail Sergeyevich Gorbachev as General Secretary of the Communist Party.
His slogans of **'glasnost'** and **'perestroika'** introduced the 'politics of change' which involved Russian renunciation of pretensions to the domination of its neighbours. This also produced **political upheavals** in the satellite states of central and eastern Europe. The year 1989 saw the reunification of East and West Germany, and only a year later, the mighty **Warsaw Pact**, an alliance of Communist countries to counter that of NATO, was dissolved. Within the USSR, **nationality conflicts** soon broke out and the first republics asserted their independence (Latvia in 1990, Esto-

Bering Strait, and the autonomous region of the Evenks in Central Siberia. Plans to set up an autonomous republic for **Germans** living in Russia were postponed for the time being, but the republic of Altai includes administrative districts with self-government by German residents. Part of the territory of the Russian Federation is the **exclave of Kaliningrad**, between Poland and Lithuania. The 1993 agreement, which was rejected by the republics of Chechnya and Tatarstan, envisages a federated democratic republic.
Russia's **bicameral parliament** consists of the **State Duma**, whose representatives are directly elected every four years, and

Economy

Russia, a gigantic country with an apparently inexhaustible supply of **raw materials** (one third of the Earth's natural gas, 12 per cent of its petroleum and one third of the coal in the world, apart from enormous supplies of gold and iron ore, the largest deposits on Earth of minerals in the Urals, uranium and immense stands of timber), has massive heavy **industry** but, like the inefficient **agricultural sector**, continues to suffer from the long-term consequences of transformation from the erratic Soviet planned economy to a market economy. Farming, which on account of the climatic conditions

Transport Infrastructure

Russia's **railway network** covers 154,000 km mainly in the southwestern part of the country. Some 40 per cent of the system is reserved for freight. The most important long-distance connection is the **Trans-Siberian Railway**, which covers more than 9,311 km and runs from Moscow to Vladivostok. There is also an extension to China, as far as Beijing.
Russia's **road network** extends over a length of 948,000 km, of which 416,000 are not public, but

Russian Orthodox churches: Despite the great iconoclasm of the eighth and ninth centuries, holy icons are still central to the rituals of Russian Orthodoxy, which has survived through eighty years of atheist, Communist rule.

reserved exclusively for military and industrial purposes. Only 336,000 km are surfaced, another 201,000 are only passable during a few months of the year. Russia has more than 630 **airports**, meaning that even remote areas of Siberia can be reached by air.

The two international airports are Sheremtevo in **Moscow and St. Petersburg**. The national airline **Aeroflot**, which is still largely state-owned, is the largest airline in the world. **Inland navigation** on the waterway whose total length is 101,000 km, of which 16,900 km are canals, is also an important means of transport. The country's most important **ports**, the gateways to the Pacific, Atlantic and North Sea, the Black Sea and the Baltic, are at Archangel (Arkhangelsk), St Petersburg, Kaliningrad, Vladivostok, Okhotsk and Rostov.

Tourism

Russia continues to attract mainly **group travel**, because since the dissolution of the state tourist organisation, when individual travel was actually forbidden the tourist sector has been in a state of flux. **Individual tourists** encounter obstacles such as an inadequate infrastructure and an occasionally crippling bureaucratic system. In addition, many areas are still forbidden to tourists. This gigantic country has innumerable attractions to offer, from **beautiful landscapes** to superb evidence of its long **cultural history**.

The main centres of tourism are the two great cities of **St. Petersburg and Moscow**. Among the most important sights of St. Petersburg, capital city of the tsars, are the 125 museums, including the **Church of the Resurrection**, the **Hermitage**, one of the greatest art museums of the world, and the **Peter and Paul Fortress**. Most visitors to this city in the far north come for the famous 'white nights' in July, when the sky never gets dark.

Further attractions are the **palaces of the tsars** in the surrounding area, **Pavlovsk** with its unique **Park, the Peterhof** and **Tsarskoe Selo**. The main attractions of **Moscow** are **Red Square** with the **Kremlin**,

St. Basil's Cathedral and the **GUM department store**. Among the tsars' residences in and around Moscow are **Arkhangelskoye, Kolomenskoye, Kuskovo** and **Ostankino**. About 200 km south of St Petersburg lies the city of **Novgorod** with its mighty sixteenth-century Kremlin as well as two monasteries and 46 churches, of which the Cathedral of St. Sophia is the most important. The Ring of Golden Cities contains monuments from a period covering more than 1000 years: **Rostov** on the Don, the old capital of **Vladimir** with its magnificent mansions, **Suzdal** with its monasteries and churches, as well as the former royal residence of **Kideksha** are the most important of the many notable sights.

Barely four per cent of the area of the country is an official conservation area. The **Komi forest** in northern Russia is one of the world's largest national parks. Polar animals inhabit the vast, untouched forests and **Tundra**. Parts of the **Taimyr peninsula** in northern Siberia are protected areas. The still largely unexplored peninsular of **Kamchatka** contains the Kronotsky National Park whose geysers and hot springs have given the peninsula the soubriquet of 'Land of Fire and Ice'. There is also great variety of animal and plant life. The island of **Wrangel** in north-eastern Siberia, inside the Arctic Circle, is home to polar bears, seals, walruses and numerous species of Arctic birds.

Lake Baikal, in the mountains of central Siberia, has also been declared a protected area. It has unique flora and fauna, including the Baikal seal. Surrounding this inland stretch of water are health resorts and mineral springs. Other popular holiday destinations are the **Baltic** resorts near Kaliningrad, the **northern Caucasus** and the **seaside towns** of the Black and Caspian Seas.

1 Moscow is the seat of government of the Russian Federation: the palace in the Kremlin is overlooked by the 'Ivan the Great' clock tower.

2 Huts for storing straw stand on stilts to protect them from the waters of the Kamenka River.

3 The brightly-coloured domes of Russian orthodox churches originate in the Byzantine tradition. This is the Pereslavl-Zalessky-Goritsky Monastery.

4 The Stalinist architecture of Moscow State University on the banks of the Moskva River.

Asia

Asia is the largest and most populous continent, with an area of 44.7 million sq. km – over a third of the Earth's total land surface – and a population of roughly 3.8 billion.

Towering mountain ranges – the Pamirs, the Karakorums, Hindu Kush and the Himalayas, the last containing the world's highest summit (Mt. Everest: 8,846 m) – form a natural barrier between northern Asia, with its sub-arctic and continental climates, and tropical or sub-tropical south Asia. The continent's wildlife is as varied as the climate. Vegetation ranges from the mosses and lichens of the tundra, to the world's oldest rainforest in Malaysia. The range of peoples, cultures, languages and religions is remarkable. Judaism, Christianity, Islam, Buddhism, Hinduism and the philosophies of Confucius and Lao Tse all originated here.

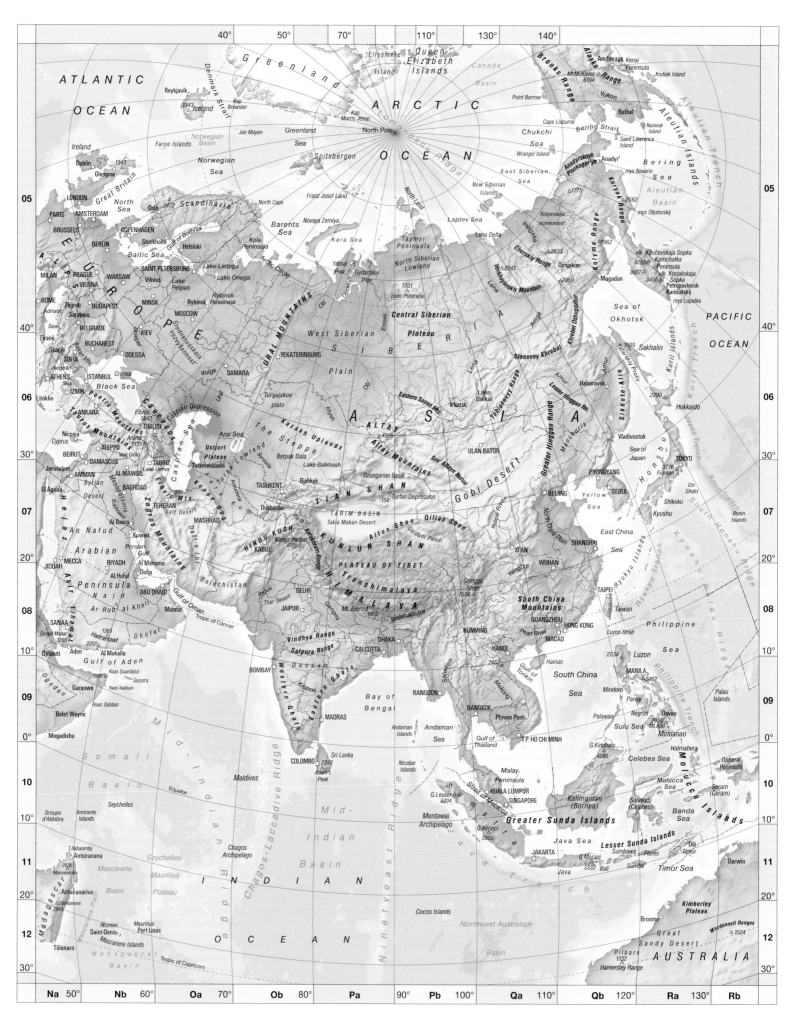

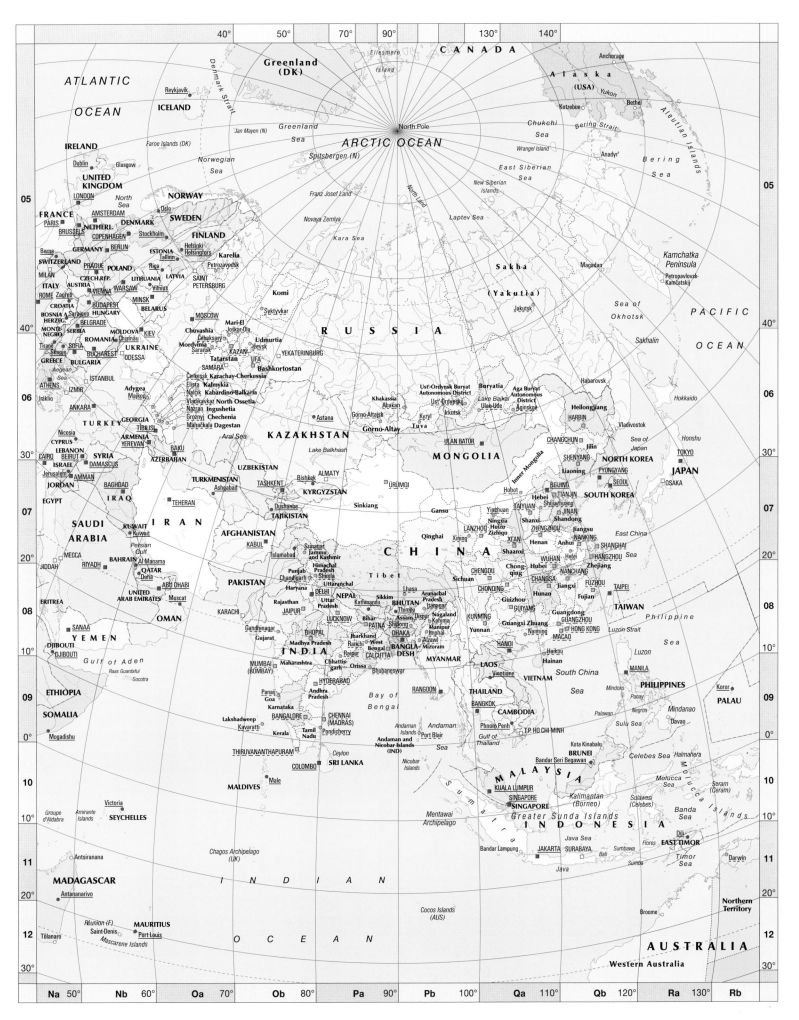

Main photograph:
Qin Shi Huangdi, First Emperor of China, regarded himself as ruler of 'all that is beneath the sky'. This grand self-image is clearly demonstrated by the impressive Terracotta Army, scuplted for the sole purpose of protecting the ruler's tomb.

The History of Asia

So many of humanity's greatest innovations first appeared in Asia. The continent saw the foundation of the world's first cities, and it is here that writing was invented. Most importantly, all of the major world religions origi-

A statue of Buddha Amitabha in Kamakura, Japan.

nated in Asia. While people in Europe were still at subsistence level, great cultures were flourishing in Asia, with formidable power structures and extensive trade routes. The stone remains of these lost kingdoms, of which two examples are the ruins of Persepolis and the Forbidden City, clearly show that the rulers saw themselves as governing the whole world. In modern times, after centuries of Western domination, the world is again looking east. Today, China has the potential to become the world's greatest economic power.

The **Babylonian Exile** was a popular theme in mediaeval illuminations. These two thirteenth-century examples depict the conquest and destruction of Jerusalem and the exile of the Jewish people.

Prehistory and early history

Evidence has been found of settlements in Asia as early as the Palaeolithic Age. Neolithic cultures developed in Mesopotamia, the Levant and Iran. Settlements based on agriculture were formed in north-western India in the fourth century BC.

In China, Neolithic cultures have been found mainly in Henan and Gansu. The Yangshao culture is considered to be the nucleus of the country that became China.

The earliest Asian cities were founded in the Bronze Age, first along the Indus, then in China. Bronze Age cultures developed in Mesopotamia, Anatolia and Syria in the second millennium BC, and the first Iron Age cultures followed in the ninth century BC.

Anatolia

The first important Anatolian culture was that of the Hittites, who invaded Anatolia around 2000 BC, and, after violent clashes with the indigenous population, established a kingdom of their own whose capital city was Kussar. The Old Hittite Kingdom, extending as far as Babylon, came into being between 1640 BC and 1387 BC Under king Suppiluliuma, the New Hittite kingdom grew into a great power from 1380 BC. The Mitani kingdom was destroyed and Hittite frontiers were extended ever further. A combined attack by the sea-faring nations ca. 1200 BC eventually destroyed the Hittites.

In the thirteenth century BC, Urartuan kingdoms were formed in Eastern Anatolia. From about 825 BC the Urartu were the dominant power in Eastern Anatolia, until the Assyrians conquered the region in 714 BC. Around 620 BC, the Scythians from southern Russia traversed the land, as did the Indo-European Armenians from 600 BC. In 610 BC, Urartu was part of the kingdom of the Medes. Gordion was the capital of the Phrygian kingdom, which was founded around 800 BC, and collapsed in the seventh century BC with the invasion of the Cimmerians. The way now lay open for the rise of the Lydian kingdom, which gradually conquered almost all the Greek cities on the Aegean coast. Together with

Sparta, Egypt and Babylon, the Greeks planned to counter the Persian threat in a preventive war. After the defeat of Pteria, Lydia became a Persian province in 546 BC. The invention of coinage is considered to be Lydia's great contribution to civilisation.

The uprising of the Greek cities against the Persians was defeated in 494 BC with the destruction of Miletus. A further punitive expedition against the Greeks failed at Marathon. A subsequent Persian campaign against Greece was postponed on the death of King Darius I, but failed when finally launched in 479 BC. It was not until 387 BC that Western Anatolia fell again to Persia in the King's Peace. After the victory of Alexander the Great over the Persian king Darius III, Asia Minor became part of Alexander's gigantic empire, which was divided after his death into the three Kingdoms of the Diadochi (successors), with Antigonus becoming ruler of Lycia and Phrygia. At the battle of Ipsus in 301 BC, Antigonus suffered a crushing defeat and Anatolia came under the control of Lysimachus. After his death and the victory of Seleucus at Kourupedion in 281 BC, the Seleucids dominated the whole of the Near East. The Celts and Galatians invaded the region in 279 BC, making it possible for Nicomedes to found the kingdom of Bithynia with its capital of Nicomedia.

In 74 BC, this kingdom passed by inheritance to the Romans. The rule of Pergamon lasted from 263 BC until 133 BC, when Attalus III bequeathed it to the Romans.

In 247 BC the Parthian empire was formed, representing a constant threat to the Seleucids as well as, later, to the Romans. The power of the Seleucids reached its height under Antiochus III, but after his defeat at the battle of Magnesia in 190 BC, their rule began to decline, and in 64 BC, the region was finally captured by the Roman general, Pompey. The whole of Anatolia now became the Roman province of Asia, and after the division of the nations it fell to Byzantium. In 1453 AD, Constantinople fell to the Turks and Anatolia was Islamised and became the capital of the Ottoman Empire, remaining so until after World War I.

After the Armistice of Mudros, the Allies occupied Istanbul, the Italians the regions of Antalya and Konya, the Greeks the region around Smyrna (Izmir), and the French, Cilicia. The Turkish nationalist movement (the Young Turks) that had begun as early as 1898, staged an uprising under General Mustafa Kemal (Kemal Attaturk) demanding a Turkish state within the original borders. In 1923, the Treaty of Lausanne established the frontiers of Turkey more or less in their present form.

The Near East

The first advanced cultures in Asia developed in Mesopotamia, the land between two rivers, the Tigris and the Euphrates. Between 3200 and 2800 BC, the Sumerians built city states, containing monumental temples, developed cuneiform script, constructed irrigation systems and used a sophisticated calendar. The city-states including Uruk, Ur, Lagash and Kish developed the Sumerian culture, backed by a well-organised priesthood and officialdom, and governed events in the third millennium BC The Sumerians experienced their final cultural heyday under Rimsin of Larsa in the eighteenth century BC. Hammurabi (1728–1686) made Babylon into the power centre of Mesopotamia. His rule was succeeded by that of the Cassites, who immigrated from Iran. From the thirteenth century to 612 BC, the Assyrians dominated the Middle East. Under Esarhaddon ca. 670 BC, their empire covered the whole of Mesopotamia, the Levant and Egypt. The Assyrians were defeated in 612 BC and were replaced by the Babylonians, whose most famous ruler, Nebuchadnezzar, built the Tower of Babel, exiled the Jewish people from their land and destroyed the Temple in Jerusalem. In 539 BC, the Babylonians were overthrown by the Medes and Persians. The Persian

King Cyrus II made Babylon into a Persian province and allowed the Jews to return to their land. The Israelite tribes conquered Canaan ca. 1500 BC and made it the Land of Israel. Around 1010 BC, King Saul was defeated in his war against the Philistines. Under Saul's successor, King David, Israel became a major power which split, after the death of King Solomon in 926 BC, into the kingdoms of Israel and Judah. The conquest and destruction of Jerusalem by Nebuchadnezzar II was followed by the Babylonian Exile. After Cyrus II's conquest of the New Babylonian Kingdom, Israel and Judah became part of the Persian empire.

Judaism could now be actively practised again, since the Persians were themselves monotheists (Zoroastrians) and this was not altered by the conquest of Alexander the Great. In 63 BC, the Romans conquered the country and called it Judaea. From 39 to 4 BC, Herod the Great was a Jewish puppet king; it was under his reign that Jesus Christ was crucified. The Jewish Revolt of 70 AD resulted in the destruction of Jerusalem by the Romans, and in 133 AD the Emperor Hadrian again expelled the Jews from their land which the Romans dubbed Palæstina.

In Persia, the rule of the Medes was followed by that of the Persians, which in the course of the sixth and fifth centuries BC absorbed Lydia, Israel and Judah, Egypt, Nubia, Libya and Anatolia. After the murder of Darius III, Persian empire fell to the forces of Alexander the Great.

The Near East experienced a decisive change through the advance of Islam from the seventh century onwards. By the time its founder, Muhammad, died in Medina in 632 AD, the new teaching had already conquered the whole of Arabia. Under Omar, the Arabs conquered Syria, Persia, Palæstina and Egypt. Under the Umayyads, in the seventh and eighth centuries, the Arab kingdom was extended to include the whole of North Africa, Spain, Kabul, Bokhara, Samarkand, Transoxiana and the Indus region.

Under the Abbasids, the kingdom disintegrated. The Arabs lost their position of supremacy, and the Persians now took control. After

Impressive reliefs adorn the palace complex of Persepolis, founded by Darius the Great, ca. 518 BC.

the death of Haroun al-Rashid in 809, the Caliphate became politically insignificant. The Mongols invaded Persia in 1256 and destroyed Baghdad in 1258.

Repeated attacks on the Byzantine Empire, the heir to the eastern half of the Roman Empire, were at first ineffectual, but the Crusaders, in spite of the temporary conquest of Jerusalem, were once again driven out of the area after a total of seven crusades.

In 1301, Sultan Osman I founded the Ottoman Empire, which at various times ruled North Africa, Syria, Mesopotamia, Arabia, the Caucasus, Anatolia, the Balkan peninsula and parts of Hungary. Starting in the late eighteenth century, the Ottoman Empire showed signs of collapse, and in 1875 it had to declare national bankruptcy.

Further to the east, the conquest of Persia was completed in 1736 by the Turkmen leader Nadir. Since the mid-nineteenth century liberal ideas had been spreading through Persia, and in 1906 a constitution was proclaimed. At the instigation of St. Petersburg, the country was divided into zones representing Russian and British interests respectively, until the constitution again came into effect in 1909.

Afghanistan, on the north-west frontier of India, founded in 1747, was the subject of British colonial aspirations, but the Afghan rulers were largely successful in preserving their independence.

The French occupied Syria in 1920 and expelled the Emir Faisal its ruler. France was granted a mandate for Syria by the League of Nations in 1923 while Britain was given the mandate for Palestine. Great Britain separated Transjordan from the rest of Palestine and installed the Hashemite Abdallah ibn Hussein. In 1926, Lebanon was separated from Syria and the regions of Hejaz and Najd were combined to form the kingdom of Saudi Arabia. In 1919, Iraq became a British mandated territory. In 1925 a constitutional monarchy was proclaimed but was later overthrown.

On 14 May 1948, after the British withdrawal from Palestine, the Jewish National Council proclaimed the state of Israel. It was immediately invaded by all its Arab neighbours, Jordan, Egypt,

Lebanon and even Iraq with which it had no borders. After four wars – in 1948, 1956, 1967 and 1973 – a process of détente began in 1974, which was continually endangered by terrorist activities. Nevertheless, a peace treaty was signed with Egypt in 1979, and with Jordan in 1994, though a solution to the conflict with the Palestinians is still a remote prospect.

In 1979, Shah Reza Pahlevi was forced to flee Iran, and the Shi'ite leader, Ayatollah Khomeini, proclaimed the Islamic Republic. Iraq's president Saddam Hussein took advantage of his neigh-

bour's military weakness in 1980 to invade Iran. The war ended in 1988 with no clear victory for either side. Iraqi troops invaded Kuwait in 1990. Following a UN ultimatum, an international army under US leadership liberated the emirate. In 2003, Iraq having failed to implement the post-Kuwait UB resolutions, the USA and its allies initiated a war against Iraq. Saddam Hussein's regime was overthrown, but the country remains embroiled in bitter sectarian fighting.

The history of Yemen is also tumultuous. In 1990, an agreement was reached for the peaceful unification of the People's Democratic Republic of Yemen (formerly Aden) and the Yemen Arab Republic to form the Republic of Yemen.

In Afghanistan, the monarchy was toppled in 1973. Soviet troops invaded in 1979. Gorbachev ended Soviet intervention in 1988, but the war against the Islamicists continued. In 1994,

the radical Taliban brought most of the country under their control. After the terrorist attacks of 11 September, 2001, for which the USA held the terrorist organisation Al Qaeda, operating in Afghanistan, responsible, the USA began a military offensive. Elections were held in 2004, but fighting and terrorism continue.

1 Palestinians staging a protest in Nablus.

2 Iran: on 12 February 1951, Shah Muhammad Reza Pahlevi married Princess Soraya. He later divorced her and married Farah Diba. In 1979, the Shah was deposed and forced to flee the country.

3 Celebrating the 'Islamic Revolution' in Tehran, overshadowed by the portrait of Ayatollah Khomeini, who until his death in 1989 was Iran's political and spiritual leader.

4 Operation Desert Storm, in 1991, liberated Kuwait from the Iraqi invaders.

Central and South Asia

*Maharajas reigned over the Indian kingdom of **Rajasthan** until 1847. Jodhpur Fort was built by the ruling Rajputs in the seventeenth century. It is constructed from yellow sandstone blocks, that are not held together by mortar.*

*The **Vietnam War** against the United States cost the lives of two million Vietnamese. Some three million were injured. The U.S. used carpet bombing and chemical weapons such as napalm and the defoliant Agent Orange leading*

Central Asia

The thinly populated steppe and desert landscapes of Central Asia and Siberia were hardly conducive to the formation of urban cultures. The Mongol Empire, united by Genghis Khan in 1206, was of supreme importance in terms of world history. In the fourteenth century, Mongol rule in Iran collapsed, and in 1368 it ended in China with the beginning of the Ming dynasty. Tamburlaine's new Mongol Empire, extending over wide regions of Inner Asia and the Near East, lasted only briefly after his death in 1405. Babur's kingdom of the Great Mughals in India survived until 1857, while the Golden Horde was defeated in 1502 in southern Russia, and the states of Kashan and Astrakhan fell in 1552 and 1557. In 1911, Outer Mongolia separated from China. Since 1990, Mongolia has been a parliamentary democracy.

In the fifteenth century, Tibet became a theocracy, with the Dalai Lama as its spiritual and political leader. In 1950, the country was occupied by Chinese troops and incorporated into China in 1951. Nepal has been able to preserve its independence since 1769, and in 1990 replaced the autocratic rule of the king with a constitutional monarchy.

After the dissolution of the USSR, several former Soviet republics declared their independence. While the process of separation was peaceful in Kyrgyzstan, Tajikistan, Kazakhstan, Turkmenistan, Georgia and Uzbekistan, Azerbaijan and Armenia went to war over the Armenian Christian exclave of Nagorno-Karabakh. The aspirations to independence of the Republic of Chechnya (part of the Russian CIS, whose inhabitants are Muslims) were forcibly suppressed in two wars from 1994 to 1996 and 1999 to 2005 by the Russian army. A diplomatic solution to the conflict is currently unlikely.

The Indian sub-continent

The excavations at Mohenjo-Daro and Harappa in the Indus valley provide evidence of an advanced civilisation in the third and fourth millennia BC, which possessed a script, planned towns and cities, sewerage and ventilated granaries. Around 1000 BC, the Aryans immigrated from Central Asia and founded the caste system. The new religions, Jainism and Buddhism, emerged in the sixth century BC. In 327 BC, Alexander the Great advanced as far as the Punjab, but had to halt his campaign there.

The first Indian empire was the Maurya dynasty founded by Chandragupta, whose domination extended through Afghanistan, Baluchistan, Sind, Kashmir, Nepal, the Ganges valley and the most of the Deccan Plateau.

After the fall of the regime no one power was able to establish itself permanently, until India experienced its Golden Age under the Gupta dynasty from 320 to 480 AD, with the flourishing of industry, art, architecture and literature. At this time, Buddhism was

Gradually the British were able to assert themselves in the face of Portuguese and French competition and subjugate the local rulers. Through the East India Company, the British gradually conquered India and Queen Victoria adopted the title of 'Empress of India' in 1876, appointing a viceroy to rule the country. From the late nineteenth century, a resistance movement was formed by the indigenous Muslims and Hindus with the foundation of the Indian National Congress. A massacre ordered in 1919 by a British general at a peaceful demonstration in Amritsar was the trigger for the first campaign of non-violent resistance organised by Mahatma Gandhi in 1920–1922. A further campaign of civil disobedience in 1930–32 led to the arrest of several hundred thousand Indians.

Laos: imposing temple statues at Wat Xieng Khwan in Vientiane.

already retreating as Hinduism advanced. Until 1000 AD, several dynasties set up various more or less short-lived regimes, when Islamic invaders first occupied northern India and then established smaller Islamic states throughout the country.

In the sixteenth century, the Great Mughals founded a vast empire which had its heyday under Akbar. Afghan invasions, increased involvement by Europe and the fall of the Mughal empire dramatically changed the power relationships during the seventeenth and eighteenth centuries.

The British government was now ready to make concessions, but the solution of the Indian question was delayed until after the end of the World War II.

The 'Transfer of Power', by which India attained independence, in August 1947, however, culminated in a bloody conflict, due to the demand for autonomy by the mainly Muslim regions in the north. They seceded under the name of Pakistan, but their borders remained disputed. Millions were resettled, but the resulting disturbances cost the lives of more than a million people.

India has had a troubled history since independence. Several prominent politicians were assassinated, including Mahatma Gandhi, Indira Gandhi and Rajiv Gandhi. The conflict over Kashmir led in 1965 to war with Pakistan. In the Tashkent Agreement, both sides renounced further use of force, but there were repeated small skirmishes and some sabre-rattling, since both India and Pakistan are believed to have atomic weapons. In 1961, India forcibly annexed the Portuguese colony of Goa, and in 1962, in a Himalayan war, China annexed some border territory.

In 1971, India helped East Pakistan gain independence. The new called itself Bangladesh and incorporated the semi-independent state of Sikkim in 1975. The Indian government intervened several times, on occasion with armed forces, in the civil conflict in its neighbouring state Sri Lanka, to the south. The conflict between Muslims and Hindus, as well as the aspirations to independence of the Sikhs in the Punjab continues to cause unrest.

South-east Asia

The kingdom of Lan Xang, which had existed since 1335 in Laos, divided into three parts in 1707. It was conquered by Siam in the nineteenth century. In the sixth century, the Khmer conquered the kingdom of Funan and in the twelfth and thirteenth centuries they ruled the greater part of Indo-china. It was they who built the temple cities of Angkor Wat and Angkor Thom.

In 207 BC, the Lak-Viet conquered the kingdom of Au-Lak, which they called Nam-Viet. In 111 BC, Vietnam came under Chinese rule, which lasted until the mid-tenth century. In 1802, the country, ruled by rival families, was successfully united by the Vietnamese emperor Gia-Long. In 1887, the French seized the areas of the present states of Cambodia, Laos and Vietnam calling them French Indochina. During World War II, the whole of Indochina was occupied by the Japanese. When they capitulated, the country's desire for self-determination was at first thwarted by the return of their former colonial rulers from France. Supported by

Pathet Lao and the Khmer Issarak, the communist Vietminh fought the French and their anti-communist Vietnamese allies. The bombing of Haiphong and the Vietminh attack on Hanoi triggered the Indo-Chinese war in 1946. After the intervention of China and several military defeats, France withdrew from Indo-China in 1954. Cambodia and Laos were now independent states; Vietnam was divided, until the time when elections were due to be held, into a Communist zone in the north and a non-Communist zone in the south.

In Laos, independence was marked by continual changes of government and civil wars. During the Vietnam war, North Vietnam moved some of its supplies through the Communist-controlled regions of Laos. The South Vietnamese attacked the country in 1971. In 1975, Laos became a Communist people's republic and it was not until 1996 that the impoverished country began to free itself from its isolation in terms of foreign affairs.

In Cambodia, Prince Norodom Sihanouk at first succeeded in keeping the country out of the Vietnam war. But the communist supply routes through Cambodia led to tensions with South Vietnam and internal conflicts. Sihanouk was toppled, General Lon Nol declared a republic and actively supported the South Vietnamese and the USA.

In 1975, the communist Khmer Rouge conquered the city of Phnom Penh and Sihanouk briefly resumed his leadership of the state. The brutal terrorist regime of Pol Pot ruled between 1976 and 1978, and more than two million people fell victim to his extremist brand of communism. In 1979, Communist opposition groups achieved power with the military support of Vietnam.

Pol Pot again retreated underground and carried on guerrilla warfare. The fall of the Khmer Rouge was not officially recognised by the UN until 1981. After the departure of the Vietnamese in 1989, Sihanouk returned from exile, and became king in 1993. It was not until 1998 that the Khmer Rouge abandoned their guerrilla warfare, but after the promise of an amnesty, some leaders of the organisation were

to terrible and largely irreversible environmental damage. After the war, thousands of Vietnamese 'Boat People' left the country.

given leading positions in the legitimate government. From 1957, the Vietcong guerrillas fought in the south of Vietnam for national unity under a socialist banner, and with the support of North Vietnam, China and the USSR. From 1960, the USA supported the south, at first with military advisers, then with troops. Neither napalm, chemical weapons, B-52 bombing of the major cities of the north, nor the deployment of elite troops could bring about victory over Ho Chi-Minh's Viet Cong guerillas. Under pressure, from their own population too, the US troops withdrew in 1973. In 1975, the south surrendered and Vietnam was officially reunified in 1976. The mass flight of the 'Boat People' and skirmishes on the Chinese border again brought the country back into the headlines. In 1978, Vietnamese troops toppled the Pol Pot regime in Cambodia. Since 1987, the government has followed a course of reform, bringing about the lifting of the American trade embargo in 1994 and achieving diplomatic recognition in 1995.

Burma, today officially called Myanmar, came into being in the eighteenth century as a result of the union of the kingdoms of Arakan and Ava. In 1885, the last king was taken into custody by the British and the country was annexed to British India, but liberated again in 1937. It achieved independence in 1947 after occupation by the Japanese in the World War II. Since then, it has been ruled by a succession of military dictators, claiming a bizarre combination of socialist and Buddhist objectives.

The kingdom of Siam was the only south-east Asian country to escape colonialisation, even though King Chulalongkorn was forced to cede large territories to France and Britain. In 1939, the Fascist government under Pibul Songgram renamed Siam as Thailand. In World War II, Thailand allied itself with Japan and annexed French and British colonies which it had to hand back at the end of the war. Since then, the political scene, in which only the figure of the king remains a constant element, has been typified by a series of coups d'état, dissolutions of parliament and disturbances,

including calls by Muslims in the south for an independent state. The country's industrial ambitions as a so-called Tiger State proved to be of only short duration in the Asian crisis.

The kingdom of Malacca was conquered by the Portuguese in 1511. In 1641 it was captured by the Dutch and from the eighteenth century the British became the leading power in the region. Malacca, Sarawak and North Borneo (later Sabah) were occupied by the Japanese in 1941, and in 1945, they were again ruled by the British. In 1957, the Federation of Malaya gained independence

and in 1963, with Singapore, Sarawak and Sabah, was extended to become Malaysia. Singapore left the Federation in 1965. Indonesian claims on the area led in 1965 to military conflict which was settled peacefully.

Indonesia and the Philippines

The Buddhist and Hindu regimes in the islands of Indonesia were succeeded from the thirteenth century by Islamic sultanates. In the sixteenth century, the Portuguese founded trading posts and Christian missions, but were driven out by the Dutch East India Company. In 1799, the Netherlands officially incorporated the islands into their colonial possessions as the Dutch East Indies, and, with one short interruption, ruled the land until 1942, when it was occupied by Japanese troops. After the Japanese surrender, Sukarno and Hatta declared the Independent Republic of Indonesia, but in two military actions in

1947 and 1948, the Dutch re-occupied their former colony, but were forced to recognise its independence at the Hague Conference in 1949. The federated United States of Indonesia were replaced in 1950 by a centralised system, while the new democracy was shaken by repeated uprisings. In 1959 Sukarno went over

1 In 1969, President Ho Chi Minh of North Vietnam was laid to rest in a grand mausoleum in Hanoi.

2 Mahatma Gandhi's personal dedication made him into a worldwide figure of peaceful resistance.

3 Jawaharlal Nehru was the first Prime Minister of independent India and followed a policy of non-alignment.

4 In 1998, protests against the Indonesian government escalated, mainly in the capital Jakarta. On 21 May, Suharto was forced to resign.

to a 'guided democracy' and led the country into a severe economic crisis and political isolation. In 1966, he was forced to give way to Suharto's 'New Order', whose liberal economic policy led to a distinct upturn n the economy, though all opposition was brutally suppressed. After the Asian crisis, Suharto could no longer hold out and was replaced by Habibie. The year 1999 also saw an end to the occupation of East Timor, which had been annexed by Indonesia after the departure of the Portuguese. In 2002, East Timor became a sovereign state.

When the Spanish took possession of the Philippines in 1521, they named the islands after their king. Colonial rule there ended when the rebel freedom fighters turned for support to the USA, which declared war on Spain in 1898. Madrid then handed over the Philippines to the United States for the sum of twenty million US dollars. The US proceeded to quell the uprisings with military force and took possession of the islands. After Japanese occupation during the World War II, the Philippines were granted their independence in 1946. In 1965, Ferdinand Marcos became president and ruled from 1972 under martial law, until he was toppled in 1986. Since then, the Philippines has had a new constitution and democtratic rule.

China

After the early Xia (twenty-first to sixteenth centuries BC) and Shang (sixteenth to eleventh centuries) dynasties, the Zhou dynasty came to power around 1050 and ruled until 256 BC. Under the Zhou, the country was organised as a feudal state and greatly extended in the years that followed. The 'Warring States' period end in 221 BC with the unification of the kingdom by King Zheng of Qin, who took the imperial title Shi Huangdi, 'First Emperor', and created a united, centrally administered state.

After his death in 210 BC Liu Bang emerged as victor of the many uprisings, and founded the Han dynasty, which lasted until 220 AD. The Han dynasty saw the invention of paper, the partial reintroduction of feudalism and

the start of trade on the Silk Road. National and civil wars repeatedly divided the country, and it was only under the Tang emperors of 618–907 that the vast Chinese empire experienced its greatest prosperity.

China was united under the foreign domination of the Mongol Yuan dynasty. In 1386, the Mongols were toppled by national uprisings and were succeeded by the twenty emperors of the Ming dynasty, in which the middle classes rose to prominence. In 1644, the Manchurians occupied the capital, Peking (Beijing) and founded the Qing dynasty.

The Mongol leader Genghis Khan practising falconry.

A phase of prosperity was followed in the eighteenth and nineteenth centuries by explosive growth in the population and the economic decline resulting from a succession of wars. The European powers did not succeed in colonising China, but in the Opium War of 1852 Britain enforced the opening of some ports to foreing trade, and acquired the island of Hong King which China considered to be of little economic importance. Further hostile action enabled the French and British to open Chinese markets even further. After

its defeat in war against Japan, China was forced to cede Taiwan and recognise the independence of Korea.

A series of agreements forced China to cede various regions to Russia, France and Britain. The German Empire leased the Bay of Jiaozhou. In 1911, the revolutionary movement deposed the imperial government and in January 1912, Sun Yat-sen became the first president of the Chinese Republic. During World War I, in which China was on the side of the Allies, various provincial warlords contended for military supremacy, causing anarchy.

In 1921, the Chinese Communist Party was founded in Shanghai. Under the leadership of Chiang Kai-shek the Kuomintang succeeded in restoring national unity. The Japanese occupied Manchuria and set up a puppet government under emperor Puyi This led to war, in which Mao Zedong's Communist partisan army only narrowly avoided defeat in the Long March of 1934/1935.

In 1937, the Japanese occupied extensive areas of the country in open war. After the Japanese surrender in 1945, the Communist People's Liberation Army, with

Soviet support, gained the upper hand in a civil war, and on 1 October Mao declared the People's Republic of China. Chiang Kai-shek fled to Taiwan and continued as president of the Republic of China on the island.

But order still did not prevail throughout the gigantic nation. Mao's 'Hundred Flowers' movement was followed by the merciless persecution of all opposition. The 'Great Leap Forward', an ambitious programme of industrialisation, resulted in the deaths from starvation of 30 million people. In 1960, the battle for leadership in the Communist camp ended with China's break with the Soviet Union. In 1964, with the explosion of its first atom bomb, China established its claim as the fifth world power.

In the 'Great Proletarian Cultural Revolution' of 1966, Mao once again destroyed internal opposition. The country's relationship with the West eased with China's membership in the UN, from which Taiwan was excluded, and the state visits of US President Nixon in 1972 and German Chancellor Helmut Schmidt in 1975. After the deaths of Chou En-lai and Mao in 1976, a power struggle broke out, which resulted in the victory of Hua Guofeng over the so-called Gang of Four. But the new 'strong man' proved to be Deng Xiaoping, who introduced basic industrial reforms and a cautious liberalisation programme.

A burgeoning democratic movement was suppressed in June 1989 on Tiananmen Square and a countrywide wave of arrests and executions aroused international protest. Anti-corruption campaigns, further liberalisation of economic life by means of the 'Socialist market economy' and the smooth return of Hong Kong and Macao led China further out of its political isolation.

The relationship between the People's Republic of China and Taiwan remains problematic, with a strong potential for conflict.

Japan

According to legend, the first Japanese emperor was descended from the sun goddess Amaterasu and founded the uninterrupted line of the ruling house.

In the fourth century, Japan came into contact with Buddhism by way of Korea, and around 550 AD it adopted Chinese characters for its language. China was also the model for the absolute bureaucratic state created in 664 by Emperor Kotuku. At the end of the twelfth century Shogun Yoritomo created a feudal state and brought in a military nobility at the cost of the loss of power of the court nobles. Henceforward, the emperor (Tenno) was merely a puppet of the powerful warlords.

In violent battles, the Shoguns and their feudal knights, the samurai, continued to strengthen their position of power. In 1600 Shogun Tokugawa Ieyasu ended the internal turmoil of the country, unified it and by means of a strict new order ensured internal peace for more than 250 years. During the time of the Shogunate, Christianity was outlawed and from 1637 Japan was almost hermetically sealed off from the outside world. Only very limited trade with the Dutch and Chinese was maintained.

As a result of US pressure, after 1854 Japan was forced to open several of its ports and agree to trade agreements with the USA and some of the European powers. The resulting xenophobic movements led to a civil war that ended with the fall of the last Shogun. In 1863, the old feudal system was abandoned and Japan was transformed into an absolute monarchy, which became a constitutional monarchy in 1889. At the same time, the army and industry were modernised, and Japan slowly advanced to the status of a regional great power.

In the war against China of 1895, Japan was able to assert its interests in Korea and gained the island of Taiwan. In 1904–05 Japanese ships sank the Russian fleet in the Russo-Japanese War; at the Peace of Portsmouth, Japan secured for itself the area around Port Arthur and the southern half of Sakhalin island.

In 1910, the Japanese annexed Korea, and in 1914 they entered World War I against the Central Powers, conquered Jiaozhou and the German South Sea Islands. In 1921, under pressure from Britain and the USA, Japan had to

On 6 August 1945, the first **atomic bomb** fell on **Hiroshima**. Three days later, a second fell on Nagasaki. The devastating effects forced Japan to capitulate, and the ceasefire was signed on 2 September on board the USS Missouri.

Tenzin Gyatso is the 14th **Dalai Lama** of Tibet. After the occupation by China in 1950, he was forced to emigrate to India in 1959. His peaceful struggle for independence for Tibet earned him the Nobel Peace Prize in 1989.

renounce supremacy in China, and an industrial crisis, a severe earthquake and battles for a universal suffrage weakened Japan's position further. In 1931, Japanese troops occupied Manchuria and created the puppet state of Manchukuo.

As a result of international protests, Japan left the League of Nations in 1933 and in 1934 announced its withdrawal from the Washington Naval Agreement, which provided for a ratio of 3 : 5 : 5 in relation to the fleets of the USA and Britain. In 1936, Japan entered the Anti-Comintern Pact with Hitler's Germany, and in 1937 abruptly initiated the Sino-Japanese War, in the course of which extensive areas of China were occupied.

On 7 December 1941, without any declaration of war, Japanese bombers attacked the American fleet at Pearl Harbor. After initial military success, Japan was forced to surrender on 2 September 1945, following the dropping of atom bombs on Hiroshima and Nagasaki.

Until 1952, General MacArthur, who was commander of the US military government, forced the emperor to renounce his divinity in a radio broadcast. Japanese war criminals were tried at the Tokyo international military tribunals and there was a thorough reform of industry. At the San Francisco Peace Treaty of 1951, Japan lost all the territories it had acquired in the previous 80 years, as well as the Kuril Islands.

Korea

The history of Korea is closely bound up with Japanese foreign policy, but despite all the attempted advances made to the country by China and Japan, it has been able to preserve its own ethnic and cultural identity and independence.

In 1876, Japan enforced trading rights with Korea. In 1895, after the Sino-Japanese war, Korea became a Japanese protectorate, and in 1910 it was annexed. After World War II, the country was divided into two zones, one Soviet-influenced and one American-influenced. North of the 38th parallel, the (Communist) Democratic People's Republic of Korea (known as North Korea) was

formed, and south of it the Republic of Korea (or South Korea), which looked to the West. In 1949 the occupying troops moved out. On 25 June 1950, North Korean troops crossed the demarcation line and conquered almost the whole of South Korea. The United Nations decided to send in a task force, which consisted chiefly of American troops under the command of General MacArthur. The North Koreans were eventually driven back as far as the Chinese border, but China intervened with a counter-offensive which pushed the UN troops back beyond Seoul. MacArthur, for his

part, was able to beat off the Chinese-North Korean units as far as the 38th parallel, and demanded expansion of the war into Chinese territory and the use of atomic weapons. As a result, he was dismissed from his post. With the armistice agreement of 1953, the 38th parallel was reinstated as a border. South Korea now changed from an agricultural nation to a prosperous industrial one, while ruled politically by military dictatorships and authoritarian regimes. Only since 1993 has Korea had a freely elected president and parliament. The country's relationship with North Korea remains tense though North Korea was ruled up to his death in 1994 by Kim Il Sung with the support of China and the Soviet Union. At present, despite talks with the South, the country, ruled by his son Kim Jong Il, is politically isolated and struggling with a disastrous economic situation of intense poverty and there are rumours of famine among the

population. This has not stopped North Korea from attempting to develop nuclear weapons with which it is threatening South Korea, and other countries, including Japan. There is an alleged alliance between North Korea and Iran in the development of these lethal weapons. North Korea remains politically isolated.

1 In July 1953, in Panmunjeom, the 38th parallel was fixed as the border between North and South Korea.

2 Mao Zedong and Lin Biao were the political leaders of the People's Republic of China, which was officially proclaimed on 1 October 1949.

3 Propaganda for the People's Liberation Army of China in the 1960s and 1970s depicting the iconic soldier-worker, Lei Feng.

4 Demonstrations for political reform began in Tiananmen Square in Beijing in 1989, but were violently suppressed.

Main photograph:
Since 1997, Hong Kong has once again been restored to Chinese sovereignty as a special administrative region. It is one of the world's most important financial centres and a hub of merchant shipping.

The Countries of Asia

The countries of Asia, inhabited by somewhere in the region of 3.8 billion people, cover one third of the Earth's landmass. This makes Asia both the largest and most populated continent in the world. All those who cross the Bosphorus with the intention of discovering Asia will be fascinated by the variety of natural geography. The continent is di-

The heart of the Middle East Conflict: the holy city of Jerusalem.

The Wat Phra Kaeo temple, part of the Royal Palace in Bangkok.

vided in two by impressive mountain ranges such as the Himalayas, the so-called 'roof of the world'. Further north lie the endless grassy steppes of Mongolia and the moss-covered tundra of Siberia. To the south sprawl evergreen rainforests. The peoples are as varied as the land. Asia contains a wider variety of cultures and religions than any other continent.

Syria

Petra, in southern Jordan, is one of the most fascinating and mysterious ruined cities in the world. In the middle of the desert, elegant pillars and bridges appear to grow out of the cliff face. This monumental piece of architecture was built by the Nabataeans, nomadic traders who combined Greek and Arabic elements in their architecture. The city dates from 300 BC and was the residence of the Nabataean King until the Romans occupied the land.

Syria

Area:	185,180 sq. km
Capital city:	Damascus

Form of government:
Presidential Republic

Administrative divisions: 13 provinces, 1 district (capital city)

Population:
18.4 million
(95 inhabitants/sq. km)

Languages:
Arabic (official), Kurdish, Armenian

GDP per capita:	US$3,500

Currency:
1 Syrian pound = 100 piastres

Natural Geography

Syria's land mass consists of 90 per cent steppe and desert terrain. The north and north-east are dominated by **steppes** and flat **plateaus** and the **Syrian Desert** covers the south-east. The **Jabal al-Nusayriyah mountain range in the west** runs parallel to the Mediterranean coast. South and east of the Anti-Lebanon lie the **Golan Heights** which have been occupied by Israel since 1967. The **Euphrates** and its tributaries flow through the north-east.

Climate

Syria is affected by two different climates. The west of the country has a **Mediterranean climate** while the east has a **dry continental climate.**

Population

Syria's population is relatively **homogeneous** in terms of ethnic origin, 90.3 per cent being **Arabs.** There are also small communities of **Kurds** and **Armenians.** The population is 90 per cent **Sunni Muslim,** but there are also minority **Alawite, Christian** and **Druze** populations. The country has a poor education system, with the result that the literacy rate is only 70 per cent.

History and Politics

The country was the centre of some of the Earth's **oldest civilisations,** being ruled consecutively by the Romans, Byzantines, Arabs and Ottomans. These various occupying powers have left wonderful archaeological remains. In 1922, the League of Nations granted France a mandate over Syria. The country first became fully independent in **1946.** During the unstable years leading up to 1970, Syria was ruled by **military governments.** Other important events include the **Union with Egypt** (United Arab Republic 1958–1961) and the **Six Day War** in 1967, when Syria attacked Israel causing it to lose the Golan Heights, at least until it chooses to sign a treaty with Israel. The constitution of 1973 caused Syria to declare itself a **Socialist Democracy,** but in fact it is a hereditary dictatorship, president Hafez al-Assad (1930–2000) was replaced by his son, Bashar al-Assad. The country has played a major role in the **Middle-East conflict.**

Economy

Economic **reform** is taking place, but only very slowly. Despite great efforts to industrialise, Syria's economy is still based on **agriculture,** which accounts for 28 per cent of GDP. Main crops are cotton, fruit and vegetables, but cultivation relies on rainfall, which can vary greatly and there is little irrigation. Manufacturing industry is based on the country's **crude oil.** Syria has not been able to make use of its large reserves, however, and oil only contributes 14 per cent of GDP, though it benefits from revenue from oil pipelines running to its major ports, Latakia and Alexandretta, from Saudi Arabia and Iran. The trade deficit is a further hindrance to the economy, and one cause of this is that there has been serious inflation, now at nine per cent. The economy has been hit in recent years by the huge increase in population. In 1972 it was only 6.6 million but in 2005 it was 18.4 million.

Transport Infrastructure

Syria's **road network** covers 40,000 km. Roads in the interior are often in poor condition. There are international airports in **Damascus** and **Aleppo,** and the main port is in **Latakia.**

Tourism

Syria's tourist infrastructure remains underdeveloped. The **historic cities** of Damascus, Aleppo and Hama and Palmyra in central Syria, are all testament to the country's varied history.

Omnipresent in Syria: a portrait of the the late President Assad.

Hafez al-Assad	King Hussein of Jordan
*Qardaha, 6.10.1930, †Damascus, 10.6.2000	*Amman, 14.11.1935, †Amman, 7.2.1999
Al-Assad joined the Ba'th Party in 1946 and became Minister of Defence in 1966. From 1971 onwards, he was President of Syria. During the Six-Day War of 1967, he cooperated with Egypt against Israel, but refused to sign a peace treaty in the 1970s, unlike Egypt, which is why the territories lost by Syria have not been regained. After the collapse of the Soviet Union, Assad worked towards a better relationship with the West.	King Hussein of the Hashemite dynasty, was crowned in 1952. During the Six-Day War against Israel in 1967, Jordan lost East Jerusalem and the West Bank. Hussein's efforts for a political solution of the Middle East conflict earned him recognition in the West, but led to tensions with the PLO. In 1974, he renounced claims to the West Bank. In 1998, he was involved in the drawing up of the Wye Treaty and in 1994 signed a peace treaty with Israel.

*The **bazaars of the Middle East** date back to the days of the caravanserai. They are the market quarters of middle-eastern cities. Open or covered alleys are lined with stalls. Some shops have several storeys, with large internal courtyards.*

Lebanon

Area:	10,452 sq. km
Capital city:	Beirut
Form of government: Republic	
Administrative divisions:	
5 provinces	
Population:	
3.8 million	
(354 inhabitants/sq. km)	
Languages:	
Arabic (official), French	
GDP per capita:	US$6,200
Currency:	
1 Lebanese pound = 100 piastres	

Natural Geography

Lebanon is a **mountainous** country (with peaks rising to 3,087 m) on the eastern Mediterranean seaboard. It has a very narrow, but fertile coast.

Climate

The mountain regions have a **continental climate** with snowy winters, but the coastal areas have a climate with **Mediterranean influences**.

Population

Arabs form the majority of the population, and there is a small **Armenian** minority. 70 per cent of the population belongs to one of the 11 recognised branches of **Islam**. 30 per cent belong to one of five **Christian denominations**.

History and Politics

After the collapse of the Ottoman Empire in 1920, Lebanon became part of the **French mandate of Syria,** until it gained independence in 1943. The Muslim and Christian populations have since been engaged in numerous **disputes** including a civil war which lasted from 1975 to 1990 and was ended in 1991 by a **peace treaty.** Since then, the country, which had been **heavily damaged by the war.** The Syrians occupied the country until early 2005, but the south of Lebanon has been occupied by foreign troops since the end of the war, first by the PLO and subsequently by Hezbollah, a guerrilla army funded by Syria and Iran.

Economy

More than **one million foreigners** work in Lebanon. The **agricultural sector** is unable to supply the country's needs. A complex irrigation system enables cultivation of fruit and vegetables. The **manufacturing sector** (paper, food) accounts for 23 per cent of GDP. The **services sector** (trade, banking) has a long history and contributes 73 per cent of GDP, making it the most important sector of the economy. Lebanon's economy is significantly in debt, though it receives funding from other Arab states.

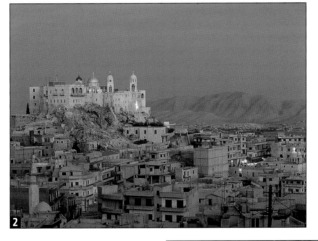

Transport Infrastructure

The majority of the road network is surfaced. **Beirut** has an international airport.

Tourism

Main points of interest are the historic cities of **Byblos** and **Baalbek,** and **Beirut**. The beaches of the Mediterranean offer many attractions.

Jordan

Area:	92,300 sq. km
Capital city:	Amman
Form of government:	
Constitutional Monarchy	
Administrative divisions:	
12 provinces	
Population: 5.7million	
(61 inhabitants/sq. km)	
Languages:	
Arabic (official), English	

GDP per capita:	US$4,800
Currency:	
1 Jordanian dinar = 1000 fils	

Natural Geography

Jordan lies on the north-west corner of the Arabian Peninsula and is divided by the 400-km-long and 10-km-wide **Great Rift Valley**.

1 The Bedouin are a nomadic people who travel with their camels across the desert regions of the Middle East.

2 Syria contains sites that are holy to both Muslims and Christians. A view of the town of Saydnaya with its famous convent.

3 Boom-town Beirut: the Corniche, the famous beach promenade, lined with high-rise blocks of shops, offices and restaurants.

4 Damascus: mosaic in the Rugaiya Mosque, built by the Iranian government for the Shi'ite community.

Young Hassidic Jews prepare themselves in the prayer room at the Wailing Wall. **Hassidism** *is a Jewish religious movement. Its adherents study the Torah (the five books of Moses) in yeshivot, religious seminaries.*

To the west, the land is **hilly**, with peaks of 600–800 m. In the east there are sheer **mountains** of up to 1,745 m, which descend to the **Arabian desert**. The **Jordan River** flows along the valley floor and into the **Dead Sea**, but it is **not navigable**, due to numerous bends. A small stretch of coast on the Gulf of Aqaba connects Jordan to the **Red Sea**, and this is Jordan's only coastal region.

Climate

Most of the country has a **desert climate** (temperatures up to 50°C in summer) with low rainfall. The **Mediterranean climate** in the west of the country means that the land there can be used for agriculture. Farm produce include grapes and olives.

Population

The population is 98 per cent **Arab**, the majority of whom are nomadic or semi-nomadic **Bedouin**. Palestinians make up 40 per cent of the population, and there are also some **1.4 million Palestinian refugees**.

History and Politics

The country was formerly known an **Transjordan** and became a British mandate in 1923. According to the **constitution,** which has been in place since 1956, the King has sole executive powers and shares legislative decisions with the national assembly. In 1994, King **Hussein** (1935–1999) concluded a **peace treaty** with Israel. Jordan's foreign policies remain a **balancing act** between the interests of the Arab countries and the West. In 1999, Hussein's son Abdullah Ibn Hussein II inherited the throne.

Economy

Up to 90 per cent of Jordan's land mass is **desert** and **mountain terrain** and unsuitable for agriculture. The country has only small oil reserves, making it one of the poorer Arab countries. The lack of development opportunities in **agriculture** (six per cent of GDP) and **industry** (30 per cent, potash, phosphorus) has meant the economy centres on the **services sector,** which contributes 65 per cent of GDP.

Transport Infrastructure

Jordan's road network is well constructed. There are international airports in **Amman** and **Aqaba**. Aqaba is the only port.

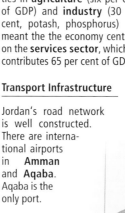

The Dome of the Rock in Jerusalem has a 31-m-high golden dome.

Tourism

Tourism is one of the most important sources of income. The main attractions for most visitors, apart from the cities of Amman and Aqaba, are the ruins of **Petra** made famous in legend and poetry as 'The Rose Red City half as old as Time'. There are other archaeological remains, especially at Jerash, and Amman, once the Roman city of Philadelphia. Aqaba on the Red Sea has many tourist attractions in the form of sandy beaches and the coral reefs offshore which can be explored by scuba divers.

*Israel is home to 200,000 **Christians**. The largest denomination is the Greek Orthodox Church, followed by the Greek Catholics. The holiest site in Jerusalem is the Church of the Holy Sepulchre containing the Tomb of Christ.*

Israel	
Area:	21,946 sq. km
Capital city:	Jerusalem
Form of government:	Republic
Administrative divisions:	
6 districts, occupied and semi-autonomous territories	
Population:	
6.2 million (282 inhabitants/sq. km)	
Languages:	
Hebrew, Arabic (both official), English	
GDP per capita:	US$22,200
Currency:	
1 new shekel = 100 agorot	

Natural Geography

In the north, the **hills of Galilee** stretch from the Mediterranean to the river Jordan. South of this is a narrow and fertile coastal plain. To the south is the **Negev desert,** which covers most of Israel's land mass. To the east, the country is bordered by the **Dead Sea** and the **Jordan Valley.**

Climate

Coastal areas have a Mediterranean climate, while the south has a **desert climate**. The summers are dry and warm, and the winters are mild and wet. Winters in the desert and mountain regions are cold.

Population

Israel has a multi-ethnic population, many of whom are **immigrants. Jews** make up some 82 per cent of the population, of whom 32 per cent are immigrants from Europe, America, Asia and Australia. Amongst the non-Jewish population, **Arabs** form the majority, with 14 per cent, but there is also a minority of **Druze.**

History and Politics

The **parliamentary republic** of Israel was proclaimed by the **Jewish National Council** in **1948** at the end of the British mandate in Palestine. A large proportion of the 650,000 Arabs living in mandatory **Palestine,** left the country when Israel's Arab neighbours invaded in an attempt to destroy it from the outset. There have been four wars

and many skirmishes and terrorist attacks between Arab states and Israel. The legalisation of the Palestine Liberation Organization (PLO) in 1993 marked the beginning of the **Middle-East Peace Process,** which ultimately aims for **Palestinian self-rule**. The peace process has had many stumbling blocks, due to Israeli settlements on the **West Bank** and Palestinian bombings. Since 2001, conflicts have escalated, with **suicide bombings** by Palestinian extremists and reprisal attacks by the Israeli army hindering a peaceful resolution. Israel unilaterally withdrew from the Gaza

Strip in 2005, but in 2006, Israel was attacked by Hezbollah, the guerilla army occupying Southern Lebanon, sparking a fifth war.

Economy

Israel's economy used to be predominantly agricultural but the country has developed into a modern **industrialised nation** with an important services sector which accounts for 81 per cent of GDP. The **manufacturing sector** consists mainly of foodstuffs, metal and steel production. **Kibbutzim** and **moshavim** (collective farms) on the mainly state-owned land produce most of Israel's food needs.

Transport Infrastructure

Israel has a very good road network. Shipping is important for **exports,** and the **ports** of Haifa, Ashdod, Ashkelon and Eilat are well-developed. The international airport is Ben-Gurion airport.

Tourism

Israel is known as the **'Holy Land'** and contains sites sacred to three world religions. These include the ruins of the Temple and remains of Jewish and Roman times, early Christian and Byzantine churches, and relicts from the Crusader periods.

1 Jerusalem: The 12th-century Church of the Holy Sepulchre is the holiest church in Christianity, built on the site of Christ's tomb.

2 Laid-back Tel Aviv: Locals relax on the beach. Hotels and bars line the promenade.

3 Dignified Tel Aviv: The port in the 7,000-year-old twin city of Jaffa retains much of its Arab architecture and past.

4 The Palestinians have developed a new self-confidence. This young woman in Bethlehem is proudly wearing traditional dress.

The Middle East Peace Process

East Jerusalem: during Friday Prayers, Muslims protest against a building project.

Photograph right: Palestinians attack Israeli soldiers in the Gaza Strip with stones.

The lands now known as Israel and Palestine, are the Holy Land for Judaism and Christianity and also the location of many sites sacred to Muslims. Although the majority of the population was Arab until the late nineteenth century, there had always been a Jewish presence here. The State of Israel was declared in 1948.

Ottoman rule over Palestine came to an end after World War I and the League of Nations gave Great Britain a mandate to rule the territory in 1922.

From the late nineteenth century the Zionist movement had produced a high level of Jewish immigration. This caused Arab riots, notably in 1939. Attempts at mediation such as the London Conference of 1939 failed to produce a solution, so the British severely restricted Jewish immigration. The result was that many Jews died who could otherwise have been saved from the Holocaust during World War II. On 29 November 1947, the UN approved the division of the territories into

a Jewish and an Arab state. The neighbouring Arab countries totally rejected this plan, but could not prevent the Declaration of the State of Israel on 14 May 1948.

On the following day, the surrounding Arab countries, as well as Iraq, attempted invaded the new state. Israel survived and was able to expand its territory beyond the area that the UN had ceded to it. Some 900,000 Arabs fled the country or were expelled by the Israeli military. The refugee camps in the neighbouring Arab countries still exist today and the Palestinians are now the world's oldest refugee population.

The Suez War followed in 1956. The Israeli army occupied Egypt's

Sinai Peninsula and the Gaza Strip, but were forced to retreat under pressure from the UN and the USA.

The Six-Day War of 1967 was the last attempted invasion of Israel by all its Arab neighbours and was led by Egypt's Gamal Abdel Nasser. It failed decisively. Israel again occupied Sinai and the Gaza Strip, as well as the Syria's Golan Heights, and the West Bank and East Jerusalem which had been seized from Palestine by Jordan in 1948. Under UN pressure, an armistice was declared on 10 June. Subsequently, the Palestine

Israeli soldiers in the city of Hebron on the West Bank.

Liberation Organisation (PLO), a new guerilla group operating outside Israel, staged terrorist operations, of which the most well known is the hostage-taking of athletes from the Israeli Olympic team in Munich in 1972, all of whom were killed.

In 1973 Egypt mounted a surprise attack, now known as the Yom Kippur War. In 1973 the Ge-

neva Conference on the Near East met and agreements were reached between Israel and Egypt as well as Israel and Syria for the withdrawal of troops. In 1974, the UN granted observer status to the PLO.

The trip to Israel in 1977 of the Egyptian President Anwar Sadat was the prelude to direct peace talks, at first bilateral, which

Photograph left: a Palestinian policeman in Jericho in front of a portrait of Yasser Arafat.

aimed at a peaceful solution to the Near East conflict. US president Jimmy Carter set up the Camp David Conference of September 1978, where the conditions for an Egyptian-Israeli peace treaty were negotiated, and this was signed in March 1979. In accordance with this, Israel withdrew from Sinai in April 1982. This positive development was overshadowed by the hostility of Libya and Syria. The situation once again intensified as a result of the Israeli bombing of the Iraqi nuclear reactor, the occupation of southern Lebanon and an alliance with the Lebanese Christian militia who were fighting Islamic factions in Lebanon, the latter backed by Syria and Iran.

In 1987, the Palestinians of the West Bank and Gaza, frustrated by a lack of progress to a resolution of their occupied status,

started the first *intifada* ('shaking off' or uprising). Hundreds of Palestinians died in the escalating violence. In 1988, Jordan abandoned its claim to the West Bank, in favour of the Palestinians.

In 1993, PLO chairman Yasser Arafat and Israeli prime minister, Yitzhak Rabin, signed an agreement in Oslo whereby the PLO agreed to recognise Israel. This was followed in May, 1994 by the Gaza-Jericho agreement which gave the Palestinians a measure of autonomy. Palestinian prisoners were released and the Palestine National Council was set up as the governing body in the West Bank and Gaza. Israeli troops moved out of the autonomous areas. In September 1995, autonomy was extended to the West Bank.

After the assassination of Yitzhak Rabin in 1995 and the election of

Benjamin Netanyahu as prime minister in 1996, the talks began to falter. The expansion of Jewish settlements in the West Bank and Gaza and the Palestinian terrorist attacks that followed led to deadlock in the peace process. The peace process eventually resumed, with the signing of the Sharm el-Sheikh agreement. Barak and Arafat came to Camp David in July, 2000 but despite some concessions by the Israelis, Arafat rejected the plan.

The visit of the new prime minister, Ariel Sharon, to Jerusalem's Temple Mount in September 2000 was the catalyst for the outbreak of the 'Second Intifada'. This produced a new wave of suicide bombings and Israeli military reprisals. Eventually, Israel made the decision to construct a con-

Students at the Islamic University in Hebron.

troversial security fence along the open border between Israel, the West Bank and Gaza.

In 2004, Arafat died. He was succeeded by the moderate Mahmoud Abbas. After encouraging their expansion for years, Ariel Sharon unexpectedly ordered a withdrawal from Jewish settlements in the Gaza Strip in 2005. The anti-Israel Hamas party won

the Palestinian elections of 2006. In July 2006, an Israeli soldier was taken hostage by Hamas in the Gaza Strip and three Israeli soldiers were kidnapped by Hezbollah. This event triggered a month-long war in which Israel bombed Lebanon and Hamas fired rockets at random at the whole of northern Israel.

Iraq

The **Kurds** live in an autonomous region in the mountainous northeast of Iraq. They represent 20 per cent of the population and are the largest minority group in the country. Here, women take up weapons along with the men to fight for an autonomous Kurdish state. This land was promised to them in 1920 by Turkey and the Allies, but the promise remains unfulfilled to this day, despite 80 years of fighting. Meanwhile, the Kurdish independence movement has splintered.

Iraq	
Area:	437,072 sq. km
Capital city:	Baghdad
Form of government:	
Presidential Republic	
Administrative divisions:	
18 provinces	
Population:	
26 million (56 inhabitants/sq. km)	
Languages:	Arabic, Kurdish is
the official language in the northern provinces	
GDP per capita:	US$3,400
Currency:	
1 Iraqi dinar = 1000 fils	

Natural Geography

The fertile **flood plains** of the **Euphrates** and **Tigris** rivers form the heartland of this state in the north eastern Arabian peninsula. Even in pre-Islamic times, artificial **irrigation systems** were built along the course of the rivers, which has produced a wide green belt parallel to both rivers. These often ended abruptly at the edge of the desert in the north east **Kurdish highlands**. In the west and south-west, semidesert and desert predominate. In the south, east of Kuwait, there is a narrow access to the **Persian Gulf** where the Tigris and the Euphrates meet at the **Shatt Al-Arab**. The Iran-Iraq war of 1980 to 1988 and the Gulf War of 1991 caused great ecological damage to the area, as did Saddam Hussein's policy of draining the marshes, from which the environment is only slowly recovering.

Climate

The arid regions have a **desert climate** with cold winters and hot, dry summers. In the northern mountains, whose peaks rise to 3,600 m, the winters are cold and snowy. In the capital city, Baghdad, which is in the plains, the average temperatures are 10°C in January and 35°C in July. This is temperate in comparison with other parts of the country.

Population

The majority of Iraqis are **Arabs**, of whom 97 per cent profess **Islam**, 60 per cent belonging to the **Shi'ite branch**. The largest minority is the **Kurds** (20 per cent) who live predominantly in an autonomous region in the mountains. There are also **Turks** and **Turkmens**. The population suffers seriously from a **shortage** of basic commodities. This can largely be attributed to the dictatorship of Saddam Hussein and the **UN Sanctions** of 1991 to 2003, the effects of which are also noticeable in the poor infrastructure (hospitals and public transport).

History and Politics

The alluvial land on the lower reaches of both rivers, one of the oldest settlements on the earth, form the heart of the **Mesopotamian kingdom**, which the Sumerians founded in the third century BC Among the great achievements of this people is the invention of the **cuneiform script**, one of the earliest forms of writing. The Sumerian civilisation was followed by that of the **Babylonians** and the **Assyrians who** ruled in the second and first centuries BC. Babylon, the capital of the powerful kingdom, was a magnet for the sciences and arts. One of the achievements of this period, **The Hanging Gardens of Babylon**, was among the Seven Wonders of the World. The **Greeks** and later the **Romans** moved into the region at the beginning of the common era and increasingly repressed the Babylonian kingdom. In the sixth century BC, Mesopotamia was conquered by the **Persians**. In the seventh century, it fell to the Abbasids whose capital was **Baghdad**, at the heart of the **Islamic Empire**. This period ended with the city's conquest and destruction by the **Mongols** in the thirteenth century. In the sixteenth century, Mesopotamia became a province of the **Ottoman Empire** who ruled it for more than 300 years.

When the Ottoman Empire disintegrated at the end of **World War I**, Mesopotamia became the British mandate of Iraq. The British installed a **monarchy** in 1921 which was eventually toppled in 1958 after rioting. Since 1961, there have been **violent conflicts** with the **Kurdish minority** who, together with the Kurds from Turkey and Iran are demanding an autonomous **Kurdistan**. Fulfilment of this demand was promised in 1920 by Turkey and its allies under the Peace Treaty of Sèvres but the promise has never been kept. Under Saddam Hussen, Kurdish settlements were attacked with **poison gas**. The monarchy was succeeded by a series of dictators, ending with **Saddam Hussein**, who waged a long and bloody war (1980–1988) against Shi'ite **Iran**. In the **First Gulf War** (1990–1991), international armed forces, led by the USA, freed **Kuwait**, which had been annexed by Iraq under Saddam Hussein.

Following the war, no-fly zones were set up for the protection of the Kurdish minorities in the north and the Shi'ites in the south. Iraq was required to fulfil various UN Resolutions, for example, recognition of the sovereignty of Kuwait and the abandonment of nuclear, biological and chemical weapons. However, the **UN weapons inspectors** were continually deceived and obstructed by the Iraqi regime. This led to air raids on Iraq by the USA and Britain, and to an extension of the **economic sanctions**, of which the general population were the principal victims. In 2002, the conflict with the USA intensified after Iraq was accused of having weapons of mass destruction, including intercontinental ballistic missiles which were capable of striking Europe and even the US. On 20 March 2003, US and British forces attacked Iraq and toppled Saddam

Baghdad: this Iraqi shopkeeper displays his wares with a smile.

The Great Mosque of Kadhimain is a Shi'ite pilgrimage centre.

Saddam Hussein

*Tikrit, 28.4.1937

After the Ba'ath Party seized power in 1968, Saddam Hussein became the most powerful Iraqi politician. He became head of state and government in 1979 and was also commander-in-chief of the armed forces. He established a totalitarian regime, and brutally eradicated any opposition. His interference with the work of the UN weapons inspectors led to conflict with the UN and USA, which ended his dictatorship in the 2003 Iraq War. He was captured by US soldiers in 2003.

Hussein's regime within a matter of weeks. In January 2005, the first free elections in over 40 years were held and a coalition government formed from the various, disparate winning factions, including Kurds. A high degree of insecurity prevails, however, and the political situation remains unstable. There are brutal terror attacks and suicide bombings, mainly from foreign militants, on a daily basis.

Economy

Iraq has the **third largest oil reserves** in the world. The country is only recovering slowly from **wars that have lasted for decades** and the **economic sanctions** imposed by the West after the Gulf War. Reconstruction will only succeed with the help of international aid. Currently, industry contributes 12 per cent to the economy, including **oil**-refining, processing and construction. Before the Iraq War, the oil economy contributed 45 per cent to GDP, industry 7 per cent, agriculture 20 per cent and the services sector 28 per cent. Only 12 per cent of the land can be cultivated and 60 per cent of this is irrigated. Cereals, tomatoes, melons and dates are the main crops.

Transport Infrastructure

Iraq's **rail network** is 2,032 km long, the **road network** is 47,000 km long, The major ports are Chur el-Amja, Basra and Umm Qasr. The Tigris, Euphrates and the Shatt al Arab are navigable. Baghdad and Basra have international airports.

Tourism

Since the wars, tourism in Iraq has come to a standstill.

Iran

Persepolis, built in approximately 400 BC, was for centuries a symbol of power of the first Persian empire of the Achaemenids, until it was burned down by Alexander the Great. Archaeological digs have not resolved the enigma of the purpose of this fortress-like residence. Some believe that it was a shrine for celebrating the Persian New Year on 21 March. However, the grandeur of the construction suggests that it may have been a royal palace.

Iran	
Area:	1,648,000 sq. km
Capital city:	Tehran
Form of government: Islamic Republic	
Administrative divisions: 28 provinces	
Population: 68 million (41 inhabitants/sq. km)	
Languages: Farsi (official), Kurdish, Turkish languages	
GDP per capita:	US$8,100
Currency:	1 rial = 100 dinars

Natural Geography

The country which lies between the **Caspian Sea** and the **Persian Gulf** is bounded in the north by the **Alborz mountains** which rise up to 5,604 m above sea level and in the south by the **Zagros mountains**. In the south-west, the country is part of the **Mesopotamian Lowland Plains**. The arid highlands in the interior of the country are riven with deep valleys. In the east, the land becomes the **Lût desert**. In the north there is the **Dasht-e-Kavir**, the **Great Salt Desert**.

Climate

Iran is a country of extremes: hot summers (up to 50°C) alternate with extremely cold winters. Generally an **arid** or a **semi-arid** climate predominates, with subtropical traces along the **Caspian seaboard**. **Rainfall** is confined mostly to the edges of the mountain ranges; subtropical vegetation is found in the north on the Caspian Sea coast.

Population

In addition to the 51 per cent **Persians**, 24 per cent **Azeris** live in the centre and in the northwest of Iran, and seven per cent of the population are **Kurds,** as well as minorities of **Lurs, Turkmens, Baluchis** and **Armenians**. Of the population, 99 per cent are **Muslims**, consisting of 89 per cent **Shi'ite** and ten per cent **Sunni**. There are also two million **refugees**, mainly from Afghanistan and Iraq. In addition to the official language of **Farsi**, Kurdish, Azerbaijani, Arabic and Armenian are also spoken. The population of Iran is very young; 44 per cent are aged under 15 years old.

The state has set up a **national insurance system** for cases of illness or unemployment. The proportion of spending on social insurance and health amounts to 15 per cent. The country has 36 universities but the **illiteracy** rate is over 40 per cent , mainly among women; there is over 50 per cent **unemployment**.

History and Politics

In 600 BC, the Persians founded an empire that extended throughout the Middle East as far as Egypt. The **Iranians** first settled the area in the second century BC.

Islamisation began in the seventh century AD when Arabs overthrew the **Sassanid Dynasty**. This introduced a period of cultural prosperity, which came to a sudden end in the thirteenth century with the **Mongol invasion**. The **Safavid-Dynasty** replaced foreign rule in the sixteenth and seventeenth centuries. In the following period, under the **New Persian Empire** whose capital was Isfahan, the economy and culture flourished, as is evidenced by the fact that many surviving buildings are regarded as the finest examples of Persian architecture.

In the nineteenth century, the country was drawn into the conflict of interests between Russia and Great Britain. **Rebellions** against the influence of the foreign powers led in 1906 to the first constitution and to the establishing of a parliament. **Shah Pahlavi**, who considered himself to be the successor to the legendary Cyrus II, ascended the Peacock throne following a coup d'etat in 1925 and founded the first Iranian kingdom. He ordered the complete reshaping of the country along **western** lines carrying out **reforms** in the educa-

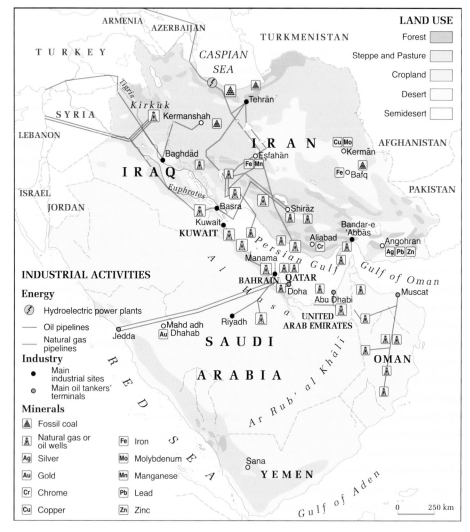

LAND USE
- Forest
- Steppe and Pasture
- Cropland
- Desert
- Semidesert

INDUSTRIAL ACTIVITIES

Energy
- Hydroelectric power plants
- Oil pipelines
- Natural gas pipelines

Industry
- Main industrial sites
- Main oil tankers' terminals

Minerals
- Fossil coal
- Natural gas or oil wells
- Ag Silver
- Au Gold
- Cr Chrome
- Cu Copper
- Fe Iron
- Mo Molybdenum
- Mn Manganese
- Pb Lead
- Zn Zinc

0   250 km

Mullahs on a PC: the computer age has reached Iran.

Mohammad Reza Pahlevi

*Tehran, 26.10.1919,
†Cairo, 27.7.1980

After his father was forced to abdicate by the Allies in 1941, the young heir to the throne was made Shah. Reza Pahlevi began a process of modernisation in Iran. His frequent disregard of Islamic traditions and brutal style of government, supported by the secret police, the SAVAK, led to massive protests and increasing opposition. In 1978, he was overthrown and forced into exile.

Ruhollah Khomeini

*Khomein, 17.5.1900,
† Tehran, 3.6.1989

This Iranian philosophy professor and cleric was the spokesperson of anti-government demonstrations and was banished from the country in 1964. After the abdication of the Shah, he returned from exile in 1979 and founded the Islamic Republic, a fundamentalist dictatorship ruled by mullahs. During his time in office, he also fought an eight-year war with Iraq. He remains a revered religious and political figure in Iran.

*The **shrine** of the Iranian Shah Nematollah Vali is the religious focal point of south-east Iran. Islamic burial shrines serve as a remembrance of great rulers, but are also a place where the faithful can come in isolation to contemplate and pray because they are open every day. In the great Friday mosques, by contrast, people come in great numbers to pray on what, for Muslims, is the most important day of the week.*

tional system, modernising agriculture and putting the state budget back on its feet. A plan to settle the nomadic tribes and to create a balance between the upper echelons of society and the masses was unsuccessful. These reforms, soon led to serious **conflicts** with the country's ruling classes, although these were subdued by force.

In 1978, the **Islamic Revolution** unsettled the country. **Ayatollah Khomeini** organised this coup from his French exile. In 1979, the second Shah was forced to flee the country and Iran was proclaimed an **Islamic Republic**. Since then, Shi'ite Islam, under Khomeini has caused a political and social transformation dominating all areas of life from the media to the judiciary. The President is elected by **Parliament** but the real rules are the twelve-man **Council of Guardians**, a team of six religious representatives and six parliamentary elected representatives. Reforms introduced by the liberal president **Sayyed Mohammed Khatami** were slow and mitigated by the strong **ultra-conservative opposition** who, with the help of the Council of Guardians, successfully opposed innovation under the religious leader **Khamenei**. The feeble attempt at reform ended with the parliamentary elections of June 2005, which was won by hardliners. The intensification of the **Iranian nuclear programme** is a central goal of the new rulers and has put the country at odds with the West, and especially the United States.

Economy

Although 38 per cent of the country's land is used for agricultural purposes, **farming** is only possible thanks to the largely underground, irrigation systems. In addition to wheat, barley, citrus fruits and sugar beet, **tobacco, tea**, **pistachios** and **dates** are grown for **export**.

Whitefish and skate, as well as sturgeon that are so important for **caviar**, are fished from the Caspian Sea. The huge **oil and gas reserves** on the Persian Gulf, the coast of the Caspian Sea as well as in the north-eastern border areas form the basis for Iran's heavy industry. The country is rich in other natural resources, including coal, copper, nickel and chromium deposits. Heavy industry contributes 85 per cent of exports; it is almost exclusively controlled by the state. Traditional industries such as **carpet-making** and also the making of copper and silver artefacts receive state support; nevertheless they are in increasing decline.

Transport Infrastructure

The country's road network covers 162,000 km. Half of the network is surfaced.

The most important **ports** are Bushehr, Bandar Imam Khomeini

and Bandar Abbas. Many remote areas are only reachable by **train**, while the **inland domestic network of air routes** is comparably well developed and extensive, due to the mountainous terrain.

Tourism

The **unstable political conditions** make the construction of a tourist infrastructure difficult. There are also strict **clothing restrictions**, which are imposed as soon as tourists land in Tehran if they have enterd the country on the Iranian airline, **Iran Air**. All women are required to wear headscarves and long dresses at all times, and since men are not allowed to shave under Islamic law, razors are banned!

All of these strict measures have been a strong deterrent to tourism, despite the fact that Iran has a rich heritage, from impressive archaeological and architectural sites to hot springs in the Zagros Mountains. In addition to the Shi'ite relics in the holy cities of **Qom** and **Mashhad**, the ancient ruined, pre-Christian cities of **Persepolis** and **Pasargadae** are world cultural treasures. The **royal mosque** in **Isfahan** with its wonderful mosaics, is an impressive example of Persian Islamic architecture.

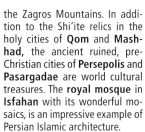

1 Nomadic tribes still live in Iran. They wander with their flocks across the mountains. Attempts to make them settle have failed.

2 Women are required to keep themselves covered. Here they prepare for Friday prayers at the King's Mosque in Isfahan.

3 Isfahan is a trade and cultural centre in which elegant restaurants serve the finest food.

4 An elegant structure: the mausoleum of Ayatollah Khomeini – founding father of the 'Islamic Republic'.

Saudi Arabia, Yemen, Oman

*Arabian mocha coffee, here being enjoyed by three men in **Bahrain**, is black, strong and sweet. In the Islamic world, the tradition of coffee-drinking, which probably originated in Ethiopia, developed much earlier than in Europe.*

Caffeine has been known and enjoyed throughout Arabia since the thirteenth century. The traditional method of preparation has changed little – coffee is brewed in a special pot from very fine grounds and poured into tiny cups.

Saudi Arabia

Area:	1,960,582 sq. km
Capital city:	Riyadh
Form of government:	Islamic Absolute Monarchy
Administrative divisions:	13 regions
Population: 26.4 million	
(11 inhabitants/sq. km)	
Language:	Arabic
GDP per capita:	US$12,900
Currency:	
1 Saudi riyal = 20 qurush =	
100 hallalah	

Natural Geography

Saudi Arabia covers most of the Arabian peninsula and the entire country is made up of **rocky** and **sandy desert**, traversed by **wadis**. The only natural vegetation can be found in the oases.

Climate

The country has a hot and extremely dry **desert climate**. The average temperatures are 2°C in January, and 31°C in July.

Population

Roughly 90 per cent of the population is **Arab**, but there are large numbers of **foreign workers, mainly** from the Indian sub-continent and the Philippines, and many from the West. The native population is exclusively Muslim, and three quarters of the population lives in the country's cities. The standard of living is high, at least for Saudi nationals.

History and Politics

The history of Saudi Arabia begins with the Prophet **Muhammad**, who not only founded the new religion of **Islam** in the seventh century AD, but also united the various Arab tribes. The region was conquered by the Mamelukes in 1269 and became part of the Ottoman Empire in 1517. After the **Ottomans,** the **al-Saud Dynasty,** which still reigns today, conquered the region, then known as Hejaz-Nejd, and created an Islamic state. The **Kingdom of Saudi Arabia** was founded in 1932. Under the political system, the king is also the head of government and 'Guardian of the Holy Places'.

Economy

The **agricultural sector**, almost exclusively date cultivation in the oases, employs 13 per cent of the population. Agriculture accounts for just under ten per cent of GDP. The vast petroleum reserves have made Saudi Arabia the world's **largest exporter of crude oil**.

Transport Infrastructure

The **road network** is well developed. There are three international airports. The country's **oil terminals** are of great importance.

Tourism

The state of Saudi Arabia is a strictly Islamic country, and the only tourists permitted to enter the country are millions of **pilgrims** to the holy places of **Mecca** and **Medina**.

Mecca, the birthplace of the Prophet Mohammed, is an important pilgrimage site for Muslims.

Yemen

Area:	527,970 sq. km
Capital city:	Sana'a
Form of government:	Republic
Administrative divisions:	17 provinces
Population: 20.7 million	
(36 inhabitants/sq. km)	
Languages:	
Arabic (official), English	
GDP per capita:	US$800
Currency:	
1 Yemen rial = 100 fils	

Natural Geography

Yemen is located on the south-western edge of the Arabian peninsula. In the north, a sandy, flat coastal strip borders the **Red Sea**, but behind this the landscape rises to form a craggy **upland**. This develops into the Rub al-Khali (Empty Quarter) one of harshest deserts in the world. South Yemen has a narrow, rainy coastal plain where most of the population lives, bordered to the north by a **plateau,** which in turn descends into a sandy desert.

Climate

Yemen's uplands receive abundant **monsoon rains**, but the southern part of the country has a **tropical desert climate**.

Population

The country is mainly populated by Yemeni **Arabs,** but one per cent of the population consists of guest workers from the Indian sub-continent. **Islam** is the state religion, no other is permitted.

History and Politics

In pre-Christian times, this was the Empire of the **Minaeans** and then the **Sabaeans**, who were overthrown by the **Abyssinians** in the seventh century. Parts of the country fell under **Ottoman** rule during the sixteenth century. The Kingdom of Yemen came into being in Northern Yemen in 1918 and became a **republic** after a **military coup** in 1962. South Yemen, formerly the British colony of Aden, became a **Socialist Republic** in 1967. **The two Yemens were eventually unified**, taking four years from 1990 to 1994.

Economy

Agriculture is restricted to the north of the country and crops include coffee, citrus fruits and dates. It contributes 15 per cent of GDP. The country's economy is based on the **export of crude oil**.

Transport infrastructure

Only ten per cent of the roads are fully made, making economic development very slow. In Yemen, there are six international **airports**.

Tourism

Main attractions for tourists include the numerous **Islamic sites** and some fascinating ancient remains of the **Sabaean kingdom**.

Oman

Area:	212,457 sq. km
Capital city:	Muscat
Form of government:	Sultanate (Absolute monarchy)
Administrative divisions:	59 provinces
Population:	
3 million	
(13 inhabitants/sq. km)	
Languages:	
Arabic (official), Farsi, Urdu	
GDP per capita:	US$13,400
Currency:	
1 Omani rial = 1000 baizas	

Natural Geography

The **Sultanate** is bordered to the north-east by the **Gulf of Oman**, to the east and the south by the **Arabian Sea** and to the west by the **barren Empty Quarter** (Rub al-Khali). The north-east coast ends in a fertile **coastal plain** about 15 km wide and the **Oman mountains**, a range of more than 600 km from the north to the south-east. The **exclave of Musandam** on the Straits of Hormuz also belongs to Oman.

Climate

Oman has an **extreme desert climate**, and temperatures in summer can soar to 50°C. The climate in the **highlands** has subtropical influences. The south and west of the country are affected by **monsoon rains**.

Population

Native **Omanis** are 74 per cent of the population. The huge **migrant worker** population includes 21 per cent from **Pakistan**. The education, social and healthcare systems were completely modernised in the 1970s, and the literacy rate has risen to 80 per cent. The **state religion** is Islam.

*Yemen's capital **Sana'a** is an impressive example of an intact Arab city. The brick decoration and the whitewashed filigree work on the facades of the clay brick buildings are very characteristic and unique.*

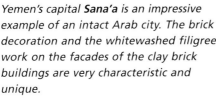

History and Politics

Oman's territory has been settled since 2500 BC. and came under Islamic rule in 634 AD.

Oman has been an **independent** state since 751. After Portuguese **colonisation** in the sixteenth century, **Ahmed bin Said** founded a dynasty in 1744 that still rules today. **Sultan Qaboos,** who rules the country as an absolute monarch, came to the throne in 1970. Since then, great advances have been made in all areas, and the Sultanate has on the whole been **stable** and **liberal** over the recent period. The country has friendly relations with the West.

Economy

Only five per cent of the land mass is used for agriculture (dates, fish, frankincense). The **crude oil sector** accounts for 40 per cent of GDP, making it the dominant branch of the economy. 70 per cent of state income is earned from this sector.

Since the crude oil reserves will run dry within three decades, the state is making attempts to **diversify** the economy.

Transport infrastructure

There are many important roads in the **north**, in the **hilly regions** and near **Salalah** in the south.

Tourism

The country has several medieval **forts** scattered throughout the land which are well worth a visit for tourists. On the coast there are facilities for water sports and diving. A particular attraction are the **turtle colonies**. Tourism is likely to be encouraged as other sources of income have to be found to replace the oil.

Kuwait

Area:	17,820 sq. km
Capital city:	Kuwait
Form of government:	
Emirate	
Administrative divisions:	
5 provinces	
Population: 2.3 million	
(123 inhabitants/sq.km)	

Language:
Arabic

GDP per capita:	US$22,100

Currency:
1 Kuwaiti dinar = 100 dirham = 1000 fils

Natural Geography

Kuwait is an **emirate** on the Persian Gulf. Ten offshore islands are also part of Kuwaiti territory. The land consists of **dry steppes** and **sandy deserts**, with some **saltwater lagoons**. Vegetation in the country is extremely sparse, consisting mainly of thorn bushes. Fauna is similarly rare. The **Gulf War** of 1991 caused severe **environmental damage.**

Climate

Summers in the country's interior are **extremely hot** (with average temperatures of 36°C) and dry – even the comparatively humid coastal regions are among the driest parts of the world, and see almost no precipitation.

Temperatures in winter can sink as low as 14°C, and there is occasional ground frost.

Population

62 per cent of those living and working in Kuwait come from neighbouring **Arab** and **Asian** countries. Kuwaitis pay no taxes and make no social security contributions. Islam is the state religion and no other is permitted.

History and Politics

Until 1716, the land was mainly uninhabited. It became a **British Protectorate** in 1899 and gained its **independence** once more in 1961.

The executive power lies in the hands of the **Emir**, who is elected from the **Al-Sabah dynasty** that has ruled since 1756. A **National Assembly** has existed since 1996, but it only has very restricted legislative influence. In May 2005, the parliament decided that from 2007, women would have the active and passive right to vote.

Economy

Only 0.2 per cent of the land mass is suitable for agricultural use, and cultivation is only possible in these areas by using artificial irrigation techniques. Most of the country's food has to be imported. Since 1946, **crude oil** has been extracted from Kuwait, and this alone is responsible for making Kuwait **one of the richest nations in the world.**

Transport Infrastructure

The road network is extensive. There is an international airport in the capital **Kuwait City** and the country has large **oil ports.**

Tourism

The **old town** of Kuwait is an attractive travel destination, as is the offshore island of **Faylakah** with its holiday resorts and beaches. Tourism may develop if the situation improves in Iraq.

Bahrain

Area:	665 sq. km
Capital city:	Al-Manama
Form of government:	Emirate
Population:	
688,000 (960 inhabitants/ sq. km)	
Language:	Arabic
GDP per capita:	US$20,500
Currency:	
1 Bahrain dinar =	
1000 fils	

Natural Geography

Bahrain is an **island state** in the Persian Gulf consisting of a total of 33 islands, of which only 13 are inhabited. The main island, Bahrain, is connected to the islands of Al Muharraq and Sitrah by causeways. The desert landscape consists of **salt marshes** and **sand dunes**.

Bahrain, Qatar

Camel racing is very popular in the land of 'black gold'. The camels are often ridden by child jockeys, specially selected from poorer neighbouring countries – their dangerous careers are cut short as the children grow in size.

Climate

The **desert climate** is slightly modified by Bahrain's position as an island. In winter, the average temperature is 19°C, and winters are warm with abundant rainfall. Summers are **extremely hot and humid** and temperatures reach an average of 36°C.

Population

Only 63 per cent of those living in Bahrain are **Bahraini** nationals. The rest of the population consists of **Arabs** from other countries in the region as well as 30 per cent of other **Asians**. There is also a substantial minority of Iranian nationals. Some 60 per cent of Bahrainis are Shi'ite **Muslims**, and 40 per cent are Sunni. Inhabitants of Bahrain pay no contributions towards the health and education systems, subsidised by the vast oil revenues.

History and Politics

As early as the third millennium BC, the city of **Dilmun** was a major trading centre between Mesopotamia, Southern Arabia and India, until it was conquered by the **Babylonians**. The Portuguese occupied the area in the sixteenth century, and this was followed by **occupation** by the **Ottomans**. Since 1783, the country has been ruled by the Sunni **Al-Khalifa** family, though it was a British protectorate from 1816 to 1971. The **Emirate** declared itself **independent** from Britain in August 1971. Bahrain introduced a **constitution** in 1973, making it the second Arab country in the Gulf to have a **Parliament**. The **Emir** abolished this constitution as well as the parliament in 1975, however, and since then, he ruled Bahrain as an **absolute** monarch.

Economy

Rich **crude oil reserves** were found in 1932, and this has long been a solid basis for the country's economy. The agricultural sector employs a mere three per cent of the working population and accounts for only one per cent of Gross Domestic Product.
The **manufacturing sector** accounts for 40 per cent of GDP. Since Bahrain's own oil reserves will soon run out, the country is increasingly developing its **services sector**, mainly off-shore banking services.

Transport Infrastructure

The road network is well constructed; causeways link the main islands to the mainland of Saudi Arabia. **Bahrain International Airport** is one of the most modern in the Middle East.

Tourism

The tourism industry is rapidly expanding and centres on the capital **Al Manama**.
Bahrain is a relatively liberal country, and attracts tourists. Attractions include numerous archaeological sites, such as the **Temples** and **tombs** of **Barbar** and the **Qal'at al-Bahrain** (Bahrain Fort).

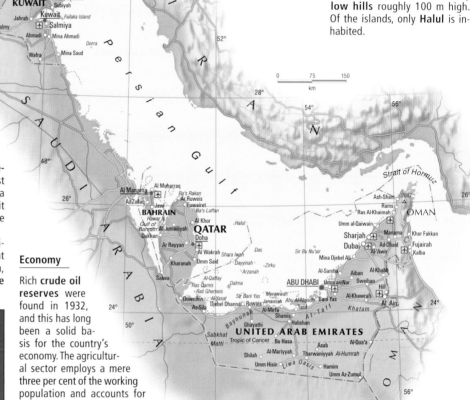

A Kuwait landmark: the Kuwait Towers are used for storing water.

Qatar	
Area:	11,437 sq. km
Capital city:	Doha
Form of government:	
Emirate (Absolute Monarchy)	
Administrative divisions:	
9 districts	
Population:	
863,100	
(71 inhabitants/sq. km)	
Language:	Arabic
GDP per capita:	US$26,000
Currency:	
1 Qatar riyal = 100 dirham	

Natural Geography

Qatar is a peninsula with offshore **coral islands** extending from the east coast of the Arabian peninsula into the **Persian Gulf**. The lowland plains are interrupted on the east coast by **low hills** roughly 100 m high. Of the islands, only **Halul** is inhabited.

Climate

Qatar has a hot and **dry climate**. The sparse desert vegetation grows only in some northern **wadis**.
Average temperatures are 17°C in January and 37°C in July. Apart from the varied **sealife**, very few animal species live in Qatar.

Population

Only 20 per cent of the population is **Qatari**. The rest are **Indians** and **Pakistanis** (35 per cent), **Arabs** from other countries (25 per cent) and **Iranians**. The social welfare, health and education systems are good and subsidised by the oil revenues. The

*The wealth of the **United Arab Emirates** is very obvious. Oil millionaires from around the world come to buy jewellery and expensive clothing here. In public, however, local women must remain completely covered and cannot go out alone.*

state religion, of 90 per cent of the population, is **Islam**.

History and Politics

The peninsula has been settled since prehistoric times,. It has been ruled by the **Al-Thani family** since the eighteenth century. Qatar was conquered by the **Ottomans** (1872–1916) and was then ruled by the **British** (until 1971), but now the head of the Al-thani family rules as an **absolute monarch**.

Economy

The entire economy is based on **crude oil**. The **natural gas reserves** are supposedly the largest in the world.

Transport Infrastructure

There is a well-constructed road network between the cities and neighbouring countries. **Doha** has an international airport.

Tourism

The country is only visited by business travellers, and is not particularly accessible to tourists. It does not have many attractions for the casual visitor.

United Arab Emirates	
Area:	82,880 sq. km
Highest altitude:	
Jabal Yibir (1,572 m)	
Capital city:	Abu Dhabi
Form of government:	
Federation of Independent Sheikhdoms	
Administrative divisions:	
7 emirates	
Population:	
2.5 million	
(63 inhabitants/sq. km)	
Language:	Arabic (official)
GDP per capita:	US$29,100
Currency:	
1 dirham = 100 fils	

Natural Geography

The country consists of a flat coastal strip along the Persian Gulf, behind which lies a **salty clay plain** and the Rub al-Khali desert. On the eastern border,

the Al-Hajar mountains rise to 1,100 m.

Climate

The **extremely hot** and **dry climate** (in summer the average temperature is 42°C) means that vegetation can only grow with intensive irrigation.

Population

Three-quarters of the residents are **migrant workers** from the Indian sub-continent. The native population enjoys a **high standard of living**.

History and Politics

The sheikhdoms of Abu Dhabi, Dubai, Sharjah, Ajman, Umm al-Qaiwain, Fujairah and Ras' al-Khaimah became **British protectorates** in the eighteenth century. After the withdrawal of the British, the Emirates joined together in 1971 to form a **federation**. According to the constitution of 1975, the seven Emirs form the **supreme council** and choose the **president** from among themselves.

Economy

Since 1962, **crude oil** has been found in the Persian Gulf. The industry employs two per cent of the working population, who contribute 50 per cent of GDP. The **services sector** has come to account for 44 per cent of Gross Domestic Product. Only three per cent of GDP in the United Arab Emirates derives from agriculture.

Transport infrastructure

The road network is well constructed. There are six international airports.

Tourism

The country offers luxury hotels, shopping and water sports.

1 Traditional and modern: The so-called 'black gold' has made Kuwait one of the richest countries in the world.

2 Omani men carrying the *khanjar* – these proud men will not be seen without their highly ornate daggers.

3 The Jumeirah Mosque in Dubai is one of the most important places of worship in the United Arab Emirates.

4 The old and the new in Dubai, the trading capital of the U.A.E. The palace of Sheikh Al Makhtum and the modern buildings reflected in the water.

Oil Fields and World Politics

Steel and smoke: at the refineries in Saudi Arabia, the atmosphere is hellish.

Photograph right: the search for new sources of oil is endless. Here, drilling in Abu Dhabi.

Crude oil, a fossil fuel, is the fundamental basis of global industry, and when it comes to oil, OPEC plays a very influential role. OPEC not only dictates prices, but, together with the USA, the organisation has the power to influence political decisions in the Arab world, to lead wars and to force peace talks.

The beginning of petroleum extraction in 1859 marked a change in the entire world economy: petroleum became the driving force of industrialisation. Up to the 1960s, seven large oil consortia dominated conditions on the world oil market. But the Arab countries, with their vast petroleum reserves, organised themselves into a pressure group.

OPEC, the Organisation of the Petroleum Exporting Countries, was founded in Baghdad on 14 September 1960. The founding members of this raw material cartel were Iran, Iraq, Kuwait, Saudi Arabia and Venezuela. They were later joined by Qatar (1961), Indonesia (1962), Libya (1962), the United Arab Emirates (1967), Algeria (1969), Nigeria (1971), Ecuador (1973) and Gabon (1973). Ecuador withdrew in 1992 as its extraction quotas were too low, as did Gabon in 1996, so that eleven member states remained.

The aim of this organisation was, and remains today, to standardise the petroleum policy of the member countries, in order to secure and, if possible, increase income from this raw material. This is brought about by fixing the quantities extracted to obtain higher prices on the world market. One of the most important measures taken after the founding of OPEC was the nationalisation of the local oil industries. In this way, its members avoided the problems of many Third World countries which, despite enormous mineral resources, are forced to sell their raw materials cheaply on the world market and in return have to import expensive finished products. The mounting debts in the Third World have largely been avoided by the OPEC states, some of which are now among the richest nations in the world.

The world was soon to learn of the political power attained by

During the Gulf War, Iraq ignited around 700 Kuwaiti oil wells.

OPEC through the leverage provided by its commodity, oil. On 13 October 1973, at a point in time when it was delivering 80 per cent of world production, OPEC announced an oil embargo. Its political aim was to persuade the importing countries to support the Arab side in the Yom Kippur war between Israel, Egypt and Syria. For the first time it became clear to the world how much it depended on 'black gold'. Admittedly the oil crisis, which in the United Kingdom led to a huge rise in oil prices and massive petrol shortages, was averted within only a few weeks. But the shock of discovering how vital this commodity was, is a lesson

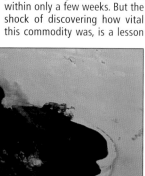

The network of pipelines is constantly being expanded – heavy labour under the desert sun.

that quickly learned. When OPEC subsequently began raising oil prices again, it became clear that its members were in possession of one of the most important raw materials for the world economy. Since then, worldwide exploration and opening up of new sources of oil has been proceeding apace. Today, some 3.5 million tonnes of crude oil are extracted annually. The largest producers are Saudi Arabia, the USA, Canada, the CIS, Iraq, Iran, the United Arab Emirates, Kuwait, Mexico, Norway, China, Venezuela and the United Kingdom. The eleven member countries of OPEC account for some three-quarters of the world's known oil reserves, while about 40 per cent of world production comes from the OPEC states.

The direct influence of the mighty oil cartel on world politics has been waning for the past 20

years or so, but the OPEC states still indirectly play a great role, since the Arab members of OPEC are important representatives of the Islamic world. In the OPEC states themselves, petroleum remains the basis of the respective national economies. In most of these countries, oil provides wealth, social validation and political stability. But in countries in which conditions are politically unstable, wars are conducted over access to petroleum, and dictatorships profit from this raw material.

The Iran-Iraq War broke out in 1980 as a result of border disputes between the OPEC partners Iran and Iraq over access to the Shat Al-Arab waterway. The Western world, together with most of the OPEC countries, sided with Iraq, since Iran had recently shocked world opinion with the Islamic revolution and the taking

of US hostages after the storming of the embassy. After eight years of war, with some 500,000 deaths, international negotiations led to an armistice agreement.

The Gulf War was triggered by the invasion of Kuwait by its neighbour Iraq on 2 August 1990. Iraq claimed one of the richest countries in the world as its 19th province. The real reason behind the annexation, however, was access to the Persian Gulf, the oil wells and the country's excellent infrastructure. A historically unique alliance of western and Arab states in 1991 liberated the little country and isolated Iraq from the international community. Twelve years later, Iraq and oil were again the focus of atten-

The Persian Gulf: tankers are used to ship 'black gold' across the world's oceans.

tion. The war conducted against Iraq on land and in the air in the spring of 2003 by the USA with British and other Western support was surrounded by speculation that the actual cause of war was the oil deposits and the possibility of reorganising the Near East from Iraq, rather than the supposed presence of weapons of

mass destruction, since the relationship between the USA and Saudi Arabia, the largest oil producer, had noticeably cooled. Control over the Gulf, a 'stupendous source of strategic power', to quote Eisenhower, had always been a foundation of US policy. Victory was quick but the fighting continues.

Kazakhstan, Kyrgyzstan

Kazakhstan is, after Russia the second largest country in the CIS. Steppes dominate the terrain which is roamed by red deer, roe deer and bears. Many Kazakhs are hunters or nomadic herdsmen, who still enjoy the traditional sport of falconry. The Kazakhs are descendants of Turkic and Mongolian nomadic tribes, who established a very influential Khanate in the fifteenth century.

Kazakhstan

Area:	2,717,300 sq. km
Capital city:	Astana
Form of government:	Republic
Administrative divisions: 19 regions, 2 municipalities	
Population: 15.2 million (6 inhabitants/sq. km)	
Languages:	Kazakh, Russian
GDP per capita:	US$8,700
Currency:	1 tenge = 100 tiin

Natural Geography

The country includes **steppe** and **desert areas** and part of the **Tianshan Mountains** (highest peak: Khan-Tengri, 6,995 m) in the south-east. The Caspian Sea forms the south-east border. The siphoning off of water from the

Population

Kazakhstan has the **most multiracial population in the CIS**: 46 per cent are Kazakhs, 34 per cent Russian, five per cent Ukrainian, three per cent of German origin, 2.3 per cent Uzbeks, together with Tatars and other ethnic groups. **Muslims** make up 47 per cent of the population, while most of the **Christians** (46 per cent) are Russian Orthodox.

History and Politics

In the mid-eighteenth century, Kazakhstan placed itself under **Russian sovereignty**, and in 1873, it was annexed by **Russia**. In 1920 it was declared an **Autonomous Socialist Republic**, which became a **Soviet republic** on joining the Soviet Union in 1925. When the Soviet Union was

gation systems. Agriculture accounts for 7 per cent of the country's GDP. One of the **world's richest deposits of copper and iron ore**, together with the large **reserves of petroleum and natural gas**, form the basis for heavy industry.
The pollution of the environment by chemicals and high levels of radioactivity resulting from the USSR's nuclear testing programme represent a major threat to the population as does the shrinking of the Aral Sea, a vast lake whose waters were used to irrigate cotton fields.

Transport Infrastructure

The thinly populated country is made accessible by a **rail network** 13,500 km in length. The 141,000 km road network is mostly surfaced. There are ap-

Kyrgyzstan

Area:	198,500 sq. km
Capital city:	Bishkek
Form of government: Presidential Republic	
Administrative divisions: 6 regions, 1 district (capital city)	
Population: 5.1 million (24 inhabitants/sq. km)	
Languages: Kyrgyz (official), Russian	
GDP per capita:	US$2,100
Currency: 1 Kyrgyzstan som = 100 tyin	

Natural Geography

Most of Kyrgyzstan lies in the **Tianshan mountains**. Three-quarters of the land area is over 1,500 m above sea level, half of which is over 3,000 m high.

Alpine-polar climate in the high mountain areas. Average temperatures in the capital range between -18°C in January up to 28°C in July.

Population

The multinational population is composed of **Kyrgyz** (52 per cent), **Russians** (18 per cent), **Uzbeks** (13 per cent), as well as Ukrainians, Germans and other ethnic groups. Three-quarters of the Kyrgyz are **Muslim**, 20 per cent are Russian Orthodox.
Since 1996, **Russian** has again become the second official language in the areas in which mainly Russians live and work.

History and Politics

Under oppression from the **Mongols** in the thirteenth century, the Kyrgyz people withdrew into the mountains. They were subsequently ruled by the **Manchus** and finally by the **Russians**.
In 1876, Kyrgyzstan was incorporated into the Russian empire. The modern state emerged for the first time after the October Revolution of 1917. In 1936, it became a **Socialist Soviet Republic** and in **1991** declared its **independence** from the Soviet Union. Changes to the **constitution of 1996** confer extensive powers on the head of state.

Economy

Kyrgyzstan is a small mountainous country in which **agriculture** is only practicable over seven per cent of the land mass but represents the most important branch of the economy. Apart from grain and fodder plants, fruit, vegetables, cotton, hemp and poppies, as well as oil-bearing plants and tobacco, are cultivated. In addition, **silkworms** are bred. The **agricultural sector** represents 35 per cent of the country's GDP.
Light industry is of great importance. Kyrgyzstan possesses substantial reserves of gold and precious **metals**, which have yet to be exploited. The country exports its **hydro-electric power** to the neighbouring states. The services sector and tourist industry are relatively underdeveloped at present.

ARAL SEA DISAPPEARENCE
1960
Syrdarja
1985
Amudarja
1992
0   100 km

Uzbekistan: modern buildings in the ancient oasis city of Tashkent.

numerous rivers and lakes for the irrigation of the land has led to **severe ecological damage**, especially the rapid shrinking of the Aral Sea.

Climate

Kazakhstan has a **continental arid climate**. Average temperatures in the capital city, Astana, range from 0°C in January to 29°C in July.

disbanded, the country declared its **independence in 1991**, and a **constitution** was drawn up in **1993**. The **bicameral parliament** consists of the **Senate** and the **Lower House**, whose representatives are directly elected.

Economy

The cultivation of **grain** and **sugar beet**, **tobacco** and **fruit** is only possible through the irri-

proximately 4,002 km of **inland waterways**. The international airports are at Alma-Ata and Astana.

Tourism

Alma-Ata ('Father of Apples') is the centre of the country's **infant tourism industry** and a major transport hub. **Winter sports** and **trekking** in the Altai mountains are possible.

The highest peak is **Mount Pobedy** (7,439 m). At 3,000 m, the landscape changes from **desert** and **semi-desert** to **mountain steppes, meadows** and **forest**. The mountain tundra adjoins the **glacier zone**, which feeds the country's lakes.

Climate

The climate is predominantly **dry and continental**, with an

*Isolated in their small, mountain republic, the people of **Kyrgyzstan** were able to escape the forced collectivisation of agriculture imposed by the Soviets. Within the protection of the 7000-m-high mountains, even their religion, Sunni Islam, managed to survive the Soviet ban. Traditional dress is still worn. The characteristic bulky headcovering of the women consists of a tightly wound white cloth; the men wear coarse felt hats.*

Transport Infrastructure

The 18,500-km-long **road network** is mainly surfaced. In addition a very dense network of buses makes access fairly easy, even to remote areas. Inland navigation is possible over about 600 km of the waterways; **Issyk-Kul** is the largest body of water in this landlocked country.

Tourism

The nature reserves and health resorts around **Issyk-Kul**, one of the world's largest inland lakes, at a height of 1,609 m, and the capital city of **Bishkek**, are the chief tourist attractions. Hiking, rambling and mountaineering will no doubt attract tourists as the country gradually develops its services sector.

Uzbekistan

Location:	Central Asia
Area:	447,400 sq. km
Capital city:	Tashkent
Form of government:	

Presidential Republic

Administrative divisions:
12 regions, 1 autonomous republic
Population: 26.8 million
(58 inhabitants/sq. km)
Languages:
Uzbek (official), Russian

GDP per capita:	US$1,900

Currency: 1 Uzbekistan sum = 100 tijin

Natural Geography

Uzbekistan includes the centre of the **Turan Basin** with the south-west of the **Kyzylkum desert**, an area 600 km long, 350 m wide.

On the south-west border, the **Amu Darya** river flows through the desert and into the Aral Sea. This makes Uzbekistan the country with the best water resources in the region. In the east, the country is bordered by the foothills of the Tianshan and Altai mountains.

Climate

The **continental climate** ensures long, hot summers with an average temperature of 32°C as well as short, extremely cold winters, during which a temperature of -38°C is not unusual. Throughout the year there is **very little precipitation**; desert and steppe areas are very extensive.

Population

The population consists of a majority of **Uzbeks** and minorities including Russians (5.5 per cent), Tajiks (five per cent), Kazakhs (three per cent), Tatars and other groups. The **Karakalpaks**, who represent 2.5 per cent of the population, were granted an autonomous republic. Of the Uzbeks, 88 per cent are **Muslims**, the majority of them of the Sunni denomination.

History and Politics

The cities of Samarkand, Bukhara and Khiva were three of the most important stages on the Silk Road. The first independent state came into being in the fourteenth century. Its **enforced incorporation** into the Autonomous Soviet Republic of Turkestan was a result of the **Russian waves of conquest** that began in 1864. On the collapse of the Soviet Union in 1991, Uzbekistan declared its independence. Its **constitution of 1992** admittedly envisages political pluralism, but the opposition is suppressed. The single-chamber parliament admits only parties that support the **president**, who alone rules the land, and has extensive authority. Displeasure with those in power culminated in May 2005 in mass demonstrations, which were ruthlessly suppressed, resulting in the deaths of several hundred people.

Economy

Uzbekistan is an agricultural country with little industry. The cultivation of **cotton** plays a central role. Uzbekistan is currently the world's third-largest exporter of cotton. The agricultural sector's share of GDP is 26 per cent. The country's manufacturing sector is equally geared towards agriculture: the largest share,

Uzbekistan is home to a mixture of people from over a dozen ethnic groups, of which just under 90 per cent are Sunni Muslim. Although the different groups share the same religion, the country has seen many internal conflicts since 1989.

apart from the manufacture of **cotton harvesting machines**, is taken up by the production of fertiliser. Of the labour force, 44 per cent are employed in farming, 20 per cent in manufacturing and 36 per cent in trade or in the services sector. A changeover from a planned economy to a competitive market economy has been the goal ever since independence was declared, but is proving difficult to achieve. There are rich reserves of **raw materials** (oil, gas, gold, silver and precious metals).

Transport Infrastructure

The majority of the 81,600 km of road network is paved. The par-

tially navigable rivers, **Amu Darya** and **Syr Darya**, are important inland waterways. The rail network is only 3,500 km long and is awaiting development. The air transport network, with an **international airport** at Tashkent, is being expanded.

Tourism

The country is as yet barely developed for tourism, but the cities of **Bokhara, Khiva, Samarkand** and **Tashkent** are centres of interest with many archaeological remains and magnificent mosques that are sure to attract tourists who will want to take 'the Golden Road to Samarkand'.

Turkmenistan	
Area:	488,100 sq. km
Capital city:	Ashgabat
Form of government:	
Presidential Republic	
Administrative divisions:	
5 regions	
Population:	
4.9 million (9 inhabitants/sq. km)	
Language:	Turkmen
GDP per capita:	US$5,900
Currency: 1 manat = 100 tenge	

Natural Geography

The territory extends from the **Caspian Sea** in the west to the border with Uzbekistan in the

east, which is bounded by the river **Amu Darya**. The flatlands of the **Karakum desert** account for 80 per cent of the land area. Striking features of the landscape include the **Kopet Dag** mountain range, which rises to 2,942 m at the border with Iran in the south, the **Ustyurt Plateau** in the north and the adjacent **Plateau of Turkmenbashi**.

The coastal strip beside the Caspian Sea is flat and sandy. The only major river is the **Amu Darya** in the north-east of the country. Since Turkmenistan includes vast **nature reserves** (for example a 260,000-ha-large bird sanctuary), there is a great variety of wildlife.

nately Islam since the seventh century, Turkmenistan came under **Russian rule** as a result of Russian expansion into Central Asia from 1877 to 1881.

In 1918, it became part of the Autonomous Soviet Republic of Turkestan, and after the dissolution of the Soviet Union in 1991 an independent member of the CIS. Even after the adoption of a new **constitution in 1992**, the old **Communist leadership** is still in place, and the president is in a position of extreme power.

Economy

Since this country was, above all, a supplier of **raw materials** and **cotton** to the Soviet Union,

Samarkand's Islamic buildings are among the most beautiful in the world.

Climate

Turkmenistan has a **continental desert climate** with very hot summers (average temperature 30°C) and cold winters (average temperature -33°C).

Population

The largest population group is represented by the **Turkmens** at 77 per cent. Of the rest, nine per cent are Uzbeks, six per cent Russians, with Kazakhs and other groups representing small minorities. Islam is the religion of 90 per cent of the population. Health and social security systems are well developed.

History and Politics

Settled by **Turkic peoples** since the fifth century, and predomi-

the manufacturing sector is today still severely underdeveloped and the economy hardly diversified. There are rich natural **resources** including natural gas, petroleum, sulphur and various mineral salts. While the desert landscape, which fortunately lacks costly and ecologically harmful irrigation, allows no farming to speak of, the most important areas of the processing industry apart from **petrochemicals** and **chemicals** are **metalworking** and the **textile industry**.

Transport Infrastructure

The 24,000-km-long road network is largely surfaced. **Air connections** are of great importance even in remote areas. Ashgabat lies on an important railway line that leads to the **Trans-Siberian-Railway**. The **Amu Darya** river is

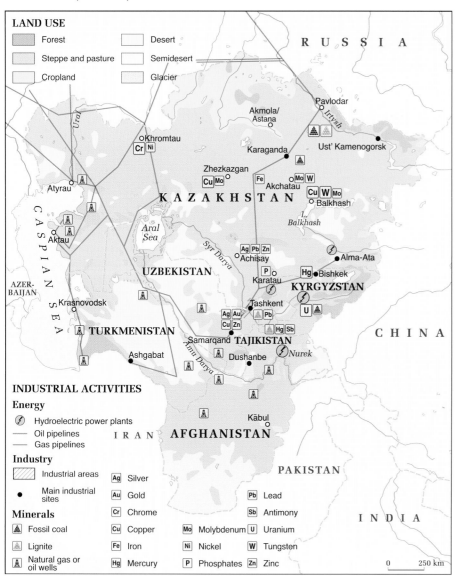

LAND USE

- Forest
- Steppe and pasture
- Cropland
- Desert
- Semidesert
- Glacier

INDUSTRIAL ACTIVITIES

Energy
- Hydroelectric power plants
- — Oil pipelines
- — Gas pipelines

Industry
- Industrial areas
- Main industrial sites

Minerals
- Fossil coal
- Lignite
- Natural gas or oil wells

- Ag Silver
- Au Gold
- Cr Chrome
- Cu Copper
- Fe Iron
- Ni Nickel
- Hg Mercury
- Mo Molybdenum
- Pb Lead
- Sb Antimony
- U Uranium
- W Tungsten
- P Phosphates
- Zn Zinc

0   250 km

*The ancient oasis city of **Bukhara** in Uzbekistan is famous for its arts and crafts: many of the goldsmiths, and silk and carpet weavers produce high-value goods, which are sold throughout the world. Bukhara was founded as a trading post on the caravan route; it was a centre of art and culture in the tenth century and attracted people from many lands. Today the city has a university and is home to more than 70 different ethnic groups.*

the most important navigable waterway.

Tourism

The centre of the country's somewhat underdeveloped tourist industry is the capital city, situated in an oasis, with **archeological sites** to be found in the surrounding area.
Turkmenistan is now being discovered by adventurous tourists.

Tajikistan

Area:	143,100 sq. km
Capital city:	Dushanbe
Form of government:	
Presidential Republic	
Administrative divisions:	
2 regions,1 district (capital city),	
1 autonomous republic	
Population:	
7.1 million (48 inhabitants/sq. km)	
Language: Tajik (official), Russian	
GDP per capita:	US$1,200
Currency:	
1 Tajik somoni = 100 diram	

Natural Geography

90 per cent of this mountainous country is **over 1,000 m** above sea level, and 70 per cent of it consists of **high mountains.** The north includes the extensive Fergana Valley; mountain ranges such as the Turkestan, Zeravshan and Gissar ranges characterise the centre of the country, and the High **Pamirs** lie to the southeast.
The mountainous regions in the west, include the 7,495-m-high **Mount Communism** and the 7,134-m-high **Mount Lenin**, the highest peaks in the CIS.

Climate

The **continental climate** is marked by dry summers (27°C) and cold winters (-20°C), replaced by a **polar climate** in the high mountainous regions.

Population

Almost the entire population lives in narrow mountain valleys, which cover barely seven per cent of the land mass. **Tajiks** represent 65 per cent of the population,

with a 25 per cent minority of Uzbeks and groups of Russians and others. A total of 85 per cent of the country's inhabitants are Muslims, 80 per cent of these being of the Sunni denomination.

History and Politics

The region, which has been settled since the first century BC, belonged to the great kingdoms of the Persians, Greeks and Macedonians and Arabs. In the ninth century, it fell to the **Mongols, and later to the Tatars and Uzbeks.** The north of the region came under **Russian rule** around 1870, and in 1918, Tajikistan became part of the Autonomous Soviet Republic of Turkestan. From 1929, the Tajik Socialist Soviet Republic continued to be an independent republic of the USSR.
After the fall of the Soviet Union in 1991, the country emerged as an independent state and member of the CIS. Since then, the multinational state has seen **three changes of government** and one **civil war**; the political situation has now somewhat stabilised.

Economy

War has had a severe effect on the nation's economy. As a result of the impenetrable mountain landscape, a poor infrastructure, and the **cultivation of cotton**, for so long the single source of revenue due to Soviet policy, Tajikistan remains the **poorest republic in the CIS** and is heavily dependent on foreign aid.
In the processing industry, apart from **wool processing** only the **foodstuffs and textile industries** are of significance. Farming still brings in 25 per cent of the GDP. The important raw materials are uranium and gold, and to a lesser extent petroleum, natural gas, lead, zinc, tungsten and tin. Up to the present day, the political regime continues to hinder economic reform.

Transport Infrastructure

The 32,000-km-long **road network** is mostly surfaced. Buses connect the remote areas. There are **international airports** at Dushanbe and Khudzhand.

Tourism

Tourism is still comparatively undeveloped. The unstable political situation means that travel is not without danger. The starting-point for tourism is the capital city, Dushanbe, from which trekking tours to the high mountain areas are organised.

1 Uzbekistan: the old town of Bukhara is the most beautiful in the Near East. Wide squares containing impressive mosques dominate the heart of the city.

2 A Kyrgyz family gathers to share a meal. Family life is of great importance in Kyrgyzstan, where many people still live a nomadic existence and travel with their clans through the country.

3 The Registan with its historic madrasah (Islamic religious school) gives the impression of stark simplicity. It is the central square in Samarkand.

Faces of Asia

Asia is the largest continent and home to more than half the world's population. Ethnic diversity and centuries-old traditions are a fascinating feature of this amazing continent.

Asia is inhabited by approximately 3.8 billion people, roughly three-fifths of the world's population. This makes it the most populous continent on Earth. More people live here than in all of the other continents combined, though some parts are more densely populated than others. Roughly 90 per cent of Asia's population lives on just one third of the land mass, mainly in the fertile plains of the great rivers, and in the coastal regions. The deserts and steppes of the Arabian peninsula and central Asia are mainly uninhabited, providing a massive contrast to the densely populated cities in the east and south-east of the continent, namely in India, China and Japan. Hundreds of ethnic groups, innumerable languages and dialects, and a wide range of traditions and customs all contribute to the varied face of the continent.

1 Hong Kong: even in this highly modern metropolis you can still see women wearing the traditional dress of the Hakka – a people of north Chinese origin, who have lived in southern China since the fourteenth century.

2 Bahrain, an ancient trading post between the Arab and Indian worlds: this man is wearing a keffiyeh, which protects him from the burning sun.

3 Thailand: a colourful example of an elaborate headdress – this girl's turban is like a flower arrangement. Among the Lisu, a minority group of northern Thailand, this costume is worn for festivities.

4 Nepal: this portrait from the only official Hindu state in the world shows an ascetic. The white-powdered forehead and the bright red stripe between the eyebrows identifies the holy man as a follower of the god Vishnu.

5 Japan: wearing the traditional make-up of a geisha, the cherry red mouth stands out against the white face. The white paint is designed to eradicate all trace of individuality, and separate the 'person of the arts' from everyday life.

6 Bhutan: In this kingdom on the southern slopes of the eastern Himalaya, Lamaism, Tibetan Buddhism, is the state religion. The photograph shows a monk from the Taktsang monastery of Gomchen. The chaplet of wooden beads is an aid to prayer and to reciting the holy texts.

7 India: The U-shaped mark on the forehead of this young girl symbolises the footprint of the god Vishnu. The elaborate face-painting and elegant make-up is donned for religious festivals and traditional dance performances.

8 Mongolia: The weathered face of this Kazakh man from Mongolia is a reflection of life on the steppes. The Kazakhs are a mainly Muslim people and a minority in this thinly populated, flat land.

9 Oman: A Bedouin from Al Qabil wears a veil and a yashmak, as well the all-enveloping burqa. In Oman, wearing the veil is considered to be an expression of female self-awareness, tradition and discretion.

10 Cambodia: joyful laughter during the daily wash – Buddhist novices at Bakong Temple in Angkor.

11 Bali: cultural tradition is brought to life in classic Indonesian dance. The grace of the movements is impressive and emphasis is placed on the hands and upper body.

12 The Indians love brightly coloured clothing and strongly-flavoured aromatic foods. This market stall in the southern Indian town of Mysore has a stunning display of coloured powders and herbs.

13 Japan: Kyoto, the former city of the emperors, is bursting with ancient traditions, and the old values are very important here. In this photograph, Shinto priests play instruments wearing their traditional ceremonial dress. Drums and flutes are some of the basic instruments used in classical, religious Japanese music.

The Religions of Asia

Golden temples, impressive stone pagodas, imposing cliff sanctuaries and modest shrines, proud minarets and elegant mosques – nowhere else is religious life as varied as in Asia. The massive continent is the birthplace of the great world religions.

Hinduism or Brahmanism, Buddhism, the national religions of China and Japan – Taoism and Shintoism – Judaism, Christianity and Islam all originated in different parts of Asia. They spread from here along the numerous trade routes, covering the whole continent, and eventually the entire world.

For those living between the Arabian peninsula and Japan, the number and variety of religious beliefs is a fundamental part of their cultural identity and their daily life, as illustrated by the handsome edifices and temple complexes. These buildings constitute the focus of ancient traditions which are still very much alive and they play host to great festivals. At the same time, the holy sites are places of devout worship and learning.

Main photograph, left: Japanese mountain ascetics (Yamabushi) in typical dress – his cap is tied on with a piece of string, and the baggy trousers reach only to the knee. At the Shogoin Temple in Kyoto, they bang the taiko, a kind of barrel-shaped drum.

1 Muslims praying in the famous eighth-century Umayyad Mosque in Damascus. The mosque is said to contain the head of John the Baptist.

2 In the Prabhat Tay Temple in Luang Prabang, Laos, a Buddhist monk prays before a statue of a reclining Buddha.

3 This man from Pushkar in Rajasthan is a Sadhu – a Hindu ascetic. The red dot on his forehead indicates the third eye of knowledge.

4 Taoist priests in Singapore hold a mass at the Hungry Ghosts Festival. Their robes are decorated with the symbols of universal unity.

Afghanistan, Pakistan

*In Pakistan, **Sharia**, Islamic law, has replaced the secular judicial system. The mosques are important social centres, such as this one, the Badshahi in Lahore, where holy men rule on matters of justice and injustice.*

Afghanistan

Area:	647,500 sq. km
Capital city:	Kabul
Form of government:	Islamic Republic
Administrative divisions:	31 provinces
Population:	30 million (44 inhabitants/sq. km)
Languages:	Pashto, Dari
GDP per capita:	US$800
Currency:	1 Afghani = 100 puls

Natural Geography

The mountainous interior is partly comprised of the **Hindu Kush mountain range** in which there are altitudes of up to 4,000 m. These areas are mainly **steppe terrain** and **stony deserts** with sparse vegetation.
The south of the country is dominated by mountainous uplands that extend into wide desert ex-

Zulfikar Ali Bhutto

*Larkana, 5.1.1928,
†Rawalpindi, 4.4.1979

The founder of the Pakistan People's Party held many ministerial posts in the 1960s but he was imprisoned from 1968-9 after conflicts with the president of the time, Ayub Khan. From 1972 to 1973 he ruled Pakistan as President and was Prime Minister, Minister of Foreign Affairs and Minister of Defence from 1973 to 1977. He was toppled by a military dictatorship in 1977. He was condemned to death and executed in 1978.

panses. The Hindu Kush mountains are often shaken by powerful **earthquakes**.

Climate

There are **great variations in climate** ranging from an arid climate to a sub-tropical climate, and even a high-alpine climate in the mountain regions.
The capital city, Kabul, has average temperatures of -3°C in January and 24°C in July.

Population

Afghanistan's population is 38 per cent **Pashto**, 25 per cent **Tajik**, 19 per cent **Hazara** and six per cent **Uzbek** with a sprinkling of other ethnic minorities.
As many as 99 per cent of the population is **Muslim**, of which the **Sunnis** are the majority (84 per cent). Afghanistan is in general an underdeveloped country. A massive 68 per cent of the population is **illiterate**, the literacy rate among women being a mere 15 per cent.
After many years of war and Taliban rule, the education, health and social systems are still in a rudimentary state. **The public health** situation is appalling with only a minority of the population having access to clean drinking water. As a result, the average life expectancy is just 43 years. Since the **war began** in 1979, almost two million people have died in direct combat. Between three

and four million children have died from **malnutrition**. Over a third of the population has fled the country and now lives in refugee camps, mostly in Iran and Pakistan.

History and Politics

The region was settled by **Persian tribes** in 2000 BC but has been under constantly changing **foreign rule** ever since. The **Emirate of Afghanistan** was

founded in 1747 but later fell under of the British sphere of influence, though the British found it impossible to control these tribes on India's North-west Frontier. In 1919, Afghanistan became a kingdom. The **republic** was founded in 1973. In order to support the Communist-leaning regime, the Red Army invaded in 1979, fighting the **Mujaheddin** guerillas for ten years, and being ultimately unsuccessful. After the last Soviet soldiers left 1989, the Afghan president, who had been installed by the Soviets, was overthrown, but the rebels then began fighting amongst themselves. In 1994, the radical Muslim **Taliban militia** joined the war and soon controlled 90 per cent of the territory, which then proclaimed an Islamic religious state ('**Islamic Emirate of Afghanistan**'). They introduced Sharia law: **television was banned** and **women** were denied education and placed under vir-

tual **house arrest**. Conflict with the USA was triggered by Afghanistan's tolerance of the Islamic extremist Osama Bin Laden and his terror organisation, Al Qaeda. After the attacks on the World Trade Center and the Pentagon in September 2001, the USA named Bin Laden and Al Qaeda responsible and launched a military attack on Afghanistan. With the support of the Northern Alliance, they were able to bring down the Taliban regime in just

under two months. From the end of 2001, the country was ruled by a transitional government under Hamid Karzai, who was confirmed president in 2002 by the Loya Jirga, a gathering of tribal and ethnic leaders. He also won recognition in the presidential elections of October 2004.

Economy

Afghanistan is one of the poorest countries in the world. Its economy is based on agriculture. Cereals, fruit and nuts are cultivated in the irrigated valleys, and livestock is reared in the mountain regions. There is also illegal cultivation of the opium poppy on a large scale. **Agriculture** accounts for 56 per cent of GDP.

Transport Infrastructure

There is no rail network and the 21,000-km-long **road network** is poor. There are **international**

The Blue Mosque in Mazar-e-Sharif, Afghanistan: doves of peace in a troubled land?

airports in Kabul and Kandahar.

Tourism

Afghanistan is **not a tourist destination**, although it was in the past. It has **historic mosques** in **Kabul**, **Kandahar**, **Herat** and at **Mazar-e Sharif**. **Bamiyan** is where the Taliban destroyed two third- and fifth-century Buddha statues in the year 2001.

Pakistan

Area:	803,940 sq. km
Capital city:	Islamabad
Form of government:	Islamic Republic
Administrative divisions:	4 provinces, 1 district (capital city), 2 territories
Population:	162.4 million (189 inhabitants/sq. km)
Languages:	Urdu (official), English, Punjabi, Sindhi
GDP per capita:	US$2,400
Currency:	1 Pakistani Rupee = 100 paisa

Natural Geography

The north of Pakistan contains sections of the **Himalayas**, the **Hindu Kush** and the **Karakoram** ranges (K2: 8,611 m). The west of the country has mountainous borders with Iran and Afghanistan. The east is dominated by the **Indus Basin**, which stretches for more than 2,000 km to the south, and ends in the **Arabian Sea**. This is where 80 per cent of the population live. Parts of the country are subject to frequent earthquakes. The Pakistani section of Kashmir was struck by a major earthquake in October 2005 in which some 80,000 people died.

Climate

The climate of Pakistan is as varied as the landscape. The mountain chains in the north-west and the north of the country have a **high-altitude climate**, while the Indus Basin has a **dry, hot climate,** which also dominates in the **steppe and desert regions**. Only four per cent of the country's land is forested.

Population

Half of the population is **Punjabi**, but there are also many **Pashtun**, **Sindhi**, **Baloch**, **Muhajir** (of Indian origin), and other ethnic minorities, including Afghans.
The official language, **Urdu**, is only the mother tongue of some eight per cent of the population, while 48 per cent speak **Punjabi**. In total, more than 20 different languages and dialects are spoken

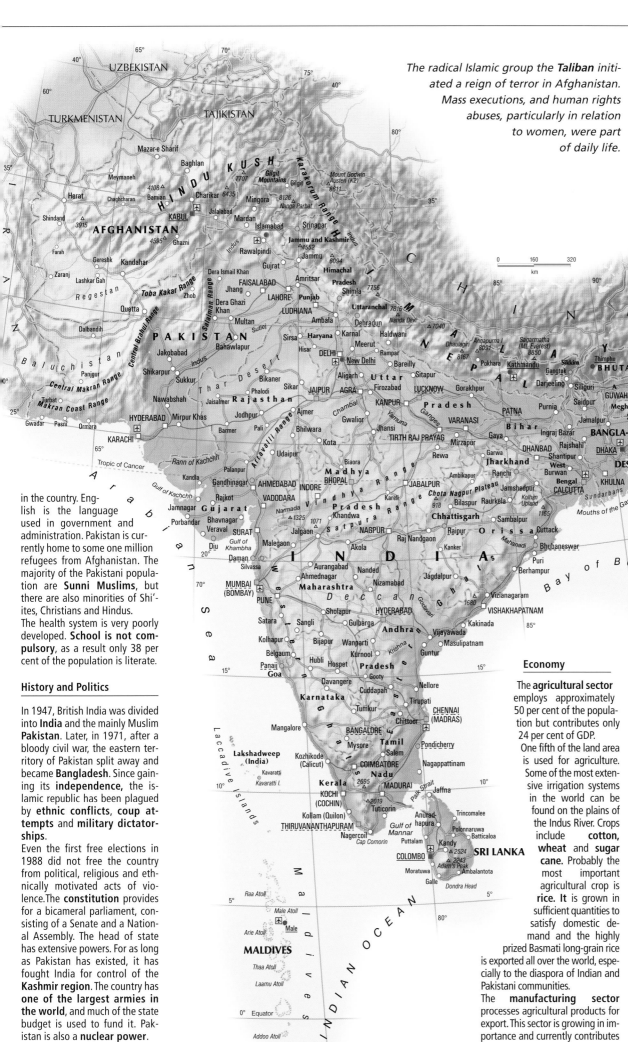

*The radical Islamic group the **Taliban** initiated a reign of terror in Afghanistan. Mass executions, and human rights abuses, particularly in relation to women, were part of daily life.*

in the country. English is the language used in government and administration. Pakistan is currently home to some one million refugees from Afghanistan. The majority of the Pakistani population are **Sunni Muslims**, but there are also minorities of Shi'ites, Christians and Hindus. The health system is very poorly developed. **School is not compulsory**, as a result only 38 per cent of the population is literate.

History and Politics

In 1947, British India was divided into **India** and the mainly Muslim **Pakistan**. Later, in 1971, after a bloody civil war, the eastern territory of Pakistan split away and became **Bangladesh**. Since gaining its **independence,** the islamic republic has been plagued by **ethnic conflicts**, **coup attempts** and **military dictatorships**.

Even the first free elections in 1988 did not free the country from political, religious and ethnically motivated acts of violence. The **constitution** provides for a bicameral parliament, consisting of a Senate and a National Assembly. The head of state has extensive powers. For as long as Pakistan has existed, it has fought India for control of the **Kashmir region**. The country has **one of the largest armies in the world**, and much of the state budget is used to fund it. Pakistan is also a **nuclear power**.

Economy

The **agricultural sector** employs approximately 50 per cent of the population but contributes only 24 per cent of GDP.

One fifth of the land area is used for agriculture. Some of the most extensive irrigation systems in the world can be found on the plains of the Indus River. Crops include **cotton, wheat** and **sugar cane**. Probably the most important agricultural crop is **rice**. **It** is grown in sufficient quantities to satisfy domestic demand and the highly prized Basmati long-grain rice is exported all over the world, especially to the diaspora of Indian and Pakistani communities.

The **manufacturing sector** processes agricultural products for export. This sector is growing in importance and currently contributes 16 per cent of GDP. The other main export apart from **wool** are textiles, clothing and **carpets**. Pakistanis living abroad make a substantial contribution to the economy by sending money home.

Transport Infrastructure

The country has good transport connections, with a **rail network** and a **road network** covering some 220,000 km, up to 60 per cent of which is surfaced. Part of

*In **Pakistan** and **India,** the markets offer a highly colourful range of products, from numerous varieties of the finest herbs to tea and exotic fruits, carpets and textiles and even livestock.*

the **Karakoram Highway** along the historic **Silk Road** leads to the Chinese border. The domestic **flight network** is also important. The main international port is in **Karachi**, the former capital.

Tourism

After **Lahore** and **Karachi**, the main places of interest are the ancient sites of **Mohenjo-Daro** and the **Hyderabad** with its relics from the colonial era.

India	
Area:	3,287,263 sq. km
Capital city:	New Delhi
Form of government: Republic	
Administrative divisions: 28 federal states, 7 union territories	
Population: 1.080 billion (319 inhabitants/sq. km)	

Mohandas Karamchand Gandhi

*Porbandar, 2.10.1869,
†New Delhi, 30.1.1948

Until 1914, Gandhi was a lawyer and a prominent member of the Indian minority in South Africa. He returned to India after World War I and organised passive resistance against British colonial rule. As president of the Indian National Congress he tried to lead India to independence through civil disobedience. He was not able to make peace between Hindus and Muslims, and India was divided into three parts. In 1948, Ghandi was assassinated by a Hindu fanatic.

Languages:
Hindi, English and 17 others
GDP per capita: US$3,400
Currency:
1 Indian Rupee = 100 paise

Natural Geography

The Indian sub-continent extends from the foothills of the **Himalayas** (Nanda Devi, 7,816 m) in the north, to the pointed triangular peninsula in the Indian **Ocean** to the south. India is divided into three different landscape zones: the mountainous zone of the Himalayas gives way to the plains of the **Indus** and **Ganges** rivers. The plains then rise in the south to form a plateau traversed by rivers. This plateau is called the **Deccan**, and has broad plains along the coasts of the peninsula. The country's vegetation is correspondingly diverse: the north and north-east are dominated by **rain forests** and **plantations**. The plains around the Indus and Ganges have sub-tropical vegetation. The **Ganges delta** has many **mangrove swamps**.
The uplands are covered in wide savannas, and there are broad steppe and desert areas in the west. India's sovereign territory also includes the **Lakshadweep Islands** and the **Andaman and Nicobar Islands**. The country has an astounding rage of fauna, including tigers, lions and many poisonous snakes. Some species are now endangered due to heavy deforestation and encroaching human habitation.
An under-sea earthquake in the Indian Ocean in December 2004 triggered a tsunami which caused great damage, mainly to the Andaman and Nicobar islands.

Climate

India has a **sub-tropical to tropical climate**, with a monsoon period. The climate in the north becomes more temperate, and mountain regions have an **alpine climate**. Average temperatures in the capital New Delhi range from 14°C in January to 31°C in July.

Population

India's population includes approximately 72 per cent **Indo-Aryan**-language speakers and 25 per cent **Dravidian-language speakers**. There are also some Himalayan and South-east ethnic groups. **Hindus** form the largest religious majority (80 per cent); **Muslims** account for 14 per cent of the population. There are also **Christian** (2.4 per cent), **Sikhs** (two per cent) minorities and groups of Buddhists, Jains and others.
Hindi is the official administrative language and the mother tongue of 30 per cent of the population and there are also 17 regional languages with official status. Since 24 languages are spoken by more than one million people and there are also many regional dialects, **English** remains a language of communication throughout the country. Despite the numerous colleges and the **204 universities,** the **literacy rate** is still very low at 52 per cent.

History and Politics

The **Indus valley civilisation**, one of the earliest advance societies, flourished in northern India between 3300 and 1000 BC. Although knowledge of this ancient culture is limited, many believe the people spoke a proto-Dravidian language. The **caste system**, an important part of Indian society today, may have been introduced by Indo-Aryan settlers after the fall of the Indus valley civilisation. The region saw the development of several great religions, including **Buddhism** in the sixth century BC, which spread through much of the **Indian empire**, first established two or three hundred years BC. In the twelfth century AD, the country became increasingly **Islamic under Mughal rule**, which reached its peak with the establishment of the **Delhi sultanate**. In 1858, after a series of battles, India became directly ruled by the **Great Britain**. **Struggles for independence** began as early as the late nineteenth century, and after World War I this movement gained momentum. A key figure was Ma-

India: the ornamental Char Minar gate in Hyderabad.

Jawaharlal Nehru

*Allahabad, 14.11.1889,
† Delhi, 27.5.1964

Nehru campaigned with Gandhi for India's independence. He became General Secretary in 1923 and President of the National Congress in 1929. He fought in all resistance movements against British rule and was imprisoned several times. After India gained independence, he became Prime Minister from 1947 until his death. On domestic issues, he followed a moderate socialist course; on an international level he advocated non-alignment.

hatma Gandhi, who lived and preached passive resistance and civil disobedience. India was finally granted independence in 1947 but part of the north seceded and became the Muslim state of Pakistan. Since then, India and Pakistan have fought several **wars** over the region of **Kashmir**, which is today divided. In 1971, India supported the creation of **Bangladesh**. Since gaining independence, India has been enjoyed relative political stability, but ethnic and religiously motivated **conflicts** between the Hindu majority and the Sikh and Muslim minority has led to internal unrest.
Under the 1950 **constitution**, India is ruled by a bicameral parliament, which consists of an upper house with delegates from the parliaments of the 25 federal states and seven union territories, and the lower house, whose representatives are elected for five-year terms. The head of state is the **president**.

Economy

India is the **second most populous country** in the world, after China, but it is also one of the countries with the **lowest incomes per capita**. Despite this, the country has highly developed armaments, nuclear and aerospace industries.
India's economy is very wide-ranging, from traditional village **agriculture,** to handicrafts and a range of modern **industries**. Roughly 67 per cent of the workforce lives directly from agriculture, which contributes one third of Gross Domestic Product. India is one of the world's **largest tea exporters**. Jute, herbs and pulses are also cultivated. Although most Indians are vegetarians for religious reasons, the country has the largest number of head of cattle in the world and is the second largest exporter of dairy products.
Extensive estuaries make India one of the largest **fishing nations** on Earth. The plentiful **natural resources** (coal, titanium, bauxite, iron ore, manganese, chrome), which are mined in small quantities, form the basis of the **heavy industry sector,** (steel and aluminium smelting, ship building and heavy machinery) which is largely in state hands. The **services sector** accounts for 42 per cent of GDP, and much of this comes from tourism.

Transport Infrastructure

India's **rail network** is a relic of the colonial era. It covers more than 62,000 km, making it the most extensive in the world. It remains to this day the country's **main form of transport**.
The **road network** covers more than two million km, half of

Mumbai, formerly known as Bombay, is the gateway to India. Some 50 per cent of India's foreign trade passes through Mumbai's huge port. The city is spread over several islands and has more than ten million inhabitants.

which is surfaced, but it still does not connect all of the populated areas. The country has 16,180 km of **inland waterways**, which are of great economic importance. The major **ports** for India's massive merchant fleet are in Kolkata (formerly Calcutta), Mumbai (formerly Bombay), Jawaharlal Nehru and Kandla. There are numerous regional airports, served by both the national airlines, and five **international airports** in New Delhi, Mumbai, Chennai (formerly Cochin), Kolkata and Bangalore.

Tourism

After **nature reserves** – the most important being the Kaziranga National Park in the northeast, which still has some 100 rare Indian rhinoceros – India offers an enormous number of **cultural attractions and places of interest**. These include the temple complexes of Khajuraho, Madurai and Mahabalipuram, and the world renowned **Taj Mahal** in Agra. The most popular holiday destinations are the beaches of **Goa** and **Kerala** and the area around **Chennai**, as well as Rajasthan's forts and desert.

up to 1,000 m (Reng Tlang: 957 m). The south-west, on the Indian border, contains part of the **Sundarbans region,** and the deltas of the **Ganges** and the **Brahmaputra** rivers.

Climate

Bangladesh has a **monsoon climate** with abundant rainfall. There are three seasons: a cool, dry winter between October and March with an average temperature of 19°C, a hot and humid summer from March to June, and the relatively cool rainy season from June to October, during

Bangladesh

Area:	144,000 sq. km
Capital city:	Dhaka
Form of government: Republic	
Administrative divisions: 6 provinces, 64 districts	
Population: 144.3 million (938 inhabitants/sq. km)	
Languages: Bengali (official), Urdu, Hindi	
GDP per capita:	US$2,100
Currency: 1 Taka = 100 poisha	

Natural Geography

Bangladesh's land mass consists entirely of **fertile lowlands,** but the unprotected, port-free coast is constantly at risk of inundation, and is often affected by severe **floods**, sometimes with catastrophic consequences.
In the east and south-east, **mountain chains** rise in the border regions, with a height of

which many thousands die in massive flooding.

Population

The vast majority of the population is **Bengali** (98 per cent) but there are also minorities of **Biharis** and other groups.
Bangladesh has **one of the highest population densities in the world**. More than 80 per cent of the population lives in rural areas, which are only partly connected by the road network and have almost no access to electricity. Social welfare is the responsibility of the family and **child labour** is very common. Public health and state provision of medical care are also seriously under-developed. The **education system** is neglected, with the result that only one third of the population can read and write. This also accounts for the huge amount of emigration, many Bangladeshis living abroad, especially in the United Kingdom.

History and Politics

Bangladesh was originally the Indian province of **East Bengal** and was part of India from its early history. Between 1757 and 1947 it was part of **British** India. As part of the division of India following independence, West Bengal became part of India,

1 Jodhpur Fort is as impregnable as a cliff wall. It is one of the most striking buildings in the 600-year-old city.

2 The Taj Mahal is a marble mausoleum for the favourite wife of Emperor Shah Jahan. At dusk and dawn, the whole structure turns a striking pink.

3 The Golden Temple of Amritsar is the centre of the monotheistic Sikh faith.

4 Dasaswamedh Ghat in Varanasi is a holy place for Hindus on the banks of the Ganges. The faithful gather here for ritual bathing.

*The people of **Bangladesh** call their country 'golden Bengal' – but the country is anything but blessed. Thousands of people drown every year in floods, and the people are forced to endure terrible poverty.*

while East Bengal became part of Pakistan.

During a period of bloody unrest after the great flood of 1970, East Bengal split from Pakistan, and proclaimed the **Republic of Bangladesh** in 1971.

After 15 years of authoritarian rule by presidents, the **first democratically elected government** took power in **1991**. The national parliament has 330 members. The **head of state** is chosen every five years by the parliament and has largely ceremonial powers.

Economy

Bangladesh has **one of the poorest national economies in the world**. **Agriculture** forms the basis of the economy and employs 63 per cent of the working population, mainly in very small operations. The sector is responsible for roughly one third of GDP.

Rice and **jute** are the most important agricultural exports. The **fishing industry** mainly exports shellfish. The **manufacturing sector** employs 18 per cent of the working population, but consists largely of small operations, which mainly process agricultural products (jute, cotton, sugar and tea) and textiles. Manufacturing accounts for approximately 18 per cent of GDP. **Heavy industry** is currently experiencing some growth, and major activi-

ties are the processing of **raw materials** (natural gas, crude oil, coal, vitreous sand and other minerals).

The **services sector** is also of increasing importance and contributes 52 per cent of GDP.

Transport Infrastructure

The 223,891-km-long **road network** is only partially paved, and the **rail network** is poorly developed. Both are of negligible importance.

The **inland waterways** consisting of a network of rivers and canals, with a length of more than 8,400 km, are the country's main transport arteries and connect to the major sea port of

Chittagong. The only international airport is in **Dhaka**.

Tourism

Bangladesh is yet to be really discovered by tourists. Important destinations are the capital city with its interesting old town, numerous **mosques** and the city of **Chittagong**. Bathing and watersports are available in Cox's Bazaar.

Part of the **Sundarbans National Park** is located in Bangladesh. The unique collection of mangrove swamps is a refuge for many rare species of tropical fauna. The best time to visit is between December and February during the dry season.

Sri Lanka

Area:	65,610 sq. km
Capital city:	Colombo

Form of government:
Socialist Presidential Republic in the Commonwealth

Administrative divisions:
9 provinces, 25 districts

Population:
20 million
(300 inhabitants/sq. km)

Languages:	Singhalese, Tamil
GDP per capita:	US$4,300

Currency:
1 Sri Lankan Rupee = 100 cents

Natural Geography

Separated from India by the **Palk Strait** and the **Gulf of Mannar**, Sri Lanka lies on the southern tip of the sub-continent. In the north and the east, the coastal strip is bordered by lowland regions, dotted with isolated hills.

In the centre of the island, there are the **Central Mountains**, that gradually rise to the 2,238-m-high **Adam's Peak** (Sri Pada) and the 2,524-m-high **Pidurutalagala**. Sri Lanka's territory also includes a further 22 smaller surrounding **islands**. The tsunami of December 2004, caused by a massive under-sea earthquake, left behind a massive swathe of destruction.

Climate

The **tropical climate** means that the country has year-round high temperatures of about 30°C. Precipitation varies according to the the seasonal monsoon rhythm. With the exception of some wetlands in the south-west of the country, Sri Lanka has an extended **dry season**, which lasts for eight months.

Population

Sri Lanka's population is 74 per cent **Singhalese** and 18 per cent **Tamil**, who are further divided into Ceylon Tamil (12.6 per cent) and Sri Lankan Tamil (5.5 per cent). Since the mid-1980s, hundreds of thousands of Tamils have left the island.

The population also consists of seven per cent Moors (Muslims) and minorities of Burghers (de-

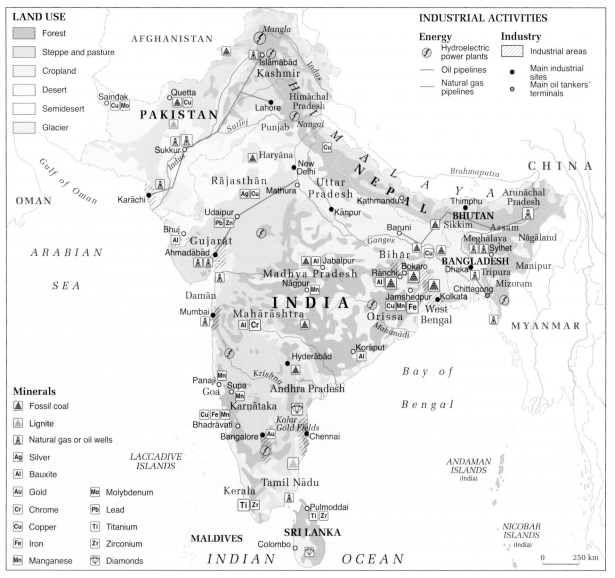

LAND USE

- Forest
- Steppe and pasture
- Cropland
- Desert
- Semidesert
- Glacier

Minerals

- Fossil coal
- Lignite
- Natural gas or oil wells
- Ag Silver
- Al Bauxite
- Au Gold
- Cr Chrome
- Cu Copper
- Fe Iron
- Mn Manganese
- Mo Molybdenum
- Pb Lead
- Ti Titanium
- Zr Zirconium
- Diamonds

INDUSTRIAL ACTIVITIES

Energy
- Hydroelectric power plants
- Oil pipelines
- Natural gas pipelines

Industry
- Industrial areas
- Main industrial sites
- Main oil tankers' terminals

AFGHANISTAN — Mangla — Islāmābād — Kashmir — Himāchal Pradesh — Saindak — Quetta — Lahore — Punjab — Nangal — PAKISTAN — Sukkur — Sutlej — Haryāna — New Delhi — Rājasthān — Mathura — Uttar Pradesh — Kathmandu — NEPAL — Brahmaputra — CHINA — Thimphu — Arunāchal Pradesh — Udaipur — Kānpur — BHUTAN — Sikkim — Assam — Baruni — Meghālaya — Nāgāland — Bhuj — Gujarāt — Ganges — Bihār — BANGLADESH — Sylhet — Ahmadābād — Jabalpur — Bokaro — Dhaka — Tripura — Manipur — Madhya Pradesh — Ranchi — Chittagong — Mizoram — Nāgpur — Jamshedpur — Kolkata — Damān — INDIA — West Bengal — Mumbai — Mahārāshtra — Orissa — MYANMAR — Mahānādi — Korāput — Hyderābād — Bay of — Krishna — Panaji — Supa — Andhra Pradesh — Bengal — Goa — Karnātaka — Kolar Gold Fields — Bhadrāvati — Bangalore — Chennai — LACCADIVE ISLANDS — ANDAMAN ISLANDS (India) — Tamil Nādu — Kerala — Pulmoddai — MALDIVES — SRI LANKA — NICOBAR ISLANDS (India) — Colombo — INDIAN OCEAN — ARABIAN SEA — Gulf of Oman — OMAN — Karāchi — Himālaya — Indus

0 ____ 250 km

*The name **Sri Lanka** means 'venerable island'. Ceylon tea, cultivated here, is famous throughout the world. The island suffers from some serious problems, including rapid population growth, internal tensions and widespread poverty.*

scendants of the Portuguese and Dutch) and Malay. In terms of religion, 69 per cent are **Buddhist**, 15 per cent Hindu and eight per cent each Christian and Muslim. Singhalese is spoken by 74 per cent of the population, and 18 per cent speak Tamil. The education and healthcare systems are well organised.

History and Politics

After settlement in the first millennium by the forefathers of the modern **Veddas**, the **Portuguese** discovered the island of Ceylon in 1505. In 1656, the Portuguese were replaced by the Dutch, who were in turn expelled by the British in 1795/1796. The island was proclaimed a British crown colony in 1802. Sri Lanka has been **independent** since 1948.
The country suffers from political instability caused by the as yet unresolved **minority problems** of the Sri Lankan Tamils and the Indian Tamils, who were in a dominant position under British rule, and who now feel disadvantaged in relation to the Singhalese. The Tamil tigers have been fighting a **civil war** in the north and east of the country in order to assert their rights. The introduction of a republican constitution in 1972 changed the country's name from Ceylon to Sri Lanka. The 1978 **constitution** is still in force today and provides for a unicameral parliament, whose representatives are elected for six-year terms and appoint the Prime Minister.
The **President** is directly elected and is both head of state and head of government. The President has wide-reaching powers.

Economy

Despite the long-running civil war, Sri Lanka's national economy shows stable **growth**.
In comparison to **agriculture** (rubber, tea, coconuts), which accounts for 18 per cent of GDP, the **manufacturing sector** is growing, though it still only contributes relatively little to GDP (18 per cent). The main sector of Sri Lanka's economy is the **trade** and **services sector** with 63 per cent of GDP. The most important exports are textiles and foodstuffs, especially tea. Cigars

(cheroots) are the traditional export of Trincomalee.

Transport Infrastructure

The island has a good transport infrastructure, with 1,501 km of **rail network** and 100,000 km of **roads,** one third of which are surfaced. The major airport and international port is in Colombo.

Tourism

The favourite tourist destinations are **Negombo**, **Trincomalee** and **Hikkaduwa**. Sri Lanka has many important cultural and historic

sites, including Kandy, once the capital, with its '**Temple of the Tooth**', **Anuradhapura** and **Polonnaruwa**, the **cave temples** of Dambulla and the old fort of **Sigiriya**. A whole 12 per cent of Sri Lanka is a **nature conservation area**. The island has superb flora and fauna and if it were not for the unrest, it would be a favourite tourist destination.

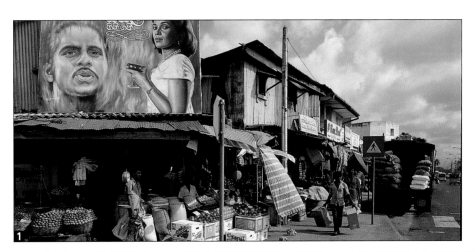

The Maldives	

Area:	298 sq. km
Capital city:	Malé
Form of government: Presidential Republic in the Commonwealth	
Administrative divisions: 19 districts (atolls) and the capital municipality	
Population: 349,100 (1,106 inhabitants/sq. km)	
Languages: Dhivehi (official), English	

GDP per capita:	US$3,900
Currency: 1 rufiyaa = 100 laari	

Natural Geography

The Maldives consist of **1,190 coral islands** grouped together both north and south of the equator to form **26 atoll groups**. The territory extends 800 km in

1 A film poster and the wares of small traders compete for attention in the streets of Colombo.

2 Elephants are vital for clearing the dense jungles. In Sri Lanka, they have been tamed for millennia, and in some places they are worshipped.

3 Buddhists, Hindus and Moslems make pilgrimages to the perahera of Kataragama in Sri Lanka. Dances accompany the celebrations, during which the gods are asked for luck.

4 Sri Lanka: the important Buddhist temple complex of Raja Maha Vihara in Kelaniya.

*The **Sadhu**, the holy men of Nepal, spend their lives in strict asceticism. The ascetic tradition is common in the many branches of Hinduism. Through abjuration, the Sadhu attempt to go beyond their connection to worldly possessions and their own mortality, and so become closer to nirvana. This is rooted in the belief that through its connection with material objects, the soul forgets its eternal being.*

one direction and 130 km in the other. The average elevation of the islands is between one and two metres above sea level and the highest point is near Wilingili (24 m). None of the islands is larger than 13 sq. km, and the main island, Malé, measures just 1.7 km by 1 km. The country has no rivers or raw materials.

Climate

The **hot, tropical climate** means that the year-round average temperature is 30°C. The two **rainy seasons** last from November to March (north-east monsoon) and from June to August (south-west monsoon).
Land animals (tortoises, geckoes and rats) are not very varied, but there is a fascinating range of **sea life** in the coral reefs.

Population

The **Maldivians**, descendants of Malay, Singhalese and Arab settlers, live on some 200 islands. One quarter of the population lives in the capital city alone.
The national language, **Dhivehi** is a dialect of Sinhala, which uses the **Arabic script**.
Since 1153, the national religion has been **Islam** and 99.9 per cent of Maldivians are **Sunni Muslims**.

History and Politics

The Maldives became a **British protectorate** in 1887, gaining **independence in** 1965. British rule in the islands was less rigid than in other parts of the empire, and the British powers respected the country's internal autonomy. The Sultanate was replaced by a republic in 1968.
The **constitution of 1975** provides for a president with extensive powers directly elected by the people. There are no political parties and no parliament.

Economy

Due to the quality of the land, **agriculture** in the Maldives is only important in terms of subsistence. Coconuts, betel nuts, cassava, onions and chilli peppers are cultivated on 13 per cent of the country's land mass.
Fishing is the most important export and is, after **tourism**, the most lucrative sector of the economy. The country obtains 60 per cent of its wealth from tourism alone, and a quarter of the population lives from the tourist industry. Roughly three-quarters of the visitors come from **Europe**.

Transport infrastructure

There is no rail network, and motorised vehicles are only permitted on Malé and Gan. The **main forms of transport** are ox-**carts** and **bicycles**. The islands are connected to each other via small craft, mainly yachts, sailing boats and motor boats. The only **international airport** is in Hulule. Domestic flights between the country's three airports are of increasing importance.

Tourism

Of the 200 inhabited islands, more that 70 are used exclusively for tourism, and this number is increasing. The **diving spots** in the Maldives are some of the most beautiful in the world, and there are diving schools on every island. The capital city Malé is also of **cultural importance**, due to its seventeenth-century mosque.

A beach on the Maldives: one of the country's many beautiful places.

Nepal	
Area:	140,800 sq. km
Capital city:	Kathmandu
Form of government:	
Constitutional Monarchy	
Administrative divisions:	

14 regions
Population:	
27.7 million (179 inhabitants/sq. km)	
Languages:	
Nepali (official), Maithili, Bhojpuri	
GDP per capita:	US$1,500
Currency:	
1 Nepalese rupee = 100 paisa	

Natural Geography

Nepal consists of a narrow strip of land 853 km long and 160 km wide on the southern slopes of the **Central Himalayas**.
The **plains of the Terai region** in the far south border the **Shivalik mountains** and the foothills of the **Lesser Himalayas**. The north of the country ends in the Great Himalayas, where **eight of the ten highest mountains in the world** are situated. Several mountains are over 8,000 m high, including **Mount Everest, the world's highest mountain,** in the extreme north of the country on the border with Tibet.
The economic and social heart of the country is the **Kathmandu Valley**, 30 km long and 25 km wide, located in the Lesser Himalayas.

Climate

In the north, the **summers are cool** and the **winters** very **severe** due to the high altitudes. In the Terai and the plains of the Ganges, as well as in the Kathmandu Valley, the climate is **subtropical.** The temperatures in Kathmandu reach an average of 0°C in January, and 24°C in July.

Population

Many different ethnic groups live in Nepal. These include the Newar, Indians, Gurung, Magar, Tamang, Bhutia, Rai, Limbu and Sherpa peoples. The population also includes refugees from neighbouring Bhutan and Tibet. **Nepali** is the official language, but a **further 20 languages** are spoken.
Nepal is the **only official Hindu state in the world**; 90 per cent of the Nepali people profess this religious belief. There are also **Buddhist** and **Muslim** minorities.

History and Politics

A single state consisting of the various principalities and clan communities of the Katmandu Valley first came into being in 1756 in the form of a **Gurkha Kingdom**. In 1792, Nepal concluded a treaty with the representatives of Great Britain.
The year 1951 saw a change in the ruling dynasty and a constitutional monarchy was introduced. The **democratic constitution** of **1959** was updated in **1962** and greater powers were assigned to the monarchy. Since the constitution of 1990, political parties have been permitted, and representatives of these parties are voted into the country's National Assembly for five-year terms.
A civil war between the government and Maoist rebels lasted for several years and resulted in the loss of some 8,000 lives. A ceasefire was agreed in early 2003, but this was broken by the Maoists in August of the same year. An extraordinary event occurred in 2001, when King Birendra's nephew Dipendra murdered the king and most of the royal family. The king is now Gyanendra.

Economy

Nepal's terrain and landscape has made it one of the most underdeveloped countries in the world. The basis of the economy is **agriculture** – mainly livestock – which employs more than 80 per cent of the population and contributes some 40 per cent of GDP.
The rich gold, copper, iron ore, slate and limestone reserves are mined for **export**. The modest **manufacturing sector** mainly processes agricultural products, including jute, sugar cane, tobacco and cereals. Other exports are **textiles** and **carpets**.

Transport Infrastructure

The **rail network** only covers a stretch of 101 km near the Indian border. Less than half of the 7,700 km of **road** is surfaced. There are irregular flight connections to the isolated high valleys. Katmandu has the only **international airport**.

Tourism

Apart from **the Himalayas**, the main attractions are the Royal Chitwan National park (Bengal tigers, rhino) and the Katmandu valley, with its **temples, monasteries** and medieval forts.

Bhutan	
Area:	47,000 sq. km
Capital city:	Thimphu
Form of government:	
Constitutional Monarchy	
Administrative divisions:	
18 districts	
Population: 2.2 million (45 inhabitants/sq. km)	
Languages:	
Dzongkha (official), Tibetan dialects	
GDP per capita:	US$1,400
Currency:	
1 Ngultrum = 100 chetrum	

*The **Sherpa**, a Himalayan people, are the pathfinders across the roof of the world. They have developed survival techniques to cope with their hostile environment and have even managed to grow crops in the most unlikely places.*

Natural Geography

The small kingdom on the southern slopes of the eastern Himalayas is largely inaccessible to the outside world. Vast **mountain chains** (Jomolhari: 7,314 m) surround the high plateau, which descends gradually into the foothills at the Indian border.

Climate

Bhutan's climate is mainly a **high altitude climate**. In the capital city, Thimphu, the average temperature in January is 4°C, and it is only 17°C in July.

Population

Buddhists comprise 75 per cent of the inhabitants of Bhutan, and a further 25 per cent are **Hindu**. The population is 63 per cent **Bhutanese**, but there are also **Gurung** and **Assamese** peoples. In 1985, a **campaign of 'Bhutanisation'** was introduced, with the intention of strengthening the traditional Buddhist culture of the population. Even today, religious and ethnic diversity is frowned upon by the majority of the dominant Buddhist population of Bhutan.

History and Politics

Though archeological exploration of Bhutan is limited, evidence of civilisation in the region dates back to at least 2000 BC. The original Bhutanese, known as Monpa, are believed to have migrated from Tibet. Since the seventeenth century, the land has been known to its own people as Drukyul, Land of the Dragon People, a reference to the dominant branch of Tibetan Buddhism that is still practiced here. The territory was initially ruled by **Indian princes**, but **Tibetan conquerors** established a **Tibetan Buddhist state** in the ninth century AD. The British invaded in 1865 and established control. A **monarchy** was established in 1907 under **British influence**, and continues to rule to this day, with a national assembly (the Tshogdu). Bhutan is represented by **India** in respect of its foreign and defence policies. The country's self-imposed **isolation** can be seen by the fact that only 6,000

visitors cross the border each year. On his 25th jubilee on 2 June 1999, the reigning monarch, King Jigme Singye Wangchuck, introduced **television** as a gift to his people.

Economy

Almost half of GNP derives from **agriculture,** which employs over 90 per cent of the working population. The country is self-sufficient in terms of food. Only very few crops (maize, wheat, cardamom) are exported. **Wood** from the extensive forests is one of the main exports. The

manufacturing sector is poorly developed and consists of small **crafts** (weaving, metal work, carvings). Technology and machinery are traditionally looked down upon.

Bhutan has only been open to **tourism since 1974,** and remains **restricted**, despite the fact that tourists bring by far the most money into the country.

Transport Infrastructure

The **first surfaced road** between India and the hitherto almost completely isolated capital city was only built in **1962**. Today, some roads connect Bhutan's larger centres of population. The mountainous landscape makes **transport connections difficult**, if not impossible. The only **international airport** is in **Paro**.

Tourism

Entry visas to Bhutan are only permitted for **group travel**.

Tourists are only allowed to stay for ten days and must pay a **daily fee** of US$200. The religious and cultural centre is **Thimphu**, but **Punakha** and **Paro** also have numerous historical sites. There are also **dzongs**, ancient monastic fortresses, which seem to cling to precariously to the mountainsides like birds' nests.

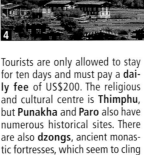

1 Those who climb to the summit of Mount Everest (8,846 m) find themselves truly on the roof of the world.

2 The eyes of the Buddha survey the four corners of the Earth: the Stupa of Swayambhunath in Kathmandu is one of the holiest Buddhist temples.

3 The atmosphere of Kathmandu's Durbar Square illustrates how religion fills the daily lives of the Nepali people.

4 Bhutan's monasteries are not just for prayer: they also play an administrative role – this is the seventeenth-century Paro Dzong.

Religious and Ethnic Conflict in South Asia

On 14 August 1947, British India was divided and became two independent nations, but this did not end the ethnic tensions in the region. The partition of British India into a Muslim state, Pakistan, and predominantly Hindu India only partially reflected the complex reality of the situation.

Following the British withdrawal from the Indian sub-continent in 1947, Pakistan was created as a separate state. This was largely through the efforts of Mohammed Ali Jinnah (1876–1948), who became Pakistan's first president but died shortly after secession. The Muslims had demanded the large provinces of Punjab and Bengal for their new state but under partition, East Punjab and West Bengal actually remained Indian. Although millions of Hindus, Muslims and Sikhs had been expelled or fled from their former homes, the transfer of populations remained incomplete. For many years, a third of the Muslim Indians still lived in the Dominion of India. Minorities of Sikhs and Hindus, though far smaller, were to be found in Pakistan but quickly decreased in number due to expulsions. Millions died in the resulting conflicts.

Even today, the effects of partition are still evident. Around 120 million Muslims live in India and since many of them have relatives in Pakistan, the Hindus often suspect them of disloyalty to the state. Relations between Sikhs and Hindus have traditionally been amicable but political disputes have led to violent between them. The Hindu Sindhis who left their homeland in Pakistan are without territory in India. In Pakistan, the Muslims from India, known as Muhajir ('immigrants' in Arabic), were seen as a possible threat to the dominance of the native Afghans, Sindhis, Pashtuns and Punjabis. Kashmir is the region in which the conflict between Hindus and Muslims was most apparent. In 1947 the future of Kashmir was a subject of debate: should it join India or Pakistan, or become independent? The predominantly Muslim population in the principality of Kashmir, which was under British patronage, were ruled by a Hindu Maharajah who was

Refugees: Hindus and Sikhs leaving Pakistan for India after partition in 1947.

under pressure to give political freedom to the Muslim majority. population. The Maharajah, however, decided to join India. The accompanying riots led to intervention by Indian troops.

Under a UN agreement, an armistice was agreed, which set what are roughly today's borders as ceasefire lines. Since then, there have been repeated clashes. In 1965, Pakistani troops crossed into Indian territory, where upon the Indian army occupied Pakistani territory in retaliation. The peace treaty of Tashkent finally restored the previous position. In 1989, there was further fierce fighting between the Muslim rebels and Indian

Main photograph: Sikh men praying in a temple in Indian Punjab.

forces in Kashmir. In 1999, there were bloody incidents and violent fighting between Indian and Pakistani border troops. The Kashmir conflict is of international significance because both India and Pakistan have nuclear weapons with corresponding delivery systems, and have more or less openly threatened to use them if they see fit.

The conflicts between West and East Pakistan led in 1971 to the third Indo-Pakistani war, in which India supported the breakaway nation of Bangladesh against West Pakistan. The borders of what had once been called West Pakistan, remained unchanged. There are indications that the conflicts between the religious groups in the respective neighbouring countries are deliberately stirred up by both governments. Officially, India and Pakistan attribute domestic un-

rest to repeated interference by a 'foreign hand'.

In neighbouring Sri Lanka to the south, disputes for control of the northern region of the island have lasted for 2,300 years. The Hindu Tamils which make up around 18 per cent of the population have felt suppressed since the end of British colonial rule in 1948. Initially, they did not enjoy equal status under Sri Lankan law. For example, Sinhala Only Act passed in 1956 declared Tamil to be a second-class language which made access to higher education more difficult for Tamils. Although the nationality laws were actually revised in 1977 and Tamil was once more declared an official language, the armed struggle continues. In 1983, a peace initiative by President Chandrika Bandaranaike Kumaratunga failed and the separatist Liberation Tigers of Tamil

Eelam ('The Tamil Tigers') were outlawed. In the open civil war that resulted, India's president Rajiv Gandhi tried to act as a mediator. In 1987, he sent an Indian peace-keeping force to monitor an agreement planned for 1988 which would have given partial autonomy to the Tamils. The soldiers were withdrawn again in 1990 following the failure of the mission. The subsequent period of peace was short-lived and fighting broke out again between the army and rebels in 1991 and 1992. In 1996, government troops captured the Tamil capital Jaffna. In the subsequent battles for the access routes to Jaffna, 860 government soldiers and 480 Tamil guerrillas died in 1999. Since 1983, at least 50,000 lives

Military presence: Indian soldiers control the high valleys in Kashmir.

have been claimed in the conflict, including victims of terrorist bombings of in busy marketplaces. The country's economy has suffered as a consequence. Investment has dwindled, and the once-booming tourist industry, which was further hit by the disastrous tsunami of December 2004, has collapsed.

Photos from left to right:
Sri Lanka: government soldiers patrol in Tantirimale near the border of the Tamil separatist region.
Kashmir: demonstrations against the occupation of the region by Indian troops.
Demonstration by radical Hindus in India.

*The **Mongolians** are a people of the steppes and live in extended families or clans. Their livestock forms the basis of their nomadic lives. Traditionally, they herded sheep, cattle, yaks and goats as well as horses, pack animals and camels.*

Mongolia	
Area:	1,565,000 sq. km
Capital city:	Ulan Bator
Form of government: Republic	
Administrative divisions:	
21 provinces, 1 district (capital city)	
Population: 2.8 million	
(2 inhabitants/sq. km)	
Languages:	
Mongolian (official),	
Kazak, Russian, minority languages	
GDP per capita:	US$2,200
Currency:	
1 tugrik = 100 mongo	

Natural geography

Mongolia is dominated in the west by the **Altai Mountains** with altitudes of up to 4,300 m and the **Khangai Mountains** with altitudes of over 3,500 m. Highlands 1,000–1,500 m above sea level occupy the eastern part of the country, at the border with China. In the north-east, these highlands are characterised by Kerulen rivers, vital for irrigation in this arid land.

Climate

The climate is **continental** and extremely **dry**: During the long winters, the average temperature ranges from -26°C to -18 °C; during the short summers, average temperatures of 17°C to 23°C are attained. In the desert the temperature can reach 50°C. The country enjoys an exceptionally high proportion of clear, **sunny** days; approximately **260** per year.

Population

Mongolians account for 90 per cent of the population. They still lead a traditional nomadic way of life to a great extent. There are also Kazakhs and Russians in addition to a small Chinese minority. The predominant religion is **Tibetan Buddhism**. There is also a minority of Muslims (four per cent). The majority of Mongolians have no professed religion.

Mongol Yuan Dynasty in 1368, the country became an insignificant territory ruled by **China**.

In 1911, **Outer Mongolia** separated from China and in 1924, the **People's Republic of Mongolia** was formed. In contrast, Inner Mongolia continued its association with China.

Following massive demonstrations, a multi-party system was introduced in 1992, during the collapse of the Soviet Union, and the **Republic of Mongolia** came into being.

Mongolia is ruled by a **unicameral parliament** whose members are re-elected every four years. The president is directly elected as head of state every four years.

Economy

The transition from a socialist planned economy to a market economy seems to have been a success. In **agriculture, traditional animal husbandry** continues to predominate (especially sheep, goats, cattle, camels and horses).

In total, the **manufacturing sector** accounts for 32 per cent of the Gross Domestic Product, whilst the **services sector** accounts for 34 per cent.

Transport

Ulan Bator is connected to the **Trans-Siberian Railway** via the country's 1,928-km-long rail network. Only a small percentage of the road network (46,470 km) is paved, predominantly around the capital city, Ulan Bator. The majority of roads are cart tracks and are mainly used by buses and HGVs.

A total of eight **airports** interconnect the populated areas which lie great distances apart. There is an international airport at Ulan Bator.

Tourism

Mongolia is hardly opened up to tourism at all. There are **few hotels** or comparable facilities. Tourists come here first and foremost to experience the **desert and go on hunting expeditions** which start out from Ulan Bator.

The capital and the ruins of the city of **Karakorum**, founded in the thirteenth century, are among the few important **historic and cultural sites**. The Mongolians themselves, many of whom still live in yurts and follow a traditional way of life are an attraction in themselves, especially as the country is rapidly modernising.

China	
Area:	9,571,300 sq. km
Capital city:	Beijing/Peking
Form of government:	
Socialist People's Republic	
Administrative divisions:	
23 provinces, 5 autonomous regions, 3 municipalities; 147 autonomous districts	
Population:	
1.3 billion	
(134 inhabitants/sq. km)	
Languages:	
Mandarin Chinese (official), dialects and minority languages	
GDP per capita:	US$6,200
Currency: 1 renminbi yuan =	
10 jiao = 100 fen	

Natural geography

As the world's **third largest country in land mass**, China contains a wide range of landscapes. From the fertile **lowlands** in the east, the landscape rises to the **Tibet Highlands** in the west and the Himalayas in the south-west. Western China is dominated by **plateaus** and **steppes** that turn into desert in the north-west and north of the country (Takla Makan, Gobi).

In the west, the Tibetan Plateau, the 'roof of the world', reaches an average altitude of 4,500 m. It is the southerly range of the Himalayas and contains **Mount Everest** (8,848 m), the world's highest mountain. The densely populated east has the **characteristics of a range of hills**. The Yellow Sea coast is flat; both of China's major rivers, the **Huanghe** (4,875 km) and the 6300-km-long **Yangtze Kiang** flow into it.

There are over 5,000 islands off the coast which is 14,500 km

Horses are very important for riding and as pack animals for the nomadic people of Mongolia.

taiga vegetation. The **mountainous desert** and **steppe vegetation** that occupies the rest of the country turns into the **Gobi Desert** in the south which lies about 1,000 m above sea level.

Four-fifths of the country consists of **grassy steppes** used as grazing land for sheep, goats and cattle. The most important stretches of water are the **Selenga** and

Social services

Social services, the health service and the education sector are all well developed.

History and Politics

Mongolia, which was long populated by nomadic horsemen, was **united** in **1206** and became the centre of a great empire which stretched **from China to Eastern Europe**. After the downfall of the

A mere one per cent of the country's land mass is usable as arable land for growing maize, wheat, fruit and vegetables. Agriculture accounts for 34 per cent of GDP.

The **rich resources** of coal, oil, copper, molybdenum, gold and tin which were exploited in Soviet times but are being phased. They still form the basis for manufacturing industry. Foodstuffs and cashmere wool are exported.

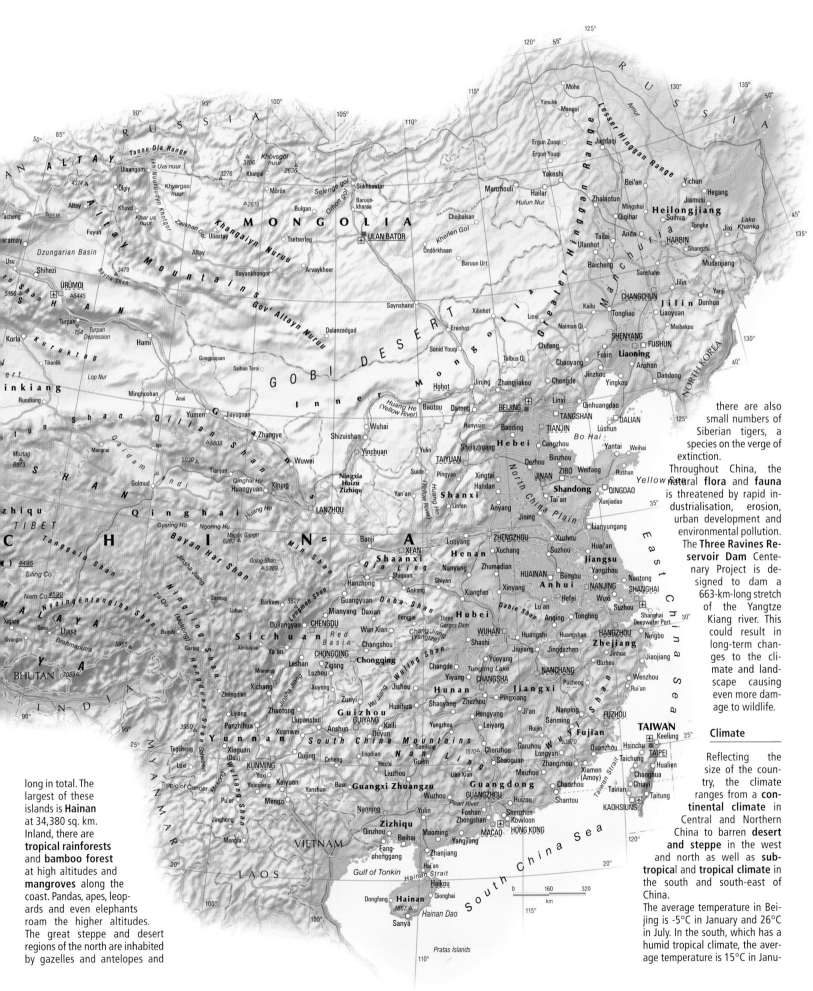

there are also small numbers of Siberian tigers, a species on the verge of extinction.

Throughout China, the natural **flora** and **fauna** is threatened by rapid industrialisation, erosion, urban development and environmental pollution. The **Three Ravines Reservoir Dam** Centenary Project is designed to dam a 663-km-long stretch of the Yangtze Kiang river. This could result in long-term changes to the climate and landscape causing even more damage to wildlife.

Climate

Reflecting the size of the country, the climate ranges from a **continental climate** in Central and Northern China to barren **desert and steppe** in the west and north as well as **subtropical** and **tropical climate** in the south and south-east of China.

The average temperature in Beijing is -5°C in January and 26°C in July. In the south, which has a humid tropical climate, the average temperature is 15°C in Janu-

long in total. The largest of these islands is **Hainan** at 34,380 sq. km. Inland, there are **tropical rainforests** and **bamboo forest** at high altitudes and **mangroves** along the coast. Pandas, apes, leopards and even elephants roam the higher altitudes. The great steppe and desert regions of the north are inhabited by gazelles and antelopes and

China

*The **Great Wall of China** stretches for a total lenghth of 10,000 km. The immense defensive structure began as a series of walls from as early as 400 BC. The wall in its current form dates from between the 13th and 16th centuries AD.*

ary and 25°C in July. The heavy rainfall decreases significantly further inland.

Population

The world's **most populous country** has no less than 40 **cities containing over one million inhabitants**. Yet over 80 per cent of Chinese still live in rural areas.

The vast majority (92 per cent) are **Han Chinese**. The most important of the approximately 50 official **ethnic groups** are Zhuang, Yi and Miao in Southern China, Hui, Manchu and Mongolian in the north and north-east and Tibetan and Uighur in the west and north-west.

It is estimated that only **15 per cent** of the population of China professes a religion. **Buddhism** and **Islam** predominate, while the proportion of Christians is approximately one per cent.

In addition to the Chinese **official language (Putonghua or Mandarin)** which is taught in the schools and used in the media, numerous Chinese dialects and minority languages are spoken. Comprehension difficulties are overcome thanks to the fact that all share the **Chinese script**.

In China, only the inhabitants of large cities or employees of large public companies are **covered by social security**. In rural areas, in particular, the provision of social security is the responsibility of

the family and village community. The **health service** is organised by the state and serves the cities predominantly. Severe environmental and air pollution is a considerable problem for public health. In vast areas of the country the quality of drinking water is poor. The soil is contaminated with chemicals and heavy metals. The **education system** is strictly organised and well developed. Primary school is attended by 98.8 per cent of children. In future, it will be compulsory for all children to attend school for nine years. China has over 600 universities and institutions of higher education. There is a charge for attendance at these institutions, however, and a political appren-

ticeship year must first be completed. In 1979, the government was decided to introduce the One Child Policy. This has led to a considerable deceleration in population growth.

History and Politics

Archaeological finds indicate that there were settlements in what is now China in the early Palaeolithic era. It is believed that Yuanmou Man lived over 600,000 years ago. Of the multiplicity of strongly regional cultures of the late Neolithic period, the **Yangshao culture** (which existed in ca. five to three millennia BC, in the province of Shaanxi) and the **Longshan culture**

(which existed in ca. 2400–1900 BC, in the province of Shandong) are among the best known due to their characteristic coloured and black ceramics.

The first historically ascertained dynasty is the **Shang** (sixteenth to the eleventh century BC) from which the first written records originate. The **Zhou** Dynasty was organised into fiefdoms. The last period of the 'Battling Empires' was that of the classical **philosophical schools**.

The Qin Dynasty began with the **unification of the empire in 221 BC.** by the king of the Qin feudal state who was the first Chinese ruler to name himself **emperor**. He unified the system of weights and measures and the

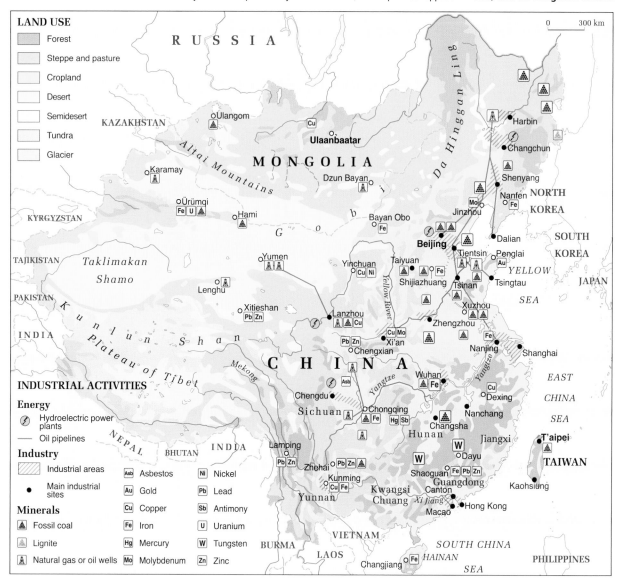

LAND USE
- Forest
- Steppe and pasture
- Cropland
- Desert
- Semidesert
- Tundra
- Glacier

INDUSTRIAL ACTIVITIES

Energy
- ⚡ Hydroelectric power plants
- — Oil pipelines

Industry
- ▨ Industrial areas
- • Main industrial sites

Minerals
- ▲ Fossil coal
- △ Lignite
- ▣ Natural gas or oil wells
- Asb Asbestos
- Au Gold
- Cu Copper
- Fe Iron
- U Uranium
- Hg Mercury
- Mo Molybdenum
- Ni Nickel
- Pb Lead
- Sb Antimony
- W Tungsten
- Zn Zinc

0   300 km

Sun Yat-sen

*Cuiheng, 12.11.1866,
†Beijing, 12.3.1925

After a coup attempt in Guangzhou, Sun Yat-sen went into exile, but returned to China in 1911 after the fall of the Manchu Dynasty and became provisional President of the Chinese Republic. He was the founder of the Kuomintang, which he formed into a potiical party with the help of the Soviets. He led a military government in 1917 and became President of Canton in south China in 1921.

Mao Zedong

*Shaoshan, 26.12.1893,
†Beijing, 9.9.1976

Mao was the son of a farmer and an assistant librarian but founded the Chinese Communist Party and was its undisputed leader after the Long March. The Communists won the civil war against the Kuomintang troops, and Mao proclaimed the People's Republic of China in 1949. As president (1954–1958), he made radical changes to China. The Cultural Revolution became an example to many Communist movements in the Third World.

*The Gate of Heavenly Peace marks the entrance to the **Forbidden City** in Beijing. The palace complex was reserved for the family of the Emperor until 1911. It was from here in Tiananmen Sqaure that Mao Zedong proclaimed the People's Republic in 1949.*

system of writing. A **central government** was formed and the empire protected by the first Great Wall. The **Han Dynasty** which followed immediately afterwards (206 BC–220 AD) began with the colonisation of the neighbouring peoples and expansion of the empire. **Paper was invented** during this period.

The empire's contacts with India and Persia flourished under the **Tang Dynasty**. In subsequent centuries, China was twice ruled by foreign invaders. The Mongolian **Yuan Dynasty** reigned from 1280 to 1368 and the Manchus of the **Qing Dynasty** ruled from 1644 to 1911.

European and American enclaves were created following the **Opium War** of 1842 when Great Britain enforced the **opening** of the **ports** that had been closed by the Chinese to foreign trade.

As a result of the Japanese Empire's victory in the **Sino-Japanese War** from 1894 to 1895, Japan annexed parts of Manchuria in 1905. Formosa (Taiwan) was also ceded to Japan.

In 1900, the **Boxer Rebellion** attacked the enclaves of foreigners but resulted in forcing further concessions from China to western countries.

In October **1911,** there was a **revolution** against the imperial government and in December 1911 the **Republic of China** was proclaimed under a military regime which was rocked by **civil war** from 1916 onwards.

The **Communist Party of China**, founded in **1921**, remained associated with the **Kuomintang**, founded in 1912, until 1927. In 1928 the **Kuomintang** established a **national government** and then fought the Communists. On the **Long March** of 1934 to 1935, the **Red Army** was compelled to retreat to the northwest. When open war broke out in 1937 against the Japanese who had founded the **puppet state of Manchukuo** in Manchuria in 1931, the two groups formed a united front.

The battles between the Kuomintang and the Communists flared up again following the capitulation of the Japanese in 1945. They did not end until 1949 with the retreat of the Kuomintang to the island of Formosa where the National Republic

of China (Taiwan) was installed. In October 1949 the **People's Republic of China** was formed under Mao Zedong. It fostered a close relationship with the **Soviet Union** until 1960. Internal battles led to the **Great Proletarian Cultural Revolution** in the 1960s which culminated in well-planned purges and civil war-like conditions.

Since 1978, the Communist leadership has been operating an **economic liberalisation policy**. However, the political system remains untouched by economic opening strategies and tolerates no opposition.

The **National People's Congress** is an indirectly elected parliament. It has in excess of 2900 members who are elected every five years; the National People's Congress appoints the **country's president** and which legislates in conjunction with a **standing** committee. The executive authority is the responsibility of the **state council** which is led by the prime minister. The state council is, in turn, elected by the **National People's Congress**. The only hitherto significant party is the **Communist Party of China** whose leaders fundamentally determine policy guidelines. The party congress elects the **Central Committee** and the **Politburo** which has 22 members and its standing committee which consists of seven members. The People's Republic of China has a seat in the **United Nations Security Council**. It also possesses **atomic weapons**.

Hong Kong and Macao have **special** political and economic

status within the People's Republic as they were the last European colonies to be restored to their mother country in 1997 and 1999 respectively.

Hong Kong and its offshore islands cover an area of 1080 sq. km. The former **British crown colony** was returned to China on 1 July 1997 after over 150 years.

1 Shanghai, the second largest and most westernised city in mainland China has a huge sea port. Foreign trade is booming, as is the leisure industry.

2 Tiantan, the 'Altar of Heaven' in Beijing: until 1911, only the Emperor, the 'Son of

Heaven' was permitted to enter. Today, the complex and the surrounding park are a favourite spot for residents of the capital to spend their leisure.

3 Hong Kong's skyline is constantly expanding. The trade and services centre is thriving, even after its return to China.

*The **cookshops**, tiny food stalls located in every back street and alley, are a favourite place for the Chinese to eat at any time of day – the choice is large, and the food is freshly prepared and very good value.*

As early as 1842, following the First Opium War, the British acquired the island of **Hong Kong Island** from China. At the time it was inhabited by 5,000 fishermen and farmers. The British acquired **Kowloon** in 1860. In 1898, Britain also leased the **New Territories** which lie to the north for a 99-year period. Hong Kong flourished under British rule in the decades that followed and became one of Asia's **most important trading centres**.

Today, Hong Kong has roughly seven million inhabitants, **95 per cent** of whom are **Chinese**. In the modern city, dominated by business and finance, the services sector contributes ca. 84 per cent of GDP, in contrast to the manufacturing sector which contributes only 16 per cent. **Agriculture** is insignificant in this densely populated region.

Macao is only separated from Hong Kong by the Pearl River estuary. The islands of Taipa and Coloane and the peninsula on the mainland are part of the region which covers an area of only 18 sq. km.

On **20 December 1999**, Macao was given back to China. The region, whose Chinese name is Aomen, has approximately 400,000 inhabitants, **95 per cent** of whom are Chinese.

The oldest European settlement in East Asia was founded as early as 1557 by the **Portuguese** who monopolised Chinese trade through this trading post. Shortly thereafter, in 1887, under Dutch rule, Portugal's claims to Macao were finally recognised by the Chinese. The city had given up its dominance to Hong Kong a long time previously.

Over half of Macao's revenue today comes from **gambling** in casinos and hotels and on racecourses. The stream of visitors from neighbouring countries and regions where gambling tends to be prohibited accounts for approximately 25 per cent of GDP, whilst the manufacturing and agricultural sectors contribute little.

China has committed itself to maintaining the existing **capitalist economic system** in both regions for a further 50 years. Both have received the status of **special administration zones** with a high degree of internal autonomy and democracy.

The regions are represented by China in matters of foreign affairs. The Beijing government also has a great influence in major matters of internal policy.

Economy

China's economic system has been in a period of upheaval since 1978. The significance of the rigid planned economy has been officially scaled down since 1993 in favour of China's **opening** up to the **global marketplace**. The collectivisation of agriculture was weakened. In the manufacturing sector, many companies were partially privatised by allowing them to be responsible for their own budgets. Enormous growth spurts originate predominantly from **commercial initiatives** which are gaining in significance through the creation of new jobs in the manufacturing and services sectors. The result is a **'Socialist market economy'** in which the key industries remain under state control, but more leeway is given to the commercial sector. The economy is hampered by **corruption** and **arbitrariness**.

As a whole, 53 per cent of the country's surface area is used for agriculture. China is the **world's largest rice producer;** Southern China is the most important centre for **rice farming**. Considerable volumes of maize, potatoes, sorghum, nuts, oilseeds, tea and cotton are also cultivated in China.

Massive deposits of raw materials form the basis of the manufacturing sector which accounts for 49 per cent of GDP. The mining sector (coal, graphite, iron ore, mineral oil, industrial minerals) employs seven per cent of the labour force. Finished goods account for the highest proportion of **exports**, mostly machinery and electronics, as well as textiles (especially cotton), finished clothing and toys.

Although the per capita income of the population has increased massively since 1978, unemployment is rising due to the extensive restructuring of the economy. Another social problem is internal migration. It is estimated that approximately 100 million migrant workers have relocated to the boom cities in the last few years.

Transport

The **rail network** which is just 65,000 km long connects all the major cities and provinces and is the country's **main means of transport**, despite the fact that only ten per cent of the network has been electrified.

The **road network** in China is over 1,118,000 km long and a fifth of it is paved. China still belongs to the least developed countries as far as private car ownership is concerned. There are only two private cars per 1,000 inhabitants.

The significant **inland navigation network** is operated on waterways with a total length of 110,600 km. This includes the **Grand Canal**, the largest man-made waterway, which runs for over 1,782 km from Beijing to Hangzhou. China has approximately 2,000 **ports**, approximately 80 of which are open to international trade. China maintains one of the world's **largest merchant fleets**. The **domestic flight network** is also well developed. There are approximately 19 **international airports** out of the country's 206 which are served by 40 Chinese airlines. The most important are located in Beijing, Shanghai, Guangzhou and Hong Kong.

Tourism

The numerous testimonies to a 5,000-year-**old culture** and a varied and **fabulous landscape** throughout China offer manifold attractions which are becoming increasingly geared towards tourism.

There are numerous sites which are worth a visit in this great empire, meaning that only the most important can be mentioned. The starting point for most visitors to China is the capital city **Beijing** which offers many historic attractions such as the **'Forbidden City'**, the Heavenly Temple, the Summer Palace and Tiananmen Square. In the vicinity are the graves of the Thirteen **Emperors** of the Ming Dynasty. The most-visited section of the **Great Wall** is near Badaling and it is the most complete. Elsewhere, parts of the Great Wall have completely disappeared and other parts are only a few feet high.

The gigantic **Yungang Grottos** and the **Hanging Monasteries** near Datong tare worth a visit. Shenyang in Manchuria was formerly called Mukden; it has the palace of Ching, the second-largest after the emperor's palace in Beijing.

Qufu, the birthplace of Confucius, honours the scholar with China's largest **Confucius Temple**. The scholar is allegedly buried here in the Kong Forest.

The **ports** of Qingdao and Tianjin, contain many relics of European and Japanese colonialisation as does Shanghai which has become China's largest city.

Hangzhou and Suzhou are located on the **Grand Canal**. Hangzhou is a unique site worth a visit with its **beautiful West Lake** famous throughout China. Neighbouring Suzhou is known as the **'Venice of the East'** because of its many bridges and canals. The city is also famous for its **Literati Gardens**.

Other important destinations include the old imperial cities of Kaifeng, Luoyang with its imposing **Longmen Grottos**, **Shaolin Monastery**, Chengde with its

Deng Xiaoping

*Xiexing, 22.8.1904,
† Beijing, 19.2.1997

This senior party member was stripped of his rank during the confusion of the Cultural Revolution, was rehabilitated in 1973, and again deposed in 1976. He regained office in 1977. As acting Chairman of the Central Commission and the military, he was a strong figure until his death. His legacy includes the bloody suppression of the democratic movement that culminated in the protests in Tiananmen Square, Beijing in 1989.

A Zhuang woman surveys the irrigated terraced paddy-fields in the province of Guangxi.

Shanghai is China's boom town: in a few short years, a completely new residential and business quarter has sprung up on the east bank of the Huangpu River, and the skyscrapers here can compete with anything in Hong Kong. Numerous infra-structural measures, for example the new underground, the city motorway and the new Pudong Bridge should solve the city's travel problems.

magnificent imperial **summer palace** and Nanjing.

At the eastern end of the historic **Silk Road** lies the old capital city of Xi'an. The city has become world-famous thanks to the discovery of the **grave** of China's **first emperor**, and the nearby massive **Terracotta Army**, part of which can be visited today.

Further sites in the city worth visiting include the museum, the **Wild Goose Pagoda** and the graves of numerous emperors.

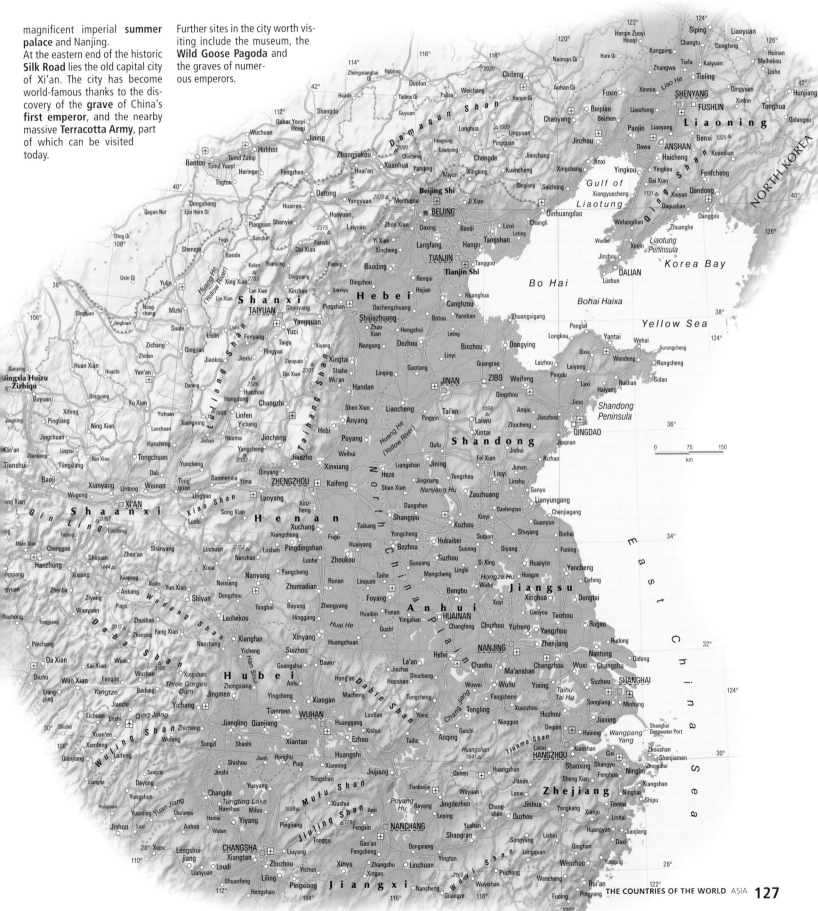

Hong Kong *was handed back to the Chinese on 1 July 1997 in a grand ceremony. Under the motto 'One Country, Two Systems', the region has been turned into an economic and political free zone for the next 50 years.*

The oasis city of **Dunhuang**, the legendary hub of the **Silk Road**, lies along the approximately 3,500-km-long historic route which takes about two-and-a-half days to cover by train. The **452 Mogao grottos** in the middle of the desert are a unique testament to **Buddhism**. The cities of Tulufan, Gaochang, Wulumuqi and Kashi were shaped by strong **Muslim** cultural influences. Kashi has an old quarter which contains the largest mosque in the province. It is worth a visit.

The main tourist centres of southern China are **Guangzhou** (formerly Canton) and the former British crown colony of **Hong Kong**, whose glittering facades attract millions of tourists annually. Haikou, the capital of the tropical island **Hainan**, has a unique western colonial architecture. Sanya has developed into a tourist centre with opportunities for **watersports** and **seaside holidays**.

Lhasa is the capital city of what is now the autonomous region of Xinjiang but was formerly the country of **Tibet**. In addition to the **Winter Palace**, the former seat of the Dalai Lama, the capital city boasts numerous temples and shrines. Once totally inaccessible, except over the Himalayas from Nepal, Tibet is slowly opening up to tourism. The country is gradually being populated by Chinese brought in to colonise it and eventually outnumber the native Tibetans.

Other worth visiting tourist destinations are the six **Gelugpa Monasteries**, the monastery town of Ganden and the town of **Rikaze**. Lhasa is the starting point for **expeditions** to the high mountains which last several weeks.

The **Yangzi** ravines and their secondary channels are among China's numerous scenic highlights. These picturesque landscapes take several days to **travel through**.

The extraordinary **craggy landscape** on the Lijiang River around **Guilin** and **Shilin** and a **strange landscape** of **limestone formations** in Yunnan are among the wonders of China. The mountainous landscape of Wuyishan with its 36 summits and 99 rocks, Emeishan, Wutaishan and Taishan are among the **holy mountains** of China which also offer unique scenic attractions. The **world's largest statue of Buddha** is in Leishan.

Further tourist destinations include the Jiuzhaigou and Huanglong nature reserves where small colonies of **giant pandas** have found refuge and those of **Wulingyuan** and **Lushan**.

China, Guilin: Cormorant fishermen at dusk.

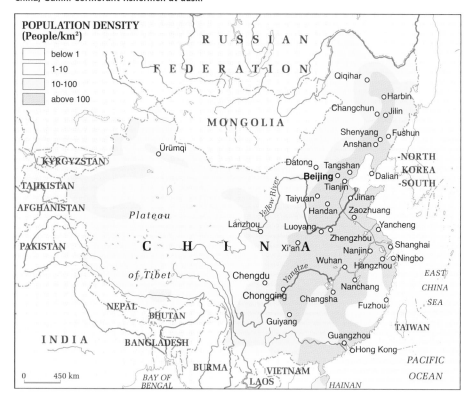

RUSSIAN FEDERATION

Qiqihar

Harbin

Changchun · Jilin

MONGOLIA

Ürümqi

Shenyang · Fushun
Anshan

KYRGYZSTAN

Datong · Tangshan
NORTH KOREA

TAJIKISTAN

Beijing · Dalian
Tianjin
SOUTH

AFGHANISTAN

Plateau
Taiyuan · Jinan
Handan · Zaozhuang

PAKISTAN

Lanzhou · Luoyang · Yancheng
Zhengzhou
C H I N A Xi'an · Nanjing · Shanghai
Wuhan · Ningbo

of Tibet
Chengdu · Hangzhou
Yangtze **EAST**
Chongqing · Nanchang **CHINA**
Changsha **SEA**
Fuzhou

NEPAL
BHUTAN
Guiyang
TAIWAN

INDIA
BANGLADESH
Guangzhou

Hong Kong
PACIFIC
0   450 km   **BURMA** **VIETNAM** *OCEAN*
BAY OF **LAOS**
BENGAL *HAINAN*

Taiwan

Area:	35,980 sq. km
Capital city:	Taipei
Form of government:	Republic

Administrative divisions:
16 counties, 5 city counties, 2 special city counties

Population:
22.8 million
(627 inhabitants/sq. km)

Languages: High Chinese (official), Taiwanese, Hakka

GDP per capita:	US$26,700

Currency:
1 new Taiwanese dollar = 100 cents

Natural geography

Situated off the south-east coast of the Chinese mainland, Taiwan belongs to the arc of islands in the South China Sea south of Japan. Densely **forested mountain** ranges with summits of over 3000 m can be found in the centre of the island. Taiwan's highest peak is **Yushan**, known as 'Jade Mountain', which is 3997 m high.

This extremely volcanic area levels out in the east, whilst in the west it turns into an 8 to 40-km-wide **coastal plain** following terraced graduations.

The Pescadors, a group of volcanic islands, belong to Taiwan but are located close to the Chinese mainland.

Climate

The climate is **sub-tropical** in the north with a good deal of precipitation. In contrast, there is a **tropical** climate in the southwest which is characterised by the winter monsoon. The average temperatures in Taipei are 15°C in January and 29°C in July.

Population

84 per cent of the population is **Taiwanese**. There are also inhabitants originating from the **Chinese mainland** (14 per cent) and Aborigines (two per cent).

The **country's** official **language** is Standard Mandarin (Guoyu).

Macao, once a Portuguese colony, is the Las Vegas of China. Since December 1999, the city is once again part of the People's Republic, but the Chinese come here to gamble as fervently as the seven million tourists who flock to Macao from around the world. The Casino Lisboa is a glamourous and often ruinous centre of the action. Every year, five million people come to this casino alone in the hope of making some quick and easy money.

Min (Taiwanese) and Hakka dialects are also spoken.

Taiwan has a well-developed **social security system** and **health service**. Over 13 per cent of the state's budget is spent on them. The country's universities and institutes of higher education, of which there are approximately 130, are the pride of the **education system**.

History and Politics

Following the first **Chinese settlement** in the ninth century and various forays from the European colonial powers – **Portugal**, which discovered the island of Formosa in 1590, **Spain** and subsequently **the Netherlands** – Taiwan again became part of the Chinese empire in 1683.

In 1895, China was obliged to relinquish the island to **Japan** in the **Treaty of Shimonoseki**. In 1945, it became the territory of the Republic of China following the surrender of the Japanese.

After defeat in the civil war on the mainland the **Chinese Nationalist government** relocated its headquarters to Taiwan in 1949 in order to continue the battle against its Communist rivals from there with the **protection of the USA**.

Relations with the People's Republic of China, which views Taiwan as its twenty-third province, remain extremely tense up to the present day. Due to pressure from mainland China, the Republic of China finds itself internationally isolated from a diplomatic viewpoint, its citizens have difficulty obtaining visas from foreign countries for travel.

The **1947 Constitution** envisages a combination of **a parliamentary** and a **presidential system**. However, the **president** has extensive powers.

Economy

Taiwan has a predominantly **capitalist** economy in which **state control** of investments, foreign trade and important branches of industry are being increasingly **privatised**. Before Taiwan was **rapidly industrialised** in the 1960s with the assistance of the USA, agriculture traditionally dominated life on this densely populated island which has a shortage of raw materials. The contribution of **agriculture** (rice, maize, soya beans, fruit, vegetables, fish and meat) to GDP is now only about three per cent.

The **highly productive manufacturing sector** is central to the Taiwanese economy. The majority of goods are manufactured for **export**. This applies, in particular, to the manufacture of electronic and high-tech goods but also to chemicals, textiles, clothing, cars and machines.

The **services sector** contributes 61 per cent to GDP and employs approximately one half of the working population. Thanks to

significant investment in neighbouring countries such as Indonesia, Thailand, the Philippines and Vietnam, labour-intensive manufacturing is increasingly being relocated abroad.

Transport

Part of the 4,600-km-long **rail network** is for freight only. The island has a dense **road network** which is surfaced with asphalt to a great extent. The country's **air links** are good. International airports are located in Taipei and Gaoxiong.

Tourism

Taipei is the tourist centre. It has an **old town** and numerous **temples**. The **National Palace Museum** houses the largest collection of Chinese paintings, artefacts and objets d'art in the world, now unique, since so much Chinese art was destroyed in mainland China during the Cultural Revolution and the Great Leap Forward. There are relics from colonial times in Gaoxiong and Tainan in the south. The mountains of Central Taiwan offer **hiking and mountain climbing**. **Gending National Park** in the south and **Yushan National Park** in the centre are the important national parks.

1 A high pass in Tibet: Tibetan Buddhists hang out colourful prayer flags in this remote region.

2 The Potala Palace, the former residence of the Dalai Lama, perches on a cliff in Lhasa. The 14th Dalai Lama has lived in exile in India since 1959.

3 Representation of a laughing Buddha in Gyantse, the third largest city in Tibet.

4 People from Taipei perform Qigong breathing exercises near the Chiang Kai-shek monument, built in remembrance of the first President of Taiwan.

From Cultural Revolution to Capitalism

Unlike other former centrally planned economies, the change in China has taken place without a major crisis and with a remarkable growth rate. The twin-track reform policies with elements of the planned and market economies could mean that China will soon play an important role in the global economic system.

For over 2,000 years, the Chinese economy was run as a feudal system based principally on agriculture. Following the Opium Wars (1839–1842 and 1856–1860), developments in industry and infrastructure under western influence were of only minor consequence for the whole empire.

On 1 October 1949, the Communist Party of China established a uniform national economic policy for the first time since the end of the empire. Under this system, the rural population formed cooperatives, which organised industrial development into a five-year plan. The key industries and the transport, trade and banking sectors were put under state control with heavy industry given absolute priority over all other sectors in accordance with the Soviet model. Despite massive growth rates, however, the Great Leap Forward proved to be a massive step back.

As the state planning system replaced the free market, companies were neither competing against each other nor were they exposed to pressure from foreign competition. Furthermore, the guaranteed prices, cheap raw materials and energy costs as well as low wages generated little incentive to produce quality goods.

At the beginning of the Cultural Revolution (1965–1969) industrial production fell dramatically. Political tussles and the deprivation of power from local party and government officials paralysed the infrastructure, planning and production. In 1971, the provinces were required to be self-sufficient, resulting in lack of economic cooperation between them.

Chairman Mao's death in 1978 triggered a radical re-shaping of economic policy. The new strong man was now Deng Xiaoping. In 1978, he set up a modernising programme and planned to reform agriculture, industry, defence and technological development. His goal was to turn China into one of the world's leading economic powers by the end of the twentieth century.

The process of reform was completed in different phases. The first phase, beginning in 1979, attacked agriculture. The old system of communes and brigades were largely abolished. Instead, households became the smallest units of agricultural production with a production quota agreed with the authorities. Any additional yields beyond this could be sold on the free market. The resulting turnover contributed to 60 per cent of the total agricultural production by the end of the 1980s.

The modernisation of the urban industrial sector followed in the mid-1980s. Heavy industry took priority over the production of consumer goods; students and teachers were sent overseas to learn modern methods of management and production. In particular, modern technological equipment was purchased from the western industrialised nations. A further important element was the ruling that state companies would now be allowed to determine how to use profits over

Despite reforms, the presence of the 'Great Chairman' Mao Zedong can still be felt.

Main photo: The 400-m-high television tower looms over the business quarter in Shanghai.

and above the designated quotas. By the late 1980s, domestic unrest in particular led to a slackening in the process of reform. The end of the Soviet Union gave the reorganisation a renewed boost. At the XIV Party Congress of the CPC, the socialist market economy initiated by Deng was encouraged.

The parallel structures of market and planned economies as well as the gradual nature of the changes to the economic system seemed to work well for Chinese politicians, because in contrast to the eastern European countries and the former USSR, the transition has gone relatively smoothly. China has registered astonishing success in the area of foreign trade. China's share in world trade has more than doubled since 1978 and the country has developed into the eleventh largest exporter in the world. The liberalisation of foreign trade

was also completed gradually. At the beginning of the 1980's, four special economic zones were established in the southern Chinese provinces of Guangdong and Fujian for controlled market economy experiments. The authorisation of local overseas trade companies, the liberalisation of the monetary system, the signing of the international trade and tariff agreements and the increasing foreign copyright and patent protection (China was a major centre of piracy) has accelerated investment from overseas companies. Above all, neighbouring Hong Kong and Taiwan have transferred labour-intensive production processes to the cheap wage area of South China. With the restoration of the British crown colony of Hong Kong to China on 1 July 1997, one of the most important economic and financial centres of Asia became

part of the People's Republic. Under the Special Administrative Region agreement, Hong Kong is supposed to be retaining its social and economic systems, as well as a measure of democracy, for at least 50 years.

The parallel structures of market and planned economies, as well as the gradual nature of the changes to the economic system, seem to have worked well for the Chinese. In contrast to the East European countries and the former USSR, there have been no notable examples of economic turmoil and collapse.

One of the most significant recent changes in China has been the dramatic increase in foreign investment in the country. Companies from around the world have

rushed into the country to take advantage of the rapid growth. The success story also has its dark side. Widespread poverty in rural areas, increased crime, inflation, environmental destruction and unemployment are all important issues. Controlling the growing gap between rich and poor may present the most serious challenge.

Photos from left to right: Since liberalisation, many small private businesses have been started in China. The daily life of a Chinese senior manager is now hardly different from that of his Western counterpart. China's textile industry is an important source of exports.

New China: the heirs of Deng Xiaoping have now moved into the twentieth-first century.

North Korea

*The cult around Kim Il-Sung, who died in 1994, survives to this day in the 'Dictatorship of the Proletariat' in **North Korea**. A constitutional amendment in 1998 made him 'Eternal President'. His son Kim Jong Il acts as president.*

 North Korea

Area:	120,538 sq. km
Capital city:	Pyongyang
Form of government:	
People's Republic	
Administrative divisions:	
9 Provinces, 2 city districts	
Population:	
22.7m (186 inhabitants/sq. km)	
Language:	Korean
GDP per capita:	US$1,800
Currency:	1 won = 100 chon

Natural Geography

In the north, the country forms part of **mainland Asia**; the east coast falls steeply to the **Sea of Japan**. North Korea is largely **mountainous** with heights of up to 2,541 m (Kuanmao): it flattens, however, in a south-westerly direction. The country's flora and fauna, which at one time were very diverse, have suffered severe damage from **massive industrialisation and pollution**.

Climate

A **cool temperate monsoon climate** predominates, with low temperatures in winter and **large amounts of rainfall** in the summer months. The temperatures in the capital city are on average -8°C in January and 24°C in July.

Population

Almost **100 per cent** of the population is **Korean**. There is a small Chinese minority.

Kim Il Sung, born Kim Song Ju

*Mangyongdae, 15.4.1912,
†Pyongyang, 8.7.1994

The Korean general led the Korean People's Revolutionary Army in 1932 against the Japanese occupying powers and became General Secretary of the Korean Workers' Party in 1946. He was Prime Minister from 1948 to 1972 and President of the Democratic People's Republic of Korea from 1972 until his death.

Religious practice is officially tolerated in North Korea, but it barely plays a role in public life. 68 per cent of the population practice no religion.

Since 1994, North Korea has been afflicted by severe **famines** as a result of crop failure, flooding and the lack of relief programmes. According to estimates from foreign relief organisations, up to three million people have starved to death in recent years. The health service is also in a disastrous condition as a result of lack of supplies. In contrast, there is **massive expenditure on weapons** (around 25 per cent of GDP), which makes North Korea one of the world's **most heavily armed countries**. There is hardly a country in the world as isolated as the Democratic People's Republic of Korea.

History and Politics

The history of both North Korea and South Korea has always been strongly influenced by the tense relationship between the neighbouring powers **Japan** and **China**. After the **occupation** of the country by Japan until 1945 and subsequently by Soviet and US troops, northern Korea was declared a **Democratic People's Republic** in 1948. A surprise invasion of South Korea by North Korean troops in 1950 started the **Korean War**. UN troops, under the leadership of the USA, launched a counter-attack. During the clashes, the North was supported by Chinese and Soviet weapons and troops.

The **armistice of 1953** set the present borders. Since then, after initial alliances with the People's Republic of China and the Soviet Union, the country has isolated itself and insisted on political, ideological and economic **independence**. Along the military buffer zone, which has existed since 1953, there have been repeated clashes with South Korea. A first historic North-South **summit** took place between the President of South Korea, Kim Tae Chung, and the President of the North Korea, Kim Jong Il in June 2000 in Pyongyang. However this resulted in further bitter clashes. North Korea's confession in 2002, that it was pursuing a nuclear weapons programme, has put pressure on the country's

relations with the US, which considers North Korea to be a 'rogue state'. This position has been reinforced by recent threats from North Korea to unleash atomic weapons on Japan and by alleged Korean cooperation with Iran in nuclear technology.

Economy

The economic policy is based on a socialist **planned economy**. In the **collectivised agricultural system**, in which 36 per cent of all those employed produce approximately 25 per cent of GDP, principal crops are rice, maize and potatoes. North Korea cannot supply its own domestic food requirements and even **feeding** the population can currently only be guaranteed by expensive

international relief action. A good 60 per cent of GDP derives from **heavy industry**, which is based on the country's **mineral resources** (coal, graphite, iron, gold, silver, lead and zinc) and the iron and **steel industry**. Machinery and **armaments are manufactured** for export. According to estimates, only 20 per cent of the labour force work in industry because of a energy shortage.

*Korean Buddhism, which contains many elements of shamanistic piety, is not a single religious entity. In **South Korea** there are 20 different schools and sects.*

developed tourist industry are the capital city, Pyongyang, which has palaces and museums. There is also the ancient capital of Kaesong close to the border with South Korea. As a result of North Korean government's isolationist policies, contact with foreigners tourism is unlikely to develop in the foreseeable future.

◐	South Korea	

Area:	98,480 sq. km
Capital city:	Seoul
Form of government:	
Presidential Republic	
Administrative divisions:	
15 provinces	
Population: 48.4m	
(485 persons per sq. km)	
Language:	Korean
GDP per capita:	US$20,300
Currency:	1 won = 100 Chon

Natural Geography

The terrain of the Republic of Korea, which lies in the **southern part** of the **Korean Peninsula**, is predominantly **mountainous**. The highest summit in the **Taebaek Mountain range** reaches a height of 1,708 m. In contrast with the flat east coast, the south and west coasts are strongly mountainous. In the south, there is a hilly, **fertile** basin through which the **Nakdong River** flows.
There are also mountain ranges on the **3500 islands,** of which around 600 are inhabited. The west of the country is covered by a 50 to 100-km-wide **coastal plain**.
The largest **rivers** in South Korea, the Han, the Pukhan, the Kum and the Nakdong, all flow into the **Yellow Sea**. Their navigability is limited.
Extensive **deciduous** and **coniferous forests** dominate the landscape. The volcanic island of **Cheju** in the **South China Sea** south of South Korea is also part of the national territory. Its highest peak, which rises to 1,950 m, is called Hallasan.

Climate

With the exception of the extreme south which is characterised by a **sub-tropical** climate, the climate is **continental** and **temperate-cool**.
In the capital city, average temperatures are 25°C in July and -5°C in January

Population

The only **minority** in South Korea is a small community of **Chinese**. Approximately half of the South Koreans are **Christians**, 47 per cent **Buddhists** and a further four per cent belong to no religious denomination.
Over **80 per cent** of the **population** live in the **cities**; of these, over a third live in the capital city, **Seoul**, one of the **largest cities** in the world with **over ten million inhabitants**.
The standard of living is high. Around 11 per cent of the state budget is spent on the **health service**. **Education** is also highly developed. Almost all **children** of school age start school; approximately half of those of the right age group is enrolled at one of more than **130 universities** in the country.

History and Politics

According to legend, the founding of a **Korean Empire** goes back to the year 2333 BC Historical support exists for 57 BC as the beginning of the era of the three **rival kingdoms** Silla, Koguryo and Paekche. In the seventh century, **Silla**, the largest of the three kingdoms, with support from the Chinese, united the whole peninsula. The **Goryeo Dynasty, founded in** 918 AD, brought the entire peninsula under its rule in 936 AD.
Following the **Mongolian conquest** of 1259 AD to 1392 AD came the **Joseon Dynasty** which was to last until 1910. During this time an administrative system was established in accordance with the Chinese model and **Confucianism** was introduced as the official state creed.

North Korea: statues protect the Emperor's tomb in Kaesong.

The Kim Il Sung Stadium in Pyongyang can seat 100,000 people.

Transport

The **rail network** covers a length of approximately 5,000 km of which 3,500 km is electrified. There are international rail connections with Russia and China. Very little of the **road network** which covers 31,000 km is surfaced; all the important cities are, linked to each other by frequent **bus services**. There are hardly any private cars. The country's domestic flight network is of little significance. The **international airport** is in Py. The

most important **sea ports** are Namp'o, Ch'ongjin and Wonsan.

Tourism

Individual trips to North Korea are not permitted. Centres of the barely

South Korea, Japan

Near the small town of **Gyeongju** lies the Solluram Grotto, in the dense forests of a national park. Built in the eighth century, it contains a 3.4-m-high granite statue of Buddha Shakyamuni, which is regarded as an important piece of Buddhist art. The surrounding temple was constructed from giant granite blocks, which together form an artificial hill.

Invasions by **Japan** in 1592 and 1597 were fended off with Chinese support. In the seventeenth century, the country began to cut itself off from the outside world, keeping contact only with China. Through its victory in the **Sino-Japanese** war of 1894/1895 Japan increased its influence, culminating in 1910 in the **annexation of Korea**.

In **World War II**, hundreds of thousands of Korean labourers were deported to Japan as forced labour and Korean women were forced into prostitution for the Japanese troops. After the capitulation of Japan in 1945, the Red Army occupied the part of Korea north of the 38th parallel.

In the south, which was controlled by the **US**, **the Republic of Korea** was set up in 1948. After the **Korean War** (1950–1953), South Korea's politics were characterised for decades by a **dictatorial regime** mainly run by generals. From the mid 1980s, however, the **democratic opposition**, which had been brutally repressed until then, gained increasing influence. The democratisation process culminated in democratic elections and the **constitution** of 1988.

The members of the **National Assembly** serve four-year terms and the **President** who has extensive powers is elected by direct popular vote for a single five-year term of office.

Due to the political troubles of the past, there is a large Korean diaspora, living mainly in the United States, especially in California. Some overseas Koreans have prospered greatly, many owning small businesses.

Economy

Over the last 30 years, economic development has been characterised by an intensive, export-orientated **industrialisation**. South Korea has developed from a producer of labour-intensive **cheap goods** in the foodstuffs, textiles and clothing industries to a supplier of its own **technologies** and proprietary goods – above all in the **motor vehicle and electronics industries**, but also in ship-building and in iron and steel production.

Industry contributes 43 per cent of GDP. The fishing industry which is intensively operated by one of the world's largest fishing fleets (fish, seafood, algae) is also a major source of exports. The **agricultural sector**, with the cultivation of cereals, as well as canimal husbandry and poultry farming, is of relatively little importance, contributing eight per cent to GDP. The **services sector**, meanwhile, contributes 51 per cent.

Transport

South Korea has an excellent, fully developed infrastructure with an extensive **rail network** (3,081 km) and a well developed **road network** (83,000 km).

The most important **sea ports** are Pusan, Ulsan ch'on. South Korea also has a busy domestic flight network and **three international airports** in Seoul (Gimpo/Kimpo Airport), Incheon (Incheon) and Busan.

Tourism

The main tourist attractions are to be found in the modern capital city of Seoul with its many places of interest, royal palaces and gardens. Other cultural and historical sites are the old **imperial cities of Kyongju** and **Suwon** and their grounds which contain numerous cultural treasures as well as the **Haeinsa Temple**. **Songnisan Park** and **Seoraksan-Park** are among the best known of the country's **national parks** which cover approximately ten per cent of the country's land mass and offer excellent mountaineering, walking and hiking opportunities in addition to magnificent landscapes.

The island of **Cheju** which has a much milder climate than the mainland and wonderful scenery

Population:	
127.4m (336 inhabitants/sq. km)	
Language:	Japanese
GDP per capita:	US$30,400
Currency:	1 yen = 100 sen

Natural Geography

The country consists of around **4,100 islands**, in an arc about 2,600 km long. The four main islands are **Kyushu** (42,073 sq. km), **Honshu** (230,862 sq. km), **Shikoku** (18,792 sq. km) and **Hokkaido** (83,511 sq. km). The **Ryukyu Islands** in the south includes **Okinawa**. The largest of the smaller islands are **Sado** (857 sq. km) and **Amamioshima** (709 sq. km).

The islands consist of approximately 75 per cent **wooded low mountain ranges**. The highest mountain is the volcanic peak of **Mount Fuji** at 3,776 m above sea level. There is massive volcanic and seismic in the land mass, due to its position at the juncture of two tectonic plates.

LAND USE
- Forest
- Steppe and pasture
- Cropland
- Barren land

La Pérouse Strait   0   150 km

RUSSIA · HOKKAIDO · CHINA · NORTH KOREA · SEA OF JAPAN · Sapporo · Muroran · Ch'ŏngjin · Kosaka · P'yŏngyang · Haeju · Kangnŭng · Seoul · Niigata · Sendai · SOUTH KOREA · Kamioka · Iwaki · Hitachi · Pusan · Korea Strait · Tokyo · OKI-SHOTŌ · Nagoya · Yokohama · Hiroshima · Kobe · Osaka · Hamamatsu · Kitakyūshū · Matsuyama · JAPAN · CHEJU-DO · SHIKOKU · Kunamoto · EAST CHINA SEA · KYŪSHŪ · PACIFIC OCEAN

INDUSTRIAL ACTIVITIES

Energy	Industry	Minerals		
— Natural gas pipelines	▧ Industrial areas	▲ Fossil coal	Cu Copper	▲ Lignite
⊘ Hydroelectric power plants	● Main industrial sites	▲ Natural gas or oil wells	Pb Lead	
☢ Nuclear power plants		Fe Iron	Zn Zinc	

Seoul, capital of South Korea, against its backdrop of mountains.

around the **Hallasan** volcano is another attraction for foreign visitors and the Koreans alike.

Japan

Area:	377,801 sq. km
Capital city:	Tokyo
Form of government: Constitutional Monarchy	
Administrative divisions: 47 prefectures	

The islands of Japan are actually a row of peaks in an underwater mountain range. It has hundreds of **volcanoes**, of which as many as 40 are active. In addition, there are over 10,000 **hot springs**. Japan is rocked daily by **earthquakes** and **seaquakes** of varying intensities.

The densest areas of population are in the wide coastal plains around Tokyo and in the area of **Kyoto** and **Osaka**.

The once rich **animal and plant world** has been almost com-

*Fish and seafood are important elements in the **cuisine** of South Korea, as it is in many of the coastal areas of south-east Asia. Ullung Island is famous for its dried cuttlefish; live fish and frogs are sold in the market in Busan.*

pletely destroyed by industrialisation and extensive use of the few areas of arable land; only a few conservation areas have been spared.

Today, over **350 Natural parks** and **27 National Parks** occupy a total of 7.5 per cent of the land. Apart from these, **paddy-fields, unirrigated crops**, forests of **cedar** and **bamboo** predominate in the countryside.

Climate

Japan lies in the pressure field between **continental artic air** and **maritime tropical air**. Due to the long north-south axis along which the country lies, it is subject to extremes of climate. The **south** is predominantly **subtropical and hot**, the **north** has **a temperate cool climate**.

Annual rainfall increases significantly in the southern most islands. While in Hokkaido, the average temperature drops in January to -3°C – against 22°C in July – the average temperature in the Okinawa prefecture is almost always 22°C.

The main island, **Honshu**, is **climatically divided**: on the side facing the Sea of Japan there are snowy winters and tropical hot winters, and on the side overlooking the Pacific Ocean, mild but dry winters alternate with hot rainy summers. In **Tokyo** the temperature in January is on average 5°C, and in July 25°C.

Population

99 per cent of the population is **Japanese**; there is also a small minority of **Ainu** (aborigines) on Hokkaido. Among the foreigners living in Japan, **Koreans** form the greatest proportion, followed by **Chinese** and **Brazilians**. The Japanese frequently belong to different religious communities at the same time: over 80 per cent are both **Buddhist** and **Shinto**, around four per cent are **Christians**. Average **life expectancy** is 80 years, the highest in the world.

In view of the corresponding **fall in the birth rate**, the increasingly **ageing population** is a major problem for Japan's **social welfare and healthcare systems**, which are amongst the most advanced on earth. Reforms, such

as the introduction of nursing care insurance and improvements in state and company pension schemes should address the problem. Japan's economic recession, which has been exacerbated by the continuing **financial crisis**, could also have an effect on the social situation in the future: the traditional rigorous **work ethic**, until now rewarded by the guarantee of **lifetime employment**, automatic promotion and closely knit company community, could eventually be replaced by the western model, based on individual performance, which will be a painful conversion.

History and Politics

Archaeological evidence indicates very early **settlements** in Japan over 20,000 years ago. However only in 350 BC when the **Yamato-Province** was formed from hundreds of small principalities did traditional history begin. In the sixth and seventh centuries AD, during the Yamato era, Chinese influence was evident in the introduction of a **bureaucratic government**, the introduction of **Buddhism**, and the adoption of Chinese cultural and technological achievements such as **Chinese script** and agricultural technology. With the **Taika-Reform** of 645 AD, a fully developed, institutionalised **empire** arose.

From the twelfth century, powerful warlords, the **Shoguns**, assumed power in the kingdom. Under the rule of the **Tokugawa-Shogun** dynasty who ruled from the sixteenth to the nineteenth centuries, the country isolated it-

self until **1853**, when the US fleet forced the **opening of the ports**. With the abolition of the last Shogun in 1868 and the restoration of the rule under a now **'divine' emperor (Tenno)**, the country was to a large extent opened up to the west and was intensively industrialised. Both the **constitution** of 1889 and

1 Red wooden torii in front of the island of Miyajima. the symbolic and spiritual entrance to the famous Itsukushima Shrine.

2 Unique aesthetic unity: the Golden Pavillion of 1398 and the landscaped gardens in the old imperial city of Kyoto.

3 Tokyo: one of the most important shrines in Japan is that of Emperor Meiji, who died in 1912, after ending the rule of the Shoguns.

4 The bright lights of the Shibuya district in Tokyo illustrate Japan's love of everything hi-tech.

Japan

Mount Fuji *rises majestically above Lake Kawaguchi. The symmetrical shape of the 3,776-m-high volcano has inspired countless poets, painters and architects. The sacred mountain is surrounded by Japan's largest area of lowland.*

the reorganisation of the military were directly **modeled on the organization of the German kingdom Prussia**. Soon after that, Japan, poor in mineral resources, began to extend its sphere of influence to the whole of east Asia, defeating the forces of **China** in 1895 and **Russia** in 1905; five years later it **annexed Korea**.

In 1931, the Japanese army occupied **Manchuria** approving the last Chinese Emperor, **Puyi**, as ruler of the puppet kingdom Manchukuo. Beginning in 1937, the **Sino-Japanese War** lasted until 1945. At the same time, Japan tried to protect and extend its conquests by entering the **Axis Pact** with **Germany** and **Italy**. With the attack on **Pearl Harbour** in 1941, the **Pacific War** began and large parts of southeast Asia were conquered. In August 1945, after the US dropped **atomic bombs** on **Hiroshima** and **Nagasaki**, the emperor announced Japan's unconditional surrender. In **1947**, with support from the USA, a new **constitution** was proclaimed which planned for **parliamentary government** under an **emperor** who had merely ceremonial functions, as a symbol of the state and the unity of the people.

The members of the House of Representatives – the **lower house** (Shugiin) – are elected every four years; the leader of the parliamentary majority in this house becomes **Prime Minister**. The House of Councillors – the **Upper House** (Sangiin) consists of delegates from regional constituencies, who each serve six year terms.

In foreign affairs, Japan maintains a **policy of pacifism**, in spite of its enormous economic strength and since 1992, has taken part on a small scale in UN peace missions.

Economy

Japan has the second **largest economy** in the world after the United States. **Agriculture** (cereals, rice and green tea grown on terraces, fruit and vegetables) is mostly a secondary occupation; Hokkaido is the centre of the extensive beef **cattle breeding industry**. As one of the world's largest **fishing nations** (fish, seafood, sea grass and seaweed), Japan maintains one its biggest fishing fleets. The fleet is partly stationed overseas and accounts for nearly **15 per cent** of the **entire world catch**.

The **country which is poor in natural resources** is industrially highly developed and strictly organised, particularly in the **metal-processing** sector. The most important **exports** are in the **ship-building and motor vehicle manufacturing industries**, the **chemicals industry**, iron and **steel** as well as the **computer industry** (telecommunications, vending machines, industrial robots and machine tools). Although all raw materials – and the majority of foodstuffs – are imported, Japan has a **positive trade balance**. The country's modern infrastructure offers employment to around 40 per cent of the labour force in the **services sector** (trade, banks, invisibles), which accounts for 60 per cent of total GDP.

Japan, which is among the world's largest creditor nations, has experienced a **major economic slowdown** since 1997 whose effects have been largely mitigated by the state but which has had a seriously detrimental effect on neighbouring countries.

Transport

In spite of its mountainous terrain, Japan has an excellent, fully developed infrastructure.

All four of the main islands are connected to each other by **tunnels** and **bridges**. The Seikan-Tunnel, which at 53.9 km is the **longest underwater railway tunnel in the world**, connects Hokkaido with Honshu; the Akashi-Kaikyo-Bridge which at 3.9 km is the world's **longest suspension bridge**, stretches from Honshu to the Awaji Island. The country's **rail network** covers a length of 23,670 km, of which 11,952 km is electrified. The 7,000 km long **Shinkansen-Network**, which links the major cities by high speed ('bullet') trains, is of great importance for

JAPANESE MEGALOPOLIS

The landmarks of Kobe under a full moon: the red port tower.

POPULATION DENSITY (People/km²)

	below 50
	50-200
	200-700
	above 700

Hirohito

*Tokyo, 29.4.1901,
†Tokyo, 5.1.1989

Hirohito became the 123rd Emperor of Japan in 1926. Under his leadership, Japanese imperialism in the Pacific collapsed, and the Japanese attacked Pearl Harbour. After the atomic bombs were dropped on Hiroshima and Nagasaki in 1945, he announced the Japanese capitulation. His role during World War II remains controversial, but he was cleared of the accusation of war crimes by a military tribunal. After Japan installed a parliament, Hirohito lost his officially divine position in Japan, but retained the throne until his death.

*The art of seduction that is never passionate: Japanese **geishas** are by no means submissive coutesans, but professionals of the disciplined and highly cultured art of entertaining men.*

individual travellers. The **road network** covers more than 1.14 million km, of which over 60,000 km are arterial roads and motorways. It is surfaced for two-thirds of its length.

The **vehicle density** of 552 vehicles per 1,000 inhabitants is among the largest in the world. In addition to numerous airports within the densely connected inland flight networks, there are three international **airports** in **Tokyo**, **Narita** and **Osaka**.

While the inland navigation routes with a total length of 1,770 km are of secondary importance, Japanese sea **ports** are among those with the **world's highest volume** of shipping. The most important international sea ports are Kobe, Hiroshima, Nagoya, Chiba, Tokyo and Sakai.

Tourism

Japan's attractions range from culturally and historically unique sites to charming landscapes and draw millions of visitors from abroad every year, despite the high cost of living and correspondingly high cost of hotel rooms and tourist facilities. There are also language difficulties; the Japanese often do not speak foreign languages and street signs are exclusively in Japanese.

The **capital city** and the **Osaka** region are regarded as the centres of tourism. Tokyo has a wealth of important museums and cultural sites; in the vicinity, there are the coastal town of **Kamakura** (famous for its large bronze Buddha) and the ancient town of **Nikko** set amidst charming mountain landscapes.

Osaka is the starting point for tours to the **old imperial cities of Kyoto** and **Nara**, which are among the highlights of touring Japan, especially the former with its important museum of Japanese artefacts and objets d'art. Kyoto also contains countless Buddhist and Shinto buildings and shrines; Nara has some of the **oldest Buddhist temples** in East Asia.

On the **Ise Peninsula**, there is the most important **Shinto relic**, along with the **Shrines of Ise**. Other towns worth seeing are Himeji, Hiroshima and Nagasaki. Opportunities for skiing, mountain-climbing and walking can be

found in the **'Japanese Alps'**. Among Japan's many areas of outstanding natural beauty, which range from landscapes, formed by lava flows and other volcanic action, there is the flora ranging from alpine to sub-tropical. Examples of such landscapes include the **Fuji-Hakone-Izu National Park**, south of Mount Fuji,

with its lakes and volcanic landscapes as well as the largely untouched **Shirakami-Sanchi mountain range** in northern Honshu. Equally charming, but less developed touristically, is **Kyushu** Island with its numerous active volcanoes, **hot springs** and well known spas such as **Beppu**.

1 Yokohama Bay is the gateway to Japan. The city of the same name has one of the world's largest harbours. Tokyo, Kanagawa and Yokohama have grown together to form one strip of urban development.

2 Imperial Kyoto: the steps lead up to the Kibune Shrine,

one of the most beautiful holy places of Shintoism.

3 A warren of streets: Tokyo is home to some eight million people, and there is a great lack of space. As a result, the face of the city is always changing. The skycrapers and motorways mirror this dynamism.

Japan: a changing economic power

The Japanese economy, once regarded as a marvel, collapsed at the end of the 1990s like a house of cards. The country today has the highest debts of any industrialised nation. In an attempt to reconstruct a viable economy, even the most traditional values of the Japanese corporate mentality are being questioned.

When the Japanese empire surrendered to the Allies in 1945, its economy was also at a low ebb. Initial measures taken included the dissolution of large and powerful businesses and the implementation of fundamental economic reforms. The newly created Ministry for International Trade and Industry (MITI) announced plans and strategies according to which production would be strictly organised almost country-wide. Lacking its own raw materials, Japan needed to be highly export-oriented, so as to create a counterbalance to the inevitable imports. Japanese industry soon concentrated on high-tech products for export. The factories were

automated to the most modern standards and were soon able to sell low-priced electronic appliances and vehicles abroad with no fear of competition.

In 1965, the country first recorded a trade surplus, and by 1968 it had become a leading industrialised nation. Responsible for this success were the more than 200,000 civil servants of the MITI. Until the 1980s, Japan was one of the world's leading motor manufacturers but its export offensives continually led to clashes with Western nations, in particular the USA. At the same time, Japan ensured that imports remained as unattractive as possible. Imported goods were subjected to high

customs duties and many products were subjected to complicated and expensive quality controls. To make Japan as independent as possible of imports, the MITI ran the domestic economy almost like a planned socialist economy.

As a result of the trade war in the 1980s, the USA began to urge Japan to improve internal demand for imported goods. The Japanese government lowered interest rates and privatised a number of state enterprises. The stock market boomed and

Japan is one of the world's largest fishing nations; here, unloading tuna in Honshu.

property prices shot up to unexpected heights.

With the enormous capital resources generated in this way, some of the country's banks rapidly rose to become the largest financial institutions in the world. They supplied credit for investments and brought huge capital resources to the West.

Today Japan is still the greatest creditor nation in the world and its government loans to the USA alone amount to more than 300 billion dollars.

This bubble had to burst, and in 1990 the severest economic crisis of the postwar years hit Japan. Stock market prices fell steeply, billions of loans proved to be

Main photograph: Yokohama is home to one of Japan's most important international ports.

Photo, left: Mount Fuji, at 3,776 m Japan's highest mountain, stands south of Tokyo.

Photo, centre: Neon signs light up the Ginza, Tokyo's shopping and leisure centre.

Photo, right: High-speed 'bullet' trains (up to 260 km/h) connect the trading centres.

irrecoverable and property was overpriced so the property market stagnated. One finance company after another went bankrupt. In addition, in 1999 the Asian crisis gripped the country; Japan had made considerable investments in the neigbouring countries, which were therefore affected by its recession. Only a rehabilitation of the banking scene at the last moment was able to prevent a crash of the Japanese money market which would certainly have spread abroad.

Since then, the Japanese economy has been in a state of flux. Japanese businesses are entering into foreign partnerships and participating in foreign concerns, and some are even being sold to foreigners. For the first time, enterprises are submitting obligatory balance sheets. Banks and insurance companies have also

faced foreign competition since 1998. The government supports these reforms with an economic programme of the equivalent of 1.4 billion euros. Today, Japan is the industrialised state with the highest debts, with a budget deficit of ten per cent of the GDP. The economic crisis has, above all, had social consequences. 'Japan Inc.', as it had been called, which made Japan into an economic miracle, was based on the traditional values of Japanese society. An important element was a close lifelong connection between firms and their employees. Jobs were guaranteed, older employees were automatically promoted and even on retirement remained loyally connected to their former workplace.

Now firms must increasingly rely on achievement and rationalisation measures in order to become flexible in the face of

competition. Labour-intensive production is increasingly outsourced to neighbouring countries where wages are lower. This is one of the triggers for the rapid rise in unemployment, which has reached a record level of 4.9 per cent.

A further problem for Japanese society is the progressive ageing of the population. Japan's life expectancy is the highest in the world, and in view of the rapidly falling birth rate, by the year 2020 one-quarter of the population will be over 65 years old. Reforms such as that of the wholly inadequate state pension funds and the introduction of health care insurance could prove to be difficult. The Japanese social system, based on outdated tradi-

Industrial boom has long been an emblem of Japan: smoking chimneys in front of Mount Fuji.

tions, is turning out to be full of holes. Japan, the former industrial powerhouse, is recovering only slowly from its massive breakdown. Only time will tell how much the inevitable changes to the world of work will affect the traditional social structures for which Japan was so often envied by other nations.

Myanmar (Burma), Thailand

Area:	678,500 sq. km
Capital city:	Yangon
Form of government:	Republic
Administrative divisions:	
7 states, 7 districts	
Population: 42.9 million	
(75 inhabitants/sq.km)	
Languages:	
Burmese (official), local languages	
GDP per capita:	US$1,800
Currency:	1 kyat = 100 pyas

Natural Geography

The country is surrounded by high mountains in the border regions, but the land becomes more open towards the coast. The **Arakan Mountains** in the southwest are covered in primeval forest, and here is the country's highest point, the 5,881-m-high **Hkakabo Razi**. In the east lies the **Ayeyarwaddy basin**, that ends in a delta on the Gulf of Martaban. This river is used to irrigate one of the largest rice growing areas in the world.

Climate

Myanmar has a variety of different climates in different regions. Near the coast, the climate is **equatorial**, but in the north it has more **sub-tropical** features. The average temperature on the plains is approximately 27°C.

Population

Myanmar is populated by a variety of different peoples, including **Burmans** (71 per cent) **Karen** (6.2 per cent), the **Shan** people (8.5 per cent), who live in a partially autonomous region, the **Rakhine** (4.3 per cent), the **Mon** (2.4 per cent) and other small ethnic minorities.
Roughly 90 per cent of the population is **Buddhist**, but there are also communities of Christians and Sunni Muslims. The Burmans live in the centre of the country, and the minorities mainly live on the border and in remote areas.

History and Politics

The **Burmans** settled and established an empire in the eighth century. The region was later conquered by the **Mongols** in the thirteenth century. The power struggles between the ruling houses ended with the country being united under a Burmese dynasty in the year 1752. Between 1866 and 1948, Burma was under **British rule**.

Following independence, the country descended into **civil war** from which the military emerged victorious. Military dictatorship since 1962 has prevented any attempts at democratisation. Since 1993, a **national assembly** controlled by the military, has ruled the country.

Economy

The dominant economic sector is **agriculture** (rice, pulses, beans). The forests are good sources of hardwoods, such as **teak,** which are a profitable export. The highest export income derives from **diamonds** and **natural gas reserves**. The **opium plantations** in the 'Golden Triangle' are a not insignificant sector of the economy.

Transport Infrastructure

The road network is only developed around the main cities. The main form of transport is the **train**; some of the rolling stock dates from the pre-war era but is still used to reach many parts of the country. In contrast, the air travel network is very good. The only international airport is in **Yangon** (formerly Rangoon).

Tourism

The main points of interest for tourists are the **Buddhist monuments** in the capital Yangon (formerly Rangoon) and the temple city of **Pagan**. **Mandalay** is also worth a visit. The Shan Plateau in the central north-west has particularly attractive landscapes. Tourists are only allowed a 14-day visa.

Myanmar: royal barge on the Lake Inle in Ywama.

Area:	513,115 sq.km
Capital city:	Bangkok
Form of government:	
Constitutional Monarchy	
Administrative divisions:	
73 provinces	
Population:	
65.4 million	
(120 inhabitants/sq.km)	
Languages:	
Thai (official), English, Chinese	
GDP per capita:	US$8,300
Currency:	1 baht = 100 stangs

Natural Geography

The west of the country is defined by extensions of the south-east Asian mountain range, which extends down into the **Malay** peninsula.
Rain**forests** cover the fertile lowlands which run from north to south. The delta of the **Menam** river is the most populated area. The **Korat plateau** in the east, gradually descends to the river **Mekong**.

Climate

Thailand has a **tropical climate** with year-round high temperatures and high humidity. The **rainy season** lasts from June to October.

Population

Up to 80 per cent of the population lives in the country. It consists of 80 per cent **Thais** with smaller groups of Chinese, Indi-

'The Golden Triangle': the border region between Myanmar, Thailand and Laos on the central Mekong plain was for a long time one of the largest opium cultivation regions of the world. While Thailand has been able to eradicate the cultivation of opium poppies, the plant is still grown in Myanmar, where the local population funds its fight against the military regime by selling the drug. After Afghanistan, Myanmar is the second largest opium producer in the world.

ans and Malays, and some mountain people. 95 per cent of the Thai people are **Buddhist**.

History and Politics

The **Thai empire** began to form in the thirteenth century, and its capital city was moved to **Bangkok** in 1782. In the nineteenth century, this empire ceded large areas to France and Great Britain. A coup d'état in 1932 led to the establishment of a **constitutional monarchy**. For many years, the formation of a modern state was hindered by repeated **attempted coups** and **unrest**. Since 1998, a new constitution has been in effect, under which legislative decisions are the responsibility of a unicameral parliament. The head of state is the **monarch**.

Economy

Agriculture employs 54 per cent of the working population. The main crops are rice, maize, cassava, sugar cane and rubber.
The **manufacturing industry** mainly produces foodstuffs, but also motor vehicle and computer components, and contributes 40 per cent of GDP. Tourism represents most of the **service sector**, which accounts for 50 per cent of GDP. The cultivation of opium **poppies** also represents a not insignificant sector of the economy.

Transport Infrastructure

Thailand has extensive and modern rail and road connections. Internal flights are also of great importance; the international airports are in **Bangkok** and **Chiang Mai**.

Tourism

Since the 1980s, Thailand has become a favourite holiday destination, despite problems with drugs, prostitution and the spread of AIDS. In addition to **Pattaya** on the Gulf of Thailand and the southern island of **Phuket**, there are numerous attractions such as the ruins of **Ayutthaya** and **Sukhothai** and the Khao-Yai national park. The Thais are also famous for their delicious food and luxury hotels.

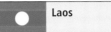

Laos

Area:	236,800 sq.km
Capital city:	Vientiane
Form of government:	
People's Republic	
Administrative divisions:	
16 provinces and 1 prefecture (capital city)	
Population:	
6.2 million (24 inhabitants/sq. km)	
Languages:	
Lao (official), minority languages	
GDP per capita:	US$1,200
Currency:	1 kip

Natural Geography

The country is surrounded by the **Xiangkhoang Plateau** (2,817 m) to the north and the 2,000 m-high **Boloven Plateau** to the south. The **Mekong** flows through the country for a distance of 1,865 km. Forests cover 40 per cent of the land area.

Climate

Laos has a **tropical monsoon climate**. The rainy season lasts from May to September; in this period, the average temperature in the capital city is 27°C.

Population

The population consist mostly of ethnic **Lao**, who can be further divided into 70 ethnic groups. There are also ethnic minorities of **Vietnamese** and **Chinese**. The population is 60 per cent **Buddhist**. Three-quarters of the people live in rural areas and only the

major cities and their surrounding areas have an electricity supply.

History and Politics

In the fourteenth century, the first Laotian kingdom was formed and Buddhism was introduced. After occupation by **Thailand** in the nineteenth century, Laos became

1 Thailand: the statues on the Grand Palace of Bangkok are demonic in appearance and are there to protect the precious Emerald Buddha inside.

2 The Buddhist leader of Laos resides in a modest residence in the former government city of Luang Prabang.

3 The grand Shwedagon Pagoda in Yangon, Myanmar is 450 m in circumference, 116 m high, coated with pure gold, and inlaid with 4,000 diamonds.

4 Thailand's capital, Bangkok: skyscrapers light up the skyline along the Chao Phraya River.

*Angkor was the former capital of **Khmer Empire**, whose influence spread far beyond Cambodia. The Angkor Wat Temple contains the mausoleum of King Suryavarman II, the glorious ruler of the Khmer in the twelfth century.*

a French protectorate, but regained **independence** in 1954. The Vietnam War spilled over into large parts of the country and Communist **revolutionary troops** conquered extensive tracts of land. In 1974, these revolutionaries became the government of the country. The **People's Democratic Republic of Laos** was proclaimed in 1975.

Economy

Laos was once a very isolated country, but since 1986, the economy has taken a successful course. **Agriculture** accounts for 80 per cent of the labour force mainly working in the paddyfields, and farming contributes 57 per cent of GDP. The forests are excellent sources of **exotic woods** (teak, ebony, rosewood) for export. The forests are endangered, however, by the slash-and-burn clearances for **the cultivation of the opium poppy**. The **manufacturing sector** is very underdeveloped. The **services**

international airport is in **Vientiane**, the capital.

Tourism

Attractions include the former royal city of **Luang Prabang** and Vientiane. Cruises on the **Mekong** are particularly popular.

Cambodia	
Area:	181,035 sq.km
Capital city:	Phnom Penh
Form of government: Constitutional Monarchy	
Administrative divisions: 21 provinces	
Population: 13.6 million (72 inhabitants/sq.km)	
Languages: Khmer (official), Vietnamese	
GDP per capita:	US$2,100
Currency: 1 riel = 10 kak = 100 sen	

under cultivation. The Tonle Sab in the central plain is the largest inland waterway in south-east Asia and also has the largest fish stocks.

Climate

The country has a humid **tropical climate** with an average temperature of 27°C. The vegetation in coastal areas is mainly **mangrove swamp**, which gives way to **monsoon forests** in the central area and to **rainforests** in the mountains.

Population

The population is 90 per cent **Khmer**, with minorities of Vietnamese (five per cent) and **Cham** and **Chinese**. The majority (85 per cent) live in rural areas, and 95 per cent of Cambodians are **Buddhist**. Only 35 per cent can read and write.
As a result of the **war**, many unexploded landmines remain scattered across the country. The in-

In 1867, the French occupied the region, defeating the Union of Indochina, and Cambodia did not regain **independence** until 1949. The French finally left Cambodia in 1954. The ruling **monarch** abdicated a year later and became president. The coup d'état in 1970 caused a **civil war**, which lasted for two years. The Communist **Khmer Rouge** emerged victorious and established a **reign of terror** that was brought down after an invasion by Vietnamese troops. After the Vietnamese withdrew in 1989, the State of Cambodia was proclaimed. An assembly charged with drawing up a constitution was voted for in 1993 under UN supervision. Cambodia became a constitutional monarchy and Prince Sihanouk became king once more. The last of the Khmer Rouge surrendered in 1998, and Cambodia became a member of ASEAN in 1999. The first free local elections took place in 2002. Sihanouk abdicated in October 2004 when he was replaced by his son, Norodom Sihamoni.

Transport Infrastructure

The rail network connects the capital with Vietnam. Only part of the road network, that covers 603 km, is paved. Shipping on the **Mekong** is very important. There are international airports in **Phnom Penh** and **Angkor**.

Tourism

The main attraction is the temple city of Angkor Wat, north of the Tonle Sab.

Vietnam	
Area:	329,560 sq.km
Capital city:	Hanoi
Form of government: Socialist Republic	
Administrative divisions: 7 regions; 52 provinces, 3 municipalities	
Population: 83.5 million (246 inhabitants/sq.km)	
Language:	Vietnamese
GDP per capita:	US$3,000
Currency: 1 dong = 10 hào = 10 xu	

Natural Geography

Vietnam lies on the east coast of south-east Asia. **Tonking** is a region in the north containing the deltas of the Red and Black Rivers. South of this is the country's central region, the **Annam**, bordered by a long, jagged coastal stretch, which is only 40 km wide at its narrowest point. **Cochin-China** is in the south, and contains one of the largest river deltas on Earth, the mouth of the Mekong River, which covers an area of approximately 70,000 sq. km.

Vietnam: magnificent gate leading into the Dai Noi citadel in Hue.

Pol Pot
*Kompong Thom, 19.5.1928, † Anlong Veng, 15.4.1998
Originally a teacher, Pol Pot became the head of Cambodia's Communist Party in 1963 and led the Khmer Rouge in the 1970–1975 civil war. From 1976 to 1979 he was Prime Minister and introduced a kind of 'primitive Communism', murdering millions of his people, mainly intellectuals. After the Vietnamese invasion, he went underground and was condemned to death in his absence. He was leader of the Khmer Rouge until 1985.

Ho Chi Minh
*Kim Lien, 19.5.1890, † Hanoi, 3.9.1969
In the 1920s, Ho Chi Minh organised the resistance to French colonial rule in Indochina. His Vietminh fought against the Japanese but after 1946, resumed the fight against the French. After the division of Vietnam, in 1954, he became the president of North Vietnam. He led the war against South Vietnam and became a symbolic figure for the student revolts in the West against the war.

sector is increasing in importance, in particular in the area of **tourism**, which has been permitted since 1988.

Transport Infrastructure

The road network is still very rudimentary, and roads are often barely passable during the rainy season. There is no rail network. The main transport artery is the **Mekong River**. The only

Natural Geography

The lowlands of the **Tonle Sab basin** and the **Mekong delta** are enclosed by the Dangrek mountain chain in the north and in the south and south-west by the Cardamom mountains.
The Mekong divides the lowlands into east and west. While the upper reaches are densely forested, further downstream there are many large areas

adequate healthcare system and an absence of any social security structure, contribute to the country low life expectancy.

History and Politics

The ancient **Kingdom of the Khmer** was founded in the seventh century AD and collapsed in the seventeenth century after repeated attacks from neighbouring countries.

Economy

Agriculture contributes 50 per cent of GDP and this sector employs 80 per cent of the labour force. Rice is the main crop. Due to the absence of infrastructure, the **manufacturing sector** only contributes 15 per cent of GDP and is relatively insignificant. Tourism is becoming an important growth factor and is sure to boost exports.

Climate

The coastal areas are affected by a **rainy season** which lasts from May to October and which sees large amounts of precipitation. The coastal regions in the south are covered in rainforest and mangroves. The climate in the north is more **sub-tropical**, with seasonal temperature variations. April is a particularly hot month with temperatures of up to 40°C.

*The tanks are abandoned but the ecological and economic cost of the **Vietnam War** is still very much in evidence today. The huge tunnel system of Cu Chi near Ho-Chi-Minh-City is one of the major memorials to the war in Vietnam.*

Temperatures in winter fall no lower than 17°C.

Population

90 per cent of the population is **Vietnamese**, but there are also minorities of **Chinese** and some **Thai** and **Khmer**. More than half the population is **Buddhist**.

History and Politics

In 1858, France occupied South Vietnam and incorporated it into its colony of **Indochina**. During World War II, the **Japanese** established a government for a short period of time, but this was abolished after their surrender. During the **Indo-Chinese War** of 1946 to 1954, the French colonial power succumbed to the Communist **Vietminh** guerrillas. The country was divided into the Communist North Vietnam and the Republic of South Vietnam. The north Vietnamese guerrillas aimed to reunite the country by force under Communist rule and this led in 1965 to an attack by the USA. The **Vietnam War** ended in 1975 with the capitulation of South Vietnam and the withdrawal of US forces. Vietnam has been reunited since 1976, but was not officially recognised by the United Nations until 1995. The **head of state** is chosen by the members of the National Assembly, who serve five-year terms of office.

Economy

Since 1986, Vietnam has been converting its economy from a socialist **state-run economy** to a **free-market economy** with some socialist orientation. **Agriculture,** which employs 65 per cent of the labour force in the cultivation of rice, cereals, soya and coffee, has been successful and contributes 28 per cent of GDP. Vietnam is currently the third largest exporter of rice. The number of private companies in the **manufacturing sector** is continually rising and produces food, machinery and chemicals for export. Despite the economic successes of recent years, Vietnam is still an underdeveloped poor country. Large **areas of land** are still **contaminated** by the defoliants dropped by the Ameri-

cans and by land mines as a result of the long years of war.

Transport Infrastructure

Road and rail connects Ho-Chi-Minh-City with Hanoi. Only 25 per cent of the **road network** is surfaced. There are **International airports** in Hanoi and Ho-Chi-

Minh-City, which was once Saigon, the capital of South Vietnam.

Tourism

Vietnam offers natural wonders such as **Halong Bay**. **Ho-Chi-Minh City** and **the ancient capital of Hué** are among the important historical sites.

1 Daily life in Cambodia: Working elephants on the Siem Reap River near Angkor Wat

2 Extensive paddy-fields dominate the plains of the 70,000-sq.-km-large Mekong delta in Vietnam. Rice is cultivated here, yielding several harvests per year.

3 Women working in front of a pagoda in Soc Trang, Vietnam. The wide hat protects the shoulders from the burning sun.

4 Nature is reclaiming its territory: powerful tree roots wind around the walls in the Cambodian temple city Angkor Wat.

The Tiger States

Main photograph: Singapore remains the symbol of the success of the Tiger States.

The bigger you are, the harder you fall: the Asian economy faced a major crisis in the late twentieth century. Predator capitalism, with its ruthless exploitation of people and the environment and highly speculative investments is now eating its own children. Once-booming economies are now struggling to recover with the help of foreign aid.

The Asian 'Tiger States' was the name originally given to the emerging nations of Hong Kong, Singapore, Taiwan and South Korea. Since the mid-1980s, Indonesia, Malaysia, Thailand and Vietnam have been added to the list of Tiger States. The second generation is known as 'Little Tigers'. While the western industrial nations and Japan had to battle against an aggravated economic crisis, the Tiger States were able to demonstrate constant economic growth of more than five per cent from the mid-1960s until well into the 1990s. The authoritarian regimes of these emerging countries created the conditions for the growth syn-

drome in south-east Asia. After the modernisation of agriculture, the manpower released from the agricultural sector could be transferred to industry. The irresistible rise in the rates of production was accompanied by repressive measures: wages were kept low and working hours and conditions resembled those of nineteenth-century Victorian England. Unions and other civil rights movements were systematically suppressed. A further drawback to the outstanding industrial record was the ruinous exploitation of the environment. No capital was set aside for the preservation of the ecosystem and the destruction of the environment took on

catastrophic proportions in south-east Asia.

The modernisation of the economy, however, enabled a new middle class to emerge, which was able to assert itself to some extent in its demands for human rights and sharing the wealth of the society with the less fortunate. Thus a purely export orientation was postponed and an increasingly domestic market was served. Gradually, labour-intensive production was transformed into capital-intensive production. The rise of the second generation

Oil for the Tigers: Malaysia has large crude oil reserves.

of Tiger States proceeded in a similar manner. Indonesia, Malaysia, Thailand and Vietnam owe their success largely to the fact that the Japanese yen was revalued in the mid-1980s in relation to the US dollar. The devaluation of the dollar and revaluation of the yen resulted in increased prices for Japanese exports. Ja-

panese firms responded to this by shifting their production to other Asian countries, whose currencies were linked to the devalued dollar, such as Indonesia and Thailand.
From the early 1990s more and more foreign capital flooded into these national economies, which sought to open themselves up to

Shipbuilding and vehicle manufacture are particularly important export industries.

American and European investment as new sources of capital. In order to attract foreign investors, portfolios were enabled and foreign banks and insurance companies were allowed to trade in hitherto closed markets.

As a further incentive to foreign investors, the rate of exchange was fixed in relation to the US dollar. So up to four billion euros of mainly US net capital per year flowed into the Tiger States. This was spent mainly on property and share speculation, both of which seemed to promise high yields. As early as 1996, however, it turned out that the building boom had reached a dead end as prices rose too high for potential purchasers. Everywhere, enormous numbers of residential and business premises stood empty. The threat of a crisis loomed in 1997, when share prices fell in South Korea by 75 per cent. The

figures for 1998 revealed the entire extent of the crisis. Indonesia was hardest hit with a reduction in GDP of 13.7 per cent. In Thailand, South Korea, Hong Kong and Vietnam things looked no better. Only in Singapore, Taiwan and the People's Republic of China, which had meanwhile joined the emerging industrial powerhouses, was the downward trend kept within limits.

The collapse of banks and insurance companies as well as the insolvency of many construction and industrial enterprises led to a rise in unemployment. Foreign trade was severely affected, due to lack of investment, venture capital and decreased buying power. Both imports and exports were falling off dramatically. In order to alleviate the consequences of the reckless financial policy of the 1990s, in 1997 to 1998, the International Monetary

Fund (IMF) alone allowed credit of US$115 billion. These funds were designed to stabilise ailing currencies and help build a new, effective banking system.

The condition laid down by the IMF was that reforms should be carried out in the financial area, such as more forceful supervision of the banks, transparency of the movement of money, smashing of monopolies, privatisation of state enterprises, dismantling of subsidies, and reduction of social benefits.

This last demand, in particular, led to the intensification of social disparities and further impoverishment of large parts of the population. In addition, more and more individuals became unemployed and foreign influence on

Singapore: Orchard Road is one of the most magnificent shopping streets in the world.

Asian industrial life increased. The success or failure of these drastic measures cannot yet be assessed. At the same time, however, a new star seems to be rising in the economic heavens of Asia. The People's Republic of China is growing in importance within the region by leaps and bounds. It already has the world's

fastest growing economy and is set to become a world power in economic terms. It could replace Japan as Asia's world power if the Chinese government succeeds in maintaining these rates of growth without falling prey to the same kinds of mistakes made by the tiger economies and Japan in particular.

Malaysia

*One country, two worlds: while the indigenous peoples of **Borneo** still hunt with blow-pipes, the city of Kuala Lumpur has moved into virtual reality. Both worlds are located in Malaysia, but that may be the only similarity.*

Malaysia

Area:	329 758 sq. km
Capital city:	Kuala Lumpur

Form of government:
Constitutional Elective Monarchy within the Commonwealth
Administrative divisions:
13 federal states (including 9 Sultanates), 2 federal territories
Population:
24 million
(66 inhabitants per sq. km)
Languages:
Bahasa Melayu (official), Chinese, Tamil, Iban, English

GDP per capita:	US$10,400

Currency:
1 Malayan ringgit = 100 sen

Natural geography

Malaysia consists of the southern part of the **Malay Peninsula** (West Malaysia) and – with the federal states of **Sabah** and **Sarawak** – the northern third of the **island of Borneo** (East Malaysia).
More than two-thirds of this predominantly mountainous country, with peaks of up to 2,000 m, is covered by a mighty **tropical rainforest**. Individual giant trees grow to a height of 60 m, with a circumference of 3 m.
West Malaysia is traversed north to south by a central **mountain range** 1,500–2,000 m in height on average, whose highest peak is **Mount Tahan** (2,190 m) in the state of Pahang. The south-east is has long **river valleys** and **alluvial plains**. The very flat

coastal areas are edged, especially in the east, by **kilometre-long white** sandy **beaches** and, in the west, by a long mangrove belt. East Malaysia's highest elevations are **Mount Murud** (2,422 m) in Sarawak and **Mount Kinabalu**, in northern Sabah, at 4,101 m the **highest mountain in south-east Asia**. **Mangrove swamps** predominate in the broad coastal plains. **Flora** and **fauna** are exceptionally varied. The largest flower in the world with a diameter of up to 1 m, the Rafflesia, grows only in Sabah.

Climate

Both parts of the country have a predominantly **moist tropical climate**, substantially determined by the **monsoons**. The average daytime temperature is 27°C, or 20°C in the uplands.

Population

Malaysia's population is composed of 64 per cent **Malays**, 27 per cent **Chinese**, and eight per cent **Indians**. The state religion is **Islam**; in addition there are Buddhists, Hindus and Christians. The official language is **Bahasa Melayu**.

History and politics

The earliest evidence of human settlement in the area of present-day Malaysia comes from Sarawak: skull fragments from the **caves of Niah** date back 35,000 years. The Malay Peninsula was

settled from the eighth to the second millenium BC by the **Orang Asli** and inhabited from the third millenium BC by **immigrants from South China**, particularly from the region of present-day **Yunnan**. The **Dayak** of Borneo are considered to be descendants of the original inhabitants, the Orang Asli.
During the first centuries AD a process of '**Indianisation**' took place in the peninsula, along with the founding of states. Up to the fourteenth century, various **Hindu** and **Buddhist** kingdoms dominated large parts of the region. The three most important of these were **Funan** (from the first century), **Srivijaya** (from the seventh century) and **Majapahit** (from the eleventh century).
Around 1400, the Malayan Prince Parameswara conquered the kingdom of **Malacca**. From this flourishing trade centre, at the time the largest city in south-east Asia, **Islam** began its

tri-
umphant
advance
through the ruling houses of Malaysia in the **fifteenth century**.
In 1511, the **Portuguese** conquered Malacca. The **Dutch** followed in 1641, and the **British** in the late eighteenth century. The British had already occupied North Borneo (now known as **Sabah**) in 1762, and leased Penang in 1786; they

settled in **Singapore** in 1819, and took control of north-west Borneo (then known as **Sarawak**) in 1842. The **Straits Settlements**, Penang, Malacca and Singapore, became **British Crown Colonies** in 1867; in the Pangkor Treaty of 1874 the Malay sultanates subjected themselves to the British rule. The **Federation of Malay States** was founded in 1896, consisting of the sultanates of Perak, Selangor, Negri Sembilan and Pahang, with Kuala Lumpur as its capital. The '**non-federated Malay states**', the sultanates of Kedah, Kelantan, Perlis and Trengganu in the north, were not ceded to the British by Thailand until 1909, and remained relatively autonomous, as did Johore in the south.
From 1941 to 1945, **Japan** occupied North Borneo and the Malay Peninsula. After Japan's surrender, the peninsula was at first ruled by a **British military government**, and Sarawak and Sabah became British

colonies. In 1946, the sultanates under the British protectorate, the Crown Colonies of Penang, Malacca and Singapore (the last of which had meanwhile become self-governing) joined together to form the **Federation of Malaya** in 1948.
After a **guerrilla war** supported by the People's Republic of China, the Federation of Malaya was granted total **independence** under the **1956 constitution** on **31 August 1957**.
The state of Malaysia, proclaimed on **16 September 1963**, resulted from the union of the **Federation of Malaya**, **Singapore** (which left the Federation in 1950), **Sabah** and **Sarawak**; Singapore became independent in 1965.
According to the constitution – last changed in 1994 – the **king** is chosen every five years by the **council of rulers**, which consists of the **nine sultans**, from among their number. The monarch is the leader of the Islamic faith, of the military and government; he approves the **prime minister** ap-

Kuala Lumpur: The Petronas Twin Towers are 450-m-high.

*Scenes from the Thaipusam Festival at the **Batu Caves** in Malaysia. Thousands of faithful climb the 272 steps to the caves to take part in the important Hindu festival. They test their faith in a trance by piercing themselves with needles.*

pointed by **parliament** and appoints some of the representatives of the **state assemblies**. Parliament is elected for a five-year term.

Economy

Malaysia is the **biggest producer of tin, rubber, palm oil** and **pepper**, as well as an important supplier of **tropical hardwoods** and of natural gas and petroleum.

The backbone of the economy, however, are the **high-tech** and **the automotive** industry. The **services sector** contributes 41 per cent of the country's GDP. The second largest source of income is **tourism**.

Transport

The well-developed, nationwide **road network** covers 93,975 km, of which 70,481 km are paved. **Buses, shared taxis** and **bicycle rickshaws** are important means of transport. Two **railway lines** run between Singapore and Thailand. Regular **flights and ferry routes** link the two parts of the country. The international airport, the **largest airport in Asia**, is at Kuala Lumpur.

Tourism

The cultural, economic and tourist centre of the country is the **capital**, Kuala Lumpur, which also proclaims its status with its 452-m-high **Petronas Twin Towers**. In addition it offers important museums and places of interest. On the coasts there are a number of

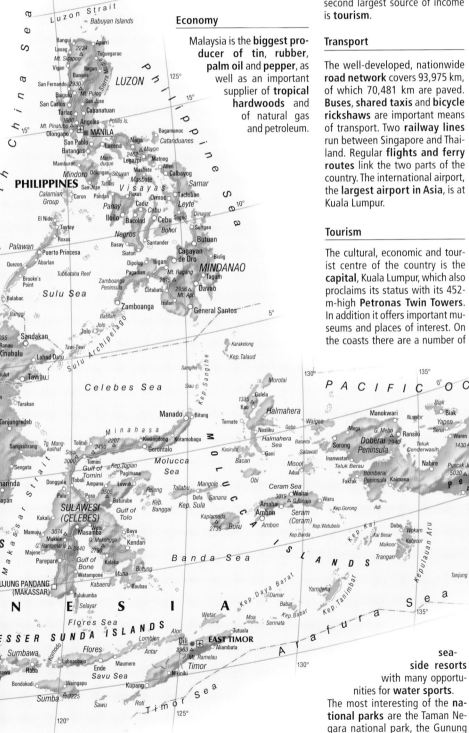

and watch these fascinating primates. The local food is a great attraction in the cities.

	**Singapore**

Area:	692,7 sq. km
Capital city:	Singapore
Form of government: Republic in the Commonwealth	
Administrative divisions: 5 districts	
Population: 4.4 million (7,176 inhabitants per sq km)	
Languages: Malayan, English, Chinese, Tamil (all official)	
GDP per capita:	US$29 700
Currency: 1 Singapore dollar = 100 cents	

Natural landscape

The group of islands on the **Malacca Straits** at the southern tip of the Malay Peninsula includes the rolling hills of the **main island of Singapore** and some **54 smaller islands**. A mere 5.5 per cent of the total land mass lies more than 31 m above sea level.

The native **fauna** and **flora** have been severely affected by human overpopulation.

Climate

Proximity to the equator ensures only **minor fluctuations in temperature** between 24°C and 31°C throughout the year.

The heavy **rainfall** of the **southwest monsoon** is concentrated between November and January.

Population

The population of this city-state is 76.4 per cent **Chinese**, 14.9 per cent **Malay**, 6.4 per cent **Indian** and 2.4 per cent other ethnic groups. Singapore has **four official and teaching languages**, Chinese (Mandarin), Malay, Tamil and English. Apart from **Buddhists** and **Muslims** there is a large number of **Christians**.

History and Politics

In **1819**, a member of the British East India Company, **Sir Thomas Stamford Raffles**, acquired Singapore from a Malay sultan. As early as 1867 it became a **British Crown Colony**.

From 1942 to 1945 Singapore was occupied by the **Japanese**. In 1946, it was granted the status of a British Crown Colony with **self-government** and became a member of the **Malay Union**, and then of the **Malay Federation** in 1948, from which it separated again in 1950.

In **1959**, Singapore was granted the status of an **autonomous state** and the country became **independent** in 1963 within the **Federation of Malaysia**. It finally became an **independent republic** in **1965**. The head of state is the **president**, who, since 1991, has been directly elected; the **unicameral parliament** is elected every five years.

Economy

As one of the **leading centres of industry and services** in the Asian region, Singapore has a highly **export-oriented economy**, which continues to record high levels of growth.

Transport

The 2,686 km **road network** is well developed. A rail and road causeway links the main island with the Malay Peninsula.

The **deepwater port** has one of the world's highest turnovers of shipping. Singapore has two **international airports** and is an important **air transport hub**.

Tourism

In addition to the attractions of the great modern city, Singapore is a model of cleanliness due to

seaside resorts with many opportunities for **water sports**.

The most interesting of the **national parks** are the Taman Negara national park, the Gunung Mulu national park and the Sepilok Orang-Utan reserve, where tourists can explore the jungle

*The immense crude oil and natural gas reserves have made the **Sultan of Brunei** one of the richest men in the world. His wealth increases by over US$ one billion a year – and he will get richer as the prices of oil and gas continue to soar.*

strictly enforced legislation. The 'fusion food' of south-east Asia is a big attraction in the cities. The offshore islands offer ideal **opportunities for scuba-diving and swimming** among the palm-fringed beaches and coral reefs.

Population:
372,000 (62 inhabitants/sq. km)
Languages:
Malay (official), English
GDP per capita: US$23 600
Currency:
1 Brunei dollar = 100 cents

Natural landscape

Two unconnected land areas on the north-west coast of Borneo, surrounded by the **Sarawak Mountains**, form the country of Brunei. **Tropical rainforest** covers 60 per cent of the land.
The coast consists mainly of **alluvial soil** with **mangrove** swamps, interspersed with **sandy coral beaches**. The **hill country** in the interior is home to a **variety of wildlife**.

Climate

Brunei has a **wet equatorial climate**; temperatures range from 24°C to 30°C and there is high humidity.

Population

The population, the majority of which consists of Malays at 64 per cent with **Indians and Chinese** at 20 per cent, benefits from a comprehensive social security system as a result of the country's enormous wealth. The citizens pay no taxes, and healthcare and education are absolutely free.
Islam, the state religion, is that of 64 per cent of the population, while only about 14 per cent are **Buddhists** and ten per cent **Christian**.

History and Politics

Trade relations with **China** in the sixth century and with the **Javanese kingdoms** in the thirteenth to the fifteenth centuries led to early **Buddhist and Hindu** influences. In the fifteenth century, **Islamicised** Malays founded the **Sultanate of Brunei**. When the Portuguese explorer, **Magellan,** landed on the coast of Brunei in 1521, the fifth sultan ruled over large areas of Borneo, the neighbouring islands and the Sulu archipelago. In 1888, Brunei became a **British protectorate**.
After the **Japanese** occupation from 1941 to 1945 the Sultanate again became a **British colony** until the **1959 constitution**, which established the country's sovereignty.
In 1984, Brunei finally became **independent**. The Sultan, enthroned in 1967, took over the running of the state in 1973, and has ruled since 1984 as an **absolute monarch**, supported by a **council**. There is no right to vote and there are no political parties.

Economy

In this small country whose ruler is one of the richest men in the world, the **economy** is of little importance. Most foodstuffs are imported. Of the country's GDP, 56 per cent derives from **petroleum and natural gas**. With its rich reserves, Brunei is one of the **largest oil exporters** in the Pacific region.

Transport

Brunei has a well-developed **road network**. The two parts of the country are linked only by a ferry. The capital city has an

	Brunei
Area:	5,765 sq. km

Capital city:
Bandar Seri Begawan
Form of government: Sultanate
Administrative divisions:
4 districts

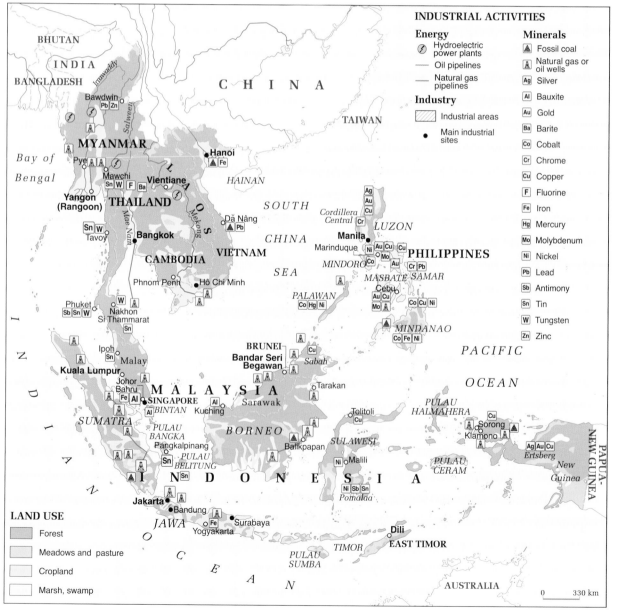

INDUSTRIAL ACTIVITIES

Energy
- Hydroelectric power plants
- Oil pipelines
- Natural gas pipelines

Industry
- Industrial areas
- Main industrial sites

Minerals
- Fossil coal
- Natural gas or oil wells
- Ag Silver
- Al Bauxite
- Au Gold
- Ba Barite
- Co Cobalt
- Cr Chrome
- Cu Copper
- F Fluorine
- Fe Iron
- Hg Mercury
- Mo Molybdenum
- Ni Nickel
- Pb Lead
- Sb Antimony
- Sn Tin
- W Tungsten
- Zn Zinc

LAND USE
- Forest
- Meadows and pasture
- Cropland
- Marsh, swamp

0   330 km

Ahmed Sukarno

*Surabaya, 6.6.1901,
†Jakarta, 21.6.1970

The founder of the Indonesian National Party (PNI) led the independence struggle against the Dutch colonial powers even before World War II. In 1945, he proclaimed the Republic of Indonesia, which was recognised by the Netherlands in 1949. He remained president until his official resignation in 1967, but from 1965 onwards was gradually disempowered by Suharto, his successor.

Bali's Kecak Dance tells the 2,000-year-old story of the kidnap of Princess Sita, who was rescued by Prince Rama with the help of a powerful army of monkeys. Narrative dances and other forms of story-telling, such as the shadow puppet theatre, are very important in Bali. The great wealth of Hindu mythology is brought to life by numerous performances and rituals. The island has more than 20,000 religious shrines.

international airport; the most important **deepwater port** and oil terminal is at Muara.

Tourism

Brunei has **no developed tourism**, but the capital with its old city, mosque and sultan's palace and the unspoiled jungle are major attractions.

Indonesia	
Area:	1,919,440 sq. km
Capital city:	Jakarta
Form of government: Presidential Republic	
Administrative divisions: 27 provinces, 3 provinces with special status	
Population: 242 million (123 inhabitants per sq. km)	
Languages: Indonesian (official), Javanese	
GDP per capita:	US$3,700
Currency:	1 rupiah = 100 sen

Natural landscape

More than **13,600 islands**, half of which are inhabited, extend in a curve more than 5,000 km long on either side of the equator. **Chains of volcanoes** run through western Sumatra and the Maluku (Molucca) islands; the highest of the **70 or so active volcanoes** is Kerinci on Sumatra at 3,805 m. The highest peak at 5,020 m is **Puncak Jaya** in the Maoke mountains of New Guinea.
More than half the land area is covered by **tropical rainforest**; in the wide **lowlands** of Sumatra and Borneo there are extensive **wetlands and freshwater swamp jungles**.
In December 2004, a violent tsunami inflicted devastating damage, particularly on Sumatra.

Climate

In the **moist tropical climate**, temperatures hardly vary throughout the year, at around 26°C.

Population

Indonesia is predominantly inhabited by **Malayan Indonesians**, of whom 45 per cent are Javanese, 14 per cent **Sundanese**, 7.5 per cent **Madurese** and there are other minorities. The largest groups of aborigines are the **Dayak** in West Kalimantan, the **Papua** in Irian Jaya and the **Balinese**. In addition there are a great number of **Chinese**, **Arabs**, **Indians** and **Pakistanis**. Some **250** different **languages** and **dialects** are spoken, of which **Javanese** predominates. The official language is **Bahasa Indonesia**, which, like English and Dutch acts as a channel of communication within this multilingual country. The **Islamic** faith is professed by 87 per cent of Indonesians, with minority groups of **Catholics**, **Protestants**, **Hindus** and **Buddhists**.

History and Politics

As early as 1000 BC, **Protomalays** emigrated from the Asian mainland to become the earliest inhabitants of Indonesia. Through of trade with **China**, beginning in the early Christian era, and later with **India**, **Buddhist** and **Hindu** influences reached Indonesia.
From the ninth to the thirteenth century the kingdom of **Srivijaya** ruled the Malay Peninsula, western Java and Sumatra. In the late twelfth century, it was separated from the Javanese kingdom of **Majapahit**, which Islamicised the country from the thirteenth to the fifteenth century. The exception was **Bali** which remained Hindu.
In 1511, **Portuguese sailors** first landed on the Maluku Islands, known as the Spice Islands or the Moluccas. They were followed by the **Spanish**, **Dutch** and **British**, who had no problem playing off the local princelings against each other. Representatives of the **Dutch East India Company**, using **Batavia** as a base, conquered the whole archipelago within three centuries, took control of the lucrative spice trade and ruled the **colony of the Dutch**

1 High-rise offices dominate the skyline of Singapore. The city has become famous for its strict laws and has lost almost all of its historic quarters.

2 The Kek Lok Si Temple on the Penang peninsula is one of the largest and most attractive Buddhist temples in Malaysia.

3 Great contrasts in Jakarta: alongside the sparkling skyscrapers of the Kuningan district, the city's slums are constantly expanding.

4 The curving terraced rice fields blend harmoniously into the hillside, a common feature of the landscape in Bali.

Indonesia, East Timor, Philippines

Rice is the staple food of south-east Asia, but its cultivation remains hard work. The rice has to be planted and harvested by hand. Ducks are used to eat the weeds that, if allowed to grow, would choke the crop.

East Indies until 1954, with short interruptions from 1811 to 1816 and 1942 to 1945 when it was occupied by the Japanese. As early as 1927, the **Partei Nasional** was founded, whose leader was **Sukarno.** He became president when Indonesia proclaimed its independence in 1945 although the colony had been returned to the Netherlands. The **Republic of Indonesia** was finally granted **independence** in **1949**, and five years later the union treaty with the Netherlands was dissolved.

Military coups, uprisings, and politically and religiously motivated unrest have since repeatedly troubled the country. The **presidential administration** of 1945 provides for a **unicameral parliament,** whose members are elected every five years. A proportion of the seats is reserved for **military personnel,** who are appointed directly by the president. The **People's Consultative Assembly,** which meets every five years, chooses the president and lays down policy guidelines. The **president** is both head of state and head of government.

Economy

About half the population works in **agriculture.** Rice, maize, cassava and sweet potatoes are the main crops for domestic requirements. Coffee, cocoa, tea and rubber are **exported.** Tropical hardwoods, rattan and copal are other important exports. More than 59 per cent of GDP is generated by agriculture and industry. The extremely rich supplies of petroleum and natural gas, coal, metals and minerals are the basis for the country's **highly developed heavy industry,** which produces exclusively for export.

Transport

There is **rail transport** on Sumatra and Java; the network, consisting mostly of narrow-gauge railway lines, is 6,458 km long. Half of the **393,000-km-long road network** is paved. The inland waterways are important arteries. Indonesia possesses a sig-nificant **merchant fleet** as well as more than 127 international ports. The domestic flight network is extensive and there are eight **international airports.**

Tourism

In addition to the sandy beaches that stretch for miles, Indonesia boasts has a plethora of outstanding cultural and historical sites. The Buddhist temple complex of **Borobudur** is considered the most important in Indian art, while the shrine of **Prambanan** is Indonesia's largest Hindu temple complex; both are on Java. Java is famous for its unique culture.

The Kutai National Park in southern Borneo is one of the **largest rainforests** in the world. The Gunung Leuser National Park in Sumatra contains countless species of birds and reptiles, as well as gibbons and **orangutans.** The island of Komodo is famous for the largest and most lethal reptile in the world, the **Komodo dragon.** The unspoiled island of Sulawesi is also famous for its jungles and wildlife.

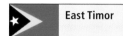
Natural landscape

This republic covers the eastern half of Timor, one of the **Lesser Sundanese Islands.** The central mountain range includes the 2,960-m-high **Mount Ramelan.** The original vegetation has been destroyed except for some jungle.

Climate

East Timor has a **tropical monsoon** climate with a short rainy season (December to March) and a dry period (May to October).

Population

The population consists predominantly of **Malays,** who are almost exclusively Roman Catholics, a relic of Portuguese colonisation.

History and Politics

East Timor was a **Portuguese colony** from 1695. The west of the island was **Dutch territory.** After World War II, the **western part** of the island was assigned to **Indonesia.** After the retreat of the Portuguese from 1975 a **civil war** broke out, and the victorious Fretilin party declared **independence.** In 1975/1976 **Indonesia annexed East Timor.** The Fretilin continued the battle against the Indonesian troops. Some 200,000 people died as a result of the Indonesian annexation policy.

In 1999, the majority of the population voted for **independence.** Indonesian troops and militias then destroyed the entire infrastructure of the country. In the autumn of 1999 the United Nations sent in a peacekeeping force and set up a caretaker government. On 20 May 2002, East Timor became independent. The Fretilin leader, **J. A. Gusmão,** was elected its first president.

Economy

The basis of the economy is the cultivation of **coffee,** rice, **manioc** and **coconut palms.** There are hopes of finding **petroleum and natural gas** in the Timor Sea. The economy is gradually recovering from the Indonesian occupation.

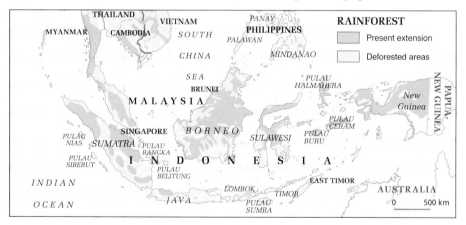

The **Sulu Islands** in the Philippines are home to several completely different peoples. As a result, the Badjao on the island of Bongao have been able to preserve their wedding rituals. The bridesmaids paint their faces white before accompanying the bride to the marriage ceremony. Life is less peaceful on other islands in the group and some are in a state of war, sadly brought to the world's attention by the taking of hostages by the Abu Sayyaf islamicist rebels.

Natural landscape

The Philippines constitute the north-eastern part of the Malay Archipelago. The country consists of some **7,100 islands**. The largest island, **Luzon**, in the north and the second largest, **Mindanao**, in the south, are separated by the **Visayas** islands, the largest of which is **Negros**. These mountainous islands are often subject to earthquakes and volcanic eruptions. Some 50 per cent of the land mass is covered with **tropical rainforest**.

Climate

The Philippines have a **dry tropical climate**; average temperatures all year round are between 25°C and 28°C.

Population

The population is composed of 30 per cent **Tagalog Filipinos**, 25 per cent **Cebuano** and **Ilocano Filipinos**, ten per cent **Binisaya**, ten per cent **Chinese**, as well as mestizos (people of mixed ancestry).
92 per cent of Filipinos are **Christian**, five per cent are **Muslim**, and in addition there are **Buddhists** and **animists**.

History and Politics

Trade relations with **China** and **India** are recorded from about 1000 AD. Islam probably began to spread only after the **arrival** of the Portuguese explorer, **Magellan**, in 1521, especially on Mindanao. **Spanish colonial rule** from the end of the sixteenth century caused almost the entire population to convert to **Roman Catholicism**.
The **opening up of trade** from 1830 and economic growth led to **efforts to gain independence** in 1896, which were ruthlessly suppressed by Spanish troops. After the **victory** of the USA in the Spanish-American War of 1898, the area came under **American rule**. In 1935, the **Commonwealth of the Philippines** was founded in preparation for independence, but freedom was won only after liberation from the **Japanese occupation** of the Philippines that occurred between 1941 and 1945.

In 1946, the area was declared a **republic**, with the **USA** securing extensive rights to construct military bases. The **dictatorship** that followed, lasting more than thirty years, which destroyed the country in both economic and social terms, only ended in 1986 when President Ferdinand. Marcos was deposed in a popular uprising.

Economy

Farming is the only source of income for 45 per cent of the population, who cultivate grain and fruit as well as cash crops such as coconut palms and copra. This has enabled the country to become the **largest producer of coconuts and related products**. The **copper** and **nickel** deposits as well as **oil wells** form the basis of industry. The main export income is derived from the sale of **electronics** and **telecommunications** equipment.

Transport

The main mode of transport other than the roads is the domestic flight network with **more than 300 airfields** and there are also good ferry links between the islands. There are nine **international airports**. The only **railway line** operates on Luzon. The **road network** covering 200,000 km is largely unpaved.

Tourism

The centre of the country is the capital city, Manila, with its interesting colonial buildings. In the north of Luzon there are the **rice**-growing terraces of Banaue, one of the many scenic beauties of the country. Popular **leisure resorts** and **beaches** are found on Cebu, Mactan, Bohol, Boracay and Negros in the Visayas group of islands. Mindanao was popular for its jungle, but has been less frequented recently due to its militant Islamic minority.

1 A sampang, a typical boat in the Philippines, floating in El Nido Bay, surrounded by the hilly landscape.

2 Farmers from the surrounding area selling their wares in a vegetable market in Jakarta. The slim profits are barely sufficient for day-to-day survival.

3 The city of Cebu is an important trading centre in the Philippines. Even after dark, the market is bustling.

4 The famous Chocolate Hills on the island of Bohol are a collection of some 1,268 conical limestone hills 40 m high.

Australia and Oceania

With a surface area of 7.6 million sq. km, Australia is the smallest continent. It was first discovered in the early seventeenth century, and was gradually settled by British colonists. Australia's native inhabitants (aborigines) were forced into reservations as a result.

Central Australia consists of deserts with scattered mountain ranges and individual mountains, the most famous of them being Uluru (formerly known as Ayers Rock), a massive monolith rising out of the sand. Just off the coast lies the Great Barrier Reef, the largest coral reef on Earth. The flora and fauna of Australia are unique, including kangaroos, duckbilled platypuses, koalas, eucalyptus (gum) trees and mimosa bushes.

Oceania consists of 10,000 islands with a total land mass of some 800,000 sq. km. The islands of Melanesia, Micronesia, Polynesia, New Zealand and Hawaii cover a vast area of 70 million sq. km. Palm-fringed beaches and blue lagoons make the islands a tropical paradise.

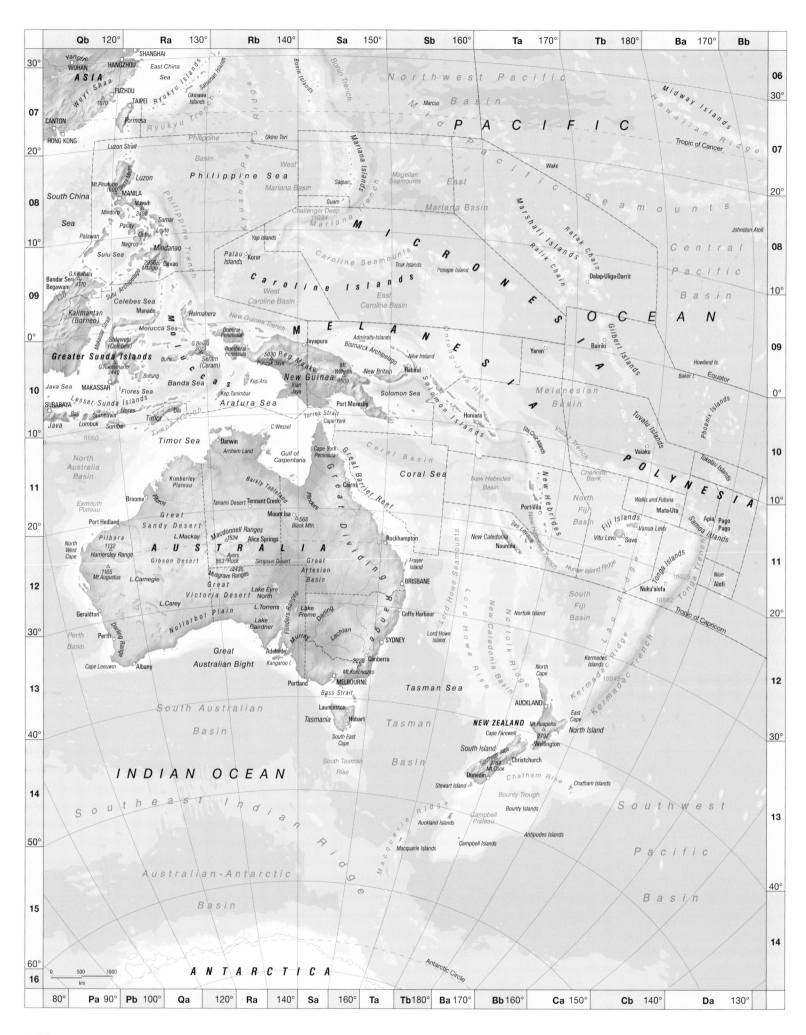

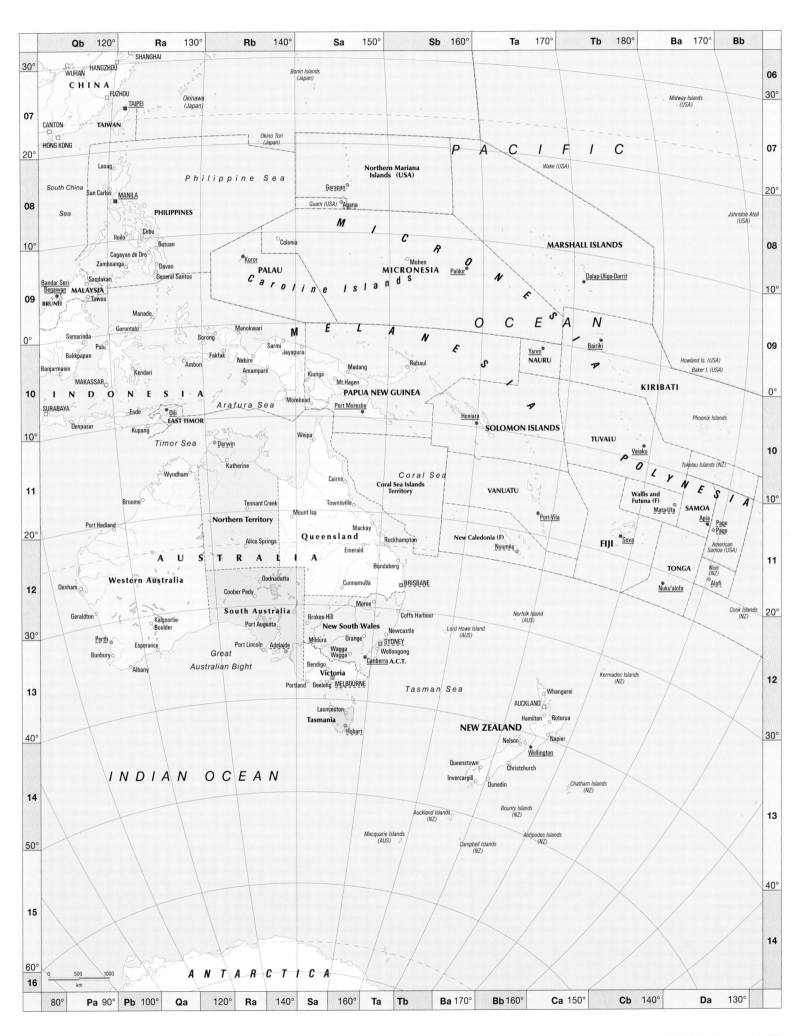

The History of Australia and Oceania

The fifth continent and the Pacific islands were discovered in the sixteenth century by European seafarers, but this remote region did not interest the colonial powers for long. It was not until the late eighteenth century that the

Polynesia: carving of the god Tiki on the Marquesas Islands.

British began to use Australia as a prison colony. At the start of the nineteenth century, Australia and New Zealand became independent, but other regions of Oceania remained under European rule. Japanese expansion before and during World War II was a great threat to this dominance. After 1945, US influence increased, and the region was now regarded as part of its sphere of interest. It was only relatively recently that many of the islands were able to assert their independence. The native peoples and their cultures had been almost completely suppressed. Only since the mid-twentieth century has the attitude of the descendants of settlers changed towards the native populations.

*Ancient rituals are still performed by the Maoris, the indigenous people, in the village of **Whakarewarewa** in the region of Rotorua on New Zealand's North Island. Since the 1980s, movements to revive Maori culture have been in the ascendant.*

Australia

As the remotest part of the world, from the European point of view, Australia was for a long time unknown to the West, but from the late Middle Ages it played an important theoretical role, since the existence was assumed of a so-called southland, terra australis incognita, as a counterpart to the northern land mass. Admittedly Spaniards and Portuguese reached the area as early as the sixteenth century, but it was not until later that the continent was recognised as a contiguous land mass.

The Aborigines, the original inhabitants of Australia, settled the continent some 60,000 years ago, and presumably it was before the arrival of the Europeans that they began to make contacts with traders from present-day Indonesia and New Guinea. They lived as hunter-gatherers and developed a complex social structure as well as a complicated mythological world of the imagination which encompassed all areas of life.

History of discovery

From the fifteenth century onwards, the Portuguese engaged in a flourishing trade with India from the west coast of Africa, which strengthened interest in the discovery of the legendary terra australis. Enthusiasm for pushing further south-east soon waned, however, since wind conditions were not conducive to voyages of reconnaissance. After the discovery of the Solomon Islands in 1567 the Spaniards hoped to take possession of gold and great territories for the Spanish crown by means of two expeditions from South America, in 1595 and 1605, but these two voyages of discovery ended in failure.

The real story of exploration first begins with the Dutch. In 1606, Willem Janzon reached the Torres Straits between the Australian mainland and New Guinea, and sighted the north coast of Australia. The Dutch governor-generals in Batavia equipped further expeditions, and in 1616 Europeans first trod on Australian soil, under the command of Dirk Hartog. Further discoveries followed, in which Abel Janzoon Tasman played the most important role. In 1642 he circumnavigated

Australia, discovering Tasmania and New Zealand in the process. On a second voyage, in 1644, he explored the north coast. Although the newly discovered land was called New Holland, the Dutch made no territorial claims to it, and soon stopped visiting the new continent.

The first British voyages of discovery proceeded in a similar manner. The descriptions by the English pirate William Dampier, who explored the west coast on two expeditions in the early eighteenth century, failed to arouse the interest of the British in further voyages. It was only the three journeys of James Cook that led to British claims to the continent. In 1770, Cook discovered Botany Bay

early nineteenth century that the Australian coasts were completely explored. Between 1801 and 1803 Matthew Flinders circumnavigated the entire continent for the first time, having first proved in 1798 with the help of the naval doctor George Bass that Tasmania was an island. At Flinders' suggestion, the continent was officially named Australia in 1817, as an allusion to the long-sought terra australis.

Colonisation

In spite of Australia's supposed unattractiveness, towards the end of the eighteenth century the country acquired a new and special socio-economic, significance for the British. After Britain's de-

James Cook claimed Australia and New Zealand for Great Britain.

and took possession of the area for the British crown at Possession Island, naming it New South Wales. His second voyage, in 1772–1775, destroyed the notions of a southland and finally provided evidence of an island continent. Also in 1772, the French made an appearance, when Marion Dufresne prepared maps and other French navigators explored the south coast. No one was prepared to challenge British supremacy, but it was not until the

feat in the American War of Independence it was no longer possible to transport convicts from the mother country's overcrowded prisons. So the plan was conceived in 1786 to build a penal colony at Botany Bay. In early 1788, Arthur Phillip arrived in Botany Bay with a first group of convicts, and on 26 January he founded – somewhat further north, the first permanent European settlement – Sydney. By 1867, prisoners had continued to be deported to Australia,

forming the driving force of the early settlement. By 1852, as many as 150,000 people had been deported to New South Wales and the colony of Tasmania that had been founded in 1803. But from 1793, the first voluntary settlers began to arrive, creating the basis of the Australian economy by sheep-rearing. The conquest of the Blue Mountains by Gregory Blaxland and William Charles Wentworth, as well as the further opening up of the interior, now allowed large herds of cattle to be kept on extended areas of grazing land.

Around 1820, stock-breeder pushed forward into Victoria and southern Queensland; the penal colony of Western Australia was founded in 1829, and South Australia in 1837. In 1851, the colony of Victoria, with its capital, Melbourne, split off from New South Wales and, in 1859, Queensland also separated from New South Wales. A gold rush in the mid-nineteenth century ensured a further great influx of immigrants.

The conflicts of interest between stock-breeder and farmers, as well as the liberal socialist views of the new urban population triggered the development of political institutions in the mid-nineteenth century. Free trade was introduced and the eastern colonies were granted new constitutions in 1850, which allowed them extensive self-determination and self-government. Free gifts of land were replaced by the regular sale of property, and governments had to answer to elected parliaments. In formal terms British colonial policy regarded the Aborigines as equals, but in practice the sheep-farmers conducted an inhumane and brutal campaign against the natives. The few survivors were finally herded together in reservations. It was not until the mid-twentieth century that the indigenous population of Australia was able to regain its original size.

The federated state

The rapid increase in population and the rapid growth of the cities led in the mid-nineteenth century to the formation of an individual Australian culture, the foundation of universities, the building of railways and a strengthening of the workers' movement. In spite of the cultural similarities between

the six colonies, their relationship was marked by fierce rivalry. The Labour Party, in particular, pursued a resolute policy of national union. The positive outcomes of referenda in all six colonies finally led to the creation of the Commonwealth of Australia, which was confirmed by the British parliament in 1900 and came into force on 1 January 1901. The new constitution consisted of a mixture of British and American elements. In order to strengthen the concept of federation, in 1908, the capital was moved from Melbourne to the newly founded Canberra. Even before the start of World War I, comprehensive social welfare legislation and general conscription were introduced.

In World War I, Australia sent about 330,000 volunteers to fight on the Allied side in the European theatres of war and confront the German colonial troops in the Pacific. In 1919, Australia received a mandate from the League of Nations to govern the former German overseas territories of Kaiser-Wilhelmsland (now part of Papua New Guinea), the Bismarck Archipelago, the Solomon Islands and Nauru.

The outbreak of World War II meant cutting the cord that connected Australia to the mother country. Since Britain was not able to protect Australia effectively against the threat of Japanese invasion, a military alliance was concluded with the USA. This did not prevent the Australians from fighting bravely in all the theatres of war, but especially against the Japanese. Fortunately, the Australian forces were able to prevent a Japanese invasion of Australia. Australia also performed a valuable role during and after World War II in supply Great Britain with desperately needed food supplies.

After 1945, the country was transformed into a highly industrialised nation of growing importance in terms of foreign policy. Emotional attachment to the British Crown continued to dwindle, even though the 'White Australia Policy', banning non-white immigration despite the fact that the country was, and still is, underpopulated, was not officially abandoned until 1973. Immigrants to Australia are still predominantly of British and Irish

*In 1808, a settlement of white colonists was discovered on **Pitcairn Island** in the South Pacific. It had been founded by the nine mutineers of the famous HMS Bounty, along with six men and twelve women from modern-day Tahiti. John Adams, the last mutineer, died in 1829, and his gravestone can still be seen. The small colony was later annexed by Great Britain. The mutiny against the infamous Captain William Bligh in 1789 has been the subject of several novels and three films.*

origin, with a substantial number from Italy, Greece, Cyprus.

New Zealand

When, in 1642, the Dutch seafarer Tasman became the first European to reach the west coast of the south island, New Zealand had some 125,000 inhabitants, who had immigrated from Polynesia from the ninth century onwards. In 1769, James Cook realised that it consisted of two islands, and claimed them for the British crown. Soon afterwards, British missionaries and whalers founded the first settlements, and systematic immigration began around 1840 under the auspices of the New Zealand Company.

In 1840, in the Waitangi Agreement with more than 550 Maori chieftains, Captain William Hobson secured British sovereignty and in return granted the Maoris rights of possession and British citizenship. In 1841, New Zealand became a British Crown Colony with Auckland as its capital.

High levels of immigration led in 1845–1848 and 1860–1872 to armed conflict between settlers and the Maori population, the latter being decimated in the battles. Gold-mining and sheep-breeding formed the main sources of income and ensured a steady influx of immigrants. In 1852 a first constitution was adopted, and in 1893 New Zealand became the first country in the world to introduce women's suffrage. In 1907, New Zealand was officially declared a dominion in the British Commonwealth.

In the 1970s, under a Labour government, the country ended its military involvement in Indochina and intensified its contacts with its Asian neighbours.

The main concern of post-war home affairs was relations with the Maoris, to whom 50,000 ha of land, unlawfully taken from them, were restored. In addition, programmes for the preservation of the art and culture of the Maoris have been set up.

Oceania

Most of the Pacific islands, after being discovered by white settlers, were subjected to frequent changes in foreign rule, which ended comparatively recently.

Palau, for example, became a presidential republic in 1947, with strong connections to the USA. Papua New Guinea was an Australian mandated territory until 1975. Since 1980, Micronesia and the Marshall Islands since 1990 have both been a republic with a Compact of Free Association with the USA. Nauru was liberated in 1968 from the trusteeship of the UN, and Kiribati from British rule in 1979. In 1978, the British Protectorate over the Solomon Islands and Tuvalu came to an end. Fiji declared independence in 1979, as did Vanuatu in 1980, Samoa in 1962, Tonga in 1970 and Palau in 1994.

1 The Sydney Opera House – designed by the architect Jörn Utzon – one of the city's tourist highlights, along with an accurate reconstruction of the legendary 'Bounty'.

2 Melbourne, the capital city from 1901 to 1911, has a population of just under three million, making it the second largest city in Australia. It is situated at the mouth of the Yarra river in Port Phillip Bay.

3 The Parliament building in the Australian capital city of Canberra was completed in 1988, a striking example of modern Australian architecture.

Main photograph:
The Caroline Islands are the largest
island group in Micronesia and consist of
963 islands and atolls, mostly of volcanic
origin. Archaeological finds indicate
early settlements.

The Countries of Australia and Oceania

Australia is the smallest continent and lies between the Indian and Pacific Oceans, entirely in the southern hemisphere. The continent is often considered to include the islands of Oceania, which are scattered over an area of

Australia: Sidney Harbour Bridge a famous landmark on the skyline.

70 million sq. km. The Australian mainland is one of uniform terrain, mainly consisting of desert, including the ancient dried-up sea in what is known as the Centre. The continent's isolated position means that it has developed unique flora and fauna, many of which have been endangered by species imported from Europe. New Zealand, on the other hand, has a hugely varied landscape, reminiscent of almost every type of European landscape. Before the arrival of the Europeans, the bird life was varied but there were no land mammals. Oceania consists of some 10,000 coral atolls or islands of volcanic origin. The climate is hot and humid.

Australia

	Australia
Area:	7,686,850 sq. km
Capital city:	Canberra

Form of government:
Parliamentary Monarchy and Federal State

Administrative divisions:
6 states, 2 territories

External territories:
Christmas Island, Cocos Islands, Norfolk Island, Lord Howe Island, Coral Sea Islands Territory, Ashmore and Cartier Islands, Heard Island, McDonald Islands

Population:
20.1 million
(2.6 inhabitants/sq. km)

Languages:
English, minority languages

GDP per capita:	US$32,000

Currency:
1 Australian dollar = 100 cents

Natural Geography

Australia is the smallest continent and the world's sixth largest country in terms of area. It measures 3,680 km from north to south, and 4,000 km from east to west. The average elevation is 300 m, and the land is approximately 70 per cent desert or semi-desert, mainly in the west and centre of the country. These regions are covered in arid grassland and are largely uninhabited. The populated areas are concentrated in the south and southeast coastal regions, which have a milder climate. Western Australia is dominated by a plateau, which includes the **Great Sandy Desert**, the **Gibson Desert** and the **Great Victoria Desert**. This tableland also contains several monadnocks, for example the famous **Uluru** (Ayers Rock), a 600 million-year-old monolith.

The central Australian basin is an arid region devoid of rivers which extends from the Gulf of Carpenteria in the north, through the Simpson Desert and as far as **Lake Eyre** (16 m below sea-level), a salt lake on the south coast and the lowest point on the continent. Hundreds more salt lakes of varying sizes can be found on the **Nullarbor Plain** in the southern part of the **Great Victoria Desert**.

The **Great Dividing Range** runs parallel to the east coast for a total distance of some 3000 km, and joins the foothills of the **Snowy Mountains** in the south. The **Great Barrier Reef** is located in Australian waters just off the mainland, and stretches 2,000 km, connecting in the north to the Torres Strait Islands. This is the largest coral reef on Earth, and with 1,500 varieties of fish, 400 different corals and more than 4,000 species of molluscs, it is also has the greatest variety of sea life.

The north of the country is only sparsely populated. It has tropical vegetation and grass savannahs, which towards the coast turn into mangrove swamps and rainforests. There are few significant water courses, those that there are include the Murray and Darling Rivers in the south. The interior of the country is extremely dry and most of the larger lakes are usually dry except after periods of heavy rainfall.

South-east of the mainland, separated by the Bass Strait, lies the island of **Tasmania** (67,800 sq. km), which has large areas of cool rainforest in the south-west. One fifth of this sparsely inhabited, mountainous island (highest point: Mount Ossa 1,617 m) is a nature conservation area.

Australia's unique plant and animal kingdoms have developed as a result of almost 50 million years of isolated evolution. All native Australian mammals are **marsupials**, of which there are a total of 300 species, including 60 different species of kangaroo. Other animals characteristic of the country include the koala and the emu. Australia also has large numbers of insects (such as compass termites), reptiles (including freshwater and saltwater crocodiles) and the birds range from parrots, cockatoos, and budgerigar. There are some very odd animal species, for example the egglaying duck-billed platypus and the Tasmanian devil. The country is also home to a many poisonous spiders and snakes. Almost all the trees are eucalyptus, Australia contains some 95 per cent of this tree variety.

Climate

In general, Australia has a desert to semi-desert climate. In the south and east of the country, the climate is more maritime, while the extreme north has a tropical climate with heavy rainfall. The precipitation declines rapidly inland from the coast, where it averages more than 1,400 mm per annum. Storms can be extremely powerful and torrential, particularly in the north and north-west of the country where the rainy season lasts from November to the end of March. Average maximum temperatures in central Australia around the Tropic of Capricorn can rise to over 50°C. In the region around Canberra, winter temperatures can fall to 2°C, and maximum summer temperatures can be over 40°C.

The damage to the ozone layer over large areas of the Antarctic is a serious environmental problem, the effects of which can be felt in Australia and New Zealand in terms of high ultra-violet radiation and increased **risk of skin cancer.** Bush fires, droughts, heavy storms and flash-floods are relatively common.

Population

92 per cent of Australians are of European descent, of which the majority have **British** and **Irish** heritage. Of the remaining population, seven per cent are of **Asian** origin, while the **Aborigines** and the even smaller group of Torres Strait Islanders have minority status, making up just one per cent of the population.

75 per cent of Australians are Christians, but there are also minorities of Jews, Muslims, Buddhists and Hindus. Just under half the total population lives in one of the three big cities, Sydney, Melbourne and Brisbane, while large areas of the country are uninhabited. Australia's population density of 2.6 inhabitants/sq. km is one of the lowest on Earth. The numerous outlying farms and homesteads are located relatively close to the few main longdistance roads which cross-cross the continent.

The standard of living is high, and the social and health systems are highly developed. The education system is also very well organised, and many children, particularly in the outback, receive longdistance lessons via the radio. There are several **universities**, the most famous being in Melbourne, Sydney and Canberra.

The unique culture of Australia's indigenous people remains threatened, but attempts are being made to integrate the native people into mainstream Australian life.

Melbourne: modern skyscrapers behind the Victorian Flinders Street Station on the banks of the Yarra.

History and Politics

More than 50,000 years ago, a land bridge existed between Asia and Australia, and there were many waves of migration from Asia to the large island continent. Divided into several clans, they wandered in complete isolation, mainly across the northern areas, around the coasts of Australia and Tasmania.

From the Middle Ages onwards, European scholars speculated about a legendary 'unknown land of the south', the **Terra Australis Incognita**, which they thought must exist in the southern hemisphere. The Dutch sailor Willem Janszoon was the first European to find the continent in 1606, when he spied Australia's

north coast. Fellow Dutchman Abel Tasman circumnavigated the continent and explored the coast of an unknown island that he named 'Van Diemen's Land' in 1642 and 1644. This was the island now known as Tasmania, later renamed in his honour. In 1770, Captain James Cook took possession of New South Wales for Great Britain. The British first used the continent as a **penal colony**. The first British settlers landed in Botany Bay in 1788 and founded Port Jackson, the heart of modern-day **Sydney**. Other cities which originated as penal colonies include Newcastle (founded in 1804) and Brisbane (1824). The first free British

settlers appeared in 1793 and founded Perth (1829), Melbourne (1835) and Adelaide (1836). From 1788 to 1865, Great Britain deported 160,000 prisoners to the continent, which was renamed Australia in 1817 after the name was popularised by Matthew Flinders, the British

explorer who circumnavigated and explored the continent. From 1851 to 1859, the first **gold rush** attracted a great wave of migration, laying the foundations of the six modern states, which fought for a greater measure of autonomy. In 1901, the six British colonies united to form the **Commonwealth of Australia,** a dominion of the British Empire. At this time, 3.8 million Australians lived in the country, and were almost exclusively of British and Irish origin. In 1927, Parliament moved to the newly established

Australia

Large **trucks** for a large country. Australia's road network runs for 913,000 km and massive lorries, like these on Stuart Highway in the Northern Territory, transport goods across long distances around the country.

capital city of **Canberra**, although Australia did not become officially independent until 1942. Since the end of World War II, Australia's population has doubled as people from a total of 120 countries have made a new home there.

The **native inhabitants** (Aborigines) of Australia have only been recognised as equal citizens and have only had citizenship and the right to vote since 1967. Their numbers plummeted in the first 100 years of European settlement from around 700,000 to just 70,000, and in the 1930s they all but disappeared. In recent years, the tribes have gradually received compensation for the denial of their traditional land rights, and have also received the right of free access to their holy places, distributed throughout the continent. Finally, in 1992 the High Court of Australia, in the so-called **'Mabo Ruling', determined** that Australia had not been an 'uninhabited land' (Terra nullius) when Great Britain had taken it over.

The Australian constitution that came into effect in 1901 provides for a **bicameral federal parliament**, consisting of the Senate (76 seats, 12 from each of the six states and two from each territory, half of which are elected every three years) and the House of Representatives (148 members, elected every three years). In addition, the six federal states and the two territories have their own parliaments.

The British monarch remains Australia's head of state and is represented by the governor-general, and the governor of each of the states. For several years, there have been discussions about a possible referendum to change Australia into a **republic**.

Australia cooperates with the US and New Zealand armed forces under the ANZUS Security Treaty of 1951.

Lord Howe Island in the south Pacific and Macquarie Island, which along with some neighbouring islands belong to the Antarctic territory of Tasmania, are also part of Australian national territory. Other territories belonging to Australia include the Ashmore and Cartier Islands, which are completely protected and upon which it is forbidden to land, Christmas Island and the Cocos (Keeling) Islands in the Indian Ocean, the Coral Sea Islands and Torres Strait Islands, the uninhabited Heard Island, which is a UNESCO World Heritage Site, the McDonald Islands in the south Pacific and Norfolk Island.

Economy

The whole country is rich in natural resources. It produces significant amounts of agricultural produce, minerals, metals and fossil fuels, and is one of the **biggest exporting nations in the world**. The most important exports are natural gas and crude oil, coal, iron ore, uranium, nickel, gold, silver, zinc, copper, sapphires and opals. Australia is the biggest exporter of bauxite, lead and uncut diamonds for industrial use.

Australia produces has the largest number of **sheep** in the world and produces the most wool. The country is also the largest exporter of beef in the world and is a major producer of dairy foods and cereals. Sugar cane, fruit, cotton and vines are also cultivated. The **manufacturing sector** is diversifying a great deal and employs 25 per cent of the working population. This sector contributes approximately 31 per cent of GDP and produces foodstuffs, tobacco, machinery, high-tech and computer equipment, cars and chemicals. The greatest contributor to GDP is the services sector (65 per cent), including the tourist sector, which employs 70 per cent of the working population.

Transport Infrastructure

Australia's **rail network** covers 38,563 km, of which 2,914 km is electrified. The rail network is concentrated in the southern part of the country. Although Australia has six rail companies, large areas of central and northern Australia have no rail service.

The **road network** has a total length of some 913,000 km, one third of which is surfaced. Large parts of the country can only be accessed by poorly maintained trails and tracks. During the rainy season in the north, many of these tracks are impassable. Australia's car ownership is 604 cars per 1,000 inhabitants, making it one of the most motorised countries in the world.

Despite 8,368 km of waterways, mainly in the south-east, **inland navigation** is of minimal importance, because most stretches of river are only navigable for small, flat craft. Australia has a **merchant fleet** of more than 600 ships, and more than 60 industrial **ports**, the most important of which are Adelaide, Brisbane, Cairns, Darwin, Fremantle, Geelong, Mackay, Melbourne and Sydney. The Tasmanian ports of Hobart, Devonport and Launceston are also significant.

Air travel is of great importance, operating from more than 400 airports and partially unsurfaced runways. Australia has nine international airports.

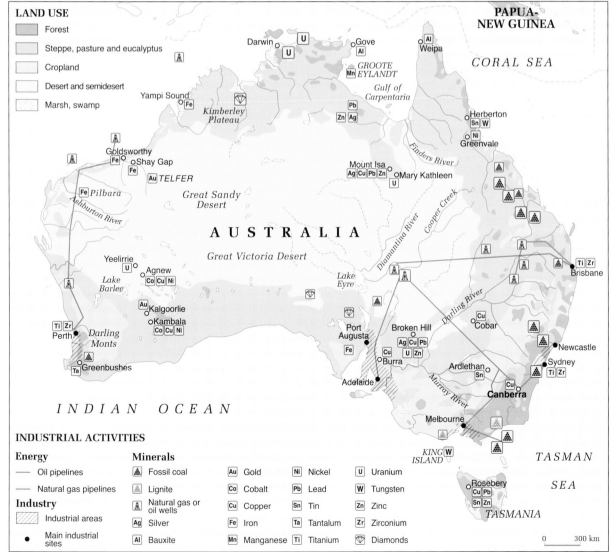

LAND USE

- Forest
- Steppe, pasture and eucalyptus
- Cropland
- Desert and semidesert
- Marsh, swamp

INDUSTRIAL ACTIVITIES

Energy
- —— Oil pipelines
- —— Natural gas pipelines

Industry
- Industrial areas
- ● Main industrial sites

Minerals

⬚ Fossil coal	Au Gold	Ni Nickel	U Uranium
⬚ Lignite	Co Cobalt	Pb Lead	W Tungsten
⬚ Natural gas or oil wells	Cu Copper	Sn Tin	Zn Zinc
Ag Silver	Fe Iron	Ta Tantalum	Zr Zirconium
Al Bauxite	Mn Manganese	Ti Titanium	Diamonds

PAPUA-NEW GUINEA

CORAL SEA

AUSTRALIA

INDIAN OCEAN

TASMAN SEA

TASMANIA

0   300 km

Australia is the world's largest producer and exporter of **wool**. When Europeans first settled there, they brought large numbers of Merino sheep, and sheep-farming quickly became a major occupation. Since then, the importance of wool has decreased. Today, wool exports contribute eight per cent of the total volume of exported goods, compared to 25 per cent 30 years ago. Almost half the wool comes from New South Wales and Western Australia.

Tourism

Millions of tourists visit Australia each year. The country has an amazing wealth of attractions, including endless sandy beaches, unparalleled natural beauty and great cities.

The focal point of the Northern Territory is the regional capital of Darwin. The city is a transport hub for flights to south-east Asia. The **Kakadu National Park** in Arnhem Land is one of Australia's greatest attractions. The cliff landscape contains indigenous cliff drawings which are thousands of years old. the landscape changes towards the coast to become a wetland full of natural wonders. The swamps contain rare plant and animal species. Uluru National Park lies in the south deep in the Outback. This is where the famous **Ayers Rock** and the **Olga Mountains**, called Kata Tjuta by the native inhabitants, are located. These are two of the most important holy sites for the Aborigines.

The densely populated coastal areas on the east coast are great centres for **watersports**. Brisbane is the capital of Queensland. The **Great Barrier Reef**, a chain of some 2,500 coral reefs and 500 islands is one of the most spectacular scuba-diving locations on Earth. Other popular holiday islands include Hinchinbrook Island, Orpheus Island, Heron Island, Hamilton Island and Fraser Island, which at 135 km long, is the largest desert island in the world.

The coast is lined with large tracts of rainforest, for example the **Daintree National Park** and the **Mount Spec National Park**, much of which is protected. Australia's interior is best explored by taking the Matilda Highway, which extends 1,500 km through the outback.

The heart of the state of New South Wales is the buzzing metropolis of **Sydney,** with its 40 beaches, numerous museums and parks and the world-famous Opera House. The most popular recreation area is the **Blue Mountains**, whose seemingly unreal colour is actually caused by large numbers of silvery-blue eucalyptus trees. The **Capital Territory** is dominated by the capital city of **Canberra**, which contains the parliament and some interesting museums.

The centre of the southern state of Victoria is **Melbourne**, Australia's second largest city. In contrast to Sydney, Melbourne seems dignified and considers itself the continent's cultural centre. The city has several museums and spacious parks, as well as many theatres and hosts many festivals and sporting events.

Some of the most attractive winter sports locations are in the **Great Dividing Range** and include the region around Mount Kosciusko, the skiing areas around Beauty, Buffalo, Buller and the Baw Baw Mountains. The centre of the state of Southern

1 The Great Barrier Reef off the north coast of Australia is over 2,000 km long and comprises several islands and atolls, making it the largest coral reef on Earth.

2 The fascinating skyline of Sydney, the largest city in Australia, with modern skyscrapers, the spectacular Sydney Opera House and Sydney Harbour bridge, completed in 1932.

3 The Pinnacles are thousands of strange limestone pillars, up to 5 m high, rising out of the yellow sand in the Nambung National Park.

*Beneath the white lighthouse on **Cape Reinga** on New Zealand's North Island the Pacific Ocean joins the Tasman Sea. Maori mythology has it that the souls of the dead flee to this part of the far north.*

Australia is Adelaide, which has a cliff-lined coast and a famous **viticultural district**. **Flinders Range** is a popular hiking area. Australia's spectacular southern coasts have colonies of penguins. The nature conservation area of **Kangaroo Island** is home to several indigenous animal species, including kangaroos, emus and koalas. The island also has impressive sea-lion colonies. The whole western part of the state is covered by the Simpson Desert. The opal settlement of **Coober Pedy** in the middle of the outback is a truly unique wonder; due to the searing heat, all of the main buildings are located underground.

Perth is the regional capital of Australia's largest state, Western Australia, which occupies the entire western third of the country. The east is characterised by desert and semi-desert and is completely uninhabited. In the north lies the wood and bushland of **Kimberley Range**. The area contains interesting cliff formations, caves and gorges, especially the sandstone cone discovered in 1982 in **Purnululu (Bungle Bungle) National Park**, and known as Wave Rock, and the spectacular Pinnacles Desert in **Nambung National Park**. The 1,106-m-high **Mount Augustus**, Aus-

tralia's highest monolith, can be found in Hamersley Range.
The **Hamersley National Park** is popular with hikers. Eighty Mile Beach is an extension of the Great Sandy Desert and extends to the Indian Ocean.
The whole of the west coast is lined with salt marshes.
Hobart is the centre of **Tasmania**, and has a historic district that is well worth visiting. In addition to the great rainforest regions (giant ferns and eucalyptus trees up to 150 m high), which are accessible by trekking routes, Tasmania has many natural won-

ders, including limestone caves and waterfalls.
The most historic site is the ruins of the penal colony of Port Arthur which was abandoned in 1877.

New Zealand	
Area:	270,534 sq. km
Capital city:	Wellington
Form of government:	
Constitutional Monarchy in the Commonwealth	
Administrative divisions:	
90 counties, 3 municipalities	
External territories:	
Cook Islands, Niue, Tokelau	
Population: 4 million (14 inhabitants/sq. km)	
Languages: English, Maori	
GDP per capita: US$24,100	
Currency: 1 New Zealand dollar = 100 cents	

Natural Geography

New Zealand consists of two islands divided by the **Cook Strait**, which is just 38 km wide at its narrowest point. The islands are located 1,500 km south-east of Australia in the south-west Pacific. The Indo-Australian and Pacific plates join beneath the islands, and are defined by a chain of mountains.
The **North Island** has active volcanoes and large thermal areas with geysers and powerful hot springs. The island is also frequently affected by earthquakes.
The South Island of New Zealand is dominated by the New Zealand Alps, a 300-km-long mountain chain which runs along the west coast. The mountains are very rugged in places. The highest point, at 3,764 m, is Mount Cook. The mountains descend steeply towards the west coast, but in the east they flatten out to form extensive wide plains.
The Fiordland in the south-west contains a vast, inaccessible primeval forest. **Milford Sound,** one of the most beautiful fjords in the world, is in this area.
Stewart Island in the **Antarctica** is a little-explored, wooded island 1,746 sq. km in area which is also part of New Zealand's national territory. New Zealand has further external territories in the south Pacific, namely the 15 Cook Islands, Niue (which is self-gov-

erned), the Chatham Islands, Tokelau (independent), the Kermadec Islands. Other islands, the Antipodes Islands, the Auckland Islands, Campbell Island and the Bounty Islands, are uninhabited.

Climate

Average temperatures in Wellington in January are 19°C. In the winter month of July they fall to an average of 10°C. Only the south-east of the country and the interior of the South Island get significant winter snowfalls. The prevailing wind is normally from the west, and rainfall is heaviest in the west of the South Island.
The country was originally covered in dense primeval forest, but since the nineteenth century, much of this has been turned into grazing land. New Zealand has **unique fauna,** including a large variety of indigenous bird and animal species, some of which are endangered. The hole in the ozone layer over the Antarctica has caused excess exposure to UV rays. Adults and especially children wear protection on the heads and necks when outdoors in summer.

Population

The population consists up to 78 per cent **European settlers** and their descendants. The proportion of **Maoris** is about ten per cent. New Zealand is a popular **country of immigration**, and Asians and Pacific Islanders make up a further 12 per cent of the population. One in four New Zealanders lives in Auckland. The population density on the North Island is 24 inhabitants/sq. km in comparison to four inhabitants/sq. km on the South Island.
New Zealand's social and health systems are exemplary. The education system is heavily based on the British model, and is also very good. The country has seven **universities** and 25 institutions of higher education.

History and Politics

The islands were settled by the Maori in the ninth century, and were discovered by Europeans in 1642. Exploration by James Cook during the period 1769/1777 prepared the way for settlement, which began in 1792. Under the

Map labels

180°
Raoul I.
Macauley I.
30°
Curtis I.
L'Esperance Rock
Kermadec Islands (New Zealand)

Three Kings Is.
North Cape
175°
Great Exhibition Bay
35°
Awanui
Kawakawa
Omapere
Whangarei
Great Barrier I.
Takapuna
Coromandel Pen.
AUCKLAND
North Island
Hamilton
Tauranga
Bay of Plenty
Te Araroa
East Cape
North Taranaki Bight
Rotorua
Opotiki
1752
Gisborne
170°
New Plymouth
Taupo
L.Taupo
TONGARIRO N.P.
Mt.Taranaki 2518
Mt.Ruapehu 2797
Napier
Hawke Bay
Hawera
Wanganui
Hastings
40°
C.Farewell
South Taranaki Bight
Palmerston North
40°
Tasman Bay
Nelson Picton
Lower Hutt
Westport
1762
Blenheim
Wellington
C.Foulwind
Greymouth
Kaikoura
NEW ZEALAND
Harihari
Mt.Cook 3764
Waipara
Pegasus Bay
MT. COOK N.P.
Christchurch
Haast
Banks Peninsula
Mt.Aspiring 3027
Ashburton
Canterbury Bight
Chatham Islands (New Zealand)
175°
Milford Sound
Cromwell
Timaru
Chatham I.
Milford Sound
Queenstown
Oamaru
South Island
Pitt I.
L.Te Anau
FIORDLAND N.P.
Te Anau
Gore
45°
Resolution I.
Dunedin
45°
Invercargill
Balclutha
175°
Foveaux Strait
Halfmoon Bay
Stewart I.
0 125 250
km
Bounty Islands (New Zealand)
Snares Islands (New Zealand)
Antipodes Islands (New Zealand)
50°
Auckland Islands (New Zealand)
50°
165°
170°
180°
Tasman Sea
Southern Alps
PACIFIC OCEAN

*New Zealand was initially settled by the **Maoris,** who probably arrived from eastern or central Polynesia in around 900 AD They are famous for their elaborate facial and body tattoos. Sticking out the tongue is part of the war dance.*

Treaty of Waitangi, signed in 1840, the Maoris waived all sovereignty rights over the land, but this did not stop further land-grabbing by white settlers. In 1863, the Maoris were finally promised **land rights**, for which they are still fighting today. New Zealand was the first country in the world to introduce **women's suffrage**. The country became an independent dominion of the British Commonwealth in 1931. The **unicameral parliament**, whose members are elected for four-year terms, choose the prime minister. Five seats are reserved for Maori representatives. New Zealand's nominal head of state is the British monarch.

Economy

The **agricultural sector** is highly developed. Main products cultivated on the North Island are cereals and fruit. The South Island is dominated by sheep-rearing, and wool and milk production.

The **manufacturing sector** enjoys a similarly successful position. The main exports include electronics, chemicals and synthetics. Large areas of forest are also cleared for timber exports. Natural reserves, including coal, natural gas and iron shale, are mined in small quantities. Large economic potential lies in the **generation of power** from hydro-electric and thermal sources.

Transport Infrastructure

The **road network** covers 93,000 km, and bus travel is of great importance. There are ferry services between the two main islands, connecting the smaller islands to each other.

The domestic **flight network** is also very important and links most of the larger towns and cities. Flying has become almost the main form of transport for New Zealanders. There are international airports in Auckland, Wellington and Christchurch. The **international sea ports** are located in Auckland, Wellington, Christchurch and Dunedin.

Tourism

New Zealand has a unique and, in some places, a largely undisturbed natural kingdom. The

country is very unpolluted, and contains numerous natural wonders. Almost one quarter of the land area is protected of which ten per cent consists of the **124 national parks**. The Tongariro National Park was founded as far back as 1887 and is a popular skiing and hiking region in the shadow of the great extinct volcanoes.

The largest park is the Fjordland National Park on the South Island. Mount Cook National Park offers mountain and glacier tours. Abel Tasman National Park and on the Coromandel Peninsula has great beaches. **Queenstown** in the Alps is a major tourist centre. The most famous attraction is the thermal region around Rotorua.

1 One of the most impressive sights in Westland National Park in the south-west of New Zealand's South Island is the 13-km-long Fox Glacier.

2 Lawn bowls, played beneath an open sky, is a popular sport in New Zealand. Competitions are held throughout the country, as here in the spa and health resort of Rotorua.

3 New Zealand's landscape is extremely varied and is reminiscent of many parts of Europe. The country's scenery is often described as a 'miniature version of the Earth'.

Papua New Guinea, Palau, Micronesia, Marshall Islands

 Papua New Guinea

Area:	462,840 sq. km
Capital city:	Port Moresby

Form of government:
Constitutional Monarchy in the Commonwealth

Administrative divisions:
19 provinces, 1 district (capital city)

Population: 5.5 million
(11 inhabitants/sq. km)

Languages:
English (official), Melanesian Pidgin English, Motu, other Papuan languages

GDP per capita:	US$2,400
Currency:	1 kina = 100 toea

Natural Geography

The archipelago covers the eastern part of the Island of **New Guinea**, the **Bismarck Island group** and numerous smaller islands.

Climate

The wet, tropical climate has a year-round even temperature of roughly 27°C.

Population

The population consists mainly of **Melanesians**, but there are also **Papuan**, Micronesian and Polynesian minorities. Roughly 34 per cent of the population profess native religions, but the large majority are Christians.

History and Politics

The eastern part of New Guinea was annexed by Germany and Great Britain in 1884. After World War I, the land was ruled by Australia. Papua-New Guinea was finally granted its **independence** in 1975.

Economy

66 per cent of the population is engaged in **agriculture** The manufacturing sector concentrates on processing the country's rich **natural resources**.

Tourism

Beautiful island tropical beaches and national parks are the country's main attractions.

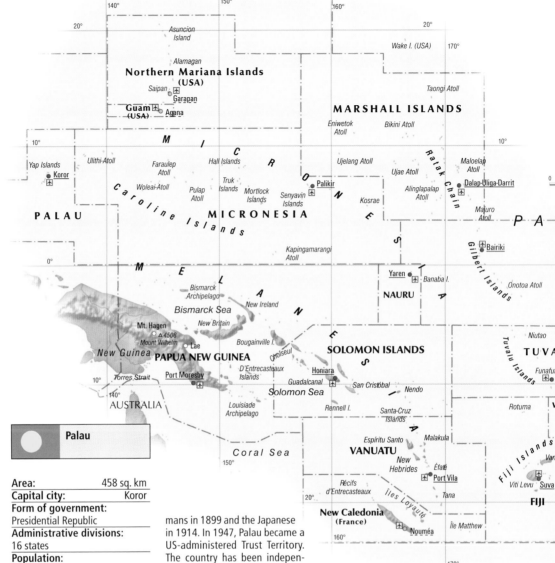

Palau

Area:	458 sq. km
Capital city:	Koror

Form of government:
Presidential Republic

Administrative divisions:
16 states

Population:
20,300 (38 inhabitants/sq. km)

Languages:
English, Palauan (both official), minority languages

GDP per capita:	US$9,000

Currency:
1 US dollar = 100 cents

Natural Geography

The 343 islands extend roughly in a line more than 200 km long in the south-west **Carolines**.

Climate

The country has a humid tropical climate, and temperatures remain in the region of 27°C year-round.

Population

The population is 84 per cent Palauan, with minorities of which the largest is **Filipino**. 33 per cent of the population profess the native religion, **Modekngei**, and 66 per cent are Christian.

History and Politics

The British controlled trade when the rich phosphate reserves attracted the interest of the Germans in 1899 and the Japanese in 1914. In 1947, Palau became a US-administered Trust Territory. The country has been independent since 1994.

Economy

Agriculture and manufacturing contribute 43 per cent of GDP. The service sector accounts for 57 per cent.

Tourism

The large number of coral islands are a great attraction for divers from around the world.

Federated States of Micronesia

Area:	702 sq. km
Capital city:	Kolonia

Form of government:
Federal Republic

Administrative divisions:
4 states

Population:
108,200 (168 inhabitants/sq. km)

Languages:
English (official), 9 Micronesian and Polynesian languages

GDP per capita:	US$2,000

Currency:
1 US dollar = 100 cents

Natural Geography

The islands are partly of volcanic origin and partly coral atolls.

Climate

The country has a hot and humid climate with high precipitation and frequent, heavy tropical cyclones. Year-round temperatures are about 25°C.

Population

The population consists of nine Micronesian and Polynesian ethnic groups, the majority of whom are Christian.

History and Politics

The islands were discovered in 1520/21 and were claimed by the Spanish for several centuries before Germany captured them in 1899. After World War I, they became part of the Japanese mandate, and after World War II, this role was taken over by the USA. Micronesia became independent in 1990.

Economy

Agriculture and **fishing** bring in just enough income to cover the country's needs. The granting of fishing licences is an important source of income. The manufacturing industry processes tuna, copra and foodstuffs for export. **Tourism** contributes significantly to the economy.

Tourism

The ruined cities of Lele in Kosrae and Nan Mandol in Pohnpei are the main attractions, along with scuba-diving.

 **Marshall Islands**

Area:	181 sq. km
Capital city:	Majuro
Form of government:	Republic

Administrative divisions:
24 districts

Population:
59,100 (311 inhabitants/sq. km)

*Due to the inaccessible landscape, many inhabitants of **Papua New Guinea** lived in complete isolation until the arrival of the Europeans. Although most of the indigenous inhabitants are today Christian, ancestor worship and occultism still play a large role. The 'Big Man' is an important political position, held only by men, which is indicated by striking body painting. The most important abilities are precise knowledge of the myths and eloquence.*

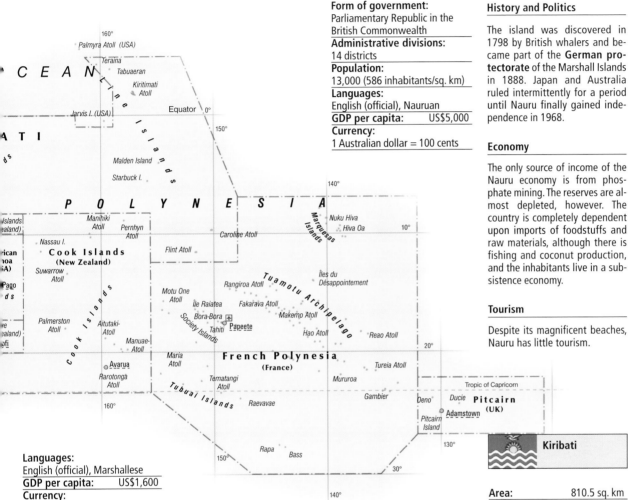

Form of government:
Parliamentary Republic in the British Commonwealth
Administrative divisions:
14 districts
Population:
13,000 (586 inhabitants/sq. km)
Languages:
English (official), Nauruan
GDP per capita: US$5,000
Currency:
1 Australian dollar = 100 cents

History and Politics

The island was discovered in 1798 by British whalers and became part of the **German protectorate** of the Marshall Islands in 1888. Japan and Australia ruled intermittently for a period until Nauru finally gained independence in 1968.

Economy

The only source of income of the Nauru economy is from phosphate mining. The reserves are almost depleted, however. The country is completely dependent upon imports of foodstuffs and raw materials, although there is fishing and coconut production, and the inhabitants live in a subsistence economy.

Tourism

Despite its magnificent beaches, Nauru has little tourism.

Population

The **Micronesian** population is 97 per cent Christian.

History and Politics

The island group was inhabited in prehistoric times, but was first discovered by Europeans in the nineteenth century. In 1892, the islands became part of a British protectorate along with the southern Ellice Islands, and were later part of the colony. After the detachment of the Ellice Islands in 1975, the territory became **independent** in 1979 it changed its name to Kiribati.

Economy

Since the country's **phosphate reserves** have been depleted, the economy has been based on coconuts for the export of copra; fishing licenses are also issued.

Tourism

The island of **Banaba** and the **Gilbert Island group** are the main tourist attractions.

Kiribati

Area: 810.5 sq. km
Capital city: Bairiki
Form of government:
Presidential Republic
Administrative divisions:
3 administrative regions and 6 districts
Population:
103,000 (121 inhabitants/sq. km)
Languages:
I-Kiribati, English (both official)
GDP per capita: US$800
Currency:
1 Australian/Kiribati dollar = 100 cents

Natural Geography

The national territory consists of 33 islands, distributed over an area of five million sq. km in the South Pacific Ocean.

Climate

The tropical climate means temperatures remain constant at 28°C. The weather is humid.

Solomon Islands

Area: 28,450 sq. km
Capital city: Honiara
Form of government:
Parliamentary Monarchy in a Commonwealth
Administrative divisions:
8 provinces, 1 district (capital city)
Population:
538,000 (18 inhabitants/sq. km)
Languages:
English (official), Pidgin English
GDP per capita: US$1,700
Currency: 1 Solomon Islands dollar = 100 cents

Natural Geography

The Solomon Islands are located in the western Pacific Ocean and form a double chain of islands, stretching over a distance of 1,450 km.

Climate

The tropical rainy climate and average year-round temperatures of

Languages:
English (official), Marshallese
GDP per capita: US$1,600
Currency:
1 US dollar = 100 cents

Natural Geography

The republic covers two atoll groups, each 1,200 km long.

Climate

The Marshall Islands have a humid and hot tropical climate. Temperatures remain constant all year round at about 25°C.

Population

Most of the Micronesian population is Christian Protestant.

History and Politics

The island group was discovered in 1529 and became a German protectorate in 1884. Japan assumed the protectorate in 1920. The UN Trust Territory mandate, administered by the USA, ended in 1980.

Economy

Coconuts, breadfruit, bananas, Taro and papaya are cultivated in a **subsistence economy**; livestock is also kept on the islands. The country has few natural resources; phosphate reserves are only mined on one atoll. The manufacturing sector processes coconut products and tuna for export. US support still forms the backbone of the economy.

Tourism

The island coral reefs provide some of the most spectacular scuba-diving experiences in the world.

Nauru

Area: 21.3 sq. km
Capital city: Yaren

Natural Geography

The small coral island is surrounded by a reef, that is exposed at low tide. A sandy beach circles the island, giving way to a strip of fertile land in the interior. The island's centre rises to a plateau 70 m high.

Climate

Nauru has a tropical climate with year-round stable temperatures of about 27°C. The rainy season lasts from November to February.

Population

The inhabitants, who speak Nauruan, are up to 60 per cent Nauruan, but there are also peoples from other Pacific islands and some immigrants from Australia, New Zealand and China.

Samoa: on the islands of the Samoan archipelago you can find what might be the oldest of the Polynesian cultures. The pre-colonial social system consisted of a complex network of family and social ties: the head of a family was also member of the village council, which in turn sent a representative to the regional council. In modern Samoa, many of the old customs and traditional structures have been retained.

27°C result in year-round precipitation, which is heaviest in the period from November to April.

Population

The islands are mainly inhabited by **Melanesians**, but there are also some **Micronesian** and **Polynesian** inhabitants. In addition to the official languages, roughly 120 different languages and dialects are spoken.

History and Politics

Discovered by Spanish seafarers in 1567, the Solomon Islands became a British protectorate in the late nineteenth century. During World War II, the Japanese occupied the islands. Great Britain gave the colony internal autonomy in 1976, and the islands became independent in 1978.

Economy

Agriculture and **dishing** generate a large share of the export income. **Forestry** is a further important source of revenue. The handicrafts made by the Solomon Islanders are a significant source of export income.

Tourism

Lagoons, waterfalls, excellent diving and sandy beaches are the main attractions for visitors. The tourist centre is the island of **Guadalcanal**.

Tuvalu	
Area:	26 sq. km
Capital city:	Vaiaku
Form of government:	
Constitutional Monarchy	
Administrative divisions:	
9 atolls	
Population:	
11,600 (423 inhabitants/sq. km)	
Languages: Tuvaluan, English	
GDP per capita:	US$1,100
Currency:	
1 Australian dollar = 100 cents	

Natural Geography

The island group consists of nine atolls and coral islands, dispersed over a distance of 560 km in the south-west Pacific. The islands are composed of coral limestone and many contain a central lagoon. Most of the islands are only a couple of metres above sea-level.

Climate

With an average year-round temperature of 29°C, the islands have tropical maritime climate.

Population

The population of the island group consists of up to 96 per cent **Polynesians,** with some Melanesians. It is almost entirely Protestant.

History and Politics

Great Britain established a Protectorate in 1892 and annexed the island group in 1916 as a crown colony. Even after gaining independence in 1978, the islands have remained a constitutional monarchy.

Economy

Tuvalu is one of the smallest countries in the world, but makes sufficient income from the export of copra and other coconut products, the issuing of fishing licenses and the sale of Tuvalu stamps to purchase foodstuffs, industrial and consumer goods. A drop in commodity prices and difficulties selling abroad have left the country dependent on development aid.

Tourism

Tuvalu is a paradise for scuba-divers and lovers of the south seas.

Vanuatu	
Area:	12,190 sq. km
Capital city:	Port Vila
Form of government:	
Republic in a Commonwealth	
Administrative divisions:	
6 provinces	
Population:	
205,000	
(16 inhabitants/sq. km)	
Languages:	
English, French, Bislama and	
Melanesian languages	
GDP per capita:	US$2,900
Currency:	
1 vatu = 100 centimes	

More than 90 per cent of Vanuatuans are Melanesian.

Natural Geography

The republic is located 2,000 km east of Australia and consists of 12 main islands and 70 smaller ones, spread over a distance of 800km from north to south. Vanuatu consists of coral atolls and volcanic islands (some of which are still active) rising abruptly out of the ocean.

Climate

With the exception of the southern islands of Eromanga and Aneityum, which are mainly dry, the islands have a tropical rainy climate with temperatures of 25°C.

Population

The majority of the population is **Melanesian,** but there are also **Micronesian**, **Asian** and **European** inhabitants. Approximately 80 per cent are Christian.

History and Politics

The island group, formerly known as the New Hebrides, has been inhabited for at least 3000 years, and was discovered by the Portuguese in 1606.
In 1906, Britain and France formed a joint administration. Vanuatu has been an independent **Republic** since 1980 and is a member of the Commonwealth. The constitution of 1980 provides for a parliament of 50 members, which is elected every four years.

Economy

Along with **fishing**, the most important contributor to the economy is **agriculture**, which employs 65 per cent of the working population. The services sector and tourism have been growing constantly in recent years.

Tourism

The attractive tropical and volcanic landscapes and the beaches are the main attractions of the well developed tourist industry, whose centres are in **Malakula** and **Pentecost**.

Fiji	
Area:	18,270 sq. km
Capital city:	Suva
Form of government: Republic	
Administrative divisions:	
4 districts; 14 provinces	
Population:	
893,400 (46 inhabitants/sq. km)	
Languages:	
English, Fijian (both official),	
Hindi	
GDP per capita:	US$6,000
Currency:	
1 Fijian dollar = 100 cents	

Natural Geography

This archipelago consists of more than 320 islands, some of which are atolls and some of which are of volcanic origin. Only 110 of the islands are inhabited.

Climate

The country has a mild, maritime tropical climate with an average temperatures of 27°C in January and 23°C in July.

Population

The population is half **Melanesian** and half **Indian**, as well as half Christian and half Hindu. There is also a minority of Muslims. The Indians were all brought to the island by the British as indentured labourers in the nineteenth and early twentieth centuries.

History and Politics

Fiji has signs of early Polynesian settlement, but the islands were discovered by Abel Tasman in 1643. Captain James Cook's visit prepared the ground for British colonisation, which began in 1874. After gaining its independence in 1970, the country remained part of the Commonwealth until 1987 when it proclaimed itself a **republic** after a military coup. A House of Representatives and a Senate, consisting mainly of members appointed by the Great Council of Chiefs, share the governing of the country.

Economy

The country has a **subsistence economy** which employs 67 per cent of the population. The sugar cane plantations and the fishing industry produce enough food for export. M**anufacturing** centres are sugar refineries, rice mills and clothing and leatherwear businesses. The extensive timber production is processed in the saw mills. Other sources of income are the mining of **gold** and **copper**. The services sector contributes around 61 per cent of GDP. Tourism is the largest source of income.

Tourism

The main destinations of the many tourists are the island resorts run by clubs, such as the **Mamanuca Islands** or the **Yasawa Islands**.

The modern-day inhabitants of **Polynesia** are not indigenous to the region, but instead moved there between 500 BC and 300 AD. Their exact origin is not known. The original social structures have been kept, and the family unit is the basis of a society with a noble class. Chiefs are selected by the elders in alternating succession. The family has a patriarchal and polygamous structure.

Samoa

Area:	2,944 sq. km
Capital city:	Apia
Form of government:	
Constitutional Monarchy	
Administrative divisions:	
11 districts	
Population:	
178,000 (62 inhabitants/sq. km)	
Languages:	
Samoan, English (both official)	
GDP per capita:	US$56,00
Currency: 1 tala = 100 sene	

Natural Geography

Samoa consists of the two larger islands Savai'i and Upolu and seven other smaller ones. They are all of volcanic origin. The island interiors are covered in rainforest, with surrounding coastal plains used for agriculture.

Climate

The country has an oceanic tropical climate with a cooler winter period from May to November (yearly average temperature: 27°C), year-round extensive periods of sunshine and short but heavy bursts of rain.

Population

The majority of the population is Protestant, and 99 per cent are indigenous **Polynesians**.

History and Politics

After early Polynesian settlement and discovery of the islands by the Dutch in 1721/1722, Samoa was in turn a British, German and American colony during the nineteenth century. After 1920, the island group came under the control of New Zealand, and became a UN-Trust Territory after World War II. The islands finally gained independence in 1961.

Economy

Roughly 80 to 90 per cent of the economic production is for the **subsistence economy.**

Tourism

Apart from the beaches and landscapes, a great attraction of the

most important archaeological findings in the Pacific area in **Letolo**.

Tonga

Area:	748 sq. km
Capital city:	Nuku'alofa
Form of government:	
Constitutional Monarchy within the Commonwealth	
Administrative divisions:	
5 areas	
Population:	
112,400 (144 inhabitants/sq. km)	
Languages:	
Tongan (official), English	
GDP per capita:	US$2,300
Currency: 1 pa'anga = 100 seniti	

Natural Geography

Tonga consists of a group of 172 islands in the South Pacific, which form two chains running from north to south. The islands to the west are mountainous and of volcanic origin, while those in the east are low coral islands.

Climate

With temperatures from 22°C to 26°C, Tonga has a tropical climate, influenced by the northwest trade winds. The rainy season lasts from December to April.

Population

The population of Tonga is very homogeneous, 98 per cent being indigenous **Polynesians.** The majority profess the Christian faith.

History and Politics

After Dutch and British expeditions in the seventeenth and eighteenth centuries, Tonga was converted to Christianity by British missionaries at the end of the eighteenth century. The islands were declared a British protectorate in 1900 and gained independence in 1970.

Economy

The country's economy is still based on **agriculture,** which employs half of the working population. Coconuts and bananas are the main export products.

Tourism

The island of **Lifuka** and the **Ha'apai** island group are the main tourist centres. Tonga is unspoiled as it has not been invaded by mass tourism or by holiday clubs as have some of the better-known Polynesian Islands. The beaches are the main attraction.

1 Kayangel Island in North Palau is an atoll of volcanic origin, 2 km wide and 6 km long, surrounded by white sandy beaches.

2 The Caroline Islands are an archipelago in the western Pacific consisting of 963 small islands and atolls. In 1994, Palau became an independent state, and the other islands have since become part of Micronesia.

3 The islands of Samoa are one of the last untouched paradises. To preserve their own identity, the tourist infrastructure is barely developed.

Africa

With an area of 304 million sq. km – roughly one fifth of the total surface of the Earth – and approximately 800 million inhabitants, Africa is the third largest continent, after Asia and America. It is dominated by the Sahara, the World's largest desert, the Kalahari desert, the river valleys of Chad, the Congo and the Zambezi. At 5,895 m, Mount Kilimanjaro is the continent's highest mountain, and Lake Victoria is Africa's largest lake. The world's longest river, the Nile, 6,671 km in length, flows south to north through Africa. Central Africa close to the equator is covered with hot and humid rain forests, bordered to the north and south first by broad savannahs, and desert areas in the lattitudes of the tropics of Cancer and Capricorn. Africa's rich wildlife is more or less confined to the extensive national parks.

Egypt has one of the oldest cultures in the world, and archaeological finds have shown that human life first emerged in sub-Saharan Africa.

Africa, physical

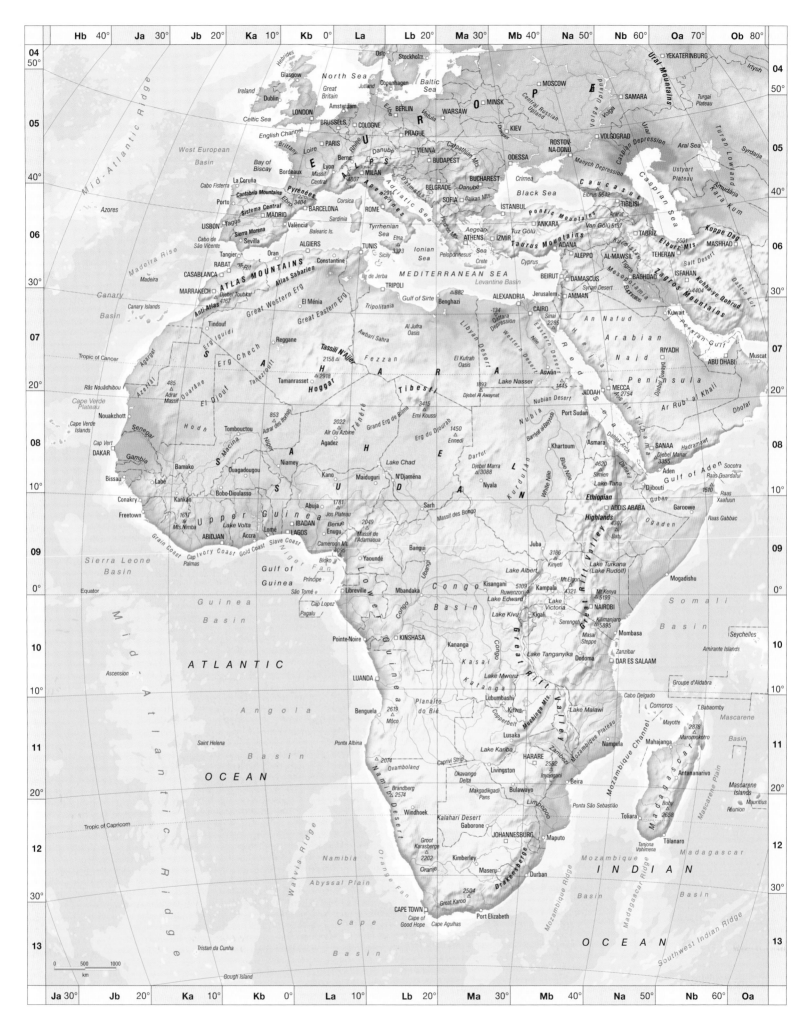

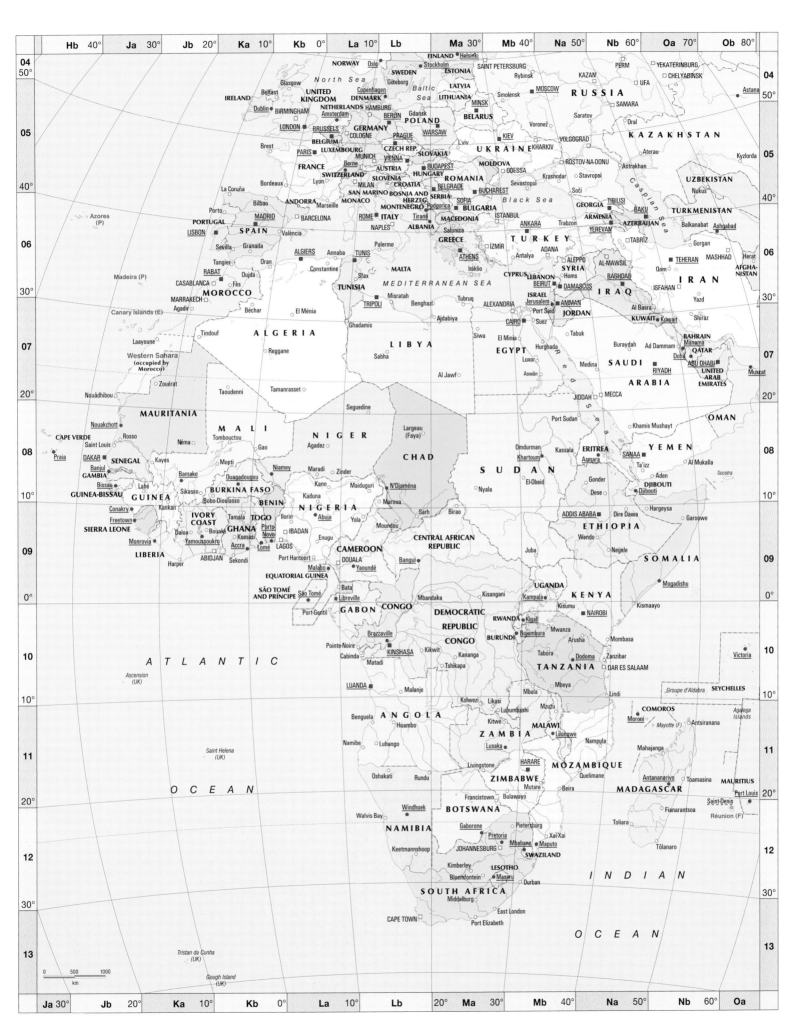

The History of Africa

The 'Dark Continent' is the cradle of mankind. It was from here that Homo sapiens spread out to settle the entire globe. One of the first great cultures developed in Egypt, but remains of other early civilisations have been discovered

The civil war in Liberia turned millions into refugees.

south of the Sahara, for example in Greater Zimbabwe. The south coast of the Mediterranean was inhabited in turn by the Phoenicians, Romans, Byzantines, Vandals and finally the Arabs, who spread Islam throughout large parts of Africa. The arrival of European explorers saw the beginning of the colonial period when most of Africa was under foreign domination. Colonialism was at its height in the nineteenth century, most African sovereign states only being established after World War II. Natural disasters, civil wars, epidemics and crop failures have also shaped the continent.

Early African History

*Sudan: Kushite Kings were buried in the pyramids at **Meroe**, the capital city of the Kingdom of Kush, in imitation of the ancient Egyptian practice. The golden age of this sub-Saharan civilisation lasted from about 300 BC to 350 AD.*

Early history

Homo sapiens is believed to have emerged in Africa more than 200,000 years ago. The species lived as hunter-gatherers, used simple stone tools and eventually spread throughout the continent as nomads or bushmen.

The growing population became differentiated into various races some 12,000 years ago, while the agrarian cultures pushed the nomads ever further into the more inhospitable regions. Bantu-speaking people came to dominate wide expanses of central and southern Africa. For the most part, the original population was organised into clans, but later great kingdoms came into being in western and central Africa.

North Africa

The first major civilisation emerged in ca. 5000 BC in the Nile delta, where the regular flooding of the river created the right conditions for an effective system of agriculture. For more than 4,000 years the Egyptian kingdom of the Pharaohs influenced world history. Its mining and smelting of iron and its forms of political organisation and administration spread to the tropical regions of Africa in the eighth century BC.

Ancient Egyptian history is divided into various kingdoms. The Old Kingdom lasted from 2755 to 2255 BC. It was during this period that the pyramids of Giza were built. These monuments are a testimony in stone to the unlimited power of the kings who ruled a well-organised theocratic state. After the collapse of the Old Kingdom, Egypt experienced a revival during the Middle Kingdom era, beginning with the twelfth dynasty in 1991 BC, but ending again with the thirteenth dynasty. Most ancient Egyptian buildings that still stand date from the New Kingdom, whose most important rulers were Sethos I and Ramses II. Impressive monuments, such as the temples of Karnak, Luxor and West Thebes, still stand. After the death of Ramses III the Egyptian kingdom fell into decline and came under the rule of various foreign monarchs including the Hyksos who devasted the country.

The foreign rule of the Persians from the twenty-eighth to the thirtieth dynasty was shaken off from time to time, but the kings of the third dynasty were the very last Egyptian Pharaohs. In 332 BC, Alexander the Great conquered Egypt and created Alexandria, named after himself, turning it into an intellectual and political capital. The last dynasty, that of the Ptolemies, ended with the defeat of Queen Cleopatra at the battle of Actium. From 30 BC to 395 CE the land of the Nile was a Roman province.

The Phoenicians set up trading posts along the Mediterranean

The Egyptian King Tutankhamun (1347–1339 BC) and his wife.

coast, which eventually developed into the mighty trading and naval power of Carthage. After the Third Punic War against the Carthaginians, the Romans gained a foothold in present-day Tunisia in 146 BC, which now became part of the Roman Empire as the province of Africa. By the first century BC they had conquered the whole of North Africa, and by the fourth century the regions west of what is now

Libya were added to the Western Roman Empire, while those to the east of it became part of the Eastern Roman Empire.

After the downfall of the Western Roman Empire in the fifth century, the Vandals, a Germanic tribe, became the dominant power on the Mediterranean coast, until they were ousted again by the Byzantines. Soon after the death of the Prophet Muhammad, in 642 AD the Arabs invaded Egypt and subsequently conquered Morocco. The population was converted to Islam, only the states of Alodia and Makuria in the Sudan were able to remain Christian for an-

other 600 years. Caravan trade through the Sahara led to the Islamisation of further parts of the continent; Muslim conquerors from the Yemen conquered Aksum, part of what is now Ethiopia, and founded Adal and Harar.

The triumphal progress of Islam seemed unstoppable and the conquest of the Iberian peninsula posed a serious threat to Christian Europe. The Mamelukes, who

conquered the Christian areas of the Sudan in the fourteenth century, became the ruling Muslim power. From the advent of the Ottoman Turks until Napoleon's Egyptian campaign in 1798 the Mamelukes ruled Egypt. In 1542, an initially successful attack on Christian Ethiopia by the Sultanate of Adal was beaten off with the assistance of Portugal.

The kingdoms of West Africa

Trade in slaves, gold, salt, cloth and household goods via the Sahara favoured the rise of larger kingdoms. The kingdom of Ghana was founded whose capital city was Kumbi Saleh zone was founded ca. 400 in what is now western Sudan. Until the eleventh century it controlled the trade routes between Morocco and the coastal forests of West Africa. The Arabs from the north became increasingly powerful, until the Almoravids, under Yusuf ibn Tashfin, gained supremacy in a Holy War in the late eleventh century. They were followed in the twelfth century by the Soso, who themselves were driven out in 1240 by the Mali people.

The kingdom of Mali was founded in the eleventh century by the Malinke and flourished in the fourteenth century under King Mansa Musa. This ruler is known to have made a pilgrimage to Mecca, Islam having been adopted earlier by the kingdom. After 1400, the Songhai empire followed that of Mali, reaching its zenith under Askia Mohammed. The capital city of Gao was conquered in 1591 by the troops of Al-Mansur from Morocco. The kingdoms that followed, Macina, Gonja Ségou and Kaarta, were unable to develop any lasting political and economic structures.

The city states of the Hausa, such as Biram, Daura, Katsina, Zaria Kano, Rano and Gobir, in the region between the river Niger and Lake Chad became powerful in the tenth century, due to shift in the great trading routes. North and east of Lake Chad, the kingdom of Kanem-Bornu established itself, continuing until 1846.

While Islam in West Africa was at first confined to the cities, the systematic advance of Islam began in the fifteenth century, and the ordinary population became

converted. The first to proselytise were the Kunta Arabs, followed in the sixteenth century by the Qadiriyyah order and later the Fulbe. In the early nineteenth century, the Hausa states were conquered by the Fulbe and theocracies ruled by a monarch, such as Macina, were founded.

The kingdoms of East Africa

Relatively little is known about the early history of East Africa. Bantu peoples settled in the interior, while the coastal regions were soon controlled by Arab traders, who in the thirteenth century founded the Zenj city states and traded in gold, slaves and ivory. Between Lake Victoria and Lake Edward some well-organised states emerged in the fourteenth century, under the rule of the Bachwezi. They lasted until about 1500, when they were conquered by invaders from the Sudan. Other states joined them, of which Bunyoro was the most important until the mid-eighteenth century, succeeded by Buganda.

The kingdoms of Central Africa

Although little reliable information exists about the early communities in Central Africa, political formations probably existed as early as the ninth century, trading in copper and ivory. In the fourteenth century, the kingdom of Congo was founded, around 1500 the Luba kingdom and about one hundred years later the Lunda kingdom. The Karanga, a Bantu people, formed the kingdom of Mwene Mutapa, which flourished due to its rich reserves of gold. In the fifteenth century it stretched from the Zambezi across the Kalahari desert, as far as the Indian Ocean and the Limpopo river.

The kingdoms of South Africa

In South Africa, by the early nineteenth century, the Bushmen had been largely driven out of the land into the enclave of the Kalahari desert by the Bantu peoples. The incursions of the Zulus, a warrior nation, triggered extensive demographic changes in southern Africa. The Ndwandwe kingdom, the kingdom of Swazi and that of the Ngoni emerged

*Kidnapping: until well into the nineteenth century the **slave trade** flourished in Africa. The European buyers had their 'goods' shipped from the west coast of Africa to plantations in the USA, Brazil and the Caribbean.*

though the last soon split into five parts. In the south of what is now Mozambique, the state of Gaza developed, and a short time later, in present-day Zimbabwe, a kingdom was created in Matabeleland.

Arrival of the Europeans

In the fifteenth century, the Portuguese navigators succeeded in circumventing the trade routes controlled by the Muslims and established trading posts on the west coast. Thus the coastal regions acquired even more importance in relation to the interior. At first, textiles, metalware and firearms were exchanged for ivory and gold, but soon the slave trade took on greater significance. Spaniards, Portuguese, British and French purchased labour for their mines and plantations in the New World. The Europeans did not usually capture the slaves directly, but made use of Arab and African intermediaries, leading to the foundation of prosperous kingdoms whose basis was the slave trade. The first of these was Benin, in the western part of present-day Nigeria. At the end of the seventeenth century the kingdoms of Dahomey and Oyo took up the dominant position, to be replaced from the eighteenth century as the great power in West Africa by the Ashanti. Prisoners captured in the many civil wars, which continued until the end of the nineteenth century, were profitably sold to the Europeans.

After the loss of its North American colonies, the relationship of Great Britain to the slave trade changed. Slavery was now outlawed, and a special colony for freed slaves was to be set up. After a failed attempt in St George's Bay, Freetown in Sierra Leone, which became a British Crown Colony in 1808, was used as a British merchant naval base in its fight against the international slave trade. In 1822 freed slaves from the USA founded the first Black African republic, Liberia.

The British fight against slavery, was not founded on purely humanitarian motives. The British crown was concerned about sovereignty on the high seas, and the capture of Spanish and Portuguese slave-ships had the useful side-effect of weakening its

sea-faring rivals on the pretext of a fight for human rights.

This policy also brought Britain into conflict with the African nations who relied on trade in human merchandise. Thus, in the mid-nineteenth century, The British fought many skirmishes against the Africans, during which they subjugated the Ashanti and some of the peoples of the Niger delta, such as the Calabar, Bonny and Brass. In 1861, the British formally took control of the island Lagos, until recently the capital of Niger.

The British campaign against the slave trade in East Africa was not quite so successful. Since the

seventeenth century, the Portuguese had fought for supremacy against indigenous Islamic rulers. Ethiopia was able to maintain its independence with Portuguese support, but by the end of the eighteenth century the Portuguese had to abandon their positions in northern East Africa. Despite the provisions forbidding slavery in agreements with Britain, it continued in this region for quite some time to come. Even to this day, a form of the slave trade persists, largely between African and the countries of the Arabian peninsula. At the Cape of Good Hope, the Dutch had been setting up bases for their trade with Indochina since 1652. The most important of these was Cape Town, at the southern tip of the continent. The Boers (Dutch for 'farmer') descendants of the original Dutch settlers, pushed ever further into the interior in search of grazing land and arable land, driving out the original inhabitants, the Bantu and the Khoikhoin.

Imperialism

From the late eighteenth century the European powers began the systematic exploration of the Dark Continent and its incorporation into their colonial empires. The continuing reconnaissance of the interior was vital to European interests.

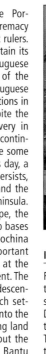

1 A wealth of elegant historical buildings are a reminder of the former glory of the Moroccan royal city, Marrakesh.

2 The pillars of Aksum, the royal city of the Ethiopian rulers, date from the fourth century, when Ethiopia became Christian under the king Ezana.

3 Djenné was an important Islamic cultural centre which in the fourteenth century became the main trading centre in the kingdom of Mali.

4 Elmina castle, built by the Portuguese in 1482, was the first slave-trading post exporting slaves from West Africa.

Modern Africa

Gamal Abd el-Nasser, the Egyptian dictator who ruled from 1954 till 1970. In 1958, he created a temporary union with Syria, known as the United Arab Republic, which soon collapsed in 1961. The Libyan leader Muammar al Ghaddafi was at one time working on plans to unify Libya with other Arab and African states.

In 1770 the British explorer James Bruce reached the source of the Blue Nile. Another British explorer, Mungo Park, followed the course of the Niger in the early nineteenth century, and the German Heinrich Barth discovered Muslim western Sudan for the Europeans. David Livingstone explored the Zambezi and in 1855 discovered the Victoria Falls. In 1863, the source of the Nile was found by John Hanning Speke, James August Grant and Samuel White Baker.

In parallel with these discoveries the great European nations competed in a frenzied imperialist race to acquire as much territory as possible to add to their colonies. The driving force was national prestige and the prospect of great gain from the exploitation of natural resources and later from the building of railways.

In 1830, France conquered Algeria, and with the occupation of Tunisia in 1881 it acquired a large continguous colonial empire in western and equatorial Africa. In 1895, it conquered the island of Madagascar and in 1911 Morocco, thus controlling the whole of the three countries (Tunisia, Morocco and Algeria) along the south coast of the Mediterranean known collectively as the Maghreb.

Disputes over the division of Africa frequently brought the European nations to the brink of war. In 1908 and 1911, the French were able to assert themselves against German gunboat diplomacy in Morocco, but had to abandon their advance into the upper Nile region in the Fashoda incident of 1898–1899 as a result of energetic British resistance. In 1806–1814, Great Britain seized the Cape Colony from the Dutch and thus began to build a major colonial dominion in South Africa. In 1843, they added Natal, in 1866–1879 Caffraria (later the Eastern Cape). The fought the first fierce battle against the Dutch in 1880–1881, capturing the Orange Free State, in 1885 added Bechuanaland and in 1890 Rhodesia. The Boer War (1899–1902) was won by the British who conquered the Dutch states along the Vaal river.

In 1910, the British consolidated their possessions in South Africa to form the Union of South Africa.

In 1882, The British occupied Egypt and from there conquered the eastern Sudan in 1896–1899 after a war with forces of the Mahdi, the Muslim ruler. In 1887–1890 they acquired Kenya, Uganda and Tanganyika in East Africa. In exchange for Heligoland, the former German island colony of Zanzibar also became British.

The Portuguese extended their coastal possessions in the west to include Angola, and in the west to Mozambique. The Congo Free State, founded in 1881–1885, which was more or less the private possession of the King of the Belgians, became Belgian Congo in 1908. The German Empire acquired Togo, Cameroon, German South-west Africa and German East Africa in 1884 to 1885. Spain retained small areas of Morocco and Western Sahara. Italy, the last colonial power in Africa, conquered Libya from the Ottomans in 1911–1912 and Abyssinia (Ethiopia) in 1936, but lost both during World War II.

Following the decisions of the Treaty of Versailles in 1919 the German colonies became man-dates of the League of Nations in 1919. The Berlin Congo conference of 1884–1885, in which German Chancellor Bismarck, had acted as an 'honest broker', achieved a balance of interests for the imperialist powers, but was not finally able to eliminate their rivalries. Navigation rights for the Congo and Niger rivers were defined, and each of the signatory powers undertook to inform the others if it wanted to acquire new territories or take over a protectorate.

Liberation movements

Political policy in Africa was determined by the European rulers; the indigenous population was not involved in decision-making. The needs of the Europeans also had significant consequences for the traditional social system of the indigenous population.

Not everyone was prepared to bow unresistingly to foreign rule. In 1870, there was an uprising in Algeria against the French, who also encountered significant resistance in western Sudan. The British suppressed armed uprisings in Matabeleland, the Ashanti region of Nigeria, the Fulbe states, Sokoto and Sierra Leone. The Germans fought from 1904 to 1908 against the Herero of south-west Africa and against the Maji Maji Rebellion in Tanganyika from 1905 to 1907.

The only successful uprising was in Ethiopia which was able to defend itself against Italian attempts at conquest in the battle of Adowa in 1896.

After World War I, the exploitation of Africa continued apace. Several colonies such as Algeria, South Rhodesia and Kenya, which had significant populations of white settlers acquired a large measure of self-rule, but the indigenous population had no voting rights or say in government. On the eve of World War II, African nationalist movements existed, but were only well-organised in Algeria and Egypt.

The new Africa

World War II led gave a boost to African self-confidence. The British and French made extensive concessions, which hastened the organisation of nationalist movements. A Pan-African Movement was founded, headed by intellectuals such as Kwame Nkrumah and Jomo Kenyatta.

Everywhere in Africa, political parties and trades unions were founded. In most places, the transition to independence was peaceful, even though the Mau-Mau, the Kikuyu guerillas in Kenya aimed to bomb their way to freedom. Ghana was the first Black African state to become independent in 1957; Guinea followed a year later. In the 'African year' of 1960, seventeen sovereign African nations came into being: Cameroon, Congo-Brazzaville, Gabon, Chad, the Central African Republic, Togo, Ivory Coast, Dahomey, Upper Volta, Niger, Nigeria, Senegal, Mali, Madagascar, Somalia, Mauritania and Congo-Leopoldville. Sierra Leone and Tanganyika followed in 1961. Tanganyika and Zanzibar united in 1964 to form Tanzania. In 1962, Uganda, Burundi and Rwanda, in 1963 Kenya and in 1965-66 Gambia declared their independence.

The white settlers of Rhodesia declared unilateral independence in 1965. Only the Europeans had political rights, leading to the country being boycotted by the UN. South Africa's apartheid policy resulted in international protests and boycotts. The black opposition united in the African National Congress.

King Mohammed V of Morocco was able to declare independence from France in 1956 and Tunisia under President Habib Bourguiba became a sovereign state in the same year, Algeria's situation was different, since it was considered a part of metropolitan France and had a huge European population. The Algerian War was fought between 1954 and 1962. In 1958, a military coup which started in Algiers toppled the fourth French republic, and France's new strong man, Charles de Gaulle, attempted a settlement, but it was not until 1962 that the People's Democratic Algerian Republic was proclaimed. The neighbouring state of Libya was under UN trusteeship and became independent in 1951 under King Mohammed

1 Democratic steps like this village court are overshadowed by **2** armed conflicts and civil wars such as those in Ethiopia. **3** Liberia is not the only country affected by hundreds of people fleeing from the war. **4** With the first free elections in 1994 democracy was introduced in South Africa.

In the 1950s, the African states began to gain independence from the European colonialists. Among the most prominent black African politicians were (from left to right) **Patrice Lumumba** (Belgian-Congo), **Julius Nyerere** (Tanzania), **Ahmed Sékou Touré** (Guinea) and **Kwame Nkrumah** (Ghana).

Idris I. He was toppled by a military coup in 1969. Since then, the country has been ruled by the 'Leader of the Revolution' the dictator Muammar Ghaddafi.

The Belgian Congo was granted independence in 1960 and its duly elected president Patrice Lumumba took office. Immediately, the provinces of Katanga (under Moîse Tshombe) and South Kasai attempted to secede, starting a brutal civil war, involving foreign powers and white mercenaries, that lasted until 1964. In the end Colonel Mobutu Sese Seko gained power in a coup d'état, supported by the West which suspected Lumumba of being too friendly with the communists.

By the end of the 1970s, almost the whole of Africa was independent. After the end of the dictatorship in Portugal, the wars in Mozambique and Angola ended, and Guinea-Bissau and Cape Verde also achieved independence. Nevertheless, these former Portuguese possessions were not to attain peace. Angola and Mozambique were granted independence in 1974 and 1975 respectively when Portugal overthrew its dictator, Salazar. However, in both countries civil war broke out as various warring factions, supported by the West and the communists with help for the former from South Africa, battled each other in a bloody struggle for power. The Angolan war lasted from 1974 to 1991 and the Mozambique war from 1975 to 1994. Both countries are still recovering from the damage and there have been setbacks in Angola due to severe flooding in recent years.

In 1975, French rule ended over the Comoro Islands, and a year later Djibouti gained independence. In 1976, Spain withdrew from its overseas province of Western Sahara, which was claimed by both Mauritania and Morocco. Mauritania withdrew its troops in 1979, but Morocco continued the war against the Polisario Front which championed a separate Sahara state. In 1992, a peace agreement provided for a referendum under UN supervision, but this has since been delayed by Morocco. Algeria has been riven by civil war after the fundamental Islamicist party the

FIS were denied power in 1991. The war broke out in 1992.

In 1980, Southern Rhodesia formally achieved independence under the name of Zimbabwe. In 1990, following the resolutions of the so-called Turnhalle Conference, Namibia, until then governed from South Africa, also became independent.

The young African states faced a whole series of major problems. The national borders ran along arbitrary colonial lines with no regard for ethnic and cultural affinities, thus hindering the establishment of genuine nation-states. Many countries replaced democ-

ratic parliamentary constitutions with one-party systems and dictatorships. The USSR encouraged this form of rule, and both West and East tried to extend their influence in Africa and conducted several 'proxy wars'.

One bright spot was the end of apartheid in South Africa and the election of the winner of the Nobel Peace Prize, Nelson Mandela, as the country's president.

Yet even today, many Africa countries are mired in strife. Ethnic conflicts, military coups and wars are still the order of the day. Among the worst were the massacres in Burundi and Rwanda in 1994. Civil wars prevail in Liberia, Sierra Leone, the Democratic Republic of Congo, Chad, Uganda, Guinea-Bissau, Somalia, the Ivory Coast and Nigeria. After Eritrea split from Ethiopia in 1993, border conflicts led to a war that ended in 2000 with the defeat of Eritrea. The border has since then been policed by UN forces. A civil war rages in Sudan against the

tribal people of the south conducted by the Janjaweed Islamic militia. Most African countries are in a state of economic depression due massive debt. Their inadequate healthcare systems are unable to cope with epidemics such as AIDS, malaria and ebola, droughts and floods. The future for Africa looks grim.

1 In the Western Sahara the Polisario Front fights against the Moroccan army for a sovereign state.

2 50 covered ox-wagons in the town of Dundee in South Africa commemorate the Battle of Blood River in 1838 between the Boers and the Zulus.

3 Confident of victory, ANC leader Nelson Mandela speaks during his election campaign in Durban in spring 1994.

4 In the early 1990s, more than 50,000 were killed and a further 300,000 died of famine in the civil war in Somalia.

Main photograph:
Preserving their culture has some negative aspects for the children of the Masai. Young girls are often engaged to be married at birth and are subject to the genital mutilation known as 'female circumcision'.

The Countries of Africa

Africa, the second largest continent in the world, after Asia, stretches from the Mediterranean in the north to the Cape of Good Hope in the south and lies between the Atlantic and Indian Oceans. The Sahara divides the conti-

A traditional method of carrying water in many African regions.

nent into two completely different regions. The north is populate by light-skinned Arabs and Berbers, the dark-skinned peoples, Bushmen, Khoikhoi and Pygmies live in the south. There is also a great difference in flora and fauna. The Mediterranean north has a desert landscape with few animal species, while the rainforests and savannahs of the south have a rich plant and animal life. Even now that they have gained their independence, most of the young African nations struggle with natural disasters, famine, poverty, disease, civil wars and ethnic conflicts.

Casablanca is the largest city and the economic centre of Morocco. The port began to prosper in the Middle Ages, and has been repeatedly destroyed and rebuilt. After the withdrawal of the French,

Morocco experienced economic difficulties, but Casablanca has recovered. An expression of the city's new self-confidence is the Grande Mosque de Hassan II with its 200-m-high minaret, which opened in 1993.

Morocco

Area:	446,550 sq. km
Capital city:	Rabat
Form of government: Constitutional Monarchy	
Administrative divisions: 16 regions	
Population: 32.7 million (69 inhabitants/sq. km)	
Languages: Arabic (official), French, Berber dialects	
GDP per capita:	US$4,300
Currency: 1 dirham = 100 centimes	

Natural Geography

The Mediterranean coast is 475 km long and lined with steep cliffs. It is bordered by a flat coastal plain which stretches for 1,050 km. A broad coastal plain then develops into the Moroccan Meseta, an area of high plains with an altitude of up to 450 m. The plains are flanked in the south and east by the **High and Middle Atlas Mountains**. The High Atlas extend 700 km, of which the highest point is the 4,165-m-high Jebel Toubkal. The Middle Atlas has peaks of up to 3,240 m in height and the Ante-Atlas in the southwest is an area of plateaus up to 2,000 m above sea level. In the north of the country, parallel to the Mediterranean coast, are the

Rif Mountains, a range of fold mountains with peaks of up to 2,456 m. High plains in the east mark the border with Algeria. The semi-desert area below the coastal plain is known as the bled.

Climate

The Atlas mountains form a barrier between the Mediterranean climate of the north-west and the Saharan-continental climate in the south and south-east. In the dry, hot summers of the northwest the temperature can rise to 29°C, and winters have high precipitation, with average temperatures of 12°C. This part of Morocco receives between 200 and 900 mm of rain per year.

The **continental climate** of the south means that temperatures can range between 0°C in winter and up to 45°C in summer. Precipitation is below 250 mm. High altitude regions receive 1,000 mm of precipitation, but above 1,000 m most of this falls as snow. A **desert climate**, with precipitation below 200 mm, predominates on the Saharan fringes.

Population

Half the population are **Berbers**, the rest Arabs. Malaki Sunnis represent 89 per cent of religious affiliation. Average life expectancy is 66 years, and the literacy rate is 44 per cent. There are minorities of Christians and Jews.

Morocco: carpets shops in the souqs of the Medina of Marrakesh.

History and Politics

In the twelfth century BC, the **Phoenicians** established trading posts on the north-west African coast. The Berber kingdom of Mauritania was established in the fourth century BC in the interior of the country. After the final defeat of **Carthage**, whose centre had been close to modern Tunis, the **Romans** began to exert influence over the region. After the collapse of the Western Roman Empire, the **Vandals** claimed it in the fifth century AD From the seventh century onwards, the **Arabs** continued to tighten their grip on Morocco, and together with allied Berber tribes conquered the Iberian peninsula, which had been occupied by the Visigoths. Islamic rule changed from the the Idrisids in the eleventh century to the Almoravids, who 100 years later gave way to the Almohads. These in turn fell to the Merinids in the thirteenth century, and finally the Wattasids in 1420.

Under the Reconquista in 1492, Spain was recaptured from the North African Moors and henceforward, the Arab empires of North Africa came under increasing European influence. Initially, the Spanish and Portuguese controlled all the most important ports, until the Alawite Dynasty, which still rules today, recaptured these cities in ca. 1670. Only Melilla, Ifni and Ceuta remained Spanish. In 1830, France attempted to bring Morocco under its influence. This resulted in a war, ending in 1844 with Moroccan defeat. The French and the Spanish divided Morocco between them in two protectorates.

Morocco gained full **independence** in 1956, except for the enclaves of Ceuta and Melilla; until 1969, Sidi Ifni remained Spanish. Sultan Mohammed V became King and was succeeded by his son Hassan II in 1961 as the head of a constitutional monarchy. In terms of foreign policy, Hassan followed a pro-European course. He died in 1999. His eldest son was then crowned Mohammed VI. The occupation by Morocco of the former Spanish colony of the Western Sahara in 1975 has developed into a long-term conflict. The most recent UN interventions failed. In

2002, there was conflict with Spain arose when Moroccan police occupied the island of Perejil in the Mediterranean.

The constitution was last amended in 1996 and provides for a **bicameral parliament** with a National Assembly and a Senate.

Economy

In 2002, Morocco had a GDP of 34.6 billion US dollars. Of this, 14 per cent derived from **agriculture**, 33 per cent from **manufacturing** and 53 per cent from the **services sector**. The most important exports are phosphate, the sale of fishing licenses and tourism. Morocco imports raw materials, machine tools and vehicles, foodstuffs and finished products. Exports include fertilisers, foodstuffs and manufactured goods.

Transport Infrastructure

The **rail network** is 1,907 km long, and the road network covers 60,513 km. International **airports** are at Rabat, Tangiers, Marrakesh, Agadir and Casablanca, where the most important **ports** are located.

Tourism

The old royal cities of Casablanca and Marrakesh and the Mediterranean beaches are Morocco's main attractions.

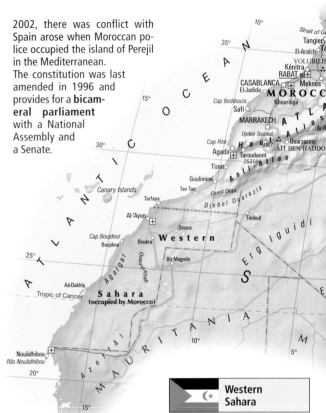

Western Sahara

Area:	266,000 sq. km
Capital city:	El Aaiún
Form of government: Republic/ annexed by Morocco since 1979	
Population: 273,000 (1 inhabitant/sq. km)	
Languages:	Arabic, Spanish
GDP per capita: no data available	
Currency: virtual currency 1 Moroccan dirham= 100 centimes	

Natural Geography

The country is almost uninhabited and consists mainly of **desert and semi-desert** with stony desert in the north, and sandy desert in the south.

Climate

The extremely **arid climate** yields an average temperature of 22°C all year round. Rainfall is limited to a couple of days a year.

Population

The small population of the Western Saha is mainly **Sahrawi,** a mixed race with Arab, Berber and black African roots. 90 per cent profess Sunni Islam.

Marrakesh was founded in 1063 by the Almoravid Dynasty. It was also the capital city of the Almohads until the end of the thirteenth century. It is one of the four Moroccan royal cities, the others being Meknes, Fés and Rabat, and possesses important examples of Islamic architecture. The Jemaa-el-Fna is the centre of one of the most beautiful souqs (markets) in Morocco. The medina of Marrakesh is a UNESCO World Heritage Site.

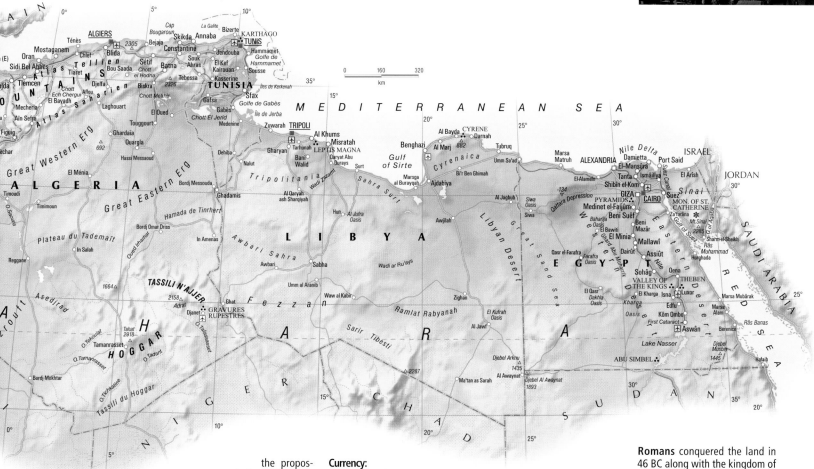

History and Politics

Since the eleventh century, the territory has been part of the Islamic empire which today rules Morocco. In 1885, the territory became Spanish, as Spanish Morocco and was declared the overseas province of Spanish Sahara in 1958. In 1973, the **Polisario Front**, a liberation movement, was established. Spain withdrew from the area in 1975 and Morocco and Mauritania were left to govern the country. Mauritania abandoned its claims to the land in 1979 in favour of the Polisario, and the land was then annexed by Morocco.

After a UN peace initiative, the Polisario and Morocco agreed to a ceasefire in 1991, to be followed by a referendum. So far, neither side can agree on how the process should continue. In 2002, the Security Council requested a UN mandate. In 2003, the UN made a new proposal, but as yet only the Polisario has agreed to it. Under the proposal, the region must enter a transitional phase with considerable autonomy, followed by a referendum in 2008. The Democratic Arab Republic of Sahara (UN name: Western Sahara) is recognised by 29 OAU states and 77 states worldwide.

Economy

The country has **phosphate reserves** and **fish stocks** in the coastal waters. Oasis agriculture and livestock-rearing is sufficient for the country's population.

Algeria	
Area:	2,381,741 sq. km
Capital city:	Algiers
Form of government:	
Presidential Republic	
Administrative divisions:	
48 districts	
Population:	
32.5 million (13 inhabitants/sq. km)	
Language:	Arabic
GDP per capita:	US$7,300

Currency:

1 Algerian dinar =
100 centimes

Natural Geography

The country consists of a narrow coastal plain with numerous bays on the Mediterranean Sea. The hinterland consists of the **Atlas Mountains** with peaks of up to 2,308 m. In the south the mountains form a plateau at an altitude of between 800 and 1,000 m, dominated by salt marshes called the 'chotts'. South of this is the **Saharan Atlas**, reaching an altitude of 2,328 m and bordering the **Sahara Desert**. The Sahara covers 85 per cent of Algeria's land mass and, apart from a narrow strip of rolling hills, the land is sandy desert with almost no vegetation. The volcanic **Ahaggar Mountains** in the southwest rise to a height of 2,918 m.

Climate

The coast and the northern slopes of the Atlas Mountains have a Mediterranean climate, with an average rainfall of 500 to 1,000 mm. The damp winter **steppe climate** of the chotts produces temperatures of 0°C in winter and 30°C in summer, with precipitation of approximately 350 mm per year. Air temperatures in the Sahara can vary by up to 20°C throughout the course of the day, with a winter average of 0°C and a summer average of more than 40°C. In summer, the area is affected by the dry **Sirocco** wind.

Population

The Algerian population is 70 per cent **Arab** and approximately 30 per cent **Berber (Kabyle)**, with a small French minority. With the exception of a few Christians, the population is almost exclusively Muslim.

History and Politics

The land was originally ruled by Berber and Moorish tribes until the **Phoenicians** established their first settlements in the twelfth century BC After the fall of **Carthage** in 149 BC, the **Romans** conquered the land in 46 BC along with the kingdom of Numidia; Numidia-Mauritania was a Roman province until the invasion of the Vandals in 429. From the seventh century onwards, several Berber and Arab kingdoms were established, until the deys, elected by the Turkish Janissaries of Algiers, took power in 1600. The Spanish, Dutch, British and French were held back until the **French** occupied Algiers in 1830 and extended their sphere of influence ever further south. In 1947, all Algerians were granted French citizenship, but this did not stop the formation of a **resistance movement**. The FLN ('Front de Libération Nationale'), under the leadership of **Ben Bella**, initiated a war against the French in 1954, until France was finally forced to recognise Algeria's **independence** in 1962. Ben Bella became the first Prime Minister of Algeria and, in 1963, the country's first President, until he was overthrown in a coup d'état by the chief-of-staff, Houari Boumedienne, in 1965.

Since the early 1990s, the conflict between the government

Algeria, Tunisia

*The **Sahara** covers more than 90 per cent of Algeria's land area. The Tuareg used to control the trade routes and participated in caravanserai trade. Today, it is very difficult for them to practice their traditional nomadic economy.*

and the **Front Islamique du Salut (FIS)** has caused severe problems. An unparalleled terror campaign against the population has cost in excess of 80,000 lives, but it is unclear who is responsible for the massacres – the Islamic fundamentalists or the military. The constitution of 1996 provides for a freely elected bicameral parliament, and although a new National Assembly was elected in 1997, an end to the violence is not in sight. In 2001, there was unrest among the Kabyles, who demanded equality and cultural autonomy. As a result, the Berber language, Tamazight, was introduced as a second official language.

Economy

In 2001, Algeria's gross national product was US$50.4 billion. Of this, **agriculture** contributed 13 per cent, **manufacturing** 49 per cent and the **service sector** 38 per cent. Main exports are crude oil and natural gas. Algeria imports food, machine parts and motorised vehicles.

Transport Infrastructure

The **rail network** covers 4,772 km, and the road network extends for 102,424 km, of which 70,650 km is surfaced. There are international **airports** in Algiers and Oran. These cities are also the main **sea ports**.

Tourism

Tourist numbers have fallen significantly due to the terrorism of the Islamic fundamentalists. The situation is improving, however.

Tunisia	
Area:	163,610 sq. km
Capital city:	Tunis
Form of government:	
Presidential Republic	
Administrative divisions:	
23 provinces	
Population:	
10 million (60 inhabitants/sq. km)	
Languages:	
Arabic (official), French	
GDP per capita:	US$7,600

Currency:
1 Tunisian dinar = 1000 millimes

Natural Geography

In the north, undulating steppes cover the foothills of the **Atlas Mountains**. The foothills of the Saharan Atlas Mountains, whose peaks rise to 1,590 m, extend as far as the coastal plains around Sfax. To the south lie salt marshes, which eventually give way to the desert dunes of the **Great Eastern Erg**, which are bordered in the east by salt marshes and the **Ksour Massif**. The north of the country has a steep coastline, but the coast in the south is sandy, with numerous lagoons. The island of **Djerba** is located off-shore in the Gulf of Sirte.

Climate

The north of the country has a **Mediterranean climate**. Precipitation is between 500 and 1,000 mm on the north coast and approximately 1,500 mm in the mountains. Average temperatures are 10°C in January and 26°C in

August. The **desert climate** of the Atlas results in temperatures of up to 45°C, and precipitation of a maximum 200 mm per year.

Population

Tunisia's population is 98 per cent **Arab** and Muslim Berbers. There are also 1.3 per cent tribal **Berbers** and a minority of Europeans – mainly French. Islam is the state religion, and 98 per cent of Muslims are Sunni. In addition, there are also Jewish, Catholic and Protestant minorities. Average life expectancy is 70, and adult literacy rate is 67 per cent.

History and Politics

The region was first settled by Berber peoples, but the **Phoenicians** established trading posts in around 1100 BC The empire of **Carthage** ruled the western Mediterranean until the **Romans** succeeded in obtaining a foothold in North Africa after the Third Punic War in 149 BC The region was conquered by the **Vandals** in 439, who ruled for over 100 years,

followed by the **Arabs**. The Habsburgs ruled for a short period from 1535, followed in 1574 by the Turks, who incorporated Tunisia into the **Ottoman Empire**.

In 1881, the French made Tunisia a protectorate. Tunisia gained full national **independence** in 1956 and, after a short period as a monarchy, became a republic in 1957. The first President, **Habib Bourguiba**, held office until 1987. His successor, **Ben Ali**, who followed a liberal path. Ben Ali retained his post as President in elections in 1994, 1999 and 2004. The constitution dates from 1959 and was last amended in 1994. It provides for election of the parliament every five years and the direct election of the President.

Economy

In 2001, GDP was US$20.1 billion, of which 16 per cent derived from **agriculture**, 28 per cent from **manufacturing** and 56 per cent from **services**. Main exports are textiles and leather, phosphates, heavy industry, energy and foodstuffs. Main imports are raw

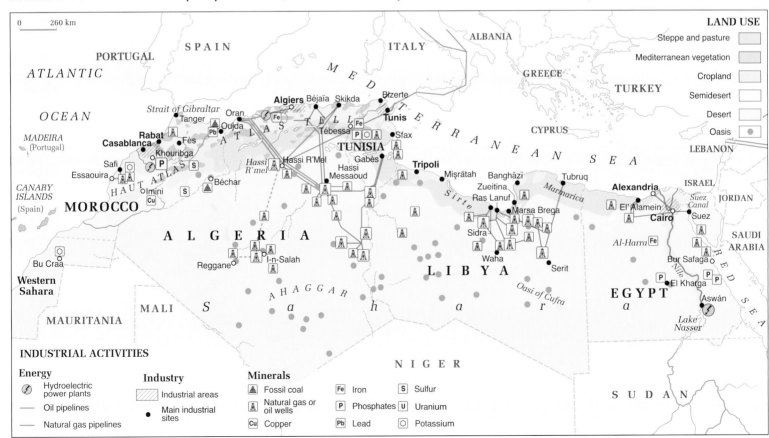

LAND USE

Steppe and pasture	
Mediterranean vegetation	
Cropland	
Semidesert	
Desert	
Oasis	

INDUSTRIAL ACTIVITIES

Energy
- Hydroelectric power plants
- Oil pipelines
- Natural gas pipelines

Industry
- Industrial areas
- Main industrial sites

Minerals
- Fossil coal
- Natural gas or oil wells
- Cu Copper
- Fe Iron
- P Phosphates
- Pb Lead
- S Sulfur
- U Uranium
- Potassium

Tunis was established by the Phoenicians in the sixth century BC, but only gained importance under the Hafsid Dynasty. Its importance increased under the Spanish Moors from the thirteenth to the seventeenth centuries. Many examples of Islamic architecture can be seen in the medina. The Great Mosque of Tunis was founded in 732, and reconstructed between the thirteenth and fifteenth centuries. The minaret was renovated in 1894.

materials and semi-manufactured products, machinery, vehicles and manufactured goods.

Transport Infrastructure

The **rail network** is approximately 2,260 km long, with some additional narrow-gauge sections for the transport of phosphates. The road network covers 20,830 km, of which 15,832 km are surfaced. There are International **airports** in Tunis, Sfax, Monastir, Tozeur, Djerba and Tabarka. Main **sea ports** are in Tunis La Goulette, Gabès and Bizerta.

Tourism

In 2001, Tunisia welcomed 5.387 million foreign visitors, bringing US$1.605 billion into the country. The excellent infrastructure and varied tourist attractions, including ruins from the Phoenician and Roman periods, as well as mosques and religious buildings make Tunisia an attractive country. Tunisians are also famous for their cuisine, considered to be the best in the Maghreb.

Libya

Area:	1,759,540 sq. km
Capital city:	Tripoli
Form of government:	
Islamic People's Republic	
Administrative divisions:	
3 provinces, 10 governorates	
Population:	
5.7 million (3 inhabitants/sq. km)	
Languages:	
Arabic (official), Berber dialects	
GDP per capita:	US$8,400
Currency:	
1 Libyan dinar = 1000 dirham	

Natural Geography

Tripolitania in the north-west consists of the coastal plains and the Al Hamadah al Hamra plateaus at an altitude of 968 m. The Sirte Basin region includes the volcanic **Al-Haruj al-Aswad** mountain (1,200 m) and has massive crude oil reserves. The **Fezzan** is an area of the hinterland consisting of sand, gravel and stony desert. **Cyrenaica** in the north-east is dominated by **Al Jabal al Akhdar** karst mountains, which descend

steeply to the coast and which become the steppes of **Marmarica** in the east and the Libyan desert in the south. With 2,286 m, Picco Bette is Libya's highest mountain, one of the northern foothills of the **Tibesti** on the border with Chad.

Climate

Almost 85 per cent of Libya's land mass is **desert** without significant precipitation, but the temperatures vary from around 0°C in winter to over 50°C in summer. On the Mediterranean coast, the average January temperature is 12°C and the average temperature in August is 26°C. Average precipitation is 300 mm. The flora and fauna of the coast are typically Mediterranean. This changes to steppe vegetation further inland, before completely disappearing in the barren desert. The most common animal species are hyenas, jackals, desert foxes and jerboa, birds of prey, snakes, scorpions, wild asses, hares and baboons.

Population

Libya's population is 97 per cent **Arab** and Muslim **Berbers**. There are minorities of Tuareg, Nilo-Saharans, Egyptians and black Africans. Islam is the state religion and that of 97 per cent of the population. There are small minorities of Catholics, Copts and other religions. Average life expectancy is 68 years.

History and Politics

In pre-Christian times, the **Phoenicians, Greeks**, and **Cartha-**ginians established settlements on the Libyan coast until the **Romans** occupied the area in the first century BC When the Roman Empire divided in two, Tripolitania became part of the Western Roman Empire, and Cyrenaica was ruled by Byzantium. The **Vandals, who succeeded the Romans** ruled for

1 Adrar is the main town in the Touat Oasis in Algeria and is an important centre of local trade.

2 Ghardaia, the main town of the Algerian oasis region Mzab. It forms a pentapolis with four other towns. Houses with terraced rooves are very typical.

3 Taghit is a typical oasis settlement on the edge of the Great Western Erg in Algeria.

4 Tunisia: The Sidi Okba Mosque or Great Mosque in Kairouan was reconstructed in the ninth century and stands out due to its marble and porphyry columns.

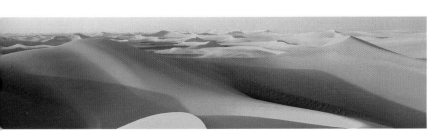

Erg is the Arabic word for a wide desert of sand-dunes such as the Libyan desert. A stony, rocky desert is called a hamada, a serir is a desert plain covered in pebbles and gravel, and fesh-fesh are deserts of fine golden sand.

some hundred years, until the **Byzantine Empire** was able to reconquer the land in the sixth century.

In 644, the **Arabs** controlled the region and converted the Berbers to Islam. In the sixteenth century, Libya became a part of the **Ottoman Empire**, and remained so until the Italo-Turkish War of 1911–1912. Italy declared Libya an Italian colony in 1934. The Sanussi, who had ruled hitherto, **resisted** the colonial rulers. In World War II, Italian and German troops fought heavy battles against the Allies on Libyan soil.

In 1945, Libya was occupied by the British and French until the UN declared the country an independent, united kingdom in 1951. King Idris al-Senussi was toppled from power in 1969 by a military coup led by **Muammar al Ghaddafi**. Although Colonel Ghaddafi no longer officially holds office, he continues to exert a

al People's Congress is the nation's highest policy-making body. The government consists of a General Secretariat of seven members. Political parties are not permitted. The voting age is 18.

Economy

GDP in 2001 totalled US$28 billion, of which **agriculture accounted** for seven per cent, **manufacturing** 44 per cent and the **services sector** 49 per cent. The main products are crude oil and natural gas, which represent 90 per cent of exports. Libya imports industrial finished products, machinery and transport equipment, chemicals, foodstuffs, luxury items and livestock.

Transport Infrastructure

The country's **road network** has a total length of some 19,189 km, more than half of which is

Egypt

Area:	1,001,450 sq. km
Capital city:	Cairo
Form of government: Presidential Republic	
Administrative divisions: 26 provinces	
Population: 77.5 million (68 inhabitants/sq. km)	
Language:	Arabic
GDP per capita:	US$4,400
Currency: 1 Egyptian pound = 100 piastres	

Natural Geography

The **Nile** is Egypt's wellspring of life. In Upper Egypt, the river has eroded a course through the limestone bedrock of the desert. Between Lake Nasser and the beginning of the delta region north of Cairo, the Nile forms a stretch of fertile land approximately

The Mediterranean coast has a flat, dune-covered landscape.

Climate

Only the area north of Cairo has a Mediterranean climate, receiving a rainfall of between 100 and 200 mm per annum. In the south it hardly ever rains, and temperatures fluctuate greatly. In the north, average temperatures are between 20°C in winter and 35°C in summer. In Aswan, temperatures range between 24°C and 41°C. In the spring, the **Khamsin**, a hot, dry sandstorm, blows across the country.

Most of the country is almost devoid of vegetation, with the exception of some tough grasses, acacia and thorn bushes. Various varieties of reed, bamboo and lotus grow on the banks of the Nile. The animal species include typical desert animals, such as the jerboa, scorpions, jackals and hye-

History and Politics

The legendary **King Menes** united the kingdoms of Upper and Lower Egypt in around 2900 BC Hieroglyphic writing, the Egyptian calendar, a distinctive cult of the dead and a polytheistic religion had already developed by the end of the first of a total of 30 Egyptian dynasties. **Ancient Egyptian** culture experienced its first golden age under the pharoahs of the fourth dynasty. The pyramids of Snofru, Cheops, Khafra and Mykerinos remain today as examples of this great civilisation.

After the collapse of the Old Kingdom between 2134 and 1991 BC there was a phase of instability, which ended when the Princes of Thebes caused Egypt to flourish once more in the **Middle Kingdom**. Foreign rule by the Hyksos lasted from 1650 until 1544 BC , followed by the

Muammar al Gaddafi

*Sirte, Sept. 1942

In 1969, Colonel Ghaddafi led a group of military officers and toppled King Idris of Libya. He has since determined the country's policies under several guises. In his 'Green Book' he promoted the main elements for the establishment of an Islamic Socialist Republic. His nationalisation of the oil industry and support for Islamic terror organisations lisolated Libya on the global stage. His policies have now changed.

SUEZ CANAL

[Map of Egypt showing: MEDITERRANEAN SEA, Port Said, Buhayrat al Manzilah, El Mansura, Jilbanah, Al Qantarah, Bahr al Baqar, Ziftá, Zagazig, Al-Mahsama, Ismâ'iliya, Ismâ'iliya, Buhayrat at Timsah, Sinai, Khamsah, Al Buhayrah al Murrah al Kubrá, Bilbays, Saba'ah, Faid, Junayfah, Cairo, Arabic Desert, Suez, G. of Suez, Nile, EGYPT, Inset map: LIBYA, EGYPT, ISRAEL, SAUDI ARABIA, SUDAN. Scale: 0 — 25 km]

Gamal Abdel Nasser

*Beni Mor, 15.1.1918, †Cairo, 28.9.1970

Nasser assisted General Naguib in overthrowing King Farouk in 1952. In 1954, he seized power from Neguib, becoming President. He soon aligned himself with the Eastern Bloc, although Communists were persecuted in Egypt. His rule saw the construction of the Aswan Dam, the nationalisation of the Suez Canal and the Six-Day War of 1967 against Israel, in which Egypt was resoundly defeated.

Mohammed Anwar Sadat

*Mit Abu al-Kaum, 25.12.1918, †Cairo, 6.10.1981

As a founder of the 'Free Officers Movement', Sadat played a decisive role in the fall of King Farouk. He became Nasser's successor and led Egypt in the Yom Kippur War against Israel in 1973. In 1978, Sadat was the first Arab leader to make peace with Israel. He was thus able to recover Sinai and reopen the Suez Canal but his moderate stance caused him to be assassinated by an extremist.

strong influence on Libyan policy. During Ghaddafi's rule, planned unions with Islamic 'brother states' have failed and the nationalisation of the oil industry and the banks have caused conflict between the Libyan ruler and the Western world. This tension was increased by direct military engagement in Chad and Libyan support of Islamic **terror organisations** abroad. Libya was even suspected of producing chemical weapons. In recent years, all this has changed and Ghaddafi is now considered a moderate in the Arab world. Under the terms of the 1977 constitution, the Gener-

surfaced. Important **sea ports** are Tripoli, Bengazi and Misurata. There are international **airports** for the main cities, Tripoli and Bengazi.

Tourism

Due to the political situation, tourism in Libya is relatively under-developed. The country is visited by 88,000 visitors per year, who spend approximately US$6 million. This is a pity, as there are some spectacular Roman and Carthaginian remains and other attractions. In recent years, tourism has been encouraged.

25 km wide. North of Cairo, the delta covers roughly 23,000 sq. km, and includes tributaries, canals and irrigation systems. West of the Nile, the **Libyan Desert**, has a monotonous sand-dune landscape broken only by a few scattered oases. The **Arabian Desert** east of the Nile is dominated by a line of mountains up to 2,000 m high, dissected by numerous wadis (dry river beds). Egypt's highest point is the 2,637 m Jabal Katrina (St. Catherine's Mount), in the **Sinai** peninsula. The **Red Sea** coast contains many coral reefs and the mountains descend right to the sea.

nas. There are just under 200 species of fish in the Nile, and a few crocodiles. The variety of birds is comparatively large.

Population

Egypt has a relatively homogeneous population, descended from the **Ancient Egyptians** and **Arabs**. There are also minorities of Sudanese, Syrians, Bedouin, Nubians, Palestinians, Berbers, Beja and Europeans. 90 per cent of Egyptians are Muslim, mostly Sunni, and the rest are Coptic, Greek Orthodox, Catholic and Protestant. Average life expectancy is 65.

establishment of the **New Kingdom**, under Amenophis Thutmosis. The New Kingdom had its age of glory in the nineteenth dynasty under Seti I and Ramses II. Most of the great Egyptian monuments date from this era.

The collapse of the kingdom began in the twenty-first dynasty when it was conquered by Ethiopians, Assyrians and, in 525 BC, by the Persians, who formed the twenty-eighth, twenty-nineth and thirtieth dynasties. The rule of the Hellenistic **Ptolemaics** began in 332 BC under Alexander the Great. This dynasty lasted until the fateful battle of

Mulid is one of the most important Islamic festivals. During the festival, people illuminate their houses with decorative lights, sing songs and collect in the mosques to remember the birth of the prophet Muhammad. The cele-brations do not follow a special liturgy, but instead, people pray as normal. On this festival, all the mosques in the Islamic world, such as this one, the Hussein Mosque in Fostat, the old part of Cairo, are particularly busy.

Actium in 30 BC, which Cleopatra VII and Mark Antony lost to Octavian. Egypt remained a **Roman province** until the collapse of the Roman Empire in 395, and then became part of **Byzantium**.

After a short period of occupation by the Persians, Arabs converted the country to Islam in 640 and it became part of the **Caliphate ruled from Baghdad**. The Egyptian Mamelukes seized power in 1250 and ruled until Egypt became part of the **Ottoman Empire** in 1517. Between 1798–1801, Napoleon led an unsuccessful campaign to conquer Egypt. In the aftermath, the Turkish governor Mehmet Ali was able to stabilise the situation, but in the mid-nineteenth century, as the Ottoman Empire declined Egypt fell increasingly under British and French influence, mainly due to the construction of the **Suez canal**.

From 1914 to 1922, Egypt was officially a **British protectorate**, and then an independent constitutional monarchy under Fuad I. In 1936, the British officially withdrew altogether under pressure from King Farouk, but they continued to maintain control of the Canal Zone.

Egypt's first attack on the newly established state of **Israel** in 1948 ended in a ceasefire. **Gamal Abdel Nasser** became President of the Republic of Egypt after a military coup. He followed his own path of 'Arabic socialism', oriented towards the Soviet Union. His effort to unite Arab nations failed in 1961 with the dissolution of the **United Arab Republic**, of which Egypt, Syria and the Yemen were members. The second war launched against Israel was the **Six Day War** of 1967. Israel captured the Sinai peninsula and the Gaza Strip from Egypt. The third attack on Israel, the Yom Kippur War of 1973, launched by Nasser's successor **Mohammed Anwar Sadat** was more successful. Sadat was the first Arab leader to make peace with Israel. Egypt was temporarily isolated within the Arab world and Sadat paid for the peace with his life in 1981 when he was assassinated by a Muslim fanatic. Under his successor, **Mohammed Hosni Mubarak**, Sinai was restored to Egypt in 1981 and the head of-fice of the Arab League was moved back to Cairo in 1990. On a domestic level, attacks by Islamic fundamentalists on tourists are a repeated source of unrest.

The constitution of 1971 was limited in 1981 by an emergency law. Of the 454, members of parliament, 444 are elected for five-year terms, and ten are named by the President. The advisory board, the Shoura, consists of 210 members, 57 of whom are chosen by the President. The head of state is directly elected every six years upon the recommendation of the parliament. The voting age is 18.

Economy

Gross Domestic Product in 2001 was US$99.6 billion, to which **agriculture** contributed 20 per cent, **manufacturing** 21 per cent and the **services sector** 59 per cent. Half of all export income derives from oil and gas. Cotton, textiles, metal products and foodstuffs are also exported. Important imports are machinery, foodstuffs, iron, steel and also cars. After the Suez canal, tourism is the main source of income in Egypt.

Transport Infrastructure

Africa's oldest **rail network** covers a total length of 4,751 km, but much of the rolling stock is outdated. Some 30 per cent of the 50,000-km-long **road network** is surfaced. The most important **sea ports** are Alexandria, Port Said and Suez. There are international **airports** at Cairo, Luxor and Alexandria. The

Suez Canal links the Mediterranean to the Red Sea.

Tourism

In 2001, four million foreign visitors spent approximately US$3.8 billion in Egypt. The best time to visit Upper Egypt is in the cooler months, from October to April.

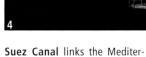 Egypt: the camel remains an important form of transport – here a camel market in the Souq al-Jamaal in Cairo.

2 Cairo has more than 500 mosques, some of which date from the ninth century. The Sultan Hassan Mosque is the most beautiful in the city.

3 Fostat, the old town of Cairo, with its narrow alleys, mosques and bazaars, is a UNESCO World Heritage Site.

4 The Isis Temple and Trajan's Kiosk on the Island of Philae were moved to the island of Agilkia during the construction of Aswan Dam.

Faces of Africa

Africa is a continent full of contrasts. More than 3,000 ethnic groups speaking approximately 1,500 different languages reflect a colourful cultural diversity, attempting to tread a path between tradition and modernity.

The Sahara acts as a natural barrier, dividing the peoples of North Africa from those of the South. For a long time, the desert acted as a virtually insurmountable barrier which meant that interbreeding only became possible at a much later stage.

The majority of North Africans are light-skinned Arabs who immigrated from the Near East in the seventh century AD and largely islamicised the indigenous Berbers. The Berbers are divided into the Riff, Guanche, Kabyle, Tuareg, Shluh, Mzab and Djerba groups. They live in extended families and traditionally breed sheep and cattle, but are increasingly cultivating agricultural crops. The languages they speak, apart from Arabic and French, are of the Hamitic group.

Black Africans predominate south of the Sahara, where they comprise approximately 70 per cent of the population. Alongside a European and Asian immigrant minority, the Pygmies in the Congo river basin, the San or Bushmen in the deserts of Botswana and Namibia and the Khoikhoi are not Hamitic. Their language is part of the Khoisan family.

The Nilo-Saharan languages are widely spoken from West Africa to Ethiopia, in the Nile valley and parts of Kenya and Uganda. The Niger-Congo language family is spoken throughout almost the whole of sub-Saharan Africa. These are often called Bantu languages. Bantu does not represent an ethnic group; the name simply means 'people'.

Ways of life are as varied as the languages. A fifth of the population of Africa lives in towns of over 20,000 inhabitants, but the vast majority lives in rural areas. Christianity and Islam are the most widespread religions. Only about 15 per cent are followers of traditional religions, in which spirits and ancestors play a significant role. Religious rites have become very mixed, however, meaning that special African forms of Islam and Christianity have developed which vary considerably from region to region. The art of black Africa is not limited to sculpture, pottery, woven textiles, beads and architecture. The human body is also a medium for works of art. Elaborate hairstyles, body painting, deco-

rative scars, piercings, masks, colourful garments and richly decorated head coverings are found all over the continent. African culture is just as rich in musical trends, which have found their way into the west via jazz and world music.

1 The Tuareg are also known as 'the veiled people', due to the face coverings worn by men as protection from the sand storms, or the 'Blue men of the desert', due to their indigo robes.

2 Coptic Christianity had its origins in Ethiopia. This faith was also established in Eritrea by the fourth century.

3 Since the Republic of Sudan's independence in 1956, conflict has smouldered between the Islamic north and the animistic and Christian south.

4 The Zulu in the eastern Republic of South Africa live in domed thatched huts, that are arranged in a circle or kraal.

5 One quarter of Eritrea's 4.3 million inhabitants are nomadic or semi-nomadic. They live mainly in the southeast of the country in the semi-desert of the Afar basin.

6 In 1992, over a quarter of the population fled from Liberia during the unrest. Since then, some have been able to return home.

7 The Bambara, Fulani, Tuareg, Soninke, Dogon, Senufo, Songhai and Malinké peoples live in Mali. Many of these ethnic groups are committed to their traditions, but this does not stop them enjoying modern appliances.

8 The Ndebele are one of the Ngni peoples and live in Zimbabwe and South Africa. The women wear traditional dress and elaborate jewellery.

Life
in Africa

Extended families and ethnic identities play an important role in many African societies. Many cultures have maintained their ancient traditions despite Western influence and dramatic economic changes.

Small pictures: Today, folk music and the colourfully dressed water-sellers in the Maghreb are mostly tourist attractions.
Women have always played an important role in the economic system. Today, they are gaining self-confidence and organising women's cooperatives throughout sub-Saharan Africa. Despite the great wealth of natural resources, many people south of the Sahara live in appalling conditions. Poverty, hunger, inadequate medical care and a dire need for education remain major problems long after the withdrawal of the colonial rulers. This is also due in part to the numerous wars and civil wars in the region, which nip in the bud any possibilities for economic and political stability. Yet African tradition and western lifestyle do not have to be at odds with each other. Nowadays, cola and supermarkets are just as much a part of daily African life as are brightly coloured clothing, myths and the traditional dances, customs and practices of the ancestors. The local witch-doctor is still accorded a high social position, while the medical facilities provided by international aid organisations are gladly used.

Large picture right:
The Ndebele are an ethnic group in southern Africa. The women traditionally wear elaborate jewellery.

Mauritania

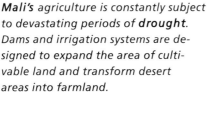
Mali's agriculture is constantly subject to devastating periods of **drought**. Dams and irrigation systems are designed to expand the area of cultivable land and transform desert areas into farmland.

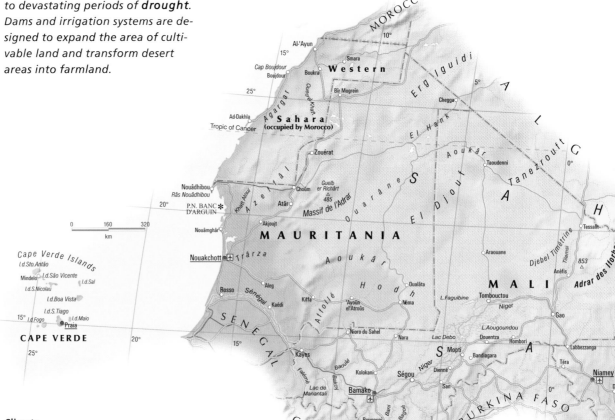

Mauritania	

Area:	1,030,700 sq. km
Capital city:	Nouakchott

Form of government:
Islamic Presidential Republic

Administrative divisions:
13 regions

Population:
3 million (2.6 inhabitants/sq. km)

Languages:
Arabic (official) and languages of Niger and the Congo

GDP per capita:	US$2000

Currency:
1 ouguiya = 5 khoums

Natural geography

Desert covers 47 per cent of the country's surface area and the coastal area is lined with sand dunes. Inland, lowland sand and rocky desert forms the Western edge of the **Sahara**. In the central part of the country is a series of sandstone plateaus 300 to 500 m above sea level; the highest peak, **Kédia d'Idjil**, has an altitude of 915 m. In the eastern part of the country, the flat stony desert turns into the sandy desert valley of **El Djouf**. Agriculture is only possible in the south of the country, on approximately one per cent of the

Climate

Practically the whole country has a dry, hot desert climate with temperatures averaging 20 to 24°C in January and 30 to 34°C in July. The average rainfall is less than 100 mm in the North, and between 300 and 400 mm annually in the South.

The **desert steppe** and the **arid savannah** of the Sahel contain grassland and shrubs; date palms grow only in the **oases**. The banks

antelopes. Ostriches, leopards and wart-hogs roam the desert steppes.

Population

Arabs and Berber Moors account for 81 per cent of the population. The b**lack Africans** consist of seven per cent Wolofs and there are five per cent Toucou-

Islam is the state religion; there is a small minority of Christians. Due to the adverse conditions of terrain and climate and lack of natural re-

History and Politics

When the Portuguese landed on the coast of Mauritania in the early fifteenth century, the once-powerful Islamic Almoravid

Moktar Ould Daddah

*Boutilimit, 20.12.1924,
†Paris, 14.10.2003

The leader of the Parti du Peuple became the ruler after Mauritania gained its independence from France in 1960 and its first president in 1961. In 1964, he established an authoritarian one-party system and was confirmed in his office three times in elections. After unsuccessfully trying to take over the former Spanish Western Sahara in 1976, the country suffered a serious economic crisis. Daddah was overthrown in a military coup in 1978.

Mauritanian women are gaining self-confidence and independence in this Islamic state.

Moussa Traoré

*Kayes, 12.9.1936

Traoré gained power through a military coup staged in Mali in 1968 and established a brutal regime of terror. In foreign policy, he was dependent on the Western, receiving support mainly from France, especially after the catastrophic droughts of the early 1970s. In 1991, he was overthrown himself in an army coup and imprisoned. After seven years, he was tried and sentenced to death, together with his wife, for abuse of power. He was subsequently pardoned.

country's surface area. The Senegal is the only river that contains water all year round and constitutes the most favourable area for human settlement.

of the Senegal are covered with baobab trees, raffia (raphia) palms and bamboo.

The savannah is a habitat for elephants, lions, hyenas and

leurs, three per cent Soninkes and one per cent Fulbes, Bambaras, Sarakolés and other ethnic groups. There are around 5,000 Europeans in the country.

sources, 31.4 per cent of Mauritanians live below the poverty line. The average life expectancy is only 53 years and the illiteracy rate is 62 per cent.

kingdom which extended as far as Spain had been defunct for 300 years. Due to the country's inhospitable terrain, the colonial powers showed little interest in

*Masks play an important role in the lives of the **Dogon** in Mali. There are a 100 different designs of these imaginative masks, symbolising ancestors, animals and spirits. Myths and stories are told through rituals and dance.*

it; consequently, Moorish sultans reigned until the end of the nineteenth century. Not until 1903 did the French declare Mauritania a protectorate and in 1920 they finally made it into a colony.

After gaining **independence** in 1960, Morocco renounced its claims to the area but these were not surrendered until 1970. Following the retreat of the Spaniards from the Western Sahara, Mauritania occupied the south and Morocco the north of this former Spanish colony. Both powers subsequently embarked in a war, supported by France, against the **Polisario National Front** independence movement . During the clashes, Mauretania's armed forces revolted and in 1979 Mauritania waived all claims to the Western Sahara.

Several coups d'état and government reshuffles ensued which resulted in a turbulent period. Tensions with Senegal led to the respective expulsions of citizens. Since 1991 a new constitution has been in place which stipulates that Islamic sharia law is now to be enforced. In 1992, the first multi-party elections were held and good relations with Senegal were restored.

The national assembly is re-elected every five years and the members of parliament, the supreme court and the head of state are elected directly by the people every six years. Voting rights are granted to those aged over 18. Although opposition parties are permitted, elections have allegedly been manipulated to ensure the ruling party wins.

Economy

The Gross Domestic Product was US$5.534 billion in 2004. **Agriculture** accounted for 25 per cent of this amount, **industry** for 32 per cent and the **services sector** for 25 per cent.

The main exports are fish, fish products and raw materials, especially iron ore and gypsum. The main imports include foodstuffs, machinery, vehicles, oil and gas and chemicals.

Transport

Of the 8,900 km of **roads** only 1,700 km are surfaced. The only stretch of **railway track**, which is 675 km long, runs from Zouîrât to Nouadhibou and is predominantly used for transporting iron ore. There are **international airports** and **sea ports** in Nouakchott and Nouâdhibou.

Tourism

Tourism in Mauritania is extremely under-developed. Several oases and the remains of ancient Islamic architecture are worth a visit. The best time to visit is between November and March.

Mali

Area:	1,240,192 sq. km
Capital city:	Bamako
Form of government:	
Presidential Republic	
Administrative divisions:	
8 regions and a capital district	

1 The Dogon in Mali build their villages on the steep slopes of the Bandiagara Highlands in a loop of Niger river. The thatched buildings serve as granaries.

2 In the market of Bamako, the capital of Mali, the wares on offer include convenience foods, grain, fish and spices. Many shoppers still barter for goods.

3 From 1907 until 1909 the great mosque of Djenné was restored, modelled on the orginal fifteenth-century design that had been destroyed.

Mali, Niger

Population: 12.2 million
(9 inhabitants/sq. km)
Languages: French (official language), Bamakan, other Mandé languages
GDP per capita: US$1000
Currency:
1 CFA franc = 100 centimes

Natural geography

The country is mainly desert, being covered by the **Sahara**, the **Sahel** and the **Sudan**. The desert in the north is flanked by the Adra mountains, rising to an altitude of up to 853 m. The river Niger flows through the south and floods vast areas on a regular basis. The highest elevation is the 1,155-m-high Hombori Tondo south of the Niger Bend. The tableland of the southwest is characterised by the valleys of the Senegal river and its tributaries.

Climate

The climate outside the desert areas is **humid and tropical**, whilst a **desert climate** prevails in the areas covered by the Sahara. Average temperatures range between 25 and 30°C in the south and 18 and 36°C in the Sahara. During the rainy season, precipitation is between 1,000 and 1,500 mm in the south, whilst it often does not rain for years in the Sahara. The grassland savannah and gallery forests of the south are replaced northwards by dry and thornbush savannah. These then turn into semi-desert and finally full desert. This is the habitat of lions, hyenas, leopards, monkeys, elephants, crocodiles, gazelles, buffalos, giraffes, hippopotamuses and many birds and reptiles.

Population

The population comprises 32 per cent **Bambaras**, 14 per cent **Fulbes**, 12 per cent **Senufos**, nine per cent **Soninkés**, seven per cent **Tuaregs**, seven per cent **Songhais**, six per cent Malinkés and smaller individual groups. Muslims account for 80 per cent of the population, 18 per cent are followers of natural religions and just over one per cent is Christian. The average life expectancy is only 50 years and the illiteracy rate is 69 per cent.

History and Politics

Following the demise of several great empires, the country broke off into smaller political units in the sixteenth century and was a French colony from 1895 to 1960. Following a failed attempt at a confederation of French Sudan and Senegal, Mali proclaimed its **independence** on 22 September 1960. After a revolt, a military dictatorship followed the first Socialist government. There has been a democratic constitution since 1992. The parliament and the head of state are elected directly every five years. Citizens of 21 years of age have the right to vote.

Economy

The Gross Domestic Product was US$5.434 billion in 2005. **Agriculture** accounted for 46 per cent of this amount, **industry** for 17 per cent and the **services sector** for 37 per cent. The main imports are machinery, vehicles, petroleum and foodstuffs. Exports include cotton and gold.

Transport

The **road network** is approximately 13,000 km long, although only around 1,800 km is paved. The majority of the roads are in the south. The **rail network** is 650 km long. The rivers Niger and Senegal are navigable at times. There is an international **airport** in Sénou.

Tourism

The infrastructure is still underdeveloped. Mali is the site of the legendary city of Timbuktu (Timbuctoo), once the centre of a flourishing empire, which is its main attraction. Bamako has interesting markets and the national museum. The best time to visit is from November to February.

Area: 1,267,000 sq. km
Capital city: Niamey
Form of government:
Presidential Republic
Administrative divisions:
8 départements
Population: 11.6 million
(8 inhabitants/sq. km)

rounded by the Central Sahara Basin on three sides. It adjoins the **Ahaggar Massif** to the North and the **Djado Plateau** and the **Tibesti Ridge** to the north-east. Numerous wadis criss-cross the **desert**. Only the River Niger and the Komadugu Yobe contain water all year round.

Climate

In the Sahara region a **desert climate** prevails, with temperatures between 17 and 34°C; precipitation is less than 50 mm.
In the Sahel, temperatures range from 22°C in January to 34°C in June. Over half of the 400 to 700 mm precipitation falls in August. Grassland dotted with clumps of trees is characteristic of the savannahs of the south, whilst in the desert vegetation is confined to the oases. Desert foxes, lizards and desert rats (jerboa) are typical desert creatures. Ostriches, elephants, buffaloes, warthogs, lions, gazelles, antelopes and hye-

cent, **Tuaregs** for 9.2 per cent and **Kanouris** for 4.3 per cent. Tubus, Arabs and Europeans form small minorities.
80 per cent of the population is Muslim, approximately 15 per cent are animists and a minority are Christians. Life expectancy is extremely low at 47 years and the illiteracy rate is exceedingly high at 86 per cent, despite the fact that primary school is compulsory.

History and Politics

Before Europeans explored the country in the late eighteenth century, several great empires and city-states existed in what is now Niger and these were converted to Islam at an early stage. The colonial powers took no interest in the country until the late nineteenth century. Niger became a French colony in 1921, an overseas territory in 1946 and an autonomous republic in 1958.
After France granted Niger **independence** in 1960, several military dictatorships succeeded the first civilian government. The first free elections took place in 1993. In 1999, there was another coup d'état led by the army. Today the country has become a **democratic presidential republic** again. In accordance with the 1999 constitution, the Parliament is elected every five years. The head of state is also elected through direct elections every five years. The right to vote is granted at 18.

Economy

The Gross Domestic Product was almost US$3.432 billion in 2005. **Agriculture** accounted for 40 per cent of this sum, **industry** for 18 per cent and the **service sector** for 42 per cent. The main imports are consumer goods, partially processed and capital goods. Uranium, peanuts, gum arabic and livestock are exported. Niger recently hit the world headlines due the possibility that the country provided the former Iraqi dictator, Saddam Hussein, with uranium for bomb-making. The lasting drought has produced a prolonged economic crisis.

Transport

The length of the **road network** is only approximately 9,700 km,

Despite catastrophic economic conditions there is a plenty on offer in the markets of Cape Verde.

Languages: French (official), Hausa and other tribal languages
GDP per capita.: US$900
Currency:
1 CFA franc = 100 centimes

Natural geography

The **Aïr** volcanic mountain range dominates the centre of the country, rising to 2,000 m and sur-

nas live in the savannah, in addition to numerous species of birds and snakes. Crocodiles and hippopotamuses live in the rivers.

Population

Hausas account for 53.6 per cent of the inhabitants of Niger. **Djermas** and **Songhays** account for 21 per cent, **Fulbes** for 10.4 per

Long period of drought and extreme temperatures are common in Niger. The sand and rock desert of Ténéré in the north of the republic is sparsely populated due to its unforgiving surroundings. However archaeological finds show that *there was a thriving hunting and herding culture in the area between 7,000 and 3,000 BC, when the climate was considerably been milder. Djado is one of the few settlements in this region, consisting of traditional mud huts.*

of which only 3,200 km are paved. There is an international **airport** at Niamey. The river Niger is partially navigable.

Tourism

The main tourist attractions are the **'W'-National Park** and the **Aïr and Ténéré National Nature Reserves**. Only around 17,000 tourists visited the country in 1996. The best time to visit Niger is between November and March.

Cape Verde

Area:	4,033 sq. km
Capital city:	Praia
Form of government: Republic	
Administrative divisions: 15 districts	
Population: 418,000 (102 inhabitants/sq. km)	
Languages: Portuguese (official), Creole	
GDP per capita:	US$6200
Currency: 1 Cape-Verde escudo = 100 centavos	

Natural geography

Only ten of a total of 18 islands within a distance of 630 km of the West African coastline are inhabited. Whilst **Sal**, **Boa Vista** and **Maio** are relatively flat and are characterised by sand dunes and salt marshes, the remaining islands have a mountainous structure and rocky coast. Pico, an extinct volcano is the highest elevation on Fogo Island, at an altitude of 2,829 m.

Climate

The passat wind, blowing from the north-east produces a **tropical climate** with temperatures ranging from 22°C in February to 27°C in September. The precipitation of 250 mm on the coast and 1000 mm at altitudes only occurs during the south-west monsoon season from August to October. In some years, however, there is no rain at all. Brushwood and thorn bushes have replaced the original vegetation which has almost completely disappeared due to bush fires and overgrazing. While the sea offers a unique variety of species of fish,

only wild goats and a few species of lizards and rodents survive on dry land, in addition to approximately 100 species of birds.

Population

71 per cent of the inhabitants of Cape Verde are **mixed race**, 28 per cent are **black** and one per cent white. Catholics account for 96.3 per cent of the population, one per cent are Anglicans and a minority are followers of animist religions. The average life expectancy is 66 years and the illiteracy rate is 28 per cent.

History and Politics

In around 1460, explorers took possession of the island for the Portuguese crown. With the end of the slave trade, the colony lost its economic significance. In July 1975 the Cape Verde islands gained **independence**. Attempts at unification with Guinea-Bissau finally collapsed in 1980. Until 1991, the system of government was of a non-aligned one-party state. When this was abolished, the first **free elections** were held. The 1992 constitution stipulates that parliament is elected every five years and that the president is directly elected every five years. The voting age is 18.

Economy

The Gross Domestic Product was US$1.128 billion in 2005. **Agriculture** accounted for 11 per cent of this amount, **industry** for 17 per cent and the **services sector** for 72 per cent. The trade balance is in deficit. In 2001, the deficit amounted to 30 per cent of GDP. External debt totalled US$300 million in 2001. Machinery, vehicles and foodstuffs are imported, while fish products and shoes are exported. One of the most important sources of foreign currency for the country are the funds sent home by expatriate Cape Verdians, of whom there are approximately 700,000, mainly in Portugal.

Transport

The country's **road network** is 2,250 km in length. Only 100 km are surfaced. Motor boats and small airlines link the various is-

lands. There is an international **airport** on Sal.

Tourism

The long, sandy beaches and the good scuba-diving, as well as the welcoming environment, make the Cape Verde Islands popular with tourists.

1 For hundreds of years camel caravans have been crossing the Sahara in the Republic of Niger, below the Aïr mountains.

2 The river Niger forms an approximately 40,000 sq. km delta in central Mali, with a labyrinth of creeks, lakes and

swamps. It has a rich flora, including the typical doum palm and the baobab.

3 There are only few settlements in the Ténéré desert in the Republic of Niger. The oasis of Iferouane is located in the shadow of the Aïr mountains.

Senegal, Gambia

*In recent years, the situation of **women in the Gambia** has improved significantly. Most of the population are Sunni Muslims. The number of women in work is rising. In spite of the questionable nature of the democratic reforms introduced in the 1996 constitution, women have become more self-confident. They are increasingly banding together in small cooperatives, running enterprises such as bakeries.*

Senegal

Area:	196,722 sq. km
Capital City:	Dakar
Form of government:	
Presidential Republic	
Administrative divisions:	
10 regions	
Population:	
11.1m (53 inhabitants/sq. km)	
Languages:	French, Wolof
GDP per inhabitant: US$1,800	
Currency:	
1 CFA-franc = 100 centimes	

Natural geography

Most of the country is covered by the Senegal and Gambian coastal lowlands. In the east, there is the mountainous region of Fouta Djallon, the source of the headwaters of the rivers of Senegal. The coastal plain is flat with the exception of the Cape Verde Peninsula, which is the result of volcanic activity on the islands.

Climate

Senegal's tropical climate is extremely dry in the north, which is often affected by **droughts**, and has an average rainfall of only 300 mm. In the south up to 1,500 mm of rain falls between April and November. The average temperature fluctuates between 27°C inland and 24.5°C on the coast.

In the coastal region, there are mangrove swamps; inland, a tropical jungle predominates, which changes into tree savannah, bush savannah and finally dry savannah to the north. The **Niokolo-Koba National Park** contains a wealth of flora and fauna, including antelopes, monkeys, hyenas, hippopotamuses, leopards, lions, elephants and buffaloes.

Population

44 per cent of the Senegalese are **Wolof**, 15 per cent **Sérer**, 11 per cent **Toucouleurs** and five per cent **Diola**. There are also minorities of Mandinka, Soninka, Malinké, Fulani, Moors, Lebanese, Syrians, French and other groups. As regards religion, 94.5 per cent are Sunni Muslims, five per cent Christians and a minority follow animist religions. The average life expectancy is only 50 years, The literacy rate is 67 per cent. More than half the population lives below the poverty line and 44 per cent live in cities.

Senegal: 78 per cent of the working population lives from farming.

History and politics

After the Portuguese discovered the mouth of Senegal River in 1444, the Dutch, French and British traded along it in gold, ivory and, above all, slaves.

In the nineteenth century, today's Senegal became a **French colony**. Soon afterwards, the Africans living in Senegal were granted French citizenship, before the country achieved **independence** on 4 April 1960. The first president was Léopold Senghor, an author whose work was extensively published in France.

An attempted federation with French Sudan (now Mali) failed in 1959, just before independence. A federation with the Gambia, known as Senegambia, lasted from 1982 to 1989.

Today, Senegal is a relatively stable democratic presidential republic. The President is elected directly every five years; parliament is also elected every five years. The voting age is 18.

Economy

In 2005, GDP amounted to US$7.97 billion of which 17 per cent derived from **agriculture**, 21 per cent from **industry** and 61 per cent from the **services sector**. Semi-manufactured products, foodstuffs, machinery, oil and vehicles are imported. Exports include fish, fish meal, peanuts and chemicals, mainly phosphates.

Transport

Only 3,600 km of the 14,000 km **road network** is paved. The **rail network** covers 1,200 km. Dakar is an important **sea port** and has an international **airport**.

Tourism

Although the tourist infrastructure is still being developed, around 300,000 tourists visit Senegal annually. Cultural centres are Dakar and Saint Louis.

Gambia

Area:	11,295 sq. km
Capital city:	Banjul
Form of government:	
Presidential Republic	
Administrative divisions:	
6 regions, 35 districts	
Population:	
1.5 m (132 inhabitants/sq. km)	
Languages:	
English (official), Mandinka, Wolof, other local languages	
GDP per inhabitant:	US$1900
Currency:	
1 dalasi = 100 butut	

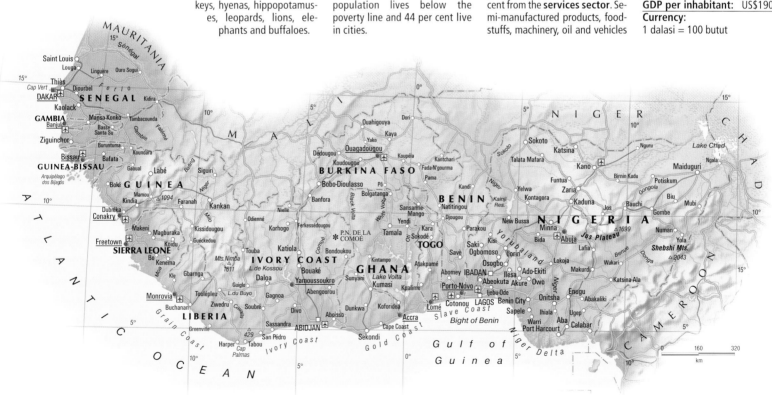

Bidjogo: The kinsmen of this small ethnic group on the coast of Guinea-Bissau, are known to be excellent fishermen, boat-builders and makers of handicrafts. Thus along with masks, they also produce cult objects, spirit containers, *fertility dolls and ancestor figures, as well as naturally styled bull masks. These are worn together with hippopotamus or colourful bird masks, during initiation ceremonies or rites of passage.*

Natural geography

The Gambia is surrounded on three sides by **Senegal**. It is a small country running beside the length of the river Gambia for 375 km from the Atlantic into the African hinterland; in parts it is only 24 km wide. The river landscape of Gambia changes from an alluvial plain to low hills and finally to a plateau which reaches a height of 200 m.

Climate

The **tropical climate** produces average temperatures of 23°C in January and 28°C in July. During the rainy season, between June and October, rainfall is 1,300 mm on the coast and 1,000 mm inland. The area at the mouth of the river Gambia is covered in mangrove swamp. In the central reaches of the river there is wet savannah and in the east dry savannah.
Both major areas of the country contain large numbers of the big animals, especially in the national parks. Typical species are crocodiles, hippopotamuses, monkeys, antelopes, wart-hogs, hyenas, jackals, leopards and many species of birds.

Population

The many ethnic groups include the **Mandinka**, the largest at 44 per cent. There are also 17.5 per cent **Fulani**, 12.3 per cent **Wolof**, seven per cent **Diola**, seven per cent **Soninke** as well as smaller minorities. 85 per cent are Muslim, ten per cent Christians and a minority of followers of natural religions. The average life expectancy is only 53 years. The literacy rate is 61 per cent.

History and politics

Portuguese explorers first discovered the Gambia in the mid-fifteenth century but handed over the trading rights to England as early as 1588. Soon trading posts were founded along the Gambia River. In 1816, the British purchased Saint Mary's Island from a local chief and established Bathurst, now the capital Banjul. This city was important early on especially for its use as a buffer against the slave trade. The Gambia was important for the trade in gold, ivory and ebony. In 1889, the official borders were established between British Gambia and French Senegal, and they still apply today.
After **independence** in 1965, Dawda K. Jawara ruled until the military coup by Yahyah Jammeh, the current president. Attempts at reunification with Senegal failed. In keeping with the 1997 constitution, 45 members of the parliament are elected directly and four members of the assembly are appointed by the president who is elected every five years. The voting age is 18 years.

Economy

In 2005, GDP was US$429 million of which 28 per cent came from **agriculture**, 15 per cent from **industry** and 58 per cent from the **services sector**. The balance of trade is alarmingly in deficit. Imports include foodstuffs, industrial goods, machinery, fuel and vehicles. Livestock, mainly cattle, peanuts, fish, skins and furs are exported.

Transport

Around 500 km of the 3,100 km **road network** is paved. The river Gambia is navigable and river transport is important. Bajul has an international **airport**.

Tourism

The Atlantic beaches are attracting more and more tourists. The best time to travel is between November and May.

Guinea-Bissau

Area:	36,125 sq. km
Capital City:	Bissau
Form of government:	
Presidential Republic	
Administrative divisions:	
3 provinces, 8 regions, 1 district (capital city)	
Population:	
1.4m (36 inhabitants/sq. km)	
Languages:	
Portuguese (official), Creole, dialects	
GDP per inhabitant:	US$900
Currency:	
1 CFA-franc = 100 centimes	

Natural geography

The Bijagos Archipelago, lies off the ragged coastline and are part of the Guinea-Bissau national territory. In the undulating hinterland, which reaches a height of 300 m, there are numerous meandering rivers, which flood large parts of the country during the rainy season.

1 The smallest socio-economic unit in Senegal is the extended family, which encompasses a large group of relatives and which is presided over by a male elder.

2 Traditionally, the most important decisions of the village community are made by the elder. This important institution has preserved its role among all the ethnic groups of Senegal.

3 Local produce is sold in the numerous markets of Senegal, though the selection is often rather limited.

*Around 85 per cent of Guinea's labour force is employed in **agriculture**, which still only contributes 24 per cent of GDP. Manioc, rice, plantains, palm kernels, bananas and pineapples constitute the main crops. The land is not very fertile, due to widespread slash-and-burn practices and primitive cultivation methods. Unfortunately, children are still widely used in the labour force, so only around 30 per cent of them attend school.*

Climate

The humid and dry tropical climates produce average temperatures of 26°C. During the rainy season, between May and October, average rainfall in the north is around 1,200 mm and 3,000 mm in the west.

The coastal vegetation consists of mangrove forests and swamps; the coastal flats and the islands are covered in evergreen rainforest. Inland, there are dry forests, which turn into tree and shrub savannah in the east. Typical fauna of the savannah are elephants, hyenas, buffaloes, antelopes and leopards. Many types of birds live on the coast, as well as crocodiles and hippopotamuses.

Population

25 per cent of the inhabitants are **Balanta**, 20 per cent **Fulani**, 12 per cent **Mandinka**, 11 per cent **Manjak** and ten per cent **Papel**. There are also other groups, including a white minority.

Over 50 per cent are followers of animist religions, 38 per cent are Muslims and eight per cent Christians – mostly Catholics. The average life expectancy is 44 years. The literacy rate is 45 per cent.

History and politics

In 1446, the Portuguese took possession of the country, calling Portuguese Guinea, and organising a lucrative **slave trade**. Portuguese rule lasted until in 1961, resistance formed against the rulers in Lisbon and a protracted liberation war began, ending in independence after the revolution of 1974 in Portugal, toppling the dictator Antonio Salazar. Repeated efforts at unification with neighbouring Cape Verde, also a former Portuguese colony, failed, leading to a series of military incursions and virtual civil war. Under the 1984 constitution which was first amended in 1996, the National Assembly and Head of State are elected directly every five years. The voting age is 18 years.

Economy

Gross Domestic Product was US$280m in 2005. Of this, 53 per cent derived from **agriculture**, 14 per cent from **industry** and 33 per cent from the services sector.

Guinea-Bissau currently has enormous foreign debts and an extremely negative balance of trade. This is due to the political unrest, coupled with the fact that the country is too small and underdeveloped to be economically viable. Food, machinery, vehicles, oil and petroleum products are imported. Cashew nuts are the most important crop contributing to 85 per cent of exports. Other exports are timber from the tropical forests, fish, coconuts and rice.

Transport

Only 300 km of the **road network** which stretches over a total length of around 5,000 km is paved. There is no rail network. The capital city, Bissau, possesses an important **sea port** and an international **airport**.

Tourism

Due the unsettled political situation, all foreigners living in the country in 1998 were evacuated. Tourism is still not possible. For climatic reasons, the best time to travel would be between December and April.

Guinea	
Area:	245,857 sq. km
Capital city:	Conakry
Form of government: Republic	
Administrative divisions: 4 super-regions, 30 regions, 1 district (capital city)	
Population: 9.4 m (29 inhabitants/sq. km)	
Languages: French (official), tribal languages	
GDP per inhabitant: US$2,200	
Currency: 1 Guinea-franc = 100 centimes	

Natural geography

The coast, which has many bays, is dotted with offshore islands. The coastal plane is 90 km wide in places. The **Fouta Djallon** plateau, which adjoins the coastal plain reaches a height of up to 1,500 m. Here lie the sources of the river Gambia and the river Senegal, as well as other rivers. The tablelands in the east are between 400 and 500 m high and are intersected by the Upper Niger and its tributaries. The highest peak of the island mountains to the south is the Mount Nimba at 1,752 m.

Climate

The tropical wet/dry climate results in average temperatures ranging from 25°C to 28°C. During the rainy season, in which there are often tremendous storms, the rainfall in the south east and on the coast reaches up to 4,000 mm, while inland only 1,300–2,000 mm.

The unspoiled **rainforest vegetation** has only been maintained in large areas of the south-east. Deforestation has produced a **moist savanna** in the west and **dry savanna** in the north-east. The coast is lined with mangrove swamps.

The once rich wildlife has only been preserved in the Nimba Reserve. The typical animals here include elephants, leopards, lions, antelopes, buffaloes, monkeys, hyenas, crocodiles, snakes, hippopotamuses, manatee and many species of birds.

Population

There are numerous ethnic groups of which the **Malinké** and **Fulani** with 30 per cent each are the most numerous. There are 15 per cent **Susu** , 6.5 per cent **Kissi** and 4.8 per cent **Kpelle**. 95 per cent of the population is Muslim and there are 1.5 per cent Christians as well as followers of various animist religions. The average life expectancy is 46 years. The literacy rate is 64 per cent, but only 17 per cent for women.

History and politics

By the time the Portuguese founded their first trading posts on the part of the coast of West Africa known as the Guinea Coast for its rich gold reserves, in the late fifteenth century, the Islamic Empire of Mali, which experienced its heyday in the fourteenth century under Mansa Musa, had long been destroyed.

The other European colonial powers became involved in the area only in the nineteenth century. The French, who were able to assert their claim over that of the British, had a long struggle against the resistance of the local population. From 1898, Guinea was a French

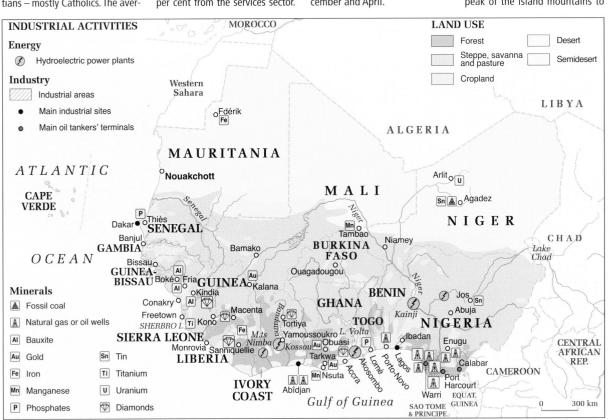

*The **Temne**, a farming people, account for a third of Sierra Leon's population and are organised around into chiefdoms, each chief usually governing several surrounding villages. Alliances and relationships within each chiefdom are of great importance to the Temne. The organisation of religious festivities is entrusted to local men's and women's associations.*

colony under the name of French Guinea (Guinée française).

After Guinea was granted **independence** in 1958, under the dictator Ahmed Sekou Touré, all opposition was brutally suppressed and two million citizens fled the country. Relations were warmest with the Soviet Union. After the death of Touré in 1984, the army staged a coup d'etat.

The new head of state, Colonel Lansana Conté, promised to introduce a multi-party system and free elections, but Guinea remains a one-party state. There are known to be human rights violations and election manipulation. The 1991 constitution provides for the election of parliament every four years and the direct election of the head of state, the president, every five years. The voting age is 18 years.

Economy

In 2005, the GDP was US$3.5 billion of which 24 per cent derived from **agriculture**, 31 per cent from **industry** and 45 per cent from the **services sector**. In spite of the great potential of the country for agricultural development and the rich deposits of bauxite, diamonds, gold and iron ore, Guinea is still dependent on international aid. Engines, machines, vehicles, consumer goods, oil and oil products and foodstuffs are all imported; coffee, rice, palm kernels, alumina, bauxite, gold and diamonds are amongst the main exports. Despite its vast natural resources, Guinea remains a very underdeveloped country.

Transport

Only one sixth of the 30,270 km long **road network** is paved. In addition to the private railway lines that are used exclusively for freight transport, there is a 660 km long state **rail link** from Conakry to Kankan. There are **sea ports** at Kamsar and Conakry and Conakry also has an international **airport**.

Tourism

Tourism is virtually non-existent. One reason is that the rulers of Guinea have agreed to allow foreign toxic waste to be dumped in their territory. The climate is at its most bearable between December and March.

Sierra Leone

Area:	71,740 sq. km
Capital city:	Freetown
Form of government:	
Republic in the Commonwealth	
Administrative divisions:	
4 provinces, 1 municipality, 147 chiefdoms	
Population: 6 million (75 inhabitants/sq. km)	
Languages: English (official), Creole	
GDP per inhabitant:	US$800
Currency: 1 leone = 100 cents	

Natural geography

The coastal plains are lined with mangrove swamps and are about 40 km wide with offshore islands, estuaries and sand banks. The partly mountainous peninsula of Sierra Leone (meaning 'lion mountain') reaches heights of up to 890 m. The plains inland border the Guinea highlands in the east, dominated by the Loma Mountains. The highest mountain is the Loma Mansa, which reaches a height of 1,948 m.

Climate

The wet/dry **tropical climate** produces temperatures between 25 and 28°C in the coastal area. During the dry season, the hot dry wind known as the **Harmattan** blows south from the Sahara. The rainfall on the Sierra Leone peninsula can amount to 5,000 mm per annum. In the east, it is 3,000 mm and in the north only 2,000 mm annually.

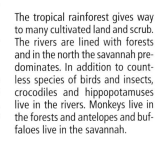

The tropical rainforest gives way to many cultivated land and scrub. The rivers are lined with forests and in the north the savannah predominates. In addition to countless species of birds and insects, crocodiles and hippopotamuses live in the rivers. Monkeys live in the forests and antelopes and buffaloes live in the savannah.

1 Play of colours: in the market of Mamou, a small town in Guinea, the local farmers sell their wares.

2 Blood diamonds: both government and the rebels in Sierra Leone have used precious stones to finance arms and mercenaries.

3 In addition to bauxite and gold, diamonds also play an important role in the Guinea economy.

4 Mobile office: because of the high illiteracy rate, professional scribes with 'offices' in the streets, have plenty of work in Freetown.

Sierra Leone, Liberia, Burkina Faso

*The agricultural sector in Burkina Faso has been consistently supported by foreign aid since the 1980s. The country's biggest asset is its **livestock**. Cattle, sheep, pigs, donkeys and poultry are reared. The supply of livestock to the capital Ouagadougou from the surrounding area is more than adequate and some traders even become wealthy enough to bring their wares to market on a motor-bike.*

Population

Among the many ethnic groups, the Mendes with 34.6 per cent and the Temnes with 31.7 per cent are the most frequently represented. In addition, there are 8.4 per cent Limba, 3.5 per cent Kuranko as well as minorities of Europeans, Asians and Lebanese. In addition to followers of local religions, 39 per cent profess Islam and eight per cent Christianity.

History and politics

After the country's discovery by the Portuguese, the Dutch and British also founded trading settlements, from which the lucrative trade in slaves, gold and diamonds was conducted in the eighteenth century. Sierra Leone became a British colony in 1808 and the first colony of freed slaves which is why the capital is called Freetown. For a long time these Creoles dominated the country due to their better education. It was declared a British protectorate in 1896.

After **independence** in 1961 conflicts broke out between the Creoles and the native population. In 1971, the status of a dominion within the Commonwealth was granted and a **Republic** declared. After a succession of military regimes the Temnes-Group All-People's Congress assumed power in 1978, suppressing all opposition. From 1990, a civil war broke out against rebels from the Revolutionary United Front (RUF) who had forced their way into the country from Liberia. The 1991 Constitution promised democratisation but this never happened due to another military coup. Following the intervention of the West African peace-keeping force ECOMOG in 1998, President Ahmad Tejan Kabbah, first elected in 1996 returned to power, but this caused the rebels to respond with attacks. Only in 1999, with the help of British forces was a peace treaty signed. The UN stationed a peace-keeping force in the country. In May 2002 Kabbah was once more elected President.

Economy

In 2005 the GNP was US$1.1bn. Of that, 42 per cent derived from **agriculture**, 27 per cent from **industry** and 31 per cent from the services sector. There are rich deposits of titanium, gold, diamonds, iron ore and bauxite but they are not well developed. The gemstone trade, mainly diamonds, principally serves the financing of the war. The agricultural sector remains weak and the arbitrary and ruthless clearing of the rainforests has led to catastrophic **environmental damage**.

Machinery, vehicles, timber and foodstuffs are imported; rutile, diamonds, bauxite and cocoa are exported.

Transport

Only around 1,200 km of the **road network** which covers 7,500 km is paved. The single **railway** line extends 84 km between Pepel and Marampa. The rivers are only navigable during the rainy season. In Freetown there is a **seaport** and somewhat further north there is an international **airport**.

Tourism

The constant civil wars and virtual absence of infrastructure make tourism almost impossible. The swampland encourages malaria which is why this part of the coast of West Africa, the Guinea Coast, was traditionally known as 'the white man's grave'. Nevertheless, if the unrest is quelled and a stable form of government achieved, the higher land of the 'lion mountain' can be relatively pleasant. Between November and March, the weather is at its best.

Liberia	
Area:	111,369 sq. km
Capital city:	Monrovia
Form of government: Presidential Republic	
Administrative divisions: 11 districts, 4 territories	
Population: 3.4m (30 inhabitants/sq. km)	
Languages: English (official), tribal languages	
GDP per inhabitant:	US$700
Currency: 1 Liberian dollar = 100 cents	

Natural geography

The 600-km-long coast is characterised by numerous sand banks, spits and lagoons as well as in parts by a rocky shoreline. A plateau landscape, which reaches heights of up to 400 m, adjoins the 10 to 50-km-wide marshy, coastal plain. In the north, there are mountains, such as the Nimba Range, including the 1,384 m high Guest House Hill.

Climate

The **tropical, rainy climate** produces average temperatures of 24 °C to 27°C on the coast and from 22°C to 28°C inland. On the coast the rainfall is 4,500 mm, inland 2,000 mm and in the mountains 3,000 mm. In summer, the **Harmattan** desert wind produces a hot, dry spell. A third of the country's area is covered by tropical rainforests, though these have been reduced by almost half due to massive deforestation and the sale of timber. On the coast, there are mangrove swamps and savannahs.

Population

Liberia contains 16 different ethnic groups. The largest are the **Kpelle** at 20 per cent, the **Bassa** at 14 per cent, the **Grebo** at nine per cent, the **Kru** at eight per cent, the **Mandinka** at six per cent and the **Loma** at six per cent. 70 per cent of the inhabitants follow animist religions, 20 per cent are Muslims and ten per cent Christians of various denominations.

History and politics

After the Portuguese occupied the Pepper Coast in 1461, several European nations founded trading posts to sell slaves and exotic woods. Nevertheless, the country remained of little interest to the colonial powers. In 1816, US philanthropists purchased a coastal strip of land from the Kru tribes and from 1822 freed American slaves settled there. In 1847, Liberia became the first independent African **Republic** with a constitution based on the US model. Under President Wilson Tubman, who ruled between 1944 and 1971 the country was once again open for foreign investors. Liberia is one of the countries that operates as a 'flag of convenience' for merchant shipping, and it became nominal port for the world's largest merchant fleet. Tubman's death was followed by several brutal **military dictatorships**. A civil war broke out that was temporarily ended in 1996. In 1997, the rebel leader, Charles Taylor, staged a coup and made himself president. In 2000, civil war broke out between government troops and the Liberian United for Reconciliation and Democracy (LURD). LURD was able to bring large parts of Liberia under its control. The fighting lasted until 2003. In August 2003, Taylor resigned and went into exile to Nigeria. With US support the West African peacekeeping force, ECOMIL, managed to stabilise the situation. In October 2003, the businessman Gyude Bryant, became head of a transitional government. In 2005, former UN Diplomat Ellen Johnson-Sirleaf was elected Head of State.

Economy

As a result of the civil war and a chaotic economic policy, the economic situation is catastrophic. Unemployment is currently over 80 per cent. Timber and diamonds continue to be exported.

Transport

Only around 750 km of the 10,000 km **road network** is paved. The **rail network** is around 520 km long and is used mainly to carry iron ore. There is an international **airport** near Monrovia.

Tourism

Liberia's tourist trade is scarcely developed. The best time to travel is between November and March.

Burkina Faso	
Area:	274,200 sq. km
Capital City:	Ouagadougou
Form of government: Republic	
Administrative divisions: 45 provinces	
Population: 13.9 m (47 inhabitants/sq. km)	
Languages: French (official), Fulani, Moorish and other tribal languages	

The mosques in Burkina Faso are made of clay, which is a typical West African construction material.

*Under president Félix Houphouët-Boigny grandiose building projects were implemented. In 1990 the **Notre-Dame-de-la-Paix** basilica, that can contain up to 18,000 people, was opened in the capital Yamoussoukro.*

GDP per inhabitant: US$1200
Currency:
1 CFA franc = 100 centimes

Natural geography

A large part of the country's land mass consists of a 250 to 350-m-high plateau and individual mountain ranges. The highest peak is the 749 m Tenakourou. The sandstone tablelands in the south-west of the country are the source of the Black Volta.

Climate

In the north-east, a dry **tropical climate** predominates; rainfall of less than 500 mm falls between June and August. The **south-west monsoon** causes rainfall of up to 1,200 mm in the south and centre of the country.
The average temperatures are 27°C to 30°C; in the north , the temperature can rise to 44°C on occasion. In the dry season, the dry hot **Harmattan** wind blows from the Sahara in the north.
In the south, moist savannahs predominate with jungle lining the rivers. In the north, there are only thorny savannahs and steppes. The national parks are well-stocked with birds, buffaloes, hippopotamuses, lions, jackals, monkeys and crocodiles.

Population

Burkina Faso has around 160 ethnic groups, including 48 per cent **Mossi**, ten per cent **Fulani** and seven per cent **Dagara** and **Lobi**. There are also groups of **Mende** as well as a European minority. Half of the population professes various animist religions, 43 per cent are Sunni Muslim and 12 per cent Christians, most of them Roman Catholic. The literacy rate is as high as 81 per cent. The average life expectancy is only 46. years.

History and politics

Europeans first began to explore the region in the early nineteenth century. Under Mossi rule, the country largely remained without foreign influence until the French claimed the region for themselves at the end of the nineteenth century. The country, under its former name of Upper Volta (Haute Volta) was declared a self-governing re-

public within the French community in 1958. After **independence** in 1960, Maurice Yaméogo became president, but he was soon overthrown in a military coup by Colonel Laminaza. One brutal dictator followed another. In addition to terror, corruption and political assassinations, a ruinous financial and economic policy resulted in a catastrophic situation. Since 1991, the former dictator Blaise Compaoré has ruled as elected head of state and has been able to achieve moderate economic advances.
The constitution was finally changed in 1997. Parliament is now directly elected every five years and the head of state, the president, every seven years. The voting age is 18.

Economy

In 2005, GDP was US$5.4 billion; of this, 35 per cent derived from **agriculture**, 17 per cent from **industry** and 48 per cent from the **service sector**.
The country has natural resources, including gold, zinc, silver, lead, nickel and manganese. Ony the gold is fully exploited. Industrial goods, food, fuel, machinery and vehicles are all imported; the most important exports are gold, cotton, peanuts, hides and skins. The economy is not helped by the fact that the country is small and landlocked. The economy is improving thanks to modernisation that has encouraged investment.

Transport

Only 1,100 km of the 16,500 km **road network** is fixed. There is a 517-km-long **railway stretch** and two international airports in the capital city and in Bobo Dioulasso.

Tourism

Tourism is developing very slowly. The best time to travel is between December and February.

Ivory Coast	
Area:	322,462 sq. km
Capital City:	Yamoussoukro
Form of government:	
Presidential Republic	

Administrative divisions:
49 departments
Population:
17.3m (52 inhabitants/sq. km)
Languages:
French (official), Dioula and other languages
GDP per inhabitant: US$1400
Currency:
1 CFA-franc = 100 centimes

1 The vicinity of Dori in the north-east of Burkina Faso is inhabited by nomadic tribes, still building their huts the traditional way.

2 The Abron belong to the Akan people of western Ghana and the eastern Ivory Coast.

3 Cotton, cocoa and wood are important exports for the Ivory Coast. There is increasing demand for other crops, especially pineapples, and although modern growing techniques are used, transport methods are often primitive, as seen here.

Ivory Coast, Ghana, Togo

*The **Ashanti** are Ghana's largest ethnic group. Until the nineteenth century they ruled a vast empire in West Africa. They are organised into a theocracy, in which the dignity of the ruler is emphasised by the amount of gold he wears.*

Natural geography

The coast is characterised by rocky cliffs in the west and lagoons in the east. A 60-km-wide coastal plain is backed by a hilly plateau. In the north and northwest, the **Nimba mountains** reach a height of 1,752 m.

Climate

In the north, a hot dry **desert climate** predominates with rainfall of 1,200–1,400 mm; in the south it is humid. Up to 2,300 mm rain falls in the mountains; 1,500 to 2,000 mm on the coast. The average temperatures range between 25°C and 28°C. Slash-and-burn forestry clearance and overgrazing have destroyed the jungle and left clearances of poor soil. Coconut palms and mangroves grow along the coast, inland, there are tropical rainforests and jungles. To the north, the moist savannah turns into a dry savannah.

Population

The population is composed of over 60 ethnic groups. In addition to 23 per cent **Baule**, 18 per cent **Bete**, 15 per cent **Senufo**, 14 per cent **Agni-Ashanti**, 11 per cent **Malinké**, ten per cent **Kru** and **Mande**, there are Dan Gouro, Kuoa, Fulani and other groups. 60 per cent are followers of animist religions, 27 per cent are Muslims and 20 per cent are Christian, mostly Catholic.

History and politics

The Portuguese in the fifteenth century and the French in the seventeenth set up trading posts along on the coast, from which they operated a flourishing trade in **ivory** and **slaves**. In the nineteenth century, the French controlled additional inland areas and operated plantations. In 1895, the Ivory Coast became part of French West Africa. Following **independence** in 1960 Félix Houphouët-Boigny took power, and remained head of state for 33 years. In 1986, he changed the official name of the country to Côte d'Ivoire. He was resented by the population for his grandiose building projects at the expense of the national economy. His successor was overthrown by a military coup d'état in 1999. In 2000, Laurent Gbagbo became president. The Ivory Coast was once considered the only stable country in the region but in September 2002, an anti-government uprising of Muslim rebels developed from a military revolt. French troops prevented the taking of Abidjan, the former capital, and the new capital, Yamoussoukro. They also supervised an armistice. The rebels were granted a share in government in the subsequent peace deal agreed in Paris in 2003. However, even the deployment of a United Nations peace-keeping force has brought no lasting stability.

Economy

In 2005, GDP was a total of US$16.5 bn. Of this, 31 per cent was derived from **agriculture**, 20 per cent from **industry** and 50 per cent from the **services sector**.

Women in Togo carrying goods on their heads.

There are large reserves of iron, nickel, copper and some oil. Foodstuffs, machinery and medicines are imported. Important exports include cocoa (the Ivory Coast is the world's largest producer), coffee, pineapples, wood and cotton.

Transport

Only 3,800 km of the 54,000-km-long road network is paved. The rail network is 665 km long. the major sea ports are Abidjan and San Pédro. The international airport is at Abidjan.

Tourism

The sandy beaches around the former capital Abidjan are increasingly popular with tourists, but political unrest has hampered expansion.

Ghana	
Area:	239,460 sq. km
Capital city:	Accra
Form of government:	
Presidential Republic	
Administrative divisions:	
10 regions, 110 districts	
Population:	
21 m (85 inhabitants/sq. km)	
Languages:	
English (official), over 70 other languages and dialects	
GDP per inhabitant:	US$2500
Currency:	
1 cedi = 100 pesewas	

Natural geography

The hinterland from the coast consists of a 20 to 100-km-wide lowland plain which joins on to the Ashanti plateau at an altitude of 700 m.

In the huge Volta river valley contains the 8,500 sq. km **Lake Volta**, one of the largest dams in the world. The **Volta** flows through a narrow gorge in the **Akwapim-Togo mountain range**, which runs along the border with Togo; the highest peak is the 885-m-high Afadjoto.

Climate

The **Harmattan,** the hot dry wind that blows south from the Sahara, and the wet **monsoon,** determine the climate of the inland tropical convergence zone. There is a rainy season between May and September, limited by the savannah climate in the north. Precipitation is between 1,100 and 1,270 mm annually. In the south there are two rainy seasons. The south-west has a rainfall of 1,250–2,100 mm annually but in the lee of the Akwapim-Togo mountain range, rainfall is only 750 mm.

Average temperatures are between 26°C and 29°C in the south; in the north, they can reach up to 43°C. Slash-and-burn deforestation, over-grazing and commercially driven timber-harvesting have led to a massive decline in the original rainforest. It has been replaced by secondary afforestation, which turns into savannah towards the north. Jungle continues to line the rivers, however. There are wild game sanctuaries in both parts of the country, populated by monkeys, antelopes, lions, leopards, buffaloes, elephants, hippopotamuses, crocodiles and many species of birds.

Population

Ghana has over 100 different population groups, the largest of which, at 52.4 per cent, are **Ashanti** and **Fanti**. There are 11.9 per cent **Ewe**, 7.8 per cent **Ga** and **Ga-Adangbe**, 1.3 per cent **Yoruba**, 15.8 per cent **Mossi**, 11.9 per cent **Guan** and 3.3 per cent **Gurma**. There are also Manda Hausa, Fulani and Europeans. As for religion, 40 per cent are Protestants, 20 per cent Catholics, 35 per cent followers of local religions and five per cent Muslim. The average life expectancy is 59 years. The literacy rate is 36 per cent.

History and politics

In 1471, Portuguese sailors landed on the Gold Coast and from then on, the Europeans traded in gold and slaves. In 1874, the Gold Coast became a British colony and in 1957 became the first country in Black Africa to gain its **independence**. At that time, the country changed its name to Ghana. The socialist course taken by the first prime minister **Kwame Nkrumah** led the country into economic ruin. The situation did not improve under the subsequent military dictatorships. One of the most important figures of recent history is Flight-lieutenant Jerry Rawlings, who served as the country's president several times. In 1991, he began democratic reforms and in 1992, a new constitution was voted in. In the presidential elections, Rawlings was confirmed in office. In 2001, the leader of the opposition, John Agyekum Kufuor, was elected President.

Economy

GDP for 2005 was US$9.4 bn of which 36 per cent derived from **agriculture**, 25 per cent from **industry** and 39 per cent from the **services sector**. The principal exports are gold, cocoa, manganese, bauxite and timber. Machinery, crude oil and finished products are amongst the main imports. Ghana is now the world's second-largest producer of cocoa. The beans were introduced by the British. Cocoa production has fallen as the trees are cut down for fuel and it takes 15 years for a tree to start producing beans.

Transport

The **rail network** covers around 1000 km and the **road network** 37,561 km, of which 9,535 km are paved. There is an international **airport** at Kotoka.

Tourism

In 1996, 300,000 tourists contributed US$248 m in foreign currency. The best times to travel are between July and September and December and March.

Togo	
Area:	56,785 sq. km
Capital city:	Lomé
Form of government:	
Presidential Republic	
Administrative divisions:	
5 Regions	
Population:	
5.7 m (77 inhabitants/sq. km)	
Languages:	

Togo

Once known as the Slave Coast, Togo took its name from a small town on Lake Togo (now known as Togoville). In the language of the Ewe, the biggest ethnic group, 'To' means water and 'Go' shore. The women washing clothes *at the river may seem romantic, yet their cheerfulness belies the wretchedness of their living conditions, including an absence of piped water. The majority of Togolese live below the poverty line.*

French (official), Kabyé, Ewe
GDP per inhabitant: US$1,600
Currency:
1 CFA franc = 100 centimes

Natural geography

The coastline is ragged, with lagoons and bays and is only 5 km long in total. The hinterland is both flat and hilly and almost 200 km wide. Mount Agou (formerly known as Mount Baumann) is the highest mountain in Togo at 986 m. North-west of the mountains, the Oti plains forms the border area with Burkina Faso.

Climate

The south is dominated by a **savannah climate** with two rainy seasons, which last from March until June and from September until October. The north only has one rainy season, from April to October. On the coastal plains, the average rainfall is 600 to 700 mm; inland it is 1,500 mm and in the north it is 1,200 mm. On the coast, the average temperatures are 27°C, and inland in the north it rises to 30°C.
Savannahs of wide grasslands with a few clumps of trees are the characteristic landscape of Togo. Mangrove swamps grow along the coast and there are palm-fringed sandy beaches. The tropical rainforest has only been preserved in the south-west Togolese mountains. In the national parks and in the game reserves, the original fauna has been able to survive. Typical animals include buffaloes, lions, leopards, hyenas, antelopes, hippopotamuses, crocodiles and a wide variety of birds and reptiles. The homes of thousands of Keto were destroyed due to coastal erosion due to the building of the Volta dam.

Population

The inhabitants belong to 40 ethnic groups. The **Ewe** are the most strongly represented with around 46 per cent. There are also **Temba, Mopa, Gurma, Kabyé, Losso, Hausa, Fulani** as well as Lebanese and French minorities. 50 per cent profess various animist religions, 35 per cent are Christians (almost exclusively Roman Catholic) and 15 per cent Sunni Muslims. The average life expectancy is 50 years. The literacy rate is 48 per cent.

History and politics

The Portuguese discovered the coast of Togo in the fifteenth century. They operated a slave trade from there, later being joined by the Danes. When slavery ended, the British and French founded trading posts. Nevertheless, large parts of the country remained under African rule, including the kingdom of **Dahomey** in the east and the **Ashanti-kingdom** in the west. German involvement began with Gustav Nachtigal and in

1884, Togo became a German colony. After World War I, France and Great Britain divided the region, which in 1922 was officially made into a mandated territory by the League of Nations. In 1946 this was reorganised into a British mandated territory in the east (British Togoland and French mandated territory in the west.
In 1956, it was agreed that the British mandated area should be annexed to Ghana and become known as the Volta region. The French mandated Togo became an **autonomous republic** on 27 April 1960.
The first president, Sylvanus Olympio, was murdered in 1963. In 1967 Etienne Gnassingbé Eyadéma overthrew the government in a bloodless coup. In spite of permitting opposition parties and a democratic constitution, he ruled the country as a dictator. After his death in 2005, his son Faure Gnassingbé became the new head of state. The parliament is directly elected every five years, as is the president.

Economy

In 2005, GNP was US$2.0 bn., of which 35 per cent derived from agriculture, 23 per cent from industry and 42 per cent from the services sector. Machinery, foodstuffs and fuel are imported. Calcium phosphate, cotton, cocoa and coffee are exported.

1 Elmina was founded in 1482 by the Portugese in the Gold Coast. The fortress is a reminder of the former slave trade.

2 A Lobi woman burning pots to make millet beer. The Lobi are ethnic Gurs, a group consisting of several million people living in West Africa.

3 In an Ashanti village near Kumasi in southern Ghana. Traditional ceremonies to honour the chiefs are still held.

4 Near Bolgatanga in northern Ghana, the old architectural style of the Mossiv people has been preserved unchanged for centuries.

Togo, Benin, Nigeria

*Most of the Beninese are followers of indigenous religions. A prevalent **ancestor cult** is based upon the belief that the ancestors must be consulted before important decisions are taken.*

Transport

The **rail network** covers 525 km and the **road network** 7,519 km, of which 2,376 km are paved. Lomé has a **major sea port** and an international **airport**.

Tourism

Tourism in Togo is barely developed. In 1996, 58,000 tourists visited the country. This is despite the beautiful scenery and hospitable people. This is because the political situation continues to give cause for concern. The best time to travel is between November and April when there is little rain.

Benin	
Area:	112,622 sq. km
Capital City:	Porto Novo
Form of government:	
Presidential Republic	
Administrative divisions:	
6 provinces, 78 districts	
Population: 7.4m	

Wole Soyinka

*Abeokuta, 13.7.1934

The playwright, poet, novelist and screenplay writer received the Nobel Prize for Literature in 1986. In his work, he attempts a synthesis of African mythology and the realities of modern life . He was engaged in the fight against military dictatorship in Nigeria and as a result was subject to constant persecution. He fled the country and was accused in absentia of treason in 1997. He returned to Nigeria from exile in 1998.

(60 inhabitants/sq. km)
Languages: French (official), Fon, Yoruba and other tribal languages
GDP per inhabitant: US$1400
Currency:
1 CFA franc = 10 centimes

Natural geography

The sandy coastline turns into a lagoon area and mangrove swamps towards the north. This is replaced by the 'terre de barre', adjoining a semi-arid plateau up to 500 m high. In the north-west, the high mountainous region of **Atacora** rises to 641 m. A steep, 300-m-high escarpment adjoins the **Pendjari lowlands**. In the north-east, the plateau falls gradually away to the Niger river valley.

Climate

In the humid savannah climate of the south, average temperatures of 27.5°C dominate; these can climb to over 40°C at times. In both the rainy seasons from March to July and from September to November, the average rainfall is 1,000–1,500 mm. In the north, on the other hand, rainfall is no more than 500 mm during the rainy season between May and September. In the dry season, the **Harmattan,** the hot Sahara wind replaces the damp **south-west monsoon.**
The largest part of the country is covered by savannah grassland with isolated clumps of trees. Of the once vast rainforest, only traces remain along the courses of the rivers and in the south-east of the country. The interesting and varied fauna is protected in nature reserves. In these areas, common species include elephants, buffaloes, antelopes, lions, monkeys, crocodiles and numerous species of birds and snakes.

Population

Of the 60 or so ethnic groups, **Kwa, Fon, Yoruba, Adja, Bariba, Som-**ba and **Gun** make up around 80 per cent. There are also Fulani, Hausa and European minorities.
60 per cent of the inhabitants of Benin are followers of various animist religions, 20.4 per cent belong to the Catholic church, the rest are divided between Islam and the Methodist church.
The average life expectancy is 55 years. The literacy rate is 63 per cent. 39 per cent of the inhabitants of Benin live in the cities. Although Porto Novo is the official capital, Cotonou, the former capital, remains the most important city.

History and politics

Since the fifteenth century, firstly the Portuguese, and then the French operated a lucrative **slave trade** from their coastal trading posts. Most of the slaves from what is now Benin were sent to Haiti. When the slave trade ended, the main focus of French activity shifted to trading in palm oil and cotton. It was only towards the end of the nineteenth century, that the French succeeded in conquering the smaller African kingdoms. Under French rule, Benin was known as **Dahomey**. In 1904, Dahomey became part of French West Africa. After **independence** in 1960 eight military and civil governments followed each other in succession, until finally, in 1972, a Communist government came to power and the country was renamed Benin in 1975.

In 1989, Communism was officially abandoned. A liberal constitution was introduced in 1990, which has provided for the election of parliament every four years and the direct election of the President every five years. The voting age is 18 years.

Economy

In 2005, GDP was US$4.3 bn, of which 36 per cent derived from **agriculture**, 15 per cent from **industry** and 49 per cent from the **services sector**.
Principal imports are industrial goods, food, machines, transport equipment and fuel. Exports include cotton, oilseed, petroleum, cement, fish products and palm oil.

Transport

Only one third of the 7,400-km-long **road network** is passable all year round. The **rail network** covers 580 km. Cotonou has a **sea port** and an international **airport**. Ships ply between the ports on the West African coast.

Lagos is both an industrial centre and Nigeria's major port. It covers four islands.

Tourism

The government has a 2001/2006 action plan for the development of tourism. There are many museums and royal palaces. The oral traditions of Benin are a unique cultural treasure, such as that of the Gèlèdè people, declared an Oral Heritage of Humanity in May 2001. The Ouidah Slave Route is an important site.

Nigeria	
Area:	923,768 sq. km
Capital City:	Abuja
Form of government:	
Presidential Federal Republic	
Administrative divisions:	
36 Federal States,	
capital city-territory	
Population:	
129m (129 inhabitants/sq. km)	
Languages:	
English (official),	
Arabic, tribal languages	
GDP per inhabitant: US$1000	
Currency: 1 naira = 100 kobo	

Natural geography

Dominated by the basins of the Niger and Benue rivers, Nigeria can be divided into four distinct geographic regions. Most of the coastline is dominated by the Niger delta, lagoons and marshes, while in the south-east it is rocky. The **coastal plain,** which is around 150 km wide, turns inland into the **Yoruba Plateau** west of the Niger, the **Oban** and the **Udi Hills** and in a southerly direction into the **Benue Plateau** east of the Niger. The Gotel and Shebshi Mountains (Dimlang 2,042 m.) lie along the border with Cameroon. The central plateau is around 1,200 m high and in the Jos Plateau rises to 1,752 m. In the north-west, the plateau sinks to the plains of Sokoto and in the north-east it leads into the alluvial plain of **Lake Chad.**

Climate

The tropical climate produces temperatures between 26°C and 29°C on the coast, from 23°C to 33°C in the north and between 21°C and 26°C in the central plateau.
In the south, the rainy season lasts from April to November; average rainfall on the coast is up to 4,000 mm. The rainy season in the north lasts from May to October; where precipitation is just under 700 mm. In the dry season, the **Harmattan,** the hot Sahara wind, determines the climate. In the north- east, which is part of the Sahel, there is semi-arid savannah. The Sudan zone, which adjoins this zone in a southerly direction consists of dry savan-

*Benin is the cradle of **Voodoo** – a religion that spread through slaves and was further developed, mainly in Haiti. It is said to have some 50 million followers worldwide. The religion, based upon rituals rather than written scriptures,* *has found an avid following in West Africa. In the former royal palace of Abomey, numerous ceremonial items are displayed. Cult objects such as these iron fetishes were produced in the forge.*

nah with thorn bushes and isolated baobab trees.

The Guinea zone is characterised by deciduous forests and savannah dotted with clumps of trees, while in the coastal region mangrove swamps predominate.

The rich variety of mammalian fauna and reptiles is seriously endangered. Only in the game reserves of Borgu and Yankari are there significant numbers of elephants, hippopotamuses, giraffes, buffaloes, lions, antelopes as well as numerous types of birds. The number of manatees in coastal waters has declined significantly.

Population

A total of 434 ethnic groups live in Nigeria, including Hausa, Fulani, Hamitic and Chad peoples, Ibo, Ibibio, Yoruba, Fulani as well as a European minority. Just under half are Christians of different persuasions, 45 per cent are Muslim. In addition, there are numerous followers of animist religions. Average life expectancy is 53 years. The literacy rate is 43 per cent. 40 per cent of Nigerians live in the cities.

History and politics

Important cultures have been established in Nigeria for 2000 years. From the eleventh century AD, the **Hausa** in the north had created their own city-states with a unique culture. Islam was soon adopted by a large percentage of the population and was already firmly established when the Portuguese discovered the Kingdom of Benin in 1472. Europeans then operated a flourishing **slave trade** with the New World until 1807. This led to wars among the different tribes as well as to extremely high population losses.

In the mid-nineteenth century, Britain declared Nigeria to be a colony, though leaving some of the traditional ruling structures in place. After the final conquest of the kingdom of Benin in 1897, the British protectorates of South and North Nigeria came into being and these merged into the Colony and Protectorate of Nigeria in 1914, Britain's largest African possession.

In 1960, Nigeria was granted its **independence** and in 1963 it became a republic within the British Commonwealth. The recent governance of the country has been characterised by coups d'état and political murders.

The Ibo region, which is predominantly Christian, attempted to break away, declared its own state, named Biafra. In 1967, a civil war broke out. By 1970, the war had cost one million lives. Biafra lost the war and was again incorporated into Nigeria.

Different military regimes have made huge profits from the rich natural resources, without allowing benefit to the population. The regime of the late General Sani Abacha was especially brutal and especially corrupt. He and his family blatantly plundered the state coffers. The regime suffered stiff opposition by pro-democracy activists but Abacha was protected by international oil concerns, attracting strong criticism against the Shell company in particular. Even after Abacha's death in a plane crash in 1992, the promised return to **democracy** did not happen. The 1999 elections under international supervision were an important step towards democracy, however. In the same year, a new constitution came into force. The widespread corruption and unrest between Christians and Muslims, which continued under the new President Olusegun Obasanjo has hindered development.

Economy

In 2005, GDP stood at US$77.3 bn, of which 30 per cent derived from **agriculture**, 45 per cent from **industry** and 25 per cent from the **services sector**. Nigeria's wealth is based on oil which accounts for 93 per cent of total exports. Machinery, chemicals, vehicles and consumer goods are imported.

Transport

The national **rail network** covers 3,557 km, the **road network** 32,105 km, of which 26,005 km is paved. There are five international **airports**. The major **sea ports** are at Lagos, the former capital, Calabar and Warri. Bonny and Burutu are oil terminals. The ports are very busy and merchant ships have to wait for days to get into harbour.

Tourism

Only 793,000 visitors came to the country in 1998; however they brought in foreign currency to the value of US$118m. The best time to travel is between October and March. Tourism is being developed around Lagos and Kano and in the national parks.

1 In the eighteenth century, villages were erected on poles in Lac Nokoué in Benin, which could only be reached by boat. This construction protected the inhabitants from their enemies.

2 The traditional kingdom of Abomey still flourishes in Benin. Some kings who, like other members of the royal family, are allowed to have several wives, continue to be important members of society.

3 The Niger delta covers an area of 25,000 sq. km, and is the largest in Africa. Its rich fish stocks provide subsistence for the local inhabitants.

Chad

Chad is one of the poorest countries in the world. 85 per cent of the population lives from agriculture. The relatively abundant supply of cattle in the market at the Faya-Largeau oasis cannot conceal widespread shortages in the region.

	Chad

Area 1,284,000 sq. km
Capital city: N'Djamena
Form of government:
Presidential Republic
Administrative divisions:
14 prefectures
Population: 9.8 million
(6 inhabitants/sq. km)
Languages:
French, Arabic (both official)
GDP per inhabitant: US$1,900
Currency: 1 CFA franc = 100 centimes

Natural geography

The West and the interior of the country consist of the Chad Basin which is flanked in the North by the **Tibesti-Massif** which is up to 3,415 m in altitude, in the South by the North Equatorial Ridge and in the east and west by the Enedi and Quadaï plateaus. Lake Chad is in the west.

Climate

In the north, the desert climate of the Sahara prevails. It is responsible for precipitation volumes be-

low 50 mm and an average

temperature of 21°C in winter and 34°C in summer. The average temperatures in the wet-dry tropical climate of the south are 25°C in January and 31°C in April. During the rainy season from May to October precipitation totals approximately 1000 mm. If you set out from the desert in the north and head in a southerly direction, you will find semi-desert, thorny, dry and wet savannah and finally, evergreen dry forests. Desert foxes, gazelles, cheetahs and hyenas live in the Sahara as well as reptiles. Antelopes, giraffes, hippopotamuses, leopards, elephants and lions live in the south.

Population

The largest groups of the 200 different ethnic groups are the **Arabs** who account for

15 per cent and **arabised populations** account for 38 per cent. The Saras and other **Tibbu Daza groups** account for 30 per cent of the population, There are also **Fulbes, Hausas** and others. Approximately half the population professes Islam, 30 per cent are Christian and 20 per cent are animists. The average life expectancy is 48 years and the illiteracy rate is 52 per cent.

History and Politics

From medieval times onwards, three powerful Islamic empires existed in the region, operating a lucrative slave trade. In the late nineteenth century, Chad became a French colony, and became part of French **Equatorial Africa** in 1910. Following independence in 1960, President Tombalbayé pursued a pro-French course. However, he was only able to maintain his rule by employing dictatorial measures. He was assassinated in 1975. The traditional north-south conflict finally culminated in a bloody civil war in which Libya took the side of the Islamic north and France the side of the Christian south. The 1996 constitution has not yet been fully put into action. However, the domestic situation is now relatively stable.

Economy

Gross Domestic Product was US$4.8 billion in 2005. **Agriculture** accounted for 39 per cent of this figure, **industry** for 14 per cent and the **services sector** for 48 per cent. Chad's agriculture aims to be self-sufficient but is unable to meet local demand. The exploitation of oil reserves increased economic growth by over ten per cent in 2002. In 2003, a pipeline to the Atlantic coast in Cameroon was put into operation. Cotton, meat, livestock, hides and skins are also exported.

Transport

Except for the approximately 200-km-long **network of roads** which are surfaced, there are only cart tracks and paths. Yaoundé has an international **airport**. Chad is landlocked.

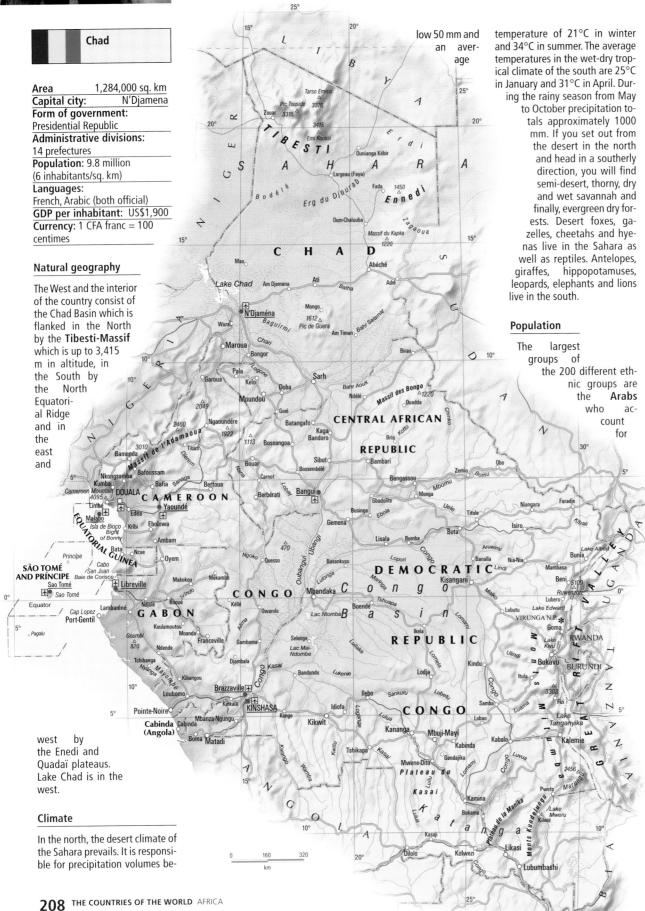

*There are more than 200 ethnic groups in **Cameroon**. The south is populated by Bantu-speaking people, the north mainly by Muslims and a range of Sudanese tribes. On the far right, a marabout – a Muslim sage.*

Tourism

The National Museum in N'jamena has collections of the Sarh culture dating back to the ninth century. Lake Chad was once the centre of Africa's lucrative salt trade but is now shrinking (literally). The lake is best seen during the August to December period, when the water level is highest and the occasional hippo or crocodile can be spotted.

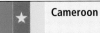
Cameroon

Area:	475,442 sq. km
Capital city:	Yaoundé
Form of government:	
Presidential Republic	
Administrative divisions:	
10 provinces	
Population:	
16.3 million (33 inhabitants/sq. km)	
Languages:	
French, English (both official languages), Bantu languages	
GDP per capita:	US$2000
Currency:	
1 CFA franc = 100 centimes	

Natural geography

To the west of a narrow lowland line called the Cameroon Line, there is the Cameroon Mountain a volcano which reaches altitudes of up to 4,000 m, west of the Adamawa mountains. These mountains rise to a height of 2,500 m and drop down in a northerly direction to Lake Chad. Several offshore islands are also of volcanic origin. The marshy coastal plain is replaced by a low-lying plateau landscape in the south which turns into the Congo Basin.

Climate

In the south, a wet-dry tropical climate prevails with precipitation volumes of 4,000 to 5,000 mm. On the coast, the average temperature is 26°C. The region surrounding Cameroon Mountain is one of the **rainiest areas** on earth with precipitation of over 10,000 mm. In the north only 500 mm of rain falls during a comparatively short rainy season and the average temperatures vary from 10°C to 40°C. In the central highlands the average temperature is

22°C and the precipitation volume is 1,500 mm. Marshes and mangrove swamps cover the coastline and the south is covered in tropical rainforest. Central Cameroon is characterised by savannah. There are many different species of the savannah in the national parks, such as baboons, giraffes, rhinoceroses, lions, elephants and buffalo. Anthropoid apes and numerous species of birds live in the rainforests.

Population

Approximately 200 ethnic groups live in Cameroon. The **Bantu-speaking minority** accounts for 40 per cent of the population, **Semi-bantus** and **Adamawas** for 20 per cent. Additionally, there are Hausas, **Fulbes**, **Pygmies** and a few Europeans. Fifty-three per cent of the population is Christian, 22 per cent Muslim and the rest are followers of animist religions. Average life expectancy is 56 years and the literacy rate is 37 per cent.

History and Politics

In addition to the **Portuguese** who landed in Cameroon around 1470, the Scandinavians, the Dutch and the British also operated a flourishing slave trade from here for over 300 years. In 1884, Cameroon became a **German colony**. Following World War I, the British and French divided the country up between themselves.
French Cameroon, as it was known, gained **independence** in 1960 and the British Cameroons followed in 1961. Cameroon was reunited, with the exception of a small area which became part of Nigeria. In the post-colonial era the country was ruled by President **Ahmadou Ahidjos** who favoured a centralist policy. Following his resignation in 1982, his successor **Paul Biya** attempted to carry through seemingly democratic reforms. As a result of the 1972 constitution, the parliament and head of state are elected every five years. Citizens have the right to vote from the age of 20.

Economy

In spite of a considerable north-south cultural and linguistic divide, which has the potential for

conflict, Cameroon is one of the richest states of sub-Saharan Africa. The country's GDP in 2005 was US$15.3 bilion. **Agriculture** accounted for 39 per cent of this figure, industry accounted for 23 per cent and the **services sector** accounted for 38 per cent. The foreign trade balance is positive. Oil, coffee, wood, bananas, cot-

1 Chad: like its neighbours, agriculture and livestock breeding suffered from the two disastrous droughts in the 1970s and 1980s in the Sahel.

2 The north of Cameroon is inhabited by semi-nomadic shepherds. Their

houses and grain stores are mostly built in a round shape from clay and stones.

3 The Arabic Tubu people live in the north and east of Chad. In the Ennedi plateau the oldest African cave paintings have been discovered.

Cameroon, Central African Republic

*The rare African **forest elephant** lives in the rainforests of West and Central Africa and reaches maximum height of 2.3 m. The extremely shy animals were only discovered in 1899. They differ from the Savannah elephants by having five toes on their front feet and four on the hind feet. Furthermore the four subspecies have round ear form rather than triangular. Their number is being estimated at only 200,000 specimen.*

ton, timber and cocoa are the main exports.

Transport

A mere 2,800 km of Cameroon's total **road network** of 71,000 km is surfaced. The **rail network** has a length of 1,115 km. The most important **port** and **airport** are at Douala.

Tourism

The tourism infrastructure is developing slowly. Yaoundé, has the Musée des Bénédictins, a collection of traditional arts and crafts housed in a Benedictine Monastery on Mont Fébé, and the newer National Museum of Yaoundé. The best time to visit is between November and April.

Central African Republic	
Area:	622,984 sq. km
Capital city:	Bangui
Form of government:	
Presidential Republic	
Administrative divisions:	
16 prefectures, capital city	
Population:	
3.8 million (6 inhabitants/sq. km)	
Languages:	
French, Sangho (both official), Bantu and Sudan languages	
GDP per capita:	US$1200
Currency:	
1 CFA franc = 100 centimes	

Natural geography

Between the Chad Basin in the North and the Congo Basin, a tropical lowland line in the South, stretches the **North Equatorial Ridge**, hilly country with an altitude of 500 to 1,000 m which also contains the headwaters for numerous rivers. In the north-west and north-east there are two mountain ranges, the Massif du Yadé and the Massif de Bongo. The Ubangi river rises by 6 m in the rainy season (June to November).

Climate

The wet-dry tropical climate is responsible for a precipitation of just under 900 mm in the north and for average temperatures of 22°C to 30°C which may rise to 40°C in summer. The average temperatures in the south range between 24°C and 28°C and the precipitation ranges between 1,500 mm and 1,800 mm. The dry savannah adjoins wet savannah in the south. Gallery forests grow along the riverbanks and evergreen tropical rainforests can be found in the extreme south. Elephants, rhinoceroses, hyenas and antelopes number roam the savannah. The forests also contain many species of primates.

Population

The largest ethnic groups include the **Bandas** (30 per cent), the **Gbayas** (24 per cent), the **Gbandis** (11 per cent), and the **Azandes** (ten per cent). In addition to **Yakomas**, **Bantus** and other peoples, there is a minority of Europeans. 57 per cent are followers of animist religions, 35 per cent are Christians and eight per cent Muslims. Average life expectancy is 49 years and the illiteracy rate is 40 per cent.

History and Politics

The original population was obliterated to a great extent in the eighteenth and nineteenth century through the slave trade. From the late nineteenth century onwards, the French established their **colonial rule** in the area of the present-day Central African Republic which was part of French Equatorial Africa.

Following formal **independence** in 1960, one military dictatorship replaced another. In 1966, Colonel **Jean-Bédel Bokassa** took power in a military coup and had himself crowned emperor in 1977. With France's assistance, he established a brutal terror regime before being overthrown in 1979. The country has been repeatedly plagued by military conflicts over power and resources ever since independence. In March 2003, the elected president, Félix Patassé, who was disliked by the people due to his political repression and poor governance was overthrown by the former General Chief of Staff François Bozizé.

Economy

In 2005 Gross Domestic Product totalled US$1.4 billion. **Agriculture** accounted for 53 per cent of this sum, **industry**, 21 per cent and the **services sector**, 26 per cent. Coffee, wood, cotton and, above all, diamonds are the principle exports.

Transport

5,000 km of the country's 24,000-km-long **road network** are passable all year round. The Ubangi river is navigable and is an important artery. The capital city, Bangui, has the only international **airport**.

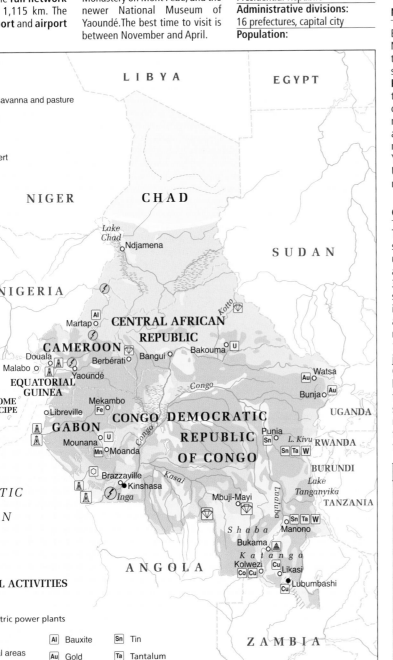

LAND USE

- Forest
- Steppe, savanna and pasture
- Cropland
- Desert
- Semidesert

LIBYA
EGYPT
NIGER
CHAD
Lake Chad
Ndjamena
SUDAN
NIGERIA
Martapo
Al
CENTRAL AFRICAN REPUBLIC
Kotto
CAMEROON
Douala
Berbérati
Bangui
Bakouma
U
Malabo
Yaoundé
Watsa
Au
EQUATORIAL GUINEA
Congo
Bunja
Au
SAO TOME & PRINCIPE
Mekambo
Fe
Libreville
CONGO DEMOCRATIC
UGANDA
GABON
Mounana
U
Punia
Sn
L. Kivu
RWANDA
Mn
Moanda
REPUBLIC
Sn Ta W
Brazzaville
OF CONGO
BURUNDI
Kasai
Kinshasa
Lake Tanganyika
Inga
Mbuji-Mayi
TANZANIA
ATLANTIC
Sn Ta W
OCEAN
Manono
Shaba
Bukama
Katanga
ANGOLA
Kolwezi
Cu
Likasi
Co Cu
Lubumbashi
Cu
ZAMBIA

INDUSTRIAL ACTIVITIES

Energy

- Hydroelectric power plants

Industry

- Industrial areas
- Main industrial sites

Al	Bauxite	Sn	Tin
Au	Gold	Ta	Tantalum
Co	Cobalt	U	Uranium
Cu	Copper	W	Tungsten

Minerals

- Fossil coal
- Natural gas or oil wells

Fe	Iron
Mn	Manganese
Diamonds	
Potassium	

0   300 km

Central African Republic, São Tomé and Príncipe, Equatorial Guinea

*The African **pygmies** were among the first to settle in the Congo basin. With a body size lesser than 1.52 m, they are the shortest people in the world. There are between 150,000 and 300,000 of them left now.*

Tourism

Tourism is extremely underdeveloped. The country's great natural diversity could be the basis for future development of the industry.

★ ★	São Tomé and Príncipe

Area:	1,001 sq. km
Capital city:	São Tomé
Form of government: Republic	
Administrative divisions: District of São Tomé, Príncipe Island (autonomous status)	
Population: 187,400 (176 inhabitants/sq. km)	
Languages: Portuguese (official), Creole	
GDP per capita:	US$1200
Currency: 1 dobra = 100 centimes	

Natural geography

Both of the main islands of São Tomé and Príncipe and the smaller, uninhabited islands belonging to the state are of volcanic origin. The **Pico de São Tomé** is 2,024 m high and the main summit of Príncipe is 948 m high.

Climate

The tropical, hot **rainy climate** is responsible for average temperatures of 25°C to 30°C which decrease to 20°C above 800 m. On average, 4,000 to 5,000 m of precipitation falls in the south-west during the rainy season which lasts from October to April. There is only 1,000 mm of precipitation in the north, however. With the exception of the areas cleared for cocoa plantations in the north, the evergreen **rainforest** is still preserved to a large extent.

Population

At the time that the country was discovered by the Europeans the islands were uninhabited. Consequently, the population consists principally of the **descendants of former slaves** originating from all over Africa, of **people of mixes race** and a few Portuguese. 93 per cent of the population are Catholics and three per cent Protestants. There are also smaller groups of followers of various animist religions. Average life expectancy is 64 years and the illiteracy rate is 40 per cent.

History and Politics

After the Portuguese discovered the islands in around 1470, they planted cocoa bushes which were cultivated by slaves. Cocoa remained the main economic factor following independence from Portugal in 1975. Since the 1990 constitution, the parliament has been directly elected every four years and the country's president every five years. Voting begins at 18.

Economy

The country is dependent to a large extent on the global market price for cocoa and payments from the donor countries of Portugal and France. The Gross Domestic Product was US$43 million in 2001. **Agriculture** accounted for 25 per cent of this figure, industry for 18 per cent and the **services sector** for 57 per cent.

Transport

The road network is approximately 300 km long in total. A regular connecting ferry service is in operation between the two main islands. An international **airport** is situated in close proximity to the capital city.

Tourism

In 1996 there were just 2000 foreign visitors to the country. The best time to visit is between June and August.

	Equatorial Guinea

Area:	28,051 sq. km
Capital city:	Malabo
Form of government: Presidential Republic	
Administrative divisions: 7 provinces	

1 The main fuel in Equatorial Guinea is still wood.

2 Cameroon's main cash crops are coffee, cocoa, cotton and bananas.

3 Agriculture in the Central African Repulic provides for the country's needs and it supplies major exports such as coffee, cotton, cattle and tobacco.

4 The Ubangi river in the south of the Central African Republic is the border with the Democratic Republic of Congo.

Equatorial Guinea, Gabon, Congo

*A medicine man talks to a **fetish**. A fetish is an object considered to have supernatural powers. Fetishes are widespread in West and Central Africa. Powerful ancestors are supposed to communicate through them.*

The practices of medicine men are based on the assumption that supernatural energies are active everywhere and men are both dependent on them and able to make use of them for their own purposes.

Population:
535 000 (18 inhabitants/sq. km)
Languages:
Spanish (official), Pidgin English, Bantu languages
GDP per capita:
US$30 000 – 50 000
Currency:
1 CFA franc = 100 centimes

Natural geography

The name of the country is misleading as it lies approximately 200 km north of the Equator. The mainland province of **Mbini** consists of a coastal plain and an inland plateau at an altitude of up to 1,200 m. The islands of **Bioko** and **Pagalu** are mountainous and together form the island province of Bioko in the Gulf of Guinea.

Climate

The tropical **rainy climate** is responsible for an average annual temperature of 25°C and an average precipitation of 2,000 mm which can, however, reach 4,000 in some regions of the country. The mangrove swamps of the coastal region are replaced by tropical rainforest inland and by savannah at higher altitude.

Population

Bantu-speaking groups account for 80 per cent of the population, **Bubis** for ten per cent and a minority are **mixed race** or white. 99 per cent of the population is **Catholic**, although in 1978, Roman Catholicism was banned. Average life expectancy is 50 years and the illiteracy rate is 50 per cent.

History and Politics

Portuguese rule began in 1472 and did not come to an end until 1778. It was ended by the Spaniards who, in the mid-twentieth century, united Bioko with the mainland region of the Spanish colony of Río Muni which the Spanish acquired in 1900. Following **independence, Francisco Macías Nguema** ruled the country using terror and oppression. After being overthrown and executed in 1979, his nephew, Lieutenant-Commander **Teodoro Obiang Nguema Mbasogo**, promised liberal reforms. However, he also proved to be a power-obsessed dictator. In 2002, he was reinstated in office for seven years. In accordance with the 1991 constitution, parliament is elected every five years and the head of state every seven years. Citizens 21 years of age and over have the right to vote.

Economy

The economy of Equatorial Guinea is today determined by its oil reserves. In the last few years, large deposits have been discovered on the coast and the mainland. Economic growth was thus in excess of 70 per cent in 2001. The oil economy accounted for 83 per cent of the GDP. Despite this fact, approximately two-thirds of the population still live below the poverty line.

Transport

The **road network** is only 180 km long on Bioko and 1,500 km long on the mainland. Regular connecting **sea** and **air services** are in operation between the islands. The **sea ports** and **airports** are at Malabo and Bata.

Tourism

Tourism is practically non-existent. The best time to visit the country is between December and February.

Gabon	

Area: 267,667 sq. km
Capital city:
Libreville
Form of government:
Presidential Republic
Administrative divisions:
9 provinces

A market women in Congo sells oil in rather strange bottles.

Population:
1.4 million (4 inhabitants/sq. km)
Languages:
French (official), Bantu languages
GDP per capita: US$5,500
Currency:
1 CFA-franc = 100 centimes

Natural geography

The country is characterised by the Ogoué and its tributaries which wend their way through valleys and gorges of a **plateau** that is part of the African Shield formation. The coastal lowland, which is up to 200 km wide, ascends to the foothills of the Lower Guinea Ridge at an altitude of 890 m. At 1,575 m, **Mont Iboundi** in the central Massif du Chaillu is the country's highest mountain. The 800-km-long coastline consists of lagoons and spits of land in the south. In the north, it is sub-divided into deltas, bays and river estuaries.

Climate

The wet-hot **tropical climate** causes only slight variations in temperature. The average monthly temperatures are approximately 26°C on the coast and 24°C inland. There are two rainy seasons, lasting from October to December and January to May respectively. In the north-west, the average precipitation is 4,000 mm. In the southerly coastal zone it is 2,500 mm and approximately 1,700 mm inland. Three-quarters of the country is covered in **tropical rainforest**. Tree-felling has, in places, transformed the once thick vegetation into secondary forest. On the coast and in the river valleys there are vast areas of **grassland**. Various species of monkeys and birds, elephants, antelopes, buffalos, crocodiles and hippopotamuses inhabit Gabon.

Population

Approximately 40 different ethnic groups live in Gabon. 54 per cent are Catholics, 40 per cent followers of traditional religions and eight per cent Protestants. Average life expectancy is 55 years and the illiteracy rate is 37 per cent.

History and Politics

Following discovery by the Portuguese, various European **colonial powers** operated a flourishing trade in exotic timber, ivory and slaves on the coast and along the navigable waterways. In 1886, Gabon became a French colony and in 1910 it became part of French Equatorial Africa. Even after gaining **independence** in 1960, the country's wealth remained to a great extent in foreign hands. Omar Bongo has been head of state since 1967. Gabon enjoys a relatively high degree of political stability. The one-party state was transformed into a multi-party democracy by the 1991 constitution which was amended in 1995. The national assembly, the senate and the head of state are directly elected every five years. Citizens can vote at 21 years of age.

Economy

Gross Domestic Product was US$6.7 billion in 2005. **Agriculture** accounted for seven per cent of this figure, **industry** for 55 per cent and the **service sector** for 38 per cent. The most significant economic factor is the exploitation of the **oil fields**, which at 88 per cent make up the lion's share of export revenue. The export of tropical timber and manganese also make a significant contribution.

Transport

Only approximately 600 km of the 7,500-km-long **road network** is surfaced. A 648-km-long **rail connection** links Libreville with Franceville. There are international **airports** in Port-Gentil and in Libreville.

Tourism

Gabon has underdeveloped tourism. The Lopé national park right in the centre of the country covers an area of 5,360 sq. km and is a promising destination for safaris and ecotourists. Another important site is the Schweitzer Hospital at Lambaréné. The best time to visit is between July and December.

Congo	

Area: 342,000 sq. km
Capital city: Brazzaville
Form of government:
Republic
Administrative divisions:
9 regions and 4 urban districts
Population:
3 million (9 inhabitants/sq. km)
Languages:
French (official) and various Bantu languages
GDP per capita: US$800
Currency:
1 CFA franc = 100 centimes

*In **Ituri primeval forest** of the Democratic Republic of Congo, ancient rituals are preserved. These Epulu women paint parts of their faces white for menstruating ceremonies. The Ngodi-Ngodi paint themselves with slaked lime and kohl.*

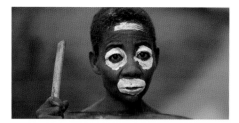

Natural geography

The coastline which is approximately 50 km wide is sandy in the north and marshy in the south. The Mayombé mountainous region reaches altitudes of up to 800 m and turns into the **Batéké Plateau** after Niari Valley which is flanked by the Monts de la Lékéti which are over 1,000 m high. The **Congo Basin** in the north-east occupies the majority of the country's surface area. The Congo and its tributaries form a flood plain here which is approximately 100,000 sq. km in area.

Climate

In the north, a tropical wet climate prevails with a virtually constant average temperature of 25°C and precipitation volumes of between 1,500 mm and 1,900 mm which are attained during the two rainy seasons from January to May and October to December. In the South, temperatures vary between 22°C and 27°C. The average precipitation of 1,300 mm falls predominantly in March and November. Mangroves grow on the coast. Wet savannah can be found in the mountains and the highlands and there are frequent floods north of the Alima. The Congo Basin is the largest **rainforest region** in Africa. Gorillas and chimpanzees inhabit the rainforest, whilst antelopes, elephants, leopards and giraffes live in the savannah.

Population

The population consists mainly of **Bantu-speaking** groups. 52 per cent are **Ba-** and **Vili-Congos**, 24 per cent are **Batekes** and **Bavilis** and 12 per cent are **M'Boshis**. In addition, there are minorities of Tékés, Sangas, pygmies, Ubangi groups and Europeans. Average life expectancy is 51 years and the illiteracy rate is 25 per cent. Half of the Congolese are Catholics and the remainder are followers of various animist religions.

History and Politics

When the Portuguese discovered the estuary of the Congo river in 1482, the interior was ruled by the kingdoms of **Congo** and **Loango** which played a part in the slave trade, assisting the European colonial powers. In 1880, the explorer **Pierre Savorgnan de Brazza** journeyed through the central Congo region and brought it under French control. Following **independence** in 1960, one military government replaced another. In 1970, **Marien Ngouabi** declared the country to be the People's Republic of Congo, a Marxist-Leninist state. Following his assassination, a military junta seized power in 1977. In 1991, the official name was changed back to the Republic of Congo. Following the adoption of a new constitution, presidential elections

were held in August 1992. These were won by **Pascal Lissouba** who also won the parliamentary elections in 1993. Following armed clashes between government troops and opposing militia, Lissouba was overthrown in 1997 by the followers of **Denis Sassou-Nguessos**. The new president succeeded in consolidating his power. Opposition candidates were not permitted to take part in the election. Sassou-Nguessos was therefore able to gain over 89 per cent of the vote for himself in the March 2002 presidential election. In the same year, there were constant clashes with rebels. In March 2003, government and militia were united, ensuring their immunity from prosecution. In October 2003, the unrest flared up again. The country is usually referred to as Congo Brazzaville, so as to avoid confusion with its neighbour, which was formerly known as the Belgian Congo, under colonial rule, then Zaïre and is now called the Democratic Republic of Congo.

Economy

Gross Domestic Product amounted to US$4.7 billion in 2005. **Agriculture** accounted for ten per cent of this sum, **industry** for 38 per cent and the **services sector** for 52 per cent. Crude oil is both the main economic factor and the most important export.

1 The widest section of the Congo river runs through the rain forest of the Congo basin.

2 Congo: apart from coffee, cocoa, manioc, rice, palm kernels, sugar cane and peanuts, and fishing are important to the economy.

3 Between Kisangani and Kinshasa the Congo river is an important navigable waterway.

4 The economy of the Congo has not yet recovered from the crisis in the 1980s. The local markets still have precious little to sell.

Congo, Democratic Republic of Congo

*The African **rainforests** are preserved in isolated areas scattered across Central Africa. They were often cleared for agricultural use. To this day many precious hardwood trees are being cut for wood processing.*

The unscrupulous deforestation also has a lasting impact on the animal kingdom. Many species once widespread in the rainforests, were deprived of living space and are now in danger of extinction.

Transport

Only approximately 550 km of the 11,000-km-long **road network** is surfaced. The two **railway lines** have a total length of 800 km. The 2,600 km of **waterways** which are navigable year round are important transport links. There are international **airports** at Pointe Noire and Brazzaville.

Tourism

The political situation has hindered significant tourism until now. The tourism infrastructure is therefore very poorly developed. The best time to visit is between June and September. However, the country is ripe for safari tourism.

Congo, Democratic Republic of

Area:	2,345 410 sq. km
Capital city:	Kinshasa
Form of government:	
Presidential Republic	
Administrative divisions:	
10 regions, 1 district (capital city)	
Population:	

Sese Seko Mobutu

*Lisala, 14.10.1930,
†Rabat, 7.9.1997

In 1960 the general commander in chief of the Force Publique assumed power in a military coup in the former Zaïre. After the reappointment of Kasavubu, he retained the supreme command of the army and became a dictator after another coup in 1965, until he was deposed in 1997, after a long and bloody civil war.

60 million (22 inhabitants/sq. km)	
Language:	French
GDP per capita:	US$800
Currency:	
1 Congo franc = 100 centimes	

Natural geography

The relatively small coastal plain which is characterised by the estuary of the Congo follows a narrow line which links the interior of the country with the Atlantic. The majority of the country consists of the **Congo Basin** which is covered in rainforest. In the north, there are vast tracts of grassy savanna. The eastern border and **Lake Tanganjika** form volcanic mountains (the Ruwenzori reaches an altitude of 5,119 m in the Margherita).

Climate

In the north, the tropical climate produces average temperatures of around 25°C which remain constant all year round and there is a precipitation volume of 2,000 mm.

In the south, the temperatures are more variable and rainfall varies between 1,200 mm and 1,500 mm, predominantly between September and May. Typical **rainforest flora** can be found in the Congo Basin along with fauna in a relatively original state. Eight to ten thousand types of plants flourish here in a complicated **ecosystem** which has hitherto only degenerated to secondary forest in small areas due to the commercial tree-felling. for timber. Among the 600 types of wood, there are numerous **valuable tropical woods**. Today, baobabs, mahogany trees, African walnut trees and limba trees still continue to flourish. Western red cedars, iroko and sable palms also grow. As the distance from the equator increases, the landscape turns into grassland savanna.

In the **mountainous regions** of the east mountain, there are mountainous forests on the slopes; the flood plains are alluvial and **marshy**.

Thatched huts on the slopes of Ruwenzori mountains.

The rich wildlife is protected predominantly in the seven great **national parks**. Okapis, gorillas and chimpanzees are some of the rainforest's inhabitants. Zebras, lions, elephants, buffaloes, rhinoceroses and giraffes live in the savanna and hippopotamuses, crocodiles and numerous fish, especially cichlids, live in the freshwater environment. There is an especially great number of species of bird.

Population

Of roughly 250 ethnic groups, **Bantu-speaking groups** are the **majority**. 18 per cent are **Lubas**, 16 per cent **Congolese**, 13 per cent **Mongos** and ten per cent **Rwandans**. There are also Sudanese groups, Pygmies and Europeans. As far as religion is concerned, 42 per cent are Catholics, 25 per cent Protestants and 15 per cent are followers of other Christian denominations. Another two per cent are Muslims or followers of animist religions. Average life expectancy is 53 years and the illiteracy rate is 33 per cent.

History and Politics

Although the **Portuguese** discovered the area of present-day Congo in 1482, the African empires of the Congo, Luba, Cuba and Lunda remained stable until the mid-nineteenth century. In 1885, the Independent Congo State was created following the Congo Conference in Berlin. The Congo became the private fiefdom of the Belgian **King Leopold II**. The slave trade was abolished. In 1908, the area finally became a Belgian colony. During World War I, Congolese troops conquered the Rwanda-Urundi area for the Allies which was granted to Belgium in 1919. Following independence from Belgium in 1960, revolts, politically motivated murders, recurring secession attempts by Katanga province and corruption affected all areas of political and economic life. In 1965, **Sese Seko Mobutu** was finally able to prevail against all adversaries and establish an authoritative, corrupt terror regime. Large sections of the population lived in poverty, and still do, despite the country's wealth. His most prominent opponent **Patrice Lumumba** who was murdered on 12 February 1961 in circumstances that remain unclear. The perpetrator has never been identified. Mobutu renamed the country **Zaïre** and ruled for over 30 years. Following a very long civil war **Laurent-Désiré Kabila** overthrew the sick dictator in 1997 and made Zaïre into the Democratic Republic of the Congo. Kabila requested that a constitution be drawn up modelled on the constitution of the USA but the promised democratisation did not happen. Politically motivated murders, corruption and armed clashes between the various tribal militia were the order of the day. In 2001, Kabila was assassinated. Shortly afterwards, his son Joseph Kabila assumed power. In 2003, a transitional constitution which the conflicting parties had agreed upon came into force. The transitional government prepared the country for free elections which were held in 2006. Although Laurent Kabila gained the largest share of the vote, he did not get the two-thirds required for the presidency.

Economy

Despite extensive **mineral resources** the country is one of the world's poorest. Currency reform and privatisation and cooperation plans have not been implemented. A budget acceptable to foreign investors does not even exist.

The Gross Domestic Product amounted to US$7.3 billion in 2005. 59 per cent of this amount derived from **agriculture** which is little developed thus far, 15 per cent was derived from **industry** and 26 per cent from the **services sector**. Machinery, semi-finished goods, foodstuffs and fuel are imported and diamonds, crude oil, copper, cobalt and coffee are some of the main exports.

Transport

The country's **rail network** is 5,138 km long, although only 858 km is electrified. 2,500 km of the country's 145,000 km **road network** is surfaced. There are international **airports** in Kinshasa, Lumbumbashi, Bukavu, Goma and Kisangani.

Tourism

Due to the political situation the tourist infrastructure is practically non-existent. However, the extraordinary wealth of wildlife and especially the gorilla colonies deep n the rainforest are promising for ecotourism. Many scientific expeditions visit the country to explore the medicinal potential of the various plant species in the rainforest. The best time to visit the area north of the equator is from December to January and for the area south of the Equator June and July.

Warlords and child soldiers

Since the end of the Cold War, the conflict patterns in Africa have changed dramatically. Radical political figures and rebels emerged, keen on their personal advantage or that of an ethnically defined clientele, exploited the population and forced civilians, often young children, to bare arms for them.

Child soldiers are still common in Angola.

The African warlords assert themselves in regions in which the state has lost its grip on power. They finance themselves through looting and stealing. The warlord regards himself as a charismatic leader, whose armed following is often press-ganged into his service. , Violence is often accompanied by drugs and initiation rituals.

The fate of children is particularly tragic under these violent circumstances. In total, up to 120,000 children are serving as soldiers in Africa.
The deployment of child soldiers has mainly practical reasons for the cynical warlords. Children require less clothing and food, are less demanding when sharing the spoils and can be sent out to minefields to create safe passages. They are also much easier

to manipulate and thus less likely to rebel against the authority of the warlord.

Above: Child soldiers from the SLA, the Sierra Leone Army.

Right: Many children in former Zaire have been trained as killers.

Sudan, Eritrea

*A camel caravan transports salt blocks from **Lake Assal** in Djibouti. The salt lake is situated 155 m below sea level and is the lowest point of Africa. Djibouti's salt pans are among the largest on earth.*

Sudan

Area:	2,505 813 sq. km
Capital city:	Khartoum
Form of government:	Republic
Administrative divisions:	
26 provinces	
Population: 40.1 million	
(14 inhabitants per sq. km)	
Languages:	
Arabic (official), English as well as Hamitic and Nilotic languages	
GDP per capita:	US$2,100
Currency:	
1 Sudanese pound = 100 piastres	

Natural geography

Sudan is the largest country in Africa. It has a flat valley landscape, interrupted only by a few isolated mountains. The highest elevation is represented by Kinyeti (3,187 m) in the south. The great Sudd swamp, a flood plain of the **White Nile**, separates the north and south of the country. Almost 60 per cent of the population lives in the Nile valley which has the best farmland. Almost one third of the country consists of sandy desert, bordered to the south by savannah and grass steppe. Rainforests are found in the mountainous regions of the south.

Climate

The climate is largely continental-tropical turning to desert in the north. At the Red Sea, temperatures of over 50°C are regularly recorded. The Khartoum region has the highest average annual temperature (32°C).

Population

Of the Sudanese population 52 per cent are predominantly **Nilotic**, falling into more than 500 different ethnic groups, while 39 per cent of the population are of **Arab origin**. 70 per cent are adherents of Islam, living mainly in the north of the country, while the Christians, who live mainly in the south and in Khartoum, make up only ten per cent of the population. One quarter of Sudanese are adherents of animist religions. The official language, Arabic, is the mother tongue of 50 per cent of the population, while the oth-

er half speak more than 100 languages, of mainly Nilotic origin.

History and Politics

The history of what is now the Sudan dates back millennia, when, as Nubia, it was part of the Egyptian empire. It was not until 1000 BC that the independent kingdom of Kush came into being. It was replaced in the fourth century BC by the Kingdom of Meroe whose rulers and converted to Christianity, and which lasted until 325 AD. The kingdom of Axum, now Ethiopia, then conquered the land. Arab tribes followed in the late thirteenth century and Islamised the country. Britain and Egypt ruled the Sudan jointly from 1820. In 1881 a bloodthirsty revolt was led by Mohammed Ahmad, the so-called 'Mad Mahdi' – the Mahdi being the renewer of faith awaited by Islam, who would restore divine order. General George Gordon quelled the revolt in 1899, since when he was known as Gordon of Khartoum.

Sudan: the El-Sheik Deffa Allah Mosque koranic school, Omdurman.

In 1956, Sudan declared its **independence** from the joint Anglo-Egyptian rule, and disputes broke out between north and south. As early as 1958 a military regime took over. In 1971, Colonel Ghaafar Numeri ruled a one-party state. In 1983, open **civil war** broke out between north and south. The war produced a prolonged **famine**, due partly to the centuries-old religious and political clashes be-

tween the Christian African south and the Islam-dominated north but aggravated by drought conditions. Even the parliamentary constitution of 1998 could not change this, since a state of emergency had been declared. A cease-fire declared in 2002 was ignored by both the military regime and the rebels. The United Nations has tried to intervene in Darfur, where the Janjaweed government-backed militia is persecuting the Christian and animist minority but without success.

Economy

60 per cent of the labour force is engaged in agriculture, largely a **subsistence economy**. The main exports are cotton, peanuts, sesame and oil seeds, as well as some 80 per cent of the worldwide production of gum arabic. The nomadic populations breed cattle. The country's **industry**, developing sluggishly only since 1956, is severely underdeveloped. It employs five per cent of the labour force population, mainly produc-

ing cotton textiles. The most significant economic area is the **services sector**, which produces 50 per cent of GDP.

Transport

The 11,610-km-long **road network** consists mainly of dirt roads, which do not allow all-year-round connections to the neighbouring countries. The Nile

waterways are important transport routes, inland navigation being possible for 5,310 km of the river's length. The major **port** is at Port Sudan, and the only international **airport** is at Khartoum.

Tourism

Tourists rarely visit this crisis area. Sites of cultural and historical interest include Dongulah and Karimah from the Nubian empire and the mosques of Khartoum.

Eritrea

Area:	121,320 sq. km
Capital city:	Asmara
Form of government:	Republic
Administrative divisions:	
10 provinces	
Population: 4.5 million.	
(35 inhabitants per sq. km)	
Languages:	
Arabic, Tigrinya (both official)	
GDP per capita:	US$1,000
Currency: 1 nafka = 100 cents	

Natural geography

This small republic is bordered to the north-east by the **Red Sea**. The narrow coastal plain expands in the north into the **Abyssinian Highlands**, where the highest point of the country, Soira (3013 m), is found, and which also includes the main settlement area as a result of its rich natural resources and cooler climate. The southern lowland at the foot of the Danakil mountains is largely desert. The Dahlak islands in the Red Sea are also part of the territory of Eritrea.

Climate

The narrow coastal strip along the Red Sea is among the hottest regions on earth, but in general a continental-tropical climate prevails. In the highlands above 1,000 m a pleasantly temperate climate prevails. Temperatures in the capital are about 15°C in January, 22°C in July.

Population

The population consists of 50 per cent **Tigrinyans**, 40 per cent **Tigre** and **Kunama**, four per cent **Afar**

(nomads) and three per cent **Saho**. 50 per cent of Eritreans are Sunni Muslims, 50 per cent Eritrean Christians. In this under-developed country, 50 per cent of the population is illiterate.

History and Politics

From 1890 to 1941, the area of present-day Eritrea was **Italian sovereign territory**, but it was captured by Great Britain during World War II and ruled by Britain until 1952. For ten years, Eritrea remained an autonomous area within Ethiopia, but it was then **annexed** as a fourteenth province, which caused an uprising. After a 30-year struggle for freedom, Eritrea gained its **independence** as a republic in 1991. The 1997 constitution has not yet come into force. In 2002, Parliament decided against the introduction of a multi-party system. In 1998, Eritrea entered a border war against Ethiopia, in which it incurred heavy losses. A cease-fire was declared in 2000. A buffer zone has so far been guarded by UN forces. In 2002, both countries agreed to the proposals of a border commission. However, in 2003 Ethiopia rejected this decision.

Economy

The civil war resulted in serious damage. Small farmers make up 80 per cent of the population, and at the present time can provide food for only 20 per cent of their fellow citizens. A redevelopment programme encourages the cultivation of coffee and tobacco for export. Of the country's GDP, 18 per cent derives from the **processing industries**, which provides items for everyday use.

Transport

The entire infrastructure is in a state of redevelopment. This applies both to the **rail network**, which was taken out of service in 1978, and to the **road network**, which consists mainly of dirt roads. The most important **port** is at Massawa; there is an international **airport** at Asmara.

Tourism

The tourist sector is inadequately developed; the main travel desti-

Eritrea's economy was heavily marred by droughts, famine and the war with Ethiopia. When the country declared its independence in 1993, much of its flora had been destroyed and most of the farmland was lying idle.

Famine was only averted because of international aid. A number of development projects have been initiated to strengthen the agricultural sector. Fode is now a centre for vegetable farming.

History and Politics

In 1884, it was part of several French protectorates on the Gulf of Aden which became French Somaliland. In 1967, the name was changed to Territory of the Afars and the Issas. As **Djibouti**, it became an **independent republic** in 1977. Rivalry between the two largest ethnic groups holds potential for future conflict.

Africa, as well as its status as a free trade area. The **services sector** generates 80 per cent of GDP.

Transport

A **railway line** links this small country with Ethiopia. The most important transshipment and transport hub and the only international **airport** is in the capital city, Djibouti.

Tourism

The tourist centres

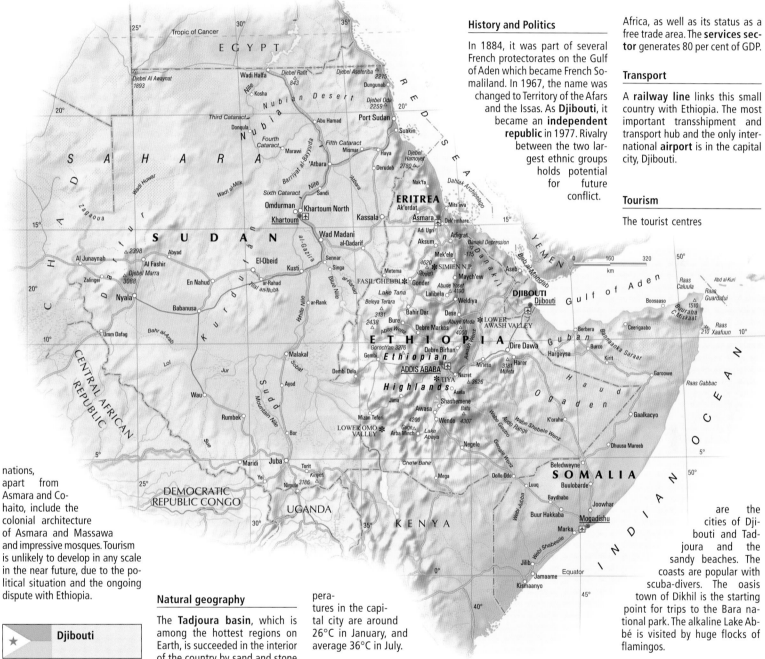

nations, apart from Asmara and Cohaito, include the colonial architecture of Asmara and Massawa and impressive mosques. Tourism is unlikely to develop in any scale in the near future, due to the political situation and the ongoing dispute with Ethiopia.

are the cities of Djibouti and Tadjoura and the sandy beaches. The coasts are popular with scuba-divers. The oasis town of Dikhil is the starting point for trips to the Bara national park. The alkaline Lake Abbé is visited by huge flocks of flamingos.

	Djibouti

Area:	23,200 sq. km
Capital city:	Djibouti
Form of government:	Republic
Administrative divisions:	
4 districts	
Population:	
477,000	
(32 inhabitants per sq. km)	
Languages:	
French, Arabic (both official), Kushite languages	
GDP per capita:	US$1,300
Currency:	
1 Djibouti franc = 100 centimes	

Natural geography

The **Tadjoura basin**, which is among the hottest regions on Earth, is succeeded in the interior of the country by sand and stone deserts (Lake Asal is 155 m below sea level), as well as steppes, which occupy 95 per cent of the land area. Abundant vegetation is found only at heights above 1,200 m in the northern foothills of the Danakil Mountains. Throughout the country there are hot springs and active volcanoes, and earthquakes are frequent.

Climate

Djibouti has an extremely hot climate with high humidity. Temperatures in the capital city are around 26°C in January, and average 36°C in July.

Population

The Issas, a Somali people, living mainly in the south of the country, constitute 60 per cent of the population, the **Afars** in the north about 35 per cent. Two-thirds, who are 94 per cent Muslim and six per cent Christian, live in the capital, the rest are nomadic shepherds. Healthcare is inadequate and infant mortality is high, so that average life expectancy is only 51 years for men.

Economy

Because of the nature of the country as well as regularly recurring droughts, agriculture only accounts for two per cent of GDP. Most foodstuffs have to be imported. The **processing industry** contributes 18 per cent to GDP. The economy is based on the country's strategic position as the route for Ethiopian exports and its position on the great international navigation routes through

	Ethiopia

Area:	1,127,127 sq. km
Capital city:	Addis Ababa
Form of government:	
Federal Republic	
Administrative divisions:	
9 regions, capital city	
Population: 73 million	
(58 inhabitants per sq. km)	
Languages:	

Ethiopia, Somalia

*South-western **Somalia** is dominated by a dry savannah. Farming consists of livestock-rearing, mainly in the river valleys of Juba and Webe Shebele. The latter disappears into the 10 to 50-km-wide dune stripe on the south coast.*

Amharic (official), 70 other languages and dialects

GDP per capita: US$800
Currency: 1 birr = 100 cents

Natural geography

Ethiopia consists of high mountains with elevations of up to 4,620 m (Ras Dashen); its plateau is shared by the **East African Rift Valley**, which leads in the north into the Danakil Depression . Here there are lakes and a few volcanoes which are still active today. Towards Sudan the mountains drop steeply away.

Climate

The northern landscape of the country consists of deserts and dry savannahs, the south-west is covered in rainforest containing many of the large mammals (rhinoceroses, elephants, buffaloes, numerous bird and reptile species). Temperatures in the capital city of Addis Ababa are only 10°C to 21°C due to its high altitude.

Population

The Ethiopians are composed of some 80 different ethnic groups, the largest of which are the **Oromo** at 40 per cent, and the **Amhara** and **Tigray-Tigrinya** at 32 per cent. Muslims make up 45 per cent of the population, 40 per cent are Ethiopian Christian, and the rest consist of other minorities. Because of the lack of healthcare, average life expectancy is only 50 years for men, while infant mortality is very high.

History and Politics

The first legendary kingdom of the **Queen of Sheba** was followed in the first century by the powerful **Aksum**, an empire that lasted for more than a thousand years, became Christian as early as the fourth century and resisted all attempts at Islamisation in the period that followed. It was not until after the end of the kingdom of the **Neguses** in the nineteenth century that a mighty state formed again, which successfully resisted European colonisation. After the last emperor, Heile Selassie, was forced to abdicate in 1974, a socialist people's republic was established, whose leader was toppled in 1991. In 1993, after a thirty-year war, the former coastal province of **Eritrea** became independent. In 1995, a parliamentary-pluralistic constitution came into force in Ethiopia. After border disputes with Eritrea, a border war began in May 2000, which was settled in June with a cease-fire agreement. In December 2000, a peace treaty was signed. The president since 2001 has been Girma Wolde Giorgis. Catastrophic drought conditions have repeatedly caused famine among the population.

Economy

Agriculture, which provides about half of the country's GDP and offers basic subsistence to 80 per cent of the population, can however hardly deliver the most basic needs in grain and pulses. Ethiopia is regularly beset by droughts and famines. The most important export is coffee. Underdeveloped industry serves the domestic market and relies on agricultural produce; an additional complication is that the largest enterprises are still state-owned.

Transport

The only **railway line** runs from Djibouti to Addis Ababa. The **road network** which covers most of Ethiopia is barely asphalted. Access to the sea, for this landlocked country is via the **ports** of Eritrea. There are international **airports** in Addis Ababa and Dire Dawa.

Tourism

Apart from the wildlife in the national parks, such as Awash, the ruins of old Aksum and the Christian sites in Addis Ababa, Lake Tana and Lalibela are among the main attractions. Tourists are gradually returning to Ethiopia.

Somalia

Area: 637,657 sq. km
Capital city: Mogadishu
Form of government: Republic
Administrative divisions: 18 provinces
Population: 8.6 million (12 inhabitants per sq. km)
Languages: Somali (official), Arabic, English, Italian
GDP per capita: US$600
Currency: 1 Somali shilling = 100 centesimi

Natural geography

Somalia, which covers the **Horn of Africa**, has a 300-km-long coastline, mainly steeply sloping and rocky at the Gulf of Aden and the Indian Ocean. The highest elevation is the 2,416-m-high **Mount Shimbiris** close to the **Gulf of Aden**. Along the flat southern coast, edged by a dune belt 10 to

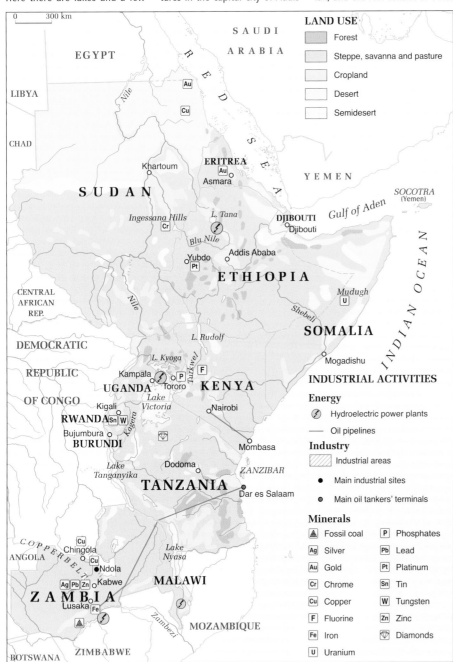

LAND USE

- Forest
- Steppe, savanna and pasture
- Cropland
- Desert
- Semidesert

INDUSTRIAL ACTIVITIES

Energy
- ⚡ Hydroelectric power plants
- Oil pipelines

Industry
- ▨ Industrial areas
- ● Main industrial sites
- ◉ Main oil tankers' terminals

Minerals

▲ Fossil coal		P	Phosphates
Ag	Silver	Pb	Lead
Au	Gold	Pt	Platinum
Cr	Chrome	Sn	Tin
Cu	Copper	W	Tungsten
F	Fluorine	Zn	Zinc
Fe	Iron	▽	Diamonds
U	Uranium		

Haile Selassie

Ras Tafari Makonnen
*Edsharsa, 23.6.1892,
†Addis Ababa, 27.8.1975

Heir to the throne since 1916, the grandson of Menelik proclaimed himself Negus (king) of Ethiopia in 1928. As emperor, he gave the country its first consitution in1931. He went into exile in England during the Italian occupation and reclaimed his throne in 1941. In 1974 he was deposed by a provisional military government.

*The famous rock temples were built at the end of the twelfth century at heights of 2,600 m, on the initiative of King **Lalibela** in the Ethiopian city named after him. The eight churches were carved directly into the tufa rock and are linked to each other through a system of passages and tunnels. The church of St. George, built in the shape of a cross, is considered the most beautiful. It is constructed inside a shaft 12 m deep and is only accessible through a gallery.*

50 km wide, lies a chain of coral reefs. The two largest rivers, the Jubba and the Shebelle, form large swamps at their mouths, but only the Jubba contains water all year round. The destruction of trees for fuel and by heavy grazing has caused the desert area to expand.

Climate

In the north-east of Somalia the climate is responsible for a desert landscape and temperatures of up to 45°C; otherwise the alternation of north-east and south-west monsoon results in seasonal climate fluctuations.
Rain falls mainly from April to June, when non-irrigated crops can be grown. Temperatures in the capital city average 26°C.

Population

Various **Somali groups** make up 85 per cent of the population; in addition there are **Bantu-speaking groups** and a small number of **Arabs**. However, exact figures are hard to obtain, for the civil war has resulted in lasting changes to the country. There is no organised health care system, life expectancy is as low as 51 and infant mortality is high. The literacy rate is only 40 per cent. The collapse of the infrastructure has caused famine.

History and Politics

After the first Muslim settlements in the seventh century, as well as Portuguese and Turkish influences in the sixteenth century, the **Sultans of Oman** ruled the region from the seventeenth to the nineteenth centuries.
From 1875 to 1884 the colonial regions of **French Somaliland** and **British Somaliland** were founded on the Gulf of Aden, followed from 1889 to 1908 by **Italian Somaliland** on the Indian Ocean.
In 1960, the **Republic of Somalia** was established. The military dictatorship of Major-General Mohammed Siad Barré.which had ruled since 1969 was toppled in 1991 after violent clashes, and Barré fled. The **civil war** which has prevailed since then between various tribal militias caused the north-east of the country to declare independence in 1991 as the **Republic of Somaliland** in the territory of the former British

Somaliland. In 1992, the United States marines tried to restore order but were unable to do so and suffered heavy casualties inflicted by the forces of the various Somali warlords. The United Nations tried to intervene as mediator in the country, where no political system currently exists. In 1995, the UN abandoned its mission having achieved nothing. In the east of the country, Puntland was declared an autonomous region in 1998. A peace conference began in the autumn of 2002. In 2003 the participants signed an agreement providing for a caretaker parliament. The present truce is, in fact,

deceptive, and the conflict with Somaliland has not been resolved.

Economy

Somalia is one of the poorest states in the world. Cattle-breeding and agriculture are among the main branches of the economy. As a result of the civil war and the catastrophic droughts, the population suffers from a chronic lack of adequate supplies of foodstuffs, water and medical care. Meanwhile economic life has shifted to the black market, smuggling and barter. Only in the breakaway province of Somaliland are conditions somewhat more stable.

Transport

The country's **road network** outside the larger cities consists of dirt roads, there are hardly any paved roads. There is no railway line, and national **air transport** is irregular. Mogadishu and Berbera are the major **ports**.

Tourism

There is no tourism due to the political situation. The capital, Mogadishu has suffered heavy damage. There are ten game reserves; the beaches on the Indian Ocean are protected by a very long coral reef and are among the longest in the world.

1 The selection offered in the markets of Hargeisa is impressive, despite the severe economic crisis in Somalia.

2 Ethiopia: in the treasure chamber of the St. Mary of Zion church in Aksum, part of its treasure is on display, including the emperor's crowns.

3 The church of Debre Berhan Selassie was founded by Emperor Yasu the Great in Gondar. It is still an important place of worship for Ethiopians.

4 Rashaida are nomads of Arab origin. They constitute 0.3 per cent of the population of Eritrea.

Kenya, Uganda

*The **Turkana** are one of the East Nile ethnic groups living in north-western Kenya. The approximately 200,000 Turkana breed cattle, camels, goats and sheep. Blood and milk are the basis of their diet. The cattle herds are significant both in economic and social terms. There is a fishing industry on Lake Turkana. The Turkana people are famous for their silver jewellery.*

Kenya

Area:	582,646 sq. km
Capital City	Nairobi

Form of government: Presidential Republic
Administrative division:
7 provinces,1 district (capital city)
Population:
33.8m (54 inhabitants/sq. km)
Languages: Kiswahili (official), English and tribal languages
GDP per capita: US$1200
Currency: 1 Kenyan-shilling = 100 cents

Natural geography

Kenya is on the east coast of Africa lying directly on the **equator** and comprises four main landscapes: dry savannah with thornbush vegetation in the north-

Jomo Kenyatta

*Ichaweri, 20.10.1892,
†Mombassa, 22.8.1978

The chairman of the Kenyan African National Union was sentenced to seven years in prison by the British colonial rulers for his leadership of the Mau-Mau-uprising. In 1961, he became its leader again and in 1963 the first prime minister of Kenya. In 1964 Kenyatta became president – an office he was to hold until his death. He rejected a multi-party system because he feared divisions along ethnic lines.

east, barren mountain foothills in the north-west around Lake Turkana, tree and thornbush savannah in the south-east and a plateau which reaches altitudes of over 3,000 m.
The savannah and vast parts of the highlands are populated with great herds of wild animals (elephants, rhinoceroses, zebras, antelopes, buffalos and giraffes) and predators (lions, cheetahs).

Climate

The climate is tropical, hot and humid, but those parts of the country visited by the monsoon also have long dry periods. The relatively mild west of the country contains most of its population. Average temperatures are approximately 20°C in Nairobi which stands at an altitude of 1,670 m.

Population

Kenya's population consists of roughly 40 Bantu-speaking groups and Nilotic tribes; the most important of these are the **Kikuyus** (who account for 22 per cent of the population), the **Luhyas** (who account for 14 per cent of the population), the **Luos** (13 per cent), the **Kalenjins** (12 per cent), the **Kambas** (11 per cent) and the **Kisiis** and the **Merus** who each account for six per cent. Over 60 per cent of Kenyans are Christians and approximately 25 per cent followers of animist religions. There are also minorities of Jews, Hindus and Muslims.

Nairobi is the economic and administrative centre of Kenya.

Average life expectancy is 46 years. The HIV/AIDS infection rate is high at approximately 15 per cent. Approximately half of the population is illiterate.

History and Politics

In 1963, the former British colony gained **independence** and declared itself a republic. **Jomo Kenyatta**, the first president, held office until 1978. A one-party system was subsequently introduced. However, in 1982 other political parties were permitted and due to pressure from foreign countries providing development aid. In 1992, the first free elections were held since 1978. In 2002, Mwai Kibaki was elected president. The parliament is elected every five years and the head of state is elected every five years through direct elections.

Economy

In the enormously productive **agricultural** sector, tea, coffee, sisal, sugar cane, fresh vegetables, legumes, cashew nuts and pineapples are the main exports. Cattle rearing also accounts for a sizeable proportion of the favourable foreign trade balance. In the **manufacturing sector**, 11 per cent of GDP is generated from the processing of foodstuffs and oil. Tourism is the most profitable branch of the economy in the services sector. It is the country's second most important foreign currency earner after agriculture.

Transport

A **railway line** traverses the country. Of the 63,800-km-long **road network** 8,800 km is surfaced. National air traffic is buoyant and includes charter flights for safaris. Three of the 29 **airports** offer connections to international airports. Nairobi is the hub of East Africa.

Tourism

Kenya's main attractions are the **national game reserves** The best known are the Masai Mara, the Amboseli and the Meru national reserves. Nairobi is the nation's centre. The port of Mombasa has an old town with Arab-influenced architecture which is worth a visit. Further tourist destinations include Lake Victoria and the Lamu Archipelago. The Olduvai Gorge where the first remains of homo sapiens were found is in Kenya.

Uganda

Area:	236,040 sq. km
Capital City	Kampala

Form of government:
Presidential Republic within the Commonwealth
Administrative division:
38 districts
Population:
26.4m (106 inhabitants/sq. km)
Languages:
Kiswahili, English (both official), Luganda

Idi Amin Dada

*Koboco 1925,
†Jeddah 16.8.2003

This former army officer became deputy chief-of-staff in 1964 and subsequently Supreme Commander of the Armed Forces of Uganda in 1966. In 1971 he overthrew President Milton Obote and established a brutal dictatorship. Around 300,000 Ugandans fell victim to his regime. After his overthrow through Tanzanian troups in 1979, he went into exile in Saudi Arabia.

GDP per capita:	US$1400

Currency:
1 Uganda shilling = 100 cents

Natural geography

The majority of the landlocked African country of Uganda which lies on the equator forms a plateau of approximately 1,000 to 3,000 m in altitude. The plateau contains the large mounds known as monadnocks.
The highest elevations in this savannah landscape are the 4,322 m Mount Elgon in the east and the 5,109 m **Ruwenzori Massif** in the west. In the south-east, half of the large **Lake Victoria** lies in Uganda. The country also possesses vast lakes and marshes such as Lake Kioga and Lake Salisbury. In contrast, the rainforests and mountain forests are dwindling. Whilst the landscape in the north is characterised by thornbush savannah, wet savannah predominates in the south.

Climate

The hot and humid tropical climate is strongly attenuated by the country's altitude. The temperatures in the capital city are approximately 22°C all year round.

Population

A total of 45 ethnic groups live in this multi-national state. **Bantuspeaking groups** constitute the majority of the population with a 50 per cent share (of which 28 per cent are Gandas). There are also Nilotic and Sudanese ethnic groups and Indian and Arabic minorities. The majority of Ugandans are Christians, 16 per cent are followers of Islam and 18 per cent believe in animistic religions.

History and Politics

A series of central African realms existed in the region of Uganda for centuries when the British conquered the country and made it into a **British protectorate** in 1894. After Uganda gained its **independence** in 1962, its fortunes were determined in the 1970s and the 1980s by conflicts between various factions fighting a civil war and the dictatorships of Idi **Amin** and Milton **Obote**, which were almost as bloodthirsty as each other. The political situation stabilised somewhat in the 1990s. The introduction of a new constitution in 1995 still failed to provide Uganda with a **multi-party democratic system**. Although political parties are now permitted, they do not as yet have the right to participate in elections. Yoweri Kaguta Museveni has been president of the country since 1986. The situation in Northern Uganda is problematical as government troops advance against the rebel movement which calls itself Lord's Resistance Army. The Ugandan army intervened in the civil war in the Democratic Republic of Congo.

*The Nilotic tribes in Kenya live nomadic lives of cattlebreeders in the savannahs and have preserved their customs and traditional clothes, which is particularly true for the **Samburu**, who pay a lot of attention to body ornaments .*

Economy

Agriculture is the most important branch of the economy and the country's greatest earner of foreign currency. Coffee is the main export. It has hitherto generated approximately 70 per cent of export revenue. Fish from Lake Victoria have become the second most important export in recent years. Tea, cotton and tobacco are also exported. In the 1990s, Uganda attained real GDP growth of approximately six per cent. In the interim, growth levelled off due to the fall in world coffee prices in particular but in 2002 it again reached 6.2 per cent. The agricultural sector feeds almost 90 per cent of the population. The manufacturing sector has produced only sufficient consumer goods for the domestic market.

Transport

The **roads** are in a poor overall condition. Only a quarter of them are passable all year round. Consequently, the 1,240-km-long **rail network** is being extended further. Domestic flights and connections by sea to neighbouring countries are also irregular. There is an international **airport** in Entebbe.

Tourism

The country's most significant sites worth visiting include both lakes and the Ruwenzori National Reserve, a paradise for rock-climbers. Part of the Virunga National Reserve belongs to Uganda; the Bwindi National Reserve is has extensive flora and local African mammalian fauna. Entebbe has a wonderful botanical gardens started in colonial times, and the spectacular Lake Victoria is dotted with lovely islands.

Rwanda

Area:	26,338 sq. km
Capital City	Kigali
Form of government:	
Presidential Republic	
Administrative division:	
11 prefectures	
Population:	
8,4m (296 inhabitants/sq. km)	
Languages: Kinyarwanda, French (both official), Kiswahili, English	

GDP per capita: US$1300
Currency:
1 Rwanda franc = 100 centimes

Natural geography

The highest elevations of this predominantly mountainous country are located in the west where they reach altitudes of up to 4,507 m in the **Virunga Volcanoes**. In central and eastern Rwanda, hilly plateaus of around 1500 m predominate.

Climate

Rainforests and wet savannah predominate up to an altitude of 2,500 m in the tropical climate which is attenuated by the altitude (average temperatures range from 19°C to 21°C). Rainforests and wet savannah turn into bamboo forests on the higher mountains. There is a wealth of animal species including lions, leopards, hippopotamuses, rhinoceroses, crocodiles and monkeys, especially in the game reserves.

Population

80 per cent of the inhabitants of this densely populated country are Hutus and 19 per cent are **Tutsis**. The country is largely reliant on foreign aid for the reconstruction of its infrastructure, the maintenance of its health service and the provision of foodstuffs. Average life expectancy is just 40 years – one of the world's lowest.

History and Politics

In the fifteenth century, the Tutsi people arrived in the region populated by the Hutus and established a feudal system.
This power structure was consolidated under German rule which began in 1885 with the charter founding German East Africa. In 1916, Rwanda came under **Belgian, colonial rule**. When the Belgians left, the Tutsis dominant position was threatened by Hutu rebellions from 1955 onwards. As a result, conflicts arose between the two groups in Rwanda and in the neighbouring country of Burundi. These culminated in a terrible genocide in 1994. in which the Hutu massacred the Tutsis, following decades of combat. According to official estimates, 800,000 people were killed from both factions. After 1997, those who had been expelled or fled in their masses returned. They had become refugees in neighbouring countries which also rejected them. In spite of a peace agreement and mediation attempts on the part of the United Nations the unrest continues.
Paul Kagame became president in 2003. There are tensions with neighbouring Uganda and also the Democratic Republic of Congo, since Rwanda gave military support to the rebels challenging Congo's president Laurent Kabila. Those mainly responsible for the massacre have largely escaped punishment.

Economy

Rwanda's economy which was completely ruined by civil war has been reconstructed since 1996 thanks to massive international assistance. The most important export is coffee which earns 80 per cent of the country's revenue, followed by tea, pyrethrum, beans, maize and bananas. The manufacturing sector is under construction and predominantly processes agricultural produce in small to medium-size enterprises.

Transport

The infrastructure was severely affected by the civil war. However, the main roads are in comparatively good condition. The international airport is located in Kigali.

Tourism

Due to the permanent unrest, Rwanda is still not considered safe to visit. One of the last few colonies of mountain gorillas live in the Virunga National Reserve.

Burundi

Area:	27,834 sq. km
Capital City	Bujumbura
Form of government:	

Presidential Republic
Administrative division:
15 Provinces
Population:
6.3m
(230 inhabitants/sq. km)
Languages:
Kirundi, French
(both official), Kiswahili

GDP per capita: 700 US$
Currency:
1 Burundi franc = 100 centimes

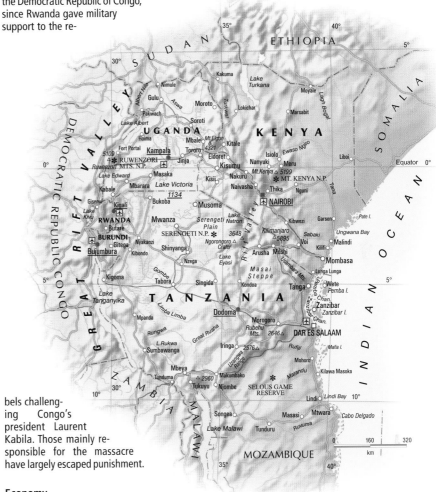

Natural geography

Lake Tanganyika constitutes the south-western border of Burundi. North-east of the lake, there are highlands with wet savannah. The country's interior forms a plateau with an average altitude of 1,500 m which is dominated by grass savannah straddling the watershed of the Congo and the Nile. There is rainforest in the north-east.

Photo safaris are an important source of income for Tanzania. Tourists can watch lions at the Ngorongoro Crater in the northern Tanzanian highland or elephants roaming wild in the Serengeti national park near Lake Victoria.

Climate

The equatorial climate is attenuated by altitude. Average temperatures range from 17°C to 22°C.

Population

The **Hutus** account for the majority of the population at 85 per cent, whilst the **Tutsis** account for 14 per cent. Both groups converse in related languages and have very similar animist religions.

History and Politics

In the fifteenth century, Tutsi tribes came from the north to settle in the area of present-day Burundi occupied by Hutu tribes. The Tutsis established a **feudalist system** which socially disadvantaged the **Hutus**.

In 1890, the country, along with Rwanda, became part of the Ger-

Julius Kambarage Nyerere

*Butiama, March 1922,
†London, 14.10.1999

As founder of the Tanganyika African National Union, he led Tanganyika to independence and became the first prime minister. After the unification of Tanganyika and Zanzibar, he became the President of the new state Tanzania. He was an advocate of a self-confident Africa and actively supported the Organisation for African Unity. In 1985, he stepped down as the President of Tanzania but continued as the chairman of the OAU. He continued to lead his party until 1990.

man colony of East Africa which was later governed by Belgium as Rwanda-Urundi. In 1962, Burundi gained **independence**. The country's situation has been determined by continually erupting conflicts between the two groups ever since. It was envisaged that the 1992 constitution would promote the resolution of ethnic conflicts; instead it led to the bloodiest war in the country's history resulting in hundreds of thousands of deaths and the flight of over one million

inhabitants to neighbouring countries. Although peace has officially reigned since 2000, civil war flares up continually. In 2001, a transitional constitution and a government composed of Tutsi and Hutu ministers were created. The peace process is repeatedly endangered due to constant violations.

Economy

Burundi is one of the world's poorest countries. Hunger and poverty-related illnesses are widespread. One of the country's problems is the reintegration of approximately 1.2 million refugees. The majority of the population is dependent on the cultivation of crops (Hutus) and cattle rearing (Tutsis) for their livelihood. Women are responsible for 70 per cent of agricultural production. Coffee is the main export. Civil war and an economic embargo by neighbouring countries

(1996–1999) have led to economic decline in all sectors. 59 per cent of the population lives below the poverty line. Burundi is not recognised by a number of countries, adding to its economic woes.

Transport

Very little of the **road network** is surfaced. **Sea** and **air connections** exist only in neighbouring countries. The capital city has an international **airport**.

Tourism

The region surrounding the capital city is the country's tourist centre and the starting point for safaris to the two national game reserves where mountain gorillas and African big game species are protected. However, tourism has come to a complete standstill due to the ongoing civil unrest.

Tanzania

Area:	945,087 sq. km
Capital City Dodoma (Seat of government: Dar es Salaam)	
Form of government: Federal Presidential Republic	
Administrative division: 25 regions	
Population: 36.7 million (38 inhabitants/sq. km)	

Language:	Swahili
GDP per capita	US$700
Currency: 1 Tanzania shilling = 100 cents	

Natural geography

Tanzania, on the **Indian Ocean**, is characterised by plateaus and mountainous country formed by tectonic fractures such as the eastern and central African rifts and volcanoes. **Mount Kilimanjaro** is Africa's highest mountain

at 5,895 m. Three great lakes are located at the country's borders (Lake Victoria, Lake Malawi and Lake Tanganyika). The islands of Zanzibar, Pemba and Mafia also belong to the country.

Climate

While the climate is tropically hot and humid in coastal areas, a moderate tropical climate prevails in the highlands. Temperatures range from 19°C to 24°C in the capital city, Dar es Salaam.

Population

Bantu tribes who are, in turn, subdivided into **130 different ethnic groups** account for 95 per cent of the inhabitants.

45 per cent of the population are Christians, 35 per cent are Muslims and 20 per cent followers of local religions. The population of the island of **Zanzibar** is of Arabic-African descent and is 99 per cent Muslim.

History and Politics

After the Portuguese occupied the coast in the early fifteenth century, **Tanganyika** became the main component of the colony of **German East Africa**. In 1920, Kenya was assigned to Great Britain under a mandate of the League of Nations and was ruled as a

confederation with Uganda and Tanganyika. In 1962, the country gained independence. In 1946, it was converted to a UN trust region. The country gained independence in 1962.

In 1964, Tanzania emerged as a federal presidential republic from the **union of Tanganyika** with the British protectorate of **Zanzibar** which had gained independence in 1963. Following an attack by Uganda, Tanzanian troops occupied Uganda in 1979 and overthrew the dictator Idi Amin. The 1977 constitution envisaged a one-party state but this was replaced by a multi-party system in 1992. Benjamin Mkapa, who had been in office since 1995, was replaced as head of state in 2005 by Jakaya Kikwete.

Economy

Tanzania is still one of Africa's poorest countries; however, privatisation programmes and a diversification of industry which has been introduced on many levels are gradually improving the situation. 57 per cent of GDP and 60 to 70 per cent of export revenue are generated from an **agrarian economy**, mainly **forestry** and **fishery**. Tanzania is well able to supply itself with food. The **manufacturing sector**, which accounts for 17 per cent of GDP, playing an increasingly important role and the significance of the services sector, especially tourism, is also increasing.

Transport

The **road network** is impassable to a great extent in the rainy season. Consequently, the **railways** have a key role to play.

The domestic flight network and the ferries to neighbouring countries offer a good service. There is an international **airport** in Dar es Salaam.

Tourism

Tanzania possesses unique natural beauty with Kilimanjaro, Lake Tanganyika and the Ngorongoro crater. The old town of Bagamoyo and the island of Zanzibar are extremely picturesque. Kilimanjaro is a favourite with mountain climbers. The best time to visit is between June and September.

The Ngorongoro caldera has a diameter of 22 km and 700-m-high walls.

The Massai

This Eastern African semi-nomadic tribe lives in the north-eastern part of Tanzania and in southern parts of Kenya. The approximately 200,000 remaining Massai have been able to preserve their traditional lifestyles up to now. Male society is strictly divided into different age groups of boys, warriors and elders; elder women have equality with elder men.

Cattle is fundamental for the Massai society.

The Massai first originated around Lake Turkana but expanded their territory as far as Lake Victoria until 1870. Their warrior caste known as the Ilmurran subjugated other nations in the area. Together with colonisation, the British also brought a cattle disease, which decimated the livestock of the Massai. This was a disaster, since the Massai believe that their rain god Ngai granted them the cattle for safekeeping when the earth and sky split. Since cattle had been given to the Massai, they believe it was permissible to steal more cattle from other tribes.

The Massai also worship cattle because it is their main source of livelihood as opposed to activities requiring schooling. Many Massai still believe that education is not important. What is im-portant is for herdsmen to search for suitable green pastures to feed the cows.

The Massai are now struggling to maintain their traditional ways of life.

Above: the Massai love colourful clothes.
Below: Richly adorned spears and painted leather shields are typical warrior dress.

Angola, Zimbabwe

*Salisbury was established in 1890 as a military settlement of the British South African pioneer colony, and from 1899 onwards developed into an important trading centre, as a result of the rail connection with Beira. In 1923, it became the capital of the British colony of Southern Rhodesia, and from 1953 to 1963 was capital of the Federation of Rhodesia and Nyasaland. In 1992, when White rule ended, the city was renamed **Harare**. It remains the capital of Zimbabwe.*

Angola

Area:	1,246,700 sq. km
Capital city:	Luanda
Form of government:	Republic
Administrative divisions:	
18 provinces	
Population:	
11.2 million	
(10 inhabitants/sq. km)	
Languages:	
Portuguese (official),	
Bantu languages	
GDP per capita:	US$2,500
Currency:	
1 kwanza = 100 iwei	

Natural Geography

To the west of the country there is a narrow coastal strip covered in rainforest. In the east, this coastal stretch meets the **Luanda Ridge** (highest point: Morro de Moco: 2,620 m) where it rises steeply to form an upland area, criss-crossed by numerous rivers. The broad steppes and humid savannahs extend to the far south-west to the fringes of the Namib Desert. The national territory also includes the northern exclave of Cabinda.

Climate

The areas in the south and along the coast have a semi-desert climate. In the capital city, average temperatures range between 21°C and 26°C. The tropical climate in the interior is milder at higher altitudes.

Population

Angola is inhabited by over 100 ethnic groups, the majority of whom are Bantu-speaking peoples. The **Ovimbundu** (37 per cent), the **Mbunda** (22 per cent) and the **Kongo** (13 per cent) are the largest groups.

History and Politics

The Portuguese explorer Diego Cão became the first European to land in the country in 1483. Portugal founded the settlement of **Luanda** in 1576 and made the country into a Portuguese colony. From 1961 onwards, various **liberation organisations** fought for sovereignty, until Angola was granted **independence** in 1975,

after the fall of the dictator Antonio Salazar in Lisbon. In the very same year, a **civil war** erupted in the country and this lasted for 27 years. The MPLA emerged victorious, with the help of Cuban troops, and proclaimed the People's Republic of Angola. The first President was Antonio Agostinho Neto. After his death in 1979, José Eduardo dos Santos took over the office of President. UNITA began its guerrilla activities. In 1990, the country's name was changed from the People's Republic to the Democratic Republic of Angola, but this did not bring an end to the conflict, because UNITA did not want to hand over its diamond-rich region in the north of Angola to the government. Hundreds of thousands of civilians fled from the disputed regions. Large areas of the country were covered in landmines. In February 2002, UNITA leader Jonas Savimbi died in battle. After this, the rebels and the government started to

foodstuffs, coffee, sisal, hemp, sugar and tobacco for export. **Manufacturing** is scarcely developed. The country has large reserves of **diamonds**, which were used as currency and 'blood diamonds' during the civil war, as well as **crude oil** and **iron ore**, but the economy is completely dependent on crude oil. 90 per cent of export income comes from the petroleum industry, and this represents 80 per cent of the national budget.

Transport Infrastructure

The whole infrastructure has been largely destroyed by the war: more than 80 per cent of the 72,000 km of **roads** are damaged and the **rail network** only operates with great restrictions, due to large numbers of landmines. The only international **airport** and the most important **port** are in Luanda. Malongo in oil-rich Cabinda is the main oil terminal.

At the Victoria Falls, the Zambezi drops 110 m into a crevasse.

negotiate and a peace treaty was signed in April 2002.

Economy

Angola's economy has been severely damaged by the prolonged civil war, and the population is largely dependent on foreign aid. **Agriculture** employs 85 per cent of the working population and produces, in addition to the basic

Tourism

Angola is not currently a tourist destination because the collapsed infrastructure makes travel outside the capital impossible. The country has many attractions from the colonial era, such as the São Miguel Fortress and was once a playground for rich South Africans. The best time to visit is between May and September.

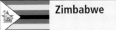

Zimbabwe

Area:	390,580 sq. km
Capital city:	Harare
Form of government:	
Presidential Republic	
Administrative divisions:	
8 provinces	
Population:	
12.7 million	
(29 inhabitants/sq. km)	
Languages:	
English (official), Bantu languages	
GDP per capita:	
US$1,900	
Currency:	
1 Zimbabwe dollar = 100 cents	

Natural Geography

The land mass is defined by the Zambezi in the north and the Limpopo basin in the south. It consists mainly of a highland region which forms part of the fringes of the Kalahari depression. In the

---

Robert Gabriel Mugabe

*Kutama, 21.2.1924

As early as 1963, Mugabe founded the Zimbabwe African National Union ZANU). After the resignation of the last White head of state, Ian Smith, Mugabe took over as Prime Minister in the renamed Zimbabwe and held office from 1980–1987. In 1981, he split with his rival, Joshua Nkomo. He became President in 1986. He kept this position in 1990, 1996 and 2002, but the elections were boycotted by the opposition. His increasingly authoritarian leadership which is leading the country to ruin, is subject to international protest.

---

east, the land rises to form the **Inyanga Mountains** with peaks of up to 2,592 m. The uplands in the interior of the country form an undulating plain with isolated hills and savannah vegetation.

Climate

The climate is defined by Zimbabwe's position on the Tropic of Capricorn; from May to October it

is the dry season. Average temperatures in the capital, Harare, range between 14°C and 21°C.

Population

The population is up to 98 per cent Bantu people, of whom the **Shona** (77 per cent) and the **Ndebele** (17 per cent) form the largest groups. Half the population adheres to syncretistic beliefs, 25 per cent are Christian, 25 per cent follow animist religions.

History and Politics

Zimbabwe first became in independent state in 1980 as a result of a long conflict over the British colony of **Rhodesia**. Rhodesia had been a British protectorate since 1891 and an autonomous colony since 1923, but in 1930/1931, the country was divided in two, known as Rhodesia and Nyasaland, a European region and an African region, much to the advantage of the Europeans.

In 1966, **ZANU** (Zimbabwe African National Union), began a guerrilla campaign against the White minority government. In 1979, talks were held in London between all parties involved and a constitution was agreed that limited the privileges of the White minority, but granted them 'protective rights'. In 1980, the country became **independent** and the name changed to Zimbabwe. In 1987, the seats reserved for Whites in parliament were abolished and the presidential system was introduced. Robert Mugabe was elected state President with executive powers. In 2000, the population voted against a law that would have enabled the government to remove land from the owners of large farms, most of whom were white, without compensation. Following this, the farms were occupied anyway and violence broke out against members of the opposition. This unrest led to an economic crisis and damaged foreign relations. As part of a land reform policy in 2002, approximately 2,600 white farmers were forcibly removed from their land.

Economy

Zimbabwe's **agriculture** is geared towards export. Its natural reserves (gold, copper, nickel, coal) and di-

*Even though only a small minority follow Islam, very few tribes in Zambia keep **pigs** for use as meat. The animals are mainly used for maintaining public hygiene, as they eat all waste and keep the villages clean.*

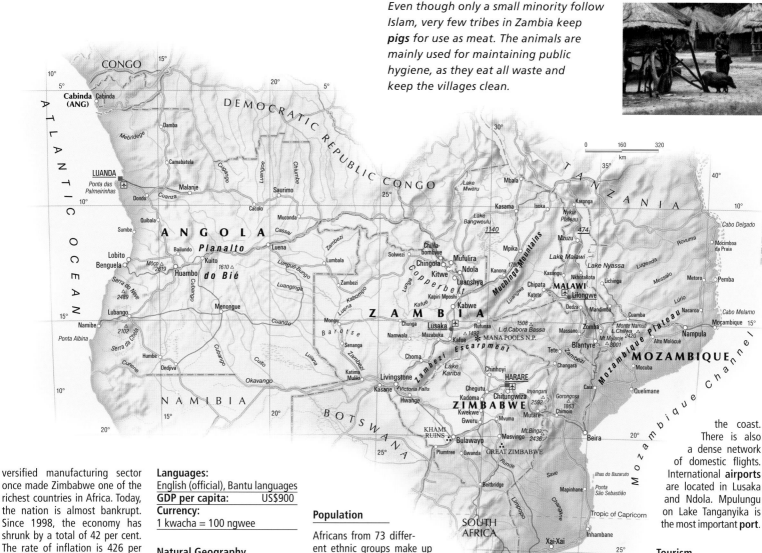

versified manufacturing sector once made Zimbabwe one of the richest countries in Africa. Today, the nation is almost bankrupt. Since 1998, the economy has shrunk by a total of 42 per cent. The rate of inflation is 426 per cent, and unemployment stands at 80 per cent. The causes include drought, incomplete conversion to a market economy, farm expropriation and loss of trust abroad.

Transport Infrastructure

The country has good **rail** and **road networks**. The domestic flight network is good. Harare has the only international **airport**.

Tourism

The main attractions are the Victoria Falls on the border with Zambia, and the fourteenth century ruined city of Great Zimbabwe.

Zambia

Area:	752,614 sq. km
Capital city:	Lusaka

Form of government:
Presidential Republic in the Commonwealth
Administrative divisions:
9 provinces
Population:
11.2 million (13 inhabitants/sq. km)

Languages:
English (official), Bantu languages

GDP per capita:	US$900

Currency:
1 kwacha = 100 ngwee

Natural Geography

Zambia lies in an area of high plains at an average height of between 1000 and 1500 m above sea level. The plains rise gradually from south to north and some individual peaks are as high as 2,300 m.
Lakes and marsh areas define the landscape in the flats of the Zambezi and Kafue rivers. The Victoria Falls are a spectacular feature and the Kariba Dam is a man-made wonder. The north-east of the country is part of Africa's **Great Rift Valley**.

Climate

The tropical climate is made slightly milder by the country's altitude and, with the exception of the hot and humid months from December to April, the savannah of the uplands is mainly arid and has suffered from severe drought.
Average temperatures in the capital city, Lusaka, are 16°C in July and 21°C in January. In the river valleys and lake areas that are covered with dense deciduous forests the climate is hot and humid year-round.

Population

Africans from 73 different ethnic groups make up 98 per cent of the population. The most widely spoken of the more than 80 languages are **Bemba**, **Nyanja**, **Kaonda** and **Lunda**. More than 50 per cent of Zambians are Christian, but there are also Sunni Muslims, small groups of Hindus, and one per cent adhere to native religions.

History and Politics

Modern-day Zambia is a republic within the British Commonwealth of Nations. The country used to be part of **Northern Rhodesia**, a British protectorate created in the year 1911 north of the Zambezi. In 1923, Northern Rhodesia became a protectorate under direct British colonial rule. Zambia gained independence and changed its name in 1964. In 1972/73, the first President, Kenneth (Kamuzu) Kaunda, created a one-party system. Internal and external pressure for democratisation finally paid off in 1990 when opposition parties were permitted.
In 1991, after elections Frederick Chiluba became president. The new constitution guarantees a **multi-party system** and provides

for simultaneous presidential and parliamentary elections.

Economy

Zambia's economy is based on the extraction and export of the largest copper reserves on Earth, and this activity alone contributes 80 per cent of foreign trade. The **agricultural sector** contributes 23 per cent of GDP and employs 86 per cent of the population. Privatisation and greater diversification should create greater opportunities in the future, and the influx of the forcibly ejected farmers from Zimbabwe may also prove an economic advantage.

Transport Infrastructure

The **road and rail systems** are well constructed. The 891 km-long Tazara Line connects the country to

the coast. There is also a dense network of domestic flights. International **airports** are located in Lusaka and Ndola. Mpulungu on Lake Tanganyika is the most important **port**.

Tourism

The main attractions are the magnificent Victoria Fall on the Zambezi, the man-made Lake Kariba covering an area of 5,000 sq. km, created by the construction of a dam and Lake Tanganyika. The large national parks are also of great interest for safaris. Zambia advertises itself as the safest tourist destination in Africa.

Malawi

Area:	118,484 sq. km
Capital city:	Lilongwe

Form of government:
Presidential Republic in the Commonwealth
Administrative divisions:
3 regions
Population:
12.1 million
(98 inhabitants/sq. km)
Languages:
Chichewa, English (both official), Tumbuka, other Bantu languages

GDP per capita:	US$600

Currency:
1 Malawi kwacha =
100 tambala

Malawi, Mozambique, Botswana

Mozambique: The 160-m-high and 330-m-long **Cabora Bassa** *dam blocks the Zambezi. This has created an immense lake with an area of 2,700 sq. km and a volume of 160 billion cu. m. The aim is to prevent the annual flood disasters and to irrigate 1.5 million ha of land. The dam has also made 500 km of the Zambezi navigable. The power station that forms part of the dam was sabotaged many times during the course of the civil war.*

Natural Geography

A large part of the country is taken up by **Lake Malawi**, which extends across the land for 550 km from north to south. The land to the west and south of the lake is mountainous, with peaks of up to 3,002 m in height (highest point: Mount Mlanje, also known as Sapitwa). Open grassland and scrub form the main vegetation. The mountain regions have areas of dense woodland. The country once had a wide range of animal life (antelopes, zebras, elephants, rhinoceros), but this is now restricted to the four protected national parks.

Climate

The climate is tropical in the north but becomes drier further south. The rainy season lasts from November to April. In Lilongwe, average temperatures are 23°C in summer and 16°C in winter.

Population

99 per cent of the population belong to **Bantu-speaking peoples**, and 58 per cent of these are **Malawi**. There are also small minorities of Arabs and Europeans. 75 per cent are Christian – mostly Protestant – but some 20 per cent are followers of native religions. The adult literacy rate is 55 per cent. Roughly one sixth of the adult population is infected with HIV positive.

History and Politics

In 1891, the region around the Lake Nyasa became a British protectorate and was joined to Rhodesia under the name of Nyasaland in 1907. Malawi gained its **independence** in 1964. The constitution of 1966 gave the President comprehensive powers, but these were restricted in 1993 after a referendum which was held due to pressure from credit-lending countries. The first free elections took place in 1994.

Economy

Malawi today remains an agricultural country: 85 per cent of the population live from **agriculture** and contribute 35 per cent of GDP. The country's self-sufficiency is repeatedly threatened by droughts. 90 per cent of exports derive from the sale of coffee. Other export goods are tea, sugar and tobacco. The fishing industry satisfies the country's own requirements.

Manufacturing industry is centred in the southern part of the country and processes domestic crops and products (tea, beer, cigarettes, textiles, shoes) for export. The tourism sector has become relatively well-developed and contributes 25 per cent of GDP.

Transport Infrastructure

The **road network** is 28,400 km long but mainly covers the south of the country and consists on the whole of dirt tracks. The **rail network** is 789 km long and connects Malawi to the international

Lake Malawi is famous for its plentiful fish stocks.

port of Beira in Mozambique. Of great importance to transport is Lake Malawi. Lilongwe has an international **airport**.

Tourism

Malawi has an extraordinary wealth of natural attractions. The main tourist centres are Lake Malawi – a lake that contains the greatest variety of fish species in the world – and Blantyre, the former colonial capital of Nyasaland, with its spectacular setting. Elephants and rhinoceros are among the animals that inhabit the Nyika and Kasungu National Parks.

Mozambique	
Area:	801,590 sq. km
Capital city:	Maputo
Form of government: Republic	
Administrative divisions: 10 provinces, Capital city	
Population: 19.4 million (22 inhabitants/sq. km)	
Languages: Portuguese (official), Bantu languages	
GDP per capita:	US$1,300
Currency: 1 metical = 100 centavos	

Natural Geography

The Indian Ocean coast has a large number of coves and bays with offshore coral reefs. Inland from the coast lie broad areas of savannah and scrubland. In the north, the land rises steeply to form a mountainous region (highest point: Monte Binga, 2,436 m). Mangrove swamps predominate in the marshes of the river deltas. The original African fauna (antelopes, gazelles, elephants and leopards) have been decimated by big game hunting.

Climate

The tropical climate is defined by heavy summer monsoon rains. Average temperatures in Maputo, the capital range between 22°C and 26°C.

Population

The population consists of Bantu peoples, of which the **Shangaan, Chokwe, Manyika** and **Sena** form the largest ethnic groups. 50 per cent follow native religions, 30 per cent are Christian and 20 per cent are Muslim.

History and Politics

The country was discovered in 1498 and occupied by the Portuguese in the sixteenth century. After a long guerrilla war, Mozambique gained **independence** from the Portuguese colonial rulers in 1975.

The liberation movement proclaimed a people's republic in the same year, and this became a parliamentary democracy with a new constitution in 1990. After a long and bloody **civil war**, a peace treaty between the right-wing rebels and the government was concluded in 1992. Free presidential and parliamentary elections were held in 1994 under the scrutiny of UN observers.

Economy

Agriculture and **fishing** contribute 35 per cent of GDP. Over half the exports income comes from the sale of crabs and prawns, which are processed by the **manufacturing industry** (13 per cent of GDP). The rich natural resources (precious and semi-precious stones, iron ore, minerals and metals) have scarcely been exploited. The wide-ranging privatisation programme in place since the 1990s has mainly been to the advantage of the **services sector**. The country's international ports also handle exports for neighbouring countries.

Transport Infrastructure

The 30,400-km-long **road network** is largely unpaved and the use of the roads is also further restricted by the large number of landmines placed on them during the civil war. Of great importance for the transport of goods to and from neighbouring countries are the 3,200-km-long **rail network** and the 3,750-km-long inland waterways. Mozambique has three international **airports** at Maputo, Beira and Nampula.

Tourism

In addition to nature reserves and the many beaches, the old trading posts and colonial cities of Maputo and Beira are also of interest to tourists. Mozambique was popular with tourists from neighbouring African countries before the civil war.

Botswana	
Area:	600,370 sq. km
Capital city:	Gaborone
Form of government: Republic	
Administrative divisions: 11 districts	
Population: 1.6 million (3 inhabitants/sq. km)	
Languages: Tswana, English (both official)	
GDP per capita:	US$10,100
Currency: 1 pula = 100 thebe	

Natural Geography

The semi-desert terrain of the **Kalahari** covers approximately 80 per cent of the country. Land suitable for the cultivation of crops can only be found in small areas in the south-east. The northern edge of the Kalahari is defined by the Okavango, an inland delta region with marsh and reed-covered areas. The north-east of the country adjoins the Makgadikgadi Pans, a large area of salt lakes.

Climate

The country has a very dry,, subtropical climate with summer temperatures reaching a high of 40°C, while winter lows can sink to 6°C. Temperatures in the capital city range between 13°C in July and 26°C in January.

Population

Up to 75 per cent of the population comes from one of eight **Bantu-speaking peoples** who speak the same language – Tswana. 12 per cent of the population are **Shona**. Small, nomadic ethnic groups live an isolated existence in the Kalahari Desert. Despite great efforts on the part of the government and international organisations, Bots-

*The **Okavango** rises in the uplands of Angola and ends in an outlet-free basin in Botswana. The marsh delta is very rich in animal life. The river constantly changes its path through the delta region.*

wana has the highest HIV infection rate in the world (38.8 per cent).

History and Politics

Missionaries from Great Britain began visiting Botswana in 1820, and the country, which had hitherto been inhospitable to foreign interests, became part of the British Empire as the protectorate of **Bechuanaland** in 1885, due to its strategically important position north of the Boer region and east of German South West Africa.
Until 1964, the country was ruled by British ambassadors in South Africa, and became **independent** as the Republic of Botswana in 1966. The parliament consists of a National Assembly and a 15-seat House of Chiefs as an advisory institution.

Economy

80 per cent of the population lives from **agriculture** in a subsistence economy, mainly growing cereals and keeping livestock. Despite this, Botswana is only able to grow about 50 per cent of its own food requirements, and agriculture only contributes four per cent of GDP. The backbone of the economy is the rich mineral reserves discovered in the 1970s. Diamond-mining in the Kalahari Desert alone contributes 70 per cent of the country's income. There are also large reserves of iron ore and coal. The mining sector employs just three per cent of the population, but contributes 35 per cent of GDP. Botswana has a customs union with South Africa and imports three-quarters of its requirements from its neighbour.

Transport Infrastructure

The populated areas of the country are well connected by **rail** and **road networks**. Gaborone is connected to the trans-African railway. The capital city also has an international **airport**.

Tourism

The range of animals in the national parks and the Kalahari Desert, inhabited by the famous Kalahari Bushmen, are attracting growing numbers of tourists. In 2003, the tourism industry contributed over US$300 million.

Namibia	
Area:	825,418 sq. km
Capital city:	Windhoek
Form of government:	
Republic in the Commonwealth	
Administrative divisions:	
13 regions	
Population:	
2 million (2 inhabitants/sq. km)	
Languages:	
English (official),	
Afrikaans, German	
GDP per capita:	US$7,800
Currency:	
1 Namibian dollar = 100 cents	

Natural Geography

The sand and rocky regions of the **Namib Desert** extend parallel to the coast. The steep terrace of the Brandberg Massif (highest point, 2,579 m) leads to an undulating upland area to the country's interior, which falls in the east to join the **Kalahari basin** at an altitude of 1,000 m. In the north, in the Ovamboland region at an altitude of 1,050 m, lies the unique **Etosha Pan**, one of the largest salt water depressions in Africa. In the northeast lies the Caprivi Strip, which stretches for 450 km to the Zambesi, and which is just 90 km wide at its broadest point.

Climate

The country has a sub-tropical climate with dry winters and hot summers. Temperatures at higher altitudes are milder, and the capital city remains approximately the same temperature year-round at 22°C. The main form of vegetation is thorny savannah.

Population

The **Ovambo** form more than 50 per cent of the population and are the largest group. Other ethnic groups in the country include the **Kavango** with nine per cent, and the **Herero** and **Damara**, each

with seven per cent. People of European origin form seven per cent of the Namibian population. 86 per cent are Christians. The official language, English, is only spoken by seven per cent of the population; Afrikaans and German are the most common languages, and Oshivambo, Herero and Nama are also spoken.

History and Politics

The first contact with white traders and missionaries took place in the mid-nineteenth century, and the region was declared the colony of **German South West Africa** in 1884. After several uprisings, the most significant German colony received the right to self-government in 1907. After the occupation by South Africa in 1915, South West Africa was transferred to South Africa by the League of Nations in 1920,

which governed the country until 1966. From 1959 onwards, resistance formed against the governing powers, and the bloody **guerrilla war** was brought to an end in 1989 with a ceasefire. **Independence** was won in 1990, and was followed by a democratic constitution. The **SWAPO** (South West African People's Organisation), founded in 1957, who had led the resistance from the very beginning, remains today the most influential political power. SWAPO candidate Hifikepunye Pohamba has been president since 2004.

Economy

The country's biggest employer is the **agricultural sector**, which employs more than 50 per cent of the population and which produces enough food for the country's needs. Livestock rearing

produces the country's most important export, beef. Despite set backs, the **fishing industry** has a lot of potential. The mainstay of the economy is **mining**, which alone contributes 20 per cent of GNP and brings in great profits, thanks to rich natural reserves (diamonds, uranium, copper, zinc and gold). The country has close economic links with South Africa.

Transport Infrastructure

Namibia has well constructed **rail** and **road networks** as well as a relatively dense domestic **flight network**. There is an international **airport** in Windhoek, and the country's **main trade port** is in Walvis Bay.

Tourism

The Namib Desert, the Etosha Pan and the national parks offer natural attractions. Those from the colonial period include the lake resorts of Lüderitz, Swakopmund and Walvis Bay.

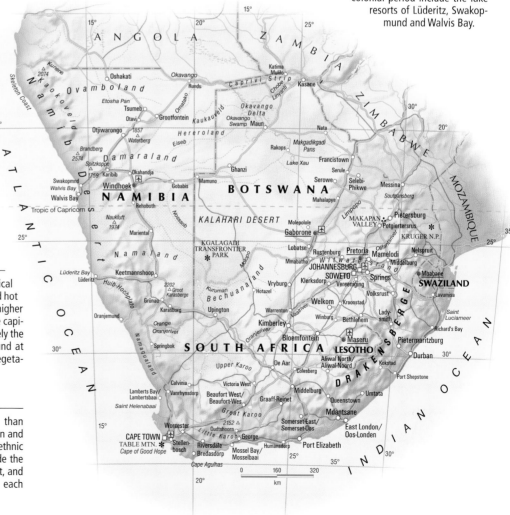

South Africa Today

ANC supporters celebrate the victory of their party.

One of the darkest chapters of modern African history was the apartheid era in South Africa. With the end of racial segregation and the election of Nelson Mandela as President, an unusual phase of freedom and liberality has begun in South Africa.

International sanctions and a failed military intervention in Angola led to a general relaxation of the strict politics of apartheid under President Botha, beginning in 1988. His successor, F. W. de Klerk, released Nelson Mandela from prison and began negotiations with the ANC, and in so doing gave the signal that fundamental changes were on the way. In the first free elections in 1994, in which all South Africans were able to vote, the ANC emerged the obvious winners and Mandela was invested as President on 10 May. Separation of powers, equality of ethnic groups and men and women, freedom of expression and freedom of religion are important elements of the constitution accepted by all groups of society. The reappraisal of the past by the Truth and Reconciliation Commission was an important catharsis in bringing the various groups of the population in racial harmony.

Main photo: at Table Mountain, apartheid is now in the past.

Top: The townships were at the heart of the resistance.

Right: Pohla Pak is a district of the Soweto township.

*The **Herero** have long been a cattle-herding people. They arrived in the region around Windhoek from northeast Africa in the seventeenth and eighteenth centuries. The elimination wars conducted by the former German colonists reduced the original population of 80,000 to just 20,000. Today, most of the Herero are Christian, and their language, a Bantu language, is taught in Namibian schools.*

South Africa

Area:	1,219,912 sq. km
Capital city:	Pretoria
Form of government: Republic	
Administrative divisions: 9 provinces	
Population: 44.3 million (35 inhabitants/sq. km)	
Languages: English, Afrikaans, Zulu, Bantu languages (all official)	
GDP per capita:	US$11,900
Currency: 1 rand = 100 cents	

Natural Geography

South Africa's landscape can be divided into three areas: the interior plateau, the Great Escarpment and the coastal seam. The extensive upland area in the country's interior, the **Karoo**, lies at an altitude of 1,000 to 1,800 m and is divided by isolated mountains. This region is bordered by the Great Escarpment, dominated in the east by the **Drakensberg Mountains**. The region contains South Africa's highest peak, Njesuthi (3,408 m). The Great Escarpment is in turn bordered by the coastal strip, which is mainly narrow and moderately craggy.

Climate

The climate is typical of the warm **sub-tropics**. In Pretoria, average temperatures are 11°C in July and 21°C in January.

Population

Three quarters of South Africans belong to the **Zulu**, **Xhosa**, **Pedi**, **Sotho**, Tswana, **Tsonga**, **Swazi**, **Ndebele** and **Venda** ethnic groups, while 13.6 per cent are of European origin. There are also nine per cent mixed race people known as coloureds (people of half-European, half-African descent) and 2.6 per cent Asians. There are a total of 11 official languages and numerous regional dialects. The HIV infection rate is 20 per cent.

History and Politics

Black settlement of South Africa dates back to the second and third centuries AD, but a Dutch Cape Colony was not established until 1652. Great Britain conquered the country in 1795 and brought many settlers to the country. From this time onwards, there were many conflicts between the Dutch **Boers** and the British. The Boer republics of **Transvaal** and the **Orange Free State** and the British crown colony of Natal were established as a result, but these regions came under full British rule after the defeat of the Dutch in the Boer War in 1901/1902. Brought together under the Union of South Africa in 1910, the colonies gained **independence** between 1926 and 1931.

The Black population suffered under the racist apartheid policies. Deeply angered, they began armed resistance in 1960, led by the African National Congress (**ANC**). In 1989, a process of protracted negotiations began between the government and the ANC, which finally ended in 1993 with the abolition of **racial discrimination**. Free elections were held place in 1994, the ANC being the clear winners. Nelson Mandela became president. The **homelands** were abolished and integrated into newly created provinces. South Africa became a member of the OAU. A new constitution was adopted in 1996. The parliament elected Thabo Mbeki as president in 1999.

Economy

After the **manufacturing industry**, the greatest contributions to GDP come from the **services sector** and **mining**. **Agriculture** makes a relatively small contribution, although this sector, together with mining, make up most of the country's export income. South Africa is the world's leading source of gold and platinum. In the 1990s, the economy improved, mainly due to the vehicle export industries.

Transport Infrastructure

South Africa has a good infrastructure and three international **airports**. The major sea **ports** are Durban, Cape Town and Port Elizabeth.

Tourism

South Africa is one of the most popular holiday destinations in the world and has a wealth of natural attractions. The country has many national parks, the most famous of which is the enormous Kruger National Park, which is an excellent game resort, offering great safaris. The Garden Route from Cape Town to Port Elizabeth is a favourite tour.

1 The Himba in Namibia occupy the so-called Kaokoland, a dry, mountainous area. They keep cattle, goats and sheep and cultivate maize and gourds.

2 The Namib Desert stretches along the Atlantic coast of Namibia. In the country's interior receives rainfall of less than 20 mm a year. Low temperatures and cloud formation are distinctive features of this coastal desert.

3 Camps Bay in Cape Town, South Africa, directly beneath the 'Twelve Apostles' mountains. The beach promenade is very popular.

Lesotho

The **Ndebele** mainly live in Zimbabwe, but the ethnic group can also be found in South Africa. Ndebele women are famous for the brightly coloured works of art with which they decorate their houses.

Lesotho

Area:	30,355 sq. km
Capital city:	Maseru
Form of government:	
Constitutional Monarchy in the Commonwealth	
Administrative divisions:	
10 districts	
Population:	
1.9 million (72 inhabitants/sq. km)	
Languages:	Sesotho, English
GDP per capita:	US$3,300
Currency: 1 loti = 100 lisente	

Natural Geography

The central region of the country and the eastern section includes part of the Drakensberg Mountains, a high mountainous region (highest point: Thabana Ntlenyana, 3,482 m). The western region lies at an altitude of between 1,000 and 1,500 m. There are almost no trees and shrubs and the main flora is grassland savannah and mountain meadows.

Climate

Lesotho has a temperate sub-tropical climate and average temperatures in the capital city are 25°C in summer and 15°C in winter. In summer, the country suffers from long, heavy periods of rainfall.

Population

The population of Lesotho is up to 99.7 per cent **Basotho**, with small European and Asian groups. 80 per cent of the Lesotho people are Christian and 20 per cent follow native religions. One third of the adult population is HIV positive.

History and Politics

The kingdom of the **Basutho** was established in the nineteenth century. Its ruler appealed to Queen Victoria for British protection in 1868. The British protectorate ended in1966, and the country was granted **independence**.

Since 1993, the country has been a constitutional monarchy. The ruler – Letsie III – only has ceremonial functions. The country has a tradition of close relations with South Africa in areas ranging from the economy to foreign policy. After a period of domestic turmoil, South African troops intervened in 1998 in order to support the government. New elections were held in 2002, and these endorsed the government.

Economy

The **agricultural sector** is poorly developed due to a lack of usable land and recurrent droughts. Main agricultural activities are the cultivation of cereals and livestock - breading. The country has almost no natural resources. The most important domestic economic factor is the **processing industry**, mainly textiles and leather processing. With the aid of foreign investment, this branch of the economy is currently being developed to make it suitable for producing exports. At least 33 per cent of GDP comes from money sent home by **migrant workers**, employed in the mines of South Africa.

Transport Infrastructure

The **road network** extends for a total of just under 5,000 km and consists mainly of dirt tracks. The capital city, Maseru, has good **rail** connections and **flight connections** to South Africa.

Tourism

The tourist centre of the country is the capital city, Maseru, with its numerous casinos and large hotels. The surrounding mountainous countryside is a well-kept secret by keen hikers. Most of the tourism is currently from neighbouring South Africa.

0   260 km

BURUNDI

KENYA

DEMOCRATIC REPUBLIC OF CONGO

Cabinda

Luanda

Porto Amboim

ANGOLA

TANZANIA

MALAWI

COMOROS

Mayotte (to France)

Cassinga

ZAMBIA

Cabora-Bassa

Kariba

Bindura

Andriamena

MADAGASCAR

Antananarivo

Cubango

Tsumeb

Hwange   Kadoma

Harare

ZIMBABWE

GREAT DYKE

Bikita

Bulawayo   Shabani

Orapa

MOZAMBIQUE

INDIAN

OCEAN

NAMIBIA

Rössing

Windhoek

BOTSWANA

Morupula

Gaborone

Messina

Jwaneng

Phalaborwa

Maputo

Mbabane

SWAZILAND

Pretoria

Johannesburg

Rosh Pinah

Oranjemund

Postmasburg

Welkom

Vereeniging

Kimberley

Bloemfontein

Richard's Bay

Okiep

Prieska

LESOTHO   Durban

LAND USE

Forest

Steppe, savanna and pasture

Cropland

Desert

Semidesert

SOUTH AFRICA

Cape Town   Mosselbaai   Port Elizabeth

INDUSTRIAL ACTIVITIES

Energy

Hydroelectric power plants

Oil pipelines

Industry

Industrial areas

Main industrial sites

Minerals

	Fossil coal		Fe	Iron		Sn	Tin
	Natural gas or oil wells		Li	Lithium		Ta	Tantalum
Ag	Silver		Mn	Manganese		Ti	Titanium
Asb	Asbestos		Ni	Nickel		U	Uranium
Au	Gold		P	Phosphates		V	Vanadium
Be	Beryllium		Pb	Lead		Zn	Zinc
Cr	Chrome		Pt	Platinum		Zr	Zirconium
Cu	Copper		Sb	Antimony			Diamonds

Sangoma are medicine men or female healers among the Zulu and the related Swazi people, who make up to 85 per cent of the population of Swaziland. They are specialists in religious rituals and are said to cure illnesses using supernatural powers. Illness is a sign of scorn from the gods and can be caused by witchcraft and magic. The healers use herbs and massages as well as spiritual techniques.

Swaziland	
Area:	17,363 sq. km
Capital city:	Mbabane
Form of government:	Constitutional Monarchy in the Commonwealth
Administrative divisions:	273 tribal areas, 55 traditional councils
Population:	1.2 million (66 inhabitants/sq. km)
Languages:	English, Siswati (both official)
GDP per capita:	US$5,300
Currency:	1 lilangeni = 100 cents

Natural Geography

The landlocked country lies between South Africa and Mozambique on the eastern slopes of the **Drakensberg Mountains.** Swaziland can be divided into four geographical areas: in the western uplands, the **Highveld,** there are plateaus and valleys at a height of between 1,000 and 1,800 m, covered in forest plantations. The **Midveld** lies at an altitude of 500 to 1,000 m and has grass and thorn bush savannah used for cereal cultivation and livestock-rearing. The Lowveld in the east is a lowland area at an altitude of 150 to 500 m and is also used for agriculture. The region is bordered by the mountainous **Lebombo Plateau** at between 500 and 800 m in altitude.

Climate

The west has a moderate, subtropical climate with high precipitation, but the east is hotter and drier. In the capital city, Mbabane, average temperatures are 12°C in July and 29°C in January.

Population

Up to 97 per cent of the population is **Swazi**. 60 per cent are Christian and 40 per cent belong to native religions. The country is troubled by an HIV infection rate of 33.4 per cent.

History and Politics

The region has been settled by the Bantu people, the Swazi, since the mid-eighteenth century. They founded their kingdom in 1815.

The first Boers entered the country in 1868, and greater numbers of British began entering the region from 1877 onwards. Swaziland was named a British protectorate in 1903 and regained its **independence** in 1968. The constitution of 1978 gave the king, Mswati III, extensive executive powers, which, despite great pressure for democratisation and an amendment to the constitution in 1992, remain largely unrestricted to this day.

Economy

The economy of Swaziland is traditionally dominated by the processing of agricultural and forestry products and further processing for the export-oriented **manufacturing industry** is becoming increasingly important. As a result of structural change, manufacturing now contribute 42 per cent of GDP. The proportion contributed by the **services sector** is 48 per cent. The importance of mining (iron ore, asbestos) has greatly reduced, but the tourism industry has potential for growth.

Transport Infrastructure

The **rail network** is only 224 km long and is mainly used to transport goods to Mozambique. The **road network** has a length of 2,885 km but is only well developed between the main centres. The rest of the roads are mainly dirt tracks.
The **air strip** in Mbabane only has connections to international destinations via Johannesburg airport in South Africa.

Tourism

Entertainment districts have developed in the capital city, which attract many tourists from South Africa. In terms of landscape, the most attractive regions are the mountains and the large wild game reserves of Mlilwane, Malolotja and Hlane.

1 Basotho men ride across a river valley in Makhaleng, Lesotho – they are members of an ethnic group that arrived in the eighteenth century.

2 The South African metropolis of Durban has an impressive skyline, great beaches and a yachting marina.

3 From Table Mountain there is a breath-taking view of Cape Town, a city in one of the best locations in the world.

4 Many Sotho, one of the Bantu-speaking people who make up most of the population of Lesotho, live in huts constructed in traditional style.

Madagascar, Comoros, Mauritius

*The population of **Madagascar** is very different from that of the African mainland. Most inhabitants are descendants of Indonesian settlers who arrived 2,000 years ago, bringing with them rice cultivation.*

Madagascar

Area:	587,041 sq. km
Capital city:	Antananarivo
Form of government:	Republic
Administrative divisions: 28 regions	
Population: 18 million (27 inhabitants/sq. km)	
Languages: Malagasy, French (both official), Howa	
GDP per capita:	US$900
Currency: 1 Madagascan franc = 100 centimes	

Natural Geography

Madagascar is the fourth-largest island in the world, and most of its land mass, apart from the coastal plains in the west, is taken up by a mountain which rises gradually to a height of 2,876 m. The summit is located to the west of a central upland area.

Climate

The country has a tropical climate with great variations in the amount of precipitation. The eastern side, bordering the Indian Ocean, has high precipitation and is typified by lush tropical rainforest. The unique flora and fauna is threatened by slash-and-burn deforestation, cyclones, spring floods and earthquakes.

Population

The majority of the **Malay-Indonesian** inhabitants, half of whom are Christian and half of whom practice native religions, belong to one of more than 20 clans. Ten per cent of the population are Muslims. The social and health systems are deficient, as are basic food supplies.

History and Politics

The island was settled early on by south Asians but was discovered by the Portuguese in 1500, who settled on the coast, along with the French. The native population successfully resisted attempts at colonisation until 1896. The French colony became **independent** in 1960, when it called itself Malgache. It reverted to the name of Madagascar in 1975. The constitution of 1992 provides for a bicameral parliament. In 2002, civil unrest was provoked by vote-rigging during the elections.

Economy

Approximately 75 per cent of the population live off **agriculture**, mainly in the form of small-scale cultivation of rice, cassava, maize, sweet potatoes, mangos, bananas and sugar cane.
The most important **exports** are coffee, vanilla, cloves, cotton, sisal hemp, peanuts and tobacco. The manufacturing industry is poorly developed but it is linked to the fishing industry, processing prawns, tuna and lobster for export. Madagascar's **natural reserves** are not insignificant, but are not yet fully exploited.

Transport Infrastructure

Only ten per cent of the **roads** are surfaced and many cross-country roads can become impassable. The main form of transport is the rail network. The domestic flight network is one of the most dense in the southern hemisphere.

Tourism

In addition to the many nature parks which are home to lemurs, numerous unique species of reptile and amphibian (frogs, chameleons) and civet cats, the capital city, Antananarivo has a large Friday market, which is a great attraction for tourists in search of local handicrafts.

Comoros

Area:	2,700 sq. km
Capital city:	Moroni
Form of government: Islamic Presidential Republic	
Administrative divisions: 3 island districts	
Population: 671,000 (338 inhabitants/sq. km)	
Languages: Comoran, French (both official), minority languages	
GDP per capita:	US$600
Currency: 1 Comoran franc = 100 centimes	

Natural Geography

The national territory consists of the three larger islands **Njazidja**

Friday mosque in Mutsumudu on the Comoros island of Anjouan.

(Grande Comore), Mwali (Mohéli) and **Nzwani (Anjouan)** and further small islands off the coast of East Africa. These are largely of volcanic origin. The highest volcano is Le Karthala (2,361 m), which is still active.
In the upper regions of the craggy mountains, the tropical rainforest is replaced by savannah. The narrow coast has mangrove swamps and coral reefs.

Climate

The tropical climate results in high levels of precipitation. The average temperature is 25°C.

Population

The **mixed population** consists of African, Arab, Indian and Madagascan settlers. The low standard of education means that half of the population can neither read nor write. The health and social systems are also completely inadequate for the needs of the inhabitants. Life expectancy of men is only 48, for women it is only 52.

History and Politics

The islands were ruled by the Persians and the Arabs in the sixteenth century. The French **colony** founded on the neighbouring island of Mayotte in 1843 was expanded to include the Comoros in 1912. The Comoros declared its **independence** in 1975. After years of instability, the foundation of an Islamic Republic in 1997 caused the two islands of Mwali and Nzwani to declare themselves independent. Colonel Azali Assoumani took power in a military coup in 1999. In 2001, a peace agreement was reached with those islands that had broken away. A new federal constitution in the same year created the Union of the Comoros.

Economy

Agriculture employs 80 per cent of the population, yet the subsistence economy does not grow enough food to adequately supply the population. Large sections of agricultural land are used for the cultivation of the main exports, vanilla, cloves, coconuts and ylang-ylang, a rich perfume. Gross domestic product in 2005 was US$402 million. Agriculture contributed 41 per cent, manufacturing 12 Muslim and the services sector 47 per cent.

Transport Infrastructure

Due to the island's landscape, it has very few **roads** and no **rail network**. Ferry and flight connections run between the islands at irregular intervals, although the transport network is improving, so as to attract tourists. There is an international **airport** in Moroni.

Tourism

Tourism suffers from a lack of infrastructure, but this is being renovated. The Comoros are home to some rare and unique species of fauna, such as the mongoose lemur. In addition to the capital city Moroni, with its Arabic architecture and mosques, the crater lakes and palm-fringed sub-tropical beaches attract many tourists, especially from the rest of Africa.

Mauritius

Area:	2,040 sq. km
Capital city:	Port Louis
Form of government:	Republic
Administrative divisions: 9 districts, 3 dependencies	
Population: 1.2 million (542 inhabitants/sq. km))	
Languages: English (official), Creole, Hindi, Urdu	
GDP per capita:	US$13,300
Currency: 1 Mauritian rupee = 100 cents	

Natural Geography

The island is of volcanic origin. Its highest point is the Piton de la Rivière Noire at a height of 882 m. The coast is lined with white beaches and numerous coves, with off-shore coral reefs. The territory also includes Rodrigues Island, the Agalega Islands and the Cargados Carajos Shoals.

Climate

The climate is sub-tropical, humid and warm. The rainy season lasts from May to October. Temperatures remain constant year-round at an average of 25°C. The original luxuriant rainforest vegetation has only been preserved in a few conservation areas.

Population

The ethnic and cultural composition of the population is very varied: 68 per cent are the descendants of **Indian plantation workers** and 27 per cent are

*The breath-taking natural beauty of the island nations of **Mauritius** and the **Seychelles** are of great importance for their economies. Magical beaches, amazing diving locations and good infrastructure attract large numbers of tourists.*

Creole. Hindus are the largest religious group, representing 52 per cent of the population, but there are also many Christians (29 per cent) and Muslims (17 per cent).

History and Politics

The island had already been discovered by early settlers in the tenth century but was occupied by the Dutch in the sixteenth century, who established a plantation there. It was at this time that the island received its current name, it is named after Prince Maurice of Nassau. In the eighteenth century, the French took over the colony and brought African slaves to the island. Under British colonial rule which began in 1810 and lasted until **independence** in 1968, Indian indentured labour was brought to the islands to work the plantations. In 1992, Mauritius ended its status as a constitutional monarchy under the rule of the British crown. The country became a republic with a president as head of state, but remained part of the Commonwealth.

Economy

The **agricultural sector** employs 14 per cent of the working population, and great importance is placed on the cultivation of sugar cane. Three-quarters of the country's food has to be imported. The cultivation of potatoes, vegetables, bananas and pineapples is under state control. The **manufacturing sector** is very much geared towards export. Main sectors include the processing of textiles, wool and sugar. The tourism industry today forms a significant part of the growing **services sector**, and employs 20 per cent of the working population.

Transport Infrastructure

The **road network** is well constructed. Port Louis has an international **airport**.

Tourism

The centre of the well-developed tourist industry is the capital city, Port Louis. The Black River Gorges and the Ile aux Aigrettes national parks, home to fruit-bats and numerous species of ex-

otic bird, are also well worth a visit. Extensive paradise beaches and diving spots can also be found on the other islands.

Seychelles

Area:	454 sq. km
Capital city:	Victoria
Form of government:	
Republic in the Commonwealth	
Administrative divisions:	
23 districts	
Population:	
81,000 (177 inhabitants/sq. km)	
Languages:	
English, French, Creole	
GDP per capita:	US$7,800
Currency:	
1 Seychelles rupee = 100 cents	

Natural Geography

The archipelago lies in the western Indian Ocean, 1600 km off the coast of East Africa. Fewer than half the islands are inhabited. Many of them are coral atolls (with a total area of 210 sq. km), but the main islands of **Mahé**, **Praslin**, **Silhouette** and **La Digue** are mountainous. On the largest island, Mahé (area: 158 sq. km), the mountains reach a height of up to 905 m and have only sparse vegetation.

Climate

The tropical-oceanic climate divides the year into a relatively cool period with little precipitation (May to September) and the north-west monsoon period (December to March) with hot temperatures and a lot of rain.

Population

The population is 98 per cent Christian, and has Asian, African and European origins. Due to the

large number of tourists, the inhabitants of the Seychelles have the highest per capita income of any African country.
90 per cent of the population live on Mahé.

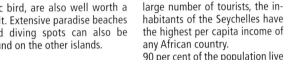

Independence in 1976 was followed by years of political instability, during which the original constitution was abandoned as the result of a coup. The presidential constitution of 1979 gives the President extensive powers.

History and Politics

The uninhabited group of 115 islands was first discovered by the Portuguese Vasco da Gama in 1501 and became a French colony in 1756. The islands became a British colony between 1794 and 1811. From 1903, the Seychelles has had the status of an autonomous British crown colony.

Economy

In addition to the traditional economic sectors of **agriculture** and **fishing, tourism** has become a very important economic factor in the Seychelles. The main exports are still fish, cinnamon and copra. There are plans to convert the country to a financial and trading centre, in the near future.

Transport Infrastructure

The Seychelles have a very well-constructed infrastructure: **ships** and **planes** connect the smaller and larger islands to each other.

Tourism

The Seychelles are well known as a tropical paradise, with palm-fringed beaches and white sand. Mahé is an island of powdery white sands and lush vegetation, rising through plantations of coconut palms and cinnamon trees to forested peaks that afford views of neighbouring islands. Other attractions include the nature reserves on Praslin and Silhouette islands and the local Creole food.

The Americas

The two continents of the Americas, including Greenland, stretch over an area of 42 million sq. km and have a population of 680 million. Mountain plateaus, such as the Grand Canyon, the Rocky Mountains and the Great Plains are typical of North America.

The Andes mountain chain (Aconcagua: 6,963 m), the Amazon basin containing the largest area of rainforest on Earth, as well as savannahs and steppes are typical of South America. The summits of the volcanic Cordillera reach heights of over 5,000 m. The paradise islands of the West Indies in the Caribbean are also of volcanic origin. Many large nature parks protect the monumental landscape and the unique flora and fauna, such as the Galapagos Islands off the west coast of South America. The original inhabitants of North America were the Native Americans who today mostly live in reservations. A mixed population has developed through immigration from Europe and Asia and the descendants of African slaves.

North America, physical

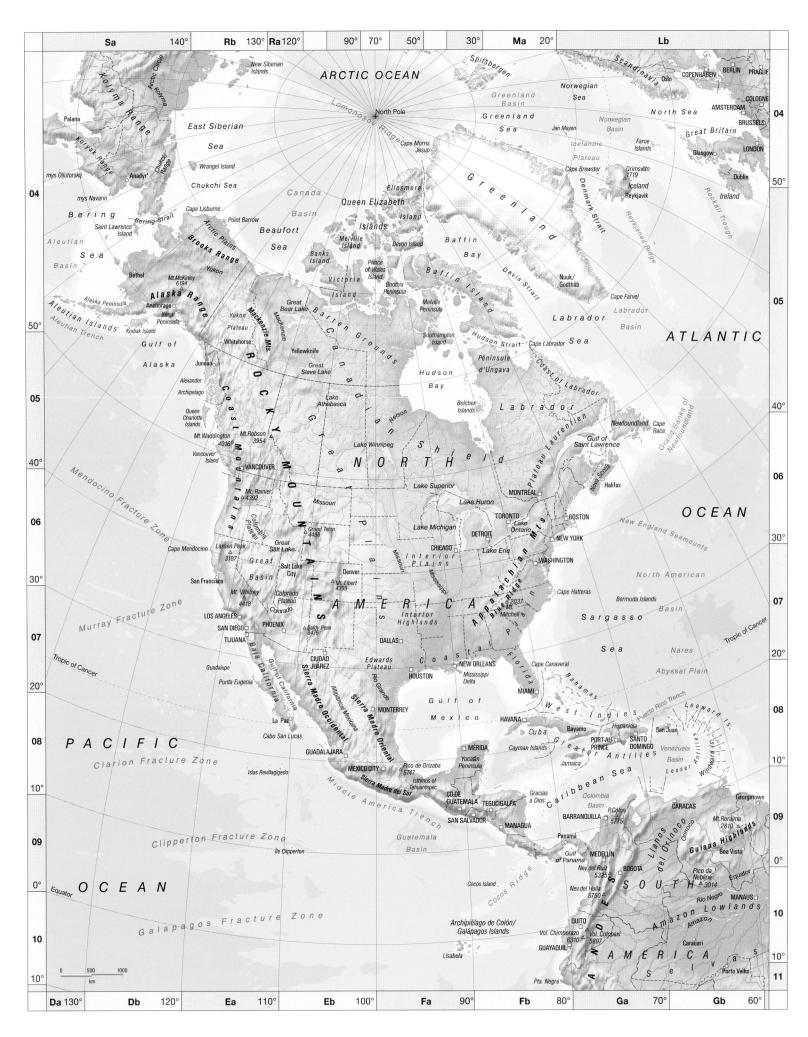

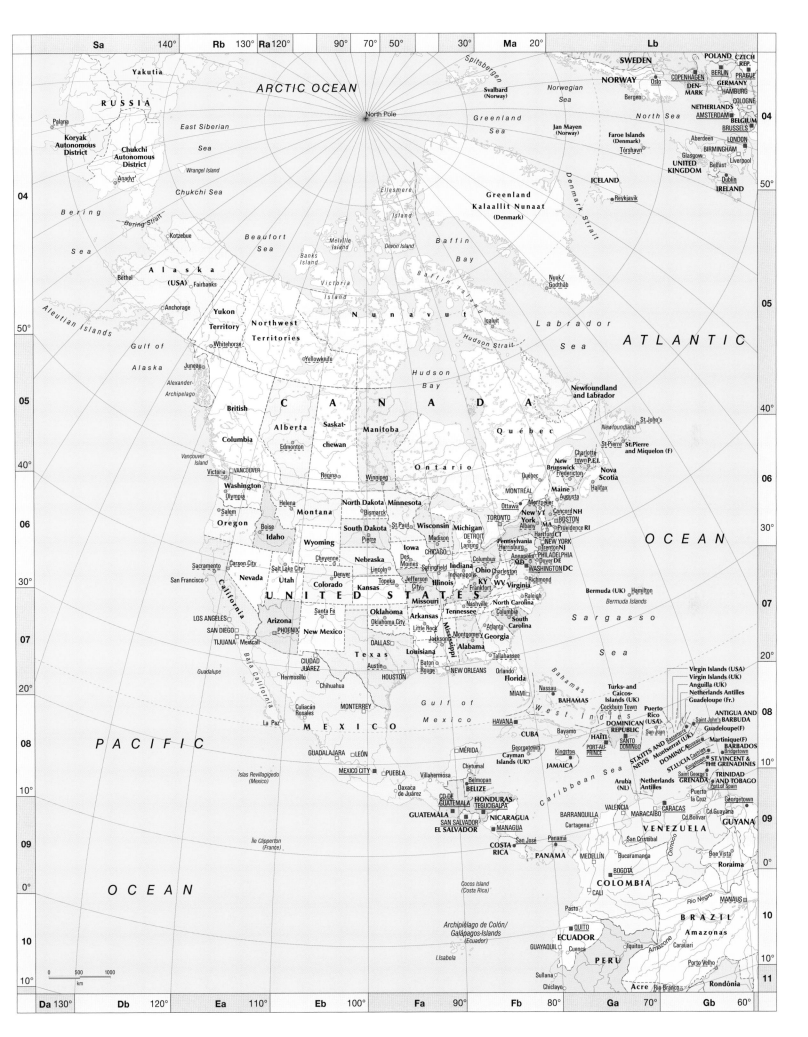

South America, physical

Eb 100° Fa 90° Fb 80° Ga 70° Gb 60° Ha 50° Hb 40° Ja 30° Jb 20°

140° Da 130° Db 120° Ea 110° Eb 100° Fa 90° Fb 80° Ga Gb 60° Ha 50° Hb 40° Ja 30° Jb 20° Ka 10° Kb 0° La 10° Lb

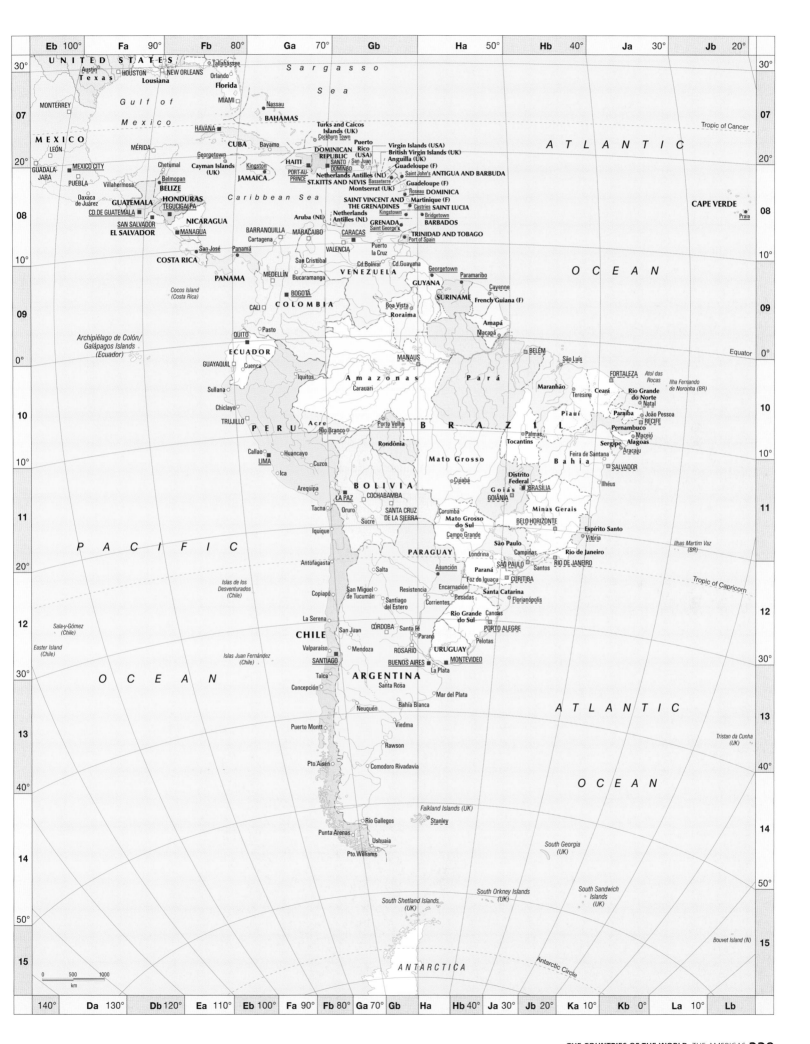

	Eb 100°	Fa 90°	Fb 80°	Ga 70°	Gb	Ha 50°	Hb 40°	Ja 30°	Jb 20°	

UNITED STATES
Austin
Texas
Tallahassee
HOUSTON
NEW ORLEANS
Orlando
Lousiana
Florida
MONTERREY
MIAMI
Gulf of
Mexico
Nassau
Sargasso Sea
BAHAMAS
MEXICO
LEÓN
MÉRIDA
Chetumal
HAVANA
CUBA
Bayamo
Turks and Caicos Islands (UK)
Cockburn Town
Puerto Rico (USA)
San Juan
Virgin Islands (USA)
British Virgin Islands (UK)
Anguilla (UK)
ATLANTIC
Tropic of Cancer
GUADALA-JARA
MEXICO CITY
PUEBLA
Villahermosa
Belmopan
Georgetown
Cayman Islands (UK)
Kingston
JAMAICA
DOMINICAN REPUBLIC
SANTO DOMINGO
HAITI
PORT-AU-PRINCE
Guadeloupe (F)
Saint John's
ANTIGUA AND BARBUDA
Basseterre
ST.KITTS AND NEVIS
Netherlands Antilles (NL)
Montserrat (UK)
Guadeloupe (F)
Roseau
DOMINICA
CAPE VERDE
Oaxaca de Juárez
GUATEMALA
HONDURAS
CD.DE GUATEMALA
TEGUCIGALPA
BELIZE
Caribbean Sea
SAINT VINCENT AND THE GRENADINES
Martinique (F)
Castries
SAINT LUCIA
Praia
SAN SALVADOR
EL SALVADOR
NICARAGUA
MANAGUA
Aruba (NL)
Netherlands Antilles (NL)
GRENADA
Saint George's
Kingstown
Bridgetown
BARBADOS
COSTA RICA
San José
BARRANQUILLA
MARACAIBO
Cartagena
CARACAS
TRINIDAD AND TOBAGO
Port of Spain
PANAMA
Panamá
VALENCIA
Puerto la Cruz
Cocos Island (Costa Rica)
MEDELLÍN
Bucaramanga
San Cristóbal
Cd.Bolívar
Cd.Guayana
VENEZUELA
Georgetown
Paramaribo
OCEAN
CALI
BOGOTÁ
COLOMBIA
GUYANA
Cayenne
SURINAME
French Guiana (F)
Boa Vista
Roraima
Amapá
Macapá
Archipiélago de Colón/
Galápagos Islands (Ecuador)
QUITO
Pasto
BELÉM
São Luís
Equator
ECUADOR
GUAYAQUIL
Cuenca
MANAUS
Amazonas
Pará
FORTALEZA
Atol das Rocas
Ilha Fernando de Noronha (BR)
Iquitos
Carauari
Maranhão
Teresina
Ceará
Rio Grande do Norte
Sullana
Chiclayo
Natal
Piauí
Paraíba
João Pessoa
TRUJILLO
PERU
Acre
Rio Branco
Porto Velho
B R A Z I L
Palmas
RECIFE
Pernambuco
Tocantins
Maceió
Callao
Huancayo
Rondônia
Sergipe
Alagoas
Aracaju
LIMA
Cuzco
Mato Grosso
Bahia
Feira de Santana
SALVADOR
Ica
Cuiabá
Distrito Federal
BOLIVIA
Arequipa
LA PAZ
COCHABAMBA
Goiás
BRASÍLIA
Ilhéus
Tacna
Oruro
SANTA CRUZ DE LA SIERRA
GOIÂNIA
Minas Gerais
Sucre
Corumbá
Mato Grosso do Sul
BELO HORIZONTE
Iquique
Campo Grande
São Paulo
Espírito Santo
Vitória
Ilhas Martim Vaz (BR)
Antofagasta
PARAGUAY
Londrina
Campinas
Rio de Janeiro
Islas de los Desventurados (Chile)
Salta
Asunción
Paraná
SÃO PAULO
Santos
RIO DE JANEIRO
Tropic of Capricorn
Sala-y-Gómez (Chile)
Copiapó
San Miguel de Tucumán
Resistencia
Encarnación
Foz do Iguaçu
Posadas
CURITIBA
Santa Catarina
Easter Island (Chile)
Santiago del Estero
Corrientes
Florianópolis
Rio Grande do Sul
Canoas
La Serena
CÓRDOBA
Santa Fe
PORTO ALEGRE
Islas Juan Fernández (Chile)
Valparaíso
San Juan
Paraná
Pelotas
CHILE
SANTIAGO
Mendoza
ROSARIO
URUGUAY
MONTEVIDEO
Talca
BUENOS AIRES
La Plata
Concepción
ARGENTINA
Santa Rosa
ATLANTIC
Neuquén
Bahía Blanca
Mar del Plata
OCEAN
Puerto Montt
Viedma
Rawson
OCEAN
Pto.Aisén
Comodoro Rivadavia
Tristan da Cunha (UK)
Falkland Islands (UK)
Río Gallegos
Stanley
Punta Arenas
Ushuaia
South Georgia (UK)
Pto.Williams
South Orkney Islands (UK)
South Sandwich Islands (UK)
South Shetland Islands (UK)
Bouvet Island (N)
ANTARCTICA
Antarctic Circle

0 500 1000
km

| 140° | Da 130° | Db 120° | Ea 110° | Eb 100° | Fa 90° | Fb 80° | Ga 70° | Gb | Ha | Hb 40° | Ja 30° | Jb 20° | Ka 10° | Kb 0° | La 10° | Lb |

The History of the Americas

It started as a mistake: the Genoese explorer Christopher Columbus set sail in 1492 to conquer India and discovered America, the 'New

The Mayan highlands: The Ruins of Chichén-Itzá in Yucatán.

World'. This proved to be a fitting name, for the 'old world' of America was destined to disappear almost without trace. The magnificent temples in the highlands of South and Central

A relict of the Spanish colonisation: the Fort El Morro in Puerto Rico.

America, some of which were thousands of years old, were flattened and replaced by churches that were no less imposing. Central and South America still suffer today from the legacy of the colonial era. By contrast, Canada and the USA emerged as wealthy democracies.

America as it was

*12 October 1492: This was the day on which the world changed. **Christopher Columbus** landed on Guanahani Island and America was 'discovered'. At the time, Columbus had no idea of the significance his discovery would have for world history. He believed he had arrived in the East Indies.*

The old empires

When European explorers landed in the New World at the end of the fifteenth century, it was a by no means 'primitive' population that they found. In Central America, a highly advanced culture, that of the Olmecs, who used a simple script and calendar system, had existed since 1500 BC.

Around 300, the Mayas succeeded the Olmecs as the rulers of Yucatán. The ruins of magnificent cities containing vast temples and the astronomical knowledge of these people bear witness to the high degree of civilisation of this Pre-Columbian culture. The Aztec empire which also originated in present-day Mexico, and the Inca empire in the Andes region are further examples of highly-developed social systems. The conquistadors and colonisers would not tolerate the co-existence of New and Old World cultures. The social structures of the original populations were therefore forcibly annihilated, their natural environment systematically destroyed and the people exterminated on a massive scale.

Discovery of a continent

There has been much speculation as to whether Punic or Roman seafarers might have succeeded in sailing to the Americas in antiquity. It is certain, however, that the Vikings established a settlement in Newfoundland at the beginning of the eleventh century which they subsequently abandoned for reasons unknown. In the fifteenth century, the Portuguese funded many voyages of discovery to locate the sea route to the allegedly fabulously wealthy countries of the East. But it was a Genoese explorer in the service of Spain who was to discover America in 1492: Christopher Columbus. In the years that followed, the Spaniards continued their voyages of discovery. They reached Oregon on the west coast and Labrador on the east coast a mere 50 years later. However, it was not only the Spanish and Portuguese who set sail for the New World. Commissioned by the English, John Cabot discovered Newfoundland in 1497 and Sir Humphrey Gilbert founded the first English settlement there in 1583. In 1524, Giovanni da Verrazano, a seafarer in French service, realised that America was a continent. In 1534–1535, the Frenchman Jacques Cartier sailed up the St. Lawrence River to what is now Montreal. In 1608, Samuel de Champlain founded Quebec.

Colonisation of Latin America

America was discovered by Europeans on 12 October 1492, when Columbus set foot on land again after ten weeks at sea. He probably landed on the small Caribbean island of Guanahani (San Salvador). A few days later he decamped to Hispaniola where he founded the first Spanish stronghold in the New World, La Navidad. On three subsequent voyages he discovered the Lesser Antilles, Puerto Rico and Jamaica and set foot on the Central American mainland.

Spain and Portugal divided the New World between themselves as early as 1494 through the Treaty of Tordesillas. This treaty envisaged that Brazil, which had been discovered by Pedro Álvares Cabral, should become the property of Portugal. The relatively accurate cartographic data circulated by Amerigo Vespucci to illustrate his discoveries, and his conviction that he had discovered a new continent, prompted the German cartographer Martin Waldseemüller to name the continent America.

The conquistadors

When the Spaniard Hernán Cortés landed on the Gulf Coast in 1519, accompanied by his small troop of followers, the Aztec empire was in its prime. Cortés was initially received courteously by Moctezuma II as it was believed that the Spaniards were the 'white gods' of prophecy. The conquest of the Aztec empire was ultimately made possible thanks to the psychological rather than the military

Map: AMERICA IN 1790

Labels on map: RUSSIAN FED., Alaska, Gulf of Alaska, Baffin Bay, Greenland, Hudson Bay, Canada, Louisiana, Vice-Royalty of New Spain, UNITED STATES, New York, ATLANTIC OCEAN, Gulf of Mexico, Havana, Mexico City, CARIBBEAN SEA, Maracaibo, Panama, Georgetown, Paramaribo, Guyana, Caienna, Vice-Royalty of New Granada, PACIFIC OCEAN, Vice-Royalty of Brazil, Lima, Vice-Royalty of Peru, Rio de Janeiro, Vice-Royalty of Rio de la Plata, Buenos Aires

Dependences
- British
- French
- Spanish
- Portuguese
- Danish
- Russian
- Dutch
- U.S. territory in 1783

0   850 km

1 'Washington Crossing the Delaware' by E.G. Leutze.
2 The bitter battles fought during the American Civil War (1861–1865) cost a total of 623,000 lives.

America's indigenous inhabitants battled in vain: Atahualpa, the last Inca king, was executed by Pizarro in 1533. Even Sitting Bull was unable to stop the advance of the white man.

effects of their firearms, as well as through the infection of the Amerindians by pathogens that were harmless to Europeans.
The Inca Empire suffered a similar fate when it was weakened by internal conflicts upon the arrival of Francisco Pizarro's army. The Spaniards eventually succeeded in an-nihilating the Inca Empire in the mid-sixteenth century.

English vs. French in Canada

After French seafarers had taken possession of the region around the St. Lawrence River, which they named 'New France', they extended their dominion to the Mississippi river. The conflict with the English colonies in Canada was decided in favour of the British and, in 1763, after the Seven Years War, the whole of Canada was surrendered. The Quebec Act of 1774 offered the Catholic French-Canadians full religious and cultural autonomy.
In 1791, two settlement areas were created which were different from a cultural and religious viewpoint: Upper Canada was dominated by the Anglo-Saxons and the province of Lower Canada was populated by the French. In 1841 they were united as a result of the Canada Union Act.

The arrival of the Pilgrim Fathers

The colonisation of the British area of North America began in 1620 with the landing of the Pilgrim Fathers on board the 'Mayflower'. Of these pious emigrants, 41 signed the 'Mayflower Compact', America's first governing document. The American colonists soon became discontented with the mother country due to a very unwise policy of severe taxation.

The United States is born

On 16 December 1773, 150 British settlers masquerading as Indians boarded three tea clippers which were anchored in Boston harbour and threw the cargo overboard in protest against unfair taxation and monopolisation of the tea trade. This was the prelude to the American Revolution. In 1776, the United States of America declared their independence. In 1789, Con-

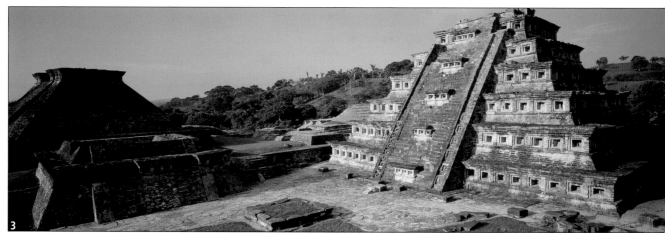

gress met in New York for the first time and on 30 April 1789, George Washington became the first President of the United States.
His successor was John Adams (1797–1801) who was, in turn, succeeded in 1800 by the spiritual father of the Declaration of Independence, Thomas Jefferson. In 1803, Jefferson doubled the young nation's territory through the Louisiana Purchase from France. Following the War of 1812 against England, which ended in a draw in 1815, the USA's self-confidence was further boosted. A foreign policy principle was subsequently formulated in 1823 by President James Monroe, with the Monroe Doctrine which rejected

1 17 years of work for eternity: Gutzon Berglum created the monumental portraits of Washington, Jefferson, Lincoln and Roosevelt in the Mount Rushmore National Monument.

2 Symbol of Christianisation: the Cathedral Metropolitana in Mexico City is the largest cathedral on the continent. This is also the burial place of Mexico's bishops.

3 El Tajin, a great ruined city on the Gulf of Mexico, dominated by the so-called Niche Pyramid, named after the 365 niches that are decorated with stucco.

Modern America

Twentieth century US Presidents: Democrat Franklin D. Roosevelt, 32nd President (1932–1945); Republican Dwight D. Eisenhower, 34the President (1953–1961); Democrat John F. Kennedy, 35the President (1961–1963); Republican Richard Nixon, 37the President (1969–1974); Republican Ronald W. Reagan, 40the President (1981–1989); Republican George Bush, 41st President (1989–1993); Democrat William J. Clinton, 42nd President (1993–2001).

European claims to American territory and advocated non-interference by the Americas in European policy matters.

Spanish and Portuguese interests in Latin America

The conquered regions of Central and South America were declared integral parts of the empire of Castile. The original inhabitants were considered to be free subjects of the Spanish crown. The Indian Council, which was resident in Spain and which ruled on financial, administrative, legal and religious affairs was an important administrative body. The Casa de la Contratación in Seville oversaw the transport of freight, goods, people and money to the colonies. Administrative units were established in Seville itself. These included Rio de la Plata, New Granada and the viceroyships of Mexico and Peru. The Portuguese established a feudal society in their South American colony, Brazil, which traded in timber, sugar and the slave trade. Brazil did not had its first gold rush in the late seventeenth century.

Colonial Christianisation

The conversion to Christianity of the indigenous people was an important component of Spanish colonial policy. While there were many forced baptisms, the Franciscans and Jesuits showed some interest in native American traditions. The Jesuit community that emerged during the seventeenth century in what is now Paraguay was an exception to this rule.

Independence in Central and South America

In 1825, Portugal was obliged to acknowledge the independence

1 These slaves, shipyard workers in Virginia photographed in 1861, were emancipated in 1865.

2 Millions of immigrants from Europe flooded America at the end of the nineteenth century.

3 The brutal regime of the Mexican dictator, Porfirio Díaz, who was supported by the United States, led to a bloody revolution in 1910.

of Brazil which became a constitutional monarchy. The demand for independence became more persistent in the Spanish territories. Under the leadership of Simón Bolívar and José de San Martin, the Spanish were expelled from the whole of South America in the 1820s. As a result of the Monroe Doctrine, the US supported these actions.

Central America was liberated from Spanish colonial rule in 1820. Mexico initially became an independent empire, then, 1823, a conservative republic.

New states of Latin America

New states emerged out of the former Spanish colonies from 1821 onwards. They formed alliances which sometimes disintegrated leading to war. Thus, the General Captaincy of Guatemala was initially part of the viceroyship of New Spain, before declaring its independence and joining the Empire of Mexico in 1822. Following the downfall of Augustin I, it seceded from Mexico and joined a Central American federation modelled on the United States, which became the first country in the Americas to abolish slavery. In 1839, the federation split into Guatemala, El Salvador, Honduras, Nicaragua and Costa Rica.

The federations and great empires of the South American continent only lasted a short time. In 1830, Bolívar's Gran Colombia disintegrated into the countries of Colombia, Venezuela and Ecuador. Paraguay, Bolivia, Uruguay. Argentina emerged from the united provinces of Rio de la Plata.

Expansion of the North American Federation

In 1846, the USA annexed Texas which had been independent

4 The Great Depression: food distribution by the Red Cross to the needy in Arkansas during the economic crisis of the 'Hungry Thirties'.

5 Boomtown New York City: Since the late nineteenth century increasing numbers of skyscrapers have been constructed and now dominate the skyline. Here are a few builders taking a lunchbreak high over the city.

for ten years after a bitter battle with its ruling colonial power, Mexico. Mexico was further obliged to surrender California, New Mexico and parts of Arizona to the USA. In the mid-nineteenth century, the prospect of owning land and the discovery of gold mobilised millions of settlers to seek their fortunes in the 'Wild West'. The Native American population which had suffered greatly at the hands of the White Men in the past resisted the newcomers but were beaten in bitter fighting.

The War of Secession

The American Civil War which lasted from 1861 to 1865 was a true acid test. The conflict between the industrialised states of the North and the agricultural South had been smouldering for a long time. The cotton barons in the South viewed slavery as the basis of their economy but it had already been abolished in the North. South Carolina quit the union in December 1860, following the election of Abraham Lincoln. Six states followed, creating the Confederate States of America. Four further states left the union but, interestingly, the 'slave states' of Maryland, Delaware, Kentucky and Missouri remained in the union. Following the capitulation of the Confederacy, slavery was abolished throughout the USA under the thirteenth amendment to the Constitution.

Further territorial expansion

In 1867, Alaska was bought from Russia and the Pacific islands of Hawaii, Samoa, Midway and the Philippines were acquired through secession and conquest legally. Guam and Puerto Rico came under US administration in 1898 after the United States won the Spanish-American War fought for the independence of Cuba. Washington ensured control of the Panama Canal by supporting Panama's attempts at independence from Colombia.

As the nineteenth century turned into the twentieth, the USA became a world player for the first time; Theodore Roosevelt acted as intermediary in the Russo-

Japanese War of 1904–1905 and President Wilson took the US into World War I in 1917.

The Crash and World War II

The period of increasing prosperity was brought to an abrupt end in 1929 by 'Black Friday', the stock market crash. Unemployment and even hunger prevailed in the USA which had previously been so wealthy. The 'New Deal' policy introduced by President Franklin D. Roosevelt slowly brought the United States out of the crisis.

Following the 1941 surprise attack on Pearl Harbor by the Japanese, the USA entered World War II which they brought to a victorious end with the release of atomic bombs on Hiroshima and Nagasaki in August 1945.

All of a sudden, the USA became the most important player on the world stage. The Soviet Union, which also aimed for world domination, confronted the USA in the 'Cold War'. This determined American foreign policy for almost half a century.

Witch hunts and citizenship

The government resorted to drastic measures to deal with actual or supposed Communists at home during the post-war McCarthy era. The atmosphere became more liberal in the late 1950s and early 1960s, raising a question that had long been ignored: equality before the law for all ethnic groups. Racial segregation in pub-lic places was only finally out-lawed under John F. Kennedy. When Kennedy was assassinated in 1963 by Lee Harvey Oswald, his successor, Lyndon B. Johnson, had to continue to bear the heavy burden of the Vietnam War.

A policy of strength

The self-assurance of the nation plummeted in the 1970s. Corruption, the political assassinations of civil rights campaigner Martin Luther King and presidential candidate Robert Kennedy, the Watergate scandal and the failure to free the Americans taken hostage in the US Embassy in Tehran contributed to the depressed mood. Ronald Reagan, who was elected in 1980, promised to return the

USA to its former greatness. However, the break-up of the Soviet bloc made the policy of aggression obsolete and Reagan left behind a catastrophic budgetary situation. The USA played the role of global policeman under George Bush. It imprisoned Noriega, the head of state of Panama and punished Saddam Hussein for the occupation of Kuwait with 'Operation Desert Storm'.

The economy stabilised under President William Clinton. During the Kosovan crisis, the USA participated in the aerial bombardment of Yugoslavia within the framework of NATO. In late 1999, the USA handed over the Panama Canal Zone to Panama. In January 2001, George W. Bush was sworn in as 43rd President of the United States. On 11 September 2001, the Islamic terrorists of al-Qaida destroyed the World Trade Center in New York and attacked the Pentagon in Washington. They demanded the extradition of Osama bin Laden, terrorist mastermind, who was supported by the Taliban regime in Afghanistan. In October 2001, the USA began a military offen-sive which led to the downfall of the Taliban though Al Qaida remained in hiding in Afghanistan. In 2002, the conflict with Iraq escalated when the US government accused the country of producing weapons of mass destruction. The USA commenced the 'Iraqi freedom' operation in 2003 with British and other Euro-pean support. This pre-emptive strike against Iraq led to the col-lapse of Saddam Hussein's regime within weeks. The USA views North Korea as a further security risk. In 2002, North Korea finally admitted to working to produce atomic weapons. Iran is doing the same, with Korean support, giving the USA major cause for concern.

1 Juan Domingo and Evita Perón celebrating after his swearing-in as Argentinian President for a second term.

2 John F. Kennedy loved to be close to the people. This trust cost him his life in Dallas in 1963.

3 Fidel Castro and Nikita Khruschev, firm friends, in the Kremlin in 1963.

Canada in modern times

Despite a strong independence movement, Canada supported the British motherland in the Boer War and in World War I. Canada only gained independence as a dominion of the British Empire in 1931 thanks to the Statute of Westminster. It did not formally gain independence from the British crown until 1982, although the Queen remains head of state. Where home affairs are concerned, French-Canadian attempts at independence have produced tensions.

Latin America in the twenty-first century

The transition from liberal democracy to brutal military dictatorship gained a new dimension through the victory of Fidel Castro in Cuba in 1953. To protect the interests of the USA, President Kennedy dabbled in the well-tried policy of US intervention, but this time it failed miserably. The economic and political crises of the 1960s led to the downfall of many civilian governments which were replaced by military juntas. An attempt at Marxism, as practiced by Salvador Allende in Chile, was foiled by General Pinochet with US assistance. In 1973, Pinochet established a terror regime that cost the lives of many of his opponents. Since the 1980s, almost all of Latin America has been in civilian hands again and democratic constitutions have been introduced. But in oil-rich Venezuela, the election of Hugo Chavez in a landslide victory in 1998 has caused concern, with his increasingly radical Marxist policies. Despite formal democratisation, South America's persistent high foreign debt, ruth-less exploitation of the environment and human rights abuses remain largely unresolved.

4 Salvador Allende visiting a factory. The Marxist policy of the Chilean President ended abruptly in 1973, when he was assassinated in a coup.

5 The dream of freedom and equality for Afro-Americans was seriously threatened by the assassination black Civil Rights activist Reverend Martin Luther King in Atlanta in 1968.

Main picture:
Manhattan's skyscrapers symbolise
for many the seemingly limitless
possibilities that the United States
of America offer.

The Countries of the Americas

From the Bering Straits in Alaska to Cape Horn at the southernmost tip of Chile, from north to south, the enormous expanse of the American continents links the Earth's two polar ice caps. A flight from west to east in North America

Rio de Janeiro, one of the most exciting cities in South America.

crosses eight time zones. The 42 million sq. km of the Americas encompasses more than a third of the Earth's land area.

With its tundra, salt deserts and tropical rainforests, The Americas are a land of variety and contrasts. This is not only true geographically: while the USA expands its political and economic supremacy, many inhabitants of the countries of Latin America live on the verge of subsistence. Their history is marked by military dictatorships and an often futile struggle for freedom and democracy.

Canada

*The **Inuit** ('people') of the Eastern Canadian Arctic, were once highly specialised at surviving in a hostile environment. They lived in isolation from other Eskimo groups and developed a unique culture and language. Nowadays the Inuit live mainly in mixed settlements. Traditional clothing, language and customs are being increasingly abandoned.*

 Canada

Area:	9,984,670 sq. km
Capital city:	Ottawa
Form of government: Parliamentary Monarchy in the Commonwealth of Nations	
Administrative divisions: 10 provinces, 2 administrative regions	
Population: 33.1 million (3 inhabitants/sq. km)	
Languages: English, French (both official)	
GDP per capita:	US$32,900
Currency: 1 Canadian dollar = 100 cents	

Natural geography

Canada is the world's second-largest country and, together with Alaska, occupies the entire northern section of the North American continent. The country stretches from the **Pacific** in the West to the **Atlantic** in the East, from the Great Lakes in the South to the islands of the North Pole.

Two great mountain chains run parallel to the coast in east and west. The **Cordillera** runs along the Pacific coast and continue into the South American Andes. The **Appalachians** in the east have been severely eroded in the course of the Earth's history and in some places are merely rolling hills. The **Canadian Shield** covers most of the country. It is a rocky plain 200 to 600 m above sea level which rises to 1,500 m in Labrador and is dotted with lakes. In the far north, the continent breaks up into a multitude of islands. The largest are **Baffin Island** with an area of 495,000 sq. km, **Victoria Island** with 212,000 sq. km and the **Queen Elizabeth Islands**. The **Canadian Archipelago** is permanently covered in snow and ice. The **Appalachians** and the **Notre Dame Mountains** which stretch to Newfoundland run parallel to the Atlantic coast.

Between the coast and the mountains there are broad **marshy plains** and deeply-cut **fjords**. The great St. Lawrence Seaway cuts deep inland to the fertile **St. Lawrence Lowland**.

Further west are the lowlands around the **Great Lakes**. Lakes Ontario, Erie, Huron and Superior share a border with the United States. The **Niagara Falls**, on the Niagara River between Lake Erie and Lake Ontario – one of the most spectacular natural sights in North America – are divided between Canada and the USA.

The **Canadian Shield** is the world's oldest **mountain range**, although it has lost a lot of height due to its age. The **Moraine Embankments** and the countless lakes are relics from the Ice Age.

In the west, they give way to a vast, flat landscape. The **Central Canadian chain of lakes** with Lake Winnipeg, Lake Athabasca, Great Slave Lake and Great Bear Lake form a transitional link to the **Great Plains**. The monotonous prairie landscape consists of debris and deposits from the Canadian Shield and contains enormous **deposits of coal, natural gas, crude oil and oil shale**.

Canada is bordered in the west by high mountains. The Northern **Rocky Mountains** are part of the same formation as the **foothills** of the **Columbia Mountains** although they divided from each other by the **Rocky Mountain Trench** through which the **Columbia River** and the **Fraser River** flow on their way to the Pacific Ocean. The **Coastal Cordillera** runs parallel to the Pacific coast. Mount Logan, in this chain, is the highest mountain in Canada, rising a height of 5,951 m. The jagged coastline contains numerou fjords running parallel to the Atlantic coast. Between the mountain chains of the Coastal Cordillera and the Rocky Mountains there are wide areas of flat land such as the **Fraser Plateau** and the **Nechako**, **Stikine**, **Nisutin**, Yukon and Porcupine plateaus.

Climate

Canada as a whole is part of the Arctic and the sub-Arctic climate zones. Consequently, the average temperature is below 0°C in more than half of the country.

In the **permafrost regions**, on King William Island for example, the annual average temperature is -17°C, while on the southern

The St. Lawrence River is the life blood of Quebec City.

Canada

'The Mounties': the Royal Canadian Mounted Police is responsible for keeping order in the southern Rocky Mountains of Alberta. However, with only three inhabitants per sq.km in **Canada**, there is not much for them to do. The Rockies, once attractive to fur-trappers, were flooded by gold-diggers in the late nineteenth century. Horses continue to be the best means of transport. They hauled the huge logs used in construction of fortifications such as Fort McLeod.

edge of Hudson Bay, at the borderline between mixed woodland and tundra, the average temperature is a more bearable - 6.6°C.

The climatic conditions only permit **year-round habitation** and agriculture in the southern parts of Canada. Whilst there is precipitation of 800 to 1,500 mm in the area of the Atlantic, the **precipitation** in the inner plains is only approximately 300 mm annually. The rainfall in the Arctic Archipelago is extremely low (just 60 mm), whilst rainfall on the western hillsides of the Coastal Cordillera can be as much as 6000 mm.

In the **tundra** of Upper Canada, moss, lichen and stunted bushes grow despite extreme climatic

there are **forests of cedars** and Douglas fir, red cedar and hemlock fir.

The **fauna**, of which there are many species, has been preserved especially in **nature reserves**. The largest national parks include the **Wood Buffalo National Park** south of the Great Slave Lake, the **Prince Albert National Park** in Saskatchewan and the **Banff** and the **Jasper National Parks** in the Rocky Mountains. **Caribou** and **musk-oxen** live in the Arctic regions, while **polar bears**, **seals** and **walruses** live along the coast.

The forests are roamed by **American elks**, **black bears** and various **species of deer**. **Grizzly bears**, **mountain goats** and **big horn sheep** live in the Cordilleras.

with 800,000 individuals, whilst European immigrants and their descendants predominate. These are **Anglo-Canadians** (28 per cent), **Franco-Canadians** (21 per cent) and Canadians of **Irish, German, Italian, Ukrainian, Dutch, Polish, Norwegian, Chinese** and South Asian origin. 45 per cent of Canadians are **Catholic** and 40 per cent **Protestant** belonging to a variety of denominations. The rest of the population is **Muslim, Orthodox, Jewish** or **Sikh**. **Schooling is compulsory** in Canada; this is regulated differently from province to province. The **illiteracy rate** is less than five per cent. There are 77 **universities**. **Medical provision** is exemplary; **average life ex-**

Cartier commenced the systematic reconnaissance and appropriation of the land for France in 1534. The first **French settlers** arrived in 1604 and in 1608 **Samuel de Champlain** founded the city of Quebec. From 1627 onwards, the country was annexed by the **Société de la Nouvelle France**, a trading company that operated a monopoly on the fur trade in particular. The land became the property of the French crown in 1674, so that French territory now stretched from Canada down to the Gulf of Mexico.

England disputed French supremacy at an early stage. The **Hudson's Bay Company,** which was formed in 1670, laid claim to all territories whose inland wa-

whole was awarded to the British crown. However, extensive cultural and religious autonomy was granted to the French settlers in the **Quebec Act** of 1774.

During the **American War of Independence**, the province of Quebec remained loyal to Great Britain. However, following the independence of the Thirteen colonies, the newly-formed **United States of America** raised claims to Quebec. The Forty-ninth Parallel was not formally acknowledged as a border until after the War of 1812.

The American Revolution led to a **migration movement** of loyalists from the former American colonies. A second **wave of immigration** – from Great Britain in particular – resulted in another significant increase in population in the mid-nineteenth century. Until 1840, the province of Quebec was divided into British-populated Upper Canada and French-populated Lower Canada as a result of the **Constitution Act** of 1791. The two predominantly autonomous administrative districts were subsequently united to form the Province of Canada. In 1887, the **Dominion of Canada** was created as a confederation of the provinces of Quebec, Ontario, New Brunswick and Nova Scotia. The regions which were controlled by the Hudson's Bay Company were annexed to the Dominion in 1869. **British Columbia** joined the federation in 1871, followed by Prince Edward Island in 1873 and Newfoundland in 1949.

An economic upturn and over-exploitation of raw materials commenced towards the end of the nineteenth century. In 1885, the transcontinental **Canadian Pacific Railway** was completed. On 16 August 1896, gold was discovered in Rabbit Creek, near Dawson, in the Yukon region. The creek was promptly renamed Bonanza Creek, and many of the locals started staking claims. Gold was found all over the place, and most of these early stakeholders became known as the 'Klondike Kings'. Since the Yukon was so remote, word spread slowly, but on 17 July, eleven months after the initial discovery, the steamship 'Portland' arrived in Seattle from Dawson carrying 'more than

Pierre Elliott Trudeau

*Montréal 18.10.1919
†Montréal 28.9.2000

This professor of constitutional and civil rights law was an MP for the Liberal Party from 1965 to 1984 and became its chairman in 1968. He was Prime Minister from 1968 until 1979 and from 1980 until 1984. The bi-lingual, charismatic politician is regarded as the architect of multi-cultural Canada thanks to his concept of bilingualism. He negotiated in the conflict between the Anglos and the French-Canadians and tried to prevent the separation of Quebec province from the rest of Canada.

Two Jack Lake, a magnificent lake in the Banff National Park in Alberta.

conditions. The **boreal coniferous forest** which extends as far as Lower Canada is almost 1000 km wide and stretches from west to east over the whole of Canada. Pines, firs and black and white spruce are the main species that grow here. **A belt of prairie** follows which alternates with mixed woodlands.

The original grassland and shrubs of the **prairies** have fallen victim to agriculture to a great extent. The **sugar maple** flourishes in the **hardwood forests** of the east. Its leaf has become the **national symbol** of Canada. In the high mountains of the west

Bison stocks have been severely reduced in the prairies and large herds can now be found only in the national parks. **Beaver, mink** and other fur-bearing animals can still be found almost anywhere. The varied **birdlife** is impressive, in Newfoundland and on the Gaspé Peninsula in particular. The rivers and lakes are full of **salmon, trout** and other species of fish.

Population

The original population, the **Native Americans, Inuits** and **Métis** are still in the minority

pectancy is 79 years. There is a fertility rate of 1.7 births per woman and, combined with a **minimal infant and child mortality rate**, the population growth is approximately one per cent. The **urban population** is 77 per cent. The most populous city is Toronto with around 4.3 million inhabitants.

History and Politics

The **Vikings** were the first Europeans to reach the east coast of Canada in approximately 1000 AD, but it was another 500 years or so before **Jacques**

ters flowed into Hudson's Bay. As a result of the **Spanish War of Succession**, Nova Scotia, New Brunswick, Newfoundland and the areas surrounding Hudson's Bay were awarded to England in the **Treaty of Utrecht** in 1713. The conflicts between the English and the French culminated in the **Seven Years War** fought in Europe between Brandenburg, Prussia and England on one side and Austria, France and Russia on the other. In 1760, the superior English fleet triumphed in the North American secondary theatre of war. Under the **Treaty of Paris** of 1763, New France as a

*A ritually painted child of the **Algonquin** tribe performing a ritual dance. This tribe, that settled along the Ottawa river before the birth of Christ, now lives in poverty at the edge of Canada's capital. Ottawa's political importance, despite its remote location, is due to the fact that it lies at the border betwen the English- and French-speaking parts of Canada. Evidence of the Native American origins of the city are now confined to the Museum of Civilisation.*

a ton of gold'. Within six months, approximately 100,000 gold-seekers set off for the Yukon. Many died or lost their enthusiasm. They had to walk most of the way, using pack animals or sleds to carry hundreds of pounds of supplies. The Canadian authorities required that all Klondikers bring a year's worth of provisions with them. Even so, starvation and malnutrition were serious problems along the trail. Cold was another serious problem. The Gold Rush eventually petered out when the rich seam of gold was depleted.

Canada's detachment process from the British motherland happened slowly and in several stages. Following World War I, in which Canada fought alongside the British, a separate Canadian delegation participated in the Versailles peace negotiations. In 1923, Canada concluded the first independent foreign trade agreement with the USA, the Halibut Treaty. However, it was not until eight years later that the subordination of the Canadian parliament to British institutions finally ended with the Statute of Westminster and the country gained **independence** as a dominion of the Commonwealth. **During World War II,** Canadian troops fought alongside the Allies and when the war ended Canada became one of the founder members of **NATO.** The constitutional law of 1982 meant final constitutional independence from Great Britain. In 1988, Canada and the USA agreed to establish a **free trade zone** which was extended to **NAFTA** in 1994 when Mexico entered into the agreement.

As far as home affairs are concerned, the dispute between the Anglo-Canadians and the Franco-Canadians has raged for decades. The French minority were granted greater **privileges** in 1969 and the French language was accorded the status of a **second official language** in 1974. Independence for Quebec province was rejected by a narrow majority in the **referendum** held in 1995.

Canada is a **parliamentary monarchy within** the British **Commonwealth** of Nations. The nominal **head of state** is **Queen Elizabeth II** who is represented by a local governor-general. The

Lower House is re-elected every five years and 75 of the 301 seats are reserved for Quebec province. The **senate** has a maximum of 112 members who are appointed by the governor-general on the recommendation of the prime minister. The **right to vote** begins at 18.

Economy

Massive **deposits of raw materials**, **huge forests**, **modern industry** and efficient **agriculture** make Canada one of the world's richest countries. In 2005, Canada's **GDP** totalled

US$ 1 trillion. Agriculture accounted for two per cent of this figure, industry for 29 per cent and the services sector for 69 per cent. Four per cent of the working population is employed in **agriculture**, 23 per cent in **industry** and 73 per cent in the **services sector**. The balance of trade is positive. Major exports are motor vehicles, machinery, timber, wheat, mineral ores, aluminium, oil, natural gas and fish products. Significant **imports** include machinery, vehicles and manufactured goods. Canada's main trading partner is the USA.

Transport

The **rail network** spans **70,000 km**. In contrast to the north which is hardly opened up at all, the **road network** is well-developed along the US border. The St. Lawrence Seaway is the longest river and is navigable, connecting the Atlantic coast with the Great Lakes.

Tourism

Canada has many tourist attractions, including **national parks** with magnificent scenery such as the Canadian side of the Niagara Falls and cosmopolitan cities such as **Quebec**, **Montreal** and **Vancouver** in British Columbia on the Pacific coast.

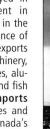 Ice floes drifting in Baffin Bay. Northern Canada is sparsely populated and barely developed.

 Savoir-vivre: Montreal is a successful synthesis of tradition and modernity in architecture, lifestyle, art and culture.

3 The Moraine Lakes such as Ten Summits in Alberta, shown here, were formed in the Rocky Mountains during the Ice Age.

4 Toronto, the prosperous metropolis of the province of Ontario, Canada's answer to the Big Apple: almost 70 nationalities co-exist peacefully here.

United States of America

Washington, D.C.: The White House is the traditional seat of the most important man in America. All the presidents have lived and worked here, with the exception of the first, George Washington, who helped to design the capital city with a French engineer, Major Pierre Charles L'Enfant. The Oval Office, the president's elegant workroom is at the heart of the White House building.

United States of America

Area:	9,631,418 sq. km
Capital city:	Washington, D.C.

Form of government:
Presidential Federal Republic
Administrative divisions:
50 federal states, 1 district
External territories:
Northern Mariana Islands, Puerto Rico, American Virgin Islands, American Samoa, Guam, 8 islands in the Pacific, 3 islands in the Caribbean
Population: 296 million
(29 inhabitants/sq. km)
Languages:
English (official), Spanish, Native American languages
GDP per capita: US$41,800
Currency :
1 US dollar = 100 cents

Natural geography

The USA can be divided into four broad geographical areas, the **coastal plain** in the east, the **Appalachians**, the **Prairies** and the **Rocky Mountains** to the west. The Atlantic coastal plain extends from the 49th to the 24th parallel, that is from the mouth of the **Hudson River** in New York as far as the coastal plain at the **Gulf of Mexico** in Florida. In the west, the coastal plain is bordered by the **Appalachian** mountain range, which extends for about 2,500 km south-west to north-east from Georgia to Maine. The Appalachians, never more than 200 km in width, were formed in the Mesozoic era and in geological terms are therefore considerably older than the **Rocky Mountains**.
The Appalachian mountain range is known by different names in different states, such as the **Great Smokies** in Tennessee and North Carolina, the **Catskills** in New York, the **White Mountains** in New Hampshire, the **Green Mountains** in Vermont, the **Blue Ridge Mountains** between West Virginia and Georgia, and the **Alleghenies** in Pennsylvania. This severely eroded rocky massif consists of ridges, valleys and plateaus The highest peak is Mount Mitchell (2,037 m) in the south.
The Missouri-Mississippi basin is the watershed of the two largest rivers in the USA and extends from the Canadian Shield in the north to the Gulf of Mexico in the south. This broad landscape reaches heights of about 400 m and slopes more steeply in the alluvial land of the **Mississippi**. The monotonous prairie landscape can be divided into four great lowlands, the Interior Plains, the Coastal Plains, the Great Plains and the Interior Highlands. The **Great Lakes** in the north form the US share of the Canadian Shield and are the largest contiguous lake district in the world. Lake Superior, Lake Michigan, Lake Huron, Lake Erie and Lake Ontario are linked to each other as well to the Atlantic by the St Lawrence Seaway, consisting of the river and a network of canals. The Cordillera runs down the west coast and is up to 1500 m wide in places. The **Rocky Mountains** are a young folded mountain range consisting of individual chains, intersected by broad valleys. The mountains reach heights of 4,000 m and extend from the Arctic Ocean to the Mexican border.
The **Columbia plateau** in the north lies in the shadow of the Cordillera, traversed by the Columbia River, the Snake River and other smaller rivers. The **Great Basin** is the largest region of North America with no outlet to the sea and is characterised by inhospitable deserts such as **Death Valley** and the salt lakes. The Colorado plateau is semi-desert tableland through which the Colorado River has carved the **Grand Canyon** to a depth of up to 1,800 m. Further west is the Pacific Mountain System, beginning in the north with the snow-capped Cascades that rise to a height of 4,000 km.

In the south lies the **Sierra Nevada** with an average height of 3,000 m. Mount Whitney, at 4,418 m is the highest mountain in the contiguous United States. Only Mount McKinley in Alaska, at 6,194 m, is higher.
The **Coastal Ranges** are only 1,500–2,000 m high and are separated by the 700 km length of the Great Valley and by the Puget-Willamette Trough.

Climate

Because of the vast size of the country and its diverse geography, including several large mountain ranges, the United States runs the gamut of climates. In the north, conditions are cool to temperate and in the interior the **continental climate** ensures sharp contrasts between summer and winter. In the Deep South, the climate is **sub-tropical** and it is **tropical** in southern Florida. In the Pacific Northwest, the states

The Capitol dominates the skyline in Washington D.C.

*The monumental **Capitol building** is where Congress, the legislative power of the USA, sits in session. The rotunda, crowned by a statue of liberty, accommodates both chambers of Congress. The 79 m-high cupola was completed in 1863 and is the second-highest building in the city after the Washington Monument.*

of Oregon and Washington to the crest of the Cascade Mountains, there is up to 3,800 mm of precipitation a year, falling as rain and snow. In summer, temperatures average over 30°C. In the central Pacific region, the Rocky Mountains and the states of California, Idaho, Montana, Wyoming and Colorado, temperatures vary from over 45°C in summer on the coast to as low as -20°C in winter in **Yellowstone National Park**. Southern California, Nevada, Utah, Arizona, New Mexico and south-west Texas have only about 250 mm of precipitation. In winter, temperatures rarely fall below freezing point, but in the summer they may rise to more than 40°C. In the mid-western states of North and South Dakota, and from Minnesota to central Texas, the thermometer in winter often shows -10°C (North Dakota) and in summer it rises to more than 40°C (Texas). Degrees of precipitation vary between 550 mm in the north and 800 mm in southern Texas. In the eastern states precipitation over the entire year amounts to between 760 mm and 1,270 mm. Summer temperatures often reach 30°C. In Florida, the summer weather is hot and sultry.

The contrasts in atmospheric pressure and temperature in the **Great Plains** often result in **tornadoes** and on the **Gulf Coast** in **hurricanes**, which regularly inflict severe damage. The extreme north-east (Vermont, New Hampshire) is covered in coniferous forest, which changes to mixed and deciduous forest further south. Spruce, fir, beech, maple, hickory and oak are the characteristic trees. In the dry interior, wide flat **prairies** extend with varying densities of vegetation. **Desert landscapes** predominate in the southwest (Arizona, New Mexico) and tropical vegetation with **mangrove swamps** in Florida.

The mountains in the west are wooded, and **Alaska** has a share of the boreal coniferous forest and tundra. There is a multiplicity of fauna. The typical inhabitants of the prairies include bison which, even after mass slaughter, even in the national parks, are now once again increasing in numbers. The national bird, the bald eagle, has become rare. In Florida, there are crocodiles and alligators, and in the north, grizzly, brown and black bears. Whales, dolphins and manatees disport themselves along the coasts, which are rich in fish. The survival of endangered species prized for their fur is to some extent ensured by the **national parks**.

Population

The USA is the classic example of a multi-cultural society, whose population is composed of ethnic groups from almost all over the globe. The native population of **Native Americans**, **Eskimos** and **Aleuts** now accounts for only one per cent of he population, while 74 per cent are **white**, 13 per cent **black**, 12 per cent **Hispanic** and four per cent of **Asian** origin.

While in the nineteenth century and the first half of the twentieth century the majority of immigrants came from Europe, the main countries of origin of non-native citizens today are Mexico, the Philippines, China, Cuba, India and Vietnam. The population of the USA is composed of 26 per cent **Catholics**, 16 per cent **Baptists**, six per cent **Methodists**, 3.7 per cent **Lutherans**, 2.6 per cent **Jews**, 1.1 per cent **Episcopalians**, 1.5 per cent **Orthodox Christians**, 1.8 per cent **Muslims** and 1.8 per cent **Presbyterians**. In addition there are sizeable minorities of **Sikhs**, **Bahai** and **Buddhists** as well as adherents of various **sects**. Average life expectancy is 77 years. The education system is regulated by the individual states, but generally speaking education is compulsory between five and 16 years old. The illiteracy rate is less than five per cent. The USA has a total of some 3,700 **universities and colleges**. With 240 Nobel prizes, the USA tops the number of prize winners, though many of the laureates were foreign-born and educated outside the US. Apart from the very highly educated elite, a large number of schoolleavers have inadequate spelling and basic arithmetic.

Of the US population, 76 per cent live in the cities, 22 per cent are under 15 years old and 13 per cent over 65. The average age is just 35 years, and the annual rate of population growth is 0.79 per cent.

History and Politics

The **Vikings** were the first Europeans to reach North America, but

United States of America

'Lady Liberty': For millions of immigrants, the **Statue of Liberty** at the entrance to New York harbour symbolised a dream come true. It is the work of the French sculptor, Frédéric-Auguste Bartholdi. The steel structure was built by Gustave Eiffel. The 46-metre-tall Statue stands on a 47-metre-high granite pedestal and was a gift from the wealthy French citizens to the USA as a symbol of liberty. It was placed on the Liberty Island in 1886.

were not able to maintain their settlements in the long term. There is evidence of **settlements** at least 12,000 years ago. After the discovery of America by **Columbus** in 1492, it was another 73 years before the Spanish started the colonisation of North America with the foundation of St Augustine in Florida.

After the English defeated the Spanish Armada in 1588, their only rivals were the French and Dutch. The French founded **Quebec** in 1608, and the Dutch founded **New Amsterdam**, the present-day New York, around 1625. In 1607, the first British colony was established with the foundation of Jamestown in Virginia, followed by other settlements in the course of the sixteenth and seventeenth centuries. British colonisation continued on a larger scale after 1620 when the **Pilgrim Fathers** landed at Plymouth Rock in what is now New England. Hardships at home, political unrest and religious persecution of the Puritans led to an endless stream of settlers.

Three main British colonies were founded. The economy of the South (Maryland, North and South Carolina, Virginia, Georgia) was based mainly on large **plantations** using **slave labour** for the growing of cotton, indigo and tobacco.

The **New England colonies** engaged in trading and had fishing industries and a merchant fleet, while the Mid-Atlantic colonies were particularly attractive to settlers from Ireland, Scotland, Germany and the Netherlands with their cultural attractions, a high degree of religious freedom and flourishing trade. The British colonial power was able to secure supplies of raw materials and markets for its own manufactured goods and the British army and navy protected the settlers from attack by the Spanish, French, Native Americans and pirates.

In the **French and Indian War**, which became part of the **Seven-Years War**, the British established their claims, but the settlers' increasing self-confidence was displayed in 1773 at the **Boston Tea Party**. This was the start of the American **War of Independence** also known as the American Revolution of 1778. In 1789, the United States constitution came into being, and **George Washington** became the country's first president. In 1800, his successor John Adams moved into the White House in the **District of Columbia**, on land seceded from Maryland, which was now separate from the state of Virginia. Under the third president, **Thomas Jefferson**, US territory expanded by 140 per cent when **Napoleon** was paid US$15 million for the 2.1 million sq. km of land between Mississippi and the Rocky Mountains, now known as the Louisiana Purchase. A further war with England, the War of 1812, ended in a deadlock in 1815, but confirmed the territorial integrity and **independence** of the USA.

In the early nineteenth century, the US extended its borders to the south, south-west and north-west. After **Texas** broke away from Mexico in 1845 a war began with **Mexico**, which ended in 1848 with the acquisition of the land north of the Rio Grande.

The discovery of gold in California in 1849 and the prospect of fertile land resulted in the westward migration of millions of settlers. Native Americans who resisted the appropriation of their land were ruthlessly suppressed and forced on long treks into small, inhospitable reservations far from their homelands. Foreign policy was formulated in 1823 through the Monroe Doctrine, which claimed hegemony for Washington on the North American continent against all European claims west of the Atlantic. Social and economic

Franklin Delano Roosevelt

*Hyde Park, 30.1.1882,
†Warm Springs, 12.4.1945

After an electoral victory over President Hoover in 1932, Roosevelt tried to steer the US out of the terrible slump that followed the Wall Street Crash. Central points of his 'New Deal' were further state help for the poor and a job creation programme. Abandoning the isolationist policies of his predecessors, he brought the United States into World War II after the Japanese attack on Pearl Harbor in 1941. This popular politician was elected for an unprecedented third term in 1940 and a fourth term in 1944.

Dwight David Eisenhower

*Denison, 14.10.1890,
†Washington, D.C., 28.3.1969

The commander-in-chief of Allied Forces Europe in World War II , was elected 34th President in 1953. Despite the aggressive policies of his Secretary of State, John Foster Dulles, his policy towards the USSR during the Suez and Hungarian crises was more defensive. With the 'Eisenhower doctrine' of 1957 he secured support for self-rule for the Arab countries which led to an intervention in Lebanon in 1958. On the home front he expanded the social system known as Modern Republicanism.

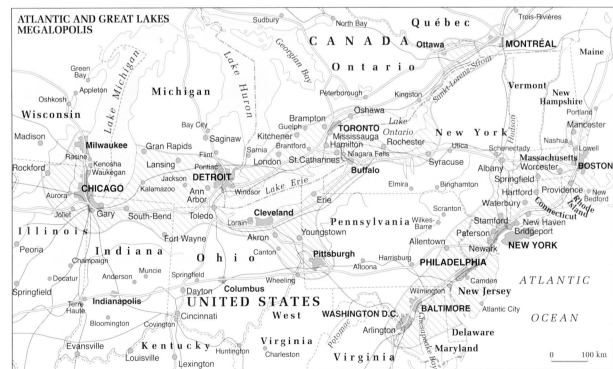

*The **Old State House** in **Boston** once served as the British Governor's office. Nowadays it is a museum of the city's history. The Georgian-style building is one of the stops on the 'Freedom Trail' a history of US Independence.*

It is here, on Boston Common that the first shots were fired in the War of Independence. Boston continues to be a centre of intellectual activity: several prestigious 'Ivy League' universities such as Harvard, are close by.

development was extremely variable and depended on the regions of the new federal state. While the farmers of New England and the industrialists and capitalists of the north favoured emancipation of the slaves, the cotton barons of the Deep South wanted to retain **slavery**. The **antagonism** between the advocates of **slavery** and the **abolitionists** intensified, culminating in 1861 in the secession of eleven states, led by South Carolina, and their union as the Confederated States. The civil war that followed lasted for four years and cost the lives of 623,000 soldiers. When the Confederacy surrendered in 1865, unity was restored and slavery abolished under the **Thirteenth Amendment** to the Constitution. **Reconstruction** was not completed until 1877 though the full emancipation of the Afro-Americans had by no means been achieved. On the contrary, a militant racism developed and the **Ku Klux Klan** came into being.

Streams of settlers from the Old World continued to decimate the native population. The extinction of the mighty herds of bison through the construction of the trans-continental railways took away the livelihoods of the native dwellers on the prairies. Occasional successes such as the rout of General Custer's cavalry at the Battle of **Little Big Horn River** in 1876 made no difference to the fate of the native population. After the defeat of the Apaches under their chief Geronimo in 1886 and the massacre of the Sioux at **Wounded Knee** in 1890, their resistance was finally broken.

The sudden rise of the USA to the status of a **world power** began around 1900. With Alaska, bought from Russians in 1867 for 7.2 million gold dollars and the annexation of Guam, Hawaii, Samoa, Puerto Rico, Midway and the Philippines, the USA extended its claims in the Caribbean and Pacific. An explosion on an American warship in the port of Havana served as an excuse for **the Spanish-American War**, which ended with the independence of Cuba in 1880. The USA now claimed worldwide authority and operated imperialist policies in the Americas, intervening in Venezuela from 1902 to 1904 securing control, disputed under international law, of the

Panama Canal zone. President **Theodore Roosevelt** entered the world diplomatic stage as a mediator in the Treaty of Portsmouth, which ended the Russo-Japanese war, and at the conferences at Algeciras and the Hague. In World War I, the US at first declared neutrality, but in 1917, after the resumption of submarine warfare by

Germany, it entered the war on the side of the Allies.

Wilson's **Fourteen Point programme** for a democratic reconstruction of Europe was not implemented at the peace conferences of 1919. The USA did not join the **League of Nations** although it had been proposed by President Wilson. During **isola-**

1 Midtown Manhattan: the architect Le Corbusier once described New York as a 'vertical city'. The buildings have to be narrow at the top for light to penetrate to street level.

2 The state of Maine is known for its spectacular coastline. The rugged rocks are topped with

old lighthouses such as this one dating from 1827.

3 Brightly illuminated Boston radiates a serene elegance, even by night. The capital of New England has around 600,000 inhabitants, small in comparison with other big cities in the US.

The USA is a leader is space travel, bio-technology and IT research.

USA – The World Superpower

Since the collapse of the Eastern Bloc, the USA has been the world's strongest economic and military power. The belief in the superiority of its political system has led the USA into many international conflicts and has enabled it to stand up confidently to international organisations such as the United Nations.

Large numbers of immigrants, growing economic power and the occupation and settlement of massive territories all enabled the USA to develop into an imperial power, which then entered into competition with the European colonial empires. In 1867, the USA purchased Alaska from Russia for the relatively low sum of 7.2 million gold dollars. Over the following decades, America acquired further territories in the Pacific and the Caribbean.

America's engagement in the affairs of other nations began with Theodore Roosevelt's attempt to broaden Washington's sphere of influence. The USA supported Panama's struggle for indepen-

dence and thus secured for itself control of the Panama Canal, which opened in 1914.

During World War I, the United States initially remained neutral, but supported the Allies by supplying weapons. By entering the war, and through his actions after the war, President Woodrow Wilson began a period of participatory politics, but this only lasted a short time. His Fourteen Points, which set out the criteria for a new order in Europe, was only partially and very slowly implemented. Although the League of Nations was a US idea, the country itself did not, in fact, join and once more resumed its isolationist-protectionist politics.

After the severe economic crisis that began in 1929, America came up with the New Deal, giving a boost to the armaments industry. America increased its export of weapons and in so doing brought itself out of global isolation.

The attack on Pearl Harbor forced the USA into war against Japan, which quickly became a battle for supremacy in the Pacific. In terms of the war in Europe, America initially remained neutral, but once more supplied weapons to the Allies. After the declaration of

Rich oil reserves are still insufficient to satisfy the USA's huge demand for energy.

war by the Germany the USA mobilised and went on to play a deciding role in the eventual defeat of Nazi-Germany.

Signs of confrontation with America's wartime ally, the USSR, began to emerge in 1945. Stalin wanted to extend his influence over all of Eastern Europe. In its fight against Communism the USA did not support democratic

systems alone, but also aided dictatorships with terrible human rights records, but this was often ignored if they the American campaign against communism.

Stemming the spread of Communism and extending its own sphere of influence was the USA's primary international aim for more than 40 years. The division of the world into American and

America's aircraft construction industry must today compete with the Airbus Consortium.

Main photo: the aircraft carrier USS 'America' – an example of America's military supremacy.

Soviet spheres of influence lead to serious crises, such as the Berlin Blockade of 1947/48 and the Korean War of 1950–1953, followed by the construction of the Berlin Wall in 1961 and the Cuban Missile Crisis of 1962.

Both sides had immense nuclear weapons potential, and the world sat under the threat of war between two superpowers. Both sides attempted to assert or further their positions of power by fighting proxy wars in Third World countries. Economic interests also played a significant role in these wars. The USA has intervened directly in many countries in its own 'back yard'. These include Guatemala, in 1954, the Dominican Republic in 1965 and in Grenada in 1983. Cuba's socialist rule under Fidel Castro, was and remains an irritation for the USA which imposes severe restrictions on any kind of trade or contact with

Cuba. The struggle for political supremacy spread to space. The USSR had the initial upper hand in space exploration, but the USA successfully countered this in 1969 by being the first to land on the moon.

The USA suffered a bitter defeat in Vietnam. After a prolonged war, the US troops were forced to retreat in 1973. The myth of an invincible America was dented.

After the collapse of the Eastern Bloc, the USA became the only superpower, and felt called upon to act as a 'global policeman'. In 1991, the USA liberated oil-rich Kuwait from the clutches of the Iraqi dictator Saddam Hussein in the Gulf War. Under President Clinton in 1993, the USA attempted to find a solution to the Middle East conflict, with some initial success. The USA also exerted its power in Europe, and stepped in to resolve the Kosovo

Crisis in 1999 caused by the break-up of Yugoslavia when NATO forces began bombing Serbian positions without a UN mandate. The terror attacks of 11 September 2001 began a new era for the USA as this was the first time an enemy had inflicted serious damage on its soil. Under President George W. Bush the USA declared war on global terrorism and its 'state supporters', beginning with an offensive against the Taliban regime in Afghanistan and continuing in 2003 with the Iraq War.

Whereas the USA received a UN mandate for its attack on Afghanistan, the attack on Iraq went ahead, despite the absence of a resolution from the UN permitting the attack.

The dollar rate and the Dow Jones Index have become measures of the global economy.

Over-production in agriculture affects the global market.

United States of America

During Prohibition, Mafia clans ruled in **Chicago**. Nowadays, it is the stockbrokers who rule the city. Chicago is one of the world's major trading centres and has the second most important commodities and futures market.

tionism, women's suffrage and Prohibition were introduced. The ban on alcohol led to brisk smuggling and the rise of organised crime. The ban on alcohol was not lifted until 1933. The economy seemed to be booming, until the Stock Market Crash of 29 October 1929, known as **Black Friday**. President Hoover was unable to deal with the starvation and misery that resulted in the 1930s, and it was only the **New Deal** devised by his successor, Franklin D. Roosevelt, that slowly led the country back from disaster.

The USA finally entered World War II after the Japanese attack on **Pearl Harbor** on 7 December 1941 and contributed substantially to the surrender of Nazi Germany on 8 May 1945. After the war, the USA abandoned its traditional foreign policy of non-intervention and became involved as an active world power. This role was imposed by the **East-West conflict**, which was to characterise world politics for more than forty years.

The Marshall Plan, instigated and funded by the United States, for the reconstruction of Europe was introduced in 1947, and at the same time the **arms race** began with the Soviet Union.

The USA took the leading role in the defence organisations of **NA-TO**, **SEATO** and **CENTO** and reacted energetically to provocation such as the Berlin blockade and the Korean crisis. Stalin's death in 1953 seemed to usher in a phase of detente, but the political climate was intensified by the **Suez Crisis** and the failed Hungarian Revolution, both in 1956. The Berlin crisis at the end of 1958 and the conflict between Taiwan and the People's Republic of China followed. From 1950, the USSR had its own **atom bomb**, and from 1953, the **hydrogen bomb**. The shooting down of a U2 reconnaissance aircraft over the USSR and the successful Communist Revolution in Cuba in 1959 shattered the myth of American invincibility. At home, the McCarthy era brought a witch-hunt for real or supposed Communists, and the **Civil Rights movement** protests emerged to fight discrimination against African-Americans.

The election victory of **John F. Kennedy** aroused great hopes, although his fame is to be sought in the legend of his vision of breaking through of new frontiers rather than in his actual success. Only by deploying federal troops was Kennedy able to end **racial segregation** in schools, already declared unconstitutional in 1954. From the point of view of foreign policy, the picture was also somewhat negative. The attempted Bay of Pigs invasion by exiled Cubans in 1961, supported by the US government, was a miserable failed. Meanwhile, the Western world was forced to accept the building of the Berlin Wall. The **Cuban Missile Crisis** of 1962 led the world to the edge of global nuclear war, but was dispelled by the end of the year. After the **assassination of Kennedy** on 22 November 1963 in Dallas, Vice-president Johnson took over, inheriting a heavy burden. The **Vietnam War** and the civil rights movement, as well as the dependence of the USA on Arab oil imports, which became

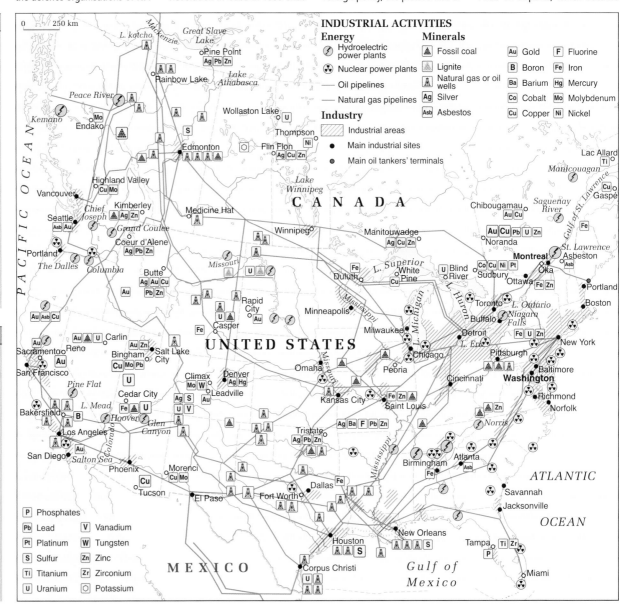

INDUSTRIAL ACTIVITIES

Energy
- Hydroelectric power plants
- Nuclear power plants
- Oil pipelines
- Natural gas pipelines

Industry
- Industrial areas
- Main industrial sites
- Main oil tankers' terminals

Minerals
- Fossil coal
- Lignite
- Natural gas or oil wells
- Ag Silver
- Asb Asbestos
- Au Gold
- B Boron
- Ba Barium
- Co Cobalt
- Cu Copper
- F Fluorine
- Fe Iron
- Hg Mercury
- Mo Molybdenum
- Ni Nickel

- P Phosphates
- Pb Lead
- Pt Platinum
- S Sulfur
- Ti Titanium
- U Uranium
- V Vanadium
- W Tungsten
- Zn Zinc
- Zr Zirconium
- O Potassium

*From the **Kennedy Space Center** on Cape Canaveral in Florida a shuttle takes off on a space mission. The United States maintains the most ambitious and spec-tacular space programmes in the world, despite massive budget cuts. Shuttles are mainly deployed as they can be re-used. One of the most interesting space missions in recent years were the expeditions to Mars, which impressive the first pictures of Mars' surface.*

evident after the Six-Day War of 1967, impelled him to decline further candidacy in 1968. The new president, **Richard Nixon**, made efforts to normalise relations with China and to reach agreements on arms limitations (the SALT talks) with the Soviet Union. Despite the massive bombing of North Vietnam and Laos, the Americans finally withdrew in defeat in 1973. Two years later, South Vietnam collapsed. Although Secretary of State **Kissinger** received the **Nobel Peace Prize**, the myth of an invincible America was shattered. As many as 57,000 Americans lost their lives in Vietnam. On the domestic front, too, trust in the government was severely shaken when in 1974, two years after Nixon's re-election, the **Watergate affair** forced the president to resign.

Under **Gerald Ford**, the policy of disarmament continued and the Conference for Security and Co-operation in Europe was created. The foreign policy aim of President **Jimmy Carter** was to improve human rights abroad. His peace mediation between Egypt and Israel and the signing of two agreements on the Panama Canal were successful. But after the invasion of Afghanistan by the Soviet Union and the botched liberation of hostages in the US embassy in Tehran, the Republican opposition called for a return to **power politics**.

The former actor **Ronald Reagan**, who succeeded Carter in office in 1981 had the backing of the neo-conservative Republicans. The strength of America was to be renewed by a massive rearmament programme, including a plan for a new space defence system (the so-called 'Star Wars') and the deployment of new medium-range missiles in western Europe. Support for anti-communist regimes, regardless of their human rights record, was another aspect of Reagan's policy. The sending of US troops to **Lebanon**, the occupation of Grenada in 1983 and military strikes against the Libyan head of state **Ghaddafi** were calculated to boost American self-confidence. In President Reagan's second term of office, which was overshadowed by the **Iran-Contra affair**, there was a rapprochement with the Soviet Union,

which announced unilateral steps towards disarmament under **Mikhail Gorbachev**. The end of the Cold War was ushered in by the **START (Strategic Arms Reduction Treaty) discussions**. When **George Bush** moved into the White House in 1989, the USA was the only remaining superpower and self-confidently took on the role of **world policeman**. In 1989, for example, US troops marched into **Panama** and took General Noriega prisoner. Later, he was sentenced to 40 years in jail for drug-dealing in the USA. In 1991, the USA led the military **offensive** in an international alliance against the Iraqi aggressor **Saddam Hussein**, who was forced to reverse Iraq's occupation of Kuwait. The military mission in Somalia to secure UN assistance however remained without result. The economic policy of '**Reaganomics**', continued by President George Bush, introducing a period of high **unemployment**, a significant foreign trade deficit and an extremely high national debt. Not least as a result of the disastrous economic situation, the Democratic challenger William J. (Bill) **Clinton** succeeded in winning the presidential election of 1993. Clinton reduced the national debt, achieved almost full employment and strengthened the competitiveness of the economy. In terms of foreign affairs, he was able to gain international esteem through his peace negotiations between **Israel** and the **PLO** in 1993. In spite of Clinton's popularity, the Republicans pressed for his impeachment due to a **sexual scandal**, though this was averted after an embar-

rassing investigation. In the spring of 1999, NATO, under the military leadership of the USA, embarked on **bombing raids** on the former Yugoslavia, in order to prevent 'ethnic cleansing' in the semi-autonomous **Kosovo** region. In June 1999 Serbian units withdrew from Kosovo and international KFOR **peace-keeping** troops moved in.

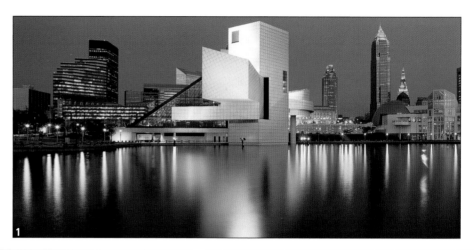

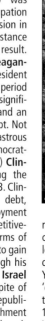

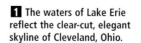 **1** The waters of Lake Erie reflect the clear-cut, elegant skyline of Cleveland, Ohio.

2 The palm-fringed boardwalk of Miami's South Beach oozes sunshine-state flair. The state has become a haven for retirees from the north seeking winter sunshine.

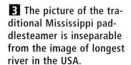 **3** The picture of the traditional Mississippi paddlesteamer is inseparable from the image of longest river in the USA.

4 An old water-mill in West Virginia. The state is still very rural despite its coal mines.

United States of America

*The **Pueblo Indians** of Arizona and New Mexico are one of many Native American communities in the south-west. In 1680, they fought against subjugation by Catholic missionaries and won. The self-confident Pueblo Indians, so-called because they farmed and lived in villages, still practice their own religion: it is based on harmony between all beings and is also expressed in arts and crafts. Many Pueblo artists are renowned world-wide.*

In 2001 George W. Bush, son of George Bush, was sworn in as 43rd president. On **11 September 2001**, suicide bombers piloting hijacked aircraft destroyed the World Trade Center in New York and attacked the Pentagon in Washington. The result was a **military offensive against Afghanistan**, whose Taliban regime was sheltering the Al Qaida terrorist organisation. The war ended with the fall of the Taliban. A further result of 11 September was the **war against Iraq**, whom the USA accused of producing weapons of mass destruction and maintaining a worldwide terrorist network. The war began in the spring of 2003 and ended Saddam Hussein's rule. At home, Bush came under pressure after no weapons of mass destruction were found, and in Iraq, terrorist attacks were being carried out daily on the US forces.

The **constitution of 1789**, last amended in 1992, provides for a bicameral Congress. The 435 members of the **House of Representatives** are directly elected every two years, and the 100 **Senators** every six years, one-third being elected every two years. The president's serves for four years, with the option of one additional term. The head of state is not elected directly, but by an electoral college of 538 delegates. The voting age is 18 years.

Economy

The US economy is the largest in the world. In 2001, the GDP was US$9,900 billion. This included **agriculture** at two per cent, **industry** at 26 per cent and the service sector at 72 per cent.
The area usable for agriculture amounts to 47 per cent of the total land mass. The **enormous ranches,** averaging 190 ha, are used for breeding poultry, cattle, pigs and sheep. All kinds of fruits, vegetables and cereals are cultivated as well as tobacco. There are vineyards in the East and West. The USA is the world's largest exporter of wheat and the third largest of rice. The country's industry produces virtually every product imaginable, the most important categories being motor vehicles, electronics, chemicals, foodstuffs and metal-processing. The chief **imports** are capital goods, motor vehicles, luxury items and oil. The main **exports** are machinery and transport equipment, raw materials, consumer goods, motor vehicles and agricultural products. The most important **natural resources** are petroleum, natural gas, anthracite and brown coal, zinc, lead, silver and gold.

Transport

The importance of the **railways** continues to decrease. The remaining 406,000 km of track are used by private companies mainly to transport freight. Passenger transport accounts for only 0.7 per cent of rail transport. Of some 6,261,200 km of roads, 60 per cent is asphalted. The **Interstate Highways** link almost all the states and there are many freeways or parkways (motorways) inside the large cities, such as New York, Chicago and Los Angeles, to assist the folow of traffic.is swift. However, due to

Two worlds in Nevada: Navajo shepherds and the glitz and glitter of Las Vegas are only kilometres apart.

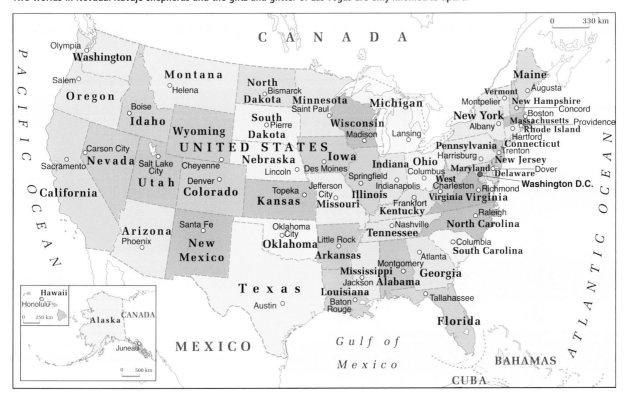

The stuff that dreams are made of is produced in **Hollywood**: a day pretending to be movie star Mae West is in high demand as well as the evergreens Micky and Minnie Mouse. Studio tours and theme parks are big attractions.

the fact that public road transport has long been neglected in favour of the private car, there is massive road congestion in the cities. The public transport network is gradually being improved, with additional subway (underground) lines being added in cities such as Washington D.C. and Los Angeles, but the problem persists.

There are 13,400 airports in the USA. Of the 180 international airports, **Chicago O'Hare**, with 60 million passengers per year, is the largest in the world, run a close second by **New York's Kennedy and Newark Airports**. The most important **seaports** are New Orleans, Houston, New York, Baltimore, Baton Rouge, Boston, Honolulu, Jacksonville, Los Angeles, Pittsburgh, Savannah, Seattle, Tampa and Toledo. **Inland navigation** is possible on 41,009 km of waterways.

Tourism

The **beaches** of Florida and California, the **surfing** spots of Hawaii, the impressive great cities, as well as the stunning landscapes, above all in the **national parks**, attracted 45.5 million tourists to the USA in 2002. In addition there is a strongly developed **domestic tourist industry**. In 2002, tourism brought in US$72.2 billion. The USA is a popular travel destination all year round; the **Indian summer** and autumn (fall) considered the most beautiful time of year, especially in New England.

States of the continental United States

New England

The name New England was coined in 1614 by the English captain John Smith. **Puritans** began to settle here from the early seventeenth century, followed by Scots and Irish. New York was at first a Dutch colony called New Amsterdam. The United States of America emerged from the earlier **New England Confederation**. Today, New England, with **Harvard University** and **MIT**, is one of the two intellectual centres of the USA, the other being Cali-

fornia. Agriculture, including livestock-rearing and the cultivation of fruit and vegetables, continue to be an important economic factor, as are fishing, timber and shipbuilding.

The Southern states

The Southern states are generally considered to be **conservative** in character and with an agriculture-based economy. The former cotton monoculture has given way to more diversified crops. In Virginia, despite massive anti-smoking campaigns, **tobacco-growing** remains important; Kentucky and

Tennessee have the most famous bourbon and rye **whiskey distilleries**, and **Cape Canaveral in Florida** is the launch site for the US space programme, under the control of Houston, Texas. The Florida **Everglades** offer breathtaking wonders of nature.

Great Lakes

The Great Lakes extend to the Canadian border and are linked by the **St Lawrence river** and numerous canals, so that giant ocean-going vessels can penetrate deep into the interior. Chicago O'Hare is the largest airport in the world and the automobile industry is centred in Detroit.

Midwest

The Midwest includes the states of Montana, North and South Dakota, Iowa, Missouri, Oklahoma, Kansas, Nebraska, Wyoming and Idaho. This area is chiefly agricultural. Of particular interest to

tourists is Wyoming, where the **Grand Teton National Park** and the **rodeos** attract many visitors. North-west of Montana lies the Glacier National Park. In South Dakota, there are the **Badlands National Park** and the Custer State Park. The Wild West is still alive near **Rapid City**, where the Indian chiefs **Crazy Horse** and

1 Denver: oil wells and an average of 300 days of sunshine a year attract newcomers to the 'mile-high' city.

2 The 2.7-km-long Golden Gate Bridge spans the San Francisco Bay, connecting

San Francisco with the famous wine-growing Sonoma Valley.

3 The vastness of Monument Valley in Arizona is legendary. The whole area is dotted with typical red sandstone outcrops called mesas and tumbleweed. This is Navajo Indian territory.

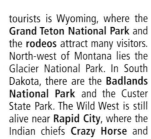

United States of America

Puerto Rico's capital city **San Juan** has preserved the character of its Spanish colonial past. Yet the picturesque views surrounding Fort Aleza conceals Puerto Rico's past when the indigenous people fought bitter battles against the Spanish colonists. The natives' defeat and the subsequent colonialisation were only possible due to Spanish imports of African slaves, who were forced to fight alongside them. Puerto Rico is now a commonwealth of the USA.

Sitting Bull were based, and where the US cavalry lost General Custer's units at the Battle of Little Big Horn. This is where the conflicts with Native Americans ended with their massacre at the Battle of **Wounded Knee**. Near Keystone, five US presidents have been immortalised in stone by monumental likenesses carved into Mount Rushmore.

South-west

The states of Arizona, New Mexico, Nevada and Utah are sparsely populated due to the inhospitable landscape. Here, too, the Wild West lives on. Abandoned ghost towns from pioneer days and the rock formations of **Monument Valley** are familiar locations in many Western films. The salt lakes can film industry, and San Francisco, with its famous **Golden Gate Bridge**, attracts tourists, as do the national parks of Yosemite, Sequoia, Kings Canyon, Joshua Tree and Death Valley, and the exclusive, resort of Malibu with its famous Getty Museum, built as a recreation of the Roman Villa of the Scrolls in southern Italy.

The **Pacific Coast of Oregon**, with its lovely mountains, waterfalls and forests has hardly been discovered by European tourists. Its attractions include the Crater Lake National Park, **Hell's Canyon** and old Portland. Apart from the busy city of Seattle, the embarkation port for Alaska, the state of Washington offers a number of impressive national parks and the beautiful Cascade Mountains, which includes Mount Hood, (3,426 m).

was sold to the USA in 1876. Before Alaska became the 49th state of the USA in 1959, it was a district until 1912, then a territory. Its main industries are fishing, logging and the processing of oil, natural gas, gold, iron, copper, tin, coal, asbestos and uranium. The capital is **Juneau**.

Hawaii

In 1798, James Cook discovered the **Sandwich Islands**, which cover an area of 28,313 sq. km and have 1.2 million inhabitants. Seven of the eight main islands are inhabited: Hawaii, Maui, Oahu, Kauai, Molokai, Lanai and Niihau. The Hawaiian state flag still features the union flag.

The capital is **Honolulu** on Oahu. In 1959, Hawaii became the 50th came a protectorate of New Zealand after World War I, and gained independence in 1962. The **government** consists of a House of Representatives and a Senate as well as a US governor. The capital is **Pago Pago** on Tutuila. The main industry is **fishing**.

Guam

The largest of the Mariana islands at 541 sq. km is Guam, with some **160,000 inhabitants**, mostly Malayan Chamorros and Filipinos.

Missions to the island from Spain began in 1668. In 1889, the Spanish ceded Guam to the USA. The Japanese occupation, from 1941, ended in 1944 with the island's reconquest by the USA. Since 1982, Guam has had internal **au-** From 1672, the region was colonised by Denmark, and St Croix was under French administration up to 1733. In 1917, Denmark sold the islands to the USA for US$25 million. Since 1927, the inhabitants have had US citizenship. The **government** consists of a 15-member parliament and a US governor. Almost all the income from the Virgin Islands derives from tourism.

US Commonwealth territories

Northern Marianas

Of these 16 volcanic and coral islands, with a total land area of 541 sq. km, only six are inhabited. The 52,284 inhabitants are predomi-

Waikiki Beach is the tourist centre of Hawaii, with an average of 80 hotels per sq. km.

Richard Milhous Nixon

*Yorba Linda, 9.1.1913,
†Park Ridge, 22.4.1994

The former senator for California was elected the 37th President of the US in 1968. Together with Secretary of State Kissinger, he tried to de-escalate the Vietnam War, limit the arms race and normalise the relations with the People's Republic of China. The Water-Gate affair forced him to resign in 1974, two years after his re-election.

---

of Utah, the **Grand Canyon**, the gambling city of Las Vegas and the national parks attract numbers of tourists, as do the mesas of New Mexico and Arizona, where many retirees come for the healthy climate. On account of the almost dust-free air, the **high-tech industry** has made its home here.

Pacific States

The states of California, Oregon and Washington are both agricultural and industrial, but tourism and, in California, the **computer industry**, play important roles. California is known as the Golden State due to its former gold rushes. **Hollywood**, a suburb of Los Angeles, is the centre of the Ameri-

States outside the continental United States

Alaska

Alaska has a land area of 1,700,138 sq. km but only 609,000 inhabitants, including **Inuit**, **Native Americans**, Aleuts, and 35,000 **members of the armed forces**. The **Alaska mountains** are in the south and include the 6,193-m-high Mount McKinley. There are fjords along the coast. The flat central plain, containing the **Yukon** and Kuskokwim rivers lies just south of the Arctic Circle. Alaska was discovered in 1741 by Bering and Chirikov and was a Russian possession until it

state of the USA. The main industry is **tourism**.

Overseas territories

American Samoa

This group of volcanic islands – Tutuila, Ta'u, Aunn'n, Olosega, Ofu and the atolls of Rose Island and Swains Island – cover a total land area of 194.8 sq. km. The population numbers **60,000 inhabitants** mainly of Polynesian descent. After its discovery by the Dutch, it was jointly ruled by Britain, Germany and the USA from 1889. Eastern Samoa became part of the USA in 1900, while Western Samoa be-

tonomy. The 15-member parliament is elected every two years, and the governor every four years. The capital is **Agana**. There is a US Army base on the island due to its **strategic importance**, and it is the main source of income. **Tourism** is also a big earner for the islands.

US Virgin Islands

The main islands, St Thomas, St Croix and St John, in this 348 sq. km island group in the **Caribbean**, have 97,120 inhabitants, of whom 80 per cent are **Black or mixed race** and 15 per cent **White**. When it was discovered by Columbus in 1493, it was inhabited by Caribs and Arawaks.

nantly Polynesian. They are US citizens but have no right to vote in US federal elections. The islands were discovered by **Magellan** in 1521 and were under Spanish rule until 1898. They were then sold to **Germany** and from 1920 they were a **Japanese mandated territory**. The Japanese used the islands as a strategic base during World War II. After 1945, the US Departments of Defense and the Interior took over the administration of the islands. In 1978, the islands adopted a constitution and in 1986 the UN trusteeship ended, and internal **autonomy** was proclaimed. Both chambers of the parliament are elected every two years, and the governor is elected every five years. The main source of income is **tourism**.

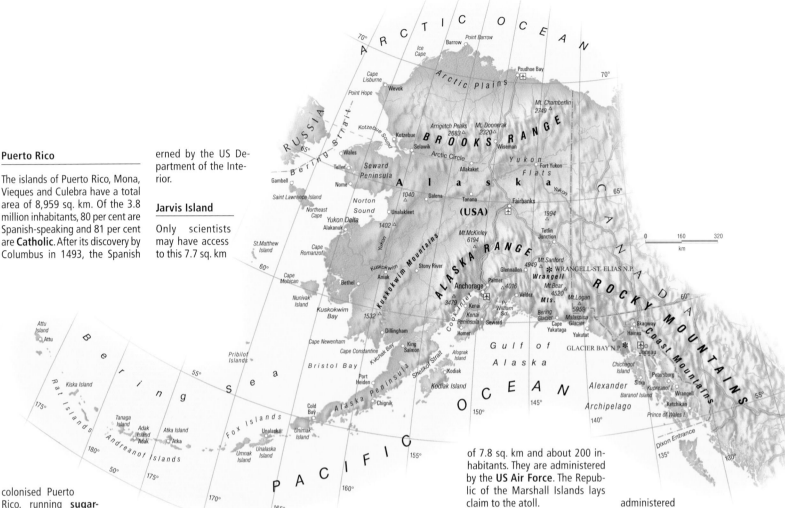

Puerto Rico

The islands of Puerto Rico, Mona, Vieques and Culebra have a total area of 8,959 sq. km. Of the 3.8 million inhabitants, 80 per cent are Spanish-speaking and 81 per cent are **Catholic**. After its discovery by Columbus in 1493, the Spanish

colonised Puerto Rico, running **sugar-cane plantations** which were worked by slaves, and exploiting the mineral resources.

After the Spanish-American war in 1898, Puerto Rico was governed by the USA. In 1917, the inhabitants were granted limited US citizenship. In 1952, Puerto Rico was granted internal **autonomy**. In 1993, the population rejected both complete independence and also annexation by the USA as its 51st state. The government consists of a directly elected governor and a parliament. The inhabitants are US citizens, but have no voting rights in federal elections. Most of Puerto Rico's income is earned from tourism and from remitances sent home by those living in the US.

United States minor outlying islands in the Pacific

Baker Island

This 2.3 sq. km atoll is **uninhabited** and may only be accessed by scientists. The US Department of the Interior is responsible for its administration.

Howland Island

This 2.3 sq. km island is **uninhabited** and may only be accessed for scientific purposes. It is gov-

erned by the US Department of the Interior.

Jarvis Island

Only scientists may have access to this 7.7 sq. km uninhabited island. The US Department of the Interior is responsible for its administration.

Johnston Atoll

The north and east islands of this 2.6 sq. km atoll were a **test area for nuclear weapons** and are off limits up to the present day. The main island has a facility for disposing of chemical weapons. The islands, with their 1,200 inhabitants, are administered by the US Department of the Interior.

Kingman Reef

This eight sq. km coral reef is **uninhabited** and is administered by the US Navy.

Midway Islands

This 5.2 sq. km coral atoll has been a US possession since 1867 and a **naval base** since 1903. In 1942, The Battle of Midway, one of the most famous sea battles in the war in the Pacific, was fought here. The 435 inhabitants all serve in the US Navy, which will shortly hand over the administration of the islands to the US Department of the Interior.

Palmyra

This six sq. km atoll is **private property**, but is administered by the US Department of the Interior.

Wake Island

The three coral islands, Wake, Wilkes and Peal, have a total area

of 7.8 sq. km and about 200 inhabitants. They are administered by the **US Air Force**. The Republic of the Marshall Islands lays claim to the atoll.

United States minor outlying islands in the Caribbean

Navassa Island

This 5.2 sq. km island is **uninhabited** but serves as a base of yachtsmen and fishermen. It is administered by the US coast-guard station.

Guantanamo Bay Naval Base

The 111.9 sq. km US naval base is on Cuban territory and has become notorious as the place in which suspected terrorists have been held without trial since 2003.

A bay surrounded by 16 glaciers: the Glacier National Park in south-eastern Alaska.

The American Way of Life

American society has long been forced to fight the claim that it has no true culture of its own. Although it is often laughed off as a cliché, the 'American Way of Life' stands for one thing above all: freedom.

When asked to describe the 'American Way of Life', most people will mention a pretty house in the suburbs and a typical family unit: mom, dad, two kids, a dog and a car. Everyone will recognise this stereotype from 1950s American television shows. Although this middle-class dream no longer represents the American dream in the twenty-first century, the world has a fixed perception of American life. The friendliness and general openness of the North American people is legendary, as demonstrated by their relaxed manners and informal dress sense. Americans really believe that everyone can make their own luck, and that hard work pays off. They expect to be allowed to live freely as they would like, and in return they are prepared to spend a lot on a good education for their children and the finest medical care that money can buy. Competition and performance are fundamentals of the American way of life. High flyers in the national sports of baseball and American football are treated as heroes, and their names are commemorated in halls of fame. In a country with seemingly endless wide-open spaces, Middle America is used to living in spacious houses on large plots of land. The suburbs around the major cities began to appear in the 1940s, as car ownership became widespread. They attracted people away from the overcrowded cities with the lure of being closer to nature and having a better quality of life (and the opportunity for barbecues). Today, the suburbs consist of a sea of family houses and swimming pools, stretching all the way to the horizon, intersected and connected only by eight-lane freeways. Given the great size of the country, Americans have a particularly close relationship with their cars. Almost nobody walks, even short distances, and petrol is cheap. There's always plenty of parking in the lots of the huge supermarkets, shopping malls and fast food restaurants. Americans have a deep conviction that everything is possible, and they have not just developed their immense country and constructed dazzling cities, such

as Las Vegas rising out of the desert sand, but they also stand at the forefront of technical advances. US inventions – or rather their mass marketing – have long dominated the modern world, ranging from the light bulb, the cinema and the industrial mass production of cars to television and the internet. Many icons of American culture have now become world-wide brands, including Coca Cola, Marlboro, Levis jeans and the billion dollar Hollywood movie industry.

1 New York, the city that never sleeps. Giant billboards in Times Square light up the night. It's life lived 24-hour-a-day, seven days a week.

2 American footballers are national heroes, and are the embodiment of fighting spirit, fair play and the belief that only the best win.

3 Las Vegas, In the middle of the Nevada Desert, is an antidote to daily life for many Americans. The city attracts 40,000 visitors a day, and it is said that the casino 'Strip' is brighter at night than in the daytime.

4 Fast cars, fast food: fast-food restaurants save time on the way to a better life.

5 A well known American cliché is that of the cowboy, casually puffing away on his Marlboro cigarette. The Wild West still exists, but the lone rangers have long gone.

6 Operation Beauty: an attractive appearance is the way to success. The cult of the body is America's new religion.

7 Rock 'n' Roll means Elvis, a Cadillac and flashy clothes. This Elvis impersonator in Las Vegas makes a living from 1950s revival.

8 An innocent world in bright colours: Walt Disney's visions of a better life are another key aspect of the American Dream.

Cities of the USA

No architectural achievement has typified twentieth-century architecture as much as skyscrapers, those contemporary cathedrals, symbols of freedom, prosperity, enthusiasm and modernity.

North America is a continent of skyscrapers. The greatest challenge posed to the city fathers has been to give the skylines of their cities a distinctive appearance. Seattle's cityscape, for example, features the distinctive Space Needle. The Queen of the Skyscrapers is still New York City, of course. 'Classic' is the word that comes to mind when pondering the densely built-up southern tip of Manhattan, whose skyline was a hundred years in the making. Chicago's impressive panorama consists of numerous contemporary architectural masterpieces. Oil brought great wealth to Texas, a fact commemorated in the almost unreal skylines of Dallas and Houston, visible from afar. St. Louis glistens, its elegant Gateway Arch towering above the Mississippi River and San Francisco is captivating with its landmark Transamerica Pyramid.

Large picture: Chicago ascends to the heavens along the banks of Lake Michigan. A view of the parade of skyscrapers from the 442-m-high Sears Tower.

1 The vitality of Philadelphia is mirrored in its skyline. The Declaration of Independence was signed here in this renowned university town in 1776.

2 Chiselled office buildings typify the skyline of the financial and lifestyle metropolis of Miami. When the offices close, the city's vibrant nightlife gets going in the bars and shops of Bayside Marketplace on the harbour.

3 Los Angeles keeps growing – both vertically and horizontally. The people who live and work in L.A. spend twice as much time commuting than do residents of other major US cities.

4 Houston owes its prosperity to petroleum. Oil dollars funded the development of masterpieces of modern high-rise architecture.

5 The invasion of fortune-hunters during California's Gold Fever transformed the fishing village of San Francisco into a modern metropolis. Today, the only fever is Stock Market Fever in the city's financial district.

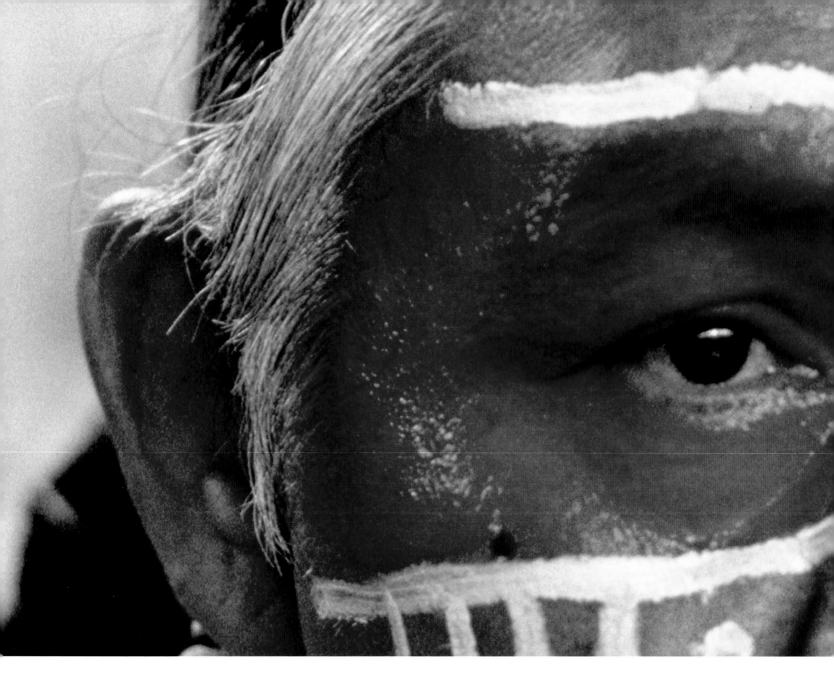

Face painting was once very prevalent among the Indians of North America – a tradition that in modern times is perpetuated mostly at powwows.

'Indian' Reservations

Today, Native Americans make up one per cent of the North American population and own a mere three per cent of their own lands, which are spread over some 270 reservations. Compared to their previous lives as hunter-gatherers and farmers, their conditions have drastically worsened due to the rule of the White Man.

The so-called 'Indians', whose name stems from an error made by Columbus after his 'discovery' of America in 1492 when he believed he had reached India, are thought to have migrated first to North and then to South America 30,000 years ago via the Bering Straits over a land bridge from Asia that existed up to 10,000 years ago. According to varying estimates, the population of the first human settlers across all of the Americas numbered between 15 and 100 million.
In 1990, the Native American population of the United States was slightly over two million, including the around 35,000 Eskimos. Approximately 600,000 In-

dians and about 30,000 Eskimos live in Canada, the numbers varying considerably due to the diversity of population registration methods. For example, some people consider themselves Indians but are not recorded in any tribal roll and are therefore not recognised as Native Americans. This is especially true of the Cherokees, a tribe to which over 300,000 people claim allegiance. Technically, the Cherokee should be the largest US American Indian tribe; but their tribal roll includes only some 70,000 members.
Current statistics concerning life expectancy, medical care, education, unemployment and living conditions attest to the fact that

Native Americans are the most disadvantaged ethnic group in the US, the country with the biggest GNP in the world and the seventh-richest industrialised nation. The living conditions of Indians residing on reservations, in particular, can be compared to conditions in third-world countries. It has been demonstrated that, in many reservations, up to 75 per cent of Native Americans live below the poverty level. In some regions, the unemployment rate is as high as 90 per cent and many are dependent on govern-

A dignified and proud Umatilla Indian attending the tribal gathering.

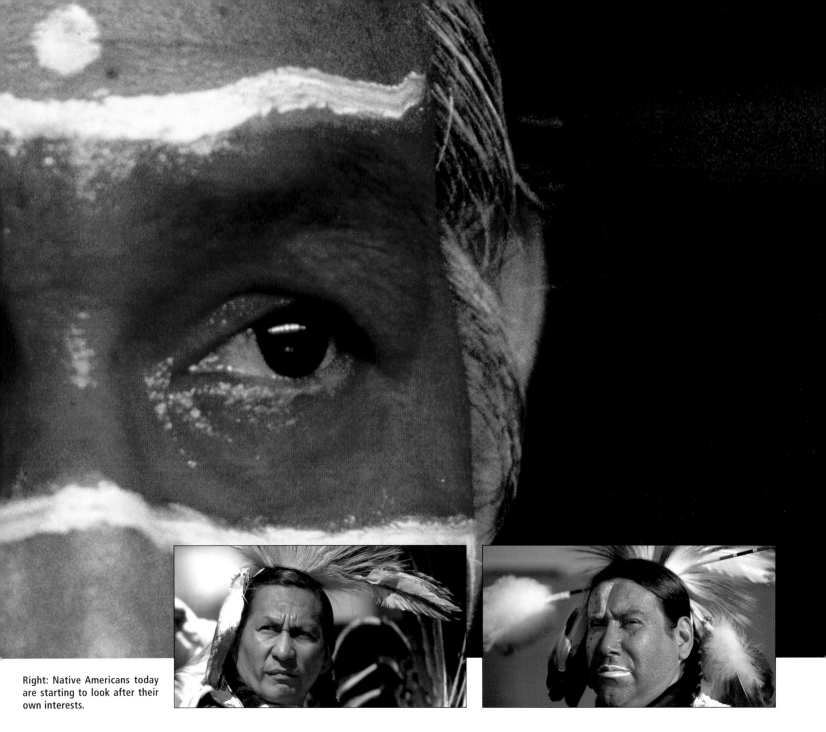

Right: Native Americans today are starting to look after their own interests.

ment assistance. As a result there is a great deal of drunkenness and other social problems. This is mostly due to the fact that there is little or no industry on reservations, and those industries that decide to use the reservations as a base cannot find another location due to the environmental pollution they cause or other risks they pose to local residents. As an example, 80 per cent of all nuclear plants are situated near reservations or are located directly on Native American lands. On some reservations, the only 'industry' is gambling. This is because certain states do not allow gambling on their territory, but the reservations are Federal land, so Native Americans derive large amount of revenue from allowing casinos to operate in the reservations. This earns revenue but is hardly conducive to social cohesion.

Despite, or perhaps because of, the inadequate social, medical and economic conditions, the original inhabitants of North America have preserved and handed down many of their traditional rituals. One example of this is powwows, which are still held annually. Originally, a powwow had social significance. Because Native Americans lived in small nomadic tribes (a way of life that also conserved their natural resources), the various tribes all met up in a large annual gathering. While the chiefs dealt with important tribal matters such as forming economic and political alliances, a myriad of feasts and ceremonies were held for the people. These habitual get-togethers were packed with traditional rites such as the sun dance, the appointing of godparents and ritual naming ceremonies.

More than ever, today's North American Indians are holding on to their traditions in order to strengthen their identities, and the powwow represents an important form of expression of Indian culture. It is a time for reunion, friendship and mutual respect, accompanied by ritualised dances and music rich in symbolism. The most important musical instrument is the drum, which forms the connection to the ancestors.

Today, there are three types of powwows. At the grand competitive powwows, the most beautiful outfits and the best dancers are awarded prizes. This form of powwow is a tourist attraction as well, and thus also a source of revenue. The spiritual powwow is

Even tribal members living in remote locations do not miss out on a powwow.

a religious forum during which various healing rituals are performed and spirits are consulted. During socio-cultural powwows, the focus is on social and cultural exchange between the various tribes. At all three types or powwow, dance is the shared, preferred Indian form of expression.

During the sun dance, a day-long cleansing dance, when the dances of pain, hunger, thirst and weariness are performed, asceticism can visions to help solve problems associated with spiritual matters. Even today, respect for nature and the spirits are at the heart of every powwow.

Mexico

Area:	1,972,550 sq. km
Capital city:	Mexico City
Form of government:	
Federal Presidential Republic	
Administrative divisions:	
5 regions; 31 federal states, 1 capital district	
Population:	
106.2 million (53 inhabitants/sq. km)	
Languages:	
Spanish (official), minority languages	
GDP per capita:	US$10, 000
Currency:	
1 Mexican peso = 100 centavos	

Natural geography

North and central Mexico are covered by the **Meseta Central**, a highland plateau with elevations of 1,300 m in the south. The substrate of the high plain is characterised by **river basins**, **mountainous ridges** and **rift valleys** and is surrounded by massive, rugged mountain ranges extending about 1,200 km towards the

Basalt formations near Durango.

coast, by the **Sierra Madre Occidental** in the west with elevations up to 3,000 m and by the equally high **Sierra Madre Oriental** in the east. The southern central highland, the **Sistema Volcánica Transversal or Cordillera Neovolcánica**, consists of a volcanic belt in which Mexico's highest mountains are situated. These are the **Citlaltépetl** (5,700 m), **Popocatépetl** (5,452 m) and the **Iztaccíhuatl** (5,286 m). The mountain ridge of the **Sierra Mixteca** links the highland with the **Sierra Madre del Sur**, a labyrinth of narrow mountain peaks and deep valleys, with summits reaching 3,000 m. The **Chiapas Highland** is connected to the **Isthmus of Tehuantepec**, the narrowest point in Mexico. Long beaches, marshes, sand banks and lagoons are typical of the Gulf coast. The lowland region reaches its widest point of 450 km at the limestone plain of the **Yucatán Peninsula**. In the north-west, the **Baja California** Peninsula, which is on average only 90 km wide, stretches over about 1,250 km, with elevations of up to 3,000 m. The most important rivers are the **Río Grande del Norte**, defining the northern border, the **Río Lerma**, which flows from its source in the Toluca high valley, feeding the **Lago de Chapala**, Mexico's largest inland lake, and emptying into the Pacific as the **Río Grande de Santiago**. In the north-eastern and Baja California deserts, the flora consists mainly of **succulents** and **cactuses**; in the southern highland steppe, there are **thorn bushes** and **agave plants**; in the evergreen tropical forest running along the coastal strip of the south-western Gulf of Mexico, there are **mangroves, bamboo, ferns** and **orchids**; the tropical rainforest in the southern Yucatán Peninsula contains **mahogany trees**, tropical **palms**, **chicle trees**, **epiphytes** and **kapok trees**.

The fauna is similarly varied. There are numerous **predators**, such as wolves, coyotes, black bears and lynxes, also **red deer and wild boars** as well as **capebaras** and various **reptiles** such as alligators, rattle snakes and iguanas and many **species of bird and insect**.

Climate

Due to the enormous expanse of land from north to south and the numerous mountains, the country has a variety of different climates. The **sub-tropical areas in** the north have **hot dry summers** and **temperate winters**, whereas the tropical **south** is hot and damp the whole year round. Central Mexico is roughly divided in terms of climate into the **Tierra caliente** (up to approximately 700 m above sea-level) with an average annual temperature of over 25°C, the Tierra templada with temperatures of 18–25°C, the Tierra fría with temperatures of 12–18°C, at the upper limit of vegetation at 4,000–4,700 m, and the Tierra helada in the perpetual snow zone. South of the central high plains, average **annual rainfall** is about 600 mm, but in many places in the north rainfall is only 250 mm. The **Baja California Peninsula** experiences similarly low levels of rainfall, whereas on average 1,000 mm falls on the Pacific coast, primarily between June and September. In the **trade winds** area on the Gulf of Mexico, rain falls evenly throughout the

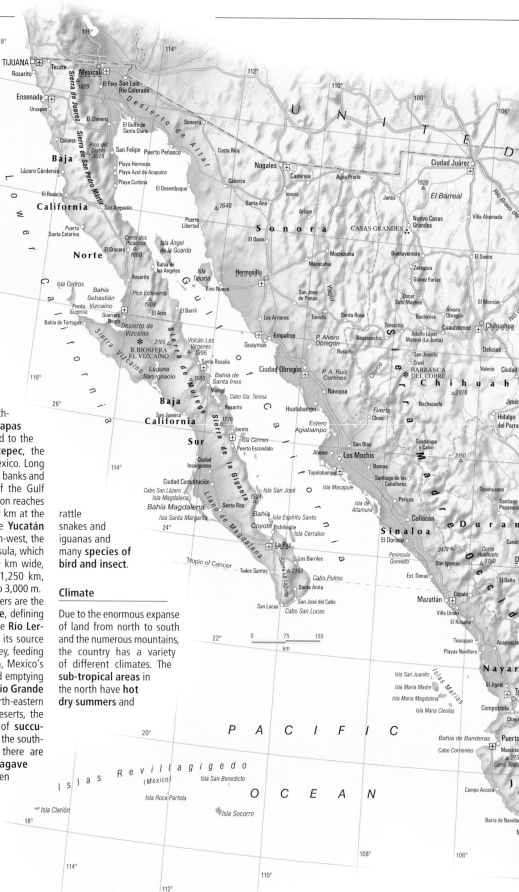

*The whole of Mexico celebrates 12 December as the day of the Virgin of **Guadalupe**. According to legend, the Virgin appeared on several occasions to the baptised Native American Juan Maria in 1531. The fervent cele-brations on this day symbolise the deep piety in Mexico, especially among the native population. The culture of Aztecs and traditional animist beliefs have been syncretised with Catholicism.*

year. This area is also within the **hurricane** belt. The highest precipitation of over 4,000 mm falls in the **Tabasco lowlands**. On the west coast, **tropical tornados** start in the **Gulf of Tehuantepec** and move northwards creating damage as far north as Southern California in the USA.

Population

Mexico's population is 60 per cent **mestiso (Spanish-Amerindian)**, 14 per cent **Amerindian** and nine per cent **white**. In addition, there are approximately **150,000 foreigners** who live permanently in the country, mostly from the United States. The urban population is 74 per cent. Average **life expectancy** is 72 years; the **illiteracy** rate is ten per cent; in-fant mortality is 2.7 per cent; **childhood mortality** at 3.2 per cent and **population growth** at around 1.6 per cent. There are on average 2.8 births per woman. **Catholics** make up 89.7 per cent of the population, **Protestants** 4.9 per cent. The rest belong to the **Jewish**, **Baha'i** and **traditional religions**.

School attendance is compulsory for children aged between six and twelve years; secondary education lasts for up to six years and is voluntary; **school enrollment quota** is more or less 100 per cent. State primary schools are free of charge.

History and Politics

There is evidence of a **hunter-gatherer culture**. dating from about 22,000 years ago. In about 3000 BC., the first permanent settlements were founded and in 1100 BC, the **Olmecs** developed the first advanced civilisation whose centre was in **La Venta** . Between 200 and 600 AD, the **Teoti-huacán** kingdom produced the first major examples of urban architecture. Their city had approximately 200,000 inhabitants. Trade and manufacturing guaranteed **relative prosperity**. The invasion of foreign peoples from the north determined Central Mexico's subsequent fate until the Spanish conquerors first made their appearance. In the twelfth century BC, the **Chicimecs** succeeded the the **Toltecs** as rulers. An advanced **Mayan** civilisation developed on the Yucatán Peninsula in 1200 BC. Between 400 BC and 300 AD, the Mayas developed a **written script** and a sophisticated **calendar system** which they were able to devise through astronomical predictions. During this period of prosperity, there were 110 religious and political centres lasted until the tenth century AD. There are varying theories concerning the decline of the Maya. The **Aztec's domination** of central Mexico began when **Tenochtitlán** was founded in 1370. In the mid-fifteenth century,

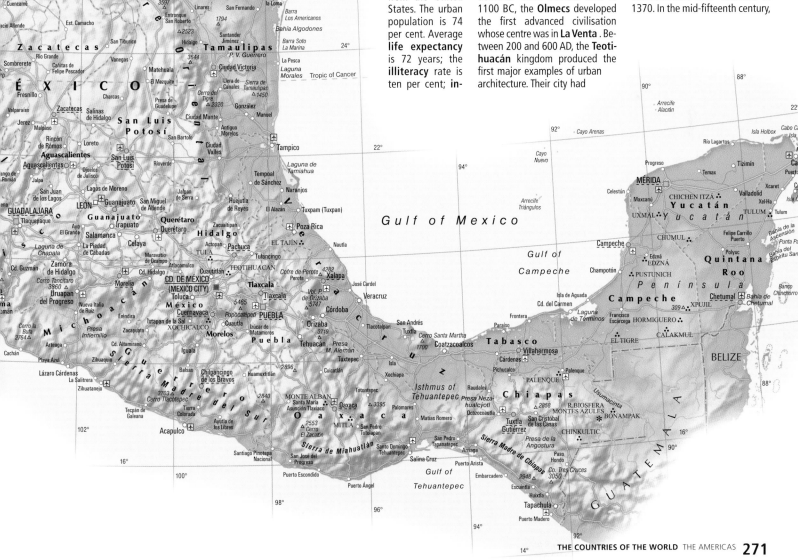

Mexico

*The cliffs of **Acapulco** rise to a height of 40 m and are rugged and magnificent. Several times a day young daredevils – the so-called 'Clavidistas' – leap from the highest rocks into La Quebrada bay. Acapulco is also famous for its night life, bars and luxury hotels. This port city in south-west Mexico was once an exclusive resort for the upper classes but it is now popular with tourists from around the world.*

King **Moctezuma I** created a territory that stretched from the Gulf to the Pacific coast. Under **Moctezuma II**, a **central administrative and legal system** was established along with a very tightly organised army. Aztec civilisation was doomed when in 1519 the Spanish explorer, **Hernán Cortez,** landed on the Gulf coast. The Spanish completely conquering the kingdom in 1547, aided by the psychological effects of **firearms** and a clever policy of alliances with **enemies of the Aztecs**. Tenochtitlán fell in 1521 and the new **capital of Mexico City** was created. In 1535, Spain appointed a viceroy to rule the colony of New Spain. More than 12 million Amerindians lost their lives in clashes with the colonists before 1570. Many of the deaths were due to **infections** and **diseases** that the Europeans brought with them. The colonial period lasted 300 years.

At the beginning of the nineteenth century, **tensions** were mounting between the Spanish motherland and the colonial population. The ideas of liberty propagated by the French Revolution and the American colonists' War of Independence coupled with brutal economic exploitation of New Spain by the Spanish crown triggered the **Mexican War of Independence** in 1810, which was led by the priests **Miguel Hidalgo** and **José Maria Morelos. Augustín de Itúrbide**, who was crowned emperor of Mexico in 1822, renounced Spain, but was deposed two years later. The new republic was marked by extreme political and economic instability. The government changed 34 times before **Antonio López de Santa Anna** became the dictator in 1854.

The **USA** attacked the country in 1846-1847 due to unpaid debts and occupied half of the country under the Peace Treaty of Guadalupe Hidalgo. The **constitutional reform** implemented by **Benito Juárez**, Minister for Justice and later President, also failed to stabilise the political situation. In 1861, Mexico was occupied by **British**, **French** and **Spanish** troops. In 1864, the French appointed **Maximilian von Hapsburg** as emperor of Mexico. As **Napoleon III** of France withdrew, his troops under pressure from the USA, Juárez seized power and had Maximilian executed in 1867. Although the dictatorship of Porfirio Díaz managed to put the economy back on its feet in the 35 years preceding 1911, he did not manage to end social tensions. The **Mexican revolution** began in 1910, led by **Pancho Villa** and **Emiliano Zapata**, and this led to the fall of Díaz in 1911.

After the civil war ended in 1920, the socialist maxims of the 1917 constitution caused owners of large land holdings to be dispossessed and mineral resources were placed under state control. In 1938, President **Lázaro Cárdenas** nationalised the oil industry and the railways. After World War II, there was a modest economic upturn, but this ended abruptly in 1982. From then on, the **Partido Revolucionario Institucional (PRI)**, which had ruled continually since 1929, gradually lost its position of power. In 1997, the PRI lost its absolute majority in Parliament and the mayor's post in Mexico City for the first time. There was a severe **economic crisis** in 1994 following the privatisation of the banks and entry into the NAFTA free trade zone.

Serious internal political concerns remain unsolved, such as: **corruption**, **nepotism**, **politically motivated homicides**, a powerful **drug mafia** and the armed struggle of the **Zapatista Army of National Liberation**, which fights for equal opportunities for the Amerindian population in the state of Chiapas.

Mexico is a **federal presidential republic** under a constitution, which has been altered several times since 1917. The 31 states (Estados) and the capital city's

Mexico city: the 'floating gardens' of Xochimilco.

On the Yucatán peninsula vendors sell tropical fruits.

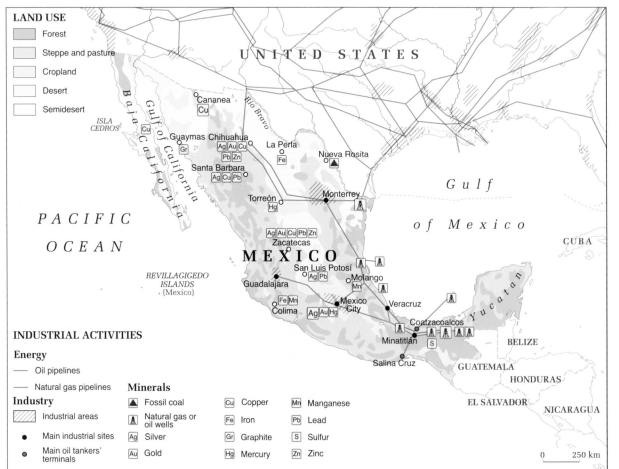

LAND USE

- Forest
- Steppe and pasture
- Cropland
- Desert
- Semidesert

INDUSTRIAL ACTIVITIES

Energy

— Oil pipelines

— Natural gas pipelines

Industry

- ▨ Industrial areas
- • Main industrial sites
- ◉ Main oil tankers' terminals

Minerals

- ▲ Fossil coal
- ⬛ Natural gas or oil wells
- Ag Silver
- Au Gold
- Cu Copper
- Fe Iron
- Gr Graphite
- Hg Mercury
- Mn Manganese
- Pb Lead
- S Sulfur
- Zn Zinc

0   250 km

*A Mexican woman making a tortilla in a special pan. The popular tortillas or tacos are eaten with spicy food in **Oaxaca**. Beans and sweetcorn are staple foods in Mexico. Cornmeal mush and thick soups as well as bread are made from slaked corn dough, known as masa harina. Cooking and raising children are women's work and in the countryside this strict Catholic division of roles has been preserved to this day.*

Federal District (Distrito Federal) have their own constitution and enjoy a relatively high degree of autonomy. The **President** is head of the government and commander-in-chief of the armed forces. He is elected directly for a six-year term. Citizens are **entitled to vote** from the age of 18. The **bicameral system** consists of a **House of Representatives** and a **Senate**. The Cámera Federal de Diputados has 500 members, of whom 300 are directly elected for a three-year term. The 128 senators are elected for six years.

Economy

In 2005, **GDP** was US$693 billion, to which **agriculture** contributed six per cent, **industry** 26 per cent and the **services sector** 68 per cent. **Unemployment** stood at only two per cent and the **rate of inflation** 6.4 per cent. Mexico's **foreign debt** amounts to US$158.3 billion. About a quarter of the labour force is employed in agriculture. The main crops are **maize**, **sugar cane**, **vegetables**, **coffee**, **cotton** and **cereals**. Further important contributors are **cattle-breeding**, **fishing** and the **timber and paper industries**. Industry employs 22 per cent of the labour force. **Cars**, **textiles**, **electronics** and **chemicals** are produced. **Petroleum**, **natural gas**, **zinc**, **salt**, **copper**, **uranium**, **manganese**, **gold** and **silver** are also significant economic contributors. The tourism sector earned US$4.647 billion. The balance of trade is even. Manufactured goods are exported, of which the major components are 21 per cent **electrical devices**, 18 per cent **motor vehicles** and **parts**, 12 per cent **machinery**, ten per cent **oil** and four per cent **chemicals**. The major **imports** are 51 per cent **machinery** and **vehicles**, 16 per cent **chemicals**, eight per cent **iron** and **steel** and four per cent **paper** and **printing products**. The USA is the major trade partner for both imports and exports. Pollution is becoming a serious problem in Mexico, due to the massive output of fumes from 130,000 factories and 2.5 million motor vehicles. The official laxity in this respect, in order to encourage foreign investment is likely to cause serious problems for the future and is certainly a deterrent to tourism. There have been two recent serious accidents caused by gas explosions, one in 1984 in Mexico City and the other in 1992 in Guadalajara. Despite public outrage, little has been done to prevent future disasters.

Transport

Although the **transport network** has been expanded in recent times, some mountainous areas are still barely accessible. **Air transport** therefore plays an important role in travel. There are 33 national and 55 international airports, the largest of them in Mexico City. The **road network** is 249,520 km long, of which 5,920 km are motorways or toll roads and 45,600 km federal highways. The remaining roads are only partly paved; the proportion of surfaced roads is around 37 per cent. The almost 21,000 km long **rail network** handles passenger and freight traffic. The 49 **seaports** on the Pacific and Caribbean coasts handle 85 per cent of exports.

Tourism

In 1996, there were 21.4 million foreign visitors to the beaches of **Acapulco**, **Puerto Vallarta** and the resorts of Cancún and the relics of pre-Columbian civilisation. Mexico City, built on a dried up crater lake, is the cultural centre of the country and has world-famous archaeological and art museums. Other notable buildings include the sixteenth-century cathedral and the Ministry of Education building which has murals by Mexico's most famous artist, Diego Rivera. Other cities that have interesting colonial architecture are Guadalajara and Monterrey. Due to its geographical location, Mexico City suffers from bad air pollution and traffic jams. The ideal **time to travel** to Mexico is between November and March when the weather is cooler.

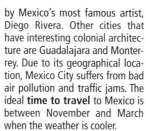

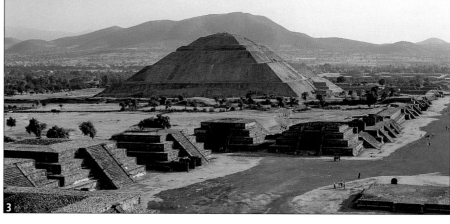

1 The Pico de Orizaba National Park is situated between Vera Cruz and Pueblais around the Pico de Orizaba mountain peak (5,700 m).

2 Mexico City: The Zócalo in the centre of the capital is the site of the oldest cathedral in Latin America. Although it is 250 years old, it blends in well with the modern surroundings.

3 The 'street of the dead' and the sun pyramid. Teotihuacán was once a huge city but the founders remain unknown.

Guatemala, Belize

Honduras: The ruined city of Copán was only excavated in the nineteenth century. It is the biggest Maya city discovered so far. The number of inhabitants has been estimated by experts at about 200,000, for whom Copán served as a ceremonial centre. Large stone figures from different eras fill the temple. The 'hieroglyphic stairs' are impressive, containing the longest known Maya text.

 Guatemala

Area:	108,889 sq. km
Capital city:	Guatemala City

Form of government:
Presidential Republic

Administrative divisions:
22 departments

Population:
14.6m (127 inhabitants/sq. km)

Languages:
Spanish (official), Mayan-languages

GDP per inhabitant: US$4,300

Currency:
1 quetzal = 100 centavos

Natural geography

The **Petén lowlands** in the north form part of the **Yucatán Peninsula**. The fertile Pacific coastline is up to 50 km wide. The **Cuchumatanes Mountains** and **Madre Mountains** are in the south. Of the 30 semi-active volcanoes, **Tajumulco volcano** at 4,220 m is the highest.

Climate

The lowlands have a **warm, humid climate** throughout the year, with average temperatures ranging between 25°C and 30°C. At altitudes between 600 m and 1500 m, the average temperature is 18°C, and at altitudes above 1,500 m it is 12°C. The **rainy season** lasts from May to October. Rainfall depends on the northeast trade wind. In the Caribbean lowlands and on the Pacific coast, precipitation is between 1,000 and 2,000 mm; in the mountains, it is up to 1,000 mm and in the plains and valleys, 6,000 mm. The north and the Caribbean lowlands are covered with evergreen rain forests, which become tropical mountain forests, pinewoods, oak wood and mixed forest at higher elevations. On the Pacific Coast, there are dry forests and the Petén Lowlands are covered in savannah with pine scrub. Among the rich variety of fauna, there are pumas, manatee, jaguars, crocodiles, monkeys, tapirs and many types of birds.

Population

60 per cent of the population is **Amerindians**; 30 per cent is mestizo; **blacks**, **zambo** and **whites** constitute the remaining ten per cent. In addition to 80 per cent **Catholics** and 19 per cent **Protestants** there is a minority of **Bahai**. The average life expectancy is 66 years. The **literacy rate** is 44 per cent. 39 per cent of Guatemalans live in overcrowded city districts and over half live below the poverty line.

History and politics

When **Pedro de Alvarado** conquered the country in 1524 for the Spanish Crown, the **Mayan** civilisation had been in decline for 600 years. In 1543, Guatemala became governed by the **Viceroy of New Spain**. After the withdrawal of the Spanish in 1821, the country came under Mexican administration and from 1823 until 1838, it was part of the **Central American Federation**. Guatemala became independent in 1847, and has since been ruled by a succession of dictators. Since the early twentieth century, most have been puppets of the powerful **United Fruit Company**. In 1944, a popular uprising, leading to a general election and democratic rule started what is known as 'The Ten Years of Spring', a period of free speech, political activity and proposed land reform under President Juan José Arévalo. In 1951, left-wing President **Arbenz Guzmán** initiated further reforms. All this ended in 1954 with the help of the CIA. Gen. Ydígoras Fuentes seized power in 1958 following the murder of Col. Castillo Armas. Left-wing guerrillas fought the government and the military, countered by extreme right-wing 'death squads'. The **civil war** lasted 36 years until the 1996 Peace Agreement with the loss of 200,000 lives. Guatemala is now a democratic presidential republic with a parliament elected every four years and a directly elected president. The voting age is 18.

Economy

In 2005, GDP was US$26,9 billion, of which 24 per cent derived from **agriculture**, 20 per cent from **industry** and 56 per cent from the **services sector**. Machinery, vehicles, consumer goods

The Mask Temples of Tikal in Northern Guatemala.

and raw materials are imported, coffee, sugar, bananas, cotton and timber are exported.

Transport

Guatemala has a 17,000-km-long **road network** and two **international airports**.

Tourism

Despite high levels of crime, in 2002, income from tourism amounted to almost US$500 million. Sites of special interest are Guatemala City, the Mayan centre of worship at **Tikal**, the colonial architecture of Antigua and Quetzaltenango and the national parks.

 Belize

Area:	22,965 sq. km
Capital city:	Belmopan

Form of government:
Constitutional Monarchy within the Commonwealth

Administrative divisions:
6 districts

Population:
279,000 (11 inhabitants/sq. km)

Languages:
English (official), Creole-English, Spanish, minority languages

GDP per inhabitant: US$6,800

Currency:
1 Belize dollar = 100 cents

Natural geography

The green, flat hills in the northwest, change into humid, marshy coastal lowlands towards the Caribbean coast. A coral reef 250 km long parallel to the coast is divided into many **coral** atolls. At 1,122 m, Victoria Peak is the highest of the **Mayan Mountains**.

Climate

A **tropical humid climate** predominates. The average rainfall is 1,400 mm in the north and west, 2,500 mm on the slopes and up to 4,000 mm in the high altitudes. The average temperature is 26°C, while in the in the mountainous regions it is 24°C. The country is frequently afflicted by devastating **cyclones**. Almost half of Belize is covered with deciduous or evergreen **forests**. Belize also has **palm savannahs** and there are **mangrove swamps** on the coast. Jaguars, armadillos, tapirs and snakes, live in the forests and crocodiles and alligators live in the fresh and salt waters.

Population

The population of Belize consists of 43.6 per cent **mestizo**, 29.8 per cent **Creole**, 11 per cent **Amerindian** and 6.6 per cent **Garifuna**. 58 per cent of the population are Catholic and 28 per cent **Protestant**, there are also **Muslims**, **Hindus**, **Jews** and **Bahai**. Life expectancy is 75 years, only seven per cent of the population is illiterate.

History and politics

Before **Columbus** discovered Belize in the early sixteenth century and Cortez turned it into a Spanish colony in 1524 and 1525, it was at the heart of the Mayan civilisation.

Around the mid-seventeenth century, **British pirates** came to Belize followed by settlers. In the subsequent period, the Spaniards and the British fought over the area. After the Spaniards were expelled from Central America in 1821, **Guatemala** imposed a turf war, whose effects are felt even today. In 1862, the colony of **British Honduras** was founded which became a Crown Colony in 1871. It was renamed **Belize** in 1973 and in 1981, it was granted **independence**. The British monarch, as head of state, is represented by a governor-general. The 1981 Constitution provides for a **bicameral parliament**. The congressmen are elected every five years, and senators are appointed every eight years by the governor-general. The voting age is 18 years.

Economy

In 2005, GDP was just under US$908m, of which 20 per cent derived from **agriculture**, 23 per cent from **industry** and 57 per cent from the **services sector**. Machinery, consumer goods and raw materials are imported. Exports include timber, sugar, citrus fruits, bananas, fruit juices and fish and shellfish.

Transport

Around 1,600 km of the 2,000 km **road network** is passable throughout the year. Stanley Field is the major **airport**; the largest **sea ports** are at Belize City and Stann Creek.

Tourism

In 2002 over 250,000 tourists visited the ancient Mayan ruins, the coral atolls and the 17 national parks with their rich wildlife. The best time to travel is from November to April.

Guatemala: In Chichicastenango old Mayan and Catholic myths have been syncretised into a unique mixture. The city was founded on the ruins of a Mayan place of worship. Once a year, thousands of Guatemalans come here to celebrate Santo Tomás Day.

and eight per cent **Protestant**. Life expectancy is 69 years; the **illiteracy rate** is 29 per cent despite compulsory schooling.

owners were the de facto rulers of El Salvador until a **rebellion of agricultural workers** took 30,000 lives in 1932. M**ilitary juntas** succeeded each other until 1967 and the economic and social situation became more and more disastrous as a result. Following an elimination match for the World Cup finals in 1969, the **'Football War'** broke out against Honduras, which dragged on until 1980. A long brutal **civil war** cost around 75,000 lives and lasted officially until 1992. Even after the peace treaty, the situation remained critical: **corruption** and **mismanagement** predominate. Under the 1983 constitution , parliament is elected every three years and the head of state is elected directly every five years. The **voting age** is 18.

is a large **foreign trade deficit**. Machinery, motorised vehicles, oil, food and timber are imported; coffee, cotton, textiles, sugar and other agricultural products are among the **exports**.

Transport

Around 10,000 km of the 13,000 km **road network** is passable all year round. Cuscatlán has the only international **airport**.

Tourism

The ruins of Tazumal and other Mayan cities and places of worship and the volcanos are the major attractions. Tourism has resumed now that the civil war has ended and it is safe to visit the country. The best time to travel is between November and February.

Natural geography

Behind the narrow Pacific coastline, a **mountain chain** joins the **volcanoes**, some of which are around 2,000 m high and still active. The capital city, San Salvador, and **Lake Ilopango**, which is 250 m deep, lie in a depression. In the north, there is a plateau 400 to 1,000 m high; in the north-west, the 2,418-m-high Montecristo peak is part of the **El Pital mountain** range.

Climate

In the **tropical humid and dry climates**, the average temperature is 25°C. During the rainy season, precipitation in the central highlands and on the coast is between 1,500 and 2,000 mm and in the mountains, up to 2,500 mm. In most places, the tropical and savannah vegetation and mangrove swamps have been cleared for agriculture. As a result, the fauna has become depleted though there are many species of birds.

Population

The inhabitants consist of 89 per cent **mestizo**, ten per cent **Amerindian** and one per cent **white**. 92 per cent are **Catholics**

History and politics

El Salvador, conquered in 1526 by **Pedro de Alvarado** for Spain, remained part of the Kingdom of Guatemala (Also known as the Captaincy General of Guatemala) until 1821. After the Spanish defeat, the country fell first to **Mexico**, then from 1823 to 1839 it was part of the **Central American Federation**. In 1859, El Salvador became an independent **republic**. The plantation

Economy

In 2005, GDP was US$16,5 bilion of which, 12 per cent derived from **agriculture**, 24 per cent from **industry** and 64 per cent from the **services sector**. Unemployment is at 50 per cent. There

*The Indians of **Guatemala** are the descendants of Mayas. The legacy can still be found in the folklore art as well as on the many markets, not just for the tourists. Many Mayan women are masters at the art of weaving. The colourful textiles, skillfully combining creativity with tradition, are produced on a hand-loom.*

Natural geography

The land mass stretches from the **Gulf of Honduras** on the Caribbean to the **Gulf of Fonseca** on the Pacific and consists of several mountain ranges of volcanic origin rising to up to 2,500 m. The Pacific coast is only 70 km long and very narrow. The Caribbean coast is characterised by estuaries, lagoons and marshes. The **Bahía Islands** and **Swan Islands** belong to the national territory.

Climate

On the side of the country facing the Pacific Ocean, a **dry, tropical climate** prevails in winter; the average temperature is 28°C; the

Ernesto Cardenal

*Granada 20.1.1925

The poet and Catholic priest was an early opponent of the Somoza dictatorship. He was unfrocked in 1985 for his liberation theory and his participation in the Sandinista government in which he served as Minister of Culture (1979–1987). In this capacity, he devoted himself to fighting illiteracy. He received a Peace Prize from the German Publishers Association for his social commitment and his literary work in 1980.

average rainfall in the highlands is 1,000–2,000 mm. In the **permanently humid Caribbean lowlands** average temperatures of 25°C predominate.
The rainfall diminishes from north to the south. On the north coast, there are **cyclones** in the summer. The Caribbean lowlands are covered by **rainforest** up to a height of 1,500 m. The inland high plateau is covered with **dry savannah, pinewoods** and **mountain forests**. In the sheltered valleys, scrub and thorn savannahs dominate. The pacific plains are covered in **forest** while the coastline is covered in mangrove swamps. Bears, leopards, panthers and pumas road the tropical

rainforests which also have plenty of reptiles and insects.

Population

Of the population, 89.9 per cent of Hondurans are **mestizos,** 6.7 per cent **Amerindians,** 2.1 per cent **blacks** and 1.3 per cent whites. 90 per cent profess Roman Catholicism. The rest are Anglican, Baptist and Bahai. Life expectancy is 70 years; the illiteracy rate is 27 per cent. 40 per cent of Hondurans are concentrated in the overcrowded cities; 80 per cent live below the poverty line.

History and politics

When Columbus landed in the area which is today's Honduras

Belize: The 'Blue hole' in lighthouse riff.

in 1502, the ancient Mayan culture had already declined to a large extent. Spanish rule ended in 1821; in 1823, Honduras became a part of the Central American Federation and in 1838 it gained its independence. It has a history of **military juntas,** with brief intervening periods of democracy. The true **rulers,** however, are to be found in the **USA.** The National Fruit Company ruled this **'banana republic'** in the back yard of the United States for centuries. In 1983, Honduras allowed the US backed right-wing **Nicaraguan contras** to operate land and sea military bases from which to attack Nicaragua. This unpopular policy

provoked a coup by junior officers. Today, the country is officially a democratic presidential republic. Parliament and President are elected directly every four years. The voting age is 18. The power of the **military** is considerable, although it has been restricted in recent years. Political assassinations are not uncommon.

Economy

In 2005, GDP was US$7.8 billions, of which 21 per cent derived from **agriculture,** 33 per cent from **industry** and 46 per cent from the **services sector.** Consumer goods, raw materials and textiles are imported, coffee, bananas and shellfish are exported as well

as valuable tropical timber such as rosewood and mahogany.

Transport

Only one tenth of the total 18,000-km-long **road network** is paved. The major long-distance connection is the legendary **Pan-American Highway** that runs the length of the continent. There are three international **airports** and several national **airports.**

Tourism

In 1995, 238,000 tourists contributed US$33 million in foreign currency. The best-known tourist

destinations are the **Caribbean beaches** and relics of the Mayan culture, especially the **Copán ruins.** The best time to travel to Honduras is from December until May.

▲ Nicaragua	
Area:	129,494 sq. km
Capital city:	Managua
Form of government: Presidential Republic	
Administrative divisions: 16 departments	
Population: 5.4m (42 inhabitants/sq. km)	
Languages: Spanish (official), Chibcha	
GDP per inhabitant:	US$2,800
Currency: 1 gold cordoba = 100 centavos	

Natural geography

Nicaragua is the largest country in central America and the most thinly populated. The **Cordillera mountain range** that includes the 2,107-m-high **Pico Mogotón** are in the north. The Caribbean lowlands contain many lagoons and marshes and are sparsely populated. In the east, they are up to 80 km wide. Many **sandbanks, islands** and **coral reefs** run parallel to the 480-km-long Caribbean coast. Lake Nicaragua, which has an area of 8,263 sq. km, and the smaller **Lake Managua** are in the Nicaragua Depression. A mountain range up to 1,800 m high containing active volcanoes runs parallel to the 346-km-long Pacific coast. Earthquakes and volcanic activity are a constant threat throughout the country.

Climate

The **tropical-humid** climate is only temperate on the Caribbean coast and in the mountainous regions. The temperatures fluctuate on average between 24°C and 28°C in the lowlands and between 17°C and 22°C in the mountainous regions. In the east, the average rainfall is 2,500–6,000 mm, in the west it is up to 2,000 mm and in the Nicaraguan Depression it is only 1,000 mm.

The **rainforest** of the Caribbean lowlands contains valuable tropical timber. In the north, there are vast pinewoods; on the Caribbean coast known as the Mosquito Coast, there are mangrove swamps and palms, while the Nicaraguan Depression contains the remains of a dry forest. **Coniferous mountain forest** begins at an altitude of 600 m; this turns into mixed woodland at an altitude of 800 m. The rich variety of **fauna** includes jaguars, pumas, monkeys, alligators, turtles, snakes and many species of birds.

Population

69 per cent of Nicaragua's population are **mestizo,** 14 per cent **whites,** nine per cent **blacks** and four per cent **Amerindians, mulattos** and **zambo.**
89 per cent of the population is **Catholic,** five per cent **Protestant** and there are also followers of different natural religions. The life expectancy is 68 years; there is 34 per cent illiteracy. 63 per cent of Nicaraguans live in the cities and 44 per cent live below the poverty line.

History and politics

In 1502, Columbus landed on the east coast of today's Nicaragua. In 1524, **Francisco de Hernández** conquered the country for the Spanish Crown. The **independence movement,** which started in 1811, expelled the Spaniards from Nicaragua in 1821. From 1823 until 1838 the country was a part of the Central American Federation. Interests of the **United Fruit Company** as well as a planned **canal** to link the two oceans placed Nicaragua increasingly in the US sphere of influence. From 1912 until 1937, the country was occupied by US troops. **Augusto Sandino** led the liberation movement that arose from the occupation. **Sandino** was murdered in 1934 by **Anastasio Somoza.** The **Somoza clan,** whose members largely acted in US interests, then ruled until 1979, exerting brutal dictatorial power. After the fall of the Somoza regime, the opposition, left-wing Sandinistas gained power under president **Daniel Ortega.** He implemented land reform and reformed the healthcare and education systems.

*Around 300 islands are scattered in the Central America's largest lake, **Lake Nicaragua**, 148 km long and 55 km wide. The Isla de Ometepe is the largest island. On the Isla de Solentiname, Ernesto Cardenal founded an artists' colony around the church.*

Democratic rights did not help the left wing junta on the road to success, due to the existence of the US-backed **contras**, a right-wing militia representing the vested interests of Nicaragua's landowners.

After a long, bloody civil war, there was an **armistice** in 1998. In 1990, free elections were held for the first time, from which the centre-right opposition emerged victorious. Under the 1987 constitution, last modified in 1995, the National Assembly is elected every five years. The period of office of the directly elected president is also five years. The **voting age is** 16 years.

Economy

In 2005, GDP was US$5,0 billions, of which 35 per cent came from **agriculture**, 21 per cent from **industry** and 44 per cent from the **services sector**.

There is a serious **foreign trade deficit**. Industrial products, consumer goods and oil are imported. Exports are mainly timber, coffee, fish and shellfish, meat, sugar and bananas.

Transport

The 15,000-km-long road network is only well-developed in the west. The 384-km-long section of the **Pan-American Highway** as well as the only east–west road linking **Matagalpa** with **Puerto Cabezas** represent the most important highways. There is a 344-km-long railway network, as well as an international **airport** in Managua.

Tourism

Tourism is starting up again now that the fighting has ended. The Mosquito Coast, where many of the locals speak English, is popular. The best time to travel is between December and February.

Costa Rica

Area: 51,100 sq. km
Capital city: San José
Form of government:
Presidential Republic
Administrative divisions:

7 provinces

Population:
4m (74 inhabitants/sq. km)
Languages:
Spanish (official), English, Creole
GDP per inhabitant: US$10,000
Currency:
1 Costa Rica colon = 100 centimos

Natural geography

In the north, the **Cordillera de Guanacaste** which reaches heights of 2,000 m, extends in a southerly direction. The **Cordillera Central**, which reaches heights of 3,000 m, adjoins the eastern side of the **Cordillera de**

Guanacaste. The **Central Valley** runs east-west in the centre of the country. South of the valley, the Cordillera's highest peak is the **Cerro Chirripó** (3,820 m). The Caribbean lowlands are characterised by a **coastline that contains many lagoons**. The mountains are volcanic and there is consequently frequent volcanic activity and earthquakes.

Climate

While the Atlantic coast has a **tropical climate** with an even temperature and rainfall of 3,000 to 4,000 mm, the **wet-dry Pacific coast** has only 2,000 to 2,500 mm of precipitation annually. In the Central Valley, the rainfall is under 2,000 mm and the average temperature is 20°C. The average annual temperature in the lowlands is 26°C, and at altitudes above 3,000 m it is on average less than 10°C. Most of the country is covered with **tropical rainforest** and in the mountain

regions there are **evergreen forests**. In the lagoons, there are mangrove swamps. The hinterland contains cabbage-palm swamps and on the Nicoya and Osa peninsula there are dry forests and savannahs. Tapirs, jaguars, pumas and monkeys are among the rich variety of **fauna**.

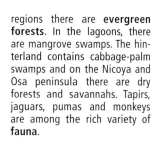

1 The impressive ruins of the Mayan city of Xunan stand on a mound overlooking the jungle in Belize. The temple city is one of the country's main attractions.

2 An important local market in Chichicastenango, northern Guatemala.

3 Guatemala: Antigua lies at the foot of three volcanos, including the Agua (3,766 m). The city has been destroyed several times in earthquakes.

4 Las Isletas: the beauty of the archipelago in Lake Nicaragua lake is deceptive, as the lake is highly polluted.

Costa Rica, Panama

Costa Rica: *This small country has several active volcanos in a chain running from north to south. The Volcan Poás National Park surrounds the active volcano of that name which is 2,700 m high. The park contains a wealth of flora and fauna. The volcano is still active, belching steam and gas from its twin crater lakes.*

Population

87 per cent of Costa Ricans are **white**, seven per cent **mestizo**, three per cent **black** and **mulatto**, two per cent **Asian** and one per cent **Native Americans**. 89 per cent of the population are Catholics, eight per cent Protestants and a minority are Bahai and Jewish. The life expectancy is 77 years and there is five per cent **literacy**. Half of the Costa Ricans live in the cities; there is **compulsory education**.

History and politics

The area was discovered by Columbus in 1502, and in 1520 it was seized by the Spanish Crown, finally becoming part of the **Kingdom of Guatemala** (also known as the Captaincy General of Guatemala). In 1821, the country separated from Spain and from 1823–29 it was part of the **Central America Federation**. After political and economic turbulence, the situation stabilised in the early twentieth century. Since 1889, the country has been a **republic**; the current constitution came into war after a brief civil war in 1949.

Costa Rica maintains no standing army and the country is regarded as **the most stable state** in the region. The civil war in Nicaragua however, had an adverse effect on northern Costa Rica. **Parliament** and the president are elected directly every four years.

Economy

The country is one of the wealthiest in **Latin America**. In 2004, the GDP was US$19.4 billion of which 15 per cent derived from **agriculture**, 24 per cent from **industry** and 61 per cent from the **services sector**. Raw materials, fuel and consumer goods are imported; exports include bananas, coffee, fish and shellfish, machinery, timber and tropical fruits.

Transport

Around 3,500 km of the 29,000 km **road network** is paved, however, only the central highlands are well developed in terms of infrastructure. The Juan Santamaria international **airport** is one of two airports in San José and there is a network of domestic airports.

Tourism

Tourism contributes considerably to the **economy**. Income from tourism represented US$1.3 bn in 2002. The Caribbean coast has long **sandy beaches**. The best time to travel is the between December and April.

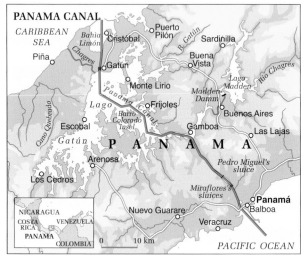

Costa Rica: the Fortuna volcano looms over green hills

Panama	
Area:	78,200 sq. km
Capital city:	Panama-City
Form of government:	
Presidential Republic	
Administrative divisions:	
9 provinces, Panama Canal Zone	
Population:	
3 million (39 inhabitants/sq. km)	
Languages:	
Spanish (official), English	
GDP per inhabitant:	US$7,300
Currency:	
1 balboa = 100 centesimos	

Natural geography

In the west, the volcanic mountain range of the **Serrenía de Tabasará** includes the 3,478 m high **Chiriquí Mountain**, close to the border with Costa Rica. In the east, there are several smaller mountain ranges reaching heights of up to 1,000 m. The

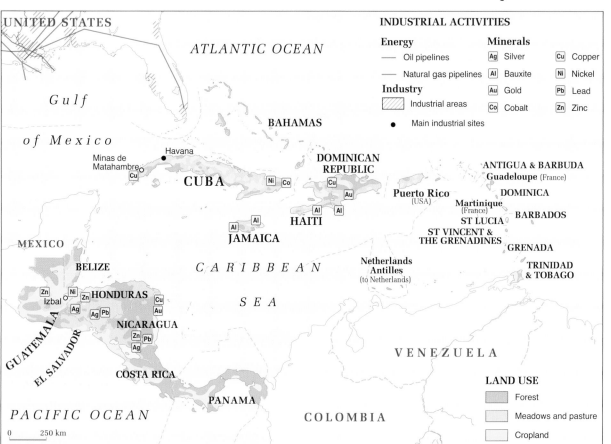

INDUSTRIAL ACTIVITIES

Energy
— Oil pipelines
— Natural gas pipelines

Industry
▨ Industrial areas
● Main industrial sites

Minerals
Ag Silver
Al Bauxite
Au Gold
Co Cobalt

Cu Copper
Ni Nickel
Pb Lead
Zn Zinc

LAND USE
Forest
Meadows and pasture
Cropland

*Bananas are one of **Costa Rica's** major exports. Most of the plantations are situated on the Caribbean coast in the east of the country. Around six per cent of export income derives from bananas and coffee, which are sent mainly to the USA. Thanks to its stable political conditions Costa Rica has become a role model for governance in Central America. There is a good education and welfare system and the economy is booming.*

open **Darien Lowlands**, which extend to the Caribbean Coast, are at the foot of these slopes. The isthmus of Panama at 46 km at its narrowest point between the Atlantic and Pacific oceans.

Climate

The **tropical climate** has constantly high temperatures and extremely high humidity. The average annual temperature is 27°C, in the mountain regions it is 20°C. The average annual rainfall is up to 4,500 mm on the Caribbean coast up to 2,000 mm on the Pacific Coast.

Evergreen **tropical rainforest** is found on the Caribbean Coast as well as on the Darien Lowlands. Cloud forest predominates at altitudes above 2,500 m. Savannahs and dry forests cover the lowlands on the Pacific cost, while the **Gulf of Panama** is covered in mangrove swamps. The fauna contains many species of birds, as well as crocodiles, alligators, pumas, ocelots, monkeys, jaguars and tapirs.

Population

65 per cent of Panama's population are **mestizo**, 13 per cent are **black** and **mulatto**, ten per cent are **Creole**, 8.3 per cent are **Indian** and two per cent are **Asian**. 96 per cent of the population are Roman Catholics, the remainder being Protestants, Muslims and Jews. Life expectancy is 74 years, there is nine per cent **illiteracy**. 65 per cent of the Panamanians live in cities.

History and politics

After Panama's discovery by Columbus, **Vasco Núñez de Balboa** reached the Pacific Ocean by land in 1513. From 1542, Panama belonged to the **Viceroyalty of Peru**. After the 1821 war of liberation, it became a part of Greater Colombia and in 1903 it became a sovereign republic. Panama's **Independence** was supported by the United States. In this way, the US secured access to the **Panama Canal** which opened in 1914. Although the 16-km-wide Canal Zone was returned to Panama in 2000, the USA retains a **right of intervention**.

The period of constantly changing **military regimes** ended in 1990 through US intervention and the arrest of the dictator **Noriega**. The country's main problems are its failing economy and corruption in all areas of public life. In 2002, President Mireya Moscoso, one of the world's few women heads of states, asked for assistance from United Nations support in the country's fight against corruption.

A presidential republic was created under the 1994 constitution. Parliament and the president are each elected for five-year terms. The voting age is 18.

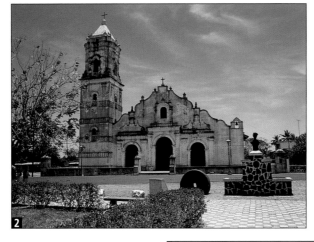

Economy

In 2001, GDP was US$9.5 billion, of which eight per cent came from **agriculture**, 19 per cent from **industry** and 73 per cent from the **services sector**. The main **imports** are oil, capital goods and food; bananas, shellfish and coffee are exported. The most important economic factors by far are income from canal transport and the flag of convenience that makes Panama the owner of one of the **world's largest merchant fleets**, most of it foreign-owned. The Smithsonian Tropical Research Institute is located here.

Transport

One third of the 8,900 km **road network** is paved. The main transport artery is the Panama Canal. The Canal Zone has the most fully developed infrastructure of the country. The international **airport** of Tocumen is east of Panama City.

Tourism

In 2002, more than half a million tourists visited Panama and spent US$626 million. These were mainly **tourists on cruise ships**. The **Milaflores locks** are an amazing sight. The best time to travel is from December until April when the weather is cooler.

1 Costa Rica: The Valle Central near Cartago is dominated by the Irazú volcano (3,432 m), that has been dormant for the last 30 years.

2 In the interior of Panama there are many examples of colonial architecture such as this baroque church in Ocú.

3 Cartago in central Costa Rica is an important pilgrimage site: the basilica contains the shrine of the patron saint of Costa Rica.

4 Ocean-going ships passing through the Panama canal: the economy of Panama is heavily dependent on income from it.

Cuba

Havana: the capital of Cuba was the 'Paris of the Caribbean' until Fidel Castro took power. Poker games would run through the night, and ice-cold Cuba Libre would comfort lonely souls. The shows in the elegant 'Club Tropicana' bring this legendary atmosphere back to life – at least for the tourists.

Cuba

Area:	110,860 sq. km
Capital city:	Havana
Form of government:	
Socialist Republic	
Administrative divisions:	
14 provinces, 1 special	
administrative district	
Population: 11.3 million	
(101 inhabitants/sq. km)	
Language:	Spanish
GDP per capita:	US$3,300
Currency:	
1 Cuban peso = 100 centavos	

Natural Geography

The **main island** mainly consists of lowlands. In the south-east there are **Sierra Maestra** mountains that are often affected by earthquakes. The highest peak, Pico Turquino, reaches a height of almost 2,000 m. The Sierra Trinidad is a smaller range of mountains in the centre of the island, and the Cordillera de Guaniguanico lies in the west.
The Havana and Matanzas **highlands** are in the north. Numerous coral atolls and reefs are located off the **coasts**.

Climate

The **wet-dry climate** is affected by the north-east trade winds. Temperatures are between 22°C and 28°C. In the interior, annual precipitation, which is at its highest between June and October, is 1,000–1,500 mm. The natural

rainforests and mountain forests have largely given way to cultivated land and palm savannahs. The fauna is not very varied and consists mainly of insectivores, reptiles and rodents. By contrast, the coastal waters are well stocked with fish.

Population

Cuba's population is 51 per cent **mixed race**, 11 per cent black and 37 per cent white. 59 per cent of the population **profess no religion**, 39 per cent are **Catholic** and the rest a Protestant minority. The average Cuban **life expectancy** is 76, and **adult literacy rate** is just over 95 per cent. Schooling is compulsory. 76 per cent of the population lives in cities.

History and Politics

The island was discovered by **Columbus** in the year 1492 and

was subsequently occupied by the **Spanish**. Spain had to defend its new overseas territory constantly against pirates and colonial competitors. Towards the end of the nineteenth century, the **USA**

supported the independence movement and used this as a pretext to declare war on Spain in 1898. The island remained under US control until 1902. Guantánamo Bay was leased by the USA as a **military base in 1903** and although the

terms of the agreement make it a perpetual automatically renewed lease, Cuba views the US presence as an illegal occupation.
After an unstable period with several changes of government, **Fulgencio Batista** came to power in 1933 and ruled the country as a dictatorship until 1958. The revolution led by **Fidel Castro** resulted in a reorganisation of the social system and the establishment of free health care and education for the masses.
Cuba's **socialist politics** and his alignment with the **USSR** led to a permanent deterioration in the country's relations with the USA. A planned invasion of exiled Cubans at the Bay of Pigs, organised by the **CIA**, failed in 1961. Plans to station Soviet nuclear

missiles on Cuba led to the **Cuban Missile Crisis** of 1962, which for a time threatened to escalate into a nuclear war. The crisis was resolved after concessions by Khrushchev, but the **embargoes** imposed on Cuba by the USA continue to cripple Cuban foreign trade to this day.
After the collapse of the Eastern Bloc, Cuba lost an important trading partner and some of its economic power. Through improved **relations with Europe,** other countries in Latin America and the Catholic Church, Castro has made efforts to bring the country out of isolation, without abandoning the principle of a socialist planned economy.

Fidel Castro

*Mayari, 13.8.1926

After the guerrilla war of 1956–1959, Fidel Castro and a small liberation movement toppled the dictator Juan Batista. Castro has ruled ever since as Prime Minister. The exclusion of the old elite and the nationalisation of manufacturing and agriculture brought Castro into a conflict with the USA which reached its peak during the Cuban Missile Crisis. Since the end of the Cold War, Castro has tried to forge closer ties with the West.

The dome of the National Capitol dominates Havana's skyline.

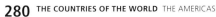

Trinidad: 'Son' was Cuba's most popular musical sound in the 1920s and is still played today by the founding fathers from back in the day. Son is a mixture of solo and chorus singing, which later developed into salsa. Since the worldwide success of the Wim Wenders film 'Buena Vista Social Club', the melancholy music is once more well-known around the globe.

Economy

The country has a GDP of US$20.7 billion, of which **agriculture** accounts for seven per cent, **manufacturing** 31 per cent, and the **services sector** 62 per cent.
The trade deficit is US$1.47 billion. Main imports are machines, fossil fuels and transport equipment. Export products are tobacco, rice, bananas, sugar and

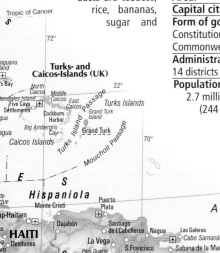

sugar products, as well as nickel ore. **Tourism** plays an increasingly important role in the economy.

Transport Infrastructure

The 4,677-km-long **rail network** is well constructed, as is the **road network,** which has a length of 27,100 km. There are five international **airports**.

Tourism

The main centres for foreign visitors are the cities of **La Habaña** (Havana), **Trinidad** and **Santiago de Cuba,** and the beaches of **Matanzas**. In 1996, the country welcomed just under one million tourists, who contributed US$1.35 billion. The largest contingent was from Canada. The best time for travel is between November and April.

 **Jamaica**

Area: 10,990 sq. km
Capital city: Kingston
Form of government:
Constitutional Monarchy in the Commonwealth
Administrative divisions:
14 districts
Population:
2.7 million
(244 inhabitants/sq. km)

Languages:
English (official), Patois
GDP per capita: US$4,300
Currency:
1 Jamaican dollar = 100 cents

Natural Geography

A massive range of fold mountains runs through the **island** from west to east. The highest mountain is **Blue Mountain Peak** with an maximum height of 2,256 m. Karstified limestone plateaus make up approximately two-thirds of the country's area. The narrow coastal strips are dominated by marshes in the south, and there are sandy beaches in the north. Much of the tropical rainforest has been cleared for cultivation.

Climate

The north-east trade winds define the **warm, tropical climate**. Temperatures scarcely fluctuate from the average of 27°C. In the northern mountainous regions, annual rainfall is 2,500–5,000 mm, but in the south it is just 800 mm. Powerful **hurricanes** often strike the country in late summer. The limestone plateaus are dominated by **savannah vegetation**, and the mountain slopes are covered in evergreen **rainforest**. Higher regions have **mountain and cloud forest**. The country has many species of birds and reptiles, and is also home to mongooses and bats, though they are not native to the island.

Population

The population is 76 per cent **Black**, 15 per cent mulatto, 1.3 per cent Indian, 0.2 per cent white and 0.2 per cent Chinese. 56 per cent are **Protestant,** five per cent **Rastafarian** and 4.9 per cent **Catholic.** There are also minorities of Baha'i, Jews and Muslims. Average life expectancy is 74, and the **adult literacy rate** is 95 per cent. Approximately half the population lives in the cities.

History and Politics

The island was discovered by **Columbus,** and the Spanish settlement that followed almost completely eradicated the indigenous Carib population. In 1670, the **English** disputed Spain's claim to the island. The country was initially an infamous **pirate stronghold,** but sugar cane and cocoa plantations made Jamaica one of the richest colonies in the British Empire. Until slavery was finally abolished in 1838, large numbers of **African slaves** were brought to work on the plantations and sugar mills.
After 1938, the government became increasingly autonomous, and Jamaica became **officially independent** in 1962. Since the 1970s, the country has fluctuated between a socialist and a market economy, following either a Cubafriendly or USA-friendly course. The **House of Representatives** is elected every five years. The **voting age** is 18.

Economy

Gross national product in 2005 stood at US$9.1 billion, of which eight per cent was derived from **agriculture,** 34 per cent from **manufacturing** and 57 per cent came from the **service sector**. The most important imports are raw materials, consumer goods, semimanufactured goods and food. Main exports are aluminium, textiles, sugar, bauxite, bananas and coffee.

Transport infrastructure

The **rail network** is 300 km long and a well constructed **road network** covers 17,000 km. The country has two international **airports** and two **sea ports**.

Tourism

In 2002, just under 1.3 million tourists came to the country, spending US$1.23 billion. The best time for visiting Jamaica is between December and April.

 Haiti

Area: 27,750 sq. km
Capital city: Port-au-Prince
Form of government:
Presidential Republic
Administrative divisions:
9 départements
Population:
8.1 million
(270 inhabitants/sq. km)
Languages:
French (official), Creole
GDP per capita: US$1,600
Currency:
1 gourde = 100 centimes

Natural Geography

Haiti covers the western third of the island of **Hispaniola** and consists of two large peninsulas around the **Gulf of Gonave**. The Massif du Nord and the Massif du Sud cover some 80 per cent of the country's land mass. Between these two mountain ranges lies the Plateau Central, the valley of the most important river, the Artibonite, and the Plaine du Cul-de-Sac which contains a salt lake, the Étang Saumâtre. Haiti is frequently struck by earthquakes.

Climate

The north-east trade winds produce a **tropical climate** and average temperatures of 25°C to 29°C. Temperatures are cooler in the uplands, where average precipitation is between 1,000 and 1,500 mm. On the plains, precipitation is just 500 mm. Powerful **hurricanes** are common in late summer.
Aggressive deforestation has meant that only ten per cent of the country is now covered in tropical **rainforest**. Cacti and thorn bushes grow on the mountain slopes, and dry or humid

Cigar-making still employs many people in Cuba. Tobacco cultivation is a job for the men, but women roll the hand-made cigars. Cuban cigars are reputed to be the finest in the world.

savannahs are found in the basins. Mangrove swamps grow along the coast. The country once had a rich variety of fauna, but all that remains today are some reptiles, rodents and bird species.

Population

Haiti's population is 95 per cent **black** and five per cent **mulatto**. Whites only represent a small minority of the population. Officially, 80 per cent are **Catholic** and ten per cent **Protestant**, but the traditional **Voodoo cult** and syncretic religions are widespread. Average **life expectancy** is just 55 years and more than half of the population of Haiti can neither read nor write. Only 32 per cent live in the cities.

History and Politics

After the island was discovered by **Columbus** in 1492, the **Spanish** struggled to establish themselves in the western region. Initially, Haiti was a **pirate stronghold**, but the French finally drove them out and became the nominal rulers in 1697.

Using **African slaves,** the colonists cultivated successful plantations and made Haiti into one of **France's** wealthiest colonies. In the aftermath of the French Revolution, the slaves demanded their right to freedom and broke away from France in 1804, under their leader Toussaint L'Ouverture. Haiti merged with the eastern part of the island, the Dominican Republic, but this union lasted for only 22 years, from 1822 to 1844.

After this, various **dictators** snatched power from each other in a series of coups, until the **USA** occupied the country in 1915. After the Americans left in 1935, Haiti remained under US financial control until 1947.

The dictatorships of François **Duvalier** and his son Jean-Claude ('Papa Doc' and 'Baby Doc') were infamous. Jean-Bertrand **Aristide** was elected President in 1990. Not long after Aristide gained power, he was overthrown by yet another military coup, and was only able to reclaim office in 1994, with the help of 20,000 US soldiers. Since 1996, there has once more been a freely elected civilian government, but Haiti remains the politically unstable and impoverished. The **bicameral parliament** is elected every four years, and the head of state every five years. The voting age is 18.

Economy

In 2005, GDP stood at US$4.3 billion, of which 42 per cent was from **agriculture**, 13 per cent came from **manufacturing** and 45 per cent from the **service sector**. Unemployment stands at 70 per cent. The country has a huge foreign trade deficit. Main imports are consumer goods, machinery, food and fuel. Haiti exports light industry products, cocoa, coffee and sugar. Large numbers of Haitians work in the sugar cane plantations of the Dominican Republic; there is a huge emigré population, living mainly in the United States.

Transport Infrastructure

Only 600 km of the 4000-km-long **road network** is surfaced. The **railway** (600 km) is used for the transport of goods. The country has seven domestic **airports** and one international airport.

Tourism

Tourist numbers have reduced dramatically due to the high HIV/AIDS infection rate and significant levels of violent crime. Tourism remains an important economic factor however. The best time to travel is between December and March.

François Duvalier

*Port-au-Prince, 14.4.1907,
†Port-au-Prince, 21.4.1971

After his election to the post of President of Haiti in 1957 – supported by the military – 'Papa Doc', so-called because he had once been a doctor, became a dictator and named himself President for the rest of his life in 1964. During his office, the mulatto elite of the country was practically removed of all their powers. In 1971, he named his son, Jean-Claude, as successor. Known as 'Baby Doc', he was toppled in February 1986, despite attempts to reform, and went into exile in France.

A former presidential palace: the Museum of the Revolution, Havana.

Dominican Republic

Area:	48,730 sq. km
Capital city:	Santo Domingo
Form of government: Presidential Republic	
Administrative divisions: 26 provinces, Capital city district	
Population: 8.9 million (179 inhabitants/sq. km)	
Language:	Spanish
GDP per capita:	US$6,500
Currency: 1 Dominican Peso = 100 centavos	

Natural Geography

The national territory comprises two-thirds of the island of **Hispaniola**. Four parallel mountain chains traverse the island from north-west to south-east. The Pico Duarte in the Cordillera Central an altitude of 3,175 m, is the country's highest mountain. Extensive areas of lowland lie between the mountain ranges. The only substantial inland lake is the saltwater lake of Lago Enriquillo. The country is frequently struck by earthquakes.

Climate

The Dominican Republic has a **tropical climate**, the effects of which vary greatly depending on the region. In the area around the capital, temperatures range between 14°C and 27°C. Precipitation fluctuates between 2,000 mm in the mountains and 600 mm on the Hoya de Enriquillo, also known as the Cul-de-Sac Depression. The humid mountain slopes are covered in evergreen **rainforest**, and **mountain woodland** grows in the rain-sheltered areas of the Cordillera. In the **savannahs** of the plains, the flora mostly comprises thornbushes and cacti. There are many bird species, manatees, alligators and Hispaniolan hutia.

Population

60 per cent of the inhabitants of the Dominican Republic are **mulattos**, 28 per cent are **white** and 11.5 per cent **black**. **Catholics** make up 90 per cent of the population and the rest consist of Protestants, Jews and Baha'i.

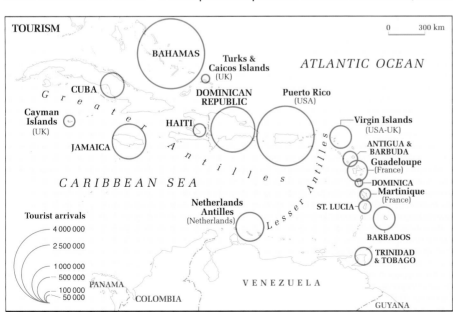

TOURISM

0 ____ 300 km

ATLANTIC OCEAN

BAHAMAS

Turks & Caicos Islands (UK)

CUBA

Great

er

Antilles

Cayman Islands (UK)

DOMINICAN REPUBLIC

Puerto Rico (USA)

HAITI

Virgin Islands (USA-UK)

JAMAICA

ANTIGUA & BARBUDA

Guadeloupe (France)

DOMINICA

Martinique (France)

CARIBBEAN SEA

Netherlands Antilles (Netherlands)

ST. LUCIA

Lesser Antilles

BARBADOS

Tourist arrivals
- 4 000 000
- 2 500 000
- 1 000 000
- 500 000
- 100 000
- 50 000

TRINIDAD & TOBAGO

PANAMA

VENEZUELA

COLOMBIA

GUYANA

Dominican Republic, Bahamas

*The Hemingway Bar in **Havana** still pays tribute to the Nobel Prize winning writer, who often came to the bar, the 'Bodeguita del Medio', to enjoy different Mojito cocktails. Ernest Hemingway lived on the outskirts of Havana, and he made the drink famous throughout the world in 1939. The writer lived in **Cuba** for 20 years. His local bar, near the Catedral de San Cristobal de La Habana was his escape and his worst enemy: Hemingway was an alcoholic.*

Average **life expectancy** is 71 years and **adult literacy rate** is 82 per cent. 63 per cent of the population lives in cities.

History and Politics

After **Columbus** discovered the island of Hispaniola, the **Spanish** killed off the native Carib and Arawak population. Spain initially lost possession of the west of the island and ceded the east to the **French** in 1795. The country first became independent in 1804 and briefly united with Haiti, only to break away shortly after. The country once more came under Spanish control, and finally gained full **independence** in 1865. From 1916 to 1924, the Dominican Republic was occupied by the **USA**. A short-lived liberal phase ended in 1930 when the dictator **Trujillo Molina** came to power. His murder in 1961 was followed by a democratic government. A series of military coups and a civil war provoked new US intervention in 1965. Since then, the country has been a **republic**. Since 2000, the country has been ruled by the social democrat PRD. The bicameral parliament and head of state are directly elected every four years. Voting is compulsory starting at 18.

Economy

GDP in 2005 was US$18.2 billion, of which 13 per cent derived from **agriculture**, 32 per cent from **manufacturing** and 55 per cent came from the **services sector**. Important exports are gold, silver, nickel, sugar cane, coffee and cocoa. The Dominican Republic imports oil, machinery and consumer goods. **Tourism** brought in US$2.7 billion in 2002, and is a significant economic factor.

Transport Infrastructure

The **road network** covers 18,000 km and is well constructed. 30 per cent of the roads are paved. The international **airport** near Santo Domingo provides good flight connections to the US mainland and to other Caribbean islands.

Tourism

In 2002, 2.8 million foreign tourists enjoyed the beaches of **Puerto Plata** and **La Romana**. The best time to visit is between November and April.

Bahamas

Area:	13,939 sq. km
Capital city:	Nassau
Form of government:	
Constitutional Monarchy in the Commonwealth	
Administrative divisions:	
18 districts	
Population:	
302,000 (21 inhabitants/sq. km)	
Language:	English
GDP per capita:	US$18,800
Currency:	
1 Bahamian dollar = 100 cents	

Natural Geography

The **island kingdom** consists of 30 larger and 700 small tropical islands and some 2,000 atolls and cays, stretching over a distance of 1,200 km. Most of the flat islands have wide, palm-fringed beaches. The country has no highlands or large rivers. Only 30 islands are inhabited.

Climate

The **sub-tropical maritime climate** combined with the cooling effects of the **Gulf Stream** mean that the country has year-round pleasant temperatures of between 22°C and 28°C. In the north-west, annual levels of precipitation are 1,200 mm, compared with 1,000 mm in the south-east. In the latter half of the year, the islands are often hit by **hurricanes**. The Bahamas are covered in **savannahs**, and the north-west also contains **woodland**, salt marshes and mangrove swamps in the bays.

Population

The population of the Bahamas is 72 per cent **black**, 14 per cent

1 Cuba: Trinidad's emblem is the tower of the San Francisco Convent and Church.

2 Old American cars, such as this one in the city of Trinidad, are often driven in Cuba.

3 Cuba: The Plaza de la Catedral lies in the centre of Havana's old town. The colonial buildings in this part of the city are a tourist attraction.

4 The cultivation of sugar cane was once the main source of income for many Caribbean states. Tourism has now caused this activity to lose importance.

Dominican Republic: The beaches of the Caribbean island are a paradise for many tourists. Merengue musicians complete the tropical dream, which enchants ever more people each year. Since 1970, tourist numbers have increased by a factor of five. Catastrophes like Hurricane George in 1998 do not change the beauty of the region. The hurricane devastated large parts of the Dominican Republic. The government estimated the damage caused at US$1.2 billion.

mulatto and 12 per cent **white**. The majority belong to diverse **Protestant denominations**, and 16 per cent are members of the **Catholic** faith. There are also minorities of Muslims, Jews and followers of native religions. Average **life expectancy** is 73 years and the **literacy rate** is 95 per cent. The proportion of city-dwellers is 86.5 per cent.

History and Politics

Columbus first set foot on American soil in 1492 when he landed on the island of **San Salvador**, today also known as Watling Island. The **Spanish** carried off almost all of the native inhabitants as **slaves** to neighbouring islands. **English settlers** first arrived in 1648, but the settlement was constantly troubled by skirmishes with pirates until the islands were made a British colony and the British fleet was based in the Bahamas. In 1973, the **crown colony** became **independent**. The Senate and the House of Representatives are elected every five years, and the 16 members of the Senate are appointed by the governor general. The voting age is 18.

Economy

The major contributor to the economy is **tourism** which accounts for half the income. There is also a flourishing invisibles sector because the particularly liberal **tax laws** attract foreign capital, making the Bahamas a trade and banking centre and the home of many 'accommodation addresses'. **Agriculture** and **manufacturing** are only partially developed. 80 per cent of imports are foodstuffs, fuel, machinery and consumer goods. Exports include aragonite, pharmaceuticals, oil, rum and shellfish.

Transport Infrastructure

The 22 inhabited islands are well served by a **road network** covering 4,100 km. There are regular **flights** between the islands, and Nassau and Freeport have international **air and sea ports**.

Tourism

The **paradise beaches** of Grand Bahama, Bimini, Cat Island and,

Rum Cay attract many visitors from the USA. The Blue Holes on the island of Andros are the world's longest and deepest submarine caves. In 2001, 4.2 million tourists spent US$1.75 billion.

St. Kitts and Nevis

Area:	261.6 sq. km
Capital city:	Basseterre
Form of government:	Federation/Constitutional Monarchy in the British Commonwealth
Administrative divisions:	14 districts
Population:	39,000 (160 inhabitants/sq. km)
Language:	English
GDP per capita:	US$8,800
Currency:	1 Eastern Caribbean dollar = 100 cents

Devon House in the Jamaican capital Kingston.

Natural Geography

St. Kitts (area: 168 sq. km) and **Nevis** (area: 93 sq. km) belong to the **Lesser Antilles volcanic arc**. Mount Liamuiga (Mt. Misery) on St. Kitts is 1,137 m high and has a crater lake. The coasts are lined with black volcanic sands. The islands have sulphurous hot springs and are hit by earthquakes.

Climate

The **tropical climate** is affected by the trade winds. The coasts have relatively constant temperatures

of about 27°C. Average **precipitation** ranges from 750 mm in the west and 1,200–1,500 mm in the east, but can be as high as 3,000 mm in the mountains. The higher altitudes are covered with **rainforests and mountain cloud forests**. The lower slopes are used for **cultivation**. The fauna includes monkeys, mongooses and 60 species of bird.

Population

86 per cent of the population is **black**, 11 per cent **mulatto** and two per cent **white**. There are 40 different Christian denominations, including **Anglicans** (36 per cent), **Methodists** (32 per cent), **Catholics** (11 per cent) and **Moravians** (nine per cent). The other religious minorities are insignificant. 41 per cent of the population lives in the three main towns. Average **life expectancy** is 70 and the **literacy rate** is 90 per cent.

History and Politics

The island group, consisting of St Christopher, Nevis and Anguilla, were discovered by **Columbus**, and the **Spanish** then shipped the native population off to work in mines in Haiti. In the seventeenth and eighteenth centuries, the **English** and **French** fought over the islands, which became British in 1783. Both islands gained **independence** in 1983 and formed a **federation**, despite a strong separatist movement in Nevis. The islands have a joint national assembly,

but Nevis also has its own parliament and prime minister. The voting age is 18. The capital, Basseterre is on St Christopher Island; the main town on Nevis is Charlestown.

Economy

GDP in 2001 was US$283 million. **Agriculture** accounted for five per cent, 23 per cent came from **manufacturing** and 75 per cent derived from the **services sector**. Main exports are cars, sugar and sugar derivatives. Imports include machinery and foodstuffs.

Transport Infrastructure

The **road network** is 300 km long. There is an international **airport** and a **deep sea port** in Basseterre. There are no direct flights to Nevis from outside the Caribbean.

Tourism

The main attractions are the beaches, hot springs and resort hotels. The tourist season is between December and April.

Antigua and Barbuda

Area:	442 sq. km
Capital city:	St. John's
Form of government:	Constitutional Monarchy in the British Commonwealth
Administrative divisions:	6 districts, 2 dependencies
Population:	68,722 (151 inhabitants/sq. km)
Languages:	English (official), Creole English
GDP per capita:	US$11,000
Currency:	1 Eastern Caribbean dollar = 100 cents

Natural Geography

This small state in the Caribbean comprises the islands of **Antigua** (280 sq. km), **Barbuda** (161 sq. km) and the uninhabited **Redonda** (one sq. km) in the **Lesser Antilles**. The islands rest on layers of coral and have large areas of karstification. The Shirley Heights in south-west of Antigua are of volcanic origin. Barbuda has a

coastline with a large number of bays and coves and offshore coral reefs. The islands have no natural waterways.

Climate

The **mild tropical climate** reaches temperatures of 23°C to 28°C. Average **precipitation** is 900 mm. The woods contain wild boar and red deer (both imported) and various species of lizard, tortoise and bird.

Population

The inhabitants are 94.4 per cent **black**, 3.5 per cent **mulatto** and 1.3 per cent **white**. The majority are **Anglican**, but there are also some 14,500 **Catholics** and some Jews. Average **life expectancy** is 75 and the **adult literacy rate** is 95 per cent. Only 36.2 per cent of the population lives in cities.

History and Politics

The islands were discovered by **Columbus** and the **Spanish** transported the native inhabitants as slaves to work in the mines of other colonies. Barbuda was settled by English colonists in 1628 and Antigua in 1632. In the seventeenth and eighteenth centuries, the **English** and **French** fought over the islands which later became a centre of the **slave trade**. From 1871–1956, Antigua and Barbuda were both British colonies. In World War II, the **USA** established marine and airforce bases on the islands which are very much resent by the inhabitants. This small state has been **independent** since 1981. The House of Representative is elected every five years, and the senators are appointed by the Governor-General who represents the head of state, Queen Elizabeth II. The voting age is 18.

Economy

In 2001, GDP was US$621 million. **Agriculture** accounted for four per cent, **manufacturing** for 18 per cent and the **services sector** for 78 per cent. Agriculture and manufacturing are underdeveloped, the most important sector of the economy is **tourism**. Finished products, raw materials and foods are

*The simple art of **Haiti** fascinated the American DeWitt Peters so much that he founded the Centre d'Art in Port-au-Prince in 1944. The centre fosters Haitian art, which is characterised by optimistic paintings in bright colours. The paintings are exported to the United States and Europe where they are very popular. Many are also on sale in the art galleries of Haiti's capital city, **Port-au-Prince**.*

imported, and export goods include crude oil products, cotton and textiles.

Transport Infrastructure

The **road network** is some 1,000 km long and well constructed. There is an international **airport** in Coolidge and St John's has a **deep-sea port**.

Tourism

Some 200,000 foreigners visit the country every year for the white beaches of **Antigua** and the beautiful reefs of **Barbuda**. There are also an additional 250,000 **cruise visitors**. The high season is between December and April.

Dominica

Area:	750 sq. km
Capital city:	Roseau
Form of government:	
Republic in the Commonwealth	
Administrative divisions:	
10 districts	
Population:	
70,000 (93 inhabitants/sq. km)	
Languages:	
English (official), Patois, Cocoy	
GDP per capita:	US$5,500
Currency:	
1 Eastern Caribbean dollar =	
100 cents	

Natural Geography

The mountainous **island** has continuous **volcanic activity**, as demonstrated by the crater lake known as Boiling Lake, discovered in 1922. There are numerous hot springs and fumaroles. Large parts of Dominica remain unexplored to this day. The mountains in the country's interior are up to 1,400 m high and have steep cliffs and ravines. The north coast has sheer cliffs some 200 m high.

Climate

The **tropical climate** is defined by the north-east trade wind that constantly blows across the region. Temperatures range between 25°C and 30°C. The coast has an annual **precipitation** of 1,800 mm, and in the mountains this can be as high as 6,500 mm.

The island is often affected by strong **hurricanes**. Almost the entire island is covered by tropical **rainforest**, which is home to many species of bird and various reptiles and rodents.

Population

91 per cent of the inhabitants are **black**, six per cent **mulatto** and **creole**, and 1.5 per cent **Indian**. There is also a small minority white population.

80 per cent are **Catholic** and 13 per cent **Protestant**. There are also minorities of Muslims, Hindus, Jews and Baha'i. Average

life expectancy is 74 years. The **adult literacy rate** is over 95 per cent, and 41 per cent live in the cities.

History and Politics

The island was discovered by **Columbus** on a Sunday ('Dominica' is Spanish for Sunday) in 1493, hence the name. The island's remote location meant that **European settlers** did not arrive until the seventeenth century. After a long period of dispute between the **British** and **French**, Dominica finally became British in 1814, and from 1967–1978 was a member of the West Indies Associated States. The country was granted **independence** in November 1978. The main towns are Portsmouth and Marigot.

Economy

GDP in 2001 was approximately US$224 million. Of this, 18 per

cent derived from **agriculture**, 19 per cent from **manufacturing** and 63 per cent from the **service sector**. Fossil fuels, consumer goods, machines and chemicals are imported; exports include agricultural products (mainly bananas, sugar cane and processed sugar), cocoa, copra, coconuts and fruit juices.

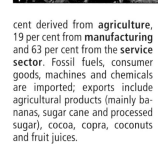

1 The coral reefs of the Bahamas are a habitat for numerous species of flora and fauna. The Bahamas are coral islands.

2 In the Caribbean, people live at a leisurely pace. The local bar is a meeting place for sharing the latest gossip.

3 The markets in Haiti are very crowded. Many visitors come by bus from the more remote regions.

4 Sun, sea, palm trees: In Samana, a sleepy town in the Dominican Republic, you can experience an original tropical paradise.

*What is today a paradise for tourists was once a hell for the African slaves of the sugar cane plantations. The **Caribbean islands** used to be in the possession of the colonial powers, who maintained their power with violence. The descendants of these slaves now form the majority of the population in many of the Caribbean states, but most still live in terrible social conditions. Medical provisions are deficient, and poverty and hunger are widespread on many islands.*

Transport Infrastructure

The **road network** has a total length of ca. 800 km and is restricted to the coastal areas. Melville Hall is the international **airport**.

Tourism

The island's unspoiled **nature** attracts increasing numbers of tourists to the country. The best time to visit is between December and April.

St. Lucia

Area:	616.3 sq. km
Capital city:	Castries
Form of government:	
Constitutional Monarchy in the British Commonwealth	
Administrative divisions:	
11 districts	
Population:	
166,300 (263 inhabitants/sq. km)	
Languages:	
English (official), French patois	
GDP per capita:	US$5,400
Currency: 1 Eastern Caribbean dollar = 100 cents	

Natural Geography

St. Lucia belongs to the **Lesser Antilles** and is of volcanic origin, as demonstrated by the two 800-m-high conical volcanos, Gros Piton and Petit Piton in the southwest of the island. The south and west have white sandy beaches with offshore coral reefs. The interior is mountainous, with up to 950 m, and is traversed by numerous rivers and streams.

Climate

The north-east trade wind defines the **tropical wet-dry climate** and produces average temperatures of 25–30°C and precipitation of 1,200 mm on the coast and up to 3,500 mm inland. The original **rainforest** now only persists at higher altitudes. On the lower slopes, it has been replaced by cultivation. The rainforests contain a variety of bird species.

Population

The population of St. Lucia is 90.3 per cent **black**, 5.5 per cent mulatto, 3.2 per cent **Asian** and 0.8 per cent **white**. 77 per cent profess the **Catholic** faith and the rest belong to **Protestant** denominations. Average **life expectancy** is 70 years and the **literacy rate** is 82 per cent. The three largest towns account for 47 per cent of the population.

History and Politics

The island was discovered by **Columbus** but the **native inhabitants** successfully resisted attempts by European seafarers to conquer them until well into the seventeenth century. After a long dispute between **England** and **France**, the island became British in 1814, and became an **independent state in the Commonwealth** in 1979, although it still maintains its links to French culture and the local patois is based on French. St. Lucia has a bicameral parliament based on the British system and Queen Elizabeth II is head of state. Compulsory voting is from the age of 21.

Economy

GDP in 2001 was approximately US$628 million, of which eight per cent derived from **agriculture**, 17 per cent from **manufacturing** and 75 per cent from the **service sector**. Main exports are agricultural products, including bananas, cocoa, sugar and citrus fruits. Imports include consumer goods, machinery, textiles and fertilisers. **Tourism**, mainly from the USA, is becoming increasingly important to the economy.

Transport Infrastructure

The 800 km-long **road network** is largely well-constructed. Two modern **ports** are being developed for foreign trade and **cruise ships**. An international **airport** is located near Vieux Fort.

Tourism

In 2002, the island welcomed more than 250,000 foreign visitors to the unspoiled countryside, including the volcanoes. The best time for travel is between mid-December and mid-April.

Palms, sand and deep blue sea: Sam Lord's Castle has one of the most beautiful beaches in Barbados.

St. Vincent and The Grenadines

Area:	389 sq. km
Capital city:	Kingstown
Form of government:	
Constitutional Monarchy in the British Commonwealth	
Administrative divisions:	
6 districts	
Population: 117,000	
(300 inhabitants/sq. km)	
Language:	
English	
GDP per capita:	US$2,900
Currency:	
1 Eastern Caribbean dollar = 100 cents	

Natural Geography

To the north of the mountainous **main island of St. Vincent** lies the **active volcano** of Soufrière (1,234 m). In the east of the country, the land becomes flatter towards the sea. The numerous smaller islands located to the south of St. Vincent are called the **Grenadines** and are also of volcanic origin. These islands are largely uninhabited.

Climate

The country has a **tropical climate** with average temperatures between 25°C and 27°C. Mountainous regions have annual levels of precipitation of 3,500 mm; this is just 1,500 mm in the lowlands. The Grenadines are noticeably drier. In summer there are often strong **hurricanes**. The island's interior is covered in evergreen rainforest which is home to an amazing variety of bird species.

Population

The inhabitants of St. Vincent and the Grenadines are 66 per cent **black**, 19 per cent **white**, 5.5 per cent **Indian** and two per cent **zambo** (mixed race with black and Indian parents). 75 per cent are **Protestant** and nine per cent are **Catholic**. Just under half of the population lives in cities. The average **life expectancy** is 73 years and the **literacy rate** is 82 per cent.

Natural Geography

History and Politics

It is most likely that **St. Vincent** was discovered by **Columbus** in 1493, but European seafarers were unable to conquer the warlike **native Caribs** and colonise the island until the seventeenth century. In the years prior to 1798 the colonial power switched between the **French** and **British** several times. From 1958–1962, the island group was part of the **West Indies Federation** and from 1969 it was an associated state in the British **Commonwealth**, before becoming **independent** in 1979. According to the 1979 constitution, part of the parliament is elected every five years and part is appointed by the Governor-General who represents Queen Elizabeth II. The voting age is 18.

Economy

GDP in 2001 was US$312 million, of which 12 per cent was derived from **agriculture**, 24 per cent from **manufacturing** and 64 per cent from the **services sector**. Main imports are machinery, consumer goods and foodstuffs. The country exports agricultural products, mainly bananas, arrowroot and cotton. **Tourism** is increasingly important to the economy.

Transport Infrastructure

Approximately half of the 400 km of **road** is well-constructed. Regional **flights** connect St. Vincent with the international **airports** of neighbouring countries but there are no direct flights from outside the Caribbean.

Tourism

The island group, and especially Mustique, is popular with tourists. **Yachts** and **cruise ships** bring many of the 200,000 foreign visitors who arrive each year. The best time to visit is between January and May.

Grenada

Area:	344 sq. km
Capital city:	St. George's
Form of government:	
Constitutional Monarchy	

*The sea is the most important source of protein for the people of the Caribbean. The **fish stocks** have been declining here for years, however, and it is ever harder to supply the increasing demand. A problem is the use of chemicals in fishing, for example the use of lead in crab fishing. This destroys the coral reef and the species living in it. The death of the smaller fish means that the larger predators also keep away from the reefs.*

Population:
89,500 (259 inhabitants/sq. km)
Languages:
English (official), Patois
GDP per capita: US$5,000
Currency:
1 Eastern Caribbean dollar =
100 cents

Natural Geography

The **main island,** like the **Grenadines** to the south, is of volcanic origin. The interior of the island is mountainous, and the highest point is Mount Saint Catherine (840 m). Numerous crater lakes, sulphurous springs and earthquakes are indications of volcanic activity. Grenada is the most southerly of the Windward Islands.

Climate

The **tropical climate** is made milder by the trade winds, and the country has an average temperature of 27°C. Annual precipitation on the coast is 1,500 mm, compared with up to 5,000 mm in more mountainous regions. The natural tropical **rainforest** has only been preserved in the mountains. The island is home to numerous species of birds, various reptiles, rodents and monkeys.

Population

The population is 82 per cent **black,** 13 per cent **mulatto,** three per cent Indian and one per cent white. 53 per cent are **Catholic** and 14 per cent **Anglican. Seventh Day Adventists** account for nine per cent of the population and seven per cent are members of the **Pentecostal Church.** Average **life expectancy** is 72, and the **literacy rate** is 91 per cent. Only 13 per cent of the population lives in cities.

History and Politics

The island was discovered by **Columbus** and was later settled by the **French,** who suppressed the indigenous people and used them, along with African **slaves,** to work their **plantations.** In 1762, Grenada was occupied by **Great Britain** and remained a Crown Colony until **independence** in 1974. Attempts at re-

form by premier **Maurice Bishop** ended in 1983 when he was murdered. The **USA** used this as an excuse to invade, but the actual reason behind the move was apparently to stop Grenada's improving relationship with the USSR. After the withdrawal of the US troops, the 1974 constitution was re-adopted with some alterations. Fifteen members of the House of representatives are directly elected, and 13 are appointed by the Governor-General. The voting age is 18.

Economy

GDP in 2001 was US$368 million. **Agriculture** accounted for ten per cent, **manufacturing** for 19 per cent, and the **services sector** for 71 per cent. The country has a serious foreign trade deficit. Imports include machinery, consumer goods, food and raw materials. Exports are based around nutmeg (25 per cent of world production), but also include cocoa, tropical fruits, rum and sugar. **Tourism** is becoming increasingly valuable to the economy.

Transport Infrastructure

The **road network** is 980 km long. There is an international **airport** at Point Saline.

Tourism

Grenada welcomes approximately 300,000 foreign visitors each year. By far the majority are **cruise ship passengers.** The best time to visit is between December and April.

 Barbados

Area:	430 sq. km
Capital city:	Bridgetown

Form of government:
Constitutional Monarchy in the British Commonwealth
Administrative divisions:
11 districts

1 The natural harbour, English Harbour, on Antigua also provides protection from hurricanes. This spot was once used to protect the British fleet.

2 An ancient sugar mill in Montpelier. On St. Kitts and Nevis hardly any sugar cane is now cultivated. The tiny island lives off tourism.

3 The church of Soufrière stands directly on the beach. Space is short on Dominica, and the island has an area of just 751 sq. km.

4 The brilliant green bay is just one of the features that makes St. George's, the capital of Grenada, one of the prettiest cities in the Caribbean.

Barbados, Trinidad and Tobago

*The Mardi Gras carnival in **Trinidad** is the most important cultural event on the island. Every year, the dazzling parades through the streets offer a spectacle to rival that of Rio de Janeiro. The exuberance with which this Roman Catholic festival to mark the beginning of Lent is celebrated on Trinidad dates back to the the time of African slavery. The elaborate costumes, often consisting of huge wheels of tulle and flowers.*

Population:
279,000 (644 inhabitants/sq. km)
Languages:
English (official), Bajan
GDP per capita: US$17,300
Currency:
1 Barbados dollar = 100 cents

Natural Geography

Barbados, the most easterly island of the West Indies, is of volcanic origin, and much of the surface consists of karst and coral limestone. The highest point is Mount Hillaby at 340 m. The east coast is dominated by cliffs but the south-east is relatively flat. The west and south coastlines are lined with broad, sandy beaches. **Coral reefs** surround most of the island.

Climate

The **tropical climate** is defined by the trade winds which constantly blow across the region. Average temperatures are a pleasant 24°C to 27°C. Average precipitation is 1,000–2,000 mm. **Hurricanes** are common in summer and autumn.
Extensive **agriculture** has eliminated all but small sections of the original **rainforest**. The country still has numerous species of birds, mongooses, monkeys and lizards. The waters are teaming with fish stocks.

Population

The population of Barbados is 92 per cent **black**, 3.2 per cent **white** and 2.6 per cent **mulatto**. **Catholics** make up five per cent of the population, and there are also minorities of Jews, Muslims and Hindus. The vast majority of the population belong to **Protestant** churches and sects.
Average **life expectancy** is 76 years and the **adult literacy rate** is over 95 per cent. Bridgetown has a branch of the **University of the West Indies**. Just under half of the population live in cities.

History and Politics

Soon after discovering the country, the **Spanish** killed or deported the native inhabitants. When European settlers arrived in 1635, the country was uninhabited.

African **slaves** were brought in to work in the **plantations**. Until **independence** in 1966, Barbados was a **British colony**. Relations with Cuba were established in 1972. The lower house of the bicameral parliament, the House of Assembly, is elected every five years and the Senate is appointed by the Governor-General. The voting age is 18.

Economy

GDP in 2005 stood at US$2.9 billion. **Agriculture** accounted for 6.4 per cent, **manufacturing** for 15.6 per cent, and the **services sector** for 78 per cent. Main imports are food, machinery, consumer goods, timber for

Beaches of white sand make Barbados a holiday paradise.

construction, paper and crude oil. **Exports** are predominately based on the island's monoculture, the cultivation of sugar cane. **Sugar**, **molasses**, **syrup** and **rum** are just some of the by-products of this branch of the economy. Diversification is finally taking place and cotton, textile, electronics and cement are now being exported. **Tourism** has become the biggest earner.

Transport Infrastructure

The **road network** is 1,700 km long and is well constructed. There is a **sea port** and an international **airport** in the capital

city, Bridgetown. The other towns – Speightstown, Holetown and Oistins – are linked by road.

Tourism

The country's sandy beaches are a great attraction, as well as the fascinating flora and fauna and the impressive caves. The high season is from December to April.

Trinidad and Tobago	
Area:	5,128 sq. km
Capital city:	Port-of-Spain
Form of government: Presidential Republic in the Commonwealth	
Administrative divisions: 8 counties, 3 municipalities, Tobago (autonomous)	
Population: 1.1 million (234 inhabitants/sq. km)	
Language:	English
GDP per capita:	US$12,700
Currency: 1 Trinidad and Tobago dollar = 100 cents	

Natural Geography

Approximately 8,000 years ago, these islands were connected to the South American mainland. On the island of **Trinidad,** three ranges of mountains extend from west to east. The El Cerro del Aripo at a height of 940 m is the highest point. Pitch Lake

is the world's largest natural reserve of **asphalt**. The Maracas Falls and the Blue Basin waterfalls 91-m-high are remarkable. The landscape in the north and south is defined by a cliff-lined, steep coast, and the flat coasts in the east and west have many lagoons and mangrove swamps. **Tobago** is dominated by a mountainous area up to 576 m high, the only flat strip of land being located in the south-west. With the exception of the cliffs in the north-east, the coast line consists of flat, sandy beaches. The country has many **coral reefs**, the most famous of which is Buccoo Reef.

Climate

The north-east trade wind gives the islands a **humid, tropical climate** with an average temperatures of between 24°C and 26°C. Most of the annual precipitation falls between July and December; amounts vary from 1,600 mm in the west to 3,800 mm in the east of Trinidad, and reaches 2,200 mm on Tobago.
Tobago is almost entirely covered by tropical **rainforest**, apart from the coastal regions. In the south and west of Trinidad there are also **savannahs** and **humid and dry woodland**.
The **animal kingdom** is very varied, including monkeys, bats, snakes, tortoises, alligators, raccoons, sloths, ocelots, peccaries, elk, the common agouti, armadillos and many species of birds and butterflies.

Population

The population is very diverse with 40.3 per cent **Indian ancestry**, 39.6 per cent **black** and 18.5 per cent **mulatto**. **Christians** account for 40.3 per cent, 3.8 per cent is **Hindu** and 5.8 per cent **Muslim**. Average **life expectancy** is 73 years and the **adult literacy rate** is higher than 95 per cent. 72 per cent of the population live in the towns, the capital Port-of-Spain, San Fernando, Arima as well as in Scarborough on Tobago.

History and Politics

Columbus discovered **Trinidad** on his third voyage in the year

1498. Until 1797, the **French, British, Dutch and pirates** of the Spanish Main challenged the Spanish governor for domination of the islands.
In 1802, the islands officially became a **British colony**, and finally gained **independence** in 1976. The European settlers who arrived in the seventeenth and eighteenth centuries brought **black African slaves** to the islands, and later also **Asian indentured labourers** to work on the plantations. This is the reason for the variety of ethnicities on both the islands.
The House of Representatives is elected every five years, and appoints the members of the Senate. An Electoral College selects the president every five years. The voting age is 18.

Economy

GDP in 2005 was US$13 billion. **Agriculture** accounted for two per cent, **manufacturing** for 42 per cent, and the **services sector** for 56 per cent. The economy has experienced a five per cent rate of growth in recent years.
Natural reserves, including crude oil, natural gas and bitumen have made the islands rich. Exports include crude oil, natural gas, bitumen (Trinidad has the largest natural asphalt reserves on Earth in the 40-ha asphalt lake known as Pitch Lake), chemicals, sugar, rum, coffee and tobacco. The country imports raw materials, capital goods and consumer items.

Transport Infrastructure

Approximately 2,800 km of the total 6,400 km of **road** is surfaced, but much of it is in poor condition. Port-of-Spain has the main **port** and an international **airport**. Both islands are connected by a regular **ferry service**.

Tourism

Approximately 250,000 foreign tourists come to the islands each year, mainly attracted by the impressive **sandy beaches** and the natural wonders, such as the waterfalls and the unique Pitch Lake. The best time to visit is between January and May.

Holiday dreams are the main export of the Caribbean.

Caribbean Paradise

The island groups of the Greater and Lesser Antilles form a large arc, over more than 3,500 km, stretching from the coasts of Florida to Venezuela and enclosing the Caribbean Sea. The Caribbean island world offers endless sandy beaches, green hills, crystal clear waters and inhabitants who live life to the full.

The Caribbean has a tropical climate, which is perfect for abundant vegetation. Bromeliaceae grow along power lines and orchids grow on the walls of houses. The interior of many of the larger islands is covered in dense primeval rainforest, interspersed with expansive plantations growing traditional products such as bananas, tobacco, coffee and sugar cane. These plantations formed the economic basis of the islands for several centuries. Soon after the islands were discovered by Columbus, the first Europeans came to establish settlements and introduced the plantation economy. They brought millions of slaves from

Africa into the region. The ancestors of these slaves now form the overwhelming majority of the Caribbean population.

In recent years, tourism has largely replaced traditional economic sectors. The unique way of life in the Caribbean, which varies from island to island depending on the mixture of African traditions and the cultural heritage of the European colonial powers, is one of the main attractions for many tourists.

The Greater Antilles are made up of Cuba, Jamaica, Hispaniola and Puerto Rico. The largest of the western Antilles is Cuba, famous for its cigars, rum and the amazing depth of musical tradition,

which has the whole world on its feet dancing. The neighbouring island of Hispaniola is divided into two countries, Haiti and the Dominican Republic. Jamaica, the home of rum and Rastafarians, is approximately 150km south of Cuba. Jamaica's greatest export is Reggae, which spread from here across the whole world.

The Lesser Antilles comprise the Windward Islands and the Leeward Islands, which run parallel to the coast of Venezuela. The Windward Islands include Barbados, Trinidad and Tobago. The islands of the Lesser Antilles are part of a curve of volcanic islands at the edge of the Caribbean Plate, and, along with

The Caribbean islands are popular with fans of water sports.

Montserrat, display much volcanic activity. Barbados is located to the east of the Caribbean arc of islands, and is largely made up of coral limestone. Some of the Caribbean islands are still overseas territories, including the British Crown Colony of the Cayman Islands and the Virgin Islands, which half belong to Great Britain and half to the

USA. Martinique and Guadeloupe are French overseas Départements, and Montserrat belongs to Great Britain. St. Kitts and Nevis, Antigua and Barbuda, Dominica, St. Lucia and St. Vincent and the Grenadines are independent states, as is Grenada, whose main export item, nutmeg, is proudly displayed on the nation's flag.

Colombia, Venezuela

The mountainous landscape of **Colombia** makes the road-building very difficult. Rivers, such as the Río Magdalena and its tributaries, have long been the traditional transport and trade routes. Floating markets have developed at the main transport hubs, where the traditional products – bananas, sugar cane and pineapples – can be traded from boat to boat.

Colombia

Area:	1,138,910 sq. km
Capital city:	Bogotá
Form of government:	Republic

Administrative divisions:
32 departments,
capital city district

Population:
42.9 million
(36 inhabitants/sq. km)

Language:	Spanish
GDP per capita:	US$7,100

Currency:
1 Colombian peso = 100 centavos

Natural Geography

One third of the land mass is covered by part of the **Andes**. The Cordillera Occidental rises to a height of up to 4,000 m. The Cordillera Central, a mountain range containing many volcanoes, ends in the north in the **Sierra Nevada de Santa Marta**. These mountains include Colombia's highest peak, the 5,775-m-high **Pico Cristóbal Colón**. Between the Cordillera Central and Oriental, the **Rio Magdalena** flows into the Caribbean Sea. The east is covered by lowland plains, extending into the **Amazonian Lowlands** in the extreme south-east.

Climate

Apart from its north Caribbean coast, Colombia lies in the **inner tropics**. Below 1,000 m, temperatures are constant at between 25°C and 30°C. At an altitude of up to 2,000 m, temperatures are about 18°C, and over 3,000 m, they drop to 10°C. There is great variation between day and night. The northern Pacific coast and the western side of the Andes has the highest rainfall, with an average 10,000 mm of annual precipitation, compared with just 300 mm on the eastern Caribbean coast. **Flora** and **fauna** vary greatly depending on altitude. Tropical rainforests can be found up to a height of 900 m, above which they are replaced by mountain and cloud forests. Above 2,500 m, the main vegetation is evergreen oaks, and above 3,200 m there is high steppe vegetation. The **snow line** is at 4,500 m. The flat plains known as 'llanos' are covered in humid or dry savannah, and towards the Pacific coast, marshy woodland is replaced by mangrove swamps. The **rainforest** contains a wide variety of flora and fauna including monkeys, anteaters, sloths, raccoons, jaguars and tapirs. The infamous piranha fish inhabit the rivers.

Population

Colombians are 58 per cent **mestizo** (of mixed Spanish and American heritage), 20 per cent **white**, 14 per cent **mulatto**, four per cent **black** and three per cent **zambo**. The literacy rate is 91 per cent, and life expectancy is 70 years. 95 per cent of the population is **Catholic**, and 73 per cent live in connurbations. Schooling is compulsory between the ages of six and twelve.

History and Politics

Alonso de Ojeda discovered the country in 1499, beginning a period of Spanish rule that only ended with the 1819 War of Liberation, led by **Simón Bolívar**. The national territory of the new Republic of Grand Colombia was gradually reduced, reaching its current size in 1903. Tensions between clerical and secular powers have defined the country's politics. The reforms of the 1930s ended in a civil war that cost a total of 200,000 lives between 1949 and 1958. Today, left-wing **guerrilla s**, brutal attacks by the **military** and the **power of the drug cartels** maintain a wave of **violence** and **corruption**. The bicameral parliament and the state president are directly elected every four years. The voting age is 18.

Economy

In 2005, GDP was US$98 billion of which 11 per cent was derived from **agriculture**, 23 per cent from **manufacturing** and 56 per cent from the **services sector**. Exports include crude oil, coffee, coal and gold. Colombia is an importer of machinery, chemicals and food.

Transport Infrastructure

The **rail network** is 3,386 km long, and the **road network** covers 106,600 km. The country has three international **airports**. The **Pan-american Highway** is only well-maintained in some places.

Tourism

Approximately 600,000 foreign visitors bring in around US$one billion annually. Attractions include Cartagena and Santa Cruz

Tunja: the Bolívar Monument in memory of the great national hero.

de Mompox, the Tieradentro and Los Katios **national parks**. The best time to visit is between December and March.

Venezuela

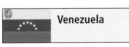

Area:	912,050 sq. km
Capital city:	Caracas

Form of government:
Federal Republic

Administrative divisions:
22 federal states,
1 federal district (Capital city)

Population:
25.3 million
(27 inhabitants/sq. km)

Language:	Spanish
GDP per capita:	US$6,400

Currency:
1 bolívar = 100 céntimos

Natural Geography

Venezuela can be divided into three geographic areas: the **mountains of the Andes**, the **Orinoco Lowland** and the **Guiana Highlands**.
In the north-west lie the Maracaibo basin and Lake Maracaibo (13,300 sq. km), an area with rich crude oil reserves. This lowland area is bordered by the **Cordillera de Mérida**, a mountain chain which is home of the country's highest peak, the 5,002-m-high **Pico Bolívar**, and the Serrania del Perija. Southeast of this region lie the Orinoco Lowlands. This grassland is up to 400 km wide and is often flooded during the rainy season.
South of the Orinoco lie the Guiana Highlands, which cover almost half of Venezuela's land area. A number of **sandstone mesas** reach altitudes of around 3,000 m. The extreme south-west is part of the Amazonian basin.

Climate

Venezuela has a **tropical, wet-dry climate**. On the slopes of the Andes, annual precipitation is around 3,000 mm, but in the Orinoco Lowlands this is just 2,000 mm. The Guiana Highlands see approximately 3,000 mm of rain, the high basins of the mountains on the Caribbean coast, which are frequently struck by earthquakes, and some Andes valleys get up to 1,000 mm of precipitation, but on the north coast rainfall is just under 400 mm. At altitudes of up to 800 m, average annual temperatures reach between 25°C and 29°C. Up to the snow line at 2,000 m, temperatures are 15°C to 25°C, and on the coast and in the lowlands, they can climb as high as 38°C.

Population

Venezuela's population is 69 per cent **mulatto** and **mestizo**, 20 per cent **white**, nine per cent **black** and two per cent **Native American**. Life expectancy is 73 years and the literacy rate is 91 per cent. 93 per cent are **Catholic** and five per cent **Protestant**, but there are also minorities of Jews, Catholics, Orthodox and Muslims. 86 per cent of the population live in the towns and cities. Schooling is compulsory between the ages of five and 15, but 11.8 per cent of the population lives below the poverty line.

History and Politics

Columbus landed on the coast in 1498. After a short period of German rule, Venezuela became a Spanish colony from 1757. In 1777, the **Captaincy General of Venezuela** was established. The struggle for liberation, led by **Simón Bolívar**, ended in 1821 with victory over the Spanish. The newly created **Republic of Grand Colombia** collapsed just nine years later. Venezuela became an **independent republic** in 1830. The country was ruled by military dictators until World War II.
The mining of the country's rich natural reserves was mainly undertaken by foreign firms until 1976, but the subsequent nationalisation of the oil and iron ore industries did not bring economic and political stability to the country. **Attempted coups** by the military, social unrest, **criminality** and high **inflation** are the norm. In 1998, the left-wing Hugo Chávez became President. The population voted for a new constitution in 1999, after which the country became known as the Bolivarian Republic of Venezuela. The presidential elections of 2000 were won by Chávez, but his autocratic leadership attracted resistance from all levels of society. Despite a general strike, the opposition did not manage to precipitate a change in leadership at the start of 2003. The strike led to a huge economic crisis, as the oil industry was almost brought to a standstill. The parliament and president are directly elected every five years.

Economy

GDP in 2005 was US$106.1 billion. **Agriculture** accounted for four per cent, **manufacturing** 47 per cent, and the **service sector** 49 per cent. 80 per cent of exports are from crude oil and natural gas. Machinery and consumer goods are the main imports.

*The small town of **Villa de Leyva** is one of Colombia's national monuments, due to the fact that almost all of the old colonial buildings have been preserved.*

Numerous churches, white-washed houses and the town hall around the 14,000-sq.-m Plaza Mayor are relics from the colonial age.

Transport Infrastructure

Venezuela has a good transport system, especially on the north coast. The **road network** is 82,700 km long, of which 32,501 km are surfaced. There is also 584 km of **railways** and seven international **airports**.

GDP per capita: US$4,000
Currency:
1 Guyana Dollar = 100 cents

Natural Geography

The **Pakaraima Mountains** the highest peak being the 2,810-m-high Mount Roraima. These descend into a hilly landscape which adjoins the coastal lowlands, which are covered in dense mangrove woodland. The southwest of the country is

3,000 mm annual precipitation, but to the country's interior, this is just 1,500 mm. Almost 90 per cent of the land area consists of evergreen **rainforest**. The hills are covered in savannah vegetation, and the coastal region has **salt marshes** and mangrove swamp. The country has a wide range of **fauna**, including deer, jaguars, crocodiles, armadillos, tapirs, anteaters and ocelots, **poisonous spiders** and **piranhas** in the rivers.

South America. In 1814, the colonial powers divided the region into three. For 150 years, the west of Guyana was the colony of British Guyana. After the **abolition of slavery** in 1834, the region was in desperate need of workers, and **indentured labour** was brought over from **India**. In 1961, the British Crown Colony was granted autonomy, and five years later earned a place as an independent constitutional monarchy in the Commonwealth.

Since 1970, Guyana has been a presidential republic. The parliament is elected every five years; the

Tourism

In 1994, approximately 113,000 foreign visitors brought US$47 million into the country, but Guyana's tourist infrastructure leaves a lot to be desired. The country is popular with trekkers, hikers, mountainclimbers and anglers. The main beauty spots are the Kaietur Falls in the Kaietur National Park.

	French Guiana

Area: 83,534 sq. km
Capital city: :
Cayenne (seat of administration)
Form of government:
Département d'outre-mer (DOM)
(French overseas region)
Population:
160,000 (2 inhabitants/sq. km)

Tourism

In 2001, 500,000 tourists brought approximately US$600 million into the country. The best time to travel is between December and April.

	Guyana

Area: 214,969 sq. km
Capital city: Georgetown
Form of government:
Presidential Republic in the Commonwealth
Administrative divisions:
10 regions
Population:
765,000 (3 inhabitants/sq. km)
Languages: English (official), Hindi, Urdu

dominated by savannah vegetation. Since the seventeenth century, the sea has been held back to create areas suitable for agricultural use.

Climate

The climate is **tropical**, and the coast is influenced by the **trade winds**. The temperatures here remain constant, but temperatures on the Atlantic coast fluctuate between 24°C and 29°C. Coastal regions see between 2,000 and

Population

Indians constitute 51.4 per cent of the population, 30.5 per cent are **black**, 11 per cent **mulatto** and **mestizo**, and 5.3 per cent Native American. Life expectancy is 64 and the literacy rate is over 95 per cent. **Protestants** constitute 34 per cent of the population, 33 per cent are **Hindu**, 20 per cent **Catholic** and eight per cent **Muslim**. The urban population is 36 per cent.

History and Politics

The British, **Dutch** and **French** all fought for the north-east corner of

winning party appoints the president. The voting age is 18.

Economy

In 2005, GDP was US$782 million, of which 42 per cent came from **agriculture**, 32 per cent from **manufacturing** and 26 per cent from the **service sector**. Guyana imports fuel and consumer goods. Main exports are gold, diamonds, sugar, bauxite and rice.

Transport Infrastructure

The road network is approximately 5,000 km long, and only paved in the coastal regions. The major towns and cities are served by **regional air transport**.

Languages:
French (official), Creole
GDP per capita: US$3,612
Currency: 1 euro = 100 cents

Natural Geography

A broad plain, 15–40 km wide, runs parallel to the coast. In the interior there are the **hills** of the Guiana Shield.

Climate

The yearly average temperature in this **humid and hot country** is 27°C. The rainy season lasts from December to July. The coastal strip consists of **savannah** and **mangrove swamps.** Most of the land is **tropical rainforest** with a wonderful range of wildlife.

The **Yanomami** live in dense forest on the Venezuelan-Brazilian border. They are today one of the most threatened peoples in the the world. Land-grabbing and slash-and-burn deforestation is destroying their habitat. Many

Yanomami die from diseases that have been brought into the country which their immune systems cannot cope with. In Yanomami mythology, men and animals are inextricably linked by 'shadow souls' and both share the same fate.

Population

More than half of the population is **Creole**, but 30 per cent is **black**, ten per cent **white**, ten per cent **Asian** or Arawak Indian who live in the rainforests in relative isolation. A significant minority consists of Hmong people who are refugees from Laos, and who work mainly supplying and selling fruit s and vegetables from their market gardens. The majority of the population are Roman Catholic. The education system is that which prevails in France and schooling is compulsory up to the age of 16.

History and Politics

The Spanish discovered what is now French Guiana in around 1500, but made no colonial claims. As a result, the **British, French** and **Dutch** fought for the land until the borders were finally established in 1814. Since the mid-nineteenth century, **slaves from Africa** and later **indentured labour from Asia** were set to work on the plantations. From 1854 to 1938, Guiana was a **French penal colony**. The prison known as **Devil's Island**, one of the offshore islands in the Isles du Salut group, became famous as the place to which Alfred Dreyfus was sent after being wrongly convicted of treason in France in 1894 and for the account of life there in the book 'Papillon' written by Henri Charrière, a former inmate. Since 1848, the French Guyanese have enjoyed **French citizenship**. The country has its own parliament, elected every six years, and also sends representatives to the National Assembly and the Senate in Paris.

Economy

Agriculture employs 11 per cent of the working population, **manufacturing** 21 per cent, and the **services sector** 68 per cent. Half of the money spent in the country are related to the scientific work performed at the **European Space Agency at Kourou**.
Coffee, rice, bananas, sugar cane and manioc are cultivated. Crab-fishing, the timber industry and gold-mining are also of economic importance. Consumer goods, machinery and vehicles are imported; exports are timber heli-copter parts, gold coins, crabs, coffee and rum. The economy is in general poorly developed and is dependent on French subsidies.

Transport Infrastructure

Of the 550-km-long **road network** 350 km of are surfaced. The interior can only be reached by **plane** or **riverboat**. There is an international airport and port at Cayenne.

Tourism

Tourism is restricted to the coastal region. The wildlife is spectacular and the countryside unspoiled so it is popular with trekkers and hikers. The best time to visit is between August and November.

Suriname

Area: 163,265 sq. km
Capital city: Paramaribo
Form of government: Presidential Republic
Administrative divisions: 9 districts, capital city district
Population: 438,000 (3 inhabitants/sq. km)
Languages: Dutch (official), Hindustani, Javanese, English
GDP per capita: US$4,700
Currency: 1 Suriname dollar = 100 cents

Natural Geography

Suriname is mainly covered by a **high plateau containing many ravines**. The **Wilhelmina Mountains**, whose highest peak is the 1,230-m-high Julianatop lie in the interior. Near the Atlantic coast

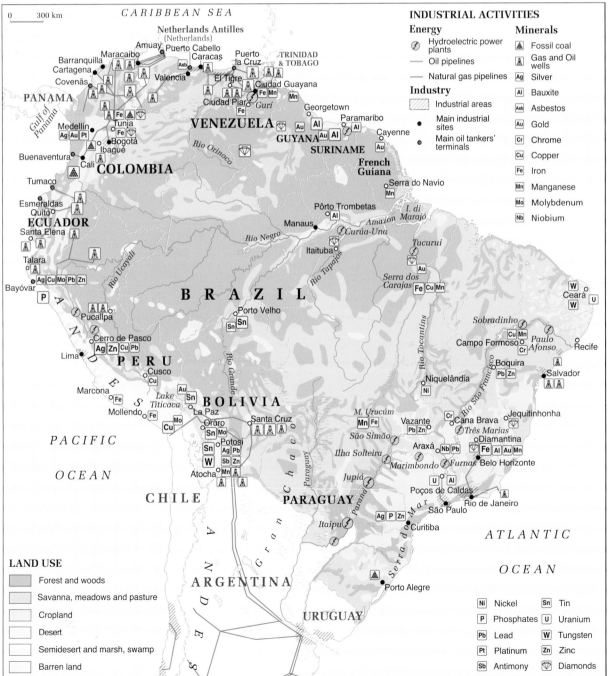

INDUSTRIAL ACTIVITIES

Energy
- ⚡ Hydroelectric power plants
- — Oil pipelines
- — Natural gas pipelines

Industry
- ▨ Industrial areas
- • Main industrial sites
- Main oil tankers' terminals

Minerals
- Ⓐ Fossil coal
- Ⓐ Gas and Oil wells
- Ag Silver
- Al Bauxite
- Asb Asbestos
- Au Gold
- Cr Chrome
- Cu Copper
- Fe Iron
- Mn Manganese
- Mo Molybdenum
- Nb Niobium

- Ni Nickel
- P Phosphates
- Pb Lead
- Pt Platinum
- Sb Antimony
- Sn Tin
- U Uranium
- W Tungsten
- Zn Zinc
- ▽ Diamonds

LAND USE
- Forest and woods
- Savanna, meadows and pasture
- Cropland
- Desert
- Semidesert and marsh, swamp
- Barren land

San Agustín is the most significant archaeological site in Colombia. Between 650 BC and 1400 AD numerous tombs were constructed here – some simple and some hill-like burial mounds, decorated with puzzling figures. The stone sculptures are mythological beings, half animal and half human. San Agustín's origins remain unknown.

there is an area of hills and a coastal plain, between 20 and 100 km wide. This area is where 80 per cent of the population lives. It is the main agricultural area.

All of the country's rivers flow northwards; the two most important are the **Courantyne** and the **Maroni**. The **Suriname river** is dammed to form the Prof. Dr. Ir. W. J. van Blommesteinmeer (Brokopondo Reservoir).

Climate

Although temperatures in the mountains can fluctuate widely, the rest of the country has a constant **tropical temperature** of around 27°C. During the **rainy season,** up to 2,500 mm of rain can fall on the mountain slopes; the coastal region only receives 1,500 mm. 85 per cent of the country is covered in rainforest, parts of which are still unexplored. Towards the coast, savannah vegetation predominates, followed by mangrove swamp and marshes along the coast.

The tropical rainforests have a rich wildlife, including jaguars, tapir, monkeys and ocelots, numerous reptiles and many species of bird. The coastal waters contain manatees and turtles.

Population

The population consists of 34.2 per cent **Indians**, 33.5 per cent **Creole**, up to 17.8 per cent **Javanese**, 8.5 per cent **black** and minorities of **Native Americans, Europeans, Lebanese** and **Chinese**. Life expectancy is 71 years and the literacy rate is 93 per cent. 27 per cent of the population are **Hindu**, 23 per cent **Catholic**, 20 per cent **Muslims** and 19 per cent **Protestant**. There is the remnant of a thriving Jewish community and the oldest synagogue in the New World. Nearly half the population lives in the cities. Schooling is compulsory from 6 to 12.

History and Politics

Columbus landed in Guiana in 1498, when the country had already been settled by Native Americans for more than 2,500 years. Colonial wars and various treaties first brought the country under **French**, then **Dutch** and finally **British rule**. In 1814, what is

now Suriname became a **Dutch colony** and in 1954, it became part of the Netherlands with equal rights and **a large measure of autonomy**.

Suriname was granted **independence** in 1975, but serious, ethnically motivated power struggles broke out. The resulting economic and political instability caused a **wave of emigration**. Since all inhabitants held a Dutch passport, one third of the population was able to move to the Netherlands. Under the 1987 constitution, the country is a presidential republic. The head of state and the bicameral parliament are elected every

five years. All citizens over the age of 18 have the right to vote.

Economy

GDP in 2005 was US$1.3 billion. **Agriculture** accounted for seven per cent, **manufacturing** for 35 per cent and the **services sector** for 58 per cent.

Despite an almost even trade balance, a large proportion of the population lives in dire **poverty.** Many can only survive from **black market dealing** and **smuggling**. The country mainly imports raw materials, processed goods and consumer products. Main exports are aluminium, prawns and rice.

Transport Infrastructure

The only paved roads are found in coastal regions. The main cities, the capital Paramaribo, Nieuw Nickerie, Brokopondo and Nieuw Amsterdam are connected by **domestic flights**. The rivers are the main form of transport.

Tourism

Tourism is expanding, and new facilities are opening up, including the Overbridge River Resort, popular with hikers and anglers. The colonial architecture of Paramaribo, including the cathedral, are also of interest. The best time of year to visit is from February to April.

1 In the Venezuelan Simón Bolívar National Park, people live at an altitude of 3,000 m. Venezuela's highest mountain Pico Bolívar (5,002 m) is in this region.

2 The east of Venezuela is largely uninhabited and rivers flow through endless jungle. The whole region around the Auyantepui (2,953 m) can only be reached by plane or boat.

3 Caracas is the political and economic centre of oil-rich Venezuela. Skyscrapers are typical of the city's skyline.

The Pre-Columbian legacy

The Spanish conquistadors were blinded by dreams of gold when they set foot in Central and South America. Some of the Pre-Columbian cultures were not only immensely rich, they had also constructed complex social structures. The history of the various peoples extends back to the fourth century BC.

When the Spanish conquerors landed on the coasts of South and Central America at the beginning of the sixteenth century they stumbled upon cultures which were highly developed. Blinded by gold and the immeasurable wealth of these people, they promptly set about destroying the great empires of the Aztecs and the Incas. These were only the last of the advanced Pre-Columbian civilisations which can be dated back to the fourth century BC.

Many of their remains and ruins, a large proportion of which are concealed in the depths of the rainforest, are still puzzling scientists. The Olmecs of the La Venta civilisation founded the oldest advanced civilisation in Central America in the rainforests of the Gulf coast of Mexico in approximately 800–400 BC. They were skillful builders and had the elements of a calendar and writing system at their disposal. This civilisation continued in the city of Teotihuacán in the Mexican highlands which was founded in approximately 100 BC and it dominated the entire Mexican highlands from 650 AD. With 150,000 inhabitants Teotihuacán was the largest city of the American continent in around 350 AD.

Further south in the region of Oaxaca and Tehuantepec, the Zapotec civilisation reached its zenith more or less simultaneously. The Zapotecs founded ceremonial sanctuaries such as Mitla and extended the city of Monte Albán, founded by the Olmecs. However, the most significant civilisation in America before European colonisation were the Mayas. Their highly-developed culture, which had an enormous influence on future empires, reached its prime between the third and ninth centuries AD.

In the wooded lowland of the Yucatán peninsula, centres such as Copán, Uxmal and Tikal were created, from which the Mayas soon dominated the surrounding area.

Teotihuacán, Mexico: a snake's head from the Quetzalcóatl pyramids.

Religion ruled the lives of these people. They offered human sacrifices to placate the gods. They also made astonishing advances in astronomy, chronology and mathematics.

It is unclear why the Mayas abandoned their cities from 900 AD onwards and returned to the northern Yucatán. They mingled with the warlike Toltecs and their civilisation flourished again in Chichén Itzá in approximately 1200 AD.

At around this time, the Aztecs emigrated to the highlands of Mexico and established a powerful empire which stretched from the Gulf Coast to the Pacific. The centre of their realm was Tenochtitlán and its remains can still be seen in the present-day capital,

Large illustration: The Inca city of Macchu Picchu in the High Andes sits in splendour like an eagle's nest.

Monuments of power: the Mexican Maya palaces of Sayil and Tulum.

Mexico City. Their flourishing economy was based on the highly-developed cultivation of arable land. They also had open-air cafés and 'floating gardens' which can be marvelled at in Xochimilco today. Religion played a dominant role in their strict, class-conscious society. The ruler of the Aztecs, Moctezuma, believed the arrival of the conquistadors in 1519 to be a confirmation of ancient prophecies about the arrival of white gods. Consequently, the Spanish conquerors found it easy to annihilate the last advanced civilisation in Central America two years later, encountering little resistance. The old state language of the Aztecs, Nahuatl is still spoken by the Native American population of Mexico.

Further south the Andes region was also inhabited by mysterious and powerful empires. The oldest architectural remains in the New World are the 4,600-year-old step pyramids in Caral in Northern Peru. The ruins of the civilisation of Chavín (1250–400 BC) and Moche (200–700 BC) can also be found in Peru. This civilisation left behind monumental pyramids and great cities.

The Nazca civilisation (200 to 600 BC) still puzzles scientists with its unique gigantic engravings on the ground running for up to 2 km in length. They were not even discovered until 1926 when they could be viewed from the air. These engravings in a desert valley may have served as a calendar for priests, places of worship where rain was prayed for, or areas for stretching out huge strips of cloth for the weaving industry. The centre of the highly-developed empire of Chimú (1000 to 1470) was the great city of Chanchán; over 100,000 people lived there in its heyday. The Chimús attained a high standard of craftsmanship but only a few pieces of jewellery have survived. The Chimús were finally taken over by the Incas, who began to conquer their neighbours with campaigns from 1438 onwards. The Incas, who ruled large parts of Columbia, Ecuador, Bolivia, Argentina, Chile and Peru founded their first capital in Cuzco and ran a strictly administered empire, in which the ruler, who was also called an 'Inca', possessed unlimited power. He stood at the centre of the cult as a descendant of the sun god. All the temples in the empire were dedicated to him. The enormous dominion of tributary empires was divided into districts overseen by governors and controlled by a uniform official

The four 'Atlantean columns' of Tula are 4.60 m high and once supported the roof of a temple.

language and a well-developed road network. Only the reports of the Spanish conquerors provide information about the overwhelming sight of the great Inca city of Cuzco. They mention gardens containing plants fashioned from gold. In 1533, the Spaniards led by Francisco Pizarro conquered the Inca Empire. The treasures were melted down or removed.

There was a sensational discovery in 1911 of an abandoned Inca city in the Peruvian highlands which was later named Machu Picchu. The city had been miraculous spared not only from the Spanish depredations but from the frequent earthquakes. Six million Indians still speak Quechua, the language of the Incas, in the Andean highland of Peru.

Brazil

*Coffee and meat are **Brazil's** most important exports. The farmers are very badly affected by fluctuations in the world market price for coffee or meat, which is a contributing factor to the growing migration to the cities.*

 Brazil

Area:	8,511,996 sq. km
Capital city:	Brasília

Form of government:
Federal Republic
Administrative divisions:
26 federal states
1 federal district (capital city)
Population:
186.1 million
(21 inhabitants/sq. km)
Languages:
Portuguese (official), regional
Indian languages

GDP per capita:	US$8500

Currency:
1 real = 100 centavos

Natural geography

The world's fifth largest country occupies almost half of the South American continent. It shares a border with all the countries of South America, with the exception of Chile and Ecuador. Some of the island groups in the west Atlantic also belong to Brazil. Brazil is divided up into three large regions with very different landscapes: the **mountainous country of Guayana** in the north, the **Amazonas lowland** in the south and the **Brazilian mountain country** in the south-east.

The mountainous region of Guayana contains the country's highest mountain the **Pico da Neblina** (altitude: 3,014 m) which stands near the Venezuelan border. This mountain range is characterised by vast plains and isolated monadnocks. It ends very abruptly in the Amazon region.
The **Amazon the world's largest river** is up to 25 km wide and over 60 m deep at its lower reaches. It traverses the world's **largest tropical forest** (an area of 4 million sq. km). Its tributaries, of which there are over 1,000, are also exceptionally full of water but are not navigable, however, due to a large number of rapids.
The tributaries have some spectacular waterfalls, notably the 115-m-high **Guaira Falls**, the **Iguazu Falls** (72 m high) and the **Paulo Alfonso Falls** on the São Francisco River (81 m high).
Brazil's mountain region is approximately five million sq. km and occupies over half of the country's land mass. The mountain range is coated in sedimentary rock which was formed in the Palaeozoic and Mesozoic eras. In the south-east, it extends out to form the coastal mountain ranges of **Serra do Mar** and **Serra da Mantiqueira** before dropping steeply down to the Atlantic Coast. In the south and south-west, the uplands turn into coastal

terms of mineral resources. It possesses immense deposits of oil, iron, manganese, gold, gemstones, bauxite, magnesium, copper, tin, zinc, chrome, tungsten, nickel and uranium. The enormous resources in terms of **tropical timber** and **hydroelectric power** have become a significant economic factor.

Climate

In the Amazonas lowland of the north there is a **tropical rainforest climate** with temperatures of approximately 27°C and precipitation volumes of 2000 mm to 4000 mm.
In the mid-west and the mountainous Guayana region there is a **savannah climate** with a dry season in winter producing daytime temperatures of 17°C to 28°C. The average precipitation is approximately 1600 mm, producing deciduous forests and open grassland. There are large swamps in Pantanal.
A savannah climate, temperatures of 23°C to 30°C and precipitation of 1250 mm are typical of the **coastal region** to the south of the Amazon estuary. The vegetation is scrubland, stunted trees and succulents.
In the coastal area and in the south-east, a **tropical rainforest**

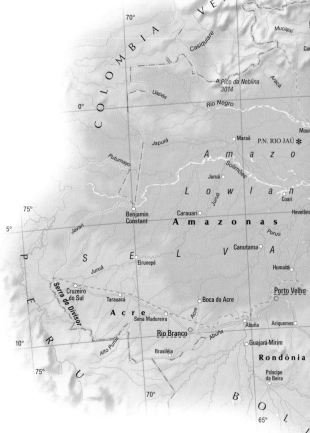

22°C and precipitation of 1330 mm favour a landscape of tall grasslands and coniferous forests. There are many cattle ranches in this area.
Recent climate problems have consisted of serious drought in

otters, monkeys, sloths and various species of birds and snakes. The Brazil has one third of the world's tropical rainforest, containing around 55,000 flowering plants,

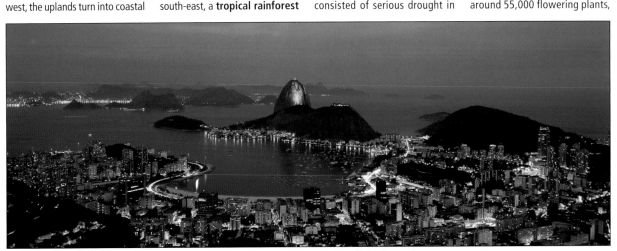

The 395-m-high Sugarloaf Mountain dominates Guanabara bay and the skyline of Rio de Janeiro.

lowlands which are bordered by lagoons. The **Pantanal** Lagoon in the West is in the mountains of the **Mato Grosso**.
Although its geological indexing is only in its early stages, Brazil is one of the world's richest countries in

climate prevails with temperatures of between 18°C and 27°C and precipitation of 1460 mm.
In the **sub-tropical wet**, **moderate climate** of the south the seasons are differentiated. Temperatures of between 14°C and

the north-east, the **El Niño** climate phenomenon and continued **deforestation**. Nevertheless, the Amazon jungle contains a wealth of **fauna**. Tapirs, wild boars, iguanas, jaguars, leopards, stags, racoons, anteaters, turtles,

the greatest variety in the world, many of which have not yet been classified, but due to deforestation, they are in danger of disappearing even before uses have been found for them.

Splendid costumes and an exuberant lust for life: no country in the world celebrates the **Carnival** as lavishly as **Brazil**. The samba schools that lead the parades, are for the men and women from the favelas – the slums of Rio de Janeiro – a chance to escape the daily misery of their district, if only for one day.

religions and **Afro-Brazilian cults**. Many Brazilians belong to several religious denominations simultaneously! Consequently, it is impossible to compile accurate statistics. Average **life expectancy** is 67 years.

Health care is non-existent for large sections of the population in spite of continually improving healthcare and this affects the youngest members of society in particular. The **infant mortality rate** is just four per cent.

Although schooling is compulsory between the ages of seven and 14, the **illiteracy rate** is 17 per cent. 80 per cent of Brazilians live in cities. Although Brazil has the world's **eighth largest national economy**, 23.6 per cent of the population still live below the poverty line.

History and Politics

The Portuguese seafarer **Pedro Álvares Cabral** landed on the Brazilian coast on 22 April 1500 and seized the region for the Portuguese crown under the 1494 Treaty of Tordesillas. In order to protect the newly acquired regions from the claims of other colonial powers, Martim Alfonso **de Sousa** started systematically populating the region in 1532 by founding **São Vicente**. Portuguese aristocrats took possession of enormous estates. The Indians who lived there were systematically enslaved or slaughtered. African slaves were shipped in to work the large plantations. The seventeenth and eighteenth centuries were the time of the great **expeditions**:

Population

People of European ancestry account for 53 per cent of the population. They can be sub-divided as follows: 15 per cent of **Portuguese descent**, 11 per cent of **Italian descent**, ten per cent of **Spanish** descent and three per cent of **German descent**. Approximately 34 per cent of the population consists of people of **mixed races**, and 11 per cent are **black**.

There are approximately 300,000 **native Brazilians** belonging to approximately 200 ethnic groups. The **Japanese**, of which there are approximately one million, constitute a further minority. Roughly 75 per cent of Brazilians are **Catholic**, ten per cent are Protestant and there are members of alternative Christian denominations such as the Pentecostal Church. Other religious minorities are **Buddhists**, **Baha'is**, **Jews**, **Muslims**, followers of **natural**

Brazil

*The justice buliding and cathedral in **Brasília:** the capital of Brazil was designed between 1956 and 1960 according to the at the time state of the art civil engineering concepts. Oscar Niemeyer was one of the main architects.*

Starting out from São Paulo, expeditions penetrated ever further into the interior of the country to capture Indians as slaves and capture fabulous treasures. The colonial area was constantly extended thanks to raids by these notorious **bandeirantes of São Paulo** – ruthless gold-seekers and slave-hunters. In 1763, the Portuguese colonial administration was relocated from São Salvador do Bahia (now known as Salvador) to **Rio de Janeiro**. Dutch and Spanish claims to the land were warded off.

The borders of modern Brazil were finally defined in the 1750 **Treaty of Madrid**. In 1789, the first revolt began against Portuguese supremacy which ended in defeat. The battle for autonomy continued for several more decades. In 1808, King Joaõ VI moved the Portuguese seat of government from Lisbon to Rio de Janeiro as Napoleonic troops had occupied Portugal. In 1821, the court returned to Lisbon.

Under the influence of the **Andrada de Silva** brothers, the king's son who had remained a prince regent and refused to acknowledge the renewed colonial status of Brazil declared the country's **independence** and was crowned Emperor **Pedro I** in 1822. Portugal finally granted Brazil its independence three years later.

The gradual emancipation of the slaves was proclaimed in the **'Golden Law'** of 1888. The monarchy was abolished and the Republic of Brazil proclaimed in 1889 through a **military coup**, facilitated by an **economic crisis** and **unrest** in the armed forces. The new rulers drew up a constitution modelled on that of the United States. In 1891, the United States of Brazil were founded. The first republican governments were despotic **military dictatorships**, but the political and economic situation stabilised from 1894 onwards.

The **export of coffee** and the stronger development of **industry** after the outbreak of **World War I** led to short-lived economic prosperity. The worldwide **postwar depression** also affected Brazil and the economic decline caused serious internal unrest which set Brazil's development back years.

In 1930, **Getulio Vargas** came to power. He used the global economic crisis to make himself an **absolute dictator** in 1937. Inspired by the fascist systems which then predominated in Europe, he abolished the constitution and all political parties.

Vargas' **role models** were undoubtedly **Mussolini** and **Hitler**. However, in 1942, under pressure from the USA, Vargas joined the coalition against Hitler. The **Estado Novo** ended in 1945 with Vargas' downfall but in 1950 he returned to power. Due to **maladministration** and **corruption** in his regime he came under greater pressure and eventually committed **suicide** in 1954.

Juscelino **Kubitschek de Olivera** attempted to remedy the economic devastation that was Vargas' legacy by making a fresh start. His government operated an ambitious **industrialisation policy** from 1956 and he decided to found a new capital for the nation, the city of **Brasília deep in the interior**. This decision was symbolic. Kubitschek de Oliveira wanted to develop the Brazilian interior which was mostly under-developed. Although his economic policy led to increases in productivity, little benefit appeared to have been gained since this economic expansion had been funded by printing money, leading to crippling inflation. Purchasing power was seriously reduced and foreign debt reached record levels.

In 1963, President **João Goulart** attempted to push through **agrarian reform** for the benefit of landless farmers and attempted to nationalise the **oil industry**. His socialist ideals were opposed by a strong conservative opposition, supported by leading senior army officers. Eventually, there was a **military** coup in 1964, backed by the USA.

A state-regulated **two-party system** replaced the hitherto multiple political parties. The **opposition** was brutally suppressed. It was not until General Ernest **Geisel**, who served as president from 1974 to 1979, that the severe **repression** of the dictatorship was slightly relaxed.

In 1973, Brazil experienced an **economic upturn** with growth rates in double figures, but another depression followed soon afterwards. In 1985, the **military** finally exited the political stage and a gradual **process of democratisation** ensued but in 1990, inflation still stood at a staggering 1,795 per cent.

Since the mid-1990s the **economic reforms** of civilian governments have borne their first fruits, but the country still suffers from a deep **social divide** between the rich and the poor, marauding death squads, drug-dealing, corruption and immense foreign debt. Luiz Inácio Lula da Silvo, ('Lula') the current left-leaning Labour president who has been in power since 2003 can rely on the widespread support of all sections of society. He appears to be leading the country into a new era of democracy and prosperity. Since the 1988 constitution was last amended in 1997, Brazil has been governed by a bicameral **parliament** consisting of a house of representatives elected every four years, and a senate elected every eight years. The president, the **head of state**, is directly elected every four years and can only serve two terms. The **right to vote** begins at 16;

São Paulo: Skyscrapers dominate the skyline of the biggest city in South America. Almost ten million people live or just survive here.

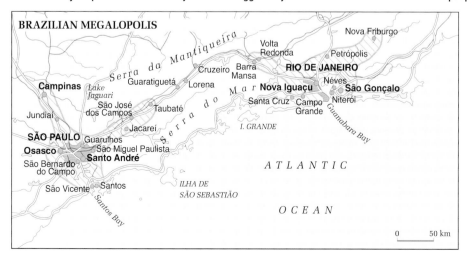

Emilio Garrastazú Médici

*Bagé 4.12.1906,
†Rio de Janeiro 9.10.1985

Médici took over the management of the Brazilian secret service in 1966. In 1969, he was appointed president by a military junta. He brutally suppressed the opposition, and introduced torture and death squads during his five-year rule. Resistance was growing and the election of 1974 put an end to his reign of terror.

*Chainsaws and slash-and-burn clearing methods are eating away at the **Brazilian rainforests**. Many Brazilians see no alternative to this. Around 10,000 sq. km of rainforest are cleared each year.*

voting is compulsory between the ages of 18 and 69.

Economy

In the last 25 years, Brazil has developed from an agrarian nation to an **emerging market country** thanks to massive **industrialisation**. The Brazilian **economic miracle** is extremely unevenly developed regionally and socially.

In 2005, **GDP** was US$619.7 billion. **Agriculture** accounted for 14 per cent of this amount, **industry** for 37 per cent and the **services sector** for 49 per cent. Brazil's main trading partners are the USA and Argentina. The trade balance surplus amounted to US$2.6 billion in 2002.

The main imports are machinery, vehicles, fuel, electrical appliances and foodstuffs. The most important **exports** are metals and metal products, vehicles and vehicle parts, soya beans and soy products, chemicals, mineral ores, paper, coffee and sugar. 14 per cent of the agricultural land is used for **crop-growing** and approximately half the total area to **cattle-rearing**; the rest lies fallow. In the fertile south **soybeans**, **sugar cane**, **coffee** and **tobacco** are grown, and there is a thriving cattle trade. In the north, the cultivation of **tropical fruits**, **cocoa plantations** and **forestry products** plays an important role. The annual **clearance** of 25,544 sq. km of jungle is liable to seriously upset **the ecological balance**.

Brazil's energy resources are largely untapped. They consist of hydro-electric power (at present there are two large dams, Itaipú on the Paraná River and Tucuruí on the Tocantins River) and the possibility of using nuclear power fuelled by the considerable deposits of uranium ore.

Transport

The **rail network** which was **privatised** in 1997 extends for 27,400 km, only 2,200 km of which is electrified. 60 per cent of freight and 65 per cent of passenger traffic are transported by road. The road network extends over 1,939,000 km but only 178,400 km are paved. Projects such as the construction of the 5000-km-long Transamazónica Highway are intended to improve Brazil's road in-

frastructure. **Rio de Janeiro** and **São Paulo** are the largest of the 22 international **airports**. Santos, Rio de Janeiro, Angra dos Reis, Praia Mole and Vitória are the largest of the 50 **sea ports**. Of the approximately 50,000 km of inland waterways, the Amazon accounts for 3,680 km. The largest inland port, **Manaus,** can be reached by large ocean-going vessels via the 1,600 km navigable stretch of the Amazon.

Tourism

Roughly 4.8 million foreign visitors came to Brazil in 2002 and

spent approximately US$3.7 billion. The most popular destinations are the coastal cities of **Rio de Janeiro**, **São Paulo**, **Salvador** and **Recife**, **Manaus** (whose famous opera house must be the most remote in the world), **Brasilia** and the **Iguazu Falls** inland. The **Copacabana** Beach in Rio de Janeiro, the **Sugarloaf Mountain** and the samba spectacle in the **Carnaval do Brasil** number among the tourist highlights. The Amazonian **rainforest** with its fascinating and unique fauna and flora, including 20 per cent of all the world's species of birds, makes Brazil a destination which is visited all year round. The tropical summer lasts from **April** to **October** and these are also the most pleasant months for touring the country.

Other attractions are Mount Roraima, Xingu National Park. Between December and May the entire Brazilian coast is warm enough for bathing.

1 The baroque coastal town of Olinda is one of Brazil's oldest and most beautiful cities. The Benedictine monastery of São Bento, surrounded by palms, is a masterpiece of late baroque architecture.

2 The Waira, an indigenous Amazon people have preserved

most of their rites and customs under the protection of the rainforest.

3 There is just one way to reach Belém and that is by boat on the Rio Pará. Almost all the wares on sale in the big market of Belém are transported via the river.

4 In Salvador de Bahia time seems to stand still. The beautiful colonial-style houses have been elaborately renovated with much attention to detail. Colourful baroque facades and splendidly-decorated church towers line the streets.

Ecuador

In the isolation of the **Galapagos Islands**, a unique ecosystem developed which helped Charles Darwin to explore the mechanisms of evolution. The 30 volcanic islands are inhabited by endemic, i.e. unique species such as these marine iguanas. The understandable fascination with the Galapagos is rather problematic: although tourism is already strictly limited, it still disrupts the fragile habitat.

Area: 283,560 sq. km
Capital city: Quito
Form of government:
Presidential Republic
Administrative divisions:
20 provinces, Galapagos Islands and undefined areas
Population:
13.3m (50 inhabitants/sq. km)
Languages:
Spanish (official), Indian dialects
GDP per inhabitant: US$3,900
Currency: 1 US-dollar = 100 cents (since 2000)

Natural geography

The smallest country in the Andes is divided into three large regions. **Fertile lowlands** between 50 km and 150 km wide extend along the Pacific Coast. Two chains of the Andes mountains surround the **Sierra region**,

José María Velasco Ibarra

*Quito 19.3.1893,
†Quito 30.3.1979

The lawyer was the dominating politician in Ecuador since 1934 and ruled altogether five times: 1934–1935, 1946 to 1947, 1952–1956, 1960–1961 and 1968 till 1972. However he could only survive one term without being overthrown by the military. In 1970 he suspended the Constitution, dissolved the parliament and ruled – supported by the conservative military – as a dictator. He was deposed in 1972.

which is up to 3,000 m high. The highland basins are separated from each other by ridges. The highest peak of the Cordillera Occidental is the extinct volcano Mt. Chimborazo which is 6,310 m high. The 5,897-m-high Cotopaxi in the Cordillera Oriental is still active. This region is under constant threat from earthquakes. The **Amazon region** in the east is barely populated and crisscrossed by many tributaries of the great river.

Climate

The coastal region is characterised by a **tropical climate**; rainfall reduces towards the south. In the north, which has an annual rainfall of over 2,500 mm, there are vast **rainforests**, which turn to **thornbush and cactus savannah**. The average temperature in Guayaquil, the regional capital, is 25.5°C. The south, which is affected by the Humboldt Current, is extremely dry with less than 300 mm rainfall. In the highlands, rainfall is low, and the average temperature of 15°C remains constant all year round, though there are considerable fluctuations between day and night.
In the Andes region, where the rainfall is up to 5,000 mm, there are mountain forests and cloud forests; above the tree line at 3,500 m this turns into mountain

meadows. The **lowlands** in the east, which are sparsely populated, are characterised by evergreen rainforests. The climate phenomenon known as **El Niño** causes severe damage to agriculture, producing **flooding** in the coastal area and droughts inland.

Population

The population of Ecuador is composed of 35 per cent **mestizo**, 25 per cent **white**, 20 per cent **Indian**, 15 per cent **mulatto** and five per cent **black**. 93 per cent of the population profess the **Catholic faith**, the remainder are **Protestants**, **Baha'i**, **Jews** and followers of native natural religions. Life expectancy is 70 years; there is ten per cent illiteracy. 60 per cent of the population lives in the cities; 30 per cent live below the poverty line. Education is compulsory for ten years.

History and politics

Before Pizarro's General **Sebastián de Benalcázar claimed** the country for the Spanish crown in 1533/1534, Ecuador was a part of the Inca Empire. The Quito Audiencia first belonged to the **Viceroyalty of Peru**, then, from the early eighteenth century, to the **Viceroyalty of New Granada**. The struggle for liberation from the Spanish ended victoriously for Bolívar's General **Antonio José de Sucre** in 1822, and Ecuador became **part of Greater Colombia**. Ecuador finally declared its **independence** in 1830. Its subsequent history is characterised by a large number of **coups** and **extreme political instability**. The republic was dedicated to the Sacred Heart of Jesus (by act of Congress) in 187. The period 1925 to 1944 was one of extreme instability when no president was able to complete his term of office. **Josémaría Velasco Ibarra** was able to stabilise the situation in 1944., but after unrest and yet another economic crisis, he was overthrown in 1972. Two military juntas followed, until the introduction of a market economy and a democratisation process were achieved in 1978. Failed economic policies, reductions in the price of oil and the climate phenomenon known as El Niño led the country into **economic**

*During the colonial period, **Lima** was the most cultured and influential city in South America. In this 'pearl of the Pacific' Peru's biggest ecclesiastical complex, the abbey-church of San Francisco was founded in the shadow of the* *dreaded Inquisition. Its yellow front shines in the sun and is regarded the most beautiful church facade in Lima. The adjoining monastery buildings are impressive, built in the splendid Mudéjar architectural style of the Spanish Moors.*

crisis from 1990 to 2000, at the climax of which the American dollar was introduced to replace the sucre, the existing currency. Under President Gustavo Noboa and, since 2003, under Lucio Gutiérrez, the country has slowly been recovering and inflation has fallen from 90 to nine per cent. GDP increased in 2002 by 3.3 per cent and is set to increase further due to high price of oil.

The 1978 **constitution**, which was last amended in 1998, provides for a parliament whose representatives are elected every four years; the president is elected directly for a period of four years. The voting age is 18 years.

Economy

In 2005, GDP was US$30.7 billion, of which 13 per cent derived from **agriculture**, 39 per cent from **industry** and 48 per cent from the **service sector**. 28 per cent of the labour forced work in agriculture, 18 per cent in industry and 53 per cent in the service sector. There is a considerable foreign debt of US$13.9 billion.

Raw materials, capital and consumer goods as well as fuel are the principal imports; crude oil, bananas, industrial products and shrimps are the main exports.

Transport

Only half the 37,000-km-long road network is passable all year round; the 1,392 km long Pan-American Highway is regarded as the most important arterial route. There is a rail network which is 1,000 km long and two international airports in Quito and Guayaquil. The major sea ports are Guayaquil, Esmeraldas, Balao, Manta and Puerto Bolívar.

Tourism

Tourism is not yet well developed on the mainland but by far the greatest place of interest is the **Galapagos** Islands which are part of the national territory. These islands are inhabited by species of fauna not seen elsewhere, such as the giant tortoises and were the inspiration for Charles Darwin's ground-breaking *Origin of the Species*. The best time to travel to mainland Ecuador is from June to October.

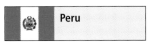

Peru	
Area:	1,285,216 sq. km
Capital city:	Lima
Form of government: Presidential Republic	
Administrative divisions: 25 regions	
Population: 27.9 m (22 inhabitants/sq. km)	
Languages: Spanish, Quechua (both official), Aymará	
GDP per inhabitant:	US$6,000
Currency: 1 new sol = 100 centimos	

Natural geography

Peru is divided into three large regions. The coastline is 2,300 km long and 50–140 km wide and interior consists of deserts and savannah. The three main chains of the Andes running parallel to the coast, the **Sierras** consist of the Cordillera Occidental whose highest peak is the 6,768 m Huascarán; the Cordillera Central and the Cordillera Oriental. **Lake Titicaca** is high in the mountains at an altitude of 3,812 m. The main rivers, the Marañón and the Ucayali, meet in the north-eastern **lowlands** of the Amazon. The Montaña region on the eastern slopes of the Andes contains the Amazon headwaters, known as the Selva.

Climate

Because of Peru's tropical location, the climate is relatively stable. In the coastal regions it is cooled by the **Humboldt Current** and on average there is only 45 mm of rainfall annually. The coastal desert continues far up the Andes slopes, where the vegetation consists mainly of cacti and thorn bushes. The montaña has a tropical hot climate with abundant rainfall. Here, and in the eastern lowlands, tropical rainfall predominates. In the Andes, rich forests of palms, tree ferns and Peruvian bark trees are found up to altitudes of 3,500 m. At up to 4,600 m, there are alpine meadows, grassland and moorland. At the higher altitudes, stone and rock outcrops, depleted of vegetation, predominate. As for the fauna, condors, alpacas, llamas and vicuñas live in the highlands; in the eastern lowlands, there are

various species of monkeys, reptiles and birds as well as jaguars, peccaries, tapirs and sloths.

Population

The population consists of 47 per cent **Amerindians**, 32 per cent **mestizos**, 12 per cent **white** and small minorities of **Japanese**,

1 Like this farmer with his cabbages, one third of Ecuador's population lives from agriculture. They sell their produce in the local markets.

2 The Quechua Indians in Peru and Ecuador have a long tradition of Alpaca breeding.

Typically colourful blankets and pullovers are made from the wool, to protect the Quechua against the cold of the high Andes.

3 The Manú river winds its way into the Amazon basin. Manú national park covers over 18,000 sq. km.

Indigenous Bolivians represent 71 per cent of the population. Although they have officially had equal rights since 1953, they still live a politically and culturally remote existence in Bolivia's highlands. Their diet consists of maize and sweet potatoes and they only visit the cities such as La Paz for the big, colourful markets in which they can sell their handicrafts, the ponchos, pottery and silver jewellery that are popular with tourists.

mulatto and **Chinese**. 89 per cent of the population are **Catholics**, three per cent are **Protestants**. There are also Jews and followers of **natural religions**. Almost half the population lives below the poverty line. Life expectancy is 68 years and there is 11 per cent il**literacy**. 71 per cent of the population lives in the cities. Education is compulsory from six to 15 years, although only 20 per

detached from the **Viceroyship of Peru**.
Simón Bolívar's and José de Sanmartin's armies achieved **independence** in 1821, which was consolidated in 1824 after the victory of Antonio José de Sucre. The discovery of deposits of **salpetre** caused an **economic upswing** that lasted until the mid-nineteenth century but ended after the country lost the **Salpetre War** against Chile in

1884. The provinces of Tarapacá and Arica were awarded to Chile. Tacna was handed back to Peru in 1929.
In the early twentieth century, the discovery of **rubber** trees and **oil reserves** once more improved the economic situation, though the majority of the population did not benefit. **Military dictatorships** ruined any plans for reform. The majority of the mineral resources were in foreign hands

until the government nationalised the mines in 1973.
The 1980s were characterised by the civil war between the **Sindero Luminos (Shining Path) Marxist guerillas** and the military. President Alberto Fujimori, elected in 1990, introduced a strong **neoliberal economic system** but his **authoritarian** and corrupt **regime** met with increasing disapproval from the population.

After accusations of bribery he fled in 2000. In 2001, Alejandro Toledo was elected president. On the basis of the poor economic situation, countrywide strikes and demonstrations against the government took place, which in 2003 led to a state of emergency being declared on several occasions.
The unicameral parliament is elected every five years, as is the president. The voting age is 18.

Ernesto »Che« Guevara Serna

*Rosario 14.6.1928,
†Higueras 9.10.1967

The Argentinian doctor together with Castro liberated Cuba from Batista's dictatorship in 1959. As the minister of industry he was crucial in the revolutionary change of Cuba. The leading figure of the armed conflict against imperialism went eventually to Bolivia in 1965 in order to found a guerilla army. However he failed both politcially and in military terms. He was arrested in 1967 and killed without a court process.

cent of schoolchildren take their school-leaving examinations.

History and politics

A civilisation had already been established in Peru by the second century BC. Between 1000 and 300 BC, **advanced civilisations** arose with monumental places of worship, such as the **Chavin de Huántar**. Between 200 and 600 AD, powerful urban centres developed which waged war against each other. The **Tiwanaku culture** was replaced by other regional cultures in around 1000 AD, of which the most powerful was the **Chimú** whose capital city was **Chan Chan**.
The **Inca culture** developed around 1200. It was brutally destroyed by the Spanish, first under Francisco Pizarro who landed in 1532/1533 and finally in 1572 by Francisco de Toledo, despite its obvious military superiority. In 1739, the **Viceroyship of New Granada** and in 1776 **the Viceroyship of Río de la Plata** were

In the wide 'Holy Valley of the Incas' near Cuzco the Inca rulers finally rest in peace.

Economy

In 2005, GDP was US$69.8 billion of which 27 per cent was derived from **agriculture**, 25 per cent from **industry** and 48 per cent from the **service sector**. Exports include lead, Peru being the biggest producer in South America. Other exports are coca, coffee, lama and vicuña wool, copper, iron and oil. Imports include machinery, vehicles and foodstuffs. The deposits of gold, silver and zinc iron remain to be exploited.

Transport

The **rail network** covers around 2,041 km and the **road network** covers 71,400 km, of which only 7,783 km is paved. There are **four international airports**.

Tourism

The Inca ruins are the most popular attractions. The best time to travel is November to April.

Bolivia

Area:	1,098,581 sq. km
Capital cities: Sucre, La Paz	
Form of government: Presidential Republic	
Administrative divisions: 9 departments	
Population: 8.8m (7.7 inhabitants/sq. km)	
Languages: Spanish, Quechua, Aymará (all official)	
GDP per inhabitant:	US$2,700
Currency: 1 boliviano = 100 centavos	

Natural geography

The 3,609–4,000-m-high **Altiplano de Bolivia (Andes highland**

Lake Titicaca (8300 sq. km) is situated between Peru and Bolivia. Taquile Island with its stone gateways lies in this 'Holy Sea of the Incas'. The Aymará live on islands in the Bolivian part. They build their boats of totora, a kind of bullrush.

plateau) forms the heartland of Bolivia. The west of the country is dominated by the Cordillera Occidental, and the north-east by the Cordillera Real including the 6,682-m-high Mount Illimani. In the south, the Cordillera Oriental and the Cordillera Central form the East Bolivian mountain range. The **lowlands** are in the east and the Chaco Boreal region is named after the river of the same name that runs through it.

Lake Titicaca and **Lake Poopó** are in the highlands. They are connected to each other by the Desaguadero river which has large salt flats at its estuary.

Climate

The climate is **tropical** throughout nearly the whole country, but the rainfall decreases from up to 2,000 mm in the north-east to 200 mm in the south-west. In the cool **Altiplano**, the rainfall, which is already low reduces further towards the south. Average temperatures fluctuate in La Paz from 8°C in July to 12°C in December. In the lowlands, savannahs and jungle predominate. The river valleys and mountainsides are covered in virgin rainforest.

Population

Around 71 per cent of the inhabitants are **Amerindians** and there are also **mestizos**, **whites** and **creoles**. As far as religion goes, 92,5 per cent of the population are Catholic, the remainder are Protestant and Baha'i. Life expectancy is 61 years; there is 17 per cent **illiteracy**.

History and politics

Settlements have been found in Bolivia dating from five centuries BC. From 200 to 800 AD, the **Aymará-Indians** developed an **advanced civilisation**. Between 1460 and 1475, the **Incas** conquered the region which the Spanish seized in 1538. Five years later, Bolivia joined the **Viceroyship of Peru** and in 1776 the **Spanish Viceroyship of the Río de La Plata**. Antonio José de Sucre led a war of liberation in 1809, which resulted in Bolivian **independence** in 1825. Since then, the country's history has been determined by wars and

domestic unrest. Since Bolivia was foundation, there have been around **200 governments**.

In several wars, Bolivia lost areas that were rich in raw materials, such as the Atacama Desert and the Gran Chaco. The **reform**s introduced by President Victor **Paz Estenssoro** came to a sudden end in 1964 after a **military coup** replaced him with a junta. The death of **Che Guevara** in battle in 1967, crushed the **left**-wing **Partisan movement**. There followed a succession of **military** coups. The reform policy, which **Gonzalo Sánchez de Lozada** introduced in 1993, seemed at first to stabilise the political situation, but the former **dictator Hugo Banzer** returned to power between 1997 and 2001. This time he was democratically elected, though in 2001 he resigned on health grounds. In 2002, Lozada was once more elected president. After demonstrations lasting for weeks against Lozada's neo-liberal economic policy, he resigned in 2003. His successor was Carlos Mesa. Evo Morales won the presidential elections held in December 2005.

The parliament consists of a house of representatives and a senate both of which are elected every five years, as is the President, who is directly elected.

Economy

In 2005, GDP was US$9.6 billion of which 17 per cent derived from **agriculture**, 31 per cent from **industry** and 52 per cent from the **services sector**. The growth rate is one per cent. Of those employed, 44 per cent work in agriculture.

The main imports are capital goods, semi-processed products, raw materials, and consumer goods. The exports are mainly zinc, gold, soya, tin, timber, natural gas and silver; the importance of the **cocaine trade** should not be underestimated.

Transport

There is a 25,000-km-long road network, much of it in poor condition. There are 4,000 km of railway. There are international airports at **La Paz**, the seat of government (Sucre is the seat of the judiciary) and at **Santa Cruz**.

Tourism

In 2001, around 600,000 tourists contributed US$156 million to the Bolivian economy. The best time to visit is between April and October. Lake Titicaca, the Andes and the various remnants of Inca culture are among Bolivia's main attractions.

1 The skyscrapers in the skyline of La Paz look like matchboxes against the backdrop of the Andes.

2 The Incas built the giant fortress of Sacsayhuamán, in order to protect the riches of their former capital of Quito. The huge,

smooth stone blocks are almost seamlessly laid one upon the other.

3 Built on relics: Cuzco has been plundered and razed to the ground. The Plaza de Armas at the heart of the old city, and the cathedral stand on the ruins of Inca temples.

Argentina: Millions of farm animals graze the vast pastures of the Pampas. Cattle and sheep are driven by gauchos across ranches the size of Luxembourg. Every second farm animal lives in the Pampas and 90 per cent of Argentinian grain is produced here. The seemingly endless stretch between the Andes and the Atlantic is only interrupted by occasional clumps of trees.

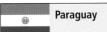

Paraguay	
Area:	406,752 sq. km
Capital city:	Asunción
Form of government:	
Presidential Republic	
Administrative divisions:	
17 Departamentos	
Population:	
6.3 million (15 inhabitants/sq. km)	
Languages:	
Spanish, Guaraní (both official)	
GDP per capita:	US$4,900
Currency:	
1 guaraní = 100 céntimos	

Natural geography

The eastern area, consisting of undulating **hills** and **plains** with elevations of up to 700 m, extends to the **Río Paraná**, the river bordering Brazil and Argentina. The west is part of the **Gran Chaco** lowlands.

Climate

The prevailing climate is **tropical** in the north and **sub-tropical** in the south. Rainfall is 2,000 mm in the east and 800 mm in the west. Sub-tropical, evergreen **rainforests** are typical of the **mountain regions** in the east. **Wet savannah** predominates in the northern lowlands of the **Oriente** region and prairie grasslands cover the southern lowlands. In the Gran Chaco, there are deciduous dry forests, quebracho forests, savannah and bush. Jaguars, vampire bats, various species of reptile, monkeys, red deer, wild boar and parrots are some of the very varied **fauna**.

Population

Paraguay's population is 90 per cent **mestizo (Spanish Amerindian)**, three per cent **Amerindian** and two per cent **Creole**. There is eight per cent illiteracy. Average life expectancy is 71 years. **Catholics** make up 94 per cent of the population and there are also **Protestants** and **Baha'i**. Just over half the population lives in the towns and cities.

History and Politics

The **Spanish first occupied** the country in 1535. In 1609, a Jesuit state was established, lasting until 1767. Following the end of Spanish colonial rule, a **free state** emerged under the dictator **Rodriguez de Francia**. The country was completely **isolated** politically and economically. In 1840, Paraguay started to open up under the rule of **Carlos Antonio López**.

During the regency of his son **Francisco Solano López**, Paraguay waged a **war** against **Uruguay**, **Brazil** and **Argentina**, which only a fraction of the population survived. The country only recovered from this blow after 1918. Although renewed hostilities with Bolivia over **oil fields** ended in victory for Paraguay, these oil reserves eventually did not prove to be worth exploiting. The country's political and economic situation rapidly became unstable. In 1954, **General Alfredo Stroessner** seized power and established a **military dictatorship** that lasted 35 years. Even since Stroessner's overthrow, subsequent governments have often found themselves facing allegations of **corruption** and **election** fraud. The **Head of State** is **elected directly** for a five-year period; the **parliament** consists of a Chamber of Deputies and a Senate. Citizens are entitled to vote from the age of 18 years.

Economy

In 2005, **GDP** was US$ 7.3 billion, to which **agriculture** contributed 27 per cent, **industry** 25 per cent and the **services sector** 48 per cent.

The relatively high **unemployment rate** remains constant at about 30 per cent due to lack of development. About 34 per cent of the labour force is employed in agriculture. Consumer goods, machinery, cars and trucks, fuel, raw materials and semi-processed products are **imported**. Cotton, soybeans, maté, vegetable oil and timber are the primary **exports**. There is a substantial **deficit in the balance of trade**.

important river harbour in this land-locked country.

Tourism

Paraguay is not a classic holiday destination. Most visitors come from the **neighbouring states** to buy cheap duty-free goods, as the trade in smuggled goods has assumed vast proportions.

Besides a lot of natural wonders, there are remains from the period when Paraguay was a **Jesuit state** on the Jesuit highway between Asunción and **Encarnación**. The best time to travel is between April and October.

Uruguay	
Area:	176,215 sq. km
Capital city:	Montevideo
Form of government:	
Presidential Republic	

POPULATION DENSITY
(People/km²)

below 1	
1-10	
10-100	
above 100	

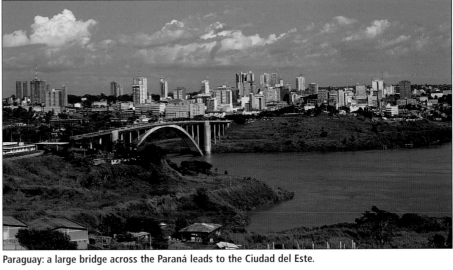

Paraguay: a large bridge across the Paraná leads to the Ciudad del Este.

Transport

The state railway consists of a 376-km-long **rail network** linking Asunción with Encarnación. The **road network** is approximately 13,000 km long, of which 705 km is part of the **Pan-American Highway**. Most of the roads are not paved.

River navigation plays an important role in the eastern region, which is almost completely surrounded by the country's river borders. Trade with neighbouring states is mainly possible via the waterways. Asunción is the most

Administrative divisions:
19 Departamentos
Population:	
3.4 million	
(19 inhabitants/sq. km)	
Language:	Spanish
GDP per capita:	US$10,000
Currency: 1 peso uruguayo =	
100 centésimos	

Natural geography

Uruguay is a country of gently undulating **hills** between the **Río de la Plata**, the Uruguay river and the **Atlantic**. Barely ten per cent of the country is at an alti-

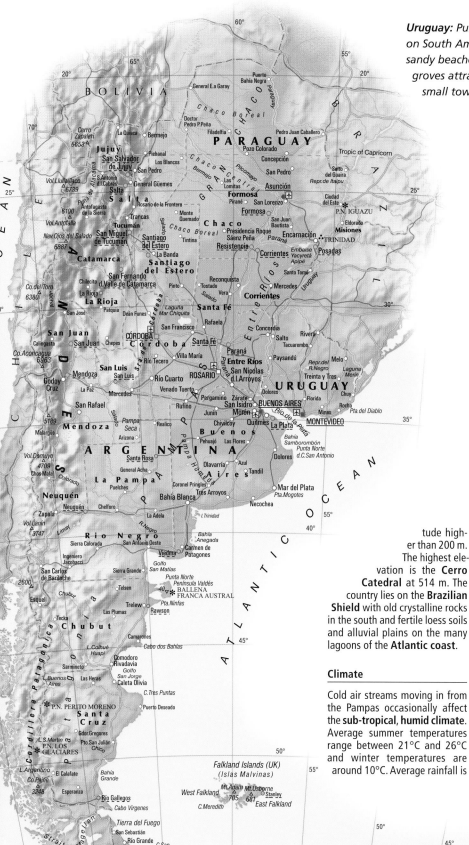

Uruguay: *Punta del Este is a popular resort on South America's Atlantic coast. Fine sandy beaches, dunes and eucalyptus groves attract thousands of tourists to the small town during the holiday season.*

1,000 mm. Uruguay's original wooded landscape has given way to vast **grassy meadows**. The **animal kingdom** has also lost a large part of its biodiversity. It is now rare to find the nandu or common rhea a flightless bird that grows to a height of 1.70 m. Jaguars, foxes, caimans, armadillos, red deer and pumas live in the north.

Population

Uruguay's population consists of 88 per cent whites, eight per cent mestizos (Spanish-Amerindian) and four per cent blacks. As many as 91 per cent live in the towns. **Life expectancy** is 74 years. Illiteracy stands at three per cent. **Catholics** make up 78 per cent of the population and there are 75,000 **Protestants** and 50,000 in the **Jewish community**. School is compulsory between the ages of six and 15.

History and Politics

tude higher than 200 m. The highest elevation is the **Cerro Catedral** at 514 m. The country lies on the **Brazilian Shield** with old crystalline rocks in the south and fertile loess soils and alluvial plains on the many lagoons of the **Atlantic coast**.

In the eighteenth century, the Portuguese and Spanish occupied in name only the country that they had discovered in 1515, as a result of what they saw as its poor mineral resources and due to bitter resistance from the **native population**. Uruguay became part of the Spanish viceroyship of the **Río de la Plata** from 1777, then part of Brazil in 1817. After a war of liberation in 1828, it declared its independence. From the beginning of the twentieth century until the 1960s, Uruguay's great prosperity was matched by exemplary social legislation. Yet free elections were only resumed in 1984 following a brutal **military dictatorship** in the 1970s. The 1967 **constitution**

Climate

Cold air streams moving in from the Pampas occasionally affect the **sub-tropical, humid climate**. Average summer temperatures range between 21°C and 26°C and winter temperatures are around 10°C. Average rainfall is

provides for a bicameral parliamentary system. The head of state who is also the head of government is elected for a five-year-term. Citizens are **entitled to vote** from the age of 18.

Economy

Some 80 per cent of Uruguay's land mass is used for **agriculture** mainly as **grazing for livestock**. Only 8.5 per cent of the labour force is employed in the **agricultural sector**. The **services sector,** at 69 per cent, contributes by far the largest amount to GDP, followed by **industry** with 23 per cent.
In addition to **export revenue**, which have increased rapidly in the last few years, **tourism** has also generated large sums of money. The main exports are beef, textiles, furs, leather and rice; the country's two most important **trading partners** are Brazil and **Argentina**.

Transport

The 2,070-km-long **rail network** is in poor condition. Of the extensive 50,900-km-long **road network**, only 6,973 km is paved.
The only international **airport** is in Montevideo, which is also the major sea port.

Tourism

In 2002, revenue from tourism amounted to US$100 million. The **spas** and beaches on the coast and the capital city of **Montevideo** are the most popular destinations. Most visitors come from Argentina. The best time to visit is in March and April, October and November.

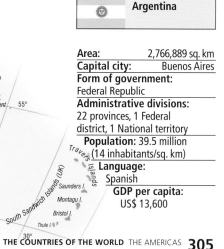

Argentina	
Area:	2,766,889 sq. km
Capital city:	Buenos Aires
Form of government:	
Federal Republic	
Administrative divisions:	
22 provinces, 1 Federal district, 1 National territory	
Population: 39.5 million (14 inhabitants/sq. km)	
Language: Spanish	
GDP per capita: US$ 13,600	

Argentina

Buenos Aires: approximately 150 years ago, the tango was born here. It is a mixture of Creole, African and Spanish elements. This passionate music, shunned by elegant and prudish society, has become the symbol of Argentina's spirit and culture.

Currency: 1 Argentinian peso = 100 centavos

Natural geography

Argentina, the 'land of silver', stretches over an expanse of 3,700 km from north to south. The northern part of the Andes forms the vast highland of the **Puna Argentina** with 5,000 m high peaks and numerous salt marshes. The **Nevado Ojos del Salado** at 6,863 m is the highest of all the massive volcanoes. The main Cordillera begins south of the Puna with the Cerro Aconcagua, the highest mountain in South America at 6,960 m. The pre-Cordillera runs parallel to this in the east with the Pampas of the Sierra on the coast. The **Patagonian Cordillera** lies adjacent in the south and contains numerous lakes and rivers. The Tierra del Fuego Cordillera stretches south of this to Cape Horn.
The wide, level **steppe landscape** of the **Pampas** is characteristic of the natural scenery.

Climate

While the **north** is hot and humid with temperatures of over 30°C in the summer, the **Tierra del Fuego** is distinguished by a **subantarctic cold** climate, the lowest temperatures dropping to -30°C and below. A sub-tropical climate predominates in central Argentina: the average temperature of Buenos Aires ranges between 10°C in winter and 23.5°C in summer. Two-thirds of the country lies in a wide **dry zone**; the rainfall is only 500–1,000 mm on the eastern plains. Precipitation can be as much as 2,000 mm in the mountain region of Misiones, in the Tierra del Fuego, in the eastern descent of the Andes in the north-west and in part of the south Cordillera.
There is **savannah and woodland** in the **area between the rivers**, with swamp forests along the river banks. **Bush forests** grow south of this area and in Patagonia there are arid, semi-desert scrubland and steppes. There are **evergreen rainforests** in the mountains of Misiones and on the eastern slopes of the Sierra in the **north-west**.
Jaguars, howler monkeys, tapirs, caiman, swamp deer and numerous species of bird live in the forests and marshes of the north. The steppe fauna includes guanacos, nandus, armadillos and chinchillas, whereas the south Andes provide an environment for pumas, condors and guemal. On the coast of Patagonia there are colonies of penguins and seals.

Population

Some 90 per cent of Argentina's population is descended from **European immigrants** and five per cent are **mestizos** (Spanish-Amerindian). In addition, there are 35,000 **Amerindians** and 2.3 million **foreigners**. Catholics make up 91 per cent of the population and Protestants two per cent. There is also a large Jewish community. Life expectancy is 73 years. **Illiteracy** is less than 3.8 per cent. **School is compulsory** between the ages of six and fourteen. 88 per cent of the population live in the cities.

History and Politics

Spanish rule over the country began when **Juan Díaz de Solís** sailed up the River Plate in 1516. In 1776, the viceroyalty of the **Río de la Plata** was created. In 1816, the **United Provinces of South America** broke away from Spain; the **civil war** that followed eventually led in 1853 to Argentina's first free **constitution**.
A military junta, supported by the rich cattle-breeders, ruled at this time. Military **conflicts** and internal **unrest** prevailed until the early twentieth century, when the economy began to expand. This upturn, which peaked in the early 1920s, led to a **wave of immigration** by European settlers. The growing **prosperity** of the country ended abruptly when the **worldwide economic crisis** hit in the 1930s.
The moderate, **democratic government** which was in power until 1930, was removed by a **military coup** followed by a **dictatorship**. The situation was unstable for over a decade.
In 1946, the people finally chose an authoritarian, neo-fascist, populist politician, President, **Juan Domingo Perón**. Both the president and his wife Maria Eva ('Evita') née Duarte enjoyed great popularity. She was almost worshipped as a saint. Evita, who had grown up in relative poverty was able to curry favour with the lower classes. She fought passionately for the poorest people in Argentina and for women's right to vote.
Perón was forced to leave the country in 1955, following his wife's death. From then on, the country alternated between **civilian** and **military regimes**. After seven years of rule by a military junta, Argentina occupied the Falkland Islands, a British possession. The last dictatorship of the generals ended in 1983,

---

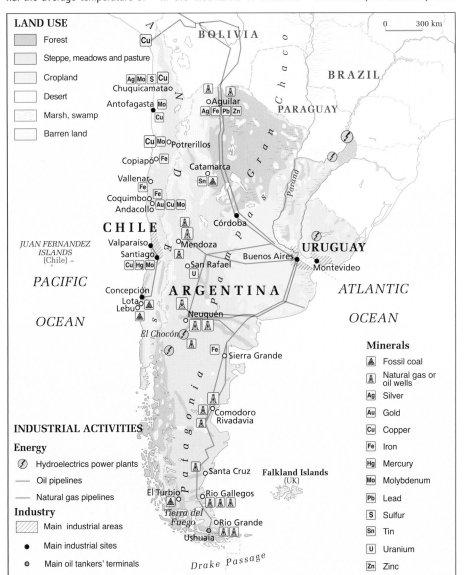

LAND USE

- Forest
- Steppe, meadows and pasture
- Cropland
- Desert
- Marsh, swamp
- Barren land

INDUSTRIAL ACTIVITIES

Energy
- ⊘ Hydroelectrics power plants
- — Oil pipelines
- — Natural gas pipelines

Industry
- Main industrial areas
- ● Main industrial sites
- ◎ Main oil tankers' terminals

Minerals
- 🄰 Fossil coal
- 🄰 Natural gas or oil wells
- Ag Silver
- Au Gold
- Cu Copper
- Fe Iron
- Hg Mercury
- Mo Molybdenum
- Pb Lead
- S Sulfur
- Sn Tin
- U Uranium
- Zn Zinc

Argentinian steaks are eaten all over the world. The meat of this country is of high quality as the cattle in the Argentinian Pampas offer optimal grazing conditions. Beef alone accounts for eight per cent of Argentina's total exports. Although the majority of livestock is for export, lamb and beef are traditionally an important part of the Argentinian diet.

following Argentina's defeat in the war with Great Britain over the islands. In spite of a few **corruption scandals** and a long-ignored aversion to deal with the past, the **democracy** that was founded in the **1994 constitution** has appeared increasingly stable. The serious economic crisis in the late 1990s, which led the country to the brink of insolvency, acted as a severe test. The Peronists are the only significant political opposition, but they are split into several factions. In the presidential elections of 2003, Néstor Kirchner beat his opponent, former president Carlos Menem.

Argentina is a **Federal Republic** consisting of 22 provinces, the **Buenos Aires district**, and the national territory of Tierra del Fuego. The bicameral **Parliament** consists of a chamber of deputies and a senate. The President is directly elected for a four-year term. Citizens are **entitled to vote** from the age of 18 years.

Economy

In 2005, GDP was US$182 billion, to which **agriculture** contributed six per cent, **industry** 31 per cent and the **services sector** 63 per cent. Agriculture employs ten per cent of the labour force, industry 24 per cent and the services sector 66 per cent.

There is a balance of trade deficit of around US$4 billion. Machinery, vehicles, consumer goods and chemical products are **imported**; agricultural produce, especially beef is an important **export**. So are grain, wool, linseed oil, coal, copper, molybdenum, gold, silver, lead, zinc, barium and uranium. The country has vast untapped reserves of oil, natural gas and hydro-electric power.

Transport

Argentina has the best transport network in South America. Of the **216,100 km of road**, 61,598 km is paved, but is often in poor condition. The **rail network** stretches for 37,910 km.

There are nine international **airports** in addition to Buenos Aires and over 100 **sea ports**. Goods are also transported over the 11,000-km-long network of **inland waterways**.

Tourism

In 2002, Argentina had 2.6 million visitors. The **beaches** of the **Atlantic coast** are popular, as is the capital city **Buenos Aires**, the **skiing areas** and **national parks** in the Andes and the large **game reserves** in the Tierra del Fuego. The best **time to travel** to **central**

Argentina is between February and May or September and November; the best time to visit the **sub-tropical regions** is between April and October. To visit the **south**, people mostly travel in the summer which lasts from December to February. The most important holiday month for Argentinians is January.

1 The Iguazú Falls are among the largest in the world. The noise is deafening: every second, almost two tonnes of water fall 74 m into the chasm.

2 The Plaza de la Republica by night. This is one of the most important squares in Buenos Aires. The 67-m-tall obelisk in the centre is a monument to the city's foundation in 1536.

3 Five hundred km of eternal ice: the Perito Moreno glacier in Patagonia is the main attraction in the Los Glaciares national park.

Chile

Easter Island: The Maio culture developed on one of the world's most isolated islands. More than 300 of their giant stone sculptures are scattered across the 160 sq. km island.

Chile

Area:	756,950 sq. km
Capital city:	Santiago de Chile

Form of government:
Presidential Republic
Administrative divisions:
12 regions, capital city region
Population:
16 million (21 inhabitants/sq. km)
Language: Spanish
GDP per inhabitant: US$11,300
Currency:
1 Chilean peso = 100 centavos

Natural geography

With a length of 4,230 km and an average width of only 176 km, the country extends along the western coast of South America.

Salvador Allende Goossens

*Valparaiso 26.7.1908,
†Santiago de Chile 11.9.1973

The Marxist politician was elected president in 1970 and enraged the landed oligarchy and the army with his nationalisation and social reforms. In 1973, the generals revolted in a coup led by Pinochet. Salvador Allende was murdered when the presidential palace was stormed. Allende was the first elected left-wing president in Latin America.

Augusto Pinochet

*Valparaíso 25.11.1915

The General led a military coup in 1973 against the Marxist president Allende. He first headed the military junta and from 1974 became president. Although he stepped down in 1990, he ensured his regime would escape prosecution for human rights violations. In 1999, he was arrested in the UK but was released in early 2000. He was re-arrested in Spain and returned to Chile to stand trial in 2004.

Two mountain ranges run through the country from the north to the south. Parallel to the **coastal cordillera (Cordillera de la costa)** which is up to 2,500 m high, the Cordillera Principal extends in the east. In the broader north section, there are active **volcanoes** such as the 6,880 m high Ojos del Salado and the Llullaillaco at 6,723 m. In the south, the heavily glaciated **Patagonian Cordillera**, which extends beyond the Strait of Magellan into the **Cordillera in the Tierra del Fuego**, joins to this main ridge of the Andes. The longitudinal valley which lies in between is divided by ridges into several valleys. The Atacama desert, the driest on earth is in the north, but the central part of the country consists of a **fertile, undulating landscape** with many lakes and in the south the north-south valley sinks below sea level. There are frequent **earthquakes** due to continuous movement of the earth's tectonic plates and many of the volcanoes are still active.

Climate

From north to the south, Chile is split into five land formations that determine the climate. The **'great north'** consisting mainly of desert, has a rainfall of less than 100 mm annually and it is relatively cold because of the **Humboldt Current,** with an annual average temperature of 16–18°C. The sparse vegetation is characterised by succulents and dwarf shrubs. In the **'little north'**, south of the Huasco river with its dwarf shrubs and succulents, the rainfall is 100–250 mm. Between Illapel and Concepción a **temperate warm climate** predominates and the rainfall is 2,000 mm. With an average annual temperature of 13–15°C, plants that prefer a temperate climate flourish. Vast deciduous and coniferous forests cover the **'small south'** up to the Gulf of Ancud. In the cool temperate, moist climate, the average temperature is

Chile's capital city Santiago de Chile at dusk.

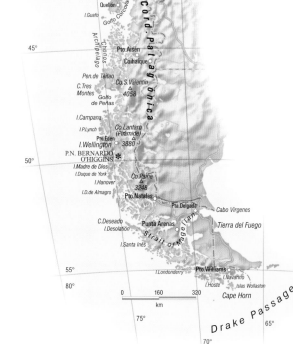

*The Valle Colchagua near Santa Cruz is one of **Chile's** famous wine-making regions. The even temperatures makes Chilean wine very low in acidity. The wine is mainly red, made from French Merlot or Cabernet vine stocks.*

12°C and average rainfall is 1,000 mm.

In the **'great south'**, on average, temperatures of 6°C to 8°C predominate and there is up to 3,000 mm rainfall. The evergreen **rainforest and cloud forest** is replaced in the far south by stunted trees and **sphagnum bogs**.

Population

The population – 84 per cent of whom live in the cities – is composed of 91.6 per cent **mestizo** and **white** and 6.8 per cent **Amerindian**. 77 per cent of Chileans are Catholic, 13 per cent Protestant. The life expectancy is 75 years. Around 15 per cent of Chile's population live below the **poverty line**.

History and politics

In 1541, the country was conquered by the **Spaniards**. In 1778, Chile became the independent **Kingdom of Chile (also known as the Captaincy General of Chile)**, and in 1818 it became a sovereign state. The **'War of the Pacific'** which ended victoriously for Chile in 1883 and the exploitation of the rich **copper deposits** made Chile into an important exporter of raw materials. The domestic situation however was characterised by many changes of government. In 1918, the **saltpetre monopoly** was disbanded, a situation which led to economic decline and social tensions. Further crises followed a brief **upturn** after World War II. The socialist reforms of the **President Salvador Allende**, elected in 1970, ground to a halt in 1973 when he was assassinated in a **military coup**. Under the cruel dictatorship of General **Augusto Pinochet**, political opponents were persecuted and tortured and over 3,000 were murdered or 'disappeared'. In 1988, Pinochet authorised a referendum after domestic and overseas pressure, which resulted in the majority of voters rejecting an extension of his rule. In 1990, free elections were held for the first time. Under the leadership of Christian Democrats Patricio Aylwin and Eduardo Frei, Social Democrat Ricardo Lagos and Michelle Bachelet, since January 2006, Chile has developed once more into a country

with a stable democracy. Chile has been a **Presidential Republic** since 1925. The constitution, which was last amended in 2000, provides for a **bicameral parliament** and an obligation to vote from the age of 18 years.

Economy

Only 23 per cent of the land mass can be used for **agricultural purposes**. The main crops are sugar cane, rapeseed, wine-grapes, fruit and sunflowers. The most important economic sector is **mining**, particularly the mining of copper, coal, iron ore, molybdenum, man-

ganese, gold and silver. Oil and gas are also exported. Of the workforce, 17 per cent are employed in agriculture, 27 per cent in industry and 56 per cent in the services sector. In 2005, **GDP** was US$115.6 billion.

All these minerals, agricultural products, timber and paper pulp are exported; finished goods, vehicles and luxury items are among the imports.

Transport

Of the 79,750 km of roads only 11,006 km are paved. The **rail network** covers around 6,782 km. There is a good **long-distance bus network**. The most important **airport** is in the capital Santiago de Chile. 90 per cent of foreign trade uses the well-developed sea routes.

Tourism

With around **1.5 million** tourists, tourism is only moderately devel-

oped in Chile. Popular tourist destinations are **Easter Island**, part of the national territory, the north Chile coast and the **lakes** around **Osorno**. Tierra del Fuego is an adventure holiday.

The **best time to travel** to **southern Chile** is January and February, for central Chile the best time to travel is from October to March.

1 Chile's 'Lake District' impresses with its snow-covered peaks and crystal clear lakes, so suitable for boat trips.

2 The port city of Valparaiso is of strategic importance to Chile. On the Plaza Sotomayor there is a monument to fallen soldiers.

3 Dirt roads cross the Atacama Desert, the most arid in the world. It is situated in Chile's 'Great North'.

4 The gigantic glaciers of Patagonia lure many tourists on take boat trips and helicopter flights.

The Arctic

Emperor penguins are the largest of the seven species of penguin in the Antarctica and grow to 115 cm tall. Like all penguins, they are ratites, flightless birds, protected from the cold with pads of fat and well adapted to life in icy waters.

Emperor penguins dive as deep as 260 m. They breed in colonies but do not make nests. They hold the single egg on their feet and warm it under a flap of skin. In the emperor penguins the male birds nurture the young.

The Arctic

Area: 26,000,000 sq. km
Territorial affinity:
Canada, Russia, USA, Denmark, Norway

Natural geography

The Arctic covers the **Arctic Ocean**, the land mass and its surrounding islands. The central Arctic region consists of pack ice – compressed sea ice broken up into fragments – up to 40 m thick. In the summer months, the polar **pack ice** extends as far as northern **Spitzbergen** in Norway, **Severny Zemlya**, the **New Siberian Islands**, **Cape Barrow** in Alaska, the islands of the **Canadian Archipelago** and the **north coast of Greenland**.
The Polar ice cap extends further over the sea during the Arctic winter, covering the **Bear Islands** north of Iceland, across the southern tip of Greenland and over the **Newfoundland Reef** roughly as far south as Halifax in Canada, as well as over parts of the **Bering Sea**, the **Sea of Japan** and the **Sea of Okhotsk** off Siberia.

Climate

Only 40 per cent of the Arctic is permanently covered in ice. Average temperatures are around 0°C in summer and -30 to -35°C in winter. The **coldest region** in the world is **Yakutsk** in the Siberian Taiga. The Russian **Vostok** (eastern) **Research Station** in Antarctica holds the record for the world's lowest temperature, -89.2 °C, recorded there on 21 July 1983. The parts of the polar regions not covered in ice are covered in **permafrost**. So are the forests of Scandinavia, Canada and Siberia within the Arctic Circle and just below it. An average temperature significantly below 0°C is required before the sub-soil freezes permanently. The **boreal coniferous forest belt** include the Siberian Taiga and the Scandinavian and Canadian coniferous forests. If the average temperature during the warmest month does not exceed 10–12°C, normal tree growth is no longer possible. Consequently, only stunted, dwarf conifers and bushes grow in the **tree and bush tundra**. The permanently frozen ground of the **Arctic tundra** adjoining the Arctic circle is treeless, the only vegetation consisting of lichen, moss, club-moss and hardy grasses. In the **summer months,** the subsoil thaws to a depth of a few tens of centimetres for a month or so and plants grow. In the **winter** a severe frost prevails with temperatures as low as -50°C.

On the coasts of Antarctica there are very few ice-free zones.

Population

Approximately two million people live in the Arctic. They consist of **northern Europeans** and **northern Asians** as well as **Inuits** (Eskimos), **Samis** (Lapps) and **Yakutians.**

History and Politics

The territory of the Arctic regions is shared between **Canada** (Arctic Archipelago), **Russia** (Siberia), **USA** (Alaska), **Denmark** (Greenland) and **Norway** (Spitzbergen, Jan Mayen Island and Bear Island). On 1 October 1996, the **Arctic Council** was formed. Due to the highly fragile nature of the Arctic eco-system, the purpose of this body is to coordinate all **development plans** in the field of mineral resources, fishing and hunting. The member countries are **Denmark, Finland, Iceland, Russia, Norway, Sweden** and the **USA**. Additionally, three **organisations of native inhabitants** have the right to make their voices heard.
From the fifteenth century onwards, **European seafarers** attempted to map out the Arctic Ocean. Their objective was to find a sea route to the Orient, the long-sought **north-west Passage**. Not until the nineteenth century did **scientific interest** also have a role to play. In 1827, the **expedition** of ships on runners led by **Sir Edward Parry** came within 900 km of the Pole. A costly rescue operation for **Sir John Franklin** who wanted to locate the **north-west Passage** in 1845 lasted 15 years and gleaned valuable geographical insights, although Parry and his crew were never found. Numerous other spectacular expeditions failed. The American **Robert E. Peary** claimed the honour of being the first person to step on to the North Pole on 6 April 1909. On 19 April 1968 the American **Ralph Plaisted** reached the North Pole on foot. In 1926, **Roald Amundsen, Lincoln Ellsworth** and **Umberto Nobile** flew over the Pole in a dirigeable airship. In 1958, the American nuclear submarine **Nautilus** dived underneath the Polar ice cap and the nuclear-powered Soviet ice-breaker 'Arctica' traversed the Pole on the surface of the water in 1977.

Economy

The economic significance of the North Pole lies in the **exploitation** of its **raw materials**. The US has found large natural oil and oil shale deposits in Alaska. **Petroleum, natural gas, zinc, silver** and **gold** are present in the Canadian Arctic, there is **zinc** in Greenland, **coal** in Norway and Russia and **iron** in Norway; **apatite, petroleum, natural gas, non-ferrous metals, gold, diamonds** and **nickel** are all present in Russia. All of the countries bordering on the Arctic Ocean have **fishing industries**. The **breeding, hunting** and **trapping of fur-bearing animals**, such as fur seals and arctic foxes is of economic importance in Canada and Russia. Small groups of native peoples make a living from the **hunting of whales and seals**, though this traditional way of life is disappearing.

Antarctica

Area:
12,500,000 sq. km, 14 million sq. km including the polar ice cap.

Natural geography

Antarctica was part of the original continent of **Gondwanaland** that split into **Antarctica, Africa, South America, Australia** and the **Near East** approximately 180 million years ago. With an average altitude of 2,040 m, the highest part of the continent lies below the Antarctic Circle. It has an area of 12.5 million sq. km – or 14 million sq. km including the **polar ice cap**. 90 per cent of the world's **freshwater ice** is stored here. This corresponds to 80 per cent of the world's total reserves of fresh water. The sea has an open link to the Atlantic and also to the Indian and Pacific Oceans. The **Ross Sea** and **Weddell Sea** divide the continent into two halves. In the

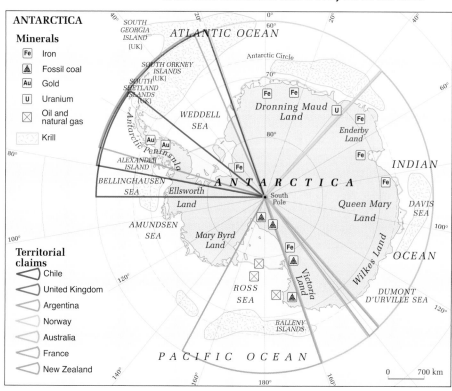

ANTARCTICA

Minerals

Fe	Iron
▲	Fossil coal
Au	Gold
U	Uranium
⊠	Oil and natural gas
░	Krill

Territorial claims
- Chile
- United Kingdom
- Argentina
- Norway
- Australia
- France
- New Zealand

SOUTH GEORGIA ISLAND (UK)
ATLANTIC OCEAN
Antarctic Circle
SOUTH ORKNEY ISLANDS (UK)
SOUTH SHETLAND ISLANDS (UK)
WEDDELL SEA
Dronning Maud Land
Enderby Land
Antarctic Peninsula
ALEXANDER ISLAND
BELLINGHAUSEN SEA
Ellsworth Land
ANTARCTICA
South Pole
INDIAN
Queen Mary Land
DAVIS SEA
AMUNDSEN SEA
Mary Byrd Land
ROSS SEA
Victoria Land
OCEAN
Wilkes Land
DUMONT D'URVILLE SEA
BALLENY ISLANDS
PACIFIC OCEAN

0   700 km

Exploration of the Antarctic: the Esperanza base is located in the Argentinian area of the Antarctic. The peninsula in the West extends the furthest into the Polar sea. Antarctica has been divided into claims but most countries do not recognise these divisions. However, the researchers have a common goal: the investigation of the importance of Antarctica for the world climate and the growing threat of a gap in the ozone layer.

East, there is a high pleateau with an area of 10.4 million sq. km which is covered in ice sheets; in the West, the great **Antarctic peninsula** with an area of 2.69 million sq. km ends in numerous islands to the north.

Western Antarctica contains glaciated fold mountains of over 4,000 m in altitude. **Mount Erebus**, an active volcano rising to a height of 4,023 m, stands on **Ross Island** in the Ross Sea. Around the Pole the inland ice which is up to 2,500 m thick forms a **plateau** approximately 3,000 m above sea level. This turns into **glaciers** and finally into **icebergs** with **drift ice** around its edges.

Climate

Central Antarctica is an extremely **cold**, **dry desert** with an annual average precipitation of 30 to 70 mm and an average temperature of between -50°C and -60°C. The conditions at the coast are somewhat less extreme with a precipitation of 200 to 400 mm and temperatures ranging from -10°C to -20°C. The continent's **violent storms**, **lack of sunshine** and persistent fog are responsible for a natural environment that is equally hostile.

Population

Antarctica is **uninhabited** apart from the scientific personnel who live there temporarily at the **42 research stations**. Approximately 1,000 scientists live in the Antarctic in summer and 4,000 scientists in the Antarctic winter.

History and Politics

Although it was assumed that there was a 'terra incognita' in the southern polar region as early as Antiquity, the British seafarer **James Cook** first reached the Antarctic Circle in 1772 to 1775. Antarctica was sighted very soon afterwards, in 1820, by three explorers, the British Edward **Bransfield**, the American Nathaniel **Palmer** and the Russian Fabian von **Bellinghausen**. Scientific research into the region did not begin in earnest until the twentieth century. On 14 December 1911, the Norwegian Roald **Amundsen** was the first explorer to reach the South Pole, several weeks before the famous expedition of the Englishman Robert Falcon **Scott**. Numerous **expeditions** followed over land and by aeroplane. Seven countries have laid claim to approximately 80 per cent of the Antarctic region but they are not recognised in international law. Argentina claims the region it calls Antárdida Argentinia (1,231,064 sq. km), Australia the Australian Antarctic Territory (5,896,500 sq. km) and the area surrounding Heard and the McDonald Islands (359 sq. km), Chile, Antártida Chileña (1,205,000 sq. km), France, Adélieland (432,000 sq. km), Great Britain, the British Antarctic Territory (1,710,000 sq. km), New Zealand, the Ross Dependency (750,310 sq. km) and Norway, Queen Maud Land (2,500,000 sq. km).

On 1 December 1959, 12 states signed a treaty to regulate the economic exploitation and other interests of Antarctica. The **Antarctic Treaty** came into force on 23 June 1961. Since then, **43 countries** have signed the treaty, 26 with consultative status, i.e. with the obligation to maintain a scientific station. These 26 countries are Argentina, Australia, Belgium, Brazil, Chile, the People's Republic of China, Germany, Ecuador, Finland, France, Great Britain, India, Italy, Japan, South Korea, New Zealand, the Netherlands, Norway, Peru, Poland, Russia, Sweden, Spain, South Africa, Uruguay and the USA. The following countries have entered into the treaty **without consultative status**: Bulgaria, Denmark, Greece, Guatemala, Canada, Colombia, North Korea, Cuba, Austria, Papua New Guinea, Romania, Switzerland, Slovakia, the Czech Republic, Turkey, the Ukraine and Hungary. Under this treaty, all claims to regions south of the 60° latitude are illegitimate. **Administration** is via consultative conferences. Under this comprehensive treaty, the whole of Antarctica is demilitarised and nuclear testing is prohibited. Within the framework of amicable scientific research work, all the parties to the treaty have free access to the territory.

Supplementary treaties ensure the preservation of flora and fauna and prohibit exploitation of the mineral deposits. **The ozone layer** in the Antarctic has been **under observation** since 1957 and has developed a worrying hole.

Economy

The exploitation of **deposits of raw materials** is not permitted under the Antarctic Treaty and **fishing** is strictly controlled.

Tourism

Tourism exists but strict **ecological conditions** apply. Tourists can visit the **penguin colonies** or bathe in **volcanic inland waters**.

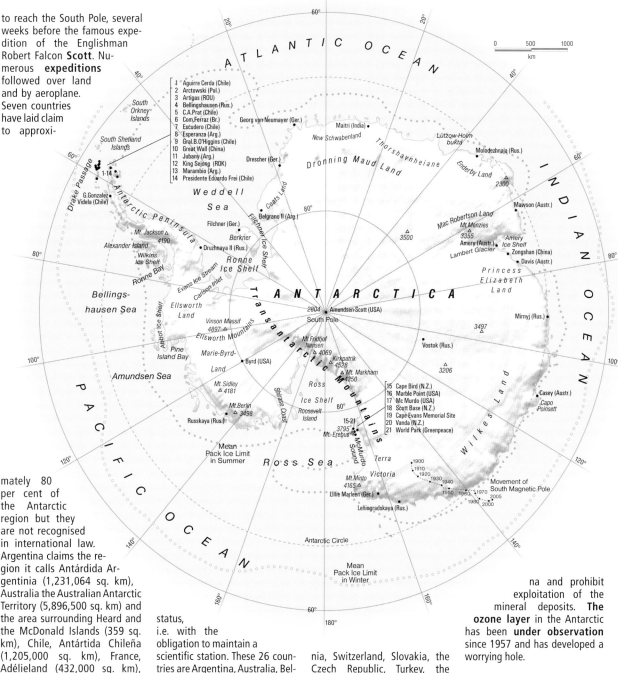

Main picture:
UN World Food Programme staff load sacks of grain for transportation to a flooded area.

Alliances and international organisations

At the Paris Peace Conference in April, 1919, the victorious Allies, though still reeling from the impact of the painful experiences of World War I, signed the Constitution of the League of

UN Secretary General Kofi Annan making a speech in New York.

Nations – the first worldwide gathering of states to secure world peace. In 1945, the League of Nations was succeeded by the United Nations Organization (UNO) whose headquarters are in New York.

The United Nations have made it their goal to maintain peace and international security and to promote peaceful international relationships based on the principles of equality of states and the right to self-determination of peoples. The UN has a staff of more than 50,000, including members of the UN's special organisations, working in nearly every country on Earth.

The UN Secretaries General : *The first Secretary General of the United Nations was Trygve Lie of Norway (1946–1952, not pictured). He was followed by Dag Hammerskjöld of Sweden (1953–1961), Sihtu U Thant of Myanmar (1962–1971, in photo with John F. Kennedy), and Kurt Waldheim*

The UN and its organizations

UN
United Nations Organization
Established: 1945
Members: 192 states
Headquarters: New York
In 1942, at the height of World War II, 26 states decided to stand together. On 24 October 1945, a total of 45 nations adopted the United Nations Charter. As a result, the allies of World War II developed a global forum, replacing the League of Nations which had been formed in 1919. The aim of the union was and is to maintain world peace and international security, and to promote human rights and basic liberties 'without distinction as to race, sex, language or religion'. The peaceful resolution of conflicts is the organisation's prima-

UN troops under P. de Cuéllar won the Nobel Peace Prize in 1988.

ry task. The United Nations is not supposed to interfere with a people's right to self-determination. Every member state of the United Nations is represented by one vote in the United Nations General Assembly (UNGA), which convenes once a year. Permanent members of the Security Council are China, France, the United

Kingdom, Russia and the USA. Ten further members are elected for two years. The Security Council acts on behalf of all the member states, and grants and renews the mandate of the UN peacekeeping forces.

ECOSOC
Economic and Social Council
Established: 1945
Members: 54 states
Headquarters: New York
Coordination of the member states in economic and social matters, under the authority of the General Assembly.

FAO
Food and Agriculture Organization
Established: 1945
Members: 190 states
Headquarters: Rome
Improvement of the state of nutrition and support for agriculture in developing countries.

IAEA
International Atomic Energy Agency
Established: 1957
Members: 137 states
Headquarters: Vienna
Control of nuclear plants and the disposal of nuclear waste. The agency also monitors compliance with the 1970 Treaty on the Non-Proliferation of Nuclear Weapons.

ICAO
International Civil Aviation Organization
Established: 1947
Members: 188 states
Headquarters: Montreal
Coordination of international civil aviation, taking health aspects into consideration.

IFAD
International Fund for Agricultural Development
Established: 1977
Members: 163 states
Headquarters: Rome
Promotion of the agrarian economy and the nutritional situation in the developing countries.

ILO
International Labour Organization
Established: 1919, re-established:** 1946
Members: 177 states
Headquarters: Geneva
Improvement of working conditions for workers throughout the world, elimination of exploitation and the development of new employment opportunities in the countries of the Third World. The modernisation of the countries of central and eastern Europe has been on its agenda since the collapse of Communism. Other campaigns include the fight against child labour and the introduction of laws to protect working women, especially pregnant and mothers of new-born babies throughout the world, and especially in the Third World.

IMO
International Maritime Organization
Established: 1948
Members: 163 states
Headquarters: London
International body handling issues of merchant shipping, safety on the high seas and protection of the maritime environment.

INCB
International Narcotics Control Board
Established: 1961
Members: 13 states
Headquarters: Vienna
Monitoring of compliance with measures for controlling narcotics.

ICJ
International Court of Justice
Established: 1945
Headquarters: The Hague
This panel of 15 judges from various states is the UN's primary judicial organ. It can only take action when both parties (states) agree with the handling of the conflict. Their judgements cannot create precedents.

IMF
International Monetary Fund
Established: 1944
Members: 184 states
Headquarters: Washington
Monitoring the international monetary system and the assignment of development aid. The IMF also produces bi-annual reports on the world's economic status.

UNCTAD
United Nations Conference on Trade and Development
Established: 1964
Members: 192 states
Headquarters: Geneva
Promotion of international trade, in particular with developing countries.

UNDP
United Nations Development Programme
Established: 1965
Headquarters: New York
Executive council for the coordination and financing of technical aid for developing countries.

UNEP
United Nations Environment Programme
Established: 1972
Headquarters: Nairobi
Administrative council for international environmental protection measures, including those outside the UN system.

UNESCO
United Nations Educational, Scientific and Cultural Organization
Established: 1946
Members: 190 states
Headquarters: Paris
This special organisation of the UN promotes the collaboration of the member states in terms of cultural interests. The organisation is constantly adding to its 'World Heritage List'. Particular support is given to education and training programmes in the developing countries.

UNFPA
United Nations Population Fund
Established: 1967
Headquarters: New York
Explanation of questions concerning family planning and health concerns for mothers and children. Also examines the connections between economic and population development.

UNHCR
United Nations High Commissioner for Refugees
Established: 1949
Headquarters: Geneva
Aid for refugees who have been persecuted for racial, religious or political reasons. The body regularly publishes current figures for numbers of refugees throughout the world, and proposes and monitors aid grants.

UNICEF
United Nations International Children's Fund
Established: 1946
Headquarters: New York
Works in approximately 160 states to ensure that mothers and children obtain the necessary food and medical care. Mainly financed through private donations. Attempts to ban the recruitment of 'child soldiers'.

UNIDO
United Nations Industrial Development Organization

of Austria (1972–1981), Javier Pérez de Cuéllar (1982–1991, photo below left) from Peru and Boutros Boutros-Ghali from Egypt (1992–1996). The seventh Secretary General is Kofi Annan of Ghana. He began his term of office in 1997 and was re-elected in June 2001.

Established: 1966
Members: 171 states
Headquarters: Vienna
Supports projects to boost industrial development.

World Bank Group
Headquarters: Washington
Comprises five institutions:

IBRD
International Bank for Reconstruction and Development
Established: 1944
Members: 184 states

IDA
International Development Association
Established: 1959
Members: 163 states

IFC
International Finance Corporation
Established: 1956
Members: 176 states

MIGA
Multilateral Investment Guarantee Agency
Established: 1985
Members: 163 states

ICSID
International Centre for Settlement of Investment Disputes
Established: 1966
Members: 154 states
The World Bank Group grants loans and gives advice about tackling poverty and promoting the economy.

WFP
World Food Programme
Established: 1961
Headquarters: Rome
The world's largest institution for food safety and emergency famine relief.

WHO
World Health Organization
Established: 1948
Members: 192 states
Headquarters: Geneva
The WHO maintains a worldwide epidemic warning service and is

involved in the furthering of medical research and provision, for example in the fight against AIDS (UNAIDS).

WIPO
World Intellectual Property Organization
Established: 1967
Members: 179 states
Headquarters: Geneva
Promotion of the protection of commercial and industrial intellectual property rights. WIPO largely finances itself through the provision of its services.

WMO
World Meteorological Organization
Established: 1985
Members: 185 states
Headquarters: Geneva
International cooperation for establishing meteorological stations and severe weather warning systems.

Other international organisations

AfDB/AsDB
African/Asian Development Bank
Established: 1963/1966
Members: 53 African and 24 non-African states/ 44 Asian and 17 non-Asian states
Headquarters: Abidjan/Mandaluyong City
Allocation and coordination of development aid funds for Africa and Asia.

AI
Amnesty International
Established: 1961
Members: approximately one million individual members in 140 countries around the world
Headquarters: London
Amnesty International is the largest voluntary human rights organisation and works for the

release of peaceful political prisoners, and for the abolition of torture and the death penalty.

AOSIS
Alliance of Small Island States
Established: 1990
Members: 39 small islands and coastal states

1 The Palace of the League of Nations in Geneva is today home to several UN sub-organisations.

2 US President George W. Bush in September 2003 at the UN General Assembly which meets annually in the Assembly Hall of the **3** UN Headquarters in New York.

Alliances and international organisations

European Union: The flags of the Member States in front of the EU buildings in Brussels and the European Parliament in Strasbourg. After expansion in 2004, the European Union now has 25 Member States with a total of 450 million inhabitants.

Headquarters: New York
Tackles problems caused by flooding and hurricanes as a result of global warming.

APEC
Asia-Pacific Economic Cooperation

The flag of the EU with 12 stars as a symbol of unity.

Established: 1989
Members: 21 countries bordering the Pacific
Headquarters: Singapore
Working to create a free trade area in the region by the year 2020.

League of Arab States
Established: 1945
Members: 22 Arab states in Africa and Asia
Headquarters: Cairo
Union of all of the independent Arab states aiming to promote collaboration in fields of culture, economy, politics and science.

ASEAN
Association of South East Asian Nations
Established: 1967
Members: Brunei, Indonesia, Malaysia, Philippines, Cambodia, Myanmar, Singapore, Thailand, Vietnam, Laos
Headquarters: Jakarta
Promotion of economic growth, social advancement and political stability. A free-trade area will be established by the year 2010.

CEFTA
Central European Free Trade Agreement
Established: 1993
Members: Poland, Slovakia, Slovenia, Czech Republic, Hungary, Bulgaria, Romania
Headquarters: none
The members created a free trade zone and had the long-term aim of accession to the EU and NATO, mostly achieved.

EFTA
European Free Trade Area
Established: 1960
Members: Iceland, Liechten-

CFA
Communauté Financière Africaine
Members: 13 states in western and central Africa
Headquarters: none
Currency union of former French colonies in Africa. The currency is the CFA Franc of the West and Central African Central bank.

Commonwealth of Nations
Established: 1931
Members: 53 states
Headquarters: London
Promotion of political, economic and cultural cooperation and the protection of democracy in the member countries. The foundation of the Commonwealth led to the process of decolonisation. By 1984, all of the colonies had gained independence, but remain associated with Great Britain.

ECO
Economic Cooperation Organization
Established: 1985
Members: Afghanistan, Azerbaijan, Iran, Kazakhstan, Kyrgyzstan, Pakistan, Tajikistan, Turkey, Turkmenistan, Uzbekistan
Headquarters: Tehran
Cooperation of Islamic neigh-

bours in terms of trade, agriculture, industry, transport, technology, science and education.

stein, Norway, Switzerland
Headquarters: Geneva
Promotion of free trade within the member countries and associated third countries.

EP
European Parliament
Established: 1952
Members: a total of 732 elected representatives from all the EU Member States
Headquarters: Strasbourg, Luxembourg, Brussels
The EP and the Council of Ministers form the EU budgetary authority and oversee the way funds are used.

CE
Council of Europe
Established: 1949
Members: 46 states
Headquarters: Strasbourg
This organisation of almost all of the European states was founded in London as the result of a private international law initiative. The aim of the organisation is to promote collaboration, preserve a shared heritage, and to protect human rights ('European Convention on Human Rights' of 1950) and the interests of minorities, as well as the strengthening of young democracies in Eastern Europe.

EU
European Union
Established: 1993
Members: Germany, France, Great Britain, Finland, Italy, Spain, Netherlands, Belgium, Austria, Sweden, Denmark, Portugal, Greece, Ireland, Luxembourg and, since May 2004, Latvia, Estonia, Lithuania, Hungary, Poland, Czech Republic, Slovakia, Slovenia, Malta and Cyprus
Headquarters: Strasbourg, Brussels, Luxembourg
The precursor to the EU developed from the European Coal and Steel Community, whose scope was widened in 1957 when it became the European Economic Community (EEC). In 1967, this organization merged with the European Atomic Energy Community (Euratom) to form the EC, which changed its name to the EU in 1993. The union strives for joint foreign and security policies and promotes collaboration in terms of economic development, domestic policies and legislation. It is above all a free trade area.

EU Commission
Established: 1993 (formerly the EC Commission)
Members: two commissioners each from Germany, France, Italy and Great Britain and one from each of the rest of the EU states.
Headquarters: Brussels
The Commission is responsible for the implementation of the budget plan, and monitors compliance with EU regulations and treaties.

EU Council of Ministers
Established: 1993 (formerly EC Council of Ministers)
Headquarters: Brussels
Council members are government ministers in the EU states (e.g. the ECOFIN Council, a meeting of the economic and finance ministers). The chairmanship of the Council rotates every six months. The Council issues directives which take precedence over national law. The Council of Europe, of which the President of the EU Commission is also a member, takes precedence over the Council of Ministers.

European Court of Justice
Headquarters: Luxembourg
The highest judicial authority in the EU handles cases of EU law. Judgements cannot be appealed by national courts.

FTAA
Free Trade Area of the Americas
Members: USA, Canada, all the Central and South American states
Headquarters: none
An agreement signed in 1994 in Miami aimed to combine the North and South American free-trade zones (NAFTA and Mercosur). By including all of the states of Central America, the organisation plans to become the world's biggest inter-country internal market.

CIS
Commonwealth of Independent States
Established: 1991
Members: Armenia, Ukraine, Azerbaijan, Georgia, Russia, Kazakhstan, Kyrgyzstan, Moldova, Tajikistan, Turkmenistan, Uzbekistan, Belarus
Headquarters: none
Union for the political, cultural, military and economic collaboration comprising twelve of the former Soviet Republics and chaired by Russia.

ICRC
International Committee of the Red Cross
Established: 1863 as the 'Committee of Five'
Members: max. 25 Swiss nationals
Headquarters: Geneva
The organization began in 1880, developing from the 'Committee of Five' for the support of wounded soldiers, and the aid organization today is a private association for the promotion of human rights and the umbrella organization of the International Red Cross. The Red Crescent and Red Magen David (Israel) are affiliated to it.

IOC
International Olympic Committee
Established: 1894

The European Parliament in Strasbourg: Sessions of the 732 members of parliament take place here in the plenary chamber. The EP is legitimised through general and direct voting and has gained more powers and increasing influence over European politics through a series of treaties. As with all parliaments, it has three fundamental areas of authority: legislation, budget and controlling powers over the executive.

Members: 201 National Olympic Committees (NOCs)
Headquarters: Lausanne
Decides the host, rules and programme of the Olympic Games.

NAM
Non-aligned Movement
Established: 1961
Members: 114 states
Headquarters: not fixed
The majority of UN members, mainly countries of the Third World, that are not members of any military pact. They work for more influence within the UN.

NATO
North Atlantic Treaty Organization
Established: 1949
Members: 19
Headquarters: Brussels
Initially a military mutual assistance pact, started by the USA in response to the threat posed by the Warsaw Pact. Since the early 1990s, the organisation has had collaboration with eastern Europe, of whom some are already members of the EU.

OECD
Organization for Economic Cooperation and Development
Established: 1961
Members: 30 states
Headquarters: Paris
Successor to the Organization for European Economic Cooperation (OEEC), founded in 1948. Its aim is the economic development and improvement of living standards for the population of the member states.

OPEC
Organization of Petroleum Exporting Countries
Established: 1960
Members: 11 states
Headquarters: Vienna
Crude oil cartel organisation working for the interests of its member states, whose economies are highly dependent on crude oil exports.

OSCE
Organization for Security and Cooperation in Europe
Established: 1975 (CSCE),

since 1995 OSCE
Members: 55 states
Headquarters: Vienna
The signing of the final communiqué in Helsinki marked the start of the work of the conference for preserving peace in Europe.

UNPO
Unrepresented Nations and Peoples Organization
Established: 1991
Members: 52 nations and peoples.
Headquarters: The Hague
The organization represents all states, peoples and national minorities which are under-represented or not represented at all by the UN.

WEU
Western European Union
Established: 1954
Members: 10 states, all both NATO and EU members
Headquarters: Brussels
Once the European arm of NATO, this defence pact will soon be dissolved due to the establishment of an EU Security and Defence Identity (ESDI).

WTO
World Trade Organization
Established: 1995
Members: 146 states and the EU Commission
Headquarters: Geneva
Replaced the 1947 GATT World Trade Agreement which was much less powerful and had fewer members. The World Trade Organization began life on 1 January 1995 and has since monitored multilateral treaties for the exchange of goods and services, as well as patent and other ownership rights. The WTO also strives for effective dispute resolution in trade conflicts and abolition of unfair competition. China is not currently a member of the WTO.

1 Protest action by Amnesty International (AI) to help the victims of human rights abuses. In one third of cases, the organisation is successful in its aim to release prisoners, suspend executions and have death sentences reduced to terms of imprisonment. It highlights injustices in the press.

2 At the bi-annual OPEC conferences, the member states decide their crude oil outputs and fix prices.

3 One of UNICEF's tasks is to ensure that 250 million people in Africa have sufficient clean water and sanitation.

United Nations

After World War II, an organisation was founded which was dedicated to the preservation of peace worldwide – the United Nations. Today almost every nation in the world is a member of the UN, which consists of very varied organisations, concerned with matters as diverse as development aid and atomic security.

The United Nations Organization emerged from the Charter of the UN Conference on International Organizations, which was signed on 26 June 1945 in San Francisco and came into force on 24 October 1945. The aims of the UN are the preservation of world peace, international security, multilateral development aid and the safeguarding of human rights and basic freedoms 'without distinction as to race, sex, language or religion'. At first all states that had fought against the Allies in World War II were excluded under an 'enemy states' clause. Today 192 nations are members. Only Taiwan, Western Sahara (occupied by Morocco) and the Vatican have not joined

the United Nations in the case of the first two because membership is opposed by their powerful enemies inside the organisation . Apart from the main headquarters in New York, the UN has offices and institutions all over the world. The official working languages are Arabic, Chinese, English, French, Russian and Spanish. The regular annual budget of the UN is supplied by contributions from member states, with the USA, Japan, Germany, France, the United Kingdom, Italy and Russia being responsible for some 70 per cent of the cost. Enormous contribution arrears, particularly on the part of the USA, are increasingly endangering the

work of the United Nations. The UN system consists of a structure of organistions that are partly independent from a legal point of view. The UN's main bodies are the General Assembly, the Security Council, the Economic and Social Council, the International Court of Justice and the Secretariat. The General Assembly (UNGA) is the central political consultation body, in which each member country has one vote.

The Security Council has the most wide-ranging responsibilities and is able to take binding decisions

UNO secretary-general Kofi Annan with the Algerian President Abdelaziz Bouteflika.

for all members. It consists of the five permanent members, the People's Republic of China, France, the United Kingdom, the USA and Russia. In addition, the Security Council has ten non-permanent members, comprising five African and Asian, two Latin American,

two Western European and one Eastern European states. They are elected for two years by the General Assembly by a two-thirds majority, five being elected each year. The permanent members have a right of veto. Decisions over procedural issues require the

Big picture: The UNO building (middle front) among a sea of houses in New York City.

At least once a year: the General Assembly in session in the Great Hall.

The conference hall of the Security Council, the central organ of the United Nations.

agreement of nine members, and further decisions must be approved by nine members including all the permanent members.

As the body mainly responsible for the safeguarding world peace and international security, the Security Council is able to appoint subordinate bodies. The UN peacekeeping forces receive a mandate for measures taken to maintain or restore peace, which involves the deployment of military or combined 'blue helmet' troops in crisis areas. Since 1948, more than 56 such measures have been taken, in which some 800,000 military personnel from 110 nations have taken part. At the present time, there are 15 blue-helmet missions, involving 37,000 soldiers and police from 89 countries. In addition, missions are carried out on behalf of the UN by member countries and organisations (such as NATO), for example KFOR, consisting of

28,000 soldiers, in Kosovo, and the ISAF in Afghanistan, with 5,500 soldiers from 30 nations.

The International Criminal Tribunal in Rwanda, sitting in Arusha (Tanzania), exists to try those responsible for the genocide and violation of human rights in Rwanda in 1994. Since 1993, the International Criminal Tribunal for the former Yugoslavia has been investigating genocide and crimes against humanity perpetrated since 1991 in the territory of former Yugoslavia.

The International Court of Justice in The Hague consists of 15 judges, who are each elected for nine years by the General Assembly and the Security Council. Only nation states are permitted as dlitigants, and both sides must agree to trial by the Court. The effectiveness of this body is however considered to be slight.

The Economic and Social Council,

ECOSOC, is the central body for economic, cultural, humanitarian and social questions. Its 54 members are elected for three years by the General Assembly. Of the subsidiary bodies, the most significant are the five regional economic commissions, which are concerned with the economic development of major regions beyond national borders.

The Secretariat, with offices in New York, Geneva, Vienna and Nairobi, is the UN's administrative body. The highest administrative official is the secretary-general. The period of office is five years, with the possibility of re-election for one further term. This high office has been occupied as follows: 1946–52 by Trygve Lie, 1953–61 by Dag Hammarskjöld, 1962–71 by Sithu U Thant, 1972–81 by Kurt Waldheim, 1982–91 by Javier Pérez de Cuéllar, 1992–96 by Boutros Boutros Ghali and since

1997 by Kofi Annan. Apart from its administrative functions, the position also has a political aspect. It is a central task of the secretary-general, for example, to stand up for world peace. In 2001, the United Nations Organization, together with its secretary-general, was awarded the Nobel Peace Prize.

Further UN organisations are the children's world relief organisation UNICEF, the world trade conference UNCTAD, UNIDO for the encouragement of industrialisation in the developing countries, UNCDF for the financial support of the developing countries, the development programme (UNDOP), the environmental programme (UNEP), the population fund (UNFPA), the Office of the High Commissioner on Human Rights (UNHCHR), the High Commissioner for Refugees (UNHCR), and the World Food Programme (WFP).

Further, there are 14 special or-

ganisations in the UN system, which work largely autonomously. They include the International Monetary Fund (IMF), the World Health Organisation (WHO), the Food and Agriculture Organisation (FAO), the International Labour Organisation (ILO), the Educational, Scientific and Cultural Organisation (UNESCO), the World Bank Group, the Industrial Development Organisation (UNIDO), the World Intellectual Property Organisation (WIPO) and the International Atomic Energy Organisation (IAEO). The United Nations occupies as building on the Hudson River in New York where it has been since its foundation. The building has not been renovated for many years and is in such dire need to drastic improvement that the organisation may need to temporarily relocate while essential renovation is carried out.

Peacekeeping missions of the United Nations

Soldiers were deployed on peacekeeping missions under the flag of the UN for the first time in June 1948. The 'Blue Helmets' were to monitor the ceasefire between Israel and its Arab neighbours. Since then, the United Nations have been involved in 60 peacekeeping operations in which more 2,200 have lost their lives.

The use of peacekeeping troops is one of humanity's most important instruments for safeguarding peace. The job of the peacekeepers ranges from the surveillance of ceasefires and peace agreements to the protection of aid workers. In the last few decades, the effectiveness of the peace missions has been discussed, following the tragic experiences of Bosnia, Somalia, Rwanda and Sierra Leone, and more effective procedures have been demanded. The catalogue of deployment opportunities must be thought over, as there are fewer interstate conflicts today that threaten world peace, but there are many more ethnic, religious and social

conflicts and internal tensions that cannot be resolved using the current terms of reference. Today, there are many more deployments enforcing peace, that are based on a 'robust' mandate from the world safety council. Under this remit, soldiers may not only use their weapons for self-defence, but also ensure the implementation of the truce or agreement.

At the time of writing, there are 15 UN peacekeeping operations, as well as the deployments that are carried out on behalf of the United Nations by organisations such as NATO. This includes SFOR in Bosnia-Herzegovina, KFOR in Kosovo and ISAF in Afghanistan.

Europe

SFOR (Stabilisation Force in Bosnia and Herzegovina): Since 1996; maintaining and securing the peace in post-war Bosnia-Herzegovina, 12,400 soldiers.

KFOR (Kosovo Force): since 1999; to protect the civilian population and UN personnel against violence. 28,000 soldiers.

UNMIK (United Nations Interim Administration Mission in Koso-

'Blue Helmet' soldiers in a ruined Bosnian village. The mission in Bosnia-Herzegovina lasted from 1995 to 2002.

UN patrols in Lebanon as part of the UNIFIL mission present since 1978.

vo): Since 1999; transitional surveillance and expansion of local administrative structures in Kosovo.

UNFICYP (United Nations Peacekeeping Force in Cyprus): Since 1964; to prevent further fighting between the Greek Cypriot and Turkish Cypriot communities.

UNOMIG (United Nations Observer Mission in Georgia): Since 1993. Monitoring ceasefire between the Government of Georgia and the Abkhaz authorities.

Middle East

ISAF (International Security Assistance Force): Since 2001; ISAF 's mission is to support the government of Afghanistan in the development of a stable democracy and creation and maintenance of internal security.

UNTSO (United Nations Truce Supervision Organisation): Since 1948. UNTSO was the first peacekeeping operation established by the United Nations. It monitors ceasefires, supervises armistice agreements and assists other UN operations in the Middle East.

UNIFIL (United Nations Interim Force in Lebanon): Since 1978, peacekeeping forces in Lebanon, 1,990 military personnel, 405 civilians. After the July/Augut 2006 crisis, this mission is soon to be expanded to police the ceasefire along the Lebanon-Israel border south of the Litani River.

UNDOF (United Nations Disengagement Force): Since 1974; the mission is charged with policing the ceasefire between Israel and Syria.

Asia

UNMOGIP (United Nations Military Observer Group in India and Pakistan): Since 1949; monitoring the ceasefire between India and Pakistan in the state of Jammu and Kashmir.

UNMIT (United Nations Mission in South East Timor): Since 2002 and soon to be expanded, UN mission in East Timor.

Africa

UNOCI (United Nations Operation in Côte d'Ivoire): Since 2004, supporting the implementation of the peace agreement.

MINURSO (United Nations Mission for the Referendum in Western Sahara): Since 1991, monitoring the ceasefire in the Western Sahara between Morocco and the Polisario National Front.

MONUC (United Nations Observer Mission in the Democratic Republic of Congo): Since 1999; UN mission to prevent a return of the civil war.

UNMEE (United Nations Mission in Ethiopia-Eritrea): Since 2000, monitoring the ceasefire between Ethiopia and Eritrea.

UNMIS (United Nations Mission in the Sudan): Since 2005; supporting implementation of the peace agreement.

ONUB (United Nations Operation in Burundi): Since 2004; it was established to support implementation of the Arusha Agreement.

UNMIL (United Nations Misssion in Liberia): Since 2003; monitoring the ceasefire.

The Americas

MINUSTAH (United Nations Stabilization Mission in Haiti): Since 2004; established to support the country's transitional government.

The World in Overview

The Earth has been continuously subjected to a variety of natural forces throughout the 4.5 billion years of its existence. Powerful geological and atmospheric phenomena have continually changed its terrain, its climate, its vegetation and, of course, the appearance of its inhabitants. About 10,000 years ago, Homo sapiens or 'modern human beings' began their exciting cultural evolution, one that has gathered momentum around the world over the last 100 years. Today, in addition to the forces of nature, the growing global population of over six billion people is having an impact on the face of our planet. Human beings are continually reshaping their environments, as a glance at the growing Chinese city Shanghai (below) illustrates. The billions of people on our planet are divided into diverse social, economic, ethnic, and economic groups. Humanity, undoubtedly, has immense scientific and creative potential but so many of the world's major problems, including disease and poverty, remain unresolved.

The Universe

People have been observing the sky since prehistoric times. Not even the latest modern technology can provide accurate information about its origin, extent or age.

The astrologers of antiquity and the Middle Ages assumed that the size of our cosmos was finite. While the Ancient Greeks believed that the fixed firmament constituted the edge of the universe, medieval scientists supposed that God's kingdom was concealed behind it. Astronomers of early modern times postulated an infinite universe – a proposition which was, however, seriously called into question in the late nineteenth century by Olbers' Paradox. Modern optical equipment and the Theory of Relativity, where Euclidean geometry is not applicable to outer space, confirm the theory that the total size of the universe is finite despite the fact that its dimensions are unimagineable.

Size and age of the universe

The radius of the universe is estimated at approximately 18,000 million light years. Relativity theory makes the probable assumption that the size of the universe is not constant but that there must be expansion and contraction. This expansion movement of the universe has been proven by both the Doppler Effect and Hubble.
The cosmos is approximately 18,000 million years old if it were to be subjected to a constant expansion speed. However, as several important parameters are not yet available for Hubble's constant and it must be supposed that expansion is initially more rapid, this figure is only approximate and serves as a point of reference only.
Modern cosmology contests this birth date for the universe and affirms a minimum age of 13,000 million years due to what is known as the CNO cycle and the measurements of red displacements of the light from distant solar systems.

Birth of the universe

The theory which is generally accepted today regarding the origin of the universe is based on a material which is initially extremely thick, but which thins as it expands. According to this 'big bang' theory, the zero hour would be a singularity with an infinitely great thickness.

The development of a universe which starts with the big bang is sub-divided into six different phases. In the Planck era, which ended 10^{-34} seconds after the big bang, no spatial structures could be determined according to Heisenberg's Uncertainty Principle and the four natural forces were still united in a single force. They differentiated themselves for the first time in the Quark era which lasted from 10^{-27} seconds. From around 10^{-36} to 10^{-33} seconds after the big bang the inflation of the universe, an abrupt expansion of the radius by a factor of 10^{50}, is believed to have taken place. Quarks and leptons were now distinguishable particles. In the Hadron era, which lasted until 10^{-4} seconds, existing matter came into being. The most important newly created particles were neutrons, pro-

Northern Firmament

The NGC 604 constellation some 2.7 million light years away.

Southern Firmament

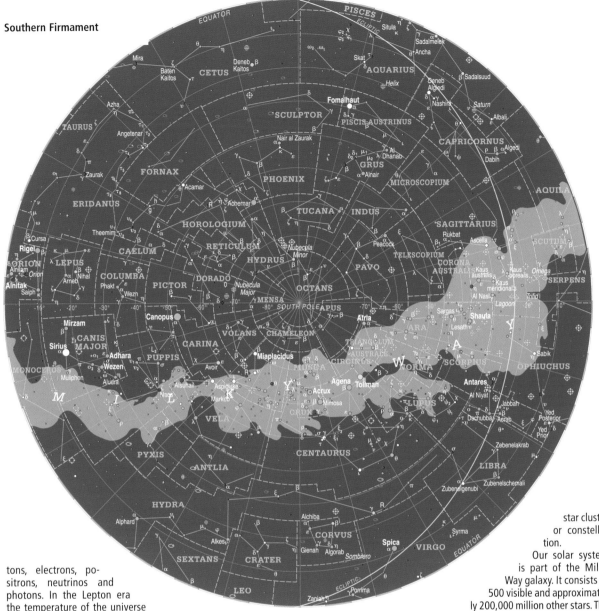

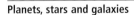

with figures. The constellation names used today and which were agreed upon in 1925 can be traced back to the Egyptians, Babylonians and Greeks. In China and other ancient Asian cultures other constellations are used. Of the 88 official constellations, 32 are in the Northern Hemisphere and 47 in the Southern Hemisphere. Nine constellations can be found in both hemispheres. Until the seventeenth century, astrology was considered to be a science designed to explore the relationship of the positions of

Southern Firmament
Translation of important constellations

Antila	Bellows
Apus	Bird of Paradise
Aquarius	Aquarius
Ara	Altar
Caelum	Etching needle
Canis mayor	Dog Star
Capricornus	Ibex
Carina	Keel
Centaurus	Centaur
Cetus	Whale
Chameleon	Chameleon
Circinus	Compasses
Columba	Dove
Corona	Southern
Australis	Crown
Corvus	Raven
Crater	Beaker
Crux	Southern Cross
Dorado	Goldfish
Eridanus	Eridanus River
Fornax	Oven
Grus	Crane
Horologium	Pendulum clock
Hydrus	Southern water snake
Indus	Indian
Lepus	Hare
Libra	Scales
Lupus	Wolf
Mensa	Table mount
Microscopium	Microscope
Musca	Fly
Norma	Goniometer
Octans	Octant
Pavo	Peacock
Phoenix	Phoenix
Phyxis	Ship compass
Pictor	Easel
Piscis	Southern
Austrinus	Fish
Puppis	Stern
Reticulum	Net
Sagittarius	Sagittarius
Scorpius	Scorpion
Sculptor	Sculptor
Scutum	Shield
Sextans	Sextant
Telescopium	Triangular
Triangulum	Stellar
Australe	Telescope
Tucana	Toucan
Vela	Ship sail
Virgo	Virgin
Volans	Flying Fish

tons, electrons, positrons, neutrinos and photons. In the Lepton era the temperature of the universe decreased to 1010°K million (Kelvin). In this phase, which lasted until approximately 20 seconds after the big bang, the universe consisted primarily of photons, leptons and hadrons. In the Radiation era which followed, the temperature of the universe decreased massively to 3000°K.

In the first four minutes after the big bang deuterium, tritium and helium were created. Matter and radiation detached themselves from each other and rays could now move freely in the universe which had been hitherto opaque. The era of matter has lasted up to the present day. The heavenly bodies that can be observed today were created.

Planets, stars and galaxies

The most explored heavenly body is our planet, Earth. As planets are only observable in reflected sunlight, we only know with some certainty our own planetary system consists of nine large planets, their moons, numerous planetoids and comets which revolve around a star, the Sun.

Stars are classified as red giants, white dwarves, neutron stars or black holes depending on their stage of development. The different classes of stars are recorded in what is known as the Hertzsprung Russel Diagram. The sudden illumination of a star where there is an extreme increase in brightness is known as a nova or a supernova. A collection of stars is called a star cluster or constellation.

Our solar system is part of the Milky Way galaxy. It consists of 500 visible and approximately 200,000 million other stars. The number of stars decreases with increasing proximity to the poles of the galaxy. Our galaxy is known as a spiral nebula due to its spiral structure. There are numerous examples of these nebulae in the vastness of the universe. In addition, elliptical and irregular galaxies exist and there are other types. Scientists are not yet able to calculate the total number of galaxies in existence. However, it is believed that there are significantly more than 100 million.

In addition to field galaxies, there are also galaxy clusters, collections of between ten and 10,000 galaxies with an average diameter of ten to 30 million light years. Super-clusters are units of several galaxy clusters. Fifty such super-clusters have been hitherto identified and they consist of a dozen galaxy clusters on average.

Constellations and astrology

Even the early astronomers associated certain groups of stars with the heavenly bodies as they concerned human being. However, modern science is unable to confirm that heavenly bodies exert their influence on individual destinies or political events and astonomers generally consider that astrology, however useful it may have been in the past for furthering knowldge, is pure superstition.

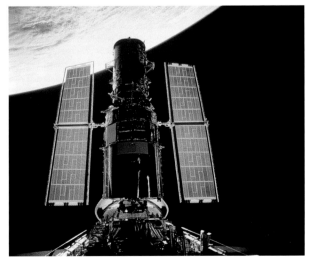

Hubble Space Telescope can reach further into space.

The Solar System

Our solar system consists of nine planets, 61 moons, approximately 50,000 planetoids, numerous inter-stellar comets and meteorites as well as inter-stellar matter. The solar wind, reaching out five billion km into the space, is considered to be an extension of our Solar System.

Excrescences on the sun's surface.

Our solar system (photo montage): generally considered to be nine planets and their moons surrounding the

The Sun

The central body of our planetary system is the Sun, a star of medium size in cosmic terms, of the G2 type, which came into existence about 4.5 billion years ago and revolves once around its own axis in around 26 days.

The diameter of the Sun is 1,392,530 km, which is 3.6 times the distance between Earth and Moon. Its total volume is 1,414 x 1,033 cu. cm, corresponding to 1,297,000 times the volume of the Earth. The mass of the Sun amounts to 99.9 per cent of the mass of the entire solar system. The average surface temperature is about 5,700°C, while the temperature at the core reaches 15 million°C and the core atmospheric pressure is 200 billion times greater than the Earth's. Inside the sun, 463 million tonnes of hydrogen melts every second to produce 460 billion tonnes of helium. The resulting energy of 380 sextillion kilowatt hours is hurled into all directions of the universe in the form of visible light.

The nine planets, with the exception of Mercury and Pluto, move around the Sun in almost circular orbits according to Kepler's laws.

The inner planets

The distances between the planets are measured in astronomical units (AU), with one AU equalling 149.6 million km and corresponding roughly to the average distance between Sun and Earth.

With an average distance of 0.39 AU, Mercury is the planet closest to the Sun, and is visible from Earth only at twilight. Its orbit around the Sun is highly eccentric and varies between 46 million and 70 million km. Its diameter is 4,900 km, its mass 0.06 times the mass of Earth. The surface temperature is +430°C on the day side and -170°C on the night side. The surface is covered with craters, which are attributable to meteorite strikes. Four-fifths of Mercury consists of a nickel-iron core; because of its small size it is unable to form an atmosphere. The Mercury year, that is, the time it takes to orbit around the Sun is the equivalent of 88 Earth days.

Venus is the planet closest to Earth and is particularly visible, as either the evening or the morning star. Its distance from the Sun is 0.72 AU, its diameter 12,100 km, its mass 0.81 the mass of the Earth. The surface of Venus, long assumed to be cool due to its cloud cover, has recently been determined at 460°C. Its atmospheric pressure varies between 15 and 22 Earth atmospheres. The dense cover of sulphurous clouds on Venus produces an extreme greenhouse effect accounting for the high temperature. It takes 225 Earth days to orbit the sun and its rotation time is 243 Earth days. To date, several probes have made soft landings on the planet, which should provide information about the atmosphere on Venus, 98 per cent of which consists of carbon dioxide. Since the atmosphere is opaque, the photographs of the probes were the first to provide an impression of the surface, which is pockmarked with craters and has mountain ranges higher than any on earth. The core of Venus consists of iron and nickel.

Earth, with its Moon, is the third planet, and the 'red planet' Mars, at a distance of 1.52 AU from the Sun, is the fourth planet. A Mars day lasts 24 hours and 37 minutes, and a Mars year is the equivalent of 688 Earth days. The diameter of Mars is 6,800 km, its mass is only 0.11 of the Earth's mass. The Viking I, Viking II and Pathfinder missions were unable to confirm the theories that life on Mars is possible. The polar caps on Mars are covered with ice like those on earth. The core of Mars consists of iron sulphides with some nickel. Violent sandstorms rage on the surface, which is pockmarked with craters and has high elevations and deep valleys more dramatic than any on earth.

The asteroid belt

Between Mars and Jupiter, there are a large number of small-to-minute planets in movement, with diameters of between 1 km and 1000 km. They separate the inner planets from the outer planets and are known as asteroids or planetoids. Of these asteroids, 75 per cent have a dark surface. They are all much too small to have an atmosphere and many are even too small to have been named by anything more than a number.

The outer planets

Jupiter is the largest planet in our solar system. It lies 5.2 AU from the Sun, and its mass is 117.9 times that of the Earth. It has a relatively constant surface temperature of -130°C and a diameter of about 142,700 km. A Jupiter day lasts nine hours and 50 minutes, and a Jupiter year is the equivalent of 4,333 Earth days. Of its 16 moons, four are larger than the dwarf planet Pluto; these were discovered by Galileo in 1610. Vol-

Pathfinder Mission on Mars: The view from 'Sojourner' over the planet's surface.

The planets according to their distance from the Sun:

Mercury (1st planet)
Maximum diameter: 4,900 km
Orbiting time: 87.9 days
Average distance from the Sun:
56.9 million km
Surface temperature: +430°C
(day side), -170°C (night side)
no moons

Venus (2nd planet)
Maximum diameter: 12,100 km
Orbiting time: 224.7 days
Average distance from the Sun:
108.2 million km
Surface temperature: 460°C
no moons

Earth (3rd planet)
Maximum diameter: 12,756 km
Orbiting time: 365.26 days
Average distance from the Sun:
149.6 million km
Surface temperature: 15°C
1 moon

Mars (4th planet)
Maximum diameter: 6,800 km
Orbiting time: 686 days
Average distance from the Sun:
227.9 million km
Surface temperature: -50°C
2 moons

Jupiter (5th planet)
Maximum diameter: 142,700 km
Orbiting time: 4,333 days
Average distance from the Sun:
778.3 million km
Surface temperature: -130°C
Rotation on own axis: 9:50'30"
16 moons (Ganymede, with a diameter of 5,270 km, is the largest moon in the solar system)

Saturn (6th planet)
Maximum diameter: 120,800 km
Orbiting time: 10,759 days
Average distance from the Sun:
1.428 million km
Surface temperature: -185°C
18 moons (the planet with the most moons); seven ring systems

Uranus (7th planet)
Maximum diameter: 51,600 km
Orbiting time: 30,685 days
Average distance from the Sun:
2872 million km
Surface temperature: -215°C
15 moons

Neptune (8th planet)
Maximum diameter: 48,600 km
Orbiting time: 60,189 days
Average distance from the Sun:
4,498 million km
Surface temperature:-110–200°C
8 moons; one ring system

Pluto (9th planet)
Maximum diameter: c. 2,300 km
Orbiting time: 90,465 days
Average distance from the Sun:
5,910 million km
Surface temperature: -230°C
1 moon

Venus

Jupiter

Neptune

Saturn

canic activity outside the Earth was first observed on Jupiter's moon Io. Jupiter consists of hydrogen, helium and methane, and is therefore gaseous in nature and has a massive core. Mighty storms rage over the extensive, dense atmosphere. They are so big they can be observed from Earth in the form of spots on the surface.

The sixth and second largest planet is Saturn, with a distance of 9.54 AU from the Sun. Its maximum diameter is some 120,800 km, its mass is 95 Earth masses. Saturn rotates once around its own axis in ten hours 14 minutes, and once around the Sun in 10,759 Earth days. It is known to have 18 moons, including Titan,

which might even be capable of supporting life. Like Jupiter, Saturn consists of a gas with an iron core. Storms rage on its surface with wind speeds up to 1,500 km per hour, and the surface temperature is -185°C. The planet's most striking feature is the multicoloured rings around it, which extend as far as 140,000 km into space. They are presumed to be the remains of an exploded moon, and consist of fragments of stone and ice, from minute particles to those of up to 10 m in diamentr.
The distance of the seventh planet, Uranus, from the Sun is 19.2 AU, and so it is invisible to the naked eye. It was discovered in 1781 by William Herschel, the Astronomer Royal to King George

III of Great Britain. Its diameter is some 51,600 km, its mass is equivalent to 14 Earth masses. The Uranus year lasts for more than 84 Earth years, the Uranus day for 17 hours and 14 minutes. The planet's atmosphere consists of molecular hydrogen, helium and methane.
Neptune, discovered in 1846, is 30 AU from the Sun, has a diameter of 48,600 km and a mass of 17.23 Earth masses. Its year lasts 165 Earth years, its day is about 19 hours. This planet can only be viewed through a telescope. It has eight moons, a surface temperature of up to -220°C and an atmosphere composed of hydrogen, helium and methane. The 'blue spot' is a storm formation the size of the Earth.

Pluto, 39.9 AU from the Sun, has only been known to exist since 1930. Pluto's status as a planet has long been the subject of debate. In 2006, the scientific organisation IAU decided to classify Pluto as a 'dwarf planet'.

Sun

The Earth

Seen from the Sun, the Earth is the third planet in our solar system. Formed 4.5 billion years ago, it is the only heavenly body on which in the course of its development, forms of organic life are known to have emerged.

The Earth and its satellite, the moon.

Our blue planet is not quite a perfect sphere. The Earth is slightly flattened at the poles and bulges slightly at the Equator. The radius at the Equator is 6,378,388 km, and at the poles 6,356,912 km. The circumference at the Equator is 40,076 km, and the corresponding mean circumference is 40,009 km. The Earth's surface measures 510,083 million sq. km. Its volume is 1,083 x 10^{12} cu. cm, its mass is 5,973 x 10^{27} g and its average density 5,515 g/cu. cm. The average temperature of the Earth's surface is around 14.5°C. The Earth takes 365 days, five hours and 48 minutes to revolve around the Sun in an ellipse, an almost circular motion. The Earth's orbiting time around the Sun is called a year. The distance varies between the aphelion at the beginning of July and the perihelion at the beginning of January from 152 to 147 million km, with the average distance being 149,597,870 km. The sidereal rotation period amounts to 23 hours, 56 minutes and four seconds, which means that in one day the Earth revolves on its own axis from west to east, with a negligible variation in rotation speed. This revolution of the Earth determines the alternation between day and night. Since the axis of rotation is not vertical along the Earth's path, but is inclined at an angle of 66 degrees and 33 minutes, the northern and southern hemispheres experience what might be called 'opposing' seasons.

A hurricane over the ocean as seen from space.

The Earth's surface

The Earth's surface consists of 71 per cent water and 29 per cent solid land. The average elevation on land is 790 m in height, and the average depth of the oceans is 3,900 m deep. The mass of the oceans is 1.4 x 1024 g, that of the earth's crust is 2.5 x 1025 g, of the earth's mantle 4.05 x 1027 g, of the core 1.90 x 1027 g, and the ice cap is 30 x 1021 g. The biomass on land is 8.7 x 1017 g and in the oceans 1.8 x 1015 g.

The surface of the Earth is divided theoretically into a network of lines parallel to the Equator and the meridians which are at right angles to them and are called longtitudes. The geographical latitude is taken from the equator to the poles, from 0 to 90 degrees. The geographical longitude extends eastward and westward from the zero meridian through Greenwich from 0 to 180 degrees. The parallels at 23 degrees and 27 minutes north and south of the imaginary line round the centre of the Earth called the equator are the tropics of Cancer and Capricorn, where the Sun is at its zenith on 22 June and 22 December.

Earth's crust and Earth's mantle

The interior of the Earth is divided into various strata. The outer stratum or layer is the Earth's crust, whose thickness varies between 8 km in the oceans and 40 km on the continents. The outermost layer of the Earth's crust, the sial layer, consists predominantly of silica and aluminium ores. Granite is the most important type of rock. The deeper layer, called the sima, contains a mixture of basalt with silica and magnesium.
Below the Earth's crust there is the mantle, which is also divided in two. Down to a depth of 1,200 km ultrabasic rocks predominate, and at greater depths. the chalcosphere, there are heavy metal sulphides and oxides. The temperature increases by 10°C approximately every 33 m in the direction of the Earth's core. In the core itself, which extends from 2,900 km to 6,370 km in depth, temperatures are estimated at 2,000°C to 5,000°C. The core probably consists of nickel and iron,; its outer part is viscous, its innermost part is firm.

EARTH'S HISTORY

The Precambrian

The history of the Earth, covering some 4.5 billion years, is divided into various eras.
In the early Precambrian, the Archaic period, the Earth first formed a solid crust. In the same era, about 3.5 billion years ago, the first life forms developed: primitive blue-green algae and bacteria, single-celled but without nuclei, whose traces have been

Compiled from hundreds of satelite photos: this recent image of the Earth displays the continents and ocea

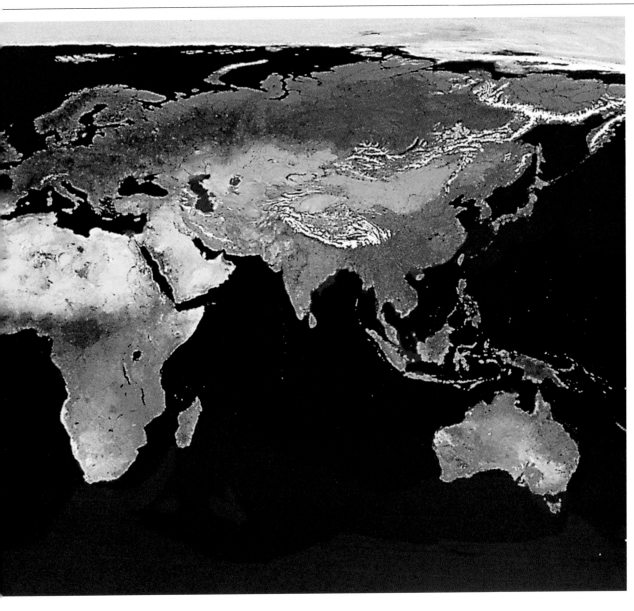

divided into the Pleistocene and the Holocene. The Pleistocene lasted until about 10,000 years ago and was marked by severe fluctuations in climate. The first hominid, Australopithecus, developed in the early Pleistocene age. The discoveries of Homo pekinensis, Homo heidelbergensis and Homo steinheimensis give clues to the development of the human race in the middle Pleistocene era. Neanderthal man lived about 72,000 years ago in the late Pleistocene. Modern Homo sapiens has existed for some 100,000 years.

The most recent era of the Neozoic is the Holocene, which began about 10,000 years ago and is marked by the retreat of the glaciers and a decline in tectonic plate movement.

Earth's atmosphere

The Earth is surrounded by a covering of gas, the so-called atmosphere, which, as a result of gravity, assists in bringing about the rotation of the planet. The atmosphere consists of 80 per cent nitrogen and about 20 per cent oxygen, with traces of carbon dioxide, argon, neon, helium, krypton, xenon, hydrogen and ozone, as well as dust, water vapour and smoke.
Our present-day atmosphere is significantly different from the original atmosphere of the Earth in its still-molten state. It presumably came into being as a result of the interplay of volcanic exhalations and photosynthesis in the stratosphere as assimilated by plant life.

The atmosphere is divided into clearly distinguishable layers. The troposphere extends 12 to 16 km over the Equator, and a good 8 km over the poles. At the tropopause, temperatures range from -40°C to -90°C. The lowest layer of the troposphere is where Earth's weather systems first develop.
The next layer is the stratosphere, which has a width of about 80 km. The mesosphere contains the ozone layer, of vital importance for us, whose destruction is now threatened by negative environmental effects. Temperatures vary considerably according to height, but are about -120°C in the mesopause and up to -2000°C in the ionosphere, which extends in height to 600 km. The boundary with interplanetary space is formed by the exosphere, which, like the ozone layer, exerts an important protective function for life on Earth, since it absorbs the primary cosmic rays that are harmful to life forms. The exosphere extends to some 100,000 km above the surface of the Earth.

discovered in chalk deposits in the Eastern Transvaal, South Africa.

Palaeozoic

The Paleozoic era is sub-divided into six periods. These can easily be distinguished by the life-forms that came into being during the period in question. The first invertebrate sea creatures developed during the Cambrian era, 590 to 500 million years ago, vertebrate fish during the Ordovician 500 to 435 million years ago, the first land plants in the Silurian 435 to 400 million years ago, the first land animals and trees in the Devonian 400 to 350 million years ago, reptiles and coal forests in the Carboniferous period 350 to 280 million years ago and coniferous forests in the Permian 280 to 225 years ago.

Mesozoic

The Mesozoic covers a period of 160 million years. It is sub-divided into Triassic, Jurassic and Cretaceous.

The development of dinosaurs and the first mammals began in the transition from the the Permian to Triassic periods. During the Jurassic period, 180 to 135 million years ago, America and the Antarctic became separated from Africa. The first great reptiles populated the continents. The first primaeval bird, archaeopteryx, made attempts at flight. In the Cretaceous period, 135 to 65 million years ago, the South Atlantic was formed, and a vegetation appeared that was similar to that of the present day. Towards the end of this era, the dinosaurs died out, and the mammals began their triumphal progress with the development of the first primates and the first hoofed animals. The first 'modern' birds conquered the skies.

Neozoic

The Neozoic era is divided into the Tertiary and Quaternary eras. The Tertiary began 65 million years ago with the Paleocene, when the Atlantic Ocean came into being.

The Polar seas formed 57 million years ago in the Eocene period. The Oligocene followed 39 million years ago, when the formation of the Alps was completed and oil, coal and amber deposits were formed. The Miocene period began 25 million years ago and produced the Gulf of Aden, California and the Red Sea. In the Pliocene, which began ten million years ago, temperatures fell rapidly, and all forms of animals and plants living today came into being. The Quaternary designates the period of the last two million years and is

The aurora borealis: a fantastic light display in the ionosphere.

The moon is the closest heavenly body to Earth and its natural 'satellite'. At a distance of approximately 384,400 km, it accompanies the blue planet on its way round the Sun.

Most of the planets in our solar system have one or more satellites. The Earth's Moon, however, at ⅟₈₁th of the Earth's mass, is incomparably larger than other moons in comparison with their central planets. Its sidereal rotation time, in relation to the Earth as a fixed star, takes 27 days, seven hours and 43 minutes. Its rotation around the Sun (Kepler's ellipse) takes 29 days, 12 hours and 44 minutes. In orbiting the Earth, the Moon rotates once around itself, so that, from Earth, only one and the same side of the Moon can ever be seen.

The average distance of the Moon to Earth is 384,400 km and it varies between 363,300 and 405,500 km. The Moon's diameter is 3,476 km and its circumference is 10,920 km. Its mass is 73.5 trillion tonnes, so that it can be calculated to have an average density of 3.34 g/cu. cm. The absence of an atmosphere is the reason for its low speed of 2.38 km/h.

Origin of the Moon

There are three theories about the origin of the Earth's satellite. Firstly, that the Moon took shape together with the Earth out of a primaeval mist. Secondly that the Moon was captured by the Earth. Thirdly that the Moon was a piece of the Earth that broke away from it. The last of these theories is the most likely. According to this hypothesis, the Moon came into being from the substance of the Earth about 4 to 4.5 billion years ago. It consisted at first of a mixture of iron sulphide, ferrous nickel and magnesium silicate as well as uranium, thorium and potassium. The chemical process which then took place resulted in the formation of an iron core and a crust of magnesium silicate. The probability of the formation of the Moon from the substance of Earth is also confirmed by the fact that the central point of the mass of the Moon has shifted from its geometric central point in the direction of Earth and that its crust is appreciably thinner on the side that is turned towards the Earth.

Surface of the moon

The characteristic moon surface derives from massive strikes from space, which noticeably declined about 3.9 billion years ago. For the last three billion years or so, no further streams of lava have broken through the surface.

Two different types of surface can be identified, even with a simple telescope. Apart from the maria (plural of mare), the name given to the great plains, the mountainous regions are also strewn with a number of craters. The occasionally powerful strikes – up to 200 km in diameter – have thrown up rubble whose precipitation has in turn created many secondary craters. The crater walls consist of material that has been thrown up from the lower depths. The great mountain formations are giant craters which have been covered by basalt lava; the mare regions are also covered by layers of laval rock of up to 50 km thick.

Phases of the Moon

In the course of its wanderings, the Moon, like the Earth, is illuminated by the Sun and thus presents a changing appearance. The phases of the Moon move from the invisible new Moon through a crescent Moon ever increasing in fullness to the half-lit so-called first quarter. The Moon then brightens to become a full Moon,

The Near Side of the Moon

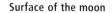
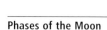

Apollo 15 taking off.

James Irwin, astronaut of the Apollo-15 mission on 30 June 1971.

The Far Side of the Moon

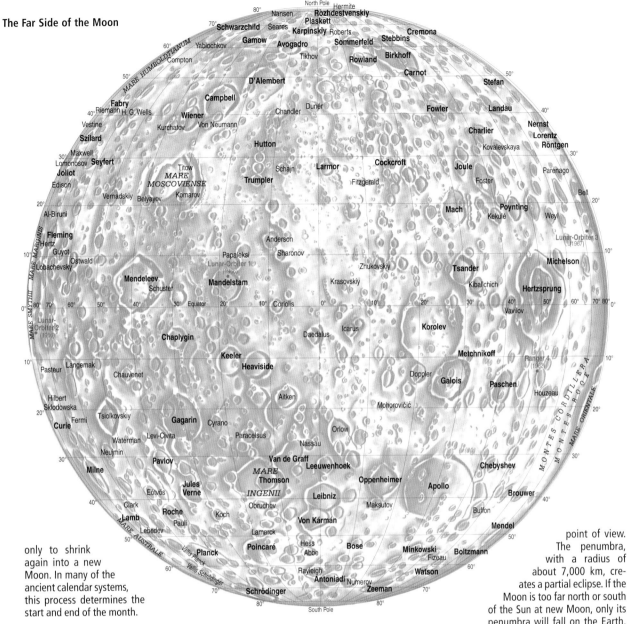

only to shrink again into a new Moon. In many of the ancient calendar systems, this process determines the start and end of the month.

Rare celestial phenomena

The changing constellation of Sun, Moon and Earth sometimes leads to two particularly spectacular celestial phenomena. Eclipses of the Sun can only occur at new Moon, and eclipses of the Moon only at full Moon. The spherical shape of Earth and Moon means that their respective shadows are in two

parts. These are an inner cone, whose tip points away from the Earth or the Sun, and an outer cone, which points towards the Sun or the Earth. The interplay of the umbra (total shadow) and the penumbra (half-shadow) makes it possible to have the different types of darkness.

Eclipses of the Moon occur when the Earth moves between Sun and Moon in such a way that the shadow of the Earth plunges the Moon's surface into darkness. In a total eclipse of the Moon, the brightly lit disc of the Moon enters entirely into the core shadow of the Earth. If the Moon moves north or south past the centre of the core shadow, the result is a partial eclipse. The fascination of a total eclipse of the Moon is, above all, the fact that the Moon never totally disappears. The Earth's atmosphere breaks up the light of the Sun and guides the red part of the Sun's light into the shadow of the Earth. For this reason the Moon often appears to be dark red in colour during a total eclipse. An eclipse of the Sun takes place when the Moon is between the Earth and the Sun. The umbra of the Moon, at 380,000 km, corresponds roughly to the distance between Earth and Moon. Thus the point of the shadow can cover an area of a maximum of 273 km in diameter, in which the Sun is in total darkness from the observer's

point of view. The penumbra, with a radius of about 7,000 km, creates a partial eclipse. If the Moon is too far north or south of the Sun at new Moon, only its penumbra will fall on the Earth. The result is a partial eclipse of the Sun. This phenomenon can only be observed in the Arctic or Antarctic. A ring-shaped eclipse of the Sun takes place when, as in the total eclipse, the umbra of the Moon falls upon the Earth, but because of the varying distance between the three heavenly bodies it cannot bridge the total distance from the Earth's surface. In this case, a slender ring of the Sun's surface is still visible around the edges of the Moon.

In a total eclipse of the Sun it is possible to see the full extent of the Sun's corona. When the Sun is distant from the Earth and the Moon is close to the Earth, a total eclipse of the Sun can be seen from the Earth that lasts for up to eight minutes.

Exploration of the Moon

The development of more and more sophisticated and precise optical instruments has enabled us to perform a fairly detailed

exploration of the Moon. Space travel contributed to the discoveries. In 1959, the Soviet Luna 2 probe made the first landing on the Moon's surface. In the same year, Luna 3 provided the first images of the side of the Moon that is permanently turned away from the Earth. The first soft landing was made by Luna 9 in 1966. With Apollo 8 came the first sighting of the far side of the Moon by the human eye. The

eventual triumph of the United States resulted in the first manned mission to the Moon. On 20 July 1969 the commander of Apollo 11, Neil Armstrong, took his famous 'giant step for mankind'. There followed six further manned missions to the moon as part of NASA's Apollo programme lasting until 1972. The excessive cost of manned space flight, and the two disasters resulting in the deaths of astronauts. The first was the break of the Challenger in mid-air on January 28, 1986 and the second happened on 1 February 2003 when the space shuttle Columbia broke up in re-entering Earth's atmosphere.

Near Side of the Moon
Translation of selected moon areas

Lacus Mortis	Lake of Death
Lacus Somniorum	Lake of Dreams
Mare Crisium *	Sea of Crises
Mare Foecunditatis	Sea of Fecundity
Mare Frigoris	Sea of Cold
Mare Humorum	Sea of Moisture
Mare Imbrium	Sea of Showers
Mare Nectaris	Sea of Nectar
Mare Nubium	Sea of Clouds
Mare Serenitatis	Sea of Serenity
Mare Spumans	Foaming Sea
Mare Tranquillitatis	Sea of Tranquility
Mare Undarum	Sea of Waves
Mare Vaporum	Sea of Vapours
Oceanus Procellarum	Ocean of Storms
Palus Nebularum	Swamp of Fog
Palus Somnii	Swamp of Dreams
Sinus Aestum	Bay of Floods
Sinus Iridium	Rainbow Bay
Sinus Medii	Central Bay
Sinus Roris	Dew Bay

* The word 'Mare' stems from a time when it was assumed that the dark areas on the moon's surface were seas.

Far Side of the Moon
Translation of selected moon areas

Mare Australe	Southern Sea
Mare Marginis	Sea of the Edge
Mare Moscovense	Moscow Sea
Mare Orientale	Eastern Sea
Mare Smythii	Smyth's Sea

'... one giant leap for mankind.'

Tectonic activity

The Earth is alive. Since its formation, the continental plates have wandered right across the planet. Volcanic erruptions and earthquakes at the edges of the plates, manifest the formidable forces at work inside the Earth. Every year, terrible disasters affect the human population due to these natural phenomena.

Mt. St. Helen's: the crater after the erruption.

VOLCANOES

Volcanic belts

A distinction is made between active and extinct volcanoes, although it is never possible to say with absolute certainty that a volcano that has been inactive for centuries will not suddenly erupt. Sixty-two per cent of all active

volcanoes are in the area of the Pacific Ocean, and the share may even be greater, since the undersea volcanoes are to a great extent still unexplored.

The Circumpacific Volcanic Belt also includes the West Pacific Volcanic Belt, which extends from the Aleutian, Kuril and Riukiu islands through the Marianas, Philippines, New Guinea and the Solomon Islands as far as Vanuatu, the former New Hebrides. This includes some 40 per cent of all the volcanoes on Earth. The island volcanoes of the Inner Pacific, on Hawaii and Samoa for example, make up three per cent of all volcanoes, and the Eastern Pacific Volcanic Belt, which includes Alaska, the USA, Mexico and Central America, contains 17 per cent of the rest.

A further volcanic belt extends from Indonesia across India and Afghanistan to the Mediterranean. The volcanic activity of the old continental masses can be seen in the Great Rift Valley system between the southern Taurus mountains in Anatolia and Lake Tanganyika in East Africa. Undersea volcanoes are mainly found at the boundaries between plates beneath the Pacific and Indian Oceans.

Plate tectonics

The reasons for the distribution of the volcanic belts are explained by the theory of plate tectonics. According to this theory, the shell of the globe of Earth and parts of its upper mantle are broken up into seven large and several smaller plates. Some of these masses drift apart, others collide, yet others slide underneath each other in what is called subduction. The volcanic belts are to be found along these tectonic lines, where the earth's crust is particularly weak and vulnerable.

Volcanic eruption on Hawaii.

Through the movements and adjustments of the earth's crust, trenches can develop, which extend deep into the earth's mantle. This allows released magma to rise to the surface, and this process is exacerbated by the release of gases. Volcanic eruptions mainly follow through vents, more rarely through trenches. In powerful eruptions, the volcanoes produce material of juvenile origin, i.e. frm when the planet was in its infancy. The liquid magma emerges either as burning liquid lava or as a solid ejected mass.

The rigidity of lava is primarily dependent on its viscosity. A thin liquid lava may pour out as a pyroclastic flow, medium viscosity results in lava lumps, and pillow lava results when fluid lava flows under water and becomes rigid.

Often, however, a volcano produces no streams of lava, but emits loose masses. These may be dust-like ashes, as well as pumicestone tufa, nut-sized lapilli, or breadcrust bombs, which may be as big as a human fist.

The structure and form of a volcano depend essentially on the type of emissions it produces, the number an frequency of its emissions, the structure of its internal magma chamber and fluctuations in the viscosity of the ejected magma. Depending on the emission products, volcanoes are

distinguished as lava, mixed, gas and loose volcanoes.

Volcanic eruptions often result in catastrophic destruction, but there are also considerably less harmful phenomena which are attributable to forms of volcanic activity. These are fumaroles, solfataras, mofettes, thermae and geysers.

Active volcanoes

The following is a list of the major active volcanoes: Etna in Sicily, Vesuvius near Naples, Stromboli in the Mediterranean, Santorini in the Cyclades, Hekla in Iceland, Pico de Teide in Tenerife, Mount Cameroon, Nyiragongo in the Congo, Semeru on Java, Krakatoa in the Sunda Strait, Fujisan on Honshu, Klyuchevskaya Sopka in Kamchatka, Mt. Saint Helens in the USA, Volcán de Colima in Mexico, Fuego in Guatemala, Mont Pelée on Martinique, Cotopaxi in Ecuador, Mount Erebus in the Antarctic and Mauna Loa on Hawaii.

EARTHQUAKES

Varieties of earthquake according to cause

Earthquakes also have their origins in the interior of the earth.

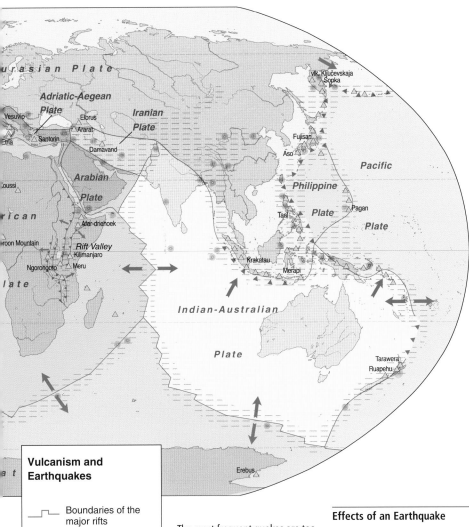

Vulcanism and Earthquakes

Boundaries of the major rifts

Deep-sea trenches (areas of active subduction)

Fault zones

Direction of horizontal movement of the big plates

Active volcanos

Earthquake zones and epicentres of strong earthquakes

A cleft in California after an earthquake of 7,5 on Richter scale.

Destroyed highway after an earthquake in Los Angeles.

The exit point is called the hypocentrum, the point vertically above the chamber on the earth's surface which is the epicentre. The sensory perception area is the name for the area in which the earthquake is felt without the need for measuring instruments. Earthquakes are caused by subterranean tensions, from which earthquake waves emerge. Quakes due to the collapse of subterranean cavities are relatively rare at only three per cent. The energy released in this way is, however, usually negligible. Volcanic earthquakes comprise about seven per cent of all earthquakes. They are caused by gas explosions in the magma chamber.

The most frequent quakes are tectonic quakes. They occur because of shifting masses and tensions in the earth's interior. These quakes release the most energy and cause the most devastation on the earth's surface. They are classified into flat, medium and deep quakes based on the depth of the magma chamber.

Earthquake strengths

The shock waves produces by earthquakes, which are classified as longitudinal and transversal waves, can be recorded with the help of a seismograph. The strength of a quake is measured according to various scales. A commonly used one is the 12-part Mercalli scale. According to this scale, quakes of a strength of 6 to 8 are considered small quakes, those of 7 to 10 are medium quakes, 8 to 11 are major quakes and 10 to 12 are world quakes. The overlaps are explained by the fact that exact differentiation between strengths of quake is not possible. While the Mercalli scale is based on subjective human perception, the Richter scale provides objective values. It is expressed in terms of magnitude. Quakes of a magnitude below 4 are regarded as weak, those of a magnitude of 8 as devastating.

Effects of an Earthquake

The results of an earthquake are felt most strongly at the epicentre. Vertical or horizontal shifts of masses can tear open kilometre-long crevasses. On the San Andreas fault line, over the last 10,000 years, shifts of masses produced by earthquakes have caused valleys to be displaced by up to 20 km. In the earthquake that destroyed San Francisco in 1906, there were horizontal movements of 6.4 m, and in the great earthquake of 1923 that struck Yokohama and Tokyo, the sea floor sank by more than 400 m in Sagami Bay, the epicentre.
If the epicentre lies over the sea floor, the result is a tidal wave (tsunami) that often reaches only 1 to 2 m in height in the open sea and therefore may pass unnoticed. Along coasts. a tsunami (the word is Japanese) can reach heights of up to 40 m. Destructive tsunamis have struck Lisbon in 1755, Tokyo and Yokohama in1923, the east coast of New Guinea in 1998 and the South-east Asia on 26 December 2004.

Earthquake disasters

The world's worst recent earthquakes: 1755 in Lisbon, the 1783 in Calabria, the 1855 earthquake in Tokyo, the 1896 earthquake on the Japanese island of Hondo, the 1906 San Francisco earthquake and great fire, the 1908 earthquake in Messina, the 1915 quake in Avezzano, Italy, the 1920 earthquake in the Chinese Province of Shanxi, the 1923 Sagamibukt earthquake in Japan, the 1935 earthquake in India, 1939 in Chile and in Anatolia, 1950 in Assam, 1960 in Agadir, Morocco and in Southern Chile, 1968 in Khurasan in Iran, 1970 in Huaráz in Peru, 1972 in Nicaragua's capital city Managua, 1976 in Guatemala and in Chinese Tangshan, 1978 in Tabas in Iran, 1980 in Campania, 1985 in Mexico City, 1995 in Kobe, 1999 in Turkey, 2003 in Iran, 2004 in South-east Asia and 2006 in Kashmir.

Climate

*Every region on Earth has a distinct climate.
Similarities in different regions enable global climate
exploration and a division into separate climatic
zones. Various factors affect the climate. In this century, the effects of human activity on the climate are becoming apparent and impossible to ignore.*

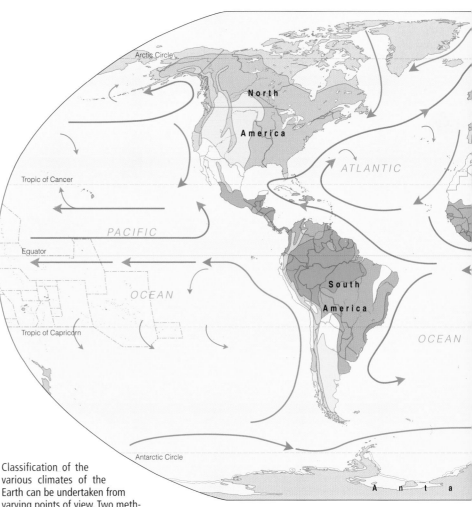

Diverse climates: ice blocks in Alaska, sand deserts in the Sahara, the Amazon rainforest.

Classification of the various climates of the Earth can be undertaken from varying points of view. Two methods predominate: genetic classification is based on the physical development of climates, and takes into account the dynamic processes in the atmosphere. Air masses, currents and fronts can be considered at almost any level of complexity. One type of classification is based on the effects produced by the climate and refers mainly to prevailing ground conditions and the animal and plant world.

Types of climate

The most useful classification is that developed by Vladimir Köppen in the early part of the twentieth century, which is based on vegetation, temperature and precipitation. His climate formula distinguishes five basic types, which are designated by capital letters. Group A denotes a tropical rainforest climate, in which the average temperature throughout the year is over 18°C.

These climates are found in the tropical convergence zone. Group B climates are found within the sub-tropical high pressure belt and are known as dry climates. Group C climates are temperate warm climates and are found in zones in which the prevailing wind is from the west. Group D climates are Boreal or snow-forest climates. Average temperatures are below -3°C in the coldest and

above 10°C in the warmest months. The Arctic climate of Group E is found above the tree-line in high mountain areas and within the Arctic Circle.

These climate zones are differentiated as climate types by the addition of further letters, as in, for example, F: Frost climate. The average temperature here is below freezing point at all times. S: In the Steppe climate there is only slight precipitation, but there is still barely even vegetation. T: In the Tundra climate the average temperature is higher than 0°C for at least one month of the year. W: An arid, desert climate typified by very slight or non-existent precipitation.

In the damp climate (f) there is precipitation throughout the year. Further lower-case letters are used: s: summer-dry, w: winter-dry, m: medium form between f and w; a: hot summers, meaning an average temperature of more than 20°C in the warmest month, b: cool summers – the average temperature during the warmest month is below 22°C and higher than 10°C for one to three months; d: severe winter, in which the average temperature in the coldest month is below -38°C; h: hot – the annual average is above 18°C; and k: cold, with the annual average below 18°C. According to these classification criteria, eight

to 11 main climate types are recognised.

Cold climates

The cold or snow climates (E) are the Tundra climate (ET) and the Frost climate (EF), in which no monthly average is above 10°C and no vegetation is found. The Tundra climate in the extreme north of Eurasia and America allows for only sparse growth of mosses, lichens and stunted shrubs. Average precipitation over the year is from 500 to 1,000 mm, temperatures are between -55°C and 25°C, but even in summer the average of 10°C is not exceeded. The Frost climate prevails in the Antarctic, in Greenland and in high mountain areas. There is no vegetation, precipitation reaches only about 100 mm, and the average temperature all year round is below freezing point.

Cold/temperate climates

Cold/temperate climates are found only in the northern hemisphere. Wintry damp/cold climates (Df) predominate in northern and western Europe as far as central Siberia and in northern North America. Vegetation consists of forests and grassy steppes,

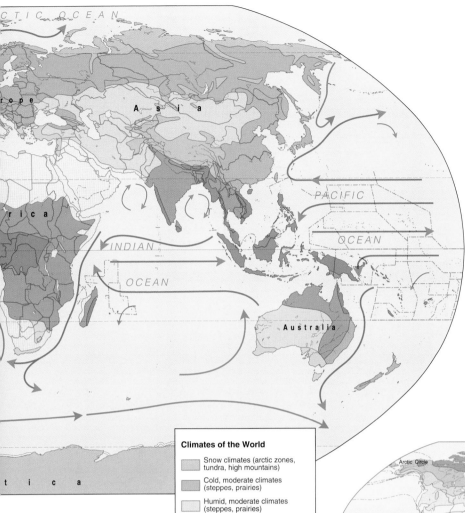

in a hot version (BWh), and in Central Asia in a cold version (BWk). Precipitation and vegetation are very uncommon in these climates.

Savannah climates

The Savannah climate (Aw), with a rainy season in the summer and a markedly dry season in the winter, is to be found mainly in South America and Africa, but also in northern Australia, Central America, India and south-east Asia. On river banks there is evergreen primaeval forest vegetation, which transmutes into looser forest conditions or a tree savannah, and finally into an open grassland savannah.

Tropical rainforest zones

Tropical rainforests (Af) are found in areas immediately adjacent to these climatic zones. The daytime temperature reaches a maximum of 35°C. Seasons cannot be distinguished; the average precipitation of about 1500 mm is distributed evenly over the whole year. The constant heat and high humidity result in an evergreen primaeval forest vegetation. Tropical rainforest is found in Amazonia, the Congo basin and the Malaysian archipelago. Similar climatic conditions (Am) are found in the monsoon forests of India and south-east Asia.

Climate changes

There have been constant changes of climate throughout history. The reasons are primarily to be found in the fluctuations of solar energy. Thus, for example, ice ages in the history of the Earth have alternated with long periods of heat.

In the last 100 years a noticeable warming of the Earth's climate has been recorded. As a result, sea levels rose by an average of 20 cm during the twentieth century. The causes of this phenomenon are no longer being sought in the cyclical fluctuations of solar eruptions. Rather, the rising air temperature in recent decades can be attributed substantially to increased industrialisation. The enormous quantities of carbon dioxide released by industry have created the so-called greenhouse effect.

Climates of the World

- Snow climates (arctic zones, tundra, high mountains)
- Cold, moderate climates (steppes, prairies)
- Humid, moderate climates (steppes, prairies)
- Damp/temperate climates (deciduous and mixed forests)
- Winter humid climates (Mediterranean vegetation)
- Arid-tropical climates (semi-deserts and deserts)
- Summer humid tropical climates (Savannah)
- Perpetually humid tropical climates (rain and monsoon forests)
- ▶ Cold sea current
- ▶ Warm sea current

precipitation is between 300 and 1000 mm and in the winter average temperatures may be down to as low as -40°C. In eastern Siberia the wintry dry/cold climate (Dw) is determined by even lower precipitation levels of 150 to 650 mm. In summer, average temperatures are 20°C, but in the winter the thermometer may fall to -50°C.

Dry/temperate climates

Dry/temperate climates are distinguished as Steppe climate (BS) on both sides of the sub-tropical desert belt, Dry Savannah with dry winters and moderately damp summers (BSw), the summer-dry steppes in higher latitudes (BSs) and the warm steppes at the edge of the desert (BSh), which become increasingly cooler the further they are from the Equator (BSk) predominate above all in North America and Central Asia. Hot Steppe climates are found in Australia, North Africa, the Kalahari Desert, Mexico, the Near East and southern Asia, as well as in the western Pampas.

Damp/temperate climates

The damp/temperate climate (Cf) is to be found in Europe, south-east Northern America, on the coasts of south-west Australia, south-east Asia, south-east Africa, in the Pampas and in south and west Patagonia. Deciduous, coniferous and mixed forests thrive at an average annual temperature between 8°C and 25°C and with average precipitation of 700 mm to 1500 mm. The warm summer-dry climate (Cs) is also referred to as the Mediterranean climate and is typified by hardwood vegetation, hot summers and damp, cool winters. Annual precipitation is between 400 mm and 750 mm. This climate type is also found in California, Chile, South Africa and southern Australia.

Desert climates

The desert climate (BW) is found in the dry belts of North Africa and southern Asia as well as Australia,

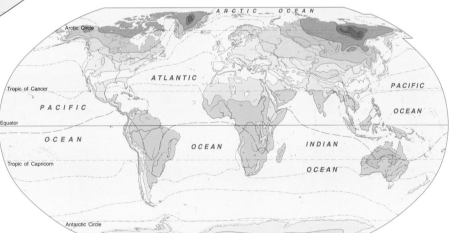

Average temperatures in January

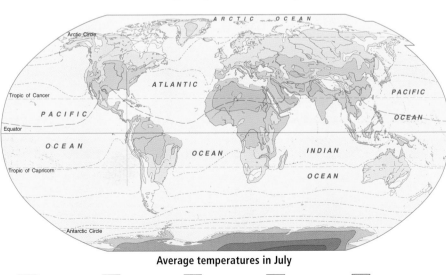

Average temperatures in July

- Below -50 °C
- -50 °C to -40 °C
- -40 °C to -30 °C
- -30 °C to -20 °C
- -20 °C to -10 °C
- -10 °C to 0 °C
- 0 °C to +10 °C
- +10 °C to +20 °C
- +20 °C to +30 °C
- Over +30 °C

Climate

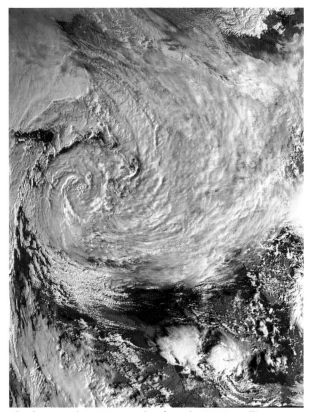

Cloud system above Europe, taken from the NOAA satellite.

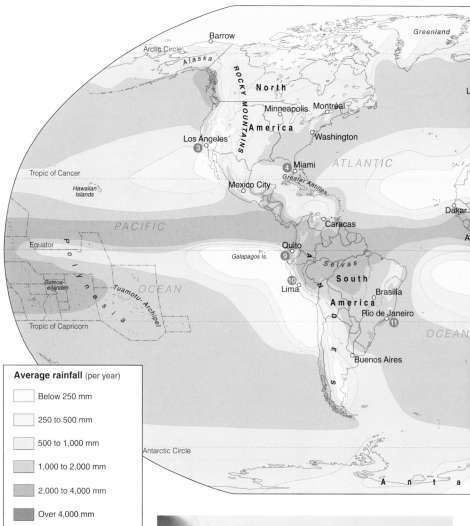

Average rainfall (per year)

- Below 250 mm
- 250 to 500 mm
- 500 to 1,000 mm
- 1,000 to 2,000 mm
- 2,000 to 4,000 mm
- Over 4,000 mm

Carbon dioxide and other trace gases have an effect on the atmosphere similar to that of the glass windows of a greenhouse. Sunlight does reach the Earth, but the rays of heat reflected by the Earth's surface are absorbed.

Whether and to what extent the increased emissions of carbon dioxide, fluorine chlorinated hydrocarbons, methane and nitrous oxide are responsible for global warming remains in dispute. At successive international climate conferences, the industrial nations have as yet been unable to agree on compulsory limitations on these emissions. The USA, in particular, has been unwilling to accept the climate protection measures proposed by the countries of the European Union. If a noticeable reduction in trace gases is not achieved in the foreseeable future, dramatic results must be expected. The melting of the ice caps could result in the submergence of smaller islands and entire coastal regions. Bangladesh would disappear altogether as would south-east England, including London.

El Niño

El Niño is a climatic phenomenon which causes severe disruption to the world's weather patterns every two to seven years. The name is Spanish and refers to the Christ Child, for this phenomenon always appears around the Christmas season, that is, in the summer of the southern hemisphere. Under normal weather conditions, there is a stable area of high pressure along the west coast of South America, with the winds moving counter-clockwise around this high. As a result, cold air moves from the south towards the Equator, and is diverted westwards by the Coriolis force. This air current is the south-east trade wind, which bounces against the north-east trade wind at the Inner Tropical Convergence zone. The trade winds travel westwards, rising as they do so, and over the west coast of Australia they encounter an area of low pressure. The strength of the winds is dependent upon the difference in pressure between high and low. These air movements also result in sea currents such as the cold Humboldt Current, which continues to warm up and finally becomes the westward-moving South Equatorial Current.

If El Niño appears, the high pressure breaks down over South America, the difference in pressure from the Australian low pressure area reduces, or even takes on negative values. The normal trade winds disappear or even blow in the opposite direction.

Air pollution, destroyed rainforest: human activity influences the global.

Increase of CO₂ emissions and global warming

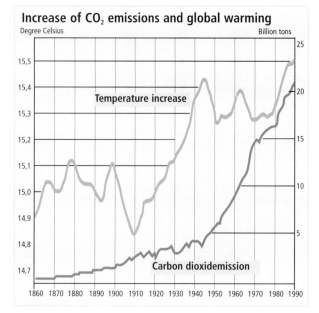

Degree Celsius — Billion tons

Temperature increase

Carbon dioxide emission

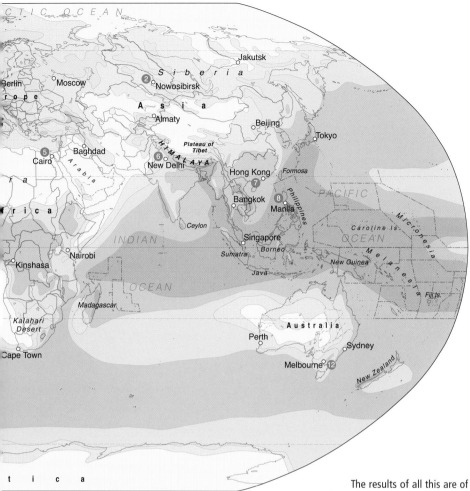

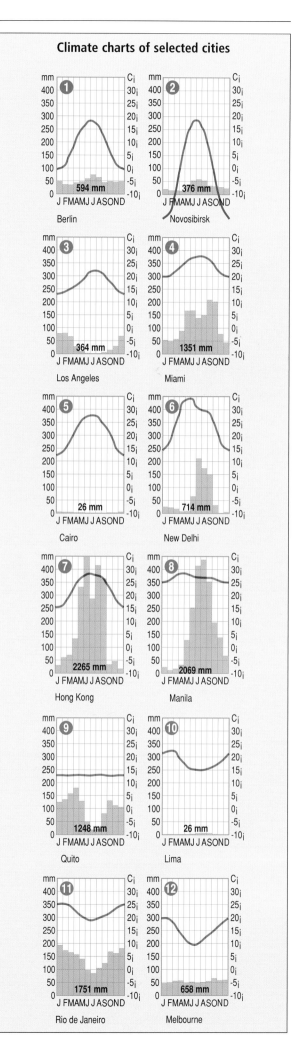

Climate charts of selected cities

1 594 mm — Berlin

2 376 mm — Novosibirsk

3 364 mm — Los Angeles

4 1351 mm — Miami

5 26 mm — Cairo

6 714 mm — New Delhi

7 2265 mm — Hong Kong

8 2069 mm — Manila

9 1248 mm — Quito

10 26 mm — Lima

11 1751 mm — Rio de Janeiro

12 658 mm — Melbourne

Tornadoes, dried out landscapes: a serious indication of global climate change.

The results of all this are of dramatic – and potentially catastrophic – dimensions for the southern hemisphere.

In South America the cold, nutrient-rich water of the Humboldt Current is displaced by warm, nutrient-poor water, which results in a drastic reduction of fish stocks. Since during an occurrence of El Niño air masses of high humidity move in from the sea, replacing the dry winds from the land, the otherwise dry west coast of South America experiences torrential rainfall. The opposite situation occurs in Australia, Africa and Indonesia. Here, because of changes in wind direction, the usual precipitation is absent. As a result, catastrophic flooding and disastrous drought conditions are both consequences of El Niño. Ominously, El Niño has been becoming more frequent in recent years. Whether this is yet another effect of global warming or merely a freak weather pattern remains to be seen. Some meteorologists claim that weather patterns are always seriously disrupted at the turn of a century, and point to similar events at the turn of the nineteenth and twentieth centuries. Weather forecasters employed by the major television and radio networks are certainly predicting an increase in catastrophic weather events, such as Hurricane Katrina, which devastated parts of the American South.

Population

One of the most serious problems facing mankind is the issue of global overpopulation. Now that the number of people living on the planet has risen above six billion, just how long can the Earth actually support its ever increasing population?

Tokyo: the world's largest city.

The population of the world increases by approximately 225,000 people every day. In October 1999, the number of people living on Earth passed the six billion mark for the first time. Although the rate of population growth has decreased, every year of the 1990s saw the number of people on the planet increase by something in the region of 81 million. It originally took 123 years for the population of the world to double from one billion to two billion, but since then population growth has accelerated in absolute terms at such a rate that it only took 11 years for the number of people to increase from five to six billion.

United Nations estimates indicate that in the year 2015, the world population will be some 7.5 billion, and that this will rise to 9.4 billion by 2050.

Population Control

Just a few years ago, the estimates for these population figures would have been significantly higher, but measures for population control have recently

shown the first signs of success. It is hoped that this trend will continue. It has been proven that epidemics, wars, natural catastrophes and malnutrition cause high mortality but have little effect on total population numbers. Only comprehensive medical welfare services and proper family planning can prevent the threat of overpopulation. In recent years, the average birth rate has fallen below three children per woman for the first time. Population development has no single global trend, however, but varies greatly from region to region.

Industrialised Nations and Developing Countries

The population in developed industrial nations is hardly increasing at all. In some countries, such as Russia, Germany, Italy and Japan, population numbers are actually decreasing. The USA is an exception among industrialised nations, and it is estimated that the US population will increase from the current 296 million to approximately 332.5 million by 2025.

The expected world population growth will take place mainly in the developing countries. By 2025, the population of Africa will grow from 840 million to 1.45 billion, and that of Asia will jump from 3.8 billion to 4.78 billion. Even within developing countries, however, the birth rate is not uniform. Increased family planning information, the availability of contraception as well as political pressure has successfully and astonishingly reduced the birthrate in China, South Korea and Singapore to around 1.8 children per woman. Even in countries with relatively limited access to contraception and family planning, the birth rate

is dropping. This is true for the countries of Latin America, Thailand and Algeria, where women give birth to an average of three children. It is only in the African states south of the Sahara that the birth rate over the past 30 years has seen only an insignificant reduction. The average birth rate in these countries can be as high as six children per woman.

Population Distribution

By the year 2025, the population of the world will rise above 8 billion people. Africa's rate of population growth, at 2.6 per cent, is by far the highest in the world. In Central and South America the growth rate pre-2025 will be 1.5 per cent, in Asia 1.4 per cent, in Oceania 1.3 per cent and in North America 0.3 per cent. For Europe no population growth is currently predicted.

In 2005, China had a population of 1.3 billion, making it the most populated country on Earth. Next came India with 1.1 billion, the USA (300 million), Indonesia (222 million), Brazil (186 million), Pakistan (158 million), Russia (143 million) Bangladesh (141 million), Nigeria (131 million), Japan (128 million) and Mexico with 101 million inhabitants.

These statistics will be significantly different by the year 2050. The UN's population predictions are: India 1640 million, China 1606 million, Pakistan 381 million, the USA 349 million, Nigeria

339 million, Indonesia 319 million, Brazil 264 million, Bangladesh 239 million, Ethiopia 194 million and Congo 164 million.

Urban Populations

Population growth in cities is much higher than in rural areas. Total population growth in 2000

was 1.4 per cent, but the population in cities grew by 2.5 per cent. Urban population growth in Africa, Asia, Central and South America is considerably higher than in the devoleped nations of Australia, North America and Europe. According to UN statistics in 2005, the most populous urban areas were: Tokyo-Yokohama (35 million), Mexico City (18.7 mil-

Population Distribution Urban/Rural

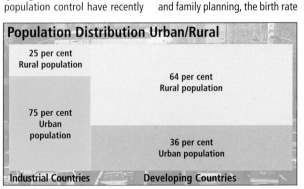

25 per cent Rural population

75 per cent Urban population

Industrial Countries

64 per cent Rural population

36 per cent Urban population

Developing Countries

Population Development (in billions)

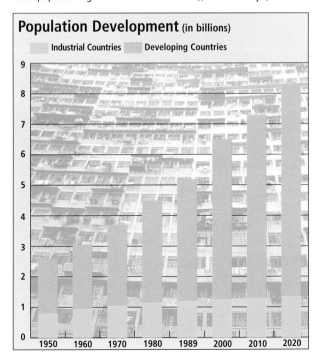

Industrial Countries   Developing Countries

1950 1960 1970 1980 1989 2000 2010 2020

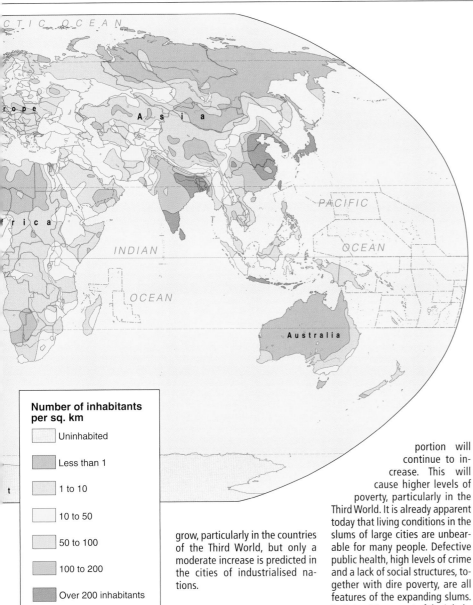

Number of inhabitants per sq. km

- Uninhabited
- Less than 1
- 1 to 10
- 10 to 50
- 50 to 100
- 100 to 200
- Over 200 inhabitants

lion), New York (18.3 million), Sao Paulo (17.9 million), Mumbai (17.4 million), Delhi (17.1 million), Calcutta (13.8 million), Buenos Aires (13 million), Shanghai (12.8 million), Jakarta (12.3 million), Los Angeles (12 million), Dhaka (11.6 million), Oskaka (11.2 million), Rio de Janeiro (11.2 million), Karachi (each 11.1 million), Beijing (10.8 million), Cairo (10.8 million), Moscow (10,5 million), Manilla (10.4 million), and Lagos (10.1 million). All of these cities continue to

The world's population centres
In the year 2005, nearly half of the world's population lived in cities.

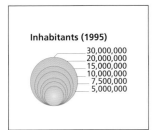

Inhabitants (1995)
- 30,000,000
- 20,000,000
- 15,000,000
- 10,000,000
- 7,500,000
- 5,000,000

grow, particularly in the countries of the Third World, but only a moderate increase is predicted in the cities of industrialised nations.

Urbanisation and Slums

According to development trends, half of the world's current population lives in cities, and this pro-portion will continue to increase. This will cause higher levels of poverty, particularly in the Third World. It is already apparent today that living conditions in the slums of large cities are unbearable for many people. Defective public health, high levels of crime and a lack of social structures, together with dire poverty, are all features of the expanding slums. In Cairo, 84 per cent of the inhabitants live in slums,; in other cities, such as Rio de Janeiro, Bombay, Lagos and Mexico City, the slums are forecast to expand. Growing urbanisation, coupled

Extremes: the empty Sahara and an overcrowded beach in China.

with a simultaneous exodus from the countryside, highlights the fact that people place all their hopes on what they believe will be a better life in the city. Of course, this hope does not always live up to expectations. Statistically, Australia's population density of two inhabitants per sq. km is exceptionally low, but this figure can be regarded in a different light if it is considered that the country has huge areas of un-inhabited land, and 90 per cent of Australians live in the cities. The population distribution in Egypt, where only four per cent of the national territory is inhabitable, is even more extreme. In many Asian countries, the situation is very similar. Statistics actually show that three quarters of the Earth's population live on a mere seven per cent of the total land mass. Urbanisation is now one of the major global issues.

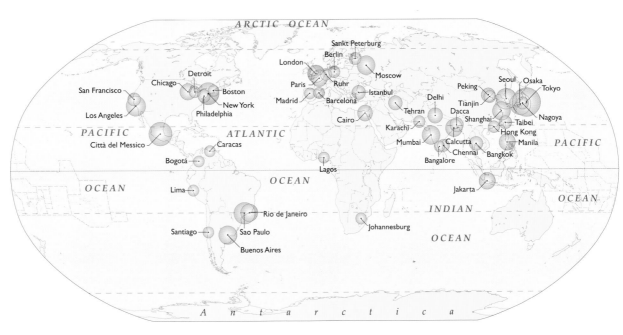

Religions

Despite modern trends towards secularisation, religion continues to play a decisive role in daily life. Religions often influence our thoughts and actions and are therefore a deciding factor in human behaviour and social interaction.

Jesus on the Cross: a holy symbol for Christians around the world.

In every age, and among every people, religious ideas have had an important influence on culture, social structures and politics. Conversely, religion has also been used to legitimise political regimes and there have been numerous alliances between important religious and political leaders. In prehistoric times, the practice of religion was mainly restricted to a family or clan group, as it is still seen today in many of the so-called animistic religions. The development of different societies saw a parallel increase in the level of organisation of religious communities, which were becoming ever larger.

Religion initially followed social barriers, so, until the end of Antiquity, religious communities were more or less confined to defined areas. It was only as a result of large movement of peoples and the missionary movements of the newly established monotheistic religions, such as Christianity and Islam, that 'global religions' took shape, and it became more difficult to classify or define a region by religion. History has shown that religion is constantly subject to change: large religious communities can disappear, new ones can emerge, and religions which were believed to be dead can suddenly experience a revival.

Judaism

The monotheistic global religions all have their origins in Judaism, which probably appeared in the second millennium BC in Egypt. In around 1280 BC, Moses led the Children of Israel into the Promised Land where the once nomadic people settled down and lived according to the rules set out in the Torah, the Five Books of Moses. After an eventful history, Jerusalem was destroyed by the Romans in the year 70 AD, and the last Jewish resistance movement led by Simeon Bar-Kokhba was defeated in the year 135 AD. Although the Jews never entirely disappeared from the Holy Land, most of the Jewish people left the region and settled mainly in Europe and and other regions of Asia. Persecutions, expulsions and pogroms by Islamic and Christian rulers led to repeated migrations of the Jews.

In most of Europe Jewish emancipation did not begin until the mid-nineteenth century, but anti-semitism remained deeply ingrained in many of the country's people. The racist policies of the Nazis in Germany led to the extermination of millions of European Jews.

The Jews of Palestine declared the creation of the state of Israel in 1948, after the UN voted in favour of partitioning the region. Predominantly Jewish Israel and its Arab neighbours have fought several wars in recent decades. Today, most of the world's Jews live in Israel and the United States.

Christianity

Christianity is the world's largest religious group. More than a quarter of the world's population profess Christianity. Christians are divided into a number of denominations. The largest of these is the Roman Catholic Church, followed by Protestant and Orthodox Christian groups. The core beliefs of all Christians centre around the life of Jesus of Nazereth, who was executed by the Romans in Jerusalem around the year 33 AD and who, according to tradition, is supposed to have risen from the dead.

Initially, early Christians saw themselves as a Jewish denomination, proclaiming the imminent return of the Messiah. The mis-

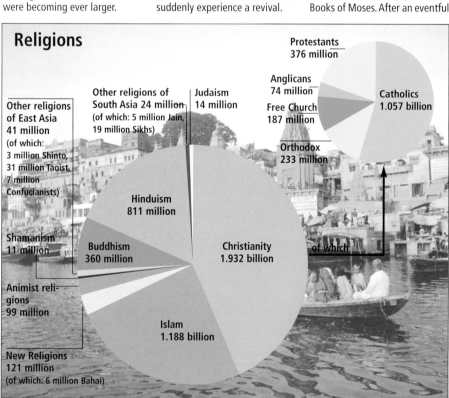

Religions

- **Other religions of East Asia 41 million** (of which: 3 million Shinto, 31 million Taoist, 7 million Confucianists)
- **Other religions of South Asia 24 million** (of which: 5 million Jain, 19 million Sikhs)
- **Judaism 14 million**
- **Shamanism 11 million**
- **Hinduism 811 million**
- **Buddhism 360 million**
- **Christianity 1.932 billion**
- **Animist religions 99 million**
- **Islam 1.188 billion**
- **New Religions 121 million** (of which: 6 million Bahai)
- **Protestants 376 million**
- **Anglicans 74 million**
- **Free Church 187 million**
- **Catholics 1.057 billion**
- **Orthodox 233 million**
- of which

Buddhism: a temple complex in Ayut

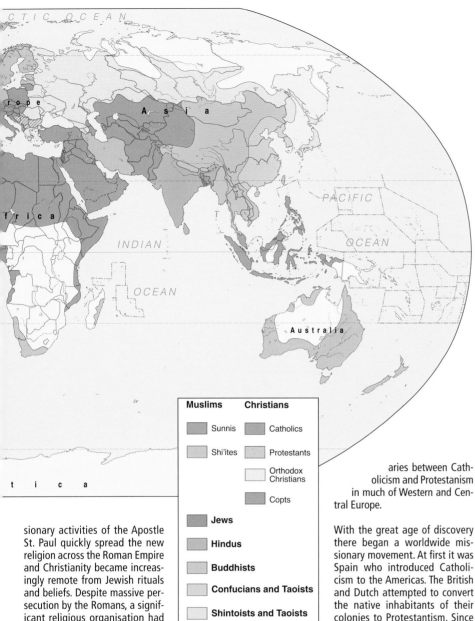

Voodoo: the main religion of Haiti is of African origin.

Legend (map)

Muslims
- Sunnis
- Shi'ites

Christians
- Catholics
- Protestants
- Orthodox Christians
- Copts

- Jews
- Hindus
- Buddhists
- Confucians and Taoists
- Shintoists and Taoists
- Animistic Religions

...land.

sionary activities of the Apostle St. Paul quickly spread the new religion across the Roman Empire and Christianity became increasingly remote from Jewish rituals and beliefs. Despite massive persecution by the Romans, a significant religious organisation had been established within 300 years, covering almost the entire known world. The strict centralist structure of the Church, with the Bishop of Rome as its head, became a power factor that could no longer be overlooked, and in the fourth century AD, Christianity was adopted by the Emperor Constantine as the state religion of the Roman Empire.

As a result of theological differences, the Church split in the year 1054, and the consequences of this division can still be seen today in the form of the Roman Catholic Church and the Orthodox denominations. The successors of the Western Roman Emperor, in particular Charlemagne, who proclaimed himself the Holy Roman Emperor, imposed Christianity on their subjects and used missionaries to spread it throughout large parts of Central and Eastern Europe. The history of Christianity has seen the formation of many new sects. The teachings of Martin Luther and other reformers led to the formation of an independent evangelical church, which did not recognise the authority of the papacy. The foundation of the Anglican church in England in 1534 was one of the most important events during this era. The Thirty Years War devastated Central Europe and determined the bound-aries between Catholicism and Protestanism in much of Western and Central Europe.

With the great age of discovery there began a worldwide missionary movement. At first it was Spain who introduced Catholicism to the Americas. The British and Dutch attempted to convert the native inhabitants of their colonies to Protestantism. Since the fall of Communism, the Orthodox faithful of Eastern Europe have once again been able to practice their faith openly.

Islam

There are more than one billion Muslims, followers of Islam, in the world. Islam is a monotheistic religion, founded by the Prophet Muhammad in the seventh century AD. The origins of the religion lie in the Arabian peninsula, where the religion's holy cities, Mecca and Medina are located. Islam's Holy Book is the Koran, the word of Allah, the Sunna, the records of speeches and acts of the Prophet and the Hadith, the interpretations and allegories of the faith. Differences of opinion as to the successor to the Prophet led to a split between the Sunnis and Shi'ites in the very early stages. Shi'a Muslims represent around 15 per cent of the total Muslim population. Islam spread very quickly across Asia and North Africa. In 713, the Moors con-quered Spain, where they remained until they were eventually repulsed in the fifteenth century. The Ottoman Turks conquered Byzantium in 1453 and made Istanbul (formerly Constantinople) a further centre of Islamic power. Islam also spread strongly throughout many countries of the lands of sub-Saharan Africa. After the collapse of the Ottoman Empire, the influence of Islam decreased, but in recent years, many Muslim states have gained increasing self-confidence.

Unfortunately, there has been increased activity by violent Islamic fundamentalists in recent years. In several countries Islamic religious states have been proclaimed which leave little room for personal freedom, women's rights or tolerance of religious minorities.

The regime in Iran, the Taliban in Afghanistan, fundamentalist terror attacks and the ruthless islamicisation of southern Sudan have unfortunately led to increased misconceptions about Islam among many non-Muslims.

Hinduism

Hinduism is mainly practised in India and has more than 800 million followers. Hindu belief is rooted in a series of ancient scriptures known as vedas. Hindus believe in re-incarnation and the continuous cycle of creation and death. Karma determines into which level of life a being is reincarnated. The doctrine of transmigration of souls has been used to legitimise the caste system, according to which every person has a specific place in society.

Buddhism

Buddhism was established by Prince Siddhartha Gautama, who lived in northern India in the sixth century BC. The aim of a good life is to escape the cycle of reincarnation through complete self-realisation, and to find release in Nirvana, 'extinction'. In fact the founder did not consider Buddhism a religion but rather a world philosopy. Nevertheless, Buddhism became the state religion of India in the third century BC and spread beyond the country's borders throughout the region, especially into what are now Pakistan, Bangladesh and Afghanistan.

The religion divided into the northern Hinayana Buddhism, and Mahayana Buddhism in the south. In India, Buddhism was suppressed by Brahmanism, but variants of the religion became established in Ceylon. It still flourishes in Tibet, Mongolia, China, Korea and Japan. Small communities have also been established in Europe and America. Buddhism has some 360 million followers around the world.

Taoism, Confucianism and Shinto

Confucianism is not strictly-speaking a religion in the true sense of the word, but it is an important form of ancestor worship practised by the Chinese. Taoism, which also has a pantheon of gods, is another major Chinese religion.

Approximately 40 per cent of the Japanese population follow Shinto, an ancient Japanese nature religion with distinctive ancestor-worship. The traditional role of the deified Tenno (the Emperors of Japan viewed as a deity) ended with the Japanese defeat in World War II, which also led to a separation of state and religion.

Animistic Religions

Animistic religions are the oldest forms of belief and are practiced today by many people in th third World. An integral part of these religions is the belief that our immediate surroundings are populated by souls. Animals, plants, stones and features of the landscape have a 'soul', and these items are then made into an object of worship. These places can also be simply regarded as a home for spirits and demons. Ancestor worship and totemism also play an important role in animistic religions. Voodoo is a successful animistic religion.

Languages

Only about 80 of the estimated 3,000 to 10,000 languages spoken in the world are official national languages. Different classifications and uncertain statistical data make exact figures as to the number of languages and their speakers impossible to ascertain.

Religious books played an important role in the spread of languages.

Number of Languages

The exact figure for the number of languages spoken in the world is a subject of constant debate. Estimates range from 3,000 to some 10,000. The main problem is that the experts cannot always agree on what is a dialect and what a language in its own right. Another issue is that even today, hitherto undiscovered languages are emerging, particularly in the Amazon Basin, Central Africa and New Guinea. The exploration of undeveloped regions has caused some native languages to completely die out in just one generation. In Brazil alone, some 800 Native American languages have been lost since the nineteenth century.

A further problem is that the definition of a language is often politically influenced. Danes, Norwegians and Swedes can talk to each other with very few problems, but Danish, Norwegian and Swedish are classified as separate languages. The situation is different in China, where there is a large number of local dialects, divided into eight main groups, the speakers of which can often only communicate using their common script. Despite this, Chinese is classified as a single language.

Number of Speakers

It is even harder to determine how many people speak each language. As a starting point, it can be said that Chinese is the mother tongue of over a billion people. English is regarded as the world's dominant language, however, despite the fact that there are only 350 million mother-tongue speakers. Add to this figure 300 million bilingual English speakers, and some 100 million people who have perfected English as a foreign language. In more than 70 countries, English is used an an official or semi-official language. In science, mass media, sport, diplomacy, technology, popular culture and the education system, English has a dominant position.

Other languages have also become widespread as a result of colonisation, such as French in Africa and Spanish in South and Central America. Due to significant demographic fluctuations, as in some West African states, it is difficult to assign a language to definitively to a particular nation. As a consequence, Creole and Pidgin are gaining increasing significance. It is hard to say if these are languages or dialects. It is also hard to ascertain reliable figures due to differences in population development. The population in Europe is stagnating, but India's population is growing at more than the average rate, which has a great effect on statistics for the languages spoken on the sub-continent.

Mother Tongues

According to estimates, the most common mother tongues are: Chinese, with around one billion speakers, followed by English (350 million), Spanish (300 million), Hindi (400 million), Arabic, Bengali and Russian (each 150 million), Portuguese (200 million), Japanese (120 million), German (100 million), French and Punjabi (each 70 million), Javanese and Bihari (65 million), Italian and Korean (60 million), Telugu and Tamil (55 million), Marathi and Vietnamese (50 million). While the number of German or Chinese mother-tongue speakers is roughly in line with the population figures for the countries where these are the official languages, the situation is completely different for Hindi, Urdu or Malay.

Official Languages

Chinese (Mandarin) is the official language of approximately one billion people, and English is the official language for roughly half that number. Next come Hindi (ca. 420 million), Spanish (380 million), Russian (290 million), Arabic (220 million), Bengali (200 million), Portuguese (180 million), Malay (155 million), Japanese and French (each approximately 125 million), German (120 million), Urdu (100 million), Italian, Korean and Vietnamese (each approximately (60 million), Farsi (55 million), Tagalog, Thai and Turkish (50 million).

Language Families

Linguists have been attempting to research the history of lan-

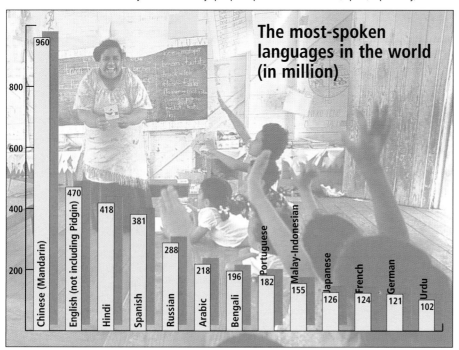

The most-spoken languages in the world (in million)

- Chinese (Mandarin): 960
- English (not including Pidgin): 470
- Hindi: 418
- Spanish: 381
- Russian: 288
- Arabic: 218
- Bengali: 196
- Portuguese: 182
- Malay-Indonesian: 155
- Japanese: 126
- French: 124
- German: 121
- Urdu: 102

Indo-European families of languages

	Germanic
	Romance
	Indo-European
	Slav
	Miscellaneous
	Sino-Tibetan languages
	Ural-Altaic languages
	African languages
	Austronesian languages
	Hamito-Semitic languages
	Dravidian
	Indian languages
	Isolated languages
	Uninhabited regions

Languages as an aid to a better future: school in Somalia.

guages and to document scientifically the linguistic similarities and differences since the eighteenth century. All attempts to classify languages involve certain risks and inaccuracies. The result has been a grouping of languages into various families.

With approximately two billion speakers, the Indo-European family of languages is the largest group. It can be further divided into Albanian (Albania, parts of the former Yugoslavia, Italy and Greece), Armenian (Armenia, parts of Turkey, the Armenian diaspora), Balto-Slavic (Baltic, Eastern Europe, CIS), Germanic (Scandinavia, Germany, USA, Canada, Australia), Celtic (Great Britain and France), Greek (Greece, parts of Cyprus), Indo-Iranian (Northern and Central India, Iran, Tajikistan, Kurdistan) and Italic (Western and Southern Europe, Romania, South and Central America).

Other significant language families include: Sino-Tibetan (China, Tibet, Indonesia, Thailand, Malaysia, Singapore), Uralic (Finland, Hungary, scattered places throughout the former USSR), Caucasian (Georgia, Armenia, Azerbaijan), Paleo-Siberian (north-east Siberia), Altaic (Uzbekistan, Turkey, Azerbaijan, Turkmenistan, Kirghizia, Mongo-

lia, parts of China, Iran and Afghanistan), Dravidian (southern and eastern India, southern and eastern Africa, northern Pakistan), and south-east Asiatic (Vietnam, Laos, Cambodia, Burma, Malaysia).

African languages can be divided into more than 1,000 Niger-Congo languages (Central Africa), more than 100 Nilo-Saharan languages (upper reaches of the Chari and the Nile) and the Khoisan languages (South Africa). Some 200 Hamito-Semitic languages are spoken in North

Africa, including Arabic, which is also spoken in large parts of the Middle East. The Austronesian family of languages cover the area between Madagascar, Taiwan, Hawaii and New Zealand, and consists of 600 different languages.

The greatest density of different languages can be found on New Guinea. The 600 languages spoken on the island belong to the Indo-Pacific family, which also includes language groups of southern Australia, Tasmania and in the Bay of Bengal. Indo-Pacific languages include: Tagalog (Philippines), Bahasa Indonesian (Malaysia, Indonesia), Malagasy (Madagascar), Tok Pisin (Papua New Guinea), Sundanese (West Java), Javanese (Java, Malaysia), Motu (Papua New Guinea), Chamorro (Micronesia, Guam), Tasmanian (Tasmania), Maori (New Zealand), Kiribatese (Gilbert Islands), Tahitian (Tahiti), Tongan (Tonga), Samoan (Samoa), Fijian (Fiji), and Rapa Nui (Easter Island).

Although there were once several thousand indigenous languages spoken in the Americas, only very few survive, of which some have only a handful of speakers. In North America there are 300 languages with scarcely more than 300,000 speakers. There are approximately 70 Meso-American Indian languages spoken in the area between Mexico and

Nicaragua. The diversity of Indian languages in South America was drastically reduced by the arrival of Portuguese and Spanish. Today, there are still approximately 100 language families, which can be divided into three main groups: Macro-Chibchan which has some 50 languages with 20,000 speakers, the 200 languages of Ge-Pano-Carib spoken by some one million people, and the Andean-Equatorial group consisting of 250 languages.

The languages of the native inhabitants of Australia, the Aborigines, are yet to be fully investigated. Before colonisation, there

China: the many dialects have a common script.

may have been some 500 languages, of which 250 still exist, but of these only five have more than 1,000 speakers.

Difficulties in Classification

Two important languages which cannot be definitively assigned to a particular family are Japanese and Korean. Both are often classed as Altaic languages, but it is difficult to prove whether or not there is actually a common root. Korean is spoken by some 50 million people, mainly in North and South Korea, but there are also minority groups of speakers in Japan, China and the former USSR. Japanese also has some Austric characteristics, as well as a series of Sino-Tibetan (Chinese) traits. Approximately 118 million people speak Japanese, mainly those living on the Japanese islands, but also Japanese in the USA and in Brazil.

Some languages do not follow any of the scientific criteria at all, and cannot even begin to be classified. Such languages include the isolated languages of the Native Americans, but also Ainu on the islands of Sakhalin, Hokkaido and the Kurile Islands. In Europe, the Basque language is a linguistic puzzle for language researchers. Some scientists suspect that the language is related to the Caucasian languages, others that it is another Ural-Altaic language like Hungarian, but this cannot be proven.

Food

In theory, the world can feed between 20 and 30 billion people. Despite this fact, of the world's 6.3 billion people, approximately 600–800 million suffer from chronic malnutrition. While the EU continues to offer rewards for the destruction of agricultural overproduction, hundreds of people in Africa starve to death every day.

Plentiful produce on a 'floating market' in Thailand.

Hunger and Overproduction

In recent years, the amount of food produced by farming in the world has risen significantly, and has more than compensated for the increased demand caused by the growth in population. It is a sad fact, however, that despite increased per capita production and the fact that in terms of pure statistics, there is more than enough food to adequately nourish everybody on the globe, uneven distribution of food supplies means that people in some regions of the world are living in conditions of starvation. Although approximately 800 million people on Earth are suffering from hunger, the EU is implementing policies to reduce the amount of food grown in its member states. Many African families do not even receive the minimum recommended calorie intake per day, but in countries such as the United Kingdom and Germany, state measures are being introduced to leave agricultural land fallow, because it is impossible to sell surplus food resulting from agricultural overproduction.

Adequate nutrition is not just about having enough food to eat. Even if a country produces sufficient foodstuffs, this does not mean that all of that country's people are adequately nourished. This is partly due to the fact that the quantities of vitamins and proteins consumed may not be sufficiently nutritious. One example of this is Mexico, where figures show that the country has a significant level of surplus food production, yet 14 per cent of the child population suffers from malnutrition.

The Causes of Regional Differences

The reasons behind these extreme regional variations in food distribution and nutritional intake are very complex. On the one hand, natural factors play an important role. Climatic conditions are not the same throughout the world. It is immediately clear that in the Sahara or in Greenland, no food can be cultivated effectively. Another important factor is that in many places, excessive cultivation, slash-and-burn or soil erosion caused by human intervention has significantly decreased the fertility of the soil.
On the other hand, many countries, particularly those in the Third World, are not in a position to be able to make the most of the land they have. Farmers in poor countries often lack modern technology, good-quality seeds or adequate fertilisers. Knowledge of efficient cultivation methods is also often shockingly inadequate. Even the political and social relationships in the developing countries contribute to the appaling conditions of the food supply network. Farmers are paid too little for their crops, which gives them no incentive to increase production. A particularly stark example can be seen in South America, where farmers in some countries cultivate plants for making drugs instead of for eating, because growing and selling cereals and fruits does not generate enough income to support their families. Distribution of land and unfair conditions for tenant-farmers also have extremely negative effects on the situation.

In many poor countries, the under-supply of food due to problems of under-production often fails to be balanced by imports, because there is simply not enough money available. There may be an adequate range and quantity of foods on the market, but the income of large sections of the population is insufficient to be able to purchase these foods. Even when harvests are good, deficient infrastructure prevents farmers from being able to profit by them. There is often no transport to carry produce from areas of over-production to areas where food is in short supply, or the poor quality of warehouses means that large quantities of food is lost to pests and disease.

Hunger in Africa and parts of Asia is also caused by war. Military operations, large waves of refugees and requisitions by the military and rebels make farming impossible and prevent food from being stored and distributed. The civil wars in Somalia, Afghanistan, Sierra Leone, Liberia, Sudan, Burkina Faso, Burundi, Rwanda and in the Democratic Republic of Congo have led to particularly serious problems of malnutrition.

Malnutrition

In North America, Australia, New Zealand, Japan, Argentina and Europe, the state of nutrition of the population is guaranteed, and good food is available and accessible to the majority of the population. In Africa, particularly in the sub-Saharan countries, the situation is catastrophic. The only exceptions are the Republic of South Africa and some of its neighbours, where agriculture is efficient. In 30 African countries, more than 30 per cent of the population is malnourished. The situation is relatively satisfactory in Mauritania, Benin, the Ivory Coast, Congo and Gabon, but the situation is worst in Sudan, Ethiopia, Somalia, Mozambique and Chad. Outside Africa, this famine situation is only matched in Haiti and Afghanistan. In Africa, 250 million people cannot afford to feed themselves adequately.

Rice cultivation: the most important method of food production in south-east Asia.

Burkina Faso: Lobi women brewing beer.

Daily calorie consumption per head

- Less than 2,000
- 2,000 to 2,500
- 2,500 to 3,000
- 3,000 to 3,500
- Over 3,500

In Somalia, the proportion of malnourished people is a shocking 72 per cent, in Ethiopia the figure is 65 per cent, and in the Democratic Republic of Congo 39 per cent. In Tanzania and Nigeria, 38 per cent of the population is malnourished.

The number of malnourished people is Asia is significantly higher, standing at 500 million, but the proportional figures are much lower. The situation is worst in Afghanistan, where 73 per cent of people are malnourished, followed by Bangladesh, where the figure is 34 per cent, India (21 per cent), Pakistan (17 per cent) and China (16 per cent).

The situation remains precarious in North Korea, where 13 per cent of the 23 million inhabitants suffer from starvation, though in that secretive society the figures can only be guessed at.

In Central and South America, there are a further 43.3 million people who do not receive enough food. In Peru, almost half of the population struggles to feed itself, in Venezuela, the figure is 20 per cent and in Columbia, 18 per cent. Approximately 150 million of the 800 million people worldwide who suffer from chronic malnourishment are children. In some countries, more than half of all children under five have their growth stunted due to malnutrition. In North Korea, the admitted figure is 60 per cent, in Zambia 59 per cent, in Burundi, 57 per cent, in Afghanistan, Ethiopia and the Yemen 52 per cent and in Nepal 51 per cent.

A Look to the Future

The United Nations Food and Agricultural Organization (FAO) believes that by 2015 the number of people going hungry in the world can be halved, but measures to increase productivity, improve distribution and increase the level of income are still insufficient. As long as dictators and military rulers in the Third World can afford to lavish expenditure on expensive weapons and mercenaries, as long as the industrial nations make more income from selling weapons than from their food supplies, as long as econom-ic factors determine whether surplus food is destroyed or delivered to needy regions, and as long there is speculation on futures as opposed to actual demand determining prices, there can be no solution to the problem.

The malnutrition situation is clearly the result of an unfair global economy that allows 15 million people to die from malnutrition every year, of whom four million are children. Many more people are undernourished, making them susceptible to disease. This despite the fact that there is more than enough food in the world to feed them.

Hunger in Sudan: 800 million people are undernourished.

The poor and needy: many mouths share a plate of millet.

Excess of the rich.

Measurements of Wealth

Measurments of GNP and GDP per capita are often cited when comparing the wealth and economic strength of nations. But these measurements are sometimes misleading as they often fail to reflect the economic, social, and geographic divisions in a society.

Rajasthan, India: women building roads.

Definition and significance

Gross National Product (GNP) refers to the total monetary value of the goods and services produced within a given period by the citizens and companies of a country, including wealth accumulated abroad. The Gross Domestic Product (GDP) on the other hand is defined as the value of all goods and services created within the political boundaries of a specific nation. The difference lies in the fact that GNP does not include the economic activity of foreigners living in a country, but it does include that of a state's citizens living or working abroad, while the opposite is true when

measurinfg the GDP of a country. It should be borne in mind, however, that these figures may be subject to significant fluctuations as a result of natural disasters, wars and other external factors. They also say nothing about the true condition of assets measured, such as the condition of buildings or machinery, or about the remaining supply of natural resources available in a country.

GDP by countries and per capita

According to recent calculations, global GDP for 2005 was estimated to be around US$ 44 trillion. This figure means that global GDP

per capita was around US$ 6,800 in 2005. However, a comparison of individual nations clearly shows that global GDP is extremely unevenly distributed. The United States of America had the highest GDP in 2005 at approximately US$12.4 trillion. Next came Japan with about US$4.6 trillion, Germany with US$2.7 trillion, China with US$2.2 trillion, the United Kingdom with US$2.1 trillion, France with US$2.1 trillion, Italy with 1.7 trillion US dollars, Canada with

US$1.1 trillion and Spain with US$1.1 trillion.

According to the International Monetary Fund estimates for 2005, Luxembourg in Western Europe has the highest per capita GDP during that year, with more than US$50,000 per capita generated in 2005, next is Norway with around US$42,000, the United States of America with US$41,300, the Republic of Ireland with just over US$40,000, Iceland with around US$35,000, Canada and Denmark both with an estimated US$34,000, Austria with US$33,400, Switzerland with US $32,500, Qatar on the Persian Gulf with US$31,500 and Belgium with slightly more than US$31,000. In contrast to these high figures, per capita GDP in the Democratic Republic of the Congo amounted to less than US$800 in 2005. The figures are similar for many of the world's poorest nations, including Ethiopia with US$800, Yemen with US$750, Burundi with US$730, Niger and Sierra Leone with around US$900 each and Malawi in southern Africa with just US$600.

National debts

These figures have only limited significance, however. For example, they do not take such factors as national debt into account.

Mexico, one of the most indebted developing countries has external debts in excess of US$ 170 billion. Dramatically high debts have also been piled up by Brazil, Russia, China, Indonesia, India, Argentina, Thailand, Poland, the Philippines, Venezuela, Nigeria and Egypt. If the assumed creditworthiness of a country is accepted as a criterion, Switzerland, Norway, the member states of the European Union, Japan, the USA, Canada, Singapore and Taiwan are flourishing, while most of the sub-Saharan African countries, together with Albania, Haiti, Cuba, Georgia, Belarus, the former Yugoslavia, Iraq, Afghanistan and North Korea are not even considered creditworthy.

Income distribution

The arithmetical average of per capita income is also distorted by the fact that income distribution patterns within a country are not taken into account. This is most clearly observable in Brazil and SouthAfrica. But an inter-European comparison also provides interesting information. For example, the level of national income in the United Kingdom and the Netherlands is roughly comparable. But the wealthiest 20 per cent of UK population make ten

Global economic growth (real increase of GDP in per cent)

Year	Value
1987	3.8
1988	4.5
1989	3.5
1990	2.4
1991	1.7
1992	2.6
1993	2.6
1994	3.8
1995	3.5
1996	3.7
1997	3.8
1998	2.7
1999	3.6
2000	4.3
2001	2.6
2002	3.0
2003	3.8

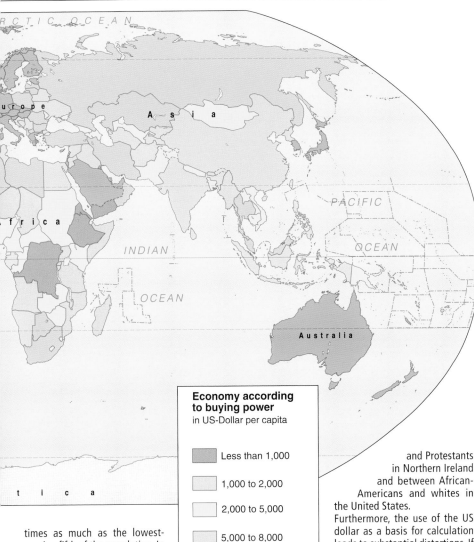

Georgian 'manufacture': a cutler at work.

Handicrafts in China: turning table-legs in Xinjiang.

Car assembly line without people: robots at work.

Economy according to buying power
in US-Dollar per capita

- Less than 1,000
- 1,000 to 2,000
- 2,000 to 5,000
- 5,000 to 8,000
- 8,000 to 15,000
- Above 15,000
- No data available

times as much as the lowest-earning fifth of the population. In the Netherlands, the discrepancy is only half as great. In Central and Eastern Europe the distribution of income is still relatively even-handed. This also applies to poorer developing countries such as Ghana and Uganda.

Wealth gaps also appear among various groups within individual countries. In the Philippines, for example, there is a dramatic difference between residents of Manila, the capital city and those of outlying areas such as Min-

danao. In Mexico, the indigenous ethnic groups are clearly under-privileged in comparison with the rest of the population, there is also a significant income and wealth gap between Catholics

and Protestants in Northern Ireland and between African-Americans and whites in the United States.

Furthermore, the use of the US dollar as a basis for calculation leads to substantial distortions. If the basis is the actual buying power of a local currency, the wealth gap alters to the disadvantage of the industrialised countries. The case of Cape Verde is a good example of this. According to its nominal GDP, Cape Verde is one of the world's poorest countries but the picture changes when living costs in the country are taken into account.

Computer production: a rapidly growing industry.

Poverty today and tomorrow

According to the criteria of the World Bank, one quarter of the world's population is living below the poverty line. By this definition, a poor person is anyone who has less than one US dollar a day at their disposal. This means that at least 1.5 billion would fall into this category.

In South Asia, 515 million people are in this situation, i.e. 43 per cent of the population, in East Asia and the Pacific region 446 million (26 per cent), in Sub-Saharan Africa 219 million (39 per cent), in Latin America and the Caribbean 110 million (24 per cent), in the Near East and North Africa 11 million (four per cent) and in Europe and Central Asia 15 million (3.5 per cent).

While poverty has noticeably

decreased in East Asia and slightly in South Asia in recent years, the income situation in Africa has remained consistently alarming. Since the collapse of the Soviet Union, most of the formerly communist countries of the Europe have experienced dramatic economic transformations. During the early and mid-1990s levels of poverty and unemployment increased rapidly in many parts of Eastern Europe, including Poland, Romania and the successor states of the Soviet Union. The situation in the region has greatly improved in recent years with many countries there now exhibiting strong growth and a decline in poverty.

Income alone, however, still does not tell the whole truth about average living conditions in a society. If life expectancy and educa-

tion are also taken into, another 300 million individuals can also be classified as destitute. Measured in terms of GDP, the wealth gap between the industrialised countries and the poorest states is in the order of 155:1. Taking into account the relative buying power of currencies, the ratio is 'only' 23:1.

Based on the high growth rates of many developing nations and the relatively slow growth of the wealthiest countries, one could assume that global income will become more evenly distributed in the future . This trend, in itself a positive one, does not however reflect the wide range of social and political challenges facing the emerging economies of the world, challenges that could threaten even the most impressive economic progress.

Life expectancy

Life expectancy of a human being depends largely on nutrition, medical care and public health in his or her environment.

Life expectancy rises with growing wealth: a family on Bali.

In the mid-1980s average life expectancy at the point of birth stood worldwide at about 62 years. By the year 2000, the average had increased by five years. Average life expectancy varies quite considerably from country to country, however. Thus people living in industrialised nations can expect to live to the age of 77, those in the emerging nations to 69 and those in the developing countries to 64.

Life expectancy by country

The statistics for the poorest developing countries, however, is still substantially lower. An inhabitant of Lesotho, for example, has an average life expectancy of only 34 years. In Sierra Leone it is 40 years, in Uganda 41, in Malawi 42, in Afghanistan and Guinea-Bissau 43, in Zambia 44, in Guinea and Gambia 45, and in Mali 46 years.

A Japanese male, on the other hand, has an average life expectancy of 81 years. In Switzerland, Sweden and Iceland, too, life expectancy is high at 80 years. Next come Australia, France, Italy, Canada, Norway and Cyprus, where the average age at death is 78. Britons, too, have quite a high life expectancy at an average of 78 years.

During the last 30 years, the difference between life expectancy in the industrialised nations on the one hand and of the developing countries on the other has decreased from 25 to about 13 years. The trend towards longer life does not, however, apply everywhere. In countries afflicted by epidemics or wars, life expectancy has actually decreased. This applies especially to the African countries south of the Sahara, where a particularly high rate of HIV-infected individuals is found, or countries such as Rwanda or the Sudan, in which whole groups of the population have been systematically massacred.

Example: Russia

Developments in the successor states of the former Soviet Union are particularly dramatic. In 1987, an average Soviet Russian expected to live to about 65 years, but by 2000 life expectancy had sunk to below 60. This downward trend particularly affected the socially disadvantaged city dweller. The reasons are, on the one hand, the objectively lower standard of healthcare and on the other the psychological uncertainty wrought by basic life changes due to political events. The planned economy system relieved the populations from the responsibility for their own lives, to some extent incapacitating them, but at least it ensured adequate nutrition and reasonably good medical care.

The social pressures inflicted by political upheaval and a dangerous tendency of many Russians to overindulge in alcohol are the causes for the drop in life expectancy. Officially, all Russian citizens today still have health insurance, but the health service has broken down completely. The technical equipment of hospitals and medical practices no longer meets even the minimum standards usual in the industrialised states. Defective equipment is no longer repaired or replaced, and money is lacking even for the basic provision of medications.

Child mortality

Substantial progress has been made in the reduction in child mortality. While 240 of every 1000 children born in 1975 died before their fifth birthday, today

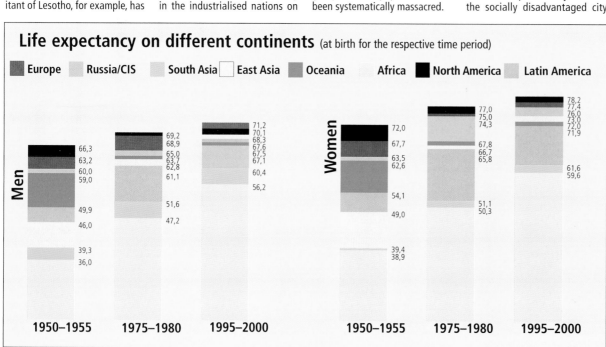

Life expectancy on different continents (at birth for the respective time period)

Europe   Russia/CIS   South Asia   East Asia   Oceania   Africa   North America   Latin America

Men

1950–1955: 66,3 / 63,2 / 60,0 / 59,0 / 49,9 / 46,0 / 39,3 / 36,0

1975–1980: 69,2 / 68,9 / 65,0 / 63,7 / 62,8 / 61,1 / 51,6 / 47,2

1995–2000: 71,2 / 70,1 / 68,3 / 67,6 / 67,5 / 67,1 / 60,4 / 56,2

Women

1950–1955: 72,0 / 67,7 / 63,5 / 62,6 / 54,1 / 49,0 / 39,4 / 38,9

1975–1980: 77,0 / 75,0 / 74,3 / 67,8 / 66,7 / 65,8 / 51,1 / 50,3

1995–2000: 78,2 / 77,4 / 76,0 / 73,0 / 72,0 / 71,9 / 61,6 / 59,6

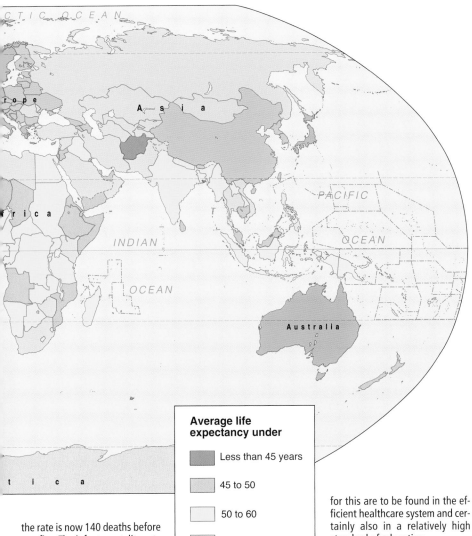

Average life expectancy under

- Less than 45 years
- 45 to 50
- 50 to 60
- 60 to 70
- 70 to 75
- Over 75 years

Extended families now often consists of three or four generations.

the rate is now 140 deaths before age five. The infant mortality rate has also declined. In 1990, 76 of every 1000 babies born died before their first birthday, the rate has now fallen to 58.

Improved nutrition, exemplary medical care, clean drinking water, and irreproachable hygiene and public health conditions allowed infant mortality in the Western industrialised nations to drop to almost zero. In Germany, Canada, Japan, Switzerland and the Netherlands, for example, it is only 0.6 per cent. In the emerging nations, child mortality is somewhat higher, in Russia for example it is 2.7 per cent, in Hungary and Poland 1.4 per cent, in Bulgaria 1.6 per cent, and in Estonia 1.9 per cent.

The so-called 'Tiger economies' of East Asia have almost reached the level of the Western countries. In Taiwan only 0.6 per cent of infants died, in South Korea 0.8 per cent, and in Singapore as few as 0.5 per cent. In Indonesia, infant mortality was significantly reduced, but still stands at about five per cent. In the Arab countries of the Near East and North Africa the rate fluctuates between about six per cent in Morocco and Egypt and 1.2 per cent in Kuwait. Similar figures are recorded for the countries of South and Central America.

In the developing countries, clear differences are to be found. Infant mortality stands at 7.6 per cent in India, 3.8 per cent in China, 6.7 per cent in Papua-New Guinea, but 17 per cent in Angola, 16.5 per cent in Afghanistan, 16.4 per cent in Sierra Leone, 15.9 per cent in the Western Sahara territory, and 15.8 per cent in Mozambique.

The proportion is similar in the death rates for children aged under five years. Here, the income and level of education of the parents plays a decisive role.

Factors determining life expectancy

The fact that it is not only the economic power of a country that is decisive for a higher or lower life expectancy is shown by the example of Cuba. Although the average Cuban makes only US$3,030 a year, the average life expectancy is 76 and infant mortality is 0.9 per cent. The reasons

for this are to be found in the efficient healthcare system and certainly also in a relatively high standard of education.

An important factor in the high mortality rate in many countries is the lack of access to clean water and hygienic sanitation. This problem is particularly acute in the slums of the big cities in developing countries. It can be assumed that more than 220 million city-dwellers worldwide are unable to obtain clean drinking water, and that for twice as many, not even the most primitive sanitary arrangements are available. Medical care is uniformly excellent in the industrialised countries. On average, there is a doctor for every 344 individuals. In the developing countries the ratio is considerably less favourable at 1:5767. This is also mirrored in expenditure on health. The industrial nations spend 36 times more per capita on healthcare than the countries of sub-Saharan Africa.

Causes of death

A glance at the causes of death show that a long life by no means implies a good life. While 41.5 per cent of people in developing countries suffer from diseases resulting from infection or parasites, in the industrialised nations such deaths account for only 1.2 per cent.

The picture changes in the case of deaths caused by the diseases of the wealthy. In the industrialised states, circulatory diseases cause 46.7 per cent of deaths, and cancer 21.6 per cent, while the corresponding rates in the developing countries are only 10.7 per cent and 8.9 per cent respectively.

Within the industrialised nations too, varying social systems affect the causes of death. These differences are not only related to industrial safety, traffic safety measures or drug use. In some societies, violent crime has become so widespread that it is a factor that has to be taken into account. For example the most frequent cause of death among males aged 18 to 60 in Washington D.C., is neither heart

attack nor cancer, but murder. The picture is similar in Los Angeles. While some parts of the city spend more on healthcare than anywhere else in the United States, the deaths of young people in Watts, Rancho Santa Fé and similarly deprived neighbourhoods inhabited by Blacks and Latinos is on the increase due to drive-by shootings in gang wars.

In the industrialised countries, death from arteriosclerosis and other heart diseases, diabetes, cancer, Parkinson's disease, Motor Neurone disease and other immune deficiencies and chronic complaints are likely to increase, while those from infections, including HIV/AIDS, are likely to decrease due to improved care.

Agriculture

Agriculture provides the crops and livestock that feed the vast majority of mankind. Productivity in individual countries and regions depends on climate, soil and water resources as well as technology and the business acumen of farmers.

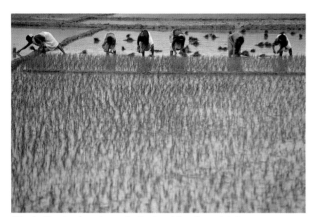

Rice is the dominant crop in East and South-east Asia.

The natural living space of plants and animals has undergone a fundamental shift through the actions of the human race. Any food plant and those usable for other purposes are now cultivated well outside their original areas of origin. It may be surprising to discover that a plant as typical of South and Central America as sugar cane was first introduced by the colonial powers. The potato is considered a staple European food, but it was first brought to Europe by the conquistadors from South America. Thanks to irrigation and fertilisation, plants have been cultivated in areas where this had previously been impossible. This also applies to new hybrids and cultures. The tomato originated from sub-tropical South America, but today it flourishes in the cold Netherlands, where it is produced in great quantities in greenhouses using large quantities of fertilisers and pesticides.

The same applies to livestock. Originally, sheep and cows were confined to Eurasia and Africa. In South America, only the llama and alpaca were known, in North America only the dog and the turkey. The aborgines of Australia reared no livestock. With the colonisation of the world, cattle, for example, were brought to South America in 1525, and it is now hard to imagine the Argentinean pampas without cattle. The largest number of wild camels is to be found in Australia, although the animals were only introduced in the mid-nineteenth century. Sheep-rearing is one of the most important branches of New Zealand's economy, but sheep were not brought there from Europe until the late eighteenth century.

Selection and improved cultivation methods have continued to increase crop yields. Farming methods aimed at unconditional yield increase also have their downside, however. Deforestation, the over-fishing of rivers, lakes and the sea, the uncontrolled use of pesticides and the unpredictable consequences of radiation and genetic engineering have led to the increasingly vocal demands for rational, responsible farming.

Forms of agriculture

The simplest form of agriculture is practised by hunter-gatherers. They live by collecting the fruits, seeds and roots of wild plants and hunting animals in the wild. A primitive economy of this kind, practised since the Neolithic period, has been preserved among some Indian tribes in the Amazon area, the Bushmen of the southern Kalahari, the Pygmies in the Congo basin, the Australian Aborigines, the Aeta in the Philippines, the Wedda in Sri Lanka and the Senoi and Sakai in Malaysia and Sumatra.
Sedentary farmers work the soil usng primitive tools and cultivate mainly ochroes, dasheen, millet, maize and pulses. When the soil is exhausted, they move on and finds a new cultivation area clearing the forest and scrub using the slash-and-burn method which is still frequently practiced in the tropics and sub-tropics.

In order to ensure that their animals are adequately fed, nomads of the steppes often cover long distances from one feeding place or watering place to another. The movement of herds of sheep, goats, cattle and camels was once an important trading connection between settled farmers. Today, total nomads such as the Tuareg and the Bedouin are found only in the Sahara and Arabia, and even they are being encouraged to settle down.

Improving the soil by ploughing was known in prehistoric Mesopotamia and was perfected in the days of ancient Rome. Along with this went the breeding of pack-animals to pull the machinery. The medieval three-field system and crop rotation, which has been practised in Europe and North America since the nineteenth century, brought further substantially higher yields from the soil and improved supplies of meat and milk. The invention of chemical fertilisers, the use of pesticides, scientific breeding methods and improved farm machinery contributed further improvements to agriculture.
The natural limits of agriculture are being pushed ever further. Nevertheless, only about ten per cent of the earth's land mass is under cultivation. In the Antarctic, Northern Canada, Siberia and Greenland, in the deserts of the

Agricultural production (in millions of tonnes)

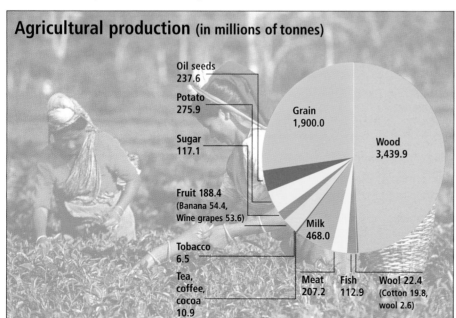

Oil seeds 237.6
Potato 275.9
Sugar 117.1
Fruit 188.4 (Banana 54.4, Wine grapes 53.6)
Tobacco 6.5
Tea, coffee, cocoa 10.9
Grain 1,900.0
Wood 3,439.9
Milk 468.0
Meat 207.2
Fish 112.9
Wool 22.4 (Cotton 19.8, wool 2.6)

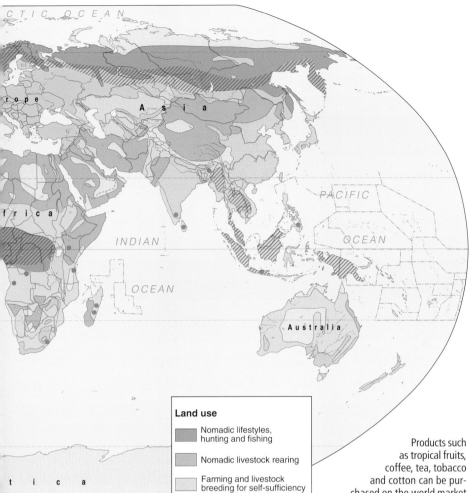

Sheep breeding in the Argentinian Pampas.

Industrial animal husbandry: a battery hen unit.

Land use

- Nomadic lifestyles, hunting and fishing
- Nomadic livestock rearing
- Farming and livestock breeding for self-sufficiency
- Industrial farming and intensive livestock breeding
- Farming for self-sufficiency
- Extensive farming and livestock breeding
- Plantations
- Timber industry

Sahara, Australia and Central Asia and in mountainous areas, agriculture is simply an impossibility. However, new irrigation systems, as well as the cultivation of plants with extremely short vegetation cycles, and particularly resistant breeds are now being used to extend the areas of cultivation.

Supplies of agricultural products

The countries of the EU employ a highly mechanised intensive farming system which is able to provide the population with an abundance of crops as well as with meat, milk and fish. Non-saleable surpluses are often produced. Output can be reduced by state programmes subsiding set-aside and reduction of cattle stock. Even major epidemics such as swine fever, BSE and foot-and-mouth disease have had no disastrous consequences for the food supply.

Products such as tropical fruits, coffee, tea, tobacco and cotton can be purchased on the world market without difficulty. The USA and Canada are the leading nations with respect to surpluses and exports. Apart from tropical fruits, their domestic market is self-sufficient in almost every agricultural product. The large surpluses are sold on the world market, where subsidy policies and agricultural trade policies, particularly those of the EU and Japan, regularly obstruct the export of North American produce.

The exporting countries of South America, especially Brazil and Argentina, supply the world market with beef, grain and fruit. Coffee and banana exports are an important economic factor for Latin America and the Caribbean.

In Africa, agricultural production in South Africa, Namibia and the Maghreb is adequate to supply the home market, leaving a modest surplus for export. As a result of adverse weather conditions, wars and a misguided agricultural policy, production in most of the sub-Saharan African countries is stagnant and in some places it has even declined.

Agriculture in India and China, on the other hand, has taken a powerful leap forward. Modernisation of machinery, improved seed supplies, expansion of the infrastructure and the building of more irrigation systems have ensured steady increases in productivity. Even the highly populated emerging countries of east, south-east and south Asia have been able to increase their agricultural production to such an extent that a satisfactory nutritional situation has been achieved.

Most of the countries of the Near East and Japan are dependent on imports of foodstuffs, but these are largely paid for by those countries oil wealth and industrial production respectively. The situation is more problematic in the case of the CIS, which has recorded a significant decline in production after the dissolution of the Soviet Union. The difficulties resulting from regime changes are also obvious in other former Eastern bloc countries, although a recovery is slowly occuring.

The most important agrarian products

One of the most important crops are cereals, and in particular wheat, rice and maize (corn). The major grower countries are China, the USA, India, Russia, Indonesia, France, Brazil and Germany. The leading exporters are the USA, Canada, the EU countries, Argentina, Australia and Thailand. India is one of the world's major rice exporters. The world's largest exporter of rice is the USA.

In 2004, around 705 million tonnes of maze, 624 miilion tonnes of grain and 608 million tonnes of rice were harvested worldwide. The major producers of these crops are also the largest consumers, which is why only a small percentage of the crops harvested are exported.

In 2003, around 90 million tonnes of fish were caught worldwide. According to official estimates the amount of fish caught exceeded international quotas by 27 million tonnes. The most important fishing nations are China, Peru, Chile, Japan, the USA, India, Russia, Indonesia and Thailand. Fish farms are becoming increasingly important. Most of the salmon now marketed comes from fish-farms. The largest meat producer worldwide is, surprisingly, China, followed by the USA, Brazil, Argentina, Russia and the EU countries. Timber and logging is a major industry in the USA, Canada, Russia and China. The wood is used for paper pulp as well as in construction and furniture production. The leading exporters are Australia, New Zealand and Chile, while cotton is exported mainly from China, the United States and India. Rubber is produced primarily in Thailand, Indonesia and Malaysia. Coffee is an important export for Brazil, Colombia, Indonesia and Kenya.

Deep-sea fishing in the Atlantic.

Cattle ranch in the USA.

Combine harvesters at work.

Mineral Resources Metals and minerals

In addition to natural resources used as a source of power, minerals and metals are important raw materials for industry. Due to dwindling reserves of metals and minerals, the industrialised nations are increasingly developing modern recycling methods.

A landscape radiacally altered by mining.

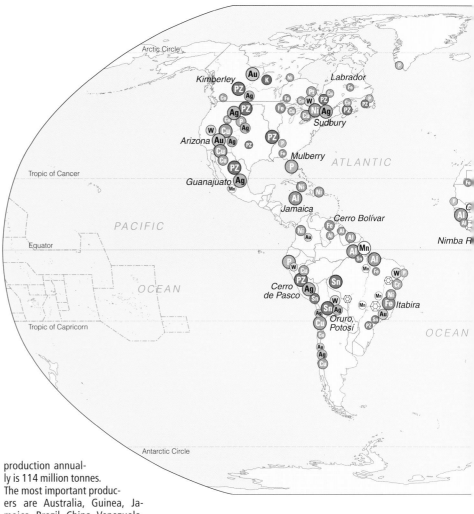

Humans learned at an early stage to extract metal from ore and use it to produce weapons, tools and jewellery. Since the deposits of such raw materials are not evenly distributed throughout the world, trading soon began in the much-coveted metals and minerals. Since the age of discovery, the colonial powers systematically exploited the resources of their overseas possessions, and not infrequently the demand for raw materials was the trigger for armed conflict. The possession of precious metals such as gold and silver meant wealth and political power. The fight for the exploitation of the deposits was conducted with corresponding bitterness. Technological progress meant that nearly all metals became indispensable for certain areas of industrial production.

Bauxite is an aluminium hydrate used in the manufacture of abrasives and fireproofing. But above all it is of importance for the production of aluminium. Worldwide production annually is 114 million tonnes. The most important producers are Australia, Guinea, Jamaica, Brazil, China, Venezuela, India, Suriname, Russia, Greece and Guyana.

Lead is used mainly for vehicle batteries, for sheet metal, water pipes, grenades and seals. In addition it is used in the chemical industry for making lead cells, in medicine for protection from x-rays, and for coating cables. Worldwide production annually amounts to just under three million tonnes. The main producers are Australia, the USA, China, Peru, Canada, Mexico, Sweden, South Africa, Morocco, Kazahstan, Ireland and Poland.

Zinc is used mainly in the building and automotive industries for galvanised steel products, but also as sheet metal for making roofs watertight, and in various combinations for pharmaceutical products, lacquers, disinfectants and conservation materials. Zinc is also a component of alloys such as brass and tombac, a zinc and copper alloy. World production of zinc amounts to some 9.3 million tonnes. The main producers are Canada, Australia, China, Peru, the USA, Mexico, Ireland, Spain, Kazakhstan, Russia, India and Brazil.

Chromium is an important finish for steel. Reserves of chromium are relatively large, but they are concentrated in comparatively few places. World production stands at 9 to 10 million tonnes annually, more than half of which originates in southern Africa and in Kazakhstan. China is also a chromium exporter.

Iron is the main material of the metal industry. The automobile industry, ship-building, armaments, building materials are all manufacturing areas that could not manage without iron, which is mostly turned into steel. Iron ore deposits in Europe are now only mined in France, Austria and Norway. Because of the pressure of competition from much cheaper iron from overseas, the European mines only survive through massive state subsides. A good trillion tonnes of iron ore are produced annually worldwide. The most important producing countries are China, Brazil, Australia, Russia, the USA, India, the Ukraine, Canada, South Africa, Sweden, Venezuela, Kazakhstan, Mauritania, North Korea, Chile and Austria.

Humanity has always had a great fascination with gold. This precious metal once had little practical use – for dental fillings, for example. However, as the supremenly inert metal, gold has important uses in the electronics industry. This is likely to increase the demand for gold. At present, however, only about five per cent of gold is employed in industry, the rest is used for the manufacture of jewellery or ends up in the treasuries, even though today most currencies are not backed by gold reserves.

A steel mill in China's Inner Mongolia province.

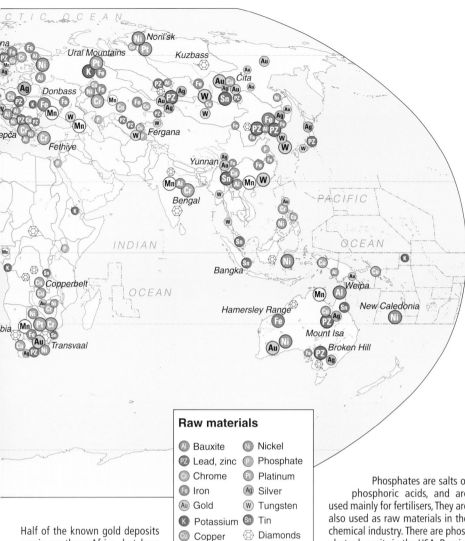

Raw materials

(Al)	Bauxite	(Ni)	Nickel
(PZ)	Lead, zinc	(P)	Phosphate
(Cr)	Chrome	(Pt)	Platinum
(Fe)	Iron	(Ag)	Silver
(Au)	Gold	(W)	Tungsten
(K)	Potassium	(Sn)	Tin
(Cu)	Copper	⬡	Diamonds
(Mn)	Manganese		

○ 1st grade resource:
over five per cent of
known world reserves

○ 2nd grade resource:
one to five percent of
known world reserves

○ 3rd grade rresource:
below one per cent of
known world reserves

Modern gold mine in Indonesia.

Diamond-prospecting in South Africa.

Half of the known gold deposits are in southern Africa, but here the noble metal is increasingly deep-mined from very large amounts of slag, while in Australia or China it can be obtained through open-cast mining. World production annually stands at a good 2500 tonnes, of which about a fifth comes from South Africa. Further important gold-mining countries are the USA, Australia, China, Russia, Canada, Brazil, Uzbekistan, Papua-New Guinea, Ghana, Chile, Peru, Colombia, Zimbabwe and the Philippines.

Potash salts are extracted from arid zones and are used mainly as fertiliser. They are also used in explosives, for the production of glass and the saponification of fats. The metallic element potassium occurs in nature only in combination. The most important deposits are in Israel, Jordan, Germany, Alsace, Canada, the USA and Russia.

World copper supplies are assessed at around 600 million tonnes. The main producers are Chile, the USA, the CIS, Canada, Indonesia, Peru, Poland, Australia and China. Annual worldwide output is ten million tonnes. Since more and more copper is being obtained from recycled materials, and substitutes for this valuable metal are being found, for example in telecommunications technology and plumbing, a noticeably lower demand is to be expected in the future.

Manganese is one of the most important finishes for steel. The manganese deposits in the oceans have not yet been fully exploited. On the mainland, the most important deposits are in South Africa, the Ukraine, Russia, Brazil, Gabon, Australia, India, China, Mexico and Ghana and Vanuatu.

Nickel is used to harden steel and make it resistant to corrosion. It is also used to make such alloys as cupro-nickel which is the favourite metal for coinage. Important deposits are found in Canada, Australia, Indonesia, New Caledonia, Cuba, Russia and Brazil.

Phosphates are salts of phosphoric acids, and are used mainly for fertilisers, They are also used as raw materials in the chemical industry. There are phosphate deposits in the USA, Russia, Estonia , Brazil, North Africa, Togo, Senegal, Israel, Jordan and China.

Platinum is used above all to produce exhaust gas catalytic converters, electronic components and to make jewellery. In 2003, South Africa extracted around 140 million tonnes, other major producers include Russia, Canada and the USA.

Silver is an important raw material in the photochemical industry. But it is also used in the electronics industry, as well as for the production of jewellery, cutlery and coins. Worldwide annual production is over 18,000 tonnes. Mexico, Peru, the USA, Australia, Chile, Canada, Poland, Kazakhstan, Bolivia, Morocco, Sweden, Russia, North Korea and South Africa are the leading producers.

Tungsten is used to soften steels at high temperatures and is employed in the armaments industry. About one quarter of world production comes from South-east Asia. Further deposits are found in the USA, Russia, Australia, Bolivia, Portugal, France and Austria.

Tin is used mainly for alloys, employed in the packaging industry. World production amounts to 160,000 tonnes per year. The most important producers are China, Indonesia, Brazil, Peru, Bolivia, Russia and Malaysia. Tin-mining was once an important industry in the United Kingdom, but cheaper imports have made it totally impractical and the last tin mine in Cornwall closed in 2001.

Diamonds are classified as gemstones or industrial diamonds. Gemstone diamonds account for about 80 per cent of total production. In 2003, 148 million carats of rough diamonds were mined. The most important deposits are found in Australia, the Russian Federation, the Democratic Republic of Congo, Botswana, South Africa, Namibia, Brazil, China, Ghana and Venezuela, most diamonds are processed and cut in India, Belgium, Holland and Israel.

Phosphate mine near Kipeme, Togo.

Energy

Worldwide energy consumption depends on various factors. Seasonal variations are crucial as are new technological advances. Thus growing ecological awareness in the wealthy industrialised countries of Europe, the collapse of communism in the former Eastern bloc industries and a massive jump in oil prices have clearly slowed the increase in energy consumption.

Electricity from wind power is becoming increasingly important.

Approximately 13.6 billion tonnes of bituminous coal units of energy are produced worldwide every year. Consumption is distributed very unevenly, however. While an inhabitant of Chad only consumed eight bituminous coal units in 2002, a US citizen used 11,391 units. Per capita consumption in the industrialised countries is therefore considerably higher than in the developing countries. The countries of Europe and North America account for one-fifth of the world's population, but consume around 60 per cent of the annual global energy requirement while Africans, who account for 13 per cent of world population, only consume three per cent of total energy. The difference is likely to get worse, rather than better, with higher energy prices.

Causes of varying energy consumption

These variations can be primarily attributed to industry structure. Countries with relatively important coal, steel and chemical industries have a significantly higher energy consumption than agricultural nations. The duration of hot spells, the degree of automation and the technical handling of energy are also factors. Thus, in some European countries efforts are being made to improve heat insulation, to use engines that are more economical, etc. Awareness of energy issues has also grown significantly in the United States recently

As deposits of energy sources are also very unevenly distributed, many countries are forced to import energy, while others produce their more than they need for their own consumption many times over and can offer the surplus on the global market.

It is not only deposits of energy sources which have a part to play; political and economic factors also determine the energy policies of individual countries. Thus, German bituminous coal-mining is only viable thanks to state subsidies and the electricity produced by coal-fired power stations is considerably more expensive than in

Denmark which is reliant on foreign imports of coal. Denmark could actually produce electricity even more cheaply by using nuclear power but it has decided to forgo the economic advantage due to the dangers associated with radiation. Other European countries face a similar dilemma.

Bituminous coal as an energy source

Indigenous resources are not always of prime importance in determining the proportion of coal in the electricity production of a country. Thus, bituminous coal-mining has declined sharply in France, Spain, Germany and Great Britain. In Belgium and the Netherlands it has been discontinued due to non-profitability.

Until the 1960s, bituminous coal was the most important energy source globally. Today, it only supplies approximately one quarter of global primary energy. A determining factor for this is the cheaper price of crude oil, natural gas and nuclear energy. In particular, Western European bituminous coal can no longer compete with these energy sources and the bituminous coal of South Africa and Australia which is considerably easier to mine and therefore cheaper. Global bituminous coal reserves total

1,000 billion tonnes. It is estimated that approximately three or four times as much as this is located in further deposits which have not yet been exploited.

A total of 3,833.3 million tonnes were mined globally in 2003. The main producers are China, the USA, CIS, India, South Africa, Australia, North Korea, Germany, Great Britain, Canada, Indonesia, Columbia, the Czech Republic, Spain, Mexico and France. The most important exporters are Australia, the USA, South Africa, Canada, Poland, Indonesia, China and Colombia, while the United Kingdom, Japan, South Korea, Italy, Germany, Belgium, Spain and Brazil import significant amounts.

Lignite

Although lignite has a lower calorific value than bituminous coal, it can be mined significantly more efficiently in open-cast mining and its primary use is in electricity production. Global reserves of approximately 4,430 billion tonnes are chiefly distributed in the former USSR, the Czech Republic, Poland, USA, China, Australia and Germany. A total of 877 million tonnes were mined globally in 2003. The main producers are Germany, Russia, the USA, Poland, the Czech Republic,

A modern solar power facility in the American Southwest.

Giants of an energy era: nuclear cooling towers.

Atomic power: a nuclear combustion chamber.

Crude oil refinery: processing the most important resource.

Energy industry

▨	Bituminous coal
▨	Crude oil
▨	Natural gas
Ⓤ	Uranium
▪	Hydroelectrical power stations

Greece, Turkey, Australia, Serbia, Montenegro, Canada, Romania, Bulgaria, India and Thailand.

Crude oil

More than one third of global energy consumption is met by crude oil, although the industrialised countries dependent on imports are attempting to exploit alternative energy sources in the wake of the recent oil crisis. The discovery of North Sea oil and thus the decreased efficiency of the OPEC cartel, the increasing scepticism of nuclear energy and advances in automation were responsible for a further increase in oil production. Alternative propellants for motor vehicles are not yet ready for roll-out. Over 3,600 million tonnes of crude oil were extracted globally in 2004. The largest producers are Saudi Arabia, the United States, Russia, Iran, Mexico, Norway, China, Venezuela, the United Kingdom, Canada, Nigeria, the United Arab Emirates, Kuwait, Indonesia, Libya, Algeria, Egypt, Oman, Brazil, Argentina, Angola, Malaysia, India, and Australia. The consumer countries are the industrialised nations, above all the USA, the CIS, Japan, the countries of the EU, China, Canada and India. While the USA is simultaneously the second largest oil producer and its greatest importer, Saudi Arabia, Iran, Russia, Norway, the United Arab Emirates, Venezuela, Nigeria and Great Britain head the list of exporting countries.

Natural gas

While natural gas, a by-product of crude oil exploration, was burned off on many occasions in the past, the value of this energy resource has since become increasingly recognised. Today, natural gas accounts for approximately one quarter of the global energy supply although roughly three-quarters is consumed in North America and Europe. USA, Japan, Germany, the Ukraine, France, Italy and Belarus are the main importers. Around the world, a total of 2,558.2 billion cu. m was extracted in 2003. The biggest suppliers are Russia, the USA, Canada, the Netherlands, Great Britain, Algeria, Indonesia, Saudi Arabia, Norway, Australia, Iran, Mexico, Venezuela, Malaysia, the United Arab Emirates, Romania, Italy and Argentina. The most significant exporters are Russia, Canada, the Netherlands, Algeria, Indonesia, Norway and Turkmenistan. In particular, Russia's natural gas reserves are huge.

Natural gas contributes a quarter of the global energy demand.

Nuclear energy

The use of nuclear energy was considered a promising alternative to fossil fuels in the 1950s and 1960s. Virtually all industrialised countries and some emerging markets banked on this future energy source. The reactor disaster at Chernobyl in 1986 and increasing awareness of the dangers involved in the eventual disposal of radioactive waste led to scepticism of this technology. Consequently, the expansion of nuclear power has almost come to a standstill. In around 12 countries (including China, Iran, Romania and North Korea) nuclear power stations are still being constructed. On 1 June 2003, 437 nuclear power stations were operating in 31 countries according to data supplied by the International Atomic Energy Organisation. In 2002, Germany ruled that it would phase out the economy's dependence on nuclear power in stages, abandoning the energy source completely by 2021. The USA produces the most nuclear power, followed by France, Japan, the UK, Russia, Canada, Germany, the Ukraine, Sweden, South Korea, India, Spain, Taiwan, Bulgaria and Switzerland. Despite international protests, in 1997 a power station of the same type as Chernobyl was connected to the grid in Slovakia. In France and Lithuania, two-thirds of electricity is produced by nuclear power. In Sweden and Belgium it amounts to roughly one half and 30 per cent in Germany.

Alternative energy sources

The proportion of hydroelectric power, wind power, solar energy and other renewable energy sources is still relatively low. However, intensive research is being carried out in this area and research-intensive technologies such as wind energy and photovoltaic systems are gaining in significance.

Industry and trade

After the oil crisis of the 1970s, the world economy clearly recovered in the last decades of the twentieth century. The industrialised nations of East Asia as well as China and India are making their mark. At the start of the twenty-first century international trade is becoming ever more important in an era of increasing globalisation.

Robots at work on a car assemby line.

Comparative growth rates

In the Western industrialised nations, the average growth rate in previous years was 2.3 per cent. Japan and the USA have fared considerably better than the countries of the European Union with growth rates of 2.4 per cent and 3.6 per cent respectively. Due to continually high unemployment, the countries of the European Union have only been able to record an average growth rate of 1.6 per cent.

A dramatic financial crisis in the East Asian region caused a global deceleration of economic development during the late 1990s. The so-called 'tiger economies' such as Singapore, Malaysia, Taiwan, and Indonesia were badly hit by the economic crisis. Japan and South Korea were also strongly affected. Most of the region's economies have now recovered and China's incredible growth is now luring more investors than ever before to East Asia.

The economies of the transition countries of Eastern Europe stabilised to a great extent and recorded impressive growth rates in places. This was not the case for Russia and many other successor countries of the former Soviet Union. This was largely due to corruption and a bureaucracy that remains hostile to investment., although export of natural resources have boosted the Russian economy in recent years.

While some countries of South America, sub-Saharan Africa, and East Asia improved their balance of trade in recent years, the economy of some of poorest nations, including several in Africa, stagnated or even deteriorated further. This remains a worrying trend.

Industrial production

Industrial production is extremely unevenly distributed in the individual countries of the world. Production in the OECD countries is still the highest. However, the growth rates in the South and South-East Asian emerging market countries are considerably greater, at 11 to 12 per cent, than the growth rates in the Western industrialised countries, where growth in 2004 was only around three per cent. Global industrial production in 2004 increased by an average of 4,5 per cent. The lower growth rates of the highly-developed industrialised nations can be attributed, in particular, to the high cost of labour and social costs. Rationalisation, automation and the transfer of production to low-wage countries are solutions adopted by Western European industry to the challenge posed by transition countries and emerging market countries. This has caused the unemployment rate to increase in most industrialised countries, despite average economic growth of two per cent. A large proportion of production has been outsourced. This is partic-

From US granaries, wheat is exported into the whole world.

Futures exchange in Chicago: hectic trading in metals, pork and many other commodities.

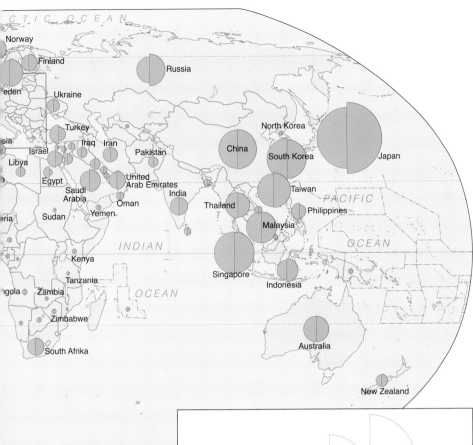

Container port: an important terminal for imports an exports.

1 5 10 25 50 100 150 250 500 700

Imports **Exports**

In US$ billions
The semi-circles correspond in each
case to 100% of imports and exports.

ularly the case in Switzerland, the Benelux countries, Germany, Scandinavia and Japan. Countries to which production is being outsourced includes India, China, Korea, South-east Asia and countries in Eastern Europe.

Branches of industry

Iron and steel production is still among the most important industries in the world. In 2003, China was the world's largest producer of pig-iron at 202,3 million tonnes. Japan, the USA, Russia, Germany, Brazil, India, South Korea, France and the United Kingdom also have are also major producers. The world-wide leading producer of steel in 2003 was China at 202.3 million tonnes, followed by the USA, Japan, Russia, Germany, South Korea, Italy, Brazil, the Ukraine, India, France, the United Kingdom and Canada.

The chemical industry is still experiencing moderate growth in the developed industrialised nations, while in the emerging market countries show strong growth rates. Chemical production has declined in Eastern Europe and Russia. Plastics are the basis of the building trade, the packaging and transport industries, the electrotechnical industry and the automobile industry, as well as being

used in the manufacture of paint and adhesives. The most significant producers are the USA, Japan, China, Germany, Taiwan, South Korea, France, the Netherlands and Italy. In 2002, 86.3 million tonnes of artificial

fertiliser were produced globally. The biggest producers by far were China, the USA, India and Russia. In 2002, around 30 million tonnes of synthetic fabric was produced around the world. Around 30 per

cent of this amount originates in China. Most of the rest is also produced in Asia. Major producers include Taiwan, the USA, South Korea, India, Indonesia, and Japan. The electronics industry is booming thanks, in particular, to increased demand for computers, electronic components and consumer electronics. In this sector, too, production is increasingly being relocated to South and South-East Asia, in particular to China, Taiwan, Hong Kong, Singapore, South Korea and Malaysia. Nevertheless, many of the leading companies in the electronic fields, especially the computer hardware and software sectors, are based in industrialised Western nations.

The automobile industry is one of the most important consumers of the electronic and mechanical components. The largest automotive manufacturer in 2003 was the USA which produced 12.1 million vehicles. Japan, Germany, France, South Korea, Spain, the United Kingdom, Italy, Canada and Mexi-

co followed. The USA and Japan are by far the leaders in the production of commercial vehicles. The globalisation of the world economy is especially apparent in the automobile industry. There are numerous of multi-national mergers and takeovers in this industry. For instance, Adam-Opel AG belongs to General Motors, Skoda, Seat and Rolls-Royce belong to Volkswagen and Chrysler and Mercedes merged to become Daimler-Chrysler. Asian countries now dominate shipbuilding but the German shipbuilding industry remains the third-largest after Japan and South Korea. Despite increases in exports from the developing countries, the Western industrialised countries and Japan remain the leaders in global trade. Germany remains the world's leading exporter; followed by the USA, Japan and China.

Major trading routes

Major industrial areas

Major industrial export routes

Major raw materials routes

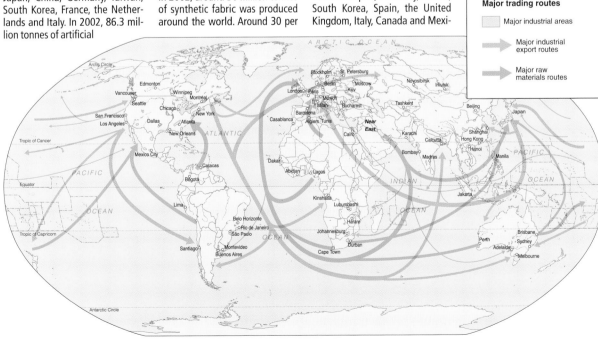

Natural Landscapes of the World

Romantic, bizarre, barren or majestic: these are attributes we tend to use to describe the Earth's natural geography that surrounds and fascinates us. These words prove that we respond emotionally to mountains, plains, coastlines and river valleys. The landscape is in constant flux, as is everything else on our planet. Heat energy released by the sun and from the Earth's interior causes continuous change in nature. This energy powers tectonic plate displacement, volcanic eruptions, the winds and the flow of rivers. It defines and delineates climate and vegetation.

Each continent has its own special features, which may consist of panoramic landscapes such as cordillera mountain chains or vast expanses of desert. Within these grandiose and largely inter-related areas there exists an almost boundless variety of natural landscapes unaltered by man. Sometimes these areas develop their own personality. We make this concession to them: by giving names to certain distinctive beauty spots, we single them out, thus distinguishing them from the mass of peaks, rivers, lakes and rock formations.

Endogenous forces involved in the earth's formation

Deep in the core of planet Earth, forces are created which have a substantial influence on its superficial shape. Mountain ranges which have folded upwards provide proof of the movement of continental plates, impelled by thermal energy from the Earth's core. Volcanic eruptions and earthquakes are further visible consequences of endogenous forces.

The shape of the Earth

The diverse forms and material of which natural landscapes consist are the visible consequences of the forces prevailing at the Earth's core. In order to understand how these forces control the processes that take place on the surface of the Blue Planet, it is necessary to envisage a rough diagram of the composition of the globe.

The San Andreas fault: the visible shift of the continental plates.

Core and crust

The Earth has a round-shaped composition as a result of its cosmic formation over a period that lasted for several millions of years. The centre of the Earth consists of a hard, thick core made of iron with a diameter of 2,440 km. Its temperature is estimated to be as high as 5,000°C. A liquid outer core

surrounds it which is at an approximate distance of 2,890 km from the Earth's surface and is 5,150 km thick. The Earth's mantle consists of rocks of medium thickness that surround the core, followed by the relatively thin crust which measures approximately 40 km in depth. The crust was formed by rocks that were lighter in weight and that rose to the Earth's surface and solidified during the planet's formation. The repeated fusion and solidification of these primaeval crusts eventually led to the formation of the continental core.

Plate tectonics

The entirety of all geological phenomena can now be explained by a single theory, the theory of plate tectonics. According to this theory, the Earth's crust is divided into various slabs which move towards each other, away from each or past each other in a continuous, dynamic process.

Lithosphere and asthenosphere

The outer shell of our planet contains two layers that can be distinguished from one another and that play a significant role in the shaping of the Earth's surface.
The hard, solid lithosphere surrounds not only the Earth's crust but also the solid parts of the Earth's outer mantle which lie directly beneath it. It floats on the malleable, viscous area of the mantle which is called the asthenosphere and consists of fused rocks. Naturally, these rocks are extremely hot and are subject to extreme pressure.
Approximately a dozen larger and a few smaller plates have now been discovered. The actual motion of the continental plates is caused by the flows of currents of hot material that pour out from the Earth's core to the surface, cool down and drop back down again in a continuous cycle.

Plate boundaries

Perhaps the most important of all the geological processes can be observed at the boundaries of the great continental plates as this is where the mechanical movements of the plates move towards each other. Massive fold mountains are formed when plates drift on top of one another where plate boundaries overlap. This is known as subduction or uplift and it leads to the formation of volcanoes.
Ridges are torn open where plates drift away from one another. As a rule, these take the form of a mountain ridge in the sea and are referred to as mid-oceanic ridges. Such a ridge has emerged on the surface of Iceland and is discernible as a crevice-shaped rift. The zones in which the Earth's surface is pressurised by the force of two plates as they move past each other are called transform faults. The friction of the plates against one another only permits sporadic movement slide which expresses itself in frequent earthquakes.

Rock deformation

It is possible to deduce which massive forces are at play in the Earth's core through the movement of plates, if the shapes of mountain ranges are studied closely. Hard rocks and sediment will be bent, folded or slanted at an angle.
In this process, three types of tectonic force act upon the rocks: pressure, distention and dissection. Pressure and compression forces are at work when plates move on top of one another; distension forces are in play when they move away from one another. Dissection forces produce deformities in rocks when two plates glide past each other.

Folding and fault tectonics

Folds form in the Earth's crust when it is compressed horizontally. The extent of the folding, the shape and altitude of a fold mountain, for example, is fundamentally dependent on two factors: on the amount of time during which the rock is subjected to the forces that are distorting it and the composition of the rock which determines the resistance it can use to counter the compression forces acting upon it.
Distension forces do not produce folds at all, but rather expand and thin out the crust, thus forming basin landscapes.

Earthquakes and volcanic eruptions

The strongest earthquakes in the last 100 years (magnitude based on Richter/Kanamori scale)	The most disastrous volcanic eruptions in human history (by number of victims)
Chile (22.5.1960) 9.5	Tambora, Sumbawa (1815) 90,000
Alaska (28.3.1964) 9.2	Miyi, Java (1793) 53,000
Indian Ocean (26.12.2006) 9.1	Pelé, Martinique (1902) 40,000
Russia (4.11.1952) 9.0	Krakatoa, Java (1883) 36,300
Ecuador (31.1.1906) 8.8	Nevado del Ruiz, Colombia
Alaska (4.2.1965) 8.7	(1985) 22,000
Sumatra (28.03.2005) 8.6	Etna, Siclly (1669) 20,000
Alaska (9.3.1957) 8.6	Laki Island (1783) 20,000
India (15.8.1950) 8.6	Unzen, Japan (1792) 15,000
China (16.12.1920) 8.6	Vesuvius, Italy (79 AD) 10,000

Volcanic sources: The water heated in the Earth's core is very rich in sulphur and minerals. The Grand Prismatic Spring in Yellowstone National Park owes its bright colours to the millions of micro-organisms that live in it. Champagne Pools is one of numerous hot springs on the North Island of New Zealand.

Fault structures occur when tensions in the rock become too great. Fault structures include fissures which may be formed locally within a plate in specific areas of tension and faults which may be caused by various forces producing distortions. When the broken edges of rock collide with one another they produce so-called 'faults'.

Tectonic forces are very strong, particularly at the plate boundaries. They not only act upon the outer plate boundaries – they can also produce faults in rock formations, even at a great distance from the actual boundary zones of the plates.

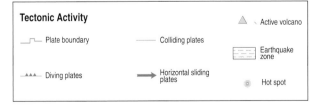

Tectonic Activity

Plate boundary	Colliding plates	△ Active volcano
Diving plates	Horizontal sliding plates	Earthquake zone
		Hot spot

Volcanic activity and earthquakes

Life is dangerous at the plate boundaries. This is where tectonic forces distort the plates most strongly and their effects can be felt particularly intensely. Volcanoes make islands explode or smother vast landscapes in pyroclastic flows of lava, fire, ashes and smoke. Earthquakes can ravage entire regions or cause mountain ranges to collapse.

Volcanic activity

The majority of the Earth's crust is composed of fused rock which rose from the Earth's core to the surface and cooled down to form volcanic rock. This process, known as volcanic activity, is a phenomenon which is almost exclusively limited to the plate boundaries. About 80 per cent of the Earth's approximately 500 volcanoes are located on the plate boundaries which are constantly colliding. This is particularly striking in what is known as the Pacific Ring of Fire which runs along the outer edges of the Pacific and Nazca Plates.

When an oceanic plate in the asthenosphere pushes up against a mainland plate and slides under it, the edges fuse in places. The molten rock, which is known as magma, now rises to the surface. The majority of the magma hardens within the Earth's crust. However, some magma vents rise as far as the Earth's surface. This produces volcanoes. The rising magma initially collects inside the volcano in what is known as a magma chamber until the pressure inside is so great that lava streams out or erupts from the volcanic crater in a massive explosion.

Volcanoes have determined the appearance of our natural landscapes in significant ways – not only where we can clearly identify them as volcanoes due to the lava fields, trails of smoke, basalt columns, remains of craters or the shape of the volcanic mountain, which usually forms a cone. Enormous eruptions which occurred several hundred thousands of years ago have produced vast landscapes of volcanic rocks, whose actual dimensions can only be calculated by using satellite pictures taken from space.

Earthquakes

The tectonic plates are subject to constant forces that cause them to distort. Where they push up against each other, the sort of faults occur that have been described above. In immediate proximity to these zones , the forces of distortion and deformation initially act upon the blocked, displaced rocky masses until resistance due to friction has been overcome. At this point, the rock breaks or fissures, and parts of the crust are displaced with explosive force.

This spontaneous jolt jars the Earth's crust so strongly that it produces what we call an earthquake. If the earthquake is strong enough, the shape of the Earth's surface may change permanently. Rift valleys can emerge. Probably the largest Rift Valley of this kind that the Earth has ever experienced runs from the shores of the Dead Sea, right down through Africa. This is the Great Rift Valley which produced the Dead Sea, the Red Sea and the Bitter Lakes of Egypt and Kenya. There are other smaller rifts of this kind and yet more may be so old that they have eroded away over time.

Hawaii: the volcanos lie over the so-called Hot Spot.

Crater Lake: the water filled caldera of a collapsed volcano.

Sunda rift: volcanic activity created numerous islands in the area.

The constant movement of wind and water – the current of a river, glaciers, marine or ground water – shapes the Earth's natural landscapes through erosion. These exogenous forces are impelled by the thermal energy inherent in solar radiation. They determine the dynamic circulation of the atmosphere and oceans.

Numerous waterfalls in the Norwegian Fjords.

Annapurna massif: a mixture of endogenous and exogenous forces.

Coastal erosion: 'The Twelve Apostles' rock formation, Australia.

The 'building blocks' of Planet Earth

The extent to which exogenous forces form and alter the appearance of natural landscapes depends, above all, on the nature of the rocks upon which they act. The key to rock composition lies in the crystalline structures of the minerals of which they consist.

Minerals

Minerals are the basic building blocks of our planet. They determine the nature, i.e. the hardness, colour and shape of rocks.
Few rocks consist of a single mineral. Notable exceptions are chalk and quartz. Most other rocks consist of several mineral ores

Rocks

Rocks are the basis of the landscape; their nature and the history of their formation also determines how the appearance of a natural landscape comes about.
There are three different groups of rocks: magmatic rocks which have been formed through volcanic activity; sedimentary rocks which can occur in loose or solid forms and are formed by erosion and weathering processes; and metamorphic rocks which have emerged through the transformation of pre-existing rocks, during the formation of a mountain range, for example.

Landscape development

Wind, water and even gravity are responsible for ensuring that the Earth's rocks remain in constant motion. That is why natural landscapes are constantly changing their appearance.

Mass movements

When great lumps of soil or rock detach themselves from outcrops due to the effect of gravity and move towards the valley, their long journey to the ocean begins. Rock falls and landslides are classed as mass movements, but streams of loose material may detach themselves almost imperceptibly from the substrate.

Water which has been absorbed by the rock also plays an important role in these processes. It reduces resistance and weakens the structure of rock and soil so it breaks up more easily.

Rivers

Rivers are probably the most diverse landscape forms among the exogenous forces. They carry away outcrops, wash up sediments in a delta and sculpt deep grooves into underground rock. The course of a river follows the shape of the surface of the landscape as it searches for the easiest route to the ocean. This route determines whether the river

runs relatively straight or flows towards the valley in torrents and waterfalls. These forms of current produce differences in the nature and volume of the method of absorption and transportation of eroded rock.
In the transverse section of a river the volume of matter transported

Water which has been absorbed is not constant. Dissolved suspensions move at a different speeds and have different effects on the landscape, depending on whether they are carried along near the surface or lie as silt on the river bed.
Sediment in suspension is deposited differently. Smaller and lighter suspended particles remain in the stream longer than larger particles. They are whirled around and deposited periodically. The river bed is exposed to a constant two-way process of erosion and sedimentation.
Rivers not only erode loose material, they can erode hard rocks. The sediments which have been carried along have an important

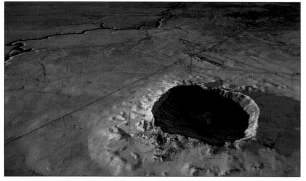

Meteor Crater in Arizona: 'alien' landscape formation.

part to play, as they serve as an abrasive.
While the forces shaping rivers on loose soil can easily be observed, where hard rock is concerned, one can merely observe the sublime legacies created over several hundred thousand years by streams that may even have run

The deepest canyons and ravines	
Grand Canyon (USA) 1,800 m	Black Canyon/Colorado (USA)
Hell's Canyon/Snake River (USA)	700 m
1,700 m	Grand Canyon du Verdon
Barranca del Cobre (Mexico)	(France) 700 m
1,400 m	Milford Sound (New Zealand)
Wu chasm at Yangtse (China)	600 m
900 m	Bryce Canyon (USA) 600 m
Vicos chasm (Greece)	Sanmen chasm at Huang He
900 m	(China) 600 m
Neretva chasms (Bosnia-Herze-	Visriviere Canyon (Namibia)
govina) 800 m	600 m
Canyon of the Black River	Vaihiria lake (Tahiti) 550 m
(Vietnam) 800 m	Wadi Dadès (Morocco) 400 m
Via Mala (Switzerland) 700 m	Wadi al-Kantara (Algeria) 400 m

completely dry by now. Deep canyons and gorges have remained as eloquent proof of the Earth's history.

The sea

The great ocean currents, the storms and the power of the tides shape not only the profile of the ocean floors which are invisible to us but even the coastline, especially at continental boundaries, which are strongly affected by the force of waves.

In the same way that rivers erode and deposit soil, the sea removes rock from the coastlines in order to re-deposit it on the ocean floor or on other coastlines as sediment. The diversity of the natural landscapes which have been shaped by sea water seemingly knows no boundaries. Long sandy beaches have been formed to which the tides carry freshly ground sand; in other places blustering breakers sculpt strange formations into cliffs.

The ocean floor is also exposed to constant sedimentation. This can be observed when ocean floors are broken up due to endogenous processes. Then the solidified sediments are exposed to the same exogenous forces as the remaining rocks and fascinating landscapes can emerge from the weathered strata of rocks of different degrees of hardness.

Glaciers

Water is also an important factor in landscape formation in the world's cold regions. There are two types of glacier: the inland ice sheets in Greenland and the Antarctic, and the moving rivers of ice that form on mountains at high altitudes. Like ocean currents, these ice sheets push through valleys towards the ocean, though their movement is almost imperceptible to the human eye.

In order to calculate the force which is concealed in the movement of glacier ice, we must take a look at the numerous landscapes which were formed in Europe, Asia and North America during the last Ice Ages. Accumulated scree has cut deep gullies in the rocky sub-soil and sculpted vast U-shaped valleys. Where secondary glaciers have

fused with a primary glacier after the ice has melted away, steep rocky cliffs have been created from which waterfalls cascade. The large stones deposited by glaciers are known as rubble. They are left behind when the ice melts that once enclosed them. Moraines are masses of stony and sandy material that have been transported by the glacier.

Wind

Winds have similar powers of erosion to rivers through accumulated dust and sand. They play an important part in the formation of the deserts in particular.

The sand is transported by the wind in the same way as a river transports water. Larger stones are propelled directly along the surface of the ground, grains of sand and pebbles are whirled upwards and propelled in leaps. When the wind dies down, the wind-borne sand particles remain in situ as sediment.

If sand and silt particles are blown away, the subsoil is also gradually worn away. Enclosed basins emerge. Rocky outcrops are eroded by wind-borne sand. This can cause a rounding of sharp edges or an outcrop can even be worn away completely.

Meteorite craters

Meteorite strikes are an exception. Although they alter the shape of the surface of the Earth, they are 'external' effects which do not originate in the oceans and the Earth's atmosphere, unlike exogenous processes.

Large meteorites have altered the appearance of vast landscapes and even whole continents within seconds, in the course of the Earth's history. There have been two recent incidents of meteorites striking the earth. The first is known as the Tunguska Incident when a large meteorite fell in a remote part of Siberia in 1908 destroying 2,000 sq. km of forest. The earlier incident was only discovered when it was realised that a 'moon crater' formation in the Arizona desert had been left by a meteor that hit the earth 50,000 years ago.

Heavily eroded rocks can be used to read the history of the Earth layer by layer, like a book.

Ahaggar: the erosive forces in the Sahara are particularly strong, resulting in unusual rock formations.

'Totem pole' in Monument Valley: the reddish colour of the sandstone is due to erosion.

Climate and Vegetation Zones

The Earth is divided into several vegetation zones, each of which contains specific varieties and groups of plants. The vegetation zones run parallel to the lines of latitude, and are roughly similar to the climatic zones. Climate is affected by geographical factors, such as latitude, altitude, ocean currents, topography and vegetation.

Polar Regions

The Earth has two polar regions, the Arctic at the North Pole, and the Antarctic at the South Pole. Both regions are characterised by snow and ice and a six-monthly cycle of polar night and polar day. The South Pole, south of the 55th parallel, consists of Antarctica, scattered islands and ice-shelves and has a surface area of just under 14 million sq. km. The mainland is mountainous, with altitudes up to 5,140 m, and is covered with a thick ice-sheet (average thickness 2,000–2,500 m), which constitutes over 90 per cent of the world's total ice mass. The climate is extremely cold and dry. The only vegetation, found on a few sub-antarctic islands, are mosses, lichen, grasses and some flowering plants. The North Pole includes the Arctic Ocean and has a land area of 11 million sq.km. Most of the North Pole consists of a 12 million sq. km pack-ice layer. The climate is more temperate than in the Antarctic, due to the effect of the sea currents. Ice-free areas have sparse vegetation.

Tundra and Taiga

The tundra lies south of the Polar region and north of the tree-line. This belt of vegetation, covering parts of northern Asia, Europe and America, is typified by short but warm summers, long, severe winters and little precipitation. The climate only allows for the sparse growth of mosses and stunted shrubs. Temperatures range from -55°C to 25°C, but even in summer, the average temperature of 10°C is rarely exceeded. The taiga region, a belt of woodland (also called boreal woodland) consisting mainly of conifers lies south of the tundra. This terrain is mostly found in Siberia and north-west Russia. Both the tundra and the taiga are covered in permafrost, meaning that the sub-soil remains permanently frozen all year round.

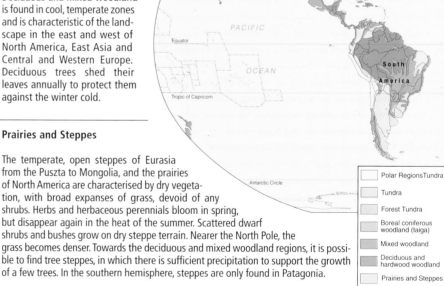

Deciduous and Mixed Woodland Zones

Deciduous and mixed woodland is found in cool, temperate zones and is characteristic of the landscape in the east and west of North America, East Asia and Central and Western Europe. Deciduous trees shed their leaves annually to protect them against the winter cold.

Prairies and Steppes

The temperate, open steppes of Eurasia from the Puszta to Mongolia, and the prairies of North America are characterised by dry vegetation, with broad expanses of grass, devoid of any shrubs. Herbs and herbaceous perennials bloom in spring, but disappear again in the heat of the summer. Scattered dwarf shrubs and bushes grow on dry steppe terrain. Nearer the North Pole, the grass becomes denser. Towards the deciduous and mixed woodland regions, it is possible to find tree steppes, in which there is sufficient precipitation to support the growth of a few trees. In the southern hemisphere, steppes are only found in Patagonia.

Humid and Dry Savannah

The savannah climate has a rainy season in summer, and a marked dry period in winter. This type of terrain is mainly found in South America and Africa, but also in northern Australia, Central America, India and southeast Asia. The amount of precipitation decreases the greater the distance north or south of the rainforest zone, and the dry periods become longer. Humid savannah can be found bordering tropical rainforest zones. Towards the poles, the length of the dry spells increases. In the equatorial regions, only the taller trees lose their leaves, and the undergrowth remains green year-round. In monsoon regions there is a severe wet-dry climate, and the whole forest loses its leaves. The dry savannah is closer to the poles than the humid savannah regions. It mainly covers large areas of Africa. This terrain is characterised by open grassland, interrupted by the odd tree, and occasional small woods. Main tree species are baobab, xerophile palms, ponytail palms and umbrella trees.

Semi-desert

Almost one third of the Earth's land surface is covered by desert or desertified areas. A large proportion of this is semi-desert. This is the transitional region between the almost vegetation-free full deserts and the steppe regions and they have average annual precipitation of 100–200 mm. After the occasional shower, semi-deserts can temporarily change in appearance and take on the character of steppe or savannah terrain, and for this reason they are also called 'desert steppes' or 'desert savannahs'. Typical semi-desert vegetation includes, thorn bushes, thorny trees, dry grasses and stunted bushes. These featureless wastes can be interrupted by oases, which appear wherever there is access to ground water. Freshwater pools or river water enables trees to grow even in the desert (date palms, poplars).

Deserts

These regions of Earth have such dry or cold climates that only certain types of flora, such as cacti and succulents, can tolerate them, and they have no landscape-defining vegetation. A distinction can be made between cold deserts and dry or hot deserts. The latter are mainly found in sub-tropical regions with high atmospheric pressure, beside oceans with cold water currents and in enclosed mountain basins. Full deserts have almost no vegetation and precipitation levels of below 100 mm annually. The aridity and significant temperature differences between day and night cause heavy erosion. Temperature differences also produce large amounts of powerful air circulation, creating dust storms and sandstorms.

Sub-tropical Zones

The sub-tropical zone is a band 2,000 km wide between the tropical and temperate zones, characterised by dry summers and mild winters. It is defined by a large number of smaller vegetation zones with alternating rainy and dry seasons. The sub-tropics contain deserts, steppes and also moist woodland.

Rainforests

Tropical rainforests extend either side of the equator in the zone of the tropics, which is constantly wet. Precipitation falls year-round, with most rain falling during the rainy seasons in spring and autumn. Maximum temperatures can reach 35°C. Temperature variations are very small. Rainforests are characterised by large numbers of plant species and most commonly three canopy levels. In the centre of the forests, relative humidity is almost 100 per cent. Rainforests affect the carbon, oxygen and nitrogen cycles of the Earth, making them an important climate regulator.

Map legend:

- Non-tropical semi-desert, desert
- Mediterranean vegetation
- Subtropical moist woodland
- Tropical semi-desert, desert
- Dry savannah
- Humid savannah
- Tropical rainforest

Mountains

Mountains are divided into low ranges and high ranges depending on altitude. They can also be classified according to the shape of the peaks (mountains ridges and mountain chains) and according to origin (volcanic and eroded mountains). Low mountain ranges are much older and have more rounded hilltops and ridges, which are often wooded to their upper reaches. High mountains ranges were formed much nearer to the present time and were caused by folding of the Earth's crust. They are characterised by sheer faces, high summits, and deep valleys. The summits of high mountain ranges have no vegetation and the peaks are mainly covered in snow and ice. The highest and most imposing mountain range on Earth is the Himalayas, between the north Indian lowlands and the Tibetan plateau. The range forms a curved arc, 2,400 km long and between 150 km and 280 km wide. The highest peaks are Mount Everest (8,846 m – the highest peak on Earth) and Kanchenjunga (8,586 m). Fold mountain ranges are continuously being formed by tectonic plate movement.

Main photograph:
Crashing waves demonstrate the power of water. Waves are generated by the wind and break over the coast when the water near the surface moves faster than the water at the base.

The Oceans

Approximately 71 per cent of the Earth's surface is covered by salt water. This vast body of water is divided by the continents to form the three great oceans: the Atlantic Ocean, between Europe, Africa and America, the Pacific

Rose fish: one of the huge number of fish species in the oceans.

Ocean between America, Asia, Australia and the Antarctic mainland, and the Indian Ocean between Africa, Asia and Australia. Mounts and ridges on the ocean floor separate peripheral seas from the oceans. These lesser seas can fall into one of two categories: marginal seas, positioned to one side of a continent, such as the North Sea, and mediterranean seas, surrounded by several continents, such as the European Mediterranean Sea; or completely land-locked within a continent, such as the Baltic Sea. Arctic cold, tropical warmth and differences in salt content all demonstrate the variety and complexity of the world's oceans and seas.

Atlantic Ocean

*In winter, the **Arctic Ocean** is completely covered in sea ice to a depth of up to 3.5 m thick. Polar bears and Arctic foxes are ideally adapted to the extreme cold. Polar bears live in the coastal and drift-ice regions of the Arctic Circle. Arctic foxes live in the tundra regions.*

Atlantic Ocean

The Atlantic Ocean is the second-largest of the Earth's three great oceans. It covers a surface area of 84.11 million sq. km, not including the lesser seas, and contains 322.98 million cu. km of water. If the lesser seas are taken into account, the surface area rises to 106.6 million sq. km and the volume to 350.91 million cu. km. Including lesser seas, the average depth is 3,293 m, and if these are not included, the average depth is 3,844 m. The deepest point in the Atlantic is the **Milwaukee Deep** in the **Puerto Rico Trench**, east of Haiti, where the waters descend to a depth of 9,219 m. Approximately one third of the **Atlantic Ocean** has a depth of between 4,000 m and 5,000 m. The continents are bordered by shallow ocean areas called continental shelves, with depths of up to 200 m.

The Atlantic Ocean originally began to form between 195 million and 135 million years ago in what is today the centre of the **North Atlantic Ocean** as the continent of North America began to separate and drift away from the

Mid-Atlantic Ridge

The floor of the Atlantic is dominated by an S-shaped ridge. This continuous underwater mountain chain stretches from the north of Iceland to Bouvet Island in the South Atlantic and divides the Atlantic into two large deep-sea basins, each further divided by more ridges. Some of the peaks of this mountain chain rise above the ocean surface in the form of mountains (examples are the Azores and Ascension Island), but most lie between 1.5 and 3 km beneath the surface. Along the centre of this ridge runs a deep rift valley, between 24 and 28 km wide. This valley is traversed by folds running from east to west, which take the form of narrow ridges and deep ravines.

African continent over the course of several million years.

The **central Atlantic** had already reached one third of its current size 150 million years ago. During the Cretaceous Period (between 144 and 65 million years ago), South America and Africa began to drift apart, forming the **South Atlantic Ocean**. It was not until much later, approximately 60 million years ago, that the **North Atlantic Ocean** was formed as the ocean floor between **Greenland** and the **Rockall Plateau** began to expand.

Most of the deposits on the bed of the Atlantic Ocean are the remains of marine life, the rest is mainly sediment from the continents. The layers of such sediments can be between several hundred metres and 9,000 m thick. The surface waters of the Atlantic contain numerous **currents**, caused by the wind and by

Satellite view of the Atlantic Ocean.

differences in water temperature and salt content. The best-known current in the North Atlantic is the **Gulf Stream**. This warm water current is only about 50 km wide, but it is very fast-moving, travelling at speeds of five knots (more than 130 km) a day.

The Gulf Stream originates off the east coast of North America. It begins with the **Florida and Antilles currents** and flows north to the **Great Banks of Newfoundland**. Under the effect of the

prevailing west winds, the current leaves the coast and crosses the ocean in the form of the North Atlantic Current. The Gulf Stream carries a lot of warmth and has a major impact on the climate of western and northern Europe, creating milder temperatures, particularly in winter. Other warm ocean currents are the **North and South Equatorial Currents** which are directed westwards by the trade winds, and the **Guinea Current** which flows between these two currents, but in the opposite direction. Cold ocean currents include the **Labrador Current**, the **East Greenland Current** in the North Atlantic and the **Falkland and Benguela Currents** in the South Atlantic.

The highest water temperatures are found around the meteorological equator and can reach 27°C to 28°C. The eastern side of the North Atlantic is free of ice all year round below latitude 77° N, but the western side of the North Atlantic is only ice-free all year-round below latitude 45° N.

The area around the meteorological equator (latitude 5° N) is characterised by light winds, but this region is bordered by the **trade wind zones** in which east winds blow constantly. These are in turn bordered by the **horse latitudes or doldrums** in which there is little wind, followed by the **west wind zones** with strong

and very changeable winds, and the **Polar regions**, within the Arctic Circle, in which the prevailing winds blow mostly eastward. Hurricanes only form in the western North Atlantic. The west wind zones have heavy rainfall, but the trade wind zones get very little. Large amounts of cloud form where the water temperature is colder than the air, for example above the **Great Bank of Newfoundland**.

In the open Atlantic, average tide fluctuations are only about 1 m, but they can be significantly greater on the ocean shelves. On the Patagonian coast, in the **Gulf of Saint Malo**, the **English Channel** and the **Bristol Channel**, tide fluctuations may be as great as between 9 and 12 m. The highest recorded tides in the world occur in the Bay of Fundy, in Canada, on the **Gulf of Maine**, where there are fluctuations of between 14 m and 15 m.

The Atlantic Ocean is very well stocked with fish (sardines, anchovies, cod, herring, shellfish), particularly in the cold water areas. More than 80 per cent of the fish caught in coastal and deep-sea fishing are taken from the North Atlantic, making it the most heavily-fished body of water on Earth. Drilling for crude oil and natural gas takes place in the relatively shallow waters of the continental shelf near the coasts, particularly in the **North Sea**, on the

Sea floor expansion

Seismic activity along the central trench of the mid-oceanic ridge causes the continuous creation of new ocean floor. Magma bubbles up from deep within the Earth and forms a new ocean bed. As a result, the floor of the ocean expands by between 1 and 5 cm a year. An extreme example of this process, known as 'sea floor expansion', is the island of Surtsey, which suddenly rose from the sea bed in 1963, as the result of an underwater volcanic eruption south of Iceland.

coast of **West Africa** and in the **Caribbean**. Shingle and gravel is dredged off the coast of north-west Europe, and this is also of economic importance. Manganese deposits can be found at a depth of 2,000 m to 6,000 m, and it should soon be possible to extract these for economic use.

Arctic Ocean

The **Arctic Ocean** includes the **Barents Sea**, **Baffin Bay** and **Hudson Bay** and is sometimes considered an extension or part of the **Atlantic Ocean**. It is located between Eurasia, America and Greenland and is the smallest of the world's oceans. It has an area of 12,173 sq. km and an average depth of 1,000 m, being 5,626 m deep at the deepest point.

The Arctic Ocean consists of four main basins (**the North American, Siberian, Eurasian and Fram Basins**), separated from each other by three great ocean ridges. The largest of these, the **Lomonosov Ridge**, stretches from north-west to south-east for a distance of over 1,750 km. The **Mid-Arctic Ridge**, a branch of the **Mid-Atlantic Ridge**, runs parallel to it. The **Alpha Ridge** is situated on the Canadian side of the Lomonosov Ridge.

The continental shelf off the coast of northern Asia is much broader than that of other oceans. In some places it is as wide as 1,600 km and it is never narrower than 480 km. The **Kara, Laptev, Chukchi, Beaufort, Lincoln** and **East Siberian Seas all form** part of this shelf.

The Atlantic Ocean joins the Arctic Ocean in the region around the Greenland Sea. This narrow channel between Greenland and Spitsbergen produces 80 per cent of the water transfer between the two oceans.

In winter, the Arctic Ocean is covered by a layer of sea-ice between 2.5 m and 3.5 m thick. In summer, the continental fringes are free of ice. The ice is in continuous motion, caused by the rotating currents (**pack-ice drift**). Most Arctic icebergs originate from glaciers. They can tower up to 80 m above the water and may be more than 1,000 m long. Another form of iceberg is found off the

Mud flats are particularly common on the *North Sea coasts* of the Netherlands, Germany, Denmark and England. They are flat, tidal areas between the mainland and the sea, which are dry at low tide but covered by the sea as the tide comes in.

shores of **Ellesmere Island** and North Greenland. These 'islands of ice' consist of very old ice masses. They are only about 5 m in height and appear to be relatively small, but they may be up to 200 m wide. The **Barents Sea**, between the coast of northern Europe, Spitsbergen and Novaya Zemlya, has a surface area of 1.4 million sq. km and is mainly ice-free in the south. **Baffin Bay** covers an area of 500,000 sq. km north of the pack-ice border and is up to 2,377 m deep. Hudson's Bay (1.4 million sq. km) is a shallow sea in the north-east of North America that extends far inland and is connected to the Arctic Ocean via the **Foxe Channel** and to the **North Atlantic** via the **Hudson Straits**. Hudson Bay is covered in ice from November to May.

The Arctic Ocean and the seas bordering it have large oil and gas reserves, but difficult conditions – extreme cold, strong winds and the constantly shifting sea-ice – prevent the extraction of these resources.

Mediterranean Sea

The Mediterranean Sea covers an area of 3.02 million sq. km and has a volume of 4.38 million cu. km. It lies in a basin approximately 4,000 km long which runs from the coasts of Israel, Lebanon and Syria in the east, to the **Straits of Gibraltar** in the west. The Straits of Gibraltar are the only natural connection between the Mediterranean and the Atlantic. Since 1869, the Mediterranean has been connected to the **Red Sea** in the east via the **Suez Canal**.

The narrow **Straits of Sicily** divides the Mediterranean into an eastern and a western half. The western Mediterranean has a broad, shallow bed covered in sediment approximately 25 million years old. The eastern section is divided by the Mediterranean ridge system, which consists of folds of deposits up to 70 million years old. The main basins of the western Mediterranean are the **Algerian-Provençal Basin** and the **Thyrrhenian Basin**, which are divided by the island chains of Corsica and Sardinia. The eastern Mediterranean is divided into the **Ionian** and **Levantine Basins**. The deepest point in the

Mediterranean is in the Ionian Basin, west of the Peloponnese (5,121 m). This is a significant depth, considering that the average depth in this part of the sea is only about 1,500 m.

The Mediterranean is very salty. Off the coast of Anatolia, the salt content can be as high as 39.5 per cent. This is caused by

heavy evaporation and only small amounts of fresh water entering the sea from the surrounding mainland. In winter, dry winds accelerate the evaporation process, increasing the salt content and cooling the surface of the water. The cold, salty water sinks and flows across the sea bed, through the Straits of Gibraltar

1 The Pont de Normandie, a cable-stayed bridge. Huge bridges like these span treacherous currents and connect, cities, islands and countries.

2 Sunset over the 'Durdle Door', a natural rock arch in the cliffs of Dorset, on the south coast of England,

formed by the power of wind and water.

3 St. James Beach in False Bay in Cape Town, South Africa. The region has a Mediterranean climate. The Cape peninsula lies on the border between the Atlantic and Indian Oceans.

The **Mid-Atlantic Ridge** is an area affected by sea floor expansion, characterised by earthquakes and strong, hot currents. Most of the volcanic islands of the Atlantic, such as Iceland and the Azores, are located on top of this submarine mountain chain. **Iceland,** the

'Island of fire and ice' in the far north is a relatively new land formation. Roughly 30 of the country's 140 volcanoes are still active today. **Surtsey**, a volcanic island off the south coast of Iceland, rose out of the sea in 1963 as the result of a submarine eruption.

and out into the Atlantic. To balance this, surface water with low salt content flows through the straits into the Mediterranean. These water currents flow east to the coast of North Africa and form the only real currents in the Mediterranean. Water exchange with the Atlantic is small. Tidal differences are also very small, usually only around 30 cm. Water exchange is also minimal in the semi-enclosed coastal bays and coves, meaning that the water near the coasts can be quite heavily polluted.

The Mediterranean climate consists of hot summers with little to no precipitation and mild winters, often with a lot of rain. Constant, but relatively mild winds predominate in summer. The eastern Mediterranean, mainly the **Aegean**, is affected by the **Etesian wind** every summer. This is a dry, north or north-westerly wind, caused by a pronounced difference in air pressure between the high pressure over the Azores and the monsoon depression of southwest Asia. In winter, the western Mediterranean is affected by areas of low pressure in the Atlantic. This can sometimes cause a warm southerly wind **(the Sirocco)** and a cold north wind **(the Mistral).**

The **Adriatic** and **Aegean Seas, the Sea of Marmara, the Ligurian, Ionian** and **Tyrrhenian Seas** and the inland **Black Sea** (423,000 sq. km.), connected to the eastern Mediterranean via the **Dardanelles, the Sea of Marmara** and the Aegean, are all extensions of the Mediterranean. The Mediterranean region has large oil and gas reserves which have to date only been exploited on the continental shelf. A lack of plankton in the upper water levels means that fish stocks in the Mediterranean are relatively restricted.

American Mediterranean Sea

This area of the Atlantic Ocean between North, Central and South America consists of the **Caribbean Sea** and the **Gulf of Mexico**. The Caribbean covers 2.64 million sq. km; it is at its deepest in the **Cayman Trough** (7,680 m). The Gulf of Mexico has an area of 1.54 million sq. km, an average depth of 1,512 m and a maximum depth of 4,029 m.

The three basins of the **Caribbean Sea (the Yucatan, Colombian and Venezuelan Basins)** are separated from the Atlantic by the **Greater and Lesser Antilles** and from each other by ocean ridges. The bed of the Caribbean Sea was probably once part of the Pacific crust that broke off as South America and Central America merged. The **Guiana Current** and a section of the **North Equatorial Current** flow past the island of St. Lucia and into the Caribbean Sea. In the west, the trade winds drive surface currents northwards away from the South American coast, where they mix with colder waters that have greater nutritional content. Surface water

Cliff-lined coast: the Algarve, Portugal's spectacular Atlantic coast.

flows from the Yucatan Basin and north into the the Gulf of Mexico, where it eventually reaches the Atlantic through the **Straits of Florida.** The heating of this water contributes to the warming of the **Gulf Stream.**

In the eastern Caribbean Basin, beyond the Lesser Antilles, the Atlantic plate is shifting, causing volcanic activity. In the west the Pacific plate is pushing below the land mass of Central America, with the result that this region is often troubled by earthquakes and volcanic eruptions.

Large oil and gas reserves occur in the region. They are found off the coasts of Louisiana and Venezuela, the Mexican states of Veracruz and Campeche and around the islands of Trinidad and Tobago.

North Sea

The North Sea is situated between the British Isles and the European mainland. It covers an area of 580,000 sq. km. The average depth is 93 m, and the deepest point is 725 m in the **Norwegian Trench**, off the coast of Norway.

Water movement in the North Sea is caused by the tides, strong winds and variations in salt content. Cold water flows into the North Sea between the Orkney and Shetland Islands and along the east coasts of Scotland and England. At the same time, warmer water from the North Atlantic Current flows in through the **English Channel**. The warm water current flows along the Dutch coast towards Denmark and Norway. It is this warm water current that keeps the North Sea ice-free in winter as far as the **German Bight** and the Dutch mud-flats, where drift-ice forms, and there

may even be pack-ice during severe winters. The tides of the North Sea are in line with those of the Atlantic Ocean, meaning that tidal fluctuations can be very high, up to 6.5 m. Salt content is 35 per cent in the northern North Sea, but reduce to 25–30 per cent in the German Bight.

The waters of the North Sea are rich in plankton so they are an important breeding ground for many species of fish. Significant oil reserves lie at a depth of 200 m in the **East Shetland Basin**.

Baltic Sea

The **Baltic Sea** is also part of the Atlantic, divided from the main body of the ocean by Scandinavia and Jutland. The sea covers an area of 420,000 sq. km and has an average depth of 55 m. The maximum depth is 469 m, just north of **Gotland**. The Baltic Sea can be further sub-divided into the **Arkonas Basin, the Great and Little Belt, the Bornholm Basin, the Gotland Sea, the Gulf of Riga, the Gulf of Finland, the Sea of Åland** and the **Gulf of Bothnia**. The Baltic is linked to the North Sea via the channels known as the **Skaggerak** and **Kattegat**. Approximately 1,400 cu m of water flows into the Baltic Sea every year, including fresh water from rivers on the mainland, salt water from the North Sea flowing in along the bed of the straits **(Great Belt, Little Belt and The Sound)** and through precipitation. Approximately the same amount of water is lost through evaporation or by water with a low salt content flowing out on the surface through the straits. The surface water temperature in summer is 13°C to 20°C in the western Baltic Sea, and 9°C to 19°C in the Gulf of Bothnia. In winter, the coastal waters of the **Gulf of Finland** and the **Gulf of Riga** are normally frozen over. Tidal fluctuations are less than 0.15 m. The shallow regions of the western Baltic and the Gulfs of Finland and Bothnia can be subject to powerful storm surges. The Baltic Sea is one of the most polluted seas in the world; in the mid-1990s, almost a quarter of the waters were classed as biologically dead. It also has the lowest salt content of any sea at 1.5 per cent.

Other Seas in the Atlantic

The **Irish Sea** between Great Britain and Ireland covers 103,000 sq. km and is up to 159 m deep. It is connected to the Atlantic via **St. George's Channel** in the south and the **North Channel** in the north. The **English Channel** links the Atlantic Ocean to the North Sea. It has an average depth of 50 m, and is only 32 km wide at its narrowest point, the **Straits of Dover** between England and France.

On the east coast of North America, the **Gulf of St. Lawrence** connects the St. Lawrence Seaway and the Great Lakes to the Atlantic Ocean.

Pacific Ocean

The Pacific Ocean is the largest ocean on the planet. It was named by Magellan, the first European to navigate its waters, because he

Amber

Amber is the 'gold of the Baltic Sea'. It is the fossilised sap of *Pinus succinifera* and other extinct conifers from the Tertiary Period. Between 30 and 50 million years ago, extensive forests covered marshes and moors, which gradually sank and were covered in layers of sedimentary rock formed from sand and dust. This process created brown coal (lignite) as well as amber. It also caused water to evaporate from the resin; oxidation and other chemical and physical processes turned the resin into a light but solid stone. Its colour ranges from pale to dark yellow to brownish-orange, and it can be opaque or transparent. Insects and leaves trapped within a piece of amber make it particularly valuable to collectors. The main amber deposits are found near Kaliningrad, an exclave of Russia surrounded by Poland and Lithuania. The area is even known informally as Yantarny Krai, the Amber region.

The **Coral Sea** is part of the South Pacific between Australia, New Guinea and the Solomon Islands. The sea contains numerous coral reefs (including the Great Barrier Reef) and coral islands. Coral provides food and habitat for a huge variety of plants and animals.

experienced calm weather there. Not including its smaller seas, the Pacific covers 166.24 million sq. km. Including lesser seas, the area is 181.34 million sq. km. This means that the ocean covers one third of the Earth's surface. In the east, the Pacific is bordered by North and South America, in the north by the **Bering Straits**, in the west by Asia, the Philippines, Indonesia, New Guinea and the Melanesian Islands, and in the south by the Antarctica. The border between the Pacific and the Atlantic in the south-east is defined as a line stretching from Cape Horn, over Cape Lookout (South Shetland Islands) to the Antarctic peninsula. The Pacific is separated from the Indian Ocean along the meridian of the southeast Cape of Tasmania (147° longitude), the western outlet of the **Bass Straits** and a line from northwest Australia running through Timor, Flores Island and the Sumba Islands to the Straits of Malacca. The Pacific is the deepest of the oceans, with an average depth of 4,188 m. Its deepest point is the 11,034-m-deep **Mariana Trench**, which stretches over 2,500 km parallel to the east coast of the Philippines. Deep sea trenches are a characteristic feature of the Pacific and can be found in the east, west and north of the ocean. The second deepest trench is the **Tonga Trench** which is 10,800 m deep. The remaining trenches are between 6,000 m and 8,000 m deep.

Ridges and mounts cover the bed of the Pacific. The global mid-oceanic ridge system, which also runs along the Atlantic and Indian Oceans, emerges in the southern Pacific as the **Indian-Antarctic Ridge** and continues as the **South Pacific Ridge** and finally the **East Pacific Ridge**. Ridges also divide the eastern part of the ocean to form the **Pacific-Antarctic Basin**, and the **Chile, Peru, Panama** and **Guatemala Basins**. A jagged ridge in the western Pacific, running from New Zealand to Japan, borders further basins which are probably synclines (downward folds) of an old continental block. The Central Pacific is divided into four large basins, separated from each other by slight rises: these are the **South, Central, Northeast and North-west Pacific Basins**. The oldest ocean crust

(100 to 135 million years old) lies in the west Pacific. The edges of the ocean are active subduction zones. The Central Oceanic Ridge is expanding at a rate of 15 cm per year, forming new sea bed. The deep sea bed east of the ridge is slowly drifting eastwards towards South America. The Australian plate is slowly moving north

beneath the Indian Plate. There is strong tectonic activity in the deep sea trenches. In the **Mariana Trench,** the Pacific Plate pushes 11 cm further below the Philippines Plate every year. Powerful earthquakes and chains of new volcanoes, such as the Pacific Ring of Fire, are a common feature along the deep sea trenches.

1 The Polynesian Island of Bora Bora is an extinct volcano which is slowly sinking into the sea, leaving an atoll behind.

2 The 'Twelve Apostles', a series of rock formations off the coast of south-east Australia, are a good example of the effects of erosion.

3 Milford Sound in New Zealand: the 16-km-long fjord on the South Island was formed in the Ice Age and is surrounded by sheer rocks. It is one of the most imposing natural wonders of the New Zealand archipelago. The photo shows Mitre Peak rising 1,692 m straight out of the water.

Pacific Ocean

Sea mammals can be found in all of the oceans. Bottle-nosed dolphins live in the seas around the Arctic Circle. Humpbacked whales migrate from their summer feeding grounds in the Antarctic to give birth to their young in the warmer waters of the South Sea and the Caribbean.

The surface currents of the Pacific Ocean consist of two main gyres. The North Pacific is dominated by the North Pacific gyre which rotates strongly clockwise. The **North Equatorial Current** is part of this gyre, and at 14,500 km long, it is the longest westward-flowing ocean current in the world. The warm and fast-moving **Kuroshio Current** lies in the west. Near Japan, the Kuroshio meets the cold **Oyashio Current**, flowing in a southerly direction, and moves away from the mainland, crossing the ocean as the **North Pacific Current**. Branches of this current flow north along the American Continent as the **Alaska Current** and south as the **California Current**. Near the equator, the Equatorial Counter-current, which flows eastwards, divides the current systems of the North and South Pacific. In the South Pacific, the South Equatorial Current, the South Pacific Current and the **Mentor Current** form a second gyre, which moves in an anti-clockwise direction. The **East Austral Current** is a western branch of this current.

The **Antarctic Circumpolar Current**, in the far south, circles the whole of the southern hemisphere. The wide, cold **Humboldt Current**, which flows north along the South American coast and joins the **South Equatorial Current** is a branch of this current.

The **Pacific Equatorial subsurface-current (Cromwell Current)** flows east some 100 m below the westward-flowing South Equatorial Current.

The two main wind systems of the Pacific Ocean are the West Wind zones, located between the 30° and 60° latitude in both the northern and southern hemispheres. The regular trade winds blow between these two zones, blowing from the east in the northern hemisphere and from the west in the southern hemisphere. Powerful tropical cyclones, called typhoons in the West Pacific and hurricanes in the South and East Pacific, are common in late summer and early autumn in the trade wind areas. The calm belt, known as the Horse Latitudes in the north and the Doldrums in both north and south, is usually only affected by light winds, but cyclones can develop at certain times of year.

In the tropics and sub-tropics, average yearly air temperatures can exceed 29°C. Most precipitation falls in the Doldrums (3,000 mm per year). The West Wind zones are also relatively wet, with more than 1,000 mm precipitation. The eastern trade wind zones are extremely dry, with less than 100 mm precipitation each year. In zones with large amounts of precipitation, the salt content of the water is relatively low (28 per cent to 34.5 per cent), but in the sub-tropics where little rain falls, salt levels can exceed 35.5 per cent.

Drift-ice, pack-ice and continental ice in the form of icebergs from the Antarctic can be found year-round in the South Pacific. Average tidal fluctuations in the open sea are approximately 1 m, but on the continental shelves, they can be much higher (9.1 m in the Gulf of Alaska).

The Pacific island chains are volcanic in nature. Islands such as New Zealand are fragments of the continental crust.

Australasian Mediterranean Sea

The Australasian Mediterranean Sea is a lesser sea of the Pacific Ocean. It includes a number of seas in the Malay Archipelago, in the region between China in the north and Australia in the south. The largest of these seas is the **South China Sea** which has a maximum depth of 4,374 m, as well as a wide continental shelf, with depths of less than 200 m. The Australasian Mediterranean Sea also includes the Java, Sulu, Philippines, Celebes, Banda,

Pacific Islands

The Pacific contains more than 10,000 islands with a total land area of 3.6 million sq. km. These include the **Malay Archipelago**, the **Philippines**, **Japan** and **New Zealand** and the island groups of **Micronesia**, **Melanesia** and **Polynesia**.

Most Pacific Island chains run from north-west to south-east, but older chains run from north to south. This difference can be explained by the movement of the Pacific Plate 40 million years ago.

Flores, Arafura and Timor Seas. The **Banda Sea** between the islands of Sulawesi (Celebes), Buru, Seram, Tanimbar, Wetar, Timor and Flores is up to 7,440 m deep. The **Celebes Sea** between Sulawesi, Borneo and Mindanao has a maximum depth of 6,220 m. The **Java Sea** is the shallowest at only 200 m.

Seas on the Pacific Rim

The Pacific rim contains a number of smaller seas off the coasts of

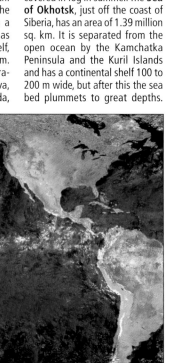

Satellite view of the Pacific Ocean.

the surrounding continents. The northernmost of these is the **Bering Sea** between the east Siberian coast, Alaska, the Aleutian Islands and the Commander Islands, which has an area of 2.26 million sq. km and a maximum depth of 4,097 m. Its northern outlet is the Bering Straits, which lead into the Chukchi Sea. The Straits are 85 km wide at their narrowest point and 50 m to 90 m deep. The northern Bering Sea is usually frozen over in winter, and is often covered in fog in summer. The **Sea of Okhotsk**, just off the coast of Siberia, has an area of 1.39 million sq. km. It is separated from the open ocean by the Kamchatka Peninsula and the Kuril Islands and has a continental shelf 100 to 200 m wide, but after this the sea bed plummets to great depths.

The average depth of the Okhotsk Basin is 971 m, but the maximum depth is 5,210 m. For seven months of the year, most of this sea is covered in drift-ice. The **Sea of Japan**, between the Japanese islands and the Asian mainland, has an area of 1 million sq. km and is up to 4,225 m deep. In the south, it is connected to the East China Sea via the Korea Straits, and to the Okhotsk Sea in the north via the Gulf of Tartary and the La-Pérouse Strait. The **East China Sea**, a shallow sea overlying a continental shelf that is strongly affected by the Yangtze

Kiang River lies between China, Taiwan, the Ryukyu Islands and Kyushu. In the Okinawa Trench, the East China Sea reaches a depth of 2,719 m. The East China Sea adjoins the **Yellow Sea**, a shallow sea with many bays between China and Korea. The yellow colour of the sea is caused by the loess soil deposited by

*The **Southern Ocean** surrounds the Antarctic and is the point at which the three great oceans meet. Most of the ocean is covered in ice in winter, some of which melts again in the summer. Certain sea creatures, such as krill,* *are found in immense numbers in the Southern Ocean and provide food for whales, seals, fish, squid and birds. Penguins live on the coasts of the southern hemisphere from the sub-tropics to the Antarctic.*

the Huang He River. The **Coral Sea**, which lies between Australia, New Guinea, the Solomon Islands and the New Hebrides connects with the **Tasman Sea** south of the Australian mainland, between Australia, Tasmania and New Zealand.

Ozone Layer

A reduction in the thickness of the ozone layer over the Antarctic was first noticed in 1979. It was caused by chloro-fluorocarbons (CFCs), mainly from aerosol sprays, carbon dioxide (CO_2) and halon, which is used as a solvent. CFCs rise into the atmosphere, where UV rays release the chlorine. The chlorine atoms alter the ozone molecules, reducing the ozone concentration in the ozone layer. As a result, unfiltered UV light, which is harmful to life forms, reaches the Earth and penetrates the surface of the oceans. In the Southern Ocean, this can cause great damage to the creation of phytoplankton and seaweed, two vital elements in the Antarctic food chain. Particularly strong depletion of the ozone layer occurs in the Antarctic spring (September to October). Due to the persistence of chlorine in the atmosphere, the ozone layer is unlikely to repair itself before the mid-twenty-first century even if remedial measures are applied.

The **Gulf of California** which separates Baja California from the Mexican mainland, and the **Gulf of Alaska,** stretching from the Alaska Peninsula and Kodiak Island in the west to the Alexander Archipelago in the east, are also part of the Pacific Ocean.

Southern Ocean

The Southern Ocean is the name given to the Antarctic regions of

the Atlantic, Indian and Pacific Oceans that surround the continent of Antarctica. The ocean covers the regions south of the Antarctic Convergence (between 50° S and 55° S), at which point the cold Antarctic water sinks beneath the warmer sub-tropical ocean waters. The Southern Ocean covers an area of approximately 38 million sq. km, of which 21 million sq. km is covered by sea-ice in winter, and 4 million sq. km of which is permanently frozen all year round. The continental shelf is narrower and deeper than other continental shelves, with depths of between 370 m and 490 m. The Southern Ocean also contains ridges.

1 Hawaii: the eight largest islands in the Pacific island group are formed by the peaks of sunken volcanoes. Black lava beaches are signs of earlier volcanic activity.

2 Dramatic steep cliffs and rumbling surf: off the coast of California, the Pacific is by no means always the 'calm ocean' that Magellan experienced.

3 Icebergs form in the Southern Ocean as pieces break away from the floating ice-shelves that surround Antarctica. Thousands form each year, and they are often larger than Arctic icebergs.

Indian Ocean

*The **Red Sea** is a long, narrow, shallow sea in the Indian Ocean containing coral reefs that are a favourite hunting ground for sharks. Most species of this cartilaginous fish are carnivores and prefer water that has been warmed by the sun. The large numbers of small fish attract most sharks in July and August. The feared grey reef sharks congregate during the winter months around Shark's Reef south of Sharm-el-Sheikh in order to breed. The area is frequented by tiger sharks, leopard sharks and hammerhead sharks.*

Indian Ocean

The Indian Ocean is the smallest of the three great oceans and lies between Africa, Asia and the Antarctic. The ocean covers an area of 73.43 million sq. km. Seas forming part of the Indian Ocean include the **Persian Gulf** and **Red Sea**, and if these are included within the scope of the ocean, its total area is 74.12 million sq. km. The Indian Ocean covers approximately 20 per cent of the Earth's ocean surface. The average depth is 3,897 m, and the deepest point is the **Java Trench**, south of Java, at 7,450 m. Over one third of the Indian Ocean is 4,000 m to 5,000 m deep. The ocean's only wide continental shelves are off the coast of north-west Australia, in the **Andaman Sea**, the **Gulf of Bengal** and in the **Arabian Sea**. The Indian Ocean is not separated from the Atlantic by any natural borders, but an imaginary 4,000 km line, following the longitude 20° E, from Cape Agulhas on the southern tip of Africa to the Antarctic, is generally accepted as the border between the two oceans.

The formation of the Indian Ocean began more than 200 million years ago, when the original supercontinent of Pangaea broke apart. Australia and Antarctica separated from Africa and drifted south-eastwards. Later, India broke away from the Antarctic Continent and drifted northwards, where it joined Eurasia approximately 30 million years ago. The separation of Australia and the Antarctic occurred 65 million years ago. The age of the ocean basin of the Indian Ocean in its current form is approximately 36 million years.

The Indian Ocean bed is dominated by a ridge running along its centre forming an inverted Y-shape. This **Central Indian Ridge** divides in the north to form the **Arabian-Indian Ridge (Carlsberg Ridge)** and the **East Indian Ridge** and extends south-eastwards as the **Indian-Antarctic Ridge**. The **South-west Indian Ridge**, the western arm of the central ridge, joins the **Mid-Atlantic Ridge** on the far side of the southern tip of Africa. These ridges divide the Indian Ocean into several deep-sea basins.

86 per cent of the deposits on the floor of the Indian Ocean consist of the remains of sea creatures and 14 per cent are the products of erosion. The flat plateaus are mainly covered in lime silt, but the deeper basins are covered in reddish-brown clay and silica silt. The Indus and the Ganges, two of the largest river systems in the world, drain into the Indian Ocean and in the course of time, they have deposited thick sediments eroded from the Himalayas. Volcanic activity in the region around Indonesia has caused the ocean floor to be covered by a thick layer of volcanic ash and other volcanic deposits.

In addition to the large islands of Madagascar and Sri Lanka, the Indian Ocean also contains numerous island groups, such as the Comoros, the Seychelles, the Maldives, the Andaman Islands and the Kerguelen Islands, which sit on an underwater plateau just below the surface of the ocean. Another example is the **Mascarene Plateau** north-east of Madagascar, which was formed when the original southern continent broke apart.

Atolls

A characteristic feature of the Indian Ocean and the Pacific are atolls – island formations caused by rings of living coral reefs. These limestone rock formations are formed by coral reefs on top of submarine mountains or volcanos and can support narrow, sandy islands. The largest atolls in the Indian Ocean are the Seychelles and the Maldives. Atolls normally have a ring structure and enclose the surface of the ocean to form a lagoon encircled by limestone sand. The atolls of the Maldives, however, have a different structure. Some of these are actually faros, or fringing reefs, where a coral bank joins an island to form a ring, enclosing a shallow lagoon. The lagoon of this type of an atoll is normally much shallower than a main lagoon. Coral reefs are rich in fish food sources and they are frequented by many species of sea creature and are a paradise for divers.

Satellite view of the Indian Ocean.

Unlike the other oceans, the surface currents in the northern Indian Ocean are affected by the seasonal monsoon winds and reverse direction twice a year. From November to April, the north-east Monsoon generates the **North Equatorial Current**, which carries water from India to the coast of Africa. Here, the current turns south and runs along the coast of Somalia to the Equator, where it joins the **South Equatorial Current** and flows east as an equatorial counter-current. In April, the North-east Monsoon is replaced by the South-west Monsoon, forming the strong **Somali Current** which flows north. From July, the monsoon current starts flowing east. At the Indonesian archipelago, the mass of water turns south and returns as part of the significantly stronger South Equatorial Current. The southern part of the ocean is dominated year-round by anti-clockwise surface water circulation, consisting of the **South Equatorial Current** flowing east, and the **West Wind Drift** flowing west. Part of the South Equatorial Current flows south between Africa and Madagascar and joins the **Agulhas Current**, the strongest westerly boundary current of the Southern Hemisphere, covering 180 km a day along the edge of the South African continental shelf.

The region south of the **monsoon zone** is subject to the standard planetary winds, just like the other oceans. The constant winds of the **south-east trade wind zone** are followed by the **Horse Latitudes** which contain light, spiralling winds, and the **West Wind zone**, where the winds can be very changeable and stormy in winter. Polar east winds are only found near Antarctica. Cyclones are most common between November and April in the region around Mauritius, and occasionally in the Arabian Sea and the Bay of Bengal.

The air temperature throughout much of the Indian Ocean is more than 25°C year-round. Precipitation in the eastern equatorial region is about 3000 mm per year, and in the West Wind belt around 1000 mm per year. It is normally only foggy around the coast of Somalia. Drift-ice, pack-ice and icebergs from the Antarctic can be found year-round. Tidal fluctuations are normally relatively low (for example, 0.18 m on the coast of Sumatra). The highest fluctuations are 4.5 m in the Ganges Delta, 5.1 m in the **Gulf of Martaban** and 8.9 m in the **Gulf of Cambay**.

The narrowness of the continental shelf around the Indian Ocean, especially along the east African coast, means that fishing plays a far less important role than in the Pacific and Atlantic Oceans and is restricted to coastal waters. The alternation of the surface ocean currents and the absence of an influx of cold water during the north-east monsoon period on the western edges of the basin also restrict the number of fish. Oil and gas reserves are only found at the northern end of the **Arabian Sea**.

Red Sea

The Red Sea is a long and thin **intercontinental sea** off the Indian Ocean between the Arabian peninsula and Africa. It is connected to the **Gulf of Aden** by the **Bab al-Mandab** and artificially to the **Mediterranean Sea** by the **Suez Canal**. It has an area of some 430,000 sq. km and a width of 145–306 km. The average depth is 538 m, and the deepest point is 2,604 m. The sea is named after a species of algae (*Trichodesmium erythraeum*) containing red pigment, which temporarily turns the deep blue surface waters a red colour. The floor of the Red Sea is covered by a broad continental shelf and a perpendicular trough, which is dissected by a valley just under 25 km wide. This valley is the result of relatively new spreading of the sea floor, as demonstrated by volcanic activity, such as fresh lava flows. The

Giant squid live in the temperate and warm regions of the oceans. The largest species is the Pacific Giant Squid, which can be up to 7 m long and weigh 70 kg. *Manta rays* can measure up to 8 m across, and are found in the tropical waters of the oceans.

Red Sea is expanding by about 1.25 cm a year.

The surface water currents change depending on the season. Between November and March, they flow north-west, towards the Gulf of Suez, before turning around and flowing south-east towards the straits of **Bab al-Mandab**. The exchange of water with the Arabian Sea is determined by the tides. Currents near the sea floor transport salt-rich water from the Red Sea through the straits and into the **Gulf of Aden**, while a surface current moving in the opposite direction carries water with low salt content into the Red Sea. Surface salt content is 37 per cent in the south, and 41 per cent in the north. Summer temperatures are normally above 30°C, and in winter they range between 20°C and 25°C.

The clear waters of the Red Sea and the lack of freshwater run-off from the surrounding dry mainland have provided ideal conditions for extensive coral reefs on both sides of the sea, which extend over a length of more than 2,000 km. The Red Sea contains some 350 species of coral. The sediments of the ocean floor are rich in heavy metals, in particular zinc, copper, lead and manganese.

Persian Gulf

This sea of the Indian Ocean between Iran, the lowlands of Iraq and the Arabian peninsula is connected to the **Gulf of Oman** by the **Straits of Hormuz**. The Persian Gulf covers an area of 239,000 sq. km and has an average depth of only 25 m. This very shallow sea has a maximum depth of 170 m.

Where the Arabian peninsula meets the Asian continental plate, an active **subduction zone** has formed in the Persian Gulf. The north-east coast of the Gulf descends steeply but the opposite side falls at a more shallow incline to form a crevasse.

Water circulation in the Persian Gulf is also determined by the **monsoon winds**. Warm, salty water flows out of the Gulf and into the Arabian Sea during the south-west monsoon season. Temperatures are relatively high,

reaching an August average of 30°C to 32°C. Average temperatures in February are 15°C to 22°C. The salt content of the water ranges from 37 per cent to more than 40 per cent in some places. According to estimates, the crude oil reserves in the Persian Gulf and the surrounding countries represent approximately

56 per cent of total world reserves. The shallowness of the sea and the warm climate means that the oil here is much easier to extract than, say, the North Sea oil which lies at greater depths in a very stormy, hostile sea. The largest gas reserves are in the adjoining Zagros Mountains of Western Iran.

1 The island group of the Seychelles in the Indian Ocean, 1,000 km east of Kenya, consists of about 90 islands which sit on an underwater shelf. Thirty of the islands are of granite and syenite and have sheer coastlines. The remaining islands are flat coral reefs.

2 The Maldives: this archipelago in the Indian Ocean consists of 20 atolls with 1087 islands, most only 2 m above sea-level. Only 220 of the islands are inhabited.

3 Thailand's coast on the Gulf of Siam, which connects to the South China Sea.

Main photograph:
The 4,478-m-high, steep pyramid-shaped peak of the Matterhorn is made of hard crystalline rock. The mountain is one of the most imposing peaks of the Swiss Alps.

Europe

In geological terms, Europe is merely the western extension of the huge continent of Eurasia, but the Urals and Caucasus Mountains and the Black Sea form a well-defined, natural frontier between the two continents. The landscape of

Southern England: the picturesque 'Durdle Door'.

the European Continent is very disparate and uneven. This means that this relatively small continent, covering just 10.5 million sq. km, has a wide range of different landscape features: mountain ranges and basins, ranges of hills and lowlands, craggy coastlines and numerous offshore islands, large and small.

The landscapes of northern Europe were mainly formed during the Ice Age. This region is adjoined by Central Europe with its low mountain ranges. The Alps and the Pyrenees form the natural borders of Western Europe. The southern European peninsulas are situated on the north coast of the Mediterranean.

Europe

Iceland: *Hveravellir lies between the enormous volcanic glaciers of Langjökull and Hofsjökull. In this region, the geothermal springs put on an impressive display. These hot springs are just one of the many indications of volcanic activity.*

This island in the North Atlantic is of volcanic origin and has a fascinating natural landscape, including several active volcanoes, hot springs, fumaroles, glaciers and fjords. The island of Surtsey lies just south of the mainland.

Iceland

Iceland is the second largest island in Europe. It is located in the North Atlantic, just south of the Arctic Circle. The island is of volcanic origin and contains more than 140 volcanoes, some 30 of which are still active. Two such volcanoes are **Hekla** and **Askja**. Signs of continued volcanic activity include geysers and solfatara, which are particularly common on the western half of the island. Glaciers and melt-water flows have also played an important role in shaping Iceland's landscape. Glaciers still cover 11,800 sq. km of the island.

On the coasts in the west, north and north-east, immense basalt promontories rise out of the sea to heights of up to 1,000 m. In the south and south-east, the coast is largely flat. The gravel moraine adjoining this flat coastal land are also a result of glaciation during the Ice Age, as are the country's many fjords, trough valleys, cirques and outwash plains. The **Fjell Plateau** is between 300 and 1,200 m high and rises to form the Iceland Plateau which is 1,200 to 2,000 m high. The uplands are dotted with sheer cliffs, which can be up to 500 m high. The highest point is **Hvannadalshnúkur** (2,119 m), and the largest glacier is **Vatnajökull** (8,410 sq. km).

Scandinavian Peninsula

This is the longest peninsula in Eu-rope and covers 750,000 sq. km, including the countries of Sweden and Norway, and by extension Denmark and Finland. The North Sea coast of **Jutland** is flat with coastal lagoons and dunes in the north and mud flats and marshes in the south. To the north of the peninsula, the landscape is dominated by the **Scandinavian Mountains**. Several rivers traverse the mountains of **Norland**. In **Sveåland** there are numerous large lakes. **Götaland** is a hilly region to the south, which also contains a large number of lakes. The region's countless **fjords** are a relic from the Ice Age.

The **Skerry coast** was formed dur-ing the Pleistocene glaciations. The Scandinavian Mountains, with their wide plateaus (fjells) and numerous glacial plateaus, run along the whole north coast of the peninsula and drop into the North Sea in the west. **Lappland** lies north of the Arctic Circle. It is a plain containing isolated mountains which adjoins the hills of the **Central Finnish Ridge,** with its many lakes.

Lappland

Lappland, home of the Lappish people, covers eastern Sweden, eastern Norway, northern Finland and parts of the **Kola Peninsula**. The landscape is characterised by wide plateaus covered in tundra and bogs, interspersed with scattered, isolated mountain peaks.

Finnmark

In the extreme north-east of Norway, the snowline has been pushed back northwards due to the Gulf Stream. This means that

Scandinavian mountains: Geirangerfjord in Norway

the region is able to support pine forests, such as those of the Stabbursdalen National Park at 70° N, the northernmost pine forest in the world.

Scandinavian Mountains

The **Scandinavian Mountains** extend over the whole of the Scandinavian Peninsula. Although some peaks reach a height of more than 2,000 m, such as Glittertind (2,470 m) and Kebnekaise (2,117 m), this is mainly a low mountain range. The etchplains in the west, which fall steeply into the sea and whose deep valleys form **fjords,** are typical features of the region.

Finnish Lake District

The **Finnish Lake District** contains approximately 55,000 lakes which date from the last Ice Age. The principle lakes are **Saimaa** and **Päijänne**.

British Isles

This island group sits on the north-west European continental shelf. It consists of the two main islands of **Great Britain** and **Ireland**, the **Shetlands** and the **Orkneys**, the Inner and Outer **Hebrides**, the **Isle of Man, Anglesey, the Isle of Wight** and numerous other smaller islands. Great Britain is divided into three geographical areas, the **Highlands** in the north and west, the **Midlands** and the **Lowlands** in the south. The Scottish Highlands are separated from the **Southern Uplands** by a deep rift, the Great Glen. The **Cheviot Hills** form the border between Scotland and England. The **Pennines** run in a north–south direction down the centre of England, and the **Cumbrian Mountains** are located in the west. The far south-west of the island consists of the granite, hilly peninsula of **Devon and Cornwall**. **Lowland Britain** consists of a flat cuesta landscape. The Midlands and Lowlands of Scotland mark the border between the Highlands and Lowland Britain. **Southern England** is characterised by ranges of hills, the Thames Valley and the Hampshire Basin. **East Anglia** and **The Fens** in the east are flat and marshy, some parts lying below sea-level. Fjord-like inlets, such as the **Firth of Forth** and **Moray Firth** are characteristic of the Scottish coast. The high cliffs on the **south coast facing the English Channel** were formed by buckling of the layers of chalk. These are the famous White Cliffs of Dover.

Ireland

Most of the island is dominated by the Irish Lowlands that rise no higher than 100 m. This region contains numerous bogs and lakes. In the north-west, the landscape rises to form the low mountain range of the **Caledonian Mountains**. The highest points are **Nephin** (807 m) and **Mount Errigal** (752 m). In the south, the Irish Lowlands are bordered by a range of mountains formed during the **Armorican period**. Ireland's highest mountain, the 1,041 m-high **Carrauntoohill,** is in this area. The **Wicklow Mountains** are up to 924 m high and form the central mass of the Leinster Mountains, a low mountain range on the island. The coasts consist mainly of deeply-fissured cliffs, with inlets that can extend far inland.

Shetland and Orkney Islands

There are over 100 islands in the **Orkneys and Sheltlands**. The largest are Mainland, Sanday, Westray and Stronsay, Yell, Unst, Fetlar, Bressai and Whalsay. The **Pentland Firth** separates the Scottish mainland from the 70 Orkney Islands. The coasts are characterised by a large number of bays and high cliffs.

Scottish Highlands

The Scottish **Highlands** are split in two by the 95-km-long **Glen More** to form the **Northern Highlands,** which are up to 1,182 m high, and the **Grampians,** which include the 1,343-m-high **Ben Nevis,** Scotland's highest mountain.

This long valley also contains many lakes, including **Loch Ness,** which in places is 229 m deep. The western Highlands end in craggy cliffs. The largest lake in the British Isles is **Loch Lomond** (70 sq. km) south of the Grampians.

Pennines

This Palaeozoic low mountain range runs from north to south and is England's watershed. The highest point is the 893-m-high **Cross Fell**. West of the Pennines lie the **Cumbrian Mountains**, whose numerous ravines and lakes are known collectively as the **Lake District**.

Wales/Cambrian Mountains

Wales mainly comprises barren hills devoid of trees. The highest point in the **Cambrian Mountains** is the egg-shaped **Mount Snowdon,** which reaches a height of 1,085 m. The plateaus, covered in meadows, drop suddenly into the sea, forming spectacular 90-m-high cliffs.

Cornwall

The steep, vertical cliffs of **Cornwall** extend into the Atlantic in the far south-west of Great Britain. The rounded peaks of the land away from the coast are traversed by narrow valleys. The mountain ridges rise in stages and are covered in moorland and marshes.

European Lowlands

The European Lowlands stretch from the Atlantic, along the North Sea and the Baltic Sea coasts and into Russia. Much of the area is characterised by dry, sandy deposits of poor soil left over from the Ice Age. It was originally covered in mixed woodland, but is today partly covered by stunted shrubs and pine heathland. The terminal moraines of Lower Saxony have a dry, loamy-sandy soil, dotted with clumps of trees.

The impressive moraines from the Wolstonian glaciation period include **Lüneburg Heath**, the **Hamburg Mountains** and **Fläming**. The southern land ridge extends from Emsland over Fläming and

The Giant's Causeway on the north coast of *Ireland* is the stuff of legends. It is up to 60 m wide in places and stretches for some 5 km. This tongue of land near the fishing village of Ballycastle consists of 40,000 symmetrical basalt columns which can be up to 6 m high. Most of the columns are regular hexagons. They were formed by crystallisation, when lava flowing into the sea cooled down very quickly. The formation continues under the water.

into the Lower Silesian Mountains. The moraines of the **Baltic land ridge** surround the Baltic Sea from **North Jutland** to **East Prussia**. The **North Sea Coast** has a barrier of dunes and tidal shallows, beginning at Calais and extending north-east as far as North Schleswig. Away from the coast, the sandy plains are covered in marshes.

French Lowlands, Brittany and Normandy

The fertile cultivated land of the **Paris Basin** is interspersed with wooded areas and sandy soil. The Seine valley is bordered in the north-west by **Brittany** and **Normandy**. The crystalline rocks of the coast have been eroded by surf to form steep cliffs and numerous islands.

Brittany's landscape actually consists of a very ancient mountain range that has now been eroded to a maximum height of 384 m in the **Monts d'Arrée**. Vegetation in the region is characterised by heathland, moorland, woodland and clumps of tall trees.

The Paris Basin adjoins the **Garonne Basin**. The extensive pine forests south of Bordeaux and the straight, flat coastline with its numerous coastal lagoons and an impressive belt of dunes dominate the landscape. The **Rhône-Saône Basin** between the **Cévennes** and the **Alps** has a distinctly Mediterranean character. The flood plains of **Languedoc**, the **Rhône Delta**, the **Riviera** and **Provence** are all part of this region.

North Sea Coast/Mud-flats

The Belgian **North Sea Coast** is flat and has no off-shore islands. This coast is lined with a wall of dunes up to 30 m high and a series of dykes, behind which lies a stretch of treeless marshland, traversed by numerous drainage ditches. This area adjoins the dry, sandy plains of **Flanders**. The North Sea coast of the Netherlands is characterised by barrier beaches and a belt of dunes that are only interrupted by the estuaries of the **Rhine** and **Meuse rivers**. The original moorland and silt landscapes have been transformed by the man-made polders (dykes) into broad, treeless stretches of pastureland , some of which is land reclaimed from the sea. The North Sea coast of Germany is flat and protected from flooding by dykes. The **North and East Frisian Islands** rise out of **tidal mud-flats**. The **small, low islands off the coast of Schleswig-Holstein** are an interesting feature. These flat, marshy islands have man-made terps (sea-walls) to provide protection from storm surges for humans and grazing animals. Between these islands and the dykes lie mud-flats, which are dry when exposed at low tide.

Central European Low Mountain Range

The **Central European Low Mountain Range** is a chain of disparate rugged massifs, beginning in western Europe. The region is bordered to the south by the Alps and the Carpathian Mountains and in the east it joins the Lublin basin and gradually merges with the Russian plateau. These highly eroded mountains date from the Variscan Orogeny. The constituent massifs have both craggy folds and flat crests. Most of the low mountain range is covered in mountain forest, but in many places, the original trees have been replaced by plantations of spruce.

Vosges and the Black Forest

The **Vosges** to the west of the Rhine extend from the Belfort Gap in the south to the Col de Saverne in the north. The **Southern Vosges** is a chain of mountains and ridges with craggy hills, covered in woodland.

The **Northern Vosges** are also densely forested and consist of large red sandstone slabs. The highest elevation is Grosser Winterberg at a height of 581 m. The highest mountain in the whole of the Vosges is Grand Ballon (1,423 m). To the east of the Rhine lies the

1 Dawn in the wild Scottish Highlands: Buachaille Etive Mór at an altitude of 1,000 m.

2 Land's End is the extreme tip of Cornwall, the peninsula in the south-west of England. These rugged cliffs are England's westernmost point.

3 Ireland: Galway Bay on the west coast of the island.

4 St. David's Head: the cliff-lined tongue of land in west Wales extends out into the Atlantic. The south coast is relatively calm, but the north is often battered by the surf.

*The Mediterranean islands **Sardinia** and **Corsica** are separated by the Strait of Bonifacio. Both islands are mainly mountainous. Corsica has numerous peaks above 2,000 m, but the highest point on Sardinia is just 1,834 m.*

Black Forest. It is 160 km long and between 22 and 60 km wide. Its romantic valleys and mountain lakes are particularly attractive. The region's numerous mineral and thermal springs, particularly around Baden-Baden, are signs of seismic activity. The Black Forest also contains the highest cascade in Germany, the Triberg Waterfalls (162 m).

German Low Mountain Range

The **Rhenish Slate Mountains** are located west of this range of low mountains. To the west of the Rhine and north of the Moselle lies the volcanic **Eifel region** with its crater lakes. South of the Moselle is the **Hunsrück**, which is mirrored to the east of the Rhine by the **Taunus**. The **Westerwald** mainly consists of areas of pastureland covering the basalt bedrock. To the north, **Bergisches Land** adjoins **Sauerland**. Further to the east lie the forest-covered red sandstone plateaus of the **Weserbergland** and

Leinebergland. To the south lie the **hills of Hesse** and the **Vogelsberg Mountains**. The **Harz Mountains** are 100 km long and 35 km wide, an isolated massif south-east of Hanover. The **Frankenwald** and **Thuringian forests** have lost some of their once impressive woodland. The **Fichtel Mountains**, on the other hand, still have dense woodland, and the region's granite hills form an undulating basin at a height of 600 m. Further east lie the **Ore Mountains, the Elbe Sandstone Mountains** and the **Lusatian Mountains**. The hills around the fringes of the **Upper Rhine Valley**, **Spessart and Odenwald**, are covered by **the Palatine Forest** and the **Black Forest**. This is followed by the cuesta of southern Germany, with the **Swabian Mountains** and the **Frankish Alb**. East of these mountains, the Naab Valley extends to the mountains on the east Bavarian border, the **Bavarian Forest** and the **Bohemian Forest**.

Rhine

The Rhine is 1,320 km long and is one of Europe's most important transport routes. It originates in the Swiss canton of Graubünden (Grisons). The two upper branches of the river join to form the Alpine Rhine which opens out into a delta in Lake Constance. The river flows out of the lake and plummets over the 20 m falls at Schaffhausen. The Thur and Aare Rivers join from the west and the Wutach from the east. The Rhine flows through the lowlands of the Upper Rhine until Bingen, where it joins the Neckar and Main. In the Rhine Gorge, the river flows through slate mountains. The Mosel, Ahr, Lahn and Sieg rivers flow down deep valleys to join the Rhine. The Lower Rhine winds through the Lower Rhine Valley in the Netherlands, before its main estuary arms, the Waal and Lek Ijssel, spill out into the North Sea.

Danube

The second longest river in Europe (2,858 km) begins as the Breg and Brigach in the eastern Black Forest. It flows through the Bavarian Forest into the Vienna Basin and from there through the lowlands of Hungary. The river divides into several branches covering a wide delta before it drains into the Black Sea.

Bavarian Forest, Bohemian Forest, Sudetenland

The **Bohemian Forest** is divided by the Cham-Further Lowland. In the south-east, a long, broad basin divides the **Bavarian Forest**, which lies between the Danube and the Regen and rises to a barren landscape at an altitude of about 1,121 m. The highest point is the **Great Arber** (1,456 m).

The **Sudetenland** extends for a length of some 300 km and is 30 km to 60 km wide. It lies between the Lusatian Mountains and the Moravian Gate. The **West Sudetenland** consists of the **Karkonosze**, the Jizera Mountains and the Bóbr-Kaczawa Mountains. It adjoins the Klodzko Valley and the Masyw Snieznika. The **East Sudetenland** consists of the Hruby Jeseník Mountains and the Nízky Jeseník. The highest peak is **Snow Mountain** in the Korkonosze at a height of 1,602 m.

Steep escarpments characterise the Rhine valley in Germany.

Massif Central

The French **Massif Central** covers some 85,000 sq. km, making them the largest connected mountain range in France. They are bordered by the **Garonne Basin**, the **Paris Basin** and the **Rhône-Saône Basin**.

The **Auvergne** is the centre of the Massif and is one of Europe's most impressive volcanic regions. The highest point of the Massif Central is in the volcanic Chaîne des Puys. It is the 1,886-m-high **Puy de Nancy** in Mont Dore. In

the karst plateaus of the **Causses** in the south, the Tarn, has carved out deep gorges.

Alps

The highest mountains in Europe cover a length of 1,200 km on the southern European mainland.

Pyrenees

This high mountain range between the Mediterranean Sea and the Bay of Biscay divides the Iberian Peninsula from the rest of mainland Europe. The **Pyrenees** are 435 km long, but only have a maximum width of some 100 km. The highest point is **Aneto** at 3,404 m. Between the passes of **Col de Somport** in the west and the 1,915-m-high **Col de Puymorens** lie the Central Pyrenees, which can reach heights of around 2,900 m in the region around Andorra, and can be over 3,350 m high in the Monte Perdido and Maldeta Massif.

The East Pyrenees adjoin the **Albères** near the Mediterranean. The highest point here is the **Pic Carlit** (2,921 m). The major high valleys are Capcir, Cerdagne and Vallespir. Although **Pic d'Anie** is 2,504 m high, the West Pyrenees between the **Irati Valley** and the 1,632-m-high **Somport Pass** is more like a low mountain chain, and descends to the coast of the Basque Country.

Iberian Peninsula

The largest and westernmost of the three southern European peninsulas is bordered by the Pyrenees in the north, the Atlantic in the west and south-west, and by the Mediterranean in the east and south-east. The heart of the peninsula is an almost circular high plateau (**meseta**), which is traversed by a range of mountains running from west to east. The **Cordillera Central** divides the plateau into the smaller North Meseta, up to 800 m high, and the South Meseta, up to 600 m high. The edges of the plateau are surrounded by chains

of high hills: in the north the **Cantabrian Mountains (Cordillera Cantábrica)**, in the east the **Sistema Ibérico** (highest point: 2,313 m) and in the south by the **Sierra Morena**. To the west, the plateau descends gradually over the **Estremadura** to the Atlantic. The **Ebro River** forms the Ebro Basin between the Pyrenees and the Sistema Ibérico, and the **Guadalquivír River** creates the **Andalusian Basin**, which opens out into a wide lowland area towards the Atlantic.

Cantabrian Mountains

The **Cantabrian Mountains** stretch to the north Spanish coast between the Pyrenees and the **Galician Hills**. Only 30 km from the coast, this range of hills reaches its highest point, the 2,648-m-high **Picos de Europa**.

Cordillera Central

The **Cordillera Central** crosses the whole of the Iberian Peninsula and divides Spain's central plateau. They are rolling hills that reach a height of 2,592 m in the **Sierra de Gredos**. These hills divide the meseta into the North Meseta, traversed by the **Douro River**, and the South Meseta, also known as **La Mancha**.

Cordillera Bética

The **Cordillera Bética** or Sistema Bética is an area of alpidic folds that run north-east from the **Straits of Gibraltar**, parallel to the coast and as far as **Cabo de la Nao**. The mountain system continues in the **Balearic Islands**. The main chain of the Cordillera Bética is the 90-km-long **Sierra Nevada** in Andalusia. One of its peaks, **Mulhacén**, is 3,478 m high, making it the highest mountain on the Iberian Peninsula.

Sierra Morena

The so-called 'brown mountains' form the southern edge of the plateau of inland Spain and receive a lot of rain. The plateaus rise so gradually that the incline is barely noticeable, but they reach heights of 1,323 m. The 400-km-long steep escarpment of the Guadalquivír Lowland is particularly impressive.

*The highest volcano in Europe is the 3,350-m-high **Etna** on the east coast of **Sicily**. The active volcano has a main crater and more than 200 smaller craters made of ash and clinker. The volcano has erupted more than 100 times in its history. Etna's plumes of smoke are a reminder of its continued activity – and unpredictable nature.*

Balearic Islands

The **Balearic** island group lies in the western Mediterranean and consists of the main island **Mallorca**, the slightly smaller **Menorca**, the Pitiusas (**Ibiza and Formentera**) and several smaller islands. The islands are the continuation of the **Cordillera Bética**. The highest peak is the 1,445 m **Puig Mayor** on Mallorca.

Apennine Peninsula

The **Apennine Peninsula** is divided into three main areas. In the north, the **Alps** form a divide from the rest of Europe. South of the Alps, the **plain of the Po River** extends as far as the **Adriatic**. In the Ice Age, this former sea bay became choked with debris carried down by rivers from the Alps and the Apennines.
Vicenza and Padua are overshadowed by the extinct volcanoes of **Colli Berici** and **Colli Euganei**, where hot sulphurous springs, the Abano Terme, rise to the surface. In the north-west, the **Apennines** extend almost all the way to the coast, where the narrow coast of the **Riviera** can be found.
The mountains surround an area of hills in a broad arc that is open towards the west. These are the **hills of Tuscany** which are also part of the Umbrian Basin. South of Monte Amiata lies Latium with its forest-covered extinct volcanoes and beautiful crater lakes. Between the volcanic hills lie plateaus formed of tufa, a volcanic rock, with few trees, surrounded by extensive, but largely dry moors and marshes.
The **Adriatic coast** has few harbours and is flat, but the west coast has numerous coves, bays and off-shore islands.

Apennines

The **Apennines** extend across the peninsula from the Alps to the north of **Sicily**, covering 1,100 km. The highest peaks are in the central section, the karstified limestone hills of the **Abruzzi**. The highest point is **Gran Sasso d'Italia** (2,912 m). The Southern Apennines are an uneven disconnected range of mountains. The crystalline massifs of **La Sila** and **Aspromonte** are in Calabria.

Corsica

The 8,680 sq. km Mediterranean island is 185 km long from north to south and is a maximum of 85 km wide. The mountainous interiis rugged and crossed by numerous valleys. The highest point is the 2,710-m-high **Monte Cinto**. The mountains in the west are granite and porphyry. In the east the mountains are younger and are made of slate. The vegetation consists of maquis shrubland, beech and conifer woodland. The west coast has many natural harbours, but the east coast is lined with marshes and coastal lagoons.

Sardinia

The interior of the 23,813 sq. km island is a plateau-like mountain terrain, with craggy peaks in the north-east, covered in maquis shrubland. The **Campidano Basin**, is a wide graben in the southwest. The highest point is **Gennargentu** (1,834 m).

Sicily

The **Straits of Messina** divide the largest island in the Mediterranean (25,426 sq. km) from the Italian mainland. In the west, **Monti Peloritani** (1,279 m), **Monti Nebrodi** (1,847 m) and **Madonie** (1,979 m) are a continuation of the Apennines. The steep cliffs are covered in maquis scrub and the remains of oak and beech woodland. South of Palermo lies a sedimentary ridge and plateau landscape, which extends into an area of hills and mountains, largely devoid of trees. On the coast of Siciliy is Europe's largest volcano, the 3,350-m-high **Etna**.

1 Bizarre limestone walls and strangely-shaped peaks rise in the southern foothills of the Pyrenees.

2 A view over the east coast of Sicily to the gradual slopes of the 3,350-m-high Mount Etna, an active volcano.

3 The Straits of Gibraltar on the south coast of the Iberian Peninsula: the cliff-lined tongue of land is connected to the mainland by alluvial plains.

4 The Dentelles de Montmirail in Provence, at the extremity of the arc of the Western Alps.

The peaks of Mont the Blanc region, the highest mountain group in Europe.

The Alps

The Alps emerged relatively recently in the earth's history, in the Cretaceous and Tertiary eras, but did not take their present form until the Quaternary. The longitudinal valleys run from Lake Constance in the north to Lake Como in the south, deep into the high mountains separating the Western from the Eastern Alps.

The Alps, Europe's highest mountain range is about 1,200 km long and between 150 and 250 km wide. The Passo dei Giovi near Genoa in the south is considered to be the frontier with the Apennines. In the north, the Alps extend as far as Lake Geneva and break off in the west towards the Rhône valley. In the north-east they push forward as far as the Danube near Vienna and in the south as far as the Plain of the Po. The Western Alps, with their many peaks of over 4,000 m in height, has a southern chain, consisting of crystalline and metamorphic rocks, and a limestone northern chain, separated from each other by a longitudinal valley. The

French limestone alps change into crystalline mountains from the 4,807-m-high Mont Blanc.

Near Nice, this crystalline zone begins with the oceanic Alpine chain, which reaches its greatest height at 3,297 m in the Aiguille de l'Argentière. To the north, the crystalline massifs extend as far as Mont Blanc and then continue along an east-west axis.

Mont Blanc is the highest mountain in Europe, and has given its name to the whole glaciated massif which rises between the longitudinal valleys of the Arve and the Dora Baltea.

The Central Alps include the Walliser Alps, the Bernese Oberland, the Gotthard massif, the Bernina

group, the Silvretta group, the Ötztal and Zillertal Alps, the Hohe and Niedere Tauern as well as the Ortler and Adamello groups. The isolated peak of the Matterhorn is the mightiest of the mountains in the Walliser Alps. Like a steep, square-cut pyramid, this giant of crystalline plutonic rock tapers upwards to a height of 4,478 m, higher by more than 1,000 m than the glacier passes that surround it. The border of the Eastern Alps is marked by the line of Lake Constance – Rhine valley – Splügen – Lake Como. The Eastern Alps are

View from Col de Lautaret over the Meije massif in the French alps.

twice as broad as the Western Alps, but markedly lower, with peaks rising to a maximum of 4,000 m.

The crystalline central Alps are flanked to the north and south by limestone areas. The mineral nature of this limestone and

dolomite rock is responsible for the particularly stark formation of this rocky landscape. On the south side it creates the beautiful Dolomites and in the north it is most impressive in the 2,962-m-high Zugspitze massif. The limestone mountains in the marginal zones

do not attain anything like the heights of the peaks in the central Alps, being on average only about 2,000 m high. The northern limestone Alps include the Dachstein massif in Austria, which has typical karst rock formations.

The nature of the Alpine landscape, so rich in relief formations, was created both by the variety of the rocks as well as by an upward thrust following the completion of folding and shifting processes in the Late Tertiary.

Massive Ice Age reshaping also contributed to the creation of the relief. The gigantic primeval glaciers created the valleys and mountain passes, the deep lakes such as Lake Constance, Lake Geneva, Lake Lucerne and the northern Italian lakes.

Typical features are the narrow gorges, wide valleys and the stepped formation of the high passes, as well as waterfalls, cirques and smaller lakes in the summit region.

The Königssee, not far from Berchtesgaden, is typical of the many charming alpine lakes. Its clear water reflects the evergreen forests and steeply towering rock faces, more than 2,000 m high, such as the 2,713 m Watzmann, which encircle the lake.

Today only the highest regions lie above the snowline. These are the plateau glaciers of Mont Blanc, the Walliser Alps and Bernina. Some glaciers still flow down into the valleys.

In its accumulation zones less snow thaws in the course of a year than new snow falls. In the ablation zones, below the snowline, the relationship is the exact opposite. The glacier tongues thaw out here, turning into mountain streams, feeding the many rivers that flow down the narrow Alpine gorges, such as the Rhine, the Rhône, the Po, the Inn, the Drau and the Save.

The snowline varies in altitude between 2,500 m and 3,400 m depending on the latitude and longitude. The Alpine zone with its extended meadows and pastures can reach an altitude of 1,600 m. They are followed lower down by a band of dense coniferous forest, replaced by deciduous trees and ending in the cultivated land at the foot of the mountains.

Some two dozen Alpine peaks are higher than 3,000 m. The highest mountains in the Alps from west to east are: Monte Viso (3,841 m), Pic de Charbonnel (3,750 m), Aiguilles de Grand Sassière (3,747 m), Mont Blanc (4,807 m), Grand Combin (4,314 m), Matterhorn (4,478 m), Dufourspitze (Pointe Dufour, 4,634 m), Weissmies (4,023 m), Monte Leone (3,553 m), Weisskugel (3,739 m), Wildspitze (3,774 m), Hochfeiler (3,510 m), Gross-Venediger (3,674 m) and Grossglockner (3,797 m).

The Alps range from France and Switzerland through Austria, Germany and Italy.

Main picture: the Aiguilles de Chamonix with Mont Blanc in the background.
Above: Mönch (4,099 m) and the Eiger (3,970 m) in the Bernese Oberland.
Below: The Langkofel (3,181 m) in the Dolomites.

*The island of **Pag** in the Adriatic Sea is 60 km long, with a area of 290 sq. km and elevations of up to 348 m. It is one of more than 600 islands that stretch along the Dalmatian Coast of the **Balkan Peninsula**. The islands are a series of parallel folds that have been submerged by the sea.*

Balkan Peninsula

The easternmost of the Mediterranean peninsulas begins in the north-west in the **Dinaric Alps**, which then extend to join the **Albanian Alps** in the south, with peaks of up to 2,700 m. These are followed by a series of disconnected mountain ranges.
The high peaks drop steeply into the **Adriatic**, leaving just a narrow coastal area. The Adriatic coast is dotted with numerous offshore islands, all with mountainous karstified terrain. The northern edge of the Balkan Peninsula is defined by the **Danube** and **Sava Rivers**. The 'Danube Lands' of Bulgaria is the name given to a region of undulating plains that rise to form a steep escarpment 150 m above the Danube. Deep valleys with vertical cliffs traverse this loess-covered landscape. The **foothills of the Balkans** begin to rise here, slowly climbing to their full height.
Parallel to the **Balkans** but located slightly to the south is the **Sredna Gora**, a **low mountain range in Bulgaria**, which adjoins the **Balkan-Turkish lowlands and hills,** traversed by the

Volga

The Volga is the longest river in Europe running for 3,530 km. It also has the largest volume of water. It originates in the Valdai Hills and initially flows north. Further downstream, the river turns south. Below Volzhskiy, the Volga branches to form the Achtuba, and the two rivers form a valley 25 km wide where they drain into the Caspian Sea.

Dnieper

The Dnieper is the third largest river in Europe (2,200 km). It rises in the north of the Central Russian Uplands, crosses the Ukraine in nine cataracts and drains into the Black Sea below Kherson.

Maritsa River. The **Thracian Massif** is divided into the **Rila, Pirin** and **Rhodope Mountains**. In the southern half of the Balkan Peninsula, the coasts are lined with numerous bays and headlands. The interior is mountainous.
Epirus is a treeless, karstified mountain region with few depressions. To the east lie the plains of **Thessaly,** dominated in the north-east by the 2,917-m-high **Mount Olympus**. Greek Macedonia consists of impassable mountains with small, enclosed valleys. The **Halkidiki Peninsula** is lined with cliffs and has three tongues of land that extend into the sea. East of this lie the undulating hills of **Thrace**. In the heart of central Greece, the **Attica Peninsula** has mountains that extend right to the coast. This region has many

Dinaric Mountains: the Plitvice Lakes are connected by waterfalls.

fertile basins and depressions. The **Isthmus of Corinth** separates central Greece from the **Peloponnese**, which, along with the numerous **Aegean Islands**, constitute southern Greece.

Balkans and Rhodope Mountains

The **Balkan Mountains** extend for 600 km and are 21–50 km wide. They run in parallel chains from the **Danube** to the **Black Sea**. Only the **High Balkans** are as high as the Alps. The **West Balkans** date from the Triassic

and Jurassic periods and reach a height of 2,168 m. The **Balkans** become significantly lower to the east, and descend to **Cape Emine**. The **Rhodope Mountains** lie between the plains of the Maritsa to the north, the Aegean coast to the south, the Mesta valley in the west and the Bulgarian-Greek border in the east. The highest peak is the 2,191 m **Golyam Perelik**.

Pindus

The **Pindus** mountain range is part of the young Dinaric-Hellenic fold mountain system that runs parallel to the **Ionian Sea** coast. The craggy mountains reach heights ranging from 2,200 m to over 2,600m. The highest point is **Smolikas** at a height of 2,637 m.

Peloponnese

The peninsula is separated from the rest of the mainland by the Gulf of **Patras** and the Gulf of **Corinth**. The interior of the peninsula consists of jagged limestone mountains which rise to 2,407 m at Mount St. Elias in the **Taygetos Mountains**. **Arcadia** is a rough highland area with an average altitude of 1,000 m.

Aegean Islands, Crete

Thassos, Samothrace, Lemnos, Lesbos, Chios, Samos, the Cyc-

lades and the **Sporades** are the major island groups in the **Aegean Sea**. The largest and southernmost of the islands is **Crete** which is mainly mountainous. The heavily karstified high ridges reach a height of 2,456 m at **Mount Ida**. The mountains fall steeply to the coast in the south, but in the north they descend to form an area of upland hills at an altitude of up to 1,500 m.

Carpathian Mountains

The **Carpathian Mountains** stretch over some 1,300 km in the shape of an arc around the north and east of the **Pannonian Plain**. Despite a maximum height of 2,655 m, the mountains have the characteristics of a low mountain chain. The Carpathian mountains are divided by basins and deep valleys to form; the **Western Carpathians** extending to the valley of the Harnad River, the **Central Carpathians** which reach as far as the region around the source of the Tisza River, the heavily wooded **Eastern Carpathians** with their thermal springs that extend as far as the Romanian Plains and the **Southern Carpathians**.

Eastern European Lowlands

The **Eastern European Lowlands** lie east of the Central European Lowlands and are bordered by the **Caucasus** in the south and the **Urals** in the east.

Baltic Ridge, Eastern European Lowlands

The **Baltic Ridge** rises to the west and south of the **Baltic Sea**. It reaches a height of up to 329 m in Eastern Pomerania.
The **Russian Plain** extends to the east of the Central European Lowland seam, running as far as the **Carpathians**, the **Crimean Mountains** and the **Caucasus Mountains**. The whole area lies on a bedrock of gneiss, granite and crystalline schist, which extends under the Caspian Sea to a depth of up to 10,000 m. This bedrock comes to the surface in the **Donets Basin**, the **Podolian**

Upland in Karelia and on the **Kola Peninsula** In Karelia and on Kola, glaciers have left behind bare hills and deep lakes. Further east and south-east lies a gently undulating young moraine landscape dotted with lakes.
The **Valdai Hills** and northern Belarus are characterised by terminal moraine plains and pine-covered sandy soil. The Smolensk-Moscow Uplands and the **Siberian Uvali** are ancient moraine landscapes, which today take the form of flat-topped ridges. In the south lie moors and extensive marshlands of the meandering rivers. The major rivers are the **Polesye,** which joins the **Pripyat** which in turn flows into the **Dnieper**. Broad marshy lowlands have also formed along the middle sections of the **Oka** and the tributaries of the **Desna**.
Numerous rivers in the landscapes of southern and central Russia have eroded countless valleys. South of the plateaus there is a belt of steppe terrain, which borders the lowland regions of the **Caspian** and **Black Seas**.

Russian Plains

The plains of southern and central Russia form part of the Eastern European Lowlands and rarely rise above 300 m. The higher plains, which run alongside the courses of the great rivers, have a regular relief. To the west, they rise gradually from a broad river plain, and fall steeply to the east. In between there is a series of high plateaus containing symmetrical hills. The forks of the numerous river systems have formed large numbers of ravines and valleys on the edges of the plains. In the **Donets Basin** and the **Podolian Uplands**, a thick layer of bedrock rises to the surface which forms the foundation of the entire Eastern European Lowlands.

Urals

The **Urals** divide the Eastern European Lowlands from the West Siberian Plain and form the boundary between Europe and Asia. They have a width of 40–150 km and stretch for 2,000 km along the 60th parallel from the tundra

*The Greek Island of **Santorini** is the southernmost of the **Cyclades**, formed by the remains of a volcanic peak which came into being almost 3,500 years ago after a violent explosion. The beaches on this unique island are covered in grey-black laval sand, and the island's interior is also covered in volcanic rock. Santorini was devastated by an earthquake in 1956.*

of the **Kara Sea coast** to the steppes of **Kazakhstan**.

The **Arctic** and **Sub-arctic Urals** lie between Mount Konstantinov at a height of 492 m in the north and the 1,425-m-high Sablya in the south. The north of the Urals consists of a series of massifs, whose rounded peaks reach a height of about 1,000 m. This region ends south of the 1,331-m-high **Mount Isherim**.

The **Middle Urals** are a series of highly eroded low mountains which gently undulate at a height of between 300 m and 700 m. The highest point is the 1,569-m-high **Konchakovski Kamen.** The 1,002 metre-high Mount Yurma marks the border. Here the mountains spread out in a fan shape into several relatively high ridges, before giving way to treeless steppe terrain. The highest point in the Southern Urals is the 1,638-m-high **Gora Yamantau**. South of the Byelaya river there is an undulating plateau with a large number of valleys, which descends to the **Ural River**. The **Mugodzhar Hills** are even lower, and it is here that the Urals give way to the hills and plains of Kazakhstan.

Caspian Basin, Caspian Sea

The **Caspian Basin** is a lowland area north of the **Caspian Sea** covering an area of some 200,000 sq. km at altitudes of between 28 m and 149 m. The Caspian Sea is the largest inland sea on Earth, covering an area of 371,800 sq. km.

Black Sea, Crimea

The **Black Sea** is part of the **European Mediterranean Sea**. It covers a total area of 423,000 sq. km and has extensive shelves at a depth of below 100 m in Odessa Bay and in the western part of the sea. The Black Sea is believed to have been created when a narrow land bridge that separated a shallow lake from the Bosphorus was subjected to massive rainfall. The sea finally broke through the land bridge and poured into the lake. The event is said to have happened within human existence and is the origin of the story of Noah's Flood and similar legends.

The 25,600 sq. km **Crimean Peninsula** is connected to the mainland by the 8-km-wide Perekop Isthmus. In the west, the Crimea narrows to form the **Tarchankut Peninsula**, and in the east to form the **Kerch Peninsula**. The north is characterised by flat, dry steppes dotted with salt lakes. The **Crimean Mountains** rise in the south; Roman Kosh is the highest peak at a height of 1,545 m. The northern slopes are partially forested. The southern slopes leading to the Black Sea and the narrow coastal stretch are covered in typically Mediterranean lush vegetation.

Caucasian Mountains

The land connecting the Black Sea and the Caspian Sea is an extensive mountain region with varied topography. The steppes of the **Caucasian foothills** rise to form the **Greater Caucasus**, which extend over 1,500 km and are between 32 km and 180 km wide. The area is divided from west to east into five regions. The **Pontic Mountains** have Mediterranean vegetation on the coast and deciduous woodland at a higher altitude.

The **Abkhazian Mountains** reach heights of up to 4,046 m at Mount Dombay-Ulgen, which is partly glaciated. The mountains reach their highest average elevation in the **Central Caucasus** between the two extinct volcanoes of **Elbrus** (5,642 m) and **Kazbek** (5,047 m). A total of 15 peaks in this region rise higher than 4,800 m.

In the **Caspian Caucasus**, the high mountains descend into the

Sumqayit (Sumgait) valley to form a gentle, wooded low mountain range. In the south, the Greater Caucasus terminate abruptly in the Transcaucasian Highlands. The **Lesser Caucasus** rise to the south of this divide. A lava plateau at an altitude between 1,500 m and 2,000 m lies at the heart of these mountains.

1 The Meteora Monastery in Thessaly was constructed on the steep, craggy, weathered peaks of the Pindus Mountains.

2 Surf in the Bay of Kolpos Merembellou in the east of Crete, the largest of the Greek islands.

3 Naxos is the largest of the Cyclades: this mountainous island is steep in the east, but the western half is fertile.

4 The Black Drina River rises in Lake Ohrid. The surrounding limestone formations, south of the Albanian Alps, are divided by deep ravines.

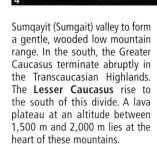

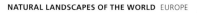

Quiver trees in Namibia:
this South African species
of aloe grows up to 10 m
high and the trunk can be
as much as 1 m thick.

Africa

The third largest continent on Earth between the Atlantic and the Indian Ocean is a compact land mass rising to an average height of 650 m. The Mediterranean and the Red Sea separate Africa from the neighbouring continents of

Europe and Asia. Basins, highlands and huge mountain ridges or uplands, characterise the African landscape. North Africa is primarily shaped by basin land-scapes with the gigantic Saharan desert covering about a third of the Af-rican land mass. Central Africa is very similar in

Victoria Falls: where the
Zambezi plunges 110 m.

terms of topography, but is covered in rain-forest, whereas highlands mostly define the face of southern Africa. The Great Rift Valley fault system is situated on the eastern side of the continent, where there are volcanoes over 5,000 m high. This is the most variable part of the continent in terms of natural geography. Few islands line the coasts, apart from the large island of Madagascar. Africa is neatly segment-ed in half by the equator, so apart from the up-lands, there are only two climates; tropical and sub-tropical.

*The wide valleys of the **Sahara** desert are known as wadis. In these valleys, when rain falls heavily, the dry river bed fills up rapidly but dries out again as soon as there is another long dry spell. The water table is near the surface, so oases are often found alongside wadis.*

The Atlas region

The **Atlas** and **Rif** mountain chains run parallel to the Mediterranean and Atlantic coasts in the north-west of the African continent, enclosing a partly fertile, partly steppe central plateau.

This plateau consists of the fertile **Sebou Basin**, the **coastal Meseta** next to the Atlantic Ocean and the barren highlands of the east Moroccan Meseta. In the north, the plateau is edged by the foothills of the **Atlas** Mountains and in the south by the **Saharan Atlas range**. The fold mountains of the Atlas-Rif system are the result of the collision of the European continental plate with the more stable African plate. This event took place in the Palaeozoic period, approximately 600 million years ago, and lasted until the Tertiary period.

Rif Mountains

The **Rif Mountains** stretch over 300 km from the **Straits of Gibraltar** to the **Cape Tres Forcas** and are composed of palaeozoic rock, which appears on the surface on the Mediterranean coast. Younger sedimentary strata cover the mountains inland. The wild and rugged peaks reach elevations of 2,448 m (**Tidighin**) and are adjacent to the **Middle Atlas** in the south.

The Atlas Mountains

The **Middle Atlas** stretches over a distance of more than 350 km and reaches an average height of 1,300 m. The eastern part, where the Middle Atlas drops in a steep escarpment, has the characteristics of a high mountain region (**Bou Naceur**, 3,340 m), whereas the western part changes into extensive high plateaus that have shifted in a stepped fashion, with protruding mountain peaks of only around 400 m.

The **High Atlas** extends over 800 km from **Cape Ghir** to the east Moroccan **Meseta**, where it branches and becomes the **Saharan Atlas**. The highest peak is the Toubkal summit (4,167 m). The range slopes away in the west and south into steep rocky cliffs up to 1,000 m high. In the north, it flattens out gently to the Meseta. In the south-east, it lies adjacent to the mountain chains of the Saharan Atlas, reaching heights of over 2,300 m.

Sahara region

The largest area of desert on Earth extends over about 12 million sq. km. The vast tableland, which is covered with sand and boulders interspersed with small oases, stretches over approximately 6,000 km along an east-west axis from the **Atlantic** to the **Red Sea** and over 2,000 km in a north-south direction as far as the Sudan.

Whereas the steppe landscape of the **Mediterranean coast** in the north only forms a narrow strip of around 100 km before merging completely with the desert, the shape of the landscape only alters gradually in the south. The semi-desert and thornbush savannah of the **Sahel** gradually change into desert in an approximately 300 m wide corridor. Only about 20 per cent of the **Sahara** is covered with sandy desert; the remaining areas are boulder and stone basins, which are covered with a layer of fine gravel (**Serirs**) on the plains and by coarse rock (**Hammadas**) on the plateaus. The stepped rims of the basins slope down to **wadis** or riverbeds, which are only filled with water after rainfall. Interior depressions, covered with huge **ergs** and closed salt lake areas (chotts), characterise other parts of the north as far as the Mediterranean coast. These interior basins extend southwards and form the **Tenere desert** and the **Libyan** and **Arabian deserts**. These areas, intersected by the **Nile Basin**, extend as far as the **Red Sea**.

The **Central Sahara** contains mountain islands and highlands, such as the **Tademait**, **Tassili** and **Djado**, ringed by high mountain ranges such as the **Ahaggar**, **Tibesti**, **Aïr**, **Iforas** and **Ennedi**. The only permanent stretch of water in the Sahara is the **Nile**. Excluding the Nile valley, about 2 million people live in the Sahara desert. They are mostly nomads and oasis farmers. The Sahara has an extreme desert climate: temperatures can reach more than 50°C during the day and sink below freezing point, even on summer nights.

Ergs

The massive dunes in the interior depressions of **West and Central Sahara**, which contain occasional high, ochre to reddish-yellow sand dunes, only occupy about one fifth of the Sahara. They have created a very definitive image of the desert, however.

The largest of these sand seas are the **Grand Erg Occidental**, which stretches over 500 km between Mauretania and the Saharan Atlas, the **Grand Erg Oriental** and the **Grand Erg du Bilma**. In addition, there are small ergs everywhere, whose drifting dunes change shape and size according to the prevailing wind, so they are continually transforming.

Ahaggar (Tassili n Ajjer)

The **Ahaggar** is the largest mountainous area in the **Central Sahara**, extending over an area of almost 300,000 sq. km.

The heart of this spectacular mountain region, which was formed about 600 million years ago and reshaped through continuous volcanic activity, is the bizarre basalt landscape of the **Atakor**, with the **Tahat** summit reaching 2,918 m. To the north and east of the Ahaggar are the

Niger

The Niger, which at 4,160 km long and with a catchment area of about 2.1 million sq. km counts as one of the longest rivers on the continent, rises in the Loma Mountains in Guinea, near the border with Sierra Leone. The river then flows in a north-easterly direction to the western Sahara and, with its tributary, the Bani, forms a large inland delta in Mali, where about 40,000 sq. km is inundated for three to six months of the year. Here the Niger loses about half of its water. It then meanders to the southeast in the Niger bend at the Upper Guinea watershed of Tosaye. At Yelwa, the Niger is stemmed by the Kainji dam. The Benue, which flows into the Niger at Lokoja, doubles the amount of water in the river, which reaches a width of between 700 m and 2,000 m at Onitsha. It finally flows in numerous branches into a delta of approximately 25,000 sq. km in the Gulf of Guinea.

Nile: this picture illustrates how much life in the surrounding desert depends on the river.

Nile

At 6,671 km, the Nile is the longest river on Earth and the most important river in Africa. It has a catchment area of approximately 3.35 million sq. km and flows from ten sources in the mountains of Burundi. It then quickly forms the Kagera, which flows into Lake Victoria after a journey of 850 km, in order to leave Uganda at Jinja as the Victoria Nile. This flows through Lake Kyoga, crosses the ridge at the eastern rim of the Central African rift via the Kabalega Falls and pours into Lake Albert. The Albert Nile, which is known as the Mountain Nile from the Sudanese border, finally reaches the marshy area of the Sudd. From here, as the White Nile it picks up the Gazelle Nile and the Sobat and joins the sediment-rich Blue Nile at Khartoum, which flows down from the Ethiopian highlands. After the confluence with the Atbara, the Nile covers the final 2,700 km as it flows through the Nubian and Libyan deserts. The first of the six famous Nile cataracts is at Aswan in Egypt. After forming a huge delta, the numerous branches of the Nile finally drain into the Mediterranean near Alexandria.

*On the edge of **Lake Chad**, which forms a type of natural border between Chad, Cameroon, Niger and Nigeria, much reed and papyrus grows. Numerous floating papyrus islands characterise further parts of the lake surface. The largest tributary to this alluvial lake is the Chari. Lake Chad is also particularly significant for its abundance of fish.*

Tassili steppes, which were formed about 250 million years ago. The sandstone strata on this high plateau have been washed away over millions of years by earlier river courses and eroded by wind and sand into unique shapes. The vast **Tassili n'Ajjer** in Algeria, containing the **Adrar** at a height of 2,158 m, looks like a fantasy moonscape.

The Tibesti Mountains, Djado Plateau

The steep gorges and bizarre weathering of the **Tibesti Mountains** in the central Sahara, which cover an area of approximately 100,000 sq. km, are one of the most impressive landscapes on the continent.

The deeply fissured high mountains jut out like a wedge with a sheer drop of about 450 m to the surrounding low plateau. The substrate of the Tibesti mountain range consists of granite and slate strata, which folded upwards in the Quaternary and Tertiary periods. In the course of these tectonic activities, several volcanoes were formed, whose cooled lava masses now sit on this substrate as mountain peaks. The massive **Emi Koussi**, which is the Sahara's highest point at 3,415 m, is one of these volcanoes. It has a diameter of 70 km at the base. Volcanic phenomena, such as fumaroles and hot springs, can also be found here. The surrounding highlands form the transition to the plateaus, including the **Djado Plateau**, which is traversed by huge wadis.

Libyan Desert

The Libyan desert in the northeastern Sahara covers an area of approximately 1.5 million sq. km. It consists of extensive tablelands with distinct tiers of strata that were separated during the Ice Age by waterways. Where the north is characterised by chalk from the Tertiary period, the south is composed primarily of sandstone. The tablelands rise in the south to several massifs and reach their highest elevation in the **Jabal al-Uwayn**at at 1,934 m. The extremely dry and inhospitable **Libyan Desert** is a gravel desert in most parts, interspersed with vast sand dunes in the

basins. From the southern slope of the **Marmarica**, the **Qattara Depression** stretches from the Siwa Oasis to the deepest point, the Qattara Basin (-133 m).

Nubian Desert

The rocky and sandy desert extending east of the **Nile** to the **Red Sea** covers about 400,000 sq. km and is uninhabited as a result of its exceptionally dry climate. The mountainous region rises in an easterly direction, reaching its highest elevation in the **coastal range** at **Jabal Oda** (2,259 m), where the incline slopes steeply to the coast.

Groundwater is only available in one dry valley in the **Nubian Desert**.

Nile Basin, Nile Delta

On its journey through the **Libyan** and the **Nubian Deserts**, the **Nile** has eroded an approximately 20-km-wide and up to 300-m-deep box canyon and forms six cataracts. Before the first of these **cataracts**, at Aswan, a 500-km-stretch of river was dammed to form the Aswan High Dam and Lake Nasser, known as Lake Nubia in the small section in the Sudan.

The extensive sedimentary deposits from the annual Nile floods are caused by the tropical monsoon rains falling on the Ethiopian Highlands which in turn feed water to the **Blue Nile**. This phenomenon has led to the formation of an extremely fertile coastal strip which widens as it flows through Egypt into the **Nile Delta**. The river branches

off into the vast Nile delta measuring approximately 24,000 sq. km. From there, the branches of the Nile, the **Rosetta** and the **Damietta** drain into the Mediterranean. This fertile area has been intensively cultivated for thousands of years and can truly be said to be the cradle of civilisation.

1 This delightful scenic route leads over the 2,260-m-high Tizi-n-Tichka Pass in Morocco's High Atlas Mountains.

2 Tafraoute, Morocco: the Anti-Atlas, lying to the south of the Atlas mountains, was formed considerably earlier than the other Atlas ranges.

3 The Wadi Dadès in Morocco's Atlas Mountains. Wadis are dry river valleys and most have steep valley walls.

4 Sahara: the Ennedi Mountains in north-eastern Chad soar to a height of 1,450 m. The plateau consists of sandstone.

Sahara

The Arabs call the large dunes of the Sahara the 'Bahr bela ma' or the 'Sea without water', as the soft rise and fall of the dune crests are reminiscent of the swell of the ocean. Alexander von Humboldt, the well-travelled natural scientist, believed in the nineteenth century that the Sahara was part of a huge desert belt, extending from the Atlantic to India.

The Sahara is the world's largest hot desert, covering over 9,000,000 sq. km an area almost as large as the United States. Only about 20 per cent of the surface of this large desert is covered with sand and a mere ten per cent of the Sahara can be described as genuine sand dunes. The aeolian shapes carved by the wind make up only a small part of this desert; most of the wealth of geological forms was and is shaped by what surface water there is.

That may sound surprising, as the Sahara is still one of the driest regions on Earth. Yet the comparatively low precipitation, which falls intermittently at the edges of

the Sahara and only rarely in the centre, has huge erosive power. The sudden torrents of rain cause flash floods, heavily eroding the stepped slopes and edges of the wadis (dry river beds) and carving deep gorges in the mountains; sand and rubble are washed into the wide dry valleys or the inner Saharan areas.

A large part of the very varied geological formations of the Sahara ultimately date from a time when the climate was wetter. Over millions of years, the region has been inundated several times and vast layers of sediment have been deposited in the basins, which are 7 km thick in places. These basins,

which are covered by stone and boulder deserts, are lined with folds where the crystalline sub-soil of the Saharan substrate has become visible. These uplifted folds were formed mainly in the centre of the Sahara and developed further through volcanic activity. The high mountains of the Ahaggar fall into this category.

The transition from the basins to the high stepped strata of the mountain regions and plateaus, such as the Tassili n Ajjer is momentous.

Bizarre sandstone rock formations in the Tassili mountains.

When Europe lay under a thick sheet of ice 1.8 million years ago, the Sahara was a fertile landscape as a result of a wet phase, known as the pluvial period. During this era, many rivers crisscrossed the steppe landscape and formed deep gorges, which are today's wadis. In the summer, large lakes

filled depressions in the landscape. The Sahara has now been a desert for approximately 40,000 years, even though shorter pluvial phases, most recently in 4,000 BC, again caused the completely arid areas to recede. The climate soon became warmer and drier again, which was how the desert began

The Ounianga Serir lake lies between the Tibesti and the Ennedi mountains.

to grow. Since then, there have been wetter and drier periods, but there is no doubt about the expanse of perpetual desert. For about 200 years, a particularly dry period has prevailed, which has intensified in the last 100 years and manifested itself as severe droughts in the southern zone, at the edge of the Sahel and in the Sahel itself. Additionally, the effect of livestock grazing has led to very evident desertification.

The north-east trade winds are a further significant force of nature that has affected the shape of the Sahara. They not only create the shifting dunes but, working in conjunction with water, they have the power to move boulders and debris. The effect of sand corrosion is particularly great in the southern Sahara, where the trade winds have an extreme effect, and this has led to the formation of strangely shaped rocky outcrops.

The hot and often sand-laden winds such as the Sirocco (known as the Ghibli in Libya), the Khamsin, the Simoom or the southerly Harmattan are also feared, as they can suddenly turn into sandstorms; these may last only a few minutes or for days on end. The Saharan winds carry the sanddust even as far as the European Alps.

Today, only a few areas in the Sahara are habitable although the area is one of the most ancient of human habitats. Archaeologists have found signs of human activity dating back 500,000 years, when the rainfall pattern allowed settlement.

Today, those who live in settled communities in the Sahara primarily inhabit the oases, which have grown up in places where favourable conditions have enabled access to the groundwater trapped in the sedimentary strata.

These desert gardens, where date palms grow in abundance and limpid pools are stocked with goldfish, are to be found primarily at the northern end of the Sahara where they create a belt of vegetation. The nomadic tribes who roam the area mostly live in the dry valleys, the highlands, plateaus with more favourable climates at the foot of the high mountains and in some of the dune landscapes that periodically contain water. Most of the inhabitants of the Sahara live around its edge, in areas such as the Sahel. It is worth noting that the different ethnic groups that live in the Sahara did not previously have a name by which to designate the whole region. They still only rarely use the Arabic word

Sunset over the mighty peaks of the Ahaggar in the South Algerian Sahara.

'sahrâ' today, which means 'yellowish' as well as 'barren'. The regional expressions for the individual landscapes that the Sahara's inhabitants employ to illustrate the variety of landscapes are symbolic. In this way, the Sahel becomes the rescuing 'shore', which is reached by travellers from the north. The Tenere desert is called the 'land out there' and the vast boulder desert of Tanezrouft 'the land of thirst'.

The variety of shapes and colours, mountains and fantastic rock formations make the Sahara into a diverse landscape, of which the sand dunes are only a small part.

Africa

*Although not far from the Equator, the summit of **Kilimanjaro** is covered in snow. Due to its immense height, the mountain massif has a variety of climates and vegetation zones. Up to a height of 3,000 m land which was previously wooded savannah, has been cleared for agricultural use. There is also mountain forest and mountain grassland, which gives way to the icy wastes of the summit.*

Sahel

The landscape of the **Sahel**, Arabic for 'shore', stretches in a 300- km-wide belt from the Atlantic coast to the **Horn of Africa**, across the whole African continent, creating a gradual transition area from the extremely dry **Sahara** and the wetland **savannah** in the south.

The Sahel consists mainly of thornbush savannah with isolated grassland that is suitable for use as grazing land for nomadic herds of livestock. However, further south, in the region of the **Niger** and **Senegal** rivers and in the area around **Lake Chad**, irrigation is possible.

Due to intensive farming and cattle-rearing, large parts of the original tree and bush vegetation have been destroyed. Overgrazing and serious drought have led to large-scale soil erosion, so that every year, several million tonnes of dust from this region is blown away – some of it ends up as far away as Europe.

Congo

The second largest river in Africa at 4,734 km, the Congo rises in the Mitumba Mountains and flows as the Lualaba across the Lunda and Central African basins, where it forms numerous rapids and lakes. The river loses only 60 m in height at the seven individual waterfalls that make up the 100 km stretch of the Stanley Falls. It flows as a lowland river 14 m wide for more than 1,700 km to Kinshasa. On its long route through the Congo basin, it absorbs many tributaries including the Lomami and the Ubangi. The Lower Guinea Basin is crossed by the Congo at Livingstone Falls (Inga Falls). Below, the valley opens up into a wide basin to the river mouth which is covered in mangrove swamp and continues as a 1,700 m deep gorge to the ocean floor in the Atlantic.

Sudan region

The area between the **Sahara** in the north and the rainforest regions in the south is around 4.5 million sq. km in size. The zone, which spreads from **Fouta Djallon** to **the Ethopian highlands** in the east, is 900 km wide on average. The difference in height is only small at 250–500 m, although in **Ouaddaï** and **Ennedi**, the plateaus that divide Niger, Chad and the White Nile basins, the elevation is greater.

The Sudan has climate and vegetation zones that are almost parallel in width. The north is covered by dry savannah, which gives way to thornbush savannah at the Sahel.

At its southern extremity, the Sudan extends into the wet savannah region.

Guinea highlands

The central **highlands of Guinea** form the western edge of the

The 3000-m-high Mulanje-Massif in the South of the Malawi lake.

Upper Guinea basin and consist of mountainous regions that overlap the **Fouta Djallon**, which rises to an altitude of approximately 1,500 m.

It reaches its greatest elevation at the northern end of the **Massif du Tamqué** (1,538 m). In the east, it turns partly into forest, partly into uplands covered in high pasture up to an altitude of around 400 m.

The **Senegal** and **Niger** rivers both have their sources in the Guinea highlands.

Niger Basin

With its tributary, the river **Bani**, the **Niger** forms a massive inland delta of around 40,000 sq. km between Ségou and Timbuktu. The delta is flooded for three to six months of the year, and leaves broad swamps that add their waters to the many smaller and larger lakes.

Chad basin

This extensive depression covers part of the **Sahara** in the north, and the **Sudan** in the south. It is surrounded by the **Tibesti** and **Ennedi** plateaus and the western edges of the **Darfur mountains** as well as the **Azande basin**, and the **Ouaddaï** highlands. The lowest point is the **Bodélé Depression** in the central south (160 m). **Lake Chad** which occupies a large proportion of the depression is a tideless lake, only 3–7 m deep, believed to be the remains of an inland sea. The circumference of the lake is constantly changing due to intense evaporation, but it is thought to be 22,000 sq. km in size today. The northern part has almost completely dried out since 1972. The only river flowing into Lake Chad is the **Chari River**, which discharges into a constantly expanding delta at the south of the lake. The shores are swamps in which reeds and papyrus flourish. On the eastern side there are many islands created by dunes. Lake Chad was once the largest lake in Africa, but that is no longer the

case, and there is a danger that it may eventualy disappear altogether due to global warming and demands on its waters.

Darfur region

This mountainous region comprises a broad, sparsely vegetated plateau, which spreads south from the **Libyan desert**, and is dominated by the volcanic highlands of the Marrah mountains in the central region. The **Darfur mountains** cover 480,000 sq. km. They consist mainly of a 600 to 1,100-m-high plateau,dominated by the Marrah mountains, which are on average 2,200 m high. This area of basalt rock rises to a peak in the Marrah at 3,088 m. The north of this sparsely-inhabited region is covered with dry savannah, while the south, in contrast, is often flooded during the rainy season.

Sudd

The swamp of the **Sudd** (Arabic for 'barrier') is an extensive floodplain of the **Nile**. It is created by the discharge of the Mountain Nile from the uplands of the **Azande basin** in a broad alluvial plain, where the river, becoming increasingly sluggish, meanders and accommodates the **Sobat River** and the **Bahr el-Ghazal** ('River of the Gazelles').

With its swamps, lagoons and side-channels, the Sudd covers an estimated area of between 100,000 and 130,000 sq. km, and is thickly overgrown with beds of reeds, papyrus and grasses. The Nile loses about 60 per cent of its water through evaporation in the Sudd, before it flows northwards as the White Nile.

Ethiopian highland

The deep **Ethiopian rift**, the continuation of the **East African rift**, divides the **Ethiopian highlands** into a western region, which stretches to the southern basin of **Lake Turkana** and falls steeply into the **Sudan**, and an eastern region, which gently slopes into the **Somali Peninsula**. The Ethiopian rift, which is interspersed with lakes and volcanoes that are still young, opens out to the north-east into the **Afar Depression**. Broad

plateaus dominate the landscape, ringed by volcanic massifs.

To the north, the Amhara highlands are riven with deep valleys. The adjacent Simien mountains reach hights of 4,620 m (Ras Dashan), while the lower Kaffa highlands stretch to the south-west. The eastern highlands are dominated by Mount Batu (4,307 m). Throughout the region, the highland escarpments and the deep river gorges (Omo, Blue Nile and Takaze) are very steep.

Somali Peninsula

This wedge-shaped peninsula, better known as the **Horn of Africa** because of its shape, is bordered to the north by the **Gulf of Aden** and to the south by the open **Indian Ocean**. The Somali Peninsula is a steep massif, dropping to the south, while to the north it slopes gradually to the sea, structured by step faults.

The highest elevation is the 2,416 m **Mount Shimbiris** in the north. Here, the coast is very steep and rocky and descends to a coastal plain up to 100 km wide. The Somali Peninsula is mainly semi-desert.

Central Africa

Central Africa consists mainly of broad plateaus, which gain height towards the east. The central **Congo basin**, which has a narrow channel to the Atlantic coast, is surrounded on all sides by deep valleys of pre-Cambrian rocks. In the west, there is the **Lower Guinea basin**, in the north the **Azande basin**, in the south the Lunda basin and in the east the margins of the **central African rift**. These scoop out the surface of the land and plunge steeply, by up to 3,000 m, at the margins. They are surrounded by huge rocky outcrops such as the Mitumba **mountains**.

The **Virunga volcanoes**, North of **Lake Kivu**, are a mountain range running east to west, with a peak at 4,507 m (**Mount Karisimbi**). The **Rwenzo Mountain range** contains the highest mountain in central Africa, the 5,109-m-high **Mount Stanley**, which is heavily

East African rifts: The African rift system was created at the end of the tertiary period, as a result of the enormous movement of the earth's crust, and is associated with intense volcanism. As a result, there are numerous cone-shaped volcanoes, such as Mount Meru and Kilimanjaro that punctuate the steppes of the East African rifts, also called Rift Valley. The steppe is a habitat for large herds of herbivores such as zebras and gnus.

glaciated around the summit. The lower slopes are grassy.

Congo basin

The landscape stretching across both sides of the Equator is drained by the **Congo River** and its tributaries, which form extensive swamps. The river basin contains an almost circular depression with a circumference of more than 1,000 km containing a lake, the **Malebo Pool,** at a height of 400 m. The area is covered in young, tertiary and quaternary sedimentary rocks.

The equatorial tropical climate of the Congo basin is covered in the largest stretch of African evergreen rainforest. The higher borderlands consist of tabular, mesozoic sandstone strata that look like a series of steps in the south, traversed by rivers and rapids.

Upper and Lower Guinea basins

The **Upper Guinea basin** runs parallel to the Atlantic coast in an east-west direction from the **Pepper Coast** to the **Niger delta.** Numerous rivers, such as the Volta river system, which cross the valley, have formed fertile alluvial plains and deltas, often reaching deep into the interior. In the **Nimba mountains,** the Upper Guinea Basin is on a plateau which reaches 1,752 m at its highest point.

The **Lower Guinea Basin** runs parallel to the Atlantic coast between **Cape Lopez** and the mouth of the **Cunene River** – a stretch of around 1,800 km. The basins rise steeply from a coastline almost 250 km long and reach heights of between 1,020 m (**Chaillu Massif**) and 2,620 m (**Moco**). Within the country, the Lower Guinea Basin slopes towards the **Congo Basin,** while they both merge into a plateau in the centre, traversed by numerous streams and rivers.

Bié Plateau

The **Bié Plateau** in the southern region of the **Lower Guinea Basin** is an almost square upland at an altitude of 1,500 m and with Mount **Moco,** rises to 2,620 m. The fertile grasslands, watered by numerous rivers, which cover a large proportion of

Angola, slope southwards to the edge of the Namibian desert. Not far from the border with Namibia, the **Cunene,** which has its source in Central Angola, cuts through the rocky outcrops and plunges 120 m at the site of the **Ruacana Waterfall.**

Muchinga Mountains, Mitumba Mountains

The **Mitumba Mountains** form the western edge of the Central African rift over 1,200 km between **Lake Tanganika** (33,000 sq. km) on the eastern border of Tanzania and the **Rwenzori**

Mountains. South of **Lake Kivu** they reach a height of over 2,400 m, then slope steeply down to the rift. The Muchinga Mountains overlook the Lunda basin highlands, at an average altitude of 1,000–1,300 m, west of the Mitumba Mountains, and rise to 1,502 m in the **Chifukunya Hills.**

East African rift system

The tectonic fault line of the East African rift system still contains active volcanos and experiences earthquakes. It stretches from the Jordan River valley in the Near East right down to the **Zambezi,** a total length of 6,000 km. It is the longest rift valley on Earth, running as far south as Mozambique in southern Africa. It is some 6,400 km long and averages 48–64 km wide. The rift has been forming for some 30 million years, as Africa and the Arabian Peninsula separate, and has produced

such massifs as Kilimanjaro and Mount Kenya. The system's main branch, the Eastern Rift Valley continues south along the Red Sea to several lakes in Kenya. It is less obvious in Tanzania, where the eastern rim has been eroded. It continues south to the Indian Ocean near Beira. The western branch terminates in Malawi.

1 In the centre of the Ngorogoro Nature Reserve there is the Ngorogoro volcano, whose crater is one of the largest on the earth with a diameter of 22 km.

2 The rocky needles at the summit of Mount Kenya are the remains of a volcanic crater.

3 Thick vegetation covers the slopes of the Rwenzori massif, which is over 5,000 m high – the highest point is covered in mist for most of the year.

4 At almost 6,000 m high, the huge Kilimanjaro massif appears to float in the distance.

Africa

*The **Etosha Plain** in the **Kalahari Desert** is dry almost throughout the year. However the smaller pools and wells that surround it provide a constant water supply to the area. They are filled from a freshwater reservoir beneath the salt plain and attract large herds of animals. During the rainy periods, the apparent desert suddenly transforms itself for a fleeting period into a green landscape. Wild animals in search of food follow the rainfall.*

The East African Rift System was formed as a result of strong movements of the earth's crust at the end of the Tertiary Era.

The **East African Rift System**, also known as the **Rift Valley**, forms the eastern part of the rift valley system. North of **Lake Turkana**, formerly known as **Lake Rudolf**, the Rift Valley continues into the **Ethiopian Rift Valley** and extends to the **Afar Depression**. It determines the shape of the landscape of large parts of Tanzania, Kenya and Ethiopia.

The western edge of the **Central African Rift Valley** is bordered by parallel faults and is an average of 40 – 50 km wide. The valleys contain finger-lakes, such as **Lake Tanganyika** which is around 650 km long, and at one point reaches 655 m below sea level; the lowest point in the African Rift Valley. Towards the south, the Central African Rift Valley continues into the **Niassa Rift**, containing **Lake Niassa** or **Malawi**.

The East African Rift Valley System marks the point at which the African continent splits and the African (Nubian) plate separates from the East African (Somalian) plate. This is most clearly illustrated in the Afar Depression (-116 m) and in a fissure in the Red Sea from which magma erupts.

Highland Lakes

In the **Ethiopian Rift Valley**, **Lake Turkana**, with an area of 8,600 sq. km, forms the closed Lake **Omo** and the **East African Rift Valley** contains a series of lakes, up to a height of 1,500 m. The **Semliki River** connects **Lake Albert** (5,300 sq. km) with **Lake Rutanzige** and **Lake Edward** (2,150 sq. km). **Lake Kivu** (2,650 sq. km), on the other hand, empties into the **Ruzizi River** which flows into Lake **Tanganyika**. **Lake Malawi** is 550 km long and covers an area of 30,800 sq. km. With a depth of 706 m, it is one of the deepest lakes on earth. It drains in the south through the Shire River into the **Zambezi**.

Between the **East African** and the **Central African Rift Valleys**, lies the vast, shallow **Lake Victoria**, which, at 69,484 sq. km is the largest lake in Africa, the largest tropical lake in the world, and the second-largest freshwater lake in the world in terms of surface area. Being relatively shallow for its size, with a maximum depth of 84 m and a mean depth of 40 m, Lake Victoria ranks as the seventh largest freshwater lake by volume.

Kilimanjaro

The volcanic massif of **Kilimanjaro** (Swahili for 'Shining Mountain') is the highest mountain in Africa. It consists of three volcanoes, Shira (4,300 m), **Mawenzi** (5,355 m) and **Kibo**. The highest point is the **Uhuru Peak** on the Kibo volcano, at a height of 5,895 m. It is the only volcano whose crater has a diameter of 2 km. The volcano is still active. Hanging glaciers about 4,300 m long flow from its snowy peaks. Beneath the glacial zone of the summit there is scree and moraine. Between 3,000 m and 4,300 m, there is a belt of trees and tall grass. Between 1,800 m and 3,000 m, cloud forests with

Victoria falls: the Zambezi plunges 110 m here.

unique varieties of flora and fauna cover the slopes; dry savannah is found below this point. Kilimanjaro was declared a National Park in 1971.

Mount Kenya

This volcano, just south of the equator, has been extinct for a long time. It is the highest mountain in Kenya and the second-highest in Africa. It has a base circumference of 153 km. The highest of the heavily eroded peaks are the **Batian** (5,200 m), the **Nelion** (5,188 m) and the **Lenana** (4,985 m).

Grasslands extend up to a height of around 3,200 m, above which there is dense rainforest, that turns into alpine vegetation at a height of 4,600 m. Above this, there is a lava field which is covered by glaciers at the summit.

Serengeti

The Serengeti is a wide savannah dotted with clumps of trees. It is at an altitude of 1,500 to 1,800 m in the highlands, south-east of Lake Victoria which occupies almost half the total area of the Serengeti. The south-east of the vast grassland, whose name in the Masai language means 'endless plains', has some afforestation along the river banks in the west. Umbrella acacias, typical of the African tree steppes, are found here. The Serengeti, which has one of the highest populations of wild game on earth, is the heartland of the Serengenti National Park in Tanzania. The Serengeti became legendary as a result of the migration of the massive herds of animals. In May and June, when the rainfall dwindles and the grassy plains have been grazed, thousands upon thousands of gnus, zebras and gazelles, followed by lions, hyenas, cheetahs as well as numerous species of birds move north-westwards, to the Masai-Mara National Reserve in south Kenya in search of water.

In the autumn, the big herds return once more to the short grass steppes of the Serengeti.

South Africa

The **South African interior** is dominated by a series of undulating plateaus, extending from the Cape Province to central Angola. The **South African Plateau** is part of this area as are the neighbouring **highlands of Zambia** and **Zimbabwe**, the **Niassa Plateau** and the **Manica Plateau** in the north-east.

The coastlines are characterised by mountain ranges and coastal plains. Such coastal mountains and escarpments are found in the **Mulanje Mountains** (3,000 m), the **Lebombo Mountains** and in the **Dragon Mountains** as well as in **Namibia**. Coastal plains are only found in **Mozambique** and in **Namibia**.

The **Kalahari Basin** forms the central depression of the South African plateau. It rises to the edge of the plateau up to the **Great Escarpment**, which accompanies the **Zambezi** plateau to Angola. Here it separates the interior from the arid coastal regions. This escarpment arose as a result of an uplift and now forms the **Dragon Mountains**, the **Stormberg**, the Sneeuberg and the **Nuweveld Mountains**. Some of the mountain ranges in this escarpment were formed by Mesozoic lava deposits.

Namib

This cold desert, whose very name means 'the empty desert', extends for a length of around 1,800 km between Port Nolloth and Namibe along the Atlantic coast. Its east-to-west width varies from 80 km to 130 km, until it meets the foot of the **Great Escarpment**. It has an area of around 50,000 sq. km. The **Kunene Region** in the north consists of a series of isolated mountains, whose highest peak is the **Brandberg Mountain** (2,579 m).

The extreme dryness is caused by the Benguela Current, which frequently produces a sea-mist. Other areas of the north are covered by pebbles and gravel and become the **Kalahari Desert**. This area is almost devoid of vegetation, while the central desert is characterised by wide stretch of dunes, which can reach a height of 300 m.

Kalahari

The dry basin landscape consists of an area of around 800,000 sq. km and consists of broad highland areas, covered by the largest continuous stretches of sand on earth. The large dunes typical of the western end, have mostly existed since the Ice Age. The only peaks in the otherwise endlessly flat dry savannah, which is 900 m high, are isolated rocky outcrops. The **Kalahari** contains numerous salt pans and the remains of glacial lakes, among them the **Makgadikgadi Pan** and the **Etosha Pan**, two of the largest on Earth. In the north, the swampy **Okavango Basin** periodically feeds the Boteti river system when conditions permit.

Okavango-Basin

The **Okavango River** springs from the **Bié Highland**, and after around 1,800 km seeps into a basin in the northern **Kalahari**. Here it forms a 240-km-wide inland delta with several branches and lagoons.

This vast marshy region, which is almost completely flooded during the rainy season extends over an area of around 16,800 sq. km. The marshland is covered in dense beds of reeds and papyrus; at the higher altitudes, there is forest and savannah.

The inland delta is the habitat of many different types of animals. During the dry season elephants, gnus, zebras, antelopes and buffaloes migrate into the savannahs. Various species of birds, such as ospreys, cormorants and cranes live in the swamps.

Zambezi-Basin (Victoria falls)

The **Zambezi River** emerges from **Luanda** and flows through Angola and western Zambia,

*The **Okavango** flows – unusually – not into another river or into open water, but sinks into the sand sea of the Kalahari. The Okavango delta is one of the most impressive landscapes in the world. The delta stretches over 17,000 sq. km and is a swamp area containing a rich variety of flora and fauna.*

forming the border between Zimbabwe and Zambia. At Maramba, the river, now 1,700 m wide, leaves the highland and thunders down into a ravine, 110 m deep and 50 m wide, at right angles to the direction of flow. This is the **Victoria Falls**.

In the **Tete Basin**, the Zambezi reaches the **Mozambique Lowlands** and finally, after a total of 2,736 km, forms a delta with its tributary the **Shire**, which is around 5 km widle, before it flows into the Indian Ocean.

South African Highland

The **South African Highland**, the centre of which has wide plains and undulating plateaus, is subdivided into three different regions: the **High Veld** (1,200 to 1,800 m), which covers the southern Cape Plateau (up to 1,855 m) and includes the **Basotho Highland**; the transition zone of the **Middle Veld** which is over 600 m high and covers large parts of the South African highland; and the hilly area of the **Low Veld**, which adjoins the flat coastal plain in the eastern **Transvaal**.

The most important waterway is the **Orange River**, whose tributaries are the **Caledon** and Vaal in the highlands. It finally drains into the **Atlantic**.

Karoo

The desert and semi-desert known as the **Karoo** form a series of basins, which extend between the **great escarpment** and the **Cape Mountains** at a height of 300–900 m. The region is split into the **Great Karoo** in the south and the **Little Karoo** in the west. This area of 395,000 sq. km covers almost a third of the Republic of South Africa, and consists of dry savannahs.

Dragon Mountain

In the **Dragon Mountains** in the **Natal**, the eastern part of the **Great Escarpment** forms a spectacular vertical rock face, rising to up to 1,000 m high. The hilly area known as **Little Berg**, which is between 1,800 and 2,000 m high, is situated close to this steep drop. The Natal-Dragon Mountains consists of massive sand-

stone strata, which are overlapped by layers of basalt and diabase. Geologically much older rocks ,such as dolomite and quartzite, form the Great Escarpment in the **Transvaal's Dragon mountains**, which rise to 2,286 m. The highest peaks are the **Thabana-Ntlenyana** (3,482 m) and the **Champagne Castle** (3,376 m).

Madagascar

The fourth largest island on the planet is separated from the east coast of Africa by the 400-km-

wide **Mozambique Channel**. It is 587,041 sq. km in area.

Over the central mountainous region which is approximately 800–1,600 m high, increasing in height in an easterly direction, there are individual island mountains and mountain massifs of volcanic origin. **Maromokotro** (2,886 m) is the highest peak. Due to the tropical climate, the **Andringitra Mountains (Pic Boby**, 2,656 m) in the south of the island has been attractively weathered.

Towards the east, the highlands drop steeply towards the coast, while in the west, at a lower altitude it becomes a relatively wide coastal plain divided by bays. There are off-shore coral reefs. This asymmetry matches the watershed, which is near the eastern edge, with the larger rivers to the west such as the **Betsiboka**. Madagascar is famous for its extensive rainforests, inhabited by several species of fauna, such as lemurs that are unique to the is-

land. The drier south-western part of the island is covered by thorn-bush savannah.

The Manambolo river has created deep canyons and gorges and has some spectacular waterfalls as it meanders through the jungle that surrounds it. The west coast has many protected harbours and broad plains.

1 The giant dunes of the Namibian desert can reach an altitude of 300 m.

2 The Ugab Terraces at the border of the South African interior Highlands: several table mountains and canyons were formed through erosion east of the southern Namib.

3 The Blyde River, a tributary of the Olifants River, cuts through the dolomite limestone of the South African Draken mountains.

4 The symbol of Cape Town is the 1,092-m-high Table Mountain, rising at the Cape of Good Hope.

Main photograph:
The vertical cliff towers of
Guilin, southern China, are
an excellent example of
karst topography.

Asia

Asia is the largest continent on Earth. Its huge variety of impressive landscapes range from the Arabian Peninsula to the Siberian lowlands, and from the 8,000-m-high mountains of the Himalayas to the tropical karst topography and

Mount Everest: the highest mountain in the world.

rainforests of south-east Asia. Mountains, plateaus, basins and lowlands are all intermingled in no apparent order.

Many of Asia's most impressive landscapes have been formed by plate tectonics. The Himalayas were created by the folding of the Earth's crust 25 million years ago when the Indian subcontinent collided with the great continent of Eurasia. The mountains and islands along the Pacific coast are also characterised by tectonic activity. It is here that the Pacific and Philippine plates are pushing beneath the Eurasian plate, causing volcanic activity, a process known as subduction.

Asia

*The **Aral Sea** between Kazakhstan and Uzbekistan, which is slightly brackish, once contained many fish. This inland sea was once the fourth largest lake in the world, but the water level has been steadily dropping in recent years.*

The effect of low precipitation and high evaporation had an effect, but the main problem is that both the rivers that feed the lake, the Amu Darya and Syr Darya, have been dammed for irrigation purposes.

West Siberian Plain and North Siberian Lowland

The fertile **West Siberian Plain** between the Ural Mountains and the Yenisei River is one of the largest areas of lowland on Earth, covering 2.6 million sq. km. The plain continues north of the Central Siberian Plateau as the North Siberian Lowland, which consists largely of moorland.

The great Ob, Irtysh, Yenisei, Lena, Aldan and Kolyma rivers flow through both regions.

The **West Siberian Plain** has several particularly distinct zones of vegetation. Tundra and permafrost cover the far north, replaced further south by the taiga. Next comes an area of forest steppe, followed by grassland steppe landscape to the south.

Central Siberian Plateau

A flat, undulating plateau rises between the **Yenisei** and **Lena** rivers and is bordered to the north by the North Siberian Lowland, and to the south by the **Eastern Sayan Mountains**. It covers an area of some 3.5 million sq. km. The plateau has an average altitude of 700 m and contains numerous lakes. To the north-west, the region rises to the **Putorana Plateau** at a height of up to 1,701 m.

Lake Baikal

Lake Baikal has a surface area of 32,500 sq. km, making it the largest mountain lake in Asia and one of the biggest freshwater lakes, by volume, on Earth. It also has one of the largest fish populations for its size. The lake is 636 km long and 79 km wide and is surrounded by densely forested mountains – the **Baikal Mountains** in the west, the **Chamar-Daban** in the south and the **Barguzin Mountains** in the east. The lake is 455 m above sea level, and its greatest depth is 1620 m, making it the deepest lake on Earth. It is fed by 336 tributaries, but the only outlet is the river **Angara**. The only large island is **Olkhon**, with an area of 730 sq. km. Lake Baikal was formed 60 million years ago in the Palaeogene Period and has some unique endemic wildlife.

Mountains of Eastern Siberia

The **mountains of Eastern Siberia** form a broad arc east of the middle and lower courses of the Lena River. The vast curve of the Verkhoyansk Range enclose the basins of the Kolyma, Yana and Indigirka rivers, an area of marshes and lakes.

The interior of this semi-circle of mountains contains high peaks such as the **Chersky Range** and low mountain ranges such as the Oymyakon Plateau. On the Pacific coast, the **Koryak Mountains** (rising to 2,562 m) merge almost seamlessly into the mountain chains of the Kamchatka Peninsula. The **Sikhote-Alin mountain system** follows the coastline south to the Sea of Japan.

Verkhoyansk Range

The **Verkhoyansk Range** in the inhospitable Sakha region in the far north-east of Russia extends in a wide arc over 1,100 km, parallel to the Lena River in the west. The mountains extend as far as the Laptev Sea. This fold mountain range has an average height of 1,000 m and a maximum height of 2,389 m. The terrain is covered in tundra vegetation, mainly mosses and lichens and is virtually uninhabited.

Chersky Range

These mountains in north-eastern Siberia stretch for 1,500 km from the lower reaches of the Yana River to the upper reaches of the **Kolyma**. The highest point is **Pobeda Peak** at 3,147 m. The chains of this highly structured fold mountain range are mainly composed of metamorphic rocks and sandstone, in which numerous rivers have carved out deep gorges and valleys. Parts of the range are covered in imposing glaciers. Forests of larches cover the slopes at medium to high altitudes.

Kolyma Mountains

This mountain chain in north-eastern Siberia has a total length of approximately 1,300 km, consisting several isolated massifs and ridges. The **Kolyma Mountains** are the watershed between the **Arctic Ocean** and the **Pacific**. Larch forests grow on the lower slopes; the higher altitudes (up to heights of 1,962 m) are covered in mountain tundra.

Kamchatka Peninsula

This peninsula is 1,200 km long and stretches between the Bering Sea and the Sea of Okhotsk. It is one of the most significant volcanic regions on Earth. A structured chain of mountains extend from north to south down the whole of the western side of **Kamchatka**. The highest point is the **Itchinskaya Sopka** volcano (3,621 m). The central part of the

Tigris and Euphrates

The **Tigris** covers a length of 1,950 km, rising in the East Taurus Mountains and flowing south-east through Iraq. Several large tributaries join the river from the east. At Kut, the Shatt al-Hai branch of the river begins to flow south. At Amara, the Tigris becomes a huge swamp, home of the Marsh Arabs and providing a unique flora and fauna.

The **Euphrates**, including the headwaters, the Murat, flows over a total distance of 3,380 km. It rises in the East Anatolian Plateau as the Kara and Murat Rivers, which merge at the Keban Reservoir. The river then passes through the uplands of Syria and Iraq down through southern Iraq, before merging into the Tigris to form the Shatt al-Arab, which drains into the Persian Gulf.

Lake Baikal has a depth of 1,620 m, making it the world's deepest lake. It also has one of the largest quantities of water and fish stocks.

Lena, Ob, Irtysh, Yenisei

The **Lena** rises in the Baikal Mountains at a height of 930 m and flows through a narrow valley that slowly broadens out. After 1,450 km, the river is joined by the Vitim. The Lena flows into the Central Yakut Plain, where it is joined by the Aldan. After some 4,400 km, the river opens into the Laptev Sea in a large delta that covers approximately 30,000 sq. km. The **Ob** is the main river of the West Siberian Plains and is formed by the confluence of the Katun and Bija Rivers, both flowing down from the Altai Mountains. In the lower reaches of the river, it divides to form two branches, the Greater and Lesser Ob, which reunite after approximately 460 km. After 3,650 km (if the largest tributary, the Irtysh, is included, the total length is 5,410 km) the Ob opens into the Kara Sea in the Gulf of Ob, which is 900 km long and 30-90 km wide. It is only free of ice for short periods of the year. The fertile Ob Basin covers 85 per cent of the West Siberian Plain. Including its tributaries and branches, the Ob has a drainage basin covering 2.975 million sq. km.

The **Irtysh** rises in the glaciers on the south-west slopes of the Altai and flows west through Lake Saissan, joining the Ob near Khanty-Mansijsk after 4,248 km. The **Yenisei** is formed by the confluence of the Greater and Lesser Yenisei Rivers which rise near the Mongolian border and flow north. After 4,130 km, the Yenisei opens into the Kara Sea in the 435 km-long Gulf of Yenisei. All of the rivers are frozen for between five and eight months of the year, and 80 per cent of the outflow is produced in summer.

*The **Dead Sea**, a terminal or sink sea between Israel and Jordan, has a salt concentration of 28 per cent, one of the highest in the world. Only certain species of algae and micro-organisms can live in it. The sea was formed by a trench and has a maximum depth of 400 m, making it the deepest basin on Earth. Irrigation in the surrounding areas, reducing the amount of water fed into it by the river Jordan, has led to a reduction in the water level of the sea.*

peninsula is up to 450 km wide. Another mountain chain on the eastern side of the peninsula runs parallel to the western chain. These mountains contain 160 volcanoes. The highest of the 29 active volcanoes is the **Klyuchevskaya Sopka** (4,750 m). The steep cliffs of the **Kamchatka Valley**, irrigated by the Kamchatka River lie between the two partially glaciated chains. The valley is dominated by taiga vegetation. In the east, the mountains drop down to a marshy coastal plain.

Sikhote-Alin

This mountain system is 1,200 km long and 250 km wide. It runs parallel to the coast from the **mouth of the Amur River** in the north to the southern tip of the **Murvyov-Amursky Peninsula** in the south.

The mountains have an average height of 800 m and comprise several low mountain chains, divided from each other by deep valleys. The chain sits on a bedrock of sandstone, schist and basalt, and the highest point is Anik Mountain (1,933 m). The mountains drop steeply down to the Sea of Japan.

Anatolia

The Anatolian region extends between the Black Sea and the Mediterranean and is divided from the European mainland by the **Sea of Marmara** and the narrow **Bosphorus**.

Extensions of the **Taurus** and **Pontic Mountains** surround the **Anatolian Plateau**, which becomes the **Armenian Highland**. This is bordered by the **Lesser Caucasus** in the north, and by the **Taurus Mountains** in the south. To the south, the Euphrates and the Tigris supply water to a fertile basin, bordered to the east by the **Zagros Mountains**, which in turn descend into the desert terrain of the **Iranian Uplands**.

Anatolian Plateau

The plateau runs along the Black Sea coast from the **Pontic Mountains** and continues parallel to the Mediterranean coast, surrounded by the **Taurus Mountains**, which rise in the east. The plateau descends towards the coast to form fertile plains. The highest peak is **Mount Ararat** at a height of 5,165 m.

The Anatolian Plateau is traversed by numerous rivers (the most important are the Euphrates and the Tigris). The area close to the Taurus Mountains contains numerous terminal lakes, including **Lake Van** at an altitude of 1,646 m.

Taurus Mountains

The **Taurus Mountain system** belongs to the Anatolian fold mountain belt and is composed mainly of limestone and metamorphic rocks, which in places are covered by a young volcanic stratum. The highest mountain in the range is **Buzul Dagı** (4,168 m). The volcanic mass of **Mount Erciyes** (3,916 m) developed to form the tufa walls and peaks of the **Goreme**.

Mesopotamia

Mesopotamia literally means the land 'between two rivers'. The region extends between the middle and lower courses of the **Euphrates** and **Tigris** rivers. It is a fertile basin, provided with ample water by the numerous tributaries and branches of the two rivers. The marshy and silt-covered mouth is dotted with lakes.

Arabian Peninsula

The Arabian Peninsula is the largest peninsula in Asia, covering an area of 3.5 million sq. km. It is a desert plateau which rises to a height of up to 3,000 m and is interspersed with wadis. The **Red Sea** separates the Arabian Peninsula from the continent of Africa. In the west, the long depression, formed by **Mesopotamia** and the Persian Gulf, forms the border with the fold mountains of northern Iran (the **Zagros Mountains**), which extend down to the far southeastern tip of the peninsula at Jabal ash-Sham (3,017 m).

The highest point on the peninsula is in the south-west (Jabal an-Nabi Shu'ayb, 3,760 m), but the mountains then drop steeply to the Red Sea. To the north, the mountains slope down more gradually in several stages. The large depression in the interior of the peninsula is covered by sandy desert and dunes.

Najd

This plateau in the north-east of the Arabian peninsula is mainly

1 Anatolia: Cappadocia's impressive landscape of strange columns and towers has been created by the erosion of soft tufa stone, interspersed with harder rocks.

2 Taurus: hot springs flow over the limestone terraces at Pamukkale. The deposits formed by the high mineral content of the water have created a staggered basin.

3 The tiny settlement of Shaharah in the north of Yemen sits at an altitude of 2,450 m. Foothills of the mountains along the Arabian Peninsula reach a height of 3,000 m.

Himalayas

Seen from the south, the Himalayas form a huge arc stretching across the top of the Indian sub-continent. The steep, thrusting mountain system contains several of the world's highest mountains and is the subject of countless myths and legends among the local peoples living in its shadow. The name 'Himalaya' derives from Sanskrit, meaning 'the snow abode'.

The Himalayas consists of four mountain chains running parallel to each other. These are the Sub-Himalayan Range, also known as the Siwalik Hills, the Lower Himalayan Range and the Great Himalayas. The fourth and most northerly mountain chain, the Gangdise Shan, is separated from the Great Himalayas by an immense valley formed by the Brahmaputra River and has peaks reaching a height of more than 7,000 m. Vast snowfields and glaciers cover some 17 per cent of the mountains and extend as far as the lower valleys, where they feed the sources of Asia's

largest rivers, the Brahmaputra, the Ganges and the Indus. The Himalayas system contains a total of 19 rivers, some of which flow south and leave the mountain system in deep gorges with sheer cliff walls that can tower up to 5 km into the sky. The immense size of the Himalayas mean that they also form a significant climate and vegetation divide. The mountains act like a wall, blocking the cold air from the north of the continent, which would otherwise provide cooler temperatures all the way to the south of the Indian sub-continent. At the same time, the mountain barrier

prevents the significant precipitation of the summer monsoon from moving northwards. Instead, the rain only affects the southern mountain slopes, and the Tibetan Plateau to the north is one of the driest regions on Earth. The southern slopes of the Himalayas are covered in lush rainforest and cloud forest, but the northern slopes are dominated by dry, alpine steppes. In the upper regions, the alpine climate gives way to a polar climate, and hurricane force winds howl over the glaciers.

It is hard to imagine that the highest mountains on Earth were

once a layer of sediment on the ocean floor, but proof comes in the form of fossilised mussel shells and other sea creatures that can be found at an altitude of several kilometres. The Himalayas are a relatively young range of alpidic fold mountains.

The story of their creation began 60 million years ago when the Indian continental plate, drifting at a speed of several centimetres a year, began to slide under the Eurasian Plate. Between 55 and 40 million years ago, a fracture formed at the site of this collision in the crust of the Indian Plate. The crust pushed further north below the sinking fracture paths and began to subduct, while the fractured layer of crust was pushed south on to the Indian sub-continent. Approximately 30 million years ago, a new fracture formed much deeper in the crust and this layer was also pushed on to the Indian sub-continent. The Himalayas began to form at the subduction zone and are still growing today at a rate of a

The lake at the foot of Cho-latse, south-west of Mount Everest, is fed by glacial water.

couple of millimetres a year. This folding process is far from complete, and the region is regularly affected by landslides, accompanied by powerful earthquakes. It is possible to imagine that Mount Everest may one day be higher than 9,000 m, but only if the mountain grows faster than the eroding forces of wind, rain, frost and ice wear it down. It is these substantial erosive powers that have formed the jagged and pointed mountain silhouettes to create the astounding raw beauty of the region.

The people living here believe that the eternally snow-covered peaks are the home of the gods. At the beginning of the twentieth century, climbers began to attempt to conquer the mountains in these remote regions, despite the fact that the area had hardly been mapped. It was not until the 1950s that news spread around

the world that the peaks had been climbed successfully for the first time. Thanks to improved equipment, a French expedition in 1950 was the first to reach the summit of Annapurna I at an altitude of over 8,000 m. After that, new peaks were conquered every year. Even the slopes of the notoriously challenging Kanchenjunga were climbed in 1955. The last of the major peaks to be reached was Sishapangma, which was eventually conquered by a Chinese expedition in 1964.

Thin air, icy cold and sudden changes in weather conditions remain a danger to mountaineers to this day, despite huge advances in equipment and clothing in recent decades. Since Sir Edmund Hillary and Sherpa Tensing Norgay first reached the top of Mount Everest in 1953, approximately 700 climbers have mastered the peak. More than 150

people have lost their lives in the attempt, either on the ascent or during the descent. At least 20 have died on the mountainside in the last few years alone.

All of the world's mountains over 8,000 m are located in the Himalayas and the connecting mountain chains. These are Mount Everest (8,863 m), K2 (8,611 m), Kanchenjunga (8,586 m), Lhotse (8,511 m), Makalu (8,481 m), Dhaulagiri (8,167 m), Manaslu (8,156 m), Cho Oyu (8,153 m), Nanga Parbat (8,126 m), Annapurna I (8,091 m), Gasherbrum I (8,068 m), Gasherbrum II (8,035 m), Broad Peak I (8,047 m) and Sisha Pangma (8046 m).

Nepal: the impressive peaks of the Annapurna massif even block the path of the clouds.

Main photograph: Mount Everest, the highest mountain on Earth.

1 The Karakoram Mountains in Pakistan include K2 which rises to 8,611 m.

2 Tibet: the Rongbuk glacier flows through the valleys of Mount Everest.

3 View of Makalu from Mount Everest.

Asia

*The Mongolian **Altai** is the highest mountain chain in Mongolia and one of the country's greatest natural wonders. The chain is approximately 1,000 km long and up to 4,362 m high. The impressive Altai mountain system also extends through Russia and the Gobi Desert, where the slopes can reach a height of up to 4,000 m.*

covered by stony and sandy desert and is enclosed by **Jabal Tuwaik** and **Jabal Shammar**, after which the land in the east descends to a sandy desert. The Al-Aramah Plateau is in the centre of this barely inhabited region.
The **Najd** lies at an altitude of between 600 m and 1000 m and is the most populated part of the peninsula, thanks to its numerous oases and wadis.

Rub al Khali

The **Great Arabian Desert** whose name in Arabic means 'Empty Quarter', covers 780,000 sq. km, making it the largest continuous stretch of sand on Earth. The desert is 1,500 km across and contains sand dunes up to 300 m high. The climate is extremely dry and there are almost no oases.

Elburz Mountains

This range of fold mountains lies south of the **Caspian Sea** in northern Iran and forms the climate and vegetation divide between the desert landscape of the **Iranian Highlands** and the coastal landscape around the Caspian. The highest peak is **Damavand** at a height of 5,670 m. On the south side of the mountains there is a dry area of mountain steppe. The northern face of the mountains is wetter and is covered in mountain forests and areas of grassland.

Iranian Highland

The highlands and the surrounding mountains are part of the Alpidic mountain chain that runs through Europe and Asia and divides here to form a northern branch, the **Elburz Mountains**, and a southern branch, the **Zagros Mountains**. The interior of the highlands is a basin with no outlets, dissected by mountain ranges. There are large inland deserts, the **Lut Desert** and the **Great Salt Desert**. The mountains in the north and west are volcanic and the area is subject to powerful earthquakes; a sign of the regions continuing tectonic activity.

Zagros Mountains

This young Alpidic fold mountain range divides the Iranian High-land from the southern basin of the Euphrates and Tigris lowlands. The mountain range is about 1,200 km long and extends from the mountains of Armenia to the **Gulf of Oman**. The peaks can rise to altitudes of over 4,500 m, and are interspersed with wide, shallow high-altitude valleys.

'The Roof of the World'

The massive arc of the most impressive and highest mountain system in the world extends for more than 2,500 km and forms a climate and vegetation divide between the **Indian Sub-continent** and the **Tibetan Plateau**. The range contains most of the highest mountains on Earth. The **Himalayas** are young alpidic fold mountains. They formed at the northern edge of the Indian Continental Plate, which collided with the Eurasian Plate approximately 60 million years ago, pushing this plate upwards from

Tibetan Plateau: the ruined Phuntsoling monastery in Central Tibet.

beneath at a speed of a couple of centimetres a year. The folding process began about 20 million years ago, and the Himalayas are continuing to grow. The **Hindu Kush, Karakorams** and **Pamirs** in the north-west all belong to this mountain system.

Pamirs, Hindu Kush, Karakorams

The highest mountain of the **Pamirs** is **Ismail Samani Peak** (7,495 m), formerly known as Communism Peak. The steep mountain folds are covered in a desert landscape and there are broad high valleys in the interior. The **Hindu Kush** is about 700 km long and heavily glaciated. The range has 20 peaks of over 7,000 m, the highest of which is the 7,690-m-high **Tirich Mir**. The **Karakorams** have four peaks of over 8,000 m, including **K2** (8,611 m), the second highest mountain on Earth.
More than a third of these mountains are covered in glaciers. The **Siachen** and **Baltoro Glaciers** contain some of the largest floes of ice outside the Arctic regions.

Himalayas

The main mountain system of the **Himalayas** is divided into four chains with steep mountain folds. The highest of these is the **Great Himalayas**, which have a maximum distance from north to south of 250 km. Nine of the world's 14 peaks rising over 8,000 m are found in this chain. To the south lies the **Lower Himalayan Range** with altitudes of about 4000 m and broad valleys. This range joins the **Sub-Himalayan Range**, also known as the Siwalik Hills, which descend to the plains of the Indus River. To the north, the **Brahmaputra River** divides the Great Himalayas from the Gangdise Shan.

Gangdise Shan

The mountain range is over 1,000 km long, with a maximum altitude of 7,088 m (**Nyainqen-tanglha Feng**). The **Gangdise Shan** only joins the **Great Hi**malayas in the west. The region has particularly low precipitation and is largely covered in steppe terrain. Only the southern slopes of the mountains are glaciated, the gentle northern slopes have a desert landscape.

Tibetan Plateau

The Tibetan Plateau is both the largest and highest plateau in the world, covering 2 million sq. km with an average altitude of 4,500 m. It is surrounded by a barrier of mountains 7,000 m to 8,000 m high. The dry and inhospitable plateau is intersected by a small number of mountain chains, and the areas in between are covered in gravel deposits or salt lakes. The north and west of the plateau is mainly gravel and scree desert, while high steppes and tree steppes are found in the east. The area to the south of the Gangdise Shan forms a trench at an altitude of just 3,600 m, and this is where most of the Tibetan people live.

Tarim Basin

This endorheic drainage basin is surrounded by the **Tian Shan, Kunlun Shan, Altun Shan** and **Pamir** mountains. It stretches from west to east over a distance of 1,500 km, and is up to 650 km wide. The altitude drops from 1,400 m in the west, to approximately 800 m in the east. The lowest point (780 m) is dominated by **Lop Nur**, a dried-up salt lake covering an area of about 25,000 sq. km.
The region has a harsh, arid continental climate. A large expanse of the **Tarim Basin** (272,000 sq. km) is covered by the **Takla-makan Desert**, with its immense sand dunes. Tributaries entering the basin from the surrounding mountains disappear or end in salt flats at the edges of this desert. The **Tarim River** only provides enough water to supply a small number of oases in the north of the desert.

Kunlun Shan, Tian Shan, Nan Shan

The **Kunlun Shan** is a late Triassic fold mountain system that stretches for more than 3,000 km and forms the northern border of the Tibetan Plateau. The Western Kunlun Shan joins the Pamirs and reaches a height of 7,546 m (**Muztagh Ata**), before dividing into two chains in the east. The Central Kunlun contains the heavily glaciated **Ulug Muztagh** (7,723 m) and the **Burhan Budai Mountains** (7,720 m). The mountain valleys contain numerous sink salt lakes. Tectonic valleys divide the chain from the Eastern Kunlun, which gradually rise to the **Qin Ling** in the east.
The **Tian Shan** stretch over 2,500 km and are bordered on all sides by deserts and semi-deserts (**Gobi Desert, Dzungaria Desert**). The mountain chain is interspersed with numerous streams and mountain valleys (**Turpan Basin**, 154 m below sea level at its lowest point) and is composed of Precambrian and Palaeozoic rock. The highest point is **the Pobeda Peak** at 7,439 m.
The **Nan Shan** is a series of high alpidic chains, with deep valleys and numerous endorheic basins, salt lakes and marshes.

Gobi Desert

This immense basin in the heart of Asia extends for some 2,000 km and has an area of approximately 1.3 million sq. km. It is surrounded by mountains on all sides. The low foothills of the **Mongolian Altai Mountains** extend far into the **Gobi Desert**, which lies at an altitude of approximately 1,000 m. Only the south-west consists of pure sandy desert (**Badain Jaran Desert**, 47,000 sq. km, **Tengger Desert**, 36,000 sq. km), the rest is steppe terrain. Water drains from the north-east, via the **Kerulen**, to the **Amur** river. The most important river is the **Etsin Gol**, which provides water for the oases in the valley.

Mongolia

This area of Central Asia is dominated in the west by the **Altai Mountains,** with altitudes of up to 4,300 m, and the **Khangai Mountains** (over 3,500 m). Plateaus at a height of 1,000 m to

Pacific Ring of Fire

The Central Oceanic Ridge is one of the main forces driving continental plate movement. Deep sea magma flows out of the side of this ridge, pushing the surrounding plates away from each other as it hardens at a speed of approximately 2 cm per year in the Atlantic and up to 18 cm per year in the South Pacific.

Magma rising from the centre of the Earth to the ocean floor forms approximately 2.5 cu. km to 3 cu. km of new oceanic crust each year. Simultaneously, the same amount of oceanic crust is forced deep underground and re-melted in the deep sea trenches at the edges of the continental plates.

Molten lava can often break through the Earth's crust at the site of these subduction zones, forming volcanoes. The arrangement of volcanoes on the Earth is by no means random. The area around the Pacific Plate alone contains some two-thirds of the 600 active volcanoes on Earth. A ring of fire covering 32,500 km and consisting of volcanic island chains and belts of volcanoes encircles the Pacific Ocean. It stretches from the Antarctic Peninsula, over Tierra del Fuego to the huge volcanic mountain chains of the Southern and Central American Cordillera.

The arc of islands that extends from the volcanoes of Alaska and across the Aleutian Islands marks the northern edge of the Pacific Plate. This string of islands continues on to the Kamchatka Peninsula in Siberia and the Kuril Islands. It is here that the Pacific Plate pushes below the Eurasian Plate. The series of volcanoes continues with further island chains, stretching from Japan to Taiwan and south to the Mariana Islands. This marks the border between the Pacific Plate and the relatively small Philippine Plate, which is itself surrounded by three further plates. The edges of the Philippine Plate form the particularly active chains of volcanoes in Indonesia and the Philippines.

The volcanic ring ends along the edge of the Indo-Australian Plate with the volcanoes of Melanesia and Fiji in the South Pacific, New Zealand and some sub-Antarctic islands. This massive Pacific Ring of Fire does not merely create volcanoes, which can suddenly spring back to life after centuries of lying dormant, 95 per cent of the world's earthquakes also originate here. Undersea activity off the coast of Indonesia caused the tsunami of December, 2004.

Main photograph: an eruption on the Kamchatka Peninsula in Eastern Siberia.

1 New Zealand: the volcanic White Island is one of a chain of active volcanoes that extends to Mount Ruapehu.

2 Mount Fuji: Japan's highest volcano is currently dormant.

*The **Yangtze Jiang,** the 'long river', rises in the Tibetan Plateau and flows into the sea at Shanghai after 6,300 km. Much of the river is navigable and is of great economic importance for China.*

The fascinating landscape of this river includes the Three Gorges in the provinces of Sichuan and Hubei. Tiger Leaping Gorge is situated on the border between Tibet and Yunnan.

1,500 m cover the east of the country. The north-east is covered in taiga vegetation. The rest of the region is dominated by mountain deserts and steppe vegetation, bounded in the south by the **Gobi Desert.** Four-fifths of the region consists of steppe and pastureland. The most important river is the **Selenga.**

Dzungaria

This tectonic trough between the **Mongolian Altai** and the **Eastern Tian Shan** is bordered by the **Gobi Desert** in the east. The border in the west consists of several mountain chains (**Djungarian Alatau**). The interior of the region is mainly covered by sandy deserts, with salt steppes and lakes around the edges (**Ulungur, Ebinur, Sayram**). The only outlet is the **Irtysh River.**

Altai Mountains

Yangtze and Huang He

The **Yangtze** is the third-longest river on Earth. It rises at the confluence of several rivers at an altitude of 5,600 m on the Qinghai Plateau. It then flows south-east through high mountain chains. The river crosses the eastern section of the Red Basin, at which point it is 500 m wide, before cutting across the Yunnan-Guizhou Plateau for a distance of 648 km between Chongqing and Yichang. The Yangtze then meanders eastwards across a great plain. At Nanjing, the 'long river' forms a massive delta, and drains into the East China Sea at Shanghai in two branches after covering a total distance of 6,400 km.
Rising in the Qinghai Plateau, the **Huang He** then winds along the southern edge of the Gobi Desert and around the Ordos Plateau into wide plains. It flows into the Yellow Sea north-west of the Shandong Peninsula after covering a total distance of 4,845 km.

The mountain system splits to form the Russian, Mongolian and Gobi Altai. The Palaeozoic mountains of the **Russian Altai** rise in the centre and east to glaciated peaks with a height of some 4,506 m. The rest of the system consists of plateaus, low mountain chains and steppe-covered valleys. The **Mongolian Altai** begins at the **Tabyn Bogdo Ola** and extends for 1,000 km. The **Gobi Altai** extends for some 500 km, rising to a height of some 3,957 m. They mark the south-eastern boundary of the mountain system.

Khangai Mountains

This range is 700 km long and has an average altitude of 2,500 m. The highest point is the 4,031-m-high Mount **Otgontenger.** The mountains consist of strata of granite, schist and sandstone. The higher altitudes have only a sparse covering of vegetation.

The southern slopes consist of steppes and the north faces are covered in dense forest.

North-east China Plain

This region is densely populated and intensively farmed. It extends along the Pacific coast from the fertile plains traversed by the **Huang He River** to the lowlands in the middle and lower reaches of the **Yangtze River.** In the plains of the lower Yangtze, the

river's waters and those of its tributaries have formed a series of natural lakes.

Shandong Peninsula

The **Shandong Peninsula** divides **Bo Hai Bay** in the north from the Yellow Sea in the south. The peninsula has numerous small bays, and the western section is part of the flood plain of the **Huang He River.** The interior is covered in hills and mountains.

Dongting Lake, Poyang Lake, Tai Lake

Dongting Lake is one of China's largest freshwater lakes and forms a natural dam, preventing the waters of the **Yangtze** from escaping and regulating the river's flow. The volume of the lake is decreasing due to the large amount of sediment deposited by the river. The lake covers an area of between 3,600 sq. km

and 4,700 sq. km. The relatively shallow **Poyang Lake** is fed by the **Gan River.** The lake also serves as a retention basin, and its surface area varies greatly, depending on the flow of water that enters it (between 3,700 sq. km and 5,070 sq. km). **Tai Lake** is fed by a labyrinth of water courses, which are connected to the **Yangtze** by the **Huangpu River** and by canals.

Yangtze Delta

At Nanjing, the **Yangtze** begins

to form a wide **delta,** 350 km long and up to 80 km wide, covering an area of more than 80,000 sq. km. It is here that the Yangtze dumps approximately 300 million tons of silt and mud into the sea each year. The area surrounding the fertile delta is one of the most heavily populated regions of China.

Central Chinese Mountains

The **Central Chinese Mountains** separate the North-east China Plain from sub-tropical South China. It consists mainly of ancient, highly eroded mountains, composed of granite.

Qin Ling Mountains

This mountain system stretches 1,550 km and forms the climate divide between the temperate north and the sub-tropical south

of China. It is also the watershed between the river systems of the **Huang He** and **Yangtze Rivers.** The Variscan fold mountain chain, composed of granite, limestone and sandstone, reaches its highest point at the 3,767-m-high **Mount Taibaishan.**

Khingan Range

Both mountain chains stretch from the **Amur River** to the region north of Beijing and form the northern edge of the central lowlands of Manchuria. The

Greater Khingan separates this lowland from the Mongolian Plateau in the west and is mainly composed of granite and basalt. The average height is 1,200 m. The mountains are covered in dense forests to an altitude of more than 2,000 m. The **Lesser Khingan** is a low mountain chain to the north-east that rises to a height of some 1,200 m. The **Amur River** flows through a deep gorge to the north-east.

Sichuan

Eastern **Sichuan** is dominated by the large Sichuan Basin (220,000 sq. km) along the middle section of the **Yangtze** River. The abundance of red sandstone in this area has given it the name of the **Red Basin.**
The fertile hills at an altitude of 400 to 800 m are interspersed with shallow valleys and are surrounded on all sides by mountains up to 3,000 m in height and by the Yunnan-Guizhou Plateau. This plateau, at a height of 1,800 to 2,000 m, is mainly composed of limestone and dominates western Sichuan and central Hunan. It is bordered by the **Sino-Tibetan Mountains** and the **Qinghai Plateau.** The Sino-Tibetan Mountains reach a maximum height of 7,556 m in the **Daxue Shan.**

Mountains of South-east China

The mountains of South-east China are very segmented and can be divided into two systems, the **Nan Ling** and the **Wuyi Shan.** They separate the **South China Lowlands** from the **Yangtze Plain** further north. The mountains rise to a height of 200 m to 1,100 m, with narrow valleys and wide basins, and they provide some of China's most attractive landscapes.
The whole region once lay beneath the sea. It has only been dry land since the Tertiary Era. The area has huge limestone strata, with an average thickness of 1,100 m, on a granite bedrock. Earth movements have misaligned and uplifted these layers, and erosion has created a magnificent karst topography. The strange karstified limestone

The Gobi Desert covers the whole southern section of Mongolia. Nomads live in this inhospitable place.

*The **Indus River** is over 3,000 km long and rises in the Gangdise Shan Mountains around the Tibetan Plateau at a height of 5,000 m. The river winds through the Himalayas cutting spectacular gorges up to 3,000 m deep before flowing out on to the shallow plains in the south-west. The Indus continues southwards across the dry landscape of Pakistan, providing much-needed water for the surrounding regions.*

towers of the **Guilin** region on the **Lijiang River** are among the strangest and most beautiful natural landscapes on Earth.

Nan Ling

The **Nan Ling mountain system** is an eastern extension of the **Altun Shan**, consisting of a series of staggered mountain chains, which form the watershed between the **Yangtze** and the **Zhujiang** to the south. The main peaks are over 1,500 m high. The highest elevation is 1,902 m. To the south, the mountains descend to form rolling hills.

Wuyi Shan

The mountain system consists of a series of chains which form the border between Fujian and Jiangxi provinces. It has peaks of up to 1,800 m. The southern end of the mountain range includes the **Shanling** with its densely forested slopes, honeycombed with limestone caves. In the north-east, the mountain terrain gives way to the dense bamboo forest of the **Xianxia Mountains**. The **Wuyi Shan** has a very attractive landscape of cliffs with several peaks and green gorges.

Taiwan

The island of Taiwan (Formosa) is separated from China by the 160-km-wide **Straits of Taiwan**. It has an area of 36,000 sq. km and is dominated by a central, young **fold mountain chain**, which runs through the island from north to south and covers approximately two-thirds of the land area. The craggy, rainforest-covered mountains have more than 60 peaks, which can reach heights of over 3,000 m. The highest point is the 3,997-m-high **Mount Yu Shan**. To the east, the mountains fall steeply, but in the west the peaks drop in terrace-like stages to form a fertile flat coastal strip between eight and 40 km wide.

In the north of the island, above the **Taipei Basin**, there is a group of extinct volcanoes which are part of the volcanic arc of the **Ryukyu Islands**. Taiwan's position on the join between the Pacific Plate and the Philippine Plate means that the island is often affected by volcanoes as the Earth's crust constantly shifts.

Japan

Japan consists of an arc of approximately 4,100 islands about 2,600 km long. The islands are actually the peaks of an underwater volcanic mountain range. The main islands of **Kyushu** (36,554 sq. km), **Shikoku** (18,260 sq. km), **Honshu** (227,414 sq. km) and **Hokkaido** (83,511 sq. km) are joined in the north by the **Sakhalin Island** and the **Kuril Is-**

lands. The **Ryukyu Islands**, including **Okinawa**, form the southern extensions of this island chain. The main islands contain numerous bays and peninsulas. Three-quarters are afforested low mountains with deep valleys and steep cliffs, interspersed with interior valleys, terraces and plateaus. Even the two largest basins and eight plains, which are traversed by rivers and open to the sea, are divided into vertical levels. These islands are the main population centres of Japan. The island chain has experienced a great deal of tectonic activity since the Neogene period and contains hundreds of volcanoes, of which 40 are still active, including **Mount Aso** (1,592 m).

Honshu

Honshu is the largest of the main Japanese islands and contains both volcanic and granite mountain chains, with narrow coastal seams and large peninsulas

(including the **Kii, Izu and Noto peninsulas**), some of which are extensions of the mountain chains. The main mountains are the **Japanese Alps**, which consist of the Akaishi, Kiso and Hida Mountains, and which reach an altitude of 3,192 m in central Japan. **Mount Fuji** rises to a height of 3,776 m and is the

1 The vegetation on the high plains of Mongolia is only suitable for grazing livestock. The yurts (tents) of the native nomads dot the landscape.

2 Green pasture as far as the eye can see: the landscape of the Chinese autonomous region of Xinjiang Uygur, also known as East Turkestan, is an important habitat for the nomadic peoples of the steppes.

3 Mountains near Lijiang: the karst cliffs in the South China region around Guilin rise almost vertically out of completely flat plains.

Asia

*The coast of **Halong Bay**, some 150 km east of the Vietnamese capital Hanoi, provides a stunning landscape. The strange array of weird columns was formed after sea levels rose at the end of the Ice Age. Amazing rock formations of towers and needles are the result of harsh erosion over the course of many hundreds of thousands of years.*

highest mountain in the country, and is part of a volcanic chain that extends over the **Izu Peninsula** and into the Sea of Japan. The largest plain on Honshu, after the 32,000 sq. km **Kanto Plain** around Tokyo, is the region of Kansai, west of the Alps. This area contains **Lake Biwa** (675 sq. km), which formed in a tectonic hollow; it is Japan's largest lake. **Kansai** is not a flat plain, but is intersected by numerous plateaus, mountains and basins. To the south-west, the mountains rise to form a narrow peninsula, which runs along the **Inland Sea** – a depression filled with sea water that separates Honshu from Sjikoku – and which ends at the Kammon Strait.

Sakhalin

This island has an area of 76,400 sq. km and is located between the Gulf of Tartary and the **Sea of Okhotsk**. It has a length of 948 km and is some 160 km wide. Only the north is mountainous; the highest point is **Mt. Lopatin** (1,609 m). The island is covered in tundra, with mixed woodland to the south.

Ganges, Indus

The **Ganges** rises in the Himalayas at a height of 4,600 m at the confluence of the Bhagirathi and the Alaknanda. The river flows through the Ganges Plain before forming a fertile delta over an area of 56,000 sq. km. After a distance of 2,700 km, the Ganges opens out into the Bay of Bengal. The **Indus** rises at a height of 5,182 m in the Gangdise Shan and flows between the Karakorams and the Himalayas in a north-westerly direction, before turning south and leaving the mountains behind. The Kabul River joins the Indus as it enters the Indus Plain. In this arid plain, the Indus feeds water to an oasis approximately 150 km wide. After 3,200 km, the river flows into the Arabian Sea, forming a delta of over 7,800 sq. km.

Indian Sub-continent

The Indian Sub-continent is bordered by the **Arabian Sea** in the west and the **Bay of Bengal** in the east, and terminates in the south in a triangular peninsula, which extends into the Indian Ocean. The north of the sub-continent is covered by part of the **Himalayan mountain system**. South-east of the Himalayas lie the **plains of the Ganges Brahmaputra**, and south-west of the Himalayas there is the **Indus Plain** (the Punjab), that gives way to the dry landscape of the **Thar Desert** in the south.
The **Indian Peninsula** is covered by the **Deccan Plateau**, which contains mountain chains with heights of up to 1,722 m, formed during the folding that produced the Himalayas. These mountain chains include the **Aravalli Range, Vindhya Range and Satpura Range**. The Deccan is surrounded by the mountains of the **Western Ghats** and the **Eastern Ghats**, which run parallel to the coast. The coastal seam in the west is very narrow, but in the east, north and south, the mountains are bordered by a

Mekong

The **Mekong** rises at an altitude of approximately 3,000 m on the Tibetan Plateau and flows south-east through deep gorges in the mountains of eastern Tibet. North of Luang Prabang, the river bends sharply to the south and then follows the northern and eastern edges of the Khorat Plateau, where it is joined by the Mun River. Despite the river's shallow gradient it creates several cataracts over this stretch, the most famous being the Khone Falls in Laos near the border with Cambodia. The Mekong forms a flood plain with several other rivers 550 km before its mouth. It then turns south and forms a wide delta before draining into the South China Sea, having covered a distance of more than 4,500 km.

broad lowland area. Both the **Ganges** and **Indus Rivers** form huge deltas.

Thar Desert

The Thar Desert is a dry landscape covering 250,000 sq. km between the **Aravalli Range** and the **Indus Plain**. It is mostly covered in steppe vegetation, with long stretches of dunes. The region has a very small population and is irrigated by a few canals. The area includes a 15,000 sq.-km-region of desert which has been created by human activity.

Ganges Plain

At Haridwar, the **Ganges** enters a wide plain covering an area of over 1 million sq. km, providing water to one quarter of the subcontinent. The Ganges meanders east across this extensive plain, at a very slight gradient. Several tributaries join the river, including the **Ghaghara, Gandak, Yamuna** and the **Son**, forming a convoluted river system and a very fertile region which is densely populated as a result.

Indonesia: Mt. Agung (3,142 m) is the highest volcano on Bali.

The Ghats

The **Western Ghats** follow the west coast of India for a distance of 1,500 km and form a fault scarp which drops steeply to the coast of the Arabian Sea.
In the south, the mountains rise to form the **Nilgiri Mountains**, with a height of more than 2,000 m, then dividing into the individual massifs of the **Southern**

Ghats, whose highest peak is **Anaimudi** (2,695 m).
The **Eastern Ghats** are a series of hill and mountain chains stretching from north to south, where they reach their highest elevation of 1,628 m, before joining the Western Ghats at the Nilgiri Mountains.

Sri Lanka

The island is separated from the Indian Sub-continent by the shallow Palk Strait and the Gulf of Mannar. Sri Lanka, formerly known as Ceylon, has an area of 65,610 sq. km, much of which is dominated by lowland and coastal plains, lined with lagoons. The only mountains are at the southern end of the interior of the island; the highest point is **Pidurutalagala** which rises to an altitude of 2,524 m. The island also has a number of isolated peaks, such as **Sigiriya** and Sri Pada, also called Adam's Peak (2,243 m). Sri Lanka is composed of Pre-Cambrian stone primarily land. Only the far north-west of the country has partially karstified limestone strata of the Tertiary Period.

South-east Asia

South-east Asia is bordered to the south and east by the South China Sea and extends into the foothills of the **mountains of East Tibet**, which run along the east coast as the **Annamitic Cordillera** (**Ngoc Linh**, 2,598 m). On the west coast, the **Bilauktaung Mountains** (2,075

m) extend into the **Malay Peninsula**. The steep mountains to the north of south-east Asia are followed by the broad **Khorat Plateau** in the centre of the region, which is surrounded by further mountain ranges, the **Dangrek Mountains** (1,328 m) and the **Cardamom Mountains**. To the south, a broad plain traversed by many rivers ends in the Mekong Delta.

Mekong Delta

The **Mekong** widens into a delta at Phnom Penh, covering an area of 70,000 sq. km. The growth of this delta to the south-west is affected by ocean currents. The water courses in the delta vary depending on the monsoon rains. To mitigate the effect of the floods, the delta has been dammed to form the **Tonle Sap Lake**.

Hoang Lien Mountain Range

The north of South-east Asia is dominated by this mountain range with deep valleys and an average height of 2,000 m. The range is an extension of the mountains of East Tibet and has numerous plateaus. The highest point is **Fansipan** (3,143 m) in the north-east.

Malay Peninsula

This peninsula between the Andaman Sea and the Gulf of Thailand is 1,500 km long from north to south. The narrowest point is the **Kra Isthmus** (40 km). The peninsula has numerous bays and is traversed by a mountain system which forms one coherent mass in the north but which separates in the south to form staggered mountain chains (**Tahan**, 2,190 m). To the south, a series of hills lead to a marshy coastal plain. This is dominated by scattered karstified pillars (**Halong Bay** and **Phang Nga Bay**). Tropical rainforest covers most of the peninsula, which gives way to mangrove swamps on the west coast.

Indonesian Islands

The **Malay Archipelago** is a chain of islands covering a distance of

New Guinea: The mountains of the second-largest island on Earth are covered in rainforest. New Guinea lies on an extension of the Indonesian island chain and also marks the start of Oceania. It is on the border between the two continents. Like many other islands between the Indian and Pacific Oceans, New Guinea is also surrounded by numerous coral reefs and offshore coral islands.

5,000 km which sits on the 200-m-deep continental shelf of the Sunda Plate at the boundary between the Indo-Australian Plate and the Philippine Plate. Several mountain chains have folded here as a result of volcanic activity since the Mesozoic Era. The islands have a bedrock of sandstone and limestone – with the exception of Borneo – but high levels of volcanic and tectonic activity gives them largely volcanic characteristics. The area beween the Pacific and Indian Oceans form the longest uninterrupted volcanic chain on Earth. Seventy of them are young volcanoes that have erupted since the year 1600. The islands are mountainous and only the larger ones – **Luzon, Mindanao, Java, Sumatra** and **Borneo** – have large flood plains. Some of the islands have offshore coral reefs.

Sumatra

Sumatra covers an area of some 425,000 sq. km and is the most westerly of the Indonesian islands. It is separated from Java by the narrow Sunda Straits. The landscape in the west is dominated by the **Barisan Mountains**. This densely forested mountain range has several active volcanoes (**Kerinci**, 3,798 m, **Merapi**, 2,891 m), and drops steeply on the west coast, but is bounded in the east by a foothill region, followed by undulating lowlands and finally a marshy coastal plain and mangroves. In the interior of the Barisan Mountains, tufa deposits have formed plateaus.

Java

The island has an area of 126,650 sq. km, with a volcanic mountain chain running its entire length, rising to heights of 3,676 m. The mountains descend to the coast of the Java Sea.

Borneo

With an area of 746,950 sq. km, mountainous Borneo is the third largest island on Earth and is composed of schist and Mesozoic rock. The highest point is **Mount Kinabalu** at 4,101 m. The foothills of the central mountains surround a basin containing numerous lakes and marshes. The coasts have few bays. The interior was once completely covered in dense rainforest but much of it has been cleared to produce grassland.

The Philippines Archipelago

The island group forms the northeastern section of the **Malay Archipelago** and comprises more than 7,100 islands. The main islands of **Luzon** (108,772 sq. km) and **Mindanao** (94,594 sq. km) alone make up some two-thirds of the total land mass. The

islands are covered in densely forested mountain chains and hills, dominated by both extinct and active volcanoes.

New Guinea

New Guinea has an area of approximately 771,900 sq. km and is covered by several parallel and densely forested mountain chains along its whole length. In the south, these mountains are bordered by a flood plain about 450 km wide, which has formed alongside the **Digul** and **Fly Rivers**. The coast has numerous bays and peninsulas and is dominated by mangrove swamps.

Mountains of New Guinea

The young fold mountain chains that run the length of the island join in the south-east to form the **Owen Stanley Range** on a peninsula, which continues in the is-

land groups to the east. In the west, the **Maoke Mountains**, are covered in dense rainforest. The **Central Range** whose highest point is **Puncak Jaya** (5,020 m) is glaciated. Tectonic activity is mainly restricted to the northern coastal mountains and the only volcanic region is in the east (**Mount Lamington**, 1,785 m).

1 Mayon on the island of Luzon in the Philippines reaches a height of 2,412 m and is an active volcano.

2 The karstified pillars in Phang Nga Bay north of the Thai city of Phuket are the result of thousands of years of erosion.

3 The active volcano of Bromo is 2,614 m high. It is in the Bromo-Tengger-Semeru National Park on Java and is part of the Tengger Caldera.

4 Rice terraces: mountain slopes in the Philippines transformed by the Ifugao into a unique agricultural landscape.

Main photograph:
The Nambung National
Park in Western Australia
with stone columns rising
in the desert.

Oceania

The smallest continent, known as Oceania or Australasia, is the 'island continent' consisting of Australia, a few large islands (such as eastern New Guinea and the two islands of New Zealand) and roughly 7,000 smaller islands scattered over the Pacific. Australia can be

Australia: the Great Barrier Reef in Queensland.

sub-divided into three major areas, the West Australian tableland which occupies approximately half the country, the adjoining central Australian lowland and the Great Dividing Range which adjoins it in the east. The island of Tasmania and the Great Barrier Reef off the north-east coast are other important physical features. New Zealand is predominantly mountainous and covered in sub-tropical and temperate forests. The Pacific islands are divided into three groups: Melanesia, Polynesia and Micronesia. The larger islands are of volcanic origin, the smaller ones are mostly coral atolls.

Oceania

'The **Twelve Apostles'** on the coast of Victoria, Australia: these huge needles, up to 40 m high, are an excellent illustration of the erosive power of wind and water. They are part of the Port Campbell National Park.

Northern Australian mountain ranges

The **Western Australian tableland** which rises west of the **MacDonnell Chain** and continues to the west coast encircles the central Australian lowland. The tableland which has an average altitude of 250 m to 800 m has its highest elevations in several mountain ranges that stretch from the West coast to the **Gulf of Carpentaria**. It is traversed by numerous rivers but only those near the coast contain more than a trickle of water all year round. **Darling Scarp (Bluff Knoll**, 1,109 m) contains the continent's oldest rocks. Inland, the plateau becomes a vast, desert-like dry landscape, the Simpson Desert, with numerous salt lakes before dropping down to form the central Australian lowland.

Hamersley Basin which adjoins the Darling Scarp in the north reaches altitudes of up to 1,236 m (**Mount Bruce**). **Mount Augustus** which has an altitude of 1,106 m is in this mountainous region and is rocks coloured red due to its iron content.

The **King Leopold Range** forms the southern border of the **Kimberley Plateau**. This mountainous country drops away in the North to form **Arnhem Land**. In the south, it adjoins the limestone **Barkley Tableland**.

Darling

The 2740 km Darling is the longest river in Australia. The headwaters originate in the Darling Downs in the Great Dividing Range. The main headwater is the MacIntyre River. The Darling carries between 340 million and 550 million cu. m of water per year on average but when there is no rain it can dry out altogether. After absorbing many tributaries originating in the Great Dividing Range, the Darling flows into the Murray near Wentworth, which in turn eventually drains into the Indian Ocean.

Kimberley Highlands

The mountain range bordering the **Kimberley Plateau** stretches from the **Joseph Bonaparte Gulf** in the north where it drops down in sheer cliffs to the **Great Sandy Desert** in the south.

The rugged landscape occupies an area of approximately 360,000 sq. km, gradually rising to a height of 936 m (**Mount Ord**). At average temperatures of 38°C, the vegetation is typical of a savannah and is suitable for rearing cattle and sheep.

Rivers have sculpted impressive caverns and remarkable gorges in the sandstone which predominates here. Millennia of erosion and weathering have produced extraordinary rock formations such as the weird limestone formation in **Purnululu** which was only discovered in 1982.

The foothills of the Kimberleys form richly structured, high cliffs close to the Indian Ocean where extensive breaker platforms made

Kimberley: eroded limestone rocks in Purnululu National Park.

of sandstone can be found upstream. The coastal area is remarkable for its significant iron ore deposits.

Arnhem Land

The peninsula between the **Timor Sea** and the **Gulf of Carpentaria** in the north of the **Northern Territory** occupies an area of approximately 80,000 sq. km.

At the scalloped edges of the coast in the lowlands of the Gulf of Carpentaria, tropical rainforests, mangrove swamps and **wetlands** are typical of the

landscape. Vast silt and mud flats and salt marshes cover the estuary. In the extremely rugged mountainous country inland on the peninsula, water channels have sculpted deep channels and gullies. Savannah and grassland can be found to the south.

Central Australian Desert

Approximately 70 per cent of the total land mass of Australia consists of desert and semi-desert formed by an inland sea that dried up 120 million years ago. The scree deposits and sandy regions stretch over massive distances from the West Australian tableland through the Central Australian Basin to the cordilleras. The **Great Sandy Desert**, the **Tanami Desert**, the **Gibson Desert**, the **Great Victoria Desert** and the **Simpson Desert** are surrounded in the north, west and east by mountain ranges and plateaus. Inland, scattered monadnocks and several mountain ranges predominate. They include the **Musgrave Ranges** and the **MacDonnell Ranges**. Uluru (Ayers **Rock**), the **Olgas** and **Mount Connor** (altitude 760 m) are among the monadnocks which emerge from the sandstone plains. The region has few waterways, and those that exist are only full after heavy rainfall, mostly evaporating into great salt-pans. Thus **Lake Eyre**, **Lake Torrens** and **Lake Gardiner** are misleading names as the 'lakes' seldom contain water. In the vast desert of

'the Centre', massive underground reservoirs lie at great depths, including the **Great Artesian Basin** whose Mesozoic sediments store large quantities of water from the last Ice Age.

Gibson Desert

This stony desert in central Western Australia between the Great Sandy Desert and the Great Victoria Desert occupies an area of approximately 330,000 sq. km. Vast sections of this treeless plain are covered in recent deposits of scree, over which larger sand dunes covered in scrub vegetation have formed. Individual monadnocks and isolated mountains, reaching altitudes of up to 600 m, tower over the seemingly endless plain.

Numerous salt-pans and salt lakes have formed, including **Lake Disappointment** which, due to the infrequent precipitation, continues to evaporate, ensuring that its salt concentration is constantly increasing.

Victoria Desert

The **Great Victoria Desert** is bordered by the Musgrave Ranges in the North, the Darling Plateau in the West and by the Stuart Ranges in the East. Sandy and scree deserts, relieved in places by bushy vegetation, cover the vast, treeless, dry region.

In the eastern and western border regions, the desert turns into salt marshes. In the south, the limestone tableland of the **Nullarbor Plain**, which contains caves carved out by underground currents, leads to the coast where it forms a spectacular, 200 m high, rugged line of cliffs.

Great Sandy Desert

The largest of the continent's four deserts is situated in the northern part of the western Australian desert and occupies an area of approximately 520,000 sq. km. It extends to the south of the Kimberley Plateau, becomes the Gibson Desert in the south and is bordered in the east by the MacDonnell Ranges. At **Eighty Mile Beach**, the western foothills of the Great Sandy Desert reach the coast of the Indian Ocean where it forms vast

stretches of dunes. The Great Sandy Desert consists primarily of extensive plains with parallel sand dunes covered in dry grasses. Only sporadically do monadnocks such as **Mount Cornish** (363 m) rise over the vast plains. In the north-west, the desert contains the artesian wells of the **Desert Basin**. Vast salt-pans lie in the south and east.

Simpson Desert

The **Simpson Desert** covers the south-east of the Northern Territory as well as parts of the states of South Australia and Queensland and has a total area of over 250,000 sq. km.

The MacDonnell Ranges form the northern border. In the east, the scree and sandy desert containing massive dunes between 30 and 60 m high becomes the **Great Artesian Basin**.

Central Australian Mountains

The **MacDonnell Ranges** are part of the mountainous regions which divide the vast plains and steppes of central Australia. They were formed approximately 600 to 900 million years ago and are one of the oldest mountain ranges in the world.

The chain of hills runs from east to west and consists of quartz and sandstone. They stretch over the sub-soil of the West Australian tableland which has an average altitude of 600 m and a length of 380 km and reach their peak at **Mount Zeil** which has an altitude of 1,510 m. The arc of the **Musgrave Ranges** to the south is approximately 210 km long and consists of granite formations. The highest peak is **Mount Woodroffe** (1,440m). The south-eastern foothills of the Musgrave Ranges form the **Petermann Ranges** which are approximately 320 km long.

The numerous monadnocks which sporadically tower over the vast desert plains and steppes are one of the most impressive wonders of nature in Australia. The most famous is the 867 m-high, massive **Uluru (Ayers Rock)** the largest monolith in the world with a breadth of approximately 9 km, and the over 30 sandstone **Olgas** which cover an area of approximately 28 sq. km.

Monoliths of Australia

On the world's driest continent, erosion, the most powerful force of nature, has created impressive geological formations. These also include the greatest monoliths on Earth.

Australia is the driest inhabited continent. It is also the flattest and has the oldest and least fertile soils, due to the fact that the centre of the country, the deserts, are a vast, dried-up sea bed. As a result, it has always been a playground for the elements of wind and water which have created spectacular and imposing monoliths over the millennia. Uluru (Ayers Rock) enchants those who visit it when its sandstone faces interspersed with mica and feldspar turn a blood-red colour at sunset. It is 3.6 km long, 2 km wide and rises 335 m above the plateau. As the rocks which consist of harder sandstone weather more slowly than the surrounding area, this monadnock now towers over the dry plain. Its lower slopes are severely eroded and wind and water have created basins and canyons on its plateau-like top. The precipitation from violent thunderstorms pours down these channels in massive cataracts during the rainy season.

This mountain is the home of the mythical rainbow snake Uluru which is why the Aborigines have given it this name.

The Olga Mountains lie not far away. These near-circular worn-down rock formations which number over 30 and which tower over the surrounding plain at altitudes of up to 460 m have been

exposed by millennia of erosion. The 'Kata Tjuta', as the Aborigines call the Olgas, have a mythological significance too. They are considered to be the fossilised heads of man-eating giants.

The third in the league of great monoliths is Mount Connor, to the east of Ayers Rock, also sacred to the aborigines. This flat-topped limestone and sandstone boulder is 3 km long and 1.2 km wide. Its lower slopes are extremely rugged and covered in scree, whilst the upper slopes consist of rocky crags. For the aborigines this is where their mythical ice man comes from.

Big picture: the Olga Mountains, called 'Kata Tjuta' by the Aborigines, form a group of approximately 30 small individual mountains in the centre of Australia.

1 Ayers Rock, called 'Uluru' by the Aborigines, looks like a red giant, especially at sunset and sunrise. This phenomenon is caused by ferric oxides in the rock surface.

2 The 'Devil's Marbles', located between Alice Springs and Darwin are approximately 1.5 million years old. The granite lumps, created by erosion, soar like monolithic peaks straight out of the flat central Australian desert.

Oceania

Mount Cook, called 'Aorangi' by the indigenous Maori, is located in the New Zealand Alps on the South Island. It is New Zealand's highest mountain at 3764 m. The surrounding National Park was founded in 1953. The many glaciers and lakes of this mountain landscape are stunning. The longest glacier on the southern hemisphere is the Tasman Glacier, stretching from Mount Cook almost 30 km into the valley.

Great Dividing Range

The **Australian Cordillera** runs parallel to the Pacific coast around the entire southern and south-eastern coast for approximately 3,000 km, starting in the north at **Cape York Peninsula**, and running north-south to the south coast at Melbourne. It then continues on to the island of **Tasmania**. It consists of a series of ranges, the Great Dividing Range, New England Range, the Blue Mountains and the Australian Alps. The mountain chain consists primarily of low mountains and is divided by several plateaus. It reaches an altitude of 1611 m in the north with **Mount Bartle Frere**. **Mount Kosciuszko**, near the capital city of Canberra, is in the southern foothills of the **Australian Alps**. At 2,230 m it is the highest mountain in the **Great Dividing Range** and in Australia as a whole.

The Australian cordillera forms the continent's main water divide. It was folded upwards through subduction as a result of seismic events in the Tertiary Era. It descends in a steep platform formation in the east and slopes downwards to form vast plains further inland.

Murray

The Murray is Australia's largest river and has water all year round. It originates in the Snowy Mountains and crosses them in its upper reaches through a series of deep gorges 320 km in length. It then crosses the Murray Darling Basin in the central Australian lowland, where, with its tributary the Murrumbidgee, it irrigates the extensive farmland through dams and artificial water courses from the Snowy River. After 2570 km, the Murray flows into Lake Alexandrina and through Encounter Bay, eventually draining into the Indian Ocean.

New South Wales

The state of **New South Wales** lies in the south-east of the continent and occupies a total area of approximately 800,000 sq. km. It can be divided geographically into four sections. First there is the coastal strip, with climates ranging from temperate on the far south coast to sub-tropical near the Queensland border. Then there are the Australian cordilleras adjoining a narrow coastal strip containing tropical rainforest, vast sandy beaches and expanses of dunes. They reach their highest point in the south at Mount Kosciuszko (altitude: 2,230 m) in the Australian Alps. In the north, the cordilleras run towards the **New England Range** (**Round Mountain**, 1,615 m) and the **Blue Mountains** (945 m).

New Zealand: The volcanic cone of Mount Taranaki (2,518 m).

The Australian cordilleraes gradually slopes down to the west and turns into the western plains which cover approximately two-thirds of the territory and are surrounded by the **Grey Range**. The **Murray River** (length: 2,570 km) which flows through the country, and its tributary the **Darling** which rises in the cordilleras, form the only large inland water systems of the Australian continent

that containwater all year round. The plains that are suitable for farming are in the Riverina area around Wagga Wagga. The far north-west consists of arid plains.

Tasmania

The island of **Tasmania**, of the south coast of Australia, was originally part of the Australian mainland. It was first formed 12,000 years ago, at the end of the last Ice Age, when the sea level rose and large parts of the country were flooded. This is when the **Bass Strait**s were formed which separate Tasmania from the mainland. The island occupies an area of 67,800 sq. km. It has a central mountainous plateau which is a continuation of the Australian Cordillera and reaches its highest point at **Mount Ossa** (1,617 m) which slopes in a south-easterly direction. The rest of the island is mountainous, with a narrow strip of flat coastal plain along its northern coast.

The island exhibits numerous Ice Age formations. It is covered with rainforest fed by rivers on which there are spectacular cascades and rapids such as the **Russell Falls**. Tasmania promotes itself as

the 'Natural State' owing to its large, and relatively unspoilt, natural environment. Forty per cent of the island consists of reserves, National Parks and World Heritage Sites.

New Zealand – North Island

The island, which occupies an area of 114,500 sq. km and is separated from the South Island by the **Cook Straits**, is 38 km wide and displays unusual scenic diversity. The **Northland** and the volcanic **Coromandel Peninsula** in the north are characterised by long, level coastlines with wide sandy beaches and expanses of dunes as well as rocky cliffs.

The volcanic region of the North Island stretches from **White Island** in the **Bay of Plenty**, a volcano which is still active, to Mount Egmont in the Eastern region of **Taranaki**.

A plateau has formed around the three volcanoes in the region of **Tongariro** in the centre of the island. Lake Taupo is approximately 600 sq. km in area. It is a crater lake, formed following a gigantic volcanic explosion. To the north of Lake Taupo lies the famous central geothermal region around **Lake Rotorua**. Here, the entire panoply of volcanic and post-volcanic phenomena can be found: small crater lakes, geysers such as the **Pohutu** and boiling-water lakes rich with colourful, shiny mineral deposits, sinter terraces and sulphurous mud flats. **Mount Tarawera** (1,111 m) has been cut in half by a 19-km-long chasm since its last eruption in 1886.

Along the east coast, the folds of the cordillera stretch from the East Cape to the southern peak. These are, the **Huiarau**, the **Ruahine**, the **Puketoi** and the **Tararua Ranges**. The northern foothills of the **Southern Alps** reach altitudes of up to 1,700 m. The southern North Island consists of low mountains and hills traversed by numerous rivers such as the **Manawatu** and the **Wanganui**. High cliffs overlook the Cook Straits at this point.

Mount Egmont, Ruapehu

Mount Egmont (2,518 m) rises in the east of New Zealand's North Island, known as **Taranaki** in Maori. It is a dormant volcano which last erupted in 1775. The snow-covered, isolated volcanic peak is located in the centre of an almost circular peninsula with a diameter of approximately 60 km formed by lava deposits.

Three further volcanic craters dominate the centre of the North Island and form the **Tongariro Highland**. **Mount Ruapehu is** the only volcano which is still active and is also the highest mountain on the North Island at 2,797 m. The other two are **Mount Ngauruhoe** (2,290 m), which last erupted in 1975, and the supposedly extinct **Mount Tongariro** (1,968 m).

This mountainous region is glaciated to a large degree and is bisected by deep gorges. Strange rock formations characterise the landscape.

New Zealand South Island

The north of the **South Island**, which occupies an area of 150,700 sq. km, is characterised by low mountain ranges such as the **Tasman Mountains** (**Mount Kendall**, 1,811 m, **Mount Anglem**, 979 m) and the picturesque ria coast of the **Marlborough Sound**. The **Freshwater River** flows through a swampy valley, rising close to the north-west coast and flowing south-east into the narrow bay of the **Paterson Inlet. The Rakeahua river** also flows into the Paterson Inlet. The **Southern Alps** are a defining factor of the South Island with their numerous peaks rising above 3,000 m, massive glaciers and beautiful high mountain landscapes. The Alps fall steeply to the west, whilst sloping downwards in the east where they become the vast lowland **Canterbury Plains**. In the south-east, there is the mountainous landscape of **Otago**, reaching altitudes of up to 1,200 m and traversed by the broad river valleys of the **Clutha** and the **Mataura**. On the Otago peninsula this mountain range drops steeply down to the Pacific. In the far south, vast plains stretch all the way to the coast.

The imposing **fjords** in the southwest of the South Island were created during the Ice Age as powerful ice currents flowing towards

*The **Palau-Islands** are situated at the western edge of Micronesia. They are atoll islands (the remains of coral reefs). Altogether there are 300 islands surrounded by extensive coral reefs.*

the ocean, sculpting granite and shale mountains and forming deep fjords, bays, inlets and numerous islands in the Tasman Sea. The mountainous region, which contains deep ravines, reaches its highest points at **Mount Irene** (1,879 m) and **Mitre Peak** (1,692 m). The numerous lakes in the east such as **Te Anau** and **Manapouri** were also formed at the end of the Ice Age. As the sheets of ice thawed, the depressions caused by the weight of the ice pressing down on them filled with water.

Southern Alps

The **Southern Alps** are the youngest mountain range in New Zealand, originating approximately 10 million years ago.
The mountains run parallel to the west coast for a distance of around 450 km from the northern foothills of the **Marlboroughs** to the southern foothills of the **Dunstan and Garvie Mountains**.
Mount Cook, New Zealand's highest mountain at 3,764 m, **Mount Tasman** (3,497 m) and **Mount Sefton** (3,157 m) are among the 16 peaks in the centre of the island that are higher than 3,000 m. Over 360 glaciers traverse the mountainous landscape, which rises again to 3,036 m in the southwest with **Mount Aspiring**.
The largest of the glaciers is the **Tasman Glacier** on Mount Cook which is 29 km long and 9 km wide. The **Hooker Glacier** and the **Mueller Glacier** are additional examples of these moving rivers of ice. Towards the west, the Southern Alps descend to the narrow coastal plain which is only 50 km wide, where further imposing ice masses, including the **Franz Josef Glacier** and the **Fox Glacier,** descend from the highest mountainous regions to 300 m above sea level. The Southern Alps gradually slope downwards in an easterly direction. The Alpine glaciers feed numerous mountain lakes on these gently descending plateaus, including the **Wakatipu**, the **Tekapo**, the **Pukaki** and the **Hawea**.

Canterbury Plains

Like the wide plains of the southern area, the alluvial **Canterbury Plains** in the east of the South

Island are also covered in Ice Age sediment. They are bounded by the foothills of the Southern Alps and the east coast of the South Island. They are situated south of Christchurch, the biggest city on the South Island. They are bounded in the north by Hundalee Hills in the Hurunui District, and in the south they merge into the plains of North Otago beyond the Waitaki River. The Canterbury Plains are formed from the alluvial shingle produced by several large rivers, notably the Waimakariri, the Rakaia, the Selwyn, and the Rangitata Rivers. The land is used for sheep-rearing but is prone to drought, especially when the prevailing wind is from the north-

west. At these times, the weather phenomenon known as the Nor'west Arch, an arch of clouds accompanied by a hot northwesterly wind, can be seen across much of the plain. The rivers of the Canterbury Plains have a distinctive braided appearance. Beyond the Waitaki, they run in narrow channels, rather than spreading across wide shingle depressions, as is the case in Canterbury, eventually draining into the Pacific Ocean.
The rivers of the Canterbury Plains carry away debris from the Southern Alps. These Alps extend to the **Banks Peninsula**, formed in the Tertiary Era, over six million years ago, following violent eruptions of two volcanoes. The Banks Peninsula once contained primaeval forest full of New Zealand's native flora and bird species, but most of it was felled or burned during the first 50 years of European occupation. What remains still provides a refuge for unique birdlife.

1 Milford Sound in the Fjordland National Park. Mitre Peak overlooks one of the most beautiful fjords in the world.

2 The steep and mountainous island of Moorea in French Polynesia is a remnant of a once active volcano. The coral reef surrounding the island is clearly seen in the limpid waters of the deep blue sea.

3 Moorea: the island has several rugged mountains up to 1000 m in altitude. The bays north of Moorea include the Baie de Cook and Baie d'Opunohu. The coastline is covered in lush, tropical vegetation.

4 Lake Rotorua in the volcanic area of the New Zealand's North Island. Its original sinter terraces were destroyed in a volcano explosion.

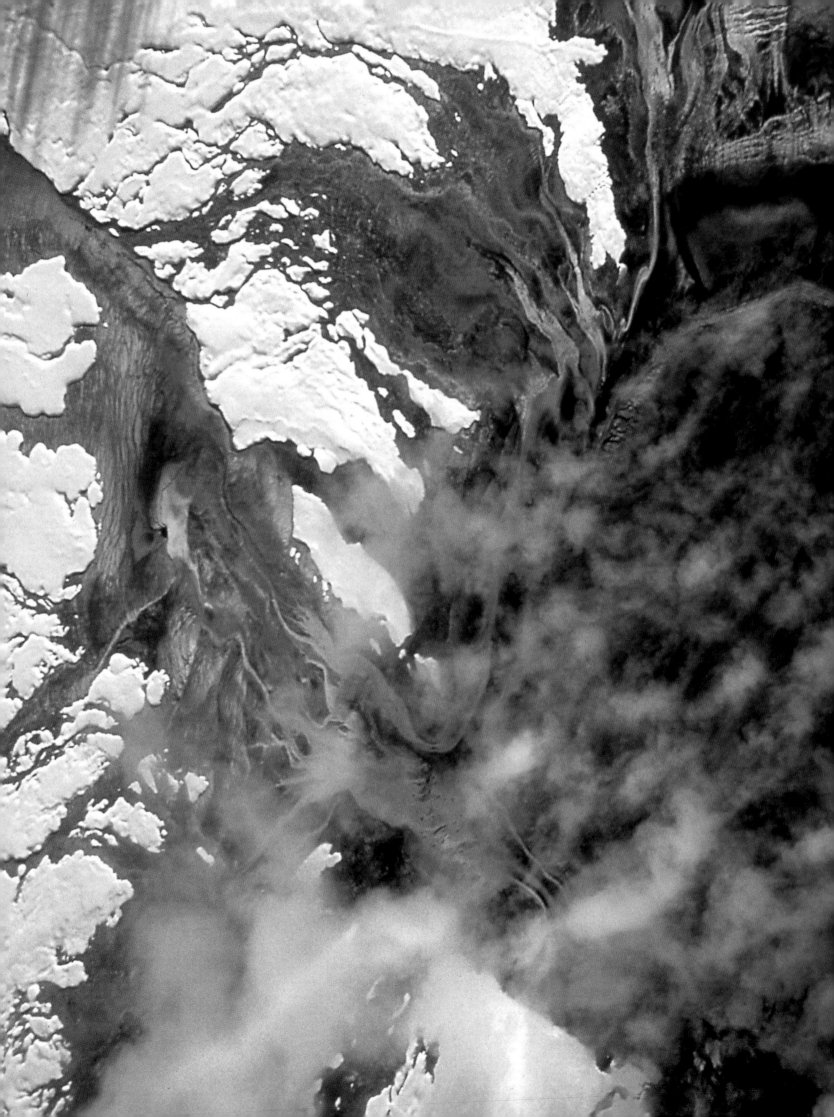

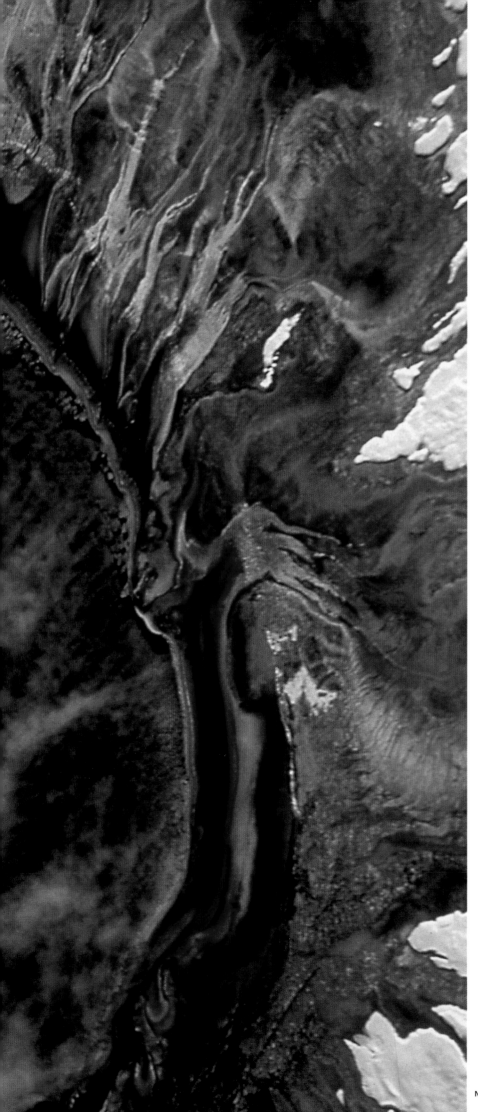

Main photograph:
The strange, bright colours
of Grand Prismatic Spring
in Yellowstone National
Park, Wyoming, are caused
by micro-organisms.

North and Central America

This continent in the northern hemisphere also includes Mexico and Greenland and covers an area of 23.5 million sq. km. Over two-thirds of the land mass consists of North America. Central America forms a land bridge between this

The Caribbean coast of the Mexican Yucatán Peninsula.

continent and the continent of South America. The great landscapes of the continent stretch between the Pacific and Atlantic Oceans and range from the glaciers of Alaska to the tropical Caribbean islands. In the north-east, the islands and hills of the Canadian Shield surround the expanse of Hudson Bay. Further south lie the Great Lakes, followed by the US Deep South, which is bordered to the west by the three parallel chains of the Cordilleras, and to the east by the Appalachians. The Cordilleras also extend through Central America, where the Yucatán Peninsula and the islands of the Greater and Lesser Antilles surround the Caribbean Sea.

North and Central America

Greenland: more than four-fifths of the island is covered with an inland ice sheet. Icebergs are created when the huge valley glaciers move seawards and calve (give birth to icebergs). In summer, above the Arctic Circle, the sun stays above the horizon even at night.

The Arctic

The **Arctic Ocean** is one of the seas of the Atlantic Ocean. It connects the land masses of the North American and the Siberian tundra and numerous islands. It is demarcated by the Arctic Circle, but it is more meaningful to take its boundary as being the 10° July isotherm or the tree line. The pack ice covering of the Arctic is relatively thin with an average thickness of only 3 m.

Depending on the definition of the Arctic, it covers an area of between 21 million sq. km and 26 million sq. km, of which 18 million sq. km consists of sea.

The types of landscape on the mainland are primarily ice and scree deserts, but tundra with permafrost subsoil also covers parts of the land mass. The North American regions of the Arctic and **Greenland** belong to the **Canadian Shield**; the northern European section belongs to the **Baltic Shield**. The regions east of the Urals are counted as the **Siberian Table**.

when winds push ice floes together and reductions in temperature cause them to freeze together.

Greenland

The largest island on Earth at 2,175,600 sq. km is separated from the North American mainland by the **Kane Basin**, **Baffin Bay**, the **Kennedy Channel**, the **Davis Straits** and **Smith Sound** in the west and from Svalbard by the Greenland Sea.

Geologically, Greenland is a continuation of the Canadian Shield. It consists of Pre-Cambrian crystalline and intrusive rocks. In the north and east, younger sedimentary and volcanic rocks overlie these ancient formations. Approximately five-sixths of the area is covered by a permanent ice cap. Only a very narrow strip of coast and the seaward **skerries**, small rocky hillocks rounded by the action of glaciation, are free of ice.

Deep **fjords** cut into the coastline. These are lined with mountain ranges rising in the west

cially near the coast, but these are mostly covered in snow and are not visible.

Massive glaciers move slowly down through the mountain ranges to the sea, where they often break off abruptly and produce icebergs. The **Humboldt Glacier** which is approximately 100 km wide and the 300 km-wide steep cliff at **Melville Bay** are particularly impressive.

The Arctic Islands

The North Polar Region also consists of numerous islands which belong geologically to the original mainland. Only Ellesmere, northern Greenland, Svalbard and Novaya Zemlya, with their alpine appearance, clearly belong to an earlier era in the Earth's history.

Greenland is the largest of the Arctic islands. The Canadian Arctic archipelago lies off the American mainland in the north. Jan Mayen is a volcanic island in the European North Sea. In 1970, the 2,277-m-high glaciated Beeren-

land and numerous other small islands. Alpine, glaciated formations predominate in the west, and ice-covered plateaus are prevalent in the eastern and central areas. There are also individual mountains, such as the 1,712-m-high Newton Peak. East of Svalbard lies the Franz Josef Land archipelago, consisting of around 60 islands. The largest of these are **Graham Bell Land**, **Wilczek Land** and **Zemlya Vilcheka** in the east and **Zemlya Aleksandry** and **Prince George Land** in the west.

The landscape here consists mainly of ice-covered plateaus approximately 300 m high, which often rise to heights of 800 m.

The **Novaya Zemlya** archipelago stretches between the Barents and Kara Seas in a 925-km-long arc. It consists of two main islands and several smaller ones. These islands consist of Palaeozoic mountains that soar to 1,547 m on the North Island and 1,292 m on the South Island. The **Kara Strait** divides the two islands. The southern areas range from flat to undulating, while glacial valleys and fjords intersect

Siberian Seas. The **Lyakhovskiye Islands** in the south, the New Siberian Islands proper (or Anzhu Islands) and the **De Long Islands** in the north-east belong to this archipelago. Arctic tundra covers **Wrangel Island** (Ostrov Vrangelya), which has elevations of up to 1,096 m and lies off the north coast of Siberia between the East Siberian Sea and the Chukchi Sea. The island of Iceland, most of which lies outside the Arctic Circle, is generally no longer regarded as part of the Arctic.

Alaska

This peninsula in the north-west of the American continent is bordered by the Arctic Sea to the north, the **Bering Sea** to the west and the Pacific to the south. The whole of **Alaska** is mountainous and based on a substrate of crystalline schist, limestone and sandstone, overlaid with subsequent strata from the Jurassic, Cretaceous and Tertiary periods. The shape of the landscape can be traced back to folding and tectonic movements in the Tertiary period. The Earth here is still moving today as is evidenced by the active volcanoes on the **Aleutian Islands** and the numerous earthquakes.

The **Brooks Range** in the north, with elevations of up to 2,816 m, is adjacent to a coastal plain of varying widths, containing many lakes and marshes. In spite of these elevations, the mountain range, with its plateau landscape, has more of the characteristics of a low mountain range.

The mountain ranges of the **Chugach Mountains** and the **Alaska Range** run parallel to the Brooks Range. The southern regions of these ranges are heavily glaciated. In the north-west, the mountains drop steeply to the **Yukon Basin**. The water-meadows cover a large area in the direction of the Bering Sea and meet at a coastal plain, which is mostly covered by the **Yukon** and **Kuskokwim** rivers as they flow into the delta.

Almost three-quarters of the area is covered in permafrost, which reaches depths of up to 400 m. Inland, tundra vegetation prevails and in the south there are pine and sitka spruce forests.

Hudson

This river in the eastern USA, is named after the English sea captain, Henry Hudson. It rises in the Adirondacks from several small lakes. The Hudson is 507 km long and flows into New York Bay. It is linked to the lower reaches of the St. Lawrence river and to the Great Lakes by several canals. Its most important tributary is the Mohawk, which joins it from the east.

Alaska: in Glacier Bay 16 glaciers flow into the sea.

Yukon

This is Alaska's main river. It is 2,554 km long but if its headwater, the Nisutlin, is taken into account it is even longer, at 3,185 km, making it one of the longest rivers in North America. It has a drainage area of some 830,000 sq. km. The Yukon rises in the Coast Mountains and flows into the Bering Sea. The estuary covers an area of 30,000 sq. km of swamps and lakes.

The only heavy glaciation is that of the ice cap covering Greenland and on some other islands; however the sea is largely frozen for large parts of the year. In the central Arctic Ocean, the ice floes freeze in winter, creating a solid ice sheet. Icebergs are mainly found on the periphery.

In the area around the coast, there are large ice-free stretches of water, but these can quickly transform themselves into massive ice sheets

to a height of 1,800 m and reaching elevations of 3,733 m on the east face. Inland, the land sinks to 250 m below sea level, giving it the shape of a huge bowl, filled with a vast sheet of ice.

The inland pack-ice rises to 3,300 m in height and has a volume of 2.5 million cu. km. Only the mountain peaks soaring above the ice break up the monotonous white scenery. There are depressions, crevasses and clefts espe-

berg volcano erupted. Bjørnøya (Bear island) lies between the European ice cap and Svalbard. It is a table-shaped rocky island rising to a height of 536 m containing numerous shallow lakes and a distinctive cliff coast.

The archipelago of Svalbard lies 565 km off the Norwegian mainland. It consists of Spitsbergen (formerly known as Vestspitsbergen), Nordaustlandet, Edgeøya, Barentsøya, Prince Charles Fore-

the centre. Around 25 per cent of the islands are covered by a vast inland ice cap.

The **Severnaya Zemlya** (or Nicholas II Land) archipelago lies off the **Taimyr** peninsula between the Kara and the Laptev Seas. Mainland ice covers barely half of the four large and several smaller islands.

The **New Siberian** Islands (**Novosibirskiye Ostrova**) stretch between the Laptev and East

Alaska

Three seas surround the Alaskan peninsula: the Arctic Sea extends to the north, to the west the peninsula is separated from Asia by the Bering Sea and it is bounded to the south by the Pacific Ocean.

High mountain ranges, rivers and lakes are the primary characteristics of the Alaska's varied landscapes. The topography of Alaska has its origin in an early period of Earth's history. In the Jurassic, Cretaceous and Tertiary periods, numerous layers of sediment were deposited on a substrate of limestone, schist and sandstone. Tectonic plate movements and folding processes then created a large variety of formations during the Tertiary period.

This process is still not complete. Active volcanoes on the Aleutian Islands and numerous earthquakes, which mostly occur on the south coast of Alaska, show that seismic activity is still at work changing the shape of the peninsula.

Alaska's interior is characterised by rolling hills, basins and deep river gorges. The two main mountain ranges run from east to west, parallel to each other. The more southerly Pacific Mountain System, which forms a large arc in southern Alaska, is part of the North American Cordillera. The central area, the Alaska Range, has summits of around 6,000 m, which extend over the Aleutian Range to the Aleutian Islands. Prince William Sound south of the Chugach Mountains is picturesque.

Numerous glaciers flow to the Pacific coast, which is dotted with islands. The jagged coastline has many inlets, peninsulas and fjords. A steep slope in the northwest marks the transition to the Yukon Basin, which is approximately 1,200 m high in the east, but flattens out to the west.

The Brooks Range, north of the Pacific Mountain System, is a trunk mountain chain, traversed by deep valleys; the mountains rise to a height of 2,816 m. The chain continues towards the Arctic Sea parallel to a coastal plain of varying widths containing many marshes and lakes.

Alaska's major rivers are the 1,287-km-long Kuskokwim, whose course follows the Kuskokwim mountains, as well as the Yukon, whose waters flow across a wide delta into the Norton Sound.

Big picture: Mount McKinley (6,194 m). The snowline begins at around 2,000 m.

1 The 5,951-m-high, glaciated Mount Logan stands on Alaska's south-east border.

2 Alaska chain: Wonder Lake at the foot of Mount McKinley is the biggest lake in the Denali National Park.

3 Autumn in the 24,000 sq. km Denali National Park.

North and Central America

*Mount Saint Helen's in Washington State was considered to be dormant, until it suddenly erupted violently in 1980, blowing off its cone and killing 60 people. Lava and ash rained down for many miles around. This is one of the volcanos formed during the Tertiary Era in the **Cascades Range**.*

The Alaska Range

The **Alaska Range** is a continuation of the **North American Cordillera** and is the highest region in this high mountain range. **Mount McKinley**, at 6,194 m, is the highest mountain in North America. The volcanic **Aleutian Range** is a continuation of the Alaska Range on the Alaskan Peninsula, finally ending in the **Aleutian Islands**.

The Yukon Basin

The northernmost of North America's intra-mountain basins is situated between the **Coast Mountains** and the **Brooks Range** and slopes gradually from a height of 1,200 m in the east as it heads west. The landscape is composed of low mountain ranges, hills and basins. The deep gorges of the river valleys are very impressive. The **Yukon** and

Colorado River

The Colorado River rises in the Rocky Mountains and flows for 2,334 km draining into the Gulf of California in Mexico. It is of great economic importance due to its dams and artificial irrigation systems. The river is renowed for the deep chasms it has cut through the Colorado plateau. The Grand Canyon is on average 1,600 m deep and between 6 km and 29 km wide. The steep sides are stepped with ledges and platforms, and broken up by many intersecting gorges.

the **Kuskokwim** rivers drain into the Yukon Basin.

The Mackenzie Mountains

The **Mackenzie Mountains** are a range in north-western Canada on the Alaskan border. They are the northern continuation of the **Rocky Mountains** and extend over a distance of 800 km. The range, which has been little explored, reaches a height of 2,900 m.

The Canadian Shield

The **Laurentian Massif** curves around from the mouth of the **Mackenzie River** in the north via the **Great Bear Lake**, the **Great Slave Lake**, **Lake Athabasca**, the **Reindeer Lake** and **Lake Winnipeg** to the **Labrador** coast. It covers an area of around 5 million sq. km.

In the west, the massif is bordered by the **Hudson Bay Basin** and in the north it ends in the islands of the Canadian-Arctic archipelago.

Whereas the southern part of the islands generally consists of flat plains mostly devoid of vegetation or of gently undulating plateau landscapes that are rarely above 400 m, the northern regions are generally mountainous.

The high **Innuitian Mountains** contain numerous glaciers.

Mount Challenger on **Ellesmere Island** rises to an altitude of 3,048 m and the range reaches to 2,600 m on **Baffin Island**. The Canadian Shield has an average altitude of 400 to 500 m and gently curves in the shape of a key around the edges. In the west, the boundaries consist of tiers of strata of the **Interior Plains** and in the east they are bounded by the Labrador coastal region. The **Torngat Mountains**, rise to an altitude of 1,700 m. The

ancient land mass consists of archaic and proterozoic rocks, mostly gneiss, granite, limestone and sandstone. The land mass is covered with rivers and dotted with lakes, the result of Ice Age glaciation. There are endless expanses of wooded hills, bare flat rocky outcrops and shallow basins.

Baffin Bay

The area of sea that was named after the British seafarer, William Baffin, is a branch of the North Atlantic and extends over an area of 689,000 sq. km between Greenland in the west and Baffin Island in the east. **Baffin Bay** is 1,450 km in length, the width varies between 110 km and 650 km. The **Davis Straits** connect the Labrador Sea and Baffin Bay; the narrow **Nares Strait** leads to the Arctic Sea. Depths of 2,100 m have been

Mount Columbia (3,747 m) at Lake Maligne in the Rocky Mountains.

measured in the middle of the Bay in the **Baffin Hollow**; elsewhere, the Bay is between 240 m and 700 m deep. The undersea shelves of Greenland and Canada line the seabed of Baffin Bay. The sediment on the sea bed consists of deposits of debris from the Ice Age.

The prevailing climate in the Bay is extremely cold and even in the height of summer the icebergs barely melt. The tidal range is between 4 m and 9 m.

Baffin Island is Canada's largest Arctic island at 688,808 sq. km. The heavily glaciated mountains reach heights of up to 2,600 m.

Newfoundland

This island in the Atlantic Ocean, measuring 108,860 sq. km, faces the wide estuary of the **St. Lawrence River** of the east coast of Canada.

The interior consists of a trunk mountain block, which rises to 814 m as the **Appalachian** foothills in the **Long Range Mountains**. The glaciers from the last Ice Age have created a low hilly relief which and contains many forests, moors, lakes, rivers and waterfalls. The rocky cliff coast is laced with numerous fjords.

Labrador

This peninsula in the north-east of North America forms the eastern part of the Canadian Shield with an area of approximately 1.6 million sq. km. Labrador was virtually uninhabited until recent times; it consists of a plateau that reaches 1,700 m in the **Torngat Mountains** in the northeast. Dense pine forests characterise this landscape with its wealth of lakes. In the north, the vegetation gradually changes into Arctic tundra. The Labrador trough, which stretches from **Ungava Bay** to **Lake Mistassini**, contains rich iron ore deposits.

Rocky Mountains

The Rockies stretch for more than 4,300 km down the west coast of North America from the Brooks Range in Alaska via Canada to New Mexico. They are part of the **North American Cordillera**, which continues down the west coast into Central and South America. They were folded upward about 150 million years ago at the transition from the Cretaceous period to the Tertiary and partly uplifted. Around 50 million years ago, the high mountain ranges were uplifted again through volcanic activity. Molten magma welled up in the Earth's crust, solidified into granite or other igneous rocks and penetrated through to the

surface as magma again after renewed amalgamation.

The **Rocky Mountains** gained their definitive appearance approximately two million years ago, when immense ice sheets cleared a path during the Ice Age and cut deep gorges into the rock, polishing mountain slopes and carving deep basins which are now mountain lakes. The Ice Age glaciers are also responsible for the trough valleys, corries, moraines and fjords typical of this mountain chain. Some parts of the Rocky Mountains are still heavily glaciated.

In total, 74 peaks have elevations of over 3,500 m and 600 mountains exceed the 2,000 m mark. **Mount Elbert** in Colorado at 4,396 m is the highest peak.

In the north, the Rocky Mountains are more densely wooded than in the south and are divided into longitudinal valleys due to numerous river resurgences. In the south, the mountains are separated into parallel chains, which include several high basins, such as the Colorado Plateau and the Great Basin.

The Coast Mountains

The **Coast Mountains** are part of the Pacific Mountain System and stretch over 1,600 km from the Alaskan border through British Columbia to the **Fraser River** in the south. Many summits are higher than 3,400 m in the **Munday**, **Tiedemann** and **Monarch Mountains**. The highest peak is **Mount Waddington** at 4,016 m. Numerous glaciers have cut deep gorges or canyons in the rock and also created the fjord landscape on the Pacific Coast.

The Cascade Mountains

The **Cascades** stretch for about 1,100 km from British Columbia in the north via the states of Washington and Oregon to California in the south.

After the mountain range had been levelled down to a trunk area in the Early Tertiary period, it was later raised again by volcanic activity. The numerous peaks of over 3,000 m are extinct volcanoes, which are partly glaciated. There is still some volcanic activity.

The **Niagara Falls** were formed during the Ice Age. The Niagara River, which marks the border between Canada and the USA, flows from **Lake Erie** into **Lake Ontario**. In the middle of its course, the river drops over a 60 m sheer cliff to form the Niagara Falls which are split in two. The semi-circular Horseshoe Falls are on the Canadian side and on the American side, the American Falls.

The highest elevations are **Mount Rainier** at 4,392 m, **Mount Adams** at 3,751 m and **Mount Hood** (3,426 m). The densely wooded mountains showa clear climate delineation. Whereas clouds from the Pacific precipitate on the western slopes, there is very little rainfall in the regions situated in the eastern lee of the range. Rainfall only increases in the higher mountain ranges of the Rocky Mountains further to the east. They are called the Cascades due to their numerous rapids and waterfalls.

The Coast Ranges

To the west of the **longitudinal valleys** of the **Willamette** River and the **Puget Sound**, the relatively short chains of the **Coast Ranges** run parallel to the Pacific coast.

In the centre, they are approximately 1,000 m high, but climb to 2,692 m in the **Diabolo Range**. Several geological faults traverse the high ranges, of which the most famous is the **San Andreas Fault**. At this point, the Pacific and American continental plates are moving past each other. The tension arising from this, which can be released without warning, means that the region is permanently at risk from earthquakes. The city of San Francisco is built at one of the most vulnerable points, meaning that its inhabitants must always be prepared for earth tremors of varying intensity.

To be convinced of the volcanic activity in the Cascade Range area, one merely has to visit **Lassen Volcanic National Park**, where bubbling fumaroles and hot springs are evidence of how thin the Earth's crust is here.

Sierra Nevada

The Great Basin is a 500,000 sq. km wide desert highland, which stretches between the Columbia Plateau in the north, the Mojave Desert in the south, the Sierra Nevada in the west and the Wasatch Range in the east. Short, sheer mountain ranges intersect the Great Basin along a north-south axis. In Mount Bonpland and the East Humboldt Range, the mountains reach elevations of 3,450 m.

The basins are situated at an altitude of between 1,000 and 1,500 m in the north; in the south they sink to below sea level in the arid Sonora Desert at the **Salton Sink**, now known as the Salton Sea. The Salton Sink is located in south-eastern California near the Arizona border. In 1905, a levee broke on the Colorado River. The river found the easiest course for the overflow which was a nearby deep natural depression known as the Salton Sink. A huge lake was created, which has no outlet and is brackish as a result. It is now known as the Salton Sea. The Salton

Sink is the eighth deepest place on earth.

Death Valley, so named for its hostile climate is a National Park. It reaches the deepest point on the land surface of the United States (-86 m) at the brackish Badwater Basin. This is also one of the hottest places on earth, a temperature of 56.7°C having been recorded there in 1913. Death Valley National Park was established in 1933, covers almost 4,800 sq. km.

Viewed from the top of the 3,368 m Telescope Peak in the Panamint Range Mountains, the floor of Death Valley spreads out almost 3.5 km below. All the great divisions of geological time, the eras and most of their sub-divisions, are represented in the rocks of the mountains that ring Death Valley. The short rivers seep away into the ground, Great salt crusts and enormous salt lakes, such as the **Salduro Flats** in western Utah make the whole region

into a highly inhospitable landscape. The **Great Salt Lake**, which is only 5m deep on average, is the remainder of a once considerably larger freshwater lake from the ice-age, whose surface area varied between 3,900 and 5,300 sq. km.

The playas of the **Mojave** and **Gila Deserts** are extremely arid.

1 Alaska chain: the Kluane National Park, at the border of Canada with Alaska, contains around 4,000 glaciers, some of which are over 10 km in width and up to 100 km long.

2 + **3** Northern Rocky Mountains: lakes formed during the ice age, partly glaciated high mountains and deep, lonely valleys are typical of the Canadian Rockies, as here in the Banff National Park.

4 The Cascade chain: Mount Rainier is 4,392 m high, covered in several glaciers.

Rocky Mountains

The 'Rockies' form the eastern section of the North American Cordillera and run along the west coast of the continent of North America. In total, 74 peaks in the Rocky Mountains reach a height of more than 3,500 m, and 600 mountains are higher than 2,000 m. The mountain range is home to many endangered animals.

The Northern Cordillera extends for 4,500 km from Alaska through Canada and along the West Coast to New Mexico. The mountains form the backbone of the North American Continent. The highest points in the region are the 4,399-m-high Mount Elbert in Colorado and Mount Robson in Canada, (3,954 m).

In geological terms, the Rocky Mountains are a relatively young chain of fold mountains. The story of the creation of the Rockies began approximately 120 million years ago, when tectonic movements of the Earth's crust caused large areas of land to fold. Powerful subterranean volcanic activity accompanied these force-

ful movements. Magma welled up from beneath the crust and solidified on the surface as granite and other plutonic rocks, or reached the Earth's surface in the form of lava.

The modern landscape of the Rocky Mountains was shaped by powerful glaciers which formed in the Ice Age that began just two million years ago. Sheets of ice, some several thousand metres thick, thrust over the mountain sides and into the valleys. They cut razor-sharp ridges into the stone, wore down prominent cliff formations, smoothed the mountain slopes and carved out deep bowls, that later filled with melt-water to form mountain lakes.

The natural landscapes of the Rocky Mountains are extremely varied and have been a favourite subject of landscape paintings since the early nineteenth century. The Grand Canyon of northwest Arizona is also part of the Rockies. This amazing sight, the most famous gorge in the world, is the result of slow erosion by the Colorado River over millions of years, eating into the stone strata of the plateau to form a canyon 400 km long, between 6 and 30 km wide and up to 1,800 m deep. The Colorado

River has numerous cataracts and rapids, making it a paradise for whitewater rafting enthusiasts.

The Rocky Mountains are also North America's main watershed. The rivers rising in the mountains, often dammed to form lakes, are an important source of water, particularly for the inhabitants of

the south-western States which have low rainfall.

In 1807, a fur hunter in the northwestern state of Wyoming stumbled across a particularly impressive landscape with dramatic vertical cliffs, rumbling waterfalls, boiling hot springs and geysers. Back in his home town of St. Louis, nobody believed his

Fantastical glacier landscape in the Glaciers National Park, Montana.

Left: catching a glimpse of an elk or grizzly bear is an unforgettable experience.

fanciful descriptions of a weird landscape. Over the following decades, other trappers also described this wondrous area in Yellowstone, in the middle of the Rocky Mountains, until eventually two official expeditions were sent to the region. Their impressive report resulted in the creation in 1872 of the world's first National Park – Yellowstone.

Since then, a series of further nature reserves have been established in the northern Rockies. They are Glacier National Park in Montana, Denali National Park in Alaska, the Grand Tetons in Wyoming and the Rocky Mountains National Park in Colorado – whose large number of mountains over 3,000–4,000 m have given it the nickname 'The Roof of the Continent'. The Guadalupe Mountains National Park in Texas and New Mexico has been created in the southern Rockies.

The Rocky Mountains offer ideal habitats for many rare and endangered mountain animals. The Bald Eagle, the national bird of the United States, rules the skies and the rare Whooping Crane finds refuge here. The dense woodland of the national parks consist mainly of spruce, fir and pine, and the forests are inhabited by elk, wapiti, bighorn sheep, mountain hares and beavers. Nocturnal animals, including foxes, pumas, lynxes and wolves, hunt their prey at night.

The symbol of the North American wilderness is the giant grizzly bear, a sub-species of the brown bear, although the grizzly is now threatened with extinction. Only some 1,000 specimens remain in North America. Before the continent was discovered by European settlers, it was inhabited by 100,000 of these 2.5-m-high bears. Their territory extended

from Alaska to Mexico and from the Pacific coast to the endless expanse of the Great Plains.

The mountain goat lives above the tree line of the Rocky Mountains, almost undisturbed by any other creature. This relative of the chamois is incredibly agile on the steep mountain rocks and dangerous cliffs. Another inhabitant of the high mountains is the marmot, which can hibernate for up to eight months of the year and which, in the short time in between, will normally only leave its burrow to collect food. The shy and nimble coyote – a relative of the fox and wolf – has only been reintroduced to the Rocky Mountains in the last few decades. This animal has adapted well to the tough living conditions of its

mountain habitat, and it will eat anything. The same cannot be said of the enormous masters of the plains: the bison. These massive wild cattle can be three metres long and have a shoulder height of 2 m, but only eat grass – though in huge quantities of up to 12 kg a day – in order to prepare for the tough, long and

strength-sapping winters of the cordillera, during which snow can block the passes as early in the year as November. During the coldest part of the year, temperatures in the valleys can sink to -20°C. Like so many other natural environments, the wilderness of the Rockies is now threatened with oil exploration.

At 3,618 m, Mount Assiniboine in Alberta is one of Canada's most beautiful mountains.

The Colorado Plateau

In the south-western United States, ancient oceans and movements of the Earth's crust have formed an immense plateau over a period of 300 million years. In the last ten to 20 million years, wind and water have transformed it further.

The Colorado Plateau is riven with deep gorges, including the famous Grand Canyon, impressive cliff formations, towering stone monoliths and curious arches. It is an indescribable collection of picturesque rock formations that only the wonders of nature could produce.

The plateau lies in the south-western United States of America and covers an area of approximately 112,000 sq. km, spanning four states – Arizona, Utah, Colorado and New Mexico.

Large sections of this breath-taking landscape are protected and are open to the public in the form of National Parks.

Main photograph:
The cliffs and mesas (table-shaped mountains) of Monument Valley are the remains of an even older landscape that has now been almost completely eroded.

1 The sandstone formations of the Arches National Park are almost surreal. They have been caused by the variations in hardness of the composite rocks, which are subject to the constant forces of erosion.

2 Sandstone arches in Arches National Park. Harder rock in the upper strata has meant that the sediment below has only been partially eroded.

3 Bryce Canyon: the reddish-pink colour of the rock is the result of weathering. The iron in the minerals of the rock is slowly oxidising.

4 The Virgin River has defined the landscape of Zion National Park and has formed a very deep gorge, which in places is very narrow.

5 Monument Valley: clearly, the Three Sisters mesas were once part of a higher plateau.

The Grand Canyon

This immense gorge on the Colorado Plateau in nothwest Arizona, has been eroded over millions of years by the Colorado River. It is one of the most impressive natural wonders in the world.

In 1540, the Spaniard López de Cárdenas was the first European to set eyes on the stunning panorama of the Grand Canyon, but the region was not properly mapped until the mid-nineteenth century. The exact formation process of the Grand Canyon has still not been fully researched. It seems likely that approximately ten million years ago, the Colorado began to search a path across the rocky plateau. Over the course of time, a gorge has developed, which is now up to 1,800 m deep, 350 km long and 30 km wide. Wind and water have both played a role in giving the cliff walls their bizarre features. The sequence of different stone layers is easy to see in the walls of the gorge, and these indicate the separate geological periods of the development of the Earth. Fossils found here have provided useful information about life millions of years ago. The deepest and most impressive section of the gorge was declared the Grand Canyon National Park in 1908 and covers an area of 4,934 sq. km.

Temperatures in the Grand Canyon can reach 50°C and only extremely resilient plants and animals can survive here. The region is home to several species of cactus and thorn bush, rattle snakes, scorpions and black widow spiders. Only a small variety of fish live in the Colorado River itself. Iguana, toads and frogs live on the river's banks. In some places, it is possible to find beavers and otters. Only the woods on the northern and southern borders of the river provide a habitat for a larger variety of plants and animals.

Main photograph:
The Grand Canyon is the most famous gorge in the world. It is divided by cliffs, protrusions, and platforms, and the cliff walls can descend in stages. The canyon also has several lesser gorges. The layers of rock are mainly red, blue and yellow in colour.

Photo right: From certain angles, the Colorado River looks like a silver stream in the Grand Canyon.

*Sierra Nevada: the 4,418-m-high **Mount Whitney** in the Californian Central Sierra Nevada, is the highest peak in the USA outside Alaska. The upper slopes of the Sierra Nevada are mainly covered with forests.*

Colorado Plateau

With an area of around 112,000 sq. km,the tableland of the **Colorado Plateau** spreads across northern Arizona, southern Utah, south-western Colorado and north-western New Mexico. The altitudes can reach between 1,500 m and 3,300 m.

The numerous plateaus are made from different strengths of rock strata that are in various stages of erosion. Mountain streams and rivers have cut deep clefts in the rock. The most famous of these is the massive Grand Canyon.

Grand Canyon

One of the greatest natural wonders on earth is the deep gorge, around 350 km long (greater than the distance from London to Paris!) that the Colorado River has cut through the Colorado Plateau in north-west Arizona.

The gorge is 1,600 m deep in the centre and ranges in width from 6 to 29 km. For a long time it was thought the canyon was created by the collapse of a rift, as it did not seem possible that the Colorado river, which is not that impressive in such a dry landscape, could have cut such a deep and wide gorge through the rock strata. In 1869, John Welsey Powell was able to prove that the rock strata on both sides of the valley belonged to the same faces, so a rift collapse could be ruled out. The Colorado needed about six million years to mould this massive depression in the rock. Geologists have found the area to be an excellent field of research, as more than 350 m years of natural history has been exposed on the sides of the gorge.

The various rock strata in the Grand Canyon stretch from the Kaibab limestone of the Permian era on the surface, through to archaic formations at the bottom of the gorge. The individual strata are only slightly sloping, and are made up of step-like escarpments. The 100 m-thick **Kaibab limestone** is the youngest and deepest stratum, deposited in the Permian era. The numerous marine fossils contained in it make it easy to recognise that this white formation was once a sea bed.

The next stratum is composed of yellow Coconino sandstone. It is associated with Supai formation with red and green sandstones, chalk and slate. The next layer consists of Redwell limestone from the Lower Carboniferous era. The gorge cuts deep into the **Archaean bedrock** that is formed from granite, gneiss and mica schist – rocks that have partly been overlaid with red sandstone, schist and chalk from the Algonkian age.

After the Colorado Plateau was uplifted in the Miocene age, erosion wore away strata from the Eocene, Cretaceous, Jurassic and Triassic eras, and the river was able to carve a course for itself deep in the base of the bedrock. The bizarre rock formations – towers, ledges and crevices, some reminiscent of a Buddhist stupa – are the result of a combination of various factors – the alternating hard and soft rock strata, vertical and horizontal erosion, extreme

Great Basin: rocks in the Death Valley.

temperature fluctuations, wind and aridity.

There are three distinct **vegetation zones**. In the dry heat of the valley, only desert plants can prosper. Above this there is a temperate zone, where the land is dominated by live-oaks and junipers. At over 2,000 m there are mixed forests containing Douglas firs and aspen. In winter, the high plateau is covered in deep snow. Both the northern rim and the southern rim of the Grand Canyon are open to the public, although

visitors are not given access to the northern rim during the winter. There are also helicopter rides over the canyon, and to nearby Lake Havasu. The 72-km-long Lake Havasu on the Colorado River was named by the Chemehuevi Indians and translates into 'Land of the Blue Green Water'.

Bryce Canyon

Another impressive natural wonder of the Colorado Plateau is **Bryce Canyon** in south-western Utah. The canyon, around 146 sq. km in size, was not formed by a river like the Grand Canyon, but is the result of erosion of the steep edges of the Pansaugunt Plateau.

Bryce Canyon was formed shortly after the Grand Canyon and **Zion Canyon**, which belong together, geomorphologically speaking. The course of natural history can also be read from these slopes. The rock strata in the west come from the Pre-Cambrian era, and get gradually younger to the east. In the Triassic there was a plateau landscape here that was made from limnic chalk, to which pillars, columns and strangely shaped blocks still bear witness. Around 60 million years ago, southern Utah was covered by a lake. Chalk, sand and alluvium were deposited on the lake bed and this was compressed into a 600 m-thick rock stratum. When several massive tectonic movements occurred 13 million years ago and squeezed the land into a

slope, the lake drained away. The formations that were piled up to 3,000 m high broke apart and were fragmented into massive blocks by the tension. This is where the work of the erosion agents began, carving the shapes that are visible today from the Pansaugunt Plateau.

The massive temperature fluctuations and the composition of the eroded materials, which are hostile to plant life, mean that there is little vegetation in the vicinity of Bryce Canyon.

A certain attraction comes not only from the breath-taking rock formations, but also from the fascinating interplay of colours. The metal oxides in the rocks create widely different impressions of colour, depending on the weather and the position of the sun. Bryce Canyon has been opened up to the public. A well signposted network of paths indicate the places of interest in this fascinating area full of natural history.

Monument Valley

Monument Valley is in the central region of the Colorado Plateau, on the border of Arizona and Utah. This 70-km by 80-km-wide valley within the Navajo Indian reservation reaches elevations of 1,600 m to 2,300 m.

The isolated rock towers and tablelands are made of De Chelley sandstone and stand 600 m above the landscape. Depending on the position of the sun, visitors to this picturesque giant can experience a fascinating show of light, shadow and every shade of red and purple.

The red sandstone dates from the late Permian era. When almost all of North America was covered with a primeval lake in the early Triassic period, a large amount of sand was deposited in Monument Valley. After the sea drained away, the uplift phase of the Colorado Plateau began, which caused the mountains to break into giant slabs in the process. Over several million years, wind and water eroded the upper stratum, which was then covered by later formations. The different strata were subjected to various weathering processes in the period following the Quaternary. The formation of the curious red rock giants is mainly the work of the

wind, which eroded the soft strata over millions of years. Only the most resilient rocks could resist the force of the wind.

The typically shaped rocks are reminiscent of sculptures, causing people to imagine all kinds of representations. They have been given names such as 'the Totem Pole', 'Big Indian', 'King's Throne' and 'Castle'. The vegetation is rather sparse, consisting of a few isolated barrel cacti, stunted bushes, succulents and some grasses. The lack of ground cover exposes the fascinating mechanism of this unique landscape. The Navajo Indians live dotted around the site in their traditional huts.

Arches National Park

More than 300 m years ago, the foundations of this 300 sq. km National Park were laid in the US state of Utah. On the bed of a primaeval sea, thick layers of salt accumulated. These later expanded into underground domes under the pressure of subsequent deposits. The surrounding rock material advanced, and fragmented under the tension into immense parallel rock strata. Precipitation and wind eroded the softer layers of rock from these blocks and created the famous **Arches** – bizarre, free-standing rock arches. The most famous of the rock arches of which there are around 200 – is the so-called Delicate Arch, which stands in isolation 50 m high on a rocky plateau.

Great Plains

With a length of over 5,000 km and a breadth of between 500 km and 1,200 km, the **Great Plains** stretch from the west of the Inner rim from the Arctic coast at the mouth of the Mackenzie River, to the Rio Grande in central Texas, where they meet the Gulf Coast. This plateau was originally covered in grassland. The phenotype changed only after the first white settlers took over the land and allowed their cattle and horses to graze on it. Large fields, on which grain is largely grown as a monoculture, determine the look of the landscape today. While the

The *Joshua Tree National Monument* in the *Great Basin* consists of two different types of desert, the *Colorado desert* and the *Mojave desert*. Joshua Trees, members of the Yucca family of succulents are found in the High Desert.

altitudes in the east are only around 400 to 500 m, the plateaus, traversed by a large number of rivers, rise westwards to heights of up to 1,600 m in the foothills of the Rocky Mountains.

Great Lakes

The five **Great Lakes** are linked together by the St Lawrence Seaway, which drains into the Atlantic. The largest group of freshwater lakes on Earth, said to contain 20 per cent of all the freshwater on the surface of the planet, were created during the last Ice Age – the lakes are the remains of massive glacial basins. On the northern shore of the Great Lakes there is the flat valley of the St Lawrence Seaway, which was shaped by Pleistocene glaciation inland, and still exhibits many glacial forms. The 100 m natural barrier around the river, rises at the lake shores into a rump landscape of a height of 300–400 m.

The banks of the Great Lakes are shaped by a steep fjord-like coast, which gives way to **Georgian Bay,** containing numerous islands and skerries formed during the last Ice Age. The Great Lakes have a total area of around 245,000 sq. km.

Lake Superior is the largest at 82,103 sq. km. It has a maximum depth of 405 m, and is drained by **St Mary's River** into **Lake Huron.** Lake Superior is free of ice for eight months of the year.

Lake Huron is at an altitude of 177 m, has an area of 61,797 sq. km; it is up to 228 m deep. **Lake Michigan**, which lies to the south-west, is 57,757 sq. km. It is linked to Lake Huron by the **Straits of Mackinaw**, and is 282 m deep. The most southerly of the Great Lakes is **Lake Erie** – 25,725 sq. km and up to 64 m deep. This lake is linked to **Lake Ontario** by the **Niagara River**. The difference between the water levels is the reason for the formation of the **Niagara Falls**. Lake Ontario, the smallest and most easterly of the Great Lakes, is 19,011 sq. km, lies 75 m above sea level; it is 244 m deep in places. The canals that connect the lakes make them navigable for ships.

Appalachians

The Appalachian central massif, formed from crystalline rocks, stretches over 2,600 km from Newfoundland to northern Alabama. The 200 to 300-km-wide mountains were created around 300 m years ago during the Appalachian mountain-building phase in the Palaeozoic era, and are therefore considerably older than the Cordillera in the west. After a period of erosion, the Appalachians were lifted again in the Triassic period, and than eroded again, so the highest elevations of the **White Mountains** and the **Green Mountains**

1 The Yosemite national park demonstrates the variety and the beauty of the Sierra Nevada. The fruitful valley is overshadowed by the granite cupola of El Capitán.

2 Aspen, Colorado: snow- and ice-covered mountains, deep ravines and forests are typical of the Rocky Mountains in this part of Colorado.

3 Big Sur on the southern coast mountains between San Simeon and Carmel in central California. The Pacific breakers hurl themselves against the rugged coastline, a surfer's paradise.

North and Central America

Great Plains: the area in the Western Plains of the USA is poor in vegetation and often described as *'The Badlands'*. The Badlands National Park in South Dakota comprises almost 100,000 ha.

It contains a fascinating stone landscape, formed through wind and water erosion of the less resistant rocks, resulting in ravines, chines, towers and pyramids.

barely reach 2,000 m. The highest peak is **Mount Mitchell** at 2,037 m. The Appalachians are divided into north and south sections by the **Hudson-Mohawk gorge**. The Northern Appalachians comprise a 750m-high plateau, which was heavily glaciated during the Ice Age but is still easily recognisable due to the glacial deposits and landfill features.

The Southern Appalachians are divided into several thinner ridges. The **Piedmont** is limited by the coastal plain fault lineson. The 100 to 400-m-high undulating plateau is dominated by the **Blue Ridge** to the west.

Until the nineteenth century, the Blue Ridge was only passable through a few mountain passes such as the **Cumberland Gap**. The spine of the Southern Appalachians is the 1,500-km-long and 150-km-wide **Great Appalachian Valley**, that comprises several parallel strata up to 600 m high.

Mississippi, Missouri

The 'Great River' river or 'Missi Sepe' as the Indians called it rises in the Itasca lake 445 m above sea level, west of a Upper Lake. It flows through almost the whole length of the Great Plains and has the drainage area of 3,221 sq. km. With the Missouri, it has a combined length of 6,020 km, making it one of the longest rivers in the world. The lower reaches begin after the absorption of its tributraries, the Missouri and Illinois rivers, near St. Louis. Because it flows so slowly, the Mississippi is very meandering and creates ox-bow lakes. It is protected in many places by high embankments called 'levees'. Strong sedimentation means that the Mississippi has a shallow bed, so that it often flows above that of its surroundings. Flooding is therefore not unusual. The Mississippi eventually drains into the Gulf of Mexico at the wide Mississippi Delta.

This landscape is traversed by a river system that features numerous rapids, particularly on the **Tennessee River** and its tributaries. A steep escarpment marks the transition from the Great Appalachian Valley to the **Appalachian Plateau**, the largest area of the Appalachians. The **Allegheny** and **Cumberland**-plateaux are shaped by deep valleys that have been eroded into the rock by numerous rivers. The terrain slopes from around 1,000 m in the east to 300 m in the west, before gradually being replaced by the grassy plains of the central lowland.

The Mississippi stores a lot of sediment in its delta.

Gulf Coast

The northern and central parts of the Gulf Coast were given their current appearance during the Cretaceous period. Low mounds, rarely higher than 200 m and made from ancient rock, shape

the landscape. Long sandy beaches, sand banks, swamps and lagoons line the Gulf. There are almost no natural harbours in this northern region of Mexico.

The coastal plain is traversed by the **Rio Grande** (Rio Bravo del Norte) and **Tamesí-Pánuco** rivers. In the central part of the Mexican state of Veracruz, the extremities of the **Sierra Madre Occidental** narrow the plains to a breadth of only 15 km, and at San Andrés Tuxtla, the flat landscape is interrupted by a rocky coastline and undulating landscape. The rivers **Usumacinta**, **Grijalva**, **Coatzacoalcos** and **Papaloapan** turn into swampland at their estuaries, covered with typical swampland vegetation of mangroves, bulrushes and reeds. Naturally, the area is prone to serious flooding and this does serious damage to shipping and the oil installations in the region.

Mississippi basin

The immense watershed of the **Mississippi** is around 3,208,000 sq. km, of which 1,365,000 sq. km are in **Missouri**, and 528,000 sq. km in **Ohio**. In the north, there are glacial plateaus along the Canadian border, with numerous lakes and marshes. In the central region, a basin covered with recent sediment has determined the landscape, while towards the coast there are flat lagoon-rich alluvial areas. To the east, the Appalachians form the catchment area with the Rocky Mountains to the west.

Florida

The peninsula of **Florida** stretches almost 700 km into the sea, and divides the Gulf of Mexico from the Atlantic.

In the central area, Florida has a breadth of 110–150 km, in the north is the 550-km-wide 'panhandle'. In the south, there is a 600-km-long chain of offshore islands, the so-called **Florida Keys** (from the Spanish 'cay' an island). The last island in the chain, Key West, is the most southerly and westerly point of the continental United States and only 150 km from Cuba.

To the east, Florida is part of the continental shelf, and is made of strong limestone strata, which uplifted from the sea during the Triassic Era. The strong sea level fluctuations determined by cold and warm fronts have led to the formation of rolling uplands stretching towards the centre of the State.

South of **Lake Okeechobee**, the largest of the almost 8,000 lakes, there is a limestone plain containing numerous springs. In the **coastal area** to the west the land is sinking, and the terrain consists of swampland with numerous backwaters and bays, while to the Atlantic side, the coast contains spits – flat tongues of land, that form a barrier against the open sea – and long flat sandy beaches.

The Florida **Everglades** in the south are a huge swamp surrounded by thick mangrove forests, in which manatees have found their most northerly retreat. The Everglades are a National Park, full of interesting

wildlife, including alligators and crocodiles.

Atlantic Coastal Plain

The fault line marks the transition to the **Atlantic Coastal Plain**. The coast has many bays and fjords and skerries are witness to the glacial formation of this northerly stretch of coastline. Further south, the coast is full of fjords and inlets, along the course of which the coast widens. In the north, the coastal rivers have formed many natural harbours, while the south has more alluvium, lagoons and swamps.

Baja California

Baja California (**Lower California**) is a thin narrow peninsula, separated from the Mexican mainland by the Gulf of California. The peninsula is 1,200 km long and 40 to 240 km wide. Its upper surface is made of rock formations from the Cretaceous and Triassic periods.

In the south, sea sedimentation and volcanic remains from the Pleistocene and Holocene periods characterise the landscape. Several chains of mountains cross the peninsula, continuing the **Californian coastal mountain range**. In the east, the mountains fall to a steep rim, while they slope more gently in the west. These crystalline mountains are over 1,500 m high, but occasionally reach heights of 3,000 m.

On both sides of the **Sierra Santa Clara** there are plateaux, broad, flat strips of desert and cactus savannah. At the narrowest corner of the Gulf of California, the Colorado River reaches the sea in a massive delta. During the dry summer months, however, the river may dry up before it reach its destination.

Mexico

Almost 80 per cent of the surface of Mexico geologically belongs to the mainland, which narrows to barely 200 km at the Isthmus of **Theuantepec**. In the north-west, the thin peninsula of **Lower California** is attached to the

*The red sky of Shenandoah National Park in the State of Virginia: the National Park stretches alongside the **Blue Ridge Mountains**, the main chine of the **Appalaches**, and is mostly afforested. It is famous for its rich flora and fauna. The park offers magnificent views, especially in the late summer and autumn when the leaves of the deciduous trees, change to yellow, red and brown.*

mainland. South of the Isthmus of Theuantepec, the **Yucatán Peninsula** and the Mexican state of Chiapas make up the **Central American landmass**. The Mexican highland forms the continuation of the North American cordillera system and rises from 1,000 m in the north to 2,000 m. Towards the coast, the highlands drop away in steep slopes. To the west of the Mexican highland plateau, the **Sierra Madre Oriental** rises to 3,500 m.

The Meseta Central lies at a height of between 1,500 m and 3,000 m and is divided up into basins by isolated mountain ridges. The largest of these is the **Bolson de Mapimi**. In the east, the highland is bordered by the **Sierra Madre Occidental**, which rises up to 4,000 km, and by **Cordillera Volcánica** in the south.

These volcanic regions include the highest mountains in Mexico, like the snow-covered 5,700-m-high **Citlaltépetl** and the only slightly lower **Ixtaccicuatl** and **Popocatépetl**.

Numerous earthquakes and active volcanoes are proof of the continuing tectonic movement in this mountain region. The most impressive proof of volcanic activity is **Paricutin**, a volcano created in 1943.

The highland of **Chiapas**, which can be up to 3,000 m high, is abutted by the Sierra **Madre del Sur** at the coast, with several volcanic cones up to 4,000 m high. To the north east, the highland flattens gradually, and ends at the Yucatán Peninsula. Mangrove forests crossing the coastal lowland of **Tabasco**, are interlaced with rivers and lagoons, which continue from the **Gulf of Campeche** to the coastal lowland of Veracruz. While the **Rio Grande** carries extremely low levels of water in the arid winter, it becomes a raging torrent in the rainy season. The biggest river within the country is the **Rio Grande de Santiago**.

Sierra Madre

The highland of Mexico is abutted by two mountain ridges – in the west the **Sierra Madre Occidental**, and to the east the

Sierra Madre Oriental. The Sierra Madre Occidental runs from north-west to south-east, is around 1,100 km long and around 160 km wide. The elevation is over 1,800 m in the middle, with the highest elevation even exceeding the 3,000 m mark. The direction of the strata in the massive mountain chain and valleys are the result of the folding in the Mesozoic era. The so-called Barrancas – ravines up to 1,500 m deep – are a tourist attraction. The Sierra Madre Oriental also originated in the Mesozoic period. South-east of the Rio Grande there is a range

of relatively low mountains which rise to a massive chain south of Monterrey with peaks of over 3,000 m.

The Sierra Madre del Sur is a craggy labyrinth of mountain ridges and deep valleys of chalk sediment. The mountains, up to 3,000 m high, are bordered to the north by the lowlands of the **Balsa-Mezcala** river systems, to the east by the **Sierra Mixteca**, and in the southwest by an intermittent coastal plain.

Mexican highlands

The **highlands of Mexico** reach a height of around 2,500 m in the south, but in the north they are only 1,100 m high. The landscape is formed by seven large basins that are interlaced with a variety of isolated mountain chains and deep fissures in the earth.

The rather monotonous landscape of the northern highlands

is shaped by deserts with dunes and desert-like steppes, that slowly give way to grasslands. The mountain ridges stretch from north to south and from north-west to south-east and are up to 800 m to 900 m higher than the basins.

In the rainy season, flat lakes develop in the basins, which

1 Portland: the east coast of the New England states dives relatively smoothly into the Atlantic behind the northern highlands of the Appalaches.

2 Allegheny plateau: Pocahonta's river flow in the plains between the northern Appalaches and the Great Lakes.

3 High Mountains, wide valleys: in the Great Smokey Mountains in Tennessee lie the highest peaks of the Appalachen.

4 Whitewater Bay: The Everglades are an extended swamp and reed area surrounded by Mangrove forests, at the southern end of Florida.

*The West Indian Island of **Saint Lucia** is one of the Lesser Antilles. It is of volcanic origin, mountainous with rugged slopes rising to a height of 1,000 m partly forested. However only the higher layers display the pristine tropical rain forest vegetation, as most of the island is covered in secondary forest. The signature mark of the island is the steep volcanic cones of Gros Piton and Petit Piton, soaring from the plain near the Soufrières Volcano.*

evaporate again in the dry season. As they have no tidal movement and no outlet, salt remains in the basins, which transform into salt marshes and salt-clay plains.

The southern highlands are shaped by precipitation and have mountains and rolling hills formed by volcanic landfill. Gentle knolls alternate here with craggy volcanic peaks and basins, and high valleys with numerous lakes in between. The region, which is generally mountainous, also has isolated swamps and hot springs.

Sonora

The parallel mountain ranges with their broad valleys and the north Pacific coastal plain in the state of Sonora were created in the mid to late Triassic period. The detrital stone formations, which surround the basins of Sonora, give way to several mountain ranges to the north east. The coast itself is flat and sandy, with rocky areas and lagoons only in certain bays. The arid landscape of the **Sonora desert** begins in the north, and stretches to California and the south east of Arizona.

Yucatán, Central America

Central America forms the mainland bridge between the North and Latin American continents. The thin strip of land with mountain ridges can be up to 500 km wide in places.

The flat rolling country in the north west of Belize is part of the limestone plateau of the **Yucatán** peninsula. It is only in the extreme south that the foothills reach the Caribbean coast. Elsewhere, there is a marshy stretch of up to 75 km between the land and sea.

On the coast, there are more than 100 small untouched coral islands, the so-called Cays. In south Belize, the outer reaches of the Central American bedrock rise to **Victoria Peak** at 1,122 m. The **Maya Mountains** are composed of gneiss, schist, shale, and granite.

The Petén plateau in northern Guatemala is also part of the Yucatán peninsula. It consists of karst formations and swamps. The almost unexploited region is covered by thick rainforest, which gives way to pinewood and eventually savannah.

South of the Yucatán peninsula the landscape changes into the mountainous region of Central America. The area around Honduras is also part of the highlands encircled by the **Cordilleras.**

The eastern lowlands of Honduras are a humid, thickly-forested alluvial region, also described as **Misquite.** On the edge of the coast there is a marshy alluvial plain with lagoons. It provides an ideal habitat for mosquitoes and has been jokingly called the 'Mosquito coast'.

The western coastal lowlands of the Pacific are also geologically a relatively young alluvial plain. The **Nicaragua basin** with **Lake Nicaragua** and **Lake Managua** divides the broader north from the smaller southern part of the bridging land.

Lesser Antilles: the Virgin Islands in the Caribbean island arc.

The area is tectonically weak and prone to earthquakes and volcanic activity. In **Costa Rica,** three consecutive mountain ranges divide the north and the Caribbean lowland, from the low landscape of Guanacaste and the rolling country of the south west. In the canal zone in Panama, the central American strip of land is at its narrowest, at 55 km.

Yucatán Peninsula

The 450-km-wide and 600-km-long **Yucatán** Peninsula lies between the Gulf of Mexico in the north and west, and the **Caribbean** to the east. The large chalk plateau with karst formations gradually rose from the sea after the end of the Triassic period, and the lifting process continues today.

The peninsula is, apart from the 150-m-high **Sierrita,** completely flat. Although there no watercourses, there are extensive dry forests in the north, and rainforests in the south. This is due to the chalk substrate, which provides sufficient water supply through the formation of natural cisterns. The Yucatan Peninsula is famous for its unspoiled landscapes and tropical wildlife.

The west coast consists of sand banks and lagoons, and in the south there are coral reefs and smaller islands such as **Cozumel,** which is popular with scubadivers.

Central American Cordilleras

In southern Guatemala, the cordillera system has two main strands – the north western **Sierra de los Cuchumatanes** and the southern **Sierra Madre.**

The Sierra Madre is made up of craggy cordilleras and extensive plateaux. Here, there are several volcanic cones, of which some are still active. The **Tajumulco**

volcano is the highest peak in Central America at 4,220 m. Although volcanism has formed numerous small mountain ridges in the Honduras region, the volcanic cones, so typical elsewhere, are missing here.

In Nicaragua, the Central American cordillera continues into the Central Cordillera, and divides into several 100 – 200-km-long ridges. Although the **Pico Mogotón** is 2,107 m high, the mountains in this range are rarely higher than 1,500 m. In the north west of Costa Rica a chain of volcanic cones forms the **Cordillera de Guanacaste,** which reaches 1,971 m with **Orosî.** Further on are the much higher and partly active volcanos of the **Cordillera Central. Irazu** is the highest peak of this mountain range at 3,432 m. The mountains in the **Cordillera de Talamanca,** which are divided by the Valle Central, are higher, peaking with **Chirripó Grande** at 3,820 m. In Panama, the **Cordillera de Talamanca** continues into the volcanic **Serrania de Tabasará** mountain range. The highest point is **Volcán Barú** at 3,478 m. At only 1,000 m high, the mountains on the Caribbean coast of Panama, like the **Cordillera de San Blas,** are considerably lower.

Caribbean Islands

The **Caribbean islands** stretch in a broad arc over 4,000km from the south coast of Florida to the north eastern coast of Venezuela. The overall area of the islands is around 234,000 sq. km.

Around 95 per cent of the islands belong to the Antilles, with the **Greater Antilles** making up 90 per cent of the land surface. The **Lesser Antilles** is made up of innumerable small islands and are divided into the Windward and Leeward islands. The **Bahamas,** as well as the **Turks and Caicos Islands** and the more **remote Cayman Islands** are also part of the Caribbean Islands. The island arc separates the Caribbean Sea from the Atlantic. Around the islands, large parts of the sea are also part of the continental shelf. The **Bahamas, Cuba** and **Trinidad** are dominated by shellow seas, which have formed since the last

Ice Age. The remaining regions of the Caribbean are deep sea, with an average depth of 4,000 to 5,000 m. In the Cayman rift, depths of 7,250 m have been measured, in the Puerto Rico rift 8,540 m, and the Milwaukee Deep 9,219 m.

In these rifts, the earth's crust is particularly thin. It is here that the epicentre of earthquakes are often located and the islands themsleves are tectonically unstable. Given the abrasion terraces formed in the coral chalk, it is possible to determine to what extent the islands are being pushed out of the water. Often it is in these coastal regions, which are rising step by step, that it is possible to recognise the channels chiselled in the chalk by the surf. Particularly impressive terrace systems can be seen in the north west part of Hispaniola and on Cape Maisi in Cuba.

The Bolsas and Bocas peculiar to the Netherlands Antilles, Cuba and Curacao are, in contrast, the result of marine flooding.

A particular attraction of the landscape lies in the many coral reefs that stretch from the north to the Bermudas. The reefs on the island coasts are clearly divided into inner reef, reef crest, reef platform and ruckriff. The bank reefs further out to the sea, which are barely under the water surface, are less clearly differentiated.

A particular feature of the Caribbean islands is the wonderful sandy beaches, which often cover the coastal rock.

Greater Antilles

The islands of **Cuba, Jamaica, Hispaniola, Puerto Rico** and other small islands make up the Greater Antilles. The North American **Cordillera** continues into this island arc, turning towards the east in Central America.

Several parallel mountain chains make up the island of Hispaniola. In the central cordillera, **Pico Duarte** reaches a height of 3,175 m. **Sierra Maestra,** with **Pico Turquino** at 1,974 m on Cuba, **Blue Mountain Peak** at 2,256 m on **Jamaica** and **El Yunque** at 1,065 m on Puerto Rico are branches of the cordillera system. Even if the mountains reach high levels, they are different from the Rocky Mountains in that the re-

Baja California (lower California) is separated by the Gulf from the continent. The desert peninsula is 1,300 km long and its mountain chain over 3,000 m high. Typical of the stark coastal landscape of the peninsula in the North West of Mexico are the numerous cacti, capable of surviving long drought periods. In Baja California alone, 120 different cacti have been counted and almost half of them can only be found there.

lief was not formed by ice-age glaciation, but by erosion from rivers and precipitation. larger plains can be only found in the Bahamas and on Cuba. Here there are low chalk plateaux with uniform formations.

Lesser Antilles

A large number of tiny islands make up the Lesse Antilles archipelago, which are divided into two island chains.

The **Leeward Islands** form an arc from the **Virgin Islands** in the north to Trinidad in the south. **Montserrat, Antigua, Guadeloupe** and **Dominica** make up the northern Leeward Islands. **Martinique, Saint Lucia, Saint Vincent** and **Grenada** are part of the Windward Islands.

The Windward Islands lie off the coast of Venezuela, and stretch from east to west from **Aruba** to the **Isla de Margarita**. The South American cordillera continues here, from Aruba to Trinidad, with the only notable heights being 920 m at **Pico San Juan** on Margarita and 941 m at Cerro del Aripo on Trinidad.

The Leeward Islands are of volcanic origin. There are still active volcanoes on Monserrat, Martinique, Guadeloupe and Saint Vincent. These pose a constant and serious threat to the population. In August 1955, the capital of the island of Monserrat was evacuated as there was a threat of an eruption. The extinct volcanoes are now mostly volcanic ruins, but like the **Quill** on Saint Eustacius, some are still complete volcanic cones. Another obvious sign of the continuing volcanism are the solfatara and fumeroles on **Saint Lucia**. Flat chalkstone regions are a distinguishing feature of the islands in the island arc of **Anguilla, Antigua** and **Barbuda**.

Although many of the Caribbean islands have been spoiled by the over-cultivation of cash crops such as sugar-cane, bananas, coffee and rice, others, such as St. Bath's and Mustique are completely unspoiled and are playgrounds for wealthy jet-setting tourists from all over the world. Geologically-speaking the Caribbean islands are only of two origins; volcanic and coral atoll. The most interesting volcano in

the Caribbean is Mont Pelée, one of several active volcanoes on the island of Martinique in the French Antilles. Martinique is an island of volcanic nature, as with all of the islands on the Lesser Antilles chain. Like the archipelagos in the 'Pacific Ring of Fire', the islands of the Lesser Antilles consist of volcanoes built up by subduction trenches; something rarely found in the Atlantic Ocean, as most of the Atlantic volcanoes are 'hot spot' volcanoes like those found in Iceland and Hawaii. Martinique's sole volcano, Mount Pelée last erupted in 1902, destroying the city

of St. Pierre, the capital, in a pyroclastic flow, and killing approximately 25,000 to 35,000 people.

The type of volcanic explosion, that occurred is known as a 'Peléean Eruption'. It is caused by a solidified volcanic dome known as a 'dike' which smashes due to the force of the magma and hot gasses that well up inside it from the magma chamber. The lavaflows down the mountain by means of gravity. The force of the Mount Pelée eruption was made worse due to the fact that there was a vee-shaped notch in the cone that directed the explosion and ensuing lava straight on to the built up area directly below the volcano.

A recent example of the Mount Pelée-type explosion can be found on another of the Lesser Antilles, the British colony of Montserrat. Montserrat has a strato volcano, Mount Souffiière that was thought to be dormant. Monterrat has suffered from mi-

nor earthquakes but the volcano suddenly erupted in 1992. Like the Mount Pelée earthquake, the eruption was caused by magma squeezing through the solidified cone of the volcano at very high pressure. The build-up started through the movement of magma through cracks deep in the rocks.

1 The summetrical giant: the 5,462-m-tall Popocatépetl is the highest active volcano in North and Central America.

2 The impressive 'Barranca del Cobre' (Copper Canyon) in the Sierra Madre. It is even bigger than the Grand Canyon in North America.

3 Crater lakes of the volcano Poás (2,700 m) in Costa Rica. The central American Cordilleras are full of volcanoes.

4 Costa Rica: the Central American Cordilleras are mostly covered by tropical mountain and rain forests.

Main photograph:
The morning light reveals
the multicoloured rock
strata of the towering
Cerro Paine in Patagonia.

South America

The steeply imposing chain of the Cordillera
continues down the Pacific coast right through
the southern part of the American double continent. With the Andes it attains its greatest
width, measuring
some 700 km west
to east at the
Tropic of Capri-
corn. Numerous
high plains link
the upper slopes
of the Cordilleras.
Lowlands adjoin it
in the east, includ-
ing both the gi-
gantic Amazon
basin and the
fertile plains of
the Pampas. The
mountain areas in
the north and east
are overgrown
with tropical vege-
tation. The north-
south axis of South America, some 7,500 km
in length, results in extreme climatic differences. The cool to temperate region of Patagonia merges into the southern latitudes of Tierra del Fuego, which is affected by the Antarctic.

Above: The Iguaçu Falls in the border triangle of Argentina, Brazil
and Paraguay cascade over an area
of some 4 km in width, in about
300 individual waterfalls and cataracts, to a depth of about 80 m.

Below: On the west coast of
South America there is continual
volcanic activity.

*The Chapada dos Guimaraes in the highlands of **Mato Grosso** adjoins the **Brazilian Highlands**. Chapadas are the extended plateaus occupying most of the Brazilian Highlands. They are mostly covered by tropical rain forests.*

Colombian Cordilleras

In Colombia, the **Andes** divide into three mountain chains at Nudo de Pasto: the **West**, **Central** and **East Cordilleras**. Deep, long valleys, the **Rio Cauca** and **Rio Magdalena**, which flow to the Caribbean, separate the mountain ranges from each other. In contrast to other high mountain areas, the Andes in Colombia do not present a steep alpine appearance. The landscape is marked by wide plateaus and ridges. The only exception are the highly glaciated, more recent volcanoes in the Central Cordilleras. The **Cordillera Occidental** has an average height of 3,000 m and consists of crystalline rock. The highest elevation of the barely saperated Cordillera Occidental is the 4,764-m-high **Cumbal**.

The **Cordillera Central** is also composed of crystalline rock, but only its southern part forms a continuous chain. Elsewhere the Cordillera Central forms ridges with an average height of 4,000 m and includes numerous young, semi-active volcanoes. These volcanic cones reach considerable heights and their glaciated peaks are well above the snowline. The tallest of these volcanoes are the 5,750-m-high **Nevado del Huila** and the 5,400 m **Nevado del Ruiz**.

Amazon

The longest river in South America has a drainage area of 7 million sq. km and an approximate length of 6,500 km. It originates in the two main headwaters of Marañón and Ucayali, springing up in the Andes. In its middle reaches it is called Solimões. It crosses the Brazilian lowlands and flows with its three main branches into the Atlantic. By the time it reaches Iquitos, the Amazon is 1.8 km wide, near Manaus it is 5 km wide and the estuary mouth is up to 250 km. The tidal flow and the Pororoca tidal wave can be felt 800 km upstream.

Further north lies the **mountainous country of Ruiz**, 2,000 to 3,000 m high. To the extreme north, the Central Cordillera ends with the isolated mountain block of the **Sierra Nevada de Santa Marta**, which slopes steeply down to the Caribbean. It contains Colombia's highest mountain, **the Pico Cristóbal Colón** (5,775 m). The **Eastern Cordillera** is on average over 5,000 m high and splits into two branches. The **Cordillera de Mérida** continues beyond Venezuela and the **Sierra de Perijá** ends on the Guajira peninsula.

These two mountain ranges on Venezuelan soil surround **Lake** derricks. It has an outlet to the Gulf of Venezuela.

The Cordillera Oriental is composed of gneiss and granite, with overlying sediment from the Mesolithic and Quaternary periods. Characteristic features are the basins situated at an altitude of 2,800 m, which resulted from primaeval lakes and were later filled with ablation rubble.

The **Rio Magdalena** flows for about 1,000 km through a rift valley between the Central and East Cordilleras into the Caribbean. Its most important tributary, the **Rio Cauca**, also flows through a rift valley between the

The Angel Falls: the total drop measures 948 m.

Maracaibo, 180 km long and up to 120 km wide. It is the largest lake in South America and believed to be the second-oldest on earth. Beneath its waters lie the largest petroleum deposits on the South American continent, so the beauty of the lake is marred by more than 5,000 oil Central and West Cordilleras. The Cauca rises in the western Central Cordillera and has cut a deep gorge in the rock as it flows northwards. The river banks are lined with thick rainforest. The river is navigable and is an important transport route for the local people.

Guayana Highlands

The **Guyana Highlands** extend over about 1.5 million sq. km between the Orinoco, the Amazon lowlands and the Atlantic Ocean. The granite bedrock consists of high, flat plateaus split by extremely steep canyons.

The rivers carve their paths through shallow valleys, repeatedly broken up by rapids, cascades and waterfalls. The most impressive of these is undoubtedly the **Angel Falls**, at 948 m the highest waterfall on Earth. The falls are named after an American pilot called Jimmy Angel, so the name has no religious connotation as one might expect.

The nearby 226-m-high **Kaieteur Falls** is the world's largest single drop waterfalls, measuring 222 m. For comparison, The drop at Kaieteur is about five times greater than Niagara Falls.

To the west, the wooded highlands rise steeply towards ragged granite plateaus. The **Serranía de Mapichí** rises up to 2,260 m and the **Sierra Marahuaca** reaches a height of 2,579 m. The northern ascent, which consists of a 400 m to 600-m-high bedrock and is surmounted by a series of individual, isolated mountains is the easiest ascent.

At a height of 1,000 to 1,400 m, there are high plateaus divided

Orinoco

The 2,575-km-long Orinoco rises in the southern mountains of Guyana and at first flows westwards. It forks into two branches. The southern Casiquiare joins the Amazon system and the northern branch continues north as the Orinoco running along the base of Guyana's mountains. After the absorption of numerous tributaries springing up in the Cordilleras, such as the Meta and Guaviare, the Orinoco turns east and eventually creates a 30,000 sq.km delta from which it drains into the Atlantic Ocean.

into steep steps, consisting of several layers of sandstone. These are composed of deposits from primaeval rivers and seas, which have developed into their present form through erosion over the course of time. They are punctured with fissures and crevasses.

Gran Sabana

The **Gran Sabana** is a treeless grassy expanse consisting of flat sandstone table mountains on average more than 1,000 m high and rising to 1,400 m in places. It is overshadowed by steeply rising table mountains, including the 2,810-m-high **Mount Roraima**, the highest on earth, which has given its name to the sandstone rock that is found here. At 2,994 m, the **Pico da Neblina,** whose northern slopes are shared by Brazil and Venezuela and whose southern slopes are in Brazil are part of the Neblina National Park. Together with the neighbouring Parima-Tapirapeco National Park in Venezuela and the **Canaima** National Park, they form a protected area of about 80,000 sq. km, probably the largest protected tropical rainforest in the world. The sandstone plateaus of the interior are typical savannah landscapes.

Selvas

About 600 million years ago, the **Amazon Basin** was a bay open to the west towards the primeval Pacific Ocean. After the Andes folded in the Tertiary era, the route to the sea was blocked and the region gradually transformed itself into a gigantic inland lake. It was not until the Quaternary Period that the waters were able to break through, this time to the Atlantic Ocean.

At 4 million sq. km, the Amazon lowland – Brazilians call it **Selvas**, 'the woods' – is the largest tropical forest on earth. But the highly sensitive ecological system is under threat. The massive deforestation of the jungle to clear land for agriculture and the associated destruction of countless plant and animal species has become a problem of global importance, transcending all national boundaries.

Amazon basin

The Amazon flood plain is, at 4 million sq. km, the largest tropical forest on earth and it extends over an area of 3,500 km between the Andes and the Atlantic Ocean; the maximum extent from north to south is 2,000 km.

The Amazon basin started out as a bay open to the primaeval Pacific, between the Guyana Highlands and Brazil. When the Andes were uplifted in the Tertiary Period, the young mountain range blocked the way to the open sea and transformed the region into a gigantic inland lake. The Palaeozoic strata were overlaid by about 800 m of sand-and-clay ablation material.

At the start of the Tertiary Era, the waters of the primaeval River Amazon managed to push through into the Atlantic. The inland lake gradually drained away, leaving the Tertiary ablation free to form solid ground wherever it

was not threatened by flooding. During the Pleistocene Era, the rivers cut deep channels through this solid ground, and later broad valley landscapes were uplifted. These flood plains are still threatened by inundation. It has therefore been the 'main task' of the Amazon River to drain its broad valley into the Atlantic.

Again in the Pleistocene Era, the funnel-shaped estuaries of the Amazon, the Tocantins, Xingu and Tapajós were formed. Almost the entire Amazon basin is covered by evergreen tropical rainforest, and the interior basin has a relatively constant tropical primaeval forest climate – humid and hot.

The eastern part, however, has a variable damp tropical climate; the weather in the area has become noticeably dryer, however, in recent years and this is having its effect on the flow of the Amazon. The usual culprit – global warming – is suspected.

The river itself, and the rainforest which extends up to its banks, are the most important landmarks of the Amazonian lowlands. As a living space for rare animal species and many plants as yet undiscovered, which might have medicinal uses, this vast forest area is of vital interest to the whole world, for which it also serves as a climate regulator and source of

fresh water. Unfortunately, its unique ecosystem is threatened by human activity. Deforestation for crop-growing and logging have already destroyed large areas of the Amazonian rainforest. In fact, development of the Amazonian basin for agriculture is a largely pointless exercise, since the soil is poor, meaning that cultivated areas soon have to be abandoned. But by the time the soil has regenerated and the original vegetation returned, decades or even centuries will have passed.

Many of the local tribes who once inhabited the rainforest have had to leave their traditional settle-

Big picture: Tropical rainforest covers most of northern Brazil. The Amazon and its tributaries flow through the thick jungle like arteries.

Small picture: The Rio Negro is the biggest tributary of the Amazon. During the rainy season it floods an area of up to 650,000 sq. km.

ment areas, either as the result of deforestation or because speculators and land-grabbers have driven them out. Of the original five million or so native inhabitants, fewer than 200,000 remain.

South America

*The volcanic **Galapagos Islands** lie out in the Pacific Ocean 1,000 km from the South American mainland to which they have never been connected. The resulting unique development of the islands' flora and fauna have made them world-famous. The landscape is typical of a volcanic island with lava formations, tufa and cinder cones dominating the bizarre crater landscape with its sparse ground cover. Tourism is heavily restricted to preserve the environment.*

Brazilian Highlands

North-eastern Brazil is typified by very varied forms of landscape. The coastal plain is between 40 and 60 km wide and was created in the Tertiary Era. Then the land rises inland to a plateau up to 300 m high, consisting of uniformly ancient sedimentary rock, which in the west has become exposed again after the ablation of more recent rock.

In the interior and in the east these more recent sedimentary deposits have still largely been preserved.

Further inland there is a table land up to 800 m high, in which sandstone plateaus have survived from the formerly underground Palaeozoic and Mesozoic sedimentary rock cover.

Paraná

The Paraná river emerges through the confluence of the Rio Paranaíba and the Rio Grande in the Brazilian Highlands. In its upper reaches, the river has many waterfalls. After the absorption of the Paraguay River, the Paraná flows southwards as a wide lowland river. Near Rosario it branches into several arms and expands into a wide, swampy delta. North of Buenos Aires it absorbs the Uruguay river to become the Río de la Plata, a mighty, 50 km to 200-km-wide estuary that drains into the Atlantic. The Paraná and its tributaries carry vast amounts of sediment. It is so silted up that it is only navigable if a path is first dredged for the boat.

In the west, the land is only about 150 m above sea level. There are many isolated mountains consisting of gneiss and granite. Particularly fascinating landscape features are the weathered granite rocks and quartzite reefs of the **São Francisco valley**.

In north-western Brazil, the upper strata have not been able to withstand erosion. Remnants are found only in the low sandstone plateaus of the **Serra do Cachimbo** and the **Serra dos Caiabis**. To the south and east, the area is bordered by the **Chapada dos Parecis**, the **Mato Grosso** and the **Serra do Roncador**.

Brazilian Uplands

The largest enclosed area of natural landscape in South America, of which there is about 6 million sq. km, is the Brazilian Uplands, the **Planalto**, which gradually rises out of the Amazon basin. The **Brazilian Uplands** is on average about 500–1,000 m high, but to the south and east it rises to almost 3,000 m. The highest elevation is the 2,890-m-high **Pico da Bandeira**. This is followed by the 2,787 m **Pico das Agulhas Negras** and the **Pico de Itambé**, which, with its 2,033 m, only just exceeds the 2,000 m boundary.

In the west, the mountainous land of Brazil is bordered by the lowlands of the **Pampas** and the **Gran Chaco**, in the east it drops steeply, often by up to 100 m, in the **Serra do Mar** to the Atlantic, leaving room for only a narrow strip of flat coastline. This is the site of one of the world's most famous beaches, the Copacabana in Rio de Janeiro with its beautiful backdrop, Sugar Loaf mountain.

The **Planalto** consists of a crystalline base, which is largely composed of gneiss, mica shale and quartzite. This massif is very old in terms of earth history and is part of the primaeval South American continent. Ablation and weathering on the Atlantic coast as well as erosion by tributaries of the Amazon have once again exposed this bedrock.

In other areas of the mountainous country, the Palaeozoic and Mesozoic strata have resisted erosion.

The varying degrees of weathering in these younger layers, consisting of sandstone, limestone and basalt, are responsible for the variety of the landscapes.

A fascinating natural spectacle can be seen in the south-east of the mountainous country. Only a few kilometres from its estuary in the **Paraná**, the **Iguaçu** tumbles over a broad horseshoe-shaped fracture some 2,700 m wide, into a gorge about 80 m in depth. This awesome sight is accompanied by the clouds of spray, shimmering in all the colours of the rainbow that are thrown up by the rushing waters.

Planalto: the Iguaçu Falls, on a tributary of the Paraná.

Mato Grosso

The **Mato Grosso** is a very old, severely eroded mountain range, which covers most of the Brazilian state after which it is named. To the west, it borders the **Serra dos Parecis** and to the south it merges with the flooded savannahs of the **Pantanal**.

The Mato Grosso plateau, which attains an average height of about 600 m, forms the border between the Amazon basin in the north and the Paraguay basin in the south.

While the very sparsely populated highland in the north of the Mato Grosso contains primaeval forests from which rubber is harvested, in the south and east the vegetation consists mainly of grass and tree savannahs. This is rich agricultural land. Cereals, cotton, tobacco and coffee are cultivated and there is also cattle-ranching.

Paraguay

The Rio Paraguay rises in the Mato Grosso mountains and flows in its upper reaches through the 100,000 sq. km wide alluvial soil of Pantanal. On its way south, it constitutes the borders of the country of Paraguay – which was named after it – with Brazil and Argentina. The river crosses the Gran Chaco and flows into the Paraná river as its main tributary, near the city of Corrientes. The total length of the Paraguay River is 2,550 km. The most important tributaries are the São Lourenço, entering from the east and the Pilcomayo and Bermejo tributaries entering from the west.

The Andes

The **Andes Cordillera** extends some 7,500 km from the Caribbean coast as far as the southernmost tip of the South American continent. This mountain range is between 200 km and 800 km wide. This mountain range piled up when the South American continental plate moved over the Pacific plate. The seismic activity continues as the massif continues to uplift. Earthquakes and volcanic eruptions are evidence of today's continuing plate movements.

The **southern Andes** is a narrow high mountain range, which in the **Tierra del Fuego** reaches a height of about 1,500 m, soon rising to 3,500 m. In central Chile and western Argentina, it towers to more than 5,000 m. This area contains **Aconcagua**. At a height of 6,960 m, this extinct volcano is not only the highest mountain in the Andes but also the highest in both South and North America. The Central Andes begins at the **Atacama desert** in Chile. Between the West and East Cordilleras lies the **Altiplano**, containing both of the famous mountain lakes, **Lake Titicaca** and **Lake Poopó**. Several mountains over 6,000 m in altitude are part of the Central Cordilleras. They include the **Sajama** (6,520 m), **Ausangate** (6,384 m) and, rising east of Lake Titicaca, **Illampu** (6,362 m).

The whole area is highly important in terms of cultural history. The ruins of the 'forgotten city' of Machu Picchu contain significant vestiges of the Inca culture. This city, which is difficult to access even today, escaped destruction by the Spanish conquistadors because of its remoteness. In 1911, the area was rediscovered and made accessible to the public.

In northern Peru, the Andes become noticeably lower and the **North Andes** begin, whose two main chains again reach 6,276 m in Ecuador. Ecuador also includes the rumbling **Cotopaxi**, the most active volcano on earth, which reaches a height of (currently) 5,897 m. Its apparently perfectly formed cone is actually composed of an older and a younger volcano. Cotopaxi, beneath which hot magma presses close to the earth's surface, is snowcovered all year round. The last eruption of the volcano took place in 1928. Fortunately, the inhabitants of the region did not suffer much from its eruption, but

Some 60 km away from the Ecuadorian capital Quito, Cotopaxi, at 5,897 m the highest active volcano in the world, is surrounded by the Cotopaxi Nature Reserve. The distinctive cone-shape of the summit is covered with snow and ice above 4,000 m. The volcanic activity on Cotopaxi, which last erupted in 1928, is caused by the collision between the Oceanic and Continental Plates.

if Mount St. Helen's, in North America, is anything to go by, that may not be the case in the future. Near the state border between Ecuador and Colombia, at the **Nudo de Pasto**, the Andes divide into three main parallel chains, of which the Central Cordillera again rises to 5,750 m (**Nevado del Huila**), but then gradually declines, as do the West and East Cordilleras.

With the **Cordillera of Mérida**, an area of foothills of the East Cordillera, the Andes continue as far as Venezuela, where they reach their most northerly point.

Atacama Desert

A large desert has formed on the western edge of northern Chile, due to the absence of rainfall. The land is buried under ablation rubble of the **Puna** or Altiplano. The surface of the **Atacama** is covered in salt crusts, the so-called 'salares', gravel and stony detritus.

The Atacama is the driest and most inhospitable desert on earth, having no oases or any underground source of water. The extremely low rainfall and the dramatic difference between day and night temperatures mean that it is virtually devoid of vegetation.

Lake Titicaca

The 8,300-sq. km-wide **Lake Titicaca** is the largest highland lake on earth, 3,812 m above sea level in the heart of the Andes between Peru and Bolivia. Since navigation is possible on the lake, it is also considered to be the highest navigable waterway in the world.

Lake Titicaca is 190 km long, an average of 50 km wide, and up to 281 m deep. On its eastern shore it is overshadowed by the peak of the 6,362-m-high **Illampu**. More than twenty rivers flow into this glacial lake. Depending on precipitation and glacier melt, these convey variable amounts of water at different seasons.

The lake is drained by the **Rio Desaguatheo** which itself drains into **Lake Poopó**, which has no outlet.

Lake Titicaca has a very irregular shape and contains 33 islands and several peninsulas. In the mythology of the local Uru Native Americans, the **Isla del Sol** in the middle of the lake plays a significant role. They believe that 'Sun Island' is the birthplace of the Sun and an important site at which to hold traditional festivals.

Lago Chucuito in the north is linked to **Lago Huinaymarca** in the south by the 80-m-deep Straits of Tiquina, thus making both lakes navigable. Although Huinaymarca has a distinctly brackish taste, it is considered to be a freshwater lake, but the waters are said to have health-giving properties.

Altiplano

The **Altiplano** is a highland at an altitude of 3,600 m to 4,200 m between the West and East Cordilleras and forms the western part of the **Puna block**.

This high plain, with no outlet, is some 700 km long and up to 200 km wide, and is covered only with sparse vegetation. The indigenous Aymarás provide themselves with all they need by the cultivation of potatoes, maize and barley. Sheep and chickens supply them with meat, milk and eggs. They produce wool from the fleece of llamas, so they are completely self-sufficient. Since the Quaternary Era, a number of 100-m-high layers of rubble have overlaid the ancient **boulders**. Mountain ranges running from north to south divide the Altiplano into individual basin landscapes. The dry steppes of the southern part of the region contain large salt-pans such as the **Salar de Uyuni**.

1 The Andes: in the East, the highlands are edged with numerous cordilleras of different heights. The Cordillera Vilcabamba near Cuzco is one of the smaller peaks.

2 Lake Titicaca, highest lake in the world. Like Lake Poopó, it is a glacial lake of a type that can be found throughout the Andean highlands.

3 Isla Pescado, Bolivia: Several salt lakes, swamps and deserts were formed in the southern part of the Andean highlands. Due to evaporation these mostly sink lakes with no outlets become clogged with evaporite minerals and eventually dry out.

4 The Salar de Uyuni, almost 3,700 m above sea level, is the largest of the many salt-pans of the Altiplano. Another problem of glacial lakes is that they turn brackish over time.

The Andes

Cordilleres Occidental: snow-covered volcano cone in the Chilean Lauca National Park.

The Andes Cordillera is the longest chain of mountains in the world extending over the entire western coastal area of the South American continent. In almost every case several 'partial Cordilleras' run parallel to each other. In the border triangle of Peru, Bolivia and Chile the mountains cover an area extending more than 700 km.

The Andes Cordillera extends in several chains throughout the entire lenth of South America, covering over 7,500 km from the Caribbean Sea in the north to Cape Horn at the southern tip of the continent. At this point the mountain range breaks up into countless small islands.

The Southern Andes consists of a narrow, high mountain range which in Tierra del Fuego rises to up to 1,500 m; further north the peaks reach as high as 3,000 to 5,000 m in central Chile and western Argentina. This part of the range contains the 6,800-m-high Tupungato and the 6,960-m-high Aconcagua, the highest mountain in the Andes and in the whole American continent. From a latitude of 27° S, the mountains expand into the Central Andes. Between the West and East Cordilleras lies the Altiplano with its outlet-free salt lakes and huge freshwater lakes such as Lakes Poopó and Titicaca. North-west of Lake Titicaca, the two chains approach each other again. In the north Peruvian gap at 5° S, the high ranges flatten out again and become narrower. This is where the North Andes begins, dividing in Ecuador into two main chains, which extend up to 6,267 m in height. Of the three main chains in Colombia, the middle one reaches average heights of about 5,000 m. The Cordillera of Mérida, the foothills of the Eastern Cordillera, extends into Venezuela.

The Andes came into being as a result of a series of geological processes. The basins of the Mesozoic were filled with deposits from primaeval rivers, which resulted in the formation of a huge mass of strata several kilometres thick. As a result of the shifting of the South American Continental Plate and the Oceanic Nazca Plate, in the course of several successive folding periods, the original rock melted and transformed under pressure. Erosion finally caused a considerable reduction in height and the formation of further deposits. The severely broken-down relief forms took shape in the early Pliocene. The shape continued to develop during the Quaternary Era through pronounced volcanism and in the south, volcanoes emerged from beneath the Ice Age glaciers.

The Andes offers a wide variety of the most varied types of landscape. The Altiplano, for example, is a basin landscape at an altitude of 4,000 m. Encircled by mountains over 5,000 m and 6,000 m high, the Puna is a desert highland

Patagonia: the 3,128-m-high summit of Cerro Torre in the Fitzroy Massif.

The 3,000-m-high, steep granite rocks dominate the Torres del Paine in the South of Chile.

Big picture: The 6,400-m-high Parinacota volcano lies in the Chilean Lauca National Park.

which came into existence in the Tertiary era. The basins of the Puna, at an altitude of up to 4,200 m, are often covered by a salt crust and at deeper points filled with a salty swamp. Within the Puna there are a number of volcanoes; at its western edge there is a concentration of younger volcanoes such as the 6,723-m-high Llullaillaco and the 6,880-m-high Ojos del Salado.

The extremely inhospitable Atacama desert turns in the Altiplano into a semi-desert covered with sparse grassland and cactus.

The high peaks of the Central Cordillera are covered with snow. The melted snow and ice irrigates the agricultural land in the valleys. The snowline above the city of Mendoza in Argentina starts at 4,500 m, but it is lower further south. In Patagonia the Ice Age has left clear traces behind. The heights here hardly reach 4,000 m,

but glaciation increases. The mountains on the Pacific coast were formed in the Quaternary by gigantic icebergs. These cut deep fjords into the land and heaped up moraine banks behind which huge lakes such as Lago Buenos Aires and Lago Argentino filled up. The glaciers are still present and can be seen in the Argentinian Los Glaciares National Park, which covers an area of 6,000 sq. km. They form the largest continuous glacial surface north of the Antarctic. One of the largest glaciers here is the 30-km-long Perito Moreno. Among the most impressive landscapes in the Andes is the Cordillera Blanca with its rugged giant mountains, glaciers, moraines and glacier lakes and the impressive double peak of Huascarán, towering to a height of 6,768 m.

The Andes in Ecuador are strongly volcanic. The heavily glaciated

Chimborazo, (6,310 m) and Cotopaxi, (5,897 m). The latter is the highest active volcano on Earth.

The great heights of the Andes as well as their enormous extent over the entire lenght of the South American continent make this mountain range the greatest climatic borderline on Earth. While the eastern foothills of the Andes are supplied with high precipitation by the trade winds, large areas of the leae side of the range are extremely arid.

Areas that can be used for agriculture are rare in the Andes. The small areas of fertile land on the slopes is therefore terraced to enable the cultivation of grain, vegetables, fruit and tobacco. The extreme altitude determines what

Los Glaciares National Park: The Perito Moreno glacier dominates the Lago Argentino with its formidable ice sheets.

crops can be grown. In the valleys, tropical fruits, such as bananas, as well as rice and cotton can be grown; the middle slopes can be used for cultivating sugar cane, coffee and tobacco. At the higher altitudes, winter wheat and potatoes are grown. The high pastures can also be used for grazing cattle.

The local Quechua population also keeps herds of llama and vicuña; native animals that are used to these high altitudes. The llamas are used as pack animals and vicuña wool is highly prized, both in its natural state and woven into cloth. Vicuña blankets made by the Quechua sell for high prices.

South America

The San Valentin glacier in Chile, surrounding the San Rafael Lake, transports ancient blocks of ice on its way to the sea. The giant San Rafael glacier, stretches from the Patagonian inland to the Chilean coast.

Cordillera Blanca

To the north of Lima, the Santa Valley separates the West Cordillera of the Andes into two parallel mountain ranges, the **Cordillera Negra** and the **Cordillera Blanca**. The Cordillera Blanca acquired its name from its many towering peaks covered in snow. One of these is **Huascarán**, at 6,768 m the highest mountain in the Peruvian Andes.

This folded mountain range came into existence in the Late Tertiary Era, but the process of uplift has still not been completed. The relief of the Cordillera Blanca was drastically reshaped in the Ice Age. Moraines, cirques and trough valleys are evidence of the power of the mighty ice sheets which poured down the west flank especially on the high mountain range. Terminal moraines dammed up the smaller lakes. Particularly impressive are the deep trough valleys at a height of around 4,000 m, such as the **Quebrada Santa Cruz** and the **Quebrada Honda**. This inhospitable region has not attracted human habitation; only in the fertile **Santa valley** have a few villages and settlements sprung up.

Gran Chaco

The **Gran Chaco** is a high plateau, some 800,000 sq. km wide, which extends over the territory of Paraguay and Argentina between Paraná in the east and the Andes in the west. The Gran Chaco lies at a height of 100 m to 400 m.

The **Chaco Boreal** in the north is succeeded by the **Chaco Central** and further south, the **Chaco Austral**. The Chaco Boreal consists of sand and clay sediment, which forms an uneven plain that tilts upwards in the west.

A few isolated elevations occasionally interrupt the monotony of the featureless landscape. The slight variations in the relief can only be recognised in the rainy season, when the hollows fill up with water and the higher ridges stand out like islands above the flooded plain.

The dry forests are succeeded in the west by thornbush and dry steppes. There are isolated grassy areas, whose meandering forms show that they are, in fact, the beds of ancient rivers that once flowed through here. In the Argentinian part of the Gran Chaco, unlike the Chaco Boreal, the land is much more fertile. About a third of the land is covered with forest. Between the forests there are open meadows containing a few isolated trees.

The sub-tropical climate results in very hot summers, and in the rainy season large areas are flooded. The main rivers that run through the Gran Chaco are the **Pilcomayo, Bermejo and Rio Salado**, which contribute only a small part of their waters to the Paraguay river.

Pantanal

The **Pantanal**, one of the planet's most spectacular wetland systems. is a flood plain more than 100,000 sq. km wide covering upper Paraguay, Bolivia and Brazil. Geologists include the Pantanal in the **Brazilian uplands**, since in terms of earth history the plain is part of the same region. It differs from the mountainous area in its landscape, but in fact it is only an

Bolivian Lowlands

From the eastern slopes of the Andes the extensive **Bolivian lowlands** change from the humid and hot Amazon basin in the north to the hot arid scrub of the Gran Chaco.

This hilly, completely featureless expanse is covered with rich vegetation, in stark contrast to the sparse highlands. In the north, there are extensive rainforests, which change towards the south into open woodland.

Adjacent to these are the grassy savannahs of the **Llanos del Mamoré**. This alluvial area also contains gallery woods and forest islands, the so-called 'montes'.

The **mountain country of Chiquitos**, which rises to an altitude of 1,400 m, is succeeded by a large swamp, which covers the flood plain of the low-lying **Paraguay** river. Dry forests and thornbush steppes mark the gradual transition to the **Chaco boreal** in the south. The main rivers are the 1,800-km-long **Rio Mamoré** and the 1,700-km-long Rio Beni, which combine to form the **Rio Madeira**.

Patagonia: the mighty Perito Moreno glacier in Los Glaciares National Park.

oval sunken area of the same terrain. In the rainy season, the 20- to 40-km-wide depression is largely submerged. Swamps, lakes and meandering rivers ensure a varied landscape.

The banks of the **Paraguay** river, which flows through the Pantanal, are covered with rainforest which flourishes in the damp, humid climate.

In the dry season, which lasts as a rule from October to April, the plateaus that adjoin the river are used by farmers from the lowlands as rich pasture in which to fatten their livestock.

The Pampas

The **Pampas** consist of a gigantic plain which stretches between the 30th and 37th southern parallels. To the west it begins at some 500 m at the foot of the Andes, and extends as far as the Atlantic in the east. In the north it gradually changes into the **Gran Chaco** and is bordered in the south by the **Patagonian tableland**. To the east, the Pampas are framed by the heights of the **Brazilian** highlands, while in the west they are dominated by the mighty **Andes**.

The Pampas are part of the central Argentinian lowlands, a geologically relatively young deposit area dating from the Quaternary Era, to which **Mesopotamia** and the Gran Chaco also belong.

The original landscape of the Pampas was determined by a treeless grass steppe, but in earlier times it may have been covered with forests.

The human race has radically altered the face of the Pampas, for the fertile steppe soil, similar to the black earth of the Ukraine, is admirably suitable as an area for agricultural use. Immigrants to the region have created an extensive cultivated area. Today the region, particularly the damp eastern Pampas, is characterised by wide grain fields and huge cattle pastures.

The cattle grazing on the Pampas, consisting of herds of Aberdeen Angus and Herefords, have become famous for the delicacy of their flesh. Alfalfa or lucerne, which is grown here and used for animal fodder also contributes to the flavour of the world-famous Argentinian beefsteaks.

The central and south-eastern region also contains grazing land for cattle herds but the grassy meadows are considerably drier and much less cultivated than those of Europe and North America, so that this area preserves its original wild appearance to a much greater extent.

Patagonia

In the south, the Pampas gradually changes into the **Patagonian tableland**. In the barrel-shaped valley of the Río Negro, crops are grown in a fertile 10 to 15-km-wide strip, where the land resembles that of the Pampas. South of the **Río Negro**, however, the landscape changes dramatically. Bitter, whirling winds, huge glaciers and icy torrential downpours such as are hardly to be met elsewhere, have created a landscape unlike any other on earth.

In the Pleistocene, huge ice sheets covered vast areas of the continent. The icy streams that flowed from the high mountains down to the Pacific cut deep trough valleys through the mountains. The **glaciers** on the Pacific side were then, as now, exposed to masses of humid air that formed over the Pacific Ocean and fell as rain over the western slopes of the Cordilleras.

As the glaciers melted, sea water penetrated the valleys, producing a maze of islands and fjords, unique in both the northern and the southern hemisphere.

The huge fjords, up to 1,200 m deep, divide the Andes along the Pacific coast into several ranges, which run parallel to the chains of the Cordilleras. In addition, a dense system of sea channels run at a ninety-degree angle, tracing the oblique course of the original fault lines.

Violent storms rage constantly in the **fjord** areas, and it rains daily, the precipitation being very violent and ice-cold. The Cordilleras here are some 4,000 m high and their countless glaciers often extend far out into the sea.

A breathtaking natural spectacle can be observed in the fjords when, with a mighty roar, amplified by echoes, huge masses of ice burst from the glacier tongues and crash into the water.

The eastern side of the **Cordilleras** are much less exposed to the force of the winds. In the low-lying, sheltered areas, forests are able to flourish, but towards the east the winds again gain strength and only a monotonous dry steppe landscape is able to withstand them. In the Pleistocene Era the glaciers, noticeably smaller than those in the western half, carved depressions into the mountainous landscape, which remained as lakes after the ice had melted. These include the **Lago Argentino, Lago Nahuel Huapi** and **Lago Buenos Aires**. An impressive spectacle can be observed at Lago Argentino. The

The beach of South Georgia one of the **Falkland islands**. These islands, known in Spanish as the Malvinas, lie some 500 km off the South American coast. The main islands, West and East Falklands, are separated by the Falkland Sound. The landscape whose sparse vegetation is only suitable for sheep-grazing, is mainly hilly. On both islands, the highest mountains rise 700 m above sea level.

enormous **Moreno glacier** shifts every couple of years to this lake in south-western Patagonia, where it forms a huge ice barrier, which can rise up to 60 m high. When the build-up of water finally bursts through the barrier, the ice smashes apart with a tremendous crash.

The stratified area slopes down in marked gradations to the Atlantic. The crystalline bedrock that was swept over it in the Ice Age is covered by low-lying sedimentary formations, tufa and layers of black basalt.

The surface has been shaped by river water into countless small **mesas** (table formations) and is strewn with the so-called Patagonian detritus, consisting of pebbles about the size of hens' eggs. The highest mountains of the Patagonian Cordilleras are the towering **San Valentín** at 4,058 m and the **San Lorenzo** at 3,706 m.

Tierra del Fuego

The sheltered east side of the Cordilleras was deeply affected by Pleistocene glaciers. The depressions created by these glaciers filled with water after the Pleistocene Era. One such water-filled sink is the **Straits of Magellan**, named after its Portuguese discoverer, Ferdinand Magellan. When Magellan sailed through the Straits in 1520, a stretch of water some 583 km long, between the Pacific and the Atlantic, he saw a number of small fires burning on the port side of the ship. He named the land on which they were burning **Tierra del Fuego** – land of fire. Tierra del Fuego has a total area of 73,746 sq. km. The rugged inhospitable landscape of **Patagonia** continues on the main island and the many smaller islands off shore. Since they experienced the same geological processes, the tableland is structured in the same way and **fjords** and straits offer the same natural spectacles. In Tierra del Fuego, the Cordilleras are much lower, reaching a maximum height in **Cerro Yogan** of only 2,469 m. The ice sheets break up only gradually. The glaciated peaks, which tower over the fjords like gigantic icebergs, are a magnificent sight.

The climate is chilly to temperate, with an annual mean temperature of 5.5°C. Storms are frequent occurrences.

Falkland Islands

The **Falkland Islands** lie 770 km north-east of Cape Horn in the South Atlantic. This island group, known in Spanish as the **Islas Malvinas**, because they were originally discovered by sailors from St. Malo in Britanny, consists of two main islands and almost 200 smaller islands. East Falkland has an area of 6,760 sq. km; West Falkland is 5,280 sq. km in area.

The stony landscape consists of treeless grassland without any notable stretches of water, extending over a hilly tableland, interspersed with stratified mountainous ridges.

Intensive sheep-rearing by the settlers in the last 150 years has almost totally destroyed the native vegetation, originally consisting of tussock grass, heather and peat moorland.

The South Sandwich Islands and South Georgia in Antarctica are included among the Falkland Islands for political purposes. All are British crown colonies. The capital of the Falkland Islands is Port Stanley. The Falkland Islanders are almost exclusively of British descent.

It is likely that valuable deposits of mineral ores and even petroleum may lie beneath the British territorial waters off the Falkland Islands, but there has been no confirmation of any finds. This is one reason why the Islands' sovereignty is hotly disputed.

1 Smoke issuing from the Caldera of the 2,840-m-high Villarrica Volcano at Lake Villarrica. Like other smaller volcanos at the southern tip of the South American Cordilleras, it is considered to be extinct.

2 The Atacama Desert lies on the coast between Chile and Peru. It is considered to be the driest in the world. The landscape is dominated by sedimentary strata at different stages of erosion.

3 Northern Patagonia is the foothills of the Pampas. It is a steppe-like dry zone, covered in stunted trees, shrubs and grass.

The climate is inhospitable and it is not suitable for farming.

4 Patagonia, Los Glaciares National Park: the mighty glaciers slide slowly down into the valley, gradually revealing the stark outline of Mount Fitzroy (3,375 m) and the other peaks behind them.

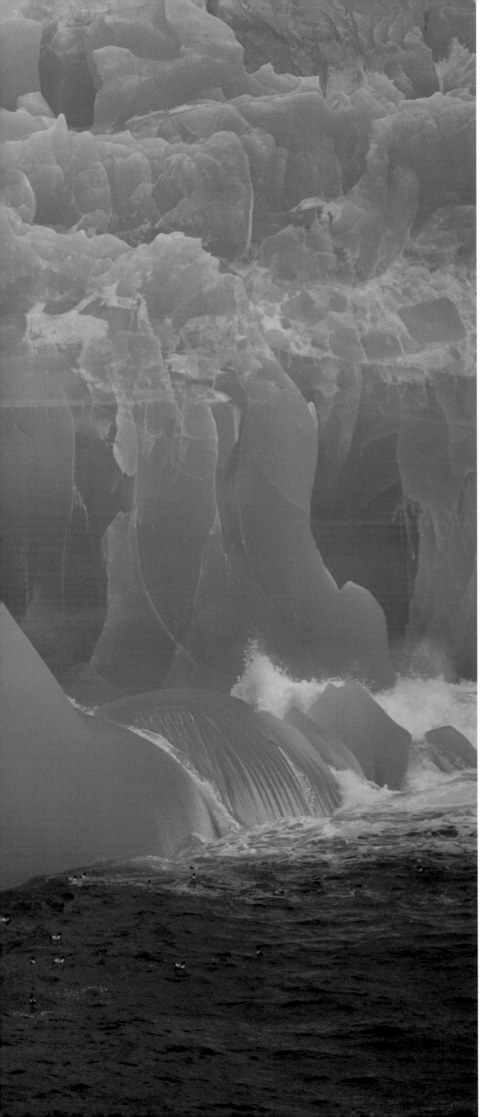

Main photograph:
The Antarctic ice desert is uninhabited by mammals. Only penguins occasionally live on parts of the immense sheet of ice.

Antarctica

Antarctica is the coldest of all the continents. More than 90 per cent of the total amount of ice on Earth amasses here around the South Pole. The land mass of the continent, which is about the same size as Europe, is covered by a

The pack-ice around the Antarctic is only solid in winter.

layer of ice approximately 2 km thick. At the centre of the continent, this ice sheet may reach a depth of 4.5 km. The immense weight of the ice pushes the submerged mountains far below sea level.

The size of the continent depends on the time of year. It can double in size in winter, due to the increased ice mass. Only the mountains on the Pacific edge are not entirely covered in ice. The Antarctic ice desert is divided into five regions, distinguishable by the characteristics of the ice sheet. These regions include two great ice shelves, that are made entirely of ice and have no solid rock foundation.

Antarctica

An iceberg is trapped by the frozen sea at Kloa Point on the Mawson Coast: icebergs are formed ('calved') when part of the inland ice mass or a valley glacier breaks off. 'Tabular icebergs' *are sheets that have broken off from the Antarctic ice-shelf. These can be several kilometres in length and they can float around the Southern Ocean for months.*

South Orkney Islands
South Shetland Islands

In addition to the main land mass of the Antarctic Continent, the territory of the Antarctic also includes several offshore subantarctic island groups. The **South Orkney Islands** lie between the **Scotia Sea** in the north and the **Weddell Sea** in the South Atlantic. The island group consists of the main islands, **Coronation** and **Laurie,** and a number of smaller islands. The whole island group covers an area of 622 sq. km.
The inhospitable islands are mainly mountainous and can reach altitudes of up to 2,100 m. The landscape is heavily glaciated. The scant vegetation consists of mosses, algae and lichen. Apart from two research stations on the islands of **Signy** and **Laurie,** the archipelago is uninhabited.
The **South Shetland Islands** lie in the **Drake Passage,** approximately 90 km north of the **Antarctic Peninsula.** The island chain is 510 km long and has an Alpine, glaciated landscape, composed mainly of volcanic stone. It covers an area of 4,622 sq. km. Seismic and volcanic activity beneath the ice sheet persists to this day. Only lichen and algae grow on the inhospitable island group, which is uninhabited, with the exception of a research station on **Deception Island.**

Filchner-Ronne Ice Shelf

The massive ice shelf in the south **Weddell Sea** is divided by **Berkner Island** into the eastern **Ronne Ice Shelf** and the western **Filchner Ice Shelf.** It is the second largest ice shelf in the Antarctic and covers an area of some 530,000 sq. km. The extensive ice shelves form when the glaciers of the mainland move towards the sea and enter it at such a shallow gradient that they do not break apart. Near the coast, the ice shelf almost sits on the ocean floor.
The ice shelf also consists of frozen precipitation and sea water and has a thickness of approximately 250 m in the far north, and up to 1,800 m in the south, where it extends more

than 840 km into the mainland. Where the sheet meets the water, the ice is still about 30 m thick. Icebergs and sheets of ice frequently break away from this huge ice shelf to form tabular icebergs with an area of more than 10,000 sq. km and drift-ice which can float out many kilometres into the Southern Ocean.

Trans-antarctic Mountains

The **Trans-antarctic Mountains** were formed through a process of uplift and denudation beginning 450 million years ago at the edge of the Antarctic Plate. The mountain range has a total length of 4,800 km and separates the continent into a smaller eastern section and a significantly larger western part.
East Antarctica has a table shape composed of Precambrian igneous and metamorphic rocks from the former great southern continent. West Antarctica is composed of younger rock.
The Trans-antarctic Mountains are completely covered by ice in

the central sections and stretch from **Victoria Land** in the south to the **Weddell Sea** to the northeast of the continent. In the north, glaciers extend from the mountains into the sea to form **Edith Ronne Land**. The glacial extensions in the east reach out far into the **Ross Sea,** forming the immense **Ross Ice Shelf** that covers an area of 540,000 sq. km.

The eastern side of the mountains contains volcanoes and areas of seismic activity, stretching from Ellsworth Land all the way to the Scotia Arc. The mountain system reaches its greatest height in the steep mountain chain along the Ross Sea (**Kirkpatrick,** 4,528 m and **Markham,** 4,350 m). At this point, the mountains drop away very steeply into the sea. The Trans-antarctic Mountains extend into Victoria Land to form an island in the centre of the Ross Ice Shelf. This island, **Mount Erebus,** is the highest active volcano on the continent. Very few places in the Antarctic are free of ice (just 1.5 per cent of the total area). These include the **Dry Valleys** in Victoria Land near the U.S. McMurdo Station on the edge of the Ross Ice Shelf. This region covers an area of some 3,000 sq. km, and was formed by strong dry winds, called katabatic winds, that blow through the region at extremely high speeds.
The Dry Valleys are subject to unusual temperature fluctuations and have seen no precipitation

Drift-ice on the coast of the Antarctic Peninsula.

for approximately two million years. The area also contains some salt lakes, such as **Lake Vanda,** formed by melting glaciers during warmer periods.

Antarctic Mountains

The Antarctic also contains other mountain chains or individual

peaks, known by the Inuit term of **Nunataks,** which protrude above the 2-km-thick layer of ice in the central Antarctic and the coastal regions. These include the **Sentinel Range** whose highest peak, **Mount Vinson** (5,140 m), is also the highest mountain on the continent, and the mountain chains that extend from the north coast to the Leopold and Astrid Coast, which can reach heights of 3,600 m and which formed 80 million years ago at the fractured edge of the former continent of Gondwanaland. In **MacRobertson Land,** the glaciers on **Mount Menzies** (3,355 m) fall steeply to form the **Amery Ice Shelf.**

Antarctic Peninsula

The **Antarctic Peninsula,** formerly called **Graham Land** or the **Palmer Peninsula,** between the Weddell Sea and the Bellingshausen Sea in West Antarctica, is some 1,300 km long and is Antarctica's largest peninsula. The peninsula forms the northernmost extension of the continent and its highest point, **Mount Jackson** (4,191 m), in the ice-free Antarctic Andes, is actually an extension of the South American Cordillera. In geological terms, it is the youngest mountain on the continent. The edge of the peninsula contains numerous volcanoes, some of which are still active, and other signs of volcanic activity.
Off the west coast of the peninsula there are some islands, including the large **Alexander Island,** and other large ice shelves. This area has relatively mild summer temperatures and is the site of a number of permanently manned scientific research stations.

Queen Maud Land

Queen Maud Land is an extensive upland area covering a large part of the north-east between 20° W and 45° E. In this region, the ice layer can be more than 4.5 km thick. The weight of this immense mass of ice has pushed the underlying mountains below sea-level. The endless ice desert is only interrupted by a small number of scattered, steep cliffs and strange peaks, rising above

the frozen white landscape. **New Swabia,** a section of land near the coast of Queen Maud Land, is covered by mountains for a length of more than 1,000 km. These include the **Mühlig Hoffmann Mountains,** maximum altitude 3,090 m, and the **Wohlthat Massif,** with a maximum altitude of 2,980 m. South of these mountains, the land rises to form the **Wegener Plateau** at more than 4,000 m above sea level. New Swabia is also the site of the German Neumayer Research Station.

Wilkes Land

Wilkes Land, along the southeast coast facing the Indian Ocean, between the **Queen Mary Coast** and the **George V Land,** covers the area between 100° E and 142° E, representing most of eastern Antarctica.
This wide, barren region is almost entirely covered by a uniform ice sheet, more than 4,700 m thick. There are outlet glaciers along the coast. **Bunger Oasis** is on in **Knox Land,** and Adélie Land, which covers some 390,000 sq. km, is located in the east.

Kerguelen Islands

The archipelago of the **Kerguelen Islands** at the southern end of the Indian Ocean, approximately 2,800 km south-east of Madagascar, comprises the main island, Kerguelen (5,800 sq. km), also called Desolation Island, and a further 300 small islands and protruding mountain peaks, which together cover an area of 7,215 sq. km. The heavily glaciated Kerguelen Island is dominated by mountain peaks, the highest of which is **Mount Ross** rising to 1,960 m. The island is of volcanic origin, and there is still some volcanic activity in the form of hot springs.

Research Stations

The Antarctic Treaty was signed by 12 countries in 1959 and states that Antarctica is a continent for conducting research, which can only be used for peace-

The Weddell Sea has a maximum depth of 5,000 m and large parts are covered in floating drift-ice and icebergs. In the south, the sea is dominated by a permanent ice shelf. It was named after the English explorer J. Weddell and forms a southern part of the Atlantic, cutting deep into the continental mass of the South Polar region and dividing it into West and East Antarctica.

ful purposes. In 1991, 40 nations signed an additional treaty. Since then, approximately 46 research stations belonging to different countries have been established in this inhospitable region. Approximately 1,200 scientists live on these stations in winter, and a further 2,500 in summer.

The main focus of the research is the circulation systems in the ocean, water and ice in the Antarctic. It is becoming increasingly important to use the ice sheet to detect traces of climate change with the aim of drawing conclusions about the current trends in the world's climate.

The following are the research stations belonging to the different nations:

USA: **McMurdo Station**, on the southernmost extension of the Ross Sea; **Amundsen Scott South Pole Station**, at the geographic South Pole; **Palmer Station**, Anvers Island

Russia: **Vostok Station**, on the inland ice of East Antarctica (Station Vostok II), it was here that the lowest temperature on Earth was recorded at -91.5°C; **Bellingshausen**, King George Island on the South Shetland Islands; **Molodezhnaya Station**; **Novolazarevskaya Station**; **Progress Station**; **Mirny Station**; **Russkaya Station**

Australia: **Davis Station**, Princess Elizabeth Land; **Casey Station**, Wilkes Land; **Mawson Station**, MacRobertson Land; **Macquarie Base**, Macquarie Island

New Zealand: **Scott Base**, Ross Island, Victoria Land, on Mount Erebus

Argentina: **Esperanza Base**; **Orcadas Base**; **San Martín Station**

Germany: **Georg von Neumayer Station**, New Swabia

Great Britain: **Halley Research Station**; **Rothera Research Station**, Adelaide Island

Italy: **Mario Zucchelli Station**, Terra Nova Bay, Ross Sea

India: **Dakshin Gangotri Station**; **Maitri Station**, Schirmacher Region

China: **Great Wall Station**, King George Island, South Shetland Islands; **Zhongshan Station**, Amery Ice Shelf

Chile: **Professor Julio Escudero Base**, King George Island, South Shetland Islands; **Capitán Arturo Prat Base**, Greenwich Island, South Shetland Islands; **Bernardo O'Higgins Station**, Antarctic Peninsula

France: **Dumont d'Urville Station**, Adélie Land

South Africa: **SANAE IV**

Japan: **Showa Station**

Brazil: **Comandante Ferraz Station**

South Korea: **King Sejong Station**, King George Island

Norway: **Troll Station**, Queen Maud Land

Finland: **Aboa Station**, Queen Maud Land

Spain: **Juan Carlos I**, Livingston Island

Ukraine: **Akademik Vernadsky Station**, Galindez Island

Poland: **Henryk Arctowski Station**

Uruguay: **General Artigas Station**, King George Island

1 Floating islands: pack-ice, drift-ice and icebergs are characteristic of the Southern Ocean. Strange 'mountains' are created which disappear within a relatively short space of time. The temperature variations between the seasons ensure the cycle is kept in motion.

2 Mount Melbourne volcano in Victoria Land, rises to a height of 2,733 m. The peaks of the Trans-antarctic Mountains are among the few places in Antarctica that are not completely covered in ice.

3 Mount Erebus (3,795 m), the world's southernmost active volcano is situated on an island in the Ross Sea. It last erupted in 2006.

4 The peaks of the Trans-antarctic Mountains, the highest range in Antarctica. Glacial ice has formed over centuries as the winter snows have gradually compacted.

Atlas

The world came into existence 4.5 billion years ago, but life did not begin until a billion years later. Our planet is not exactly spherical, but rather the shape of a squashed balloon. The poles are slightly flattened and there is a bulge at the Equator which has a circumference of 40,076 km. The surface of the Earth consists of 71 per cent water and only 29 per cent solid land; that is why the Earth is known as the 'Blue Planet'. The land area is divided into five landmasses: Europe, Africa, Asia, Australasia and the Americas. These were formed in the Mesozoic Era when the land, consisting of plates that combined to form a supercontinent known as Pangaea, broke apart. These plates are still constantly moving, and this is what causes volcanic eruptions and earthquakes. Kilimanjaro, at 5,895 m the highest mountain in Africa, is a silent witness to the violent focres occurring beneath the Earth's surface.

Legend

Bodies of water

River
Intermittent river
Waterfall, rapids
Freshwater lake
Reservoir
Salt lake
Salt pan
Swamp
Coral reef

Political and other boundaries

International boundary
National capital
Disputed international boundary
Administrative boundary
Administrative capital

Topography

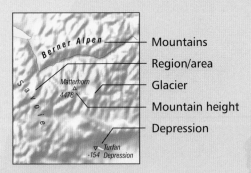

Mountains
Region/area
Glacier
Mountain height
Depression

Color tints

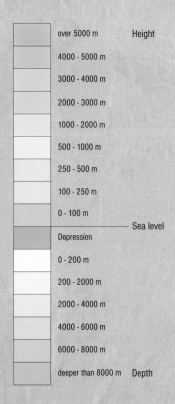

over 5000 m   Height
4000 - 5000 m
3000 - 4000 m
2000 - 3000 m
1000 - 2000 m
500 - 1000 m
250 - 500 m
100 - 250 m
0 - 100 m
                     Sea level
Depression
0 - 200 m
200 - 2000 m
2000 - 4000 m
4000 - 6000 m
6000 - 8000 m
deeper than 8000 m   Depth

Special symbols

✈	International Airport
✈	National Airport
△5445 ▽-154	Elevation above/below sea level
	Wall
	Motorway
	Primary highway
	Railway

Classification of cities and towns

▫ DALIAN	Town over 1 million inhabitants
○ Colorado Springs	Town 100,000 - 1 million inhabitants
○ Dodge City	Town 10,000 - 100,000 inhabitants
○ Brady	Town under 10,000 inhabitants
• Georg von Neumayer (Ger.)	Research station

Type faces

INDIAN OCEAN	Ocean
Gulf of Mexico	Gulf, bay
Java Trench	Undersea landscapes, trenches
L. Torrens *Yamuna*	Lake, river
Great Plains	Region/area
ANDES	Mountains
Aconcagua	Mountain
North Cape	Cape
Greater Antilles *Mauritius*	Islands, Island
BRAZIL	Sovereign state
North Dakota	State/province

Place locator

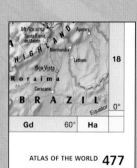

Search for the name of the sought after area/city in the alphabetically arranged map index. The place names are followed by the page numbers of relevant maps as well a number-letter combination indicating the area's location in the map. Letters indicate the east-west position and numbers the north-south position of an area.

Example:
Boa Vista 477 Gd18
Page 477
Map section Gd18

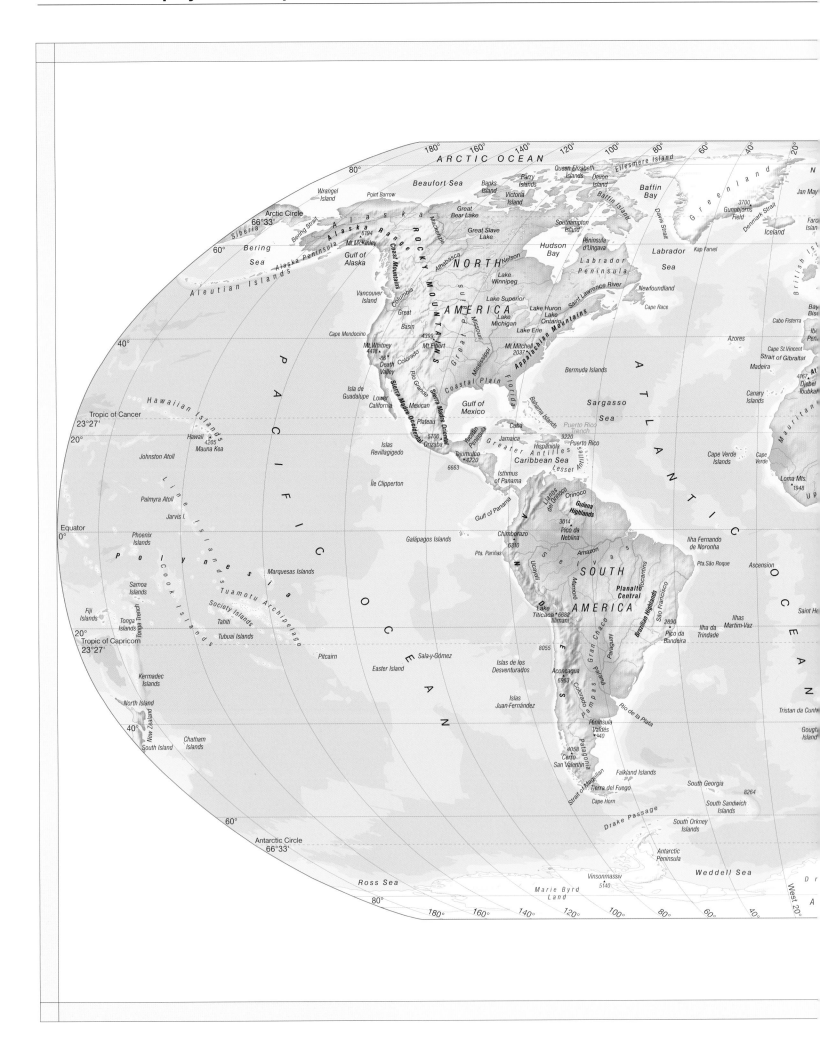

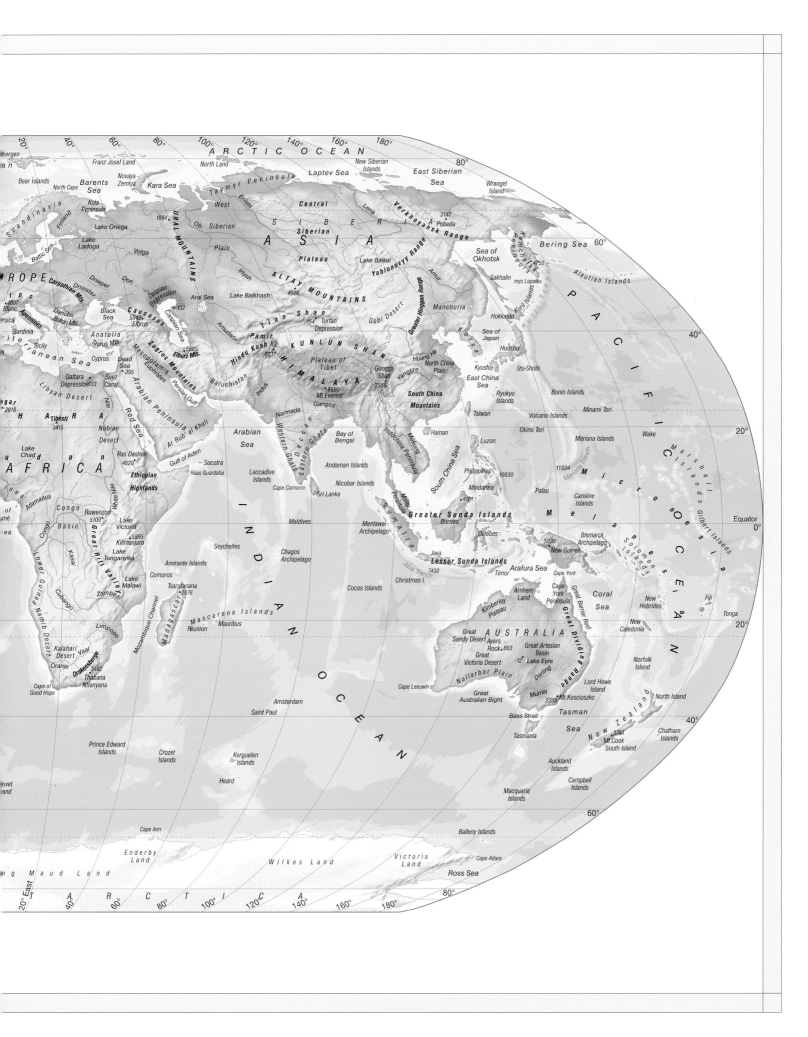

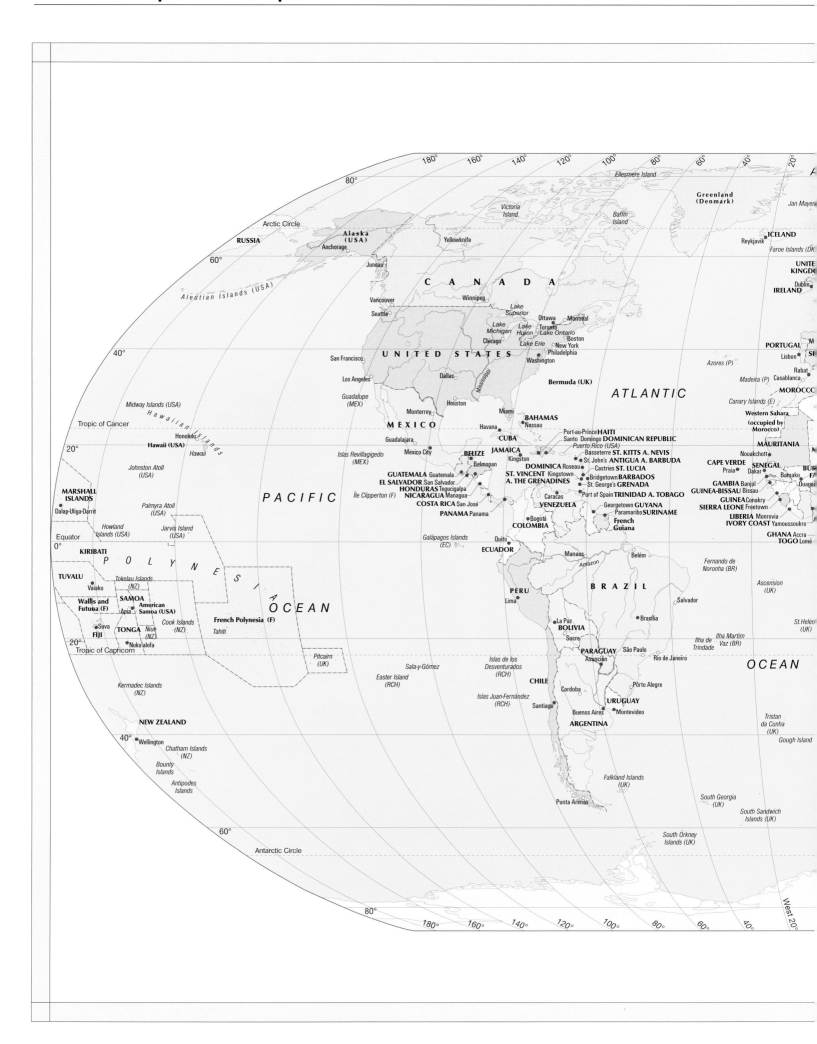

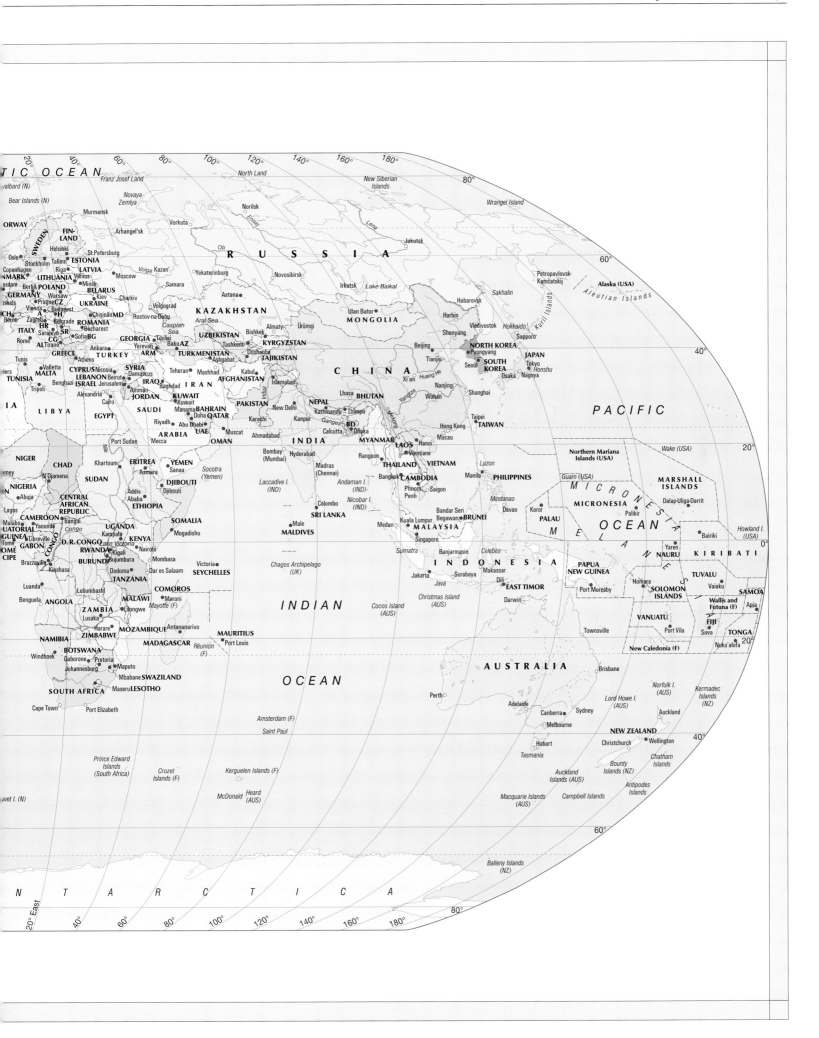

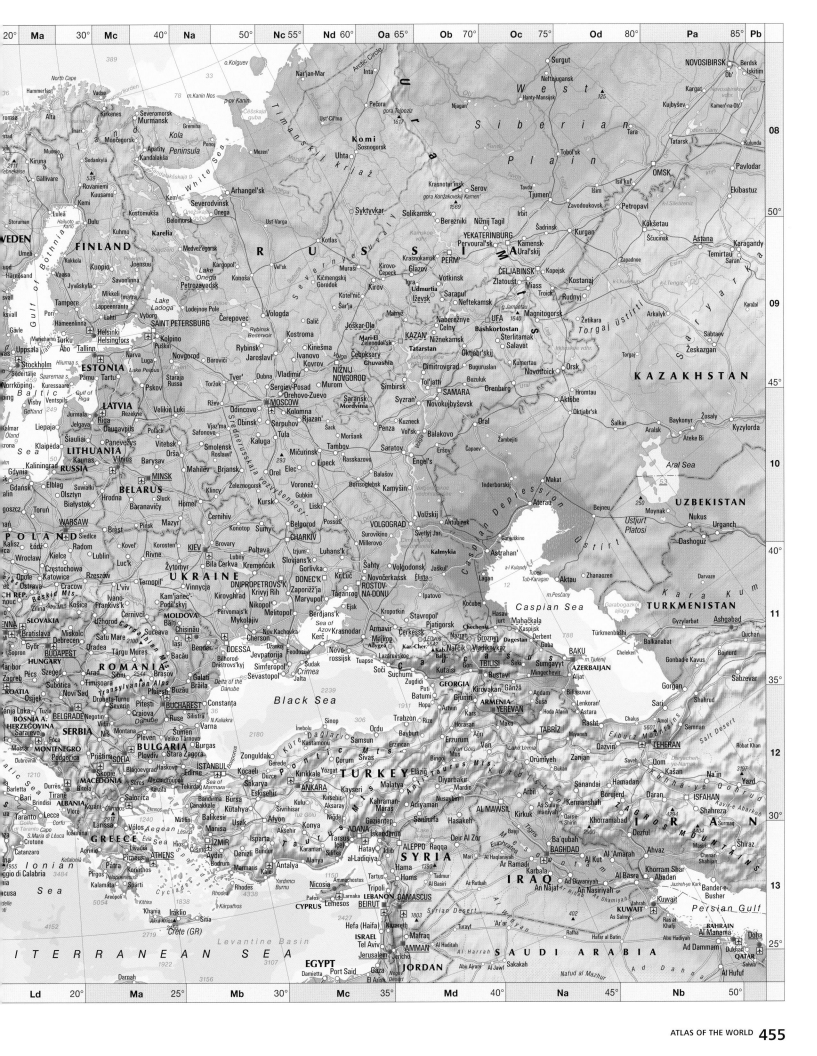

O C E A N

Chukchi Sea

Alaska (USA)

Bristol Bay

Wevek
Cape Lisburne
Kotzebue Sound
Seward Peninsula
Bethel
Wrangel Island
Wales
Nome
Alakanuk
Kuskokwim Bay
Cape Newenham

Ušakovskoye
Uelen
Lavrentija
Northeast Cape
Saint Lawrence Island (USA)
Nunivak Island

Proliv Longa
Koljučinskaja guba
Mys Šmidta
Providenija
Gambell

East Siberian Sea

New Siberian Islands

Čaunskaja guba

hrebet Pekul'nej

B e r i n g

Pribilof Islands

o.Novaja Sibir'
Pevek
ostrov Ajon
Pallavaam
UgoΓnye Kopi
Nagornyj
Anadyr'
St.Matthew Island (USA)

S e a

o.Kotel'nyj

Anadyrskoye Ploskogor'ye
1887
m. Navarin

Laptev Sea

pr.Sannikova
o.Bol. Ljahovskij
1775 Bilibino
Chukchi
Arctic Circle
1651
3795

pr.Dmitrija Lapteva
Čerskij
Anjujskij hrebet
Autonomous District
Koryak Range
A l e u t i a n

o.Bol.Begičev
'Sagastyr
Olenëkskij zaliv
Janski zaliv
Kolymskaja nizmennost'
Olojskij hrebel
1797
g. Ledjanaja
2562
B a s i n

Saskylah
Lena Delta
m.Buor-Haja
Čekurdah
Omolon
1503
Kamenskoe
Apuka
m. Oljutorskij

kraž Čekanovskogo
guba Buor-Haja
Jano-Indigirskaja nizmennost'
Jukagirskoe ploskogor'e
1613
Koryak
Korf
Oljutorskij zaliv

Olenëk
Žigansk
Deputatskij
Cherskiy Range
Momskij hrebel
2243
Zyrjanka
1411
1814
1483
Autonomous District
Sirsova Ridge

Sakha
Menkerja
Bataga
2533
Honuu
Sejmčan
1962
Karaginskij
Ossora
o.Karaginskij
Attu I. (USA)

2247
Lazo
2690
Ust'-Nera
Susuman
Jagodnoe
zaliv
Šelihova
Sredinnyj
o. Ozernoj

Siktjah
Janskoe ploskogor'e
Ojmjakon
m. Tajgonos
Komandorskie o-va

Udačnyj
(Yakutia)
2081
2120
hrebet Suntar-Hajata
Tomtor
Ust'-Omčug
m. Tolstoj
Ust'-Kamčatsk
Agattu I. (USA)

Viljujskoe plato
Sangar
Handyga
2959
Kamchatka Peninsula
4750
vlk. Ključevskaja Sopka
m. Kamčatskij

Central'nojakutskaja ravnina
Viljujsk
2184
Magadan
m. Južnyj
3607
m.Kronockij

Njurba
Jakutsk
Ust'-Maja
Okhotsk
m. Alevina
vlk. Korjakskaja Sopka

Mirnyj
ravnina
Kerdem
Amga
3456
Petropavlovsk-Kamčatskij

Prilenskoe plato
Ulu
2460
PACIFIC

Viljujskoe vdhr.
Lensk
Olëkminsk
Sea of Okhotsk
m. Lopatka
OCEAN

Čagda
o. Paramušir

Aldanskoe nagor'e
2243
1890
hrebet Dzhugdzhur
m. Elizavety
o. Onekotan

1702
Patomskoe nagor'e
Aldan
1906
o. Šiaškotan

Stanovoy Nagor'ye
Olëkma
Čul'man
2067
Šantarskie Ostrova
Čumikan

g.Skalistyj Golec
Nerjungri
2384
Kurill Islands
o. Rassua

2467
Stanovoy Khrebet
Nikolaevsk-na-Amure
o. Simušir

Buryatia
Stanovik
3067
hr. Tukuringra
Verhnezejskaja ravnina
Sakhalin
o. Urup

2630
Olëkminskij Range
Skovorodino
1609
Poronajsk
m. Terpenija

Yablonovyy Range
Čita
Mogoča
Zejsko-Bureinskaja ravnina
Uglegorsk
o. Iturup

Ulan-Udė
Mohe
Šimanovsk
Bureinskij hrebet
Vanino
Južno-Sahalinsk

Aga Buryat Autonomous District
Yimutu
Zeja
Komsomol'sk-na-Amure
Holmsk
o. Kunašir

Čita
Mangui
Blagoveščensk
Amur
Habarovsk
La Perouse Strait

Aginskoe
Jagdaqi
Birobidžan
Jewish Autonomous Region
Wakkanai
Abashiri

Borzja
Ergun Zuoqi
Bei'an
Bikin
Asahikawa
2290
Kushiro

Ergun Youqi
Yichun
Dal'nerečensk
Asahi dake
Obihiro

Manzhouli
Yakeshi
Zhalantun
Hegang
Dal'negorsk
SAPPORO
Tomakomai

Hailar
Bei'an
Jiamusi
Rudnaja Pristan'
HOKKAIDO

Chojbalsan
Qiqihar
Mingshui
Jixi
JAPAN

Ondörhaan
Tailai
Anda
Suihua
Lake Khanka

Baruun Urt
Ulanhot
Heilongjiang
Tonghe
Spassk-Dal'nij

HARBIN
Shangzhi

CHINA
Heilongjiang

Greater Hinggan Range

Lesser Hinggan Range

Sikhote-Alin'

Tatarskiy Proliv

Kuril Trench

Komandorskie o-va

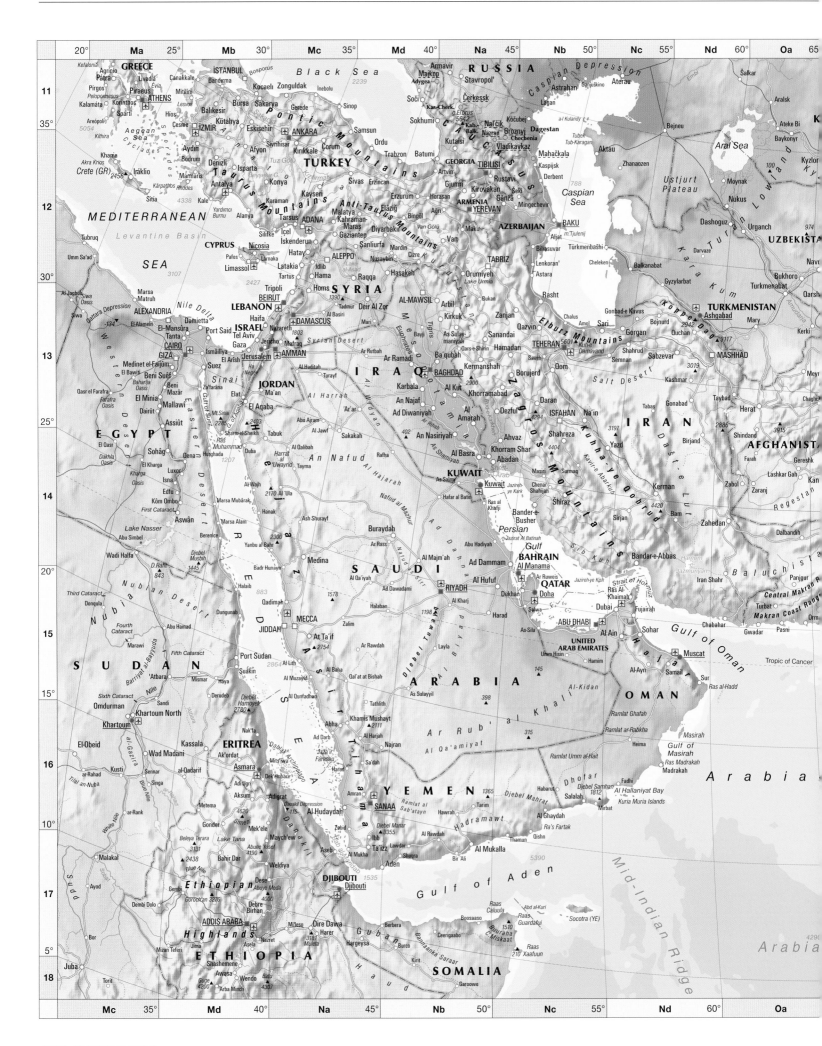

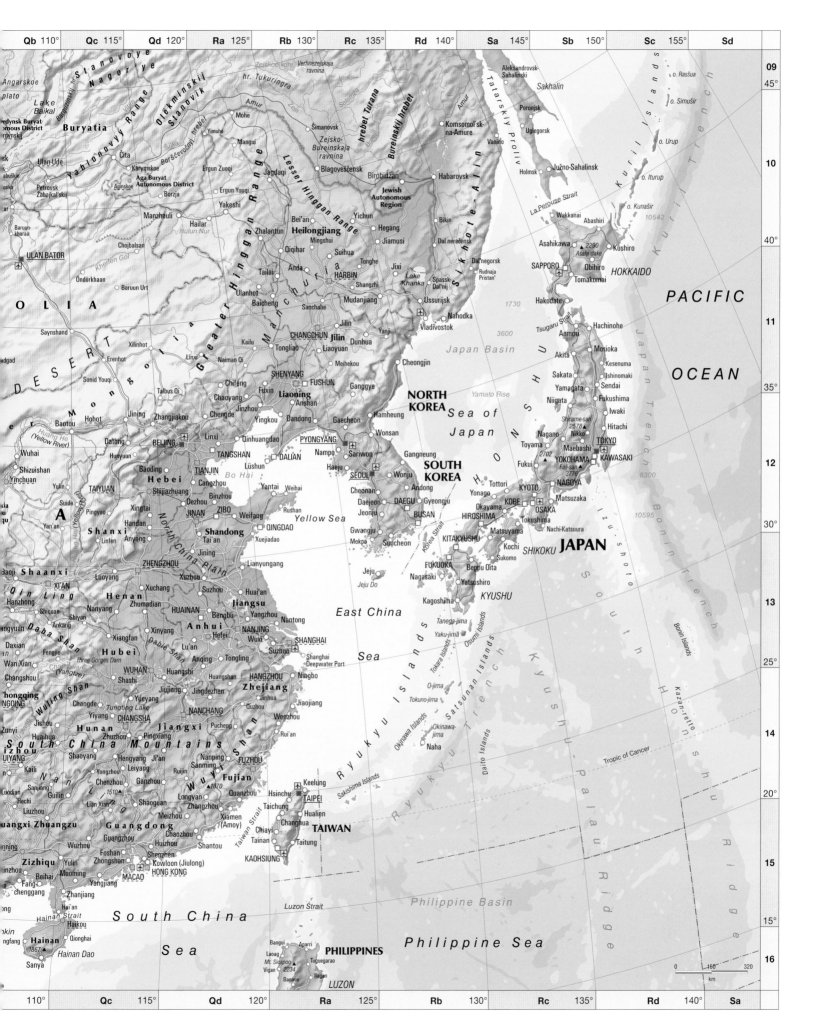

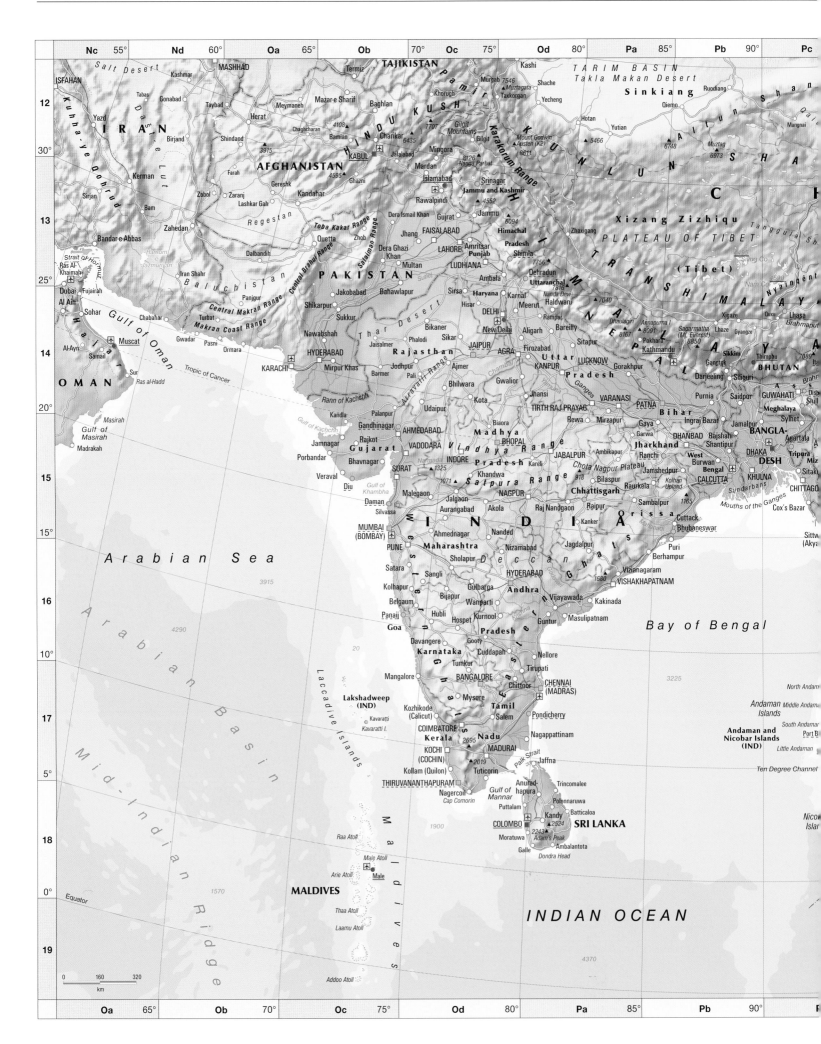

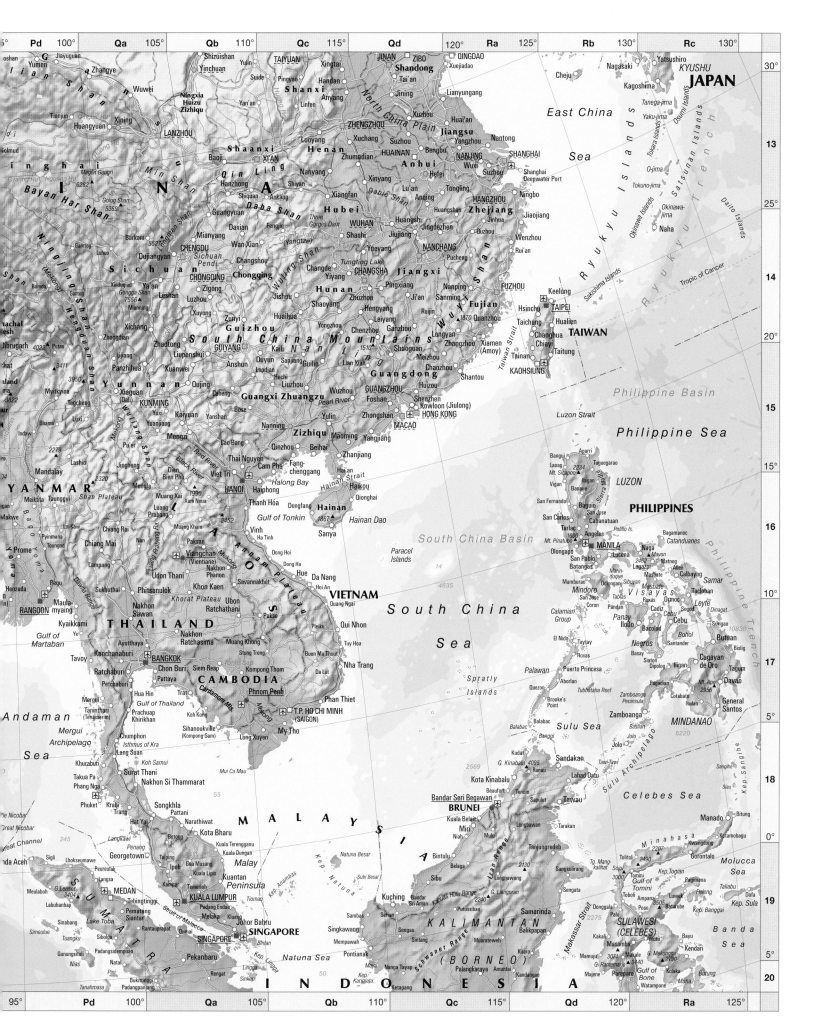

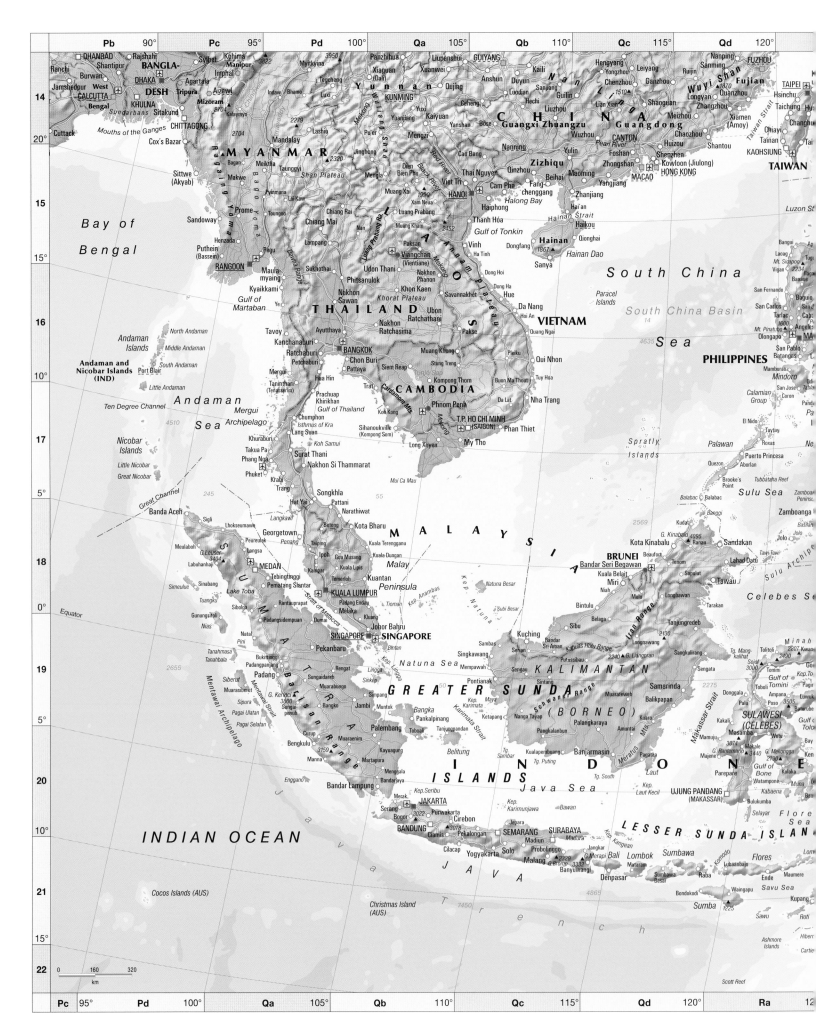

Australia, New Zealand

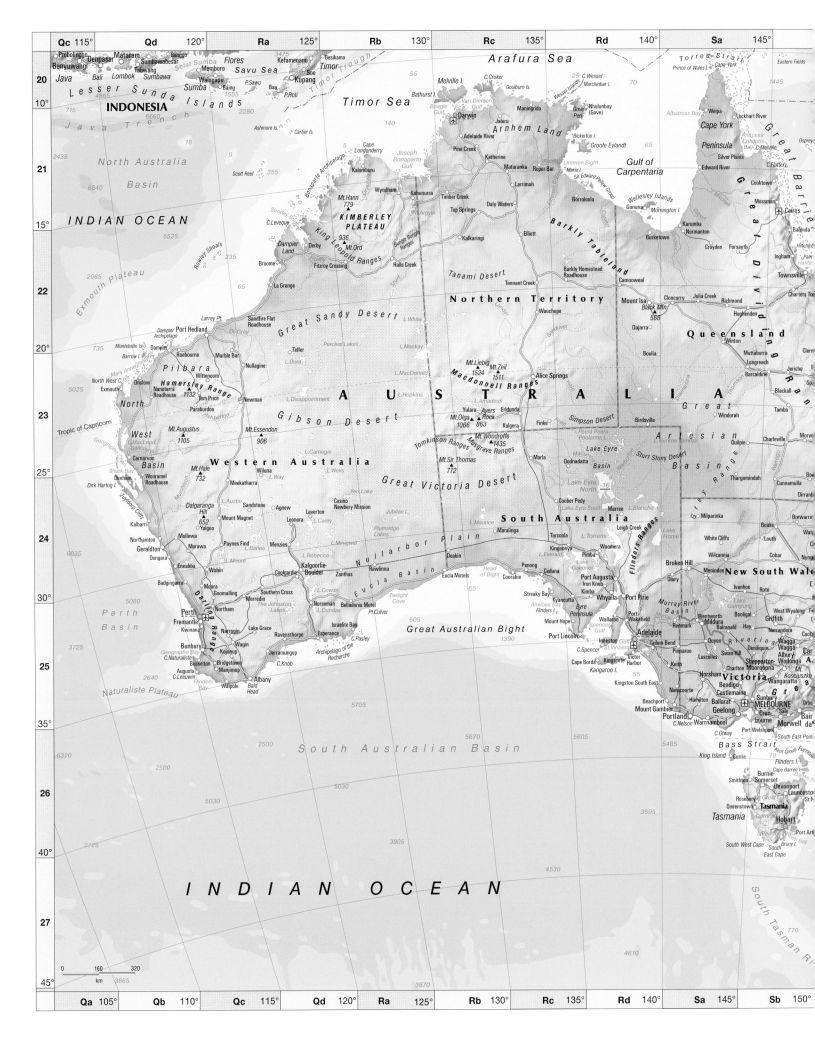

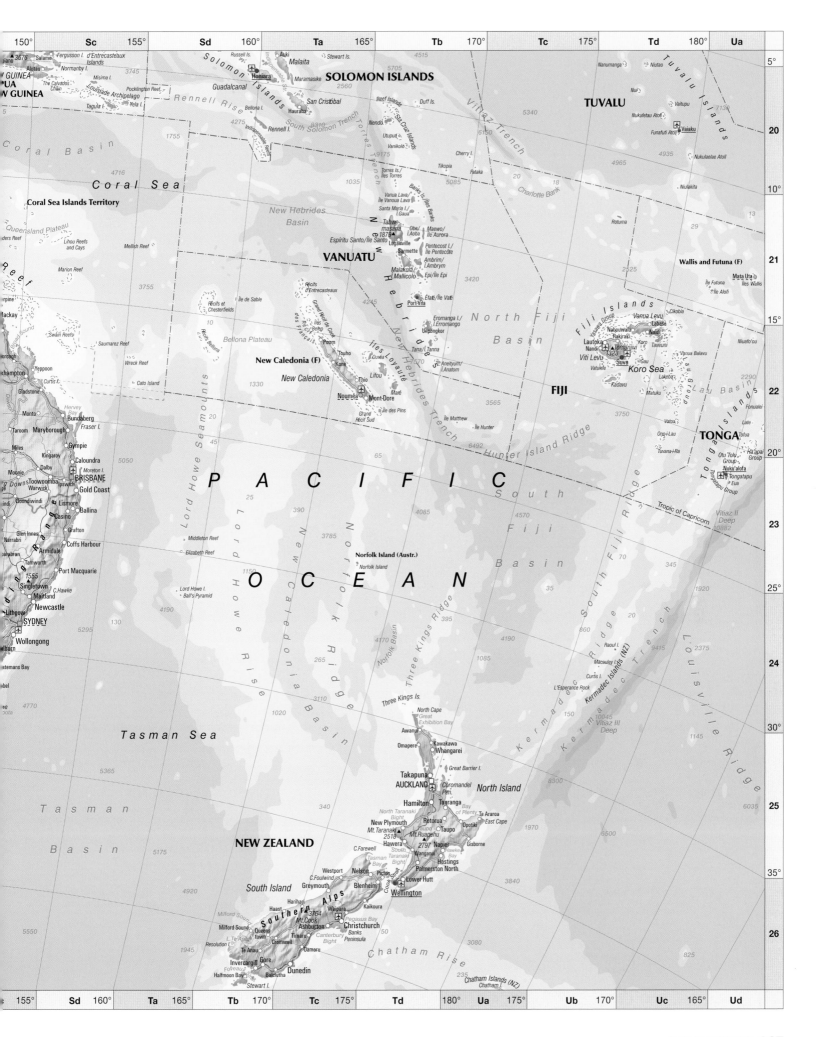

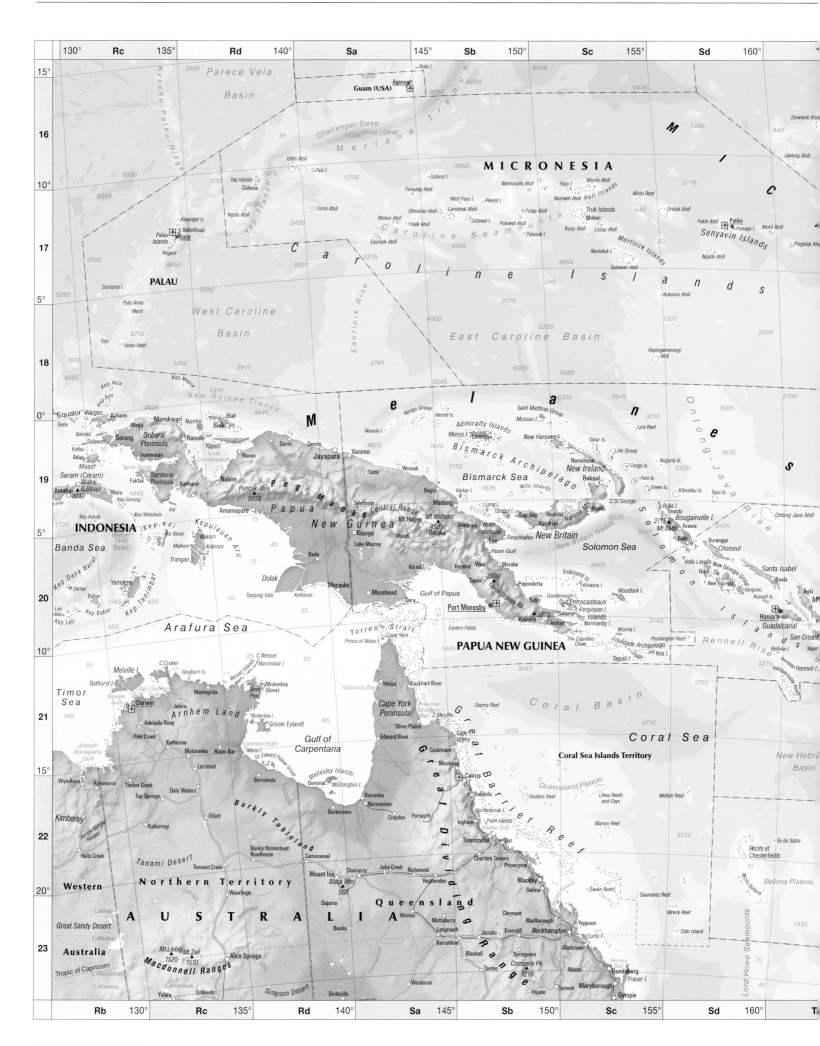

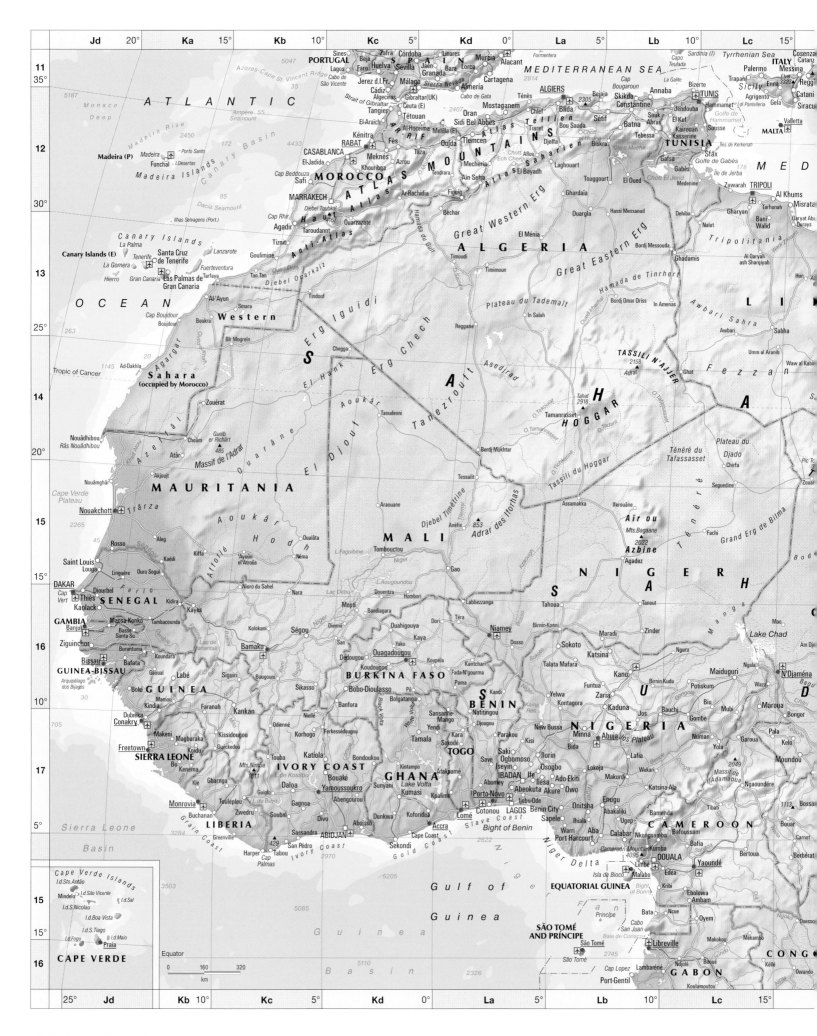

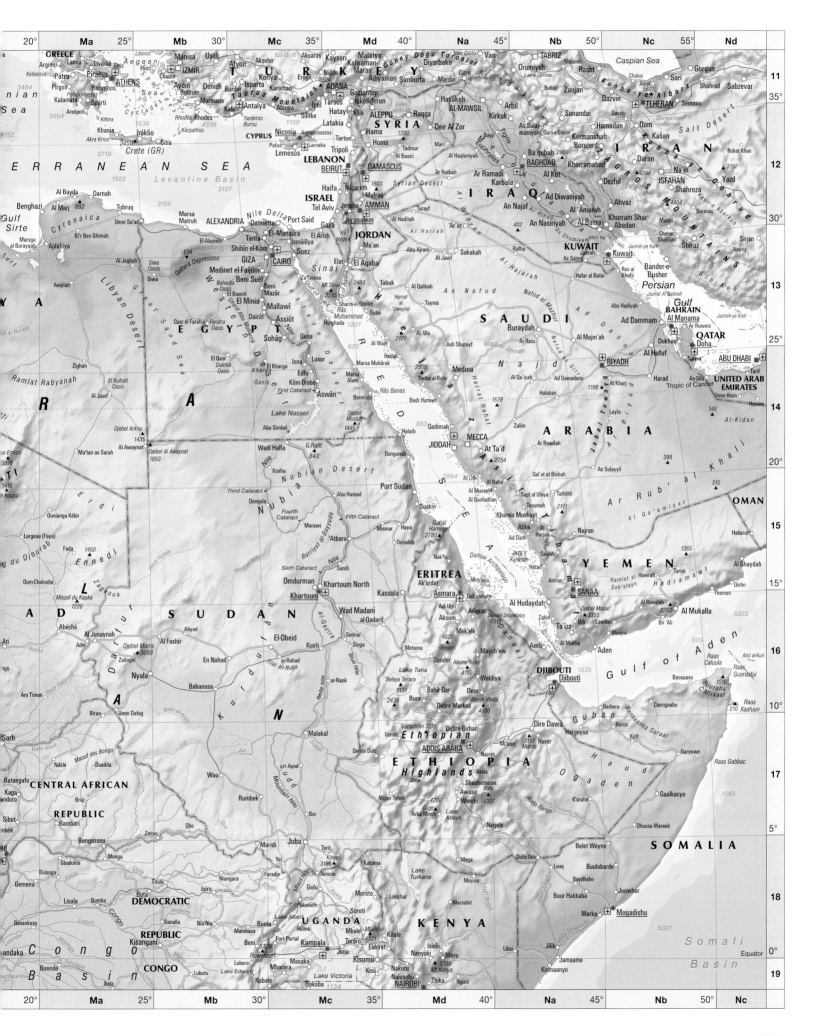

GREECE
Lésvos
Argíni
Lamía
Lívadhiá
Pátra
Piraeus
Kefaloniá
Peloponnese
Kalamata
ATHENS
Spárti
Khaniá
Akra Krios
Sitía
Crete (GR)

Manisa
Uşak
Afyon
İZMIR
Aydın
Denizli
Burdur
Isparta
Antalya
Marmaris
Fethiye
Kale
Rhodes
Kárpathos

Akşehir
Konya
Karaman
Silifke
İçel
Tarsus
ADANA
İskenderun
Hatay
Antakya
Kırıkkale
Kilis

Aksaray
Kayseri
Niğde
Kahraman
Maraş
Gaziantep
ALEPPO
Raqqa
Latakia
Tartus
Tripoli

Kırşehir
Malatya
Adıyaman
Şanlıurfa
Mardin
Deir Al Zor
Hama
Homs
Tadmur
Al Basiri

Diyarbakır
Cizre
Hasakeh
AL-MAWSIL
Kirkuk
Mari
Ba'qubah
BAGHDAD

Van Gölü
Van
Orumiyeh
Lake Ormia
Arbil
As Sulaymaniyah
Qars-e Shirin
Khorramabad

TABRIZ
Mıyaneh
Rasht
Zanjan
Bukan
Sanandai
Hamadan
Borujerd
ISFAHAN

Caspian Sea
Chalus
Amol
Qazvin
TEHERAN
Qom
Kašan
Shahreza
Daran

Gorgan
Sari
Shahrud
Sabzevar
Semnan
Robat Khan
Na'in
Yazd

CYPRUS
Nicosia
Lemesós
Larnaca
Pafos
Ammochostos

LEBANON
BEIRUT
DAMASCUS
Haifa
Nazareth
ISRAEL
Tel Aviv
Jerusalem
Jericho
AMMAN

Syrian Desert
Ar Rutbah
Ar Ramadi
Al Kut
Karbala
An Najaf
Ad Diwaniyah

IRAQ
Al Hillah
An Nasiriyah
Al Amarah
Al Basra
Abadan
Khorram Shar

IRAN
Dezful
Ahvaz
Shahijan
Masjed
Shiraz
Neyriz
Sirjan

Al Marj
Darnah
Tubruq
Marsa Matruh
ALEXANDRIA
Port Said
Damietta
Gaza
JORDAN
Ma'an

Benghazi
Al Bayda
Gulf of Sirte
Ajdabiya

Suez
CAIRO
GIZA
Beni Suef
Sinai
El Aqaba
Elat
Tabuk

Siwa Oasis
Qattara Depression
Bahariya Oasis

EGYPT
El Minia
Mallawî
Assiût
Sohâg

LIBYAN DESERT

SAUDI
Buraydah
Ar Rass
Ad Dammam
BAHRAIN
Al Manama
QATAR
Doha
ABU DHABI

Medina
RIYADH
Al Kharj
Harad
UNITED ARAB
EMIRATES
Tropic of Cancer

JIDDAH
MECCA
At Ta'if
ARABIA

Aswân
Lake Nasser
Abu Simbel

Wadi Halfa
Nubian Desert
Nubia
Dongola
Abu Hamad

Port Sudan
Suakin

OMAN
Ar Rub' al Khali

SUDAN
Omdurman
Khartoum North
Khartoum
Kassala

ERITREA
Ak'ordat
Asmara

YEMEN
SANAA
Al Hudaydah
Ta'izz
Al Mukalla
Aden

Darfur
Abéché
Al Junaynah
El Fashir
Nyala

Wad Madani
al-Qadarif
Sennar
El-Obeid
Kusti

Gonder
Bahir Dar
Aksum
Mek'ele

DJIBOUTI
Djibouti
Gulf of Aden
Berbera
Boosaaso

CENTRAL AFRICAN
REPUBLIC

Malakal
Wau
Rumbek

ETHIOPIA
Highlands
ADDIS ABABA
Nazret
Jima
Awasa

Dire Dawa
Harer
Hargeysa

Gaalkacyo

Juba
Torit
Bor

SOMALIA

UGANDA
Kampala
Lake Victoria
KENYA
NAIROBI

DEMOCRATIC
REPUBLIC
CONGO
Kisangani

Mogadishu
Somali
Basin
Equator

Northern South America

| Ec 105° | Ed 100° | Fa 95° | Fb 90° | Fc 85° | Fd 80° | Ga 75° |

Chile
Basin
328

22

20°
3763
4123
2992

Islas de los Desventurados (RC)

23
5532 483
Sala-y-Gomez-Fracture Zone
222
497

Tropic of Capricorn
3826

25°
Sala y Gómez (RC)
3947

Roggeveen Basin

Rapa-Nui (RC)
Easter Island
Islas Juan-Fernández (RC) 430

Isla Robinsón Crusoe
(Isla Más a Tierra)
24
1510
I.Alejandro Selkirk
1800 4025

P   A   C   I   F   I   C

30°
Restinga de Sefton

2980
12

25
4400

Chile
2726 4387 4612
Valdivia Fracture Zone
2674

35°
2923
R i s e
3543

4688

26

O   C   E   A   N

40°
4295

3342
Mornington
Abyssal Plain

27
4764

45°

28
South East Pacifi

0 160 320
km

| Da 135° | Db 130° | Dc 125° | Dd 120° | Ea 115° | Eb 110° | Ec 105° | Ed 100° | Fa 95° | Fb 90° | Fc 8 |

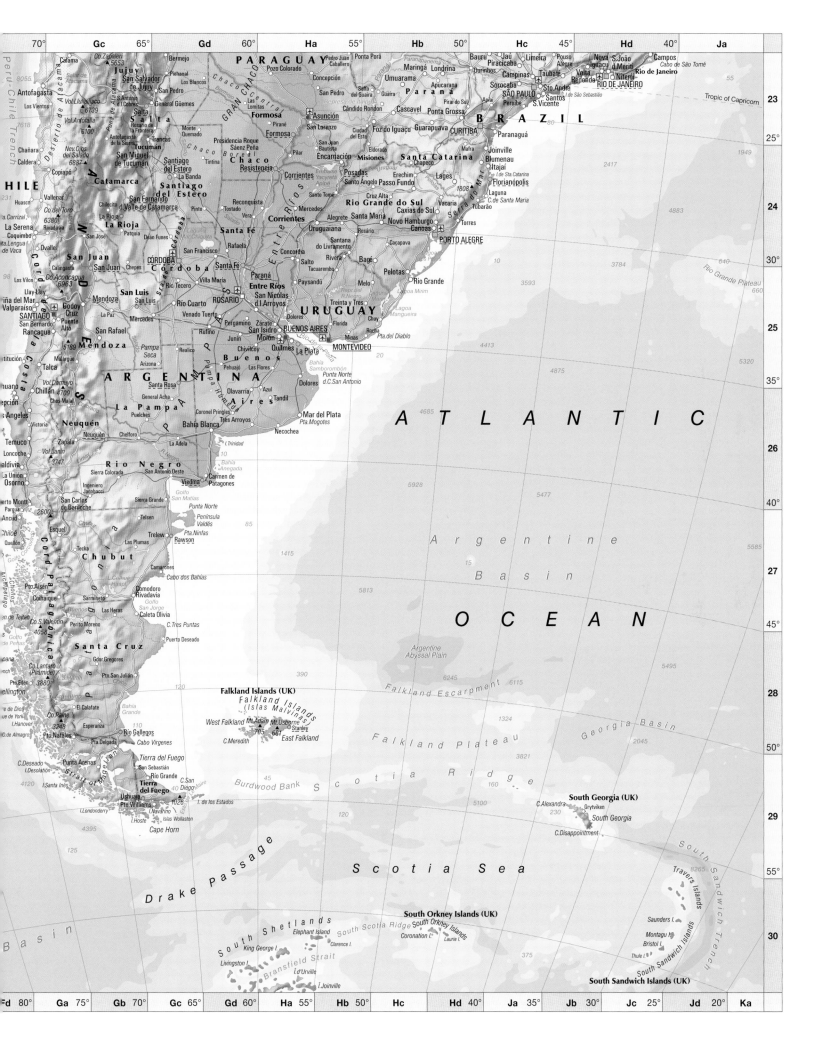

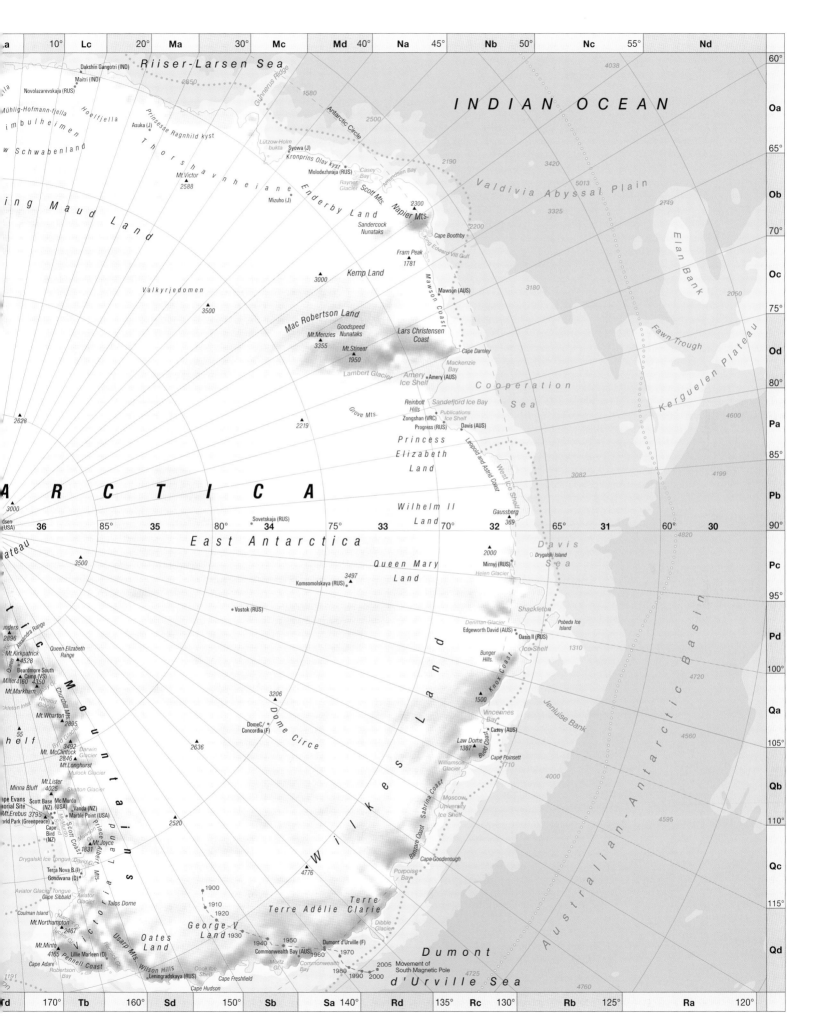

Riiser-Larsen Sea

Dakshin Gangotri (IND)
Maitri (IND)

INDIAN OCEAN

4038

Oa

Novolazarevskaja (RUS)

Mühlig-Hofmann-fjella

Hoelfjella

Prinsesse Ragnhild kyst

imbulheimen

w Schwabenland

Thorshavnheiane

Gunnerus Ridge

2650

1580

Antarctic Circle

2500

Valdivia Abyssal Plain

2190

3420

5013

Ob

Asuka (J)

Lützow-Holm bukta

Syowa (J)

Kronprins Olav kyst

Molodezhnaja (RUS)

Casey Bay

Amundsen Bay

2200

3325

2749

Mt.Victor
2588

Mizuho (J)

Enderby Land

Rayner Glacier

Scott Mts.

Napier Mts.

2300

King Edward VIII Gulf

Cape Boothby

Elan Bank

Oc

Ving Maud Land

Sandercock Nunataks

Fram Peak
1781

Mawson Coast

Mawson (AUS)

3180

2060

Valkyrjedomen

Kemp Land

3000

75°

3500

Mac Robertson Land

Goodspeed Nunataks

Mt.Menzies

Lars Christensen Coast

Cape Darnley

Fawn Trough

Kerguelen Plateau

Od

3355

Mt.Stinear
1950

Mackenzie Bay

Lambert Glacier

Amery Ice Shelf

Amery (AUS)

Cooperation Sea

80°

2628

Grove Mts.

Reinbolt Hills

Sandefjord Ice Bay

Publications Ice Shelf

4600

Pa

Zongshan (VRC)

2219

Progress (RUS)

Davis (AUS)

Princess

Elizabeth

Land

Leopold and Astrid Coast

West Ice Shelf

3082

4199

85°

Pb

3000

Wilhelm II

Gaussberg

Gaussberg
369

Land

4820

lsen
(USA)

36

85°

35

80°

Sovetskaja (RUS)

34

75°

33

70°

32

31

60°

30

90°

East Antarctica

Davis Sea

Pc

ateau

3500

Queen Mary

2000

Mirnyj (RUS)

Drygalski Island

Helen Glacier

3497

Land

Komsomolskaya (RUS)

95°

Vostok (RUS)

Shackleton

Pd

nders

2896

Mt.Kirkpatrick

Queen Elizabeth Range

4528

Denman Glacier

Edgeworth David (AUS)

Pobeda Ice Island

Oasis II (RUS)

1310

Beardmore South Camp (VS)

Miller 4160   4350

Mt.Markham

Bunger Hills.

Ice Shelf

4720

Qa

3206

Wilkes Land

1500

4560

keton Inlet

Mt.Wharton
2895

Dome Circe

Vincennes Bay

Churchill Mts.

55

3492

Casey (AUS)

helf

Byrd Glacier

Mt.McClintock
2846

Darwin Glacier

2636

Law Dome
1387

Budd Coast

Cape Poinsett
1710

Jenluise Bank

4000

Qb

Mt.Longhurst

Mulock Glacier

Mt.Lister
4025

Moscow University Ice Shelf

Minna Bluff

Skelton Glacier

Williamson Glacier

4595

pe Evans
rorial Site

Scott Base (NZ)

Mc Murdo (USA)

Vanda (NZ)

Mt.Erebus 3795

Marble Point (USA)

2520

orld Park (Greenpeace)

Cape Bird (NZ)

Mt.Joyce
1831

Banzare Coast

Sabrina Coast

Qc

Drygalski Ice Tongue

David G.

Prince Albert Mts.

W

4776

Terre

Cape Goodenough

Porpoise Bay

Terra Nova B.(I)

Gondwana (D)

Aviator Glacier Tongue

1900

Terre Adélie Clarie

Dibble Glacier

115°

Cape Sibbald

Aviator Glacier

Talos Dome

1910

Coulman Island

1920

George V

Mt.Northampton
2467

Land

1930

Dumont d'Urville (F)

Qd

Marin

Mt.Minto
4165

Lillie Marleen (D)

Oates Land

Mt.Wilson Hills

1940

1950

Commonwealth Bay (AUS)

1960

Dumont

Cape Adare

Robertson Bay

Pennell Coast

Cook Ice Shelf

Leningradskaya (RUS)

Cape Freshfield

Mortz

Commonwealth Bay

1970

2005

1980

Movement of South Magnetic Pole

1990   2000

d'Urville Sea

4725

4760

1191

Cape Hudson

Australian-Antarctic Basin

	Fb 80°	Ga 70°	Gb 60°	Ha 50°	Hb 40°	Ja 30°	Jb 20°	Ka 10°	Kb 0°	La 10°	Lb

Southampton Island
Baffin Island
Godthåb/ Nûk
Greenland
Iceland
Faroe Islands
Norwegian Sea
Scandinavia

03 60°
Hudson Strait
Labrador Sea
Uummannarsuaq/ Kap Farvel
Iceland Basin
90
Shetland Islands
British Isles
North Sea
Vänern
03 60°

Hudson Bay
Péninsule d'Ungava
Coast of Labrador
Labrador Basin
Reykjanes Ridge
21
Ireland
Great Britain
Berlin

04 50°
Labrador Peninsula
Cape St. Charles
London
Rhine
Elbe
04 50°

James Bay
Les Laurentides
NORTH AMERICA
English Channel
EUROPE
Danube

5080
West European Basin
Paris
Loire
Mont Blanc 4810
Alps
Apennines

05 40°
Lake Superior
Québec
Gulf of Saint Lawrence
Newfoundland
Grand Banks of Newfoundland
4636
Bay of Biscay
5120
Cabo Fisterra
Pyrénées 3404
Rhône
Ebro
Corsica
Sardinia
Rome
05 40°

Lake Michigan
Lake Huron
Saint Lawrence River
Halifax
Saint Pierre and Miquelon
69
Iberian Basin
Duero
Madrid
Toledo
Baleares 2890

Chicago
Lake Ontario
Lake Erie
Boston
Nova Scotia
5943
Lisbon
Sierra Nevada
Mediterranean Sea
Sicily

St. Louis
Ohio
Washington D.C.
New York
Cape Cod
Azores
Azores-Cape St. Vincent Ridge
Cabo de São Vicente
Strait of Gibraltar
Algiers

06 30°
Tennessee
Appalachian Mountains
Cape Hatteras
North American
770
Canary
Madeira
Rabat
Casablanca
Atlas Mountains
Tripoli
06 30°

Mississippi
Coastal Plain
Jacksonville
Bermuda Islands 4755
Basin
Canary Islands
Great Western Erg
Great Eastern Erg

New Orleans
Cape Canaveral
Sargasso Sea
Basin
6690
A T L A N T I C
Canary Basin
Sahara
Erg Chech
Hoggar 2918 Tahat
Tassili N'Ajjer
Fezzan
Tibesti

07 20°
Mexican Basin
Gulf of Mexico
Miami
Straits of Florida
1708
Tropic of Cancer
Cap Blanc
Nouakchott
3415 Emi Koussi
07 20°

Mérida
Yucatán Peninsula
Havana
Cuba
Florida
Bahama Islands
9219 Milwaukee Deep
Cape Verde Plateau
Senegal
Niger
2022 Aïr ou Azbine
2818

Cayman Trench
Jamaica
Puerto Rico Trench
Cape Verde Islands
Cap Vert Dakar
Bamako
Niamey
Lake Chad

08 10°
Guatemala
7680
Greater Antilles
Puerto Rico
Guadeloupe
Dominica
Cape Verde
6390
Ouagadougou
N'Djamena
08 10°

San Salvador
Lago de Nicaragua
Caribbean Sea
Lesser Antilles
Barbados
Guiana Basin
Loma Mts. 1948
Sierra Leone
Abuja
Benue

6682
Managua
San José
Punta Gallinas
Maracaibo
Caracas
Trinidad
Sierra Leone Rise
Conakry
Upper Guinea
Lagos
Cameroon Mountain 4095

09
Cocos Island
Panama
Orinoco
Georgetown
Paramaribo
2432
Sierra Leone Basin
Monrovia
Yamoussoukro
Accra
Bioko
Libreville
09

Bogotá
Nev. del Huila 3901
Llanos del Orinoco
Guiana Highlands
Mt. Roraima 2810
4478
Romanche Gap
C. Palmas
Abidjan
4369
Gulf of Guinea
5212
São Tomé
Lower Guinea

Cocos Ridge
Quito
Chimborazo 6310
3750
Pico da Neblina 3014
Marajó
Equator
6537
7858
Guinea Basin
Cap Lopez
Pagalú (Annobón)

10 0°
Galápagos Islands
Pta. Negra
Amazon Lowland
Iquitos
Manaus
Belém
Fortaleza
Fernando de Noronha
Cabo de São Roque
Ascension
Brazzaville
Kinshasa
Congo
10 0°

4146
Huascarán 6601 6708
Madeira
Pôrto Velho
Tapajós
Natal
Recife 5512
Brazil Basin
Luanda

11 10°
Peru Basin
Lima
Yungas
SOUTH AMERICA
Central
Planalto
Sertão
São Francisco
Salvador
Saint Helena
Angola
Benguela
11 10°

Lake Titicaca
La Paz
Altiplano
Brasília
Brazilian Highlands
C. Fria

4124
6867
Atacama
8055
Pantanal
Paraguay
Belo Horizonte
Pico da Bandeira 2890
53
147
5590
Windhoek

12 20°
Islas de los Desventuradas
6887 Nev. Ojos del Salado
Gran Chaco
Asunción
Paraná
Rio de Janeiro
São Paulo
Serra do Mar
Vitória Seamount
Tropic of Capricorn
O C E A N
231
Namib Desert
12 20°

Rio Grande Plateau

13 30°
PACIFIC
6963 Aconcagua
Córdoba
Uruguay
Pôrto Alegre
638
3749
232
Walvis Ridge
Cape Town
Cape of Good Hope
13 30°

3884
Islas Juan Fernández
Santiago
Chile
Río de la Plata
Montevideo
Pampas
Buenos Aires
Tristan da Cunha
Cape Basin
5605 1285

OCEAN
Chile Basin
Bahía Blanca
5267
Argentine
Gough
426

14 40°
Chile Rise
Chiloé
Chonos Archipelago
San Valentín 4058
Río Negro
Península Valdés 40
Basin
4287
14 40°

Patagonia
6881

15 50°
Punta Arenas
Strait of Magellan
Falkland Islands
South Scotia Ridge
South Georgia
8264 Meteor Deep
15 50°

Tierra del Fuego
Cape Horn
Drake Passage

0 700 1400 km

90°	Fb 80°	Ga 70°	Gb 60°	Ha 50°	Hb 40°	Ja 30°	Jb 20°	Ka 10°	Kb 0°	La 10°	Lb

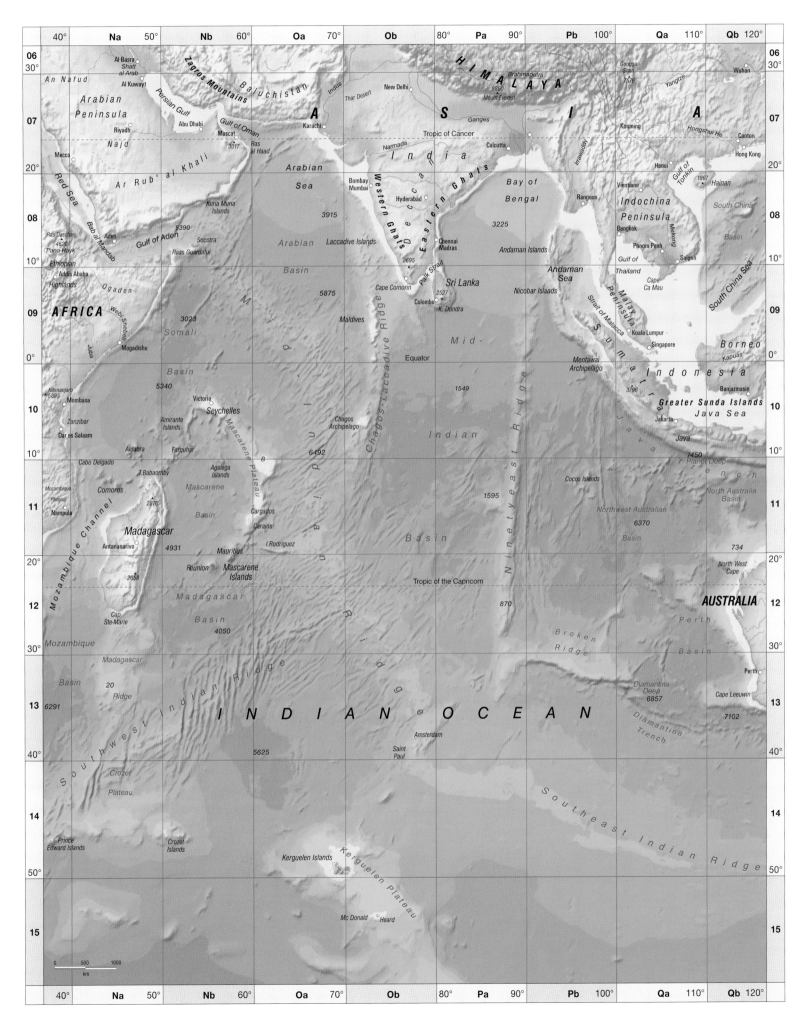

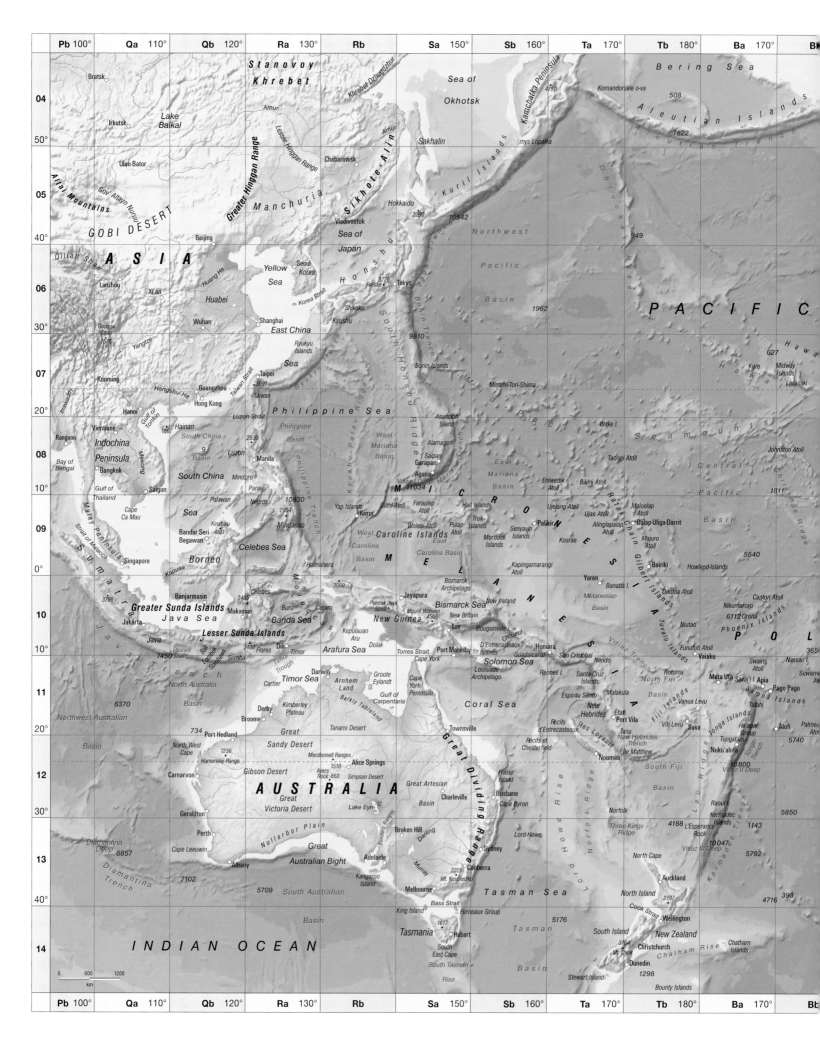

Pb 100° Qa 110° Qb 120° Ra 130° Rb Sa 150° Sb 160° Ta 170° Tb 180° Ba 170° B

Bering Sea

Stanovoy Khrebet

Bratsk

Sea of Okhotsk

Komandorskie o-va 508

Aleutian Islands

Kamchatka Peninsula 4750

04

Amur

Lesser Hinggan Range

Khrebet Dzhugdzhur

7822

Aleutian Trench

50°

Irkutsk Lake Baikal

Amur

Chabarowsk

mys Lopatka

Kuril Islands

949

Ulan Bator

Sikhote-Alin

Greater Hinggan Range

Sakhalin

Obruche

05

Altai Mountains

Gov' Altayn Nuruu

Manchuria

Vladivostok

Hokkaido 2290

10542

Northwest

40°

GOBI DESERT

ASIA

Beijing

Sea of Japan

Honshu

Japan Trench

Pacific

Qilian Shan

Lanzhou

Yellow Sea

Seoul Korea

Basin 1962

PACIFIC

06

Gongga Shan 7576

Xi'an

Huabei

Fusan 3776 Tokyo

Bonin Trench

30°

Wuhan

Huang He

Shanghai

Shikoku

Kyushu

South Honshu Ridge

9810

627 Hawa

Yangtze

East China

Ryukyu Islands

Bonin Islands

Kure Midway Islands

07

Kunming

Taipei 3997

Sea

Ryukyu Trench

Minami-Tori-Shima

Mid Pacific Seamounts

Lisianski

20°

Hongshui He

Guangzhou

Taiwan Strait

Taiwan

Philippine Sea

Asuncion Island

Wake I.

Central

Hanoi Hong Kong

Gulf of Tonkin

Luzon Strait

Alamagan

Johnston Atoll

08

Rangoon

Vientiane

Hainan 1867

Philippine Basin

West Mariana Basin

Saipan Garapan

Taongi Atoll

Christmas Ridge

Indochina Peninsula

South China 2930 Basin

Luzon

Agaña

East Mariana Basin

Eniwetok Atoll

Bikini Atoll

1811

10°

Bay of Bengal

Bangkok

Mekong

Gulf of Thailand

Saigon

9 Basin

Manila

Mindoro

Vitiaz 11034

Mariana Trench

Pacific Basin

Irrawaddy

South China

Palawan

Negros

Panay

10830

2954

Yap Islands

Ujelang Atoll

Ujae Atoll

Maloelap Atoll

09

Cape Ca Mau

Sea

Bandar Seri Begawan

Kinabalu 4101

Mindanao

Koror

Ulithi-Atoll

Faraulep Atoll

Hall Islands

Truk Islands

Alinglapalap Atoll

Dalap-Uliga-Darrit

Singapore

Strait of Malacca

Woleai-Atoll

Pulap Atoll

Senyavin Islands

Palikir

Majuro Atoll

5540

0°

Malay Peninsula

Kapuas

Borneo

Celebes Sea

Halmahera

West Caroline Basin

East Caroline Basin

Mortlock Islands

Kosrae

Bairiki

Howland-Islands

Sumatra

3798

Banjarmasin

Celebes

3455

Buru

3000

Caroline Islands

Kapingamarangi Atoll

Yaren

Banaba I.

Onotoa Atoll

Canton Atoll

10

Greater Sunda Islands

Makassar

Moluccas

Ceram

Jayapura

Bismarck Archipelago

New Ireland

Melanesian Basin

Nikumaroro

6112 Orona

Phoenix Islands

Jakarta

Java Sea

Banda Sea

Puncak Jaya 5050

Mount Wilhelm 4508

Bismarck Sea

New Britain

Bougainville I.

Niutao

POL

10°

Java

Planet Deep

Lesser Sunda Islands

Dili

Flores

Kepulauan Aru

Dolak

New Guinea

Lae

Choiseul

Honiara

Vitiaz Trench

Tuvalu Islands

Funafuti Atoll

Vaiaku

365

7450

Bali Lombok Sumbawa Sumba

Timor

2400

Timor

Arafura Sea

Torres Strait

Port Moresby

D'Entrecasteaux Islands

Solomon Sea

Guadalcanal San Cristobal

Nendo

North Fiji

Rotuma

Swains Atoll

Nassau

11

Darwin

Timor Sea

Cape York

Louisiade Archipelago

Rennell I.

Santa-Cruz Islands

Basin

Mata Uta Savai'i I. Apia

Suware

Cartier

Arnhem Land

Groote Eylandt

Cape York Peninsula

Coral Sea

Espíritu Santo

Malakula

Vanua Levu

Fiji Islands

Pago Pago

Samoa Islands

6370

North Australia Basin

Derby

Kimberley Plateau

Gulf of Carpentaria

Townsville

New Hebrides

Éfaté Port Vila

Viti Levu

Suva

Tahiti

Alofi Palme

20°

Northwest Australian

734 Port Hedland

Broome

Great Sandy Desert

Récifs d'Entrecasteaux

Iles Loyauté

New Hebrides Trench

Tonga Islands

Tongatapu

Ha'apai Group

5740

Basin

North West Cape

1236

Macdonnell Ranges

Tanami Desert

Récifs et Chesterfield

Ile Matthew

Nuku'alofa

12

Carnarvon

Hamersley Range

Gibson Desert

Avers Rock 868 1510

Alice Springs

Simpson Desert

Great Artesian Basin

Fraser Island

Noumea

South Fiji Basin

Vitiaz II Deep 10800

30°

Geraldton

AUSTRALIA

Great Victoria Desert

Lake Eyre -12

Charleville

Brisbane Cape Byron

Howe Rise

Norfolk

Norfolk Ridge

4188 L'Esperance Rock

Raoul I. Kermadec Islands

1143

5850

13

Diamantina Deep 6857

Perth

Cape Leeuwin

Nullarbor Plain

Broken Hill Darling

Lord-Howe

Three Kings Ridge

North Cape

Vitiaz III Deep 10047

5792

Albany

Great Australian Bight

Adelaide

Murray

Sydney

Canberra 2228

Auckland

Kermadec Trench

40°

Diamantina Trench

7102

Kangaroo Island

5709

South Australian

Mt. Kosciuszko

Melbourne

Tasman Sea

North Island

2797

4716 393

14

INDIAN OCEAN

King Island

Tasmania

Furneaux Group

1617

Hobart

5176

Tasman

South Island

Mt Cook 3764

New Zealand

Christchurch

Chatham Rise

Chatham Islands

South East Cape

South Tasman Rise

Basin

Dunedin 1298

Cook Strait Wellington

Bounty Islands

Stewart Island

0 600 1200 km

Pb 100° Qa 110° Qb 120° Ra 130° Rb Sa 150° Sb 160° Ta 170° Tb 180° Ba 170° Bb

The index to place names explained

All of the places named on the maps in the atlas section are listed in the index to place names. The place names are listed alphabetically. Special symbols and letters including accents and umlauts are ignored in the order of the index. For example, the letters Á, Ä, Â are all categorized under A, and è, °, Î are all treated as the standard Latin letter Z. Written characters consisting of two letters joined together (ligatures) are treated as two separate characters in the index: for example, words beginning with the character Æ would be indexed under AE.

The most commonly used abbreviations in the atlas are also used in the index. These abbreviations are listed and explained on this page (below). Generic geographic terms (sea, bay, etc.) and word articles (the, le, el, etc.) were used in the order of the index: for example, the Gulf of Mexico is listed under G and Le Havre, France is listed under L. Virtually all of the places listed in the atlas have a country reference; these nations are identified by their international license (registration) plate codes. The various international license codes are identified on page 276. In the case of communities and areas that are located on or between the borders of two or more nations, the license plate codes of the various nations are listed and separated by a slash.

The names of areas and geographic features that cannot be assigned to specific states, such as the Atlantic Ocean, are followed by the page number of a map featuring the area and the number of the map grid box in which the area is depicted on the map.

Abbreviations

Abb.	Abbey, abbaye (French), abbadia (Span.), abbazia (Ital.)	Gt.	Great-	Nac.	Nacional (Span.), Nacional'-nyj, -aja, -oe (Russian) = national	Sel.	Selat (Indonesian) = strait
Aborig.	Aboriginal (indigenous inhabitants of Australia)	Hr.	Hrebet (Russian) = high	Naz.	Nazionale (Ital.) = national	Sg.	Song (Vietnamese) = river
Ad.	Adas (Turkish) = island	Ht.	Haut (French) = high-	Nev.	Nevado (Span.) = snow-covered mountain peaks	Sk.	Shuiku (Chinese) = reservoir
Ág.	Ági -os, -a, -i (Greek) = saint	Hte.	Haute (French) = high-			Sra.	Sierra (Span.), serra (Port./Ital.) = mountain range
Ban.	Banjaran (Malaysian) = mountain range	Hts.	Haut -s, -es (French) = high-	Niž.	Niž-e, -nij, -naja, -neje (Russian) = lower-	St./St	Saint (English and French), sankt (German, Dutch)
Bol'.	Bol'-šoj, -šaja, -šoe (Russian) = large-	I.	Isla (Span.), ilha (Port.) = island	Nižm.	Nižmennost' (Rus.) = plain		
C.	Cape, cap (French), cabo (Span./Port.), capo (Ital.)	Î.	Île (French) = island	Nva.	Nueva (Span.) = new-	Sta.	Santa (Span./Port./Ital.) = saint
		Ind.	Indian/ Native Americans, First Nation	Nvo.	Nuevo (Span.) = new-	Star.	Star -o, -yj, -aja, -oe (Russian) = old-
Can.	Canal	Is.	Islands	o.	Ostrov (Rus.) = island	Ste	Sainte (French) = saint
Cast.	Castle, castel (French.), castillo (Span.), castelo (Port.), castello (Ital.)	Îs.	Îles (French) = islands	P.	Port (English and French), puerto (Span./Port.), porto (Ital.) = harbor	Sth.	South, southern
Cd.	Ciudad (Span.), cidade (Port.) = city	Jaz.	Jazovir (Bulg.) = reservoir	Peg.	Pegunungan (Indonesian) = mountain	Sto.	Santo (Span./Port.) = saint
Co.	Cerro (Span.) = mountain, hill	Jct.	Junction	Pen.	Peninsula, péninsule (franz.), península (Span.), penisola (Ital.)	Str.	Street, Strait, stretto (Italian), stræde (Danish), stret (Norwegian)
Conv.	Convento (Span.) = monastery	Jez.	Jezioro (Pol.), jezero (Czech/Slovak./Serb./Croat./Slov.) = lake				
Cord.	Cordillera (Span.) = mountain range			Pk.	Peak	t.	tau (Kaz.) = mountain
Corr.	Corrente (Port.), corriente (Ital./Span.) = river	Kan.	Kanal (Turk./Rus.), kanaal (Dutch), kana (Pol.) = canal	p-ov.	Poluostrov (Rus.) = peninsula	T.	Take (Jap.) = peak, summit
		Kep.	Kepulauan (Malaysian) = archipelago	Pres.	Presidente (Span./Port.) = president	Tel.	Teluk (Indonesian) = bay
Cr.	Creek	Kg.	Kampong (Malaysian), kampung (Khmer) = village	Prov.	Provincial, Province	Tg.	Tanjung (Indonesian) = cape
D.	Dake (Jap.) = mountain			Pse.	Passe (French) = pass	Vdhr.	Vodohranilišče (Russian) = reservoir
D.	Danau (Indonesian) = lake	Kör.	Körfezi (Turk.) = gulf, bay	Pso.	Paso (Span.), passo (Ital.) = pass	Vel.	Velik -o, -ij, -yki, -oe (Rus.) = large-
Dağ.	Dağlar, dağlari (Turkish) = mountain range	L.	Lake, lac (French), lago (Ital./Span./Port.), loch, lough (Gaelic)	Pt.	Point	Verh.	Verhn -ee, -ie, -ij, -jaja (Rus.) = mountain
Ea.	Estancia (Span.) = estate	M.	Mys (Rus./Ukr.) = cape	Pta.	Punta (Span./Port.) = point		
Emb.	Embalse (Span.), embassament (catalonian) = reservoir	Mal.	Malo, -yj, -aja, -oe (Rus.) = small	Pte.	Pointe (French) = point	Vill.	Village
		Mt.	Mount, mont (French)	Pto.	Punto (Ital.) = point	vlk.	Vulkan (Rus.) = volcano
Ens.	Ensenada (Span./Port.) = small bay	Mta.	Montagna (Ital.), montaña (Span.) = mountain range	R.	River, rivière (French), río (Span.), ribeiro, rio (Port.), rîu (Romanian), reka (Bulgarian)	Vol.	Volcano, volcan (French), volcán (Span.)
Erm.	Ermita (Span.) = hermitage	Mte.	Monte (Ital./Span./Port.), montagne (French) = mountain			Vul.	Vulkan (German.), Vulcano (Ital./Romanian) = volcano
Est.	Estación (Span.) = train station	Mtes.	Montes (Span./Port.), montagnes (French) = mountains	Ra.	Range	Y.	Yama (Jap.) = mountain, mountain range
Faz.	Fazenda (Port.) = estate			Rep.	Republic, république (French), república (Span./Port.), republicca (Ital.)		
Fl.	Fleuve (French) = river	Mți.	Munții (Romanian) = mountain range	Repr.	Represa (Port.) = dam	Zal.	Zaliv (Russian), zalew (Polish) = bay
Fs.	waterfalls	Mti.	Monti (Ital.) = mountain range	Res.	Reservoir, réservoir (French)	Zap.	Zapovednik (Russian) = nature reserve
g.	gawa (Jap.) = river	Mtn.	Mountain	Resp.	Respublika (Russian) = republic	Zp.	Zapadn -e, -ji, -aja, -noe (Russian) = west, western
G.	Gora (Russian), góra (Polish), gunung (Indonesian) = mountain	Mtns.	Mountains	s.	San (Jap.) = mountain		
Gde.	Grande (Span./French) = large	Mts.	Mountains, Monts (French)	S.	San (Span./Ital.), são (Port.) = saint		
Geb.	Gebirge (German), gebergte (Dutch) = mountain range	N.	North, Northern, Norte (Ital./Span./Port.), Norra (Swedish), Nørdre (Norwegian), Nørre (Danish), Nord (German)	Sanc./Sanct.	Sanctuary		
Grd.	Grand (French) = large			Sd.	Sound, sund (German, Danish, Norwegian, Swedish)		

International license (registration) plate code

A	Austria	ES	El Salvador	MH	Marshall Islands	SR	Serbia
AFG	Afghanistan	EST	Estonia	MK	Macedonia	SK	Slovakia
AG	Antigua and Barbuda	ET	Egypt	MNG	Mongolia	SLO	Slovenia
AL	Albania	ETH	Ethiopia	MOC	Mozambique	SME	Suriname
AND	Andorra	F	France	MS	Mauritius	SN	Senegal
ANG	Angola	FIN	Finland	MV	Maldives	SOL	Solomon Islands
ARM	Armenia	FJI	Fiji	MW	Malawi	SP	Somalia
AUS	Australia	FL	Liechtenstein	MYA	Myanmar (Burma)	STP	São Tomé and Príncipe
AZ	Azerbaijan	FSM	Micronesia	N	Norway	SUD	Sudan
B	Belgium	G	Gabon	NAM	Namibia	SY	Seychelles
BD	Bangladesh	GB	Great Britain	NAU	Nauru	SYR	Syria
BDS	Barbados	GCA	Guatemala	NEP	Nepal	TCH	Chad
BF	Burkina Faso	GE	Georgia	NIC	Nicaragua	TG	Togo
BG	Bulgaria	GH	Ghana	NL	Netherlands	THA	Thailand
BH	Belize	GNB	Guinea-Bissau	NZ	New Zealand	TJ	Tajikistan
BHT	Bhutan	GQ	Equatorial Guinea	OM	Oman	TLS*	East Timor
BIH	Bosnia and Herzegovina	GR	Greece	P	Portugal	TM	Turkmenistan
BOL	Bolivia	GUY	Guyana	PA	Panama	TN	Tunisia
BR	Brazil	H	Hungary	PAL	Palau	TO	Tonga
BRN	Bahrain	HN	Honduras	PE	Peru	TR	Turkey
BRU	Brunei	HR	Croatia	PK	Pakistan	TT	Trinidad and Tobago
BS	Bahamas	I	Italy	PL	Poland	TUV	Tuvalu
BU	Burundi	IL	Israel	PNG	Papua New Guinea	UA	Ukraine
BY	Belarus	IND	India	PRK*	Korea, North	UAE	United Arab Emirates
C	Cuba	IR	Iran	PY	Paraguay	USA	United States of America
CAM	Cameroon	IRL	Ireland	Q	Qatar		
CDN	Canada	IRQ	Iraq	RA	Argentina	UZ	Uzbekistan
CG	Montenegro	IS	Iceland	RB	Botswana	V	Vatican City
CH	Switzerland	J	Japan	RC	Taiwan	VN	Vietnam
CHN*	China	JA	Jamaica	RCA	Central Africa Republic	VU	Vanuatu
CI	Cote d'Ivoire	JOR	Jordan	RCB	Republic of the Congo	WAG	Gambia
CL	Sri Lanka	K	Cambodia	RCH	Chile	WAL	Sierra Leone
CO	Colombia	KIR	Kiribati	RDC	Dem. Republic of the Congo	WAN	Nigeria
COM	Comoros	KNA*	Saint Kitts and Nevis	RG	Guinea	WD	Dominica
CR	Costa Rica	KS	Kyrgyzstan	RH	Haiti	WG	Grenada
CV	Cape Verde	KSA	Saudi Arabia	RI	Indonesia	WL	Saint Lucia
CY	Cyprus	KWT	Kuwait	RIM	Mauritania	WS	Samoa
CZ	Czech Republic	KZ	Kazakhstan	RL	Lebanon	WV	Saint Vincent and the Grenadines
D	Germany	L	Luxembourg	RM	Madagascar		
DARS	Western Sahara	LAO	Laos	RMM	Mali	YE	Yemen
DJI	Djibouti	LAR	Libya	RN	Niger	YV	Venezuela
DK	Denmark	LB	Liberia	RO	Romania	Z	Zambia
DOM	Dominican Republic	LS	Lesotho	ROK	Korea, South	ZA	South Africa
DY	Benin	LT	Lithuania	ROU	Uruguay	ZW	Zimbabwe
DZ	Algeria	LV	Latvia	RP	Philippines		
E	Spain	M	Malta	RSM	San Marino		
EAK	Kenya	MA	Morocco	RUS	Russia		
EAT	Tanzania	MAL	Malaysia	RWA	Rwanda		
EAU	Uganda	MC	Monaco	S	Sweden		
EC	Ecuador	MD	Moldova	SD	Swaziland		
ER	Eritrea	MEX	Mexico	SGP	Singapore		

* Some countries do not have official vehicle registration codes. In these cases, the international three-letter code (ISO 3166) is shown.

Symbols used in the index

▣	Mountains	⬟	River	▣	National Park	◌	Town/City
▲	Mountain	▨	Fall/Rapids	▤	Submarine relief	◁	Desert
◉	Landscape	▱	Lake	▪	State	▨	Oasis
▧	Volcano	▱	Ocean/Bay	▢	Province		
◪	Glacier	▥	Coral Reef	◉	Capital		
▤	Cape	◿	Island	◉	Province capital		

Dimitrovgrad – Gotland

Dimitrovgrad RUS 455 Nb08
Dinagat RP 465 Rb16
Dinan F 454 Kd09
Diourbel SN 470 Ka16
Dipolog RP 465 Ra17
Dire Dawa ETH 471 Na17
Dirk Hartog Island AUS 466 Qc24
Dirranbandi AUS 466 Sb24
Disko Bugt DK 475 Hb05
Disko Ø DK 475 Hb05
Dispur IND 462 Pc13
Diu IND 462 Oc14
Divinópolis BR 479 Hd23
Divo CI 470 Kc17
Dixon Entrance CDN 474 Db08
Diyarbakır TR 458 Na11
Djambala RCB 472 Lc19
Djebel Al Awaynat SUD 471 Mb14
Djebel Arknu LAR 471 Ma14
Djebel Hamoyet SUD 471 Md15
Djebel Mahrat YE 458 Nc15
Djebel Manar YE 458 Na16
Djebel Marra SUD 471 Ma16
Djebel Musbih ET 471 Mc14
Djebel Ouarkziz MA 470 Kc13
Djebel Rafit SUD 471 Mc14
Djebel Samhan OM 458 Nc15
Djebel Timétrine RMM 470 Kd15
Djebel Toubkal MA 470 Kc12
Djebel Tuwayq KSA 458 Nb14
Djelfa DZ 470 La12
Djerem CAM 470 Lc17
Djibouti DJI 471 Na16
Djibouti DJI 471 Na16
Djougou DY 470 La17
Dniepr UA 455 Mc09
Dniestr UA 455 Ma09
Dnipropetrovs'k UA 455 Mc09
Doba TCH 470 Ld17
Doberai Peninsula RI 465 Rc19
Doctor Pedro P.Peña PY 479 Gd23
Dodge City USA 476 Fa11
Dodoma EAT 473 Md20
Dofa RI 465 Rb19
Doha Q 458 Nc13
Dolak RI 465 Rd20
Dollo Odo ETH 471 Na18
Dolores RA 481 Ha26
Dolores ROU 481 Ha25
Dolphin and Union Strait CDN 474 Ea05
Dombås N 454 Lb06
DomeC/ Concordia 483 Ra34
Dome Circe 483 Ra33
Dominica WD 477 Gd15
Dominican Republic DOM 477 Gb15
Don' RUS 455 Na09
Dondo ANG 472 Lc20
Dondra Head CL 462 Pa17
Donec'k UA 455 Md09
Donga WAN 470 Lc17
Dongara AUS 466 Qc24
Dongfang CHN 461 Qb15
Donggala RI 464 Qc19
Dong Ha VN 463 Qb15
Donghae 461 Rc11
Dong Hoi VN 463 Qb15
Donqula SUD 471 Mc15
Dori BF 470 Kd16
Dortmund D 454 Lb08
Dosso RN 470 La16
Dothan USA 477 Fc12
Douala CAM 470 Lb18
Douentza RMM 470 Kd15
Douglas GB 454 Kd08
Douglas USA 476 Ec12
Douglas Range 482 Gb32
Dourados BR 479 Hb23
Dove Bugt DK 475 Ka03
Dover GB 454 La08
Dover USA 477 Ga11
Drakensberge ZA 472 Mb25
Drake Passage 481 Gc30
Drammen N 454 Lc07
Drescher 482 Ka33
Dresden D 454 Lc08
Drobeta-Turnu Severin RO 455 Ma10
Droning Ingrid Land DK 475 Hc06
Droning Louise Land DK 475 Jc03
Dronning Maud Land 482 Kc34
Drumheller CDN 474 Eb08
Drummondville CDN 475 Gb09
Družnaja II 482 Gc33
Družnaja III 482 Kb33
Dryden CDN 475 Fb09
Drygalski Ice Tongue 483 Tb34
Drygalski Island 483 Pc32
Drysdale AUS 466 Rb22
Dry Tortugas USA 477 Fd14
Duba KSA 458 Md13
Dubai UAE 458 Nd13
Dubawnt Lake CDN 475 Ed06
Dubbo AUS 466 Sb25
Dublin IRL 454 Kc08
Dubna RUS 455 Md07
Dubréka RG 470 Kb17
Dubrovnik HR 455 Ld10
Dubuque USA 476 Fb10
Ducie GB 489 Db12
Dudinka RUS 456 Pb04
Dujiangyan CHN 460 Qa12
Dukhan Q 458 Nc13
Duluth USA 476 Fb09
Dumai RI 464 Qa18
Dumont d'Urville 483 Rd32
Dumont d'Urville Sea 483 Rc31
Duncan Mountains 482 Ca36
Duncansby Head GB 454 Kd07
Dundalk IRL 454 Kc08
Dundas DK 475 Gc03
Dundee GB 454 Kd07
Dunedin NZ 467 Tc28
Dunfermline GB 454 Kd07
Dungunab SUD 471 Md14
Dunhua CHN 461 Rb10
Dunkwa GH 470 Kd17
Durango MEX 476 Ec14
Durango USA 476 Ec11
Durant USA 476 Fa12
Durban ZA 473 Mc24
Durrës AL 455 Ld10
Dushanbe TJ 459 Ob11
Düsseldorf D 454 Lb08
Duyun CHN 461 Qb13
Džankoj UA 455 Mc09
Dzaoudzi F 473 Nb21
Dzungarian Basin CHN 456 Pb09

E

Eagle Pass USA 476 Ed13
East Cape NZ 467 Td26
East Caroline Basin 468 Sb18
East China Sea 461 Ra12
Easter Island RCH 480 Ec24
Eastern Desert ET 471 Mc13
Eastern Fields PNG 466 Sb21
Eastern Ghats IND 462 Od16
Eastern Sayan Mountains RUS 456 Pd08
East Falkland GB 481 Ha29
East London ZA 472 Mb25
East Mariana Basin 488 Sb08
East Saint Louis USA 477 Fc11
East Siberian Sea RUS 457 Tb05
East Timor TLS 465 Rb20
Eau Claire USA 476 Fb10
Eauripik Atoll FSM 465 Sa17
Eauripik Rise PAL 465 Sa18
Ebola RDC 471 Ma18
Ebolowa CAM 470 Lc18
Ebon Atoll MH 469 Tb18
Ecuador EC 478 Ga19
Edéa CAM 470 Lc18
Eden AUS 467 Sb26
Edfu ET 471 Mc14
Edgeworth David 483 Qa32
Edinburgh GB 454 Kd07
Edirne TR 455 Mb10
Edmonton CDN 474 Eb08
Edmundston CDN 475 Gc09
Edward, Mount 482 Gc34
Edward River AUS 466 Sa21
Edwards Plateau USA 476 Ed12
Edward VII Peninsula 482 Ca34
Éfaté/ VU 467 Tb22
Égvekinot RUS 457 Ua05
Egypt ET 471 Mb13
Eights Coast 482 Fa33
Eirunepé BR 478 Gb20
Eiseb NAM 472 Ld23
Eivissa E 454 La11
Eivissa = Ibiza E 454 La11
Ejsk RUS 455 Md09
Ekibastuz KZ 456 Oc08
El-Alamein ET 471 Mb12
Elan Bank 483 Ob30
El Aqaba JOR 458 Md13
El-Araïch MA 470 Kc11
El Arish ET 471 Mc12
Elat ET 471 Mc13
Elâzığ TR 458 Md11
El Banco CO 478 Gb17
El Bawiti ET 471 Mb13
El Bayadh DZ 470 La12
Elblag PL 455 Ma08
Elbląg PL 455 Ld08
El Bordo CO 478 Ga18
Elbrus RUS 458 Na10
El'brus RUS 455 Na10
Elburz Mountains IR 458 Nc11
El Cajon USA 476 Ea12
El Calafate RA 481 Gb29
El Callao YV 479 Gd17
El Centro USA 476 Ea12
El Djouf RIM 470 Kc14
El Dorado MEX 476 Ec14
Eldorado RA 481 Hb24
El Dorado USA 476 Fb12
Eldoret EAK 471 Md18
Elec RUS 455 Md08
Elephant Island GB 481 Ha31
Elephant Island 482 Hb31
Eleuthera Island BS 477 Ga13
El Hank RIM 470 Kc14
Elista RUS 455 Na09
Elizabeth City USA 477 Ga11
Elizabeth Reef AUS 467 Sd25
El-Jadida MA 470 Kc12
El Kef TN 470 Lb11
El Kharga ET 471 Mc13
Elko USA 476 Ea10
El Kufrah Oasis LAR 471 Ma14
Ellef Ringnes Island CDN 475 Ed03
Ellesmere Island CDN 475 Fc02
Elliot Lake CDN 477 Fd09
Elliott AUS 466 Rc22
Ellsworth Land 482 Fc33
Ellsworth Mountains 482 Fc34
El–Mansûra ET 471 Mc12
El Ménia DZ 470 La12
El Minia ET 471 Mc13
El Nido RP 464 Qd16
El-Obeid SUD 471 Mc16
El Oued DZ 470 Lb12
El Paso USA 476 Ec12
El Qasr ET 471 Mb12
El Salvador ES 477 Fc16
El Sombrero YV 478 Gc17
El Sueco MEX 476 Ec13
El Tigre YV 478 Gd17
Elx E 454 Kd11
Ely USA 476 Eb11
Embalse Yacyretá Apipé RA 481 Ha24
Embi KZ 458 Nd09
Emerald AUS 466 Sb23
Emi Koussi TCH 471 Ld15
Emmen NL 454 Lb08
Emporia USA 476 Fa11
Encarnación PY 481 Ha24
Ende RI 464 Ra20
Enderbury Atoll KIR 469 Ub19
Enderbyland 483 Na32
Eneabba AUS 466 Qd24
Enggano RI 464 Qa20
English Channel GB/F 454 Kd08
English Coast 482 Gb33
Enid USA 476 Fa11
Enisej RUS 456 Pb04
Enisejsk RUS 456 Pc07
Enisejskij zaliv RUS 456 Pa04
Eniwetok Atoll MH 468 Ta16
En Nahud SUD 471 Mb16
Ennedi TCH 471 Ma15
Ensenada MEX 476 Ea12
Entrecasteaux Islands PNG 468 Sc20
Entre Rios RA 481 Ha25
Entre Rios RA 481 Ha25
Enugu WAN 470 Lb17
Epi VU 467 Tb22
Equatorial Guinea GQ 470 Lb18
Erdi TCH 471 Ma15
Erebus, Mount 483 Tc34
Erechim BR 481 Hb24
Erenhot CHN 461 Qc10
Erfurt D 454 Lc08
Erg Chech DZ 470 Kd13
Erg du Djourab TCH 471 Ld15
Erg Iguidi RIM/DZ 470 Kc13
Ergun Youqi CHN 457 Ra08
Ergun Zuoqi CHN 457 Ra08
Erie USA 477 Ga10
Erikub Atoll MH 469 Tb17
Eritrea ER 471 Md15
Erldunda AUS 466 Rc24
Eromanga Island VU 467 Tb22
Eršov RUS 455 Nb08
Ertis KZ 456 Pa08
Erzin RUS 456 Pd08
Erzincan TR 458 Md10
Erzurum TR 458 Na11
Esbjerg DK 454 Lb07
Escanaba USA 477 Fc09
Escudero 482 Ha30
Escuintla GCA 477 Fb16
Eskişehir TR 455 Mc11
Esmeraldas EC 478 Ga18
Esperance AUS 466 Ra25
Esperanza RA 481 Gb29
Esperanza 482 Ha31
Espírito Santo BR 479 Hd22
Espiritu Santo VU 467 Tb22
Esquel RA 481 Gb27
Essej RUS 456 Qa05
Essequibo GUY 479 Ha17
Estância BR 479 Ja21
Estevan CDN 475 Ed09
Estonia EST 455 Ma07
Estrecho de Le Maire RA 481 Gc30
Estreito BR 479 Hc20
Ethiopia ETH 471 Md17
Ethiopian Highlands ETH 471 Md17
Etna I 454 Lc11
Etosha Pan NAM 472 Ld22
Eucla Basin AUS 466 Rb25
Eucla Motels AUS 466 Rb25
Eugene USA 476 Dd10
Euphrates IRQ 458 Na12
Eureka USA 476 Dd10
Evans Ice Stream 482 Ga34
Evans Strait CDN 475 Fd06
Evansville USA 477 Fc11
Evenki Autonomous District RUS 456 Pc05
Everett USA 474 Dd09
Évia GR 455 Ma11
Évora P 454 Kc11
Ewaso Ngiro EAK 471 Md18
Exmouth AUS 466 Qc23
Exmouth Plateau AUS 466 Qd22
Exuma Sound BS 477 Ga14
Eyre Peninsula AUS 466 Rd25

F

Fachi NG 470 Lc15
Fada TCH 471 Ma15
Fada-N'gourma BF 470 La16
Fadhi OM 458 Nd15
Fairbanks USA 474 Cc06
Faisalabad PAK 462 Oc12
Fais Island FSM 465 Sa17
Fakaofo Atoll NZ 469 Ub20
Fakarava F 489 Cb11
Fakfak RI 465 Rc19
Falémé RMM 470 Kb16
Falkland Escarpment 481 Hb28
Falkland Islands GB 481 Gd29
Falkland Plateau 481 Hb29
Falls City USA 476 Fa10
Falun S 455 Ld06
Fangchenggang CHN 461 Qb14
Faraday 482 Gd32
Faradje RDC 471 Mb18
Farafangana RM 473 Nb23
Farafra Oasis ET 471 Mb13
Farah AFG 458 Oa12
Faranah RG 470 Kb16
Faraulep Atoll FSM 465 Sa17
Fargo USA 476 Fa09
Farmington USA 476 Ec11
Faro P 454 Kc11
Faroe Islands DK 454 Kc06
Farquhar Group SY 473 Nc20
Fawn Trough 483 Oc30
Fayetteville USA 477 Ga11
Fayetteville USA 476 Fb11
Fayu Island FSM 468 Sc17
Feira de Santana BR 479 Ja21
Fengjie CHN 461 Qb12
Feni Islands PNG 468 Sc19
Feodosija UA 455 Md09
Fergana Valley UZ 460 Oc10
Fergus Falls USA 476 Fa09
Fergusson Island PNG 468 Sc20
Ferkessédougou CI 470 Kc17
Ferlo SN 470 Kb16
Ferrara I 454 Lc10
Ferraz, Com. 482 Ha31
Ferreira Gomes BR 479 Hb18
Ferreñave PE 478 Ga20
Fès MA 470 Kc12
Fezzan LAR 470 Lc13
Fezzan 470 Lc13
Fianarantsoa RM 473 Nb23
Fifth Cataract SUD 471 Mc15
Figuig MA 470 Kd12
Fiji FIJ 467 Td22
Fiji Islands FIJ 467 Td22
Filadelfia PY 478 Gd23
Filchner 482 Hb34
Filchner Ice Shelf 482 Hd35
Fimbulheimen 483 Lb33
Fimbul Ice Shelf 482 Kd33
Finke AUS 466 Rd24
Finke AUS 466 Rc24
Finland FIN 455 Ma06
Finschhafen PNG 468 Sb20
Firozabad IND 462 Od13
First Cataract ET 471 Mc14
Fisher Strait CDN 475 Fd06
Fishguard GB 454 Kc08
Fitzroy AUS 466 Ra22
Fitzroy Crossing AUS 466 Rb22
Fizi RDC 473 Mb19
Flagstaff USA 476 Eb11
Flensburg D 454 Lb08
Fletcher Promontory 482 Fd34
Flinders AUS 466 Sa22
Flinders Bay AUS 466 Qd25
Flinders Island AUS 466 Rc25
Flinders Island AUS 466 Sb26
Flinders Ranges AUS 466 Rd25
Flinders Reef FSM 467 Sb22
Flin Flon CDN 475 Ed08
Florence I 454 Lc10
Florence USA 477 Fd12
Florence USA 477 Fc12
Florencia CO 478 Ga18
Flores GCA 477 Fc15
Flores P 454 Jb11
Flores RI 464 Ra20
Flores Sea RI 464 Ra20
Floriano BR 479 Hd20
Florianópolis BR 481 Hc24
Florida ROU 481 Ha25
Florida USA 477 Fd13
Florida Keys USA 477 Fd14
Foca BIH 455 Ld10
Foggia I 455 Ld10
Fontur IS 454 Kb05
Forbes AUS 466 Sb25
Ford Ranges 482 Cc34
Formentera E 454 La11
Formosa RA 481 Ha24
Formosa RA 481 Ha24
Formosa do Rio Preto BR 479 Hc21
Formosa = Taiwan RC 461 Ra14
Forrestal Range 482 Hb35
Forsayth AUS 466 Sa22
Fortaleza BR 479 Ja19
Fort-Chimo CDN 475 Gc07
Fort Chipewyan CDN 474 Eb07
Fort Collins USA 476 Ec10
Fort-de-France F 477 Gd16
Fort Frances CDN 475 Fb09
Fort Good Hope CDN 474 Dc05
Fort Hope CDN 475 Fc08
Fort Lauderdale USA 477 Fd13
Fort Liard CDN 474 Dd06
Fort McMurray CDN 474 Eb07
Fort McPherson CDN 474 Db05
Fort Myers USA 477 Fd13
Fort Nelson CDN 474 Dd07
Fort Peck Lake USA 474 Ec09
Fort Pierce USA 477 Fd13
Fort Portal EAU 471 Mc18
Fort Resolution CDN 474 Eb06
Fort Rupert CDN 475 Ga08
Fort Saint John CDN 474 Dd07
Fort Saskatchewan CDN 474 Eb08
Fort Severn CDN 475 Fc07
Fort Simpson CDN 474 Dd06
Fort Smith CDN 474 Eb06
Fort Smith USA 476 Fb11
Fort Stockton USA 476 Ed12
Fort Vermillion CDN 474 Ea07
Fort Wayne USA 477 Fc10
Fort Worth USA 476 Fa12
Fort Yukon USA 474 Cd05
Foshan CHN 461 Qc14
Fosheim Peninsula CDN 475 Fd03
Fossil Bluff 482 Gc33
Fourth Cataract SUD 471 Mc15
Foveaux Strait NZ 467 Tb28
Fowler Ice Rise 482 Ga34
Foxe Basin CDN 475 Ga05
Foxe Channel CDN 475 Fd05
Foxe Peninsula CDN 475 Ga05
Fox Islands USA 474 Bc08
Foz do Iguaçu BR 481 Hb24
Frakes, Mount 482 Ea34
Fram Basin 485 Mc02
Fram Peak 483 Nd32
Franca BR 479 Hc23
France F 454 La09
Franceville G 472 Lc19
Francistown RB 472 Mb23
Frankfort USA 477 Fd11
Frankfurt D 454 Lb08
Franklin Bay CDN 474 Dc04
Franklin Strait CDN 475 Fa04
Franz Josef Land RUS 485 Na02
Fraser Island AUS 467 Sc24
Fraser Plateau CDN 474 Dd08
Fredericton CDN 475 Gc09
Frederikshåb DK 475 Hb06
Frederikshavn DK 454 Lc07
Frederikstad N 454 Lc07
Freeport BS 477 Ga13
Freetown WAL 470 Kb17
Freiburg D 454 Lb09
Fremantle AUS 466 Qd25
French Guiana F 479 Hb18
Fresnillo MEX 476 Ed14
Fresno USA 476 Ea11
Fridtjof Nansen, Mount 482 Bd36
Frobisher Bay CDN 475 Gc06
Frozen Strait CDN 475 Fd05
Fuerteventura E 454 Kb13
Fujairah UAE 458 Nd13
Fujian CHN 461 Qd13
Fuji-san J 461 Sa11
Fukui J 461 Rd11
Fukuoka J 461 Rc12
Fukushima J 461 Sa11
Fulda D 454 Lb08
Funafuti Atoll TUV 469 Td20
Funchal P 454 Kc11
Fundación CO 478 Gb16
Fundão BR 479 Hd22
Funtua WAN 470 Lb16
Furneaux Group AUS 466 Sb26
Fushun CHN 461 Ra10
Fuxin CHN 461 Ra10
Fuyun CHN 456 Pb09
Fuzhou CHN 461 Qd13

G

Gaalkacyo SP 471 Nb17
Gabès TN 470 Lb12
Gabon G 472 Lc19
Gaborone RB 472 Mb23
Gadsden USA 477 Fc12
Gaecheon PRK 461 Rb11
Gaferut Island FSM 468 Sb17
Gafsa TN 470 Lb12
Gagnoa CI 470 Kc17
Gainesville USA 477 Fd13
Galápagos Fracture Zone 489 Cb10
Galápagos Islands EC 478 Fc18
Galati RO 455 Mb09
Galela RI 465 Rb18
Galena USA 474 Ca06
Galič RUS 455 Na07
Galle CL 462 Pa17
Gällivare S 455 Ma05
Gallup USA 476 Ec11
Galveston USA 476 Fb13
Galveston Bay USA 476 Fb13
Galway IRL 454 Kc08
Galway Bay IRL 454 Kb08
Gama BR 479 Hc22
Gambell USA 474 Bb06
Gambia WAG 470 Ka16
Gambie SN 470 Kb16
Gambier F 489 Da12
Gamboma RCB 472 Ld19
Gamtog CHN 460 Pd12
Gandajika RDC 472 Ma20
Gander CDN 475 Hb09
Gandhinagar IND 462 Oc14
Ganges IND 463 Pa13
Gangesebene IND 462 Pa13
Ganggye PRK 461 Rb10
Gangneung ROK 461 Rb11
Gangtok IND 462 Pb13
Gani RI 465 Rb19
Gansu CHN 460 Pd11
Gănžă AZ 458 Nb10
Ganzhou CHN 461 Qc13
Gao RMM 470 La15
Gaoual RG 470 Kb16
Garabogazköl ajlagy TM 458 Nc10
Garanhuns BR 479 Ja20
Garapu BR 479 Hb21
Garden City USA 476 Ed11
Gardner KIR 469 Ub19
Garoowe SP 471 Nb17
Garoua CAM 470 Lc17
Garry Lake CDN 475 Ed05
Garsen EAK 473 Na19
Gartog CHN 460 Pd13
Garwa IND 462 Pa14
Gary USA 477 Fc10
Gascoyne AUS 466 Qc23
Gastonia USA 477 Fd11
Gau FIJ 467 Td22
Gaussberg 483 Pb32
Gävle S 455 Ld06
Gaya IND 462 Pa14
Gaza IL 458 Mc12
Gaziantep TR 458 Md11
Gbadolite RDC 471 Ma18
Gbarnga LB 470 Kc17
Gdańsk PL 455 Ld08
Gdingen PL 455 Ld08
Gebe RI 465 Rb18
Geelong AUS 466 Sa26
Gela I 454 Lc11
Gembi ETH 471 Md17
Gemena RDC 471 Ld18
Genale Wenz ETH 471 Na17
General Acha RA 481 Gd26
General E.a Garay PY 479 Gd23
General Güemes RA 478 Gc23
General Santos RP 465 Rb17
Geneva CH 454 Lb09
Genoa I 454 Lb10
Geographe Bay AUS 466 Qd25
Geographe Channel AUS 466 Qc23
George ZA 472 Ma25
Georgetown GUY 479 Ha17
Georgetown MAL 464 Qa17
Georgetown UK 477 Fd15
Georgetown USA 477 Ga12
George VI Ice Shelf 482 Gc33
George V Land 483 Sb33
Georgia GE 458 Na10
Georgia USA 477 Fd12
Georgia Basin 481 Ja29
Georgian Bay CDN 477 Fd09
Georgievka KZ 456 Pa09
Georg von Neumayer 482 Kc33
Geraldton AUS 466 Qc24
Geralzinho BR 479 Hd22
Gerede TR 455 Mc10
Gereshk AFG 459 Oa12
German Bight D 454 Lb08
Germany D 454 Lc08
Getafe E 454 Kd10
Getz Ice Shelf 482 Dd33
Ghadamis LAR 470 Lb12
Ghana GH 470 Kd17
Ghanzi RB 472 Ma23
Ghard Abu Muharrik ET 471 Mb13
Ghardaïa DZ 470 La12
Gharyan LAR 470 Lc12
Ghat NG 470 Lc14
Ghazni AFG 459 Ob12
Gibraltar GB 454 Kc11
Gibraltar GB 454 Kc11
Gibson Desert AUS 466 Ra23
Gijón E 454 Kc10
Gilbert AUS 466 Sa22
Gilbert Islands KIR 469 Tc18
Gilette USA 476 Ec10
Gilgit PAK 460 Oc11
Gilgit Mountains PAK 460 Oc11
Gillam CDN 475 Fb07
Girona E 454 La10
Gisborne NZ 467 Td26
Gisenyi RWA 473 Mb19
Gitega BU 473 Mc19
Giza ET 471 Mc13
Gizo SOL 468 Sd20
Gjoa Haven CDN 475 Fa05
Gjumri ARM 458 Na10
Glace Bay CDN 475 Ha09
Gladstone AUS 467 Sc23
Glasgow GB 454 Kd07
Glendale USA 476 Eb12
Glendive USA 476 Ed09
Glen Innes AUS 467 Sc24
Glennallen USA 474 Cc06
Goa IND 462 Oc16
Gobabis NAM 472 Ld23
Gobi Desert CHN/MNG 460 Qa10
Godavari IND 462 Pa15
Godhavn DK 475 Hb05
Godoy Cruz RA 481 Gc25
Gods Lake CDN 475 Fb08
Gods Lake Narrows CDN 475 Fb08
Godthåb DK 475 Hb06
Goianésia BR 479 Hc22
Goiânia BR 479 Hc22
Goiás BR 479 Hc21
Goiás BR 479 Hb22
Gold Coast AUS 467 Sc24
Gold Coast GH 470 Kd18
Golden CDN 474 Ea08
Golfe de Gabès TN 470 Lc12
Golfe de Hammamet TN 470 Lc11
Golfe du Lion F 454 La10
Golfküstenebene USA 476 Fa12
Golfo Corcovado RCH 481 Gb27
Golfo de Batabanó C 477 Fd14
Golfo de Fonseca HN 477 Fc16
Golfo de Guayaquil EC 478 Fd19
Golfo de Honduras HN 477 Fc15
Golfo de los Mosquitos PA 477 Fd17
Golfo de Papagayo CR 477 Fc16
Golfo de Peñas RCH 481 Gb28
Golfo San Jorge RA 481 Gc28
Golfo San Matías RA 481 Gd27
Golf von Thailand THA 463 Qa16
Golmud CHN 460 Pd11
Golog Shan CHN 460 Qa12
Goma RDC 473 Mb19
Gombe EAT 473 Mc19
Gombe WAN 470 Lc16
Gómez Palacio MEX 476 Ed13
Gonabad IR 458 Nd12
Gonaïves RH 477 Gb15
Gonbad-e Kavus IR 458 Nd11
Gonder ETH 471 Md16
Gondwana 483 Tc33
Gongola WAN 470 Lc16
Gongpoquan CHN 460 Pd10
Gonzalez Videla, G. 482 Gd31
Goodenough Island PNG 468 Sc20
Goodspeed Nunataks 483 Oa33
Goomalling AUS 466 Qd25
Goondiwindi AUS 467 Sc24
Goose Bay CDN 475 Gd08
Gooty IND 462 Od16
gora Beluha RUS 456 Pb09
gora Blednaja RUS 456 Oa03
Gorakhpur IND 462 Pa13
gora Konžakovskij Kamen' RUS 456 Nd07
gora Ledjanaja RUS 457 Tc06
gora Narodnaja RUS 456 Oa05
gora Pajer RUS 456 Oa05
gora Skalistyj Golec RUS 457 Qd07
gora Tel'posiz RUS 456 Oa06
Gore NZ 467 Tb28
Goré TCH 470 Ld17
Gorgan IR 458 Nc11
Gorlivka UA 455 Md09
Gorno-Altajsk RUS 456 Pb08
Gorno-Altay RUS 456 Pb08
Goroch'an ETH 471 Md17
Goroka PNG 468 Sb20
Gorongosa MOC 473 Mc22
Gorontalo RI 464 Ra18
gory Byrranga RUS 456 Pc04
Götaland S 454 Lc07
Göteborg S 454 Lc07
Gotland S 455 Ld07

Nandi – Pécs

Nandi FIJ 467 Td22
Nanga Parbat PAK 460 Oc11
Nanga Tayap RI 464 Qb19
Nanjing CHN 461 Qd12
Nan Ling CHN 461 Qb13
Nanning CHN 461 Qb14
Nanping CHN 461 Qd13
Nansen Sound CDN 475 Fb02
Nantes F 454 Kd09
Nantong CHN 461 Ra12
Nantucket Island USA 477 Gc10
Nanumanga TUV 469 Td20
Nanumea Atoll TUV 469 Td20
Nanuque BR 479 Hd22
Nanutarra Roadhouse AUS 466 Qd23
Nanyang CHN 461 Qc12
Nanyuki EAK 471 Md18
Napier NZ 467 Td26
Napier Mountains 483 Nc32
Naples I 454 Lc10
Naples USA 477 Fd13
Napo PE 478 Gb19
Nara RMM 470 Kc15
Naracoorte AUS 466 Sa26
Narathiwat THA 464 Qa17
Narbonne F 454 La10
Nares Strait CDN 475 Gb03
Nar'jan-Mar RUS 455 Nc05
Narmada IND 462 Oc14
Narrabri AUS 467 Sb25
Narrandera AUS 466 Sb25
Narrogin AUS 466 Qd25
Narsarsuaq DK 475 Hc06
Narva EST 455 Mb07
Narvik N 455 Ld05
Naryn KS 460 Od10
Naryn KS 460 Od10
Nashville USA 477 Fc11
Nassau BS 477 Ga13
Nassau I. NZ 469 Uc21
Nata RB 472 Mb23
Natal BR 479 Ja20
Natal RI 464 Pd18
Natchez USA 476 Fb12
Natitingou DY 470 La16
Natuna Besar RI 464 Qb18
Natuna Sea RI 464 Qb18
Naturaliste Plateau AUS 466 Qc25
Naukluft NAM 472 Ld23
Nauru NAU 469 Tb19
Nauru NAU 469 Tb19
Nauta PE 478 Gb19
Navoiy UZ 458 Ob10
Navojoa MEX 476 Ec13
Nawabshah PAK 459 Ob13
Nawakshut RIM 470 Ka15
Nayarit MEX 476 Ed14
Nazareth IL 458 Md12
Nazca PE 478 Gb21
Nazran RUS 458 Na10
Nazran RUS 455 Na10
Nazret ETH 471 Md17
Ncue GQ 470 Lc18
Ndélé RCA 471 Ma17
Ndende G 472 Lc19
N'Djaména TCH 470 Ld16
Ndjolé G 472 Lc19
Ndola Z 473 Mb21
Ndzuani COM 473 Na21
Nebraska USA 476 Ed10
Necochea RA 481 Ha26
Needles USA 476 Eb12
Neftejugansk RUS 456 Oc06
Negele ETH 471 Md17
Negele ETH 471 Md17
Negotin SR 455 Ma10
Negros RP 464 Ra16
Neiva CO 478 Ga18
Nellore IND 462 Pa16
Nelson CDN 475 Fa07
Nelson NZ 467 Tc27
Nelspruit ZA 473 Mc24
Néma RIM 470 Kc15
Nendo SOL 467 Tb21
Nenets Autonomous District RUS 456 Nd05
Nepal NEP 460 Pa13
Nerjungri RUS 457 Ra07
Netherlands NL 454 La08
Netherlands Antilles NL 478 Gc16
Nettiling Lake CDN 475 Gb05
Neue Hebriden VU 467 Tb22
Neuquén RA 481 Gc26
Neuquén RA 481 Gc26
Nevada USA 476 Ea11
Nevada USA 476 Fb11
Nevado Ampato PE 478 Gb22
Nevado Ausangate PE 478 Gb21
Nevado Cololo Keasani BOL 478 Gc21
Nevado Coropuna PE 478 Gb22
Nevado de Colima MEX 476 Ed15
Nevado del Huila CO 478 Ga18
Nevado del Ruiz CO 478 Ga17
Nevado Ojos del Salado RCH/RA 481 Gc24
Nevado Sajama BOL 478 Gc22
New Albany USA 477 Fc11
New Amsterdam GUY 479 Ha17
Newark USA 477 Gb10
New Braunfels USA 476 Fa13
New Britain PNG 468 Sb20
New Britain Trench PNG 468 Sc20
New Brunswick CDN 475 Gc09
New Bussa WAN 470 La17
New Caledonia F 467 Ta23
New Caledonia F 467 Ta23
New Caledonia Basin 467 Ta24
Newcastle AUS 467 Sc25
Newcastle upon Tyne GB 454 Kd07
New Delhi IND 462 Od13
New England Seamounts 477 Gd11
Newfoundland CDN 475 Ha09
Newfoundland and Labrador CDN 475 Ha07
Newfoundland Basin 486 Hb05
New Georgia SOL 468 Sd20
New Georgia Group SOL 468 Sd20
New Glasgow CDN 475 Gd09
New Guinea RI/PNG 465 Rd20
New Guinea Trench RI 465 Rd18
New Hampshire USA 477 Gb10
New Hanover Island PNG 468 Sc19
New Haven USA 477 Gb10
New Hebrides VU 469 Tb21
New Hebrides Basin VU 467 Ta22
New Hebrides Trench 467 Tb22
New Ireland PNG 468 Sc19
New Jersey USA 477 Gb11
Newman AUS 466 Qd23
New Mexico USA 476 Ec12
New Orleans USA 477 Fc13
New Plymouth NZ 467 Tc26
Newry GB 454 Kc08
New Schwabenland 483 Lb33
New Siberian Islands RUS 457 Sa03
New South Wales AUS 466 Sa25
New York USA 477 Gb10
New York USA 477 Gb10
New Zealand NZ 467 Tb27
Ngala WAN 470 Lc16
Ngaoundére CAM 470 Lc17
Ngatik Atoll FSM 468 Sd17
Ngazidja COM 473 Na21
Ngoko RCB 470 Ld18
Ngoring Hu CHN 460 Pd12
Ngorongoro Crater EAT 473 Md19
Ngulu Atoll FSM 465 Rd17
Nguni EAK 473 Md19
Nguru WAN 470 Lc16
Nha Trang VN 463 Qb16
Nhulunbuy AUS 466 Rd21
Niagara Falls USA 477 Ga10
Niah MAL 464 Qc18
Niamey RN 470 La16
Niangara RDC 471 Mb18
Nia-Nia RDC 471 Mb18
Nias RI 464 Pd18
Nicaragua NIC 477 Fc16
Nice F 454 Lb10
Nickerson Ice Shelf 482 Cc34
Nicobar Islands IND 462 Pc17
Nicosia CY 455 Mc11
Nicoya CR 477 Fc16
Niellé CI 470 Kc16
Nieuw Nickerie SME 479 Ha17
Niger RMM 470 Kd15
Niger RN 470 Lb15
Niger Delta WAN 470 Lb18
Niger Fan 470 La18
Nigeria WAN 470 Lb17
Nihoa USA 489 Bb07
Niigata J 461 Rd11
Nikiniki RI 465 Ra20
Nikko J 461 Rd11
Nikolaevsk-na-Amure RUS 457 Sa08
Nikopol' UA 455 Mc09
Nikumaroro KIR 469 Ub19
Nikunau Island KIR 469 Td19
Nile ET 471 Mc13
Nile Delta ET 471 Mc12
Nîmes F 454 La10
Nimmitabel AUS 467 Sb26
Nimrod Glacier 483 Sd35
Nimule SUD 471 Mc18
Ningbo CHN 461 Ra13
Ningjing Shan CHN 460 Pd12
Ningxia Huizu Zizhiqu CHN 461 Qb11
Ninigo Group PNG 468 Sa19
Niobrara USA 476 Fa10
Nioro du Sahel RMM 470 Kc15
Niort F 454 Kd09
Nipigon CDN 475 Fc09
Niquelândia BR 479 Hc21
Niš SR 455 Ma10
Nitchequon CDN 475 Gb08
Niterói BR 479 Hd23
Niue NZ 469 Uc22
Niulakita TUV 467 Td21
Niutao TUV 469 Td20
Nizamabad IND 462 Od15
Nižnevartovsk RUS 456 Od06
Nižnij Novgorod RUS 455 Na07
Nižnij Tagil RUS 456 Oa07
Nižnjaja Tunguska RUS 456 Pc06
Njagan' RUS 456 Ob06
Njombe EAT 473 Mc20
Njurba RUS 457 Qd06
Nkhotakota MW 473 Mc21
Nkongsamba CAM 470 Lb18
Nogales MEX 476 Ec12
Nogales USA 476 Eb12
Nome USA 474 Bc06
Nomwin Atoll FSM 468 Sc17
Nonacho Lake CDN 474 Ec06
Nonouti Atoll KIR 469 Tc19
Nordkap N 455 Mb04
Norfolk USA 477 Ga11
Norfolk USA 476 Fa10
Norfolk Basin 467 Tc25
Norfolk Island AUS 467 Tb24
Norfolk Island AUS 467 Tb24
Norfolk Ridge 467 Tb24
Noril'sk RUS 456 Pb04
Norman USA 476 Fa11
Normanby Island PNG 468 Sc21
Normandia BR 478 Gd18
Normandie F 454 Kd09
Normanton AUS 466 Sa22
Norman Wells CDN 474 Dc05
Norrköping S 455 Ld07
Norseman AUS 466 Ra25
Northam AUS 466 Qd25
Northampton, Mount 483 Tb33
Northamton AUS 466 Qc24
North Andaman IND 462 Pc16
North Battleford CDN 474 Ec08
North Bay CDN 475 Ga09
North Cape NZ 467 Tc25
North Carolina USA 477 Ga11
North China Plain CHN 461 Qd11
North Dakota USA 475 Ed09
Northeast Cape USA 474 Bc06
Northeast Pacific Basin 489 Da05
Northern Indian Lake CDN 475 Fa07
Northern Mariana Islands USA 465 Sb15
Northern Territory AUS 466 Rc23
North Island NZ 467 Td26
North Korea PRK 461 Rb11
North Land RUS 456 Pb03
North Platte USA 476 Ed10
North Platte USA 476 Ed10
North Pole 485 La0
North Saskatchewan CDN 474 Eb08
North Sea 454 La07
North Siberian Lowland RUS 456 Pb04
North Taranaki Bight NZ 467 Tc26
North West Basin AUS 466 Qc23
North West Cape AUS 466 Qc23
Northwest Pacific Basin 488 Sb05
North West River CDN 475 Gd08
Northwest Territories CDN 474 Dd06
Norton USA 476 Fa11
Norton Sound USA 474 Bd06
Norway N 454 Lb06
Norway House CDN 475 Fa08
Norwegian Basin N 454 Kd05
Norwegian Bay CDN 475 Fb03
Norwegian Sea 454 La04
Nosliku RI 465 Rb18
Nosssob NAM 472 Ld23
Nosy Be RM 473 Nb21
Nosy Mitsio RM 473 Nb21
Nosy Ste-Marie RM 473 Nb22
Notre Dame Bay CDN 475 Ha09
Nottingham GB 454 Kd08
Nouâdhibou RIM 470 Ka14
Nouakchott RIM 470 Ka15
Nouâmghâr RIM 470 Ka14
Nouméa F 467 Tb23
Nova Alvorada BR 479 Hb23
Nova Iguaçu BR 479 Hd23
Novara I 454 Lb09
Nova Scotia CDN 475 Gd10
Novaya Zemlya RUS 456 Nc04
Novgorod RUS 455 Mc07
Novi Sad SR 455 Ld09
Novočerkassk RUS 455 Na09
Novo Hamburgo BR 481 Hb24
Novokujbyševsk RUS 455 Nb08
Novokuzneck RUS 456 Pb08
Novolazarevskaja 483 Lc33
Novorossijsk RUS 455 Md10
Novosibirsk RUS 456 Pa08
Novosibirskoe vdhr. RUS 456 Pa08
Novotroick RUS 456 Nd08
Novyj Port RUS 456 Oc05
Novyj Urengoj RUS 456 Od05
Nubia SUD 471 Mc15
Nubian Desert SUD 471 Mc14
Nueltin Lake CDN 475 Fa06
Nueva Gerona C 477 Fd14
Nueva Rosita MEX 476 Ed13
Nuevitas C 477 Ga14
Nuevo Casas Grandes MEX 476 Ec12
Nuevo Laredo MEX 476 Fa13
Nuevo León MEX 476 Ed13
Nuguria Islands PNG 468 Sc19
Nui TUV 469 Td20
Nuku'alofa TO 467 Ua23
Nukufetau Atoll TUV 469 Td20
Nukulaelae Atoll TUV 469 Td20
Nukunonu Atoll NZ 469 Ub20
Nukuoro Atoll FSM 468 Sd18
Nukus UZ 458 Nd10
Nullagine AUS 466 Ra23
Nullarbor Plain AUS 466 Rb25
Numan WAN 470 Lc17
Numfor RI 465 Rc19
Nunavut CDN 475 Ec05
Nunivak Island USA 474 Bc07
Nuoro I 454 Lb10
Nürnberg D 454 Lc09
Nusaybin TR 458 Na11
Nuuk/ DK 475 Hb06
Nyainqêntanglha Shan CHN 460 Pc12
Nyakanzi EAT 473 Mc19
Nyala SUD 471 Ma16
Nyanga G 472 Lc19
Nyngan AUS 466 Sb25
Nzega EAT 473 Mc19

O

Oahu USA 489 Ca07
Oakland USA 476 Dd11
Oakley USA 476 Ed11
Oak Ridge USA 477 Fd11
Oamaru NZ 467 Tc28
Oasis II 483 Qa32
Oates Land 483 Sd33
Oaxaca MEX 476 Fa15
Oaxaca de Juárez MEX 476 Fa15
Ob' RUS 456 Ob06
Obe VU 467 Tb22
Obe VU 467 Tb22
Obi RI 465 Rb19
Obihiro J 461 Sa10
Obinsk RUS 455 Md07
Obo RCA 471 Mb17
Obskaya Guba RUS 456 Oc05
Ocala USA 477 Fd13
Ocampo MEX 476 Ec13
Ocaña CO 478 Gb17
Oceanside USA 476 Dd11
Ocotal NIC 477 Fc16
Ocotlán MEX 476 Ed14
Odense DK 454 Lc07
Odessa UA 455 Mc09
Odessa USA 476 Ed12
Odienné CI 470 Kc17
Odincovo RUS 455 Md07
Odiongan RP 464 Ra16
Oeno GB 489 Da12
Ogaden ETH 471 Na17
Ogasawara-shoto J 461 Sa13
Ogbomoso WAN 470 La17
Ogden USA 476 Eb10
O'Higgins, Gral.B. 482 Ha31
Ohio USA 477 Fd10
Ohio USA 477 Fd11
Ohotsk RUS 457 Sa07
Oiapoque F 479 Hb18
O-jima J 461 Rb13
Ojinaga MEX 476 Ed13
Ojmjakon RUS 457 Sa06
Okahandja NAM 472 Ld23
Okavango ANG/NAM 472 Ld22
Okavango Delta RB 472 Ma22
Okavango Swamp RB 472 Ma22
Okayama J 461 Rc12
Okhotsk RUS 457 Sa07
Okinawa Islands J 461 Rb13
Okinawa-jima J 461 Rb13
Oklahoma USA 476 Fa11
Oklahoma City USA 476 Fa11
Oktjabr'sk KZ 455 Nd09
Oktjabr'skij RUS 455 Nc08
Ólafsvik IS 454 Jd06
Öland S 455 Ld07
Olary AUS 466 Sa25
Olavarría RA 481 Gd26
Ólbia I 454 Lb10
Old Crow CDN 474 Da05
Olëkma RUS 457 Ra07
Olëkminsk RUS 457 Ra06
Olëkminskij Stanovik RUS 457 Qd08
Olenëk RUS 457 Ra04
Olenëk RUS 457 Qc05
Olenëkskij zaliv RUS 457 Ra04
Ölgiy MNG 460 Pc09
Olifantsrivier ZA 473 Mb23
Olimarao Atoll FSM 468 Sb17
Ólimpos GR 455 Ma10
Olinda BR 479 Jb20
Oljutorskij zaliv RUS 457 Tb07
Olmos PE 478 Ga20
Oloj RUS 457 Ta05
Olojskij hrebet RUS 457 Ta05
Olomouc CZ 455 Ld09
Olongapo RP 464 Ra16
Olympia USA 474 Dd09
Olympic Peninsula USA 474 Dd09
Omaha USA 476 Fa10
Oman OM 458 Nd14
Omapere NZ 467 Tc26
Omatako NAM 472 Ld22
Omdurman SUD 471 Mc15
Ometepec MEX 476 Fa15
Omolon RUS 457 Sc05
Omolon RUS 457 Ta05
Omsk RUS 456 Oc07
Ondjiva ANG 472 Ld22
Öndörhaan MNG 461 Qc09
Onega RUS 455 Md06
Onega RUS 455 Md06
Onežskaja guba RUS 455 Md06
Onitsha WAN 470 Lb17
Ono-i-Lau FJI 467 Ua23
Onotoa Atoll KIR 469 Td19
Onslow AUS 466 Qd23
Ontario CDN 475 Fb08
Ontario CDN 475 Fb08
Ontong Java Atoll SOL 468 Sd20
Ontong-Java Rise PNG 468 Sd19
Oodnadatta AUS 466 Rd24
Oos-Londen ZA 472 Mb25
Opole PL 455 Ld08
Opotiki NZ 467 Td26
Oradea RO 455 Ma09
Oral KZ 455 Nc08
Oran DZ 470 Kd11
Orange AUS 466 Sb25
Orange NAM 472 Ld24
Orange Fan 472 Lc25
Oranje Gebergte SME 479 Ha18
Oranjemund NAM 472 Ld24
Oranjerivier ZA 472 Ld24
Oranjestad NL 478 Gb16
Orbost AUS 466 Sb26
Ordu TR 458 Md10
Örebro S 455 Ld07
Oregon USA 476 Dd10
Orehovo-zuevo RUS 455 Md07
Orel RUS 455 Md08
Orenburg RUS 456 Nd08
Orhon gol MNG 460 Qa09
Orillia CDN 477 Ga10
Orinoco YV 478 Gc17
Orinoco Delta YV 479 Gd17
Orissa IND 462 Pa14
Oristano I 454 Lb10
Orixininá BR 479 Ha19
Orizaba MEX 476 Fa15
Orkney Islands GB 454 Kd07
Orlando USA 477 Fd13
Orléans F 454 La09
Ormara PAK 458 Oa13
Ormoc RP 465 Ra16
Orocue CO 478 Gb18
Oroluk Atoll FSM 468 Sd17
Orona KIR 469 Ub19
Orša BY 455 Mc08
Orsk RUS 456 Nd08
Oruro BOL 478 Gc22
Oš KS 460 Oc10
Osaka J 461 Rd12
Oshakati NAM 472 Ld22
Oshawa CDN 477 Ga10
Oshkosh USA 476 Fc10
Osijek HR 455 Ld09
Öskemen KZ 456 Pa08
Oslo N 454 Lc06
Osnabrück D 454 Lb08
Osogbo WAN 470 La17
Osorno RCH 481 Gb27
Osprey Reef AUS 466 Sb21
Ossora RUS 457 Ta07
Osterinsel RCH 476 Ec24
Östersund S 455 Ld06
ostov Bol. Ljahovskij RUS 457 Sa04
ostov Kotel'nyj RUS 457 Rd03
ostov Novaja Sibir' RUS 457 Sb03
Ostrava CZ 455 Ld09
ostrov Ajon RUS 457 Tb05
ostrov Arga-Muora-Sise RUS 457 Ra04
ostrova Sergeja Kirova RUS 456 Pb03
ostrov Belyj RUS 456 Oc04
ostrov Bol. Begičev RUS 457 Qc04
ostrov Bol'ševik RUS 456 Qa03
ostrov Iturup RUS 461 Sb10
ostrov Karaginskij RUS 457 Ta07
ostrov Kolgujev RUS 455 Nb05
ostrov Komsomolec RUS 456 Pc02
ostrov Kunašir RUS 461 Sb10
ostrov Oktjabr'skoj Revoljucii RUS 456 Pd02
ostrov Onekotan RUS 457 Sc09
ostrov Paramušir RUS 457 Sd08
ostrov Rasšua RUS 457 Sc09
ostrov Šiaškotan RUS 457 Sc09
ostrov Simušir RUS 457 Sc09
ostrov Urup RUS 457 Sc09
ostrov Vajgač RUS 456 Oa04
Osumi Islands J 461 Rc12
Otavi NAM 472 Ld22
Oti CI 470 La17
Otjiwarongo NAM 472 Ld23
Otra N 454 Lb07
Ottawa CDN 475 Ga09
Ottawa Islands CDN 475 Fd07
Otuzco PE 478 Ga20
Ouadda RCA 471 Ma17
Ouagadougou BF 470 Kd16
Ouahigouya BF 470 Kd16
Oualâta RIM 470 Kc15
Ouarâne RIM 470 Kc14
Ouargla DZ 470 Lb12
Ouarzazate MA 470 Kc12
Oubangui RDC 471 Ld18
Oudtshoorn ZA 472 Ma25
Oued Drâa MA 470 Kc13
Oued Irharhar DZ 470 Lb13
Oued Moulouya DZ 470 Kd12
Oued Saoura DZ 470 Kd13
Oued Tadant DZ 470 Lb14
Oued Tafassasset DZ 470 Lb14
Oued Tamanrasset DZ 470 La14
Oued Tekouiat DZ 470 La14
Oued Tichkatine DZ 470 La14
Oujda MA 470 Kd12
Oujda MA 470 Kd12
Oulu FIN 455 Mb06
Oum-Chalouba TCH 471 Ma15
Ounianga Kébir TCH 471 Ma15
Ourense E 454 Kc10
Ourinhos BR 479 Hc23
Ouro Preto BR 479 Hd23
Ouro Sogui SN 470 Kb15
Ouvéa F 467 Tb23
Ovalle RCH 481 Gb25
Ovamboland NAM 472 Lc22
Oviedo E 454 Kc10
Owando RCB 472 Ld19
Owensboro USA 477 Fc11
Owen Sound USA 477 Fd10
Owen Stanley Range PNG 468 Sb20
Owo WAN 470 Lb17
Oxford GB 454 Kd08
Oxnard USA 476 Dd11
Oyem G 470 Lc18
Ozark Plateau USA 476 Fb11
ozero Beloe RUS 455 Md06
ozero Čany RUS 456 Od08
ozero Il'men' RUS 455 Mc07
ozero Tajmyr RUS 456 Qa04

P

Paamiut DK 475 Hc06
Pachucade Soto MEX 476 Fa14
Pacific Ocean 488 Tb06
Padang RI 464 Qa19
Padang Endau MAL 464 Qa18
Padangpanjang RI 464 Qa19
Padangsidempuan RI 464 Pd18
Padilla BOL 478 Gd22
Padova I 454 Lc09
Padre Island USA 476 Fa13
Paducah USA 477 Fc11
Pafos CY 455 Mc12
Pagadian RP 465 Ra17
Pagai Selatan RI 464 Qa19
Pagai Ulatan RI 464 Pd19
Pagalu STP 472 Lb19
Pagatan RI 464 Qc19
Pagimana RI 464 Ra19
Päijänne FIN 455 Mb06
Painted Desert USA 476 Eb11
Pakin Atoll FSM 468 Sd17
Pakistan PAK 459 Ob13
Paksan LAO 463 Qa15
Pakse LAO 463 Qb15
Pakwach EAU 471 Mc18
Pala TCH 470 Lc17
Palangkaraya RI 464 Qb19
Palanpur IND 462 Oc14
Palau PAL 465 Rc17
Palau Islands PAL 465 Rc17
Palawan RP 464 Qd16
Palembang RI 464 Qa19
Palermo I 454 Lc11
Pali IND 462 Oc13
Palikir FSM 468 Sd17
Paljavaam RUS 457 Tc05
Palk Strait IND/CL 462 Od17
Palma de Mallorca E 454 La11
Palmar Sur CR 477 Fd17
Palmas BR 479 Hc21
Palmer USA 474 Cc06
Palmer Land 482 Gc33
Palmer Station 482 Gd31
Palmerston Atoll NZ 469 Ud22
Palmerston North NZ 467 Td27
Palmira CO 478 Ga18
Palm Islands AUS 466 Sb22
Palm Springs USA 476 Dd11
Palmyra USA 489 Bb09
Palpa PE 478 Ga21
Palu RI 464 Qc19
Pama BF 470 La16
Pamir TJ 460 Oc11
Pampa del Tamarugal RCH 478 Gb23
Pampa Húmeda RA 481 Gd26
Pampas RA 481 Gd26
Pampa Seca RA 481 Gc26
Pamplona CO 478 Gb17
Pamplona E 454 Kd10
Panaij IND 462 Oc15
Panama PA 477 Fd17
Panamá PA 477 Ga17
Panama Canal PA 477 Ga17
Panama City USA 477 Fc12
Panay RP 464 Ra16
Pandan RP 464 Ra16
Panevežys LT 455 Ma07
Pangkalanbun RI 464 Qb19
Pangnirtung CDN 475 Gc05
Pangjur PAK 458 Oa13
Pankalpinang RI 464 Qb19
Pantanal BR 479 Ha22
Pantanal Matogrossense BR 479 Ha22
Pantoja PE 478 Ga19
Panzhihua CHN 460 Qa13
Papantla MEX 476 Fa14
Papua RI 465 Rd19
Papua New Guinea PNG 468 Sa20
Pará BR 479 Hb19
Paraburdoo AUS 466 Qd23
Paracatu BR 479 Hc22
Paracel Islands 464 Qc15
Paraguay PY 479 Ha23
Paraguay PY 479 Ha23
Paraíba BR 479 Ja20
Paraiso do Tocantins BR 479 Hc21
Parakou DY 470 La17
Paramaribo SME 479 Ha17
Paraná BR 479 Hb23
Paraná BR 479 Hb23
Paraná BR 479 Hb23
Paraná RA 481 Gd25
Paraná RA 481 Gd25
Paranã BR 479 Hc21
Paranaguá BR 481 Hc24
Paranaíba BR 479 Hb22
Paranaíba BR 479 Hb22
Paranapanema BR 479 Hb23
Paratinga BR 479 Hd21
Pardo BR 479 Hb23
Pardo BR 479 Hd22
Parent CDN 475 Gb09
Parepare RI 464 Qc19
Pargua RCH 481 Gb27
Parika GUY 479 Ha17
Paris F 454 La09
Paris USA 476 Fa12
Parkersburg USA 477 Fd11
Parma I 454 Lc10
Parnaíba BR 479 Hc20
Parnaíba BR 479 Hd19
Parnaíba BR 479 Hd19
Pärnu EST 455 Ma07
Parry Islands CDN 474 Ea03
Paru BR 479 Hb19
Pasadena USA 476 Dd11
Pasadena USA 476 Fa13
Pascagoula USA 477 Fc12
Pasni PAK 458 Oa13
Passau D 454 Lc09
Passo Fundo BR 481 Hb24
Passos BR 479 Hc23
Pasto CO 478 Ga18
Patagonia RA 481 Gb28
Pate Island EAK 473 Na19
Paterson USA 477 Gb10
Patna IND 462 Pb13
Patomskoe nagor'e RUS 457 Qc07
Patos BR 479 Ja20
Patos de Minas BR 479 Hc22
Patquia RA 481 Gc25
Patras GR 455 Ma11
Pattani THA 464 Qa17
Pattaya THA 463 Qa16
Patu BR 479 Ja20
Pau F 454 Kd10
Paulatuk CDN 474 Dd05
Paulistana BR 479 Hd20
Paulo Alfonso BR 479 Ja20
Pavlodar KZ 456 Od08
Paynes Find AUS 466 Qd24
Paysandú ROU 481 Ha25
Peace River CDN 474 Ea07
Peace River CDN 474 Ea07
Pearl River CHN 461 Qc14
Peary Channel CDN 475 Ed03
Peary Land DK 475 Jb02
Peawanuck CDN 475 Fc07
Pebas PE 478 Gb19
Pečora RUS 455 Nc05
Pečora RUS 456 Nd05
Pečorskoe more RUS 456 Nc04
Pecos USA 476 Ed12
Pecos USA 476 Ed12
Pécs H 455 Ld09

Pedro Alfonso – Rosso

Pedro Alfonso BR 479 Hc20
Pedro Juan Caballero PY 479 Ha23
Peel Sound CDN 475 Fa04
Peera Peera Poolanna Lake AUS 466 Rd24
Pegasus Bay NZ 467 Tc27
Pegu MYA 463 Pd15
Pegunungan Maoke RI 465 Rd19
Pehuajó RA 481 Gd26
Pekalongan RI 464 Qb20
Pekanbaru RI 464 Qa18
Peleng RI 465 Ra19
Pelolas BR 481 Hb24
Peloponnesus GR 455 Ma11
Pelotas BR 481 Hb25
Pematang Siantar RI 464 Pd18
Pemba MOC 473 Na21
Pemba Channel EAT 473 Md20
Pemba Island EAT 473 Md20
Pembroke CDN 475 Ga09
Penang MAL 464 Qa17
Pendleton USA 476 Ea09
Peniche P 454 Kc11
Peninsula de Teitao RCH 481 Ga28
Península Valdés RA 481 Gd27
Péninsule de Gaspésie CDN 475 Gc09
Péninsule d'Ungava CDN 475 Ga06
Pennell Coast 483 Tb33
Pennsylvania USA 477 Ga10
Penny Strait CDN 475 Fa03
Penong AUS 466 Rc25
Pensacola USA 477 Fc12
Pensacola Mountains 482 Hb35
Pentecost Island VU 467 Tb22
Penticton CDN 474 Ea09
Penza RUS 455 Na08
Penza RUS 455 Nb08
Penžinskaja guba RUS 457 Ta06
Peoria USA 476 Fc10
Percival Lakes AUS 466 Ra23
Pereira CO 478 Ga18
Pergamino RA 481 Gd25
Périgueux F 454 La09
Perito Moreno RA 481 Gb28
Perm' RUS 456 Nd07
Pernambuco BR 479 Ja20
Pernambuco Abyssal Plain 479 Jb20
Pernhyn Atoll KIR 489 Ca10
Perpignan F 454 La10
Persian Gulf 458 Nb13
Perth AUS 466 Qd25
Perth GB 454 Kd07
Perth Basin AUS 466 Qc25
Peru PE 478 Ga21
Peru Basin 478 Fd21
Peru-Chile Trench 478 Fd20
Perugia I 454 Lc10
Peruibe BR 479 Hc23
Pervomajs'k UA 455 Mc09
Pervoural'sk RUS 456 Nd07
Pescara I 454 Lc10
Petchaburi THA 463 Pd16
Peter I Island 482 Fb32
Petermann Gletscher DK 475 Gd02
Petersburg USA 474 Db07
Petras, Mount 482 Dc34
Petrolina BR 479 Hd20
Petropavl KZ 456 Ob08
Petropavlovka RUS 456 Qb08
Petropavlovsk-Kamčatskij RUS 457 Sd08
Petrovsk Zabajkal'skij RUS 457 Qb08
Petrozavodsk RUS 455 Mc06
Peureulak RI 464 Pd18
Pevek RUS 457 Tc05
Phalodi IND 462 Oc13
Phang Nga THA 464 Pd17
Phan Thiet VN 463 Qb16
Philadelphia USA 477 Ga11
Philippine Basin 465 Rb15
Philippines RP 464 Qd16
Philippine Sea 465 Rb16
Philippine Trench RP 465 Rb16
Philippine Trench 465 Rb16
Phitsanulok THA 463 Qa15
Phnom Penh K 463 Qa16
Phoenix KIR 469 Ub19
Phoenix USA 476 Eb12
Phoenix Islands KIR 469 Ub19
Phuket THA 464 Pd17
Piaui BR 479 Hd20
Pico P 454 Jc11
Pico Cristóbal Colón CO 478 Gb16
Pico da Bandeira BR 479 Hd23
Pico da Neblina BR/YV 478 Gc18
Pico de Itambé BR 479 Hd22
Picos BR 479 Hd20
Picton NZ 467 Tc27
Pic Touside TCH 470 Ld14
Piedras Negras MEX 476 Ed13
Piehanal RA 478 Gd23
Pielinen FIN 455 Mb06
Pierre USA 476 Ed10
Pietermaritzburg ZA 473 Mc24
Pietersburg ZA 473 Mb23
Pikelot Island FSM 468 Sb17
Pikiutdleq/Køge Bugt DK 475 Hd06
pik Sedova RUS 456 Nd04
Pilar PY 481 Ha24
Pilbara AUS 466 Qd23
Pilcomayo PY 479 Ha23
Pilsen CZ 454 Lc09
Pimba AUS 466 Rd25
Pimenta Bueno BR 479 Gd21
Pinar del Río C 477 Fd14
Pindaré BR 479 Hc19
Pine Bluff USA 476 Fb12
Pine Creek AUS 466 Rc21
Pine Island Bay 482 Ed33
Pine Island Glacier 482 Ed34
Pingelap Atoll FSM 468 Ta17
Pingxiang CHN 461 Qc13
Pingyao CHN 461 Qc11
Pinheiro BR 479 Hc19
Pini RI 464 Pd18
Pinnaroo AUS 466 Sa26
Pinsk BY 455 Mb08
Pinto RA 481 Gd24
Piracicaba BR 479 Hc23
Piraeus GR 455 Ma11
Pirai do Sul BR 479 Hc23
Pirámide RCH 481 Gb28
Piranè RA 481 Ha24
Pirapora BR 479 Hd22
Pirgos GR 455 Ma11
Piripiri BR 479 Hd19
Pisco PE 478 Ga21
Pitcairn GB 489 Da12
Pitcairn Island GB 489 Da12
Piteşti RO 455 Ma10
Pittsburgh USA 477 Ga10
Piura PE 478 Fd20
Pjasina RUS 456 Pb04
Pjasinskij zaliv RUS 456 Pa04
Pjatigorsk RUS 455 Na10
Placentia Bay CDN 475 Hb09
Plainview USA 476 Ed12
Planalto Central BR 479 Hc21
Planalto do Bié ANG 472 Ld21
Planalto do Mato Grosso BR 479 Ha21
Plasencia E 454 Kc10
Plateau de la Manika RDC 472 Mb21
Plateau du Djado RN 470 Lc14
Plateau du Kasai RDC 472 Ma20
Plateau du Tademaït DZ 470 La13
Plateau Laurentien CDN 475 Gb09
Plateau Laurentien CDN 475 Gb09
Plateau of Tibet CHN 460 Pa12
plato Putorana RUS 456 Pd05
Pleiku VN 463 Qb16
Pleven BG 455 Ma10
Ploieşti RO 455 Mb10
Plovdiv BG 455 Ma10
Plumridge Lakes AUS 466 Rb24
Plumtree ZW 472 Mb23
Plymouth GB 454 Kd08
Plymouth UK 477 Gd15
Po I 454 Lc10
Pô BF 470 Kd16
Pobeda Ice Island 483 Pd31
Pobedy Peak CHN/KS 460 Pa10
Pocatello USA 476 Eb10
Pocklington Reef PNG 468 Sd21
Podgorica CG 455 Ld10
Podkamennaja Tunguska RUS 456 Pd06
Point Barrow USA 474 Ca04
Pointe-à-Pitre F 477 Gd15
Pointe du Raz F 454 Kd09
Pointe-Noire RCB 472 Lc19
Point Hope USA 474 Bc05
Poitiers F 454 La09
Pokhara NEP 460 Pa13
Polack BY 455 Mb07
Poland PL 455 Ld08
Polar Plateau 482 Eb36
Polillo Islands RP 464 Ra16
Polonnaruwa CL 462 Pa17
Poltava UA 455 Mc09
poluostrov Kanin RUS 455 Na05
Polynesia 488 Ba10
Pomio PNG 468 Sc20
Ponape Island FSM 468 Sd17
Ponca City USA 476 Fa11
Ponce USA 477 Gc15
Pondicherry IND 462 Od16
Pond Inlet CDN 475 Ga04
Ponoj RUS 455 Md05
Ponoj RUS 455 Na05
Ponta Albina ANG 472 Lc22
Ponta da Beira BR 479 Ja22
Ponta Delgada P 454 Jc11
Ponta Delgada RCH 481 Gc29
Ponta de Pedras BR 479 Hc19
Ponta Grossa BR 481 Hb24
Ponta Porã BR 479 Ha23
Ponta São Sebastião MOC 473 Md23
Pontes e Lacerda BR 479 Ha22
Pontianak RI 464 Qb19
Pontic Mountains TR 455 Mc10
Poole GB 454 Kd08
Popayan CO 478 Ga18
Poplar Bluff USA 476 Fb11
Popocatépetl MEX 476 Fa15
Popondetta PNG 468 Sb20
Porangatu BR 479 Hc21
Porbandar IND 462 Ob14
Pori FIN 455 Ma06
Porlamar YV 478 Gd16
Poronajsk RUS 461 Sa09
Porpoise Bay 483 Rb32
Portage la Prairie CDN 475 Fa08
Port Alberni CDN 474 Dd09
Port Arthur AUS 466 Sb27
Port Arthur USA 476 Fb13
Port Augusta AUS 466 Rd25
Port-au-Prince RH 477 Gb15
Port Blair IND 462 Pc16
Port Elizabeth ZA 472 Mb25
Port-Gentil G 472 Lb19
Port Harcourt WAN 470 Lb18
Port Hardy CDN 474 Dc08
Port Harrison CDN 475 Ga07
Port Hedland AUS 466 Qd23
Port Heiden USA 474 Ca07
Port Hope Simpson CDN 475 Ha08
Portland AUS 466 Sa26
Portland USA 474 Dd09
Portland USA 477 Gb10
Port Lavaca USA 476 Fa13
Port Lincoln AUS 466 Rd25
Port Louis MS 473 Nd23
Port Macquarie AUS 467 Sc25
Port-Menier CDN 475 Gd09
Port Moresby PNG 468 Sb20
Port Nelson CDN 475 Fb07
Porto P 454 Kc10
Porto Alegre BR 481 Hb25
Porto de Moz BR 479 Hb19
Port of Spain TT 477 Gd16
Porto Nacional BR 479 Hc21
Porto-Novo DY 470 La17
Porto Santo P 454 Ka12
Porto Velho BR 478 Gd20
Portoviejo EC 478 Fd19
Port Pirie AUS 466 Rd25
Port Radium CDN 474 Ea05
Port Said ET 471 Mc12
Port Shepstone ZA 473 Mc25
Port Sudan SUD 471 Md15
Portugal P 454 Kc10
Port-Vila VU 467 Tb22
Port Wakefield AUS 466 Rd25
Port Welshpool AUS 466 Sb26
Posadas RA 481 Ha24
Posadas RA 481 Ha24
Poso RI 464 Ra19
Posse BR 479 Hc21
Possoš' RUS 455 Md08
Potenza I 455 Ld10
Potgiertersrus ZA 473 Mb23
Potiskum WAN 470 Lc16
Potosí BOL 478 Gc22
Poum F 467 Ta23
Pouso Alegre BR 479 Hc23
Powell River CDN 474 Dd09
Poza Rica MEX 476 Fa14
Poznań PL 455 Ld08
Pozo Colorado PY 479 Ha23
Prachuap Khirikhan THA 463 Pd16
Prague CZ 454 Lc08
Praslin SY 473 Nd19
Prat, C.A. 482 Ha31
Prescott USA 476 Eb12
Presidencia Roque Sáenz Peña RA 481 Gd24
Presidente Eduardo Frei 482 Ha30
Presidente Epitácio BR 479 Hb23
Presidente Prudente BR 479 Hb23
Presidio USA 476 Ed13
Presque Isle USA 475 Gc09
Preto BR 479 Hc22
Pretoria ZA 472 Mb24
Priangarskoe plato RUS 456 Pd07
Pribilof Islands USA 474 Bb07
Prilenskoe plato RUS 457 Ra06
Prince Albert CDN 474 Ec08
Prince Albert Mountains 483 Sd34
Prince Albert Peninsula CDN 474 Ea04
Prince Albert Sd. CDN 474 Ea04
Prince Charles Island CDN 475 Ga05
Prince Edward Island CDN 475 Gd09
Prince George CDN 474 Dd08
Prince of Wales Island AUS 466 Sa21
Prince of Wales Island CDN 475 Fa04
Prince of Wales Island USA 474 Db07
Prince of Wales Strait CDN 474 Ea04
Prince Olav Mountains 482 Ba36
Prince Patrick Island CDN 474 Dd03
Prince Regent Inlet CDN 475 Fb04
Prince Rupert CDN 474 Db08
Princess Charlotte Bay AUS 466 Sa21
Princess Elizabeth Land 483 Od33
Prince William Sound USA 474 Cc06
Principe STP 470 Lb18
Principe da Beira BR 478 Gd21
Prinsesse Ragnhild kyst 483 Mb33
Priština SR 455 Ma10
Probolinggo RI 464 Qb20
Progress 483 Od32
Prokop'evsk RUS 456 Pb08
proliv Dmitrija Lapteva RUS 457 Sa04
proliv Karskie Vorota RUS 456 Nd04
proliv Longa RUS 457 Td04
proliv Sannikova RUS 457 Rd04
proliv Vil'kickogo RUS 456 Qa03
Prome MYA 463 Pd15
Proserpine AUS 467 Sb23
Provence F 454 Lb10
Providence USA 477 Gb10
Providenija RUS 457 Ub06
Provo USA 476 Eb10
Prudhoe Bay USA 474 Cc04
Prut RO 455 Mb09
Prypjac' BY 455 Mb08
Pskov RUS 455 Mb07
Publications Ice Shelf 483 Od32
Pucallpa PE 478 Gb20
Pucari PNG 468 Sa20
Pucheng CHN 461 Qd13
Puebla MEX 476 Fa15
Puebla MEX 476 Fa15
Pueblo USA 476 Ed11
Puelches RA 481 Gc26
Puente Alto RCH 481 Gb25
Pu'er CHN 460 Qa14
Puerto Acosta BOL 478 Gc22
Puerto Aisén RCH 481 Gb28
Puerto Ángel MEX 476 Fa15
Puerto Armuelles PA 477 Fd17
Puerto Ayacucho YV 478 Gc17
Puerto Bahía Negra PY 479 Ha23
Puerto Barrios GCA 476 Fb15
Puerto Cabello YV 478 Gc16
Puerto Cabezas NIC 477 Fd16
Puerto Carreño CO 478 Gc17
Puerto Cortés HN 477 Fc15
Puerto Cumarebo YV 478 Gc16
Puerto Deseado RA 481 Gc28
Puerto Eden RCH 481 Gb28
Puerto Escondido MEX 476 Fa15
Puerto Grether BOL 478 Gd22
Puerto Inírida CO 478 Gc18
Puerto la Cruz YV 478 Gd16
Puerto Limón CR 477 Fd16
Puerto Maldonado PE 478 Gc21
Puerto Montt RCH 481 Gb27
Puerto Natales RCH 481 Gb29
Puerto Peñasco MEX 476 Eb12
Puerto Plata DOM 477 Gb15
Puerto Princesa RP 464 Qd17
Puerto Rico USA 477 Gc15
Puerto Rondón CO 478 Gb17
Puerto San Julián RA 481 Gc28
Puerto Suarez BOL 479 Ha22
Puerto Vallarta MEX 476 Ec14
Puerto Williams RCH 481 Gc30
Pukapuka Atoll NZ 469 Uc21
Pulap Atoll FSM 468 Sb17
Pulo Anna PAL 465 Rc18
Pulusuk Island FSM 468 Sb17
Puluwat Atoll FSM 468 Sb17
Puna de Atacama RA 478 Gc23
Puncak Jaya RI 465 Rd19
Pune IND 462 Oc15
Punjab IND 462 Od12
Puno PE 478 Gb22
Punta Abreojos MEX 476 Eb13
Punta Arenas RCH 481 Gb29
Punta Burica CR 477 Fd17
Punta Carreta PE 478 Ga21
Punta Carrizal RCH 481 Gc24
Punta Coconho BR 479 Ja19
Punta Coles PE 478 Gb22
Punta da Estaca de Bares E 454 Kc10
Punta del Diablo ROU 481 Hb25
Punta Eugenia MEX 476 Ea13
Punta Galera EC 478 Fd18
Punta Gallinas CO 478 Gb16
Punta Lengua de Vaca RCH 481 Gb25
Punta Mala PA 477 Ga17
Punta Mogotes RA 481 Ha26
Punta Naranjas PA 477 Fd17
Punta Negra PE 478 Fd20
Punta Ninfas RA 481 Gd27
Punta Norte RA 481 Gd27
Punta Norte d.C.San Antonio RA 481 Ha26
Punta Prieta MEX 476 Eb13
Puntarenas CR 477 Fd17
Punta Santo Tomás MEX 476 Ea12
Punto Fijo YV 478 Gb16
Puri IND 462 Pb15
Purnia IND 462 Pb13
Purus BR 478 Gb20
Purwakarta RI 464 Qb20
Puškin RUS 455 Mc07
Putao MYA 463 Pd13
Puthein MYA 463 Pc15
Putončany RUS 456 Pc06
Puttalam CL 462 Od17
Putumayo CO/PE 478 Gb19
Putussibau RI 464 Qc18
Pweto RDC 473 Mb20
Pyinmana MYA 463 Pd15
Pyongyang PRK 461 Rb11
Pyrénées F/E 454 La10

Q

Qaanaaq/ DK 475 Gc03
Qadimah KSA 458 Md14
Qaidam Pendi CHN 460 Pc11
Qal'at al Bishah KSA 458 Na14
Qars-e-Shirin IR 458 Nb12
Qarshi UZ 458 Ob11
Qaryat Abu Qurays LAR 470 Ld12
Qasr el Farafra ET 471 Mb13
Qatar Q 458 Nc13
Qattara Depression ET 471 Mb12
Qazvin IR 458 Nb11
Qena ET 471 Mc13
Qeqertarsuaq/ DK 475 Hb05
Qiemo CHN 460 Pb11
Qilian Shan CHN 460 Pd11
Qingdao CHN 461 Ra11
Qingdao
Qinghai CHN 460 Pd11
Qinghai Hu CHN 460 Qa11
Qinhuangdao CHN 461 Qd11
Qin Ling CHN 461 Qb12
Qinzhou CHN 461 Qb14
Qionghai CHN 461 Qc15
Qiqihar CHN 461 Ra09
Qishn YE 458 Nc15
Qom IR 458 Nc12
Quang Ngai VN 463 Qb15
Quanzhou CHN 461 Qd13
Quaqortoq DK 475 Hc06
Quaqtaq CDN 475 Gc06
Quchan IR 458 Nd11
Québec CDN 475 Ga08
Québec CDN 475 Gb09
Queen Alexandra Range 483 Tb35
Queen Charlotte Islands USA 474 Db08
Queen Charlotte Sound CDN 474 Dc08
Queen Charlotte Strait CDN 474 Dc08
Queen Elizabeth Islands CDN 475 Ea02
Queen Elizabeth Range 483 Sb35
Queen Mary Land 483 Pc33
Queen Maud Gulf CDN 475 Ed05
Queen Maud Mountains 482 Cb36
Queensland AUS 466 Sa23
Queenstown AUS 466 Sb27
Queenstown NZ 467 Tb27
Queenstown ZA 472 Mb25
Quelimane MOC 473 Md22
Quellón RCH 481 Gb27
Querétaro MEX 476 Fa14
Querétaro MEX 476 Ed14
Quesnel CDN 474 Dd08
Quesso RCB 470 Ld18
Quetta PAK 459 Ob12
Quezaltenango GCA 476 Fb16
Quezon RP 464 Qd17
Quibala ANG 472 Lc21
Quibdó CO 478 Ga17
Quilmes RA 481 Ha25
Quilon IND 462 Od17
Quilpie AUS 466 Sa24
Quimper F 454 Kd09
Quincy USA 476 Fb10
Qui Nhon VN 463 Qb16
Quintana Roo MEX 477 Fc15
Quito EC 478 Ga19
Qujing CHN 460 Qa13
Qullai Kommunizm TJ 460 Oc11
Qurghonteppa TJ 459 Ob11
Quxu CHN 460 Pc13
Quyen AUS 466 Sa26
Quzhou CHN 461 Qd13

R

Raa Atoll MV 462 Oc17
Raas Caluula SP 471 Nc16
Raas Gabbac SP 471 Nc17
Raas Guardafui SP 471 Nc16
Raas Xaafuun SP 471 Nc16
Raba RI 464 Qd20
Rabat MA 470 Kc12
Rabaul PNG 468 Sc19
Radom PL 455 Ma08
Rafaela RA 481 Gd25
Rafha KSA 458 Na13
Ragaing Yoma MYA 463 Pc14
Raiatea F 489 Ca11
Raipur IND 462 Pa14
Rajasthan IND 462 Oc13
Rajkot IND 462 Oc14
Raj Nandgaon IND 462 Pa14
Rajshahi BD 462 Pb14
Rakahanga Atoll NZ 469 Ud20
Rakiraki FIJ 467 Td22
Rakops RB 472 Ma23
Raleigh USA 477 Ga11
Ralik Chain MH 469 Ta16
Rama NIC 477 Fd16
Ramlat al Sab'atayn YE 458 Nb16
Ramlat ar-Rabkha OM 458 Nd14
Ramlat Ghafah OM 458 Nd14
Ramlat Rabyanah LAR 471 Ld14
Ramlat Umm al-Hait OM 458 Nc15
Rampar IND 462 Od13
Ranau MAL 464 Qd17
Rancagua RCH 481 Gb25
Ranchi IND 462 Pb14
Rangiroa F 489 Cb11
Rangoon MYA 463 Pd15
Rann of Kachchh IND 462 Ob14
Ransiki RI 465 Rc19
Rantauprapat RI 464 Pd18
Rapa-Nui RCH 480 Ec24
Rapid City USA 476 Ed10
Raqqa SYR 458 Md11
Rarotonga NZ 489 Ca12
Ras al Khafji KSA 458 Nb13
Ras Al-Khaimah UAE 458 Nd13
Râs Banas ET 471 Md14
Ra's Fartak YE 458 Nc15
Rasht IR 458 Nb11
Ras Madrakah OM 458 Nd15
Râs Muhammad ET 471 Mc13
Rasskazovo RUS 455 Na08
Ratak Chain MH 469 Tc16
Ratchaburi THA 463 Pd16
Raufarhöfn IS 454 Ka05
Raurkela IND 462 Pa14
Ravenna I 454 Lc10
Ravensthorpe AUS 466 Qd25
Rawaki KIR 469 Ub19
Rawalpindi PAK 462 Oc12
Rawlinna AUS 466 Rb25
Rawlins USA 476 Ec10
Rawson RA 481 Gc27
Rayner Glacier 483 Nb32
Realico RA 481 Gd26
Reao Atoll F 489 Da11
Récif des Français F 467 Ta22
Recife BR 479 Jb20
Récifs Bellona F 467 Sd23
Récifs d'Entrecasteaux F 467 Ta22
Récifs et Chesterfields F 467 Sd22
Reconquista RA 481 Ha24
Recovery Glacier 482 Jb35
Red Basin CHN 461 Qb12
Red Deer CDN 474 Eb08
Redding USA 476 Dd10
Red Lake CDN 475 Fb08
Red River USA 475 Fa09
Red River USA 476 Fa12
Red River VN 463 Qa14
Red Sea 458 Md14
Reedy Glacier 482 Ca36
Reef Islands SOL 467 Tb21
Regensburg D 454 Lc09
Regestan AFG 458 Oa12
Reggane DZ 470 La13
Réggio di Calabria I 455 Ld11
Regina CDN 475 Ed08
Rehoboth NAM 472 Ld23
Reims F 454 La09
Reinbolt Hills 483 Oc32
Reindeer Lake CDN 475 Ed07
Rengat RI 464 Qa19
Renmark AUS 466 Sa25
Rennell Island SOL 468 Ta21
Rennell Rise SOL 468 Sd21
Rennes F 454 Kd09
Rennick Glacier 483 Ta33
Reno USA 476 Ea11
Represa de Itaipu BR 479 Hb23
Represa de Tucuruí BR 479 Hc19
Represa Tres Marias BR 479 Hc22
Republican USA 476 Fa10
Repulse Bay CDN 475 Fc05
Requena PE 478 Gb20
Réservoir de LG Deux CDN 475 Ga08
Réservoir Manicouagan CDN 475 Gc08
Resistencia RA 481 Ha24
Resolute CDN 475 Fb04
Resolution Island NZ 467 Tb28
Réunion F 473 Nd23
Revelstoke CDN 474 Ea08
Rewa IND 462 Pa14
Reykjavík IS 454 Jd06
Reynosa MEX 476 Fa13
Rezekne LV 455 Mb07
Rhinelander USA 476 Fc09
Rhode Island USA 477 Gb10
Rhodes GR 455 Mb11
Rhodes GR 455 Mb11
Rhône F 454 Lb10
Ribeirão Preto BR 479 Hc23
Riberalta BOL 478 Gc21
Richard's Bay ZA 473 Mc24
Richfield USA 476 Eb11
Richmond AUS 466 Sa23
Richmond USA 477 Ga11
Rifstangi IS 454 Ka05
Riga LV 455 Ma07
Riiser-Larsen Ice Shelf 482 Ka33
Rijeka HR 454 Lc09
Rimouski CDN 475 Gc09
Riobamba EC 478 Ga19
Rio Branco BR 479 Gd18
Rio Branco BR 478 Gc20
Rio Bravo MEX 476 Fa13
Rio Bravo del Norte MEX 476 Ed13
Rio Cuarto RA 481 Gd25
Rio das Mortes BR 479 Hb21
Rio de Janeiro BR 479 Hd23
Rio de Janeiro BR 479 Hd23
Rio de la Plata RA 481 Ha25
Rio Gallegos RA 481 Gc29
Rio Grande BR 481 Hb25
Rio Grande USA 476 Ed13
Rio Grande MEX 476 Ed14
Rio Grande RA 481 Gc29
Rio Grande do Norte BR 479 Ja20
Rio Grande do Sul BR 481 Hb24
Riohacha CO 478 Gb16
Rio Negro BR 478 Gc19
Rio Negro BR 478 Gd19
Rio Negro RA 481 Gc27
Rio Negro RA 481 Gc26
Rio Tecero RA 481 Gd25
Rio Verde BR 479 Hb22
Rio Verde de Mato Grosso BR 479 Hb22
Rivadavia RCH 481 Gc24
Rivera ROU 481 Ha25
Riverina AUS 466 Sa26
Riversdale ZA 472 Ma25
Riverton USA 476 Ec10
Rivière-du-Loup CDN 475 Gc09
Rivne UA 455 Mb08
Riyadh KSA 458 Nb14
Rjazan' RUS 455 Md08
Road Town UK 477 Gd15
Roanoke USA 477 Ga11
Robertson Bay 483 Tb33
Rocas Alijos MEX 476 Ea14
Rocha ROU 481 Hb25
Rochester USA 477 Ga10
Rochester USA 476 Fb10
Rockall GB 454 Kb07
Rockall Plateau 454 Ka07
Rockall Trough 454 Kb08
Rockefeller Plateau 482 Da34
Rockford USA 476 Fc10
Rockhampton AUS 467 Sc23
Rock Springs USA 476 Ec10
Rocky Mount USA 477 Ga11
Rocky Mountains CDN 474 Db06
Rocky Mountains USA 474 Eb09
Rodriguez MS 473 Oa22
Roebourne AUS 466 Qd23
Roes Welcome Sound CDN 475 Fc06
Roma AUS 467 Sb24
Romania RO 455 Ma09
Rome I 454 Lc10
Rondônia BR 478 Gd21
Rondonópolis BR 479 Hb22
Rongelap Atoll MH 469 Tb16
Rongerik Atoll MH 469 Tb16
Rønne DK 454 Lc07
Ronne Bay 482 Gb33
Ronne Ice Shelf 482 Gd34
Ronuro BR 479 Hb21
Roosevelt BR 478 Gd20
Roosevelt Island 482 Bc34
Roper AUS 466 Rc21
Roper Bar AUS 466 Rc21
Roraima BR 479 Gd18
Røros N 454 Lc06
Rosario MEX 476 Ec14
Rosario RA 481 Gd25
Rosário BR 481 Ha25
Rosario de la Frontera RA 481 Gc24
Rosario Oeste BR 479 Ha21
Roseau WD 477 Gd15
Rosebery AUS 466 Sb27
Rose Hill MS 473 Nd23
Roslawl' RUS 455 Mc08
Ross Ice Shelf 483 Bd35
Rosslare IRL 454 Kc08
Rosso RIM 470 Ka15

Index of Topics

Picture credits

II-III.1: Premium/Sekai Bunka, 2: Premium/Winz/Panorama Images; IV-V.1: Premium/Sekai Bunka, 2: Premium/Sekai Bunka/Weld; VI-VII.1: Premium/Roda, 2: Premium/Sekai Bunka, VIII-IX.1 Premium/Sekai Bunka, 2: Premium/Panorama Images/Weld; X-XI.1,2: Premium/Panorama Images/Frerck.

XII: Mauritius/AGE; Premium (3); Pix Wien; Premium. XIII: Pictor; Das Fotoarchiv/Cristofori; Premium (2); dpa; Premium. Inhalt: Atlas XIV: Premium; IFA Bilderteam.

4: Mauritius/AGE; 5.1, 5.2: Premium; 6 t.: AKG; 6.1, 3, 4: Interfoto; 6.2, 6: AKG/Lessing; 7 t., 7.1, 2, 3: Premium; 8 t., 8 b., 9. t. l., t. r., 9.1, 2, 3: AKG; 10: LOOK/Wohner; 11.1: Getty Images/Bavaria; 11.2: Premium; 12 t.: Getty Images/stone/Cornish; 12 b.: laif/Gonzalez; 14 t.: /Miliken; 14 b.: Huber/Giovanni; 15 t., 15.1, 2, 3, 4: Premium; 16 t.: Getty Images/stone; 16 b.: Mauritius/Sipa; 18 t.: Huber; 18 b.: Huber/Mehlig; 19 t.: Pictor; 19.1: Getty Images/Bavaria; 19.2,3: Premium; 20 t.: transglobe/Simons; 20.1, 2: Getty Images/stone/Ehlers; 21: Getty Images/Bavaria/Icelandic; 22 t. l., t. r.: Huber/Giovanni; 22 b., 23: Premium; 24/25: AKG; 25.1:Getty Images/stone/Vikova, 25.2: dpa; 25.3: Sipa image/Nicolas; 26 t.: Getty Images/stone/Craddock, 26 b.: /Viennaslide-Jahn; 27: /Hanson; 28 t.: /Truchet; 28 b.: Premium; 29 t.: Getty Images/stone/Butcher; 29.1, 2, 3: Premium; 30 t.: Huber; 30.b.: /Giovanni; 31 t.: /Radelt, 31.1: /Gräfenhain; 31.2: Getty Images/stone/Renaut; 31.3: /Cornish; 31.4: /Busselle; 32/33, 32.1: Premium; 32.2: Getty Images/stone/Rosenfeld; 33.1, 2: /Premium; 33.3: Getty Images/stone/Loucel; 34 t.: /Braley; 34 b.: /Everts; 35: Transglobe/Winter; 36 t.: Mauritius/Keine; 36 b., 37 t., 37.1: Premium; 37.2: Getty Images/stone/Huber; 37.3: Huber/Giovanni; 37.4: Premium; 38 t. l.: LOOK/Wothe; 38 t. r.: stone/Stadler; 38.1: Bavaria/Dressler; 38.2: Huber; 38.3, 4: H. Hartmann; 39 t. l., t. r.: Huber/Schmid; 40 t.: Premium; 40 b.: Wandmacher; 41 t., 41.1, 2, 3: Premium; 42 t.: stone/Uthoff; 42 b.: Premium; 43 t.: Getty Images /Bavaria/Photo Shot; 43 b. stone/Benn; 44 t. l., t. r., 44 b., 45 t. l., t. r., 45.1: Premium; 45.2: stone/Grandadam; 45.3: Premium; 46 t.: stone/Benn; 46 b.: Premium; 47: stone/Huber; 48 t.: Huber/Simione; 48 b.: Premium; 49 t.: stone/Merten; 49.1, 2, 3: Premium; 49.4: stone/Layda; 50.1: Premium; 50.2: stone/Layda; 50.3: Premium; 50.4: stone/Sumen; 50.5: /Armand; 50.1, 51.2: Premium; 51.3: Corbis/Murat Taner/zefa; 51.4, 5: Premium; 52 t.: Huber/Schmid; 52 b.: stone /Cassidy; 54 t.: Mauritius/Vidler; 54 t. Huber/Schmid; 55 t. l., t. r.: Wrba; 55.1: stone/Cornish; 55.2: /Layda; 55.3: Huber/Giovanni; 56: stone/Jecan; 57 t.: Transglobe/Tschanz-Hofmann; 57 b.: Premium; 58 t.: stone/Dickinson; 58 b., 59 t.: Premium; 59.1: Getty Images/Bavaria/Scholz; 59.2: Huber/Krammisch; 59.3: stone/Evans; 60 t.: /Shaw; 60 b., 61, 62 t. l.: Freyer; 62 t. r.: Transglobe/Tschanz-Hofmann; 62 b.: stone/Everts; 63 t.: Transglobe/Tschanz-Hoffmann; 63.1, 2, 3: Freyer; 63.4: Mauritius/Rossenbach; 64 t. l.: Wrba; 64 t. r., 65 t., 65.1,2,3: Premium; 65.4: Huber/Mehlig; 66 t.: Premium; 66 b.: stone/Pritchard; 67: Premium; 68 t.: Huber/Schmid; 68 b.: Premium; 69 t. l.: stone/Yeowell; 69 t. r.: zefa/Mollenhauer; 69.1: Premium; 69.2: stone/Yeowell; 69.3: Huber/Schmid; 69.4: stone/Weinberg; 70 t.: Premium; 70 b.: Huber/Damm; 71: stone/Garsmeur; 72 t.: Premium; 72 b.: stone/Carrasco; 73 t. l.: /Frishman; 73 t. r., 73.1: Premium; 73.2, 3: Huber/Gräfenhain; 73.4: Premium; 74/75: Premium; 78: Huber; 79: Premium; 80 t. l.; t. r.: AKG/Lessing; 80 b.: zefa/Maroon; 81 t.: DAS FOTOARCHIV/Quinones: 81.1: / Bakshandagi; 82.2: AKG/AP; 81.3: DAS FOTO-ARCHIV/Coyne; 81.4: /Morris; 82 t. and b.: Premium; 83 t.1: DAS FOTOARCHIV/Olson; t. 2: Ellison; t. 3: Morris; 83.1: Laif/Celentano; 83.2: AKG; 83.3: DAS FOTOARCHIV/Lannois; 83.4: Sasse; 84 t. 1, t. 2: Owen; 84 t. 4, 84 b.: AKG; 85 t.: DAS FOTOARCHIV/Sheridan; 85.1: K.U. Müller; 85.2, 3: sipa-press; 85.4: AKG/AP/Widener; 86, 87.1, 87.2: Premium; 88 t.: Eld/Laif; 88 b.: Pictor; 89 t. l., t. r.: DAS FOTOARCHIV/Scalarandis; 89.1: Pictor; 89.2: Kirchner/Laif; 89.3: DAS FOTOARCHIV/Sasse; 89.4: Krause/Laif; 90 t. l., t. r.: DAS FOTOAR-CHIV/Bolesch; 90 b., 91 t. l.: Künzig; 91 t. r.: Krause/Laif; 91.1: Huber/Schmid; 91.2: DAS FOTOARCHIV Künzig; 91.3: Krause/Laif; 91.4, 92 b.: DAS FOTOARCHIV/Künzig; 92/93: DAS FOTOARCHIV/Abbady; 93.1: DAS FOTOARCHIV/ Bakshandagi; 93.2: Hilger/Laif; 93.3: DAS FOTOARCHIV/Künzig, 94 t.: Bolesch, 94.1: Wallace; 94.2: Wheeler; 96 t.: zefa/Maroon; 96 b.: DAS FOTOARCHIV/Turnley; 97 t., 97.1, 2: IFA/Tschanz; 97.3, 4: Schmidt; 98 t.: Mauritius/Cotton; 98 b.: stone/Turner; 99 t. l., t. r.: Krause/Laif; 100 t. l.: DAS FOTOARCHIV/Sasse; t. r.: Riedmiller; 100 b.: corbis/TSM/O'Rourke; 101 t. l., t. r.: DAS FOTOARCHIV/Sasse; 101.1: stone/Willis; 101.2: DAS FOTOARCHIV/Riedmiller; 101.3, 4: Sasse; 102/103: Premium/NGS; 102 b.: Krause/Laif; 103.1: IFA/TPL; 103.2: Premium/NGS; 103.3: DAS FOTOARCHIV/Sclarandis; 104 t.: zefa/Anderle; 104 b.: Mauritius/O'Brien; 105: zefa/Minden/Lanting; 106 t. l., t. r.: Negre/Metis/Laif; 106 b.: Prem/Maibrug; 107 t.: DAS FOTOARCHIV/Stark; 107.1: Mauritius/O'Brien; 107.2: zefa/Minden-Lanting; 107.3: Mauritius/O'Brien; 108.1: Pictor; 108.2: Premium/Stanfield/NGS, 108.3: Premium/Held/Stock Image; 108.4: DAS FOTOARCHIV/Schmidt; 108.5: Premium/Cobb/NGS; 108.6: Premium/Standfield/NGS; 108.7: Premium/Held/Stock Image; 108.8: DAS

FOTOARCHIV/Christoph; 108.9: DAS FOTOARCHIV/Riedmiller; 109.1: Getty/stone/Hellier: 109.2: /Chesley; 109.3: Mauritius/Visa Image; 109.4: Pictor; 110: Getty/stone/DeVore; 111.1: Krause/Laif; 111.2: Getty/stone/Chesley; 111.3, 4: NN; 112 t. l.: DAS FOTOARCHIV/Bolesch: 112 t. r.: /Christoph; 112 b.: Getty/stone/Stahl; 113: DAS FOTOARCHIV/Pettersson, 114 t. l., t. r.: Bolesch; 114 b.: Huber/Laif; 115 t.: Premium; 115.1: Getty/stone/Allison; 115.2: corbis/TSM-Burgess; 115.3: DAS FOTOARCHIV/Bolesch; 115.4: Getty/stone/Sutherland; 116 t. l., t. r.: DAS FOTOARCHIV/Stark; 117 t. l.: Eisermann; t. r.: Schmidt; 117.1-4: Eisermann; 118 t.: Schmidt; 118 b.: corbis/TSM/Steel; 119 t. l., t. r.: DAS FOTOARCHIV/Morrow, 119.1: Premium; 119.2: Getty/stone/Sitton; 119.3: K. U. Müller; 120/121: AKG/Nou; 120 1: DAS FOTOARCHIV/Eisermann; 120.2: AKG/AP; 121.1: Villalion/Impact Visual/Laif; 121.2: DAS FOTOARCHIV/Simon; 121.3: Laif; 122 t. l., t. r.: DAS FOTOARCHIV/Christoph; 122 b.: Getty/stone/Harris; 124, 125 t., 125.1, 2, 3: Premium; 126 t. l., t. r.: FAN/Schindel; 126 b.: Getty/stone/Su; 127: Premium; 128 t. l.: DAS FOTOARCHIV/Turnley; 128 t. r.: Morris; 128 b.: Premium; 129 t.: DAS FOTOARCHIV/Sasse; 129.1, 2, 3: K. U. Müller; 129.4: Mauritius/Blokhuis; 130/131: DAS FOTOARCHIV/Sasse; 130.1: sipa /Savoure; 130.2: sipa; 131.1, 2: sipa/Savoure; 131.3: DAS FOTOARCHIV/Sasse; 132, 133 t.: DAS FOTOARCHIV/Sasse; 133.1: Stark; 133.2: Portnoy; 134 t.: Sasse; 134 b.: stone; 135 t. l., t. r.: DAS FOTOARCHIV/Sasse; 135.1: Premium; 135.2: stone; 135.3: Pictor; 135.4: stone/Ehlers; 136 t.: stone; 136 b.: Matsumoto; 137 t.: DeVore; 137.1, 2, 3: Premium; 138/139: IFA/Aberham; 138.1: Premium-Katayama/Panorama Images; 138.2: IFA/Arakaki; 139.1: Premium/Vidler/Nawrocki Stock;139.2: /Chesley/NGS; 139.3: IFA/Arakaki; 140: Premium; 141 t.: stone/Strachan; 141.1: Premium; 141.2: stone/Renaut; 141.3: Kavanagh; 141.4: DAS FOTOARCHIV/Tack; 142 t. l., t. r.: Kirchner/Laif; 142 b.: Huber/Damm; 143 t. l., t. r.: Celentano/Laif; 143.1: Premium; 143.2: Krause/Laif; 143.3: DAS FOTOAR-CHIV/Raymer; 143.4: Premium; 144/145: Premium; 144.1: DAS FOTOARCHIV/Sasse; 144.2: corbis/TSM;145.1, 2 ,3: DAS FOTOARCHIV/Sasse; 146 t.: stone/Chesley; 146 t. r., 146.b., 147 t. l., t. r.: DAS FOTOARCHIV/Sasse; 148 t. l., t. r.: Portnoy; 149 t.: stone/Cheysley; 149.1: Premium; 149.2: DAS FOTOARCHIV/Müller; 149.3: Sasse; 149.4: stone/Austen; 150 t. l.: stone/Chesley; 150 t. r.: stone/Waugh; 151 t.: DAS FOTOARCHIV/Christoph; 151.1: Huber/Giovanni; 151.2: DAS FOTOARCHIV/Petterson; 151.3: Tack; 151.4: Huber/Giovanni; 152/153: Huber/Simeone; 156: Pix-APL/La Motta; 157: DAS FOTOARCHIV/Stark; 158 t. l., t. r.: Laif/Emmler; 158 b.: AKG; 159 t.: DAS FOTOARCHIV/Berge; 159.1: FAN/Mross; 159.2, 3: Premium; 160: corbis/TSM/Faulkner; 161: Premium, 162 t.: Pict corbis/TSM/Lloyd; 163 b.: Premium; 164 t.: FAN/Heinrichson; 165 t.: DAS FOTOAR-CHIV/Cohen; 165.1, 2, 3, 166 t., 167 t. l.: Premium; 167 t. r.: Pix/IFA; 167.1, 2, 3: Premium; 168, 169: DAS FOTOARCHIV/Cohen; 170 t.: stone/Hiser; 170 b.: /Strachan; 171 t.: DAS FOTOARCHIV/Wheeler; 171.1: stone/Chesley; 171.2: corbis/TSM/Nachoum; 171.3. DAS FOTOARCHIV/Wheeler; 172/173: Pictor; 176: Huber/Damm; 177: Laif/Uluntuncok; 178 t. l., t. r.: Riehle; 178 b.: DAS FOTOARCHIV/Schwertberger; 179 t. l., t. r.: AKG; 179.1 Premium; 179.2: Laif/Uluntuncok; 179.3: Premium; 179.4: DAS FOTOARCHIV/Stark; 180 t. l., t. r.: AKG; 180 1: DAS FOTOARCHIV/Mayer; 180.2, 3, 4: Laif/Uluntuncok; 181 t. 1, t. 2, t. 3: AKG; 181.1: Laif/Bindrim; 181.2: Emmler; 181.3: Uluntuncok; 181.4: Püschner; 182: DAS FOTOARCHIV/Cristofori; 183: stone/Jecan; 184 t.: Laif/Specht; 184 b.: Premium; 185 t.: Mauritius/Doug Scott; 186 t. l., t. r., 187 t.: Laif/Gartung; 187.1: Pix/Transworld Photo; 187.2, 3, 4: Laif/Gartung; 188: stone/Molenkamp; 189 t.: Laif/Krause; 189.1, 3: Laif/Riedmiller; 189.2: Premium; 189.4: stone/Press; 190.1: Laif/Gartung; 190.2, 3: Laif/Uluntuncok; 190.3: Mau/Visa Images; 191.1: Laif/Neumann; 191.2: Laif/Uluntuncok; 191.3: Shriley; 191.4: Premium/Matthews; 192.1: Laif/Uluntuncok; 192.2: Laif/Emmler; 192.3: Laif/Riehle; 192.4: Laif/Uluntuncok; 192.5: Laif/Emmler; 192.6: FAN; 192.7, 8: Laif/Uluntuncok; 192.9: Laif/Gartung; 192.10: DFA/Christoph; 192.11: Laif/Uluntuncok; 192.12, 13: Laif/Emmler; 192.14: Laif/Riehle; 192.15: Focus/Y.Gellte; 193: Laif/Emmler; 194 t.: Laif/Uluntuncok; 194 b.: Boisseaux-Chical; 195 t.: Pix/Havlicek; 195.1: stone/Rothfeld; 195.2: Premium/Hilger; 195.3: Mau/De Foy; 196 t.: Pictor; 196 b.: Pix/Bagni; 196 t.: mediacolors; 196.1: Buck; 196.2: Transglobe/Spreckels; 196.3: mediacolors; 198 t.: DAS FOTOARCHIV/Stark; 198.1: Laif/Huber; 199 t.: Pictor; 199.1, 2, 3: Laif/Huber; 200: Sprague; 201 t.: Pictor; 201.1, 3: Laif/Hoogte, 201.2: Herzau, 201.4: Uluntuncok; 202 t.: Bessard/RFA; 202 b.: DAS FOTOARCHIV/Müller, 203 t. l., t. r.: Bolesch; 203.1: Mueller; 203.2, 3: Martel, 204 t. l., t. r.: Christoph; 204 b.: Pix/Berger; 205.1 DAS FOTOARCHIV/Stark, 205.2, 3: Christoph; 205.4: IFA/BCI; 206 t. l., t. r.: DAS FOTOARCHIV/Christoph; 206 b.: Pix/Havi; 207 t., 207.1, 2: DAS FOTOAR-CHIV/Christoph; 207.3: Pix/Havi; 208: Laif/Gartung; 209 t. l., t. r.: DAS FOTOARCHIV/Christoph; 209.1: Pix/Aberham; 209.2: DAS FOTOARCHIV/Christoph; 209.3: Pix/Aberham; 210: Mauritius/Weimann, 211 t. l., t. r.: De Foy; 211.1, 2, 3: Laif/Uluntuncok; 211.4: mediacolor's; 212 t., 212 b.: Pix/Bitsch; 213 t. l., t. r.:

Original edition: © 2006 Verlag Wolfgang Kunth GmbH & Co KG, Munich, Germany
www.kunth-verlag.de
English edition: © 2006 Verlag Wolfgang Kunth GmbH & Co. KG, Munich, Germany

Translation: American Pie Translations, London, Great Britain

Cover design: Derrick Lim

Map relief MHM ® Copyright © Digital Wisdom, Inc.

Distribution of this edition:

GeoCenter International Ltd
Meridian House, Churchill Way West
Basingstoke, Hampshire RG21 6YR
Great Britain
Tel.: (44) 1256 817 987
Fax: (44) 1256 817 988
sales@geocenter.co.uk
www.insightguides.com

Printed in Slovakia

The information and facts presented in the book have been extensively researched and edited for accuracy. The publishers,
authors, and editors, cannot, however, guarantee that all of the information in the atlas is entirely accurate or up to date at the
time of publication. The publishers are grateful for any suggestions or corrections that would improve the content of this work.